US Army Order of Battle 1919–1941

Volume 2

The Arms: Cavalry, Field Artillery, and Coast Artillery, 1919–41

by

Lieutenant Colonel (Retired) Steven E. Clay

Combat Studies Institute Press
US Army Combined Arms Center
Fort Leavenworth, KS

Library of Congress Cataloging-in-Publication Data

Clay, Steven E., 1957-
US Army order of battle, 1919-1941 / Steven E. Clay.
p. cm.
Includes bibliographical references.
1. United States. Army--Organization--History--20th century--Encyclopedias. I. Title. II. Title: United States Army order of battle, 1919-1941.

UA25.C59 2010
355.30973'09041--dc22

2010022326

Contents

Follow-on volumes include—

Explanatory Notes

Example Unit Entry (battalions, regiments, brigades)

Unit Title and Type ↓ *Parenthetical* ↓ *Component and Geographic Allotment* ↓

308th Cavalry Regiment (62d Cavalry Division) **Organized Reserve Maryland/Pennsylvania**

HQ—Cumberland, MD, 1921–22; Pittsburgh, PA, 1923–41 ← *Headquarters Location*

Demobilized 22 December 1918 at Camp Kearny, CA, as the 65th and 66th Field Artillery Regiments, and on 21 December 1918 as the 22d Trench Mortar Battery. All elements reconstituted in the Organized Reserves on 15 October 1921 and consolidated as the 308th Cavalry, assigned to the 62d Cavalry Division, and allotted to the Third Corps Area. Organized 10 November 1921 with regimental headquarters at Cumberland, MD. Regiment relocated about October 1922 to western Pennsylvania. Regimental headquarters concurrently organized at Pittsburgh. Reorganized 1 July 1929 as a three-squadron regiment. Concurrently, entire regiment relocated to Pittsburgh, PA. Typically conducted its Inactive Training Period meetings at the 107th Field Artillery's Hunt Armory at the Post Office Building in Pittsburgh. Members built the 308th Cavalry Club in 1928 on property owned by the Aspinwall Hospital in Aspinwall, PA, and conducted some Inactive Training there. Facilities included equestrian, pistol, and saber training areas. Conducted regular equestrian training with the horses of the 107th Field Artillery. Conducted summer training with the 3d Cavalry Regiment at Fort Myer, VA, and at Fort Belvoir, VA. Trained with the units of the 52d Cavalry Brigade at Mount Gretna, PA, in July 1928. Conducted cavalry Citizens Military Training Camp (CMTC) training at Fort Myer as an alternate form of training. Designated mobilization training station was the York Concentration Area, PA. Location 7 December 1941—Pittsburgh, PA. ← *Unit Service Narrative*

Organization Day: 24 February. Chosen to commemorate the regiment's organization on 24 February 1918.

Status: Disbanded 11 November 1944 as the 66th Tank Destroyer Battalion. ← *Unit status as of 2001*

Events: 301 ← *Events in which the unit participated 1919–41 (see appendix B).*

Commanders, 308th Cavalry Regiment

Col. John J. Boniface	24 February 1918–25 April 1918
Col. Hugh D. Berkeley	26 April 1918–24 September 1918
Demobilized/Inactive	21 December 1918–10 November 1921
Lt. Col. Elmer J. Kingsbury	10 November 1921–October 1922
Col. Josiah L. Reese	October 1922–15 September 1926
Col. Jean H.A. Day	15 September 1926–ao October 1926
Col. Josiah L. Reese	ao March 1927–25 February 1930
Col. George H. Cherrington	25 February 1930–January 1941
Unknown	January 1941–5 May 1941
Lt. Col. John H. Schenkel	5 May 1941–6 November 1941

Purposes and Scope

The purposes of *US Army Order of Battle 1919–1941* are threefold. The first is to fill a void in the published record of US Army units documented by *Order of Battle of the United States Land Forces in the World War* published by the Center of Military History and Mr. Shelby L. Stanton's *Order of Battle, U.S. Army World War II*. The second is to provide Army command historians, unit historians, and other individuals who are trying to research specific unit histories a basic overview of what these units were doing in the interwar period, where the units were located, and who commanded them. The third is to provide a private individual who had a relative who served during this period, and who wishes to know what that service may have consisted of, an account of the major activities in which the relative's unit was involved. The scope of the work covers units from the size of separate battalions from all arms and services to field armies, as well as the actual order of battle of each as applicable.

Each unit is represented by a unit entry block. The entries contain a host of information that is standardized in its presentation as far as possible. Each entry includes the unit title and type, the headquarters to which the unit was assigned, the geographical area to which the unit was allotted (if National Guard or

Organized Reserve), the unit's headquarters location, the unit's physical location (or the unit's headquarters location if dispersed) on 7 December 1941, a unit service narrative, the unit's organization day, the unit's status as of 2001, and a chronological listing of the unit's commanding officers. Depending on the type of unit, additional information may include a listing of subordinate units and their years of assignment; "snapshot" orders of battle for divisions, corps, and armies for selected years; and the subordinate components of nonstandard units such as harbor defense commands. Also included in this work are the headquarters, a unit service narrative, commanders, and a "Major posts, camps, stations, airfields, and National Guard and Organized Reserve training facilities" section for each of the nine corps areas and three overseas departments. Though these were not tactical headquarters in the traditional sense, their importance to this period, and to this project, were such that I felt compelled to add their information.

Unit Title and Type

The unit title, in most cases, is the designation by which the unit was known for most of the 1919–41 period. In some cases, most notably the Air Service/Air Corps units, several unit titles followed by dates are given due to numerous redesignations.

Parentheticals

Titles are often followed by parenthetical information. Typically, the first of these will be the unit type or weapon, such as **(Antiaircraft)** or **(75-mm G)**. These designations will always be in boldface type. The notation (C) will follow some units. This indicates the unit was designated as a "Colored" unit and manned by African American personnel. The term "Colored" and the designation **(C)** were the standard usage of the period in mobilization documents and elsewhere and are used here for historical purposes. These designations too will always be in boldface type. Some units held the same designation at different times, but are not the same organization. These titles will be followed by a Roman numeral in parentheses, e.g., (I), (II), etc., to clearly differentiate the separate units. These designations will always be in standard type. The final example of parenthetical information is the major headquarters to which the unit was assigned, for example: (1st Division). This is typically the brigade, division, corps, or army to which the unit was assigned. For National Guard units, these reflect planned mobilization assignments for wartime and do not necessarily reflect actual peacetime command and control relationships. In some cases, again most often Air Service/Air Corps units, the organization was assigned to several different headquarters from 1919 to 1941. In those cases, I have attempted to designate that headquarters to which the unit was assigned for the longest period or, in some instances, the headquarters to which it was assigned in the initial mobilization plans of 1921–23. Admittedly, there are a few instances where these two examples will not apply, but in each of these exceptional cases, the rationale was different and it is not feasible to explain every reason. The headquarters designations will also be in standard type.

Component and Geographic Allotment

National Guard and Organized Reserve units are identified in this section of the unit entry. The state or states of allotment are also identified. In some cases, the unit was allotted for organization to more than one state. In those instances, the states of allotment will be identified with the conjunction "and" as such: **Alabama, Mississippi, and Louisiana National Guard**. Typically, the state to which the headquarters was allotted will appear first. In other cases, usually Organized Reserve units, the organization was withdrawn from allotment to one state or geographical area, and reallotted to another. In those instances, the initial state or states of allotment and the follow-on state or states will be differentiated with a slash "/", indicating the first, second, etc., areas of allotment as such: **Organized Reserve Missouri and Kansas/South Dakota**. In some cases for National Guard or Organized Reserve units, an organization was constituted but never allotted to a given state. In those instances, only the component (i.e., **National Guard** or **Organized Reserve**) is listed. Regular Army units that were generally in an inactive status between 1921 and 1939 are shown as **Regular Army Inactive** (RAI). The vast majority of RAI units were organized with Reserve personnel during this period and thus are differentiated in this manner from Organized Reserve units and active Regular Army units. Many Organized Reserve units were withdrawn from the Reserve and allotted to the Regular Army between 1927 and 1940. These units are all listed herein as Organized Reserve units as that is the component in which they were originally allotted. Active Regular Army units below division level and which headquarters were active for the majority of 1919 to 1941 will have no component listed.

Headquarters Location

The city or post and state or overseas location where the unit's headquarters was physically and permanently located, roughly between January 1919 and 7 December 1941, is listed here. Generally speaking, temporary locations are not included unless the absence from the permanent location was for 6 months or longer. The location and relocation dates for Regular Army and National Guard units are generally accurate, having been determined from unit data cards for the Regular Army and state annual or biennial reports and various other documents for National Guard units. While the majority of the initial organization dates and locations for Organized Reserve (O.R.) units are generally accurate, the relocation dates were somewhat problematic for these units. The primary document used to determine O.R. headquarters locations are 3"x5" index cards located at the Center of Military History at Fort McNair in Washington, DC. These cards were the methodology by which the Army tracked O.R. units in the interwar period. They usually (though not always) contain dates and headquarters location for the relocation of the units, but the relocation dates themselves are often that of the actual document that notified the individual who kept the cards rather than the actual date of the relocation. The date provided on the index card has typically been used as the date of relocation in the absence of the actual date. Those dates, however, while generally accurate, can be as much as a year off. In those instances where the actual relocation date has been located in other kinds of documents, the actual date has been used.

Unit Service Narrative

The service narrative generally provides an overview of the unit's permanent changes of station, assignment and reassignment to major commands, allotment to and withdrawal from component (Regular Army [R.A.], National Guard [N.G.], O.R.), allotment to corps area or overseas department, initial organization date and location, training activities and locations, activation and inactivation, and the location of the unit (or of the unit headquarters if the unit was dispersed) on 7 December 1941. Special events and activities, awards, and deployments are also covered. For R.A. units, support to the Civilian Conservation Corps and training support to O.R. units are covered. For N.G. units, callups for state emergencies of battalion-size or larger, dates of Federal recognition, dates of induction into Federal service, summer training camp locations, and mobilization training stations are covered. For O.R. units, locations for Inactive Training Period meetings, summer training camp locations, mobilization training stations, and Reserve Officers' Training Corps (ROTC) feeder units are covered. Regular Army Inactive (RAI) units are covered similarly to O.R. units with the addition of information on Active Associate units and affiliation with ROTC units. Dates provided for unit movements are generally the dates of arrival at the new location by the unit headquarters, unless specifically given as a departure date from the losing duty station. Subordinate elements of the unit may have arrived before or after that date.

Organization Day

The War Department's General Order #24, dated 10 June 1922, established the concept of "Organization Day" (sometimes referred to as "Regimental Day") for US Army units. The Organization Day was not necessarily the date on which the unit was organized. It could also be a special date in its history such as its baptism of fire in combat. In instances where an Organization Day had been adopted, the unit's chosen date for Organization Day, an explanation of the date's significance, and the date of adoption are given, if known.

Status

The unit's status (active, inactive, disbanded, etc.) and designation as of 2001 is given if known.

Events

The numbers represent events of significance in which the unit participated between 1919 and 1941. The details of each event number are located in appendix B.

Commanders

Where known, the unit's commanders and their inclusive dates of command are provided for regiment-size units and above, and selected battalion-size units. The dates of command are for the period 1 January 1919 to 7 December 1941, or the end date of command for the last pre-World War II commander, whichever is later. For infantry, cavalry, field artillery, coast artillery, and engineer regiments, the commanders for the World War I period are also provided if known, because those commander lists were not previously provided in the Center of Military History's *Order of Battle of the United States Land Forces in the World War*. For some N.G. units, the commanders will have a state abbreviation in parentheses following their name (e.g., (GA) for the state of Georgia) in those instances where the unit was a multistate organization to identify from which state the commander was assigned. If the commander of a N.G. or O.R. unit was an R.A. officer, the name will be followed by the abbreviation (R.A.). If the commander of a N.G. or R.A. unit was an O.R. officer, the name will be followed by the abbreviation (O.R.). If the name is not followed by an abbreviation, the commander is of the component or state to which the unit headquarters was allotted. If a commander is not known for a given period, the entry "Unknown" and the inclusive dates (at least month and year) are provided. In some instances, especially for O.R. units, the inclusive dates for a given commander are not known. In those cases, the entry "ao" (for "as of") followed by a month and year indicates the earliest or latest date known for that commander to be in command of the unit indicated. The example below indicates that Colonel William J. Smith was known to be in command from at least July 1937 to at least April 1940.

Example: Col. William J. Smith ao July 1937–ao April 1940

Additionally, a single asterisk (*) beside a commander's name indicates he was an R.A. officer in command of an RAI unit. Two asterisks (**) indicates a Reserve officer who was in command of an RAI unit. Note that relatively few O.R. brigades and no RAI brigades were assigned a brigadier general as commanding general. These headquarters functioned as such on few occasions, usually at a command post exercise or occasionally during annual training. The brigade was strictly a tactical command during this period and exercised no administrative duties or responsibilities. Those duties were performed at the division and regimental levels. For that reason, O.R. and RAI brigades were generally "commanded" by majors or lieutenant colonels whose duties were primarily limited to planning, conducting, or supervising training in the brigade headquarters during the inactive training period. More often than not, personnel assigned to brigade headquarters simply conducted their inactive training with one of the subordinate regiments. At summer training, the senior regimental commander often served as the brigade commander when the brigade headquarters was intended to function as such. When assignment of Reserve officers to RAI regiments began in 1926, only a single reserve major (later changed to a lieutenant colonel) was authorized as the commander though the regiment could acquire its full quota of captains and lieutenants from the officer's Reserve Corps. In 1927, the command of these regiments was, in many cases, passed to selected Active Duty R.A. colonels and lieutenant colonels who, for the most part, were the professors of Military Science and Tactics at the college or university with which the RAI unit was affiliated. This practice seems to have effectively ended on 1 October 1933, though in some instances it was ended earlier, after which command was exercised by the senior Reserve officer assigned. Most units not affiliated with an educational institution were commanded by Reserve officers, though in a few cases they were commanded by R.A. officers who were assigned as an additional duty. This practice also seems to have ended on 1 October 1933. In many instances, brigades and regiments were commanded by captains and even lieutenants. Those organizations seem to have served more as Reserve pool units for mobilization assignment purposes than actual functional units. This was usually because the assigned personnel were geographically dispersed so as to prevent regular assembly for inactive training periods. Nonetheless, the senior officer assigned acted as the commanding officer during summer training unless a higher ranking officer was temporarily attached to assume command for the camp period.

Example Major Command Unit Entry (divisions, corps, armies)

Major command unit entries generally follow the same pattern as those for smaller unit entries with the exceptions detailed below.

Unit Title and Type ↓ | Nickname ↓ | *Component and Geographic Allotment of Entire Division* ↓

39th DIVISION

"Delta Division"

Louisiana, Mississippi, Alabama, Florida, and Arkansas National Guard

HQ—*Not organized,* 1921–23 ← *Headquarters Location*

The 39th Division headquarters arrived at Newport News, VA, aboard the S.S. *Matoika* on 31 December 1918 after 4 months of overseas service and was demobilized 23 January 1919 at Camp Beauregard, LA. In accordance with the National Defense Act of 1920, the division was allotted to the states of Louisiana, Alabama, Mississippi, Florida, and Arkansas and assigned to the IV Corps in 1921. The division's designated mobilization training station was Camp McClellan, AL. The division headquarters was not reorganized before the adjutants general of the several states from which the division was drawn petitioned the War Department to change the designation of the division to be formed as the 31st Division as that was the organization in which most of the states' units served in World War I. The request was approved and the subordinate elements assigned to the 39th Division were withdrawn and assigned to the 31st Division, less the Arkansas elements, effective 1 July 1923.

Unit Service Narrative

Status: Headquarters and Headquarters Company currently active at Little Rock, AR, as HHC, 39th Infantry Brigade.

Division Commanders

No commanders assigned

39th DIVISION
Organization 1923

UNIT:	**HQ LOCATION:**
Headquarters	*Alabama N.G.**
Headquarters, Special Troops	*Alabama N.G.**
Headquarters Company	Mobile, AL
39th Military Police Company	*Florida N.G.**
39th Signal Company	*Alabama N.G.**
114th Ordnance Company (M)	Jacksonville, FL
39th Tank Company (L)	Ozark, AL
Motorcycle Company No. 114	*Florida N.G.**
77th Infantry Brigade	Montgomery, AL
154th Infantry Regiment	Jacksonville, FL
167th Infantry Regiment	Gadsden, AL
78th Infantry Brigade	New Orleans, LA
155th Infantry Regiment	Vicksburg, MS
156th Infantry Regiment	New Orleans, LA
64th Field Artillery Brigade	*Louisiana N.G.**
114th Ammunition Train	Elba, AL
116th Field Artillery Regiment	*Florida N.G.**
141st Field Artillery Regiment	*Alabama N.G.**
114th Engineer Regiment	*Mississippi N.G.**
114th Medical Regiment	*Louisiana N.G.**
39th Division Train, Q.M.C.	*Mississippi N.G.**
39th Division Air Service	Birmingham, AL

Organization/ Order of Battle

*Indicates state of headquarters allocation; headquarters not organized or inactive.

Nickname

Many divisions adopted nicknames in the World War I period or, in a few cases, the nickname was adopted after the division was constituted or reconstituted in 1921. The nicknames are shown as illustrated.

Component and Geographic Allotment

For corps and armies, only the state to which the headquarters was allotted are listed. For divisions, every state that was allotted a unit in the division's order of battle is listed. The state to which the headquarters was originally allotted and organized will be listed first.

Organization/Order of Battle

Each division, corps, and field army has one or two "snapshot" orders of battle provided to illustrate how the command was organized at the time indicated. The 1939 order of battle provided for the R.A.'s 1st through 9th Divisions represent those divisions' final organization before the change to the "triangular" tables of organization in October 1939. Unit designations in italics indicate an inactive unit or a "not organized" or "not initiated" unit. Unit headquarters locations in italics represent the state of allotment for National Guard Inactive (NGI) units and the corps area of allotment for RAI and Organized Reserve Inactive (ORI) units. Partially active units (i.e., the headquarters was inactive, but some subordinate elements were active) are also shown in italics. For partially active units, the unit headquarters mobilization station/post is also shown in italics.

Division Commanders and Chiefs of Staff

Note that about half of the O.R. divisions actually had at least one general officer assigned as division commander sometime during this period, and none had a general assigned for the entire period. In most cases, one of the R.A. brigade commanders in the corps area was assigned as the commanding general of one of the three O.R. divisions as an additional duty. This practice seems to have been most widely used in the Second, Fourth, Fifth, and Seventh Corps Areas. In some cases, the corps area commander assigned that duty to himself. In two instances, those of the 77th and 95th Divisions, Reserve divisions were actually commanded by a Reserve officer. Generally speaking, the division's chief of staff exercised routine command in the name of the corps area commander or the assigned division commander. Thus, the names of the R.A. chiefs of staff assigned to O.R. divisions have been included in this *Order of Battle*.

Terminology and Abbreviations

The military and ethnic terminology and abbreviations used in this work are those that were used from 1919 to 1941; therefore, at the beginning of each volume is a Key to Abbreviations. See Appendix A, "Glossary of Terms," for definitions of the terminology used in this *Order of Battle*.

The National Guard

The N.G. poses several problems in preparing a work such as this because the rules by which the Center of Military History (and the states themselves) trace each unit's lineage do not always mirror those for the R.A. and O.R./US Army Reserve. For example, when a unit in the O.R. was relocated from one community to another, the unit retained its history and designation. In the case of the N.G., however, when a unit designation was relocated to a unit in another community, the history of the unit was retained in the organization located in the first community. Also, if a unit was demobilized (i.e., disbanded) in one community, and then in another community a unit is organized with the same designation, there was, in theory, no relation between the two units other than the fact that they happened to have shared the same designation. For example, the 120th Ammunition Train was organized at Bristow, OK, in May 1923. The unit in Bristow was disbanded in May 1924. A new 120th Ammunition Train was organized at Sperry, OK, in June 1924 and later reorganized as Headquarters Battery, 160th Field Artillery in June 1926. Another new 120th Ammunition Train was organized at Haskell, OK, also in June 1926, and later reorganized as Battery B,

160th Field Artillery in January 1927. In theory, there were three different organizations with the designation "120th Ammunition Train" and as such, each should merit a separate Unit Entry in this *Order of Battle*. To complicate matters, regimental, brigade, and division headquarters appear not to have been considered state- or community-specific units. For example, the Headquarters, 108th Cavalry at New Orleans, LA, was withdrawn from the state of Louisiana on 15 March 1929 and allotted to the state of Georgia and reorganized at Hinesville, GA. There appears to have been no loss of identity or history in the transfer of that unit designation between states, much less between communities in the same state. It is the same unit with the same lineage. Additionally, the Center of Military History does not consider N.G. units "constituted," even though the Federal designations of those units were clearly "placed on the rolls of the army" (this is especially pertinent since the vast majority of N.G. units used Federal designations and not state designations during the period) and allotted to the various states in 1920–21 in accordance with the guidelines laid out in the 1920 amendment to the National Defense Act of 1916. The methodology appears to assume that the designation does not exist (at least on the rolls of the Army) until the day the unit is organized and federally recognized, even though letters and memorandums allotting the unit designation to a state, mobilization plans, and numerous other documents clearly refer to the existence of the unit designation before it was actually organized. In light of these pre-existing designations, for the purposes of this *Order of Battle*, I have chosen to consider the designation of N.G. units to have been constituted in the same manner as R.A. and O.R. units (i.e., when the designation of a unit was placed on the rolls of the Army). Therefore, those units that have a clearly differentiated identity (in other words, separate battalions, regiments, divisions, etc.) are treated as one and the same organization in the Unit Entries. Only in rare instances are two (or more) N.G. units with the same designation treated as separate and distinctly different organizations. The Unit Entries for these units generally makes the purpose for differentiation self-evident.

Key to Abbreviations

(AA)	antiaircraft
(C)	Colored
(CA)	civilian airfield
(CC)	civilian college
(H)	heavy
(HD)	horse drawn
(HP)	heavy ponton
(HT)	heavy tractor
(HTA)	heavier-than-air
(L)	light
(LP)	light ponton
(LT)	light tank
(LTA)	lighter-than-air
(M&H)	medium & heavy
(M)	medium
(MA)	military airfield
(MC)	military college
(Mecz)	mechanized
(MI)	military institute
(MT)	medium tank
(Mtd)	mounted
(Mtzd)	motorized
(NGF)	National Guard Aviation Facility
(PS)	Philippine Scouts
(RO)	railway operating
(RY)	railway
(S&F)	sound and flash
(TD)	tractor/truck drawn
(Topo)	topographic
(WS)	water supply
2d Lt.	second lieutenant
A.A.	Active Associate
AA	antiaircraft
AAB	Army Air Base
Abn	airborne
AC	Air Corps
Adj.	adjutant
Adm.	airdrome
Admin	administration
AEF	American Expeditionary Force
AFG	American Forces, Germany
AFHRA	Air Force Historical Research Agency
AIT	advanced individual training
AK	Alaska
AL	Alabama
amb.	ambulance
ammo.	ammunition
ao	as of
AP	airport
AR	Arkansas
Armd.	armored
Armt	armament
Ars.	arsenal
Arty.	Artillery
AS	air service
Ash.	airship
Atk.	attack
ATS	army transport service
Aux	auxiliary
Avn.	aviation
AZ	Arizona
B.A.G.	Branch Assignment Group
Bkry	bakery
Bln.	balloon
Bn.	battalion
Bomb.	bombardment
Brig.	brigade
Brig. Gen.	brigadier general
Btry	battery
C.A.	coast artillery
C.A.C.	Coast Artillery Corps
C.G.	commanding general
C.O.	commanding officer
C.S.A.	Confederate States of America
C.W.S.	Chemical Warfare Service
C.Z.	Communications Zone
CA	California
Camo	camouflage
Capt.	Captain
CARL	Combined Arms Research Library
CARS	Combat Arms Regimental System
CASC	Corps Area Service Command
CASU	Corps Area Service Unit
Cav.	cavalry
Cbt	combat
CCC	Civilian Conservation Corps
CCX	Command and Communications Exercise
CD	Coast Defenses
Chem.	Chemical
CIA	Central Intelligence Agency
CM	civilian master
Cmd	command
Cmpl.	Complement
CMTC	Citizens Military Training Camp
CO	Colorado
Co.	company
Col.	colonel
Coll	collecting
Commo	communications
Comp.	composite
Conv	convalescent
Cos.	companies
Cpl.	Corporal
CPX	command post exercise
CST	common skills training
CT	Connecticut
Ctr.	Center
CZ	Canal Zone
DC	District of Columbia
DE	Delaware
Dent	dental
Dep	depot

Dept.	department
Det.	detachment
Disch.	Discharge
Dispry.	Dispensary
Dist.	District
Div. Arty.	division artillery
Div.	division
DNG	Deferred National Guard
Doc	document
DT	dump truck
e.g.	for example
EEN&T	eyes, ears, nose & throat
elmts	elements
Engr.	engineer
Engrs.	Engineers
ERC	Enlisted Reserve Corps
etc.	and so forth
Evac	evacuation
F.A.	field artillery
Fin.	Finance
FL	Florida
Fld	field
G	gun
G.O.	General Order
G.P.F.	Grande Puissance Filloux
GA	Georgia
Gen.	General
G-H	gun, horse drawn
GHQ	General Headquarters
GHQR	General Headquarters Reserve
Gonio	goniological
G-P	gun, portee
Gp.	group
GS	general support
GUTC	General Unit Training Camp
H	howitzer
Haw Div	Hawaiian Division
HB	heavy bridge
HD	Harbor Defenses
HHB	headquarters and headquarters battery
HHC	headquarters and headquarters company
HHD	headquarters and headquarters detachment
HHS	headquarters and headquarters squadron
HHSC	headquarters and headquarters and service company
HHT	headquarters and headquarters troop
HI	Hawaii
HM	heavy maintenance
Hosp.	hospital
Hosp Ctr	hospital center
HQ	headquarters
Hv	heavy
i.e.	that is
I.G.	inspector general
IA	Iowa
ID	Idaho
IL	Illinois
IN	Indiana
Induct.	Induction
Inf.	Infantry
Instr.	Instructor
Intel	intelligence
KKK	Ku Klux Klan
KS	Kansas
KY	Kentucky
LA	Louisiana
Lab	laboratory
LB	light bridge
LM	light maintenance
Lt.	lieutenant
Lt. Col.	lieutenant colonel
Lt. Gen.	lieutenant general
LUTC	Local Unit Training Camp
M. Rep. Bn.	Motor Repair Battalion
M. Rep. Sec	Motor Repair Section
M. Rep.	motor repair
M.C.	Medical Corps
M.P.	military police
M.T. Cmd.	motor transport command
M.T. Co.	motor transport company
M.T.	motor transport
M.T.C.	Motor Transport Corps
MA	Massachusetts
Maint	maintenance
Maj.	major
Maj. Gen.	major general
Man'g	maneuvering
Max-Fac	maxillo-facial
MD	Maryland
ME	Maine
mecz	mechanized
Med.	Medical
Met	meteorology
MG	machine gun
MGM	Metro-Goldwyn Mayer
MI	Michigan
Mil.	Military
Misc	miscellaneous
MN	Minnesota
MO	Missouri
mob.	Mobilization
MR	military reservation
MS	Mississippi
MT	Montana
Mtcyl	motorcycle
mtz	motorized
N.G.	National Guard
NC	North Carolina
NCO	noncommissioned officer
ND	North Dakota
NE	Nebraska
NGI	National Guard Inactive
NGR	National Guard Reserve
NH	New Hampshire
NJ	New Jersey
NM	New Mexico

No.	number
NV	Nevada
NY	New York
NYPOE	New York Port of Embarkation
O.R.	Organized Reserve
Obsn.	observation
Ofc.	Office
OH	Ohio
OK	Oklahoma
Opns	operations
OR	Oregon
ORC	Officers Reserve Corps
Ord.	ordnance
Org.	organization
ORI	Organized Reserve Inactive
OV	overseas
P.M.O.	Provost Marshal Office
P2D	Provisional 2d Division
PA	Pennsylvania
PC Div.	Panama Canal Division
Pers	personnel
PG	Proving Ground
Ph Div.	Philippine Division
PI	Philippine Islands
PID	Provisional Infantry Division
PL	Public Law
Plt.	Platoon
PMS&T	Professor of Military Science and Tactics
POE	port of embarkation
Port	portee
PR	Puerto Rico
Prof Sv	professional services
Prov.	provisional
Purs.	pursuit
Q.M.	quartermaster
Q.M.C.	quartermaster corps
R&I	Reception and Integration
R.A.	Regular Army
R.A.T.C.	Regular Army Training Center
Rad.	radio
RAI	Regular Army Inactive
RAR	Regular Army Reserve
Rcn.	reconnaissance
Rct.	Recruit
Rctg.	Recruiting
Rec'g	receiving
Recep.	Reception
Recr.	Recreation
Regt.	regiment
Repl.	Replacement
Res	reserve
RI	Rhode Island
Rmt	remount
Roent	roentgenology
ROK	Republic of Korea
ROTC	Reserve Officers' Training Corps
RP	Republic of Panama
Rpr	repair
S.C.	Signal Corps
S.R.	sound ranging
S.S.	steam ship
San.	sanitary
SC	South Carolina
SCF	Southern Coastal Frontier
Sch. B&C	School for Bakers and Cooks
Sch.	School
SD	South Dakota
sec	section
Secr	secret
Sect.	sector
Sel	selective
Sep.	separate
SFPOE	San Francisco Port of Embarkation
Sig.	signal
Sp. Tps.	special troops
Sp.	Special
spt.	support
Sq.	squadron
SSD	Selective Service Detachment
Sta.	station
Sup	supply
Sup Dep	supply depot
Surg.	surgeon/surgical
Sv	service
T/O	table of organization
TA	Territory of Alaska
Tact.	Tactical
TH	Territory of Hawaii
Tm	team
TN	Tennessee
Tn.	train
Tng.	Training
Tp.	troop
Tr Mtr	trench mortar
Trans	transportation
Trk	truck
TX	Texas
U.S.A.C.S.	U.S. Army Cable Ship
U.S.A.J.M.P.	U.S. Army Junior Mine Planter
U.S.A.M.P.	U.S. Army Mine Planter
U.S.A.T.	U.S. Army Transport
U.S.A.T.S.	U.S. Army Transport Service
U.S.C.G.C.	U.S. Coast Guard Cutter
U.S.C.G.T.	U.S. Coast Guard Tender
U.S.D.B.	United States Disciplinary Barracks
U.S.L.H.T.	U.S. Light House Tender
U.S.M.C.	United States Marine Corps
U.S.S.	United States Ship
U.S.V.	United States Volunteers
US	United States
USARS	United States Army Regimental System
USN	United States Navy
UT	Utah
V.C.	Veterinary Corps
VA	Virginia
VI	Virgin Islands

VM	Vickers-Maxim
VT	Vermont
WA	Washington
Wag	wagon
WDGMP	War Department General Mobilization Plan
WDGS	War Department General Staff
WI	Wisconsin
WPD	War Plans Division
WV	West Virginia
WX	weather
WY	Wyoming
XC	cross-country
Z.I.	Zone of the Interior

Military Map and Illustration Symbols

These symbols are used in the maps, tables of organization, and other illustrations presented in this *Order of Battle*. They reflect the common symbols in use from 1919 to 1941.

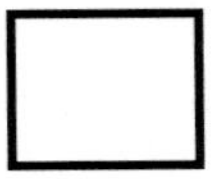	Unit	E	Engineer unit
	Train or motorized unit	ST	Special Troops unit
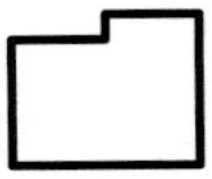	Railway unit		Mine Planter
	Infantry unit	Q	Quartermaster unit
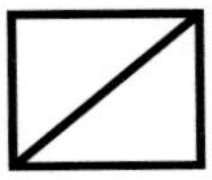	Cavalry unit		Transport unit
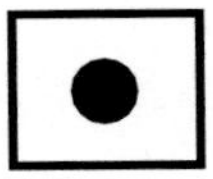	Artillery unit	P	Military Police unit
	Ammunition unit	S	Signal Corps unit
	Tank unit		Ordnance unit
	Air service/air corps unit	G	Chemical Warfare unit
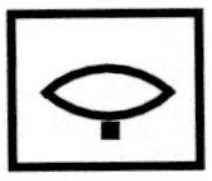	Airship unit	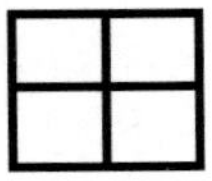	Medical unit
	Balloon unit	V	Veterinary unit

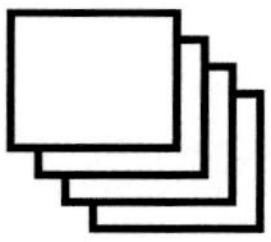	multiple units of the same size and type
	machine gun
	animal drawn
	laboratory
●	squad
●●	detachment/section
●●●	platoon/flight
I	company
II	battalion/squadron
III	regiment/group
X	brigade
XX	division
XXX	corps
XXXX	army
XXXXX	GHQ or army group

Part III

Cavalry Organizations

1919–41

Chapter 12

Cavalry Divisions

USASC Photo, NA II

Elements of the 1st Cavalry Division on maneuver near Toyavale, TX, 1938.

Like the infantry division, in 1919 the Superior Board analyzed the organization of the 1917 cavalry division proposed for employment with the American Expeditionary Force (AEF) in World War I. Only one of these divisions was formed during the war, the 15th Cavalry (Cav.) Division (Div.), and it served along the Mexican border from November 1917 to May 1918 until it was demobilized. A very large division, the 15th consisted of 3 brigades of 3 regiments each, and topped out at over 18,000 officers and men. Considered too large and unwieldy for cavalry operations, the Superior Board rejected the idea of retaining that organization and instead recommended a "square" division consisting of two brigades of two regiments each, plus various division support units. Ultimately, the Army adopted a modified form of this division.

As approved in 1921, the new cavalry division was substantially different from the 15th Cav. Div. The size of the new division was set at 7,463 officers and men, a reduction of over 10,000 troops from the 1917 model. Additionally, the division was to include a battalion-size special troops unit, which included a signal troop, ordnance company, veterinary troop, and the division headquarters (HQ) troop (a tank company would be added in 1927). The table of organization (T/O) also included a field artillery battalion, a division air service, an engineer battalion (mounted), two machine gun squadrons, and a quartermaster train.

Postwar Plans for Cavalry Divisions

The postwar War Plans Division (WPD) mobilization plans called for 12 cavalry divisions. Two of those divisions were allotted the Regular Army (R.A.), four in the National Guard (N.G.), and six in the Organized Reserve (O.R.). For mobilization purposes, each field army was assigned two cavalry divisions.

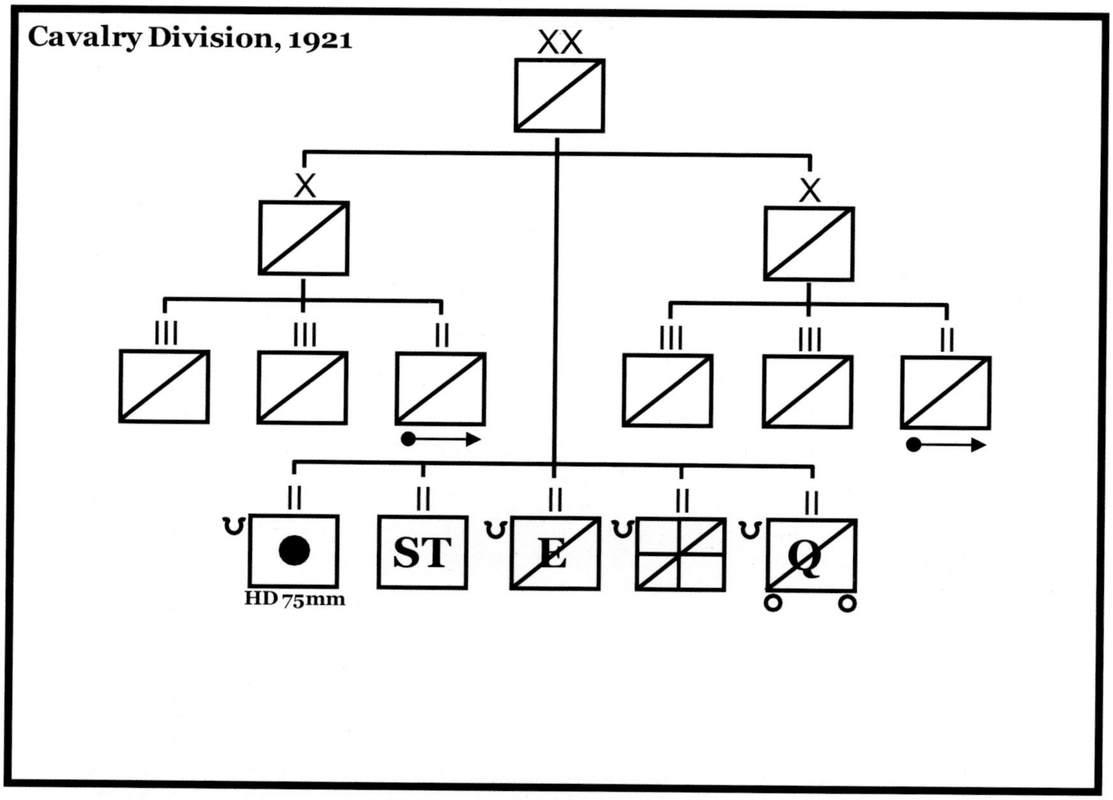

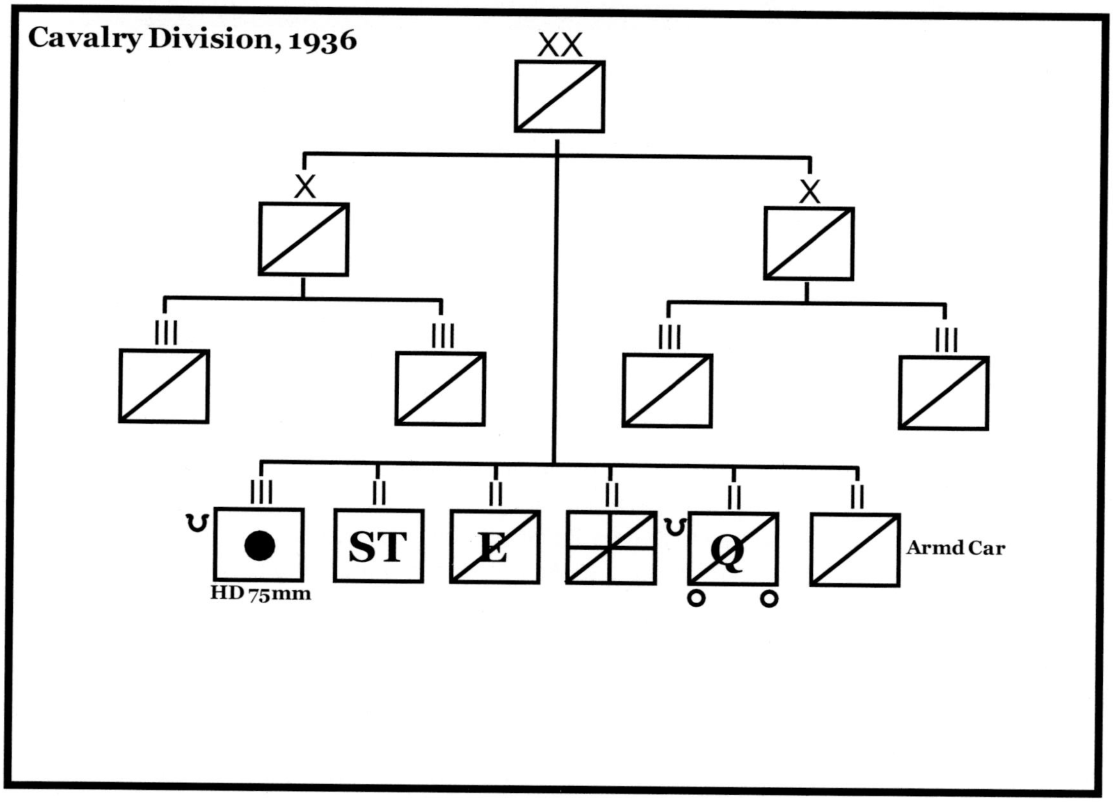

Cavalry Division organization, 1921 and 1936.

Regular Army

Organization

The postwar R.A. cavalry divisions initially consisted of the 1st and 2d Cav. Divs. Due to budget limitations, only the 1st Cav. Div. was fully activated. It was organized in August 1921 at Fort Bliss, TX, where the bulk of the division's were located. One brigade, the 1st Cav. Brigade (Brig.), was deployed in posts along the Mexican border from Camp Harry J. Jones, AZ, to Fort Clark, TX. The brigade was relocated to posts entirely within Texas in 1923. Originally, this brigade consisted of one white cavalry regiment and one black regiment, the 10th Cav. However, under existing War Department policies of the time, units of the two races were not to be brigaded. Thus in 1923, the 10th Cav. was relieved from assignment to the 1st Cav. Div. and the 1st Cav. Regiment (Regt.) was assigned in its stead. The only other change to the division's subordinate regiments in the interwar period was the assignment of the 12th Cav. in early 1933 when the 1st Cav. was relieved and transferred to Fort Knox to form the basis for the 7th Cav. Brig. (Mecz).

The 2d Cav. Div. was not organized in 1921; however, all of its cavalry regiments were already active, as were a number of its other subordinate elements. The mobilization HQ for the division was Fort Riley, KS, where a number of the division's active units were located. Virtually all of the division's inactive elements, less the division HQ itself, were organized with Reserve personnel as Regular Army Inactive (RAI) units in the Seventh Corps Area in 1926 and 1927. Additionally, War Department instructions issued in August 1927 changed a number of regimental assignments and detailed further mobilization requirements for various installation activities in the Seventh Corps Area to provide the division with personnel on mobilization. Though it participated in command post exercises (CPXs) in the 1920s and 1930s as an RAI unit, the division HQ would not be activated until 1941.

Also in August 1927, the Army constituted the 3d Cav. Div. Like the 2d Cav. Div., this division's subordinate regiments were also already active in the R.A. Most of the other subordinate units were soon organized as RAI organizations in the Fourth, Sixth, Seventh, and Eighth Corps Areas (though predominantly in the Seventh). The division was disbanded in 1940.

Training

Given that the 1st Cav. Div. was concentrated in west Texas, it was able to assemble for training easier than most of the other stateside divisions. The first division-level maneuver was conducted in the fall of 1923 near Marfa, TX. The next, however, was not conducted until 4 years later at roughly the same location. The division was able to conduct additional maneuvers on the average of about one every 2 or 3 years from that point on. It also participated in a number of corps area and army CPXs, as well as the large Third Army Maneuvers in the late 1930s and early 1940s.

In the spring of 1929, the division was deployed along the Mexican border in Arizona and New Mexico in response to fighting along the border during the Escobar-Topete Revolution. The division, along with a brigade from the 2d Div., was sent there to protect public and private property and to prevent any of the fighting from spilling over onto US soil. Though not a training event per se, the deployment gave the division staff and subordinate units an opportunity to conduct a short-notice deployment and division-level operations under almost wartime conditions.

Like the 2d Div. for the infantry branch, the 1st Cav. Div. performed the role as the test-bed organization to develop the new cavalry division tables of organization in 1938. Those tests once again validated the square organization of the cavalry division and led to the adoption of only a few changes. These included a special weapons troop and three squadrons of three troops each for the cavalry regiment, but no major changes to the division structure. The strength of the cavalry division, however, was increased to 10,680 officers and men.

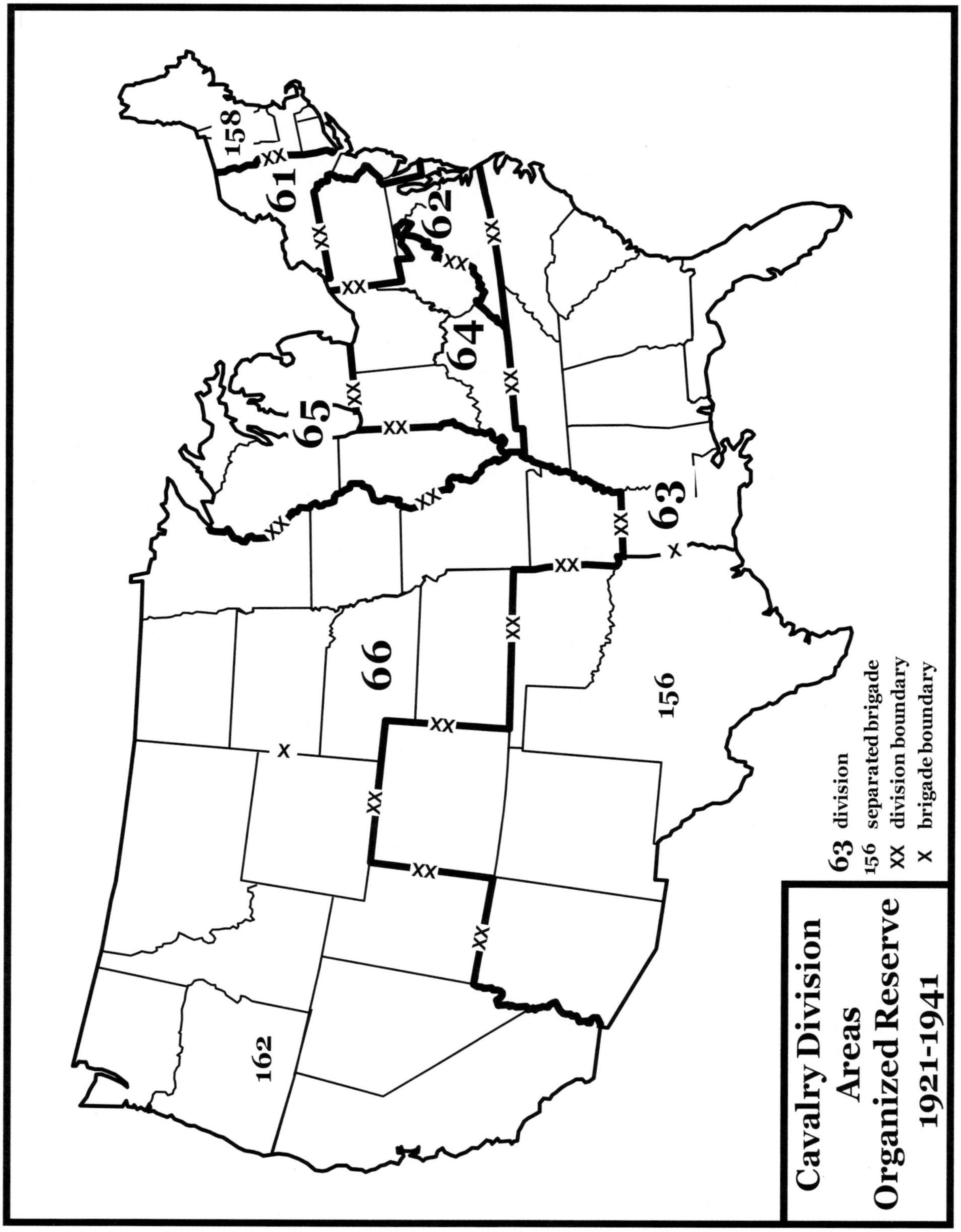

Cavalry Division Areas, Organized Reserve, 1921–41.

National Guard

Organization

The postwar mobilization plans called for four N.G. cavalry divisions, numbered 21 through 24. By the spring of 1921, most of the division subordinate units had been allotted to states and efforts to organize the divisions were soon underway. Under the rules of organization, division HQ could not be federally recognized until at least 75 percent of subordinate units had themselves been federally recognized. That requirement, coupled with a 2-year suspension of the Federal recognition of new units due to shortfalls in the Army's budget, prevented the Federal recognition of the 22d Cav. Div. HQ in Wisconsin until 1925. That status lasted just over 5 years. In 1929, due to further budget cuts, the Secretary of War directed that division-level cavalry HQ would no longer be funded until further notice. As a result, Federal recognition of the 22d Cav. Div. was withdrawn and its HQ was inactivated in June 1930. No other N.G. cavalry division HQ had been organized during this period.

By 1927, the Militia Bureau (soon to be renamed the National Guard Bureau) had determined that the geographically scattered nature of the N.G. cavalry divisions prevented them from being effectively trained. Most infantry divisions belonged to two or three states. Components of the 23d Cav. Div., however, belonged to 11 different states. Even the most concentrated division, the 21st, was composed of units from six different states. The Militia Bureau decided to limit Federal recognition to any new higher-level cavalry HQ to the brigade level (and later to the elimination of the one existing cavalry division HQ). The bureau also devised a plan where each corps area would have one cavalry brigade HQ within its jurisdiction to command and control the existing cavalry units. Therefore, a ninth brigade HQ, the 59th, was constituted and allotted to the state of Massachusetts in the First Corps Area. Massachusetts never organized the HQ, so it was reallotted to New Jersey in 1937 and quickly organized.

In 1935, the War Department reauthorized the formation of Guard cavalry division HQ. The following January, the HQ of the 24th Cav. Div., the most geographically dispersed of all N.G. divisions, was federally recognized at Topeka, KS. Though this division was the most geographically separated, it was also the division that had suffered the least from the various reorganizations, unit changes, and state allotments to its subordinate units. It was essentially the same organization as originally allotted in 1921, less the T/O changes that all the divisions experienced. Due to the failure of the various states involved in the remaining three divisions to agree on the final allotment of units and staff positions, the next division HQ was not federally recognized until 1939. By July 1940, all three of the remaining cavalry divisions were federally recognized, but their existence was short-lived. On 1 November, all four were disbanded when the WPD determined that large numbers of horse cavalry were not needed for future conflicts.

Training

Until 1936, the training of N.G. cavalry divisions was focused on brigade level and lower. Though the staff of the 22d Cav. Div. conducted its training at Camp Douglas, WI, from 1925 to 1929, the remainder of the division was not assembled there for the training and those subordinate units that were at Camp Douglas conducted their own camps separate from the division HQ.

Not until 1936 was a N.G. cavalry division able to assemble its staff at a camp for training with subordinate units. During that summer, the new 24th Cav. Div. assembled its entire HQ at Camp Guernsey, WY, for training with the 115th Cav. Each year thereafter until 1940, the HQ assembled at the camp of one its subordinate regiments or brigades for the purposes of training its staff and HQ personnel on division-level wartime tasks.

In September 1936, several states that composed the 23d Cav. Div. sent officers from subordinate units to Camp Bullis, TX, to participate in the Third Army CPX being held there. Brigadier (Brig.) General

(Gen.) Louis S. Davidson, the commander of the Texas 56th Cav. Brig. acted as the division commander, and the remaining officers provisionally formed the division staff and HQ for the CPX.

In March 1940, the division commanders and staffs of the 22d, 23d, and 24th Cav. Divs. each traveled to Fort Bliss, TX, for 4 days of training with the division commander and staff of the 1st Cav. Div. The training was designed to prepare these commands for their respective field army maneuvers coming up that summer. Though none of the divisions were able to fully assemble all of their subordinate units for the training, each was able to assemble enough to make a viable cavalry force for their respective maneuvers. The 1940 maneuvers were the last hurrah for the N.G. cavalry divisions. They were all disbanded by October 1940.

Organized Reserve

Organization

In developing the structure for the postwar Army, the WPD planned for six divisions of O.R. cavalry. These consisted of the 61st through 66th Cav. Divs. These divisions were assigned to the Fourth, Fifth, and Sixth Armies for mobilization. Like N.G. divisions, most of the O.R. units were scattered across numerous states. The one exception was the 61st Cav. Div., which was located wholly within New York with the exception of one regiment in New Jersey. Once the allotment was complete and a local board of officers determined the location of the division HQ as well as the division's subordinate elements, organization of the divisions began. A small R.A. staff was assigned to each division HQ. These staffs advertised the organization of their respective divisions in local papers, radio spots, and other means. The staff, which had been provided a list of names and addresses of former and current Officer Reserve Corps (ORC) and National Army officers, also began contacting and recruiting these men for the new divisions until they were organized.

As with the infantry divisions, a corps area commander typically functioned as the commanding general for O.R. cavalry divisions. These duties were generally administrative in nature, but even then, the vast majority of the divisions' training and administration was supervised by each division's R.A. chief of staff. In many cases, the chief of staff also functioned as the acting division commander for CPXs and other training exercises, though at times one of the O.R. brigadier generals assigned to the 61st and 65th Cav. Divs. would function as such.

In general, O.R. cavalry divisions and regiments were provided for in the same manner as infantry organizations. However, the 156th, 158th, and 162d Cav. Brigs., each located in different corps areas than their parent divisions, possessed a small R.A. staff at the brigade level, which infantry divisional brigades did not have. The cavalry staffs were typically organized as follows:

Division Staff:

Chief of Staff	colonel
Adjutant General/G1	lieutenant colonel
Assistant Chief of Staff, General Staff G3	lieutenant colonel
Assistant Chief of Staff, General Staff G3	major
Assistant Chief of Staff, G4	lieutenant colonel
Senior NCO	staff sergeant
Administrative Sergeant	sergeant
Supply NCO	sergeant
Enlisted clerk	corporal
Enlisted clerk/driver	private

Geographically Separated Brigade:

Chief of Staff	colonel
Adjutant General/S1	major

Assistant Chief of Staff, S3	lieutenant colonel
Enlisted clerk/driver	sergeant

Regiment:

Executive officer*	lieutenant colonel
Enlisted clerk/driver	sergeant

*Redesignated "unit instructor" in 1926.

Note: Ranks shown are highest authorized. Actual assigned personnel frequently held ranks lower, and sometimes higher, than those shown.

Unlike their R.A. and N.G. counterparts, the organization of Reserve division HQ and all the division's subordinate units was generally achieved by the end of 1922. Of course, for Reserve divisions all this really meant was that the unit was organized by the initial assignment of personnel. Most divisional subordinate organizations achieved somewhere near full strength in authorized officers by the mid-1920s and by then were considered functional units. Organizationally, the Reserve divisions went through the same interwar reorganizations as those in the other two components. Other than that, the composition of Reserve division subordinate units was constant from 1921 to 1941.

Training

The training of O.R. divisions posed a much greater challenge than those of the R.A. or N.G. due to the lack of equipment, horses, enlisted personnel, and funding. In any given year, for example, the War Department had only enough funds to send about 25 percent of O.R. personnel to summer camps. Still, the Reserve division staffs made the effort to conduct some level of adequate training for staffs and subordinate units at the camps and during the Inactive Training Period.

Like their infantry division counterparts, Reserve cavalry division staffs began to attend camps as a unit after 1924. In most cases, however, Reserve division staffs were only able to assemble at a summer camp about once every 4 or 5 years. When one did, the HQ most often participated in CPXs for training. During those years that the HQ did not go to camp as a unit, individual staff officers were trained in one of several ways for annual training. The most preferred was assignment to a R.A. or N.G. division staff during that unit's own summer training period. Another method was for staff officers to be ordered to duty during other times of the year to work on a R.A. division staff while in garrison, a corps area staff, or at times even the Reserve division's own Active Duty staff.

Organization (T/O)

The first significant modification to the cavalry division T/O after 1921 was the consolidation of the ambulance company and the veterinary troops into a medical squadron in 1925. A new T/O issued in 1928 dictated further major changes. This T/O eliminated the machine gun squadron in each brigade and returned one machine gun troop to each regiment. It also added an armored car squadron and a division air service consisting of a HQ and an observation squadron. The mounted engineer battalion was motorized and redesignated as an engineer squadron. The field artillery battalion was expanded to form a regiment, and a tank company was added to the special troops. Additionally, the strength of the new division was increased to 9,595 officers and men. An additional change came in 1936 when the quartermaster train was largely motorized and redesignated as a quartermaster squadron.

The final prewar revision to the cavalry division was defined in a new division T/O issued in November 1940. A summary of the changes consisted of the addition of a weapons troop to the brigade, the reorganization and redesignation of the armored car squadron as a reconnaissance squadron, the elimination of the tank company and the addition of a divisional antitank troop, the elimination of the special troops HQ, and the reorganization of the field artillery regiment to consist of two horse-drawn 75-mm pack howitzer battalions and one truck-drawn 105-mm howitzer battalion. The reorganized division now consisted of 11,676 officers and men.

1928 Cavalry Division table of organization and equipment.

Cavalry Division T/O: 401W Approved: 1 July 1928 Units:	Division Headquarters	Special Troops	Cavalry Brigades (2)	Separate Battalion, Horse Artillery	Engineer Battalion (Mounted)	Division Air Service	Armored Car Squadron (added 1929)	Medical Squadron	Quartermaster Train	Total	Medical Dept. Det. (attached)	Chaplains (attached)	Aggregate
Officers	25	15	150	20	15	32	18	10	6	291	27	7	325
Warrant Officers	--	--	4	--	--	--	--	--	--	4	--	--	4
Enlisted	--	376	2918	500	330	152	260	162	221	4,919	130	--	5049
Aggregate	25	391	3,072	520	345	184	278	172	227	5,214	157	7	5,378
Equipment													
Horses	--	185	3,338	640	310	--	--	122	15	4,610	127	--	4,737
Mules, draft	--	16	256	85	120	--	--	54	525	1,056	32	--	1,088
Airplane	--	--	--	--	--	13	--	--	--	13	--	--	13
Ambulance, animal-drawn	--	--	--	--	--	--	--	6	--	6	--	--	6
Ambulance, motor	--	--	--	--	--	--	--	6	--	6	1	--	7
Aparejos	--	--	--	--	--	--	--	--	200	200	--	--	200
Car, armored	--	--	--	--	--	--	36	--	--	36	--	--	36
Car, motor, cross-country	--	5	18	--	--	--	14	--	--	37	--	--	37
Car, motor, 7-passenger	--	1	--	--	--	--	--	--	--	1	--	--	1
Car, motor, 5-passenger	--	6	2	--	1	2	--	--	2	13	--	--	13
Cart and reel	--	--	--	1	--	--	--	--	--	1	--	--	1
Cart, reel, battery	--	--	--	3	--	--		--	--	3	--	--	3
Cart, wire	--	3	2	--	--	--		--	--	5	--	--	5
Motorcycle, solo	--	--	--	--	--	--	--	--	1	1	--	--	1
Motorcycle, with side car	--	9	--	2	8	8	--	5	2	34	10	--	44
Tank, fighting, light	--	24	--	--	--	--		--	--	24	--	--	24
Tractors, 5-ton	--	1	--	--	--	--	--	--	1	2	--	--	2
Trailer, cargo, 1½ -ton	--	--	--	--	--	5	--	--	--	5	--	--	5
Trailer, kitchen	--	2	--	--	--	1	--	--	1	4	--	--	4
Trailer, photographic, 5-ton	--	--	--	--	--	2	--	--	--	2	--	--	2
Trailer, stockroom, 4-ton	--	--	--	--	--	--		--	1	1	--	--	1
Trailer, tank, 1½ -ton	--	--	--	--	--	2	--	--	--	2	--	--	2
Trailer, tank, water, 300-gallon	--	1	--	--	--	--	--	--	--	1	--	--	1
Trailer, tire press, 5-ton	--	--	--	--	--	--	--	--	1	1	--	--	1
Truck, artillery, repair	--	1	--	--	--	--	--	--	--	1	--	--	1
Truck, cargo, ¾-ton	--	11	--	--	--	--	--	--	3	14	--	--	14
Truck, cargo, 1½-ton	--	16	16	--	--	12	--	7	28	79	--	--	79
Truck, cargo, 3-ton	--	3	--	--	--	--	9	--	1	10	--	--	10
Truck, radio, Air Service	--	--	--	--	--	1	--	--	--	1	--	--	1
Truck, field lighting	--	--	--	--	--	1	--	--	--	1	--	--	1
Truck, light repair	--	2	--	--	--	--	1	--	--	3	--	--	3
Truck, machine shop, 3–5-ton	--	--	--	--	--	1	--	--	1	2	--	--	2
Truck, photographic	--	--	--	--	--	2	--	--	--	2	--	--	2
Truck, radio, repair	--	--	--	--	--	1	--	--	--	1	--	--	1
Truck, radio	--	--	2	--	--	--	--	--	--	2	--	--	2
Truck, tank, gas, ¾-ton	--	--	--	--	--	3	3	--	--	6	--	--	6
Truck, tank, water, ¾-ton	--	--	--	--	--	1	--	--	--	1	--	--	1
Truck, small arms repair	--	3	--	--	--	--	--	--	--	3	--	--	3
Truck, tank, 3–5-ton	--	--	--	--	--	3	--	--	--	3	--	--	3
Truck, tank, 750-gallon	--	1	--	--	--	--	--	--	3	4	--	--	4
Truck, tank, gas	--	--	--	--	--	--	?	--	--	?	--	--	?
Truck, water tank, 300-gallon	--	1	--	--	--	--	--	--	--	1	--	--	1
Truck, w/reinf springs, 5½-ton	--	24	--	--	--	--		--	--	24	--	--	24
Truck, wrecking	--	--	--	--	--	--	--	--	1	1	--	--	1
Wagon, battery	--	--	--	4	--	--	--	--	--	4	--	--	4

1928 Cavalry Division table of organization and equipment (Cont.)

Wagon, escort	--	3	64	17	9	--	--	6	62	161	7	--	168
Wagon, medical	--	--	--	--	--	--	--	--	--	--	1	--	1
Wagon, spring	--	2	26	4	4	--	--	3	--	39	--	--	39
Wagon, store	--	--	--	4	--	--	--	--	--	4	--	--	4
Wagon, tool	--	--	--	--	13	--	--	--	--	13	--	--	13
Bolo	--	--	64	--	--	--	--	--	--	64	--	--	64
Caisson, 75-mm	--	--	--	24	--	--	--	--	--	24	--	--	24
Gun, 37-mm	--	10	--	--	--	--	--	--	--	10	--	--	10
Gun, 75-mm	--	--	--	24	--	--	--	--	--	24	--	--	24
Machine-gun, .30 cal.	--	14	40	--	--	--	36	--	--	80	--	--	80
Machine-gun, anti-aircraft	--	--	--	7	--	3	--	--	--	10	--	--	10
Machine-gun, flexible	--	--	--	--	--	26	--	--	--	26	--	--	26
Machine-gun, synchronized	--	--	--	--	--	26	--	--	--	26	--	--	26
Pistol	25	391	3,072	520	82	184	276	--	94	4,644	--	--	4,644
Rifle	--	125	2,124	--	263	--	80	--	133	2,725	--	--	2,275
Rifle, automatic	--	--	--	--	6	--	--	--	--	6	--	--	6
Rifle, machine	--	--	96	--	--	--	--	--	--	96	--	--	96
Saber	9	13	1,720	--	--	--	--	--	--	1,742	--	--	1,742
Submachine gun	--	--	--	--	--	--	36	--	--	36	--	--	36

1st CAVALRY DIVISION

HQ—Fort Bliss, TX, 1921–41

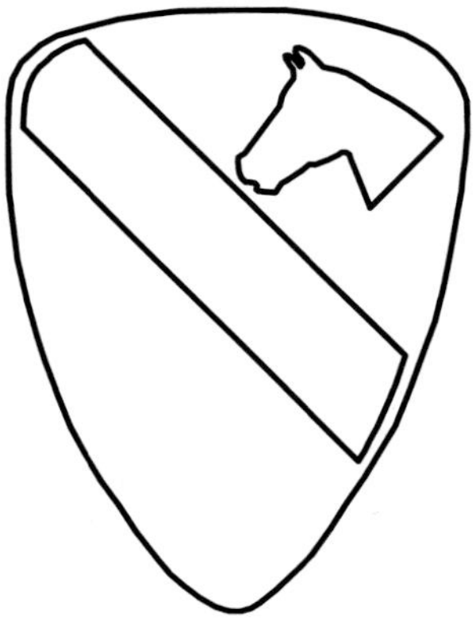

The 1st Cav. Div. was constituted in the R.A. on 20 August 1921 and activated at Fort Bliss, TX, on 13 September 1921. The division was allotted to the Eighth Corps Area and assigned to the Third Army. The division was formed around the remnants of the World War I-era 15th Cav. Div., which had been formed initially to protect the border with Mexico and was to deploy to France as the AEF cavalry force, but was disbanded in 1918 because not enough shipping was available to transport it to Europe. Unlike most other stateside divisions, the 1st Cav. Div. had an actual peacetime military mission to patrol the turbulent Mexican border and prevent incursions similar to Pancho Villa's raid on Columbus, NM, in 1916. The division's units manned posts that stretched along the Rio Grande River from Fort Bliss at El Paso to Fort Brown at Brownsville. In the early 1920s, the division garrisoned a series of platoon- and troop-size border camps from which regular patrols were dispatched to intercept bandits crossing the river to raid for cattle. By 1925, however, most of these camps were dismantled and the patrols were then conducted from the main garrisons, but less frequently as World War II approached. When not engaged in actual patrols, the 1st Cav. Div. engaged in periodic brigade- and division-level maneuvers. The first division maneuver was conducted in the early fall of 1923 near Marfa, TX. That exercise was the largest gathering of cavalry in the United States since the Civil War. Due to budget constraints, the division did not deploy its entire strength to the field again until 1927 when Marfa was again the site selected for the maneuvers. The 1929 exercise was slated for April, but was postponed due to the troubles caused by the Escobar-Topete Revolution. To ensure that US borders were secure, the entire division was deployed to border patrol camps with the bulk of the division joining the 10th Cav., 25th Inf., and elements of the 2d Div. manning posts in Arizona and New Mexico. During a fire fight between rebels and Mexican Army troops, which occurred across the border from Naco, AZ, Maj. Gen. George Van Horn Moseley, the division commander, crossed the border under fire and warned the Mexican commander to cease small-arms fire across the border into the United States or be prepared for retaliation from the 1st Cav. Div. The warning was heeded and the US troops remained disinterested and undisturbed bystanders during the remainder of the fight. The revolution was short-lived, and all units were back at home stations by the end of May. The maneuvers scheduled for April were conducted in October near Fillmore Pass, NM. Maneuvers were held near the Hueco Mountains in 1931 and 1932, but the depression and the management of Civilian Conservation Corps (CCC) camps prevented the possibility of division exercises in 1933 and for the next 2 years. The 1st Cav. Div. was given responsibility for the construction and operation of the Arizona–New Mexico CCC District. Though not a military program, the CCC camps were conducted in a loose military manner and gave hundreds of thousands of young men a taste of army life while performing work in the nation's forests. At its height, the 1st Cav. Div. was responsible for 62,500 of these young men. The next division maneuvers were held in April 1936, once again near Marfa, and again in May 1938, near Balmorhea, TX. The Balmorhea exercise was closely followed by the August 1938 Third Army Maneuver. For the Third Army Maneuver, the 1st Cav. Div. did not operate as a full division due to the lack of funds needed to concentrate it. Instead, the elements at Fort Bliss were opposed by the New Mexico N.G.'s 111th Cav. near the Ora Grande Mountains in New Mexico, while the 1st Cav. Brig. supported the VIII Corps' attacks against the 36th Div. at Camp Bullis, TX. The 1939 division maneuvers were conducted at Balmorhea against the 9th Inf. Regt. from Fort Sam Houston. For the August 1940 Third Army Maneuvers, the 1st Cav. Div. traveled to the Kisatchie National Forest in Louisiana. In that exercise, the division was the "eyes and ears" of the VIII Corps and operated against the newly formed 23d Cav. Div. After returning to home stations, the 1st Cav. Div. was relieved of the border posts by the Texas N.G.'s 56th Cav. Brig. and assembled at Fort Bliss in February 1941 for further training. After conducting a series of exercises, the division was sent again to Louisiana to participate in the 1941 Louisiana Maneuvers in August and September. The last exercise pitted the Second and Third Armies against one another. In the culminating battles, the 1st Cav. Div. successfully conducted a night crossing of the Sabine River and captured the Second Army fuel depot at Zwolle, LA, thereby preventing the refueling of Maj. Gen. George S. Patton's tanks and ensuring victory for the Third Army. After the maneuver, the division returned to its home station at Fort Bliss. Location 7 December 1941—Fort Bliss, TX.

Status: Active at Fort Hood, TX, as the 1st Cav. Div. Though the division retains the traditional title of "cavalry," it is an armored division.

Events: 30, 65, 80, 83, 97, 127, 146, 175, 206, 217, 250, 259, 284, 295, 296, 300, 315, 328

Division Commanders

Maj. Gen. Robert L. Howze	13 September 1921–7 June 1925
Brig. Gen. Joseph C. Castner	8 June 1925–29 March 1926
Brig. Gen. Edwin B. Winans	3 April 1926–19 October 1927
Brig. Gen. Samuel D. Rockenbach	19 October 1927–26 October 1927
Maj. Gen. George Van Horn Moseley	26 October 1927–29 August 1929
Brig. Gen. Charles J. Symmonds	29 September 1929–3 October 1930
Brig. Gen. George C. Barnhardt	3 October 1930–9 December 1930
Brig. Gen. Walter C. Short	9 December 1930–21 December 1930
Brig. Gen. Ewing E. Booth	21 December 1930–7 March 1932
Brig. Gen. Walter C. Short	7 March 1932–17 March 1933
Maj. Gen. Frank R. McCoy	17 March 1933–26 September 1933
Brig. Gen. Walter C. Short	26 September 1933–2 April 1934
Brig. Gen. Hamilton S. Hawkins	2 April 1934–6 July 1936
Brig. Gen. Ben Lear	6 July 1936–4 September 1936
Brig. Gen. Francis Le J. Parker	4 September 1936–1 October 1936
Maj. Gen. Ben Lear	1 October 1936–21 November 1938
Maj. Gen. Kenyon A. Joyce	21 November 1938–October 1940
Maj. Gen. Robert C. Richardson Jr.	November 1940–April 1941
Maj. Gen. Innis Palmer Swift	April 1941–August 1944

1st CAVALRY DIVISION
Organization 1921

UNIT:	LOCATION:
HQ	Fort Bliss, TX
HQ, Sp. Tps.	Fort Bliss, TX
HQ Troop	Fort Bliss, TX
1st Sig. Troop	Fort Bliss, TX
27th Ord. Co. (M)	Fort Bliss, TX
Vet. Co. No. 15	Fort Bliss, TX
1st Cav. Brig.	Camp Harry J. Jones, AZ
1st Cav. Regt.	Camp Harry J. Jones, AZ
10th Cav. Regt.	Fort Huachuca, AZ
1st MG Sq.	Camp Harry J. Jones, AZ
2d Cav. Brig.	Fort Bliss, TX
7th Cav. Regt.	Fort Bliss, TX
8th Cav. Regt.	Fort Bliss, TX
2d MG Sq.	Fort Bliss, TX
82d F.A. Bn. (Horse)	Fort Bliss, TX
8th Engr. Bn. (Mounted)	Fort Bliss, TX
Amb. Co. No. 43	Fort Bliss, TX
1st Cav. Div. Train, Q.M.C.	Fort Bliss, TX

1st CAVALRY DIVISION
Organization 1940

UNIT:	LOCATION:
HQ	Fort Bliss, TX
HQ, Sp. Tps.	Fort Bliss, TX
HQ Troop	Fort Bliss, TX
1st Sig. Troop	Fort Bliss, TX
27th Ord. Co. (M)	Fort Bliss, TX
10th Tank Co. (L)**	Fort Bliss, TX
1st Cav. Brig.	Fort Clark, TX
5th Cav. Regt.	Fort Clark, TX
12th Cav. Regt.	Fort Brown, TX
2d Cav. Brig.	Fort Bliss, TX
7th Cav. Regt.	Fort Bliss, TX
8th Cav. Regt.	Fort Bliss, TX
1st Rcn. Sq.	Fort Bliss, TX
82d F.A. Regt.	Fort Bliss, TX
8th Engr. Sq.	Fort McIntosh, TX
1st Med. Sq.	Fort Bliss, TX
16th Q.M. Sq.	Fort Bliss, TX

**Indicates unit was organized with O.R. personnel as an RAI unit.

2d CAVALRY DIVISION

HQ—*Not organized,* 1921–41; Fort Riley, KS, 1941

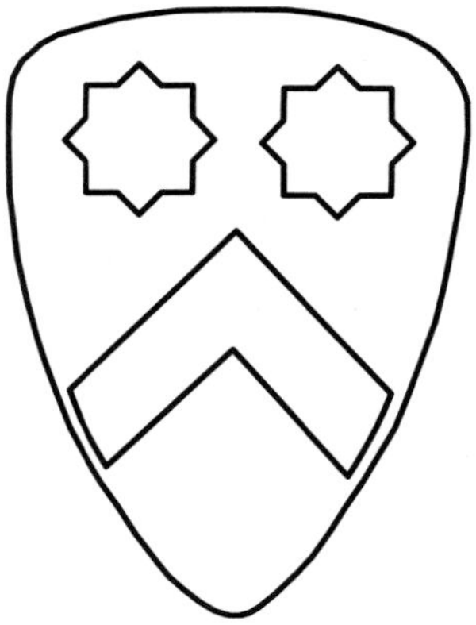

The 2d Cav. Div. was constituted in the R.A. on 20 August 1921, allotted to the Seventh Corps Area, and assigned to the Second Army. Though not activated until 1 April 1941, many of the units of the division were active from 1921 to 1940, and many others were active in the O.R. as RAI units. The active elements of the division in the 1920s and 1930s consisted mainly of the cavalry regiments; Troop A, 9th Engrs.; the various artillery units assigned during the period; and elements of the quartermaster train (later the 17th Q.M. Sq.). The division's designated mobilization station was Fort Riley, KS, where many of the units were concentrated in the 1920s and 1930s, and where they conducted their annual summer training. On 15 August 1927, under special instructions from the War Department, the division was reorganized to consist of the 2d, 4th, 12th, and 14th Cav. Regts., the 4th F.A. Bn., and the 16th Obsn. Sq. Other active elements assigned were the 14th Ord. Co., and the 5th, 6th, and 7th Pack Trains. The division Headquarters and Headquarters Troop (HHT), 3d and 4th Cav. Brig. HHTs, 2d Signal Troop, and 8th Pack Train were to be formed from unit and post support personnel at Fort Riley. The quartermaster (Q.M.) train HQ, 27th and 28th Wagon Cos., and the 2d Med. Sq. were to be formed from post support personnel at Fort Leavenworth. The rest of the units were to be activated from existing units at Fort Riley and RAI units in the O.R. After RAI units were authorized to be manned by Reserve personnel in 1926, units of the 2d Cav. Div. began to be organized in the Seventh Corps Area with most being concentrated in the Kansas City area. The 3d and 4th MG Sqs. (which were to be formed from cadre from the 2d MG Troop at Fort Riley), division special troops, and later, the inactive elements of the 2d Armd Car Sq. were all organized with reservists in Kansas City. These units conducted their summer training at Fort Riley, and therefore had a relatively close association with the division units located there. Thus, in the event of mobilization, the 2d Cav. Div. was most likely to be the first inactive division to be able to completely mobilize. Like many of the inactive R.A. divisions, the 2d Cav. Div. HQ was organized provisionally from time to time for CPXs, particularly those involving the exercises of the I Cav. Corps. As part of the general buildup of the US Army prior to World War II, the War Department directed the activation of the division at Fort Riley in the fall of 1940, where the majority of the division's active units were already concentrated. The first major element activated was the 3d Cav. Brig. on 15 October 1940, followed by the 4th Cav. Brig. (Colored) on 21 February 1941, and the division HQ on 1 April 1941. After conducting a series of premaneuver exercises, the division was sent to Louisiana to participate in the 1941 Louisiana Maneuvers in August and September. The last exercise of the maneuver pitted the Second Army against the Third Army. The major cavalry battle of the maneuver pitted the 2d Cav. Div. against the 1st Cav. Div. in the vicinity of East Texas and near Zwolle, LA. The division returned to Fort Riley in October 1941. Location 7 December 1941—Fort Riley, KS.

Status: Inactive in the R.A. as the 2d Cav. Div.

Events: 264, 328

Division Commanders

Col. Bruce Palmer*	1 October 1933–1 July 1935	*No C.G. designated*	1 July 1937–1 April 1941
Col. Charles F. Martin*	1 July 1935–1 July 1936	Brig. Gen. Terry de la Mesa Allen	1 April 1941–12 June 1941
Col. Albert E. Phillips*	1 July 1936–1 July 1937	Maj. Gen. John Millikin	12 June 1941–July 1942

*Designated C.G. for mobilization purposes.

2d CAVALRY DIVISION
Organization 1925

UNIT:	LOCATION:
HQ	*A.A.-6th Cav. Regt.*
HQ, Sp. Tps.	*A.A.-6th Cav. Regt.*
HQ Troop	*A.A.-6th Cav. Regt.*
2d Sig. Troop	*Eighth Corps Area*
13th Ord. Co. (M)	*A.A.-27th Ord Co.*
Veterinary Co. No. 16	*A.A.-Surgeon General*
3d Cav. Brig.	*A.A.-6th Cav Regt*
4th Cav. Regt.	Fort DA Russell, WY
10th Cav. Regt.	Fort Huachuca, AZ
3d MG Sq.	*A.A.-1st MG Sq.*
4th Cav. Brig.	*A.A.-6th Cav. Regt.*
12th Cav. Regt.	Fort Brown, TX
13th Cav. Regt.	Fort DA Russell, WY
4th MG Sq.	*A.A.-2d MG Sq.*
84th F.A. Bn. (Horse)	*A.A.-82d FA Bn.*
9th Engr. Bn. (Mounted)*	Fort Riley, KS
Amb. Co. No. 46	*A.A.-Surgeon General*
2d Cav. Div. Train, Q.M.C.	*A.A.-Q.M. General*

2d CAVALRY DIVISION
Organization 1940

UNIT:	LOCATION:
*HQ****	*Kansas City, KS*
HQ, Sp. Tps.**	Kansas City, KS
HQ Troop**	Kansas City, KS
2d Sig. Troop**	Des Moines, IA
14th Ord. Co. (M)	Fort Riley, KS
3d Cav. Brig.	Fort Riley, KS
2d Cav. Regt.	Fort Riley, KS
14th Cav. Regt.	Fort Riley, KS
4th Cav. Brig. (C)**	Des Moines, IA
9th Cav. Regt. (C)	Fort Riley, KS
10th Cav. Regt. (C)	Fort Leavenworth, KS
2d Rcn. Sq.**	Des Moines, IA
3d F.A. Regt.*	Fort Riley, KS
9th Engr. Sq.*	Fort Riley, KS
2d Med. Sq.**	Kansas City, KS
17th Q.M. Sq.**	Fort Riley, KS

*Indicates unit was partially inactive. HQ location shown was mobilization location.
**Indicates unit was organized with O.R. personnel as an RAI unit.
***Indicates unit was not organized. HQ location shown was mobilization location.

3d CAVALRY DIVISION

HQ—*Not organized,* 1927–40

The 3d Cav. Div. was constituted in the R.A. on 15 August 1927; allotted to the Fourth, Sixth, Seventh, and Eighth Corps Areas; and assigned to the Second Army. The division was reassigned to the General Headquarters Reserve (GHQR) as a result of the US Army reorganization of 1933. The 3d Cav. Div.'s designated mobilization station was Fort Des Moines, IA, where many of the division's units were organized with Reserve officers as RAI units and where most of them conducted their annual summer training camps. The 3d Cav. Div. consisted largely of RAI units though many of the units of the division were active during the period 1921–40. Unlike the 2d Cav. Div., the division's active units were not concentrated in one or two areas, but were spread from coast to coast. The active elements of the division in the 1920s and 1930s consisted only of the cavalry regiments; the remainder of the units were to be activated from RAI units in the O.R. Like the 2d Cav. Div., however, RAI units of the 3d Cav. Div. were predominantly located in the Seventh Corps Area with most being initially concentrated in the Kansas City area. These units conducted their summer training at Fort Riley and were under the peacetime control of the HQ, 66th Cav. Div. for administrative and training purposes. In 1933, several of the division's RAI units were transferred to the Third Corps Area, but by the late 1930s, most of the division's RAI units were relocated to Des Moines, IA.

Status: Disbanded 10 October 1940.

Division Commanders

Col. E. Kearsley Sterling*	1 October 1933–1 July 1935
Col. Edward M. Offley*	1 July 1935–1 July 1936
Col. Charles R. Mayo*	1 July 1936–1 July 1937
No C.G. designated	1 July 1937–10 October 1940

*Designated C.G. for mobilization purposes.

3d CAVALRY DIVISION
Organization 1928

UNIT:	LOCATION:
*HQ****	*Seventh Corps Area*
HQ, Sp. Tps.**	Kansas City, KS
HQ Tp.**	Kansas City, KS
3d Sig. Tp.	*Seventh Corps Area*
16th Ord. Co. (M)	*Fourth Corps Area*
13th Tank Co.**	Oshkosh, WI
5th Cav. Brig.**	Kansas City, KS
10th Cav. Regt. (C)	Fort Huachuca, AZ
11th Cav. Regt.	Presidio of Monterey, CA
5th MG Sq.**	Kansas City, MO
6th Cav. Brig.**	Kansas City, KS
3d Cav. Regt.	Fort Myer, VA
6th Cav. Regt.	Fort Oglethorpe, GA
6th MG Sq.**	Kansas City, MO
84th F.A. Bn. (Horse)**	Fort Collins, CO
12th Engr. Bn. (Mounted) **	Chicago, IL
3d Medical Sq.**	St. Louis, MO
*3d Cav. Div. Train, Q.M.C.****	*Seventh Corps Area*
*44th Obsn. Sq. ****	*Seventh Corps Area*

3d CAVALRY DIVISION
Organization 1939

UNIT:	LOCATION:
*HQ****	*Seventh Corps Area*
HQ, Sp. Tps.**	Des Moines, IA
HQ Tp.**	Des Moines, IA
3d Sig. Tp.**	Des Moines, IA
16th Ord. Co. (M)**	Little Rock, AR
13th Tank Co.**	St. Louis, MO
5th Cav. Brig.**	Des Moines, IA
9th Cav. Regt. (C)	Fort Riley, KS
10th Cav. Regt. (C)	Fort Leavenworth, KS
6th Cav. Brig.**	Des Moines, IA
3d Cav. Regt.	Fort Myer, VA
6th Cav. Regt.	Fort Oglethorpe, GA
3d Rcn. Sq.**	Des Moines, IA
84th F.A. Regt.**	Fort Riley, KS
12th Engr. Sq.**	Kansas City, KS
3d Medical Sq.**	Des Moines, IA
18th Q.M. Sq.**	St. Louis, MO

*Indicates unit was partially inactive. HQ location shown was mobilization location.
**Indicates unit was organized with O.R. personnel as an RAI unit.
***Indicates unit was not organized. HQ location shown was mobilization location.

21st CAVALRY DIVISION

New York, Pennsylvania, New Jersey, Rhode Island, Massachusetts, and Virginia National Guard

HQ—*Not organized,* 1921–40; Manhattan, NY, 1940

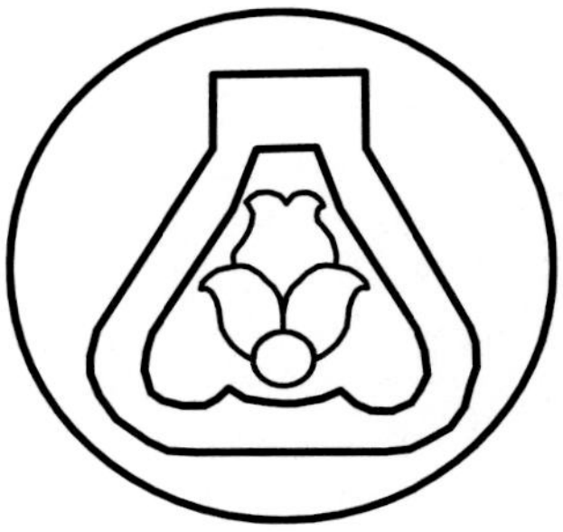

The 21st Cav. Div. was constituted in 1921; originally allotted to the states of New York, Pennsylvania, New Jersey, and Virginia; and assigned to the First Army. From 1922 to 1938, the division's subordinate units generally held separate summer camps at locations within their respective states: the 51st Cav. Brig. at Pine Camp, NY, for New York units; the 102d Cav. at Sea Girt, NJ; the 52d Cav. Brig. at Mount Gretna, PA, 1921–35 and Indiantown Gap, 1936–40. The 52d held its first full brigade camp in 1923, during which the Pennsylvania Cavalrymen held a brigade review for Gen. John J. Pershing. The 51st held its first full brigade camp in June 1928 when the 121st Cav. participated for the first time. Staggered camps were the rule of thumb for both brigades. This meant that one regiment would be followed immediately by the second so that the horses of both regiments could be pooled to mount an entire regiment. In that period of tight budgets, N.G. cavalry troops were authorized only half the number of horses (32) than that of men (about 65) per troop. The brigade HQ would arrive for the last week of the first regiment, and remain for the first week of the second regiment. This allowed the brigade commander and his staff to work with both regiments to discern strengths and weaknesses of his units. In March 1925, plans were developed to assemble the entire 21st Cav. Div. at Sea Girt for maneuvers. The plan never came to fruition, however, due to a lack of money and the idea was not pursued again until the late 1930s. Although the division HQ was not officially formed until 1940, the combined staffs of the 51st and 52d Brigs. formed the division HQ in a provisional status for First Army CPXs on several occasions. The staffs participated in the CPXs at Camp Dix in 1931 and 1934, at Fort Devens in 1936, and in the I Cav. Corps CPX at Fort Knox, KY, in 1934. Although the 21st Cav. Div. did not participate in the First Army maneuvers in 1935, 1939, and 1940, several of its subordinate units did. The 101st Cav. participated in the 1939 maneuver and the 21st Rcn. Sq. participated in the 1940 maneuver, but as the "eyes and ears" of the 22d Cav. Div. The primary reason that the division did not play a part in those major maneuvers was that it did not have a staff organized, nor a commander appointed, until the summer of 1940. This state of affairs was due, in part, to the failure of the representative states' adjutants general to agree on the division's final allotments. The division was reorganized in the fall of 1938 when the 52d Cav. Brig. was relieved from assignment and New Jersey's 59th Cav. Brig. assigned in its stead. Also, that fall the Secretary of War authorized the various states to begin final negotiations for the formation of the HQ of the remaining N.G. cavalry divisions (less the 24th, already organized). Final allotments were made in January 1939 and the division HQ, less several staff positions were allotted to the state of New York. The Secretary of War authorized the formation of the 21st Cav. Div. on 30 April 1940 and the division HQ was organized and federally recognized on 5 July 1940, making it the last N.G. cavalry division to be formed. On that date, Maj. Gen. Nathaniel H. Egleston (formerly the C.G., 51st Cav. Brig.) was appointed division commander. However, only 3 months later the division was directed to be broken up. The 21st Cav. Div. was inactivated on 1 October 1940.

Status: Disbanded effective 1 November 1940.

Events: 174, 175

Division Commander

Maj. Gen. Nathaniel H. Egleston (NY)	5 July 1940–1 October 1940

21st CAVALRY DIVISION
Organization 1922

UNIT:	LOCATION:
HQ	*Not allotted*
HQ, Sp. Tps.	*Not allotted*
HQ Troop	*Rhode Island N.G.***
21st Sig. Troop	*Not allotted*
125th Ord. Co. (M)	*Not allotted*
Veterinary Co. No. 121	*Not allotted*
51st Cav. Brig.	New York City, NY
HQ Troop	West New Brighton, NY
101st Cav. Regt.	Brooklyn, NY
102d Cav. Regt.	Newark, NJ
51st MG Sq.	New York City, NY
52d Cav. Brig.	Wayne, PA
HQ Troop	Philadelphia, PA
103d Cav. Regt.	Philadelphia, PA
104th Cav. Regt.	Harrisburg, PA
52d MG Sq.	Curtin, PA
165th F.A. Bn. (Horse)	*Virginia N.G.***
125th Engr. Bn. (Mounted)	*Pennsylvania N.G.***
Amb. Co. No. 165	*Not allotted*
21st Cav. Div. Train, Q.M.C.	*Not allotted*

21st CAVALRY DIVISION
Organization 1940

UNIT:	LOCATION:
HQ	New York City, NY
HQ, Sp. Tps.	West New Brighton, NY
HQ Troop	West New Brighton, NY
21st Sig. Troop	West New Brighton, NY
125th Ord. Co. (M)	*Connecticut N.G.***
21st Tank Co. (L)	*New York N.G.***
51st Cav. Brig.	*New York N.G.***
HQ Troop	*New York N.G.***
101st Cav. Regt.	Brooklyn, NY
121st Cav. Regt.	Rochester, NY
59th Cav. Brig.	Newark, NJ
HQ Troop	Newark, NJ
102d Cav. Regt.	Newark, NJ
110th Cav. Regt.	Boston, MA
21st Rcn. Sq.	Boston, MA
112th F.A. Regt.	Trenton, NJ
125th Engr. Sq.	*New York N.G.***
121st Med. Sq.	*New York N.G.***
121st Q.M. Sq.	Boston, MA

*Indicates unit partially organized; designated HQ location for mobilization shown.
**Indicates state of HQ allocation; HQ location not designated.

22d CAVALRY DIVISION

Wisconsin, Pennsylvania, Ohio, Illinois, Indiana, Michigan, Kentucky, Louisiana, and West Virginia National Guard

HQ—*Not organized,* 1921–25; Milwaukee, WI, 1925–30; *Inactive*, 1930–40; Harrisburg, PA, 1940

The 22d Cav. Div. was constituted in 1921; originally allotted to the states of Wisconsin, Ohio, Illinois, Michigan, Kentucky, Louisiana, and West Virginia; and assigned to the Second Army. By 1927, it had been reallotted to the states of the Fifth and Sixth Corps Areas only. The HQ was allotted to the Wisconsin N.G., which began appointing officers to the division staff in 1922, but it was not until 25 March 1925 that the division HQ was federally recognized. Col. Frank Caldwell, a R.A. officer, was offered command, but declined, not wanting to accept a dual commission in the Wisconsin N.G. Concurrently, Lt. Col. Robert M. Beck was also offered command of the 53d Cav. Brig., but declined for the same reason. A division commander was never appointed and the division was headed instead by Col. James T. Hale, the division chief of staff. In 1929, due to budget constraints, the Secretary of War directed that only brigade-level HQ would be funded in cavalry divisions until further notice. As a result, the first HQ of the 22d Cav. Div. was disbanded on 30 June 1930. During most of the period of the division's existence, training was conducted at regimental level and below. This was particularly true of the armory training period which ran roughly from August to May, and was conducted at troop level. The armory training consisted of the weekend drills typical of N.G. units of the time. Interspersed were periods of Active Duty at the call of the state. Regiments, or elements thereof, were called out from time-to-time by state governors for emergencies or to establish martial law in an unruly area. The best training for units of the 22d Cav. Div. was provided by the annual 2-week summer camps. The 53d Cav. Brig. and 105th Cav. conducted their camps at Camp Williams, WI, while the 106th Cav. was split between Camp Grayling, MI (1st Sq.) and Camp Grant, IL (HQ and 2d Sq.). The units of the 53d Brig. trained together for the first time in 1936 when it was assembled at Camp Williams for the Second Army Maneuvers that summer. Prior to 1935, the 54th Cav. Brig. HQ and the 107th Cav. trained at Camp Perry, OH, while the 123d Cav. trained at Fort Knox, KY. During the summer of 1935, the 107th Cav. came to train at Fort Knox followed immediately by the 123d Cav. The brigade HQ overlapped the camps of the two subordinate regiments. This system was similar to that practiced by the brigades of the 21st Cav. Div. By 1937, however, the regiments of the 54th Brig. were training concurrently at Fort Knox as the brigade made progress toward higher levels of collective training. The 22d Cav. Div. was reorganized in February 1939 when the

HQ was withdrawn from Wisconsin and allotted to Pennsylvania. Concurrently, the 53d Brig. was assigned to the 23d Cav. Div. and Pennsylvania's 52d Cav. Brig. was assigned to the 22d Div. This brigade, along with the newly activated 166th F.A., 22d Sig. Tp., and 122d Q.M. Sq. (all from the Pennsylvania N.G.) took to the field at Indiantown Gap for 1 week in November 1939 as part of an increase in training periods directed by the War Department. These units made up over half of the division, and while the training was conducted primarily at troop- and squadron-level, the training gave many brigade officers (soon to be assigned to the new division staff) an opportunity to conduct something akin to division-level planning. On 3 January 1940, the HQ, 22d Cav. Div. was once again federally recognized, this time at Harrisburg, PA. Two months later, the new commander, Maj. Gen. Edward J. Stackpole Jr., assembled his new staff at Fort Bliss, TX, to train with the staff of the 1st Cav. Div. from 10 to 12 March 1940. This training was designed to prepare the staff for the upcoming First Army Maneuvers near Canton, NY, in August 1940. The training was apparently worth the effort as the 22d Div. was later able to perform well above the expectations for a brand new division. During the First Army Maneuvers, the division was short one brigade because funds were not available to move the 54th Cav. Brig. to New York. The 21st Rcn. Sq. (21st Cav. Div.) was attached to the division for the maneuver to replace the missing 22d Sq. of Ohio. The final exercise of the maneuver pitted the Blue First Army (II and III Corps) against the invading Black I Corps. The 22d Div. was placed on the right flank of the First Army facing the 26th "Yankee" Div. In a typical cavalry "end-run" on the final night and day of the exercise, the cavalry units of the 22d Div. moved in behind the Yankee Div. cutting the lines of communication of the 51st Inf. Brig. Although the performance of the 22d Cav. Div. was quite impressive, the results were not convincing enough to save the division from the planners at GHQ. On 23 September 1940, the 22d Cav. Div. was inactivated.

Status: Disbanded effective 1 November 1940.

Events: 148, 159, 174, 175, 301

Division Commander

Maj. Gen. Edward Stackpole Jr. (PA)	3 January 1940–31 October 1940

Chief of Staff

Col. James T. Hale (WI)*	25 March 1925–30 June 1930

*Designated C.G. for mobilization purposes.

22d CAVALRY DIVISION
Organization 1922

UNIT:	LOCATION:
HQ	Milwaukee, WI
HQ, Sp. Tps.	*Milwaukee, WI****
HQ Tp.	Madison, WI
22d Sig. Tp.	*Indiana N.G.***
126th Ord. Co. (M)	*Milwaukee, WI****
Vet. Co. No. 126	*Ohio N.G.***
53d Cav. Brig.	*Racine, WI****
HQ Tp.	Janesville, WI
105th Cav. Regt.	Milwaukee, WI
106th Cav. Regt.	*Springfield, IL**
53d MG Sq.	London, KY
54th Cav. Brig.	*Ohio N.G.***
HQ Troop	Cincinnati, OH
107th Cav. Regt.	Cincinnati, OH
108th Cav. Regt.	New Orleans, LA
54th MG Sq.	Monticello, KY
166th F.A. Bn (Horse)	*Milwaukee, WI****
127th Engr. Bn. (Mounted)	*Wisconsin N.G.***
Amb. Co. No. 166	*Kenosha, WI****
22d Cav. Div. Tn., Q.M.C.	*Phillips, WI****

22d CAVALRY DIVISION
Organization 1940

UNIT:	LOCATION:
HQ	Harrisburg, PA
HQ, Sp. Tps.	Harrisburg, PA
HQ Tp.	Bloomsburg, PA
22d Sig. Tp.	Philadelphia, PA
126th Ord. Co. (M)	*Ohio N.G.***
22d Tank Co. (L)	*Ohio N.G.***
52d Cav. Brig.	Harrisburg, PA
HQ Tp.	Philadelphia, PA
103d Cav. Regt.	Tyrone, PA
104th Cav. Regt.	Harrisburg, PA
54th Cav. Brig.	Cleveland, OH
HQ Troop	Akron, OH
107th Cav. Regt.	Cleveland, OH
123d Cav. Regt.	Louisville, KY
22d Rcn. Sq.	Cincinnati, OH
166th F.A. Regt.	Harrisburg, PA
126th Engr. Sq.	*Kentucky N.G.***
122d Med. Sq.	*Pennsylvania N.G.***
122d Q.M. Sq.	Harrisburg, PA

*Indicates unit partially organized, designated HQ location for mobilization shown.
**Indicates state of HQ allocation, HQ location not designated.
***Indicates designated HQ location, unit not organized.

23d CAVALRY DIVISION **"Dixie Cavalry"** **Texas, Louisiana, Alabama, Georgia, Tennessee, North Carolina, Illinois, New Mexico, West Virginia, Wisconsin, and Massachusetts National Guard**

HQ—*Not organized,* 1921–39; New Orleans, LA, 1939–40

The 23d Cav. Div. was constituted in 1921; originally allotted to the states of Texas, Louisiana, Alabama, Georgia, Tennessee, North Carolina, New Mexico, and Massachusetts; and assigned to the Third Army. By 1927, it had been reallotted to the states of the Fourth and Eighth Corps Areas only. Although formal activation of the division did not occur until 1939, many of the units that made up the division began organizing or were already in existence when it was constituted. The first of the units to be assigned to the division was the 56th Cav. Brig., which was originally raised by the Texas N.G. for service along the Mexican border in World War I. In 1921, the brigade commander, Brig. Gen. Jacob F. Wolters, was designated by the War Department to be the division commander of the 23d Cav. Div. on mobilization, a designation he retained until his retirement in 1934. The 56th Brig. consisted of the 111th and 112th Cav. Regts. and the 56th MG Sq. Through the 1920s, divisional units continued to be activated, beginning with the HQ Troop, 23d Cav. Div., which was organized and federally recognized at Birmingham, AL, on 12 April 1921. Additionally, the 55th MG Sq., the 109th Cav., the 110th Cav., and HQ Troop, 55th Cav. Brig. were organized. These last units constituted the bulk of the 55th Cav. Brig., although the brigade HQ itself was not organized until 1936 due to budget constraints. In the early years, training of division units centered primarily on armory drills and, of course, the annual summer camp. Armory drill periods gave the units the opportunity to train at the squad-, platoon-, and rarely, troop-level. Troop-, squadron-, and regimental-level training was generally reserved for summer camp. By 1932, however, both the 55th and 56th Cav. Brigs. were conducting brigade-level exercises each summer. The bulk of the division's units, being located in the Fourth Corps Area, trained each summer at Fort Oglethorpe, GA, with the 6th Cav. Regt., while the 56th Cav. Brig. and the 141st F.A. trained at Camp Wolters, TX, and Camp Beauregard, LA, respectively. Since the 23d Cav. Div.'s brigades were able to concentrate their subordinate units for summer camp, they were consistently rated among the best, if not the best, N.G. cavalry units by R.A. evaluators. Commanders and staff officers of the major units in the division had several opportunities to work together before the division's activation. The first of these was in September 1936, when officers of the division participated in the Third Army CPX at Camp Bullis, TX. The provisional 23d Div. staff was made up of officers primarily from the 55th and 56th Cav. Brigs. During the CPX, the R.A. officers working with the 23d Div. gave the provisional staff high praise for their performance. The next opportunity came in August 1938 when the entire 23d Cav. Div. participated in the Third Army Maneuvers. Due to cost constraints, however, the Third Army could not be assembled in one location so the 23d did not train as a division. The bulk of the division participated in the Fourth Corps Area portion of the exercise in Mississippi's DeSoto National Forest under control of the 55th Cav. Brig. The 56th Cav. Brig. participated in the Eighth Corps Area exercise at Camp Bullis, near San Antonio, TX. The Third Army commander was so satisfied with the performance of the 23d Div. units, he recommended that the N.G. horse divisions should be retained in the army structure and mobilized as such in time of war. On 18 October 1939, at long last the division HQ was organized and federally recognized at New Orleans and the 23d Cav. Div. formally came into existence with Maj. Gen. James F. Edmonds appointed as the first, and ultimately the only, commander. Gen. Edmonds and his staff almost immediately began preparations for the 23d Cav. Div. to take part in the 1940 Louisiana Maneuvers. In January 1940, Gen. Edmonds assembled the division staff at Roberts Field in Birmingham, AL, for the additional training directed by the War Department for all N.G. units that winter. During that training, the division staff, the division HQ Tp., and HHT, 55th Cav. Brig. participated in a CPX. Two months later, Edmonds and the division staff traveled to Fort Bliss, TX, to train with the staff of the 1st Cav. Div. from 17 to 20 March 1940. This training was specifically designed to prepare the staff for that summer's maneuvers. During the Louisiana Maneuvers, the 23d Cav. Div. was assigned the mission to provide reconnaissance for the IV Corps and, during the exercise, it operated against the VIII Corps and the Regulars of the 1st Cav. Div. in the Kisatchie National Forest. Subsequent reports stated that the 23d did a credible job despite facing the more experienced R.A. troops and the difficulties caused by the rental horses provided to the N.G. units. The efforts of the 23d Cav. Div. during the exercise were good, but not good enough to save it from the Army's troop basis planners. Its performance notwithstanding, the 23d Cav. Div. was inactivated 6 October 1940.

Status: Disbanded effective 1 November 1940.

Events: 217, 300

Division Commanders

Brig. Gen. Jacob F. Wolters (TX)* June 1921–November 1934
Brig. Gen. Louis S. Davidson (TX)* November 1934–August 1938
Maj. Gen. James E. Edmonds (LA) October 1939–October 1940

*Designated C.G. for mobilization purposes.

23d CAVALRY DIVISION
Organization 1922

UNIT:	LOCATION:
HQ	*Texas N.G.***
HQ, Sp. Tps.	*Alabama N.G.***
HQ Tp.	Birmingham, AL
23d Sig. Tp.	*Not allotted*
127th Ord. Co. (M)	*Not allotted*
Vet. Co. No. 123	Samson, AL
55th Cav. Brig.	*Not allotted*
HQ Tp.	*North Carolina N.G.***
109th Cav. Regt.	Chattanooga, TN
110th Cav. Regt.	Boston, MA
55th MG Sq.	Andalusia, AL
56th Cav. Brig.	Houston, TX
HQ Troop	Brenham, TX
111th Cav. Regt.	Santa Fe, NM
112th Cav. Regt.	Fort Worth, TX
56th MG Sq.	Houston, TX
167th F.A. Bn. (Horse)	*Louisiana N.G.***
126th Engr. Bn. (Mounted)	*West Virginia N.G.***
Amb. Co. No. 167	*Alabama N.G.***
23d Cav. Div. Train, Q.M.C.	*Not allotted*

23d CAVALRY DIVISION
Organization 1940

UNIT:	LOCATION:
HQ	New Orleans, LA
HQ, Sp. Tps.	New Orleans, LA
HQ Tp.	New Orleans, LA
23d Sig. Tp.	Birmingham, AL
127th Ord. Co. (M)	*Wisconsin N.G.***
23d Tank Co. (L)	*Illinois N.G.***
53d Cav. Brig.	Madison, WI
HQ Tp.	Stanley, WI
105th Cav. Regt.	Nekoosa, WI
106th Cav. Regt.	Chicago, IL
55th Cav. Brig.	New Orleans, LA
HQ Tp.	Birmingham, AL
108th Cav. Regt.	Hinesville, GA
109th Cav. Regt.	Chattanooga, TN
23d Rcn. Sq.	Springfield, IL
141st F.A. Regt.	New Orleans, LA
127th Engr. Sq.	Huntsville, AL
123d Med. Sq.	*Alabama N.G.**
123d Q.M. Sq.	*Illinois N.G.**

*Indicates unit partially organized, designated HQ location for mobilization shown.
**Indicates state of HQ allocation, HQ location not designated.

24th CAVALRY DIVISION

Kansas, Iowa, South Dakota, Idaho, Minnesota, Wyoming, Washington, and Colorado National Guard

HQ—*Not organized,* 1921–36; Topeka, KS, 1936–40

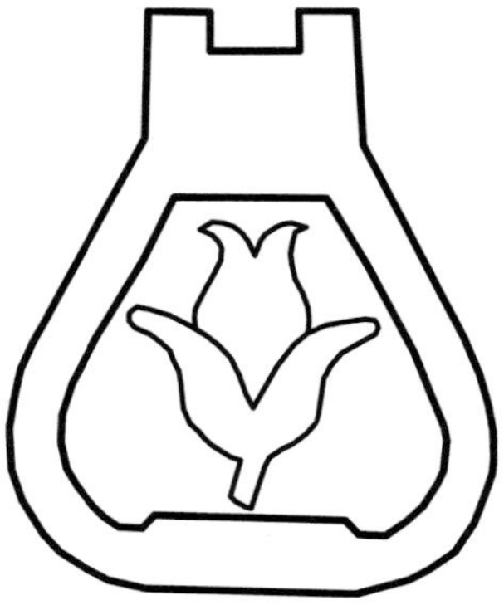

The 24th Cav. Div. was constituted in 1921; originally allotted to the states of Kansas, Iowa, South Dakota, Idaho, Minnesota, Wyoming, Washington, and Colorado; and assigned to the Third Army. It was reassigned to the Fourth Army as a result of the army reorganization of 1932. Organizationally, the 24th Cav. Div. was unique in that it was the only N.G. cavalry division to maintain the same brigades and regiments from beginning to end. It was the least affected by reorganizations and as a partial result, organized its HQ a full 3 years before the other division. As constituted, the 24th Div. consisted of the 57th and 58th Cav. Brigs. The 57th included Iowa's 113th Cav. and Kansas' 114th Cav. The 57th MG Sq., while constituted, assigned to the brigade, and allotted to the state of South Dakota, was never organized. The 58th consisted of Wyoming's 115th Cav., Idaho's 116th Cav., and the 58th MG Sq. of Washington and Wyoming. In addition to the combat units, the support units were constituted as inactive units and assigned to the division in 1921. These included the 24th Sig. Tp., 128th Ord. Co. (Maint), 168th F.A. Bn. (Horse), 128th Engr. Bn. (Mtd), and 24th Div. Q.M. Train. The 124th Med. Sq. was constituted and assigned in 1924. In July 1926, the 168th F.A. Bn. was organized from the 1st Bn., 158th F.A., which was formerly assigned to the 45th Div. One other unique fact about the 24th Cav. Div. was the organization in 1939 of a division aviation section. This section consisted of the 120th Obsn. Sq., 120th Photo Section, and a Medical Department Detachment, all from Colorado and formerly assigned to the 45th Div. All of the armory drill periods were designed to prepare the troops for the annual 2-week summer camp. Unfortunately, the camps for the units of the division were spread out all over the western United States, which made it difficult to assemble units larger than a regiment. For example, the division HQ troop trained at Camp Murray, WA; the 57th Brig. and the 113th Cav. at Camp Dodge, IA; the 114th Cav. at Fort Riley, KS; the 115th Cav. at Pole Mountain, WY; the 58th Brig. and 116th Cav. at Boise Barracks, ID; and the 168th F.A. trained at Fort Logan, CO. On 28 January 1936, the HQ of the 24th Cav. Div. was federally recognized at Topeka, KS, under the command of Maj. Gen. William K. Herndon. Realizing the difficulties he faced in training his division, Gen. Herndon immediately set out to assemble the entire organization at Fort Riley, KS, for the 1936 summer camp. Unfortunately, the funds for the movement of all the troops, horses, and equipment were not available, and the plan was shelved. Instead, Gen. Herndon developed a plan to assemble the division staff (the members of which came from the several states that comprised the division) for training. His idea included the provision that the staff would hold their camp with a different regiment each year, at least until funds came available to bring the division together. Enough funds were available to support this plan, which was implemented beginning the summer of 1936. The division staff assembled for training that summer at Camp Guernsey, WY, with the 115th Cav. For the 1937, 1938, and 1939 camps, the entire division HQ trained at Camp Dodge, IA; Camp Guernsey; and Boise Barracks, ID, respectively. In 1940, Herndon and the division staff traveled to Fort Bliss, TX, to train with the staff of the 1st Cav. Div. 24–27 March. This training was specifically designed to prepare the staff for that summer's maneuvers. Although these efforts were a step in the right direction, the closest the 24th Div. ever came to operating as a full division was during the Fourth Army Maneuvers in July and August 1940. For the Ninth Corps Area Maneuver, Gen. Herndon was able to concentrate the division HQ, the HQ troop, the 58th Cav. Brig. complete, and the 24th Rcn. Sq. at Centralia, WA. In this exercise, the division (-) was the cavalry force for the provisional Blue Corps, consisting of the 3d Div., the 40th Div., and miscellaneous coast artillery and support units. While the bulk of the division was training in Washington, a large portion of it was finishing its participation in the Seventh Corps Area Maneuver near Camp Ripley, MN, in July and early August. In that exercise, the 57th Cav. Brig., reinforced by the 24th Sig. Tp. and the 4th Cav. Regt. (Horse and Mecz), constituted the reconnaissance and screening force for the provisional Red VII Corps. The 168th F.A. and the 120th Obsn. Sq. were not part of the Fourth Army Maneuvers. Being located in the Eighth Corps Area, they participated in the Third Army's Louisiana Maneuvers that August. The results of the large-scale maneuvers of 1935–40, coupled with events in Poland and France, convinced army planners that the day of employing large bodies of horse cavalry were numbered. As a result, like the other three N.G. cavalry divisions, the 24th was inactivated in October 1940.

Status: Disbanded effective 1 November 1940.

Events: 304

Division Commanders

Maj. Gen. William K. Herndon (KS) 28 January 1936–1 October 1940

24th CAVALRY DIVISION
Organization 1922

UNIT:	LOCATION:
HQ	*Iowa N.G.***
HQ, Sp. Tps.	*Iowa N.G.***
HQ Tp.	*Iowa N.G.***
24th Sig. Tp.	*Iowa N.G.***
128th Ord. Co. (M)	*Iowa N.G.***
Vet. Co. No. 124	*Iowa N.G.***
57th Cav. Brig.	*South Dakota N.G.***
HQ Tp.	*South Dakota N.G.***
113th Cav. Regt.	Iowa City, IA
114th Cav. Regt.	Topeka, KS
57th MG Sq.	*South Dakota N.G.***
58th Cav. Brig.	*Wyoming N.G.***
HQ Tp.	*Wyoming N.G.***
115th Cav. Regt.	Douglas, WY
116th Cav. Regt.	Boise, ID
58th MG Sq.	*Washington N.G.***
168th F.A. Bn. (Horse)	*South Dakota N.G.***
128th Engr. Bn. (Mtd)	*Minnesota N.G.***
Amb. Co. No. 168	*South Dakota N.G.***
24th Cav. Div. Train, Q.M.C.	*Iowa N.G.***

24th CAVALRY DIVISION
Organization 1940

UNIT:	LOCATION:
HQ	Topeka, KS
HQ, Sp. Tps.	*Iowa N.G.***
HQ Tp.	Tacoma, WA
24th Sig. Tp.	Sioux City, IA
128th Ord. Co. (M)	*Iowa N.G.***
24th Tank Co. (L)	*Not allotted*
57th Cav. Brig.	Des Moines, IA
HQ Tp.	Des Moines, IA
113th Cav. Regt.	Des Moines, IA
114th Cav. Regt.	Topeka, KS
58th Cav. Brig.	Boise, ID
HQ Tp.	Nampa, ID
115th Cav. Regt.	Cheyenne, WY
116th Cav. Regt.	Boise, ID
24th Rcn. Sq.	Torrington, WY
168th F.A. Regt.	Denver, CO
128th Engr. Sq.	*Colorado N.G.***
124th Med. Sq.	*Colorado N.G.***
124th Q.M. Sq.	*Iowa N.G.***
120th Obsn. Sq.	Denver, CO

*Indicates unit partially organized, designated HQ location for mobilization shown.
**Indicates state of HQ allocation, HQ location not designated.

61st CAVALRY DIVISION — "The Foragers" — Organized Reserve New York and New Jersey

HQ—New York City, NY, 1921–41

The 61st Cav. Div. was constituted 15 October 1921, allotted to the Second Corps Area, and assigned to the Fourth Army. The division HQ was initiated in December 1921 by Maj. Frederick S. Snyder at the Federal Building in Rochester, NY. The HQ was relocated to the Army Building in New York City in January 1922 and finally to 39 Whitehall Street in New York City in April 1922. To maintain communications with the officers of the division, Col. William F.H. Godson, the division chief of staff, established a newsletter titled the "Forager" after the division's nickname. In accordance with early mobilization plans, the Syracuse Concentration Area was designated as the division's mobilization station. The division tables of organization remained unchanged from its formation until 1 July 1929 when the machine gun squadrons were deleted. The 151st MG Sq. was reorganized and redesignated as the 461st Armd Car Sq. The personnel of the 152d MG Sq. were reassigned to one of the cavalry regiments in New York City. Other changes to the division organization were the addition of the 461st Tank Co. (Light), and the expansion of the 461st F.A. Bn. into a regiment (and concurrently redesignated the 861st). Additionally, when the field armies were activated and army areas reallocated in 1933, the division was relieved from the Fourth Army and assigned to the First Army. The 61st Cav. Div. boasted its share of interesting personalities, some of whom gained fame later on in World War II. For example, Maj. Terry de la Mesa Allen, later to become the first commanding general of the 2d Cav. Div., and also commanded the famed "Big Red One" in World War II, was the executive officer of the 303d Cav. in New York City. The first commanding officer of the 301st Cav. Regt. was Col. William J. Donovan. Col. Donovan won the Medal of Honor in World War I and was the US District Attorney in Syracuse, NY. However, Col. Donovan would become even more famous for organizing and heading the Office of Strategic Services (OSS) during World War II, the forerunner of the Central Intelligence Agency (CIA). The Inactive Training Period for the 61st Cav. Div. usually ran September to May. The 151st Cav. Brig. and other "upstate" units conducted their training events on Tuesday evenings and were the first in the division to begin a regular schedule of marksmanship training. In fact, the 151st MG Sq. competed regularly in rifle matches against the 26th Inf. at Plattsburg Barracks, though they rarely bested the Regulars. The division HQ, 152d Cav. Brig., and other New York City units had their inactive meetings on the first and third Mondays of each month at the Army-Navy Club in Manhattan. Riding classes were conducted on Thursday evenings at the 101st Cav. Armory and correspondence courses were done on the officer's own time. The division held consolidated summer training camps for the first 2 years (1922–23) at Camp Dix, NJ. After that, the division support units generally went to other camps designed for their respective arm or service. For example, the 401st Engrs. usually trained with the 1st Engr. Regt. at Fort Du Pont, DE, the 461st F.A. Bn. trained with the 2d Bn., 7th F.A. at Madison Barracks, and the 361st Med. Sq. trained with the 1st Med. Regt. at Carlisle Barracks, PA. From 1924 to 1934, the cavalry units trained at Fort Ethan Allen, VT. The training plan was normally developed by the division's R.A. instructors and executed with the assistance of the 1st Sq., 3d Cav. and the 7th F.A., both stationed at Fort Ethan Allen. In 1935, however, the 152d Cav. Brig. was sent to train at Fort Myer, VA, with the 62d Cav. Div. and the 3d Cav. The event was so successful that the whole division traveled down to train with the 62d Div. in 1937 and 1939. For the intervening years of 1936 and 1938, the division went to Jericho, VT, near Fort Ethan Allen to train. The division staff also had the opportunity to function as a staff during several Second Corps Area and First Army CPXs held in 1929, 1931, 1934, and 1936. Due to the lack of equipment and enlisted personnel, units of the 61st Cav. Div. did not participate as organized units in the First Army maneuvers of 1935, 1939, and 1940. However, hundreds of individual officers and many enlisted men from the 61st participated as umpires or by being assigned to R.A. or N.G. cavalry units to bring them up to authorized war strength. The 1940 maneuver in upstate New York was the division's last major training event, for although the 61st was not officially disbanded until January 1942, it had almost ceased to exist by then. Most of the assigned personnel had already been called to Active Duty, leaving only a shell of the former organizations. Location 7 December 1941—Manhattan, NY.

Status: Disbanded 30 January 1942.

Events: 61, 91, 280

Division Commanders

Maj. Gen. George B. Duncan (R.A.)*	15 September 1922–1 October 1925

*Concurrently Commander, Second Corps Area.

Chiefs of Staff

Maj. Frederick S. Snyder, Cav.	23 August 1921–October 1921
Maj. Louis A. O' Donnell, Cav.	October 1921–20 January 1922
Col. William F.H. Godson, Cav.	20 January 1922–28 February 1924
Col. George Vidmer, Cav.	1 March 1924–7 September 1928
Col. Julian R. Lindsey, Cav.	7 September 1928–2 February 1932
Col. William M. Connell, Cav.	2 February 1932–October 1935
Col. George M. Russell, Cav.	October 1935–28 August 1938
Col. John K. Brown, Cav.	28 August 1938–January 1942

61st CAVALRY DIVISION
Organization 1922

UNIT:	HQ LOCATION:
HQ	Manhattan, NY
HQ, Sp. Tps.	Rochester, NY
HQ Tp.	Manhattan, NY
61st Sig. Tp.	Buffalo, NY
581st Ord. Co. (M)	Oleon, NY
Vet. Co. No. 501	Salamanca, NY
151st Cav. Brig.	Rochester, NY
301st Cav. Regt.	Syracuse, NY
302d Cav. Regt.	Newark, NJ
151st MG Sq.	Albany, NY
152d Cav. Brig.	Manhattan, NY
303d Cav. Regt.	Manhattan, NY
304th Cav. Regt.	Brooklyn, NY
152d MG Sq.	Manhattan, NY
461st F.A. Bn. (Horse)	Manhattan, NY
401st Engr. Bn. (Mtd)	Schenectady, NY
Amb. Co. No. 501	Belmont, NY
61st Cav. Div. Train, Q.M.C.	Rochester, NY

61st CAVALRY DIVISION
Organization 1940

UNIT:	HQ LOCATION:
HQ	Manhattan, NY
HQ, Sp. Tps.	Rochester, NY
HQ Tp.	Manhattan, NY
61st Sig. Tp.	Buffalo, NY
581st Ord. Co. (M)	Buffalo, NY
461st Tank Co. (L)	New York City, NY
151st Cav. Brig.	Rochester, NY
301st Cav. Regt.	Rochester, NY
302d Cav. Regt.	Newark, NJ
152d Cav. Brig.	Manhattan, NY
303d Cav. Regt.	Manhattan, NY
304th Cav. Regt.	Manhattan, NY
461st Rcn. Sq.	Albany, NY
861st F.A. Regt.	New York City, NY
401st Engr. Sq.	New York City, NY
361st Med. Sq.	Albany, NY
461st Q.M. Sq.	Rochester, NY

62d CAVALRY DIVISION

Organized Reserve Maryland, Virginia, Pennsylvania, and District of Columbia

HQ—Hagerstown, MD, 1921–24; Towson, MD, 1924–40; Baltimore, MD, 1940–41

The 62d Cav. Div. was constituted on 15 October 1921, allotted to the Third Corps Area, and assigned to the Fourth Army. The division HQ was initiated on 7 September 1921 at 27 West Washington Street in Hagerstown, MD, by Lt. Col. William R. Taylor. The division was officially activated shortly thereafter and began to flourish rapidly. From an original strength of 70 officers and no enlisted men on 31 December 1921, by 31 July 1925, the 62d Cav. Div. boasted 355 officers and 43 enlisted men and all authorized units had been activated. The division HQ was relocated to York and Allegheny Avenues in Towson, MD, on 30 June 1924. It was moved one final time on 27 September 1940 to the Hurst Building in Baltimore, MD, where it remained until its inactivation in 1942. The division tables of organization remained unchanged from its formation until 1 July 1929, when the MG Sqs. were eliminated and absorbed into other units. Other changes to the division organization were the addition of the 462d Armd. Car Sq., 462d Tank Co. (L), and the expansion of the 462d F.A. Bn. into a regiment (and concurrently redesignated the 862d). Additionally, when the field armies were activated and army areas reallocated in 1933, the division was relieved from the Fourth Army and assigned to the First Army. The 62d Cav. Div. had a number of interesting personalities assigned to or associated with it during the years between the wars. For example, the first postwar commander of the 306th Cav. was Col. John B.P. Clayton Hill, a Congressman from the state of Maryland. In February 1938, Col. Bruce C. Clark assumed the duties of the division chief of staff, a job he held until 1940. Additionally, Cols. Jonathan Wainwright and George S. Patton were frequent guests to divisional social events and various training events during the period they were regimental commanders of the 3d Cav. at Fort Myer, VA, in the late 1930s. The Inactive Training Period for the 62d Div. usually ran September to May. Most of the units held their training meetings at the armory of the N.G. unit in the city where they were located. The 306th Cav., being located close to the 3d Cav. at Fort Myer, made frequent use of that regiment's mounts and the 307th Cav. established a relationship with the cavalry ROTC unit at the Virginia Military Institute from which many of the officers of the regiment were commissioned. The 308th Cav. had a similar relationship with Valley Forge Military Academy. The division generally held its summer training camps at Fort Myer and was always supported with men and horses from the 3d Cav. For most of the period between the wars, the cavalry regiments of the division alternated each summer between participating in the regular training camp at Fort Myer and conducting the training of the cavalry elements of the Citizen's Military Training Camp (CMTC) at Fort Belvoir. For at least two camps (1926 and 1928), the 305th and 308th Regts. attended summer training with the regiments of the 52d Cav. Brig. at Mount Gretna, PA. The division support units generally went to other camps designed for their respective arm or service. For example, the 402d Engr. Sq. usually trained with the 13th Engr. Regt. at Fort Humphreys, VA, and a few years with the 1st Engrs. at Fort DuPont, DE. The 462d F.A. Bn. trained with the 6th F.A. at Fort Hoyle, MD, and the 362d Med.Sq. trained with the 1st Med. Regt. at Carlisle Barracks, PA. Beginning in 1930 the level of training of the division began to accelerate and become more varied as the division staff became more experienced in their duties and in spite of the problems brought on by the depression. In July of that year, the division, brigade, and regimental staffs participated in the Third Corps Area CPX at Fort Meade, MD. As the depression began to deepen, however, the R.A. groaned under the weight of maintaining readiness with inadequate funding while still operating the camps of the Civilian Conservation Corps (CCC). In 1934, the War Department directed the Regulars to hand over the camps to the stewardship of Reserve Officers. The 62d Cav. Div. responded with a flood of volunteers. By November 1935, 87 officers of the division were on Active Duty working with the CCC. In 1937, the 152d Cav. Brig. was sent to train at Fort Myer with the 62d Cav. Div. and the 3d Cav. The event was so successful that the entire 61st Cav. Div. came to Fort Myer to train with the 62d in 1937 and 1939. The focus of the 1939 camp was to prepare the officers of those two divisions for the First Army maneuver scheduled for the following summer. During those maneuvers, the officers of the 62d were assigned duties with the units of the 22d Cav. Div. as well as the 3d Cav. The 1940 maneuver in upstate New York was the division's last major training event, for although the 62d was not officially disbanded until January 1942, it had almost ceased to exist by then due to the call to Active Duty of most of its officers. Location 7 December 1941—Towson, MD.

Status: Disbanded 30 January 1942.

Events: 109, 247, 281

Division Commanders

Maj. Gen. James K. Parsons (R.A.)*	1 April 1938–October 1940

*Concurrently Commander,Third Corps Area.

Chiefs of Staff

Col. Thomas B. Dugan, Cav.	7 September 1921–15 October 1921
Lt. Col. William R. Taylor, Cav.	15 October 1921–1 July 1922
Col. George T. Langhorne Cav.	1 July 1922–November 1923
Lt. Col. William R. Pope, Cav.	November 1923–15 August 1924
Col. Guy S. Norvell, Cav.	15 August 1924–June 1926
Maj. John M. Thompson, Cav.	June 1926–23 August 1926
Maj. Phillip Gordon, Cav.	23 August 1926–March 1927
Maj. Stephen C. Reynolds, Q.M.C.	March 1927–16 September 1927
Col. George T. Bowman, Cav.	16 September 1927–30 June 1933
Col. Charles R. Mayo, Cav.	June 1933–July 1933
Col. John D. Long, Cav.	1 July 1933–17 May 1937
Col. Osmun Latrobe, Cav.	17 May 1937–23 July 1938
Col. Bruce C. Palmer, Cav.	2 September 1938–September 1940
Col. John C. F. Tillson Jr., Cav.	September 1940–December 1941

62d CAVALRY DIVISION
Organization 1922

UNIT:	HQ LOCATION:
HQ	Hagerstown, MD
HQ, Sp. Tps.	Hagerstown, MD
HQ Troop	Hagerstown, MD
62d Sig. Troop	Washington, DC
582d Ord. Co. (M)	Hagerstown, MD
Vet. Co. No. 502	Hagerstown, MD
153d Cav. Brig.	Baltimore, MD
305th Cav. Regt.	Philadelphia, PA
306th Cav. Regt.	Baltimore, MD
153d MG Sq.	Baltimore, MD
154th Cav. Brig.	Richmond, VA
307th Cav. Regt.	Richmond, VA
308th Cav. Regt.	Cumberland, MD
154th MG Sq.	Norfolk, VA
462d F.A. Bn. (Horse)	Baltimore, MD
402d Engr. Bn. (Mounted)	Baltimore, MD
Amb. Co. No. 502	Winchester, VA
62d Cav. Div. Train, Q.M.C.	Towson, MD

62d CAVALRY DIVISION
Organization 1940

UNIT:	HQ LOCATION:
HQ	Towson, MD
HQ, Sp. Tps.	Towson, MD
HQ Troop	Towson, MD
62d Sig. Troop	Towson, MD
582d Ord. Co. (M)	Towson, MD
462d Tank Co. (L)	Baltimore, MD
153d Cav. Brig.	Baltimore, MD
305th Cav. Regt.	Philadelphia, PA
306th Cav. Regt.	Baltimore, MD
154th Cav. Brig.	Richmond, VA
307th Cav. Regt.	Richmond, VA
308th Cav. Regt.	Pittsburgh, PA
462d Rcn. Sq.	Washington, DC
862d F.A. Regt.	Baltimore, MD
402d Engr. Sq.	Baltimore, MD
362d Med. Sq.	Baltimore, MD
462d Q.M. Sq.	Winchester, VA

63d CAVALRY DIVISION

Organized Reserve Texas, Oklahoma, Colorado, Arizona, Alabama, Georgia, Louisiana, Tennessee and North Carolina

HQ—New Orleans, LA, 1922–23; Fort Oglethorpe, GA, 1923–27; Chattanooga, TN, 1927–41

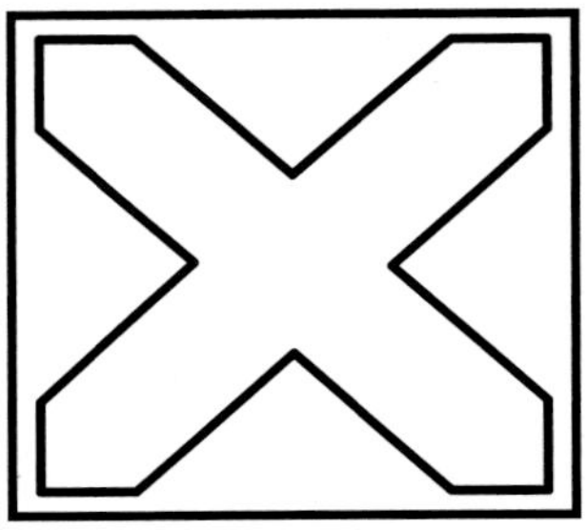

The 63d Cav. Div. was constituted on 15 October 1921, allotted to the Fourth and Eighth Corps Areas, and assigned to the Fifth Army. The division HQ was initiated on 7 July 1922 at Poland and Dauphin Streets in New Orleans, LA, by Col. James H. Hornbeck. The division HQ was moved to Fort Oglethorpe, GA, on 10 October 1923 because that post provided a more central location from which to control the division's scattered units. Originally, Camp Beauregard had been designated as the mobilization station for the division HQ, but it was changed to Fort Oglethorpe when the HQ moved there. The division HQ was relocated once again on 8 July 1927 when it was moved to the Pound Building in Chattanooga, TN, where it remained until the beginning of World War II. Except for the 156th Cav. Brig., which was to mobilize at Fort Clark, TX, and the 403d Engr. Sq. and division quartermaster train, which were to form at Camp Beauregard, LA, the division's remaining units were to mobilize at Fort Oglethorpe. The division tables of organization remained unchanged from its formation until 1 July 1929, when the MG Sqs. were eliminated and absorbed into other units. Other changes to the division at that time were the addition of the 463d Armd. Car Sq., 463d Tank Co. (L), and the expansion of the 463d F.A. Bn. into a regiment (and concurrently redesignated the 863d). Additionally, when the field armies were activated and army areas reallocated in 1933, the division was relieved from the Fifth Army and assigned to the Third Army. The division's Inactive Training Period usually ran September to May. Many of the units held their training meetings at N.G. armories or trained with ROTC units in the city where the majority of their officers were located. Units in the Chattanooga and Atlanta areas were fortunate in that they participated in a marksmanship training program at the Catoosa Training Area and Range, near the Chickamauga National Battlefield. Division units held their summer training camps at a wide variety of posts throughout the south and were able to establish consistent training partnerships with the R.A. units at those locations. The 6th Cav. at Fort Oglethorpe provided support to the units of the 155th Cav. Brig. in terms of horses, equipment, and training expertise. The 156th Cav. Brig. and 311th Cav. trained with the 1st Cav. Brig. and the 5th Cav., respectively, at Fort Clark, TX, while the 312th Cav. and 156th MG Sq. trained at Fort Bliss and were supported with men and horses from the 7th Cav. and the 2d MG Sq. As an alternate form of training, the cavalry regiments of the 155th Cav. Brig. occasionally conducted the training of the cavalry elements of the Citizen's Military Training Camp (CMTC) at Fort Oglethorpe. In July 1935, virtually the entire division, save the 156th Cav. Brig., trained the various branches of the CMTC at Fort Oglethorpe. Under the guiding eyes of the men of the 6th Cav. and the Regulars assigned to the division, the CMTC provided one of the few opportunities the 63d Cav. Div. had to operate its various echelons of HQ simultaneously. The 1930s saw the level of training in the division accelerate and become more varied as experience levels increased in the staff officers of the HQ, as well as in the officers of the units. For example, in May 1936, the brigade and regimental staffs of the 156th Brig. participated in the Third Army CPX at Camp Bliss, TX. The training objective of the CPX was to begin the process of preparing staffs of the R.A., N.G., and O.R. units for the army-level maneuvers scheduled for the summer of 1938. In the same vein, the division and brigade staffs participated in a 2-week, division-level CPX held at the Chickamauga Battlefield in May 1937. Due to the lack of horses, equipment, and enlisted men, the 63d Cav. Div. did not participate in the 1938 Third Army maneuver as an organized division. Instead, the members of the division reinforced R.A. or N.G. units to bring them up to wartime strength in officers or by acting as umpires. In general, the eastern elements of the division reinforced the 55th Cav. Brig., 127th Engr. Sq., and the 141st F.A. of the 23d Cav. Div., all of which participated in the Fourth Corps Area portion of the maneuvers held in the DeSoto National Forest in Mississippi. Concurrently, the 156th Cav. Brig. reinforced the Texas N.G.'s 56th Cav. Brig. and the 1st Cav. Brig. of the 1st Cav. Div., which participated in the maneuver at Camp Bullis, TX, as part of the Eighth Corps Area concentration. In all, over 300 officers from the division participated in the Third Army maneuver that year. The next major event in the life of the division was the 1940 Third Army maneuver held near the Kisatchie National Forest in central Louisiana in August 1940. Once again, the officers of the 63d reinforced the 1st and 23d Cav. Divs., but also provided a substantial number of officers to the 31st Div. as well. The 1940 maneuver in central Louisiana was the division's last major training event. Shortly thereafter, most of the division's assigned personnel were called to Active Duty during the build-up of the US Army in 1940–41. Location 7 December 1941—Chattanooga, TN.

Status: Disbanded 30 January 1942.

Events: 217, 255, 300

Division Commanders

Maj. Gen. Frank R. McCoy (R.A.)*	3 October 1929–1 February 1932

*Concurrently Commander, Fourth Corps Area.

Chiefs of Staff

Col. James J. Hornbrook, Cav.	18 September 1922–26 August 1927
Col. Oren B. Meyer, Cav.	26 August 1927–7 October 1929
Maj. Frank S. Besson, C.E.	7 October 1929–7 April 1930
Col. Oscar Foley, Cav.	7 April 1930–26 July 1935
Lt. Col. Fred H. Gallup, Cav.	26 July 1935–October 1935
Col. Robert Blaine, Cav.	October 1935–June 1937
Col. Daniel D. Tompkins, Cav.	24 June 1937–25 July 1940
Col. George B. Hunter, Cav.	25 July 1940–January 1942

63d CAVALRY DIVISION
Organization 1922

UNIT:	HQ LOCATION:
HQ	New Orleans, LA
HQ, Sp. Tps.	Chattanooga, TN
HQ Troop	Chattanooga, TN
63d Sig. Troop	New Orleans, LA
583d Ord. Co. (M)	Rome, GA
Vet. Co. No. 503	Jasper, TN
155th Cav. Brig.	Chattanooga, TN
309th Cav. Regt.	Asheville, NC
310th Cav. Regt.	Knoxville, TN
155th MG Sq.	Memphis, TN
156th Cav. Brig.	Dallas, TX
311th Cav. Regt.	San Antonio, TX
312th Cav. Regt.	Oklahoma City, OK
156th MG Sq.	Denver, CO
463d F.A. Bn. (Horse)	Charlotte, NC
403d Engr. Bn. (Mounted)	New Orleans, LA
Amb. Co. No. 503	Dublin, LA
63d Cav. Div. Train, Q.M.C.	Lake Charles, LA

63d CAVALRY DIVISION
Organization 1940

UNIT:	HQ LOCATION:
HQ	Chattanooga, TN
HQ, Sp. Tps.	Chattanooga, TN
HQ Troop	Chattanooga, TN
63d Sig. Troop	New Orleans, LA
583d Ord. Co. (M)	Rome, GA
463d Tank Co. (L)	Anniston, AL
155th Cav. Brig.	Chattanooga, TN
309th Cav. Regt.	Atlanta, GA
310th Cav. Regt.	Athens, GA
156th Cav. Brig.	San Antonio, TX
311th Cav. Regt.	San Antonio, TX
312th Cav. Regt.	Oklahoma City, OK
463d Rcn. Sq.	Memphis, TN
863d F.A. Regt.	Charlotte, NC
403d Engr. Sq.	New Orleans, LA
363d Med. Sq.	Chattanooga, TN
463d Q.M. Sq.	Vicksburg, MS

64th CAVALRY DIVISION **"Arrowhead"** **Organized Reserve Kentucky, Indiana, Ohio, West Virginia, New Hampshire, Vermont, Connecticut, and Massachusetts**

HQ—Lexington, KY, 1921–22; Louisville, KY, 1922–41

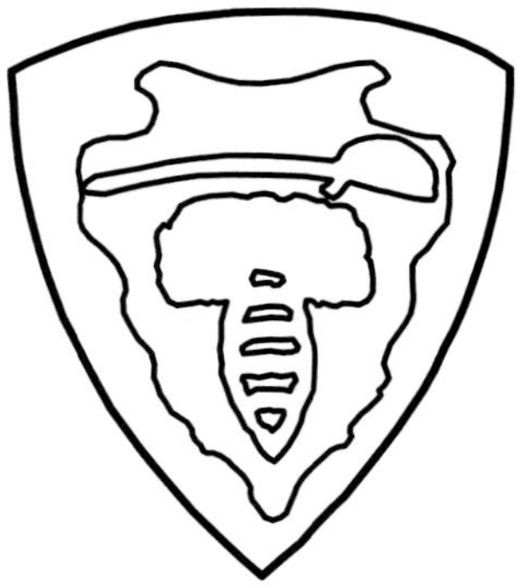

The 64th Cav. Div. was constituted 15 October 1921, allotted to the First and Fifth Corps Areas, and assigned to the Fifth Army. The division HQ was initiated 22 October 1921 at the Post Office Building in Lexington, KY, by Lt. Col. Richard W. Walker. The division HQ was moved to Louisville, KY, on 14 March 1922 to provide a more central location for the command and control of the cavalry units in the Fifth Corps Area. On official activation, the division began to flourish rapidly. By the end of 1922, the division was 62 percent complete. By 1926, the 64th Cav. Div. boasted 336 officers and 47 enlisted men and all authorized units had been activated. The tables of organization in the division remained unchanged until 1 July 1929 when the MG Sqs. were eliminated and absorbed into other units. Other changes to the division organization were the addition of the 464th Armd. Car Sq., 464th Tank Co. (L), and the expansion of the 464th F.A. Bn. into a regiment (and concurrently redesignated the 864th). Additionally, when the field armies were activated and Army areas reallocated in 1933, it was relieved from the Fifth Army and assigned to the Second Army. The Inactive Training Period for the "Arrowhead" Division usually ran September to May and many of the units held their training meetings at N.G. armories or trained with ROTC units near where the majority of their officers were located. The 313th Cav., for example, frequently conducted training at the Culver Military Academy in Culver, IN. The academy was the source for many of the regiment's officers, even though it only had a junior ROTC unit. The 316th Cav. often trained with the cavalry ROTC unit at Norwich University in Vermont. As a result of their relationship, many of the cadets from that school accepted commissions in all the units of the 158th Brig., and especially in the 316th. Elements of the 315th Cav. trained with the horses and equipment at the armory of the 2d Sq., 110th Cav. in Providence, RI. The division's units held their summer training camps at a wide variety of posts throughout the eastern United States. The units were able to establish training partnerships with the R.A. units at those locations. In the case of the 157th Cav. Brig. and its subordinate regiments, the 6th Cav. at Fort Oglethorpe provided support in terms of horses, equipment, and training expertise for their summer training, while the 157th MG Sq. trained with the 53d and 54th MG Sqs. of the Kentucky N.G. each summer at Fort Knox. The 158th Cav. Brig. trained each year with the 1st Sq., 3d Cav. at Fort Ethan Allen, VT. As an additional form of training, the cavalry regiments of the 157th Cav. Brig. occasionally conducted the training of the cavalry elements of the CMTC at Fort Oglethorpe. The 157th alternated the responsibilities of CMTC training each year with the regiments of the 155th Brig. of the 63d Div. The 158th Brig. conducted cavalry CMTC training at Fort Ethan Allen. The division's support units established training affiliations with R.A. units as well and generally went to other camps designed for their respective arm or service. For example, the 404th Engr. Sq. usually trained with the 13th Engrs. from Fort Humphreys, VA, the 464th F.A. Bn. trained with the units of 3d F.A. at Fort Knox, and the 464th Armd. Car Sq. trained with the 1st Cav. Regt. (Mecz) at Fort Knox. Additionally, the 364th Med. Sq. trained at the Fort Ben Harrison post hospital, and the division quartermaster train (later the 464th Q.M. Sq.) attended summer training at the Jeffersonville Q.M. Depot in Jeffersonville, IN. Throughout the 1930s, the 64th Cav. Div. participated in the various army and corps area CPXs at Fort Knox. The training objective of these CPXs was to prepare the staffs of R.A., N.G., and O.R. units for the 1937 Second Army maneuver. Due to the lack of horses, equipment, and enlisted men, the 64th Cav. Div. did not participate in the Second Army maneuver as an organized division. Instead, the members of the division (minus the 158th Brig.) reinforced R.A. or N.G. units to bring them up to wartime strength in officers or by acting as umpires. In general, elements of the division reinforced the 7th and 54th Cav. Brigs., which participated in the Fifth Corps Area portion of the maneuvers held at Fort Knox. In all, over 200 officers from the division participated. The next major event for the division was the Second Army maneuver held in central Wisconsin in August 1940. This time, the officers of the 64th reinforced the 1st Sq., 14th Cav., but also provided a substantial number of officers to the 38th Div. as well. The 1940 maneuver in Wisconsin was the division's last major training event, for although the 64th was not officially disbanded until January 1942, it had almost ceased to exist by then. Most of the assigned personnel had already been called to Active Duty, leaving only a shell of the former organizations. Location 7 December 1941—Louisville, KY.

Status: Disbanded 30 January 1942.

Events: 264

Division Commanders*

Brig. Gen. Julian R. Lindsey	1 March 1932–31 May 1934	Col. Bruce Palmer	10 September 1935–27 June 1936
Brig. Gen. Guy V. Henry	31 May 1934–24 July 1935	Brig. Gen. Daniel Van Voorhis	27 June 1936–8 October 1938
Col. James P. Barney	24 July 1935–10 September 1935	Col. Charles L. Scott	8 October 1938–1 November 1938
Brig. Gen. Adna R. Chaffee	1 November 1938–15 July 1940		

*These officers were concurrently Commanders, 7th Cav. Brig. (Mecz).

Chiefs of Staff

Lt. Col. Richard W. Walker, Cav.	22 August 1921–9 July 1924	Col. George Williams, Cav.	16 October 1929–3 July 1931
Col. Kirby Walker, Cav.	8 November 1924–20 November 1927	Col. George H. Baird, Cav.	3 July 1931–6 August 1934
Col. John R. R. Hannay, Q.M.C.	20 November 1927–October 1929	Col. Frederick D. Griffith, Cav.	6 August 1934–16 February 1938
Col. N. Butler Briscoe, Cav.	16 February 1938–January 1942		

64th CAVALRY DIVISION
Organization 1922

UNIT:	HQ LOCATION:
HQ	Louisville, KY
HQ, Sp. Tps.	Louisville, KY
HQ Troop	Louisville, KY
64th Sig. Troop	Louisville, KY
584th Ord. Co. (M)	Covington, KY
Vet. Co. No. 504	Cox Creek, KY
157th Cav. Brig.	Princeton, KY
313th Cav. Regt.	Earlington, KY
314th Cav. Regt.	Lexington, KY
157th MG Sq.	Hazard, KY
158th Cav. Brig.	Boston, MA
315th Cav. Regt.	Providence, RI
316th Cav. Regt.	Northfield, VT
158th MG Sq.	Boston, MA
464th F.A. Bn. (Horse)	Lexington, KY
404th Engr. Bn. (Mounted)	Lexington, KY
Amb. Co. No. 504	Fort Thomas, KY
64th Cav. Div. Train, Q.M.C.	Lexington, KY

64th CAVALRY DIVISION
Organization 1940

UNIT:	HQ LOCATION:
HQ	Louisville, KY
HQ, Sp. Tps.	Hinton, WV
HQ Troop	Huntington, WV
64th Sig. Troop	Louisville, KY
584th Ord. Co. (M)	Covington, KY
464th Tank Co. (L)	Harrodsburg, KY
157th Cav. Brig.	Charleston, WV
313th Cav. Regt.	Culver, IN
314th Cav. Regt.	Dayton, OH
158th Cav. Brig.	Franconia, NH
315th Cav. Regt.	Boston, MA
316th Cav. Regt.	Providence, RI
464th Rcn. Sq.	Wheeling, WV
864th F.A. Regt.	Columbus, OH
404th Engr. Sq.	Richmond, KY
364th Med. Sq.	Paris, KY
464th Q.M. Sq.	Winchester, KY

65th CAVALRY DIVISION **"Chevaliers"** **Organized Reserve Illinois, Wisconsin, and Michigan**

HQ—Chicago, IL, 1922–41

The 65th Cav. Div. was constituted on 15 October 1921, allotted to the Sixth Corps Area, and assigned to the Sixth Army. The division HQ was initiated on 11 February 1922 at 405 West Van Buren Street in Chicago, IL, by Maj. William C. Christy. The HQ was relocated on 12 June 1930 to the Burnham Building, 160 North La Salle Street in Chicago. The tables of organization in the division remained unchanged until 1 July 1929 when the MG Sqs. were eliminated and their personnel absorbed into other units. Other changes to the division organization were the addition of the 465th Armd. Car Sq., 465th Tank Co. (L), and the expansion of the 465th F.A. Bn. into a regiment (and concurrently redesignated the 865th). Additionally, when the field armies were activated and army areas reallocated in 1933, the division was relieved from the Sixth Army and assigned to the Fourth Army. The Inactive Training Period for the "Chevaliers" usually ran September to May and many of the units held their training meetings at N.G. armories in the city where they were located. The 317th and 318th Regts., for example, frequently conducted training with the horses and equipment from the "Black Horse Troop" of the 106th Cav. in Chicago. The 319th Cav. often trained with the Michigan elements of the 106th Cav. in Detroit, as did the 160th MG Sq. The 320th Cav. trained with troops of the 105th Cav., Wisconsin N.G. The division's units held their summer training camps primarily at Camp Custer, MI; Fort Des Moines, IA; and Fort Sheridan in Chicago. In the case of most of the division's units, the 1st Sq., 14th Cav. at Fort Sheridan usually provided support in terms of horses, equipment, and training expertise for their summer training, whether it was at Fort Sheridan or Camp Custer. For more than a few summers, the 159th Brig. was sent to Fort Des Moines to conduct training with the 14th Cav. (-). During those years, the cavalry regiments of the 159th Cav. Brig. also conducted the training of the cavalry elements of the CMTC at Fort Des Moines. The 159th alternated the responsibilities of CMTC training each year with the regiments of the 66th Div. The division's support units established training affiliations with R.A. units as well and generally went to other camps designed for their respective arm or service. For example, the 405th Engr. Sq. usually trained at Fort Sheridan and Camp Custer; the 465th F.A. Bn. trained with the units of the 1st Bn., 14th F.A., and later the 3d F.A., both at Fort Sheridan; and the 465th Armd. Car Sq. trained with the 14th Cav. at Fort Sheridan. Additionally, the 365th Med. Sq. trained at the medical officers training camp at Fort Snelling, MN. During the 1930s, the level of training accelerated and became more varied as experience levels increased in the staff officers of the HQ, as well as those in subordinate units. Throughout the 1930s, the units and staffs of the 65th Cav. Div. participated in various army and corps area CPXs. The training objective of these CPXs was to prepare the staffs of the R.A., N.G., and O.R. units for the 1937 Second Army maneuver. The first of these major exercises was the Sixth Corps Area CPX held at Camp Custer in May 1932. Three years later, the 318th Cav. participated in a staff exercise with the 33d Div. at Camp Grant. The exercise was planned and supervised by Col. George C. Marshall, the senior instructor to the Illinois N.G. at the time. This was followed by a 65th Cav. Div. CPX during April 1936 in Chicago and finally by the Second Army maneuver in August 1937. Due to the lack of horses, equipment, and enlisted men, the 65th Cav. Div. did not participate in the 1937 Second Army maneuver as an organized division. Instead, the members of the division reinforced R.A. or N.G. units to bring them up to wartime strength in officers or by acting as umpires. In general, elements of the division reinforced the 14th Cav. and the 53d Cav. Brig., which participated in the Sixth Corps Area portion of the maneuvers held at Camp Custer. In all, over 200 officers from the division participated. The next event in the life of the division was the Second Army maneuver held in central Wisconsin in August 1940. This time, the officers of the 65th Div. reinforced the 1st Sq., 14th Cav., but also provided a substantial number of officers to the 33d Div. as well. The 1940 Second Army maneuver was the division's last major training event. Over the next year, most of the division's assigned personnel were called to Active Duty during the buildup of the US Army in 1940–41. Location 7 December 1941—Chicago, IL.

Status: Disbanded 30 January 1942.

Events: 124, 148, 156, 159, 174, 175, 214, 264

Division Commanders

Brig. Gen. Hugh S. Johnson	ao August 1924-ao September 1924

Chiefs of Staff

Maj. William C. Christy, Cav.	11 February 1922–4 June 1922
Lt. Col. Charles O. Thomas Jr., Cav.	4 June 1922–8 September 1924
Col. John G. Winter, Cav.	8 September 1924–13 June 1925
Col. Alvin C. Gillem, Cav.	13 June 1925–December 1927
Lt. Col. William A. Cornell, Cav.	December 1927–26 May 1928
Col. George T. Langhorne, Cav.	26 May 1928–31 July 1931
Col. Edward Davis, Cav.	1 August 1931–10 June 1936
Col. Robert C. Rodgers, Cav.	10 June 1936–3 January 1938
Col. Edward Davis, Cav.	3 January 1938–5 February 1940
Lt. Col. James A. Kilian, Cav.	5 February 1940–January 1942

65th CAVALRY DIVISION
Organization 1922

UNIT:	HQ LOCATION:
HQ	Chicago, IL
HQ, Sp. Tps.	Chicago, IL
HQ Troop	Wilmette, IL
65th Sig. Troop	Evanston, IL
585th Ord. Co. (M)	Chicago, IL
Vet. Co. No. 505	Chicago, IL
159th Cav. Brig.	Chicago, IL
317th Cav. Regt.	Chicago, IL
318th Cav. Regt.	Chicago, IL
159th MG Sq.	Evanston, IL
160th Cav. Brig.	Detroit, MI
319th Cav. Regt.	Detroit, MI
320th Cav. Regt.	Milwaukee, WI
160th MG Sq.	Ann Arbor, MI
465th F.A. Bn. (Horse)	Galesburg, IL
405th Engr. Bn. (Mounted)	Chicago, IL
Amb. Co. No. 505	Aurora, IL
65th Cav. Div. Train, Q.M.C.	Streator, IL

65th CAVALRY DIVISION
Organization 1940

UNIT:	HQ LOCATION:
HQ	Chicago, IL
HQ, Sp. Tps.	Chicago, IL
HQ Troop	Chicago, IL
65th Sig. Troop	Chicago, IL
585th Ord. Co. (M)	Chicago, IL
465th Tank Co. (L)	Chicago, IL
159th Cav. Brig.	Chicago, IL
317th Cav. Regt.	Chicago, IL
318th Cav. Regt.	La Grange, IL
160th Cav. Brig.	Detroit, MI
319th Cav. Regt.	Detroit, MI
320th Cav. Regt.	Milwaukee, WI
465th Rcn. Sq.	Detroit, MI
865th F.A. Regt.	Chicago, IL
405th Engr. Sq.	Chicago, IL
365th Med. Sq.	Chicago, IL
465th Q.M. Sq.	Chicago, IL

66th CAVALRY DIVISION | **Organized Reserve Nebraska, Kansas, Iowa, Missouri, Utah, California, South Dakota, and North Dakota**

HQ—Omaha, NE, 1922–30; Fort Omaha, NE, 1930–33; Kansas City, MO, 1933–41

The 66th Cav. Div. was constituted on 15 October 1921, allotted to the Seventh and Ninth Corps Areas, and assigned to the Sixth Army. The division HQ was initiated in January 1922 and established in the Army Building in Omaha, NE, by Col. William L. Luhn. The HQ was moved several times during the period 1922–41, the first time to 22d and Hickory Streets in Omaha in March 1924, then to Fort Omaha about July 1930. The final move was made in August 1933 to 3614 Main Street in Kansas City, MO, ostensibly because of the heavy concentration of division officers in that city. The 66th Cav. Div. suffered from having its units spread out over a wide geographical area. Similar to the N.G.'s 24th Cav. Div., the division's organizations were located across the states of the old west. The bulk of the division was located east of the Rocky Mountains with only the units of the 162d Cav. Brig. being west of the Continental Divide. The tables of organization in the division remained unchanged until 1 July 1929 when the MG Sqs. were deleted. Other changes to the division organization were the addition of the 466th Tank Co. (L), and the expansion of the 466th F.A. Bn. into a regiment (and concurrently redesignated the 866th). Additionally, when the field armies were activated and army areas reallocated in 1933, the division was relieved from the Sixth Army and assigned to the Fourth Army. The 66th Cav. Div. boasted its share of interesting personalities. One example was Col. Julian Gaujot, who earned the Medal of Honor in 1911 near Agua Prieta, Mexico. The most famous alumnus of the 66th Cav. Div., however, was 2d Lt. Ronald Reagan, the 39th President of the United States. Commissioned in the cavalry in 1936, he was assigned to Troop B, 322d Cav. in Des Moines. When he moved to California to pursue his acting career in the late 1930s, he was reassigned to HQ Troop, 323d Cav. The division's Inactive Training Period ran roughly September to June. The Kansas City units had their training meetings each Tuesday evening for 2 hours at the Ambassador Hotel or at Fort Leavenworth. Classes were usually taught by the R.A. unit instructors, or frequently by instructors from the Command and General Staff School. Riding classes were conducted at Fort Leavenworth using horses from the 10th Cav. The Des Moines units also conducted their training events on Tuesday evenings and were able to use the mounts from the 14th Cav. as well as the Fort Des Moines riding hall to perform their equestrian instruction. The officers of the 162d Brig., not being in close proximity to Regular or N.G. cavalry units had to own their horses or pay out of their pockets to rent horses. The division, less the 162d Cav. Brig., held consolidated summer training camps for the first 2 years (1922–23) at Fort Des Moines. After that, the division support units generally went to other camps designed for their respective arm or service. For example, the 406th Engrs. usually trained with the 9th Engrs. at Fort Riley, the 466th F.A. Bn. trained with the 14th F.A. at Fort Riley, and the 366th Med. Sq. trained at the medical officers training camp at Fort Snelling. The 161st Cav. Brig. units (less the 322d Cav.) usually trained at Fort Riley, but occasionally trained at Fort Des Moines. The 322d trained at Fort Des Moines, but also went to Fort Riley for several summers. The 323d Cav. went to Del Monte, CA, near the Presidio of Monterey to train with the 11th Cav. Fort D.A. Russell, WY, was the summer training site of the 324th Cav. until the 13th Cav. was transferred to Fort Riley in 1926, after which the regiment traveled to Fort Meade, SD, to train with the 4th Cav. In addition to the summer training camps, the units of the 66th Cav. Div. also conducted the training at the CMTC. The 321st Cav. usually supervised the cavalry camps at Forts Riley and Leavenworth, and the 322d at Fort Des Moines. The 323d and 324th ran the camps at Del Monte and Fort Meade, respectively. Because of the lack of assigned enlisted personnel, horses, and equipment, the 66th Cav. Div. did not participate as an organized unit in the Fourth Army maneuvers of 1937 and 1940. However, hundreds of officers and many enlisted men from the 66th participated as umpires or by being assigned to R.A. or N.G. cavalry units to bring them up to authorized war strength. The 1940 maneuvers at Camp Ripley, MN, and Fort Lewis, WA, were the division's last major training events. For these maneuvers, the division provided over 250 officers to fill out units of the 24th Cav. Div., and the R.A.'s 2d, 4th, 11th, and 14th Cav. Regts. Many were also employed as umpires. Location 7 December 1941—Kansas City, MO.

Status: Disbanded 30 January 1942.

Events: 233, 236

Division Commanders

Col. Julian E. Gaujot, Cav. (R.A.)	11 February 1928–June 1934

Chiefs of Staff

Col. William L. Luhn, Cav.	25 October 1921–26 January 1928
Lt. Col. Frederick G. Turner, Cav.	26 January 1928–11 February 1928
Col. Julian E. Gaujot, Cav.	11 February 1928–June 1934
Maj. Harold Thompson, Cav.	June 1934–11 December 1934
Col. Hugh H. Broadhurst, Cav.	11 December 1934–11 June 1936
Col. Robert C. Rodgers, Cav.	10 June 1936–3 January 1938
Col. Hugh H. Broadhurst, Cav.	11 January 1938–July 1940
Lt. Col. Roy E. Craig, Cav.	August 1940–September 1940
Col. John A. Robenson, Cav.	September 1940–January 1942

66th CAVALRY DIVISION
Organization 1922

UNIT:	HQ LOCATION:
HQ	Omaha, NE
HQ, Sp. Tps.	Omaha, NE
HQ Troop	Omaha, NE
66th Sig. Troop	Omaha, NE
586th Ord. Co. (M)	Omaha, NE
Vet. Co. No. 506	Omaha, NE
161st Cav. Brig.	Kansas City, MO
321st Cav. Regt.	Kansas City, MO
322d Cav. Regt.	Des Moines, IA
161st MG Sq.	Junction City, KS
162d Cav. Brig.	Salt Lake City, UT
323d Cav. Regt.	San Francisco, CA
324th Cav. Regt.	Thermopolis, WY
162d MG Sq.	San Francisco, CA
466th F.A. Bn. (Horse)	Wichita, KS
406th Engr. Bn. (Mounted)	Des Moines, IA
Amb. Co. No. 506	Williston, ND
66th Cav. Div. Train, Q.M.C.	Sioux Falls, SD

66th CAVALRY DIVISION
Organization 1940

UNIT:	HQ LOCATION:
HQ	Kansas City, MO
HQ, Sp. Tps.	Kansas City, MO
HQ Troop	Kansas City, MO
66th Sig. Troop	Kansas City, MO
586th Ord. Co. (M)	Kansas City, MO
466th Tank Co. (L)	St. Paul, MN
161st Cav. Brig.	Kansas City, MO
321st Cav. Regt.	St. Louis, MO
322d Cav. Regt.	Des Moines, IA
162d Cav. Brig.	San Francisco, CA
323d Cav. Regt.	Los Angeles, CA
324th Cav. Regt.	San Francisco, CA
466th Rcn. Sq.	Kansas City, MO
866th F.A. Regt.	Topeka, KS
406th Engr. Sq.	Des Moines, IA
366th Med. Sq.	Wichita, KS
466th Q.M. Sq.	Rapid City, SD

Chapter 13

Cavalry Brigades

USASC Photo, NA II

Halftracks of the 7th Cavalry Brigade (Mechanized) in the field at Fort Knox, KY, during the 1936 Second Army maneuvers.

Cavalry brigades provided command and control for assigned or attached cavalry units and other elements attached for operations. Their mission was to plan, coordinate, and conduct operations to provide reconnaissance and security for the ground force to which they were assigned or attached. Cavalry brigades could also be used both defensively and offensively. When employed in the former mode (defense), they were usually to be deployed in an economy of force or delay role. In the latter (offense), cavalry brigades were employed in reconnaissance missions, raids, or pursuit and exploitation of routed enemy formations.

Organization

In 1921 cavalry brigades were organized to consist of a headquarters (HQ), HQ company, and two cavalry regiments and a machine gun squadron. The major change to the cavalry brigade occurred in 1928 and 1929 when the machine gun squadrons were eliminated and a machine gun troop added to each of the cavalry regiments.

The vast majority of cavalry brigades in the interwar period were divisional brigades, but there were two separate brigades. The organization of the one separate National Guard (N.G.) brigade mirrored that of the divisional brigades. The other separate brigade, the 7th Cavalry (Cav.) Brigade (Brig.) (Mechanized [Mecz]), was a completely different animal. The creation of the 7th Brig. was a result of the tests of the experimental Mechanized Force in 1928 and 1931 and General (Gen.) Douglas MacArthur's 1931 directive to begin mechanizing and motorizing the US Army "as far as is practicable." This brigade was initially organized in 1932 at Fort Knox from the remnants of the defunct Mechanized Force. Over the next several years, it was slowly built up to the point where it consisted of two mechanized cavalry regiments and various

Cavalry Brigade, 1921

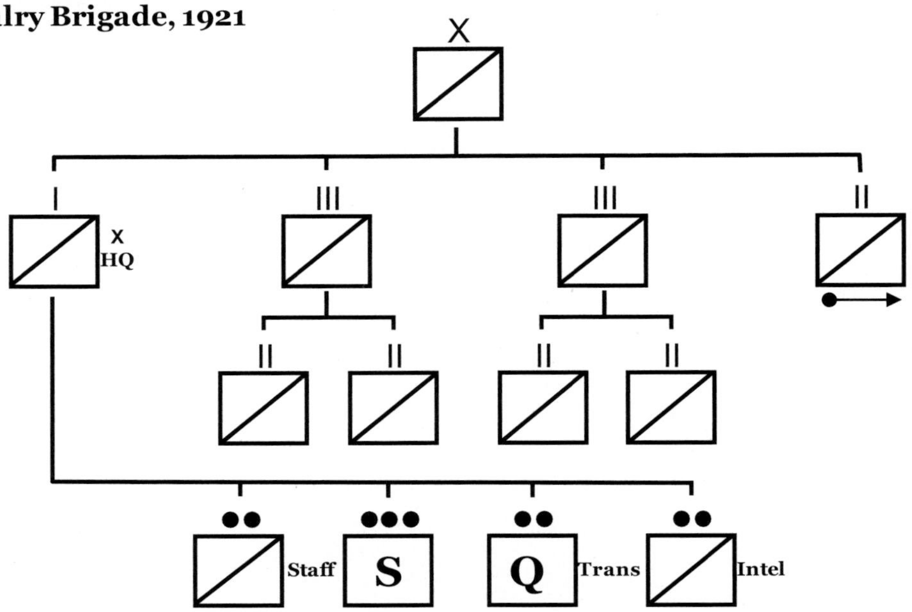

T/O:	421W
Approved:	3 February 1921
Commander:	Brig. Gen.
Officers:	147
W. O.	3
Enlisted:	2,653
Total:	2,803

For personnel and key equipment details see T/O 401w, Cavalry Division

Cavalry Brigade (Mechanized), 1936

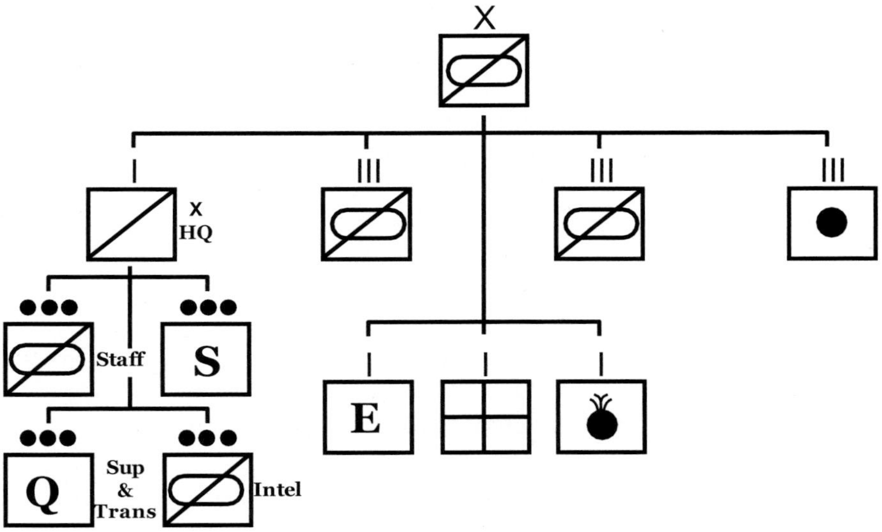

T/O:	422 (Mecz)
Approved:	1 Januray 1936
Commander:	Brig. Gen.
Officers:	112*
W. O.	2*
Enlisted:	1,589*
Total:	1,703*

*Totals include the brigade headquarters, headquarters troop, and two mechanized cavalry regiments only.

Key Equipment*:

Cars, scout	10
Cars, armored	38
Cars, combat	112
Mortars	12
Machine guns, .30 cal.	622
Machine guns, .50 cal.	194
Submachine guns	266

Cavalry Brigade organization, 1921 and 1936.

support elements by 1936. Over that period and on to 1940, when it was reorganized and redesignated as the 1st Armored (Armd.) Division (Div.) , the brigade was one of the most active organizations in the Army, traveling as far west as Fort Riley, KS, and as far north as New York State to participate in various Army training and publicity activities.

Until 1940, the 1st and 2d Cav. Brig. were the only R.A. cavalry brigades in active service. However, the brigades of the 2d and 3d Cav. Divs. were all active as RAI units at various times in the 1920s and 1930s. Though active as Reserve organizations, these brigades did not function as command and control HQ. They were typically used only as mobilization assignment units and rarely functioned as units in the inactive training period or during summer training. During 1940 and 1941, the 3d and 4th Cav. Brigs. were both activated as "Colored" organizations in the all-black 2d Cav. Div.

There were eight N.G. brigades constituted in 1921, assigned two each to the four Guard cavalry divisions. Between 1921 and 1927, the National Guard Bureau, various state Adjutants General, and War Department made several adjustments to the allotment and assignments of the 16 N.G. cavalry regiments. In the latter year, the 59th Cav. Brig. was constituted and allotted to the First Corps Area to provide each corps area with a cavalry brigade HQ. Over the next 2 years, four new Guard cavalry regiments were created, which in turn required several changes to regimental assignments to the nine brigades. In 1938, during the efforts to organize the remaining three inactive N.G. cavalry divisions (the 24th Div. was organized in 1936) the 56th Cav. Brig. was relieved from the 23d Cav. Div. and became a separate brigade in the mobilization plan. As such, it was the only one of the nine N.G. cavalry brigades federalized for Active Duty in World War II. The other eight were disbanded along with the four divisions in the fall of 1940.

Twelve brigades were constituted in the Organized Reserve (O.R.) in 1921, all of which were divisional brigades. Unlike the Guard brigades, the divisional assignments of the Reserve brigades remained constant through the interwar period. All of the divisional brigades functioned as units and a few functioned, at times, as actual HQ in the inactive training period. Those brigades were generally commanded by a Reserve senior colonel or brigadier general. Three of the brigades, the 156th, 158th, 162d Brigs., each located in different corps areas than their parent divisions, possessed a small Regular Army (R.A.) staff at the brigade level that infantry divisional brigades did not have. These staffs generally performed the same functions as the cavalry division staffs. This system was eliminated for the 158th Cav. Brig. by 1934 and thereafter the brigade was attached to the 94th Div. (and at times to the 76th Div.) for the purposes of administration, logistics, and training. The staffs were typically organized as follows:

Geographically Separated Cavalry Brigade:

Chief of Staff	colonel
Adjutant General/S1	major
Assistant Chief of Staff, S3	lieutenant colonel
Enlisted clerk/driver	sergeant

Training

Both active R.A. cavalry brigades were concentrated along the Mexican border between 1919 and 1941. The 2d Brig. was assembled entirely at Fort Bliss, TX, while the 1st Brig. was distributed in posts on or near the Rio Grande River between Marfa and Fort Brown. This disposition, while not ideal for training purposes, was necessary to satisfy the 1st Cav. Div.'s real world mission of policing the troublesome Mexican border. The division was able to assemble both brigades at one location for training only a few times before 1940. However, both brigades deployed to the field for a brigade- or division-level maneuver most years after 1926. The 1st Cav. Brig. usually trained with the 2d Div. at locations in south Texas and the 2d Cav. Brig. usually trained with the balance of the 1st Cav. Div. at locations in west Texas.

The Regular Army Inactive (RAI) cavalry brigades of the 2d Cav. Div. frequently attended summer camps in the 1920s and 1930s. In both cases, however, the brigades were largely pool organizations and rarely functioned as organized units in the Inactive Training period. At summer training, the personnel of these brigades were typically integrated into the training of subordinate regiments. The same was true for the brigades of the 3d Cav. Div. There is no evidence that the 6th Brig. was ever ordered to camp as a unit, though it is likely that its members attended camp as individuals attached to other units.

N.G. cavalry brigade headquarters and headquarters companies (HHC) typically performed their drills during the Inactive Training period at their home armories 1 night a week or on the weekend, depending on the planned training. The HQ and staff usually focused on staff skills while the various sections of the HQ troop focused on support tasks. Occasionally N.G. brigade HQ participated in division or higher level CPXs as part of their inactive training. All cavalry brigades were assigned to multistate divisions and generally attended camp within their home state. Six of the nine brigades were themselves multistate organizations and thus, their camps were generally split between the two or three states of their subordinate regiments. Several multistate brigades were able to assemble the subordinate units from other states at a brigade camp in a few instances in the interwar years. Except for the army-level maneuvers in the late 1930s and early 1940s, however, combined camps for multistate brigades were rare.

Though most O.R. brigades functioned as units, their Inactive Training assemblies tended to be conducted with one of their subordinate regiments or with another HQ. Only occasionally did these brigades hold training periods that were conducted solely with the brigade's assigned personnel. Most of these brigades functioned as actual command and control HQ during summer training camps where they participated in a division or corps area CPX. Usually, if a senior officer was not already assigned to command the brigade, the senior regimental commander temporarily filled in as commander for the camp. More often, the brigade's personnel would attend the summer training attached to one of the brigade's subordinate regiments. For a number of brigades in the 1930s, the HQ was placed in charge to control the conduct of its two subordinate regiments as they took turns training the candidates of the CMTC.

HHT, 1st Cavalry Brigade (1st Cavalry Division)

HQ—Fort Brown, TX, 1919; *Demobilized,* 1919–21; Camp Harry J. Jones, AZ, 1921–23; Fort Clark, TX 1923–41; Fort Bliss, TX, 1941

Subordinate elements—1st Cav. Regt., 1921–33; 10th Cav. Regt., 1921–23; 5th Cav. Regt., 1923–41; 12th Cav. Regt., 1933–41; 1st MG Sq., 1921–28

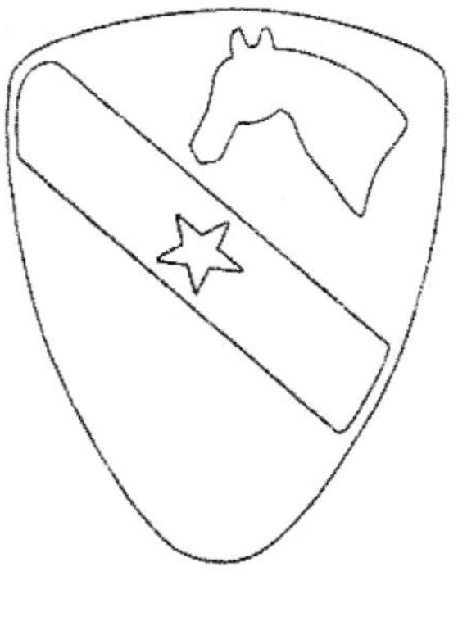

Demobilized on 14 July 1919 at Fort Brown, TX. Reconstituted in the R.A. on 20 August 1921 and assigned to the 1st Cav. Div. HQ organized on 1 September 1921 at Camp Harry J. Jones, AZ. HQ troop concurrently organized by reorganization and redesignation of H Troop, 1st Cav. Departed Camp Jones on 28 December 1922 on an overland march to Fort Clark, TX, and arrived there on 3 February 1923 for permanent station. Assumed the security mission for the Texas border from Fort Clark to Fort Brown, TX, 1923–41. Entire brigade participated in filming the movie "Rough Riders" at Camp Bullis, TX, 17 August–17 September 1926. Units of the brigade maintained habitual summer training relationships with units of the 156th Cav. Brig. from 1922 to 1940. Transferred to Fort Bliss, TX, on 6 February 1941. Location 7 December 1941—Fort Bliss, TX.

Current Status: Active at Fort Hood, TX, as HHC, 1st Brig., 1st Cav. Div.

Events: 30, 42, 55, 65, 80, 83, 97, 105, 125, 147, 183, 206, 242, 250, 258, 282, 284, 288, 295, 296, 300, 315, 328

Commanders, 1st Cavalry Brigade

Brig. Gen. James A. Ryan	25 February 1918–12 May 1918
Col. Farrand Sayre	15 November 1918–13 July 1919
Demobilized/Inactive	14 July 1919–31 August 1921
Col. Edwin B. Winans	1 September 1921–October 1921
Col. Alvord V.P. Anderson	October 1921–28 April 1922
Brig. Gen. William H. Hay	28 April 1922–9 May 1923
Col. Walter C. Short	9 May 1923–18 October 1923
Brig. Gen. William H. Hay	18 October 1923–6 November 1923
Lt. Col. Oliver P. M. Hazzard	6 November 1923–14 July 1924
Brig. Gen. Ewing E. Booth	14 July 1924–8 April 1925
Brig. Gen. Edwin B. Winans	15 September 1925–5 March 1926
Brig. Gen. Leroy Eltinge	5 March 1926–September 1929
Brig. Gen. Hamilton S. Hawkins	September 1929–1 April 1934
Col. Wallace B. Scales	1 April 1934–8 March 1935
Col. Guy Kent	8 March 1935–3 May 1935
Col. Stephen W. Winfree	3 May 1935–18 June 1935
Brig. Gen. Evan H. Humphrey	18 June 1935–3 April 1936
Col. Kerr T. Riggs	3 April 1936–28 January 1937
Brig. Gen. Kenyon A. Joyce	28 January 1937–21 December 1938
Col. Donald A. Robinson	21 December 1938–16 January 1939
Brig. Gen. Jonathan Wainwright	16 January 1939–September 1940
Brig. Gen. John Millikin	October 1940–June 1941
Brig. Gen. Karl S. Bradford	June 1941–November 1943

HHT, 2d Cavalry Brigade (1st Cavalry Division)

HQ—Fort Bliss, TX, 1919; *Demobilized,* 1919–21; Fort Bliss, TX, 1921–41

Subordinate elements—7th Cav. Regt., 1921–41; 8th Cav. Regt.,1921–41; 2d MG Sq., 1921–28

Demobilized on 9 July 1919 at Fort Bliss, TX. Reconstituted in the R.A. on 20 August 1921 and assigned to the 1st Cav. Div. HQ organized on 14 September 1921 at Fort Bliss. HQ troop concurrently organized by reorganization and redesignation of H Troop, 7th Cav. Units of the brigade maintained habitual summer training relationships with units of the 156th Cav. Brig. from 1922 to 1940. Reserve officers assigned to the brigade headquarters or headquarters troop (HHT) conducted summer training with the brigade at Fort Bliss. Location 7 December 1941—Fort Bliss, TX.

Current Status: Active at Fort Hood, TX, as HHC, 2d Brig., 1st Cav. Div.

Events: 3, 30, 65, 80, 83, 97, 127, 146, 206, 250, 259, 284, 295, 296, 300, 315, 328

Commanders, 2d Cavalry Brigade

Col. Selah R.H. Tompkins	27 December 1917–24 February 1918
Brig. Gen. Robert L. Howze	24 February 1918–12 May 1918
Unknown	13 May 1918–8 July 1919
Demobilized/Inactive	9 July 1919–31 August 1921
Col. Walter C. Short	September 1921–May 1922
Brig. Gen. Joseph C. Castner Jr.	May 1922–July 1923
Col. Fitzhugh Lee	July 1923–August 1923
Brig. Gen. Joseph C. Castner Jr.	August 1923–6 June 1925
Col. Samuel McP. Rutherford	6 June 1925–10 August 1925
Brig. Gen. Charles D. Rhodes	10 August 1925–15 December 1925
Col. Samuel McP. Rutherford	15 December 1925–7 August 1926
Brig. Gen. Charles J. Symmonds	7 August 1926–30 April 1927
Col. Samuel McP. Rutherford	30 April 1927–6 September 1927
Brig. Gen. Samuel D. Rockenbach	6 September 1927–28 August 1928
Col. William M. Connell	28 August 1928–18 September 1928
Brig. Gen. Walter C. Short	18 September 1928–30 September 1933
Brig. Gen. George Vidmer	1 October 1933–16 August 1935
Col. Joseph A. Baer	16 August 1935–26 October 1935
Col. Frank T. Keller	26 October 1935–2 July 1936
Brig. Gen. Ben Lear	2 July 1936–6 July 1936
Col. Frank T. Keller	6 July 1936–4 September 1936
Brig. Gen. Ben Lear	4 September 1936–25 October 1926
Brig. Gen. Robert McC. Beck Jr.	25 October 1936–28 February 1938
Col. John K. Herr	28 February 1938–12 March 1938
Col. Innis P. Swift	12 March 1938–6 September 1938
Brig. Gen. Robert C. Richardson	6 September 1938–2 February 1939
Brig. Gen. Innis P. Swift	2 February 1939–11 April 1941
Brig. Gen. Karl S. Bradford	11 April 1941–June 1941
Col. John K. Brown	June 1941–27 November 1941
Brig. Gen. Harry H. Johnson (TX)	27 November 1941–6 January 1942

*Concurrently commanding the 1st Cav. Div. for all or part of the period listed.

HHT, 3d Cavalry Brigade (2d Cavalry Division)

HQ—*Inactive,* 1919–26; Fort Bliss, TX, 1926–33; Kansas City, MO, 1933; *Inactive,* 1933–37; Des Moines, IA, 1937–40; Fort Riley, KS, 1940–41

Subordinate elements—4th Cav. Regt., 1923–33; 10th Cav. Regt., 1924–27; 2d Cav. Regt., 1927–41; 13th Cav. Regt., 1933–36; 4th Cav. Regt., 1936–40; *3d MG Sq.,* 1921–28

Demobilized on 15 July 1919 at Harry J. Jones, AZ. Reconstituted in the R.A. on 20 August 1921 and assigned to the 2d Cav. Div. HQ, 1st Cav. Div. designated Active Associate, 1922–24. The 6th Cav. Regt. designated Active Associate, 1924–27. The brigade HQ was organized on 24 June 1926 with O.R. personnel as an RAI unit at Fort Bliss, TX. Under special instructions from the Adjutant General, the HQ troop was withdrawn from the Eighth Corps Area on 15 August 1927 and allotted to the Seventh Corps Area; brigade HQ remained allotted to the Eighth Corps Area. In accordance with the special instructions, the HQ troop was to be organized from enlisted personnel assigned to the Cavalry School at Fort Riley, KS, to ensure rapid organization of the 2d Cav. Div. for mobilization purposes. HQ troop organized in 1927 with O.R. personnel as an RAI unit in the Seventh Corps Area. It was subsequently withdrawn from the Eighth Corps Area on 1 March 1933, allotted to the Seventh Corps Area, and organized with O.R. personnel as an RAI unit at Kansas City, MO. Officers assigned to the HHT were from Kansas and Missouri. The HQ was once again withdrawn from the Seventh Corps Area on 1 October 1933 and allotted to the Ninth Corps Area. However, Fort Riley remained the designated mobilization training station for the brigade HHT. Apparently, the HQ was never organized in the Ninth Corps Area. The HQ was withdrawn from the Ninth Corps Area on 5 June 1936 and allotted to the Seventh Corps Area. HHT organized by December 1937 with O.R. personnel as an RAI unit with HQ at Des Moines, IA. Conducted summer training with the 2d Cav. Brig. at Fort Bliss, TX, 1927–33, and with the 14th Cav. at Fort Des Moines, IA, 1937–40. Reserve personnel relieved on 15 October 1940. Concurrently the HHT activated at Fort Riley, KS. Location 7 December 1941—Fort Riley, KS.

Current Status: Active at Fort Hood, TX, as HHC, 3d Brig., 1st Cav. Div.

Events: 328

Commanders, 3d Cavalry Brigade

Col. George H. Morgan	21 December 1917–14 February 1918	Capt. Robert Colvin**	26 March 1931–1 March 1933
Brig. Gen. DeRosey C. Cabell	14 February 1918–29 April 1918	*Inactive*	1 March 1933–30 June 1933
Col. George H. Morgan	29 April 1918–12 May 1918	Col. Selwyn D. Smith*	1 July 1933–1 July 1935
Unknown	13 May 1918–14 July 1919	*Inactive*	1 July 1935–ao December 1937
Demobilized/Inactive	15 July 1919–24 June 1926	Unknown	ao December 1937–30 September 1940
Capt. George S. Danhour**	24 June 1926–26 April 1929	Col. Arthur H. Wilson	1 October 1940–24 November 1940
Capt. Claude B. Keever**	16 April 1926–24 June 1926	Brig. Gen. Terry de la M. Allen	24 November 1940–31 March 1941
		Brig. Gen. John D. Coulter	1 April 1941–15 July 1942

*Designated commander for mobilization purposes.
**RAI commanders: junior officers.

HHT, 4th Cavalry Brigade (2d Cavalry Division)

HQ—*Not organized,* 1921–27; Fort Bliss, TX, 1926–32; Kansas City, MO, 1932–33; *Inactive,* 1933; Presidio of Monterey, CA, 1933–36; *Inactive,* 1936–37; Des Moines, IA, 1937–41; Fort Riley, KS, 1941

Subordinate elements—12th Cav. Regt., 1923–33; 13th Cav. Regt., 1923–27; 14th Cav. Regt., 1927–40; 11th Cav. Regt., 1933–40; 9th Cav. Regt., 1940–41; 10th Cav. Regt., 1940–41; *4th MG Sq.,* 1921–28

Constituted in the R.A. on 20 August 1921 and assigned to the 2d Cav. Div. HQ, 1st Cav. Div. designated Active Associate, 1922–24. The 6th Cav. Regt. designated Active Associate, 1924–27. The brigade HQ was organized on 24 June 1926 with O.R. personnel as an RAI unit at Fort Bliss, TX. Under special instructions from the Adjutant General, the HQ troop was withdrawn from the Eighth Corps Area on 15 August 1927, and allotted to the Seventh Corps Area; brigade HQ remained allotted to the Eighth Corps Area. In accordance with the special instructions, the HQ troop was to be organized from enlisted personnel assigned to the Cavalry School at Fort Riley, KS, to ensure rapid organization of the 2d Cav. Div. for mobilization purposes. The brigade HQ was withdrawn from the Eighth Corps Area on 1 May 1932, allotted to the Seventh Corps Area, and organized with O.R. personnel as an RAI unit at Kansas City, MO. The brigade HHT were subsequently withdrawn from the Seventh Corps Area on 1 March 1933 and allotted to the Ninth Corps Area. Organized by December 1933 with O.R. personnel as an RAI unit at the Presidio of Monterey. The Presidio of Monterey designated as the mobilization training station for the brigade HHT, 1932–36. Withdrawn from the Ninth Corps Area on 5 June 1936, and allotted to the Seventh Corps Area. Inactivated on 12 July 1936 at the Presidio of Monterey by relief of personnel. Fort Riley again designated as the mobilization training station for the brigade HHT. Organized with O.R. personnel as an RAI unit by December 1937 with HQ at Des Moines, IA. Conducted summer training with the 2d Cav. Brig. at Fort Bliss, TX, 1927–33, the 11th Cav. at the Presidio of Monterey, 1934–35, and with the 14th Cav. at Fort Des Moines, IA, 1937–40. O.R. personnel relieved in early 1941. Activated 21 February 1941 as a "Colored" brigade at Fort Riley, KS, with a cadre of personnel from the 9th Cav. Location 7 December 1941—Fort Riley, KS.

Events: 328

Commanders, 4th Cavalry Brigade

Capt. Bernard A. Kellner**	24 June 1926–26 April 1929	Unknown	ao December 1937–January 1941
Capt. Adolphus A. Hunt**	26 April 1929–1 March 1933	*Inactive*	January 1941–21 February 1941
Inactive	1 March 1933–ao December 1933	Brig. Gen. Benjamin O. Davis Sr.	21 February 1941–19 June 1941
Unknown	ao December 1933–12 July 1936	Col. Duncan G. Richert	19 June 1941–30 October 1941
Inactive	12 July 1936–ao December 1937	Brig. Gen. Harry D. Chamberlain	30 October 1941–5 April 1942

**RAI commanders: O.R. officers.

HHT, 5th Cavalry Brigade (Colored) (3d Cavalry Division) **Regular Army Inactive**

HQ—Seventh Corps Area at large, 1927–39; Des Moines, IA, 1939–41

Subordinate elements—10th Cav. Regt., 1927–40; 11th Cav. Regt., 1927–33; 9th Cav. Regt., 1933–40; 5th MG Sq., 1927–28

Constituted in the R.A. on 15 August 1927, assigned to the 3d Cav. Div., and allotted to the Seventh Corps Area. Organized by December 1927 with O.R. personnel as an RAI unit in the Seventh Corps Area at large. Maintained training affiliation with the 2d Cav. and conducted summer training at Fort Riley, KS. Reorganized on 18 August 1933 as a "Colored" brigade HQ located by 1939 at Des Moines, IA. Disbanded 10 October 1940.

Commanders, 5th Cavalry Brigade

Unknown	ao December 1927–1 July 1933	Unknown	30 June 1935–ao December 1938
Col. Copley Enos*	1 July 1933–30 June 1935	1st Lt. George H. McNay**	ao December 1938–26 June 1939
	Unknown	30 June 1935–10 October 1940	

*Designated commander for mobilization purposes.
**RAI commanders: O.R. officers.

HHT, 6th Cavalry Brigade (3d Cavalry Division) **Regular Army Inactive**

HQ—Seventh Corps Area at large, 1927–32; *Inactive,* 1932–39; Des Moines, IA, 1939–40

Subordinate elements—3d Cav. Regt., 1927–40; 6th Cav. Regt., 1927–40; 6th MG Sq., 1927–28

Constituted in the R.A. on 15 August 1927, and assigned to the 3d Cav. Div., and allotted to the Seventh Corps Area. Organized in 1927 with O.R. personnel as an RAI unit in the Seventh Corps Area at large. Maintained training affiliation with the 14th Cav. and conducted summer training at Fort Des Moines, IA, 1928–31. Withdrawn from the Seventh Corps Area on 1 May 1932, and allotted to the Third Corps Area. Organized by July 1933 with O.R. personnel as an RAI unit in the Third Corps Area at large. Withdrawn from the Third Corps Area on 1 June 1936 and allotted to the Seventh Corps Area. Organized by December 1939 with O.R. personnel as an RAI unit at Des Moines, IA. Disbanded 10 October 1940.

Commanders, 6th Cavalry Brigade

Unknown	ao December 1927–1 May 1932	Unknown	30 June 1935–1 June 1936
Inactive	1 May 1932–ao July 1933	*Inactive*	1 June 1936–ao December 1939
Col. Charles E. Stodter*	1 July 1933–30 June 1935	Unknown	ao December 1939–10 October 1940

*Designated commander for mobilization purposes.

HHT, 7th Cavalry Brigade (Mechanized) (I Cavalry Corps)

HQ—Fort Knox, KY, 1932–40

Subordinate elements—1st Cav. Regt., 1933–40; 4th Cav. Regt., 1933–36; 13th Cav. Regt., 1936–40; 68th F.A. Regt., 1933–40; 7th Rcn. and Support Sq., 1939–40; 4th Med. Sq., 1939–40; 19th Ord. Co., 1936–40; 7th Sig. Tp., 1939–40; 47th Engr. Tp., 1940

Constituted in the R.A. on 16 January 1932 and assigned to the I Cavalry Corps. HQ activated at Camp Knox, KY, on 1 March 1932. HQ troop activated at Fort Knox, KY, on 22 October 1934. Assigned the peacetime duty of reinforcing security at the US Gold Depository at Fort Knox, KY. Subordinate units escorted shipments to the depository from New York from January to March 1937. Performed flood relief assistance at West Point, KY, during the Ohio River flood of February 1937. Conducted a 350-mile motor march to Fort Oglethorpe, GA, and return 21–24 March 1938. Entire brigade participated in the New York World's Fair 1–4 September 1939. Reorganized and redesignated HHC, 1st Armd. Div. on 1 July 1940.

Current Status: Active at Fliegerhorst Kaserne, Hanau, Germany, as HHC, 1st Armd. Div.

Events: 171, 174, 175, 185, 190, 213, 214, 220, 230, 234, 253, 264, 269, 277, 279, 280, 295, 296, 302, 328, 330

Commanders, 7th Cavalry Brigade (Mechanized)

Brig. Gen. Julian R. Lindsey	1 March 1932–31 May 1934	Col. Bruce Palmer	10 September 1935–27 June 1936
Brig. Gen. Guy V. Henry	31 May 1934–24 July 1935	Brig. Gen. Daniel Van Voorhis	27 June 1936–8 October 1938
Col. James P. Barney	24 July 1935–10 September 1935	Col. Charles L. Scott	8 October 1938–1 November 1938
Brig. Gen. Adna R. Chaffee	1 November 1938–15 July 1940		

HHT, 51st Cavalry Brigade (21st Cavalry Division) **New York National Guard**

HQ—*Not organized,* 1921–22; Manhattan, NY, 1922–36; Brooklyn, NY, 1936–40

Subordinate elements—101st Cav. Regt., 1921–40; 102d Cav. Regt., 1921–28; 121st Cav. Regt., 1928–40; 51st MG Sq., 1921–28

Constituted in the N.G. on 6 December 1921, assigned to the 21st Cav. Div., and allotted to the state of New York. HQ troop organized on 24 March 1922 by redesignation of F Troop, 101st Cav. at West New Brighton, NY. HQ organized on 8 May 1922 and federally recognized at New York City, NY. HQ relocated on 24 February 1936 to Brooklyn, NY. Conducted annual summer training at Camp Devens, MA, 1922; Camp Dix, NJ, 1923; Fort Ethan Allen, VT, 1924–25; and most years at Pine Camp, NY, 1926–38. HQ troop redesignated HQ Troop, 21st Cav. Div. on 1 October 1939. A new HQ troop organized in 1940 at New York City. HQ troop reorganized and redesignated HQ Btry., 102d C.A. Brig. on 1 October 1940. HQ disbanded at New York City on 1 November 1940.

Events: 91, 175, 234, 280, 286

Commanders, 51st Cavalry Brigade

Brig. Gen. Mortimer D. Bryant	8 May 1922–19 January 1933	Brig. Gen. Nathaniel H. Egleston	21 January 1933–5 July 1940

HHT, 52d Cavalry Brigade (21st Cavalry Division) **Pennsylvania National Guard**

HQ—Wayne, PA, 1921–25; Philadelphia, PA, 1925–26; Columbia, PA, 1926–33; Harrisburg, PA, 1933–40

Subordinate elements—103d Cav. Regt., 1921–40; 104th Cav. Regt., 1921–40; 52d MG Sq., 1921–28

Constituted in the N.G. in 1921, assigned to the 21st Cav. Div., and allotted to the state of Pennsylvania. HQ troop organized on 21 July 1920 as E Troop, 1st Cav. at Philadelphia, PA; redesignated HQ Troop, 52d Cav. Brig. on 1 June 1921. HQ organized on 6 August 1921, and federally recognized at Wayne, PA. HQ successively relocated as follows: to Philadelphia, PA, in 1925; to Columbia, PA, on 12 March 1926; to Harrisburg, PA, on 1 July 1933. Conducted annual summer training at Mount Gretna, PA, 1921–35, and at Indiantown Gap, PA, 1936–39. Entire brigade called up to perform relief duties in connection with the flooding of the Schuylkill and Susquehanna Rivers in the spring of 1936. Relieved from assignment to the 21st Cav. Div. about October 1938 and assigned to the 22d Cav. Div. The HQ was consolidated with HQ, 22d Cav. Div. on 23 September 1940, and reorganized and redesignated as HQ, 73d F.A. Brig. at Harrisburg, PA. The HQ troop was concurrently reorganized and redesignated as Troop A, 104th Cav.

Current Status: Inactive in the Pennsylvania N.G. as Headquarters and Headquarters Battery (HHB), XXII Corps Artillery.

Events: 102, 203, 301

Commanders, 52d Cavalry Brigade

Brig. Gen. John P. Wood	6 August 1921–15 February 1926	Brig. Gen. Edward J. Stackpole	3 June 1933–16 January 1940
Brig. Gen. Edward C. Shannon	16 February 1926–24 March 1933	Col. George J. Shoemaker	16 January 1940–1 October 1940

HHT, 53d Cavalry Brigade (22d Cavalry Division) **Wisconsin and Illinois National Guard**

HQ—*Not organized*, 1921–25; Stanley, WI, 1925–28; Milwaukee, WI, 1928–32; Chicago, IL, 1932–38; Madison, WI, 1938–40

Subordinate elements—105th Cav. Regt., 1921–40; 106th Cav. Regt., 1921–40; 53d MG Sq., 1921–28

Constituted in the N.G. in 1921, assigned to the 22d Cav. Div., and allotted to the state of Wisconsin. HQ organized on 21 March 1925 and federally recognized at Stanley, WI. HQ relocated to Milwaukee, WI, on 27 June 1928. HQ troop organized on 1 April 1929 by redesignation of HQ Troop, 105th Cav. at Stanley. HQ withdrawn from the state of Wisconsin on 14 August 1932, and allotted to the state of Illinois. HQ organized on 15 August 1932 and federally recognized at Chicago, IL. HQ troop remained at Stanley, WI. Conducted annual summer training most years at Camp Douglas, 1922–27, and Camp Williams, WI, 1928–39. Designated mobilization training station was Camp Williams. Relieved from assignment to the 22d Cav. Div. about October 1938 and assigned to the 23d Cav. Div. HQ withdrawn from the state of Illinois on 21 December 1938, and allotted to the state of Wisconsin. HQ concurrently organized at Madison, WI. HQ troop reorganized and redesignated on 23 September 1940 as HQ Co., 107th Q.M. Regt. Brig. HQ disbanded on 30 September 1940 at Milwaukee, WI.

Events: 148, 159, 214, 264, 302

Commanders, 53d Cavalry Brigade

Maj. John C.P. Hanley (WI) (Acting)	21 March 1925–June 1928	Col. Walter J. Fisher (IL)	15 August 1932–22 June 1938
Maj. Charles S. Mercein (WI) (Acting)	June 1928–31 August 1929	Brig. Gen. Francis M. Allen (IL)	5 July 1938–18 December 1938
Brig. Gen. James J. Quill (WI)	1 September 1929–14 August 1932	Brig. Gen. Ralph M. Immell (WI)	19 December 1938–30 September 1940

HHT, 54th Cavalry Brigade (22d Cavalry Division) **Ohio National Guard**

HQ—*Not organized,* 1921–23; Cincinnati, OH, 1923–29; Cleveland, OH, 1929–40

Subordinate elements—107th Cav. Regt., 1921–40; 108th Cav. Regt., 1921–27; 123d Cav. Regt., 1929–40; 54th MG Sq., 1921–28

Constituted in the N.G. in 1921, assigned to the 22d Cav. Div., and allotted to the state of Ohio. HQ troop organized on 1 February 1922 by redesignation of D Troop, 107th Cav. at Cincinnati, OH. HQ organized on 6 July 1923 and federally recognized at Cincinnati, OH. HHT called up to perform strike duty at coal mines near Middleport, OH, 26 July–16 August 1923. HQ troop redesignated E Troop, 107th Cav. on 1 October 1927 at Cincinnati. Concurrently, a new HQ troop organized by redesignation of E Troop, 107th Cav. at Akron, OH. HQ relocated on 21 May 1929 to Cleveland, OH. Entire brigade called up to perform relief duties in connection with the flooding of the Ohio River in January–March 1937. Conducted annual summer training most years at Camp Perry, OH, 1922–39, and some years at Camp Knox, KY. HHT disbanded on 1 November 1940 at Cleveland and Akron, respectively.

Events: 175, 213, 230, 264, 302

Commanders, 54th Cavalry Brigade

Brig. Gen. Paul L. Mitchell 18 November 1924–28 December 1926 Brig. Gen. Dudley J. Hard 28 December 1926–17 December 1935
Brig. Gen. Newell C. Bolton 10 February 1936–30 September 1940

HHT, 55th Cavalry Brigade (23d Cavalry Division) **North Carolina/Alabama and Louisiana National Guard**

HQ—*Not organized,* 1921–36; New Orleans, LA, 1936–40

Subordinate elements—109th Cav. Regt., 1921–40; 110th Cav. Regt., 1921–27; 108th Cav. Regt., 1927–40; 55th MG Sq., 1921–28

Constituted in the N.G. in 1921 and assigned to the 23d Cav. Div. HQ troop allotted to the state of North Carolina on 1 September 1926. HQ troop organized on 19 May 1927 at Statesville, NC, by redesignation of D Troop, 109th Cav. HQ troop reorganized and redesignated on 19 May 1929 as MG Troop, 109th Cav.; unit requirement remained allotted to North Carolina. HQ troop withdrawn from North Carolina in March 1933 and allotted to the state of Alabama. HQ troop organized on 15 April 1933 at Birmingham, AL, by redesignation of HQ Troop, 23d Cav. Div. (organized as the "Birmingham Sabers" and federally recognized on 12 April 1921 as HQ Troop, 23d Cav. Div.). HQ allotted to the state of Louisiana on 20 May 1936. HQ concurrently organized and federally recognized at New Orleans, LA. Conducted annual summer training most years at Fort Oglethorpe, GA, 1933–39. HQ troop called up for the following state emergencies: hurricane relief duty in Bibb and Shelby Counties in May 1933; coal miners strike in Jefferson, Bibb, and Walker Counties, 25 February–2 May 1934. HHT assembled at Roberts Field, Birmingham, AL, 14–21 January 1940, with HQ, 23d Cav. Div. to conduct additional 2-week annual training directed by the War Department for all N.G. units. HQ consolidated with HQ, 23d Cav. Div., and HQ, 108th Cav., and the consolidated unit reorganized and redesignated as HQ, 105th C.A. Bn. on 6 October 1940 at New Orleans, LA.

Events: 217, 255, 300

Commanders, 55th Cavalry Brigade

Brig. Gen. James E. Edwards (LA) 20 May 1936–19 January 1940 Brig. Gen. Raymond Fleming (LA) 20 January 1940–30 September 1940

HHT, 56th Cavalry Brigade (23d Cavalry Division) **Texas National Guard**

HQ—Houston, TX, 1921–34; Dallas, TX, 1934–35; San Antonio, TX, 1935–40; Fort Bliss, TX, 1940–41; Fort McIntosh, TX, 1941

Subordinate elements—111th Cav. Regt., 1921–29; 112th Cav. Regt., 1921–41; 124th Cav. Regt., 1929–41; 56th MG Sq., 1921–29

Constituted in the N.G. in 1921, assigned to the 23d Cav. Div., and allotted to the state of Texas. HQ organized on 20 July 1921 by redesignation of HQ, 1st Texas Cav. Brig. (organized on 23 August 1918 and federally recognized at Houston, TX) as HQ, 56th Cav. Brig. Concurrently federally recognized at Houston. HQ troop organized on 30 July 1921 by redesignation of HQ Troop, 3d Texas Cav. at Brenham, TX. HQ troop redesignated A Troop, 56th MG Sq. on 19 April 1924 at Brenham; concurrently, a new HQ troop organized at San Antonio, TX, by redesignation of A Troop, 56th MG Sq. HQ relocated to Dallas, TX, on 30 November 1934, and to San Antonio, TX, on 1 March 1935. The brigade, or elements thereof, was called up to perform the following state duties: HHT to perform martial law in connection with lawless conditions in Mexia, TX, 12 January–1 March 1922; HQ troop to perform escort duty in Houston, TX, 11–12 May 1925; HHT and six subordinate troops to perform martial law in connection with lawless conditions in Borger, TX, 28 September–18 October 1929; entire brigade to perform martial law in four counties in east Texas in connection with preventing "hot oil" production in the great East Texas Oilfield near Kilgore, TX, 17 August 1931 (elements remained on Active Duty until 17 December 1932). Relieved from assignment to the 23d Cav. Div. about October 1938, and assigned to Third Army as a separate brigade in the protective mobilization plan. Conducted summer training at Camp Mabry, TX, 1921–23; Camp Stanley, TX; 1924–26; and Camp Wolters, TX, 1927–39. For at least 2 years, in 1932 and 1933, the brigade's subordinate regiments also trained some 26 company-grade cavalry officers of the 156th Cav. Brig. at Camp Wolters. Designated mobilization training station was Fort Brown, TX, 1921–33, and Fort Bliss, TX, 1933–40. Inducted into active Federal service at San Antonio on 18 November 1940. Transferred to Fort Bliss, TX, arrived there 27 November 1940, and attached to the 1st Cav. Div. HHT transferred to Fort McIntosh, TX, on 30 January 1941. Concurrently, the remainder of the brigade relieved 1st Cav. Brig. units of the Rio Grande border posts and the Mexican Border Patrol. HHT assumed command and control of the Eastern Sector, Southern Land Frontier of the Southern Defense Command. Returned to Fort Bliss on 26 May 1941 for preliminary maneuver training with the 1st Cav. Div. in June–July 1941. After the Louisiana Maneuvers in September–October 1941, returned to Fort McIntosh. Location 7 December 1941—Fort McIntosh, TX.

Current Status: Active in the Texas N.G. at Fort Worth, TX, as HHC, 56th Brig., 36th Inf. Div. (Mecz).

Events: 80, 217, 258, 259, 300, 315, 328

Commanders, 56th Cavalry Brigade

Brig. Gen. Jacob F. Wolters	1 June 1921–20 November 1934	Brig. Gen. Walter B. Pyron	20 August 1938–13 September 1941
Brig. Gen. Louis S. Davidson	23 November 1934–20 August 1938	Brig. Gen. Charles H. Gerhardt (R.A.)	13 September 1941–6 January 1942

HHT, 57th Cavalry Brigade (24th Cavalry Division) **South Dakota/Iowa and Kansas National Guard**

HQ—*Not organized,* 1921–30; Des Moines, IA, 1930–40

Subordinate elements—113th Cav. Regt., 1921–40; 114th Cav. Regt., 1921–40; *57th MG Sq.,* 1921–29

Constituted in the N.G. in 1921, assigned to the 24th Cav. Div., and allotted to the state of South Dakota. HQ withdrawn from the state of South Dakota in 1930 and allotted to the state of Iowa. HQ organized on 16 April 1930, and federally recognized at Des Moines, IA. HQ troop withdrawn from the state of South Dakota on 27 January 1932 and allotted to the Iowa N.G. Conducted annual summer training most years at Camp Dodge, IA, 1930–39. For at least 2 years, in 1938 and 1940, the brigade's subordinate units also trained some 44 company-grade officers of the 66th Cav. Div. at Camp Dodge, Fort Riley, KS, and Camp Ripley, MN. HQ troop organized on 3 April 1939 and federally recognized at Des Moines. HQ disbanded on 15 September 1940 at Des Moines. HQ troop reorganized and redesignated Service Company, 109th Q.M. Regt. on 16 September 1940.

Events: 303

Commanders, 57th Cavalry Brigade

Brig. Gen. Park A. Findley (IA) 16 April 1930–June 1935
Brig. Gen. William K. Herndon (KS) 30 July 1935–28 January 1936
Brig. Gen. Raymond A. Yenter (IA) 24 March 1936–30 September 1940

HHT, 58th Cavalry Brigade (24th Cavalry Division) **Wyoming/Idaho National Guard**

HQ—*Not organized,* 1921–26; Cheyenne, WY, 1926–31; Boise, ID, 1931–40

Subordinate elements—115th Cav. Regt., 1921–40; 116th Cav. Regt., 1921–40; *58th MG Sq.,* 1921–29.

Constituted in the N.G. in 1921, assigned to the 24th Cav. Div., and allotted to the state of Wyoming. HQ troop organized on 15 March 1926 and federally recognized at Casper, WY. HQ organized 21 April 1926 and federally recognized at Cheyenne, WY. HQ troop redesignated HQ Troop, 115th Cav. on 1 June 1929. New HQ troop concurrently organized and federally recognized at Casper. HQ withdrawn from the state of Wyoming on 19 February 1931 and allotted to the state of Idaho. Concurrently organized and federally recognized at Boise, ID. HQ Troop withdrawn from state of Wyoming on 1 January 1939 and allotted to the state of Idaho. HQ Troop organized on 30 June 1939 and federally recognized at Nampa, ID. Conducted annual summer training most years at Pole Mountain, WY, 1926–33, and Boise Barracks, ID, 1936–39. HHT reorganized and redesignated HHB, 148th Field Artillery, 1 October 1940.

Events: 304

Commanders, 58th Cavalry Brigade

Brig. Gen. Burke H. Sinclair (WY) 21 April 1926–7 May 1929
Brig. Gen. William R. Taylor (ID) 19 February 1931–22 May 1936
Brig. Gen. Mervin G. McConnell (ID) 23 May 1936–1 October 1940

HHT, 59th Cavalry Brigade (21st Cavalry Division) **Massachusetts/New Jersey National Guard**

HQ—*Not organized,* 1927–37; Newark, NJ, 1937–40

Subordinate elements—102d Cav. Regt., 1928–40; 122d Cav. Regt., 1928–37; 110th Cav. Regt., 1937–40

Constituted in the N.G. in 1927 and allotted to the state of Massachusetts as a separate brigade. Designated mobilization station was Alston, MA, 1927–37. Withdrawn from the state of Massachusetts in 1937 and allotted to the state of New Jersey. HQ organized on 12 June 1937 and federally recognized at Newark, NJ. HQ troop allotted to the state of New Jersey on 1 January 1939. HQ troop organized on 1 April 1939 and federally recognized at Newark. Conducted annual summer training at Sea Girt, NJ, in 1937, and at Indiantown Gap, 1938–39. HQ consolidated with State Staff, New Jersey N.G. in September 1940. HQ troop consolidated with HQ Troop, 102d Cav. on 1 October 1940.

Commanders, 59th Cavalry Brigade

Brig. Gen. Lewis B. Ballantyne 21 June 1937–30 September 1940

HHT, 151st Cavalry Brigade (61st Cavalry Division) **Organized Reserve New York**

HQ—*Not initiated,*1921–22; Rochester, NY, 1922–41

Subordinate elements—301st Cav. Regt., 1921–41; 302d Cav. Regt., 1921–41; 151st MG Sq., 1921–28

Constituted in the O.R. on 15 October 1921, assigned to the 61st Cav. Div., and allotted to the Second Corps Area. HHT initiated on 6 February 1922 at Rochester, NY. Maintained a training affiliation with the 1st Sq., 3d Cav. Conducted summer training most years at Fort Ethan Allen, VT, 1923–40, and at Fort Belvoir, VA, 1937–1939. Subordinate regiments conducted training of CMTC at Fort Ethan Allen with assistance from the 1st Sq., 3d Cav. Location 7 December 1941—Rochester, NY.

Current Status: Disbanded 30 January 1942.

Events: 91

Commanders, 151st Cavalry Brigade

Capt. Frank J. Liddell	6 February 1922–6 June 1922	Maj. Edward H. Gilman	16 December 1937–24 September 1938
Brig. Gen. Brice P. Disque	6 June 1922–14 April 1937	Lt. Col. Richard N. Armstrong	24 September 1938–20 May 1941

HHT, 152d Cavalry Brigade (61st Cavalry Division) **Organized Reserve New York**

HQ—*Not initiated,* 1921–22; New York City, NY, 1922–41

Subordinate elements—303d Cav. Regt., 1921–41; 304th Cav. Regt., 1921–41; 152d MG Sq., 1921–28

Constituted in the O.R. on 15 October 1921, assigned to the 61st Cav. Div., and allotted to the Second Corps Area. HHT initiated in February 1922 at Manhattan, NY. Conducted summer training most years at Fort Ethan Allen, VT, 1923–40, with the 1st Sq., 3d Cav., and at Fort Belvoir, VA, 1937 and 1939, with the 3d Cav. Regt. Subordinate regiments conducted training of CMTC at Fort Ethan Allen with assistance from the 1st Sq., 3d Cav. Location 7 December 1941—New York City, NY.

Current Status: Disbanded 30 January 1942.

Events: 91

Commanders, 152d Cavalry Brigade

Maj. Frederick W. Wurster	3 March 1922–17 March 1922	Lt. Col. Charles W. Jacobsen	23 July 1935–15 April 1937
Brig. Gen. Lincoln C. Andrews	17 March 1922–27 November 1931	Brig. Gen. Brice P. Disque	15 April 1937–June 1939
Unknown	27 November 1931–23 July 1935	Unknown	June 1939–7 December 1941

HHT, 153d Cavalry Brigade (62d Cavalry Division) **Organized Reserve Maryland**

HQ—*Not initiated,* 1921–22; Baltimore, MD, 1922–41

Subordinate elements—305th Cav. Regt., 1921–41; 306th Cav. Regt., 1921–41; 153d MG Sq., 1921–28

Constituted in the O.R. on 15 October 1921, assigned to the 62d Cav. Div., and allotted to the Third Corps Area. HHT initiated in September 1922 at Baltimore, MD. Typically conducted Inactive Training Period meetings at the Post Office Building in Baltimore. Conducted summer training most years at Fort George G. Meade, MD, 1923–40, and some years at Fort Myer, VA, or Fort Belvoir, VA, with the 3d Cav. Regt. Subordinate regiments conducted training of CMTC at Fort Myer and Fort Belvoir with assistance from the 3d Cav. Regt. Location 7 December 1941—Baltimore, MD.

Current Status: Disbanded 30 January 1942.

Commanders, 153d Cavalry Brigade

Col. William M. Winter	September 1922–2 July 1924	Maj. Edmund P. Rutan	ao June 1930–18 March 1931
Unknown	2 July 1924–ao March 1925	Maj. Max Livingston Jr.	18 March 1931–13 June 1935
Maj. James F. Tompkins	ao March 1925–ao October 1928	Maj. Henry P. Ames	13 June 1935–23 January 1938
Unknown	ao October 1928–ao June 1930	Maj. Edwin P. Rutan	23 January 1938–1 August 1938
Lt. Col. Edward B. Harry	1 August 1938–ao August 1941		

HHT, 154th Cavalry Brigade (62d Cavalry Division) **Organized Reserve Virginia**

HQ—*Not initiated* 1921–22; Richmond, VA, 1922–41

Subordinate elements—307th Cav. Regt., 1921–41; 308th Cav. Regt., 1921–41; 154th MG Sq., 1921–28

Constituted in the O.R. on 15 October 1921, assigned to the 62d Cav. Div., and allotted to the Third Corps Area. HHT initiated in 1922 at Richmond, VA. Typically conducted Inactive Training Period meetings at the Parcel Post Building in Richmond. Conducted summer training most years at Fort George G. Meade, MD, 1923–40, and some years at Fort Myer, VA, or Fort Belvoir, VA, with the 3d Cav. Regt. Subordinate regiments conducted training of CMTC at Fort Myer and Fort Belvoir with assistance from the 3d Cav. Regt. Location 7 December 1941—Richmond, VA.

Current Status: Disbanded 30 January 1942.

Commanders, 154th Cavalry Brigade

Unknown	ao December 1922–ao March 1925	Lt. Col. John H. Schenkel	ao May 1931–ao December 1937
Maj. John C. Butler	ao March 1925–30 June 1930	Unknown	ao December 1937–ao June 1938
Col. John P. Hill	30 June 1930–1 August 1930	Maj. John P. Dean	ao June 1938–10 January 1940
Lt. Col. John C. Butler	1 August 1930–ao June 1933	Maj. Moderwell K. Salen	10 January 1940–ao January 1941
Unknown	ao June 1933–ao May 1934	Unknown	ao January 1941–7 December 1941

HHT, 155th Cavalry Brigade (63d Cavalry Division) **Organized Reserve Tennessee**

HQ—*Not initiated,* 1921–22; Chattanooga, TN, 1922–41

Subordinate elements—309th Cav. Regt., 1921–41; 310th Cav. Regt., 1921–41; 155th MG Sq., 1921–28

Constituted in the O.R. on 15 October 1921, assigned to the 63d Cav. Div., and allotted to the Fourth Corps Area. HHT initiated on 31 August 1922 at Chattanooga, TN. Conducted summer training at Camp McClellan, AL, 1923–24, and most years at Fort Oglethorpe, GA, 1925–40, with the 6th Cav. Regt. Subordinate regiments conducted training of CMTC at Fort Oglethorpe and Camp McClellan with assistance from the 6th Cav. Regt. Brigade HQ planned and conducted training of Cavalry CMTC at Fort Oglethorpe with the 309th and 310th Cav. Regts. in 1939. Designated mobilization training station was Fort Oglethorpe, GA. Location 7 December 1941—Chattanooga, TN.

Current Status: Disbanded 30 January 1942.

Commanders, 155th Cavalry Brigade

Maj. Ellsworth Wilson	31 August 1922–5 September 1930	Lt. Col. Richmond A. Mead	5 September 1930–ao November 1937
Unknown	ao November 1937–7 December 1941		

HHT, 156th Cavalry Brigade (63d Cavalry Division) **Organized Reserve Texas**

HQ—*Not initiated,* 1921–22; Dallas, TX, 1922–25; San Antonio, TX, 1925–41

Subordinate elements—311th Cav. Regt. 1921–41; 312th Cav. Regt. 1921–41; 156th MG Sq. 1921–28

Constituted in the O.R. on 15 October 1921, assigned to the 63d Cav. Div., and allotted to the Second Corps Area. Withdrawn from the Second Corps Area on 14 November 1921 and allotted to the Eighth Corps Area. HHT initiated on 5 September 1922 at Dallas, TX. Relocated on 15 October 1925 to San Antonio, TX. Participated in the annual Army Day parade in San Antonio using horses of the Peacock Military Academy. Typically conducted Inactive Training Period meetings at the Smith-Young Tower in San Antonio. Conducted summer training most years at Fort Clark, TX, 1923–35, with the 1st Cav. Brig. and 5th Cav. For at least 2 years, in 1932 and 1933, some 26 company-grade cavalry officers of the brigade and its subordinate regiments trained with the 56th Cav. Brig. at Camp Wolters, TX. Subordinate regiments conducted cavalry CMTC training at Fort Bliss with assistance from the 7th and 8th Cav. Regts. Brigade HQ planned and controlled the training of cavalry CMTC conducted by the 311th and 312th Cav. Regts. at Fort Bliss, TX, 1936–39. Brigade units provided 152 officers, to the 1st Cav. Div. (134), the 56th Cav. Brig. (10), and the 111th Cav. (8) to participate in the 1938 Third Army maneuver at Camp Bullis. A contingent of brigade officers traveled to Fort Knox, KY, in September 1939 to observe the maneuvers of the 7th Cav. Brig. in the Fifth Corps Area maneuver there. Designated mobilization training station was Fort Brown, TX, 1921–40. Location 7 December 1941—San Antonio, TX.

Current Status: Disbanded 30 January 1942.

Events: 146, 217, 258, 259, 261, 300

Commanders, 156th Cavalry Brigade

Lt. Col. Harry B. Rhodes	5 September 1922–ao September 1936	Unknown	ao September 1936–7 December 1941

HHT, 157th Cavalry Brigade (64th Cavalry Division) **Organized Reserve Kentucky/West Virginia**

HQ—*Not initiated,* 1921–22; Princeton, KY, 1922–31; Lexington, KY, 1931–37; Charleston, WV, 1937–41

Subordinate elements—313th Cav. Regt., 1921–41; 314th Cav. Regt., 1921–41; 157th MG Sq., 1921–28

Constituted in the O.R. on 15 October 1921, assigned to the 64th Cav. Div., and allotted to the Fifth Corps Area. HHT initiated in August 1922 at Princeton, KY. Relocated to Lexington, KY, on 9 July 1931. Relocated to Charleston, WV, on 5 April 1937. Conducted summer training most years at Camp Knox, KY, with the 6th Cav. Regt., 1923–32, and with the 1st Cav. Regt. (Mecz), 1933–40. Subordinate regiments conducted training of CMTC at Camp Knox with assistance from the 1st and 6th Cav. Regts. Location 7 December 1941—Charleston, WV.

Current Status: Disbanded 30 January 1942.

Commanders, 157th Cavalry Brigade

Maj. John S. Walton	August 1922–ao September 1924	Unknown	ao July 1930–ao June 1934
Unknown	ao September 1924–ao June 1930	Col. George T. Smith	ao June 1934–ao June 1937
Maj. Lewis S.N. Phillipp	ao June 1930–ao July 1930	Unknown	ao June 1937–7 December 1941

HHT, 158th Cavalry Brigade (64th Cavalry Division) **Organized Reserve Massachusetts/ New Hampshire**

HQ—*Not initiated,* 1921–22; Boston, MA, 1922–38; Franconia, NH, 1938–41

Subordinate elements—315th Cav. Regt., 1921–41; 316th Cav. Regt., 1921–41; 158th MG Sq., 1921–28

Constituted in the O.R. on 15 October 1921, assigned to the 64th Cav. Div., and allotted to the Fifth Corps Area. Withdrawn from the Fifth Corps Area on 14 November 1921 and allotted to the First Corps Area. HHT initiated in April 1922 at Boston, MA. Attached to the 76th Div. on 17 October 1929 for organization, administration, and training. Relieved from attachment to the 76th Div. on 27 January 1930 and attached to the 94th Div. Relocated to Franconia, NH, on 9 September 1938. Conducted summer training most years at Fort Ethan Allen, VT, 1922–40, with the 1st Sq., 3d Cav. Subordinate regiments conducted training of CMTC at Fort Ethan Allen with assistance from the 1st Sq., 3d Cav. Location 7 December 1941—Franconia, NH.

Current Status: Disbanded 30 January 1942.

Commanders, 158th Cavalry Brigade

Lt. Col. Wickliffe P. Draper	April 1922–23 February 1923	Maj. Alfred G. Boudreau Jr.	July 1927–January 1931
Maj. Frank L. Hiller	23 February 1923–ao October 1924	Lt. Col. Wickliffe P. Draper	January 1931–4 January 1935
Unknown	ao October 1924–ao September 1926	Maj. George B. Morse	4 January 1935–ao September 1936
Col. Jean H. A. Day	ao September 1926–July 1927	Lt. Col. Clarence H. Griffith	ao March 1937–ao August 1938
Unknown	ao August 1938–7 December 1941		

HHT, 159th Cavalry Brigade (65th Cavalry Division) **Organized Reserve Illinois**

HQ—*Not initiated,* 1921–22; Chicago, IL, 1922–41

Subordinate elements—317th Cav. Regt., 1921–41; 318th Cav. Regt., 1921–41; 159th MG Sq., 1921–28

Constituted in the O.R. on 15 October 1921, assigned to the 65th Cav. Div., and allotted to the Sixth Corps Area. HHT initiated in September 1922 at Chicago, IL. Conducted a brigade command post exercise at Chicago, IL, in August 1932 with subordinate regiments, the 65th Sig. Tp., and the Signal Corps ROTC unit from the University of Illinois. Participated in the 65th Cav. Div. CPX in Chicago in April–May 1936. Typically conducted Inactive Training Period meetings at the Post Office Building in Chicago. Conducted regular equestrian training with the horses of the 1st Sq., 14th Cav. at Fort Sheridan, IL. Conducted summer training most years at Fort Sheridan, 1922–40, with the 1st Sq., 14th Cav. Subordinate regiments conducted training of CMTC at Fort Sheridan with assistance from the 1st Sq., 14th Cav. Location 7 December 1941—Chicago, IL.

Current Status: Disbanded 30 January 1942.

Events: 156, 162

Commanders, 159th Cavalry Brigade

Capt. Michael McShane	2 October 1922–14 January 1923	Maj. Roy M. McKerchar	ao July 1932–June 1934
Capt. Andrew W. Marsh	15 January 1923–4 March 1923	Capt. E.F. Williams	June 1934–30 January 1936
Brig Gen. Robert E. Wood	5 March 1923–ao August 1927	Maj. Edwin Hancock	30 January 1936–24 May 1937
Maj. Adam R. Wachs	ao June 1928–ao August 1930	Lt. Col. William N. Leonard	24 May 1937–17 December 1937
Unknown	ao August 1930–ao July 1931	Lt. Col. Roy M. McKerchar	17 December 1937–July 1939
Capt. Theodore H. Clark	ao July 1931–ao June 1932	Col. Walter E. Palmer	July 1939–ao January 1940
Unknown	ao January 1940–7 December 1941		

HHT, 160th Cavalry Brigade (65th Cavalry Division) **Organized Reserve Michigan**

HQ—*Not initiated,* 1921–22; Detroit, MI, 1922–41

Subordinate elements—319th Cav. Regt., 1921–41; 320th Cav. Regt., 1921–41; 160th MG Sq., 1921–28

Constituted in the O.R. on 15 October 1921, assigned to the 65th Cav. Div., and allotted to the Sixth Corps Area. HHT initiated on 6 June 1922 at Detroit, MI. The brigade established a unique radio communications system in July 1929 throughout Michigan in conjunction with civilian stations for the purposes of training and informing unit personnel. Conducted summer training most years at Fort Sheridan, IL, and some years at Camp Custer, MI, 1922–40, with the 1st Sq., 14th Cav. Subordinate regiments conducted training of CMTC at Fort Sheridan and Camp Custer with assistance from the 1st Sq., 14th Cav. Location 7 December 1941—Detroit, MI.

Current Status: Disbanded 30 January 1942.

Commanders, 160th Cavalry Brigade

Lt. Col. Frederick M. Alger	6 June 1922–1 February 1923	Maj. John B. Saunders	ao September 1930–ao January 1931
Brig Gen. Hugh S. Johnson	19 September 1923–ao June 1929	Unknown	ao January 1931–ao June 1939
Unknown	ao June 1929–ao September 1930	Maj. Charles P. Rydberg	ao June 1939–ao January 1940
Unknown	ao January 1940–7 December 1941		

HHT, 161st Cavalry Brigade (66th Cavalry Division) **Organized Reserve Missouri/Nebraska**

HQ—*Not initiated,* 1921–22; Kansas City, MO, 1922–37; Omaha, NE, 1937–41

Subordinate elements—321st Cav. Regt., 1921–41; 322d Cav. Regt., 1921–41; 161st MG Sq., 1921–28

Constituted in the O.R. on 15 October 1921, assigned to the 66th Cav. Div., and allotted to the Seventh Corps Area. HHT initiated on 13 April 1922 at Kansas City, MO. Relocated to Omaha, NE, on 22 July 1937. Conducted summer training most years at Fort Riley, KS, with the 2d Cav. Regt., 1922–40, and some years at Fort Des Moines, IA, with the 1st Sq., 14th Cav. Subordinate regiments conducted training of CMTC at Fort Leavenworth, KS, Fort Des Moines, and Fort Riley with assistance from the 2d Cav. or the 1st Sq., 14th Cav. Location 7 December 1941—Omaha, NE.

Current Status: Disbanded 30 January 1942.

Commanders, 161st Cavalry Brigade

Unknown	13 April 1922–21 May 1924	Maj. John R. Stiles	June 1931–ao January 1932
Capt. J.M. Carter	21 May 1924–ao June 1924	Unknown	ao January 1932–14 December 1937
Unknown	ao June 1924–ao March 1931	Lt. Col. Roland E. Murphy	14 December 1937–19 June 1939
Capt. Gordon M. Baker	ao March 1931–June 1931	Maj. Hayden D. Hughes	28 September 1939–August 1941

HHT, 162d Cavalry Brigade (66th Cavalry Division) **Organized Reserve Utah/California**

HQ—*Not initiated,* 1921–22; Salt Lake City, UT, 1922–37; Presidio of San Francisco, CA, 1937–41

Subordinate elements—323d Cav. Regt., 1921–41; 324th Cav. Regt., 1921–41; 162d MG Sq., 1921–28

Constituted in the O.R. on 15 October 1921, assigned to the 66th Cav. Div., and allotted to the Seventh Corps Area. Withdrawn from the Seventh Corps Area on 14 November 1921 and allotted to the Ninth Corps Area. HHT initiated on 13 April 1922 at Salt Lake City, UT. Relocated to San Francisco, CA, on 14 May 1937. Conducted summer training most years at Fort D.A. Russell, WY, 1922–36, with the 13th Cav. and some years at Fort Meade, SD, with the 4th Cav. Conducted summer training at Del Monte, CA, 1938–40, with the 11th Cav. Regt. Subordinate regiments conducted training of CMTC at Del Monte and the Presidio of Monterey with assistance from the 11th Cav. Location 7 December 1941—San Francisco, CA.

Current Status: Disbanded 30 January 1942.

Commanders, 162d Cavalry Brigade

Capt. David McK. Wilson	13 April 1922–23 November 1922	Unknown	ao September 1926–ao June 1929
Lt. Col. Lewis Forester	23 November 1922–13 August 1923	Col. Harry O. Willard	ao June 1929–ao June 1932
Maj. Ridgely Nichols	13 August 1923–8 August 1925	Unknown	ao June 1932–16 April 1937
Maj. Leighroy Miller	8 August 1925–1 September 1925	Capt. William A. Panton	16 April 1937–ao June 1937
Lt. Col. Harry R. Leech	1 September 1925–ao September 1926	Unknown	ao June 1937–7 December 1941

Chapter 14

Cavalry Regiments

National Archives

A troop of the 13th Cavalry on a long distance march returns to Fort Riley, KS, in 1927.

The mission of cavalry regiments was to plan and conduct operations to provide reconnaissance and security for the ground force to which they were assigned or attached. Cavalry regiments could also be used both defensively and offensively. When employed in the former mode (defense), they were usually to be deployed in an economy of force or delay role. In the latter mode (offense), cavalry regiments were employed in reconnaissance missions, raids, or in pursuit and exploitation of routed enemy formations.

Organization

As with the infantry, the regiment was considered the base cavalry unit for combat, training, and administrative operations in the interwar period. The cavalry regiment as reorganized in 1921 consisted of a headquarters (HQ), HQ troop, and two rifle squadrons of two troops each.

All 17 of the Regular Army (R.A.) cavalry regiments remained active until 1921 when the 15th, 16th, and 17th were inactivated as part of the postwar drawdown of the Army. Shortly thereafter, a new regiment, the 26th Cavalry (Cav.), was constituted in the R.A. and organized in the Philippines as a Philippine Scout Regiment. Initially, 8 of the 15 active regiments were brigaded together in the 1st and 2d Cav. Divisions

Cavalry Regiment, 1921

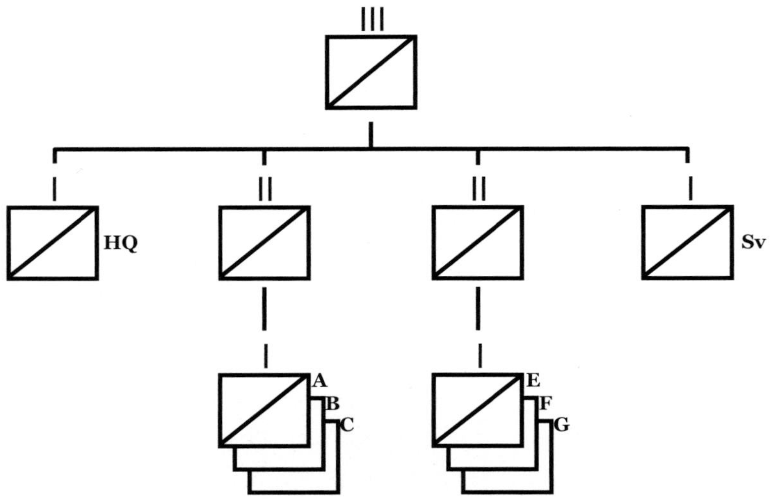

T/O: 423W
Effective: 4 April 1921
Commander: Col.
Officers:
W. O. 1
Enlisted:
Total:

Cavalry Regiment (Mechanized), 1936

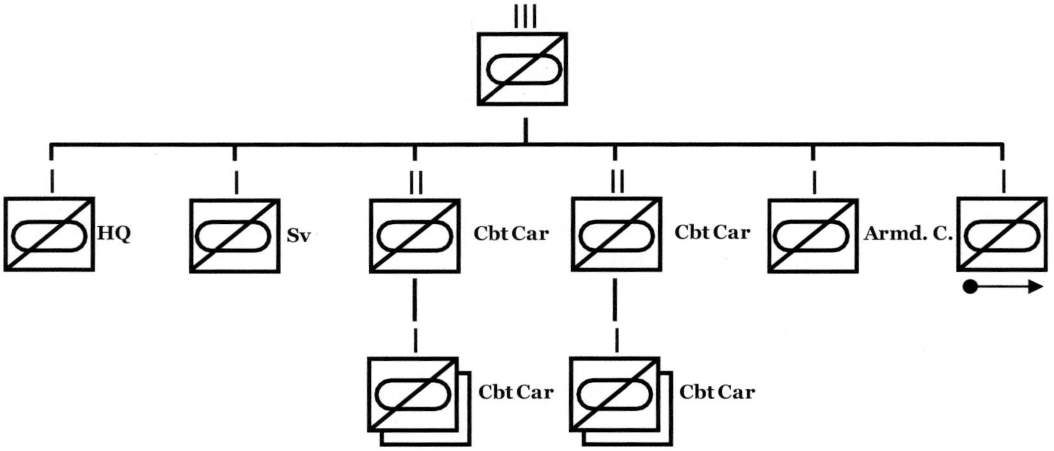

T/O: 423P
14 October 1935
Commander: Col.
Officers: 52
W. O. 1
Enlisted: 764
Total: 817

Key Equipment:	
Cars, scout	2
Cars, armored	19
Cars, half track	25
Cars, combat	56
Mortars	6
Machine guns, .30 cal.	302
Machine guns, .50 cal.	93
Submachine guns	127

Cavalry regiment organization, 1921 and 1936.

(Divs.). Four more were made divisional regiments upon the constitution of the 3d Cav. Div. in 1927. Two regiments, the 9th and 10th Cav., remained "Colored" organizations and were brigaded together initially in the 5th Cav. Brigade (Brig.) in 1933 and later in the 4th Cav. Brig. in 1940.

Other than a number of divisional assignment shifts, the number and basic organization of cavalry regiments remained relatively constant until late 1932 when the 1st Cav. Regiment (Regt.) was ordered to turn in its horses, travel by motor convoy to Fort Knox, KY, and reorganize itself into a mechanized cavalry regiment under the recently organized 7th Cav. Brig. (Mecz). This new regiment consisted of two squadrons consisting of two troops each, a HQ troop, service troop, armored car troop, and a machine gun troop. The two squadrons were mounted in "combat cars," which was essentially cavalry-speak for "light tank." The cavalry combat cars were not appreciably different from the new light tanks being manufactured for the infantry. The remainder of the squadron was mounted in some type of motorized or mechanized vehicle. The 1st Cav. was joined in the mechanized brigade in 1936 by the 13th Cav. and together would later form the basis for the new 1st Armored (Armd.) Div. in 1940.

Horse regiments changed relatively little until 1939 when the Army adopted a new table of organization for the separate "corps reconnaissance regiment." This regiment was a hybrid organization that attempted to combine horses with portee trucks and other mechanized elements to enhance the capability of the horse on the modern battlefield. Four R.A. and seven National Guard (N.G.) regiments would adopt this organization during 1939 and 1940. The "horse and mechanized" concept was an unsuccessful arrangement, however, and was abandoned shortly after the beginning of the war.

Three of the inactive R.A. regiments were organized as Regular Army Inactive (RAI) units in the interwar period. These regiments were functional organizations and were among the most active Reserve units in the Army. Initially assigned as separate regiments under the General Headquarters Reserve (GHQR) in the War Plans Division's various mobilization plans, they were reassigned to the I Cavalry Corps in 1927. Two of the three (the 15th and 17th) were reorganized and redesignated as horse and mechanized corps reconnaissance regiments in 1940; however, none of the three were activated for service until after the attack on Pearl Harbor.

Based on the new mobilization plans for the postwar era, 16 cavalry regiments were allotted to the N.G. to create the four Guard cavalry divisions contemplated. An additional separate regiment, the 117th Cav. was allotted to the states of Colorado and New Mexico. Of the others, several regiments were organized almost immediately when allotted in 1921 and the remainder were slowly built between then and 1927 when the 106th Cav. was finally federally recognized. These were not the only cavalry organizations in the N.G., however. Besides several machine gun squadrons, there were numerous separate cavalry squadrons and troops (which retained state designations) scattered around the country that had no real role to play in the Army's mobilization structure. For the most part, these units had historical significance to the state's military history and were authorized for Federal recognition by special allotment. Most of these units would be integrated into four new regiments allotted to the N.G. in 1928 and 1929. The number and organization of the N.G. cavalry regiments changed drastically in the fall of 1940 when the Guard cavalry divisions were eliminated from the force structure. At that point, of the existing 19 regiments, 7 were reorganized into horse and mechanized regiments, 6 were converted to field artillery regiments, and 4 were converted to coast artillery regiments or separate coast artillery battalions. Only two, the Texas National Guard's 112th and 124th Cav. Regts. remained traditional horse-mounted organizations, and both were federalized as part of the 56th Cav. Brig. for service in World War II.

Twenty-four cavalry regiments were constituted in 1921 and all were organized in the Organized Reserve (O.R.) by the following year. All of these regiments were brigaded together in six cavalry divisions and there were no nondivisional regiments in the Reserve. All of these were also functional and active units, but as with most Reserve organizations, the more concentrated the regiment, the more active and cohesive they were. The divisional and brigade assignments remained constant for these units throughout the interwar period, though the geographical location of the commands shifted, in some cases significantly, during this period. The most notable movements of the geographical location of these regiments were those of the three separated brigades, the 156th, 158th, and 162d Cav. Brigs. The movement of these units was due to a number of reasons, but primarily from the shifting densities of cavalry officers produced by Reserve Officers' Training Corps (ROTC) programs and the availability of field grade officers to command the organizations.

Training

R.A. cavalry regiments maintained a training cycle similar to that of the infantry regiments (see Chapter 9, Infantry Regiments, for a general description). Given the lack of funding, cavalry regiments, like most Army units, were able to go to the field, at best, for 2 to 3 weeks a year. Most of that time was usually spent in brigade, division, or corps area maneuvers in the summer or fall.

As with the infantry, N.G. cavalry regiments followed an annual training pattern that generally resembled their R.A. counterparts. One of the limiting aspects of training Guard units in this period, however, was the number of horses authorized to be maintained by each troop. A cavalry troop in this period was authorized about 65 officers and men, but only 32 horses. Thus, it became difficult or impossible to mount the entire unit for training, unless horses could be borrowed or rented. A solution was to put the troop through training by platoon. For example, one platoon would conduct skills training that required no horses while the other platoon rode the horses.

Like their infantry counterparts, Guard cavalry regiments were often called up for state emergencies, which contributed to their level of readiness. One of the most notable events was the mobilization of the 56th Cav. Brig. in 1931. The entire brigade was mobilized in September to establish martial law in the great east Texas oil field. Elements of the brigade's 112th and 124th Cav. Regts. remained on Active Duty there for 15 months in an effort to keep the area from devolving into violence over oil production quotas. Most other N.G. cavalry regiments experienced multiple calls to active service to support state authorities in the interwar period.

Summer training camps were generally conducted at the regimental level and in two cases at the brigade level. On the other hand, several regiments were multistate organizations and rarely had the opportunity to train as a complete unit. Most regiments, however, were located within a single state and throughout the 1920s and 1930s, the level of training in virtually all regiments progressed to higher levels as each unit gained in experience and cohesiveness. By the late 1920s, the regiments of the 56th Cav. Brig. were participating in a brigade-level exercise during the second week of each summer's camp. These regiments were also conducting coordinated air-ground reconnaissance efforts with the 111th Observation (Obsn.) Squadron (Sq.). The regiments of Pennsylvania's 52d Brig. were also known to participate in brigade-level exercises occasionally at Indiantown Gap. The best training for all of these regiments, of course, was the various army-level maneuvers in the late 1930s. During these maneuvers, the cavalry regiments were employed in more realistic roles with actual divisions and corps for which they conducted a variety of cavalry missions.

The training of O.R. cavalry regiments was difficult, especially given the added cavalry requirement of maintaining equestrian skills. Most Reserve regiments were able to address these requirements through a variety of means. Many O.R. regiments coordinated with nearby R.A. and N.G. cavalry and field artillery units to borrow their horses for equestrian training. Since unit horses needed to be exercised on a regular basis, these arrangements often made for a welcome and symbiotic relationship between the components. Other regiments coordinated with cavalry ROTC units, which were authorized to maintain horses. Since many of the cadets from these programs would end up with commissions in the same O.R. regiment, these arrangements also made for excellent affiliations between the units. In one case, that of the 319th Cav. located in Detroit, the officers and R.A. instructors in the regiment concluded an agreement with a nearby horse farm to provide free stabling for the units' horses. Of course, the unit's horses were not Government issue, but were owned by the officers or had been donated to, or purchased by, the unit for training purposes.

Reserve cavalry regiments conducted nonequestrian training meetings in places such as post office buildings, Federal buildings, chamber of commerce buildings, schools, ROTC buildings, R.A. installations, and N.G. armories, among others. Other than the equestrian events, the opportunity for O.R. units to conduct meaningful skills training during the inactive training period was far more limited than for R.A. and N.G. units. Therefore, most training for Reserve cavalry regiments from September to May was largely indoor events such as lectures, demonstrations, and troop schools.

Generally, summer training camps were conducted in ways similar to those of Reserve infantry regiments (see Chapter 9, Infantry Regiments, for a general description). One thing that made some cavalry camps distinctly different was the propensity to conduct the camps as brigade groups rather than at the regimental level. Given the comparatively small size of cavalry regiments combined with the fact that only about a quarter of a regiment's assigned officers were provided the opportunity to attend a camp each year, it made sense to train the brigade's officers in a single group. In this way, the two regiments would often form the leadership for a half-strength provisional regiment for the training.

HHD, Mechanized Cavalry Regiment

HQ—Fort Eustis, VA, 1931; Camp Knox, KY, 1931–32

Subordinate units—Supply Platoon, Signal Platoon

Organized provisionally in the R.A. on 1 November 1931 at Fort Eustis, VA, from assets of the discontinued Experimental Mechanized Force. Discontinued on 1 July 1932 at Camp Knox, KY, when personnel and equipment were absorbed by the newly organized Detachment, 1st Cav. Regt. (Mecz).

Commanders, Mechanized Cavalry Regiment

Col. Daniel Van Voorhis	1 November 1931–1 July 1932

Detachment 1st Cavalry Regiment (Mechanized)

HQ—Camp Knox, KY, 1932–33

Subordinate units—Sq. HQ, Combat Car Troop, Machine Gun (MG) Troop, Troop A, 2d Armd. Car Sq.

Organized in the R.A. on 1 July 1932 at Fort Knox, KY, from Headquarters and Headquarters Detachment (HHD), Mecz Cav. Regt. Discontinued on 16 January 1933 at Camp Knox, KY, when personnel and equipment were absorbed by the newly arrived 1st Cav. Regt. (Mecz).

Commander, Detachment 1st Cavalry Regiment (Mechanized)

Col. Daniel Van Voorhis	1 July 1932–16 January 1933

1st Cavalry Regiment (1st Cavalry Division)

HQ—Camp Harry J. Jones, AZ, 1919–22; Camp Marfa, TX (Fort D.A. Russell, TX), 1923–33; Fort Knox, KY, 1933–40

Stationed at Camp Harry J. Jones in Douglas, AZ, as of June 1919. Assigned 20 August 1921 to the 1st Cav. Div. Transferred to Camp Marfa, TX, by making an overland march from 26 December 1922 to 23 January 1923. Conducted a 700-mile round-trip march from Camp Marfa to participate in 1st Cav. Brig. maneuvers near Fort Clark, TX, in January 1926. Participated in the making of Famous Players—Lasky Corporation's movie "Rough Riders" in August 1926 at Camp Stanley, TX. Regiment held its last horse-mounted review in December 1932 at Fort D.A. Russell, TX. Relieved from the 1st Cav. Div. on 3 January 1933 and assigned to the 7th Cav. Brig. (Mecz). Transferred by making a 1,450-mile motorized march 2–16 January 1933 from Fort D.A. Russell, TX, to Fort Knox, KY. Reorganized and redesignated 1st Cav. Regt. (Mecz) on 16 January 1933 at Fort Knox. Regiment maintained habitual summer training relationships with the 157th Cav. Brig., 313th and 314th Cav. Regts., and the 463d Armd. Car Sq. at Fort Knox, 1933–40. Redesignated 1st Armd. Regt. on 15 July 1940.

Organization Day: 2 March. Chosen to commemorate the regiment's organization on 2 March 1833 as the 1st Regiment of Dragoons.

Status: Assigned to the US Army Regimental System (USARS) as the 1st Cav.

Events: 30, 65, 83, 97, 165, 171, 175, 185, 190, 213, 214, 217, 220, 230, 253, 269, 277, 280, 295, 296, 302, 328, 330

Commanders, 1st Cavalry Regiment

Col. Edmund S. Wright	9 October 1916–18 August 1917	Col. Conrad S. Babcock	6 August 1926–5 August 1929
Col. John C. Waterman	18 August 1917–23 September 1918	Col. John S. Fair	10 August 1929–31 January 1931
Col. Frank B. Edwards	23 September 1918–25 January 1919	Lt. Col. Joseph C. King	31 January 1931–30 March 1931
Col. Julien E. Gaujot	25 January 1919–21 May 1919	Col. William A. Austin	30 March 1931–16 January 1933
Col. Hamilton S. Hawkins	22 May 1919–31 July 1919	Col. Daniel Van Voorhis	16 January 1933–1 March 1934
Col. Guy H. Preston	15 December 1919–7 September 1920	Lt. Col. Adna R. Chaffee	1 March 1934–29 June 1934
Col. Francis Le J. Parker	18 September 1920–13 January 1921	Maj. William G. Simmons	29 June 1934–12 July 1934
Lt. Col. Julien E. Gaujot	13 January 1921–February 1921	Maj. Isaac G. Walker	12 July 1934–30 July 1934
Col. Alvord V.P. Anderson	February 1921–12 August 1923	Maj. Ralph C. Sasso	30 July 1934–25 August 1934
Col. LeRoy Eltinge	12 August 1923–29 May 1924	Col. Bruce Palmer	25 August 1934–1 July 1938
Lt. Col. Arthur Poillon	29 May 1924–11 September 1924	Col. Adna R. Chaffee	1 July 1938–31 October 1938
Col. Charles E. Stodter	11 September 1924–10 March 1926	Lt. Col. Jack W. Heard	31October 1938–12 November 1938
Lt. Col. Arthur Poillon	10 March 1926–6 August 1926	Col. Henry W. Baird	12 November 1938–15 July 1940

2d Cavalry Regiment (2d Cavalry Division)

HQ—Fort Riley, KS, 1919–41

Arrived at the port of New York on 29 June 1919 on the U.S.S. *Rijndam*. Transferred the same day to Camp Mills, NY, where emergency service personnel were discharged. Transferred to Fort Riley, KS, and arrived there on 6 July 1919. Served as the Cavalry School training and demonstration regiment and provided support to the Cavalry Board, 1921–41. Assigned to the 2d Cav. Div. on 15 August 1927. Participated in the making of Pathe Films movie "His First Command" in August 1929 at Fort Riley. Conducted a mounted forced march of 100 miles in 23.5 hours on 16–17 May 1932. Partially motorized in 1933. Supported the construction and supervision of Civilian Conservation Corps (CCC) camps in Kansas and Nebraska in 1933–34 until leadership of camps was assumed by Reserve officers. Elements of the regiment participated in the Texas Centennial celebrations in Fort Worth, TX, from 27 June to 14 October 1936. Troop G was winner of the Goodrich Trophy for 1927 and 1937. Regiment maintained habitual summer training relationships with the 321st and 322d Cav. Regts. and the 161st MG Sq. at Fort Riley. Annually sent a troop to Fort Leavenworth to support the training of the cavalry Citizens Military Training Camp (CMTC) there. Assigned Reserve officers conducted summer training with the regiment at Fort Riley. Location 7 December 1941—Fort Riley, KS.

Regimental Day: 23 May. Chosen to commemorate the regiment's organization on 23 May 1836 as the 2d Regiment of Dragoons.

Status: Active at Fort Polk, LA, as the 2d Armd. Cav. Regt.

Events: 156, 171, 177, 188, 236, 269, 303, 328

Commanders, 2d Cavalry Regiment

Col. Arthur Thayer	11 September 1917–12 August 1919	Col. Alexander M. Miller	4 August 1928–31 March 1931
Col. Edwin B. Winans	12 August 1919–1 December 1919	Lt. Col. Edward M. Offley	31 March 1931–1 April 1932
Col. John S. Winn	1 December 1919–12 June 1922	Maj. Benjamin F. Hoge	1 April 1932–30 June 1932
Col. Charles A. Romeyn	12 June 1922–1 June 1924	Col. Selwyn D. Smith	30 June 1932–15 July 1935
Col. George W. Williams	1 June 1924–23 July 1926	Maj. Robert O. Annin	31 July 1935–29 August 1935
Col. Llewellyn W. Oliver	3 July 1926–10 May 1928	Col. Dorsey R. Rodney	29 August 1935–1 September 1937
Lt. Col. John K. Herr	10 May 1928–14 June 1928	Col. Arthur W. Holderness	1 September 1937–17 April 1939
Maj. Elkin A. Franklin	14 June 1928–1 July 1928	Lt. Col. Thoburn K. Brown	17 April 1939–9 August 1939
Lt. Col. Willis V. Morris	1 July 1928–4 August 1928	Col. Harry D. Chamberlain	9 August 1939–3 April 1941
	Col. John T. Cole	3 April 1941–30 June 1942	

3d Cavalry Regiment (3d Cavalry Division)

HQ—Fort Myer, VA, 1919–41

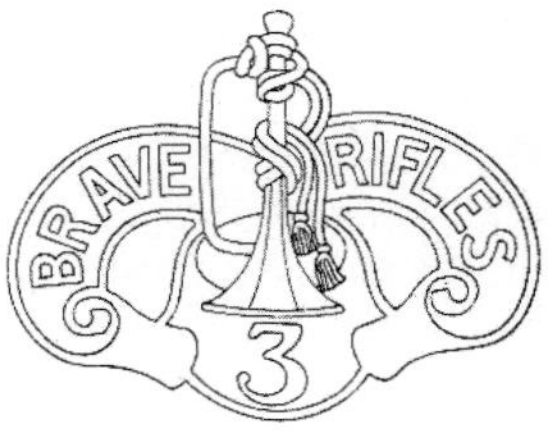

Arrived at the port of Boston on 30 June 1919 on the U.S.S. *Finland*. Transferred the same day to Camp Mills, NY. Transferred in July 1919 to Camp Devens, MA, where emergency service personnel were discharged. Regimental HQ and 3d Sq. transferred in July 1919 to Fort Myer, VA; 1st and 2d Sqs, concurrently transferred to Fort Ethan Allen, VT. The 3d Sq. inactivated at Fort Myer in September 1921 and 2d Sq. concurrently transferred to Fort Myer. Performed duties of ceremonial guard for the District of Washington and funeral escort for Arlington National Cemetery. Provided funeral escort for the burial of the Unknown Soldier on 11 November 1921 as well as for the funerals of Howard H. Taft, Woodrow Wilson, Warren G. Harding, William Jennings Bryan, Maj. Gen. Leonard Wood, and Lt. Gen. Nelson A. Miles, among other notables, during the period 1921–41. The regiment, less 1st Sq., participated in the inaugural parades of Presidents Calvin Coolidge, Herbert Hoover, and Franklin D. Roosevelt. Regiment maintained habitual summer training relationships with the regiments of the 62d Cav. Div. (305th–308th Cav. Regts.) at Fort Myer, VA, or Fort Belvoir, VA, while the 1st Sq. trained the regiments of the 61st Cav. Div. (301st–304th Cav. Regts.) and the 158th Brig. of the 64th Cav. Div. (315th and 316th Cav. Regts.) at Fort Ethan Allen, VT. Supported training of ROTC and CMTC camps at Fort George G. Meade, MD, (less 1st Sq.) and Fort Devens (1st Sq.) each summer. Assigned Reserve officers conducted summer training with the regiment at Fort Belvoir. Assigned to the 3d Cav. Div. on 15 August 1927. The 1st Sq. participated in flood relief duty near Waterbury, Winooski, and Montpelier, VT, 5-21 November 1927. Winners of the Goodrich Trophy were F Troop (1926) and E Troop (1929). Relieved on 1 December 1939 from the 3d Cav. Div. Location 7 December 1941—Fort Myer, VA.

Organization Day: 19 May. Chosen to commemorate the regiment's organization on 19 May 1846 as the Regiment of Mounted Rifles.

Status: Active at Fort Carson, CO, as the 3d Armd. Cav. Regt.

Events: 4, 62, 64, 66, 67, 78, 95, 98, 137, 151, 155, 176, 190, 240, 280, 281, 301, 330

Commanders, 3d Cavalry Regiment

Col. Augustus P. Blocksom	11 April 1913–22 June 1917	Lt. Col. ClarenceLininger	20 March 1930–25 April 1930
Col. Francis H. Beach	22 June 1917–24 July 1919	Col. Harry N. Cootes	25 April 1930–25 May 1933
Col. Lloyd M. Brett	24 July 1919–22 February 1920	Maj. George S. Patton	25 May 1933–30 May 1933
Col. William C. Rivers	22 February 1920–March 1923	Maj. Alexander D. Surles	30 May 1933–8 June 1933
Maj. Herbert E. Mann	March 1923–9 April 1923	Col. Kenyon A. Joyce	8 June 1933–15 June 1936
Col. Hamilton S. Hawkins	9 April 1923–5 August 1926	Maj. Arthur P. Thayer	16 June 1936–11 July 1936
Maj. Adna C. Chaffee	5 August 1926–24 August 1926	Col. Jonathan M. Wainwright	11 July 1936–1 November 1938
Col. William J. Glasgow	24 August 1926–22 March 1927	Lt. Col. John Millikin	1 November 1938–December 1938
Maj. Adna R. Chaffee	22 March 1927–19 June 1927	Col. George S. Patton Jr.	December 1938–24 July 1940
Lt. Col. Berkley T. Merchant	19 June 1927–7 September 1927	Col. William W. Gordon	24 July 1940–18 September 1941
Col. Guy V. Henry	7 September 1927–20 March 1930	Col. Howell M. Estes	18 September 1941–July 1942

4th Cavalry Regiment (2d Cavalry Division)

HQ—Fort Ringgold, TX, 1919–20; Fort Brown, TX, 1920–21; Fort McIntosh, TX, 1921–24; Fort D.A. Russell, WY, 1924–27; Fort Meade, SD, 1927–41.

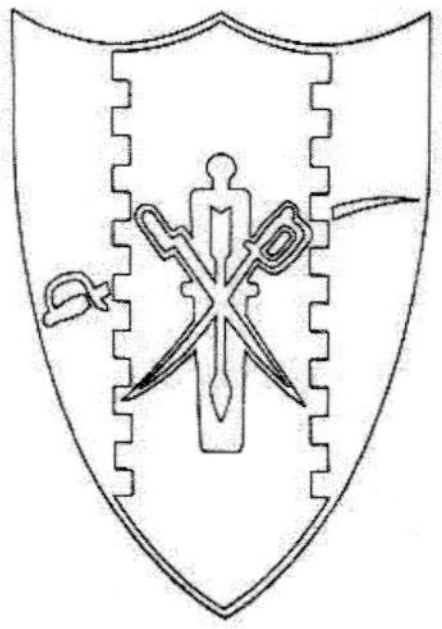

Stationed at Fort Ringgold, TX, as of June 1919. Regiment, less 2d and 3d Sqs., transferred on 9 April 1920 to Fort Brown, TX. Concurrently, 2d Sq. transferred to Mercedes, TX, and 3d Sq. transferred to McAllen, TX. The 2d Sq. transferred on 23 September 1921 to McAllen. Regiment, less 1st Sq., transferred on 12 November 1921 to Fort McIntosh, TX. Concurrently, 1st Sq. transferred to Fort Sam Houston, TX. Assigned to the 2d Cav. Div. on 24 March 1923. The 1st Sq. transferred on 6 May 1924 to Fort Meade, SD. Regiment, less 1st Sq., transferred to Fort D.A. Russell, WY, on 22 October 1924. The 1st Sq. participated in the making of Universal Studio's movie "Deadwood Dick" in August 1925. Regiment, less 1st Sq., conducted a 410-mile mounted march in September 1926 to Torrington and Douglas, WY, and return. Regiment, less 1st Sq., conducted a 350-mile mounted march 16–30 June 1927 on permanent change of station from Fort D.A. Russell to Fort Meade, SD. President Calvin Coolidge reviewed the regiment on 29 June 1927 while on the march through Rapid City, SD. The regiment provided the presidential guard during Coolidge's vacation in the Black Hills during the summer of 1927. Relieved from the 2d Cav. Div. on 1 March 1933 and assigned to the 7th Cav. Brig. (Mecz). In April 1933, the regiment assumed command and control of the South Dakota CCC District until mid-1934. Relieved from the 7th Cav. Brig. (Mecz) on 18 August 1936 and assigned to the 2d Cav. Div. Reorganized and redesignated 4th Cav. Regt. (Horse and Mecz) on 1 February 1940. Regiment maintained habitual summer training relationships with the 323d Cav. Regt. at Fort D.A. Russell, 1924–26, and the 324th Cav. Regt. at Fort Meade, 1927–40. Assigned Reserve officers conducted summer training with the regiment at Fort Meade. Relieved from the 2d Cav. Div. about 1 November 1940 and assigned to the Second Army. Location 7 December 1941—Fort Meade, SD.

Regimental Day: 3 March. Chosen to commemorate the regiment's constitution on 3 March 1855 as the 1st Cav.Regt.

Status: Assigned to the USARS as the 4th Cav.

Events: 162, 175, 233, 236, 260, 285, 295, 296, 303, 328

Commanders, 4th Cavalry Regiment

Col. Lloyd M. Brett	12 January 1917–26 August 1917	Lt. Col. Leonard W. Prunty	29 December 1927–April 1928
Col. Frederick T. Arnold	31 August 1917–29 September 1917	Col. William L. Luhn	April 1928–7 March 1931
Col. John W. Heard	29 September 1917–1 October 1918	Maj. Edward F. Shaifer	7 March 1931–20 May 1931
Unknown	1 October 1918–31 January 1919	Col. Otto W. Rethorst	20 May 1931–28 June 1933
Col. James N. Munro	31 January 1919–31 March 1919	Col. William R. Pope	28 June 1933–14 July 1935
Col. George W. Kirkpatrick	1 April 1919–11 May 1919	Lt. Col. Richard E. Cummins	14 July 1935–19 August 1935
Lt. Col. Albert B. Dockery	11 May 1919–22 July 1919	Col. Robert McC. Beck Jr.	19 August 1935–1 October 1936
Col. De Rosey C. Cabell	22 July 1919–23 September 1920	Lt. Col. Edwin O'Connor	1 October 1936–6 October 1936
Col. Howard R. Hickok	23 September 1920–10 January 1924	Col. John A. Barry	6 October 1936–4 January 1937
Maj. Harry L. King	10 January 1924–9 February 1924	Lt. Col. Edwin O'Connor	4 January 1937–25 March 1937
Lt. Col. Edward A. Keyes	9 February 1924–22 April 1924	Col. Stanley Koch	25 March 1937–2 December 1937
Col. Edwin E. Booth	22 April 1924–21 July 1924	Lt. Col. Edwin O'Connor	3 December 1937–14 December 1937
Capt. Rexford Willoughby	21 July 1924–30 September 1924	Maj. Arthur T. Lacey	14 December 1937–5 January 1938
Col. Thomas Q. Donaldson	30 September 1924–21 December 1924	Col. Robert C. Rodgers	6 January 1938–5 October 1940
Maj. Emmet Addis	21 December 1924–3 January 1925	Col. Howell M. Estes	5 October 1940–January 1941
Col. Osmun Latrobe	3 January 1925–29 December 1927	Col. John B. Coulter	January 1941–31 October 1941
Col. Joseph B. Tully	21 November 1941–16 November 1944		

5th Cavalry Regiment (1st Cavalry Division)

HQ—Fort Bliss, TX, 1919; Camp Marfa, TX, 1919–21; Fort Clark, TX, 1921–41

Stationed at Fort Bliss, TX, as of June 1919. Transferred to Camp Marfa, TX, and arrived there on 21 September 1919. Entire regiment, less Troops A and C, transferred to Fort Clark, TX, on 17 October 1921. Concurrently, Troop A transferred to Camp Eagle Pass and Troop C to Camp Robert F.L. Michie at Del Rio, TX. Assumed responsibility of the Fort Clark command sector of the Mexican Border Patrol. Assigned on 18 December 1922 to the 1st Cav. Div. Camps Michie and Eagle Pass were abandoned in July 1923 and 16 August 1923, respectively, and the regiment was consolidated at Fort Clark. Participated in the making of Lansky's Famous Players movie "Rough Riders" in August 1926 near San Antonio, TX. Troop B was winner of the Draper Award for 1929. Machine Gun Troop was winner of the Goodrich Trophy for 1932. Regiment maintained habitual summer training relationships with the HQ, 156th Cav. Brig. and 311th Cav. Regt., 1922–40. Assigned Reserve officers conducted summer training with the regiment at Fort Clark. Location 7 December 1941—Fort Bliss, TX.

Regimental Day: 3 March. Chosen to commemorate the regiment's constitution on 3 March 1855 as the 2d Cav.Regt.

Status: Assigned to the US Army Regimental System (USARS) as the 5th Cavalry.

Events: 30, 42, 55, 65, 83, 97, 105, 125, 147, 183, 206, 250, 284, 288, 295, 296, 300, 315

Commanders, 5th Cavalry Regiment

Col. George H. Cameron	3 April 1917–8 July 1917	Lt. Col. Henry E. Mitchell	29 July 1931–7 January 1932
Col. John W. Heard	8 July 1917–October 1917	Col. Thomas L. Sherburne	7 January 1932–22 June 1933
Col. Edward Anderson	October 1917–1 October 1918	Lt. Col. Joseph C. King	22 June 1933–13 October 1933
Col. W. G. Heaton	1 October 1918–27 January 1919	Col. Wallace B. Scales	13 October 1933–8 March 1935
Col. James J. Hornbrook	10 March 1919–26 May 1920	Col. Charles B. Armory Jr.	8 March 1935–20 December 1935
Col. Oren B. Meyer	26 May 1920–10 February 1921	Col. Robert C. Richardson	20 December 1935–1 June 1938
Col. James J. Hornbrook	10 February 1921–5 August 1921	Maj. Roy E. Blunt	4 June 1938–24 July 1938
Col. William D. Forsyth	5 August 1921–28 October 1923	Col. George S. Patton Jr.	24 July 1938–5 December 1938
Lt. Col. John T. Sayles	28 October 1923–17 February 1924	Lt. Col. John A. Robenson	5 December 1938–10 December 1938
Col. Wallace B. Scales	17 February 1924–25 May 1928	Col. Cuthbert P. Stearns	10 December 1938–26 June 1940
Lt. Col. Albert H. Mueller	28 May 1928–1 July 1928	Lt. Col. Harry A. Flint	26 June 1940–September 1940
Maj. Kinzie Edmunds	1 July 1928–22 September 1928	Col. Henry J. M. Smith	September 1940–ao April 1941
Col. Samual F. Dallam	22 September 1928–15 July 1931	Lt. Col. Harrison Herman	ao November 1941–December 1941
Col. Lucian K. Truscott	December 1941–May 1942		

6th Cavalry Regiment (3d Cavalry Division)

HQ—Fort Oglethorpe, GA, 1919–41

Arrived at the port of Newport News on 29 June 1919 on the U.S.S. *Kroonland* after performing occupation duties near Gievres and Vendome, France. Transferred to Camp Stuart, VA, and arrived there on 30 June 1919, where emergency service personnel were discharged. Transferred to Fort Oglethorpe, GA, and arrived there on 3 July 1919. Assigned to the 3d Cav. Div. on 15 August 1927. Troop E awarded the Draper Award for 1929. Conducted a 1,500-mile march during July–October 1929 through Georgia, South Carolina, and Tennessee. In April 1933, the regiment assumed command and control of CCC District C, Fourth Corps Area until mid-1934. Supported the construction and supervision of CCC camps in Georgia, Tennessee, and Alabama, 1933–39. The regiment provided the presidential guard and escort during President Roosevelt's visits to Gainesville, GA, and Chattanooga, TN, during 1938. Relieved on 1 December 1939 from the 3d Cav. Div. Concurrently, reorganized and redesignated 6th Cav. Regt. (Horse and Mecz). Regiment maintained habitual summer training relationships with the 155th Cav. Brig. of the 63d Cav. Div. (309th and 310th Cav. Regts.), the 157th Brig. of the 64th Cav. Div. (313th and 314th Cav. Regts.), and the 55th Brig. of the 23d Cav. Div. (108th and 109th Cav. Regts.). Assigned Reserve officers conducted summer training with the regiment at Fort Oglethorpe. Assigned to the IV Corps in October 1940. Location 7 December 1941—Fort Oglethorpe, GA.

Regimental Day: 4 May. Chosen to commemorate the regiment's organization on 4 May 1861 as the 3d Cav. Regt.

Status: Assigned to the USARS as the 6th Cav.

Events: 94, 96, 121, 143, 184, 209, 228, 255, 293, 296, 300, 325, 328

Commanders, 6th Cavalry Regiment

Col. Joseph A. Gaston	1 May 1914–2 June 1917	Lt. Col. Henry T. Bull	17 August 1929–2 September 1929
Col. John D. L. Hartman	2 July 1917–29 September 1917	Col. Evan H. Humphrey	2 September 1929–4 August 1931
Col. Alonzo Gray	29 September 1917–April 1918	Col. Gordon Johnston	4 August 1931–15 November 1933
Col. Michael M. McNamee	April 1918–7 September 1919	Lt. Col. Walton Goodwin Jr.	15 November 1933–3 January 1934
Col. James B. Erwin	7 September 1919–15 December 1919	Col. Walter S. Grant	3 January 1934–27 March 1935
Col. Frederick S. Foltz	15 December 1919–17 June 1921	Lt. Col. Kinzie B. Edmunds	27 March 1935–15 June 1935
Col. Robert R. Wallach	20 June 1921–27 December 1921	Col. Llewellyn B. Oliver	16 June 1935–1 December 1936
Col. Robert J. Fleming	27 December 1921–1 July 1925	Col. Charles Burnett	1 December 1936–4 May 1937
Lt. Col. Oscar A. McGee	1 July 1925–15 August 1925	Col. George Dillman	4 May 1937–16 August 1939
Col. George C. Barnhardt	15 August 1925–23 June 1927	Lt. Col. John A. Weeks	16 August 1939–16 September 1939
Lt. Col. Harry N. Cootes	23 June 1927–5 September 1927	Col. John Millikin	16 September 1939–6 October 1940
Col. Thomas A. Roberts	5 September 1927–17 August 1929	Lt. Col. John A. Considine	7 October 1940–19 July 1942

7th Cavalry Regiment (1st Cavalry Division)

HQ—Fort Bliss, TX, 1919–41

Stationed at Fort Bliss, TX, as of June 1919. The 3d Sq. demobilized on 20 August 1921. Assigned to the 1st Cav. Div. on 5 September 1921. The 1st Sq. transferred in September 1921 to Camp Marfa, TX. The 1st Sq. transferred on 30 January 1923 to Fort Bliss. A provisional squadron consisting of Troops C, E, and F traveled to the site of Custer's Last Stand in June 1926 to commemorate the 50th anniversary of the Battle of the Little Big Horn. The regiment, minus 2d Sq., was deployed on 11 April 1929 to Hachita, NM, to conduct border patrols as a result of the Escobar-Topete Revolution. The 2d Sq. was deployed to Slaughter's Ranch and Douglas, AZ. The regiment (-) relieved the 2d Sq., 10th Cav. at Naco, AZ, on 25 April 1929 where it remained on patrol until 13 May 1929. Winners of the Goodrich Trophy were A Troop (1928) and E Troop (1931). Regiment maintained a habitual summer training relationship with the 312th Cav. Regt., 1924–40. Assigned Reserve officers conducted summer training with the regiment at Fort Bliss. Location 7 December 1941—Fort Bliss, TX.

Organization Day: 25 June. Chosen to commemorate the regiment's participation in the Battle of the Little Big Horn, 25 June 1876.

Status: Assigned to the USARS as the 7th Cav.

Events: 3, 30, 65, 83, 97, 127, 146, 206, 250, 259, 284, 295, 296, 300, 315, 328

Commanders, 7th Cavalry Regiment

Col. James B. Erwin	24 December 1915–21 August 1916	Lt. Col. Charles McH. Eby	1 July 1929–23 October 1929
Col. Selah R. H. Tompkins	22 August 1916–14 February 1917	Maj. Robert W. Strong	23 October 1929–7 February 1930
Col. James B. Erwin	28 February 1917–21 March 1917	Col. Charles F. Martin	7 February 1930–17 November 1930
Maj. Edmund Leary	21 March 1917–19 May 1917	Lt. Col. Frank Keller	17 November 1930–5 January 1931
Col. Selah R.H. Tompkins	19 May 1917–19 February 1920	Col. Ola W. Bell	5 January 1931–14 March 1933
Col. Charles A. Hedekin	20 February 1920–10 April 1920	Lt. Col. William W. Gordon	14 March 1933–25 October 1933
Col. Charles J. Symmonds	16 April 1920–31 December 1920	Col. Joseph A. Baer	25 October 1933–26 October 1935
Lt. Col. Frank T. McNarney	31 December 1920–30 April 1921	Col. John K. Herr	26 October 1935–11 March 1938
Col. Walter C. Short	1 May 1921–7 July 1923	Lt. Col. Benjamin F. Hoge	11 March 1938–6 June 1938
Col. Fitzhugh Lee	8 July 1923–10 July 1927	Lt. Col. Harding Polk	6 June 1938–20 July 1938
Col. Selah R.H. Tompkins	10 July 1927–17 July 1927	Col. William W. West	20 July 1938–19 July 1940
Lt. Col. Howard R. Smalley	17 July 1927–18 November 1927	Col. Frederick Gilbreath	19 July 1940–1 May 1941
Col. William M. Connell	18 November 1927–30 June 1929	Col. Frederic W. Boye	1 May 1941–15 May 1941
Col. Thoburn K. Brown	15 May 1941–6 May 1942		

8th Cavalry Regiment (1st Cavalry Division)

HQ—Camp Marfa, TX, 1919; Fort Bliss, TX, 1919–41

Stationed at Camp Marfa, TX, as of June 1919. Transferred to Fort Bliss, TX, and arrived there on 9 October 1919. Assigned to the 1st Cav. Div. on 15 September 1921. Winners of the Goodrich Trophy were E Troop (1924) and A Troop (1930). Regiment maintained habitual summer training relationships with the 312th Cav. Regt. and ROTC units from New Mexico Military Institute, University of Arizona, and New Mexico A&M College. Assigned Reserve officers conducted summer training with the regiment at Fort Bliss. Location 7 December 1941—Fort Bliss, TX.

Organization Day: 21 September. Chosen to commemorate the regiment's organization on 21 September 1866.

Status: Assigned to the USARS as the 8th Cav.

Events: 3, 11, 30, 65, 83, 97, 127, 146, 206, 250, 259, 284, 295, 296, 300, 315, 328

Commanders, 8th Cavalry Regiment

Col. John W. Heard	October 1916–6 February 1917	Lt. Col. George M. Russell	1 June 1928–5 September 1928
Col. William D. Beach	6 February 1917–3 October 1917	Maj. John C. F. Tillson	5 September 1928–2 August 1929
Col. George T. Langhorne	3 October 1917–5 August 1921	Col. William R. Smedberg	2 August 1929–27 May 1932
Col. James H. Reeves	5 August 1921–11 May 1923	Col. Carl H. Muller	27 May 1932–1 July 1934
Lt. Col. C. Emery Hathaway	21 May 1923–8 September 1923	Lt. Col. Arthur H. Wilson	1 July 1934–29 June 1935
Col. Abraham C. Lott	8 September 1923–15 October 1924	Col. Frank T. Keller	29 June 1935–1 January 1937
Lt. Col. Edward A. Keyes	15 October 1924–13 November 1924	Col. Innis P. Swift	1 January 1937–19 October 1939
Col. Samuel McP. Rutherford	13 November 1924–1 June 1928	Col. Joseph P. Aleshire	19 October 1939–14 October 1940
Col. John K. Brown	14 October 1940–14 February 1942		

9th Cavalry Regiment (C) (3d Cavalry Division)

HQ—Camp Stotsenberg, PI, 1919–22; Fort Riley, KS, 1922–41

Stationed at Camp Stotsenberg, PI, as of June 1919. Departed Manila on 12 October 1922 on the U.S.A.T. *Logan* and arrived on 11 November 1922 at San Francisco, CA. Transferred to Fort Riley, KS, and arrived there on 15 November 1922. The regiment absorbed just over 200 troopers of the Cavalry School Detachment (Colored) on 1 December 1922. From 1922 to 1940, the regiment served as the Cavalry School support and demonstration regiment. Assigned to the 3d Cav. Div. on 18 August 1933. Supported and supervised the training of the Colored CMTC at Fort Riley, 1934–36 and 1938. Relieved from the 3d Cav, Div, on 10 October 1940 and assigned to the 2d Cav. Div. Location 7 December 1941—Fort Riley, KS.

Organization Day: 28 July. Chosen to commemorate the regiment's date of constitution on 28 July 1866.

Status: Assigned to the USARS as the 9th Cav.

Events: 171, 177, 188, 269, 324, 328

Commanders, 9th Cavalry Regiment

Col. Thomas B. Dugan	21 October 1916–4 August 1917	Lt. Col. Ralph M. Parker	27 June 1927–14 July 1928
Col. Michael N. McNamee	1 October 1917–3 May 1918	Col. William V. Morris	31 August 1928–16 July 1929
Col. Alfred E. Kennington	13 August 1918–September 1919	Lt. Col. Robert M. Campbell	16 July 1929–2 June 1930
Col. John W. Heard	September 1919–15 October 1920	Maj. Henry J. M. Smith	2 June 1930–22 August 1930
Col. Alfred E. Kennington	15 October 1920–13 November 1920	Lt. Col. Robert M. Campbell	31 August 1930–10 January 1932
Col. Charles D. Rhodes	13 November 1920–9 January 1921	Lt. Col. William W. West Jr.	10 January 1932–9 August 1932
Lt. Col. Richard B. Goring	9 January 1921–4 April 1921	Maj. Thomas McF. Cockrill	10 August 1932–5 September 1932
Col. Edward Anderson	4 April 1921–26 October 1922	Lt. Col. William C. Christy	9 September 1932–16 September 1935
Capt. Richard B. Trimble	26 October 1922–17 November 1922	Lt. Col. John P. Wheeler	16 September 1935–1 July 1936
Maj. Joseph F. Richmond	17 November 1922–2 June 1923	Lt. Col. Cuthbert P. Stearns	2 July 1936–10 February 1938
Lt. Col. Walter J. Scott	2 June 1923–22 August 1924	Lt. Col. George S. Patton Jr.	10 February 1938–22 July 1938
Lt. Col. Kerr T. Riggs	22 August 1924–20 June 1925	Lt. Col. Terry De La M. Allen	22 July 1938—29 June 1939
Lt. Col. Walter J. Scott	20 June 1925–19 August 1926	Col. Stephen W. Winfree	29 June 1939–1 October 1940
Lt. Col. Kerr T. Riggs	19 August 1926–27 June 1927	Col. Duncan G. Richart	7 January 1941–November 1941
	Col. George I. Smith	December 1941–6 February 1943	

10th Cavalry Regiment (C) (3d Cavalry Division)

HQ—Fort Huachuca, AZ, 1919–31; Fort Leavenworth, KS, 1931–41; Fort Riley, KS, 1941

Stationed at Fort Huachuca, AZ, as of June 1919. Assigned to the 1st Cav. Div. on 20 August 1921. Relieved on 18 December 1922 from the 1st Cav. Div. Assigned to the 2d Cav. Div. on 24 March 1923. Regiment maintained a habitual summer training relationship with the Arizona elements of the 311th and 312th Cav. Regts. at Fort Huachuca. Conducted joint maneuvers with the 25th Infantry (Inf.) Regt. each fall near Fort Huachuca. Relieved from the 2d Cav. Div. on 15 August 1927 and assigned to the 3d Cav. Div. The regiment, minus 2d Sq., was deployed to Nogales, AZ, in March 1929 to conduct Mexican Border patrols in response to the Escobar-Topete Revolution. Concurrently, the 2d Sq. was deployed to Naco, AZ, where it was later relieved by 7th Cav. A short time later, the regiment was consolidated at Nogales where it remained on patrol until mid-May 1929. Regiment, less 2d Sq. and MG Troop, transferred on 12 October 1931 to Fort Leavenworth, KS. Concurrently, 2d Sq. transferred to the US Military Academy at West Point, NY, and MG Troop to Fort Myer, VA. Troop F replaced MG Troop at Fort Myer in 1939. Relieved on 10 October 1940 from the 3d Cav. Div. Entire regiment consolidated at Fort Leavenworth on 1 February 1941 and assigned to the 2d Cav Div. Transferred on 12 March 1941 to Fort Riley, KS. Location 7 December 1941—Fort Riley, KS.

Organization Day: 28 July. Chosen to commemorate the regiment's date of constitution on 28 July 1866.

Status: Assigned to the USARS as the 10th Cav.

Events: 83, 110, 218, 240, 263, 281, 328

Commanders, 10th Cavalry Regiment

Col. De Rosey C. Cabell	5 February 1917–15 February 1918	Lt. Col. George Grunert	20 April 1926–20 August 1926
Col. Frederick T. Arnold	1 March 1918–10 July 1918	Col. Louis C. Scherer	21 August 1926–6 May 1928
Col. George B. Rodney	10 July 1918–29 October 1918	Lt. Col. Otto W. Rethorst	6 May 1928–9 July 1928
Col. Cornelius C. Smith	29 October 1918–22 February 1919	Col. Douglas McCaskey	9 July 1928–27 December 1929
Col. William A. Cornell	22 February 1919–28 March 1919	Lt. Col. Lewis Brown Jr.	27 December 1929–10 August 1930
Lt. Col. Frederick S. Snyder	28 March 1919–12 April 1919	Col. Thomas L. Sherburne	10 August 1930–10 October 1931
Col. George P. White	12 April 1919–22 August 1919	Maj. Joseph F. Richmond	12 October 1931—1 July 1932
Col. Guy Carlton	22 August 1919–14 November 1919	Maj. Pearson Menoher	1 July 1932–9 June 1934
Col. Oren B. Meyer	14 November 1919–1 May 1920	Lt. Col. Edgar W. Taulbee	15 June 1934–14 June 1935
Col. Francis C. Marshall	1 May 1920–3 August 1920	Lt. Col. N. Butler Briscoe	14 June 1935–15 February 1938
Col. Edwin B. Winans	3 August 1920–20 December 1922	Maj. Murray H. Ellis	15 February 1938–15 August 1938
Lt. Col. Hu B. Myers	20 December 1922–30 December 1923	Lt. Col. William H. W. Young	15 August 1938–28 January 1941
Col. James C. Rhea	30 December 1923–19 April 1926	Col. Paul R. Davison	28 January 1941–2 May 1942

11th Cavalry Regiment (3d Cavalry Division)

HQ—Presidio of Monterey, CA, 1919–41; Camp Seeley, CA, 1941

Stationed at Presidio of Monterey, CA, as of July 1919. Assigned to the 3d Cav. Div. on 15 August 1927. Participated in the making of Warner Brother's movie "Across the Pacific" in August 1926 and in Tiffany Production's movie "Troopers Three" in 1929. Relieved from the 3d Cav. Div. on 1 May 1932 and assigned to the 2d Cav. Div. In April 1933, the regiment assumed command and control of the Monterey CCC District until mid-1934. Supported the construction and supervision of CCC camps in northern California, 1933–39. Participated in the opening ceremonies for the Golden Gate Bridge in June 1937. Participated in the making of Warner Brother's movie "Sergeant Murphy" with cavalryman 2d Lt. Ronald Reagan in 1937. Maintained habitual summer training relationships with the 162d Cav. Brig., 323d Cav. Regt., and the 162d MG Sq. at Del Monte, CA. Relieved on 10 October 1940 from the 2d Cav. Div. Assigned about November 1940 to the Fourth Army. Transferred on 7 November 1941 to Camp Seeley, CA. Location 7 December 1941—Camp Seeley, CA.

Organization Day: 5 May. Chosen to commemorate the regiment's participation in the Battle at Ojo Azures, Mexico, 5 May 1916.

Status: Active at Fort Irwin, CA, as the 11th Armd. Cav. Regt.

Events: 112, 134, 144, 231, 289, 304, 318

Commanders, 11th Cavalry Regiment

Col. James Lockett	August 1917–15 June 1919	Lt. Col. Joseph A. Baer	2 August 1928–8 October 1928
Col. Nathaniel F. McClure	19 August 1919–4 February 1920	Col. Roger S. Fitch	8 October 1928–11 October 1930
Col. James B. Erwin	16 February 1920–11 July 1920	Lt. Col. Jerome G. Pillow	11 October 1930–3 January 1931
Lt. Col. Alvin C. Gillem	11 July 1920–9 December 1920	Col. Ben Lear	3 January 1931–30 June 1933
Col. John M. Jenkins	9 December 1920–1 July 1923	Col. Ralph M. Parker	30 June 1933–5 February 1936
Col. Joseph E. Cusack	1 July 1923–1 September 1923	Maj. Richard W. Cooksey	5 February 1936–29 February 1936
Lt. Col. Howard C. Tatum	1 September 1923–16 September 1923	Col. Troup Miller	29 February 1936–1 May 1938
Col. Herbert J. Brees	16 September 1923–10 June 1925	Lt. Col. William H. W. Young	1 May 1938–15 June 1938
Lt. Col. Howard C. Tatum	10 June 1925–1 July 1925	Lt. Col. James E. Slack	15 June 1938–28 June 1938
Lt. Col. William W. Gordon	1 July 1925–9 September 1925	Col. Homer N. Groninger	28 June 1938–1 November 1940
Col. Leon B. Kromer	9 September 1925–2 August 1928	Lt. Col. John T. McLane	1 November 1940–27 November 1940
	Col. Harold M. Raynor	27 November 1940–31 December 1941	

12th Cavalry Regiment (2d Cavalry Division)

HQ—Camp Furlong, NM, 1919–20; Camp Robert F.L. Michie, TX, 1920–21; Fort Brown, TX, 1921–41

Stationed at Camp Furlong, NM, less 1st Sq. at Corozal, CZ, and 2d Sq. at Camp Shannon, Hachita, NM. Regiment, less 1st Sq., transferred on 11 April 1920 to Camp Robert F.L. Michie at Del Rio, TX. Regiment, less 1st Sq., transferred in October 1921 to Fort Brown, TX. Concurrently, 1st Sq. transferred from Camp Gaillard, CZ, to Fort Ringgold, TX. Assumed responsibility of the Fort Brown Command sector of the Mexican Border Patrol. The 2d Sq. transferred in 1922 to Fort Ringgold. The 1st Sq. concurrently transferred to Fort Brown. Assigned to the 2d Cav. Div. on 24 March 1923. Provided the honor guard on 4 December 1929 for Mexican president Ortiz Rubio's visit to Brownsville, TX. Regimental polo team frequently participated in matches against the team from the 17th Mexican Cavalry from Matamoros, Mexico, in 1930s. Relieved from the 2d Cav. Div. on 3 January 1933 and assigned to the 1st Cav. Div. Assigned Reserve officers conducted summer training with the regiment at Fort Brown or with units of the 2d Cav. Brig. at Fort Bliss. Location 7 December 1941—Fort Bliss, TX.

Organization Day: 29 June. Chosen to commemorate the date of the regiment's completion of organization on 29 June 1901.

Status: Assigned to the USARS as the 12th Cav.

Events: 11, 55, 65, 83, 97, 105, 147, 183, 206, 250, 284, 288, 295, 296, 300, 315

Commanders, 12th Cavalry Regiment

Col. Horatio G. Sickel	ao March 1917–27 August 1917	Maj. Geoffrey Keyes	19 September 1930–5 November 1930
Col. George E. Stockle	27 August 1917–20 October 1917	Col. Francis W. Glover	5 November 1930–23 January 1933
Col. Daniel L. Tate	28 November 1917–January 1918	Col. Guy Kent	23 January 1933–3 May 1935
Col. George E. Stockle	January 1918–6 December 1918	Col. Stephen W. Winfree	3 May 1935–23 June 1935
Col. G.W. Biegler	13 December 1918–19 September 1919	Maj. John M. Thompson	23 June 1935–1 July 1935
Col. William C. Rivers	19 September 1919–2 March 1920	Maj. Frederic W. Whitney	1 July 1935–30 August 1935
Col. Lawrence T. Fleming	2 March 1920–29 March 1920	Maj. John M. Thompson	31 August 1935–18 September 1935
Col. Sedgwick Rice	29 March 1920–1 October 1923	Col. Kerr T. Riggs	18 September 1935–25 June 1937
Col. John M. Morgan	1 October 1923–28 September 1925	Lt. Col. Frederic W. Whitney	25 June 1937–16 August 1937
Lt. Col. Emund A. Buchnan	28 September 1925–2 October 1925	Col. Donald A. Robinson	16 August 1937–9 May 1939
Col. William T. Johnston	2 October 1925–7 June 1929	Lt. Col. James C. V. Crowley	9 May 1939–26 June 1939
Lt. Col. Stanley Koch	7 June 1929–27 September 1929	Col. Arthur E. Wilbourne	26 June 1939–20 September 1939
Col. Daniel Van Voorhis	27 September 1929–9 September 1930	Col. John A. Robenson	20 September 1939–17 June 1940
Maj. Oliver I. Holman	9 September 1930–19 September 1930	Col. Arthur E. Wilbourne	17 June 1940–10 June 1941
	Col. Wilferd M. Blunt	15 June 1941–6 January 1942	

13th Cavalry Regiment (2d Cavalry Division)

HQ—Fort Clark, TX, 1919–20; Fort D.A. Russell, WY, 1920–27; Fort Riley, KS, 1927–36; Fort Knox, KY, 1936–41

Regiment, less 2d Sq., stationed at Fort Clark, TX, as of June 1919. The 2d Sq. stationed at Fort Ringgold, TX. Regiment transferred on 13 October 1920 to Fort D.A. Russell, WY. Assigned to the 2d Cav. Div. on 24 March 1923. Provided the escort for President Warren G. Harding on 25 June 1923 on his visit to Cheyenne, WY. Regiment maintained habitual summer training relationships with the 115th and 324th Cav. Regts., 1922–26, at the Pole Mountain Military Reservation, WY. Participated in the making of the movie "Pony Express" near Cheyenne in July 1925 and of Pathe Films movie "His First Command" at Fort Riley in August 1929. Conducted a 625-mile march from Fort D.A. Russell to Fort Riley, KS, 18 June–18 July 1927, on a permanent change of station. Relieved on 5 August 1927 from the 2d Cav. Div. Assigned on 1 May 1932 to the 2d Cav. Div. Relieved from the 2d Cav. Div. on 18 August 1936 and assigned to the 7th Cav. Brig. (Mecz). Transferred on 6 September 1936 to Fort Knox, KY. Reorganized and redesignated 13th Cav. (Mecz) in September 1936. 3d Sq. activated 1 July 1940 at Fort Knox. Reorganized and redesignated 13th Armd. Regt. on 15 July 1940 and assigned to the 1st Armd. Div.

Organization Day: 1 May. Chosen to commemorate the regiment's organization on 1 May 1901.

Status: Assigned to the USARS as the 13th Armor.

Events: 13, 79, 130, 152, 166, 171, 177, 188, 213, 230, 253, 269, 277, 280, 295, 296

Commanders, 13th Cavalry Regiment

Col. Henry J. Slocum	1 July 1916–15 May 1917	Lt. Col. William W. Overton	11 May 1929–30 September 1929
Col. Samuel G. Jones	21 May 1917–3 August 1917	Col. Walter S. Grant	30 September 1929–21 May 1931
Col. Charles A. Hedekin	4 August 1917–3 January 1918	Col. Alexander B. Coxe	21 May 1931–22 May 1933
Col. Fred J. Herman	3 January 1918–18 March 1919	Maj. Arthur H. Truxes	22 May 1933–31 May 1933
Col. Edward Anderson	19 March 1919–24 February 1921	Col. Charles F. Martin	31 May 1933–31 May 1936
Col. Roy B. Harper	24 February 1921–1 October 1923	Maj. James A. Kilian	31 May 1936–29 June 1936
Col. John C. Boniface	1 October 1923–21 June 1925	Maj. William E. Shipp	29 June 1936–29 August 1936
Col. Henry R. Richmond	21 June 1925–19 July 1927	Capt. John H. Claybrook	29 August 1936–6 September 1936
Col. Aubrey Lippincott	19 July 1927–11 May 1929	Col. Charles L. Scott	6 September 1936–23 September 1939
Col. Jack W. Heard	24 September 1939–15 July 1940		

14th Cavalry Regiment (2d Cavalry Division)

HQ—Fort Sam Houston, TX, 1919–20; Fort Des Moines, IA, 1920–40; Fort Riley, KS, 1940–41

Stationed at Fort Sam Houston, TX, as of June 1919. Transferred on 30 April 1920 to Fort Ringgold, TX. Regiment, less 3d Sq., transferred to Fort Des Moines, IA, and arrived there on 19 August 1920. Concurrently, 3d Sq. transferred to Camp Dodge, IA, where it was inactivated on 10 September 1921. The 1st Sq. transferred on 2 September 1921 to Fort Sheridan, IL. Regiment assigned to the 2d Cav. Div. on 15 August 1927. In April 1933, the regiment assumed command and control of the Iowa CCC District until mid-1934. The 1st Sq. participated during May–November 1933 in the "Century of Progress" exhibition in Chicago, IL. The entire regiment was assembled for the first time since 1920 at Rock Island, IL, in January 1935 for regimental maneuvers and a mounted tactical march. Regiment, less 1st Sq., performed flood relief duties along the Mississippi and Ohio Rivers during January–February 1937. Transferred on 28 May 1940, less 1st Sq., to Fort Riley, KS. The 1st Sq. transferred on 20 October 1940 to Fort Riley. Regiment maintained habitual summer training relationships with the 161st Cav. Brig. and the 322d Cav. Regt. at Fort Des Moines, 1922–40. The 1st Sq. maintained habitual summer training relationships with the regiments of the 65th Cav. Div. (317th–320th Cav. Regts.) at Fort Sheridan. Assigned Reserve officers conducted summer training at Fort Des Moines and Fort Sheridan. Location 7 December 1941—Fort Riley, KS.

Organization Day: 5 March. Chosen to commemorate the regiment's organization on 5 March 1901.

Status: Assigned to the USARS as the 14th Cav.; 1st Sq. active at Fort Lewis, WA, as an element of the 2d Inf. Div.

Events: 32, 50, 123, 150, 172, 207,214, 233, 237, 256, 274, 285, 302, 303

Commanders, 14th Cavalry Regiment

Col. Augustus C. McComb	ao March 1917–May 1918	Lt. Col. Arthur G. Hixson	5 September 1928–24 September 1928
Col. James E. Shelly	May 1918–19 March 1919	Col. Edgar A. Sirmyer	24 September 1928–20 April 1931
Col. Lawrence J. Fleming	19 March 1919–23 November 1919	Lt. Col. George H. Baird	20 April 1931–1 July 1931
Col. Robert A. Brown	23 November 1919–3 October 1922	Lt. Col. Talbot Smith	1 July 1931–13 September 1931
Col. Harry La T. Cavanaugh	3 October 1922–20 April 1924	Col. Charles E. Stodter	13 September 1931–14 August 1934
Capt. James K. Cockrell	20 April 1924–13 June 1924	Lt. Col. Butler N. Briscoe	14 August 1934–26 August 1934
Maj. Murray B. Rush	13 June 1924–15 August 1924	Col. Clarence Lininger	26 August 1934–25 June 1936
Col. Frank R. Caldwell	15 August 1924–18 January 1925	Col. John C. Pegram	25 June 1936–1 August 1939
Lt. Col. A.H. Davison	18 January 1925–24 April 1925	Lt. Col. Edward J. Dwan	1 August 1939–4 November 1939
Lt. Col. David H. Biddle	24 April 1925–23 October 1925	Col. Arthur H. Wilson	4 November 1939–8 January 1941
Col. Julian R. Lindsey	23 October 1925–5 September 1928	Lt. Col. John T. Pierce	8 January 1941–July 1942

15th Cavalry Regiment (Separate) **Regular Army Inactive**

HQ—Fort D.A. Russell, WY, 1919–21; *Inactive,* 1921–27; Kansas City, MO, 1927–41

Arrived at the port of New York on 19 June 1919 on the U.S.S. *Panaman*. Transferred the same day to Camp Mills, NY, where emergency service personnel were discharged. Transferred to Fort D.A. Russell, WY, and arrived there on 26 June 1919. Sent in October 1919 to quell coal miner's strikes in Sheridan, Rock Springs, and Thermopolis, WY. Inactivated on 18 October 1921 at Fort D.A. Russell. Active Associate was 13th Cav., 1922–25, and 14th Cavalry, 1925–27. Allotted to the Seventh Corps Area on 28 February 1927. Organized about June 1927 with O.R. personnel from the 66th Cav. Div. as an RAI unit in Kansas City, MO. Typically conducted Inactive Training Period meetings at the 110th Engineers (Engrs.) armory or the Organized Reserve Center building at 20th and Vine Streets in Kansas City. Conducted summer training with the 2d Cav. Regt. at Fort Riley, KS, 1930–40. Conducted cavalry CMTC at Fort Leavenworth, KS, some years as an alternate form of training. Reorganized and redesignated 15th Cav. Regt. (Horse and Mecz) (Corps Reconnaissance) on 1 July 1940. Location 7 December 1941—Kansas City, MO.

Organization Day: 2 February. Chosen to commemorate the regiment's date of constitution on 2 February 1901.

Status: Assigned to the USARS as the 15th Cav.; 5th Sq. active at Fort Knox, KY, as an element of the 1st Armd. Training (Tng.) Brig.

Commanders, 15th Cavalry Regiment

Col. William H. Hay	15 September 1916–30 October 1917
Col. Melvin W. Rowell	January 1918–31 May 1918
Col. Mortimer O. Bigelow	28 July 1919–6 August 1919
Col. Charles A. Hedekin	20 October 1919–12 February 1920
Col. Roy B. Harper	12 February 1920–31 March 1920
Col. Thomas B. Dugan	4 April 1920–8 August 1921
Lt. Col. George B. Rodney	8 August 1921–21 September 1921
Col. Roy B. Harper	21 September 1921–18 October 1921
Inactive	19 October 1921–ao June 1927
Unknown	ao June 1927–June 1930
Maj. Merle E. Hollicke**	June 1930–7 July 1931
Maj. Ralph W. Page**	7 July 1931–ao January 1934
Unknown	ao January 1934–7 December 1941

**RAI commanders: O.R. officers.

16th Cavalry Regiment (Separate) **Regular Army Inactive**

HQ—Fort Brown, TX, 1919–20; Fort Sam Houston, TX, 1920–21; *Inactive,* 1921–26; Fort Myer, VA, 1926–38; *Inactive,* 1938–41

Stationed at Fort Brown, TX, as of June 1919. Transferred to Fort Sam Houston, TX, and arrived there on 30 April 1920. Inactivated on 12 November 1921 at Fort Sam Houston. Active Associate was 4th Cavalry, 1921–25, and 3d Cavalry, 1925–27. Organized on 17 March 1926 with O.R. personnel as an RAI unit at Fort Myer, VA. Inactivated on 21 February 1938 at Fort Myer by relief of personnel. Conducted summer training with the 3d Cav. Regt. at Fort Myer, 1928–37. Location 7 December 1941—*Inactive*.

Status: Assigned to the USARS as the 16th Cav.; HQ, 1st, 2d 3d, and 4th Sqs. active at Fort Knox, KY.

Commanders, 16th Cavalry Regiment

Col. William S. Scott	1 July 1916–1 May 1917
Col. Farrand Sayre	30 May 1917–12 October 1918
Lt. Col. Samuel B. Arnold	12 October 1918–11 November 1918
Col. James N. Munro	11 November 1918–1 February 1919
Col. Frank Keller	1 February 1919–28 February 1919
Unknown	28 February 1919–May 1919
Col. Farrand Sayre	May 1919–3 August 1920
Lt. Col. Daniel Van Voorhis	3 August 1920–6 November 1920
Col. Walter C. Short	6 November 1920–10 May 1921
Lt. Col. Lewis Foerster	10 May 1921–5 August 1921
Maj. Guy K. Wyman	5 August 1921–18 October 1921
Col. Howard R. Hickok	18 October 1921–12 November 1921
Inactive	12 November 1921–17 March 1926
Capt. Arthur Matz**	17 March 1926–28 February 1927
Maj. Harding Polk*	28 February 1927–28 April 1927
Maj. Albert J. Myer**	28 April 1927–20 June 1927
Lt. Col. Frederick T. Arnold**	20 June 1927–ao August 1927
Maj. Albert J. Myer**	ao August 1927–22 April 1930
Lt. Col. James F. Tompkins**	22 April 1930–19 October 1936
Maj. Ralph S. Koser**	19 October 1936–21 February 1938
Inactive	21 February 1938–7 December 1941

*RAI commanders: R.A. officers.
**RAI commanders: O.R. officers.

17th Cavalry Regiment (Separate) **Regular Army Inactive**

HQ—Schofield Barracks, TH, 1919–21; Presidio of Monterey, CA, 1921; *Inactive,* 1921–27; Portland, OR, 1927–41; *Inactive,* 1941

Stationed at Schofield Barracks, TH, as of June 1919. Transferred on 15 September 1921 to the Presidio of Monterey, CA. Inactivated on 26 September 1921 at the Presidio of Monterey. Active Associate was the 11th Cav., 1921–27. Allotted to the Ninth Corps Area on 28 February 1927. Organized by June 1927 as an RAI unit with O.R. personnel from the 2d Sq., 323d Cav. Regimental HQ established at Portland, OR. Concurrently, 1st Sq. organized at Corvallis, OR, and 2d Sq. organized at Seattle, WA. Conducted summer training at Fort Lewis, WA, 1930–40. Reorganized and redesignated 17th Cav. Regt. (Horse and Mecz) (Corps Reconnaissance) on 1 July 1940. Inactivated in January 1941 at Portland by relief of personnel. Location 7 December 1941—*Inactive.*

Status: Assigned to the USARS as the 17th Cav.

Commanders, 17th Cavalry Regiment

Col. Willard A. Holbrook	1 July 1916–August 1917	Unknown	ao June 1927–13 October 1927
Col. George H. Morgan	13 October 1917–1 January 1919	Maj. Harley C. Dagley*	13 October 1927–31 August 1928
Col. John D. L. Hartman	1 March 1919–4 July 1921	Maj. Paul McCormick**	31 August 1928–14 December 1933
Col. George F. Hamilton	4 July 1921–1 September 1921	Maj. Charles P. Rydberg**	14 December 1933–30 August 1934
Inactive	1 September 1921–ao June 1927	Maj. Ayres W. Johnson**	30 August 1934–January 1941

*RAI commanders: R.A. officers.
**RAI commanders: O.R. officers.

26th Cavalry Regiment (PS) (Separate)

HQ—Fort Stotsenberg, PI, 1922–41

Constituted in the R.A. on 1 October 1922 and assigned to the Philippine Department. Concurrently activated at Fort Stotsenberg, PI, by transfer of personnel from the 25th Field Artillery (F.A.) (PS), and with equipment and horses from the 9th Cav. when that regiment transferred to Fort Riley, KS. Reorganized on 1 December 1927 as a three-squadron regiment. Troops C and G inactivated on 6 March 1928 at Camp Stotsenberg. Concurrently, the 2d MG Troop was redesignated MG Troop, 26th Cav. Conducted river crossing operations in May 1933 on the Rio Grande and Hagonoy Rivers. Troops C and G activated on 15 March 1941 at Camp Stotsenberg. The 26th Cav. was the primary reconnaissance force for the Philippine Department and was assigned the task to perform the covering force mission from Lingayan Gulf to the Bataan Peninsula. Location 7 December 1941—Fort Stotsenberg, PI.

Organization Day: 1 October. Chosen to commemorate the regiment's organization on 1 October 1922.

Events: 27, 35, 41, 52, 68, 82, 100, 118, 139, 169, 179, 198, 223, 245, 270

Commanders, 26th Cavalry Regiment (Philippine Scouts)

Col. Edward Anderson	11 October 1922–16 January 1923	Col. William H. Cowles	11 November 1933–23 August 1934
Maj. John A. Considine	16 January 1923–3 April 1923	Lt. Col. Robert M. Cheney	23 August 1934–2 October 1934
Lt. Col. Alvan C. Gillem	3 April 1923–30 August 1924	Col. E. Kearsley Sterling	2 October 1934–22 July 1936
Col. Harry LaT. Cavanaugh	30 August 1924–17 June 1926	Maj. Gordon J. F. Heron	22 July 1936–30 October 1936
Lt. Col. Isaac S. Martin	17 June 1926–14 September 1926	Col. George Grunert	30 October 1936–24 December 1936
Col. John D. Long	14 September 1926–4 October 1929	Lt. Col. Edgar A. Taulbee	24 December 1936–3 July 1937
Col. Robert J. Fleming	4 October 1929–13 October 1931	Col. Clarence A. Dougherty	3 July 1937–17 July 1939
Col. Archibald F. Commiskey	13 October 1931–23 August 1934	Col. Robert Blaine	17 July 1939–13 July 1941
	Col. Clinton A. Pierce	14 July 1941–24 January 1942	

101st Cavalry Regiment (21st Cavalry Division) **New York National Guard**

HQ—Brooklyn, NY, 1921–41; Fort Devens, MA, 1941

Constituted in the N.G. on 30 December 1920, assigned to the 21st Cav. Div., and allotted to the state of New York. Organized on 1 June 1921 by redesignation of the 1st NY Cav. Regt. (demobilized on 2 April 1919 at Camp Upton, NY, as the 105th MG Battalion (Bn.); reconstituted on 1 June 1921 as the 1st NY Cav. Regt.) as the 101st Cav. Regimental HQ organized on 11 July 1921 and federally recognized at Brooklyn, NY. Subordinate squadron HQ organized and federally recognized as follows: 1st Sq. organized on 6 June 1921 at Brooklyn, NY; 2d Sq. organized on 1 June 1921 at Buffalo, NY. The entire 2d Sq. transferred on 15 February 1928 to the new 121st Cav. and a new 2d Sq. organized from the 51st MG Sq. at Manhattan, NY. Reorganized on 25 May 1929 as a three-squadron regiment; new 3d Sq. organized at Manhattan. The 2d Sq. participated in a review on 7 June 1930 for Gov. Franklin D. Roosevelt at Van Cortlandt Park. Regiment provided escort to Prince and Princess Takamatsu of Japan on 11 April 1931 during their visit to New York City. Conducted additional week-long winter training directed by the War Department at Plattsburg Barracks, NY, in December 1939. Conducted summer training at Fort Ethan Allen, VT, 1921–25 (less 1923); Camp Dix, NJ, 1923; and Pine Camp, NY, 1926–39. Reorganized and redesignated as 101st Cav. Regt. (Horse and Mecz) on 1 October 1940 and relieved from the 21st Cav. Div. Assigned to the VI Corps on 30 December 1940. Inducted into active Federal service on 27 January 1941 at Brooklyn. Transferred to Fort Devens, MA, and arrived there on 4 February 1941. Location 7 December 1941—Fort Devens, MA.

Status: Assigned to the USARS as the 101st Cav.; 1st Bn. active at Staten Island, NY, as an element of the 42d Inf. Div., and Troop E active at Geneva, NY, as an element of the 27th Inf. Brig. (Sep.).

Events: 280, 330

Commanders, 101st Cavalry Regiment

Col. Mortimer D. Bryant	11 July 1921–8 May 1922	Col. James R. Howlett	17 June 1922–9 October 1939
Col. Gilbert E. Ackerman	9 October 1939–1 August 1943		

102d Cavalry Regiment (21st Cavalry Division) **New Jersey National Guard**

HQ—Newark, NJ, 1921–41; Fort Jackson, SC, 1941

Constituted in the N.G. in 1921, assigned to the 21st Cav. Div., and allotted to the state of New Jersey. Organized on 17 August 1921 by redesignation of the 1st Regt., NJ Cav. (organized and federally recognized on 29 April 1921) as the 102d Cav. Regimental HQ organized and federally recognized at Newark, NJ. Subordinate squadron HQ organized and federally recognized as follows: 1st Sq. organized on 17 August 1921 at West Orange, NJ; 2d Sq. organized at Westfield, NJ. Relieved in May 1927 from the 21st Cav. Div. Reorganized on 15 March 1929 as a three-squadron regiment; new 3d Sq. organized at Newark. Assigned to the 59th Cav. Brig. on 12 June 1937. Further assigned to the 21st Cav. Div. on 1 April 1939. Regiment or elements thereof called up for the following state duties: escort for Gen. John J. Pershing at Camp Merritt on 31 May 1924; escort to President Calvin Coolidge on 4 July 1926 at the opening of the Camden-Philadelphia Bridge; march unit in President Herbert Hoover's inaugural parade in 1929; New Jersey representative military unit at the celebration of the 150th Anniversary of the surrender of Yorktown in 1931. Conducted summer training at Sea Girt, NJ, 1921–36, and Indiantown Gap, PA, 1937. Relieved on 1 October 1940 from the 21st Cav. Div. Reorganized and redesignated 102d Cav. Regt. (Horse and Mecz) on 16 November 1940. Assigned to the I Corps on 30 December 1940. Inducted into active Federal service on 6 January 1941 at Newark. Transferred to Fort Jackson, SC, and arrived there on 16 January 1941. Location 7 December 1941—Fort Jackson, SC.

Status: Assigned to the USARS as the 102d Armor; 1st Bn. active at Port Murray, NJ, as an element of the 42d Inf. Div.

Events: 137, 330

Commanders, 102d Cavalry Regiment

Col. Lewis Ballentine	29 April 1921–12 June 1937	Col. Henry L. Moeller	12 June 1937–6 January 1941
Col. Donald W. McGowan	6 January 1941–September 1944		

103d Cavalry Regiment (21st Cavalry Division) **Pennsylvania National Guard**

HQ—Philadelphia, PA, 1921–37; Tyrone, PA, 1937–40

Constituted in the N.G. in 1921, assigned to the 21st Cav. Div., and allotted to the state of Pennsylvania. Organized on 1 June 1921 by redesignation of the 1st Cav. Regt., PA N.G. (demobilized on 3 April–24 May 1919 at Camp Dix, NJ, as elements of the 28th Div.; reconstituted, organized, and federally recognized on 16 October 1919 at Philadelphia, PA, as the 1st Cav. Regt., PA N.G.) as the 103d Cav. Regimental HQ organized and federally recognized at Philadelphia. Subordinate squadron HQ organized and federally recognized as follows: 1st Sq. organized on 1 June 1921 at Altoona, PA; 2d Sq. organized on 1 June 1921 at Philadelphia. Reorganized on 1 April 1929 as a three-squadron regiment; new 3d Sq. organized at Valley Forge, PA. Entire regiment called up to perform relief duties in connection with the flooding of the Schuylkill and Susquehanna Rivers in the spring of 1936. Conducted summer training at Mount Gretna, PA, 1921–35, and Indiantown Gap, PA, 1936–39. Regimental HQ relocated on 1 June 1937 to Tyrone, PA. Relieved from the 21st Cav. Div. in January 1939 and assigned to the 22d Cav. Div. Reorganized on 18 June 1939 with 1st Sq. redesignated 1st Sq., 104th Cav. and new 1st Sq. organized with HQ at Altoona, PA. Relieved from the 22d Cav. Div. on 23 September 1940, converted and redesignated as the 190th F.A. Regt.

Events: 203, 301

Commanders, 103d Cavalry Regiment

Col. George Thayer	6 August 1921–10 May 1923	Col. Milton G. Baker	1 September 1935–10 June 1937
Col. Arthur C. Colahan	10 May 1923–31 August 1935	Col. Benjamin C. Jones	10 June 1937–2 February 1940
Col. Samuel B. Wolfe	2 February 1940–23 September 1940		

104th Cavalry Regiment (21st Cavalry Division) **Pennsylvania National Guard**

HQ—Harrisburg, PA, 1921–41; Indiantown Gap, PA, 1941

Constituted in the N.G. in 1921, assigned to the 21st Cav. Div., and allotted to the state of Pennsylvania. Organized on 1 June 1921 by the conversion and redesignation of the 8th Inf. Regt., PA N.G. (demobilized in May 1919 at Camp Dix, NJ, as elements of the 112th Inf. and other units in the 28th Div.; reconstituted and federally recognized on 16 October 1919 as the 8th Inf. Regt., PA N.G.) as the 104th Cav. Regimental HQ organized and federally recognized at Harrisburg, PA. Subordinate squadron HQ organized and federally recognized as follows: 1st Sq. organized at Tyrone, PA; and 2d Sq. organized on 20 July 1921 at Carlisle, PA. Reorganized on 15 March 1929 as a three-squadron regiment; new 3d Sq. organized at Harrisburg. The regiment, or elements thereof, called up to perform the following state duties: entire regiment to perform strike duty at coal mines at Ebensburg and Cokeburg, PA, 21 July–7 September 1922; Troops B and E for duty near Clarion, PA, to search for a downed airmail pilot from 6–11 October 1925; entire regiment to perform relief duties in connection with the flooding of the Schuylkill and Susquehanna Rivers in the spring of 1936. Conducted summer training at Mount Gretna, PA, 1921–35, and Indiantown Gap, PA, 1936–39. Relieved from the 21st Cav Div in January 1939 and assigned to the 22d Cav. Div. Relieved on 1 October 1940 from the 22d Cav. Div. Reorganized and redesignated 104th Cav. Regt. (Horse and Mecz) on 23 September 1940. Assigned to the II Corps on 30 December 1940. Inducted into active Federal service on 17 February 1941 at Harrisburg. Transferred on 1 March 1941 to Indiantown Gap Military Reservation. Location 7 December 1941—Indiantown Gap, PA.

Organization Day: 21 July. Chosen to commemorate the regiment's Federal recognition as the 104th Cav. on 21 July 1921.

Status: Assigned to the USARS as the 104th Cav.; 1st Sq. active at Philadelphia, PA, as an element of the 28th Inf.Div.

Events: 203, 301, 330

Commanders, 104th Cavalry Regiment

Col. Edward J. Stackpole	21 June 1921–23 March 1933	Col. George J. Shoemaker	23 March 1933–16 January 1940
Col. Albert H. Stackpole	21 March 1940–1 December 1943		

105th Cavalry Regiment (22d Cavalry Division) **Wisconsin National Guard**

HQ—Milwaukee, WI, 1921–29; Nekoosa, WI, 1929–40

Constituted in the N.G. in 1921, assigned to the 22d Cav. Div., and allotted to the state of Wisconsin. Organized on 1 April 1921 by redesignation of the 1st Cav. Regt., WI N.G. (demobilized on 16 May 1919 at Camp Grant, IL, as elements of the 120th F.A.; reconstituted and federally recognized on 16 October 1919 as the 1st Cav. Regt., WI N.G.; elements organized during October 1919–March 1921 in Wisconsin) as 105th Cav. Regimental HQ organized on 24 May 1921 and federally recognized at Milwaukee, WI. Subordinate squadron HQ organized and federally recognized as follows: 1st Sq.organized on 1 April 1921 at Milwaukee; 2d Sq. organized on 1 June 1921 at Milwaukee. Reorganized on 15 March 1929 as a three-squadron regiment; new 3d Sq. organized on 28 March 1929 at Watertown, WI. Regimental HQ relocated on 1 September 1929 to Nekoosa, WI. The regiment, or elements thereof, called up to perform the following state duties: entire regiment to perform riot control during the "Milk Strike" at Shawano, WI, 15–20 May 1933; entire regiment to perform strike duty during the labor disturbances at Kohler, WI, 28 July–20 August 1934. Conducted summer training at Camp Williams, WI, 1921–39. Designated mobilization training station was Camp Sparta, WI. Relieved in January 1939 from the 22d Cav. Div. Assigned to the 23d Cav. Div. on 1 April 1939. Relieved from the 23d Cav. Div. on 1 October 1940, and converted and redesignated as the 126th F.A. Regt.

Status: Assigned to the USARS as the 126th F.A.; 1st Bn. active at Kenosha, WI, as an element of the 57th F.A.Brig.

Events: 214, 302

Commanders, 105th Cavalry Regiment

Col. James J. Quill	24 May 1921–1 September 1929	Col. John C.P. Hanley	1 September 1929–1 October 1940

106th Cavalry Regiment (22d Cavalry Division) **Illinois and Michigan National Guard**

HQ—*Not organized,* 1921–27; Chicago, IL, 1927–40; Camp Livingston, LA, 1940–41

Constituted in the N.G. in 1921, assigned to the 22d Cav. Div., and allotted to the states of Illinois and Michigan. Subordinate squadron HQ organized and federally recognized as follows: 1st Sq. organized on 6 July 1922 at Detroit, MI; 2d Sq. organized on 20 October 1922 at Springfield, IL. Regimental HQ organized on 9 July 1927 and federally recognized at Chicago, IL. The 2d Sq. called up to perform the following state duties: coal miner strike duty at Clinton, IL, 7 August–21 September 1922, and Hillsboro, IL, 22–26 August 1923; tornado relief work at Carbondale, IL, 18 March–13 April 1925. Reorganized on 10 April 1929 as a three-squadron regiment by the redesignation of 1st Sq. at Detroit as the 3d Sq., and new 1st Sq. organized at South Haven, MI. HQ, 2d Sq. concurrently relocated to Urbana, IL. Entire regiment assembled for the first time in July

1936 for summer training at Camp Williams, WI. For at least 1 year, in 1937, the regiment also trained 18 company-grade cavalry officers of the 65th Cav. Div. at Camps Grant and Grayling. Relieved in January 1939 from the 22d Cav. Div. Assigned to the 23d Cav. Div. on 1 April 1939. Regiment, less 1st and 3d Sqs., conducted summer training most years at Camp Grant, IL, 1922–39. The 1st Sq. and 3d Sqs. conducted summer training most years at Camp Grayling, MI, 1923–39. Designated mobilization training station for the entire regiment was Camp Sparta, WI. The 1st and 3d Sqs. relieved from the regiment on 1 September 1940, converted and redesignated 1st Bn., 177th F.A. Regt. and 2d Bn., 210th C.A. Regt., respectively. Concurrently, the 106th Cav. reorganized entirely in the state of Illinois by the assignment and redesignation of the 23d Reconnaissance (Rcn.) Sq. as the new 1st Sq. Relieved from the 23d Cav. Div. on 1 October 1940 and concurrently redesignated 106th Cav. Regt. (Horse and Mecz). Inducted into active Federal service on 25 November 1940 at Urbana. Transferred to Camp Livingston, LA, on 3 January 1941 and assigned to the V Corps. Location 7 December 1941—Camp Livingston, LA.

Status: Assigned to the USARS as the 106th Cav.; no active elements.

Events: 214, 302, 320, 328

Commanders, 106th Cavalry Regiment

Col. Walter J. Fisher (IL)	9 June 1927–13 May 1935	Col. Kenneth Buchanan (IL)	9 December 1939–ao May 1940
Col. Harold T. Weber (IL)	13 May 1935–9 December 1939	Col. Charles R. Johnson (R.A.)	ao January 1941–30 January 1942

107th Cavalry Regiment (22d Cavalry Division) — Ohio National Guard

HQ—Cincinnati, OH, 1921–27; Cleveland, OH, 1927–41; Camp Forrest, TN, 1941

Constituted in the N.G. in 1921, assigned to the 22d Cav. Div., and allotted to the state of Ohio. Subordinate squadron HQ organized and federally recognized as follows: 1st Sq. organized on 20 December 1921 at Cincinnati, OH; 2d Sq. organized on 13 April 1921 at Akron, OH. Regimental HQ organized on 17 February 1922 and federally recognized at Cincinnati, OH. Regimental HQ relocated in June 1927 to Cleveland, OH. Reorganized on 30 June 1929 as a three-squadron regiment; new 3d Sq. organized at Barberton, OH. The regiment, or elements thereof, called up to perform the following state duties: escort for Marshal Ferdinand Foch on his visit to Cleveland, OH, in 1921; coal miner strike duty at Middleport and St. Clairsville, OH, 26 July–16 August 1922; tornado relief duty at Lorain and Sandusky, OH, 28 June–16 July 1924; martial law in connection with civil disorders and KKK riots in Niles, OH, 2–5 November 1924; escort for General of the Armies John J. Pershing on his visit to Cleveland in 1927; escort for President Herbert Hoover on his visit to Cleveland on 2 October 1930; coal miner strike duty at Cadiz, OH, 16 April–17 August 1932; riot control during a workers' strike at the Auto-Lite plant at Toledo, OH, 23 May–2 June 1934; and for disaster relief duty during the Ohio River flood of January–March 1937. Conducted summer training at Camp Perry, OH, 1921–34, 1936, 1938–39, and at Fort Knox, KY, in 1935 and 1937. Reorganized and redesignated 107th Cav. Regt. (Horse and Mecz) on 1 November 1940. Concurrently, the 22d Rcn. Sq. redesignated as the new 1st Sq. and relieved from the 22d Cav. Div. Assigned to the VII Corps on 30 December 1940. Inducted into active Federal service on 5 March 1941 at Cleveland. Transferred on 16 March 1941 to Camp Forrest, TN. Participated in MGM Pictures' movie "The Bugle Sounds" in June 1941 while participating in the Louisiana Maneuvers. Location 7 December 1941—Camp Forrest, TN.

Status: Assigned to the USARS as the 107th Armd. Cav.; 1st Bn. active at Stow, OH, and 2d Sq. active at Kettering, OH, as elements of the 38th Inf. Div.

Events: 213, 230, 302, 320, 324, 328, 330

Commanders, 107th Cavalry Regiment

Col. Paul L. Mitchell	17 February 1922–6 July 1923	Col. Joseph J. Johnston	1 January 1927–10 July 1927
Col. Willard O. Lathrop	7 July 1923–18 November 1924	Col. Newell C. Bolton	11 July 1927–10 February 1936
Col. Dudley J. Hard	19 November 1924–28 December 1926	Col. Woods King	10 February 1936–1 January 1944

108th Cavalry Regiment (22d Cavalry Division) **Louisiana and Georgia National Guard**

HQ—*Not organized,* 1921–23; New Orleans, LA, 1923–36; Hinesville, GA, 1936–40

Constituted in the N.G. in 1921, assigned to the 22d Cav. Div., and allotted to the states of Louisiana and Georgia. Subordinate squadron HQ organized and federally recognized as follows: 1st Sq. organized on 6 March 1922 at Atlanta, GA; 2d Sq. organized on 21 June 1922 at Jennings, LA. Regimental HQ organized on 10 November 1923 and federally recognized at New Orleans, LA. Relieved from the 22d Cav. Div. on 19 February 1927 and assigned to the 23d Cav. Div. Reorganized on 15 March 1929 as a three-squadron regiment; new 3d Sq. organized at New Orleans. HQ, 108th Cav. Regt. withdrawn from the state of Louisiana on 29 June 1936, allotted to the state of Georgia, and organized at Hinesville, GA. Regiment, less Georgia elements, called up to perform relief and guard duties associated with the flooding of the Mississippi River, 26 April–19 June 1927. Conducted summer training most years at Fort Oglethorpe, GA, 1921–39; and at Camp McClellan, AL, 1924, 1926–28, and 1933. Designated mobilization training station was Fort Oglethorpe. Relieved from the 23d Cav. Div. on 1 October 1940 and disbanded. Elements used to form the 101st and 105th Sep. Bns., C.A. (AA).

Events: 255, 300

Commanders, 108th Cavalry Regiment

Col. James E. Edmonds (LA)	27 February 1927–19 May 1936	Col. Joseph B. Fraser (GA)	29 June 1936–6 October 1940

109th Cavalry Regiment (23d Cavalry Division) **Tennessee, North Carolina, and Alabama National Guard**

HQ—*Not organized,* 1921–23; Chattanooga, TN, 1923–26; Nashville, TN, 1926–36; Chattanooga, TN, 1936–40

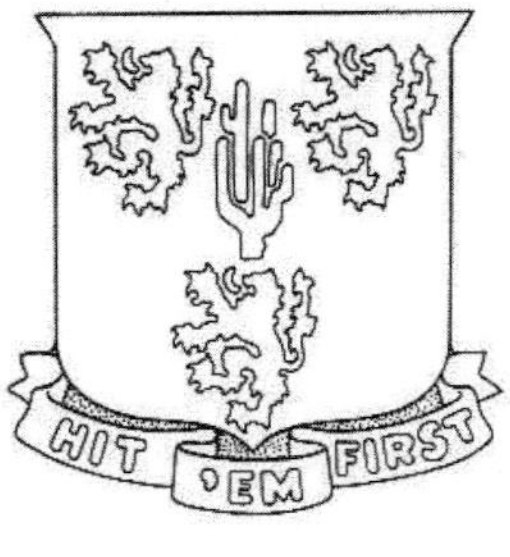

Constituted in the N.G. on 2 November 1921, assigned to the 23d Cav. Div., and allotted to the states of Tennessee, North Carolina, and Alabama. Subordinate squadron HQ organized and federally recognized as follows: 2d Sq. organized on 4 August 1921 at Hickory, NC; 1st Sq. organized on 20 April 1923 at Chattanooga, TN. Regimental HQ organized on 6 June 1923 and federally recognized at Chattanooga. Regimental HQ successively relocated as follows: to Nashville, TN, on 25 January 1926; and to Chattanooga on 28 October 1936. Reorganized on 30 March 1929 as a three-squadron regiment. Concurrently, the 2d Sq. at Hickory, NC, redesignated 3d Sq. and a new 2d Sq. organized and federally recognized at Nashville. The 3d Sq. converted and redesignated 2d Bn., 105th Engr. Regt. on 26 February 1938. Concurrently, the 3d Sq. and MG Troop withdrawn from the state of North Carolina and allotted to the state of Tennessee. The new 3d Sq. organized on 2 April 1938 and federally recognized at Nashville. The regiment, or elements thereof, called up to perform the following state duties: Troop G called up to preserve order at the trial of a Negro prisoner in Halifax, NC, 23–24 June 1927; 3d Sq.n performed strike duty at textile mills at Gastonia, NC, in April 1929; MG Troop and 3d Sq. performed strike duty at textile mills at Marion, NC, in August 1929; MG Troop and 3d Sq. performed strike duty at textile mills at Concord, Spindale, and Lincolnton, NC, 6–24 September 1934. Designated mobilization training station was Fort Oglethorpe, GA. Conducted summer training most years at Fort Oglethorpe, 1921–39, and at Camp McClellan, AL, in 1924. Relieved from the 23d Cav. Div. on 1 October 1940 and converted and redesignated as the 181st F.A. Regt.

Status: Assigned to the USARS as the 181st F.A.; 1st Bn. active at Chattanooga, TN, as an element of the 196th F.A. Brig.

Events: 255, 300

Commanders, 109th Cavalry Regiment

Col. J. Perry Fyffe (TN)	6 June 1923–19 January 1926	Col. Henry Dickinson (TN)	19 January 1926–14 September 1936
Col. Ira R. Summers (TN)	14 September 1936–1 October 1940		

110th Cavalry Regiment (23d Cavalry Division) **Massachusetts, Rhode Island, and Connecticut National Guard**

HQ—*Not organized* 1921–24; Boston, MA, 1924–37; West Hartford, CT, 1937–40; Boston, MA, 1940

Constituted in the N.G. in 1921, assigned to the 23d Cav. Div., and allotted to the state of Massachusetts. HQ, 1st Sq. organized on 28 November 1921 and federally recognized from existing units at Boston, MA. Regimental HQ organized on 3 July 1924 and federally recognized at Boston. Provided the escort to President Coolidge during his visit to Cambridge, MA, in May 1925. Relieved from the 23d Cav. Div. on 19 February 1927 and assigned to the 22d Cav. Div. Concurrently, 2d Sq. withdrawn from the state of Massachusetts and allotted to the state of Rhode Island. The 2d Sq. organized on 24 February 1927 from 1st Sq., Cav., RI N.G. with HQ federally recognized at Providence, RI. Relieved on 15 March 1929 from the 22d Cav. Div. The 2d Sq. converted and redesignated 2d Bn., 103d F.A. Regt. on 1 April 1929. A new 2d Sq. was organized on 7 June 1929 and federally recognized at Allston, MA. Reorganized on 10 June 1937 as a three-squadron regiment. Concurrently, 1st Sq. redesignated 3d Sq. and a new 1st Sq. organized by redesignation of the 1st Sq., 122d Cav. Regt. at New Haven, CT. HQ, 110th Cav. Regt. concurrently withdrawn from the state of Massachusetts, allotted to the state of Connecticut, and organized at West Hartford, CT. Assigned to the 59th Cav. Brig. on 12 June 1937. Further assigned on 1 April 1939 to the 21st Cav. Div. Connecticut elements (regimental headquarters and headquarters troop [HHT] and 1st Sq.) converted and redesignated 208th C.A. Regt. (AA) on 16 May 1940. Concurrently, 3d Sq. redesignated 1st Sq.; regimental HQ withdrawn from the state of Connecticut, allotted to the state of Massachusetts, and reorganized at Boston. Connecticut elements called up to perform the following state duties: flood relief at Hartford, CT, 19 March–1 April 1936; hurricane relief in the vicinity of Rockville, CT, 22–27 September 1938. Conducted summer training at Quonset Point, RI, 1921–31, and at Fort Devens, MA, 1932–39. Relieved from the 21st Cav. Div. on 9 October 1940 and converted and redesignated as the 180th F.A. Regt.

Events: 301

Commanders, 110th Cavalry Regiment

Col. Dana T. Gallup (MA)	3 July 1924–11 December 1934	Col. Philip L. Brown (MA)	11 December 1934–9 October 1940

111th Cavalry Regiment (23d Cavalry Division) **New Mexico and Colorado National Guard**

HQ—*Not organized,* 1921–24; Santa Fe, NM, 1924–34; Silver City, NM, 1934–39; Deming, NM, 1939–40

Constituted in the N.G. in 1921, assigned to the 23d Cav. Div., and allotted to the states of New Mexico and Colorado. HQ, 2d Sq. organized on 1 November 1921 and federally recognized at Denver, CO, from existing units. The 2d Sq. subsequently redesignated on 1 February 1922 as the 1st Sq., 117th Cav. Regt. Concurrently, the 2d Sq., 111th Cav. withdrawn from the state of Colorado and allotted to the state of New Mexico. A new 2d Sq. organized on 3 August 1923 and federally recognized at Santa Fe, NM. HQ, 1st Sq. organized on 1 March 1924 and federally recognized at Santa Fe from existing units. Regimental HQ organized on 3 March 1924 and federally recognized at Santa Fe. Reorganized on 15 March 1929 as a three-squadron regiment. New 3d Sq. organized on 14 July 1929 and federally recognized at Carlsbad, NM. Concurrently, regiment relieved from the 23d Cav. Div. Regiment called up to preserve order during a coal miner strike in Gallup, NM, during June–August 1922, and again at Gallup during May–August 1933. Regimental HQ successively relocated as follows: to Silver City, NM, on 10 October 1934; to Deming, NM, on 1 September 1939. Conducted summer training at Fort Bliss, TX, 1921–28, and at Camp Maximilliano Luna, Las Vegas, NM, 1929–39. For at least 1 year, in 1933, the regiment also trained eight company-grade cavalry officers of the 156th Cav. Brig. at Camp Luna. Designated mobilization training station, less 2d Sq., was Fort MacIntosh, TX, 1922–33 (2d Sq. at Fort Ringgold, 1922–33), and Fort Bliss, TX, 1934–40. Converted and redesignated on 26 April 1940 as the 207th C.A. Regt. (AA) (later redesignated the 200th C.A. Regt. [AA]).

Status: HHT active in the New Mexico N.G. as Headquarters and Headquarters Battery (HHB), 111th Air Defense Artillery (Arty.) Brig/ and the remainder of the regiment assigned to the USARS as the 200th Air Defense Arty.; 1st Bn. active at Roswell, NM; 2d Bn. active at Rio Rancho, NM; 3d Bn. active at Belen, NM, and 4th Bn. active at Rio Rancho, NM.

Events: 259, 300

Commanders, 111th Cavalry Regiment

Lt. Col. Fitz W. Thompson	1 November 1921–6 March 1924	Col. Clyde E. Ely	25 January 1933–23 July 1939
Col. Norman L. King	6 March 1924–9 January 1933	Col. Charles G. Sage	23 July 1939–26 April 1940

112th Cavalry Regiment (23d Cavalry Division) — Texas National Guard

HQ—Dallas, TX, 1921–25; Fort Worth, TX, 1925–38; Dallas, TX, 1938–40; Fort Clark, TX, 1940–41

Constituted in the N.G. in 1921, assigned to the 23d Cav. Div., and allotted to the state of Texas. Regimental HQ organized on 20 July 1921 at Dallas, TX, by redesignation of the 1st Texas Cav. Regt. (constituted on 20 February 1920; organized and federally recognized on 16 December 1920) as the 112th Cav. Subordinate squadron HQ concurrently organized at Dallas. Regimental HQ successively relocated as follows: to Fort Worth, TX, on 19 July 1925; to Dallas about August 1938. The regiment, or elements thereof, called up to perform the following state duties: to perform martial law during the reduction of the Borger, TX, criminal ring in September–October 1929; to restore order after the race riot in Sherman, TX, in May 1930; and to perform patrolling and production regulation in the East Texas Oilfields during September 1931–December 1932. Elements of the regiment were also called up to perform emergency relief duties at the Oak Cliffs, TX, tornado 30–31 July 1933, and the New London, TX, school explosion in March 1937. Conducted summer training at Camp Mabry, TX, 1921–23; Camp Stanley, TX, 1924–26; and most years at Camp Wolters, TX, 1927–39. Designated mobilization training station was Fort Brown, TX, 1922–33, and Fort Bliss, TX, 1933–40. Relieved from the 23d Cav. Div. on 1 April 1939 as part of the 56th Cav. Brig. (Sep.). Reorganized on 23 July 1939 as a three-squadron regiment; new 3d Sq. organized at Dallas, TX. HHT, 3d Sq. inactivated on 1 October 1940 and Troops I and K assigned to 1st and 2d Sqs. as Troops C and G, respectively. Inducted into active Federal service at home stations on 18 November 1940 as an element of the 56th Cav. Brig. (Sep.). Transferred to Fort Bliss, arrived there on 28 November 1940, and assigned to the Third Army. Transferred on 5 February 1941 to Fort Clark, TX. On arrival, relieved of the Fort Clark Command sector of the Mexican Border Patrol. Location 7 December 1941—Fort Clark, TX.

Status: Assigned to the USARS as the 112th Armor; 1st Bn. active at Dallas, TX, 2d Bn. active at Fort Worth, TX, 3d Bn. active at Brownwood, TX, 4th Bn. active at Bryan, TX, and 5th Bn. active at Marshall, TX, as elements of the 36th Inf. Div. (Mecz).

Events: 315, 328

Commanders, 112th Cavalry Regiment

Col. Lloyd E. Hill	20 January 1921–18 July 1925	Col. Walter B. Pyron	20 January 1937–21 August 1938
Col. Eugene DeBorgory	18 July 1925–25 November 1927	Col. Clarence E. Parker	21 August 1938–6 September 1941
Col. Laurence E. McGee	25 November 1927–20 January 1937	Col. Harry H. Johnson	6 September 1941–26 November 1941
	Col. Julian W. Cunningham (R.A.)	27 November 1941–November 1943	

113th Cavalry Regiment (24th Cavalry Division) **Iowa National Guard**

HQ—Iowa City, IA, 1921–29; Des Moines, IA, 1929–41; Camp Bowie, TX, 1941

Constituted in the N.G. in 1921, assigned to the 24th Cav. Div., and allotted to the state of Iowa. Regimental HQ organized on 1 June 1921 at Iowa City, IA, by redesignation of the 1st Regt., Iowa Cav. (constituted in 1920; organized and federally recognized on 3 May 1921 at Iowa City) as the 113th Cav. Subordinate squadron HQ concurrently organized as follows: 1st Sq. organized on 27 September 1921 at Des Moines, IA; 2d Sq. organized on 5 May 1921 at Ottumwa, IA. Reorganized on 11 April 1929 as a three-squadron regiment; new 3d Sq. organized at Iowa City. The regiment, or elements thereof, called up to perform the following state duties: entire regiment performed riot control duties during the Cedar County/Burlington, IA, "Cow War," 21 September–25 November 1931; regimental HQ, MG Troop, and Troops B, E, and F performed martial law at Newton, IA, in connection with labor troubles at the Maytag washing machine plant, 6–15 August 1938. Conducted summer training at Camp Dodge, IA, 1921–27 and 1929–40, and at Fort Riley, KS, 1927–28. For at least 2 years, in 1939 and 1940, the regiment also trained 20 company-grade officers of the 66th Cav. Div. at Camp Dodge and Camp Ripley, MN. Reorganized and redesignated 113th Cav. Regt. (Horse and Mecz) about 16 September 1940 and concurrently relieved from the 24th Cav. Div. Assigned to the VIII Corps on 30 December 1940. Inducted into active Federal service on 13 January 1941 at Des Moines. Transferred on 25 January 1941 to Camp Bowie, TX. Location 7 December 1941—Camp Bowie, TX.

Status: Assigned to the USARS as the 113th Cav.; 1st Sq. active at Camp Dodge, IA, as an element of the 34th Inf. Div.

Events: 303, 317, 328

Commanders, 113th Cavalry Regiment

Col. Ralph P. Howell	3 May 1921–15 October 1923	Col. Ray A. Yenter	25 April 1930–23 March 1936
Col. Park A. Findley	15 October 1923–15 April 1930	Col. Maxwell A. O'Brien	2 April 1936–30 January 1942

114th Cavalry Regiment (24th Cavalry Division) **Kansas and South Dakota National Guard**

HQ—*Not organized,* 1921–25; Topeka, KS, 1925–26; Rosedale, KS, 1926–34; Topeka, KS, 1934–40

Constituted in the N.G. in 1921, assigned to the 24th Cav. Div., and allotted to the states of Kansas and South Dakota. Partially organized on 4 November 1921 by redesignation of the 1st Sep. Sq., KS Cav. (reconstituted on 8 September 1919; HQ organized on 10 November 1919 and federally recognized at Topeka, KS) as the 1st Sq. The 2d Sq. withdrawn from the state of South Dakota on 2 July 1923 and allotted to the state of Kansas. Troop C organized in May 1924 composed entirely of Indian students from the Haskell Indian Institute at Topeka. The 2d Sq. organized on 26 July 1924 and federally recognized with HQ at Yates Center, KS. Regimental HQ organized on 10 January 1925 and federally recognized at Topeka. Regimental HQ successively relocated as follows: to Rosedale, KS, on 2 March 1926; to Topeka on 27 January 1934. Reorganized on 15 April 1929 as a three-squadron regiment; new 3d Sq. organized and federally recognized at Lawrence, KS. The regiment, or elements thereof, called up to perform the following state duties: 1st Sq. to perform strike duty at the Pittsburg, KS, coal fields, 14 December 1921–26 February 1922; 1st Sq. to perform strike duty at the Missouri-Kansas-Texas Railroad shops at Parsons, KS, 9 July–20 September 1922; elements to perform tornado relief duty at Augusta, KS, 13–16 July 1924; Troops A, B, and G to perform riot duty at Coffeyville, KS, 18–20 May 1927; four troops to perform road patrols and bridge blocks in connection with the Kansas State Penitentiary breakout, 19–20 January 1934; Troops A and F to perform riot control during labor troubles at copper mines in Baxter Springs, KS, 8–27 June

1934. Conducted summer training at Fort Riley, KS, 1922–39. For at least 2 years, in 1939 and 1940, the regiment also trained 24 company-grade officers of the 66th Cav. Div. at Fort Riley and Camp Ripley, MN. Relieved from the 24th Cav. Div. on 1 October 1940, and converted and redesignated as the 127th F.A. Regt.

Status: Assigned to the US Army Regimental System (USARS) as the 127th Field Artillery; 1st Battalion active at Ottawa, KS, as an element of the 130th Field Artillery Brigade.

Events: 226, 303

Commanders, 114th Cavalry Regiment

Col. William K. Herndon	10 January 1925–30 July 1935	Col. Paul A. Cassady	30 July 1935–1 October 1940

115th Cavalry Regiment (24th Cavalry Division) **Wyoming National Guard**

HQ—*Not organized,* 1921–24; Sheridan, WY, 1924; Cheyenne, WY, 1924–41; Fort Lewis, WA, 1941

Constituted in the N.G. in 1921, assigned to the 24th Cav. Div., and allotted to the state of Wyoming. Organized on 1 May 1922 by redesignation of federally recognized elements of the 1st Regt., WY Cav. (demobilized during March–June 1919 as elements of the 148th F.A., 116th Ammo. Train, and the 146th and 148th MG Bns.; reconstituted on 12 June 1919 as the 1st Regt., WY Cav.) as the 115th Cav. Regt. Subordinate squadron HQ concurrently organized as follows: 1st Sq. organized at Cheyenne, WY; 2d Sq. organized at Sheridan, WY. Regimental HQ organized on 24 January 1924 and federally recognized at Sheridan. Regimental HQ relocated on 11 April 1924 to Cheyenne, WY. Troop C at Riverton, WY, composed entirely of Sioux Indians. Reorganized on 1 June 1929 as a three-squadron regiment; new 3d Sq. organized at Casper, WY. Elements called up to perform railway strike duty, 23 July–27 August 1922, and strike duties near the Sheridan coal mines, August 1922. Troop I participated in Columbia Pictures movie "The End of the Trail" in 1932. Entire regiment participated in Paramount Pictures movie "The Plainsman" in 1936. Conducted a 12-day mounted training march through the mountains between Sand Creek and Mountain Home in the summer of 1933, during which Col. Mentzer suffered a heart attack and died. Conducted summer training at Fort D.A. Russell, WY (Pole Mountain Reservation), 1922–37, and at Camp Guernsey, WY, 1938–40. Reorganized and redesignated 115th Cav. Regt. (Horse and Mecz) on 1 November 1940 with redesignation of the 24th Rcn. Sq. as the new 2d Sq. Concurrently relieved from the 24th Cav. Div. Assigned to the IX Corps on 30 December 1940. Inducted into active Federal service on 24 February 1941 at Cheyenne, WY. Transferred on 10 March 1941 to Fort Lewis, WA. Location 7 December 1941—Fort Lewis, WA.

Status: Assigned to the USARS as the 49th F.A.; 1st Bn. active at Sheridan, WY, as an element of the 115th F.A. Brig. HQ, 115th Cav. active at Cheyenne, WY, as HHB, 115th F.A. Brig.

Events: 304, 309, 314, 326

Commanders, 115th Cavalry Regiment

Col. Roche S. Mentzer	9 September 1921–August 1933	Col. Rhodolph L. Esmay	1 March 1937–February 1941
Col. Burke H. Sinclair	August 1933–30 June 1936	Col. Ralph S. Grier	February 1941–October 1941
Lt. Col. Roscoe Lamb	1 July 1936–28 February 1937	Col. Charles B. Hazeltine (R.A.)	25 October 1941–ao December 1941

116th Cavalry Regiment (24th Cavalry Division) **Idaho and Utah National Guard**

HQ—*Not organized,* 1921–22; Boise, ID, 1922–29; Weiser, ID, 1929–30; Boise, ID, 1930–40

Constituted in the N.G. in 1921, assigned to the 24th Cav. Div., and allotted to the states of Idaho and Utah. Regimental HQ organized on 1 May 1922 at Boise, ID, by redesignation of HQ, 1st Regt., ID Cav. (organized and federally recognized on 29 October 1920 at Boise) as the 116th Cav. Subordinate squadron HQ organized and federally recognized as follows: 2d Sq. organized on 1 January 1922 at Salt Lake City, UT, from the 1st Sq., 1st Regt., Utah Cav.; 1st Sq. organized on 1 May 1922 at Pocatello, ID, from the 1st Sq., 1st Regt., ID Cav. The 2d Sq. converted and reorganized as the 1st Bn., 222d F.A. Regt. on 29 September 1924. Concurrently, the 2d Sq., 116th Cav. withdrawn from the state of Utah and allotted to the state of Idaho, but not immediately reorganized. Reorganized on 15 March 1929 as a three-squadron regiment. Concurrently, the regimental HQ relocated to Weiser, ID, and 2d Sq. reorganized at Caldwell, ID. New 3d Sq. organized on 26 April 1929 at Weiser. Regimental HQ relocated on 9 December 1930 to Boise. The 2d Sq. performed martial law duties to counter striking miners in the Clearwater National Forest near Pierce, ID, 3–23 August 1936. Conducted summer training at Boise Barracks, ID, 1921–35, and at Camp Bonneville, ID, 1936–39. Relieved on 16 September 1940 from the 24th Cav. Div. on 16 September 1940. Concurrently converted and redesignated 183d F.A. Regt.

Status: Assigned to the USARS as the 116th Armd. Cav.; 2d Bn. active at Twin Falls, ID, and 3d Bn. active at La Grande, OR, as elements of the 116th Armd. Brig.

Events: 304

Commanders, 116th Cavalry Regiment

Lt. Col. Ronald E. Fisher	3 May 1921–10 August 1921	Col. William S. Titus	11 June 1923–4 October 1926
Lt. Col. John F. Wall	1 October 1921–11 February 1922	Col. James Harris	2 January 1927–11 November 1930
Col. DeWitt P. Olson	11 February 1922–11 June 1923	Col. Samuel D. Hays	11 November 1930–16 September 1940

117th Cavalry Regiment (Separate) **Colorado National Guard**

HQ—*Not organized,* 1922–31

Constituted in the N.G. on 1 February 1922 and allotted to the state of Colorado. Concurrently, 2d Sq., 111th Cav. (federally recognized on 14 June 1921 as 1st Sep. Cav. Sq., CO N.G.; redesignated on 1 November 1921 as 2d Sq, 111th Cav.) redesignated 1st Sq., 117th Cav. The 1st Sq. redesignated 117th Sep. Cav. Sq. on 12 September 1931 and remainder of the regiment demobilized.

Commanders, 1st Squadron, 117th Cavalry Regiment

Maj. Christopher F. Cusack	14 June 1921–1 December 1922	Maj. George M. Corbett	30 September 1923–1 January 1925
Maj. Walter H. McComb	4 January 1923–30 September 1923	Maj. John Finch	1 January 1925–12 September 1931

121st Cavalry Regiment (21st Cavalry Division) **New York National Guard**

HQ—Rochester, NY, 1928–40

Constituted in the N.G. on 15 March 1928, assigned to the 21st Cav. Div., and allotted to the state of New York. Regimental HQ organized on 22 March 1928 and federally recognized at Rochester, NY. Subordinate squadron HQ organized and federally recognized as follows: 1st Sq. organized on 28 February 1928 (from three separate troops of NY Cav.) with HQ at Albany, NY, 2d Sq. organized on 28 February 1928 (from the 2d Sq., 101st Cav. Regt.) with HQ at Buffalo, NY. Reorganized on 15 April 1929 as a three-squadron regiment; new 3d Sq. organized with HQ at Syracuse, NY. Conducted summer training at Pine Camp, NY, 1928–39. Relieved from the 21st Cav. Div. on 30 September 1940 and elements used to form the 101st Antitank Bn., 102d Sep. Bn., C.A. (AA), and part of the 209th C.A. Regt. (AA).

Commanders, 121st Cavalry Regiment

Col. Kenneth C. Townson	28 March 1928–11 March 1935	Col. Charles N. Morgan	11 March 1935–23 September 1940

122d Cavalry Regiment (Separate) **Connecticut and Rhode Island National Guard**

HQ—New Haven, CT, 1930–35; West Hartford, CT, 1935–37

Constituted in the N.G. on 15 March 1929 and allotted to the states of Connecticut and Rhode Island. Entire regiment, less 2d Sq. and MG Troop, allotted to the state of Connecticut. The 2d Sq. and MG Troop allotted to the state of Rhode Island. Subordinate squadron HQ organized and federally recognized as follows: 1st Sq. organized on 3 May 1929 at New Haven, CT, by redesignation of 1st Sep. Sq., CT Cav.; 2d Sq. organized 1 April 1929 at Providence, RI, by redesignation of 1st Sep. Sq., RI Cav. Regimental HQ organized on 8 January 1930 and federally recognized at New Haven, CT. The 2d Sq. converted and redesignated 2d Bn., 103d F.A. on 8 January 1930. Concurrently a new 2d Sq. constituted and allotted to the state of Connecticut. Regimental HQ relocated on 22 July 1935 to West Hartford, CT. Entire regiment called up to perform flood relief duty in March 1936. Conducted summer training at Niantic, CT, 1930–36. Regiment disbanded on 10 June 1937. Concurrently, HQ, MG Troop, and 1st Sq. redesignated as elements of the 110th Cav. Regt.

Commanders, 122d Cavalry Regiment

Lt. Col. William H. Welch (CT)	6 July 1929–16 December 1934	Lt. Col. Philip S. Wainwright (CT)	17 December 1934–18 May 1936
Lt. Col. Louis S. Tracy (CT)	18 May 1936–9 June 1937		

123d Cavalry Regiment (22d Cavalry Division) **Kentucky National Guard**

HQ—Louisville, KY, 1929–40

Constituted in the N.G. on 15 March 1929, assigned to the 22d Cav. Div., and allotted to the state of Kentucky. Regimental HQ organized on 1 April 1929 and federally recognized at Louisville, KY. Subordinate squadron HQ organized and federally recognized on 1 May 1930 as follows: 1st Sq. at Frankfort, KY; 2d Sq. at Springfield, KY; and 3d Sq. at Covington, KY. Subordinate troops organized from existing troops of the demobilized 53d and 54th MG Sqs. The regiment, or elements thereof, called up to perform the following state duties: 3d Sq. for preservation of order at a criminal trial at Elizabethtown, KY, 28 April–2 May 1931; entire regiment to perform riot control at the coal miners' strike in Harlan County, KY, 6 May–30 June 1931; entire regiment to perform flood relief duties along the Ohio River, January–February 1937; several elements to perform strike duties in eastern Kentucky during May–June 1939. Conducted summer training at Fort Knox, KY, 1929–40. Relieved on 1 November 1940 from the 22d Cav. Div. Concurrently regimental HQ disbanded; Subordinate elements used to form the 103d and 106th Sep. Bns., C.A. (AA).

Events: 213, 230, 302

Commanders, 123d Cavalry Regiment

Col. Henry J. Stites	1 April 1929–May 1939	Lt. Col. John A. Polin	May 1939–1 November 1940

124th Cavalry Regiment (23d Cavalry Division) **Texas National Guard**

HQ—San Antonio, TX, 1929–40; Fort Bliss, TX, 1940–41; Fort Brown, TX, 1941

Constituted in the N.G. on 13 February 1929, assigned to the 23d Cav. Div., and allotted to the state of Texas. Regimental HQ organized on 15 March 1929 and federally recognized at San Antonio, TX. Subordinate squadron HQ concurrently organized and federally recognized as follows: 1st Sq. organized on 15 March 1929 at Fort Worth, TX; 2d Sq. organized on 15 March 1929 at Houston, TX. Subordinate troops organized from existing troops of the demobilized 56th MG Sq. and the 2d Sq., 112th Cav. Regt. The regiment, or elements thereof, called up to perform the following state duties: to perform martial law during the reduction of the Borger, TX, criminal ring in September–October 1929; to restore order after the race riot in Sherman, TX, in May 1930; and to perform patrolling and production regulation in the East Texas Oilfields during September 1931–December 1932. Awarded the Pershing Trophy (cavalry) 5 years in a row (1935–39). Relieved from the 23d Cav. Div. on 1 April 1939 as part of the 56th Cav. Brig. Reorganized on 23 July 1929 as a three-squadron regiment; new 3d Sq. organized at Houston, TX. HHT, 3d Sq. inactivated on 1 October 1940 and Troops I and K assigned to 1st and 2d Sqs. as Troops C and G, respectively. Conducted summer training at Camp Wolters, TX, 1929–39. Designated mobilization training station was Fort Bliss, TX. Inducted into active Federal service on 18 November 1940 at San Antonio as an element of the 56th Cav. Brig. (Sep). Transferred to Fort Bliss and arrived there on 28 November 1940. Assigned to the Third Army. Regiment, less 2d Sq., transferred on 5 February 1941 to Fort Brown, TX. Concurrently, 2d Sq. transferred to Fort Ringgold. On arrival, relieved the 12th Cav. of the Fort Brown Command sector of the Mexican Border Patrol. Location 7 December 1941—Forts Brown and Ringgold, TX.

Status: Assigned to the USARS as the 124th Cav.; 1st Sq. active at Waco, TX, as an element of the 36th Inf. Div. (Mecz).

Events: 300, 315, 328

Commanders, 124th Cavalry Regiment

Col. Louis S. Davidson	15 March 1929–29 November 1934	Col. Calvin B. Garwood	29 November 1934–May 1942

301st Cavalry Regiment (61st Cavalry Division) **Organized Reserve New York**

HQ—Syracuse, NY, 1921–28; Rochester, NY, 1928–41

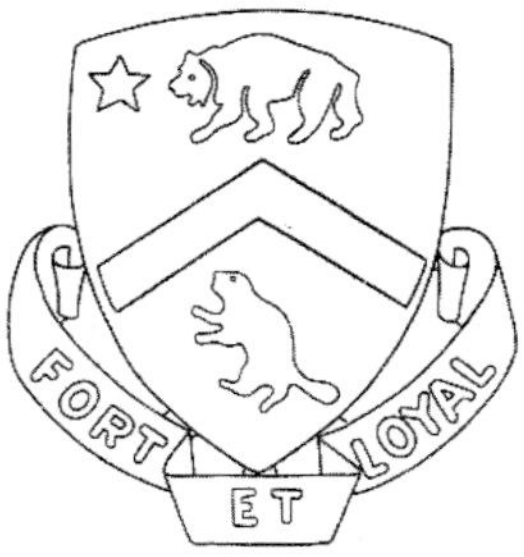

Demobilized on 15 February 1919 at Camp Kearny, CA, as the 46th and 47th F.A. Regts. and the 16th Trench Mortar Btry. All elements reconstituted in the O.R. on 15 October 1921 and consolidated as the 301st Cav., assigned to the 61st Cav. Div., and allotted to the Second Corps Area. Initiated on 15 October 1921 with regimental HQ at Syracuse, NY. Subordinate squadron HQ concurrently initiated as follows: 1st Sq. at Rochester, NY; 2d Sq. at Utica, NY. Regimental HQ relocated on 30 July 1928 to Rochester. The 2d Sq. relocated on 25 August 1928 to Buffalo, NY. Reorganized on 2 July 1929 as a three-squadron regiment; new 3d Sq. initiated with HQ at Buffalo. Conducted summer training with the 1st Sq., 3d Cav. Regt. at Fort Ethan Allen, VT, and with the 3d Cav. at Fort Belvoir, VA. Conducted cavalry CMTC training at Fort Ethan Allen some years as an alternate form of training. Typically conducted Inactive Training Period meetings at the Culver Road Armory in Rochester. Conducted regular equestrian training at the Culver Road Armory with the horses of the 121st Cav. Designated mobilization training station was the Syracuse Concentration Area, NY. Location 7 December 1941—Rochester, NY.

Status: Disbanded 11 November 1944 as the 542d Signal (Sig.) Aircraft Warning Regt.

Commanders, 301st Cavalry Regiment

Col. Sterling P. Adams	2 February 1918–28 August 1918	Col. William J. Donovan	1 March 1922–19 June 1925
Demobilized/Inactive	15 February 1919–15 October 1921	Col. Nathan C. Shiverick	19 June 1925–18 August 1932
Lt. Col. Nathan C. Shiverick	15 October 1921–1 March 1922	Col. Carl H. Loebs	19 August 1932–11 August 1936
Col. Russell R. Ward	11 August 1936–ao December 1941		

302d Cavalry Regiment (61st Cavalry Division) **Organized Reserve New Jersey**

HQ—Newark, NJ, 1921–41

Demobilized on 20 December 1918 at Camp Kearny, CA, as the 64th F.A. Regt. and the 29th Trench Mortar Btry, and as the 48th F.A. Regt. in February 1919. All elements reconstituted in the O.R. on 15 October 1921 and consolidated as the 302d Cav., assigned to the 61st Cav. Div., and allotted to the Second Corps Area. Initiated on 17 December 1921 with regimental HQ at Newark, NJ. Subordinate squadron HQ concurrently initiated as follows: 1st Sq. at Newark; 2d Sq. at Morristown, NJ. Conducted summer training with the 1st Sq., 3d Cav. Regt. at Fort Ethan Allen, VT, and with the 3d Cav. at Fort Belvoir, VA. Typically conducted Inactive Training Period meetings at the armory of the Essex Troop in Newark. Conducted regular equestrian training at various armories with the horses of the 102d Cav. Designated mobilization training station was the Syracuse Concentration Area, NY. Location 7 December 1941—New York City, NY.

Status: Disbanded 11 November 1944 as the 62d Tank Destroyer Bn. Reconstituted in the US Army Reserve on 1 January 1971 as the 302d Cav., a training regiment.

Commanders, 302d Cavalry Regiment

Col. George B. Pritchard	2 February 1918–26 August 1918	*Demobilized/Inactive*	February 1919–17 December 1921
Col. Hobart B. Brown	17 December 1921–June 1941		

303d Cavalry Regiment (61st Cavalry Division) **Organized Reserve New York**

HQ—*Not initiated,* 1921–22; Manhattan, NY, 1922–41

Demobilized on 13 February 1919 at Camp Travis, TX, as the 52d and 53d F.A. Regts. and the 18th Trench Mortar Btry. All elements reconstituted in the O.R. on 15 October 1921 and consolidated as the 303d Cav., assigned to the 61st Cav. Div., and allotted to the Second Corps Area. Initiated on 17 January 1922 with regimental HQ at Manhattan, NY. Subordinate squadron HQ concurrently initiated as follows: 1st Sq. at Manhattan; 2d Sq. at White Plains, NY. Reorganized on 2 July 1929 as a three-squadron regiment; new 3d Sq. initiated at Manhattan. Conducted summer training with the 1st Sq., 3d Cav. Regt. at Fort Ethan Allen, VT, and with the 3d Cav. at Fort Belvoir, VA. Conducted regular equestrian training with the horses of the 101st Cav. in Manhattan. Designated mobilization training station was the Syracuse Concentration Area, NY. Location 7 December 1941—Manhattan, NY.

Status: Disbanded 10 March 1952 as the 303d Armd. Cav. Regt.

Commanders, 303d Cavalry Regiment

Lt. Col. Charles S. Haight	26 January 1918–4 February 1918
Col. Samuel McP. Rutherford	4 February 1918–13 August 1918
Demobilized/Inactive	13 August 1918–16 January 1922
Col. Latham R. Reed	17 January 1922–13 February 1931
Col. Arthur M. Wolff	13 February 1931–June 1941

304th Cavalry Regiment (61st Cavalry Division) **Organized Reserve New York**

HQ—Brooklyn, NY, 1921–41

Demobilized at Camp Stanley, TX, as the 43d F.A. Regt. and the 25th Trench Mortar Btry on 17 February 1919 and 11 December 1918, respectively, and the 54th F.A. Regt. on 13 February 1919 at Camp Travis, TX. All elements reconstituted in the O.R. on 15 October 1921 and consolidated as the 304th Cav., assigned to the 61st Cav. Div., and allotted to the Second Corps Area. Initiated on 7 October 1921 with the entire regiment at Brooklyn, NY. Reorganized on 2 July 1929 as a three-squadron regiment; new 3d Sq. initiated at Brooklyn. Conducted summer training with the 1st Sq., 3d Cav. Regt. at Fort Ethan Allen, and with the 3d Cav. at Fort Belvoir, VA. Conducted regular equestrian training with the horses of the 101st Cav. in Manhattan. Designated mobilization training station was the Syracuse Concentration Area, NY. Location 7 December 1941—Brooklyn, NY.

Status: Disbanded 11 November 1944 as the 63d Tank Destroyer Bn.

Commanders, 304th Cavalry Regiment

Col. Lincoln C. Andrews	16 February 1918–12 April 1918
Lt. Col. Fitzhugh Lee	12 April 1918–17 May 1918
Col. Edward P. Orton	17 May 1918–15 August 1918
Demobilized/Inactive	15 August 1918–6 October 1921
Maj. Thompkins McIlvane	7 October 1921–11 April 1922
Col. Robert L. Bacon	11 April 1922–28 December 1923
Col. Leonard Sullivan	29 December 1923–13 June 1928
Col. John R. Kilpatrick	ao October 1928–June 1941
Lt. Col. John F. Coneybear	June 1941–ao December 1941

305th Cavalry Regiment (62d Cavalry Division) **Organized Reserve Pennsylvania**

HQ—Philadelphia, PA, 1921–41

Demobilized on 17 February 1919 at Camp Stanley, TX, as the 44th and 45th F.A. Regts. and the 15th Trench Mortar Btry. All elements reconstituted in the O.R. on 15 October 1921 and consolidated as the 305th Cav., assigned to the 62d Cav. Div., and allotted to the Third Corps Area. Initiated in December 1921 with the entire regiment at Philadelphia, PA. Reorganized on 11 December 1929 as a three-squadron regiment; new 3d Sq. initiated at Philadelphia. Typically conducted Inactive Training Period meetings at the 103d Cav. armory or the First City Troop armory in Philadelphia. Conducted regular equestrian training with the horses of Valley Forge Military Academy in Wayne, PA. Often participated as a mounted unit in Philadelphia's Army Day parade. Conducted summer training with the 3d Cav. Regt. at Fort Myer, VA, and at Fort Belvoir, VA. Trained with the units of the 52d Cav. Brig. in July 1928 at Mount Gretna, PA. Conducted cavalry CMTC training at Fort Myer as an alternate form of training. Designated mobilization training station was the York Concentration Area, PA. Location 7 December 1941—Philadelphia, PA.

Organization Day: 17 April. Chosen to commemorate the regiment's organization on 17 April 1918.

Status: Disbanded 18 October 1943.

Commanders, 305th Cavalry Regiment

Col. Albert E. Sexton	2 February 1918–15 August 1918	Col. William I. Forbes	15 September 1926–23 November 1932
Demobilized/Inactive	17 February 1919–December 1921	Col. Matthew F. James	23 November 1932–March 1936
Col. John C. Groome	December 1921–29 March 1926	Lt. Col. Robert D. McCullough	March 1936–10 September 1936
Col. Jean H.A. Day	29 March 1926–15 September 1926	Col. Vincent A. Carroll	10 September 1936–January 1941
	Lt. Col. Robert D. McCullough	January 1941–26 August 1941	

306th Cavalry Regiment (62d Cavalry Division) **Organized Reserve Maryland and District of Columbia**

HQ—Baltimore, MD, 1921–41

Demobilized on 8 February 1919 at Fort Sill, OK, as the 49th and 50th F.A. Regts. and the 17th Trench Mortar Btry. All elements reconstituted in the O.R. on 15 October 1921 and consolidated as the 306th Cav., assigned to the 62d Cav. Div., and allotted to the Third Corps Area. Initiated in November 1921 with regimental HQ at Baltimore, MD. Subordinate squadron HQ concurrently initiated as follows: 1st Sq. at Baltimore; 2d Sq. at Washington, DC. Reorganized on 1 July 1929 as a three-squadron regiment; new 3d Sq. initiated at Baltimore; MG Troop initiated at Washington, DC. Both units organized with personnel from the disbanded 153d MG Sq. Troop F was one of the few O.R. organizations to achieve 100-percent strength in enlisted men in the interwar period. Conducted regular equestrian training with the horses of the 3d Cav. at Fort Myer, VA, and the 6th F.A. at Fort Hoyle, MD. Regimental commander, Col. John C.P.T. Hill, was a US Congressman from the state of Maryland. Often participated as a mounted unit in the annual Army Day parade in Washington, DC. The regiment, less 2d Sq. and MG Troop, typically conducted Inactive Training Period meetings at the Post Office Building in Baltimore; the 2d Sq. and MG Troop typically conducted Inactive Training Period meetings at the Munitions Building in Washington. Conducted summer training with the 3d Cav. Regt. at Fort Myer and at Fort Belvoir, VA. Conducted cavalry CMTC training at Fort Myer as an alternate form of training. Primary ROTC feeder school was the Virginia Military Institute. Designated mobilization training station was the York Concentration Area, PA. Location 7 December 1941—Baltimore, MD.

Organization Day: 6 February. Chosen to commemorate the regiment's organization on 6 February 1918.

Status: Inactivated 15 May 1959 at Washington, DC, as the 306th Armd. Group (Gp.).

Commanders, 306th Cavalry Regiment

Col. George O. Cress	26 January 1918–6 August 1918	Col. John B.P. Clayton Hill	November 1921–18 December 1937
Demobilized/Inactive	8 February 1919–November 1921	Lt. Col. William H. Skinner	18 December 1937–15 January 1938
Col. Mathew F. James	15 January 1938–March 1941		

307th Cavalry Regiment (62d Cavalry Division) **Organized Reserve Virginia**

HQ—*Not initiated,* 1921–22; Richmond, VA, 1922–41

Demobilized at Fort Sill, OK, as the 51st and 55th F.A. Regts. on 8 February 1919 and 10 February 1919, respectively; and the 27th Trench Mortar Btry on 4 December 1918 at Camp Bowie, TX. All elements reconstituted in the O.R. on 15 October 1921 and consolidated as the 307th Cav., assigned to the 62d Cav. Div., and allotted to the Third Corps Area. Initiated on 6 March 1922 with regimental HQ at Richmond, VA. Subordinate squadron HQ concurrently initiated as follows: 1st Sq. at Richmond; 2d Sq. at Norfolk, VA. Reorganized on 1 July 1929 as a three-squadron regiment; new 3d Sq. and MG Troop initiated with personnel from the disbanded 154th MG Sq. at Norfolk. The regiment, less 3d Sq., typically conducted its Inactive Training Period meetings at the Parcel Post Building in Richmond; the 3d Sq. typically conducted its Inactive Training Period meetings at the Post Office Building in Norfolk. Conducted regular equestrian training with the horses of the Deep Run Hunt Club in Richmond. Conducted summer training with the 3d Cav. Regt. at Fort Myer, VA, and at Fort Belvoir, VA. Conducted cavalry CMTC training at Fort Myer as an alternate form of training. Primary ROTC feeder school was the Virginia Military Institute. Designated mobilization training station was the York Concentration Area, PA. Location 7 December 1941—Richmond, VA.

Status: Disbanded on 11 November 1944 as the 65th Tank Destroyer Bn.

Commanders, 307th Cavalry Regiment

Col. Llewellyn W. Oliver	23 January 1918–17 August 1918	Col. Matthew F. James	March 1936–18 December 1937
Demobilized/Inactive	8 February 1919–6 March 1922	Lt. Col. John C. Butler	18 December 1937–March 1938
Lt. Col. James G. Earnest	6 March 1922–23 March 1924	Maj. Max Livingston Jr.	March 1938–May 1938
Col. Delphe T.E. Casteel	23 March 1924–17 August 1926	Lt. Col. Robert B.H. Begg	May 1938–July 1940
Lt. Col. William H. Clifford	17 August 1926–13 January 1934	Lt. Col. Max Livingston Jr.	July 1940–ao January 1941
Lt. Col. Robert B.H. Begg	13 January 1934–March 1936	Unknown	ao January 1941–7 December 1941

308th Cavalry Regiment (62d Cavalry Division) **Organized Reserve Maryland/Pennsylvania**

HQ—Cumberland, MD, 1921–22; Pittsburgh, PA, 1923–41

Demobilized on 22 December 1918 at Camp Kearny, CA, as the 65th and 66th F.A. Regts., and on 21 December 1918 as the 22d Trench Mortar Btry. All elements reconstituted in the O.R. on 15 October 1921 and consolidated as the 308th Cav., assigned to the 62d Cav. Div., and allotted to the Third Corps Area. Initiated on 10 November 1921 with regimental HQ at Cumberland, MD. Regiment relocated about October 1922 to western Pennsylvania. Regimental HQ concurrently reorganized at Pittsburgh. Reorganized on 1 July 1929 as a three-squadron regiment. Concurrently, entire regiment relocated to Pittsburgh. Typically conducted its Inactive Training Period meetings at the 107th F.A.'s Hunt Armory or at the Post Office Building in Pittsburgh. Members built the 308th Cav. Club in 1928 on property owned by the Aspinwall Hospital in Aspinwall, PA, and conducted Inactive Training there. Facilities included equestrian, pistol, and saber training areas. Conducted regular equestrian training with the horses of the 107th F.A. Conducted summer training with the 3d Cav. Regt. at Fort Myer,

VA, and at Fort Belvoir, VA. Trained with the units of the 52d Cav. Brig. at Mount Gretna, PA, in July 1928. Conducted cavalry CMTC training at Fort Myer as an alternate form of training. Designated mobilization training station was the York Concentration Area, PA. Location 7 December 1941—Pittsburgh, PA.

Organization Day: 24 February. Chosen to commemorate the regiment's organization on 24 February 1918.

Status: Disbanded 11 November 1944 as the 66th Tank Destroyer Bn.

Events: 301

Commanders, 308th Cavalry Regiment

Col. John J. Boniface	24 February 1918–25 April 1918	Col. Jean H. A. Day	15 September 1926–ao October 1926
Col. Hugh D. Berkeley	26 April 1918–24 September 1918	Col. Josiah L. Reese	ao March 1927–25 February 1930
Demobilized/Inactive	21 December 1918–10 November 1921	Col. George H. Cherrington	25 February 1930–January 1941
Lt. Col. Elmer J. Kingsbury	10 November 1921–October 1922	Unknown	January 1941–5 May 1941
Col. Josiah L. Reese	October 1922–15 September 1926	Lt. Col. John H. Schenkel	5 May 1941–6 November 1941

309th Cavalry Regiment (63d Cavalry Division) **Organized Reserve North Carolina/Georgia**

HQ—*Not initiated,* 1921–22; Asheville, NC, 1922–34; Atlanta, GA, 1934–41

Demobilized at Fort Sill, OK, as the 51st and 55th F.A. Regts. on 7 February 1919 and 10 February 1919, respectively, and the 19th Trench Mortar Btry on 12 February 1919. All elements reconstituted in the O.R. on 15 October 1921 and consolidated as the 309th Cav., assigned to the 63d Cav. Div., and allotted to the Fourth Corps Area. Initiated on 29 April 1922 with regimental HQ at Asheville, NC. Subordinate squadron HQ concurrently initiated as follows: 1st Sq. at Charlotte, NC; 2d Sq. at High Point, NC. Reorganized on 1 July 1929 as a three-squadron regiment. Regimental HQ relocated on 1 March 1934 to Atlanta, GA. Concurrently, the entire regiment was relocated to northwest Georgia. Conducted summer training with the 6th Cav. Regt. at Fort Oglethorpe, GA. Conducted cavalry CMTC training at Fort Oglethorpe as an alternate form of training. Provided 23 officers to the 108th Cav. and 12 officers to the 109th Cav. for the 1938 Third Army Maneuver. Primary ROTC feeder school was the University of Georgia. Designated mobilization training station was Fort Oglethorpe. Location 7 December 1941—Atlanta, GA.

Status: Disbanded 11 November 1944 as the 544th Signal Aircraft Warning Regiment.

Commanders, 309th Cavalry Regiment

Col. Mathew C. Smith	21 February 1918–17 August 1918	Lt. Col. John W. Moore	26 April 1930–2 August 1934
Demobilized/Inactive	12 February 1919–29 April 1922	Col. Harold D. Coate	2 August 1934–25 January 1936
Col. Warren A. Fair	29 April 1922–December 1929	Col. Alexander G. Conoley	25 January 1936–ao May 1940
	Unknown	ao May 1940–7 December 1941	

310th Cavalry Regiment (63d Cavalry Division) **Organized Reserve Tennessee/Georgia**

HQ—*Not initiated,* 1921–22; Knoxville, TN, 1922–29; Athens, GA, 1929–41

Demobilized on 10 February 1919 at Camp Jackson, SC, as the 58th and 59th F.A. Regts. and the 20th Trench Mortar Btry. All elements reconstituted in the O. R. on 15 October 1921 and consolidated as the 310th Cav., assigned to the 63d Cav. Div., and allotted to the Fourth Corps Area. Initiated on 2 February 1922 with regimental HQ at Knoxville, TN. Subordinate squadron HQ concurrently initiated as follows: 1st Sq. at Chattanooga, TN; 2d Sq. at Nashville, TN. Reorganized on 1 July 1929 as a three-squadron regiment. Regimental HQ relocated on 22 October 1929 to Athens, GA. Concurrently, the entire regiment was relocated to northeast Georgia. Conducted summer training with the 6th Cav. Regt. at Camp McClellan, AL, and Fort Oglethorpe, GA. Conducted cavalry CMTC training at Fort Oglethorpe, GA, as an alternate form of training. Primary ROTC feeder school was the University of Georgia. Designated mobilization training station was Fort Oglethorpe. Location 7 December 1941—Athens, GA.

Status: Disbanded 18 October 1943.

Commanders, 310th Cavalry Regiment

Col. Julius T. Conrad	6 April 1918–24 September 1918
Demobilized/Inactive	10 February 1919–2 February 1922
Col. J. Perry Fyffe	2 February 1922–25 June 1923
Col. Richard H. Kimball	25 June 1923–18 January 1926
Lt. Col. Robert D. McDonald	18 January 1926–December 1929
Col. Warren A. Fair	December 1929–April 1933
Unknown	April 1933–ao July 1939
Lt. Col. Hugh D. Blanchard	ao July 1939–ao August 1939
Unknown	ao August 1939–7 December 1941

311th Cavalry Regiment (63d Cavalry Division) **Organized Reserve Texas and Arizona**

HQ—*Not initiated,* 1921–22; San Antonio, TX, 1922–41

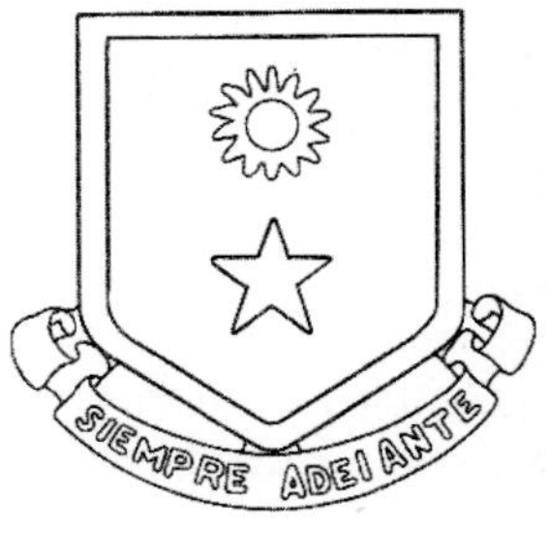

Demobilized on 22 December 1918 at Camp Knox, KY, as the 67th and 68th F.A. Regts. and the 23d Trench Mortar Btry. All elements reconstituted in the O.R. on 15 October 1921 and consolidated as the 311th Cav., assigned to the 63d Cav. Div., and allotted to the Second Corps Area. Withdrawn from the Second Corps Area on 14 November 1921 and allotted to the Eighth Corps Area. Initiated on 23 August 1922 with regimental HQ at San Antonio, TX. Subordinate squadron HQ concurrently initiated as follows: 1st Sq. at San Antonio; 2d Sq. at Fort Worth, TX. Reorganized on 1 July 1929 as a three-squadron regiment; new 3d Sq. initiated at Tucson, AZ. Officers of the regiment organized the Cavalry Club of the Southwest in San Antonio in February 1932. The 2d and 3d Sqs. relocated in March 1937 to Houston and Dallas, respectively. Senator Morris Sheppard (D-TX) invested as the honorary colonel of the regiment in February 1938. Provided 40 officers to the 1st and 56th Cav. Brigs. for the 1938 Third Army Maneuver at Camp Bullis. Several officers of the regiment traveled to Fort Knox, KY, in September 1939 to observe the maneuvers of the 7th Cav. Brig. in the annual Fifth Corps Area maneuver. Dallas-Fort Worth elements typically conducted Inactive Training Period meetings at the Federal Building and the Army and Navy Club at the Jefferson Hotel in Dallas. San Antonio elements typically conducted Inactive Training Period meetings at the Smith-Young Tower in San Antonio. San Antonio elements conducted regular equestrian training with the horses of the Peacock Military Academy and often participated as a mounted unit in San Antonio's annual Army Day parade. Conducted summer training with the 5th Cav. Regt. at Fort Clark, TX. Primary ROTC feeder schools were Texas A&M, the New Mexico Military Institute, and the University of Arizona. Designated mobilization training station was Fort Brown, TX. Location 7 December 1941—San Antonio, TX.

Status: Disbanded 18 October 1943.

Commanders, 311th Cavalry Regiment

Col. George W. Kirkpatrick	15 February 1918–21 August 1918	Lt. Col. Byron L. Barger	June 1925–1 October 1926
Demobilized/Inactive	22 December 1918–23 August 1922	Col. Calvin S. Harrah	1 October 1926–ao May 1933
Lt. Col. Byron L. Barger	23 August 1922–25 October 1922	Unknown	ao May 1933–ao July 1936
Col. Thomas H. Barton	26 October 1922–June 1925	Lt. Col. Harry B. Rhodes	ao July 1936–ao March 1937
	Lt. Col. Homer E. Carrico	ao June 1937–August 1941	

312th Cavalry Regiment (63d Cavalry Division) **Organized Reserve Oklahoma, Arizona, Colorado and New Mexico**

HQ—*Not initiated,* 1921–22; Oklahoma City, OK, 1922–41

Demobilized at Camp Jackson, SC, as the 60th and 61st F.A. Regts. in February 1919 and January 1919, respectively, and the 28th Trench Mortar Btry on 17 December 1918. All elements reconstituted in the O.R. on 15 October 1921 and consolidated as the 312th Cav., assigned to the 63d Cav. Div., and allotted to the Second Corps Area. Withdrawn from the Second Corps Area on 14 November 1921 and allotted to the Eighth Corps Area. Initiated on 23 August 1922 with regimental HQ at Oklahoma City, OK. Subordinate squadron HQ concurrently initiated as follows: 1st Sq. at Oklahoma City; 2d Sq. at Douglas, AZ. The 2d Sq. relocated to Flagstaff, AZ, in 1925 and to Ponca City, OK, on 22 August 1929. Reorganized on 1 July 1929 as a three-squadron regiment; new 3d Sq. initiated at Denver, CO, with personnel of the disbanded 156th MG Sq. The 2d Sq. relocated in March 1937 to Tucson, AZ, and subordinate troops reorganized in Arizona, New Mexico, and west Texas with personnel from the 3d Sq., 311th Cav. (3d Sq., 311th Cav. concurrently relocated to Dallas, TX, and reorganized there). Officers in central and western Oklahoma conducted regular equestrian training at the Fort Reno Remount Depot at Fort Reno, OK. The 3d Sq. typically conducted Inactive Training Period meetings at the Kitteridge Building or the Argonaut Hotel in Denver. Regiment, less 2d Sq., conducted summer training with the 7th Cav. Regt. at Fort Bliss, TX. The 2d Sq. conducted summer training with the 10th Cav. Regt. at Fort Huachuca, AZ, 1929–36. Provided 30 officers to the 1st Cav. Div. and the 111th Cav. for the 1938 Third Army Maneuver at Fort Bliss. Several officers of the regiment traveled to Fort Knox, KY, in September 1939 to observe the employment of the 7th Cav. Brig. in the annual Fifth Corps Area maneuver. Primary ROTC feeder schools were the Oklahoma Military Academy, the University of Arizona, and the New Mexico Military Institute. Designated mobilization training station was Fort McIntosh, TX, less 2d Sq., which was to mobilize at Fort Ringgold, TX. Location 7 December 1941—Oklahoma City, OK.

Status: Disbanded 11 November 1944 as the 548th Sig. Aircraft Warning Regt.

Commanders, 312th Cavalry Regiment

Col. Francis Le J. Parker	18 April 1918–11 June 1918	Lt. Col. Ralph O. Baird	ao August 1935–ao September 1935
Demobilized/Inactive	17 December 1918–23 August 1922	Unknown	ao September 1935–ao November 1937
Maj. Phil M. Hunt	23 August 1922–22 September 1922	Col. Calvin S. Harrah	ao November 1937–ao January 1938
Lt. Col. Donald R. Bonfoey	22 September 1922–December 1923	Unknown	ao January 1938–ao May 1940
Col. Karl E. Linderfelt	December 1923–ao May 1933	Lt. Col. Ralph O. Baird	ao May 1940–ao June 1940
Unknown	ao May 1933–ao August 1935	Unknown	ao June 1940–7 December 1941

313th Cavalry Regiment (64th Cavalry Division) **Organized Reserve Kentucky and Indiana**

HQ—*Not initiated,* 1921–22; Earlington, KY, 1922–25; Louisville, KY, 1925–37; Culver, IN, 1937–41

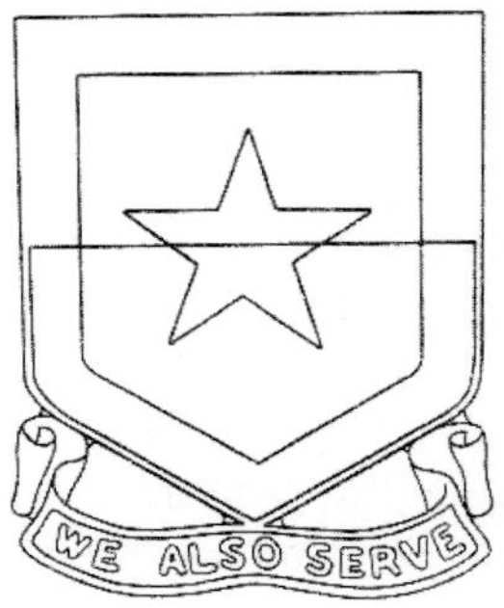

Demobilized on 21 December 1918 at Camp Knox, KY, as the 69th and 70th F.A. Regts. and the 26th Trench Mortar Btry. All elements reconstituted in the O.R. on 15 October 1921 and consolidated as the 313th Cav., assigned to the 64th Cav. Div., and allotted to the Fifth Corps Area. Initiated in January 1922 with regimental HQ at Earlington, KY. Subordinate squadron HQ concurrently initiated as follows: 1st Sq. at Paducah, KY; 2d Sq. at Morganfield, KY. Regiment relocated on 15 April 1925 as follows: regimental HQ to Louisville, KY; 1st Sq. to Central City, KY; and 2d Sq. to Madisonville, KY. Reorganized on 1 July 1929 as a three-squadron regiment. Entire regiment relocated 9 July 1931 to Louisville. Regiment relocated on 5 April 1937 as follows: regimental HQ and 1st Sq. to Culver, IN, 2d Sq. and MG Troop to Indianapolis, IN, and 3d Sq. to Vincennes, IN. Conducted annual contact camps at Culver Military Academy at Culver, IN. Conducted summer training with the 6th Cav. Regt. at Camp Knox, KY, and at Fort Oglethorpe, GA. Primary ROTC feeder school was the Culver Military Academy. Location 7 December 1941—Culver, IN.

Status: Disbanded 18 October 1943.

Commanders, 313th Cavalry Regiment

Col. Kenzie W. Walker	28 March 1918–23 August 1918	Maj. Louis S. N. Phillipp	ao June 1933–ao June 1934
Demobilized/Inactive	21 December 1918–January 1922	Col. Arthur C. Earnshaw	ao June 1935–ao July 1937
Col. Robert Rossow	January 1922–ao June 1931	Unknown	ao July 1937–ao September 1939
Unknown	ao June 1931–ao June 1933	Col. Robert Rossow	ao September 1939–ao June 1940
Unknown	ao June 1940–7 December 1941		

314th Cavalry Regiment (64th Cavalry Division) **Organized Reserve Kentucky/Ohio**

HQ—*Not initiated,* 1921–22; Lexington, KY, 1922–25; Cynthiana, KY, 1925–31; Lexington, KY, 1931–37; Columbus, OH, 1937–39; Dayton, OH, 1939–41

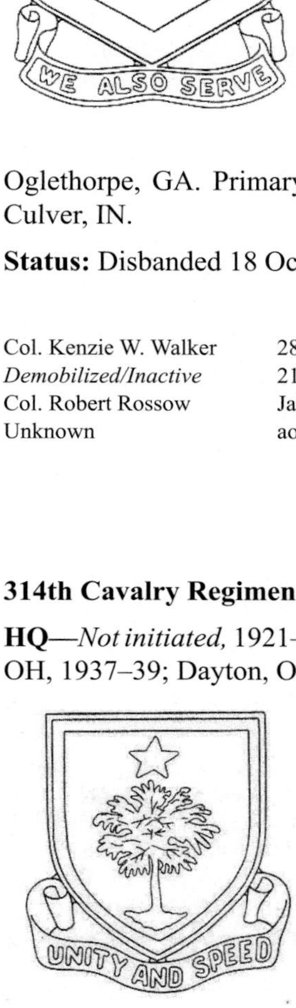

Demobilized at Camp Jackson, SC, as the 62d and 63d F.A. Regts. on 19 January 1919 and 17 January 1919, respectively, and the 21st Trench Mortar Btry on 2 January 1919. All elements reconstituted in the O.R. on 15 October 1921 and consolidated as the 314th Cav., assigned to the 64th Cav. Div., and allotted to the Fifth Corps Area. Initiated in January 1922 with regimental HQ at Lexington, KY. Subordinate squadron HQ concurrently initiated as follows: 1st Sq. at Middletown, KY; 2d Sq. at Lexington. Regiment relocated on 15 April 1925 as follows: regimental HQ to Cynthiana, KY; 1st Sq. to Lexington; and 2d Sq. to Richmond, KY. Reorganized on 1 July 1929 as a three-squadron regiment. Entire regiment relocated on 9 July 1931 to Lexington. Entire regiment relocated on 5 April 1937 to Columbus, OH. Entire regiment relocated on 22 May 1939 to Dayton, OH. Conducted summer training with the 6th Cav. Regt. at Camp Knox, KY, and at Fort Oglethorpe, GA. Primary ROTC feeder school was the Culver Military Academy. Location 7 December 1941—Columbus, OH.

Status: Disbanded 11 November 1944 as the 545th Sig. Aircraft Warning Regt.

Commanders, 314th Cavalry Regiment

Col. Cornelius C. Smith	6 April 1918–15 October 1918	Col. O. H. McGee	15 April 1925–ao August 1927
Demobilized/Inactive	2 January 1919–January 1922	Unknown	ao August 1927–ao May 1933
Lt. Col. Otto Miller	January 1922–20 April 1922	Maj. Lewis A. Maury	ao May 1933–June 1934
Maj. John H. Terry	20 April 1922–16 October 1922	Unknown	ao June 1934–ao June 1935
Col. George T. Smith	16 October 1922–15 April 1925	Col. Paul H. M. Converse	ao June 1935–ao January 1941
Unknown	ao January 1941–7 December 1941		

315th Cavalry Regiment (64th Cavalry Division) **Organized Reserve Rhode Island, Connecticut, Vermont, New Hampshire, and Massachusetts**

HQ—*Not initiated,* 1921–22; Providence, RI, 1922–40; Boston, MA, 1940–41

Demobilized on 30 January 1918 at Camp Knox, KY, as the 71st and 72d F.A. Regts. and the 24th Trench Mortar Btry. All elements reconstituted in the O.R. on 15 October 1921 and consolidated as the 315th Cav., assigned to the 64th Cav. Div., and allotted to the Fifth Corps Area. Withdrawn from the Fifth Corps Area on 14 November 1921 and allotted to the First Corps Area. Initiated on 19 January 1922 with regimental HQ at Providence, RI. Subordinate squadron HQ concurrently initiated as follows: 1st Sq. at Hartford, CT; 2d Sq. at New Haven, CT. Band initiated in 1923 at Providence. The regiment was relocated on 15 April 1926 as follows: regimental HQ remained in Providence; 1st Sq. to Providence; and 2d Sq. to Boston, MA. The regimental area at this time included all of Rhode Island, eastern Massachusetts, and the southern halves of Vermont and New Hampshire. Reorganized on 1 July 1929 as a three-squadron regiment; new 3d Sq. initiated at Boston with personnel of the disbanded 158th MG Sq. Concurrently, 2d Sq. relocated back to New Haven. Attached to the 76th Div. on 17 October 1929 for organization, administration, and training. Relieved from attachment to the 76th Div. on 27 January 1930 and attached to the 94th Div. Reorganized about January 1940 with HQ at Boston and all subordinate units allocated to Massachusetts. Senator Henry Cabot Lodge was assigned to the regiment as an officer in the late 1930s. Rhode Island elements typically conducted Inactive Training Period meetings at the Armory of Mounted Commands in Providence; Connecticut elements typically conducted Inactive Training Period meetings at the University Club in Hartford; Massachusetts elements typically conducted Inactive Training Period meetings at the Post Office Building or the Army and Navy Club in Boston. Vermont and New Hampshire elements conducted annual contact camps at Norwich University in the fall or winter. Conducted summer training with the 1st Sq., 3d Cav. Regt. at Fort Ethan Allen, VT. Participated in a mounted march in July 1924 with 1st Sq., 3d Cav. from Fort Devens, MA, to Fort Ethan Allen. Conducted cavalry CMTC training at Fort Ethan Allen some years as an alternate form of training. Primary ROTC feeder schools were Massachusetts State College and Norwich University. Location 7 December 1941—Boston, MA.

Status: Disbanded 18 October 1943.

Commanders, 315th Cavalry Regiment

Col. Walter C. Short	7 April 1918–2 August 1918	Col. Norman S. Case	6 March 1930–April 1938
Demobilized/Inactive	30 January 1919–19 January 1922	Lt. Col. Harold C. Thomas	April 1938–18 January 1940
Col. Herbert R. Dean	19 January 1922–6 March 1930	Unknown	18 January 1940–7 December 1941

316th Cavalry Regiment (64th Cavalry Division) **Organized Reserve Vermont, New Hampshire, Rhode Island, and Connecticut**

HQ—*Not initiated,* 1921–22; Northfield, VT, 1922–26; Hartford, CT, 1926–40; Providence, RI, 1940–41

Constituted in the O.R. on 15 October 1921, assigned to the 64th Cav. Div., and allotted to the Fifth Corps Area. Withdrawn from the Fifth Corps Area on 14 November 1921 and allotted to the First Corps Area. Initiated on 6 July 1922 with regimental HQ at Northfield, VT. Subordinate squadron HQ concurrently initiated as follows: 1st Sq. at Burlington VT; 2d Sq. at Manchester, NH. The regiment was relocated on 15 April 1926 as follows: regimental HQ to Hartford, CT; 1st Sq. to Waterbury, CT; and 2d Sq. to New Haven, CT. The regimental area at this time included all of Connecticut, western Massachusetts, and the northern halves of Vermont and New Hampshire. Reorganized on 1 July 1929 as a three-squadron regiment; new 3d Sq. initiated at Montpelier, VT. Attached to the 76th Div. on 17 October 1929 for organization, administration, and training. Relieved from attachment to the 76th Div. on 27 January 1930 and attached to the 94th Div. The regiment was relocated about January 1940 as follows: regimental HQ to Providence, RI; 1st Sq. to Hartford; 2d Sq. to Providence; and 3d Sq. remained at Montpelier. The regiment's Vermont elements typically conducted Inactive Training Period meetings at the Meade Building in Rutland; Connecticut elements at the University Club in Hartford and the A Troop Armory in New Haven; and Rhode Island elements at the Armory of Mounted Commands in Providence. Vermont and New Hampshire elements conducted annual contact camps at Norwich University in the fall or winter. The regiment conducted summer training with the 1st Sq., 3d Cav. Regt. at Fort Ethan Allen, VT. Conducted cavalry CMTC training at Fort Ethan Allen some years as an alternate form of training. Primary ROTC feeder school was Norwich University. Location 7 December 1941—Providence, RI.

Status: Disbanded 11 November 1944 as the 541st Sig. Aircraft Warning Regt.

Commanders, 316th Cavalry Regiment

1st Lt. Martin H. Gleason	6 July 1922–6 August 1922	Col. Clifford L. Cheney	30 April 1926–27 January 1930
Maj. Walter V. Longwell	6 August 1922–September 1922	Col. John H. K. Davis	27 January 1930–29 December 1934
1st Lt. Martin H. Gleason	September 1922–ao December 1922	Lt. Col. Joseph T. Marinan	30 December 1934–18 January 1940
Unknown	ao December 1922–ao April 1924	Lt. Col. Harold C. Thomas	18 January 1940–ao August 1940
Col. Frank B. Edwards	ao April 1924–15 April 1926	Unknown	ao August 1940–7 December 1941

317th Cavalry Regiment (65th Cavalry Division) — Organized Reserve Illinois

HQ—*Not initiated,* 1921–22; Chicago, IL, 1922–41

Constituted in the O.R. on 15 October 1921, assigned to the 65th Cav. Div., and allotted to the Sixth Corps Area. Initiated on 8 August 1922 with the entire regiment at Chicago, IL. Sponsored the Military Tournaments at Soldier's Field in Chicago in June 1926 and 1927. Reorganized on 1 July 1929 as a three-squadron regiment; new 3d Sq. initiated at Chicago. Typically conducted Inactive Training Period meetings at the Post Office Building in Chicago. Conducted regular equestrian training with the horses of the 1st Sq., 14th Cav. at Fort Sheridan, IL. Conducted summer training with the 14th Cav. at Fort Sheridan and some years at Fort Des Moines, IA. Primary ROTC feeder school was the University of Illinois. Designated mobilization training station was Camp Grant, IL. Location 7 December 1941—Chicago, IL.

Status: Disbanded 18 October 1943.

Events: 156

Commanders, 317th Cavalry Regiment

Maj. Ira G. Holcomb	8 August 1922–5 January 1923	Col. Tryggve A. Siqueland	6 January 1923–7 February 1937
Lt. Col. Lawrence M. Graham	8 February 1937–March 1941		

318th Cavalry Regiment (65th Cavalry Division) — Organized Reserve Illinois

HQ—Chicago, IL, 1921–25; La Grange, IL, 1925–37; Chicago, IL, 1937–41

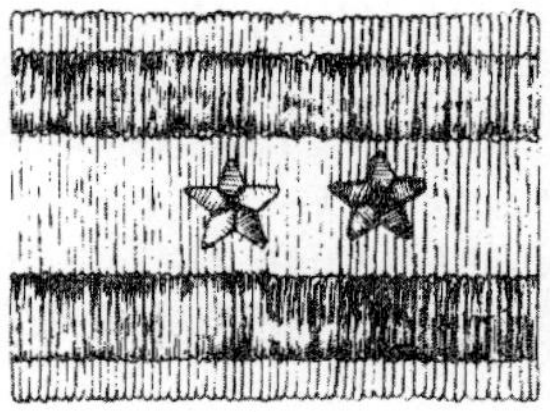

Constituted in the O.R. on 15 October 1921, assigned to the 65th Cav. Div., and allotted to the Sixth Corps Area. Initiated on 6 June 1922 with the entire regiment at Chicago, IL. Band initiated in 1923 at Chicago, IL. Regiment relocated on 2 June 1925 as follows: regimental HQ to La Grange, IL; 1st Sq. to Hinsdale, IL; and 2d Sq. to Elgin, IL. Reorganized in July 1929 as a three-squadron regiment; new 3d Sq. initiated at Chicago. Regiment relocated on 27 September 1932 as follows: regimental HQ remained at La Grange; 1st Sq. to Lemont, IL; 2d Sq. to Oak Park, IL; and 3d Sq. to Aurora, IL. Entire regiment relocated on 28 July 1937 back to Chicago. Typically conducted Inactive Training Period meetings at the Post Office Building in Chicago. Conducted regular equestrian training with the horses of the 1st Sq., 14th Cav. at Fort Sheridan, IL, and with the horses of the 106th Cav. in Chicago. Conducted summer training with the 14th Cav. Regt. at Fort Sheridan and some years at

Fort Des Moines, IA. Conducted cavalry CMTC training at Fort Sheridan some years as an alternate form of training. Primary ROTC feeder school was the University of Illinois. Designated mobilization training station was Camp Grant, IL. Location 7 December 1941—Chicago, IL.

Status: Disbanded 11 November 1944 as the 546th Sig. Aircraft Warning Regt.

Events: 158

Commanders, 318th Cavalry Regiment

Col. Harvey L. Jones	6 June 1922–1 August 1925	Lt. Col. William A. Peterson	12 May 1926–ao July 1940
Lt. Col. Charles Powers	1 August 1925–12 May 1926	Unknown	ao July 1940–7 December 1941

319th Cavalry Regiment (65th Cavalry Division) **Organized Reserve Michigan**

HQ—*Not initiated,* 1921–22; Detroit, MI, 1922–41

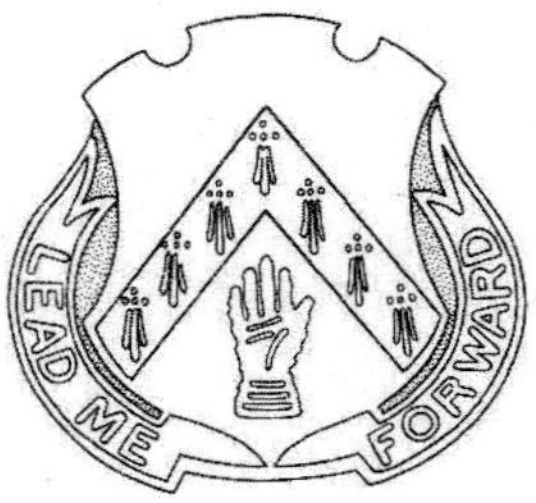

Constituted in the O.R. on 15 October 1921, assigned to the 65th Cav. Div., and allotted to the Sixth Corps Area. Initiated in April 1922 with regimental HQ at Detroit, MI. Subordinate squadron HQ concurrently initiated as follows: 1st Sq. at Detroit; 2d Sq. at Lansing, MI. Reorganized in July 1929 as a three-squadron regiment; new 3d Sq. initiated at Flint, MI. The 2d Sq. relocated on 3 December 1930 to Kalamazoo, MI; 3d Sq. concurrently relocated to Jackson, MI. Officers of the regiment organized the 319th Cav. Club of Detroit in 1930. Members built the club on property owned by a horse farm near the city. Entire regiment relocated on 28 July 1937 to Detroit. Conducted regular equestrian training with the horses of the 1st Sq., 106th Cav. in Detroit. Conducted summer training with the 14th Cav. Regt.at Fort Sheridan, IL, and some years at Fort Des Moines, IA. Conducted cavalry CMTC training at Fort Sheridan some years as an alternate form of training. Primary ROTC feeder school was the Michigan State College of Agriculture and Applied Science. Designated mobilization training station was Camp Grant, IL. Location 7 December 1941—Detroit, MI.

Status: Disbanded 11 November 1944 as the 70th Tank Destroyer Bn.

Commanders, 319th Cavalry Regiment

Unknown	April 1922–6 June 1922	Maj. James E. Murphy	May 1934–ao May 1936
Lt. Col. Wesson Seyburn	6 June 1922–ao January 1923	Lt. Col. John D. Saunders	ao June 1936–ao August 1937
Unknown	ao January 1923–ao June 1924	Unknown	ao August 1937–ao July 1939
Col. Pearle A. Davis	ao June 1924–June 1929	Maj. Howell S. White	ao July 1939–ao August 1939
Lt. Col. Harold D. Coate	June 1929–May 1934	Unknown	ao August 1939–7 December 1941

320th Cavalry Regiment (65th Cavalry Division) **Organized Reserve Wisconsin and Illinois**

HQ—*Not initiated,* 1921–22; Milwaukee, WI, 1922–41

Constituted in the O.R. on 15 October 1921, assigned to the 65th Cav. Div., and allotted to the Sixth Corps Area. Initiated on 21 September 1922 with regimental HQ at Milwaukee, WI. Subordinate squadron HQ concurrently initiated as follows: 1st Sq. at Milwaukee and 2d Sq. at Rock Island, IL. Reorganized in July 1929 as a three-squadron regiment; new 3d Sq. initiated at Milwaukee. Typically conducted Inactive Training Period meetings at the 105th Cav. armory in Milwaukee. Conducted regular equestrian training with the horses of the 105th Cav. Conducted summer training with the 14th Cav. Regt. at Fort Des Moines, IA, and Fort Sheridan, IL. Designated mobilization training station was Camp Grant, IL. Location 7 December 1941—Milwaukee, WI.

Status: Disbanded 11 November 1944 as the 71st Tank Destroyer Battalion.

Commanders, 320th Cavalry Regiment

Lt. Col. August M. Krech	21 September 1922–11 March 1924	Col. Arthur C. Earnshaw	2 June 1926–October 1931
Col. Robert W. Lea	11 March 1924–2 June 1926	Col. August M. Krech	October 1931–1 February 1941
Unknown	1 February 1941–7 December 1941		

321st Cavalry Regiment (66th Cavalry Division) — Organized Reserve Missouri and Arkansas

HQ—*Not initiated,* 1921–22; Kansas City, MO, 1922–36; St. Louis, MO, 1936–41

Constituted in the O.R. on 15 October 1921, assigned to the 66th Cav. Div., and allotted to the Seventh Corps Area. Initiated in January 1922 with regimental HQ at Kansas City, MO. Subordinate squadron HQ concurrently initiated as follows: 1st Sq. at St. Louis, MO; 2d Sq. at Little Rock, AR. The 1st Sq. relocated on 26 May 1926 to Sedalia, MO; 2d Sq. concurrently relocated to St. Joseph, MO. Reorganized in July 1929 as a three-squadron regiment; new 3d Sq. initiated at St. Louis. Concurrently, 1st Sq. relocated to Kansas City, MO. Arkansas elements inactivated on 10 December 1931 and entire regiment relocated to Kansas City, MO. Regimental HQ relocated about 24 April 1936 to St. Louis, MO. Kansas City elements conducted regular equestrian training with the horses of R.A. units at Fort Leavenworth, KS. Kansas City elements typically conducted Inactive Training Period meetings, 1922–36, at the 110th Engrs. armory or the Organized Reserve Center building at 20th and Vine Streets in Kansas City. Conducted summer training with the 14th Cav. Regt. at Fort Des Moines, IA, and the 2d Cav. Regt. at Fort Riley, KS. Conducted cavalry CMTC training at Fort Des Moines some years as an alternate form of training. Designated mobilization training station was Fort Francis E. Warren, WY. Location 7 December 1941—St. Louis, MO.

Status: Disbanded 11 November 1944 as the 547th Sig. Aircraft Warning Regt.

Commanders, 321st Cavalry Regiment

Lt. Col. Francis D. Ross	January 1922–9 September 1925	Unknown.	ao November 1928–ao December 1930
Col. Edward S. Person	9 September 1925–ao November 1928	Col. James E. McMahon	ao December 1930–14 December 1937
Unknown.	14 December 1937–7 December 1941		

322d Cavalry Regiment (66th Cavalry Division) — Organized Reserve Iowa, Minnesota, and North Dakota

HQ—*Not initiated* 1921–22; Des Moines, IA, 1922–41

Constituted in the O.R. on 15 October 1921, assigned to the 66th Cav. Div., and allotted to the Seventh Corps Area. Initiated on 11 March 1922 with regimental HQ at Des Moines, IA. Subordinate squadron HQ concurrently initiated as follows: 1st Sq. at Des Moines; 2d Sq. at Minneapolis, MN. Band initiated in 1923 at Des Moines. Reorganized in July 1929 as a three-squadron regiment; new 3d Sq. initiated at Minneapolis. Concurrently, 2d Sq. relocated to North Dakota. Minnesota elements inactivated on 10 December 1931 and entire regiment concurrently reorganized at Des Moines. 2d Lt .Ronald Reagan assigned on 17 June 1937 to Troop B. Typically conducted Inactive Training Period meetings at Fort Des Moines, the Hotel Savary, and the Federal Building in Des Moines. Conducted regular equestrian training with the horses of the 14th Cav. at Fort Des Moines. Conducted summer training with the 14th Cav. Regt. at Fort Des Moines and with the 2d Cav. Regt. at Fort Riley, KS. Conducted cavalry CMTC training at Fort Des Moines in 1929 and 1935 and at Fort Leavenworth in 1933 as an alternate form of training. Designated mobilization training station was Fort Francis E. Warren, WY. Location 7 December 1941—Des Moines, IA.

Status: Disbanded on 11 November 1944 as the 62d Tank Destroyer Bn. Reconstituted in the US Army Reserve on 1 January 1971 as the 322d Cav., a training regiment.

Commanders, 322d Cavalry Regiment

Capt. Harry Stimpel	11 March 1922–April 1922	Lt. Col. Roland E. Murphy	ao February 1931–14 December 1937
Col. Harry H. Polk	April 1922–ao February 1927	Col. James E. McMahon	14 December 1937–ao January 1938
Unknown.	ao February 1927–ao February 1931	Unknown	ao January 1938–7 December 1941

323d Cavalry Regiment (66th Cavalry Division) **Organized Reserve California, Oregon, Washington, and Nevada**

HQ—*Not initiated,* 1921–22; San Francisco, CA, 1922–24; San Diego, CA, 1924–34; Los Angeles, CA, 1934–41

Constituted in the O.R. on 15 October 1921, assigned to the 66th Cav. Div., and allotted to the Seventh Corps Area. Withdrawn from the Seventh Corps Area on 14 November 1921 and allotted to the Ninth Corps Area. Initiated on 4 March 1922 with regimental HQ at San Francisco, CA. Subordinate squadron HQ concurrently initiated as follows: 1st Sq. at Sacramento, CA; 2d Sq. at Portland, OR (two troops organized in Washington). Regimental HQ relocated in 1924 to San Diego, CA. Concurrently, Oregon and Washington elements inactivated; 1st and 2d Sqs. relocated to Los Angeles, CA. Reorganized in July 1929 as a three-squadron regiment. Entire regiment relocated 28 January 1930 to San Diego. Many unit personnel participated in earthquake relief operations, 14–22 March 1933, in the Los Angeles area. Entire regiment relocated in 1934 to Los Angeles. Conducted regular equestrian training with the horses of Troop B, 11th Cav. at Camp L.J. Hearn, CA, 1924–29. Conducted summer training with the 11th Cav. Regt. at Presidio of Monterey, CA. Conducted cavalry CMTC training at Presidio of Monterey, CA, as an alternate form of training. Lt. Ronald Reagan assigned to HQ Troop in 1939 on moving to California. Designated mobilization training station was Fort Francis E. Warren, WY. Location 7 December 1941—Los Angeles, CA.

Status: Disbanded 11 November 1944 as the 549th Sig. Aircraft Warning Regt.

Commanders, 323d Cavalry Regiment

Maj. Eugene A. DeHermida	4 March 1922–29 September 1922	Lt. Col. Cortez J. Cobler	6 October 1936–12 February 1938
Col. Charles M. Tobin	29 September 1922–ao September 1926	Maj. Verne Austin	12 February 1938–10 October 1938
Unknown.	ao September 1926–ao June 1929	Maj. John F. Snider	10 October 1938–ao January 1940
Col. Jack Hastie Jr.	ao June 1929–6 October 1936	Unknown.	ao January 1940–7 December 1941

324th Cavalry Regiment (66th Cavalry Division) **Organized Reserve Wyoming, Utah, Idaho, and Montana/California**

HQ—*Not initiated,* 1921–22; Thermopolis, WY, 1922–24; Salt Lake City, UT, 1924–37; San Francisco, CA, 1937–41

Constituted in the O.R. on 15 October 1921, assigned to the 66th Cav. Div., and allotted to the Seventh Corps Area. Withdrawn from the Seventh Corps Area on 14 November 1921 and allotted to the Ninth Corps Area. Initiated on 4 March 1922 with regimental HQ at Thermopolis, WY. Subordinate squadron HQ concurrently initiated as follows: 1st Sq. at Billings, MT; 2d Sq. at Salt Lake City, UT. HQ relocated on 4 March 1924 to Salt Lake City. Band initiated in 1928 at Cedar City, UT, making it the only O.R. cavalry band west of the Mississippi River. Reorganized in July 1929 as a three-squadron regiment; new 3d Sq. initiated at Boise, ID. Montana, Idaho, and Utah elements inactivated 14 May 1937 and entire regiment concurrently relocated to San Francisco, CA. Conducted summer training with the 13th Cav. Regt. at Fort D.A. Russell, WY, and the 4th Cav, Regt. at Fort Meade, SD. For summer training in August 1930, the regiment conducted a mounted march with the 4th Cav. along the route of Lt. Col. George A. Custer's 1874 Black Hills expedition. Designated mobilization training station was Fort Francis E. Warren, WY. Location 7 December 1941—San Francisco, CA.

Status: Disbanded 11 November 1944 as the 75th Tank Destroyer Bn.

Commanders, 324th Cavalry Regiment

Maj. Timothy J. McCoy	4 March 1922–30 October 1922
Col. Harry O. Williard	31 October 1922–ao November 1922
Unknown	ao November 1922–ao September 1925
Col. Frederic Jorgenson	ao September 1925–ao June 1939
Unknown.	ao June 1939–7 December 1941

Chapter 15

Cavalry Squadrons

USASC Photo, NA II

Troops of the 10th Cavalry under review by General of the Armies John J. Pershing at Fort Myer, VA, February 1932.

The mission of cavalry squadrons was to plan and conduct operations to provide reconnaissance and security for the ground force to which they were assigned or attached. Cavalry squadrons could also be used both defensively and offensively. When employed in the former mode (defense), they were usually to be deployed in an economy of force or delay role. In the latter mode (offense), cavalry squadrons were employed in reconnaissance missions, raids, or in pursuit and exploitation of routed enemy formations.

Organization

A total of 29 cavalry squadrons were constituted or reconstituted in the three components of the Army in the interwar period. Of these, 12 were allotted to the Regular Army (R.A.), three were allotted to the National Guard (N.G.), and 14 were allotted to the Organized Reserve (O.R.). The organization of these squadrons was not appreciably different from that for regimental squadrons.

The two of the three N.G. squadrons, the 1st Squadrons of Rhode Island and Connecticut, were special allotments from the War Department and held no role in the early mobilization plans. Both were eventually integrated into the 110th and 122d Cavalry (Cav.) Regiments (Regts.), respectively. The third squadron, the 117th of Colorado, was originally intended to be part of the 111th Cav. with New Mexico. It was later withdrawn to form an additional regiment. That plan never came to fruition, and it was later redesignated as a separate squadron. The 117th was eventually converted to field artillery in 1933.

The 14 O.R. squadrons were all originally allotted to the Fourth and Eighth Corps Areas. In 1927, the seven squadrons allotted to the Eighth Corps Area were withdrawn and allotted to the Seventh Corps Area. All 14 were demobilized in 1928 and replaced in the mobilization plans by 12 "Colored" Regular Army Inactive (RAI) cavalry squadrons, all of which were allotted to the Eighth Corps Area. Though these units were not to be organized until M-Day, at least six were inexplicably organized with Reserve personnel for about 8 months in 1935, then inactivated in November of that year. None of these squadrons were activated for service in World War II.

Training

There is no evidence that any of the six organized RAI squadrons ever held training meetings or attended a camp in their brief existence. The three N.G. squadrons carried on drills in a fashion similar to any Guard unit of their day. Each attended summer camps at their respective state training areas, but none participated in any major maneuvers of the period. Given the geographical dispersion of their personnel, it is unlikely that any of the Reserve squadrons ever functioned as a unit during the inactive training period, or held unit meetings. However, the Reserve squadrons of the Fourth Corps Area attended camps at Fort Oglethorpe, GA, for a number of summers and those of the Eighth Corps went to camps held at Fort Bliss, TX.

1st Separate Squadron, Cavalry **Connecticut National Guard**

HQ—*Not organized,* 1922–23; New Haven, CT, 1923–27

Arrived at the port of Boston on 6 April 1919 on the S.S. *Agamemnon* as the 101st Machine Gun (MG) Battalion (Bn.), an element of the 26th Division (Div.). Demobilized on 29 April 1919 at Camp Devens, MA. Reconstituted in the N.G. in 1922 as the 1st Separate (Sep.) Squadron (Sq.) Cavalry (Cav.) and allotted to the state of Connecticut. Organized on 9 March 1923 and federally recognized with headquarters (HQ) at New Haven, CT. Conducted summer training at Niantic, CT, 1923–28. Redesignated on 3 May 1929 as the 1st Sq., 122d Cav.

Status: Assigned to the Combat Arms Regimental System (CARS) as elements of the 242d Artillery (Arty.); no active elements.

Commander, 1st Separate Squadron, Cavalry

Maj. William H. Welch	9 March 1923–3 May 1929

1st Squadron, Cavalry (Separate) **Rhode Island National Guard**

HQ—*Not organized,* 1921–22; Providence, RI, 1922–27

Arrived at the port of Boston on 16 April 1919 on the S.S. *Patricia* as the 103d MG Bn., an element of the 26th Div. Demobilized on 30 April 1919 at Camp Devens, MA. Reconstituted in the N.G. on 22 August 1921 as the 1st Sq. Cav. and allotted to the state of Rhode Island. Organized on 29 May 1922 and federally recognized with HQ at Providence, RI. The squadron, or elements thereof, was called up to perform the following state duties: strike duty at Pawtuxet, RI, 20 February–14 October 1922; strike duty at Manville, RI, 31 August–3 September 1926. Conducted annual summer training at Charleston, RI, 1921–26. Redesignated on 24 February 1927 as the 2d Sq., 110th Cav.

Status: Assigned to the US Army Regimental System (USARS) as elements of the 103d Field Artillery (F.A.); 1st Bn. active at Providence, RI, as an element of the 103d F.A. Brig.

Commander, 1st Squadron, Cavalry

Maj. Samuel A. Hall	29 May 1922–24 February 1927

28th Cavalry Squadron (Separate) (Colored) (GHQR) **Regular Army Inactive**

HQ—*Not organized,* 1928–41

Constituted in the R.A. on 5 September 1928, allotted to the Eighth Corps Area, and assigned to the General Headquarters Reserve (GHQR). Attached to the Third Army. Designated mobilization training station was Fort Huachuca, AZ. Location 7 December 1941—*Not organized.*

29th Cavalry Squadron (Separate) (Colored) (GHQR) **Regular Army Inactive**

HQ—*Not organized,* 1928–41

Constituted in the R.A. on 5 September 1928, allotted to the Eighth Corps Area, and assigned to the GHQR. Attached to the Third Army. Designated mobilization training station was Fort Huachuca, AZ. Location 7 December 1941—*Not organized.*

30th Cavalry Squadron (Separate) (Colored) (GHQR) **Regular Army Inactive**

HQ—*Not organized,* 1928–41

Constituted in the R.A. on 5 September 1928, allotted to the Eighth Corps Area, and assigned to the GHQR. Attached to the Third Army. Designated mobilization training station was Fort Huachuca, AZ. Location 7 December 1941—*Not organized.*

31st Cavalry Squadron (Separate) (Colored) (GHQR) **Regular Army Inactive**

HQ—*Not organized,* 1928–41

Constituted in the R.A. on 5 September 1928, allotted to the Eighth Corps Area, and assigned to the GHQR. Attached to the Third Army. Designated mobilization training station was Fort Huachuca, AZ. Location 7 December 1941—*Not organized.*

32d Cavalry Squadron (Separate) (Colored) (GHQR) **Regular Army Inactive**

HQ—*Not organized,* 1928–41

Constituted in the R.A. on 5 September 1928, allotted to the Eighth Corps Area, and assigned to the GHQR. Attached to the Third Army. Designated mobilization training station was Fort Huachuca, AZ. Location 7 December 1941—*Not organized.*

33d Cavalry Squadron (Separate) (Colored) (GHQR) **Regular Army Inactive**

HQ—*Not organized,* 1928–41

Constituted in the R.A. on 5 September 1928, allotted to the Eighth Corps Area, and assigned to the GHQR. Attached to the Third Army. Designated mobilization training station was Fort Huachuca, AZ. Location 7 December 1941—*Not organized*.

43d Cavalry Squadron (Separate) (Colored) (GHQR) **Regular Army Inactive**

HQ—*Not organized,* 1928–35; Fort Huachuca, AZ, 1935; *Inactive* 1935–41

Constituted in the R.A. on 5 September 1928, allotted to the Eighth Corps Area, and assigned to the GHQR. Squadron organized on 12 February 1935 at Fort Huachuca, AZ, as an RAI unit with O.R. personnel. Inactivated about November 1935 at Fort Huachuca by relief of personnel. Location 7 December 1941—*Inactive*.

Commanders, 43d Cavalry Squadron

Unknown 12 February 1935–November 1935

44th Cavalry Squadron (Separate) (Colored) (GHQR) **Regular Army Inactive**

HQ—*Not organized,* 1928–35; Fort Huachuca, AZ, 1935; *Inactive,* 1935–41

Constituted in the R.A. on 5 September 1928, allotted to the Eighth Corps Area, and assigned to the GHQR. Squadron organized on 12 February 1935 at Fort Huachuca, AZ, as an RAI unit with O.R. personnel. Inactivated about November 1935 at Fort Huachuca by relief of personnel. Location 7 December 1941—*Inactive*.

Commanders, 44th Cavalry Squadron

Unknown 12 February 1935–November 1935

45th Cavalry Squadron (Separate) (Colored) (GHQR) **Regular Army Inactive**

HQ—*Not organized,* 1928–35; Fort Huachuca, AZ, 1935; *Inactive,* 1935–41

Constituted in the R.A. on 5 September 1928, allotted to the Eighth Corps Area, and assigned to the GHQR. Squadron organized on 12 February 1935 at Fort Huachuca, AZ, as an RAI unit with O.R. personnel. Inactivated about November 1935 at Fort Huachuca by relief of personnel. Location 7 December 1941—*Inactive*.

Commanders, 45th Cavalry Squadron

Unknown 12 February 1935–November 1935

46th Cavalry Squadron (Separate) (Colored) (GHQR) **Regular Army Inactive**

HQ—*Not organized,* 1928–35; Fort Huachuca, AZ, 1935; *Inactive,* 1935–41

Constituted in the R.A. on 5 September 1928, allotted to the Eighth Corps Area, and assigned to the GHQR. Squadron organized on 12 February 1935 at Fort Huachuca, AZ, as an RAI unit with O.R. personnel. Inactivated about November 1935 at Fort Huachuca by relief of personnel. Location 7 December 1941—*Inactive*.

Commanders, 46th Cavalry Squadron

Unknown 12 February 1935–November 1935

47th Cavalry Squadron (Separate) (Colored) (GHQR) **Regular Army Inactive**

HQ—*Not organized,* 1928–35; Fort Huachuca, AZ, 1935; *Inactive,* 1935–41

Constituted in the R.A. on 5 September 1928, allotted to the Eighth Corps Area, and assigned to the GHQR. Squadron organized on 12 February 1935 at Fort Huachuca, AZ, as an RAI unit with O.R. personnel. Inactivated about November 1935 at Fort Huachuca by relief of personnel. Location 7 December 1941—*Inactive.*

Commanders, 47th Cavalry Squadron

Unknown	12 February 1935–November 1935

48th Cavalry Squadron (Separate) (Colored) (GHQR) **Regular Army Inactive**

HQ—*Not organized,*1928–35; Fort Huachuca, AZ, 1935; *Inactive,* 1935–41

Constituted in the R.A. on 5 September 1928, allotted to the Eighth Corps Area, and assigned to the GHQR. Squadron organized on 12 February 1935 at Fort Huachuca, AZ, as an RAI unit with O.R. personnel. Inactivated about November 1935 at Fort Huachuca by relief of personnel. Location 7 December 1941—*Inactive.*

117th Separate Cavalry Squadron **Colorado National Guard**

HQ—Denver, CO, 1921–33

Constituted in the N.G. on 1 February 1922 as the 1st Sq., 117th Cav., and allotted to Colorado. Concurrently organized by redesignation of 2d Sq., 111th Cav. (federally recognized on 14 June 1921 as 1st Sep. Cav. Sq., Colorado N.G. at Denver, CO; redesignated 2d Sq., 111th Cav. on 1 November 1921). The 1st Sq. redesignated 117th Sep. Cav. Sq. on 12 September 1931 and remainder of the regiment demobilized. Squadron called up to perform flood duty at Pueblo, CO, 3 June–2 July 1921, and strike duty at the Columbine Mine near Boulder, CO, 21 November 1927–6 April 1928. Conducted summer training at Golden, CO, 1922–33, and Fort D.A. Russell, WY, 1924. For at least 1 year, in 1933, the squadron also trained eight company-grade cavalry officers of the 156th Cav. Brig. at Camp West. Designated mobilization training station was Golden. Converted and redesignated 2d Bn., 168th F.A. Regt. on 1 August 1933.

Commanders, 117th Separate Cavalry Squadron

Maj. John Finch	12 September 1931–7 April 1932	Maj. Raymond W. Combs	7 April 1932–1 August 1933

501st Cavalry Squadron (ZI) **Organized Reserve Georgia**

HQ—*Not initiated,* 1923–24; Cartersville, GA, 1924–28

Constituted in the O.R. in July 1923, assigned to the Zone of the Interior, and allotted to the Fourth Corps Area. Initiated in April 1924 with HQ at Cartersville, GA. Squadron conducted summer training with the 6th Cav. Regt. at Fort Oglethorpe, GA, 1924–28. Designated mobilization station was Fort Oglethorpe, GA. Withdrawn from Fourth Corps Area on 5 September 1928 and demobilized.

Commanders, 501st Cavalry Squadron

Unknown	April 1924–3 March 1925	Unknown	ao April 1925–6 June 1928
Capt. William T. Ward	3 March 1925–ao April 1925	Lt. Col. Harry P. Cooper	6 June 1928–5 September 1928

502d Cavalry Squadron (ZI) **Organized Reserve North Carolina**

HQ—*Not initiated,* 1923–24; Greensboro, NC, 1924–28

Constituted in the O.R. on 2 July 1923, assigned to the Zone of the Interior, and allotted to the Fourth Corps Area. Initiated on 23 October 1924 with HQ at Greensboro, NC. Squadron conducted summer training with the 6th Cav. Regt. at Fort Oglethorpe, GA, 1924–28. Designated mobilization station was Fort Oglethorpe, GA. Withdrawn from Fourth Corps Area on 5 September 1928 and demobilized.

Commanders, 502d Cavalry Squadron

Lt. Col. Percy K. Hexter	23 October 1924–ao September 1925	Unknown	ao September 1925–5 June 1928
Maj. Frank Wideman	5 June 1928–5 September 1928		

503d Cavalry Squadron (ZI) **Organized Reserve Tennessee**

HQ—*Not initiated,* 1923–24; Johnson City, TN, 1924–28

Constituted in the O.R. on 2 July 1923, assigned to the Zone of the Interior, and allotted to the Fourth Corps Area. Initiated in November 1924 with HQ at Johnson City, TN. Squadron conducted summer training with the 6th Cav. Regt. at Fort Oglethorpe, GA, 1924–28. Designated mobilization station was Fort Oglethorpe, GA. Withdrawn from Fourth Corps Area on 5 September 1928 and demobilized.

Commanders, 503d Cavalry Squadron

Unknown	November 1924–6 June 1928	Maj. William A. Collett	6 June 1928–5 September 1928

504th Cavalry Squadron (ZI) **Organized Reserve Alabama**

HQ—*Not initiated,* 1923–24; Tuscaloosa, AL, 1924–28

Constituted in the O.R. on 2 July 1923, assigned to the Zone of the Interior, and allotted to the Fourth Corps Area. Initiated in October 1924 with HQ at Tuscaloosa, AL. Squadron conducted summer training with the 6th Cav. Regt. at Fort Oglethorpe, GA, 1924–28. Designated mobilization station was Fort Oglethorpe, GA. Withdrawn from Fourth Corps Area on 5 September 1928 and demobilized.

Commanders, 504th Cavalry Squadron

Unknown	October 1924–5 September 1928

505th Cavalry Squadron (ZI) **Organized Reserve Texas/Kansas**

HQ—*Not initiated,* 1923–24; Fort Bliss, TX, 1924–27; Hutchinson, KS, 1927–28

Constituted in the O.R. on 2 July 1923, assigned to the Zone of the Interior, and allotted to the Eighth Corps Area. Initiated on 8 October 1925 with HQ at Fort Bliss, TX. Attached to the 156th Cav. Brig. on 3 November 1925 for administration, training, and control. Withdrawn from the Eighth Corps Area on 1 January 1927 and allotted to the Seventh Corps Area. HQ reorganized on 10 August 1927 at Hutchison, KS. Squadron conducted summer training with the 7th and 8th Cav. Regts. at Fort Bliss, TX, 1926–27. Withdrawn from Seventh Corps Area on 5 September 1928 and demobilized.

Commanders, 505th Cavalry Squadron

Unknown	8 October 1925–1 January 1927	Unknown	10 August 1927–5 June 1928
Inactive	1 January 1927–10 August 1927	Maj. John W. Moore	5 June 1928–5 September 1928

506th Cavalry Squadron (ZI) **Organized Reserve Texas/Nebraska**

HQ—*Not initiated,* 1923–24; Fort Bliss, TX 1925–27; Hastings, NE 1927–28

Constituted in the O.R. on 2 July 1923, assigned to the Zone of the Interior, and allotted to the Eighth Corps Area. Initiated by June 1925 with HQ at Fort Bliss, TX. Attached to the 156th Cav. Brig. on 3 November 1925 for administration, training, and control. Withdrawn from the Eighth Corps Area on 1 January 1927 and allotted to the Seventh Corps Area. HQ reorganized on 10 August 1927 at Hastings, NE. Squadron conducted summer training with the 7th and 8th Cav. Regts. at Fort Bliss, TX, 1926–27. Withdrawn from Seventh Corps Area on 5 September 1928 and demobilized.

Commanders, 506th Cavalry Squadron

Maj. Gaston L. Holmes	ao June 1925–1 January 1927	*Inactive*	1 January 1927–10 August 1927
Unknown	10 August 1927–5 September 1928		

507th Cavalry Squadron (ZI) **Organized Reserve Texas/Minnesota**

HQ—*Not initiated,* 1923–25; Fort Bliss, TX, 1925–27; Minneapolis, MN, 1927–28

Constituted in the O.R. on 2 July 1923, assigned to the Zone of the Interior, and allotted to the Eighth Corps Area. Initiated on 8 October 1925 with HQ at Fort Bliss, TX. Attached to the 156th Cav. Brig. on 3 November 1925 for administration, training, and control. Withdrawn from the Eighth Corps Area on 1 January 1927 and allotted to the Seventh Corps Area. HQ reorganized on 10 August 1927 at Minneapolis, MN. Squadron conducted summer training with the 7th and 8th Cav. Regts. at Fort Bliss, TX, 1926–27. Withdrawn from Seventh Corps Area on 5 September 1928 and demobilized.

Commanders, 507th Cavalry Squadron

Maj. Giddings Stone	8 October 1925–1 January 1927	*Inactive*	1 January 1927–10 August 1927
Unknown	10 August 1927–5 September 1928		

508th Cavalry Squadron (ZI) **Organized Reserve Texas/Arkansas**

HQ—*Not initiated,* 1923–25; Fort Bliss, TX, 1925–27; Searcy, AR, 1927–28

Constituted in the O.R. on 2 July 1923, assigned to the Zone of the Interior, and allotted to the Eighth Corps Area. Initiated on 8 October 1925 with HQ at Fort Bliss, TX. Attached to the 156th Cav. Brig. on 3 November 1925 for administration, training, and control. Withdrawn from the Eighth Corps Area on 1 January 1927 and allotted to the Seventh Corps Area. HQ reorganized on 10 August 1927 at Searcy, AR. Squadron conducted summer training with the 7th and 8th Cav. Regts. at Fort Bliss, TX, 1926–27. Withdrawn from Seventh Corps Area on 5 September 1928 and demobilized.

Commanders, 508th Cavalry Squadron

Unknown	8 October 1925–5 June 1928	*Inactive*	1 January 1927–10 August 1927
Unknown	10 August 1927–5 September 1928		

509th Cavalry Squadron (ZI) **Organized Reserve Mississippi**

HQ—*Not initiated,* 1923–24; Holly Springs, MS, 1924–28

Constituted in the O.R. on 2 July 1923, assigned to the Zone of the Interior, and allotted to the Fourth Corps Area. Initiated in November 1924 with HQ at Holly Springs, MS. Squadron conducted summer training with the 6th Cav. Regt. at Fort Oglethorpe, GA, 1924–28. Designated mobilization station was Fort Oglethorpe, GA. Withdrawn from Fourth Corps Area on 5 September 1928 and demobilized.

Commanders, 509th Cavalry Squadron

Unknown	November 1924–5 June 1928

510th Cavalry Squadron (ZI) **Organized Reserve Louisiana**

HQ—*Not initiated,* 1923–24; Shreveport, LA, 1924–28

Constituted in the O.R. on 2 July 1923, assigned to the Zone of the Interior, and allotted to the Fourth Corps Area. Initiated on 30 April 1924 with HQ at Shreveport, LA. Squadron conducted summer training with the 6th Cav. Regt. at Fort Oglethorpe, GA, 1924–28. Designated mobilization station was Fort Oglethorpe, GA. Withdrawn from Fourth Corps Area on 5 September 1928 and demobilized.

Commanders, 510th Cavalry Squadron

Unknown	30 April 1924–5 June 1928

511th Cavalry Squadron (ZI) **Organized Reserve South Carolina**

HQ—*Not initiated,* 1923–24; Union, SC, 1924–28

Constituted in the O.R. on 2 July 1923, assigned to the Zone of the Interior, and allotted to the Fourth Corps Area. Initiated on 30 April 1924 with HQ at Union, SC. Squadron conducted summer training with the 6th Cav. Regt. at Fort Oglethorpe, GA, 1924–28. Designated mobilization station was Fort Oglethorpe, GA. Withdrawn from Fourth Corps Area on 5 September 1928 and demobilized.

Commanders, 511th Cavalry Squadron

Unknown	30 April 1924–5 June 1928

512th Cavalry Squadron (ZI) **Organized Reserve Texas/Arkansas**

HQ—*Not initiated,* 1923–25; Fort Bliss, TX, 1925–27; Jonesboro, AR, 1927–28

Constituted in the O.R. on 2 July 1923, assigned to the Zone of the Interior, and allotted to the Eighth Corps Area. Initiated on 9 October 1925 with HQ at Fort Bliss, TX. Attached to the 156th Cav. Brig. on 3 November 1925 for administration, training, and control. Withdrawn from the Eighth Corps Area on 1 January 1927 and allotted to the Seventh Corps Area. HQ reorganized on 3 August 1927 at Jonesboro, AR. Squadron conducted summer training with the 7th and 8th Cav. Regts. at Fort Bliss, TX, 1926–27. Withdrawn from Seventh Corps Area on 5 September 1928 and demobilized.

Commanders, 512th Cavalry Squadron

Maj. Ralph Levy	9 October 1925–1 January 1927	*Inactive*	1 January 1927–3 August 1927
Unknown	3 August 1927–5 September 1928		

513th Cavalry Squadron (ZI) **Organized Reserve Texas/Nebraska**

HQ—*Not initiated,* 1923–25; Fort Bliss, TX, 1925–27; Scottsbluff, NE, 1927–28

Constituted in the O.R. on 2 July 1923, assigned to the Zone of the Interior, and allotted to the Eighth Corps Area. Initiated on 9 October 1925 with HQ at Fort Bliss, TX. Attached to the 156th Cav. Brig. on 3 November 1925 for administration, training, and control. Withdrawn from the Eighth Corps Area on 1 January 1927 and allotted to the Seventh Corps Area. HQ reorganized on 3 August 1927 at Scottsbluff, NE. Squadron conducted summer training with the 7th and 8th Cav. Regts. at Fort Bliss, TX, 1926–27. Withdrawn from Seventh Corps Area on 5 September 1928 and demobilized.

Commanders, 513th Cavalry Squadron

Maj. Robert J. Carson	9 October 1925–1 January 1927	*Inactive*	1 January 1927–3 August 1927
Unknown	3 August 1927–5 September 1928		

514th Cavalry Squadron (ZI) **Organized Reserve Texas\Kansas**

HQ—*Not initiated,* 1923–25; Fort Bliss, TX, 1925–27; Pittsburg, KS, 1927–28

Constituted in the O.R. on 2 July 1923, assigned to the Zone of the Interior, and allotted to the Eighth Corps Area. Initiated on 9 October 1925 with HQ at Fort Bliss, TX. Attached to the 156th Cav. Brig. on 3 November 1925 for administration, training, and control. Withdrawn from the Eighth Corps Area on 1 January 1927 and allotted to the Seventh Corps Area. HQ reorganized on 3 August 1927 at Pittsburgh, KS. Squadron conducted summer training with the 7th and 8th Cav. Regts. at Fort Bliss, TX, 1926–27. Withdrawn from Seventh Corps Area on 5 September 1928 and demobilized.

Commanders, 514th Cavalry Squadron

Unknown	9 October 1925–1 January 1927	*Inactive*	1 January 1927–3 August 1927
Unknown	3 August 1927–5 September 1928		

Chapter 16

Machine Gun Squadrons

USASC Photo, AOM

A machine gun troop from the 1st Cavalry Division in the field in west Texas.

The mission of machine gun squadrons was to provide heavy machine gun support to cavalry organizations in offensive and defensive operations.

Organization

In the interwar period, 26 machine gun squadrons were constituted in the three components of the Army. Of these, 6 were allotted to the Regular Army (R.A.), 8 were allotted to the National Guard (N.G.), and 12 were allotted to the Organized Reserve (O.R.). The organization was a result of an analysis of the World War I cavalry division and its subordinate units. Unlike the infantry, which eliminated the machine gun battalion and incorporated those weapons into the regimental structure, the cavalry went in the opposite direction. The branch eliminated the machine gun troop in the regiment and combined those troops into a brigade machine gun squadron due to the belief that those weapons would slow the movement of the regiments they were to support.

The machine gun squadron consisted of a headquarters (HQ), HQ troop, and three line troops. Each troop consisted of 5 officers and 110 enlisted men manning or protecting six .50-caliber heavy machine guns. Each squadron boasted 18 heavy machine guns, which provided a powerful punch on the battlefield. This table of organization remained in effect until the elimination of these squadrons in 1928.

Two of the six R.A. machine gun squadrons, the 1st Cavalry (Cav.) Division's (Div.) 1st and 2d Squadrons (Sqs.), were organized in 1921. Those of the 2d and 3d Cav. Divs. were organized only briefly

Machine Gun Squadron, 1921

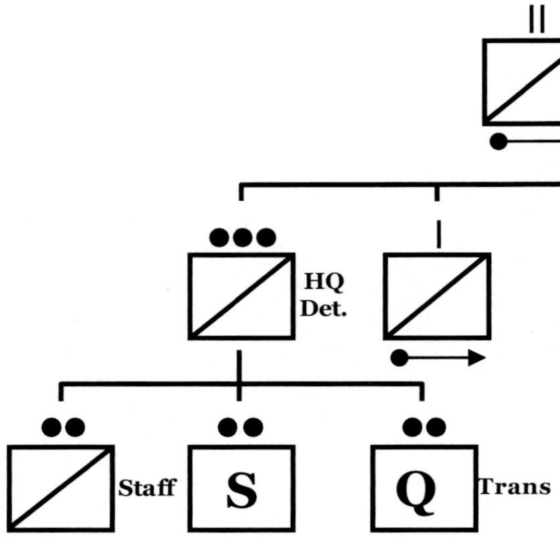

T/O:	430W
Approved:	3 February 1921
Commander:	Maj.
Officers:	21
W. O.	--
Enlisted:	171
Total:	192

Key Equipment:	
Machine guns, .50 cal.	18
Horses & Mules	562
Wagons	19
Rifles	180

Machine gun squadron, 1921.

as Regular Army Inactive (RAI) units in 1927 before being demobilized the following year. Six of the eight N.G. machine gun squadrons were fully organized in the early 1920s. Of the other two, one was partially organized and the other remained totally inactive. All 12 of the Reserve squadrons were organized during 1921 and 1922.

After about 7 years of experimentation with the machine guns squadron as a separate organization, the Cavalry branch determined that it was tactically unnecessary and undesirable to maintain the machine gun troops as separate units. Thus, in 1928, the squadrons were eliminated and the machine troop was returned to each cavalry regiment. The squadron HQ for R.A. squadrons was demobilized and the subordinate troops returned to their original regiments. In the N.G., most of the squadrons were either integrated into new or existing cavalry regiments as those units' recently authorized third squadrons or were demobilized. All of the O.R. squadrons were demobilized and the personnel used to form the third squadrons or machine gun troops of existing cavalry regiments or one of the new armored car squadrons authorized for the cavalry division. One, the 151st Machine Gun (MG) Squadron (Sq.), was initially demobilized, then reconstituted a short time later and consolidated with the new armored car squadron for the 61st Cav. Div.

Training

The 1st and 2d MG Sqs. generally participated in the events of their respective brigades. Since the standard procedure for machine gun squadrons was to attach troops to the regiments of the brigade, and rarely functioned as a cohesive, pure unit, most of the other training events for these units were conducted at the troop- and platoon-level. Much of that, not surprisingly was range firing and crew drills. RAI machine gun squadrons were active for such a short period that it is unlikely that they functioned as units.

N.G. machine gun squadrons conducted the usual training activities in the inactive training period. Much of the machine gun-related training was focused on weapons functions and assembly, crew drills, and lectures and demonstrations on theoretical machine gun employment. Due to the lack of local availability of machine gun-capable ranges, machine gun units were generally required to conduct their annual firing exercises at the summer training camps, though they might have the chance to participate in maneuver training during the second week of camp.

Most O.R. machine gun squadrons were functional organizations, though a few, mainly in the west, were too geographically dispersed to enable them to effectively assemble as units. Few of these squadrons had an opportunity to work with their primary weapon except at summer training camps. In a few instances, organizations were able to work with weapons loaned by nearby R.A. or N.G. units. Most, however, spent their inactive training periods conducting theoretical employment of the units in various tactical scenarios or conducting general skills training or troop schools. Most of the practical work with machine gun, as well as tactical training, was performed at the summer training camps.

1st Machine Gun Squadron (1st Cavalry Division)

HQ—Camp Harry J. Jones, AZ, 1921–22; Fort Clark, TX, 1923–28

Constituted in the R.A. on 20 August 1921. Organized on 1 September 1921 at Camp Harry J. Jones in Douglas, AZ, from D Troop, 1st Cav. (redesignated as HQ Detachment), and the machine gun troops from the 1st, 5th, and 12th Cav. Regts. Assigned to the 1st Cav. Div. on 13 September 1921. Transferred to Fort Clark, TX, by making an overland march from 26 December 1922 to 23 January 1923. Participated in 1st Cav. Brigade (Brig.) maneuvers near Fort Clark, TX, in January 1926. Participated in the making of Lansky's Famous Players movie "Rough Riders" near San Antonio, TX, 17 August–20 September 1926. Headquarters and headquarters troop (HHT) demobilized on 1 February 1928. Concurrently, Troops A, B, and C reorganized and redesignated as MG Troop (Tp.), 1st, 12th, and 5th Cav. Regts, respectively.

Events: 30, 42, 65, 127

Commanders, 1st Machine Gun Squadron

Capt. Hugh D. Blanchard	27 September 1921–26 January 1922	Capt. Harold A. Fellows	30 June 1926–9 September 1926
Lt. Col. Emmet R. Harris	26 January 1922–3 June 1924	Maj. Sumner M. Williams	9 September 1926–16 January 1928
Maj. Francis C.V. Crowley	3 June 1924–30 June 1926	Maj. John F. Wall	16 January 1928–1 February 1928

2d Machine Gun Squadron (1st Cavalry Division)

HQ—Fort Bliss, TX, 1921–28

Constituted in the R.A. on 26 August 1921 and organized at Fort Bliss, TX, from H Troop, 8th Cav. (redesignated as HQ Detachment), and the machine gun troops from the 7th, 8th, and 13th Cav. Regts. Assigned to the 1st Cav. Div. on 13 September 1921. The squadron maintained a habitual summer training relationship with the 156th MG Sq. Participated in 2d Cav. Brig. maneuvers northwest of El Paso, TX, in August 1926. HHT demobilized on 1 February 1928. Concurrently, Troops A, B, and C reorganized and redesignated as MG Troop, 7th, 8th, and 13th Cav. Regts., respectively.

Events: 30, 65

Commanders, 2d Machine Gun Squadron

Maj. Pearson Menoher	13 September 1921–13 December 1922	Maj. Alexander M. Milton	9 July 1924–25 September 1925
Maj. Duncan G. Richart	13 December 1922–2 July 1924	Maj. Vaughn W. Cooper	25 September 1925–5 August 1926
Maj. John B. Johnson	1 September 1926–1 February 1928		

3d Machine Gun Squadron (2d Cavalry Division)

HQ—*Not organized,* 1921–27; Tucson, AZ, 1927; *Inactive,* 1927–28

Constituted in the R.A. on 26 August 1921 and allotted to the Eighth Corps Area. Component troops were assigned and redesignated as follows: M Troop, 5th Cav. as HQ Detachment; MG Troop, 2d Cav. as A Troop; Troop D, 3d Cav. as B Troop; and Troop D, 8th Cav. as C Troop. Active associates were HQ, 1st Cav. Div., 1922–25, and 1st MG Sq., 1925–27. Assigned to the 2d Cav. Div. on 24 March 1923. Affiliated with the University of Arizona ROTC at Tucson on 10 June 1927 and organized with R.A. personnel assigned to the Reserve Officers' Training Corps (ROTC) Detachment and Reserve officers commissioned from the program. Under special instructions issued by the Adjutant General on 15 August 1927, the squadron was to be partially organized on mobilization from the 1st MG Troop stationed at Fort Riley, KS. Concurrently, the squadron was withdrawn from the Eighth Corps Area and allotted to the Seventh Corps Area. Demobilized 1 February 1928.

Commanders, 3d Machine Gun Squadron

Lt. Col. Howard C. Tatum*	10 June 1927–15 August 1927

*RAI commanders: R.A. officers who were concurrently PMS&T at the University of Arizona.

4th Machine Gun Squadron (2d Cavalry Division)

HQ—*Not organized,* 1921–27; Roswell, NM, 1927; *Inactive,* 1927–28

Constituted in the R.A. on 26 August 1921 and allotted to the Eighth Corps Area. Component troops were assigned and redesignated as follows: D Troop, 14th Cav. as HQ Detachment; MG Troop, 11th Cav. as A Troop; MG Troop, 15th Cav. as B Troop; and MG Troop, 14th Cav. as C Troop. Active associates were HQ, 1st Cav. Div., 1922–25, and 2d MG Sq., 1925–27. Assigned to the 2d Cav. Div. on 24 March 1923. Affiliated with the New Mexico Military Institute ROTC at Roswell, NM, on 10 June 1927 and organized with R.A. personnel assigned to the ROTC. Detachment and Reserve officers commissioned from the program. Under special instructions issued by the Adjutant General on 15 August 1927, the squadron was to be partially organized on mobilization from the 1st MG Troop stationed at Fort Riley, KS. Concurrently, the squadron was withdrawn from the Eighth Corps Area and allotted to the Seventh Corps Area. Demobilized on 1 February 1928.

Commanders, 4th Machine Gun Squadron

Lt. Col. Edward A. Keyes*	10 June 1927–15 August 1927

*RAI commanders: R.A. officers who were concurrently PMS&T at the New Mexico Military Institute.

5th Machine Gun Squadron (3d Cavalry Division)

HQ—*Not organized,* 1921–24; *Demobilized,* 1924–27; Kansas City, MO, 1927–28

Constituted in the R.A. on 26 August 1921 and allotted to the Eighth Corps Area. Component troops were assigned and redesignated as follows: M Troop, 15th Cav. as HQ Detachment; Troop D, 16th Cav. as A Troop; MG Troop, 16th Cav. as B Troop; and Troop H, 14th Cav. as C Troop. Active associate HQ, 1st Cav. Div., 1922–24. Demobilized on 23 April 1924. Reconstituted on 15 August 1927, assigned to the 3d Cav. Div., and allotted to the Seventh Corps Area. Organized by October 1927 as an RAI unit with O.R. personnel from the 66th Cav. Div. at Kansas City, MO. Demobilized on 1 February 1928.

Commanders, 5th Machine Gun Squadron

Unknown	ao October 1927–1 February 1928

6th Machine Gun Squadron (3d Cavalry Division)

HQ—*Not organized,* 1921–24; *Demobilized,* 1924–27; Kansas City, MO, 1927–28

Constituted in the R.A. on 26 August 1921 and allotted to the Eighth Corps Area. Component troops were assigned and redesignated as follows: D Troop, 12th Cav. as HQ Detachment; MG Troop, 6th Cav. as A Troop; Troop D, 6th Cav. as B Troop; and MG Troop, 4th Cav. as C Troop. Active associate HQ, 1st Cav. Div., 1922–24. Demobilized on 23 April 1924. Reconstituted on 15 August 1927, assigned to the 3d Cav. Div., and allotted to the Seventh Corps Area. Organized by October 1927 as an RAI unit with O.R. personnel from the 66th Cav. Div. at Kansas City, MO. Demobilized on 1 February 1928.

Commanders, 6th Machine Gun Squadron

Unknown	ao October 1927–1 February 1928

51st Machine Gun Squadron (21st Cavalry Division) **New York National Guard**

HQ—Brooklyn, NY, 1921–28

Constituted in the N.G. on 30 December 1920, assigned to the 21st Cav. Div., and allotted to the state of New York. Organized on 1 June 1921 by redesignation of Sq. A, New York Guard as the 51st MG Sq. HQ federally recognized on 22 November 1921 at Brooklyn, NY. Provided escort for Marshal Joffre of France on 26 April 1922 during his visit to New York. Hosted the annual National Horse Show, 1921–25, at the squadron's Brooklyn armory. Conducted annual summer training at Fort Ethan Allen, VT, in 1921, 1924, and 1925; Sq. A Farm, near New York City, in 1922; Camp Dix, NJ, in 1923; and at Pine Camp, NY, in 1926–27. Redesignated 2d Sq., 101st Cav. on 15 February 1928.

Commander, 51st Machine Gun Squadron

Maj. Nathaniel H. Egleston	13 December 1921–15 February 1928

52d Machine Gun Squadron (21st Cavalry Division) **Pennsylvania National Guard**

HQ—Bellefonte, PA, 1921–27; Tyrone, PA, 1927–29

Constituted in the N.G. on 1 June 1921, assigned to the 21st Cav. Div., and allotted to Pennsylvania. HQ organized on 6 August 1921 and federally recognized at Bellefonte, PA. HQ troop relocated in 1926 to Columbia, PA. HQ relocated on 21 November 1927 to Tyrone, PA. Squadron called up to perform coal miner strike duty at Ebensburg and Cokeburg, PA, 21 July–7 September 1922, and to search for a downed Army mail plane near Clarion, PA, 6–11 October 1925. Conducted annual summer training at Mount Gretna, PA, 1921–28. Squadron HQ demobilized in March 1929. Subordinate troops concurrently absorbed into the 103d and 104th Cav. Regts.

Commanders, 52d Machine Gun Squadron

Maj. Hugh L. Curtin	6 August 1921–15 February 1928	Maj. Benjamin C. Jones	12 July 1927–1 April 1929

53d Machine Gun Squadron (22d Cavalry Division) **Kentucky National Guard**

HQ—London, KY, 1921–27; Lexington, KY, 1927–29

Constituted in the N.G. on 1 June 1921, assigned to the 22d Cav. Div., and allotted to Kentucky. HQ organized on 30 July 1921 and federally recognized at London, KY. The squadron, or elements thereof, called up to perform the following state duties: strike duty in the coal fields at the Anderson Steel and Newport Rolling Mills near Newport, KY, 2 February–31 March 1922; strike duty at Madisonville, KY, 8 July–30 August 1922, and strike duty near Newport, KY, 2 February–24 April 1923; and to preserve order at a criminal trial in Lexington, KY, 1–2 February 1926. Squadron HHT disbanded on 15 January 1927 at London. Reconstituted and federally recognized on 21 February 1927 at Lexington, KY. Conducted annual summer training at Fort Knox, KY, 1922–28. Subordinate troops absorbed into the 123d Cav. Regt. on 1 April 1929. Squadron HHT detachment demobilized on 30 June 1929.

Commander, 53d Machine Gun Squadron

Maj. James K. Dillion	30 July 1921–1 April 1929

54th Machine Gun Squadron (22d Cavalry Division) **Kentucky National Guard**

HQ—Monticello, KY, 1922–24; Frankfort, KY, 1924–28

Constituted in the N.G. on 1 June 1921, assigned to the 22d Cav. Div., and allotted to Kentucky. HQ organized on 29 November 1922, and federally recognized at Monticello, KY. HHT disbanded on 10 April 1924 at Monticello. Reconstituted on 3 July 1924 and organized at Frankfort, KY. The squadron, or elements thereof, called up to perform the following state duties: strike duties in the coal fields at the Anderson Steel and Newport Rolling Mills near Newport, KY, 2 February–31 March 1922; strike duties at Madisonville, KY, 8 July–30 August 1922; strike duties near Newport, 2 February–24 April 1923; strike duties at the Straight Creek Mining District, 8 April–14 May 1924; strike duties at the Dix River Dam,10–17 November 1924; to preserve law and order at Sand Cave, KY, 2 February–18 March 1925, during the rescue attempt to save the celebrated cave explorer Floyd Collins; criminal trials in Lexington, KY, 1–2 February 1926, and Louisville, KY, 22–28 April 1926; and to preserve order at the rape trial of two Negro men at Madisonville, 23–26 November 1927. Conducted annual summer training at Fort Knox, KY, 1922–28. Subordinate troops absorbed into the 123d Cav. Regt., 1 April 1929. Squadron HHT demobilized on 30 June 1929.

Commanders, 54th Machine Gun Squadron

Maj. Wallace G. Drummond	29 November 1922–10 April 1924	Maj. Carl D. Norman	3 July 1924–1 April 1929

55th Machine Gun Squadron (23d Cavalry Division) **Alabama National Guard**

HQ—Andalusia, AL, 1922–29

Constituted in the N.G. on 1 June 1921, assigned to the 23d Cav.Div., and allotted to the state of Alabama. HQ organized and federally recognized on 31 January 1922 at Andalusia, AL. Conducted annual summer training at Camp McClellan, AL, and Fort Oglethorpe, GA, 1922–28. Designated mobilization training station was Fort Oglethorpe. Squadron reorganized and redesignated 1st Bn., 117th F.A. Regt., on 15 March 1929.

Commanders, 55th Machine Gun Squadron

Maj. William A. Jeffery	31 January 1922–15 March 1929

56th Machine Gun Squadron (23d Cavalry Division) **Texas National Guard**

HQ—Houston, TX, 1921–29

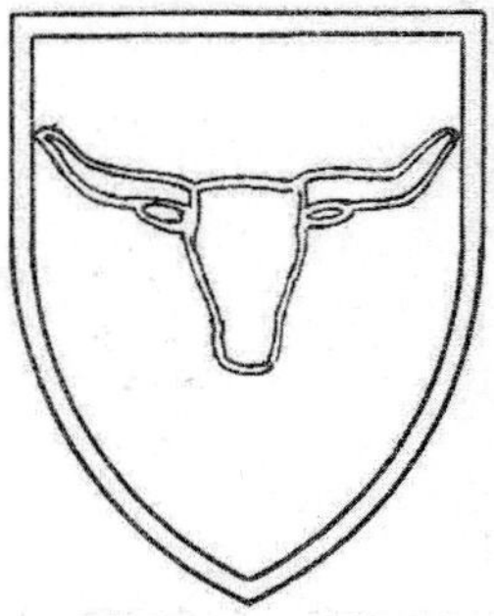

Constituted in the N.G. on 1 June 1921, assigned to the 23d Cav. Div., and allotted to the state of Texas. Squadron organized on 4 June 1921 by redesignation of 1st MG Sq., TX N.G. (organized and federally recognized on 3 February 1921) at Houston, TX. Conducted annual summer training at Camp Mabry, TX, 1921–22; Camp Stanley, TX, 1923–25; and Camp Wolters, TX, 1926–28. Squadron HHT demobilized on 15 March 1929 and subordinate troops absorbed into the 112th and 124th Cav. Regts.

Commanders, 56th Machine Gun Squadron

Maj. O'Brien Stevens	3 February 1921–22 March 1922	Maj. Calvin B. Garwood	23 March 1922–15 March 1929

57th Machine Gun Squadron (24th Cavalry Division) **South Dakota National Guard**

HQ—*Not organized,* 1921–29

Constituted in the N.G. on 1 June 1921, assigned to the 24th Cav. Div., and allotted to the state of South Dakota. No elements ever organized. Squadron withdrawn from the N.G. in April 1929 and demobilized.

58th Machine Gun Squadron (24th Cavalry Division) **Washington and Wyoming National Guard**

HQ—*Not organized,* 1921–29

Constituted in the N.G. on 1 June 1921, assigned to the 24th Cav. Div., and allotted to the states of Wyoming and Washington. Squadron, less Troop A, was allotted to the state of Washington; Troop A allotted to the state of Wyoming. Troop A organized on 11 June 1921 and federally recognized at Newcastle, WY. Troop B organized on 18 August 1921 and federally recognized at Tacoma, WA. Troop A conducted annual summer training at Pole Mountain, WY, 1922–28, and Troop B at Camp Murray, WA, 1922–24. Squadron, less Troop A, withdrawn from the state of Washington on 29 September 1924 and allotted to the state of Wyoming. Troop B redesignated HQ Troop, 24th Cav. Div. on 1 November 1924. Squadron demobilized about April 1929. Troop A redesignated on 1 June 1929 as MG Troop, 115th Cav.

151st Machine Gun Squadron (61st Cavalry Division) **Organized Reserve New York**

HQ—*Not initiated,* 1921–22; Albany, NY, 1922–28

Constituted in the O.R. on 15 October 1921, assigned to the 61st Cav. Div., and allotted to the Second Corps Area. Initiated on 7 February 1922 with HQ at Albany, NY. Typically conducted Inactive Training Period meetings at the armory of Troop B, 121st Cav. in Albany. Conducted regular equestrian training at the Troop B armory. Conducted summer training with the 1st Sq., 3d Cav. Regt. at Fort Ethan Allen, VT, 1924–28. Relieved from the 61st Cav. Div. on 20 December 1928 and withdrawn from the O.R. Personnel concurrently reassigned to the 461st Armored (Armd.) Car Sq. Reconstituted on 11 September 1929 and consolidated with the 461st Armd. Car Sq.

Commanders, 151st Machine Gun Squadron

Maj. Ernest Miller 27 June 1922–25 June 1923
Maj. Gilbert V. Schenk 25 June 1923–February 1928
Maj. Edgar C. Niles February 1928–20 December 1928

152d Machine Gun Squadron (61st Cavalry Division) **Organized Reserve New York**

HQ—*Not initiated,* 1921–22; Manhattan, NY, 1922–28

Constituted in the O.R. on 15 October 1921, assigned to the 61st Cav. Div., and allotted to the Second Corps Area. Initiated on 23 February 1922 with HQ at Manhattan, NY. Squadron was organized with many personnel who were former members of Squadron A, New York N.G. Conducted summer training with the 1st Sq., 3d Cav. Regt. at Fort Ethan Allen, VT, 1924–28. Relieved from the 61st Cav. Div. on 20 December 1928 and withdrawn from the O.R.

Commanders, 152d Machine Gun Squadron

1st Harry G. Kettner 6 February 1922–23 February 1922
Maj. Harold H. Donaldson 23 February 1922–18 April 1922
Maj. James B. Spencer 19 April 1922–May 1926
Lt. Col. Hartley W. Bartlett May 1926–March 1928
Maj. John F. Coneybear March 1928–20 December 1928

153d Machine Gun Squadron (62d Cavalry Division) **Organized Reserve Maryland and District of Columbia**

HQ—Baltimore, MD, 1921–28

Constituted in the O.R. on 15 October 1921, assigned to the 62d Cav. Div., and allotted to the Third Corps Area. Initiated on 21 November 1921 with HQ at Baltimore, MD. Conducted summer training with MG Troop, 3d Cav. Regt. at Fort Myer, VA, 1924–28. Relieved from the 62d Cav. Div. on 20 December 1928 and withdrawn from the O.R. Personnel concurrently reassigned to the 3d Sq. and the MG Troop of the 306th Cav..

Commanders, 153d Machine Gun Squadron

Maj. William R. Tyree	21 November 1921–6 October 1926	Maj. John C. Butler	6 October 1926–20 December 1928

154th Machine Gun Squadron (62d Cavalry Division) **Organized Reserve Virginia**

HQ—*Not initiated,* 1921–22; Norfolk, VA, 1922–28

Constituted in the O.R. on 15 October 1921, assigned to the 62d Cav. Div., and allotted to the Third Corps Area. Initiated in January 1922 with HQ at Norfolk, VA. Typically borrowed machine guns from M Co., 183d Inf. to perform crew training during the inactive training period. Conducted summer training with MG Troop, 3d Cav. Regt. at Fort Myer, VA, 1924–28. Primary ROTC feeder school was the Virginia Military Institute. Relieved from the 62d Cav. Div. on 20 December 1928 and withdrawn from the O.R. Personnel concurrently reassigned to the 3d Sq. and the MG Troop of the 307th Cav.

Commanders, 154th Machine Gun Squadron

Capt. Allen C. Gottschalt	January 1922–1 September 1922	Maj. James R. Mullen	1 September 1922–20 December 1928

155th Machine Gun Squadron (63d Cavalry Division) **Organized Reserve Tennessee**

HQ—*Not initiated,* 1921–22; Memphis, TN, 1922–27; Nashville, TN, 1927–28

Constituted in the O.R. on 15 October 1921, assigned to the 63d Cav. Div., and allotted to the Fourth Corps Area. Initiated on 3 August 1922 with HQ at Memphis, TN. HHT relocated in 1927 to Nashville, TN. Conducted summer training with troops of the 53d and 54th MG Sqs. at Camp Knox, KY, or with MG Troop, 6th Cav. Regt. at Fort Oglethorpe, GA, 1923–28. Designated mobilization training station was Fort Oglethorpe, GA. Relieved from the 63d Cav. Div. on 20 December 1928 and withdrawn from the O.R.

Commanders, 155th Machine Gun Squadron

Capt. Louis H. Bell	25 September 1922–ao January 1923	Unknown	ao January 1923–20 December 1928

156th Machine Gun Squadron (63d Cavalry Division) **Organized Reserve Colorado**

HQ—*Not initiated,* 1921–22; Denver, CO, 1922–28

Constituted in the O.R. on 15 October 1921, assigned to the 63d Cav. Div., and allotted to the Eighth Corps Area. Initiated on 12 September 1922 with HQ at Denver, CO. Conducted summer training with the 2d MG Sq. at Fort Bliss, TX, 1923–28. Typically conducted Inactive Training Period meetings at the Kitteridge Building or the Argonaut Hotel in Denver. Relieved from the 63d Cav. Div. on 20 December 1928 and withdrawn from the O.R. Personnel concurrently reassigned to the 3d Sq. and the MG Troop of the 312th Cav.

Commanders, 156th Machine Gun Squadron

Capt. Howard R.K. Tompkins	12 September 1922–22 November 1922	Maj. Howard R.K. Tompkins	ao December 1924–ao January 1926
Maj. Clyde E. Ely	22 November 1922–ao January 1924	Maj. Alphonse Entringer	ao August 1926–ao January 1927
Maj. Ralph Levy	ao August 1927–20 December 1928		

157th Machine Gun Squadron (64th Cavalry Division) **Organized Reserve Kentucky**

HQ—*Not initiated,* 1921–22; Hazard, KY, 1922–25; Ashland, KY, 1925–28

Constituted in the O.R. on 15 October 1921, assigned to the 64th Cav. Div., and allotted to the Fifth Corps Area. Initiated in January 1922 with HQ at Hazzard, KY. HHT relocated on 15 April 1925 to Ashland, KY. Conducted summer training with the 53d and 54th MG Sqs. at Camp Knox, KY. Relieved from the 64th Cav. Div. on 20 December 1928 and withdrawn from the O.R. Personnel concurrently reassigned to the 464th Armd. Car Sq.

Commanders, 157th Machine Gun Squadron

Maj. Homer H. McRee	January 1922–20 December 1928

158th Machine Gun Squadron (64th Cavalry Division) **Organized Reserve Massachusetts**

HQ—*Not initiated,* 1921–22; Boston, MA, 1922–28

Constituted in the O.R. on 15 October 1921, assigned to the 64th Cav. Div., and allotted to the Fifth Corps Area. Initiated in April 1922 with HQ at Boston, MA. Typically conducted Inactive Training Period meetings at the 110th Cav.'s Commonwealth Armory in Boston. Conducted regular equestrian training with the horses of the 110th Cav. in Boston. Conducted summer training with the 1st Sq., 3d Cav. Regt. at Fort Ethan Allen, VT, 1923–28. Relieved from the 64th Cav. Div. on 20 December 1928 and withdrawn from the O.R. Personnel concurrently reassigned to the 3d Sq. and the MG Troop of the 315th Cav.

Commanders, 158th Machine Gun Squadron

Capt. John Kenney	April 1922–ao January 1923	Maj. Howard S. Patterson	ao August 1924–ao November 1925
Maj. Louis H. Bell	ao August 1923–ao January 1924	Maj. Louis H. Bell	ao April 1926–20 December 1928

159th Machine Gun Squadron (65th Cavalry Division) **Organized Reserve Illinois**

HQ—*Not initiated,* 1921–22; Chicago, IL, 1922–25; Evanston, IL, 1925–29

Constituted in the O.R. on 15 October 1921, assigned to the 65th Cav. Div., and allotted to the Sixth Corps Area. Initiated 6 June 1922 with HQ at Chicago, IL. HHT relocated on 28 July 1925 to Evanston, IL. Typically conducted Inactive Training Period meetings at the 65th Cav. Div. HQ in Chicago. Conducted summer training with the 14th Cav. Regt. at Camp Custer, MI, 1922–24, and Fort Sheridan, IL, 1925–28. Relieved from the 65th Cav. Div. on 20 December 1928 and withdrawn from the O.R.

Commanders, 159th Machine Gun Squadron

Maj. William L. Elkin	6 June 1922–6 January 1923	Lt. Col. Hartley W. Bartlett	20 June 1924–ao September 1925
Capt. Albert G. Duncan	6 January 1923–20 June 1924	Maj. Charles A. Ellis	ao May 1926–ao May 1927
	Maj. William N. Leonard	ao April 1928–20 December 1928	

160th Machine Gun Squadron (65th Cavalry Division) **Organized Reserve Michigan**

HQ—*Not initiated,* 1921–22; Ann Arbor, MI, 1922–23; Lansing, MI, 1923–25; Pontiac, MI, 1925–27; Highland Park, MI, 1927–28

Constituted in the O.R. on 15 October 1921, assigned to the 65th Cav. Div., and allotted to the Sixth Corps Area. Initiated 6 June 1922 with HQ at Ann Arbor, MI. HHT relocated as follows: to Lansing, MI, on 4 May 1923; to Pontiac, MI, on 2 June 1925; and to Highland Park, MI, on 7 January 1927. Typically conducted Inactive Training Period meetings at the Highland Park High School or the Northwood Club in Highland Park. Conducted summer training with the 14th Cav. Regt. at Camp Custer, MI, 1922–25, and Fort Sheridan, IL, 1926–28. Relieved from the 65th Cav. Div. on 20 December 1928 and withdrawn from the O.R. Personnel concurrently reassigned to the 465th Armd. Car Sq.

Commanders, 160th Machine Gun Squadron

Maj. Daniel Zimmerman	6 June 1922–ao July 1922	Maj. William N. Leonard	28 November 1926–ao July 1927
Maj. Bruce E. Anderson	ao December 1922–28 November 1926	Unknown	ao July 1927–ao November 1928
Capt. John A. Broberg	ao November 1928–20 December 1928		

161st Machine Gun Squadron (66th Cavalry Division) **Organized Reserve Kansas**

HQ—*Not initiated,* 1921–22; Junction City, KS, 1922–26; Independence, KS, 1926–28

Constituted in the O.R. on 15 October 1921, assigned to the 66th Cav. Div., and allotted to the Seventh Corps Area. Initiated in March 1922 with HQ at Junction City, KS. HHT relocated on 26 May 1926 to Independence, KS. Conducted summer training with the 1st MG Troop and 2d Cav. Regt. at Fort Riley, KS, and the 4th Cav. Regt. at Fort Meade, SD. Relieved from the 66th Cav. Div. on 20 December 1928 and withdrawn from the O.R.

Commander, 161st Machine Gun Squadron

Maj. Chauncey Dewey	March 1922–20 December 1928

162d Machine Gun Squadron (66th Cavalry Division) **Organized Reserve California**

HQ—*Not initiated,* 1921–22; Fresno, CA, 1922–28

Constituted in the O.R. on 15 October 1921, assigned to the 66th Cav. Div., and allotted to the Ninth Corps Area. Initiated in March 1922 with HQ at Fresno, CA. Conducted summer training with the 11th Cav. Regt. at Presidio of Monterrey, CA, or Del Monte, CA. Relieved from the 66th Cav. Div. on 20 December 1928 and withdrawn from the O.R.

Commanders, 162d Machine Gun Squadron

Capt. Zygmunt S. Leymal	March 1922–1 March 1923	Lt. Col. Eugene A. DeHermida	1 March 1923–16 July 1925
Lt. Col. Jack Hastie Jr.	16 July 1925–20 December 1928		

Chapter 17

Armored Car and Reconnaissance Squadrons

USASC Photo, NA II

Vehicles from the 1st Armored Car Squadron at Fort Bliss, TX, about 1934.

The mission of armored car squadrons was to provide rapid, motorized reconnaissance support to cavalry organizations in offensive and defensive operations.

Organization

The armored car squadron was the cavalry's initial effort to adopt motorization in its attempts to modernize the branch for future conflict. The squadron consisted of a headquarters (HQ), a HQ troop, and three line troops each equipped with 12 armored cars. One of these organizations was authorized for each cavalry division in 1928 for an initial total of 13 in the force structure. An additional squadron for the I Cavalry Corps was constituted in 1933 and another, the 7th Reconnaissance (Rcn.) and Support (Spt.) Squadron (Sq.) was constituted as a component of the 7th Cavalry (Cav.) Brigade (Brig.) (Mechanized [Mecz]) in 1940. The designation of the armored car organization was changed to "reconnaissance squadron" in 1939.

In the Regular Army (R.A.), both the 1st and 2d Sqs. were limited to one active troop, of which only the former had a lengthy stint as an active unit. Troop A, 2d Sq. was active for only about 4 years. The remaining units of both squadrons, as well as the 3d Armored (Armd.) Car Sq., were organized as Regular Army Inactive (RAI) units. None of the four Guard squadrons were active until 1939, when the 21st, 22d, and 24th Rcn. Sqs. were organized, followed by the 23d a few months later in 1940. These squadrons were either disbanded or integrated into the new corps reconnaissance regiments created after the disbandment

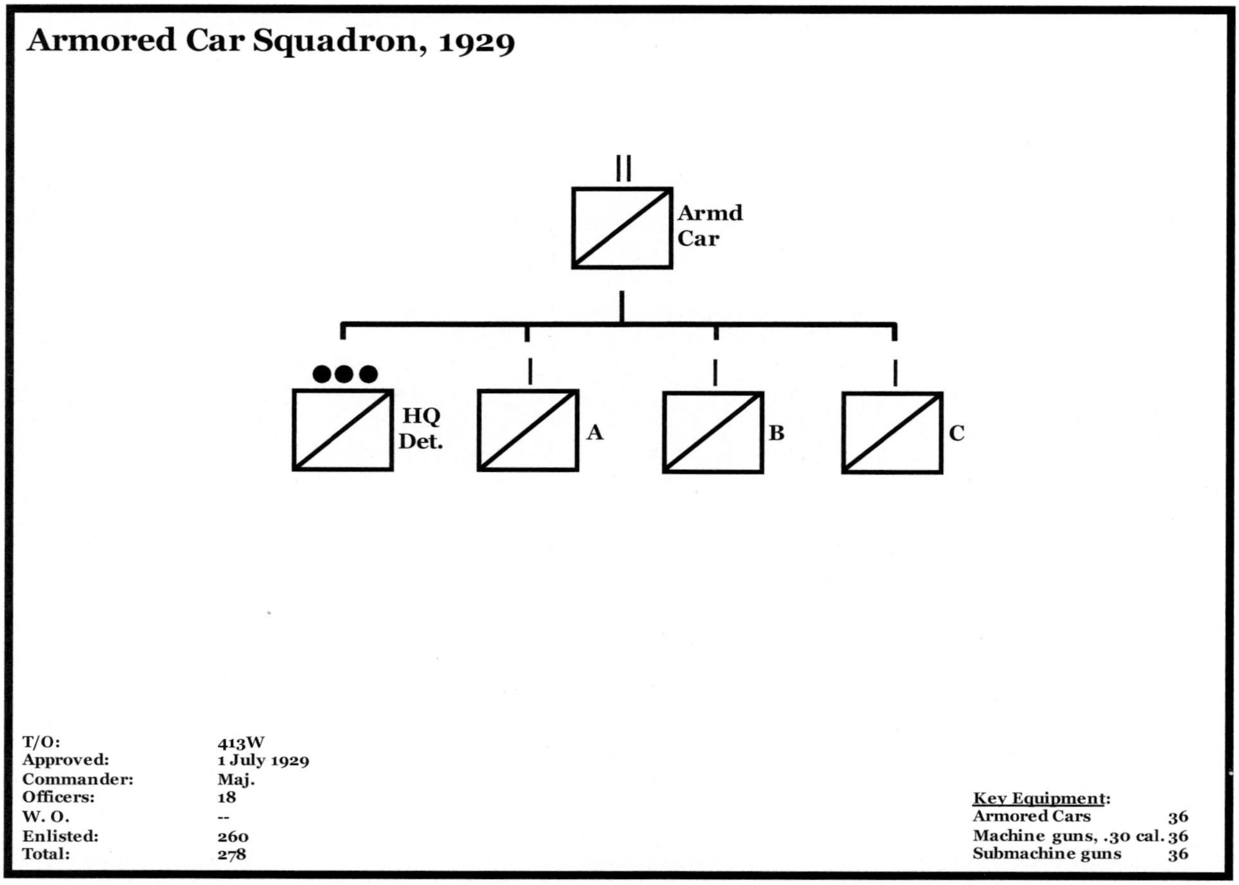

Armored car squadron organization, 1929.

of the four Guard cavalry divisions in the fall of 1940. All six of the O.R. squadrons were organized in 1928 and remained active until the beginning of World War II.

Training

The active troops of the 1st and 2d Sqs. participated in some of the most well-publicized Army maneuvers of the interwar period, and along with the Mechanized Force and 7th Cav. Brig. (Mecz), significantly contributed to the development of the motorized and mechanized tactical doctrine and training of the Army's armored and mechanized forces that were to follow in World War II. All four of the National Guard (N.G.) reconnaissance squadrons certainly spent most of their short periods of existence in organizing and equipping themselves. Each, however, participated in one of the major field army maneuvers in 1940 before being converted to other types of units. The Reserve squadrons conducted mostly theoretical classes on the employment of armored car units or attended nonmission specific training with other organizations. In most cases, the units attended camp with the motorized elements of R.A. cavalry regiments or other types of mechanized or armored units, such as the 1st Tank Company (Co.) at Miller Field, NY. Several of the squadrons had the opportunity to attend training at least once with units of the 7th Cav. Brig. at Fort Knox, KY.

1st Armored Car Squadron (1st Cavalry Division)
1st Reconnaissance Squadron (1939–41)
91st Reconnaissance Squadron (1941)

HQ—*Not organized,* 1928–32; Fort Bliss, TX, 1932–41

Constituted in the R.A. on 16 October 1928 as the 1st Armored (Armd.) Car Squadron (Sq.), and assigned to the 1st Cav. Division (Div.). Concurrently, the 1st Armd. Car Troop (organized as Provisional Platoon, 1st Armd. Car Troop at Aberdeen Proving Grounds, MD, on 15 February 1928; redesignated 1st Armd. Car Troop on 10 June 1928) redesignated Troop A, 1st Armd. Car Sq. Remainder of squadron allotted to the Eighth Corps Area. Troop A transferred to Fort George G. Meade, MD, on 29 August 1928; to Fort Holabird, MD, on 1 October 1928; and finally to Fort Bliss, TX, arriving there on 10 November 1928. The squadron, less Troop A, was organized on 30 June 1932 with Organized Reserve (O.R.) personnel as an RAI unit with HQ at Fort Bliss. Reserve officers assigned to the squadron conducted summer training with Troop A at Fort Bliss. Redesignated 1st Rcn. Sq. on 1 March 1939. The remainder of the squadron was activated on 3 January 1941, less Reserve personnel, at Fort Bliss. Redesignated 91st Rcn. Sq. on 8 May 1941. Location 7 December 1941—Fort Bliss, TX.

Events: 83, 105, 125, 146, 147

Commanders, 1st Armored Car Squadron

1st Lt. Benjamin H. Pochyla**	30 June 1932–ao January 1933	Unknown	ao January 1933–1 March 1939

**RAI commanders: O.R. officers.

Troop A (active 1928–39)

Capt. Harold G. Holt	15 February 1928–27 November 1932	Maj. John C. McDonald	9 March 1933–24 January 1935
1st Lt. Hubert W. Ketchum Jr.	27 November 1932–9 March 1933	Capt. Rogers A. Gardner	24 January 1935–19 November 1937
Capt. Claude W. Feagin	19 November 1937–1 July 1939		

2d Armored Car Squadron (2d Cavalry Division)
2d Reconnaissance Squadron (1939–41)
92d Reconnaissance Squadron (1941)

HQ—*Not organized,* 1928–31; Des Moines, IA, 1931–41; Fort Riley, KS, 1941

Constituted in the R.A. on 16 October 1928 and assigned to the 2d Cav. Div. The 1st Provisional Platoon, Troop A, 2d Armd. Car Sq. (Troop A constituted on 17 September 1928 as the 2d Armd. Car Troop; redesignated Troop A, 2d Armd. Car Sq. on 16 October 1928) organized on 28 February 1929 at Fort Holabird, MD. The 1st Provisional Platoon transferred on 1 May 1929 to Fort George G. Meade, MD. Platoon expanded and reorganized on 13 August 1930 as Troop A. Troop A was attached to the Mechanized Force at Fort George G. Meade, MD, 1930–31, as the reconnaissance element. Remainder of squadron allotted to the Seventh Corps Area. Organized by March 1931 with O.R. personnel as an RAI unit with HQ at Des Moines, IA. Troop A transferred to Camp Knox, KY, on 10 November 1931, with the remnants of the inactivated mechanized force and attached to the mechanized cavalry regiment. Attached to the 7th Cav. Brig. (Mecz) on 1 March 1932. Troop A inactivated at Fort Knox on 16 January 1933 and personnel transferred to the 1st Cav. Regt. (Mecz). Typically conducted Inactive Training Period meetings at Fort Des Moines and the Federal Building in Des Moines. Reserve officers assigned to the squadron conducted summer training with the 2d Cav. Regt. at Fort Riley, KS, 1932–40. Redesignated 2d Rcn. Sq. on 1 March 1939. Entire squadron activated in April 1941, less Reserve personnel, at Fort Riley, KS, as an element of the 2d Cav. Div. Redesignated 92d Rcn. Sq. on 8 May 1941. Location 7 December 1941—Fort Riley, KS.

Events: 98, 128, 301

Commanders, 2d Armored Car Squadron

Capt. John Bullock**	ao March 1931–ao April 1931	Capt. F. M. Seeley**	ao July 1933–ao January 1934
Unknown	ao April 1931–ao July 1933	Unknown	ao January 1934–ao March 1937
Maj. George E. Westman**	ao March 1937–April 1941		

**RAI commanders: O.R. officers.

Troop A (active 1929–33)

Capt. Lawrence C. Frizzell	31 May 1929–30 June 1929	Capt. Lawrence C. Frizzell	3 July 1929–25 April 1930
Maj. Clarence C. Benson	30 June 1929–3 July 1929	Capt. Charles H. Unger	28 February 1929–16 January 1933

3d Armored Car Squadron (3d Cavalry Division)
3d Reconnaissance Squadron (1939–40)

HQ—*Not organized,* 1928–31; Des Moines, IA, 1931–40

Constituted in the R.A. on 16 October 1928, assigned to the 3d Cav. Div., and allotted to the Seventh Corps Area. Organized by March 1931 with O.R. personnel as an RAI unit with HQ at Des Moines, IA. Typically conducted Inactive Training Period meetings at Fort Des Moines and the Federal Building in Des Moines. Conducted summer training with the 2d Cav. Regt. at Fort Riley, KS, 1936–40. Redesignated 3d Rcn. Sq. on 1 March 1939. Disbanded on 10 October 1940.

Commanders, 3d Armored Car Squadron

Maj. William A. Heap**	ao March 1931–ao June 1934	Unknown	ao June 1934–ao March 1937
Maj. Edward M. Brown**	ao March 1937–10 October 1940		

**RAI commanders: O.R. officers.

4th Armored Car Squadron (I Cavalry Corps)
4th Reconnaissance Squadron (1939–40)

HQ—Omaha, NE, 1933–41

Constituted in the R.A. on 1 October 1933, allotted to the Seventh Corps Area, and assigned to the I Cavalry Corps. Organized about December 1933 with O.R. personnel as an RAI unit with HQ at Omaha, NE. Conducted summer training with the 14th Cav. at Fort Des Moines, IA, 1934–40. Redesignated 4th Rcn. Sq. on 1 March 1939. Disbanded on 10 October 1940.

Commanders, 4th Armored Car Squadron

Unknown	December 1933–22 November 1937	Capt. Verne J. Chadsey**	22 November 1937–16 February 1938
Unknown	16 February 1938–10 October 1940		

**RAI commanders: O.R. officers.

7th Reconnaissance and Support Squadron (Mechanized) (7th Cavalry Brigade)

HQ—Fort Knox, KY, 1940

Constituted in the R.A. on 22 April 1940 and assigned to the 7th Cav. Brig. Activated on 1 June 1940 at Fort Knox, KY. Reorganized and redesignated 1st Rcn. Bn. (Armd.) on 15 July 1940 and assigned to the 1st Armd. Div.

Events: 295, 296, 302

Status: Active in the R.A. at Badingen, Germany, as the 1st Sq., 1st Cav.

Commander, 7th Reconnaissance and Support Squadron

Maj. Harrison H.G. Heiberg — 1 June 1940–1 November 1940

121st Armored Car Squadron (21st Cavalry Division)
21st Reconnaissance Squadron (1939–40)

Massachusetts and Connecticut/ New York National Guard

HQ—*Not organized,* 1928–39; Boston, MA, 1939–40; New York City, NY, 1940

Constituted in the N.G. on 19 December 1928 as the 121st Armd. Car Sq. and assigned to the 21st Cav. Div. Redesignated 21st Rcn. Sq. in January 1939 and allotted to the states of Massachusetts and Connecticut. HQ organized on 1 July 1939 and federally recognized at Boston, MA. Withdrawn from the states of Massachusetts and Connecticut on 1 July 1940 and concurrently allotted to the state of New York. Organized on 1 July 1940 at New York City, NY, and federally recognized on 9 August 1940. Squadron disbanded on 30 September 1940.

Events: 301

Commander, 21st Reconnaissance Squadron

Maj. Harold A. Rose 1 July 1939–30 September 1940

122d Armored Car Squadron (22d Cavalry Division)
22d Reconnaissance Squadron (1939–40)

Michigan/Ohio National Guard

HQ—*Not organized,* 1928–39; Cincinnati, OH, 1939–40

Constituted in the N.G. on 19 December 1928 as the 122d Armd. Car Sq., assigned to the 22d Cav. Div., and allotted to the state of Michigan. Detroit, MI, designated as HQ on organization, but the unit was never organized at that location. Withdrawn from the state of Michigan on 15 September 1939, redesignated 22d Rcn. Sq., and allotted to the state of Ohio. HQ concurrently organized and federally recognized at Cincinnati, OH. Squadron redesignated 1st Sq., 107th Cav. (H&M) on 1 November 1940.

Status: Active in the Ohio N.G. as Headquarters and Headquarters Detachment (HHD), 512th Engr. Bn.

Events: 302

Commander, 22d Reconnaissance Squadron

Maj. William W. Johnson 15 September 1939–1 November 1940

123d Armored Car Squadron (23d Cavalry Division)
23d Reconnaissance Squadron (1939–40)

Illinois National Guard

HQ—*Not organized,* 1928–40; Springfield, IL, 1940

Constituted in the N.G. on 19 December 1928 as the 123d Armd. Car Sq. and assigned to the 23d Cav. Div. Redesignated 23d Rcn. Sq. on 1 January 1940 and allotted to the state of Illinois. HQ organized and federally recognized on 16 January 1940 at Springfield, IL. Squadron redesignated 2d Sq., 106th Cav. (H&M) on 1 September 1940.

Status: Active in the Illinois N.G. as the 106th Cavalry; Troop E active at Rocks Falls, IL, as an element of the 33d Infantry Brigade.

Events: 302

Commander, 23d Reconnaissance Squadron

Maj. Mark Plaisted 15 January 1940–1 September 1940

124th Armored Car Squadron (24th Cavalry Division) **Wyoming National Guard**
24th Reconnaissance Squadron (1939–40)

HQ—*Not organized,* 1928–39; Torrington, WY, 1939–40

Constituted in the N.G. on 19 December 1928 as the 124th Armd. Car Sq. and assigned to the 24th Cav. Div. Allotted to the state of Wyoming on 1 February 1939. Redesignated 24th Rcn. Sq. on 1 April 1939. HQ concurrently organized and federally recognized at Torrington, WY. Squadron HQ disbanded on 26 October 1940, remainder of the squadron absorbed as elements of the 115th Cav. Regt. (H&M).

Events: 304

Commander, 24th Reconnaissance Squadron

Maj. Andrew W. Willis	7 April 1939–26 October 1940

461st Armored Car Squadron (61st Cavalry Division) **Organized Reserve New York**
461st Reconnaissance Squadron (1939–41)

HQ—Albany, NY, 1928–41

Constituted in the O.R. on 20 December 1928, assigned to the 61st Cav. Div., and allotted to the Second Corps Area. Initiated on 20 December 1928 with HQ at Albany, NY, by transfer of personnel from the 151st Machine Gun (MG) Sq. Consolidated on 11 September 1929 with the reconstituted 151st MG Sq. (constituted on 15 October 1921 and organized in February 1922 with HQ at Albany, NY; demobilized on 20 December 1928; reconstituted on 11 September 1929). Conducted summer training at numerous locations to include Fort George G. Meade, MD; Fort Ethan Allen, VT; Miller Field, NY; and Fort Knox, KY, 1929–41. Redesignated 461st Rcn. Sq. on 1 March 1939. Location 7 December 1941—Albany, NY.

Status: Disbanded 30 January 1942.

Events: 173

Commanders, 461st Armored Car Squadron

Lt. Col. Edgar C. Niles	20 December 1928–ao October 1933	Maj. Albert O. Dodge	24 July 1940–18 December 1940
Maj. Frank A. Willard	ao June 1934–23 November 1939	Capt. Robert S. Johnson	18 December 1940–15 November 1941
Capt. Arthur Matz	23 November 1939–24 July 1940	Maj. Frank A. Willard	15 November 1941–ao December 1941

462d Armored Car Squadron (62d Cavalry Division) **Organized Reserve District of Columbia,**
462d Reconnaissance Squadron (1939–41) **Pennsylvania, and Virginia**

HQ—*Not initiated,* 1928–29; Philadelphia, PA, 1929–32; Washington, DC, 1932–41

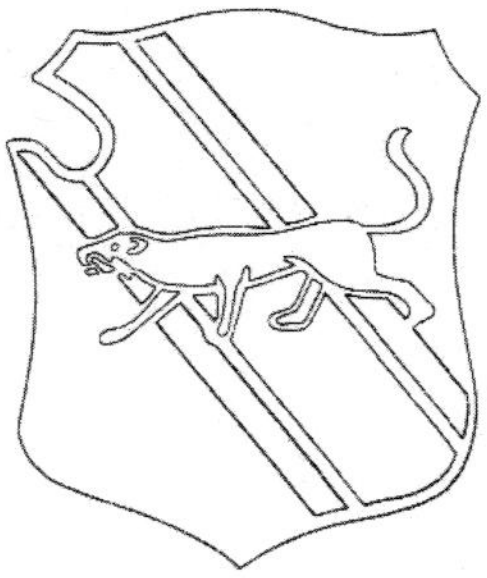

Constituted in the O.R. on 20 December 1928, assigned to the 62d Cav. Div., and allotted to the Third Corps Area. Initiated on 4 January 1929 with HHD at Philadelphia, PA, Troop A at Philadelphia, Troop B at Richmond, VA, and Troop C at Pittsburgh, PA. HHD relocated on 4 January 1932 to Washington, DC. Typically conducted Inactive Training Period meetings at the Munitions Building in Washington. Conducted summer training most years with the 3d Cav. Regt. at Fort Myer, VA, and some years with the 1st Cav. Regt. at Fort Knox, KY. Redesignated 462d Rcn. Sq. on 1 March 1939. Location 7 December 1941—Washington, DC.

Status: Disbanded 30 January 1942.

Commanders, 462d Armored Car Squadron

Maj. William L. Covington	20 December 1928–ao February 1934	Unknown	ao February 1934–ao April 1935
Maj. William J. Yetton	ao April 1935–ao August 1941		

463d Armored Car Squadron (63d Cavalry Division) **Organized Reserve Tennessee/North Carolina**
463d Reconnaissance Squadron (1939–41)

HQ—Memphis, TN, 1928–31; Asheville, NC, 1931–41

Constituted in the O.R. on 20 December 1928, assigned to the 63d Cav. Div., and allotted to the Fourth Corps Area. Initiated on 20 December 1928 at Memphis, TN, by transfer of personnel from the 309th Cav. HHD relocated on 10 November 1931 to Asheville, NC. Conducted summer training most years with the 6th Cav. Regt. at Fort Oglethorpe, GA, and some years with the 1st Cav. Regt. (Mecz) at Fort Knox, KY. Redesignated 463d Rcn. Sq. on 1 March 1939. Location 7 December 1941—Asheville, NC.

Status: Disbanded 30 January 1942.

Commanders, 463d Armored Car Squadron

Maj. Jefferson B. Osborn	20 December 1928–ao June 1932	Unknown	ao June 1933–ao June 1935
Capt. Wilton B. Carson	ao May 1933–ao June 1933	Maj. John C. Carter	ao June 1935–ao August 1936
Maj. Joel W. Clayton	ao June 1937–ao January 1941		

464th Armored Car Squadron (64th Cavalry Division) **Organized Reserve Kentucky/West Virginia**
464th Reconnaissance Squadron (1939–41)

HQ—Ashland, KY, 1928–37; Wheeling, WV, 1937–41

Constituted in the O.R. on 20 December 1928, assigned to the 64th Cav. Div., and allotted to the Fifth Corps Area. Initiated on 20 December 1928 at Ashland, KY, by transfer of personnel from the demobilized 157th MG Sq. HHD relocated on 5 April 1937 to Wheeling, WV. Conducted summer training with troops of the 6th Cav. Regt. and 1st Cav. Regt. (Mecz) at Fort Knox, KY. Redesignated 464th Rcn. Sq. on 1 March 1939. Location 7 December 1941—Wheeling, WV.

Status: Disbanded 30 January 1942.

Commanders, 464th Armored Car Squadron

Maj. Bruce M. McDill	28 December 1928–ao June 1936	Maj. Harry E. Erickson	ao June 1937–ao June 1938
Unknown	ao June 1938–7 December 1941		

465th Armored Car Squadron (65th Cavalry Division) **Organized Reserve Michigan**
465th Reconnaissance Squadron (1939–41)

HQ—Detroit, MI, 1928–41

Constituted in the O.R. on 20 December 1928, assigned to the 65th Cav. Div., and allotted to the Sixth Corps Area. Initiated on 20 December 1928 at Detroit, MI, by transfer of personnel from the demobilized 160th MG Sq. Conducted summer training with the 14th Cav. Regt. at Fort Sheridan, IL, and some years with the 1st Cav. Regt. (Mecz) at Fort Knox, KY. Redesignated 465th Rcn. Sq. on 1 March 1939. Location 7 December 1941—Detroit, MI.

Status: Disbanded 30 January 1942.

Commanders, 465th Armored Car Squadron

Maj. James E. Murphy	28 December 1928–24 April 1934	Maj. Paul H. Todd	24 April 1934–ao January 1935
Unknown	ao January 1935–7 December 1941		

466th Armored Car Squadron (66th Cavalry Division) **Organized Reserve Missouri**
466th Reconnaissance Squadron (1939–41)

HQ—*Not initiated,* 1928–29; Kansas City, MO, 1929–41

Constituted in the O.R. on 20 December 1928, assigned to the 66th Cav. Div., and allotted to the Seventh Corps Area. Initiated on 1 July 1929 at Kansas City, MO. Conducted summer training with Troop A, 2d Armd. Car Sq. and 2d Cav. Regt. at Fort Riley, KS. Conducted cavalry CMTC at Fort Leavenworth, KS, in 1933 as an alternate form of summer training. Redesignated 466th Rcn. Sq. on 1 March 1939. Location 7 December 1941—Kansas City, MO.

Status: Disbanded 30 January 1942.

Commanders, 466th Armored Car Squadron

Unknown	1 July 1929–ao March 1931	Unknown	ao July 1934–ao March 1936
Capt. Edward S. Fonda	ao March 1931–April 1931	Maj. A.C. Bradley	ao March 1936–ao September 1936
Maj. Thomas C. Swanson	April 1931–ao July 1934	Unknown	ao September 1936–7 December 1941

Part IV

Field Artillery Organizations

1919–41

Chapter 18

Field Artillery Major Commands

USASC Photo, NA II

Reserve officers calculating firing data on the field artillery range at Camp Custer, MI.

There were two types of major artillery commands in the interwar army. These were the 6 army and 18 corps artillery headquarters. As their names imply, these headquarters provided command and control of artillery assigned or attached to them for various missions and operations at the army and corps level.

The army artillery consisted only of the army artillery headquarters and an army ammunition train. All other artillery and other support organizations that served as army artillery assets would be typically attached from the General Headquarters Reserve (GHQR). These assets were to be attached to the army artillery in the numbers and type needed for specific operations and transferred to other armies as the operational situation required. The intent was to achieve maximum use and effect from available artillery assets. An army that was assuming a defensive posture, for example, would require less artillery than one that was planning for an offensive. In such a situation, the General Headquarters (GHQ) would order the transfer of artillery and other assets from the defending army to the army that was soon to launch an offensive. As only divisional and corps artillery brigades had assigned ammunition trains, the army ammunition trains provided the resupply of ammunition to the attached GHQR artillery brigades and other assets attached to the army.

The corps artillery consisted of a corps artillery headquarters and a corps artillery brigade. The mission of the corps artillery was to coordinate the operations of the corps and divisional artillery brigades, as well as any GHQR artillery assets attached from the army artillery or directly from the GHQR.

Army Artillery, 1921

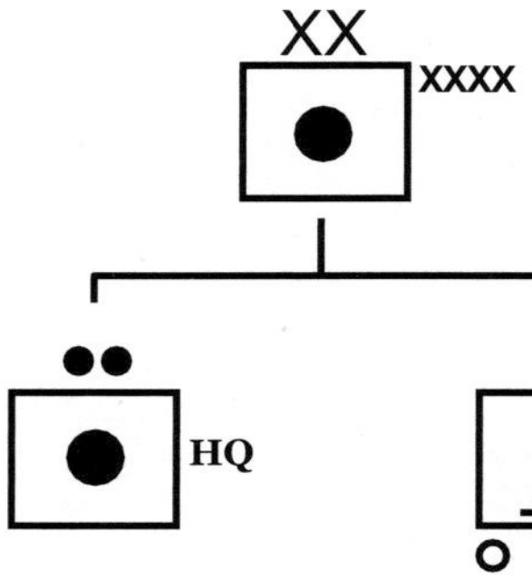

T/O:	254W
Approved:	13 September 1921
Commander:	Maj. Gen.
Officers:	63
W. O.	4
Enlisted:	648
Total:	715

The army artillery has no assigned units other than one army ammunition train. All other artillery assets are attached from the from the General Headquarters Reserve in the types and numbers needed for the mission at hand and reallocated to other armies or corps as needed.

<u>Key Equipment</u>:

Car, various	18
Trucks, various	191

Army artillery organization, 1921.

Corps Artillery, 1930

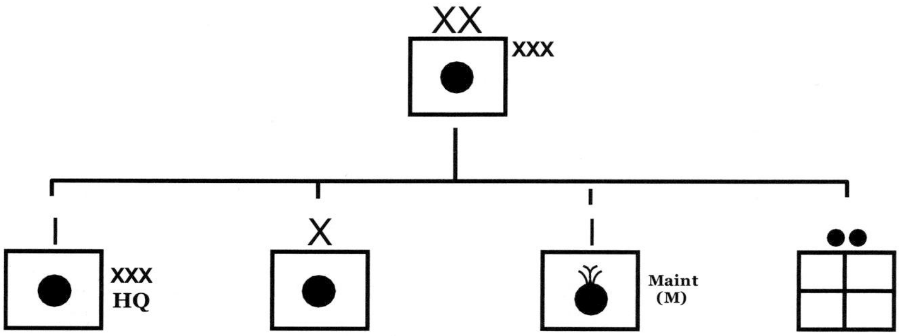

T/O:	118W
Effective:	1 July 1930
Commander:	Maj. Gen.
Officers:	327
W. O.	3
Enlisted:	6,360
Total:	6,690

<u>Key Equipment</u>:

Cars, various	158
Tractors, various	259
Trucks, various	687
Guns, 155-mm or 6-in	24
Howitzers, 155-mm	48
Machine guns, AA	83

Corps artillery organization, 1930.

All of the army and corps artillery headquarters, less those for the II and V Corps, were constituted in the Organized Reserve (O.R.) in 1921. The II and V Corps headquarters were constituted in the National Guard (N.G.) and allotted to the states of New York and Ohio, respectively. All army and corps artillery headquarters were withdrawn from their respective corps areas in September 1928 and presumably demobilized

First Army Artillery Headquarters (First Army) **Organized Reserve New York**

HQ—Manhattan, NY, 1921–28; *Inactive,* 1928–41

Subordinate elements—201st Coast Artillery (C.A.) Brigade (Brig.) (AA), 336th Ammunition (Ammo.) Train, 212th C.A. Regiment (Regt.) (AA), 213th C.A. Regt. (AA), 533d C.A. Regt. (AA), 386th Ordnance (Ord.) Company (Co.) (M)

Constituted in the O.R. on 15 October 1921, assigned to the First Army, and allotted to the Second Corps Area. Headquarters (HQ) initiated in February 1922 in Manhattan, NY. Withdrawn from the O.R. on 18 October 1927 and allotted to the Regular Army (R.A.). Withdrawn from the Second Corps Area on 5 September 1928.

Status: Disbanded on 20 March 1950.

Commanders, First Army Artillery Headquarters

Unknown	February 1922–5 September 1928

Second Army Artillery Headquarters (Second Army) **Organized Reserve Illinois**

HQ—Chicago, IL, 1922–28

Subordinate elements—202d C.A. Brig. (AA), 370th Ammo. Train, 525th C.A. Regt. (AA), 534th C.A. Regt. (AA), 535th C.A. Regt. (AA), 403d Ord. Co. (M)

Constituted in the O.R. on 15 October 1921, assigned to the Second Army, and allotted to the Sixth Corps Area. HQ initiated on 6 March 1922 in Chicago, IL. Withdrawn from the O.R. and Sixth Corps Area on 5 September 1928.

Commanders, Second Army Artillery Headquarters

Maj. Gordon Strong	6 March 1922–6 January 1923	Unknown	6 January 1923–5 September 1928

Third Army Artillery Headquarters (Third Army) **Organized Reserve Nebraska**

HQ—Lincoln, NE, 1922–28

Subordinate elements—203d C.A. Brig. (AA), 337th Ammo. Train, 536th C.A. Regt. (AA), 537th C.A. Regt. (AA), 538th C.A. Regt. (AA), 380th Ord. Co. (M)

Constituted in the O.R. on 15 October 1921, assigned to the Third Army, and allotted to the Seventh Corps Area. HQ initiated in May 1922 in Lincoln, NE. Withdrawn from the O.R. and Seventh Corps Area on 5 September 1928.

Commanders, Third Army Artillery Headquarters

Unknown	May 1922–5 September 1928

Fourth Army Artillery Headquarters (Fourth Army) **Organized Reserve Pennsylvania**

HQ—Erie, PA, 1922–28

Subordinate elements—198th C.A. Brig. (AA), 361st Ammo. Train, 521st C.A. Regt. (AA), 522d C.A. Regt. (AA), 523d C.A. Regt. (AA), 388th Ord. Co. (M)

Constituted in the O.R. on 15 October 1921, assigned to the Fourth Army, and allotted to the Third Corps Area. HQ initiated on 1 October 1922 in Erie, PA. Withdrawn from the O.R. and Third Corps Area on 5 September 1928.

Commanders, Fourth Army Artillery Headquarters

Unknown	1 October 1922–31 October 1923	Col. Charles E. N. Howard	31 October 1923–10 October 1927
Unknown	10 October 1927–5 September 1928		

Fifth Army Artillery Headquarters (Fifth Army) **Organized Reserve Indiana**

HQ—Indianapolis, IN, 1922–28

Subordinate elements—199th C.A. Brig. (AA), 362d Ammo. Train, 206th C.A. Regt. (AA), 524th C.A. Regt. (AA), 525th C.A. Regt. (AA), 384th Ord. Co. (M)

Constituted in the O.R. on 15 October 1921, assigned to the Fifth Army, and allotted to the Fifth Corps Area. HQ initiated in 1922 in Indianapolis, IN. Withdrawn from the O.R. and Fifth Corps Area on 5 September 1928.

Commanders, Fifth Army Artillery Headquarters

Unknown	ao December 1922–5 September 1928

Sixth Army Artillery Headquarters (Sixth Army) **Organized Reserve Missouri**

HQ—Kansas City, MO, 1922–28

Subordinate elements—200th C.A. Brig. (AA), 363d Ammo. Train, 527th C.A. Regt. (AA), 528th C.A. Regt. (AA), 529th C.A. Regt. (AA), 387th Ord. Co. (M)

Constituted in the O.R. on 15 October 1921, assigned to the Six Army, and allotted to the Seventh Corps Area. HQ initiated in March 1922 in Kansas City, MO. Withdrawn from the O.R. and Seventh Corps Area on 5 September 1928.

Commanders, Sixth Army Artillery Headquarters

Unknown	March 1922–5 September 1928

I Corps Artillery Headquarters (I Corps) **Organized Reserve Massachusetts**

HQ—Boston, MA, 1921–28

Subordinate elements—*81st Field Artillery (F.A.) Brig.,* 1921–23; 194th F.A. Brig., 1923–28; 360th Ord. Co. (M), 1921–28; *131st Ammo. Train,* 1921–23; *101st Observation (Obsn.) Battalion (Bn.),* 1921–23; 313th Obsn. Bn., 1923–28; 26th F.A. Regt. (RAI), 1923–28; *171st F.A. Regt.,* 1921–23; 172d F.A. Regt., 1921–28; *173d F.A. Regt.,* 1921–23; 192d F.A. Regt., 1921–28; 392d F.A. Regt., 1923–28

Constituted in the O.R. on 15 October 1921, assigned to the I Corps, and allotted to the First Corps Area. HQ initiated in February 1923 in Boston, MA. Withdrawn from the O.R. and Seventh Corps Area on 5 September 1928.

Commanders, I Corps Artillery Headquarters

Col. Harry L. Morse	February 1923–22 August 1925	Col. Harry L. Morse	23 January 1926–28 February 1927
Unknown	22 August 1925–23 January 1926	Unknown	28 February 1927–5 September 1928

II Corps Artillery Headquarters (II Corps) **New York National Guard**

HQ—*Not organized*, 1921–28

Subordinate elements—15th F.A. Brig. (RAI), 1923–28; 361st Ord. Co. (M), 1921–28; 132d Ammo. Train, 1921–24; 331st Ammo. Train, 1924–27; 15th Ammo. Train (RAI), 1927–28; *102d Obsn. Bn.,* 1921–23; 314th Obsn. Bn., 1923–27; 29th F.A. Regt. (RAI), 1923–28; 30th F.A. Regt. (RAI), 1923–28; 80th F.A. Regt. (RAI), 1923–28; 81st F.A. Regt. (RAI), 1923–28; 106th F.A. Regt., 1921–28; 258th F.A. Regt., 1921–28

Constituted in the N.G. on 15 October 1921, assigned to the II Corps, and allotted to the state of New York. Governor's Island, NY, designated as HQ on organization, but the unit was never organized at that location. Withdrawn from the Second Corps Area on 5 September 1928.

III Corps Artillery Headquarters (III Corps) **Organized Reserve Pennsylvania**

HQ—Norristown, PA, 1922–28

Subordinate elements—*82d F.A. Brig.,* 1921–23; 190th F.A. Brig., 1923–28; 362d Ord. Co. (M), 1921–28; 14th Ammo. Train, 1923–33 (RAI); 310th Obsn. Bn., 1921–28; 28th F.A. Regt. (RAI), 1921–28; 108th F.A. Regt., 1921–28; 176th F.A. Regt., 1921–28; 440th F.A. Regt., 1921–28

Constituted in the O.R. on 15 October 1921, assigned to the III Corps, and allotted to the Third Corps Area. HQ initiated on 18 April 1922 in Norristown, PA. Withdrawn from the O.R. and Seventh Corps Area on 5 September 1928.

Commanders, III Corps Artillery Headquarters

2d Lt. Charles A. Cressman	18 April 1922–ao October 1922	Unknown	October 1922–5 September 1928

IV Corps Artillery Headquarters (IV Corps) **Organized Reserve Georgia**

HQ—Atlanta, GA, 1922–28

Subordinate elements—13th F.A. Brig., 1923–28; 363d Ord. Co. (M), 1921–28; *133d Ammo. Train,* 1921–23; 13th Ammo. Train, 1923–28; 311th Obsn. Bn., 1921–23; 1st Obsn. Battery (Btry), 1923–28; 5th F.A. Regt. (RAI), 1923–28; 17th F.A. Regt. (RAI), 1923–28; 22d F.A. Regt. (RAI), 1923–28; 23d F.A. Regt. (RAI), 1923–28; 177th F.A. Regt., 1921–23; 178th F.A. Regt., 1921–23; 441st F.A. Regt., 1921–28

Constituted in the O.R. on 15 October 1921, assigned to the IV Corps, and allotted to the Fourth Corps Area. HQ initiated on 22 March 1922 in Atlanta, GA. Withdrawn from the O.R. and Fourth Corps Area on 5 September 1928.

Commanders, IV Corps Artillery Headquarters

Maj. Spencer Tunnell Jr.	22 March 1922–20 January 1925	Maj. James B. Conyers	20 January 1925–5 September 1928

V Corps Artillery Headquarters (V Corps) **Ohio National Guard**

HQ—*Not organized*, 1921–27

Subordinate elements—*83d F.A. Brig.,* 1921–23; 184th F.A. Brig., 1923–28; 364th Ord. Co. (M), 1921–28; *134th Ammo. Train,* 1921–23; 345th Ammo. Train, 1923–28; *103d Obsn. Bn.,* 1921–23; 315th Obsn. Bn., 1923–28; 29th F.A. Regt. (RAI), 1923–28; 150th F.A. Regt., 1921–28; *179th F.A. Regt.,* 1921–28; *180th F.A. Regt.,* 1921–23; 181st F.A. Regt., 1921–28; *194th F.A. Regt.,* 1921–23; 442d F.A. Regt., 1923–28

Constituted in the N.G. on 15 October 1921, assigned to the V Corps, and allotted to the state of Ohio. Withdrawn from the Ohio National Guard on 22 June 1927.

VI Corps Artillery Headquarters (VI Corps) **Organized Reserve Illinois**

HQ—Chicago, IL, 1922–28

Subordinate elements—*84th F.A. Brig.,* 1921–23; 184th F.A. Brig., 1923–28; 365th Ord. Co. (M), 1921–28; *135th Ammo. Train,* 1921–23; 346th Ammo. Train, 1923–28; 15th Obsn. Bn., 1923–28; 121st F.A. Regt., 1921–28; 123d F.A. Regt., 1921–28; 182d F.A. Regt., 1921–28; 442d F.A. Regt., 1921–23

Constituted in the O.R. on 15 October 1921, assigned to the VI Corps, and allotted to the Sixth Corps Area. HQ initiated on 15 March 1922 in Chicago, IL. Withdrawn from the Sixth Corps Area on 5 September 1928.

Commanders, VI Corps Artillery Headquarters

Maj. Robert W. Fernald	6 March 1922–6 January 1923	Maj. Harry C. Boardman	6 September 1923–11 January 1924
Maj. Gordon Strong	6 January 1923–6 September 1923	Unknown	11 January 1924–5 September 1928

VII Corps Artillery Headquarters (VII Corps) **Organized Reserve Minnesota**

HQ—Minneapolis, MN, 1922–28

Subordinate elements—14th F.A. Brig., 1923–28; 18th Ord. Co. (M), 1921–28; *136th Ammo. Train,* 1921–23; 335th Ammo. Train, 1923–27; 14th Obsn. Bn., 1923–28; 26th F.A. Regt. (RAI), 1923–28; 27th F.A. Regt. (RAI), 1923–28; 28th F.A. Regt. (RAI), 1923–28; *127th F.A. Regt.,* 1921–23; 185th F.A. Regt., 1921–28; *195th F.A. Regt.,* 1921–23; 443d F.A. Regt., 1921–28

Constituted in the O.R. on 15 October 1921, assigned to the VII Corps, and allotted to the Seventh Corps Area. HQ initiated in March 1922 in Minneapolis, MN. Withdrawn from the Seventh Corps Area on 5 September 1928.

Commanders, VII Corps Artillery Headquarters

Unknown	March 1922–5 September 1928

VIII Corps Artillery Headquarters (VIII Corps) **Organized Reserve Texas**

HQ—San Antonio, TX, 1922–28

Subordinate elements—*85th F.A. Brig.,* 1921–23; 187th F.A. Brig., 1923–28; 9th Ord. Co. (M), 1921–28; 15th Ammo. Train (RAI), 1923–28; 312th Obsn. Bn., 1921–23; 308th Obsn. Bn., 1923–28; *187th F.A. Regt.,* 1921–23; *188th F.A. Regt.,* 1921–23; 189th F.A. Regt., 1921–28; 410th F.A. Regt., 1923–28

Constituted in the O.R. on 15 October 1921, assigned to the VIII Corps, and allotted to the Eighth Corps Area. HQ initiated on 26 July 1922 in San Antonio, TX. Conducted summer training at Fort Sam Houston, TX. Withdrawn from the Eighth Corps Area on 5 September 1928.

Commanders, VIII Corps Artillery Headquarters

Maj. William G. Tobin	26 July 1922–ao May 1925	Unknown	ao December 1926–ao February 1928
Maj. Alfred G. Ranney	ao December 1925–ao December 1926	Maj. Frank H. Hicks	ao February 1928–5 September 1928

IX Corps Artillery Headquarters (IX Corps) **Organized Reserve California**

HQ—San Francisco, CA, 1922–28

Subordinate elements—*86th F.A. Brig.,* 1921–23; 189th F.A. Brig., 1923–28; 400th Ord. Co. (M), 1921–28; 332d Ammo. Train, 1923–28; 311th Obsn. Bn., 1921–28; 117th F.A. Regt., 1923–27; 178th F.A. Regt., 1923–28; *190th F.A. Regt.,* 1921–28; *191st F.A. Regt.,* 1921–23; *196th F.A. Regt.,* 1921–28

Constituted in the O.R. on 15 October 1921, assigned to the IX Corps, and allotted to the Ninth Corps Area. HQ initiated on 28 January 1922 in San Francisco, CA. Withdrawn from the Ninth Corps Area on 5 September 1928.

Commanders, IX Corps Artillery Headquarters

Lt. Col. Frederick W.H. Peterson	28 January 1922–1 May 1922	Col. William H. Williams	1 May 1922–ao May 1927
Unknown	ao May 1927–5 September 1928		

XI Corps Artillery Headquarters (XI Corps) **Organized Reserve Massachusetts**

HQ—Boston, MA, 1921–28

Subordinate elements—180th F.A. Brig., 1921–28; 351st Ord. Co. (M), 1921–28; 341st Ammo. Train, 1921–28; 301st Obsn. Bn., 1921–28; 388th F.A. Regt., 1921–28; 389th F.A. Regt., 1921–28; 390th F.A. Regt., 1921–28; 431st F.A. Regt., 1921–28

Constituted in the O.R. on 15 October 1921, assigned to the XI Corps, and allotted to the First Corps Area. HQ initiated on 28 November 1921 in Boston, MA. Withdrawn from the First Corps Area on 5 September 1928.

Commanders, XI Corps Artillery Headquarters

Col. John F. J. Herbert	28 November 1921–January 1924	Col. Henry O. Silsbee, II	January 1924–5 September 1928

XII Corps Artillery Headquarters (XII Corps) **Organized Reserve New Jersey**

HQ—Manhattan, NY, 1922–28

Subordinate elements—181st F.A. Brig., 1921–28; 352d Ord. Co. (M), 1921–28; 342d Ammo. Train, 1921–28; 302d Obsn. Bn., 1921–28; 306th F.A. Regt.; 309th F.A. Regt., 1921–28; 391st F.A. Regt., 1921–28; 432d F.A. Regt., 1921–28

Constituted in the O.R. on 15 October 1921, assigned to the XII Corps, and allotted to the Second Corps Area. HQ initiated on 15 March 1922 in Manhattan, NY. Withdrawn from the Second Corps Area on 5 September 1928.

Commanders, XII Corps Artillery Headquarters

Maj. Cornelius O'Connor	15 March 1922–28 November 1922	Col. Neil G. Finch	28 November 1922–17 May 1923
Col. John T. Delaney	17 August 1923–5 September 1928		

XIII Corps Artillery Headquarters (XIII Corps) **Organized Reserve Pennsylvania**

HQ—Altoona, PA, 1923–28

Subordinate elements—182d F.A. Brig., 1921–28; 353d Ord. Co. (M), 1921–28; 343d Ammo. Train, 1921–28; 303d Obsn. Bn., 1921–28; 394th F.A. Regt., 1921–28; 395th F.A. Regt., 1921–28; 396th F.A. Regt., 1921–28; 433d F.A. Regt., 1921–28

Constituted in the O.R. on 15 October 1921, assigned to the XIII Corps, and allotted to the Third Corps Area. HQ initiated on 17 March 1923 in Altoona, PA. Withdrawn from the Third Corps Area on 5 September 1928.

Commanders, XIII Corps Artillery Headquarters

Capt. William W. Eaton	17 March 1923–ao January 1924	Unknown	ao January 1924–5 September 1928

XIV Corps Artillery Headquarters (XIV Corps) **Organized Reserve Alabama**

HQ—Birmingham, AL, 1922–28

Subordinate elements—183d F.A. Brig., 1921–28; 354th Ord. Co. (M), 1921–28; 343d Ammo. Train, 1921–28; 303d Obsn. Bn., 1921–28; 397th F.A. Regt., 1921–28; 398th F.A. Regt., 1921–28; 399th F.A. Regt., 1921–28; 434th F.A. Regt., 1921–28

Constituted in the O.R. on 15 October 1921, assigned to the XIV Corps, and allotted to the Fourth Corps Area. HQ initiated on 22 March 1922 in Birmingham, AL. Withdrawn from the Fourth Corps Area on 5 September 1928.

Commanders, XIV Corps Artillery Headquarters

Capt. John P. Walker	22 March 1922–10 May 1923	Lt. Col. Hugh B. Hooper	10 May 1923–5 September 1928

XV Corps Artillery Headquarters (XV Corps) **Organized Reserve Ohio**

HQ—Cleveland, OH, 1922–28

Subordinate elements—184th F.A. Brig., 1921–23; 191st F.A. Brig., 1923–28; 355th Ord. Co. (M), 1921–28; 345th Ammo. Train, 1921–23; 333d Ammo. Train, 1923–28; 305th Obsn. Bn., 1921–28; 400th F.A. Regt., 1921–28; 401st F.A. Regt., 1921–28; 402d F.A. Regt., 1921–28; 435th F.A. Regt., 1921–28

Constituted in the O.R. on 15 October 1921, assigned to the XV Corps, and allotted to the Fifth Corps Area. HQ initiated in 1922 in Cleveland, OH. Withdrawn from the Fifth Corps Area on 5 September 1928.

Commanders, XV Corps Artillery Headquarters

Unknown	ao December 1922–5 September 1928

XVI Corps Artillery Headquarters (XVI Corps) **Organized Reserve Wisconsin**

HQ—Milwaukee, WI, 1922–28

Subordinate elements—185th F.A. Brig., 1921–23; 192d F.A. Brig., 1923–28; 356th Ord. Co. (M), 1921–28; 346th Ammo. Train, 1921–23; 334th Ammo. Train, 1923–28; 306th Obsn. Bn., 1921–28; 403d F.A. Regt., 1921–28; 404th F.A. Regt., 1921–28; 405th F.A. Regt., 1921–28; 436th F.A. Regt., 1921–28

Constituted in the O.R. on 15 October 1921, assigned to the XVI Corps, and allotted to the Sixth Corps Area. HQ initiated in October 1922 in Milwaukee, WI. Withdrawn from the Sixth Corps Area on 5 September 1928.

Commanders, XVI Corps Artillery Headquarters

Unknown	October 1922–5 September 1928

XVII Corps Artillery Headquarters (XVII Corps) **Organized Reserve Nebraska**

HQ—Omaha, NE, 1922–28

Subordinate elements—186th F.A. Brig., 1921–28; 357th Ord. Co. (M), 1921–28; 347th Ammo. Train, 1921–28; 307th Obsn. Bn., 1921–28; 406th F.A. Regt., 1921–28; 407th F.A. Regt., 1921–28; 408th F.A. Regt., 1921–28; 437th F.A. Regt., 1921–28

Constituted in the O.R. on 15 October 1921, assigned to the XVII Corps, and allotted to the Seventh Corps Area. HQ initiated in April 1922 in Omaha, NE. Withdrawn from the Seventh Corps Area on 5 September 1928.

Commanders, XVII Corps Artillery Headquarters

Unknown	April 1922–5 September 1928

XVIII Corps Artillery Headquarters (XVIII Corps) **Organized Reserve Texas**

HQ—San Antonio, TX, 1923–28

Subordinate elements—187th F.A. Brig., 1921–23; 358th Ord. Co. (M), 1921–28; 348th Ammo. Train, 1921–28; 308th Obsn. Bn., 1921–23; 312th Obsn. Bn., 1923–28; 393d F.A. Regt., 1923–28; 409th F.A. Regt., 1921–28; 410th F.A. Regt., 1921–23; 411th F.A. Regt., 1921–28; 438th F.A. Regt., 1921–28

Constituted in the O.R. on 15 October 1921, assigned to the XVIII Corps, and allotted to the Eighth Corps Area. HQ initiated by March 1922 in San Antonio, TX. Conducted summer training most years at Fort Sam Houston, TX. Withdrawn from the Eighth Corps Area on 5 September 1928.

Commanders, XVIII Corps Artillery Headquarters

Lt. Col. Ralph B. Fairchild	ao March 1922–5 September 1928

XIX Corps Artillery Headquarters (XIX Corps) **Organized Reserve California**

HQ—San Francisco, CA, 1922–28

Subordinate elements—188th F.A. Brig., 1921–28; 359th Ord. Co. (M), 1921–28; 349th Ammo. Train, 1921–28; 309th Obsn. Bn., 1921–28; 412th F.A. Regt., 1921–28; 413th F.A. Regt., 1921–28; 414th F.A. Regt., 1921–28; 439th F.A. Regt., 1921–28

Constituted in the O.R. on 15 October 1921, assigned to the XIX Corps, and allotted to the Ninth Corps Area. HQ initiated on 28 January 1922 in San Francisco, CA. Withdrawn from the Ninth Corps Area on 5 September 1928.

Commanders, XIX Corps Artillery Headquarters

Brig. Gen. Thornwell Mullally	28 January 1922–26 July 1922
Col. Ralph J. Faneuf	26 July 1922–17 May 1924
Brig. Gen. Adrian S. Fleming	17 May 1924–ao September 1925
Unknown	ao September 1925–ao January 1928
Lt. Col. George C. Ferch	ao January 1928–5 September 1928

Chapter 19

Field Artillery Brigades

USASC Photo, NA II

The 1st Artillery Brigade on occupation duty in Germany, 1919.

Field Artillery (F.A.) brigades provided command and control for assigned or attached field artillery regiments and other elements attached for operations. Their mission was to plan, coordinate, and conduct indirect and direct fire support for the ground gaining arms. The divisional brigades provided the direct support to the infantry and cavalry, while the corps and General Headquarters Reserve (GHQR) brigades provided counterbattery and deep interdiction fires.

Organization

Field Artillery brigades in this period consisted of several distinct types. There were divisional, corps, light, portee, and medium and heavy (M&H) brigades. Each type of brigade was designed to consist of at least a headquarters (HQ), HQ battery (Btry), and two or more field artillery regiments. In 1921, the divisional brigades were reorganized to consist of only two light 75-mm howitzer (H) horse-drawn regiments. The division's 155-mm H equipped medium artillery regiment was moved to the corps artillery brigade giving that unit four regiments: three 155-mm H regiments and one 155-mm gun (G) regiment. These brigades retained these respective structures until 1929 when the 155-mm H regiment was returned to the divisional brigades on the Army's adoption of a newer, more mobile, truck-drawn 155-mm H artillery piece. The corps brigades were correspondingly reduced by one 155-mm H regiment. The light, portee, and M&H brigades were assigned to the GHQR. The first two types of GHQR brigades consisted of a HQ, HQ Btry, and three 75-mm truck-drawn or portee transport battalions. The M&H brigades did not appear to

Field Artillery Brigade, Infantry Division, 1921

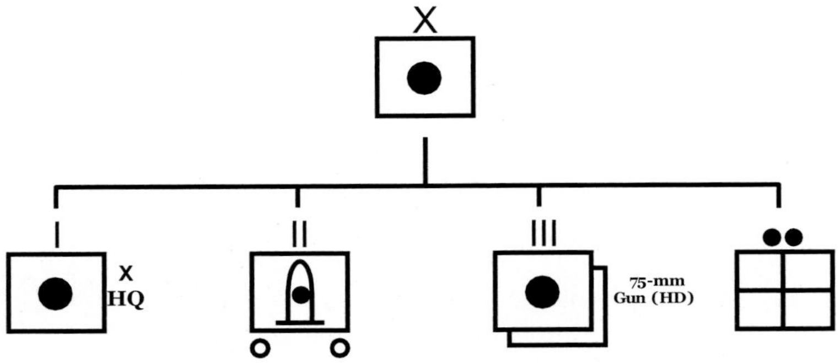

T/O:	31W
Approved:	20 January 1921
Commander:	Brig. Gen.
Officers:	169
W. O.	4
Enlisted:	3,227
Total:	3,400

<u>Key Equipment</u>:	
Cars, various	10
Horses & Mules	3,432
Trucks, various	36
Guns, 75-mm	48
Wagons	151
Machine guns, AA	42

Field Artillery Brigade, Medium & Heavy, GHQR, 1921

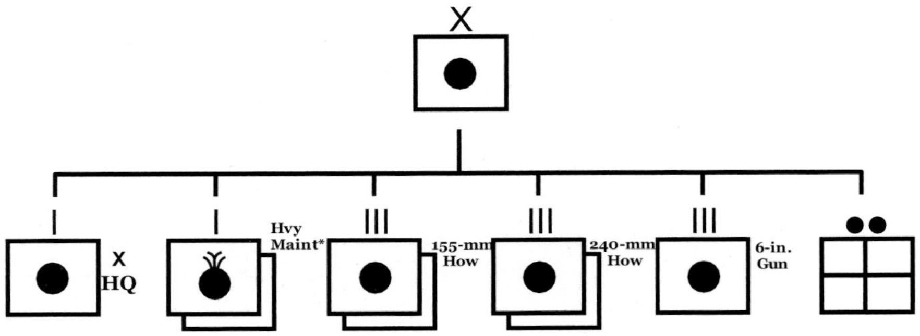

T/O:	
Approved:	
Commander:	Brig. Gen.
Officers:	
W. O.	
Enlisted:	
Total:	

<u>Key Equipment</u>:	
Cars, various	
Tractors, various	
Trucks, various	
Howitzers, 155-mm	48
Howitzers, 240-mm	48
Guns, 6-in.	24
Machine guns, AA	

* The two ordnance companies (HM) are attached units only.

Field artillery brigade organizations, 1921.

Field Artillery Brigade, Light, GHQR, 1921

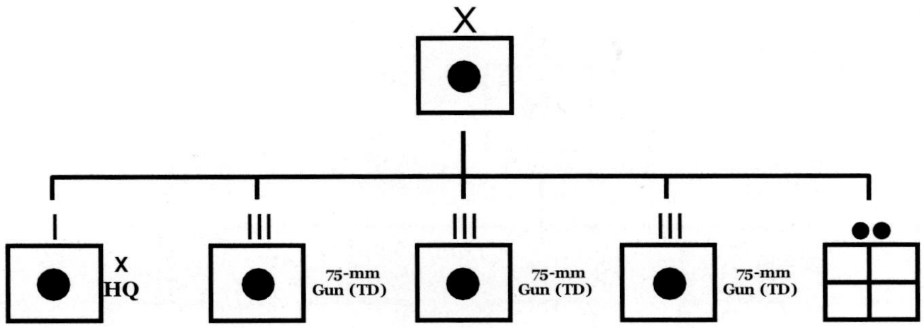

T/O:	517 1/2W
Approved:	15 December 1921
Commander:	Brig. Gen.
Officers:	219
W. O.	5
Enlisted:	3,612
Total:	3,836

Key Equipment:	
Cars, various	87
Trucks, various	131
Guns, 75-mm	72
Machine guns, AA	36

Field Artillery Brigade, Portée, GHQR, 1921

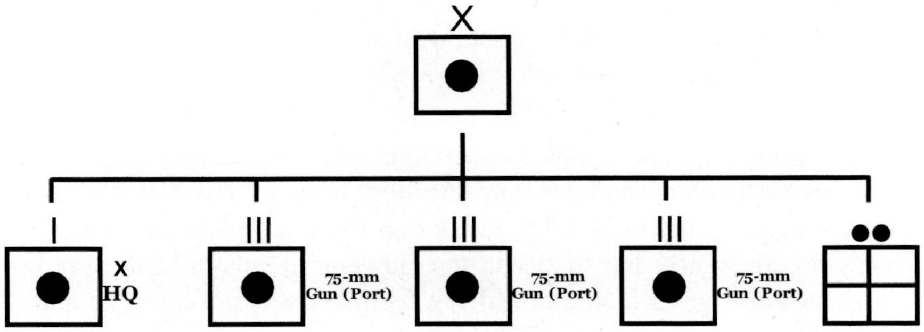

T/O:	522W
Approved:	29 November 1921
Commander:	Brig. Gen.
Officers:	219
W. O.	2
Enlisted:	2,622
Total:	2,843

Key Equipment:	
Cars, various	78
Tractors, 3-Ton	18
Trucks, various	242
Guns, 75-mm	72
Machine guns, AA	36

Field artillery brigade, organizations, 1921.

Field Artillery Brigade, Corps Artillery, 1930

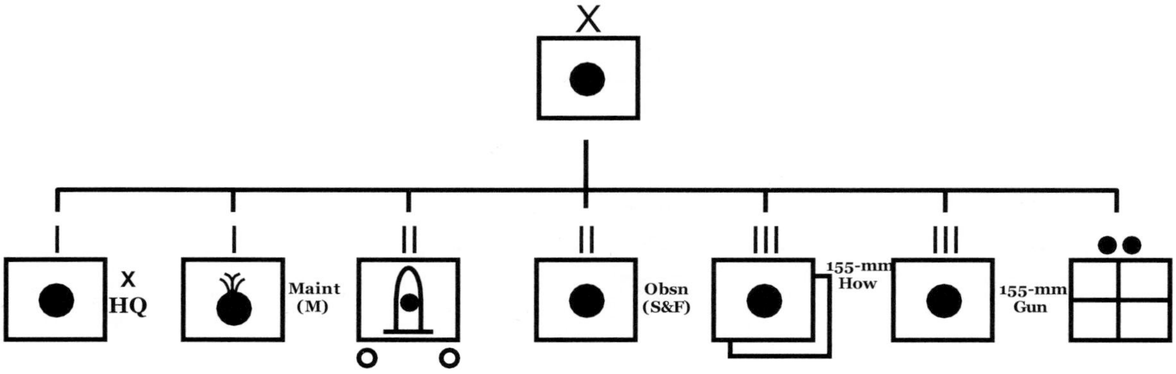

T/O:	131W
Approved:	1 July 1930
Commander:	Brig. Gen.
Officers:	314
W. O.	3
Enlisted:	6,312
Total:	6,629

Key Equipment:	
Cars, various	153
Tractors, various	259
Trucks, various	705
Guns, 155-mm or 6-in	24
Howitzers, 155-mm	48
Machine guns, AA	83

Field artillery brigade, corps artillery, 1930.

have a standardized table of organization (T/O), but typically consisted of two 155-mm H, two 240-mm H, and one 6-inch G regiments, and two attached ordnance companies (heavy maintenance). All of the M&H regiments were truck-drawn. The GHQR brigades were controlled by the General Headquarters (GHQ) and attached to, or withdrawn from, the army artillery based on current and future operational requirements.

For most of the period between 1921 and 1939, there were only five active Regular Army (R.A.) artillery brigades—four with active divisions and one corps artillery brigade. The 11th F.A. Brigade (Brig.) in Hawaii had the distinction of being the only fully active and three-regiment divisional brigade after 1921. War Department planners apparently felt that with the Hawaiian Division's mission being to hold fixed locations on Oahu, the mobility of its medium artillery regiment was not an issue and the division was authorized to retain it. The other three active divisional brigades not only lost their medium regiment, but were also eventually forced to inactivate parts of their existing regiments as well. The one active corps artillery brigade, the 13th at Fort Bragg, also inactivated bits and pieces of its active regiments. By 1930, however, the Army was able to begin reorganizing its artillery organizations and through efficiencies, was able to reactivate the 4th and 6th F.A. Brig. HQs in 1935 and 1934, respectively. In October 1939, all of the divisional brigade headquarters and headquarters batteries (HHBs) were disbanded in accordance with the triangular division T/O.

Each of the inactive R.A. divisional brigades were organized as Regular Army Inactive (RAI) units at various times during 1926 or later. Like almost all brigade and higher RAI commands, these units did not function as actual HQ and only a few were functional units. Most of the brigade HQ were essentially pool units or were used for mobilization assignments. Only a few of the corps artillery brigades and none of the GHQR brigades were organized as RAI units after 1926, although a significant increase in the number of RAI field artillery brigades in these categories were constituted in 1933.

There were 18 divisional and 6 corps brigades constituted or reconstituted in the National Guard (N.G.) in 1920–21. All of the divisional brigades were organized in the interwar period, but none of the corps brigades. In 1923, all six of the corps brigades were designated as Deferred National Guard (DNG) units, placed on the deferred list, and transferred to the Organized Reserve (O.R.). All but one were demobilized between 1927 and 1933. Six more N.G. corps brigades were constituted and organized during 1940–41 as part of the mobilization for World War II.

Not including the six DNG brigades, there were 62 field artillery brigades constituted in the O.R. in the 1920s. Of these, 27 were divisional brigades, 17 were corps brigades, 5 were light brigades, 6 were portee brigades, and 7 were M&H brigades. All of the divisional and corps brigades and most of the others were organized at some point in the interwar period. Many of the corps brigades were demobilized in 1933 and replaced in the Army's mobilization plans by RAI brigades. Some GHQR brigades were never organized and many were demobilized or inactivated by 1933, but not replaced in the mobilization plans.

Most of the Reserve divisional brigades (and a few of the others) were functional units. A number of divisional and corps brigades occasionally functioned as command and control HQ during the inactive training period. On the other hand, few of the GHQR brigades were functional units. Most were pool units used for mobilization assignments. The most active brigades were generally commanded by a Reserve senior colonel or brigadier general, though most possessed lieutenant colonels or majors as acting commanders, but who exercised no control over the brigade's subordinate regiments.

Training

The training of R.A. field artillery brigades was conducted in a variety of venues in the interwar period and as with all units in this period, the venues were dictated by budgetary constraints and other available resources. Though the desire of the three stateside infantry division commanders was to assemble their divisions and brigades at least once a year for collective maneuver training, this was not possible given the lack of training dollars. This was particularly true for the 1st and 3d F.A. Brigs., which were spread up and down the east and west coasts, respectively. The 2d F.A. Brig. was luckier as it was largely concentrated at Fort Sam Houston, TX, throughout most of this period.

N.G. field artillery brigade headquarters and headquarters batteries (HHB) typically performed their drills during the inactive training period at their home armories one night a week or on the weekend depending on the planned training. The HQ and staff usually focused on staff skills while the various HQ battery sections focused on support tasks. Occasionally, N.G. brigade HQ participated in division or higher-level command post exercises (CPXs) as part of their inactive training. Brigades assigned to single state divisions generally attended summer training at the same time as the rest of the division. For maneuver training at summer camp, multistate brigades usually attended camp with their parent division, while brigade regiments from other states trained with units of their own state. Several multistate divisions were able to assemble subordinate brigades from other states at a division camp in a few instances in the interwar years. Except for the army-level maneuvers in the late 1930s and early 1940s, however, combined camps for multistate divisions were uncommon. In many states, N.G. brigades rotated maneuver and live-fire training on a biennial basis. For example, for maneuver training one year, the Texas N.G.'s 61st F.A. Brig. would attend camp at Camp Hulen with the rest of the 36th Division (Div.). The following year, the brigade would go to Camp Bullis, TX, near San Antonio to conduct live-fire training. For many Guard brigades, maneuver and live-fire training were conducted at the same installation but rotated every other year.

Though most O.R. divisional brigade HHB functioned as units, their inactive training assemblies tended to be conducted with one of their subordinate regiments or with another HQ. Only occasionally did these brigades hold training periods that were conducted solely with the brigade's assigned personnel. Most of the brigades functioned as actual command and control HQ during summer training camps only if they participated in a division or corps area CPX. Usually, if a senior officer was not already assigned to command the brigade, the senior regimental commander temporarily filled in as commander for the camp. More often the brigade's personnel would attend the summer training attached to one of the brigade's subordinate regiments. In some cases, the brigade HHB personnel would be attached directly to R.A. or N.G. field artillery brigades for the summer training period or during major maneuvers.

In the case of the other types of O.R. field artillery brigades, few functioned as units and fewer were ever ordered to camp as units. Most often, the personnel of those brigades were ordered to camp as individuals attached to subordinate regiments or other brigades.

HHD, Provisional Field Artillery Brigade, Philippine Division (Philippine Division)

HQ—Fort McKinley, PI, 1941

Subordinate elements—1st Battalion (Bn.), 23d F.A., 1941; 24th F.A. (PS), 1941; 1st Bn., 86th F.A., 1941; 1st Bn., 88th F.A., 1941; 2d Bn., 88th F.A., 1941

Organized provisionally in the R.A. on 18 June 1941 at Fort McKinley, Philippines, and assigned to the Philippine Division. Organized to provide command and control for the artillery units of the Philippine Division in anticipation of the reactivation of the division's 12th F.A. Brig. Location 7 December 1941—Fort McKinley, Philippines.

Commander, Provisional Field Artillery Brigade

Brig. Gen. Ernest P. King	18 June 1941–4 November 1941

HHD, Fort Bragg Provisional Field Artillery Brigade (GHQR)

HQ—Fort Bragg, NC, 1941

Subordinate elements—4th, 6th, and 97th F.A. Bns.; 47th, 72d, 79th, and 112th F.A. Regiments (Regts.); and 3d and 7th Observation (Obsn.) Bns., 1941

Organized provisionally in the R.A. on 1 August 1941 at Fort Bragg, NC, and assigned to the GHQR. Organized to relieve the 13th F.A. Brig. of the responsibility of administrative and tactical control of the GHQR F.A. units at Fort Bragg. Attached to the First Army. Location 7 December 1941—Fort Bragg, NC.

Status: Disbanded on 8 July 1942 as Headquarters and Headquarters Battery (HHB), 12th F.A. Brig.

Events: 330

Commanders, Provisional Field Artillery Brigade

Col. John T. Kennedy	August 1941–20 November 1941	Col. Walter W. Hess Jr.	20 November 1941–June 1942

HHD, 1st Provisional Field Artillery Brigade **Organized Reserve Illinois**

HQ—Taylorville, IL, 1932–37

Subordinate elements—75th F.A. (RAI), 1935–37; 403d F.A., 1932–35; 497th F.A., 1932–37; 567th F.A.(RAI), 1932–37

Organized provisionally in the O.R. in February 1932 with HQ at Taylorville, IL, in accordance with Sixth Corps Area letter dated 8 February 1932. Reorganized in accordance with Special Order #6, HQ, Illinois Reserve District, dated 8 January 1935, which relieved the 403d F.A. and assigned the 75th F.A. (RAI). Established to provide command and control for the nondivisional field artillery units of the Illinois Reserve District. Discontinued in June 1937.

Commander, 1st Provisional Field Artillery Brigade

Col. George G. Seaman	February 1932–June 1937

HHB, 1st Field Artillery Brigade (1st Division)

HQ—Camp Zachary Taylor, KY, 1919–20; Camp Dix, NJ, 1920–22; Montauk, LI, NY, 1922; Fort Hoyle, MD, 1922–39

Subordinate elements—6th and 7th F.A. Regts. and 1st Ammunition (Ammo.) Train (Tn.), 1919–39; 5th F.A., 1919–20 and 1929–39

Arrived at the port of Hoboken on 5 September 1919 on the U.S.S. *Zeppelin* as an element of the 1st Div. after 9 months of occupation duty near Coblenz, Germany. Participated in the 1st Div. victory parade down 5th Avenue in New York City on 10 September 1919 and in Washington, DC, on 17 September 1919. Temporarily posted to Camp George G. Meade, MD, where emergency personnel were discharged. Transferred on 4 October 1919 to Camp Zachary Taylor, KY. Transferred on 26 September 1920 to Camp Dix, NJ. Transferred in May 1922 to Montauk, LI, NY. Entire brigade, less the 7th F.A., transferred on 18 October 1922 to Fort Hoyle, MD. Participated in the division parade down 5th Avenue in New York City on 3 September 1924 during the massive reunion of the Society of the 1st Div. Brigade units provided training assistance each summer to artillery elements of the 76th, 94th, and 97th Divs., and XI Corps at Fort Ethan Allen, VT; 77th, 78th, and 98th Div., and XII Corps at Pine Camp, NY, and Camp Dix, NJ; and 79th, 80th, and 99th Divs., and XIII Corps at Fort Hoyle, MD. Subordinate regiments typically participated in brigade-level field training in late summer and early fall at Pine Camp and Camp George G. Meade, MD, before returning to home stations. Disbanded 16 October 1939 at Fort Hoyle.

Status: Active in the R.A. in Germany as HHB, 1st Infantry (Inf.) Div. Artillery (Arty.).

Events: 38, 60, 63, 66, 72, 89, 98, 106, 109, 153, 155, 168, 191, 240, 280, 287, 292, 296, 301, 323, 330

Commanders, 1st Field Artillery Brigade

Brig. Gen. William S. McNair	May 1919–June 1919
Brig. Gen. Augustine McIntyre	June 1919–September 1919
Col. Upton Birnie	September 1919–January 1920
Col. Samuel C. Harrison Jr.	January 1920–September 1920
Brig. Gen. Dwight Aultman	September 1920–16 September 1921
Col. Henry L. Newbold	16 September 1921–18 October 1921
Brig. Gen. Edgar Russell	18 October 1921–6 December 1922
Lt. Col. Albert U. Faulkner	6 December 1922–8 February 1923
Brig. Gen. Harold B. Fiske	8 February 1923–22 December 1924
Col. Alfred A. Starbird	22 December 1924–2 March 1925
Brig. Gen. Edgar T. Collins	2 March 1925–15 March 1926
Brig. Gen. Henry G. Learnard	15 March 1926–5 March 1927
Col. Augustine McIntyre	5 March 1927–23 May 1927
Brig. Gen. Frank R. McCoy	23 May 1927–6 August 1927
Col. Harry G. Bishop	6 August 1927–October 1927
Brig. Gen. Frank R. McCoy	October 1927–23 December 1927
Col. Harry G. Bishop	23 December 1927–January 1929
Brig. Gen. Frank R. McCoy	January 1929–1 May 1929
Col. William S. McNair	1 May 1929–13 June 1929
Brig. Gen. James B. Gowen	13 June 1929–23 August 1932
Col. Laurin L. Lawson	23 August 1932–24 September 1932
Brig. Gen. Ernest D. Scott	24 September 1932–12 September 1936
Col. William P. Ennis	12 September 1936–16 May 1938
Col. Benjamin F. Miller	16 May 1938–31 October 1938
Brig. Gen. James L. Collins	31 October 1938–3 May 1939
Col. Raymond E. Lee	3 May 1939–1 July 1939
Col. Rene E. DeR. Hoyle	1 July 1939–16 October 1939

HHD, 2d Provisional Field Artillery Brigade **Organized Reserve Illinois**

HQ—Chicago, IL, 1932–36

Subordinate elements—14th F.A. (RAI), 1932–33; 22d F.A. (RAI), 1932–36; 78th F.A. (RAI), 1932–36

Organized provisionally in the O.R. in February 1932 with HQ at Chicago, IL, in accordance with Sixth Corps Area letter dated 8 February 1932. Established to provide command and control for the field artillery units of the 6th Div. organized with O.R. personnel. Discontinued on 8 May 1936.

Commanders, 2d Provisional Field Artillery Brigade

Col. Martin H. Foss	8 February 1932–8 May 1936

HHB, 2d Field Artillery Brigade (2d Division)

HQ—Camp Travis, TX, 1919–23; Fort Sam Houston, TX, 1923–39

Subordinate elements—12th F.A., 1919–39; 15th F.A., 1919–29, 1930–39; 17th F.A., 1930–39; 2d Ammo. Tn., 1919–39

Arrived at the port of New York on 6 August 1919 on the U.S.S. *Leviathan* as an element of the 2d Div. after 7 months of occupation duty near Coblenz and Heddesdorf, Germany. Transferred on 16 August 1919 to Camp Travis, TX (a subpost of Fort Sam Houston). Transferred in December 1923 to Fort Sam Houston proper. Brigade units provided training assistance each summer to artillery elements of the 90th Div. and XVIII Corps at Camp Bullis, Camp Stanley, and Fort Sam Houston. Reserve officers assigned to the brigade HHB conducted summer training with the brigade at Camp Bullis, TX, or Fort Sam Houston. Participated in the annual 2d Div. maneuvers typically held in May at Camp Bullis, TX. Disbanded on 7 October 1939 at Fort Sam Houston.

Status: Active in the R.A. at Camp Stanley, South Korea, as HHB, 2d Inf. Div. Arty.

Events: 45, 47, 55, 70, 74, 80, 147, 163, 242, 258, 282, 288, 295, 296, 298, 300, 317

Commanders, 2d Field Artillery Brigade

Col. Joseph R. Davis	ao January 1920–16 March 1920	Brig. Gen. Samuel D. Rockenbach	9 September 1928–31 January 1933
Col. Jacob A. Mack	16 March 1920–21 April 1920	Col. Joseph S. Herron	31 January 1933–15 June 1933
Brig. Gen. George V.H. Moseley	21 April 1920–3 July 1921	Col. James H. Bryson	15 June 1933–26 October 1933
Maj. Fred A. Turner	3 July 1921–12 October 1921	Brig. Gen. Francis LeJ. Parker	26 October 1933–1 May 1934
Lt. Col. Laurin L. Lawson	12 October 1921–14 December 1921	Col. James H. Bryson	1 May 1934–19 July 1934
Brig. Gen. Dennis E. Nolan	14 December 1921–20 November 1922	Brig. Gen. Herbert J. Brees	19 July 1934–23 January 1935
Brig. Gen. Paul B. Malone	20 November 1923–21 February 1928	Col. James H. Bryson	23 January 1935–9 March 1935
Col. Ernest D. Scott	21 February 1928–14 May 1928	Brig. Gen. Robert C. Foy	9 March 1935–7 March 1937
Col. Philip S. Golderman	14 May 1928–15 June 1928	Brig. Gen. Leslie J. McNair	7 March 1937–4 April 1939
Col. Ernest D. Scott	15 June 1928–9 September 1928	Col. Benjamin H. Bailey	4 April 1939–8 May 1939
	Brig. Gen. James L. Collins	8 May 1939–7 October 1939	

HHB, 3d Field Artillery Brigade (3d Division)

HQ—Camp Pike, AR, 1919–21; Fort Lewis, WA, 1921–39

Subordinate elements—10th F.A., 1919–39; 76th F.A., 1919–39; 18th F.A., 1930–39; 3d Ammo. Tn., 1919–39

Arrived at the port of Hoboken on 20 August 1919 on the U.S.S. *America* as an element of the 3d Div. after 8 months of occupation duty in Mayen, Germany. Transferred on 25 August 1919 to Camp Pike, AR. Transferred on 11 August 1921 to Camp Lewis, WA. Brigade units provided training assistance each summer to artillery elements of the 96th Div. and XIX Corps at Fort Lewis. Responsible for the support and administration of the Fort Lewis Civilian Conservation Corps (CCC) District, 1933–39. Typically participated in 3d Div. maneuvers at Fort Lewis. Disbanded on 16 October 1939 at Fort Lewis.

Status: Active in the R.A. at Fort Stewart, GA, as HHB, 3d Inf. Div. Arty.

Events: 57, 135, 145, 161, 208, 226, 238, 251, 273, 289, 294, 304, 306, 309, 314, 326, 328

Commanders, 3d Field Artillery Brigade

Brig. Gen. William M. Cruikshank	23 April 1919–April 1921	Brig. Gen. Ernest D. Scott	10 December 1931–17 August 1932
Brig. Gen. Robert Alexander*	April 1921–18 June 1927	Col. Francis W. Clark	17 August 1932–13 October 1932
Col. Philip R. Ward	18 June 1927–5 January 1928	Brig. Gen. Henry W. Butner*	13 October 1932–1 August 1934
Col. Fred E. Buchan	5 January 1928–17 April 1928	Col. Francis W. Clark	1 August 1934–27 September 1934
Brig. Gen. Charles R. Howland*	17 April 1928–23 May 1929 Brig.	Gen. Charles M. Bundel	27 September 1934–9 June 1936
Brig. Gen. Henry G. Learnard	31 May 1929–3 August 1931	Col. Frank S. Bowen	9 June 1936–4 July 1937
Col. Richard H. McMaster	3 August 1931–10 December 1931	Brig. Gen. Thomas E. Merrill*	4 July 1937–12 April 1939

Col. William H. Peck	12 April 1939–16 October 1939

*Concurrently commanding the 3d Div. for all or a portion of the period indicated.

HHB, 4th Field Artillery Brigade (4th Division)

HQ—Camp Dodge, IA, 1919–20; Camp Lewis, WA, 1920–21; *Inactive,* 1921–26; Fort Bragg, NC, 1926–35; Fort Sill, OK, 1935–39

Subordinate elements—1st F.A., 1933–39; *2d F.A.,* 1923–27; *9th F.A.,* 1930–33; *16th F.A.,* 1919–23, 1927–33; 77th F.A.,1919–23, 1930–39; *83d F.A.,* 1933–39; *85th F.A.,* 1923–30; 4th Ammo. Tn. (RAI), 1919–39

Arrived at the port of New York City on 31 July 1919 on the U.S.S. *Zeelandia* as an element of the 4th Div. after 7 months of occupation duty in Adenau and Ahrweiler, Germany. Transferred on 8 August 1919 to Camp Dodge, IA. Transferred on 11 August 1920 to Camp Lewis, WA. Inactivated on 21 September 1921 at Camp Lewis. The 3d F.A. Brig. was assigned as the Active Associate (A.A.), 1921–25. The 1st Bn., 2d F.A. was assigned as the A.A., 1925–27. HHB organized on 1 June 1926 with O.R. personnel as an RAI unit at Fort Bragg, NC. Designated mobilization training station was Fort Bragg, 1927–35. Withdrawn from the Fourth Corps Area on 1 January 1935 and activated at Fort Sill, OK. Provided command and control for field artillery units assigned to Fort Sill to support the activities and training of the Field Artillery School, 1935–39. Participated in a live-fire exercise 7–31 August 1935 at the target and maneuver range near Fort Francis E. Warren, WY. Reserve officers assigned to the brigade HHB conducted summer training with the brigade at Fort Sill, 1937–39. Disbanded on 14 November 1939 at Fort Sill.

Status: Active in the R.A. at Fort Hood, TX, as HHB, 4th Inf. Div. Arty.

Events: 310, 330

Commanders, 4th Field Artillery Brigade

Col. Wright Smith	January 1919–7 August 1919	Capt. John M. Browning**	12 September 1929–ao June 1932
Brig. Gen. Edwin B. Babbitt	8 August 1919–20 August 1920	Unknown	ao June 1932–31 December 1934
Col. Otho B. Farr	20 August 1920–21 September 1921	Brig. Gen. Henry W. Butner	1 January 1935–10 May 1936
Inactive	21 September 1921–1 June 1926	Col. Augustine McIntyre	10 May 1936–21 July 1938
Capt. John K. Dunn**	1 June 1926–27 July 1928	Col. Edward H. DeArmond	21 July 1938–5 August 1938
2d Lt. Clarence A. Smith**	27 July 1928–12 September 1929	Col. Augustine McIntyre	5 August 1938–14 November 1939

**RAI commanders: O.R. officers.

HHB, 5th Field Artillery Brigade (5th Division) **Regular Army Inactive**

HQ—Camp Gordon, GA, 1919–20; Camp Jackson, SC, 1920–21; *Inactive,* 1921–28; Indianapolis, IN, 1928–39

Subordinate elements—*3d F.A.,* 1923–30; 19th F.A. (RAI), 1919–39; 20th F.A. (RAI), 1919–23; 1930–39; 21st F.A. (RAI), 1919–21; 1930–39; 5th Ammo. Tn. (RAI), 1919–39

Arrived at the port of New York on 21 July 1919 on the U.S.S. *Agamemnon* as an element of the 5th Div. after 6 months of occupation duty in Luxembourg. Transferred on 25 July 1919 to Camp Bragg, NC. Transferred on 27 November 1920 to Camp Jackson, SC. Transferred on 3 September 1921 back to Camp Bragg. Inactivated on 5 September 1921 at Camp Bragg. Concurrently, personnel and equipment of HQ Battery (Btry) transferred to HHB, 13th F.A. Brig. The 1st F.A. Brig. was assigned as the A.A., 1921–25. The 1st Bn., 3d F.A. was assigned as the A.A.,1925–27. HHB organized on 27 February 1928 with O.R. personnel as an RAI unit at Indianapolis, IN. Designated mobilization training station was Fort Benning, GA, 1923–27, and Camp Knox, KY, 1927–39. Conducted summer training most years at Camp Knox. Subordinate regiments conducted training of Citizens Military Training Camp (CMTC) at Fort Benjamin Harrison, IN. Disbanded on 16 October 1939 at Indianapolis.

Status: Inactive in the R.A. as HHB, 5th Inf. Div. Arty.

Events: 293, 296, 302, 316, 328

Commanders, 5th Field Artillery Brigade

Brig. Gen. William C. Rivers	14 October 1918–13 March 1919	Maj. John E. Hatch	7 September 1920–22 November 1920
Brig. Gen. Adrian S. Fleming	2 April 1919–14 April 1919	Lt. Col. Albert U. Faulkner	22 November 1920–13 December 1920

Brig. Gen. Daniel F. Craig	15 April 1919–25 June 1919	Col. Richard H. McMaster	13 December 1920–3 September 1921
Col. Leo J. Ahern	22 July 1919–December 1919	*Inactive*	4 September 1921–27 February 1928
Col. Albert U. Faulkner	December 1919–16 February 1920	2d Lt. Emerson L. Burrell**	27 February 1928–2 August 1928
Col. Leo J. Ahern	16 February 1920–1 March 1920	2d Lt. Joseph L. Schecter**	2 August 1928–ao September 1928
Col. William S. McNair	1 March 1920–7 September 1920	Unknown	ao September 1928–16 October 1939

**RAI commanders: O.R. officers.

HHB, 6th Field Artillery Brigade (6th Division)

HQ—Camp Grant, IL, 1919–21; Camp Knox, KY, 1921; *Inactive,* 1921–26; Chicago, IL, 1926–39

Subordinate elements—*3d F.A.,* 1919–23, 1930–39; *14th F.A.,* 1923–27; *18th F.A.,* 1927–30; 22d F.A. (RAI), 1930–39; 78th F.A. (RAI), 1919–39; 6th Ammo. Tn. (RAI), 1919–39

Arrived at the port of New York on 20 June 1919 on the U.S.S. *Kaiserin Augusta Victoria* as an element of the 6th Div. after 6 months of occupation duty near Aignay-le-Duc, France, and Bad Bertrich, Germany. Transferred on 24 June 1919 to Camp Grant, IL. Transferred on 27 September 1921 to Camp Knox, KY. Inactivated on 17 November 1921 at Camp Knox. Concurrently, personnel and equipment transferred to the 3d F.A. The 2d F.A. Brig. was assigned as the A.A., 1921–25. The 1st Bn., 14th F.A. was assigned as the A.A., 1925–27. Designated mobilization training station was Fort Sheridan, IL, 1925–35. HHB organized on 1 June 1926 with O.R. personnel as an RAI unit at Chicago, IL. Typically conducted Inactive Training Period meetings at the Post Office Building or at the Pure Oil Building in Chicago. Conducted summer training most years at Camp McCoy, WI, and some years at Camp Custer, MI. Conducted summer training at Camp Williams, WI, in 1928 with HHB, 57th F.A. Brig. Subordinate regiments conducted training of CMTC at Fort Snelling, MN, or Camp McCoy. HQ Battery activated on 1 December 1934, less Reserve personnel, at Fort Sheridan, IL. Brigade HQ activated on 21 September 1935, less Reserve personnel, at Chicago. Active brigade units provided training assistance each summer to artillery elements of the 85th, 86th, and 101st Divs. and XVI Corps at Camp McCoy or Camp Custer. Disbanded on 2 October 1939 at Fort Sheridan.

Status: Inactive in the R.A. as HHB, 6th Inf. Div. Arty.

Events: 162, 214, 264, 293, 296, 303, 316, 328

Commanders, 6th Field Artillery Brigade

Brig. Gen. Edward A. Millar	April 1918–22 June 1919	Capt. William S. Redhed**	ao October 1928–ao June 1929
Brig. Gen. Lucien G. Berry	22 June 1919–12 September 1920	Capt. Joseph J. Donahue**	ao June 1930–ao June 1932
Brig. Gen. Samuel D. Sturgis	12 September 1920–September 1921	Unknown	ao June 1932–21 September 1935
Inactive	17 November 1921–1 June 1926	Maj. Gen. Charles D. Herron	21 September 1935–8 September 1937
Capt. Joseph A. Blake Jr.**	2 June 1926–10 September 1926	Brig. Gen. Walter F. Prosser	18 November 1937–29 June 1939
Capt. William S. Redhed**	10 September 1926–September 1927	Col. James P. Marley	10 September 1937–18 November 1937
Maj. Ralph A. Kimble**	September 1927–ao January 1928	Col. William H. Dodds	29 June 1939–2 October 1939

**RAI commanders: O.R. officers.

HHB, 7th Field Artillery Brigade (7th Division) — **Regular Army Inactive**

HQ—Camp Funston, KS, 1919–21; Camp George G. Meade, MD, 1921; *Inactive,* 1921–27; Sioux City, IA, 1927–39

Subordinate elements—*9th F.A.,* 1923–27; 14th F.A. (RAI), 1923–27; 77th F.A. (RAI), 1923–30; 79th F.A. (RAI), 1919–23, 1930–39; 80th F.A. (RAI), 1919–23, 1930–39; 7th Ammo. Tn. (RAI), 1919–39

Arrived at the port of New York on 23 June 1919 on the U.S.S. *Imperator* as an element of the 7th Div. after 6 months of occupation duty near the Puvenelle Sector and the Colombey-les-Belles Training Area, France. Transferred on 29 June 1919 to Camp Funston, KS. Transferred to Camp George G. Meade, MD, arriving there on 8 January 1921. Inactivated on 30 September 1921 at Camp George G. Meade. Concurrently, personnel and equipment transferred to the 1st F.A. Brig. The 1st F.A. Brig. was assigned as the A.A., 1921–25. The 1st Bn., 9th F.A. was assigned as the A.A., 1925–27. HHB organized by June 1927 with O.R. personnel as an RAI unit at Sioux City, IA. Conducted summer training most years at Fort Riley, KS, and some years at Camp McCoy, WI; Camp Ripley, MN; or Fort Des Moines, IA. Disbanded on 16 October 1939 at Sioux City.

Status: Inactive in the R.A. as HHB, 7th Inf. Div. Arty.

Events: 314, 326

Commanders, 7th Field Artillery Brigade

Brig. Gen. Dwight Aultman	May 1919–20 June 1919	Lt. Col. Robert F. Woods	14 December 1920–24 March 1921
Col. John W.B. Corey	21 June 1919–September 1919	Maj. Nelson E. Margetts	24 March 1921–31 March 1921
Col. Edward A. Millar	September 1919–20 April 1920	Col. Wright Smith	31 March 1921–30 September 1921
Col. Edgar A. Sirmyer	20 April 1920–September 1920	*Inactive*	30 September 1921–ao June 1927
Col. Brook E. Payne	September 1920–13 December 1920	Unknown	ao June 1927–ao June 1938
	Capt. Ralph R. Edwards**	ao June 1938–16 October 1939	

**RAI commanders: O.R. officers.

HHB, 8th Field Artillery Brigade (8th Division) — **Regular Army Inactive**

HQ—Camp Knox, KY, 1919–21; Camp Bragg, NC, 1921–22; *Inactive,* 1922–26; Lynchburg, VA, 1926–39

Subordinate elements—*2d F.A.,* 1919–22; *16th F.A.,* 1923–27, 1933–39; 20th F.A. (RAI), 1923–30; 28th F.A. (RAI), 1930–39; 81st F.A. (RAI), 1919–22, 1930–39; *83d F.A.,* 1919–22, 1930–39; 8th Ammo. Tn. (RAI), 1919–22, 1923–39

Arrived at the port of New York on 18 January 1919 on the U.S.S. *President Grant* as an element of the 8th Div. after 2 months of duty at Ploermel, France. Transferred on 22 January 1919 to Camp Knox, KY, and relieved from the 8th Div. Transferred on 30 November 1921 to Camp Bragg, NC. Inactivated on 7 January 1922 at Camp Bragg. Concurrently, personnel and equipment transferred to 13th F.A. Brig. The 13th F.A. Brig. was assigned as the A.A., 1922–25. The 1st Bn., 16th F.A. was assigned as the A.A., 1925–27. Assigned to the 8th Div on 24 March 1923. HHB organized on 22 April 1926 with O.R. personnel as an RAI unit at Lynchburg, VA. Designated mobilization training station was Fort Myer, VA, 1923–25; Camp George G. Meade, MD, 1925–33; and the Roanoke Concentration Area, VA, 1933–39. Disbanded on 16 October 1939 at Lynchburg.

Status: Inactive in the R.A. as HHB, 8th Inf. Div. Arty.

Events: 330

Commanders, 8th Field Artillery Brigade

Brig. Gen. George G. Gatley	13 August 1919–13 August 1920	2d Lt. Stanton F. Blaine**	22 April 1926–28 February 1927
Col. Manus McCloskey	13 August 1920–13 January 1921	1st Lt. Marion P. Nichols*	28 February 1927–ao March 1927
Maj. Howard M. Randell	13 January 1921–26 January 1921	Unknown	ao March 1927–8 October 1930
Brig. Gen. William Lassiter	26 January 1921–September 1921	Capt. Atreus H. Kratzke**	8 October 1930–5 September 1934
Brig. Gen. Robert Alexander	September 1921–December 1921	1st Lt. Stanton F. Blain**	5 September 1934–18 February 1935
Inactive	7 January 1922–22 April 1926	Unknown	18 February 1935–16 October 1939

*RAI commanders: R.A. officers.
**RAI commanders: O.R. officers.

HHB, 9th Field Artillery Brigade (9th Division) — **Regular Army Inactive**

HQ—Camp McClellan, AL, 1919; *Inactive,* 1923–28; Indianapolis, IN, 1928–33; Andover, MA, 1933–37; Lawrence, MA, 1937–40

Subordinate elements—*9th F.A.,* 1927–30; *18th F.A.,* 1923–27; *21st F.A.,* 1923–30; 25th F.A. (RAI), 1930–39; 26th F.A. (RAI), 1930–39; 27th F.A. (RAI), 1930–33; *36th F.A.,* 1929–30; and 9th Ammo. Tn. (RAI), 1923–39

Stationed at Camp McClellan, AL, where it was demobilized on 5 February 1919, as an element of the 9th Div. Reconstituted on 24 March 1923, assigned to the 9th Div., and allotted to the First Corps Area. The 13th F.A. Brig. was assigned as the A.A., 1923–25. The 1st Bn., 18th F.A. was assigned as the A.A., 1925–27. Withdrawn from the First

Corps Area on 19 February 1927 and allotted to the Fifth Corps Area. HHB organized on 20 March 1928 with O.R. personnel as an RAI unit at Indianapolis, IN. Withdrawn from the Fifth Corps Area on 18 August 1933 and allotted to the First Corps Area. HHB organized by June 1935 with O.R. personnel as an RAI unit at Andover, MA. Relocated in 1937 to Lawrence, MA. Disbanded on 1 July 1940 at Lawrence.

Status: Inactive in the R.A. as HHB, 9th Inf. Div. Arty.

Events: 330

Commanders, 9th Field Artillery Brigade

Inactive	24 March 1923–20 March 1928
2d Lt. William Long**	20 March 1928–10 August 1928
1st Lt. Howard D. Porter**	10 August 1928–ao September 1928
Unknown	ao September 1928–ao April 1938
1st Lt. Leland L. Currier**	ao July 1938–August 1939
Maj. John J. Kennedy**	August 1939–1 July 1940

**RAI commanders; O.R. officers

HHB, 10th Field Artillery Brigade (Panama Canal Division)

HQ—*Not organized,* 1930–41

Subordinate elements—*2d F.A.,* 1930–38; *87th F.A.,* 1930–38

Constituted in the R.A. on 28 May 1930, assigned to the Panama Canal Division, and allotted to the Panama Canal Department. Consolidated on 12 October 1936 with the 10th F.A. Brig., 10th Div. (a World War I unit organized in August 1918 at Camp Funston, KS, demobilized in February 1919 at Camp Funston; reconstituted on 12 October 1936). Location 7 December 1941—*Inactive.*

Status: Disbanded 11 November 1944.

HHB, 11th Field Artillery Brigade (Hawaiian Division)

HQ—Schofield Barracks, TH, 1921–41

Subordinate elements—8th F.A., 1921–41; 11th F.A., 1921–41; 13th F.A., 1921–41; and 11th Ammo. Tn., 1921–40

Constituted in the R.A. on 28 February 1921, assigned to the Hawaiian Division, and allotted to the Hawaiian Department. HQ organized on 1 March 1921 at Schofield Barracks, TH. HQ Btry organized on 29 April 1921 by transfer of men from the 8th, 11th, and 13th F.A. Regts. Some 1,000 officers and men from HHB, 11th F.A. Brig. and subordinate units conducted fire fighting operations in the Paumalu-Pupukea Forest Reserve, 31 August–1 September 1934. Redesignated 24th Div. Arty. on 26 August 1941.

Organization Day: 1 March. Chosen to commemorate the brigade's organization on 1 March 1921.

Status: Inactive in the R.A. as HHB, 24th Inf. Div. Arty.

Events: 33, 37, 48, 75, 88, 120, 138, 141, 158, 189, 211, 224, 248, 276, 297, 312

Commanders, 11th Field Artillery Brigade

Lt. Col. Wright Smith	28 February 1921–14 March 1921
Lt. Col. George M. Brook	14 March 1921–19 April 1921
Col. Tiemann N. Horn	19 April 1921–5 November 1922
Brig. Gen. Henry Jervey*	30 August 1921–24 February 1922
Brig. Gen. Grote Hutcheson	6 November 1922–19 July 1924
Col. Otho B. Farr	19 July 1924–24 October 1924
Brig. Gen. George V. H. Moseley	24 October 1924–14 October 1927
Brig. Gen. Allston Hamilton	14 October 1927–19 Jule 1930
Col. Ernest D. Scott	19 July 1930–24 October 1930
Brig. Gen. Henry W. Butner	24 October 1930–23 September 1932
Brig. Gen. James B. Gowen	23 September 1932–17 February 1934
Brig. Gen. Thomas E. Merrill	14 February 1934–23 March 1937
Col. Laurin L. Lawson	23 March 1937–28 May 1937
Brig. Gen. Robert C. Foy	28 May 1937–13 March 1939
Col. Donald C. McDonald	13 March 1939–30 June 1939
Brig. Gen. Donald C. Cubbison	30 June 1939–1 July 1940
Brig. Gen. Maxwell Murray	26 July 1940–26 August 1941

HHB, 12th Field Artillery Brigade (Philippine Division)

HQ—Fort McKinley, PI, 1922; *Inactive,* 1922–41

Subordinate elements—24th F.A., 1922–41; *25th F.A.,* 1921–30; *23d F.A.,* 1930–41; and *12th Ammo. Tn.,* 1921–40

Constituted in the R.A. in January 1922, assigned to the Philippine Division, and allotted to the Philippine Department. Organized in January 1922 at Fort McKinley, PI. Inactivated on 30 September 1922 at Fort McKinley. The 1st Bn., 24th F.A. was assigned as the A.A., 1922–27. Location 7 December 1941—*Inactive.*

Commanders, 12th Field Artillery Brigade and Fort Stotsenberg*

Brig. Gen. Johnson Hagood	January 1922–25 March 1924
Brig. Gen. Charles J. Symmonds	25 March 1924–20 June 1926
Brig. Gen. Lucius R. Holbrook	September 1926–15 June 1929
Brig. Gen. Frank C. Bolles	15 June 1929–10 June 1931
Brig. Gen. Herbert J. Brees	18 June 1931–23 June 1934
Brig. Gen. Francis LeJ. Parker	23 June 1934–1 May 1936
Brig. Gen. John L. DeWitt	1 May 1936–26 October 1936
Brig. Gen. Evan H. Humphrey	22 January 1937–30 April 1938
Brig. Gen. Walter S. Grant	11 May 1938–31 October 1938
Brig. Gen. Francis W. Honeycutt	31 October 1938–September 1940
Brig. Gen. Ernest P. King	October 1940–December 1941

*These general officers were the commanding generals of Fort Stotsenberg, PI, where the Philippine Division artillery elements were stationed. Only Brig. Gen. Hagood commanded the 12th F.A. Brig. during its brief Active Duty existence. The remaining officers were designated as commanding general of the brigade for mobilization purposes.

HHB, 13th Field Artillery Brigade (IV Corps)

HQ—Fort Bragg, NC, 1921–41

Subordinate elements—5th F.A., 1921–30; 17th F.A., 1921–30 and 1939–41; *21st F.A.,* 1921–23; 22d F.A.,(RAI) 1923–29; 23d F.A. (RAI), 1923–30; 29th F.A. (RAI), 1929–40; 30th F.A. (RAI), 1930–33; 36th F.A. (RAI), 1930–41; 178th F.A., 1923–29 and 1939–41; 441st F.A., 1921–24; 13th Ammo. Tn., 1921–40; 1st Obsn. Btry, 1922–29; 1st Obsn. Bn., 1929–41; 4th Ordnance (Ord.) Company (Co.), 1930–40; 363d Ord. Co., 1921–30

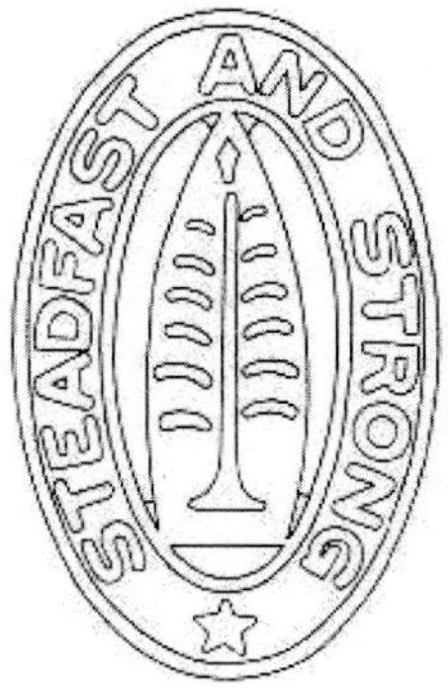

Constituted in the R.A. on 13 January 1921. Activated on 13 May 1921 at Camp Bragg, NC. Assigned to the IV Corps on 2 July 1923. Brigade units provided training assistance each summer at Fort Bragg to artillery elements of the 81st, 82d, and 87th Divs., XIV Corps, and O.R. GHQR 240-mm howitzer regiments. Responsible for the support and administration of CCC District A, Fourth Corps Area, 1933–39. Relieved from the IV Corps on 1 November 1940 and assigned to the I Corps. Location 7 December 1941—Fort Bragg, NC.

Status: Active in the R.A. at Smith Barracks, Wiesbaden, Germany, as HHB, V Corps Arty.

Events: 1, 121, 255, 293, 296, 300, 330

Commanders, 13th Field Artillery Brigade

Lt. Col. Robert C. Foy	13 May 1921–20 September 1921
Brig. Gen. Albert J. Bowley	20 September 1921–28 March 28
Col. Thomas E. Merrill	28 March 1928–13 May 1928
Col. Henry W. Butner	16 May 1928–20 August 1929
Brig. Gen. Lucius R. Holbrook	20 August 1929–5 October 1930
Col. Albert U. Faulkner	5 October 1930–2 January 1931
Brig. Gen. Herbert J. Brees	2 January 1931–23 May 1931
Col. Albert U. Faulkner	23 May 1931–June 1931
Brig. Gen. Manus McCloskey	June 1931–1 April 1938
Col. Joseph A. Rogers	1 April 1938–11 May 1938
Brig. Gen. William Bryden	11 May 1938–23 May 1940
Col. John R. Starkey	23 May 1940–13 September 1940
Brig. Gen. Francis W. Honeycutt	13 September 1940–21 September 1940
Col. George R. Allin	21 September 1940–13 November 1940
Brig. Gen. John A. Crane	13 November 1940–August 1941

HHB, 14th Field Artillery Brigade (VII Corps)

HQ—*Inactive,* 1923–28; Cleveland, OH, 1928–41

Subordinate elements—26th F.A. (RAI), 1928–29; *27th F.A.,* 1928–30; 28th F.A. (RAI), 1928–30; 33d F.A. (RAI), 1930–40; 34th F.A. (RAI), 1930–33; 35th F.A. (RAI), 1930–41; 79th F.A. (RAI), 1928–30; 185th F.A., 1923–28; *195th F.A.,* 1924–27; 443d F.A., 1923–24; 14th Ammo. Tn. (RAI), 1928–40; *335th Ammo. Tn.,* 1923–28; *14th Obsn. Btry,* 1923–29; 14th Obsn. Bn. (RAI), 1929–41; 18th Ord. Co., 1921–30; 22d Ord. Co., 1933–40

Stationed at Camp Custer, MI, as an element of the 14th Div. Demobilized at Camp Custer on 18 February 1919. Reconstituted in the R.A. on 24 March 1923, assigned to the VII Corps, and allotted to the Fourth Corps Area. The 13th F.A. Brig.assigned as A.A., 1923–27. Withdrawn from the Fourth Corps Area on 19 February 1927 and allotted to the Fifth Corps Area. HHB organized on 6 February 1928 with O.R. personnel as an RAI unit at Cleveland, OH. Relieved from the VII Corps on 1 October 1933 and assigned to V Corps. Designated mobilization training station was Fort Bragg, NC, 1923–41. Location 7 December 1941—Cleveland, OH.

Status: Active in the R.A. at Fort Sill, OK, as HHB, III Corps Arty.

Commanders, 14th Field Artillery Brigade

2d Lt. William A. Freeman**	6 February 1928–ao March 1928	Unknown	ao July 1935–ao January 1938
Unknown	ao March 1928–ao June 1935	Capt. Charles M. Pettit**	ao January 1938–ao April 1938
2d Lt. Franklin C. Salisbury**	ao June 1935–ao July 1935	Unknown	ao April 1938–7 December 1941

**RAI commanders: O.R. officers.

HHB, 15th Field Artillery Brigade (II Corps)

HQ—*Inactive,* 1923–30; Greensboro, NC, 1930–33; *Inactive,* 1933–36; Los Angeles, CA, 1936–41

Subordinate elements—*29th F.A.,* 1923–29; *30th F.A.,* 1923–30; 31st F.A. (RAI), 1930–40; 32d F.A. (RAI), 1930–32 and 1933–40; 80th F.A. (RAI), 1923–30; 81st F.A. (RAI), 1923–30; 86th F.A. (RAI), 1930–41; 106th F.A., 1923–29; 258th F.A., 1923–27; 441st F.A., 1924–41; 15th Ammo. Tn. (RAI), 1927–40; 132d Ammo. Tn., 1923–24; 331st Ammo. Tn., 1924–27; *15th Obsn. Btry,* 1923–29; 15th Obsn. Bn. (RAI), 1929–41; 361st Ord. Co., 1921–30; 18th Ord. Co., 1933–41

Stationed at Camp Stanley, TX, as an element of the 15th Div. Demobilized at Camp Stanley on 18 February 1919. Reconstituted in the R.A. on 24 March 1923, assigned to the II Corps, and allotted to the Fourth Corps Area. The 13th F.A. Brig. assigned as A.A., 1923–27. HHB organized by February 1930 with O.R. personnel as an RAI unit at Greensboro, NC. Withdrawn from the Fourth Corps Area on 1 October 1933, allotted to the Ninth Corps Area, and assigned to the IX Corps. HHB organized on 7 June 1936 with O.R. personnel as an RAI unit at Los Angeles, CA. Designated mobilization training station was Fort Bragg, NC, 1923–33. Location 7 December 1941—Los Angeles, CA.

Status: Inactive in the R.A. as HHB, XIII Corps Arty.

Commanders, 15th Field Artillery Brigade

2d Lt. Eugene J. Honeycutt**	ao February 1930–18 March 1930	*Inactive*	1 October 1933–7 June 1936
Unknown	18 March 1930–1 October 1933	Unknown	7 June 1936–7 December 1941

**RAI commanders: O.R. officers.

HHB, 16th Field Artillery Brigade (I Cavalry Corps)

HQ—*Not organized,* 1929–30; Tulsa, OK, 1930–34; *Inactive,* 1934–41; Tulsa, OK, 1941

Constituted in the R.A. on 14 January 1929, assigned to the I Cavalry Corps, and allotted to the Eighth Corps Area. HHB organized on 29 April 1930 with O.R. personnel as an RAI unit at Tulsa, OK. The 16th F.A. Brig. had no artillery units permanently assigned. The intent was for units to be attached from corps or army level brigades on an "as needed" basis for specific limited missions assigned to the I Cavalry Corps. Attached to the 95th Div. for administration and training. Conducted summer training at Fort Sill, OK, with the 1st F.A. Inactivated on 24 October 1934 at Tulsa by relief of personnel. Personnel concurrently reassigned to HHB, 18th F.A. Brig. Fort Bliss, TX, designated as HQ on reorganization, but the unit was never organized at that location. Withdrawn from the Eighth Corps Area on 5 June 1936 and allotted to the Sixth Corps Area. Chicago, IL, designated as HQ on reorganization, but the unit was never organized at that location. Consolidated on 15 October 1936 with the 16th F.A. Brig. (a World War I unit organized on 12 September 1918 at Camp Kearney, CA, as an element of the 16th Div.; demobilized on 15 February 1919 at Camp Kearney; reconstituted on 15 October 1936). Designated mobilization training station was Fort Sill, 1929–34, and Fort Bliss, 1934–36. Reorganized by February 1941 with O.R. personnel as an RAI unit with HQ at Tulsa. Location 7 December 1941—Tulsa, OK.

Status: Inactive in the R.A. as HHB, I Corps Arty.

Commanders, 16th Field Artillery Brigade

Capt. Adrian H. Lindsey**	29 April 1930–2 December 1931	*Inactive*	25 October 1934–ao February 1941
Capt. Richard C. Prater**	2 December 1931–24 October 1934	Unknown	ao February 1941–7 December 1941

**RAI commanders: O.R. officers.

HHB, 17th Field Artillery Brigade (VII Corps)

HQ—*Not organized,* 1933–34; St. Louis, MO, 1934–41

Subordinate elements—44th F.A. (RAI), 1933–41; 45th F.A. (RAI), 1933–41; 91st F.A. (RAI), 1933–41; 17th Ammo. Tn. (RAI), 1933–40; 7th Obsn. Bn. (RAI), 1933–41; 24th Ord. Co., 1933–41

Constituted in the R.A. on 1 October 1933, assigned to the VII Corps, and allotted to the Seventh Corps Area. HHB organized by December 1934 with O.R. personnel as an RAI unit at St. Louis, MO. Consolidated on 12 October 1936 with the reconstituted 17th F.A. Brig. (a World War I unit organized on 19 August 1918 at Camp Bowie, TX, as an element of the 17th Div.; demobilized on 8 February 1919 at Fort Sill, OK; reconstituted on 12 October 1936). Location 7 December 1941—St. Louis, MO.

Status: Active in the R.A. at Fort Sill, OK, as HHB, 17th F.A. Brig.

Commanders, 17th Field Artillery Brigade

Unknown	ao December 1934–7 December 1941

HHB, 18th Field Artillery Brigade (VIII Corps)

HQ—*Not organized,* 1933–34; Oklahoma City, OK, 1934–40; Fort Sill, OK, 1940–41

Subordinate elements—46th F.A. (RAI), 1933–40; 51st F.A. (RAI), 1933–40; 92d F.A. (RAI), 1933–40; 18th Ammo. Tn. (RAI), 1933–40; 8th Obsn. Bn. (RAI), 1933–40; 25th Ord. Co., 1933–40; 77th F.A., 1940–41; 142d F.A., 1941; 349th F.A., 1940–41; 2d Obsn. Bn., 1940–41

Constituted in the R.A. on 1 October 1933, assigned to the VIII Corps, and allotted to the Eighth Corps Area. HHB organized on 24 October 1934 with O.R. personnel (transferred from the inactivated 16th F.A. Brig.) as an RAI unit at Oklahoma City, OK. Designated mobilization station was Fort Sill, OK, 1933–40. Conducted summer training at Fort Sill, OK, with the 1st F.A. Consolidated on 10 October 1936 with the 18th F.A. Brig. (a World War I unit organized on 21 August 1918 at Camp Travis, TX, as an element of the 18th Div.; demobilized on 12 February 1919 at Camp Travis; reconstituted on 10 October 1936). Activated on 1 June 1940 at Fort Sill, OK, and assigned to the VIII Corps. Location 7 December 1941—Fort Sill, OK.

Status: Inactive in the R.A. as HHB, VI Corps Arty.

Events: 317, 328

Commanders, 18th Field Artillery Brigade

Capt. Richard C. Prater**	24 October 1934–ao November 1934
Unknown	ao November 1934–1 June 1940
Brig. Gen. George R. Allin	14 June 1940–January 1941
Brig. Gen. Leroy P. Collins	February 1941–11 November 1941
Brig. Gen. Vincent Meyer	11 November 1941–June 1942

**RAI commanders: O.R. officers.

HHB, 19th Field Artillery Brigade (I Corps)

HQ—*Not organized,* 1933–35; Andover, MA, 1935–37; Springfield, MA, 1937–41

Subordinate elements—37th F.A. (RAI), 1933–40; 38th F.A. (RAI), 1933–40; 88th F.A. (RAI), 1933–40; 19th Ammo. Tn. (RAI), 1933–40; 314th Obsn. Bn. (RAI), 1933–41; 8th Ord. Co., 1933–40

Constituted in the R.A. on 1 October 1933, assigned to the I Corps, and allotted to the First Corps Area. HHB organized by June 1935 with O.R. personnel as an RAI unit at Andover, MA. Consolidated on 10 October 1936 with the 19th F.A. Brig. (a World War I unit organized on 21 August 1918 at Camp Bowie, TX, as an element of the 19th Div.; demobilized on 13 February 1919 at Fort Sill, OK; reconstituted on 10 October 1936). Typically conducted Inactive Training Period meetings at the Post Office Building in Boston, MA. Relocated in 1937 to Springfield, MA. Relieved from the I Corps on 1 November 1940. Location 7 December 1941—Springfield, MA.

Status: Inactive in the R.A. as HHB, XI Corps Arty.

Commanders, 19th Field Artillery Brigade

Unknown	ao June 1935–ao June 1939
1st Lt. William F. McGonagle	ao June 1939–ao August 1939
Unknown	ao August 1939–7 December 1941

HHB, 20th Field Artillery Brigade (II Corps)

HQ—*Not organized,* 1933–37; Albany, NY, 1937–41

Subordinate elements—39th F.A. (RAI), 1933–40; 40th F.A. (RAI), 1933–40; 258th F.A., 1933–41; 342d Ammo. Tn. (RAI), 1933–40; 2d Obsn. Bn. (RAI), 1933–41

Constituted in the R.A. on 1 October 1933, assigned to the II Corps, and allotted to the Second Corps Area. Consolidated on 10 October 1936 with the 20th F.A. Brig. (a World War I unit organized on 3 November 1918 at Camp Jackson, SC, as an element of the 20th Div.; demobilized on 28 February 1919 at Camp Jackson; reconstituted on 10 October 1936. HHB organized on 22 April 1937 with O.R. personnel as an RAI unit at Albany, NY. Designated mobilization training station was Fort Bragg, NC. Location 7 December 1941—Albany, NY.

Status: Disbanded on 18 October 1943.

Commanders, 20th Field Artillery Brigade

1st Lt. Clinton McNeely**	22 April 1937–28 April 1937
Capt. Norman E. Gillespie**	28 April 1937–ao May 1937
Unknown	ao May 1937–ao July 1939
Capt. John J. Condon**	ao July 1939–28 March 1941
Capt. Norman E. Gillespie**	28 March 1941–27 March 1941

**RAI commanders: O.R. officers.

HHB, 21st Field Artillery Brigade (III Corps)

HQ—*Not organized,* 1933–41

Subordinate elements—41st F.A. (RAI), 1933–40; 42d F.A. (RAI), 1933–40; 89th F.A. (RAI), 1933–41; 343d Ammo. Tn. (RAI), 1933–40; 3d Obsn. Bn. (RAI), 1933–41; 46th Ord. Co., 1933–41

Constituted in the R.A. on 1 October 1933, assigned to the III Corps, and allotted to the Third Corps Area. Consolidated on 10 October 1936 with the 21st F.A. Brig. (a World War I unit organized in October 1918 at Camp Sheridan, AL;

demobilized in December 1918 at Camp Sheridan; reconstituted on 10 October 1936). Philadelphia, PA, designated as HQ on organization, but the unit was never organized at that location. Location 7 December 1941—*Not organized.*

Status: Disbanded 18 October 1943.

HHB, 22d Field Artillery Brigade (VI Corps)

HQ—Chicago, IL, 1933–39; Raleigh, NC, 1939–41

Subordinate elements—43d F.A. (RAI), 1933–41; 90th F.A. (RAI), 1933–41; 182d F.A., 1933–40; 22d Ammo. Tn. (RAI), 1933–40; 306th Obsn. Bn. (RAI), 1933–41; 23d Ord. Co., 1933–41

Constituted in the R.A. on 1 October 1933, allotted to the Sixth Corps Area, and assigned to the VI Corps. HHB concurrently organized with O.R. personnel as an RAI unit at Chicago, IL. Consolidated on 14 October 1936 with the 22d F.A. Brig. (a World War I unit organized in September 1918 at Camp George G. Meade, MD; demobilized in October 1918 at Camp Meade; reconstituted on 14 October 1936). Conducted summer training most years at Camp McCoy, WI. Withdrawn from the Sixth Corps Area on 9 January 1939 and allotted to the Fourth Corps Area. HHB organized about April 1939 with O.R. personnel as an RAI unit at Raleigh, NC. Location 7 December 1941—Raleigh, NC.

Status: Inactive in the R.A. as HHB, XII Corps Arty.

Commanders, 22d Field Artillery Brigade

Brig. Gen. Henry J. Reilly**	1 October 1933–24 February 1938	*Inactive*	9 January 1939–ao April 1939
Unknown	24 February 1938–9 January 1939	Unknown	ao April 1939–7 December 1941

**RAI commanders: O.R. officers.

HHB, 23d Field Artillery Brigade (GHQR)

HQ—*Not organized,* 1933–41

Subordinate elements—66th F.A. (RAI), 1933–41; 72d F.A. (RAI), 1933–41; 73d F.A. (RAI), 1933–41; 566th F.A. (RAI), 1933–40; 570th F.A. (RAI), 1933–41; 12th Obsn. Bn. (RAI), 1933–41

Constituted in the R.A. on 1 October 1933, allotted to the Second Corps Area, and assigned to the GHQR. New York City designated as HQ on organization, but the unit was never organized at that location. Consolidated on 15 October 1936 with the 23d F.A. Brig., Corps Arty. (a World War I unit organized in October 1918 at Camp Sheridan, AL; demobilized in December 1918 at Camp Sheridan; reconstituted on 15 October 1936). Location 7 December 1941—*Not organized.*

Status: Disbanded on 18 October 1943.

HHB, 24th Field Artillery Brigade (GHQR)

HQ—*Not organized,* 1933–34; Milwaukee, WI, 1934–37; *Inactive,* 1937–41

Subordinate elements—67th F.A. Regt. (RAI), 1933–41; 68th F.A. Regt. (RAI), 1933–34; 69th F.A. Regt. (RAI), 1933–41; 75th F.A. Regt. (RAI), 1933–41; 567th F.A. Regt. (RAI), 1933–41; 13th Obsn. Bn. (RAI), 1933–41

Constituted in the R.A. on 1 October 1933, allotted to the Sixth Corps Area, and assigned to the GHQR. HHB organized by May 1934 with O.R. personnel as an RAI unit at Milwaukee, WI. Consolidated on 10 October 1936 with the 24th F.A. Brig., 18th Div. (a World War I unit organized in September 1918 at Camp Knox, KY; demobilized in February 1919 at Camp Knox; reconstituted on 10 October 1936). Inactivated by June 1937 at Milwaukee by relief of personnel. Location 7 December 1941—*Inactive.*

Status: Disbanded on 18 October 1943.

Commanders, 24th Field Artillery Brigade

Maj. Maurice G. Jewett**	ao May 1934–ao June 1935	Unknown	ao June 1935–ao June 1937
Inactive	ao June 1937–7 December 1941		

**RAI commanders: O.R. officers.

HHB, 25th Field Artillery Brigade (GHQR)

HQ—*Not organized,* 1933–34; Davenport, IA, 1934–35; St. Paul, MN, 1935–41

Subordinate elements—47th F.A. Regt. (RAI), 1933–41; 70th F.A. Regt. (RAI), 1933–41; 99th F.A. Regt. (RAI), 1933–41; 100th F.A. Regt. (RAI), 1933–41; 128th F.A. Regt., 1933–41; 17th Obsn. Bn. (RAI), 1933–36

Constituted in the R.A. on 1 October 1933, allotted to the Seventh Corps Area, and assigned to the GHQR. HHB concurrently organized with O.R. personnel as an RAI unit at Davenport, IA. Relocated on 22 March 1935 to St. Paul, MN. Location 7 December 1941—St. Paul, MN.

Status: Disbanded on 18 October 1943.

Commanders, 25th Field Artillery Brigade

Lt. Col. Oliver A. Dickinson*	1 October 1933–30 June 1935	Unknown	30 June 1935–7 December 1941

*Designated commander for mobilization purposes.

HHB, 26th Field Artillery Brigade (GHQR)

HQ—*Not organized,* 1933–34; Harrisburg, PA, 1934–38; *Inactive,* 1938–41; Camp Roberts, CA, 1941

Subordinate elements—57th F.A. Regt. (RAI), 1933–41; 58th F.A. Regt. (RAI), 1933–41; 578th F.A. Regt. (RAI), 1933–41; 580th F.A. Regt. (RAI), 1933–41; 30th F.A. Regt., 1940–41; 40th F.A. Regt., 1940–41; 85th F.A. Regt., 1940–41; 147th F.A. Regt., 1940–41

Constituted in the R.A. on 1 October 1933, allotted to the Third Corps Area, and assigned to the GHQR. HHB organized by December 1934 with O.R. personnel as an RAI unit at Harrisburg, PA. Inactivated by June 1938 at Harrisburg by relief of personnel. Assigned on 24 January 1941 to the III Corps. Activated on 1 June 1941 at Camp Roberts, CA. Embarked at the port of San Francisco for transfer to Sumac, Java; departed on 21 November 1941 on the U.S.S. *Republic.* Location 7 December 1941—At sea en route to Australia.

Status: Disbanded on 18 October 1943.

Commanders, 26th Field Artillery Brigade

Unknown	ao December 1934–ao June 1938	*Inactive*	ao June 1938–1 June 1941
Brig. Gen. Marshal MacGruder	August 1941–May 1942		

HHB, 27th Field Artillery Brigade (GHQR)

HQ—*Not organized,* 1933–35; Fourth Corps Area, 1935–36; *Inactive,* 1936–38; Vincennes, IN, 1938–41

Subordinate elements—*63d F.A. Regt.,* 1933–41; 94th F.A. Regt. (RAI), 1933–41; 434th F.A. Regt. (RAI), 1933–41

Constituted in the R.A. on 1 October 1933, allotted to the Fourth Corps Area, and assigned to the GHQR. HHB organized on 21 June 1935 with O.R. personnel as an RAI unit in the Fourth Corps Area. Withdrawn from the Fourth Corps Area on 5 June 1936 and allotted to the Fifth Corps Area. Inactivated on 15 November 1936 in the Fourth Corps Area by relief of personnel. HHB organized by July 1938 with O.R. personnel as an RAI unit at Vincennes, IN. Location 7 December 1941—Vincennes, IN.

Status: Disbanded on 18 October 1943.

Commanders, 27th Field Artillery Brigade

2d Lt. John R. Chadwick**	21 June 1935–28 February 1936	*Inactive*	15 November 1936–ao July 1938
1st Lt. Otha B. Carter**	29 February 1936–15 November 1936	1st Lt. Joseph G. Cors**	ao July 1938–ao August 1938
Unknown	ao August 1938–7 December 1941		

**RAI commanders: O.R. officers.

HHB, 28th Field Artillery Brigade (GHQR)

HQ—*Not organized,* 1933–34; Indianapolis, IN, 1934–41

Subordinate elements—440th F.A. Regt. (RAI), 1933–41; 489th F.A. Regt. (RAI), 1933–41; 492d F.A. Regt. (RAI), 1933–41

Constituted in the R.A. on 1 October 1933, allotted to the Fifth Corps Area, and assigned to the GHQR. HHB organized by June 1934 with O.R. personnel as an RAI unit at Indianapolis, IN. Location 7 December 1941—Indianapolis, IN.

Status: Disbanded 18 October 1943.

Commanders, 28th Field Artillery Brigade

Capt. Ira L. Thurston**	ao June 1934–ao July 1937	Unknown	ao July 1937–7 December 1941

**RAI commanders: O.R. officers.

HHB, 29th Field Artillery Brigade (GHQR)

HQ—*Not organized,* 1933–37; Elizabeth, NJ, 1937–41

Subordinate elements—48th F.A. Regt. (RAI), 1933–41; 49th F.A. Regt. (RAI), 1933–41; 50th F.A. Regt. (RAI), 1933–41

Constituted in the R.A. on 1 October 1933, allotted to the First Corps Area, and assigned to the GHQR. Withdrawn from the First Corps Area on 5 June 1936 and allotted to the Second Corps Area. HHB organized on 21 December 1937 with O.R. personnel as an RAI unit at Elizabeth, NJ. Location 7 December 1941—Elizabeth, NJ.

Status: Disbanded on 18 October 1943.

Commanders, 29th Field Artillery Brigade

Capt. Philip C. Keiper**	21 December 1937–1 May 1941	1st Lt. Robert B. Arnold**	1 May 1941–7 December 1941

**RAI commanders: O.R. officers.

HHB, 45th Field Artillery Brigade (GHQR)

HQ—*Not organized,* 1933–41

Subordinate elements—52d F.A. Regt. (RAI), 1933–41; 53d F.A. Regt. (RAI)

Constituted in the R.A. on 1 October 1933, allotted to the Eighth Corps Area, and assigned to the GHQR. Withdrawn from the Eighth Corps Area on 5 June 1936 and allotted to the Sixth Corps Area. Chicago, IL, designated as HQ on organization, but the unit was never organized at that location. Location 7 December 1941—*Inactive.*

HHB, 46th Field Artillery Brigade (GHQR)

HQ—*Not organized,* 1933–38; Los Angeles, CA, 1938–41; Camp Livingston, LA, 1941

Subordinate elements—54th F.A. Regt. (RAI), 1933–41; 55th F.A. Regt. (RAI), 1933–41; *190th F.A. Regts.,* 1933–40; *196th F.A. Regt.,* 1933–36; 144th F.A. Regt., 1936–40; 350th F.A. Regt., 1941; 351st F.A. Regt., 1941; 353d F.A. Regt., 1941

Constituted in the R.A. on 1 October 1933, allotted to the Ninth Corps Area, and assigned to the GHQR. HHB organized by June 1938 with O.R. personnel as an RAI unit at Los Angeles, CA. Inactivated in January 1941 at Los Angeles by relief of Reserve personnel. Attached to the Third Army on 24 January 1941. Redesignated 46th F.A. Brig. (Colored) and activated on 10 February 1941 at Camp Livingston, LA. Assigned to the Third Army. Location 7 December 1941—Camp Livingston, LA.

Status: Inactive in the R.A. as HHB, 46th Arty. Group (Gp.).

Commanders, 46th Field Artillery Brigade

Unknown	ao June 1938–January 1941	Unknown	10 February 1941–5 April 1941
Inactive	January 1941–5 April 1941	Brig. Gen. George H. Paine	5 April 1941–15 September 1943

HHB, 51st Field Artillery Brigade (26th Division) **Massachusetts National Guard**

HQ—Allston, MA, 1921–41; Camp Edwards, MA, 1941

Subordinate elements—101st and 102d F.A. Regts., 1921–41; 172d F.A. Regt. (designated as the brigade 155-mm Howitzer regiment for mobilization purposes), 1929–40; 180th F.A. Regt., 1940–41; 101st Ammo. Tn., 1921–40

Arrived at the port of Boston on 6 April 1919 on the S.S. *Mongolia* as the 51st F.A. Brig., an element of the 26th Div. Demobilized on 29 April 1919 at Camp Devens, MA. Reconstituted in the N.G. in 1921, assigned to the 26th Div., and allotted to the state of Massachusetts. HQ organized on 20 April 1921 and federally recognized at Allston, MA, as HQ, 1st F.A. Brig., Massachusetts N.G. HQ Btry organized on 30 June 1921 and federally recognized at Allston. Redesignated on 30 September 1921 as HHB, 51st F.A. Brig. Converted on 1 June 1933 from horse drawn to truck drawn. Called up in September 1938 to provide command and control for units performing hurricane and flood relief duties in the Merrimack Valley. Conducted annual summer training at Camp Devens, MA, 1921–33; Underhill Range, VT, 1934 and 1936; and at the Massachusetts State Reservation at Falmouth, MA, 1937–38. Inducted into active Federal service at Allston on 16 January 1941 and moved to Camp Edwards, MA, where it arrived on 24 January 1941. Location 7 December 1941—Camp Edwards, MA.

Status: Active in the Massachusetts N.G. at Rehoboth, MA, as HHB, 42d Inf. Div. Arty.

Events: 190, 280, 301, 330

Commanders, 51st Field Artillery Brigade

Brig. Gen. John H. Sherburne	20 April 1921–10 September 1921	Brig. Gen. Daniel Needham	15 December 1930–16 November 1934
Brig. Gen. Richard K. Hale	10 September 1921–9 September 1926	Brig. Gen. Roger W. Eckfeldt	16 November 1934–16 November 1939
Brig. Gen. Erland F. Fish	10 September 1926–14 November 1930	Brig. Gen. William F. Howe	16 November 1939–12 February 1942

HHB, 52d Field Artillery Brigade (27th Division) **New York National Guard**

HQ—Brooklyn, NY, 1921–40; Jamaica, NY, 1940; Fort McClellan, AL, 1940–41

Subordinate elements—104th and 105th F.A. Regts., 1921–42; 106th F.A., 1929–42; 102d Ammo. Tn., 1921–40

Arrived at the port of New York on 3 March 1919 on the U.S.S. *America* as the 52d F.A. Brig., an element of the 27th Div. Demobilized on 1 April 1919 at Camp Upton, NY. Reconstituted in the N.G. on 30 December 1920, assigned to the 27th Div., and allotted to the state of New York. HQ organized on 20 January 1921 and federally recognized at Brooklyn, NY, as HQ, F.A. Brig., New York N.G. Redesignated on 1 June 1921 as HHB, 52d F.A. Brig. HQ Btry organized on 30 November 1921 and federally recognized at Brooklyn. Converted on 1 February 1933 from horse drawn to tractor drawn. Further reorganized on 1 June 1933 to truck drawn. Conducted annual summer training most years at Pine Camp, NY, 1922–38; and some years at Camp Welsh, NY; Tobyhanna, PA; or Madison Barracks, NY. HHB relocated on 1 February 1940 to Jamaica, NY. Inducted into active Federal service at Jamaica on 15 October 1940 and moved to Fort McClellan, AL, where it arrived on 25 October 1940. Location 7 December 1941—Fort McClellan, AL.

Events: 91, 190, 280, 286, 301, 316, 324, 328

Commanders, 52d Field Artillery Brigade

Brig. Gen. DeWitt C. Weld Jr.	20 January 1921–1 August 1922	Brig. Gen. Elmore F. Austin	15 March 1927–8 May 1928
Col. Elmore F. Austin	1 August 1922–23 June 1923	Brig. Gen. William F. Schohl	14 May 1928–11 August 1938
Brig. Gen. William O. Richardson	23 June 1923–2 October 1925	Brig. Gen. Charles G. Blakeslee	25 August 1938–October 1940
Brig. Gen. Robert W. Marshall	3 October 1925–17 January 1927	Brig. Gen. Ralph M. Pennell (R.A.)	October 1940–8 October 1941
		Col. Remond F. Kernan	1 November 1941–1 September 1942

HHB, 53d Field Artillery Brigade (28th Division) **Pennsylvania National Guard**

HQ—Wilkes-Barre, PA, 1921–23; Pittsburgh, PA, 1923–26; Wilkes-Barre, PA, 1926–39; Pittsburgh, PA, 1939–41; Indiantown Gap, 1941

Subordinate elements—107th and 109th F.A. Regts., 1921–42; 108th F.A., 1929–42; 103d Ammo. Tn., 1921–40

Arrived at the port of New York on 8 May 1919 on the S.S. *Magnolia* as the 53d F.A. Brig., an element of the 28th Div. Demobilized on 22 May at Camp Dix, NJ. Reconstituted in the N.G. in 1921, assigned to the 28th Div., and allotted to the state of Pennsylvania. HQ organized on 15 December 1921 and federally recognized at Wilkes-Barre, PA. Concurrently, HQ Btry organized and federally recognized at Coraopolis, PA. HQ successively relocated as follows: to Pittsburgh, PA, on 23 July 1923; Wilkes-Barre on 15 December 1926; and Pittsburgh on 23 May 1939. Converted on 1 January 1935 from horse drawn to truck drawn. Conducted annual summer training at Tobyhanna, PA; Mount Gretna, PA; or Indiantown Gap, PA, 1922–39. Inducted into active Federal service at Pittsburgh, PA, on 17 February 1941 and moved to Indiantown Gap Military Reservation where it arrived on 26 February 1941. Location 7 December 1941—Indiantown Gap Military Reservation.

Status: Active in the Pennsylvania N.G. at Harrisburg, PA, as HHB, 28th Inf. Div. Arty.

Events: 191, 203, 281, 301, 330

Commanders, 53d Field Artillery Brigade

Brig. Gen. Asher Miner	15 December 1921–22 July 1923	Brig. Gen. Robert M. Vail	17 November 1938–22 May 1939
Brig. Gen. Churchill B. Mehard	23 July 1923–14 December 1926	Brig. Gen. William R. Dunlap	23 May 1939–23 November 1940
Brig. Gen. William S. McLean Jr.	19 February 1927–17 November 1938	Brig. Gen. Eric F. Wood	23 November 1940–7 February 1942

HHB, 54th Field Artillery Brigade (29th Division) **District of Columbia/Maryland and Virginia National Guard**

HQ—*Inactive,* 1921–31; Baltimore, MD, 1931–39**;** Norfolk, VA, 1939–41; Fort George G. Meade, MD, 1941

Subordinate elements—110th and 111th F.A. Regts., 1921–42; 176th F.A., 1929–42; *104th Ammo. Tn.,* 1921–40

Arrived at the port of Newport News on 21 May 1919 on the U.S.S. *Orizaba* as the 54th F.A. Brig., an element of the 29th Div. Demobilized on 26 May at Camp Lee, VA. Reconstituted in the N.G. in 1921, assigned to the 29th Div., and allotted to the District of Columbia. Withdrawn from the District of Columbia on 7 July 1923 and allotted to state of Maryland. HQ organized on 10 July 1931 and federally recognized at Baltimore, MD. HQ Btry organized on 8 June 1932 and federally recognized at Richmond, VA. Converted on 1 January 1935 from horse drawn to truck drawn. Conducted annual summer training at Tobyhanna, PA, and Indiantown Gap, PA, 1931–39. HQ withdrawn from the state of Maryland on 8 August 1939 and allotted to the state of Virginia. HQ organized on 1 October 1939 and federally recognized at Norfolk, VA. Inducted into active Federal service at Richmond on 3 February 1941 and moved to Fort George G. Meade, MD, where it arrived on 6 February

1941. Transferred on 14 September 1941 to the A.P. Hill Military Reservation. Location 7 December 1941—Fort George G. Meade, MD.

Status: Active in the Maryland N.G. at Virginia Beach, VA as HHB, 54th F.A. Brig.

Events: 191, 281, 301, 330

Commanders, 54th Field Artillery Brigade

Brig. Gen. James C. McLanahan (MD) 10 July 1931–December 1938 Brig. Gen. William H. Sands (VA) 9 August 1939–28 February 1942

HHB, 55th Field Artillery Brigade (30th Division) **Georgia National Guard**

HQ—*Inactive,* 1921–23; Savannah, GA, 1923–40; Camp Jackson, SC, 1940–41

Subordinate elements—115th and 118th F.A. Regts., 1921–42; 113th F.A., 1929–42; 105th Ammo. Tn., 1921–40

Arrived at the port of Charleston on 22 March 1919 on the U.S.S. *Finland* as the 55th F.A. Brig., an element of the 30th Div. Demobilized on 10 April 1919 at Fort Oglethorpe, GA. Reconstituted in the N.G. in 1921, assigned to the 30th Div., and allotted to the state of Georgia. HQ organized on 19 June 1923 and federally recognized at Savannah, GA. HQ Btry organized on 17 April 1925 at Savannah by redesignation of A Btry, 118th F.A. Converted on 15 July 1933 from horse drawn to truck drawn. Conducted annual summer training at Fort Bragg, NC, 1923–28, and Camp Jackson, SC, 1929–39. Inducted into active Federal service at Savannah, GA, on 16 September 1940 and moved to Camp Jackson, SC, where it arrived on 19 September 1940. Location 7 December 1941—Camp Jackson, SC.

Status: Inactive in the Georgia N.G. as HHB, 118th F.A. Brig.

Events: 255, 300, 316, 330

Commanders, 55th Field Artillery Brigade

Brig. Gen. Robert J. Travis (GA) 19 June 1923–February 1941 Brig. Gen. Godfrey Cheshire (NC) February 1941–November 1941
Brig. Gen. Arthur McK. Harper (R.A.) November 1941–5 February 1942

HHB, 56th Field Artillery Brigade (31st Division) **Louisiana and Florida National Guard**

HQ—*Inactive,* 1921–24; New Orleans, LA, 1924–34; Jacksonville, FL, 1934–40; Camp Blanding, FL, 1940–41

Subordinate elements—116th and 117th F.A. Regts., 1921–41; 178th F.A., 1930–32; 114th F.A., 1932–41; 106th Ammo. Tn., 1921–40

Arrived at the port of Hoboken on 22 January 1919 on the U.S.S. *Manchuria* as the 56th F.A. Brig., an element of the 31st Div. Demobilized on 14 January 1919 at Camp Gordon, GA. Reconstituted in the N.G. in 1921, assigned to the 31st Div., and allotted to the state of Florida. HQ withdrawn from the Florida N.G. in 1924 and allotted to the state of Louisiana. HQ organized on 12 July 1924 and federally recognized at New Orleans, LA. HQ Btry organized on 27 January 1927 and federally recognized at Avon Park, FL. HQ called up to provide command and control for units performing flood relief duties in the Mississippi River Valley, 26 April–19 June 1927. Converted on 16 July 1933 from horse drawn to truck drawn. HQ withdrawn from the state of Louisiana on 3 October 1934 and allotted to the state of Florida. HQ reorganized on 4 October 1934 and federally recognized at Jacksonville, FL. HQ conducted annual summer training at numerous locations to include Camp Bragg, NC; Camp Beauregard, LA; Camp McClellan, AL; Fort Oglethorpe, GA; Camp Jackson, SC; and Camp Shelby, MS. HQ Btry conducted annual summer training most years at Camp Jackson, 1927–39, except 1930 at Camp McClellan, AL, and 1935 at Camp Beauregard, LA. HHB assembled at Camp Shelby, MS, in December 1939 to conduct additional 2-week annual training directed by the War Department for all N.G. units. Inducted into active Federal service at Avon Park, FL, on 25 November 1940 and moved to Camp Blanding, FL, where it arrived on 14 December 1940. Location 7 December 1941—Camp Blanding, FL.

Events: 56, 255, 300, 325, 328, 330

Commanders, 56th Field Artillery Brigade

Brig. Gen. Allison Owen (LA)	12 July 1924–3 October 1934	Brig. Gen. Sumpter Lowry (FL)	4 October 1934–27 February 1942

HHB, 57th Field Artillery Brigade (32d Division) **Wisconsin and Michigan National Guard**

HQ—*Inactive,* 1921–25; Milwaukee, WI, 1925–40; Camp Beauregard, LA, 1940–41; Camp Livingston, LA, 1941

Subordinate elements—119th and 120th F.A. Regts., 1921–42; 121st F.A., 1929–42; 107th Ammo. Tn., 1921–40

Arrived at the port of Boston on 5 May 1919 on the U.S.S. *Wilhelmina* as the 57th F.A. Brig., an element of the 32d Div. Demobilized on 7 May 1919 at Camp Devens, MA. Reconstituted in the N.G. in 1921, assigned to the 32d Div., and allotted to the state of Wisconsin. HQ organized on 21 March 1925 and federally recognized at Milwaukee, WI. HQ Btry organized on 24 March 1931 and federally recognized at Whitefish Bay, WI. Converted on 17 January 1934 from horse drawn to tractor drawn. Converted on 1 January 1935 from tractor drawn to truck drawn. Conducted annual summer training most years at Camp McCoy, WI, 1925–39. The brigade and its subordinate regiments conducted joint summer training in 1928 at Camp McCoy with the 6th F.A. Brig. (RAI). For at least 1 year, in 1937, the brigade's subordinate regiments also trained 26 company-grade F.A. officers of the 101st Div. at Camp McCoy. Inducted into active Federal service at Whitefish Bay, WI, on 15 October 1940 and moved to Camp Beauregard, LA, where it arrived on 21 October 1940. Transferred on 15 February 1941 to Camp Livingston, LA. Location 7 December 1941—Camp Livingston, LA.

Status: Active in the Wisconsin N.G. at Milwaukee, WI, as HHB, 57th F.A. Brig.

Events: 213, 302, 320, 328

Commanders, 57th Field Artillery Brigade

No commander assigned	21 March 1925–December 1926	Col. Alvin A. Kuchenmeister (WI)	18 September 1940–14 October 1940
Brig. Gen. Irving A. Fish (WI)	December 1926–December 1938	Brig. Gen. William S. Wood (WI)	15 October 1940–October 1941
Col. Joseph H. Lewis (MI)	January 1939–18 September 1940	Brig. Gen. Ellerbe W. Carter (KY)	30 December 1941–16 January 1942

HHB, 58th Field Artillery Brigade (33d Division) **Illinois National Guard**

HQ—*Inactive,* 1921–26; Chicago, IL, 1926–41; Camp Forrest, TN, 1941

Subordinate elements—122d and 124th F.A. Regts., 1921–42; 123d F.A., 1929–42; *108th Ammo. Tn.,* 1921–40

Arrived at the port of Hoboken on 24 May 1919 on the U.S.S. *America* as the 58th F.A. Brig., an element of the 33d Div. Demobilized on 8 June 1919 at Camp Grant, IL. Reconstituted in the N.G. in 1921, assigned to the 33d Div., and allotted to the state of Illinois. HQ Btry organized on 16 April 1926 and federally recognized at Chicago, IL. HQ organized on 29 May 1926 and federally recognized at Chicago. Converted on 13 December 1938 from horse drawn to truck drawn. Conducted annual summer training at Camp Knox, KY, 1926–27; Camp McCoy, WI, 1928–30 and 1935–39; and Camp Grant, IL, 1931–34. Conducted joint summer training in 1928 with the 487th F.A. Regt. at Camp McCoy. For at least 1 year, in 1937, the brigade's subordinate regiments also trained 46 company-grade F.A. officers of the 86th Div. at Camp McCoy. Inducted into active Federal service in Chicago, IL, on 5 March 1941 and moved to Camp Forrest, TN, where it arrived on 12 March 1941. Location 7 December 1941—Camp Forrest, TN.

Status: As HHB, 33d Div. Arty. consolidated with HQ Co., 33d Inf. Brig. on 1 February 1968 and consolidated unit active in the Illinois N.G. at Chicago, IL, as HHC, 33d Area Support Gp.

Events: 213, 302, 316, 324, 328

Commanders, 58th Field Artillery Brigade

Brig. Gen. Henry J. Reilly*	19 March 1921–5 July 1922	Brig. Gen. Frank R. Schwengel	29 May 1926–January 1936
Brig. Gen. Kellogg M. Patterson*	10 August 1923–May 1926	Brig. Gen. Samuel T. Lawton	19 March 1936–16 May 1940
Brig. Gen. Charles C. Haffner	17 May 1940–12 February 1942		

*Designated C.G. for mobilization purposes; not federally recognized as such.

HHB, 59th Field Artillery Brigade (34th Division) **Minnesota National Guard**

HQ—*Inactive,* 1921–24; Minneapolis, MN, 1924–41; Camp Claiborne, LA, 1941

Subordinate elements—125th and 151st F.A. Regts., 1921–42; 185th F.A., 1930–42; *109th Ammo. Tn.,* 1921–40

Arrived at the port of Hoboken on 4 January 1919 on the U.S.S. *Powhatan* as the 59th F.A. Brig., an element of the 34th Div. Demobilized on 24 June 1919 at Camp Dodge, IA. Reconstituted in the N.G. in 1921, assigned to the 34th Div., and allotted to the state of Minnesota. HQ Btry organized on 17 June 1921 as HQ Btry, 1st F.A. Brig. and federally recognized at Minneapolis, MN. Redesignated HQ Btry, 59th F.A. Brig. on 21 November 1921. HQ organized on 28 July 1924 and federally recognized at Minneapolis, MN. Converted on 1 September 1930 from horse drawn to tractor drawn. Further reorganized on 15 August 1933 to truck drawn. Conducted annual summer training at Camp Knox, KY; Camp McCoy, WI; and Fort Snelling, MN, 1924–30; and most years at Camp Ripley, MN, 1931–39. For at least 3 years, 1938–40, the brigade's subordinate units also trained 62 company-grade officers of the 88th Div. at Camp Ripley and Camp Grafton, SD. Inducted into active Federal service at Minneapolis, MN, on 10 February 1941, and moved to Camp Claiborne, LA, where it arrived on 20 February 1941. Location 7 December 1941—Camp Claiborne, LA.

Events: 235, 303, 320, 328

Commanders, 59th Field Artillery Brigade

Brig. Gen. George E. Leach (MN)	28 July 1924–23 June 1940	Col. Stewart G. Collins (MN)	September 1941–October 1941
Brig. Gen. Charles A. Green (MN)	24 June 1940–September 1941	Brig. Gen. LeRoy P. Collins (R.A.)	October 1941–30 January 1942

HHB, 60th Field Artillery Brigade (35th Division) **Kansas National Guard**

HQ—*Inactive,* 1921–23; Topeka, KS, 1923–41; Camp Joseph T. Robinson, AR, 1941

Subordinate elements—130th and 161st F.A. Regts., 1921–42; 142d F.A., 1936–40; 127th F.A., 1940–42; *110th Ammo. Tn.,* 1921–40

Arrived at the port of New York on 18 April 1919 on the U.S.S. *Von Steuben* as the 60th F.A. Brig., an element of the 35th Div. Demobilized on 29 June 1919 at Camp Pike, AR. Reconstituted in the N.G. in 1921, assigned to the 35th Div., and allotted to the state of Kansas. HQ organized on 7 June 1923 and federally recognized at Topeka, KS. HQ Btry organized on 11 June 1923 and federally recognized at Topeka. Converted on 1 July 1933 from horse drawn to truck drawn. HQ Btry called up to perform emergency relief duties in Topeka, 4–6 June 1935. Conducted summer live-fire and maneuver training most years at Fort Riley, KS, 1922–39. For at least 1 year, in 1939, the brigade's subordinate units also trained 37 company-grade officers of the 89th Div. at Fort Riley and Camp Ripley, MN. Inducted into active Federal service at Topeka, KS, on 23 December 1940 and moved to Camp Joseph T. Robinson, AR, where it arrived on 5 January 1941. Location 7 December 1941—Camp Joseph T. Robinson, AR.

Status: Active in the Kansas N.G. at Hutchinson, KS, as HHB, 130th F.A. Brig.

Events: 236, 303, 316, 324, 328

Commanders, 60th Field Artillery Brigade

Brig. Gen. Willie McD. Rowan (KS)	7 June 1923–24 August 1930	Brig. Gen. George H. Wark (KS)	10 February 1933–16 August 1941
No commander assigned	24 August 1930–10 February 1933	Col. Edward H. DeArmond (R.A.)	16 August 1941–5 November 1941
Brig. Gen. Charles P. George (R.A.)	5 November 1941–1 March 1942		

HHB, 61st Field Artillery Brigade (36th Division) — Texas National Guard

HQ—*Inactive,* 1921–24; San Antonio, TX, 1924–40; Camp Bowie, TX, 1940–41

Subordinate elements—131st and 132d F.A. Regts., 1921–42; 133d F.A., 1929–42; *111th Ammo. Tn.,* 1921–40

Arrived at the port of New York on 4 June 1919 as the 61st F.A. Brig., an element of the 36th Div. Demobilized on 19 June 1919 at Camp Bowie, TX. Reconstituted in the N.G. in 1921, assigned to the 36th Div., and allotted to the state of Texas. HQ organized on 17 March 1924 and federally recognized at Fort Worth, TX. Concurrently, HQ Btry organized and federally recognized in San Antonio. Converted on 30 June 1933 from horse drawn to truck drawn. Conducted annual summer training at Camp Stanley, TX, Camp Bullis, TX, and Camp Hulen, TX, 1924–39. For at least 2 years, in 1932 and 1933, the brigade's subordinate regiments also trained 26 company-grade F.A. officers of the 90th Div. at Camp Bullis and Camp Hulen. Designated mobilization training station was Camp Stanley. Inducted into active Federal service at San Antonio, TX, on 24 November 1940, and moved to Camp Bowie, TX, where it arrived on 7 January 1941. Location 7 December 1941—Camp Bowie, TX.

Status: Inactive as HHB, 36th Inf. Div. Arty.

Events: 258, 300, 317, 324, 328

Commanders, 61st Field Artillery Brigade

Brig. Gen. Claude V. Birkhead	17 March 1924–18 September 1936	Brig. Gen. Holman Taylor	19 September 1936–8 April 1938
Brig. Gen. Robert O. Whiteaker	9 April 1938–31 January 1942		

HHB, 62d Field Artillery Brigade (37th Division) — Ohio National Guard

HQ—*Inactive,* 1921–22; Columbus, OH, 1922–37; Cleveland, OH, 1937–40; Camp Shelby, MS, 1940–41

Subordinate elements—134th and 135th F.A. Regts., 1921–42; 136th F.A., 1929–42; 112th Ammo. Tn., 1921–40

Arrived at the port of Newport News on 23 March 1919 on the U.S.S. *New Hampshire* as the 62d F.A. Brig., an element of the 37th Div. Demobilized on 23 June 1919 at Camp Sherman, OH. Reconstituted in the N.G. in 1921, assigned to the 37th Div., and allotted to the state of Ohio. HQ Btry organized on 26 April 1922 and federally recognized at Dayton, OH. HQ organized on 26 July 1922 and federally recognized at Columbus, OH. Converted on 1 January 1935 from horse drawn to truck drawn. Called up to provide command and control for units performing flood relief duties in the Ohio River Valley during January–March 1937. HQ relocated on 1 June 1937 to Cleveland, OH. Conducted annual summer training most years at Camp Knox, KY, 1922–39. Inducted into active Federal service at Dayton, OH, on 15 October 1940, and moved to Camp Shelby, MS, where it arrived on 22 October 1940. Location 7 December 1941—Camp Shelby, MS.

Status: HQ consolidated with HQ, 74th Inf. Brig. on 17 November 1947 and currently active in the Ohio N.G. at Columbus, OH, as HHC, 16th Engr. Brig.; HQ Btry active as HHB, 371st Support Gp.

Events: 213, 220, 302, 320, 324, 328

Commanders, 62d Field Artillery Brigade

Brig. Gen. Harold M. Bush	26 July 1922–13 November 1935	Brig. Gen. William L. Marlin	22 December 1936–7 October 1940
Brig. Gen. Gilson D. Light	20 November 1935–21 December 1936	Brig. Gen. Leo M. Kreber	15 October 1940–16 January 1942

HHB, 63d Field Artillery Brigade (38th Division) **Kentucky National Guard**

HQ—*Inactive,* 1921–23; Louisville, KY, 1923–41; Camp Shelby, MS, 1941

Subordinate elements—138th and 139th F.A. Regts., 1921–42; 150th F.A., 1929–42; 113th Ammo. Tn., 1921–40

Arrived at the port of Newport News on 19 December 1918 as the 63d F.A. Brig., an element of the 38th Div. Demobilized on 18 January 1919 at Fort Benjamin Harrison, IN. Reconstituted in the N.G. in 1921, assigned to the 38th Div., and allotted to the state of Kentucky. HQ Btry organized on 14 February 1923 and federally recognized at Louisville, KY. HQ organized on 5 March 1923 and federally recognized at Louisville. Converted on 1 January 1935 from horse drawn to truck drawn. Called up to provide command and control of flood relief duties along the Ohio River in north central Kentucky during January–February 1937. Conducted annual summer training most years at Camp Knox, KY, 1922–39. Inducted into active Federal service at Louisville, KY, on 17 January 1941, and moved to Camp Shelby, MS, where it arrived on 28 January 1941. Location 7 December 1941—Camp Shelby, MS.

Status: As HHB, 38th Div. Arty. consolidated with HHB, 138th F.A. Gp. on 22 April 1947 and consolidated unit active in the Kentucky N.G. as HHC, 149th Brig., 35th Inf. Div. (Mecz).

Events: 213, 220, 302, 320, 328

Commander, 63d Field Artillery Brigade

Brig. Gen. Ellerbe W. Carter 5 March 1923–October 1941

HHB, 64th Field Artillery Brigade (39th Division) **Louisiana National Guard**

HQ—*Inactive,* 1921–23

Subordinate elements—116th and 141st F.A. Regts, 1921–42; *114th Ammo. Tn.,* 1921–23

Arrived at the port of New York on 18 April 1919 on the U.S.S. *Kaiserin Auguste Victoria* as the 64th F.A. Brig., an element of the 39th Div. Demobilized on 1 May 1919 at Camp Shelby, MS. Reconstituted in the N.G. in 1921 and assigned to the 39th Div. Allotted to the state of Louisiana, but the HQ was not organized before the brigade was withdrawn on 1 July 1923. Designated mobilization station was Camp McClellan, AL.

Status: Inactive as HHB, 39th Inf. Div. Arty.

HHB, 65th Field Artillery Brigade (40th Division) **Utah National Guard**

HQ—*Inactive,* 1921–31; Salt Lake City, UT, 1931–41; Camp San Luis Obispo, CA, 1941

Subordinate elements—143d and 145th F.A. Regts., 1921–42; 222d F.A., 1931–42; *115th Ammo. Tn.,* 1921–40

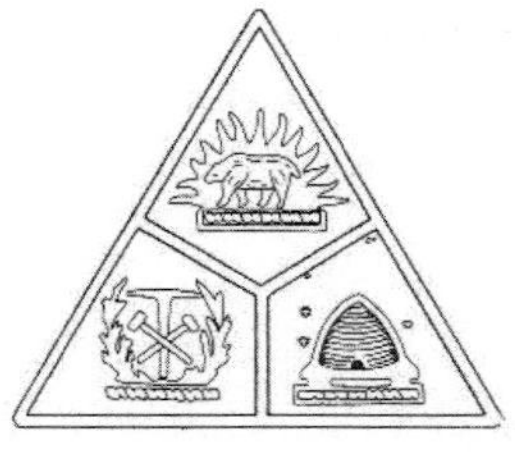

Arrived at the port of New York in December 1918 on the U.S.S. *Mallory* as the 65th F.A. Brig., an element of the 40th Div. Demobilized on 30 June 1919 at Camp Lewis, WA. Reconstituted in the N.G. in 1921, assigned to the 40th Div., and allotted to the state of Utah. HQ organized on 14 May 1931 and federally recognized at Salt Lake City, UT. Converted on 30 November 1934 from horse drawn to truck drawn. HQ Btry organized on 28 April 1936 and federally recognized at Payson, UT. Conducted annual summer training most years at Camp W.G. Williams, UT, 1931–39. Inducted into active Federal service at Salt Lake City, UT, on 3 March 1941 and moved to Camp San Luis Obispo, CA, where it arrived on 18 March 1941. Location 7 December 1941—Camp San Luis Obispo, CA.

Status: Active in the Utah N.G. as HHB, XI Corps Arty.

Events: 231, 304, 314, 326

Commanders, 65th Field Artillery Brigade

Brig. Gen. William G. Williams (UT)	14 May 1931–13 November 1936	Brig. Gen. Albert E. Wilfong (UT)	26 December 1939–7 April 1941
Brig. Gen. Carl A. Badger (UT)	13 November 1936–26 December 1939	Brig. Gen. Harcourt Hervey (CA)	8 April 1941–5 February 1942

HHB, 66th Field Artillery Brigade (41st Division) — Washington National Guard

HQ—*Inactive,* 1921–29; Seattle, WA, 1929–40; Camp Murray, WA, 1940–41; Fort Lewis, WA, 1941

Subordinate elements—146th and 148th F.A. Regts., 1921–42; 218th F.A., 1930–42; *116th Ammo. Tn.,* 1921–40

Arrived at the port of Brooklyn on 15 June 1919 as the 66th F.A. Brig., an element of the 41st Div. Demobilized on 28 June 1919 at Camp Lewis, WA. Reconstituted in the N.G. in 1921, assigned to the 41st Div, and allotted to the state of Washington. HQ organized on 29 March 1929 and federally recognized at Seattle, WA. Converted on 1 January 1935 from horse drawn to truck drawn. HQ Btry organized on 22 April 1936 and federally recognized at Seattle. Conducted annual summer training at Camp Murray, WA, 1929–39. Inducted into active Federal service at Seattle, WA, on 16 September 1940, and moved to Camp Murray, WA, where it arrived on 20 September 1940. Transferred on 20 March 1941 to Fort Lewis, WA. Location 7 December 1941—Fort Lewis, WA.

Status: As HHB, 41st Div. Arty. consolidated with HQ Co., 41st Inf. Div. on 1 March 1963 and consolidated unit active in the Washington N.G. as HHC, 81st Inf. Brig.

Events: 238, 304, 309, 314, 326

Commanders, 66th Field Artillery Brigade

Brig. Gen. Harry G. Winsor	29 March 1929–November 1932	Brig. Gen. Alvin H. Hankins	July 1934–29 September 1934
No commander assigned	November 1932–July 1934	Brig. Gen. Albert H. Beebe	10 October 1934–25 September 1940
Brig. Gen. Marshall G. Randol (R.A.)	25 September 1940–14 February 1942		

HHB, 68th Field Artillery Brigade (43d Division) — Rhode Island and Maine National Guard

HQ—*Not organized,* 1920–30; Providence, RI, 1930–41; Camp Blanding, FL, 1941

Subordinate elements—103d and 152d F.A. Regts ,1921–42; 192d F.A., 1930–41; *118th Ammo. Tn.,* 1921–40

Constituted in the N.G. on 19 October 1920 as an element of the 43d Div. and allotted to the state of Rhode Island. HQ organized on 7 March 1930 and federally recognized at Providence, RI. Converted on 1 June 1933 from horse drawn to truck drawn. HQ Btry allotted to the state of Maine and organized on 1 May 1936 at Bar Harbor, ME, by redesignation of HQ Btry and Combat Tn., 2d Bn., 152d F.A. HQ called up to provide command and control for following state emergencies: units performing riot control duties during a textile workers' strike at Saylesville, Bristol, and Woonsocket, RI, 10–14 September 1934; flood relief duties along the Pawtuxet River at Norwood, RI, 24–26 July 1938; and for hurricane relief duty at Providence, Westerly, and Newport, RI, 21–25 September 1938. Conducted annual summer training at numerous locations to include Niantic, CT, Camp Keyes, ME, Camp Devens, MA, Quonsett Point, RI, and Fort Ethan Allen, VT, 1930–39. Inducted into active Federal service at Providence on 24 February 1941 and moved to Camp Blanding, FL, where it arrived on 19 March 1941. Location 7 December 1941—Camp Blanding, FL.

Status: Active in the Rhode Island N.G. at Providence, RI as HHB, 103d F.A. Brig.

Events: 190, 280, 301, 325, 328, 330

Commanders, 68th Field Artillery Brigade

Brig. Gen. Herbert R. Dean (RI)	7 March 1930–23 February 1937	Brig. Gen. Harold R. Barker (RI)	24 February 1937–19 February 1942

HHB, 69th Field Artillery Brigade (44th Division) **New Jersey National Guard**

HQ—*Not organized,* 1920–29; Camden, NJ, 1929–40; Fort Dix, NJ, 1940–41

Subordinate elements—112th F.A. Regt., 1921–40; 156th F.A. Regt., 1921–42; 157th F.A., 1936–42; 165th F.A. Regt., 1940–42; *119th Ammo. Tn.,* 1921–40

Constituted in the N.G. on 19 October 1920 as an element of the 44th Div. and allotted to the state of New Jersey. HQ organized on 20 February 1929 and federally recognized at Camden, NJ. HQ Btry organized on 19 July 1929 and federally recognized at Camden. Converted on 25 February 1936 from horse drawn to truck drawn. Conducted annual summer training most years at Sea Girt, NJ, 1929–39. Inducted into active Federal service at Camden, NJ, on 16 September 1940, and moved to Fort Dix, NJ, where it arrived on 24 September 1940. Location 7 December 1941—In transit between North Carolina and Fort Dix, NJ.

Status: As HHB, 44th Div. Arty., consolidated on 1 August 1946 with HQ Co., 57th Inf. Brig.; consolidated unit active in the New Jersey N.G. at Fort Dix, NJ, as HHC, 50th Brig., 42d Inf. Div.

Events: 91, 190, 280, 301, 330

Commanders, 69th Field Artillery Brigade

Brig. Gen. Samuel G. Barnard 20 February 1929–30 July 1938
Brig. Gen. Edward C. Rose 6 August 1938–16 September 1941
Brig. Gen. Archibald V. Arnold (R.A.) 16 September 1941–20 February 1942

HHB, 70th Field Artillery Brigade (45th Division) **Oklahoma National Guard**

HQ—*Not organized,* 1921–23; Tulsa, OK, 1923–29; Oklahoma City, OK, 1929–40; Fort Sill, OK, 1940–41; Camp Barkeley, TX, 1941

Subordinate elements—158th and 160th F.A. Regts, 1921–42; 189th F.A., 1930–42; 120th Ammo. Tn., 1921–40

Constituted in the N.G. in 1921 as an element of the 45th Div. and allotted to Oklahoma. HHB organized on 3 August 1923 and federally recognized at Tulsa, OK. HQ Btry relocated on 1 December 1928 to Oklahoma City, OK, by redesignation of HQ Btry and Combat Tn., 2d Bn., 160th F.A. HQ relocated on 17 January 1929 to Oklahoma City. Converted on 2 August 1933 from horse drawn to truck drawn. Conducted summer training most years at Fort Sill, OK, 1924–39. For at least 1 year, in 1933, the brigade's subordinate regiments also trained 30 company-grade F.A. officers of the 95th Div. at Fort Sill. Designated mobilization training station was Fort Sill. Inducted into active Federal service at Oklahoma City on 16 September 1940, and moved to Fort Sill, OK, where it arrived on 24 September 1940. Transferred on 3 March 1941 to Camp Barkeley, TX. Location 7 December 1941—Camp Barkeley, TX.

Events: 258, 300, 317, 328

Commanders, 70th Field Artillery Brigade

Brig. Gen. Alva J. Niles 2 August 1923–August 1928
Brig. Gen. William S. Key 18 August 1928–2 February 1937
Brig. Gen. Raymond S. McLain 2 April 1937–11 February 1942

HHB, 71st Field Artillery Brigade (VI Corps) **New York National Guard**

HQ—New York City, NY, 1940–41; Fort Ethan Allen, VT, 1941

Subordinate elements—186th, 187th, and 258th F.A. Regts., 1940–41

Constituted in the N.G. on 1 September 1940, assigned to the First Army, and allotted to the state of New York. Organized on 15 September 1940 at New York City, NY, by redesignation of HHC, 93d Inf. Brig. as HHB, 71st F.A. Brig. Assigned on 30 December 1940 to the VI Corps. Inducted into active Federal service at New York City, NY, on 3 February 1941, and moved to Fort Ethan Allen, VT, where it arrived on 18 February 1941. Location 7 December 1941—Fort Ethan Allen, VT.

Status: HQ inactive in the New York N.G. as HQ, II Corps Arty; HQ Btry inactive as HQ Btry, XVII Corps Arty.

Events: 330

Commanders, 71st Field Artillery Brigade

Brig. Gen. Joseph A. S. Mundy (NY)	15 September 1940–3 February 1941	Col. Chester B. McCormick (R.A.)	17 February 1941–April 1941
Col. Lewis L. Leavell (NY)	4 February 1941–17 February 1941	Col. Lewis L. Leavell (NY)	April 1941–3 May 1941
Brig. Gen. Karl A. Baehr (R.A.)	3 May 1941–February 1943		

HHB, 72d Field Artillery Brigade (V Corps) **Michigan National Guard**

HQ—Lansing, MI, 1940–41; Fort Leonard Wood, MO, 1941

Subordinate elements—119th, 177th, and 182d F.A. Regts., 1940–41

Constituted in the N.G. on 18 September 1940 and allotted to the state of Michigan. HQ Btry organized on 27 September 1940 and federally recognized at Lansing, MI. HQ organized on 18 October 1940 and federally recognized at Lansing. Attached on 30 December 1940 to the Second Army. Inducted into active Federal service at Lansing on 7 April 1941, assigned to the V Corps, and moved to Fort Leonard Wood, MO, where it arrived on 2 June 1941. Location 7 December 1941—Fort Leonard Wood, MO.

Events: 324

Commander, 72d Field Artillery Brigade

Brig. Gen. Joseph H. Lewis (MI)	18 September 1940–December 1941

HHB, 73d Field Artillery Brigade (V Corps) **Pennsylvania National Guard**

HQ—Philadelphia, PA, 1940–41; Camp Shelby, MS, 1941

Subordinate elements—141st, 166th, and 190th F.A. Regts., 1940–41

Constituted in the N.G. on 1 September 1940 and allotted to the state of Pennsylvania. HQ organized on 23 September 1940 at Philadelphia, PA, by consolidation of HQ, 22d Cav. Div.; HQ, 52d Cav. Brig.; and HQ, 122d Medical (Med.) Squadron (Sq.) and redesignation as HHB, 73d F.A. Brig. HQ Btry organized on 17 October 1940 at Philadelphia by redesignation and reorganization of the 22d Signal (Sig.) Troop (Tp.). Assigned on 30 December 1940 to the V Corps. Inducted into active Federal service in Philadelphia on 13 January 1941 and moved to Camp Shelby, MS, where it arrived on 18 January 1941. Location 7 December 1941—Camp Shelby, MS.

Status: Inactive in the Pennsylvania N.G. as HHB, XXII Corps Arty.

Commanders, 73d Field Artillery Brigade

Brig. Gen. Edward J. Stackpole (PA)	1 November 1940–20 November 1940
Brig. Gen. Frank A. Warner (PA)	20 November 1940–6 December 1940
Brig. Gen. William March (PA)	6 December 1940–April 1942

HHB, 74th Field Artillery Brigade (IV Corps) **Georgia National Guard**

HQ—*Not organized,* 1940–41; Camp Blanding, FL, 1941

Subordinate elements—172d and 179th F.A. Regts., 1940–41

Constituted in the N.G. on 1 September 1940, and allotted to the state of Georgia. HQ Btry organized in the fall of 1940 at Gainesville, GA. Assigned on 30 December 1940 to the IV Corps. HQ Btry inducted into active Federal service at Gainesville in February 1941 and moved to Camp Blanding, FL, where it arrived in late February 1941. HQ activated in Federal service on 24 February 1941 at Camp Blanding, FL, and assigned to the IV Corps. Location 7 December 1941—Camp Blanding, FL.

Events: 330

Commanders, 74th Field Artillery Brigade

Brig. Gen. Ira T. Wyche (R.A.)	1 May 1941–16 April 1942

HHB, 75th Field Artillery Brigade (VII Corps) **Tennessee National Guard**

HQ—*Not organized,* 1940–41; Camp Forrest, TN, 1941

Subordinate elements—168th, 181st, and 191st F.A. Regts., and 14th Obsn. Bn., 1940–41

Constituted in the N.G. on 30 October 1940 and allotted to the state of Tennessee. HQ Btry concurrently organized at Lebanon, TN. Assigned on 30 December 1940 to the VII Corps. HQ Btry called to active Federal service on 24 February 1941 and transferred to Camp Forrest, TN. HQ activated soon thereafter at Camp Forrest. Location 7 December 1941—Camp Forrest, TN.

Events: 324

Commanders, 75th Field Artillery Brigade

Col. Edward H. DeArmond (R.A.)	24 February 1941–March 1941
Brig. Gen. Raymond Yenter (IA)	March 1941–December 1941
Col. Ralph Hospital (R.A.)	December 1941–June 1942

HHB, 76th Field Artillery Brigade (IX Corps) **California National Guard**

HQ—Santa Paula, CA, 1940–41; Fort Francis E. Warren, WY, 1941

Subordinate elements—144th, 183d, and 188th F.A. Regts., 1940–41

Constituted in the N.G. on 1 September 1940 and allotted to the state of California. HHB organized on 16 December 1940 at Santa Paula, CA. Inducted into active Federal service at Santa Paula, assigned to the IX Corps, and transferred to Fort Francis E. Warren, WY, where it arrived on 1 April 1941. Location 7 December 1941—Fort Francis E. Warren, WY.

Events: 326

Commanders, 76th Field Artillery Brigade

Col. Samuel D. Hays (CA)	16 December 1940–1 May 1941
Brig. Gen. Lloyd E. Jones (R.A.)	1 May 1941–December 1941

HHB, 81st Field Artillery Brigade (I Corps) **Massachusetts National Guard**

HQ—*Not organized,* 1921–23

Subordinate elements—172d, *173d*, and 192d F.A. Regts., *131st Ammo. Tn., 101st Obsn. Bn.*, and 360th Ord. Co., 1921–23

Constituted in the N.G. as the 81st F.A. Brig. in 1921, assigned to the I Corps, and allotted to the state of Massachusetts. Placed on the deferred list on 2 July 1923, transferred to the O.R. as a DNG unit, and redesignated as the 194th F.A.

Brig. Withdrawn as a DNG unit on 11 January 1927 and allotted permanently to the O.R. as the 194th F.A. Brig. Concurrently withdrawn from the First Corps Area and allotted to the Fifth Corps Area.

HHB, 82d Field Artillery Brigade (III Corps) **Pennsylvania National Guard**

HQ—*Not organized,* 1921–23

Subordinate elements—108th, 176th, and 440th F.A. Regts., 132d Ammo. Tn., 310th Obsn. Bn., and 362d Ord. Co., 1921–23

Constituted in the N.G. as the 82d F.A. Brig. in 1921, assigned to the III Corps, and allotted to the state of Pennsylvania. Placed on the deferred list on 2 July 1923, transferred to the O.R., and redesignated as the 190th F.A. Brig. Withdrawn from the state of Pennsylvania on 30 October 1923.

HHB, 83d Field Artillery Brigade (V Corps) **Indiana National Guard**

HQ—*Not organized,* 1921–23

Subordinate elements—179th, 180th, and 181st F.A. Regts., *134th Ammo. Tn., 103d Obsn. Bn.*, and 364th Ord. Co., 1921–23

Constituted in the N.G. as the 83d F.A. Brig. in 1921, assigned to the V Corps, and allotted to the state of Indiana. Placed on the deferred list on 2 July 1923, transferred to the O.R., and redesignated as the 191st F.A. Brig.

HHB, 84th Field Artillery Brigade (VI Corps) **Michigan National Guard**

HQ—*Not organized,* 1921–23

Subordinate elements—121st, 123d, 182d, and 442d F.A. Regts., *135th Ammo. Tn., 15th Obsn. Bn.*, and 365th Ord. Co., 1921–23

Constituted in the N.G. as the 84th F.A. Brig. in 1921, assigned to the VI Corps, and allotted to the state of Michigan. Placed on the deferred list on 2 July 1923, transferred to the O.R., and redesignated as the 192d F.A. Brig.

HHB, 85th Field Artillery Brigade (VIII Corps) **Colorado National Guard**

HQ—*Not organized,* 1921–23

Subordinate elements—*187th, 188th*, and 189th F.A. Regts., 312th Obsn. Bn., and 9th Ord. Co., 1921–23

Constituted in the N.G. as the 85th F.A. Brig. in 1921, assigned to the VIII Corps, and allotted to the state of Colorado. Placed on the deferred list on 2 July 1923, transferred to the O.R. as a DNG. unit, and redesignated as the 193d F.A. Brig. Withdrawn as a DNG. unit on 11 January 1927 and allotted permanently to the O.R. as the 193d F.A. Brig. Concurrently withdrawn from the Eighth Corps Area and allotted to the Seventh Corps Area.

HHB, 86th Field Artillery Brigade (IX Corps) **California National Guard**

HQ—*Not organized,* 1921–23

Subordinate elements—113th, 178th, *190th,* and *196th* F.A. Regts., 311th Obsn. Bn., and 18th Ord. Co., 1921–23

Constituted in the N.G. as the 86th F.A. Brig. in 1921, assigned to the IX Corps, and allotted to the state of California. Placed on the deferred list on 2 July 1923, transferred to the O.R., and redesignated as the 189th F.A. Brig.

HHB, 151st Field Artillery Brigade (76th Division) **Organized Reserve Connecticut**

HQ—New Haven, CT, 1921–41

Subordinate elements—302d and 355th F.A. Regts. and 301st Ammo. Tn., 1921–41; 364th F.A. Regt., 1929–41

Constituted in the O.R. on 24 June 1921, assigned to the 76th Div., and allotted to the First Corps Area. Initiated in November 1921 at New Haven, CT. Consolidated on 12 October 1936 with the 151st F.A. Brig. (a World War I unit constituted in the National Army on 5 August 1917; organized on 29 August 1917 at Camp Devens, MA; arrived at the port of Hoboken on the U.S.S. *Matsonia* on 3 February 1919; transferred to Camp Devens, MA, where it was demobilized on 5 May 1919; reconstituted on 12 October 1936). Typically conducted Inactive Training Period meetings at Artillery Hall in New Haven, CT. Conducted summer training most years at Camp Devens, MA, or Fort Ethan Allen, VT. Location 7 December 1941—New Haven, CT.

Status: Inactive in the US Army Reserve as HHC, 76th Regt. (CST).

Commanders, 151st Field Artillery Brigade

Maj. James W. Gilson	November 1921–12 November 1924	Maj. Roland S. Hotchkiss	ao June 1929–ao July 1932
Maj. Donald S. Babcock	12 November 1924–21 December 1926	Unknown	ao July 1932–ao June 1938
Unknown	21 December 1926–ao June 1928	1st Lt. Dwight P. Keller	ao June 1938–ao June 1939
Capt. John McD. Herbert	ao June 1928–ao October 1928	Unknown	ao June 1939–ao March 1941
Capt. William O. Thompson	ao March 1941–7 December 1941		

HHB, 152d Field Artillery Brigade (77th Division) **Organized Reserve New York**

HQ—Manhattan, NY, 1921–41

Subordinate elements—304th and 305th F.A. Regts. and 302d Ammo. Tn., 1921–41; 306th F.A. Regt., 1929–41

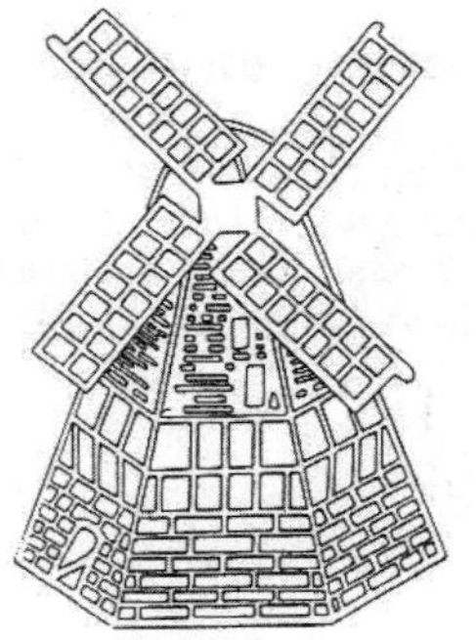

Constituted in the O.R. on 24 June 1921, assigned to the 77th Div., and allotted to the Second Corps Area. Initiated on 28 September 1921 at Manhattan, NY. Consolidated on 12 October 1936 with the 152d F.A. Brig. (a World War I unit constituted in the National Army on 5 August 1917; organized on 5 September 1917 at Camp Upton, NY; arrived at the port of Hoboken on 25 April 1919 on the U.S.S. *Mount Vernon*; transferred to Camp Upton, where it was demobilized on 9 May 1919; reconstituted on 12 October 1936). Conducted summer training most years with units of the 1st F.A. Brig. at Camp Dix, NJ, and some years at Fort Slocum, NY, or Fort Hoyle, MD. Subordinate regiments conducted training of CMTC at Madison Barracks, NY, with assistance from the 5th and 7th F.A. Regts. Location 7 December 1941—Manhattan, NY.

Status: Inactive in the US Army Reserve as HHB, 77th Inf. Div. Arty.

Events: 153, 168

Commanders, 152d Field Artillery Brigade

Maj. Lewis Sanders	28 September 1921–27 January 1922	Col. James E. Austin	May 1929–10 October 1937
Lt. Col. Jack A. Rainier	27 January 1922–15 March 1922	Col. Lewis Sanders	10 October 1937–30 January 1941
Col. Dallas S. Townsend	15 March 1922–26 July 1922	Lt. Col. Gustavus G. Reiniger	30 January 1941–3 May 1941
Brig. Gen. Henry L. Stimson	26 July 1922–May 1929	Lt. Col. John H. Allen	3 May 1941–ao December 1941

HHB, 153d Field Artillery Brigade (78th Division) **Organized Reserve New Jersey**

HQ—Bayonne, NJ, 1921–37; Englewood, NJ, 1937–41

Subordinate elements—307th and 308th F.A. Regts. and 303d Ammo. Tn., 1921–41; 471st F.A. Regt., 1929; 309th F.A. Regt., 1929–41

Constituted in the O.R. on 24 June 1921, allotted to the Second Corps Area, and assigned to the 78th Div. Initiated on 23 November 1921 at Bayonne, NJ. Consolidated on 12 October 1936 with the 153d F.A. Brig. (a World War I unit constituted in the National Army on 5 August 1917; organized on 4 September 1917 at Camp Dix, NJ; arrived on 14 May 1919 at the port of Brooklyn on the S.S. *Pesaro*; transferred to Camp Dix where it was demobilized on 21 May 1919; reconstituted on 12 October 1936). Relocated on 5 April 1937 to Englewood, NJ. Conducted summer training most years with units of the 1st F.A. Brig. at Camp Dix, NJ, and some years at Sea Girt, NJ. Subordinate regiments conducted training of CMTC at Madison Barracks, NY, with assistance from the 5th and 7th F.A. Regts. Location 7 December 1941—Englewood, NJ.

Status: Inactive in the US Army Reserve as HHC, 78th Regt. (CST).

Events: 168

Commanders, 153d Field Artillery Brigade

1st Lt. Charles L. Gulick	23 November 1921–25 January 1922	Unknown	ao January 1923–ao June 1929
Lt. Col. Leigh K. Lydecker	25 January 1922–ao March 1922	Maj. Roy M. Hunter	ao June 1929–11 April 1932
Lt. Col. Lewis Sanders	ao October 1922–ao January 1923	Col. Dallas S. Townsend	11 April 1932–ao June 1941
Unknown	ao June 1941–7 December 1941		

HHB, 154th Field Artillery Brigade (79th Division) **Organized Reserve Pennsylvania**

HQ—Philadelphia, PA, 1921–41

Subordinate elements—310th and 311th F.A. Regts. and 304th Ammo. Tn., 1921–41; 312th F.A. Regt., 1929–41

Constituted in the O.R. on 24 June 1921, assigned to the 79th Div., and allotted to the Third Corps Area. Initiated on 9 December 1921 at Philadelphia, PA. Consolidated on 12 October 1936 with the 154th F.A. Brig. (a World War I unit constituted in the National Army on 5 August 1917; organized on 29 August 1917 at Camp George G. Meade, MD; arrived at the port of Hoboken on 26 May 1919 on the U.S.S. *Princess Matoika*; transferred to Camp Dix, NJ, where it was demobilized on 30 May 1919; reconstituted on 12 October 1936). Conducted summer training most years with the 6th F.A. at Fort Hoyle, MD, and with the 16th F.A. at Fort George G. Meade, MD. Subordinate regiments conducted training of CMTC at Fort Hoyle with assistance from the 6th F.A. Regt. Location 7 December 1941—Philadelphia, PA.

Status: Inactive in the US Army Reserve as HHB, 79th Inf. Div. Arty.

Commanders, 154th Field Artillery Brigade

Capt. J. B. Gribbel	9 December 1921–6 May 1922	Unknown	ao June 1930–ao May 1931
Lt. Col. Daniel M. Bates	6 May 1922–June 1925	Maj. Fred L. Poechrer	ao May 1931–ao April 1934
Col. Joseph W. Keller	June 1925–September 1925	Lt. Col. Colbert C. McLain	ao August 1934–ao August 1935
Lt. Col. Daniel M. Bates	September 1925–ao November 1925	Col. Joseph W. Keller	ao April 1936–August 1938
Unknown	ao November 1925–ao March 1927	Lt. Col. Virgil O. Barnard	August 1938–June 1941
Capt. Curtis S. Fisher	ao March 1927–ao June 1930	Maj. Lavern G. Whitmer	June 1941–7 August 1941

HHB, 155th Field Artillery Brigade (80th Division) **Organized Reserve District of Columbia**

HQ—Washington, DC, 1921–41

Subordinate elements—313th and 314th F.A. Regts. and 305th Ammo. Tn., 1921–41; 315th F.A. Regt., 1929–41

Constituted in the O.R. on 24 June 1921, assigned to the 80th Div., and allotted to the Third Corps Area. Initiated on 4 November 1921 at Washington, DC. Consolidated on 12 October 1936 with the 155th F.A. Brig. (a World War I unit constituted in the National Army on 5 August 1917; organized on 27 August 1917 at Camp Lee, VA; arrived at the port of Newport News on 28 May 1919 on the U.S.S. *Zeppelin*; transferred to Camp Lee where it was demobilized on 1 June 1919; reconstituted on 12 October 1936). Typically conducted Inactive Training Period meetings at the Munitions Building in Washington. Conducted summer training most years with the 6th F.A. at Fort Hoyle, MD, and with the 16th F.A. at Fort George G. Meade, MD. Subordinate regiments conducted training of CMTC at Fort Hoyle with assistance from the 6th F.A. Regt. Location 7 December 1941—Washington, DC.

Status: Inactive in the US Army Reserve as HHC, 80th Regt. (CST).

Commanders, 155th Field Artillery Brigade

Lt. Col. Vincent A. Carroll	4 November 1921–15 May 1923	Unknown	ao May 1932–ao January 1934
Brig. Gen. William Chamberlaine	15 May 1923–8 June 1925	Maj. Fred A. Carter	ao January 1934–15 February 1935
Lt. Col. Vincent A. Carroll	8 June 1925–30 April 1930	Lt. Col. Ernest S. Cox	15 February 1935–ao August 1935
Col. Elisha F. Riggs	30 April 1930–August 1930	Maj. Leonard D. Densmore	ao April 1936–3 June 1936
Lt. Col. James H. Beazley	August 1930–26 February 1932	Brig. Gen. Albert L. Cox	3 June 1936–June 1940
Lt. Col. James A. Anderson	26 February 1932–ao May 1932	Lt. Col. Edwin S. Bettelheim	June 1940–1 March 1941

HHB, 156th Field Artillery Brigade (81st Division) **Organized Reserve North Carolina**

HQ—*Not initiated,* 1921–22; Raleigh, NC, 1922–41

Subordinate elements—316th and 317th F.A. Regts. and 306th Ammo. Tn., 1921–41; 318th F.A. Regt., 1929–41

Constituted in the O.R. on 24 June 1921, assigned to the 81st Div., and allotted to the Fourth Corps Area. Initiated in October 1922 at Raleigh, NC. Consolidated on 12 October 1936 with the 156th F.A. Brig. (a World War I unit constituted in the National Army on 5 August 1917; organized on 29 August 1917 at Camp Jackson, SC; arrived at the port of Newport News on 1 June 1919 on the U.S.S. *Cap Finisterre*; transferred to Camp Lee, VA, where it was demobilized on 11 June 1919; reconstituted on 12 October 1936). Conducted summer training most years with units of the 13th F.A. Brig. at Fort Bragg, NC, 1922–40. Subordinate regiments conducted training of CMTC at Fort Bragg. Location 7 December 1941—Raleigh, NC.

Status: Inactive in the US Army Reserve as HHB, 81st Inf. Div. Arty.

Commanders, 156th Field Artillery Brigade

Brig. Gen. Albert L. Cox	10 November 1922–26 March 1934	Maj. T.A. Cox Jr.	ao December 1937–ao January 1938
Unknown	26 March 1934–ao December 1937	Unknown	ao January 1938–7 December 1941

HHB, 157th Field Artillery Brigade (82d Division) **Organized Reserve South Carolina**

HQ—*Not initiated,* 1921–22; Columbia, SC, 1922–27; Spartanburg, SC, 1927–41

Subordinate elements—319th and 320th F.A. Regts. and 307th Ammo. Tn., 1921–41; 452d F.A. Regt., 1928–29; 321st F.A. Regt., 1929–41

Constituted in the O.R. on 24 June 1921, assigned to the 82d Div., and allotted to the Fourth Corps Area. Initiated on 14 January 1922 at Columbia, SC. Relocated on 8 July 1927 to Spartanburg, SC. Consolidated on 12 October 1936 with the 157th F.A. Brig. (a World War I unit constituted in the National Army on 5 August 1917; organized on 2 September 1917 at Camp Gordon, GA; arrived at the port of New York on 6 May 1919 on the U.S.S. *Black Arrow*; transferred to Camp Upton, NY, where it was demobilized on 23 May 1919; reconstituted on 12 October 1936). Conducted summer training most years with units of the 13th F.A. Brig. at Fort Bragg, NC, 1922–40. Subordinate regiments conducted training of CMTC at Fort Bragg. Location 7 December 1941— Spartanburg, SC.

Status: Active in the R.A. at Fort Bragg, NC, as HHB, 82d Airborne (Abn) Div. Arty.

Commanders, 157th Field Artillery Brigade

Capt. Gilbert P. Kearns	14 January 1922–ao February 1922	Capt. Frederick T. Parker	ao October 1936–5 November 1936
Unknown	ao February 1922–ao October 1936	Unknown	5 November 1936–7 December 1941

HHB, 158th Field Artillery Brigade (83d Division) **Organized Reserve Ohio**

HQ—*Not initiated,* 1921–22; Columbus, OH, 1922–41

Subordinate elements—322d and 323d F.A. Regts. and 308th Ammo. Tn., 1921–41; 324th F.A. Regt., 1929–41

Constituted in the O.R. on 24 June 1921, assigned to the 83d Div., and allotted to the Fifth Corps Area. Initiated on 4 February 1922 at Columbus, OH. Consolidated on 12 October 1936 with the 158th F.A. Brig. (a World War I unit constituted in the National Army on 5 August 1917; organized on 30 August 1917 at Camp Sherman, OH; arrived at the port of Hoboken on 13 May 1919 on the U.S.S. *Von Steuben*; transferred to Camp Sherman, where it was demobilized on 24 May 1919; reconstituted on 12 October 1936). Conducted summer training most years at Camp Knox, KY, 1922–40. Subordinate regiments conducted training of CMTC at Fort Benjamin Harrison, IN, or Camp Knox. Location 7 December 1941—Columbus, OH.

Status: Inactive in the US Army Reserve as HHB, 83d Inf. Div. Arty.

Commanders, 158th Field Artillery Brigade

Brig. Gen. Charles X. Zimmerman	4 February 1922–13 November 1926	Unknown	13 November 1926–7 December 1941

HHB, 159th Field Artillery Brigade (84th Division) **Organized Reserve Indiana**

HQ—*Not initiated,* 1921–22; Indianapolis, IN, 1922–41

Subordinate elements—325th and 326th F.A. Regts. and 309th Ammo. Tn., 1921–41; 403d F.A. Regt., 1929–41

Constituted in the O.R. on 24 June 1921, assigned to the 84th Div., and allotted to the Fifth Corps Area. Initiated on 30 November 1921 at Indianapolis, IN. Consolidated on 12 October 1936 with the 159th F.A. Brig. (a World War I unit constituted in the National Army on 5 August 1917; organized on 7 November 1917 at Camp Zachary Taylor, KY; arrived at the port of Hoboken on 17 January 1919 on the U.S.S. *Wilhelmina*; transferred to Camp Zachary Taylor, KY, where it was demobilized on 26 January 1919; reconstituted on 12 October 1936). Conducted summer training most years at Camp Knox, KY, 1922–40. Conducted summer training at Camp Knox with HHB, 62d F.A. Brig. in 1928 and 1930. Subordinate regiments conducted training of CMTC at Fort Benjamin Harrison, IN. Location 7 December 1941—Indianapolis, IN.

Status: Inactive in the US Army Reserve as HHC, 84th Regt. (CST).

Commanders, 159th Field Artillery Brigade

2d Lt. V.E. Tharpe	30 November 1921–June 1922	Col. Robert L. Moorhead	November 1922–ao April 1923
Maj. Azra W. Koontz	June 1922–November 1922	Col. F.W. Glover	ao July 1924–August 1924
Unknown	August 1924–7 December 1941		

HHB, 160th Field Artillery Brigade (85th Division) **Organized Reserve Michigan**

HQ—*Not initiated,* 1921–22; Holland, MI, 1922–23; Detroit, MI, 1923–41

Subordinate elements—328th and 329th F.A. Regts. and 310th Ammo. Tn., 1921–41; 330th F.A. Regt., 1929; 403d F.A. Regt., 1929–41

Constituted in the O.R. on 24 June 1921, assigned to the 85th Div., and allotted to the Fifth Corps Area. Initiated in October 1922 at Holland, MI. Relocated on 12 January 1923 to Detroit, MI. Consolidated on 12 October 1936 with the 160th F.A. Brig. (a World War I unit constituted in the National Army on 5 August 1917; organized on 25 August 1917 at Camp Custer, MI; arrived at the port of New York on 2 April 1919 on the U.S.S. *Leviathan*; transferred to Camp Custer where it was demobilized on 16 April 1919; reconstituted on 12 October 1936). Conducted summer training most years at Camp Custer, MI, and some years at Camp McCoy, WI, or Camp Grayling, MI, 1922–40. Location 7 December 1941—Detroit, MI.

Status: Inactive in the US Army Reserve as HHC, 85th Regt. (CST).

Commanders, 160th Field Artillery Brigade

Unknown	October 1922–ao September 1925	Maj. George A. Ivanick	5 October 1927–ao October 1930
Maj. Charles Cromby	ao September 1925–5 October 1927	Unknown	ao October 1930–7 December 1941

HHB, 161st Field Artillery Brigade (86th Division) **Organized Reserve Illinois**

HQ—*Not initiated,* 1921–22; Chicago, IL, 1922–41

Subordinate elements—331st and 332d F.A. Regts. and 311th Ammo. Tn., 1921–41; 333d F.A. Regt., 1929; 404th F.A. Regt., 1929–41

Constituted in the O.R. on 24 June 1921, assigned to the 86th Div., and allotted to the Sixth Corps Area. Initiated on 6 March 1922 at Chicago, IL. Consolidated on 12 October 1936 with the 161st F.A. Brig. (a World War I unit constituted in the National Army on 5 August 1917; organized on 23 August 1917 at Camp Grant, IL; arrived at the port of Hoboken on 3 January 1919 on the U.S.S. *Siboney*; transferred to Camp Grant where it was demobilized on 20 January 1919; reconstituted on 12 October 1936). Conducted summer training most years at Camp Custer, MI, and some years at Camp McCoy, WI, or Fort Sheridan, IL, 1922–40. Subordinate regiments conducted training of CMTC at Camp McCoy. Location 7 December 1941—Chicago, IL.

Status: Inactive in the US Army Reserve as HHB, 86th Inf. Div. Arty.

Events: 161

Commanders, 161st Field Artillery Brigade

Maj. Calvin D. Allen	6 March 1922–July 1922	Col. Noble B. Judah	September 1930–September 1937
Brig. Gen. Henry J. Reilly	July 1922–September 1930	Col. Edward N. Wentworth	September 1937–June 1941

HHB, 162d Field Artillery Brigade (87th Division) **Organized Reserve Louisiana**

HQ—*Not initiated,* 1921–22; New Orleans, LA, 1922–41

Subordinate elements—334th and 336th F.A. Regts. and 312th Ammo. Tn., 1921–41; 335th F.A. Regt., 1929–41

Constituted in the O.R. on 24 June 1921, assigned to the 87th Div., and allotted to the Fourth Corps Area. Initiated on 19 December 1921 at New Orleans, LA. Consolidated on 12 October 1936 with the 162d F.A. Brig. (a World War I unit constituted in the National Army on 5 August 1917; organized 1 September 1917 at Camp Pike, AR; arrived at the port of Hoboken, NJ, in February 1919; transferred to Camp Dix, NJ, where it was demobilized on 1 March 1919; reconstituted on 12 October 1936). Conducted summer training most years at Fort Bragg, NC, and some years at Fort Sam Houston, TX, 1922–40. Subordinate regiments conducted training of CMTC at Fort Bragg. Location 7 December 1941—New Orleans, LA.

Status: Inactive in the US Army Reserve as HHB, 87th Inf. Div. Arty.

Commanders, 162d Field Artillery Brigade

Maj. James A. Blount	19 December 1921–ao September 1925	Col. Richard H. Miller	ao November 1937–ao January 1938
Unknown	ao September 1925–ao November 1937	Unknown	ao January 1938–7 December 1941

HHB, 163d Field Artillery Brigade (88th Division) **Organized Reserve Iowa**

HQ—*Not initiated,* 1921–22; Des Moines, IA, 1922–41

Subordinate elements—337th and 338th F.A. Regts. and 313th Ammo. Tn., 1921–41; 339th F.A. Regt., 1929–41

Constituted in the O.R. on 24 June 1921, assigned to the 88th Div., and allotted to the Seventh Corps Area. Initiated in April 1922 at Des Moines, IA. HQ Btry relocated on 3 April 1928 to Carroll, IA. Consolidated on 12 October 1936 with the 163d F.A. Brig. (a World War I unit constituted in the National Army on 5 August 1917; organized on 25 August 1917 at Camp Dodge, IA; arrived at the port of Hoboken, NJ, in January 1919; transferred to Camp Dodge, where it was demobilized on 21 January 1919; reconstituted on 12 October 1936). Conducted summer training at numerous locations to include Fort Snelling, MN; Fort Des Moines, IA; Camp McCoy, WI; Camp Ripley, MN; and Fort Riley, KS, 1922–40. Subordinate regiments conducted training of CMTC at Fort Snelling. Location 7 December 1941—Des Moines, IA.

Status: Inactive in the US Army Reserve as HHB, 88th Inf. Div. Arty.

Commanders, 163d Field Artillery Brigade

Maj. L. S. Miller	April 1922–August 1924	Capt. Oscar L. Nay	ao June 1928–ao May 1929
Maj. Cecil M. Harris	August 1924–ao September 1925	Maj. Chester W. Wilson	ao April 1930–ao October 1930
Unknown	ao September 1925–ao February 1927	Unknown	ao October 1930–ao June 1938
Maj. Einer Johnson	ao February 1927–ao July 1927	Maj. Charles R. Snowden	ao June 1938–ao July 1938
Unknown	ao July 1938–7 December 1941		

HHB, 164th Field Artillery Brigade (89th Division) **Organized Reserve Nebraska**

HQ—*Not initiated,* 1921–22; Lincoln, NE, 1922–41

Subordinate elements—340th and 341st F.A. Regts. and 314th Ammo. Tn., 1921–41; 342d F.A. Regt., 1929–41

Constituted in the O.R. on 24 June 1921, assigned to the 89th Div., and allotted to the Seventh Corps Area. Initiated in February 1922 at Lincoln, NE. Consolidated on 12 October 1936 with the 164th F.A. Brig. (a World War I unit constituted in the National Army on 5 August 1917; organized on 5 September 1917 at Camp Funston, KS; arrived at the port of Hoboken on 27 May 1919 on the U.S.S. *Prinz Frederich Wilhelm*; transferred to Camp Funston, where it was demobilized on 5 June 1919; reconstituted on 12 October 1936). Conducted summer training most years at Fort Des Moines, IA, and some years at Fort Riley, KS; Fort Robinson, NE; and Fort Crook, NE, 1922–40. Subordinate regiments conducted training of CMTC at Fort Des Moines. Location 7 December 1941—Lincoln, NE.

Status: Inactive in the US Army Reserve as HHC, 89th Regt. (CST).

Commanders, 164th Field Artillery Brigade

Unknown	February 1922–ao October 1937	Maj. Charles A. Anderson	1 November 1937–26 July 1939
Maj. W.F. Bruett	ao October 1937–1 November 1937	Maj. Roy Stockwell	26 July 1939–ao August 1941

HHB, 165th Field Artillery Brigade (90th Division) **Organized Reserve Texas**

HQ—Dallas, TX, 1921–25; Waco, TX, 1925–41

Subordinate elements—343d and 344th F.A. Regts. and 315th Ammo. Tn., 1921–41; 345th F.A. Regt., 1929–41

Constituted in the O.R. on 24 June 1921, assigned to the 90th Div., and allotted to the Eighth Corps Area. Initiated on 12 December 1921 at Dallas, TX. Relocated on 10 July 1925 to Waco, TX. Consolidated on 12 October 1936 with the 165th F.A. Brig. (a World War I unit constituted in the National Army on 5 August 1917; organized on 25 August 1917 at Camp Bowie, TX; arrived at the port of New York on 6 June 1919 on the U.S.S. *Madawaska*; transferred to Camp Bowie, where it was demobilized on 20 June 1919; reconstituted on 12 October 1936). Conducted summer training most years with units of the 2d F.A. Brig. at Fort Sam Houston, TX, Camp Stanley, TX, or Camp Bullis, TX, 1922–40. Designated mobilization training station was Fort Sill, OK. Subordinate regiments conducted training of CMTC at Camp Bullis. Location 7 December 1941—Dallas, TX.

Status: Inactive in the US Army Reserve as HHB, 90th Inf. Div. Arty.

Commanders, 165th Field Artillery Brigade

Lt. Col. Cornelius E. Lombardi	12 December 1921–23 January 1922	Maj. Frank M. Hicks	ao January 1927–April 1930
Maj. Arthur M. Risdon	23 January 1922–22 February 1923	Unknown	April 1930–ao June 1935
Maj. Ray Stockwell	22 February 1923–ao March 1926	Maj. James C. Oehler	ao June 1935–ao July 1935
Unknown	ao March 1926–ao January 1927	Unknown	ao July 1935–7 December 1941

HHB, 166th Field Artillery Brigade (91st Division) **Organized Reserve California**

HQ—San Francisco, CA, 1921–41

Subordinate elements—346th and 347th F.A. Regts. and 316th Ammo. Tn., 1921–41; 348th F.A. Regt., 1929–41

Constituted in the O.R. on 24 June 1921, assigned to the 91st Div., and allotted to the Ninth Corps Area. Initiated on 4 November 1921 at San Francisco, CA. Consolidated on 12 October 1936 with the 166th F.A. Brig. (a World War I unit constituted in the National Army on 5 August 1917; organized on 5 September 1917 at Camp Lewis, WA; arrived at the port of New York on 30 March 1919 on the S.S. *Aquitania*; transferred to Camp Kearny, CA, where it was demobilized on 19 April 1919; reconstituted on 12 October 1936). Conducted summer training most years at Del Monte, CA, 1922–40. Subordinate regiments conducted training of CMTC at the Presidio of Monterey. Location 7 December 1941—San Francisco, CA.

Commanders, 166th Field Artillery Brigade

Unknown	4 November 1921–17 January 1922	Unknown	ao July 1928–ao July 1933
Brig. Gen. William C. Davis	17 January 1922–13 February 1926	Maj. Harold M. Sutherland	ao July 1933–11 February 1937
Maj. William L. Roach	14 February 1926–ao June 1926	Maj. William L. Roach	11 May 1937–20 December 1938
Maj. Charles G. Osgood	ao January 1927–ao July 1928	Col. Ralph J. Faneuf	20 December 1938–13 May 1939
Lt. Col. George C. Ferch	13 May 1939–June 1941		

HHB, 169th Field Artillery Brigade (94th Division) **Organized Reserve Massachusetts**

HQ—Boston, MA, 1921–41

Subordinate elements—301st and 356th F.A. Regts. and 319th Ammo. Tn., 1921–41; 357th F.A. Regt., 1929; 390th F.A. Regt., 1929–41

Constituted in the O.R. on 24 June 1921, assigned to the 94th Div., and allotted to the First Corps Area. Initiated on 23 December 1921 at Boston, MA. Consolidated on 12 October 1936 with the 169th F.A. Brig. (a World War I unit constituted in the National Army on 5 August 1917; not organized; demobilized on 18 December 1918; reconstituted on 12 October 1936). Typically conducted Inactive Training Period meetings at the University Club in Boston. Conducted summer training most years at Camp Devens, MA, 1922–40. Subordinate regiments conducted training of CMTC at Fort Ethan Allen, VT. Location 7 December 1941—Boston, MA.

Status: Inactive in the US Army Reserve as HHB, 94th Inf. Div. Arty.

Commanders, 169th Field Artillery Brigade

Brig. Gen. John H. Sherburne Jr.	23 December 1921–ao June 1938	Maj. Clinton W. Stephenson	ao February 1939–13 March 1939
Unknown	ao June 1938–ao February 1939	Maj. John H. Carleton	13 March 1939–ao January 1940
Unknown	ao January 1940–7 December 1941		

HHB, 170th Field Artillery Brigade (95th Division) **Organized Reserve Oklahoma**

HQ—Oklahoma City, OK, 1921–41

Subordinate elements—358th and 359th F.A. Regts. and 320th Ammo. Tn., 1921–41; 360th F.A. Regt., 1929–41

Constituted in the O.R. on 24 June 1921, assigned to the 95th Div., and allotted to the Eighth Corps Area. Initiated on 26 October 1921 at Oklahoma City, OK. Consolidated on 12 October 1936 with the 170th F.A. Brig. (a World War I unit constituted in the National Army on 5 August 1917; organized on 3 September 1918 at Camp Knox, KY; demobilized on 22 December 1918 at Camp Knox; reconstituted on 12 October 1936). Conducted summer training most years with the 1st F.A. at Fort Sill, OK, 1922–40. Subordinate regiments conducted training of CMTC at Fort Sill. Designated mobilization training station was Fort Sill. Location 7 December 1941—Oklahoma City, OK.

Status: Inactive in the US Army Reserve as HHC, 95th Regt. (CST).

Commanders, 170th Field Artillery Brigade

Maj. Percy DuP. Whitaker	26 October 1921–26 November 1921	Lt. Col. Harold B. Fell	ao September 1927–ao February 1928
Maj. Emmet C. Choate	26 November 1921–13 September 1922	Unknown	ao February 1928–ao November 1937
Maj. Orrin C. Fowler	13 September 1922–ao July 1925	Lt. Col. Thomas B. Matthews	ao November 1937–ao January 1938
Unknown	ao July 1925–ao September 1927	Unknown	ao January 1938–7 December 1941

HHB, 171st Field Artillery Brigade (96th Division) **Organized Reserve Oregon**

HQ—*Not initiated,* 1921–22; Portland, OR, 1922–41

Subordinate elements—361st and 362d F.A. Regts. and 321st Ammo. Tn., 1921–41; 363d F.A. Regt., 1929–41

Constituted in the O.R. on 24 June 1921, assigned to the 96th Div., and allotted to the Ninth Corps Area. Initiated in September 1922 at Portland, OR. Consolidated on 12 October 1936 with the 171st F.A. Brig. (a World War I unit constituted in the National Army on 5 August 1917; organized on 21 September 1918 at Camp Kearny, CA; demobilized on 20 December 1918 at Camp Kearny; reconstituted on 12 October 1936). Conducted summer training most years at Fort Lewis, WA, 1922–40. Subordinate regiments conducted training of CMTC at Fort Lewis. Location 7 December 1941—Portland, OR.

Status: Inactive in the US Army Reserve as HHB, 96th Inf. Div. Arty.

Commanders, 171st Field Artillery Brigade

Unknown	September 1922–ao May 23	Maj. Francis Rotch Jr.	2 March 1937–21 October 1938
Maj. Robert B. Kuykendall	ao May 1923–ao January 1925	Maj. Enno G. Fruewald	21 October 1938–January 1939
Unknown	ao January 1925–2 March 1937	Lt. Col. Laurence Solan	January 1939–ao June 1939
Unknown	ao June 1939–7 December 1941		

HHB, 172d Field Artillery Brigade (97th Division) **Organized Reserve New Hampshire**

HQ—*Not initiated,* 1921–22; Concord, NH, 1922–41

Subordinate elements—303d and 365th F.A. Regts. and 322d Ammo. Tn., 1921–41; 366th F.A. Regt., 1929; 389th F.A. Regt., 1929–41

Constituted in the O.R. on 24 June 1921, assigned to the 97th Div., and allotted to the First Corps Area. Initiated on 6 July 1922 at Concord, NH. Consolidated on 12 October 1936 with the 172d F.A. Brig. (a World War I unit constituted in the National Army on 5 August 1917; organized on 20 October 1918 at Camp Jackson, SC; demobilized on 22 December 1918 at Camp Jackson; reconstituted on 12 October 1936). Conducted summer training most years at Camp Devens, MA, 1923–40. Location 7 December 1941—Concord, NH.

Status: Inactive in the US Army Reserve as HHB, 97th Inf. Div. Arty.

Commanders, 172d Field Artillery Brigade

1st Lt. John H. Batchelder	6 July 1922–5 January 1923	Capt. Hollie L. Whittlemore	ao July 1931–ao June 1936
Maj. Thomas N. Troxell	5 January 1923–ao June 1926	Unknown	ao June 1936–ao May 1937
Unknown	ao June 1926–ao July 1929	Lt. Col. Leon W. Hilliard	ao May 1937–ao July 1939
Maj. Earle A. Reed	ao July 1929–ao August 1930	Unknown	ao July 1939–7 December 1941

HHB, 173d Field Artillery Brigade (98th Division) **Organized Reserve New York**

HQ—Syracuse, NY, 1921–41

Subordinate elements—367th and 368th F.A. Regts. and 323d Ammo. Tn., 1921–41; 472d F.A. Regt., 1929; 369th F.A. Regt., 1929–41

Constituted in the O.R. on 24 June 1921, assigned to the 98th Div., and allotted to the Second Corps Area. Initiated on 3 December 1921 at Syracuse, NY. Consolidated on 12 October 1936 with the 173d F.A. Brig. (a World War I unit constituted in the National Army on 5 August 1917; not organized; demobilized on 30 November 1918; reconstituted on 12 October 1936). Conducted summer training at numerous locations to include Camp Dix, NJ, Madison Barracks, NY, Pine Camp, NY, and Plattsburg Barracks, NY, 1922–40. Subordinate regiments conducted training of CMTC at Madison Barracks. Location 7 December 1941—Syracuse, NY.

Status: Inactive in the US Army Reserve as HHC, 98th Regt. (CST).

Events: 168

Commanders, 173d Field Artillery Brigade

Maj. George C. Mather	3 December 1921–19 August 1922	Maj.Thomas J. Shea	22 September 1930–June 1934
Maj. Charles C. Haffner Jr.	2 January 1923–28 February 1924	Lt. Col. Sidman P. Poole	June 1934–August 1939
Maj. Julius T. A. Doolittle	7 March 1924–5 December 1927	Col. Guido F. Verbeck	August 1939–27 July 1940
Col. Charles B. Sayre	5 December 1927–ao June 1929	Lt. Col. Sidman P. Poole	27 July 1940–18 November 1940
Unknown	18 November 1940–7 December 1941		

HHB, 174th Field Artillery Brigade (99th Division) **Organized Reserve Pennsylvania**

HQ—*Not initiated,* 1921–22; Pittsburgh, PA, 1922–41

Subordinate elements—370th and 371st F.A. Regts. and 324th Ammo. Tn., 1921–41; 372d F.A. Regt., 1929–41

Constituted in the O.R. on 24 June 1921, assigned to the 99th Div., and allotted to the Third Corps Area. Initiated on 2 December 1921 at Pittsburgh, PA. Consolidated on 12 October 1936 with the 174th F.A. Brig. (a World War I unit constituted in the National Army on 5 August 1917; never organized and demobilized on 30 November 1918; reconstituted on 12 October 1936). Conducted summer training most years with the 16th F.A. at Fort George G. Meade, MD, or Fort Hoyle, MD, 1922–40. Subordinate regiments conducted training of CMTC at Fort Hoyle. Location 7 December 1941—Pittsburgh, PA.

Status: Inactive in the US Army Reserve as HHB, 99th Inf. Div. Arty.

Commanders, 174th Field Artillery Brigade

Maj. J.R. Black	2 December 1921–ao January 1922	Maj. Frederick A. Ulam	July 1934–ao July 1935
Unknown	ao January 1922–ao June 1930	Unknown	ao July 1935–ao July 1937
Lt. Col. John J. Daub	ao June 1930–July 1934	Col. Edwin C. Carter Jr.	ao July 1937–ao September 1938
Unknown	ao September 1938–7 December 1941		

HHB, 175th Field Artillery Brigade (100th Division) **Organized Reserve West Virginia/Kentucky**

HQ—*Not initiated,* 1921–22; Parkersburg, WV, 1922–37; Louisville, KY, 1937–41

Subordinate elements—374th and 375th F.A. Regts. and 325th Ammo. Tn., 1921–41; 373d F.A. Regt., 1929–41

Constituted in the O.R. on 24 June 1921, assigned to the 100th Div., and allotted to the Fifth Corps Area. Initiated on 6 December 1921 at Parkersburg, WV. Relocated on 5 April 1937 to Louisville, KY. Conducted summer training most years at Camp Knox, KY, 1922–40. Location 7 December 1941—Louisville, KY.

Status: Inactive in the US Army Reserve as HHC, 100th Regt. (CST).

Commanders, 175th Field Artillery Brigade

Maj. Elliot B. Hopkins	6 December 1921–29 September 1923	Col. Elliot B. Hopkins	June 1931–ao June 1934
Brig. Gen. Frank E. Bamford	29 September 1923–June 1931	Unknown	ao June 1934–7 December 1941

HHB, 176th Field Artillery Brigade (101st Division) **Organized Reserve Wisconsin**

HQ—*Not initiated,* 1921–22; Milwaukee, WI, 1922–41

Subordinate elements—376th and 377th F.A. Regts. and 326th Ammo. Tn., 1921–41; 378th F.A. Regt., 1929; 572d F.A. Regt., 1929–41

Constituted in the O.R. on 24 June 1921, assigned to the 101st Div., and allotted to the Sixth Corps Area. Initiated on 21 November 1921 at Milwaukee, WI. Conducted summer training most years at Camp Custer, MI, and some years at Camp McCoy, WI, 1922–40. Location 7 December 1941—Milwaukee, WI.

Status: Active in the R.A. at Fort Campbell, KY, as HHB, 101st Abn Div. Arty.

Commanders, 176th Field Artillery Brigade

1st Lt. Hurley Fellows	21 November 1921–6 January 1922	Unknown	ao October 1924–ao September 1925
2d Lt. Paul T. Hegner	7 August 1923–11 March 1924	Maj. John B. Ritter	ao September 1925–ao September 1927
1st Lt. Hurley Fellows	11 March 1924–16 September 1924	Unknown	ao September 1927–ao June 1929
Capt. Olin G. Dryer	16 September 1924–ao October 1924	Maj. Otto J. Longbecker	ao June 1929– ao June 1932
Unknown	ao June 1932–7 December 1941		

HHB, 177th Field Artillery Brigade (102d Division) **Organized Reserve Missouri**

HQ—Kansas City, MO, 1921–41

Subordinate elements—379th and 380th F.A. Regts. and 327th Ammo. Tn., 1921–41; 381st F.A. Regt., 1929–41

Constituted in the O.R. on 24 June 1921, assigned to the 102d Div., and allotted to the Seventh Corps Area. Initiated on 21 November 1921 at Kansas City, MO. Conducted summer training most years at Fort Riley, KS, 1922–40, and some years at Camp Ripley, MN, or Jefferson Barracks, MO. Location 7 December 1941—Kansas City, MO.

Status: Inactive in the US Army Reserve as HHB, 102d Inf. Div. Arty.

Commanders, 177th Field Artillery Brigade

Maj. Milton M. Leach	21 November 1921–6 January 1922	Brig. Gen. Karl D. Klemm	6 January 1922–15 November 1925
Unknown	15 November 1925–7 December 1941		

HHB, 178th Field Artillery Brigade (103d Division) **Organized Reserve Colorado**

HQ—Denver, CO, 1921–41

Subordinate elements—382d and 383d F.A. Regts. and 328th Ammo. Tn., 1921–41; 384th F.A. Regt., 1929–41

Constituted in the O.R. on 24 June 1921, assigned to the 103d Div., and allotted to the Eighth Corps Area. Initiated on 26 October 1921 at Denver, CO. Typically conducted Inactive Training Period meetings at the Albany Hotel in Denver. Conducted summer training at numerous locations to include Fort Logan, CO, Fort Bliss, TX, Fort Francis E. Warren, WY, Pole Mountain Military Reservation, WY, and Camp George West, CO, 1922–40. Location 7 December 1941—Denver, CO.

Status: Inactive in the US Army Reserve as HHB, 103d Inf. Div. Arty.

Commanders, 178th Field Artillery Brigade

Lt. Col. Percy D. Whittaker	26 October 1921–March 1922	Maj. H. R. Crile	ao August 1928–September 1928
Maj. Canton O'Donnell	March 1922–ao August 1922	Maj. G. A. Bonnett	September 1928–January 1929
Unknown	ao August 1922–ao August 1924	Maj. H. O. Nichols	January 1929–September 1930
Capt. Edwin L. Glasier	ao August 1924–November 1924	Maj. D. M. Sinseng	September 1930–ao May 1931
Maj. Howard L. Hackstaff	November 1924–ao September 1925	Unknown	ao May 1931–ao October 1937
Unknown	ao September 1925–ao August 1928	Maj. Forrest M. Carhartt	ao October 1937–ao June 1938
Unknown	ao June 1932–7 December 1941		

HHB, 179th Field Artillery Brigade (104th Division) **Organized Reserve Wyoming**

HQ—Casper, WY, 1922–1941; *Inactive,* 1941

Subordinate elements—385th and 386th F.A. Regts. and 329th Ammo. Tn., 1921–41; 387th F.A. Regt., 1929–41

Constituted in the O.R. on 24 June 1921, assigned to the 104th Div., and allotted to the Ninth Corps Area. Initiated in January 1922 at Casper, WY. Conducted summer training most years with the 76th F.A. at Fort Francis E. Warren, WY, and some years at Fort Douglas, UT, or Fort Lewis, WA, 1922–40. Conducted summer training at Fort Riley with the units of the 60th F.A. Brig. in 1931. Inactivated on 21 January 1941 at Casper by relief of personnel. Location 7 December 1941—*Inactive.*

Status: Inactive in the US Army Reserve as HHC, 104th Regt. (AIT).

Commanders, 179th Field Artillery Brigade

Brig. Gen. Burke H. Sinclair	31 July 1922–20 April 1926	Col. William H. Edelblute	ao July 1929–ao June 1934
Unknown	20 April 1926–ao July 1929	Unknown	ao June 1934–21 January 1941

HHB, 180th Field Artillery Brigade (XI Corps) **Organized Reserve Massachusetts**

HQ—Boston, MA, 1921–29; *Inactive,* 1929–41

Subordinate elements—388th F.A. Regt., 1921–41; 389th F.A. Regt., 1921–29; 390th F.A. Regt., 1921–29; 431st F.A. Regt., 1921–41; 357th F.A. Regt., 1929–41; 301st Obsn. Bn., 1921–27; 315th Obsn. Bn., 1930–41; 341st Ammo. Tn., 1921–27; 330th Ammo. Tn., 1933–40; and 351st Ord. Co., 1921–28

Constituted in the O.R. on 29 July 1921, assigned to the XI Corps, and allotted to the First Corps Area. Initiated on 3 November 1921 at Boston, MA. Inactivated on 8 October 1929 at Omaha by relief of personnel. Conducted summer training at Fort Devens, MA, 1922–29. Designated mobilization station was Camp Devens, MA. Location 7 December 1941—*Inactive.*

Status: Disbanded 26 January 1943.

Commanders, 180th Field Artillery Brigade

Col. Robert E. Goodwin	3 November 1921–February 1922	Unknown	ao February 1924–ao November 1927
Maj. Thomas J. Coolidge	February 1922–January 1924	Lt. Col. Ralph H. Whitney	ao November 1927–November 1929
Col. John F. J. Herbert	January 1924–ao February 1924	*Inactive*	November 1929–7 December 1941

HHB, 181st Field Artillery Brigade (XII Corps) **Organized Reserve New York**

HQ—*Not initiated,* 1921–22; Manhattan, NY, 1922–37; *Inactive,* 1937–41

Subordinate elements—306th F.A. Regt., 1921–29; 309th F.A. Regt., 1921–29; 391st F.A. Regt., 1921–41; 432d F.A. Regt., 1921–41; 353d F.A. Regt., 1929–40, 352d F.A. Regt., 1929–40; 302d Obsn. Bn., 1921–41, 332d Ammo. Tn., 1933–41; 342d Ammo. Tn., 1921–33; 352d Ord. Co., 1921–33

Constituted in the O.R. on 29 July 1921, assigned to the XII Corps, and allotted to the Second Corps Area. Initiated on 15 March 1922 at Manhattan, NY. Conducted summer training most years as individuals at Madison Barracks, NY, or Pine Camp, NY, 1922–36. Designated mobilization training station was Pine Camp, NY. Inactivated by February 1937 at Manhattan by relief of personnel. Location 7 December 1941—*Inactive.*

Status: Disbanded 26 January 1943.

Commanders, 181st Field Artillery Brigade

Maj. Alexander Maxwell	15 March 1922–12 March 1923	Maj. Ira Richards Jr.	23 February 1926–7 December 1927
Brig. Gen. Avery D. Andrews	12 March 1923–23 February 1926	Unknown	7 December 1927–February 1937
Inactive	February 1937–7 December 1941		

HHB, 182d Field Artillery Brigade (XIII Corps) **Organized Reserve Pennsylvania**

HQ—*Not initiated,* 1921–22; Altoona, PA, 1922–39; *Inactive,* 1939–41

Subordinate elements—394th F.A. Regt., 1921–41; 395th F.A. Regt., 1921–41; 396th F.A. Regt., 1921–41; 433d

F.A. Regts., 1921–41; 303d Obsn. Bn., 1921–41; 343d Ammo. Tn., 1921–33; 333d Ammo. Tn., 1933–40; 353d Ord. Co., 1921–41

Constituted in the O.R. on 29 July 1921, assigned to the XIII Corps, and allotted to the Third Corps Area. Initiated in August 1922 at Altoona, PA. Conducted summer training most years as individuals at Fort Hoyle, MD, 1923–38. Inactivated by April 1939 at Altoona by relief of personnel. Location 7 December 1941—*Inactive.*

Status: Disbanded 26 January 1943.

Commanders, 182d Field Artillery Brigade

1st Lt. William C. Emory	August 1922–ao October 1922	Unknown	ao October 1922–7 December 1941

HHB, 183d Field Artillery Brigade (XIV Corps) **Organized Reserve Tennessee/Alabama**

HQ—*Not initiated,* 1921–22; Nashville, TN, 1922–29; Auburn, AL, 1929–41

Subordinate elements—397th F.A. Regt., 1921–29; 398th F.A. Regt. (I), 1921–29; 398th F.A. Regt. (II), 1929–33; 399th F.A. Regt., 1921–28; 434th F.A. Regt., 1921–33; 344th Ammo. Tn., 1921–40; 334th Ammo. Tn. (attached 1929–33); 304th Obsn. Bn., 1921–41, and 354th Ord. Co., 1921–28

Constituted in the O.R. on 29 July 1921, assigned to the XIV Corps, and allotted to the Fourth Corps Area. Initiated on 10 March 1922 at Nashville, TN. Relocated on 10 October 1929 to Auburn, AL. Maintained a habitual training affiliation with the 13th F.A. Brig. Conducted summer training most years as individuals at Fort Bragg, NC, 1923–41. Designated mobilization station was Camp Jackson, SC. Location 7 December 1941—Auburn, AL.

Status: Disbanded 26 January 1943.

Commanders, 183d Field Artillery Brigade

Maj. Hugh B. Hooper	10 March 1922–ao March 1922	Unknown	ao March 1922–7 December 1941

HHB, 184th Field Artillery Brigade (XV Corps) **Organized Reserve Ohio**

HQ—*Not initiated,* 1921–22; Cincinnati, OH, 1922–30; *Inactive,* 1930–41

Subordinate elements—400th F.A. Regt., 1921–23; 401st F.A. Regt., 1921–23 and 1933–41; 402d F.A. Regt., 1921–23; 435th F.A. Regt., 1921–23; 150th F.A. Regt., 1923–29; 455th F.A. Regt., 1933–41; 574th F.A. Regt., 1933–41; 345th Ammo. Tn., 1921–33; 341st Ammo. Tn., 1933–40; 305th Obsn. Bn., 1921–23 and 1927–41; 315th Obsn. Bn., 1923–27; 355th Ord. Co., 1921–23; 364th Ord. Co., 1923–33; 355th Ord. Co., 1933–41

Constituted in the O.R. on 29 July 1921, assigned to the XV Corps, and allotted to the Fifth Corps Area. Initiated about January 1922 at Cincinnati, OH. Relieved from the XV Corps on 2 July 1923 and assigned to the V Corps. Inactivated by March 1930 at Cincinnati by relief of personnel. Relieved from the V Corps on 1 October 1933 and assigned to the XV Corps. Conducted summer training most years as individuals at Camp Knox, KY, 1922–29. Location 7 December 1941—*Inactive.*

Status: Disbanded on 26 January 1943.

Commanders, 184th Field Artillery Brigade

Unknown	January 1922–March 1930	*Inactive*	December 1930–7 December 1941

HHB, 185th Field Artillery Brigade (XVI Corps) **Organized Reserve Illinois**

HQ—*Not initiated,* 1921–22; Chicago, IL, 1922–30; *Inactive,* 1930–36; Chicago, IL, 1936–41

Subordinate elements—403d F.A. Regt., 1921–23; 404th F.A. Regt., 1921–23; 405th F.A. Regt., 1921–23; 436th F.A. Regt., 1921–23 and 1933–41; 121st F.A. Regts., 1923–29; 123d F.A. Regt., 1923–29; 182d F.A. Regt., 1923–33; 330th F.A. Regt., 1929–41; 333d F.A. Regt., 1929–41; 346th Ammo. Tn., 1921–41; 306th Obsn. Bn., 1921–23; 15th Obsn. Bn., 1923–27; 318th Obsn. Bn., 1933–41; 356th Ord. Co., 1921–23 and 1933–41; 365th Ord. Co., 1923–33

Constituted in the O.R. on 29 July 1921, assigned to the XVI Corps, and allotted to the Sixth Corps Area. Initiated on 6 March 1922 at Chicago, IL. Relieved from assignment to the XVI Corps on 2 July 1923 and assigned to the VI Corps. Inactivated by December 1930 at Chicago by relief of personnel. Relieved from assignment to the VI Corps on 1 October 1933 and assigned to the XVI Corps. Reorganized by June 1935 at Chicago, IL. Conducted summer training most years as individuals at Fort Sheridan, IL, 1922–40. Designated mobilization training station was Fort Knox, KY. Location 7 December 1941—Chicago, IL.

Status: Disbanded on 26 January 1943.

Commanders, 185th Field Artillery Brigade

2d Lt. Walter H. Hinsch	6 March 1922–15 December 1922	*Inactive*	December 1930–ao June 1935
Maj. George C. Mather	16 December 1922–6 January 1923	Unknown	ao June 1935–8 May 1936
Maj. Noble M. Coe	6 January 1923–22 October 1925	Col. Martin H. Foss	8 May 1936–4 February 1937
Maj. James B. Bereth	29 October 1925–11 March 1926	Unknown	5 February 1937–27 January 1938
Lt. Col. George Richardson	9 April 1926–16 June 1926	Maj. Frank E. Gould	27 January 1938–24 February 1938
Maj. Willard J. Stanton	26 September 1926–ao June 1929	Brig. Gen. Henry J. Reilly	24 February 1938–11 May 1939
Unknown	ao June 1929–December 1930	Col. Martin H. Foss	11 May 1939–June 1941

HHB, 186th Field Artillery Brigade (XVII Corps) **Organized Reserve Missouri/Minnesota**

HQ—*Not initiated,* 1921–22; St. Louis, MO, 1922–26; Duluth, MN, 1926–33

Subordinate elements—406th F.A. Regts., 1921–33; 407th F.A. Regts., 1921–33; 408th F.A. Regt., 1921–28; 437th F.A. Regts., 1921–33; 347th Ammo. Tn., 1921–33; 307th Obsn. Bn., 1921–33; 357th Ord. Co., 1921–33

Constituted in the O.R. on 29 July 1921, assigned to the XVII Corps, and allotted to the Seventh Corps Area. Initiated in March 1922 at St. Louis, MO. Relocated on 26 May 1926 to Duluth, MN. Conducted summer training most years as individuals at Camp McCoy, WI. Demobilized on 1 October 1933.

Commanders, 186th Field Artillery Brigade

Unknown	March 1922–1 October 1933

HHB, 187th Field Artillery Brigade (XVIII Corps) **Organized Reserve Texas/Minnesota/North Dakota**

HQ—*Not initiated,* 1921–23; Dallas, TX, 1923–25; Fort Worth, TX, 1925–27; Minneapolis, MN, 1927–31; Fargo, ND, 1931–41

Subordinate elements—409th F.A. Regt., 1921–23; 410th F.A. Regt., 1921–27; 411th F.A. Regt., 1921–23; 438th F.A. Regt., 1921–33; *188th F.A. Regt.,* 1923–33; 189th F.A. Regt., 1923–30; 406th F.A. Regt., 1933–41; 437th F.A. Regt., 1933–41; 348th Ammo. Tn., 1921–23; 347th Ammo. Tn., 1933–41; 308th Obsn. Bn., 1921–33; 307th Obsn. Bn., 1933–41; 358th Ord. Co., 1921–23; 9th Ord. Co., 1923–28; 388th Ord. Co., 1928–41

Constituted in the O.R. on 29 July 1921, assigned to the XVIII Corps, and allotted to the Eighth Corps Area. Initiated on 16 February 1923 at Dallas, TX. Relieved from assignment to the XVIII Corps on 2 July 1923 and assigned to the VIII Corps. Conducted summer training most years at Fort Sam Houston, TX, 1923–27. Withdrawn from the Eighth Corps Area on 13 January 1927 and allotted to the Seventh Corps Area, but remained assigned to the VIII Corps. Initiated on 10 August 1927 at Minneapolis, MN. Relocated on 12 October 1931 to Fargo, ND. Relieved from assignment to the VIII Corps on 1 October 1933 and assigned to the XVII Corps. Location 7 December 1941—Fargo, ND.

Status: Disbanded on 26 January 1943.

Commanders, 187th Field Artillery Brigade

1st Lt. Edward L. Brown	16 February 1923–13 January 1927	*Inactive*	13 January 1927–10 August 1927
Unknown	10 August 1927–7 December 1941		

HHB, 188th Field Artillery Brigade (XIX Corps) **Organized Reserve California/Texas**

HQ—*Not initiated,* 1921–22; San Francisco, CA, 1922–29; *Inactive,* 1929–37; Waco, TX, 1937–41

Subordinate elements—412th F.A. Regt., 1921–28; 413th F.A. Regt., 1921–28; 414th F.A. Regt., 1921–28; 439th F.A. Regt., 1921–28; 409th F.A. Regt., 1933–41; 411th F.A. Regt., 1933–41; 349th Ammo. Tn., 1921–28; 335th Ammo. Tn., 1933–40; 309th Obsn. Bn., 1921–28; 359th Ord. Co., 1921–28; 358th Ord. Co., 1933–41

Constituted in the O.R. on 29 July 1921, assigned to the XIX Corps, and allotted to the Ninth Corps Area. Initiated on 28 February 1922 at San Francisco, CA. Relieved from the XIX Corps on 2 July 1923 and assigned to the IX Corps. Inactivated on 15 October 1929 at San Francisco by relief of personnel. Withdrawn from the Ninth Corps Area on 1 October 1933 and allotted to the Eighth Corps Area. Concurrently relieved from the IX Corps and assigned to the XVIII Corps. Reorganized by December 1937 at Waco, TX. Location 7 December 1941—Waco, TX.

Status: Disbanded on 26 January 1943.

Commanders, 188th Field Artillery Brigade

Brig. Gen. Thornwell Mullally	28 February 1922–23 December 1926	*Inactive*	15 October 1929–ao December 1937
Maj. Herman Laprohan	23 December 1926–15 October 1929	Unknown	ao December 1937–7 December 1941

HHB, 189th Field Artillery Brigade (IX Corps) **Organized Reserve California**

HQ—San Francisco, CA, 1923–33

Subordinate elements—190th F.A. Regt., 1923–28; 196th F.A. Regt., 1923–28; 412th F.A. Regt., 1928–33; 413th F.A. Regt., 1928–33; 414th F.A. Regt., 1928–33; 439th F.A. Regt., 1928–33; 332d Ammo. Tn. (I), 1923–28; 331st Ammo. Tn. (II), 1928–33; 311th Obsn. Bn., 1923–33; and 400th Ord. Co., 1923–33

Constituted in the N.G. as the 86th F.A. Brig. in 1921, assigned to the IX Corps, and allotted to the state of California. Placed on the deferred list on 2 July 1923, transferred to the O.R. as a DNG unit, redesignated as the 189th F.A. Brig., and reassigned to the IX Corps. Initiated by December 1923 at San Francisco, CA. Demobilized on 1 October 1933.

Commanders, 189th Field Artillery Brigade

Unknown	ao December 1923–1 October 1933

HHB, 190th Field Artillery Brigade (I) (III Corps) **Organized Reserve Pennsylvania**

HQ—*Not initiated,* 1923–27

Subordinate elements—108th F.A. Regt., 1923–27; 176th F.A. Regt., 1923–27; 440th F.A. Regt., 1923–27; 331st Ammo. Tn. (I), 1923–27; 310th Obsn. Bn., 1923–27; and 362d Ord. Co., 1923–27.

Constituted in the N.G. as the 82d F.A. Brig. in 1921, assigned to the III Corps, and allotted to the state of Pennsylvania. Placed on the deferred list on 2 July 1923, transferred to the O.R. as a DNG unit, redesignated as the 190th F.A. Brig., and reassigned to the III Corps. Philadelphia, PA, designated as HQ on initiation, but the unit was never organized at that location. Withdrawn from the N.G. on 17 September 1927.

HHB, 190th Field Artillery Brigade (II) (III Corps) **Organized Reserve New York**

HQ—*Not initiated,* 1928–29; New York City, NY, 1929–33

Subordinate elements—108th F.A. Regt., 1928–29; 176th F.A. Regt., 1928–30; 440th F.A. Regt., 1928–33; 310th Obsn. Bn., 1928–33; and 362d Ord. Co., 1928–33

Constituted in the O.R. on 5 September 1928, assigned to the III Corps, and allotted to the Second Corps Area. Initiated on 2 July 1929 at New York City, NY. Demobilized on 1 October 1933.

Commanders, 190th Field Artillery Brigade

Unknown	2 July 1929–1 October 1933

HHB, 191st Field Artillery Brigade (V Corps) **Organized Reserve Ohio/Georgia**

HQ—*Not initiated,* 1923–29; Savannah, GA, 1929–33

Subordinate elements—400th F.A. Regt., 1923–33; 401st F.A. Regt., 1923–33; 402d F.A. Regt., 1923–33; 435th F.A. Regt., 1923–33; 333d Ammo. Tn., 1923–28; 305th Obsn. Bn., 1923–27; and 355th Ord. Co., 1923–29

Constituted in the N.G. as the 83d F.A. Brig. in 1921, assigned to the V Corps, and allotted to the state of Ohio. Placed on the deferred list on 2 July 1923, transferred to the O.R. as a DNG unit, redesignated as the 191st F.A. Brig., and assigned to the XV Corps. Withdrawn from the Fifth Corps Area on 5 September 1928 and allotted to the Fourth Corps Area. Initiated on 22 October 1929 at Savannah, GA. Demobilized on 1 October 1933.

Commanders, 191st Field Artillery Brigade

Unknown	22 October 1929–1 October 1933

HHB, 192d Field Artillery Brigade (XVI Corps) **Organized Reserve Michigan/Kentucky**

HQ—Sixth Corps Area 1923–28; *Inactive,* 1928–33

Subordinate elements—403d F.A. Regt., 1923–29; 404th F.A. Regt., 1923–29; 405th F.A. Regt., 1923–28; 436th F.A. Regt., 1923–33; 306th Obsn. Bn., 1923–33; 334th Ammo. Tn., 1923–28; 356th Ord. Co., 1923–33

Constituted in the N.G. as the 84th F.A. Brig. in 1921, assigned to the VI Corps, and allotted to the state of Michigan. Placed on the deferred list on 2 July 1923, transferred to the O.R. as a DNG unit, redesignated as the 192d F.A. Brig., and assigned to the XVI Corps. Initiated in 1923 in the Sixth Corps Area at large. Withdrawn from the Sixth Corps Area on 5 September 1928 and allotted to the Fifth Corps Area, but remained assigned to the XVI Corps. Designated mobilization stations were Camp Custer, MI, 1923–28, and Camp Knox, KY, 1928–33. Demobilized on 1 October 1933.

Commanders, 192d Field Artillery Brigade

Unknown	ao December 1923–5 September 1928	*Inactive*	5 September 1928–1 October 1933

HHB, 193d Field Artillery Brigade (XVIII Corps) **Organized Reserve Texas/Minnesota/South Dakota**

HQ—*Not initiated,* 1923–27; St. Paul, MN, 1927–31; Brookings, SD, 1931–33

Subordinate elements—393d F.A. Regt., 1923–33; 409th F.A. Regt., 1923–33; 411th F.A. Regt., 1923–33; 348th Ammo. Tn., 1923–33; 312th Obsn. Bn., 1923–33; 358th Ord. Co., 1923–33

Constituted in the N.G. as the 85th F.A. Brig. in 1921, assigned to the VIII Corps, and allotted to the state of Colorado. Placed on the deferred list on 2 July 1923, transferred to the O.R. as a DNG unit, redesignated as the 193d F.A. Brig., and assigned to the XVIII Corps. Withdrawn as a DNG unit on 11 January 1927 and allotted permanently to the O.R. as the 193d F.A. Brig. Concurrently withdrawn from the Eighth Corps Area and allotted to the Seventh Corps Area. Brigade remained assigned to the XVIII Corps. Initiated on 3 August 1927 at St. Paul, MN. Relocated on 12 October 1931 to Brookings, SD. Demobilized on 1 October 1933.

Commanders, 193d Field Artillery Brigade

Unknown	3 August 1927–1 October 1933

HHB, 194th Field Artillery Brigade (I Corps) **Organized Reserve Connecticut/Kentucky**

HQ—First Corps Area, 1923–27; *Inactive,* 1927–33

Subordinate elements—172d F.A. Regt., 1923–29; 192d F.A. Regt., 1923–29; 392d F.A. Regt., 1923–33; 330th Ammo. Tn., 1923–27; 313th Obsn. Bn., 1923–33; 360th Ord. Co., 1923–33

Constituted in the N.G. as the 81st F.A. Brig. in 1921, assigned to the I Corps, and allotted to the state of Massachusetts. Placed on the deferred list on 2 July 1923, transferred to the O.R. as a DNG unit, redesignated as the 194th F.A. Brig., and reassigned to the I Corps. Initiated in 1923 in the First Corps Area at large. Withdrawn from the N.G. on 11 January 1927 and allotted permanently to the O.R. as the 194th F.A. Brig. Concurrently withdrawn from the First Corps Area and allotted to the Fifth Corps Area. Brigade remained assigned to the I Corps. Camp Knox, KY, designated as HQ on reorganization, but the unit was never organized at that location. Designated mobilization station was Camp Knox. Demobilized on 1 October 1933.

Commanders, 194th Field Artillery Brigade

Unknown	ao December 1923–11 January 1927	*Inactive*	11 January 1927–7 December 1941

HHB, 195th Field Artillery Brigade (XIX Corps) **Organized Reserve Washington/California**

HQ—*Not initiated,* 1928–30; Seattle, WA, 1930–37; *Inactive,* 1937–41

Subordinate elements—190th F.A. Regt., 1928–33; 196th F.A. Regt., 1928–33; 426th F.A. Regt., 1928–33; 413th F.A. Regt., 1933–41; 439th F.A. Regt., 1933–41; 349th Ammo. Tn., 1928–40; 309th Obsn. Bn., 1928–41; 359th Ord. Co., 1928–33; 389th Ord. Co., 1933–41

Constituted in the O.R. on 5 September 1928, assigned to the XIX Corps, and allotted to the Ninth Corps Area. Initiated on 7 April 1930 at Seattle, WA. Inactivated on 2 March 1937 at Seattle by relief of personnel. Los Angeles, CA, designated on 14 May 1937 as HQ on reorganization, but the unit was never organized at that location. Location 7 December 1941—*Inactive.*

Status: Disbanded on 26 January 1943. Reconstituted on 7 December 1949 and consolidated with HHB, XXIX Corps Arty. Inactive in the R.A. as HHB XXIX Corps Arty.

Commanders, 195th Field Artillery Brigade

Unknown	7 April 1930–2 March 1937

HHB, 207th Field Artillery Brigade (M&H) (GHQR) **Organized Reserve Mississippi/South Carolina**

HQ—*Not initiated,* 1921–25; Jackson, MS, 1925–29; Greenville, SC, 1929–41

Subordinate elements—427th F.A. Regt., 1921–41; 559th F.A. Regt., 1921–41; 560th F.A. Regt., 1921–41

Constituted in the O.R. in July 1923, assigned to the GHQR, and allotted to the Fourth Corps Area. Initiated in November 1925 at Jackson, MS. Relocated on 22 October 1929 to Greenville, SC. Conducted summer training most years at Fort Bragg, NC, 1924–40. Designated mobilization station was Camp Jackson, SC. Location 7 December 1941—Greenville, SC.

Status: Disbanded on 26 January 1943.

Commanders, 207th Field Artillery Brigade

Unknown	November 1925–7 December 1941

HHB, 211th Field Artillery Brigade (M & H) (GHQR) **Organized Reserve New York/New Jersey**

HQ—*Not initiated,* 1921–22; Brooklyn, NY 1922–37; *Inactive,* 1937–41

Subordinate elements—489th F.A. Regt., 1921–41; 490th F.A. Regt., 1921–41; 495th F.A. Regt., 1921–33; 496th F.A. Regt., 1921–41; 561st F.A. Regt., 1921–33; 526th and 528th Ord. Cos., 1921–41

Constituted in the O.R. on 15 October 1921, assigned to the GHQR, and allotted to the Second Corps Area. Initiated by December 1922 at Brooklyn, NY. Inactivated by March 1937 at Brooklyn by relief of personnel. Newark, NJ, designated as HQ on reorganization on 5 April 1937, but the unit was never organized at that location. Designated mobilization training station was Pine Camp, NY. Location 7 December 1941—*Inactive.*

Status: Disbanded on 26 January 1943.

Commanders, 211th Field Artillery Brigade

Unknown	ao December 1922–March 1937

HHB, 213th Field Artillery Brigade (75-mm G MTZ) (GHQR) **Organized Reserve Pennsylvania**

HQ—*Not initiated,* 1921–22; Scranton, PA, 1922–33

Subordinate elements—471st F.A. Regt., 1921–33; 472d F.A. Regt., 1921–33; 473d F.A. Regt., 1921–33; 396th Ord. Co., 1921–33

Constituted in the O.R. on 15 October 1921, assigned to the GHQR, and allotted to the Third Corps Area. Initiated on 6 March 1922 at Scranton, PA. Demobilized on 1 October 1933.

Commanders, 213th Field Artillery Brigade

1st Lt. Frank E. Williams	6 March 1922–ao January 1924	Unknown	ao January 1924–1 October 1933

HHB, 214th Field Artillery Brigade (75-mm G MTZ) (GHQR) **Organized Reserve Ohio/Kentucky**

HQ—*Not initiated,* 1921–26; Cincinnati, OH, 1926–30; *Inactive,* 1930–41

Subordinate elements—474th F.A. Regt., 1921–33; 475th F.A. Regt., 1921–33; 476th F.A. Regt., 1921–33; 407th Ord. Co., 1921–33

Constituted in the O.R. on 15 October 1921, assigned to the GHQR, and allotted to the Fifth Corps Area. Initiated in 1926 at Cincinnati, OH. Inactivated by March 1930 at Cincinnati by relief of personnel. Camp Knox, KY, designated on 9 July 1931 as HQ on reorganization, but the unit was never organized at that location. Designated mobilization station was Camp Knox, KY. Demobilized on 1 October 1933.

Commanders, 214th Field Artillery Brigade

Unknown	ao December 1926–March 1930	*Inactive*	March 1930–1 October 1933

HHB, 215th Field Artillery Brigade (M&H, MTZ) (GHQR) **Organized Reserve Indiana**

HQ—*Not initiated,* 1921–22; Lafayette, IN, 1922–30; *Inactive,* 1930–41

Subordinate elements—491st F.A. Regt., 1921–27; 492d F.A. Regt., 1921–41; 499th F.A. Regt., 1921–41; 500th F.A. Regt., 1921–41; 562d F.A. Regt., 1921–33; 533d and 535th Ord. Cos., 1921–41

Constituted in the O.R. on 15 October 1921, assigned to the GHQR, and allotted to the Seventh Corps Area. Initiated by December 1922 at Lafayette, IN. Inactivated by March 1930 at Lafayette by relief of personnel. Designated mobilization station was Camp Knox, KY. Location 7 December 1941—*Inactive.*

Status: Disbanded on 26 January 1943.

Commanders, 215th Field Artillery Brigade

Unknown	ao December 1922–March 1930	*Inactive*	March 1930–7 December 1941

HHB, 216th Field Artillery Brigade (M&H) (GHQR) **Organized Reserve Illinois**

HQ—*Not initiated,* 1921–24; Chicago, IL, 1924–29; *Inactive,* 1929–41

Subordinate elements—493d F.A. Regt., 1921–41; 494th F.A. Regt., 1921–41; 497th F.A. Regt., 1921–41; 498th F.A. Regt., 1921–41; 563d F.A. Regt., 1921–33; and 534th and 536th Ord. Cos., 1921–33

Constituted in the O.R. on 15 October 1921, assigned to the GHQR, and allotted to the Sixth Corps Area. Initiated on 4 July 1924 at Chicago, IL. Inactivated by December 1929 at Chicago by relief of personnel. Withdrawn from the Sixth Corps Area on 1 October 1933, and allotted to the Seventh Corps Area. Location 7 December 1941—*Inactive.*

Status: Disbanded on 26 January 1943.

Commanders, 216th Field Artillery Brigade

Maj. William J. Wrona	4 July 1924–ao June 1929	*Inactive*	ao December 1929–7 December 1941

HHB, 217th Field Artillery Brigade (75-mm G MTZ) (GHQR) **Organized Reserve South Dakota**

HQ—*Not initiated,* 1921–22; Aberdeen, SD, 1922–41

Subordinate elements—477th F.A. Regt., 1921–41; 478th F.A. Regt., 1921–41; 479th F.A. Regt., 1921–41; 398th Ord. Co., 1921–41

Constituted in the O.R. on 15 October 1921, assigned to the GHQR, and allotted to the Seventh Corps Area. Initiated in August 1922 at Aberdeen, SD. Location 7 December 1941—Aberdeen, SD.

Status: Disbanded on 26 January 1943.

Commanders, 217th Field Artillery Brigade

Unknown	August 1922–7 December 1941

HHB, 218th Field Artillery Brigade (75-mm G PORT) (GHQR) **Organized Reserve New York**

HQ—*Not initiated,* 1921–25; Albany, NY, 1925–37; Buffalo, NY, 1937–38; *Inactive,* 1938–41

Subordinate elements—568th F.A. Regt., 1921–33; 569th F.A. Regt., 1921–41; 570th F.A. Regt., 1921–33; 371st Ammo. Tn., 1921–23; 393d Ord. Co., 1921–41

Constituted in the O.R. on 15 October 1921, assigned to the GHQR, and allotted to the Second Corps Area. Initiated in August 1925 at Albany, NY. Relocated on 20 November 1937 to Buffalo, NY. Inactivated on 4 January 1938 at Buffalo by relief of personnel. Location 7 December 1941—*Inactive.*

Status: Disbanded on 26 January 1943.

Commanders, 218th Field Artillery Brigade

Unknown	August 1925–11 May 1937	Capt. William S. Bailey	11 May 1937–4 January 1938
Inactive	4 January 1938–7 December 1941		

HHB, 219th Field Artillery Brigade (M & H) (GHQR) **Organized Reserve Pennsylvania**

HQ—Middletown, PA, 1921–30; *Inactive,* 1930–41

Subordinate elements—573d F.A. Regt., 1921–41; 578th F.A. Regt., 1921–33; 580th F.A., 1921–33; 372d Ammo. Tn., 1921–23; 529th and 530th Ord. Cos., 1921–41

Constituted in the O.R. on 15 October 1921, assigned to the GHQR, and allotted to the Third Corps Area. Initiated on 15 December 1921 at Middletown, PA. Inactivated about June 1930 at Middletown by relief of personnel. Location 7 December 1941—*Inactive.*

Status: Disbanded on 26 January 1943.

Commanders, 219th Field Artillery Brigade

2d Lt. Harry E. Smith	15 December 1921–28 March 1922	Unknown	ao January 1924–9 April 1926
Capt. Samuel B. Stilwell	28 March 1922–ao January 1924	Brig Gen. Richard C. Marshall Jr.	9 April 1926–June 1930
Inactive	June 1930–7 December 1941		

HHB, 220th Field Artillery Brigade (75-mm G PORT) (GHQR) — Organized Reserve Kentucky

HQ—*Not initiated,* 1921–41

Subordinate elements—*223d F.A. Regt.* (DNG), 1921–27; *224th F.A. Regt.* (DNG), 1921–27; 421st F.A. Regt., 1923–27; 422d F.A. Regt., 1923–27; 571st F.A. Regt., 1921–41; 574th F.A. Regt., 1927–41; 373d Ammo. Tn., 1921–23; 395th Ord. Co., 1921–41

Constituted in the O.R. on 15 October 1921, assigned to the GHQR, and allotted to the Fifth Corps Area. Lexington, KY, designated as HQ on initiation, but the unit was never organized at that location. Designated mobilization station was Camp Knox, KY. Location 7 December 1941—*Not initiated.*

Status: Disbanded on 26 January 1943.

HHB, 221st Field Artillery Brigade (75-mm G MTZ) (GHQR) — Organized Reserve Wisconsin

HQ—*Not initiated,* 1921–26; Racine, WI, 1926–27; Milwaukee, WI, 1927–30; *Inactive,* 1930–33

Subordinate elements—*216th F.A. Regt.* (DNG), 1921–23 and 1927–33; *217th F.A. Regt.* (DNG), 1921–23; 415th F.A. Regt., 1923–27; 416th F.A. Regt., 1923–27; 425th F.A. Regt., 1923–27; 567th F.A., 1921–33; 374th Ammo. Tn., 1921–23; 391st Ord. Co., 1921–33

Constituted in the O.R. on 15 October 1921, assigned to the GHQR, and allotted to the Sixth Corps Area. Initiated on 26 January 1926 at Racine, WI. Relocated on 7 January 1927 to Milwaukee, WI. Inactivated by December 1930 at Milwaukee by relief of personnel. Designated mobilization station was Camp McCoy, WI. Demobilized on 1 October 1933.

Commanders, 221st Field Artillery Brigade

Capt. Lewis A. Eaton	26 January 1926–11 March 1926	Unknown	9 April 1926–December 1930
Maj. James Bereth	11 March 1926–9 April 1926	*Inactive*	December 1930–1 October 1933

HHB, 222d Field Artillery Brigade (75-mm G MTZ) (GHQR) — Organized Reserve New York

HQ—*Not initiated,* 1921–25; Albany, NY, 1925–33

Subordinate elements—*219th F.A. Regt.* (DNG), 1921–27; *220th F.A. Regt.* (DNG), 1921–27; 566th F.A., 1921–33; 390th Ord. Co., 1921–33

Constituted in the O.R. on 15 October 1921, assigned to the GHQR, and allotted to the Third Corps Area. Withdrawn from the Third Corps Area on 9 February 1922 and allotted to the Second Corps Area. Initiated in November 1925 at Albany, NY. Demobilized on 1 October 1933.

Commanders, 222d Field Artillery Brigade

Unknown	November 1925–1 October 1933

HHB, 223d Field Artillery Brigade (75-mm G PORT) (GHQR) — Organized Reserve Illinois

HQ—*Not initiated,* 1921–23; Chicago, IL, 1923–30; *Inactive,* 1930–33

Subordinate elements—*225th F.A. Regt.* (DNG), 1921–23; *226th F.A. Regt.* (DNG), 1921–27; 423d F.A. Regt., 1923–27; 572d F.A., 1921–29; 408th Ord. Co., 1921–33

Constituted in the O.R. on 15 October 1921, assigned to the GHQR, and allotted to the Second Corps Area. Initiated on 2 April 1923 at Chicago, IL. Inactivated by December 1930 at Chicago by relief of personnel. Demobilized on 1 October 1933.

Commanders, 223d Field Artillery Brigade

1st Lt. Harold K. Crabbe	2 April 1923–1 May 1923	Maj. Harold D. Squires	20 January 1926–9 April 1926
Capt. Walter B. Croan	1 May 1923–ao April 1923	Maj. James B. Bereth	9 April 1926–19 May 1928
2d Lt. Carl E. Johnson	ao December 1923–5 January 1924	Capt. Lewis A. Eaton	19 May 1928–ao June 1929
Unknown	4 January 1924–20 January 1926	Unknown	ao June 1929–December 1930
	Inactive	December 1930–1 October 1933	

HHB, 224th Field Artillery Brigade (75-mm G MTZ) (GHQR) **Organized Reserve Missouri/Iowa/Arkansas**

HQ—*Not initiated,* 1921–24; St. Louis, MO, 1924–26; Davenport, IA, 1926–31; Little Rock, AR, 1931–33

Subordinate elements—218th F.A. Regt. (DNG), 1921–23 and 1927–33; *221st F.A. Regt.* (DNG), 1921–27; 222d F.A. Regt. (DNG), 1921–23 and 1925–30; 417th F.A. Regt., 1923–33; 420th F.A. Regt., 1923–25; 406th Ord. Co., 1921–33

Constituted in the O.R. on 15 October 1921, assigned to the GHQR, and allotted to the Seventh Corps Area. Initiated in January 1924 at St. Louis, MO. Relocated on 26 May 1926 to Davenport, IA. Relocated on 12 October 1931 to Little Rock, AR. Demobilized on 1 October 1933.

Commanders, 224th Field Artillery Brigade

Unknown January 1924–1 October 1933

HHB, 225th Field Artillery Brigade (75-mm G PORT) (GHQR) **Organized Reserve New Jersey**

HQ—*Not initiated,* 1921–25; Elizabeth, NJ, 1925–33

Subordinate elements—480th F.A. Regt., 1921–33; 481st F.A. Regt., 1921–33; 482d F.A. Regt., 1921–33; 394th Ord. Co., 1921–33

Constituted in the O.R. on 15 October 1921, assigned to the GHQR, and allotted to the Second Corps Area. Initiated in December 1925 at Elizabeth, NJ. Demobilized on 1 October 1933.

Commanders, 225th Field Artillery Brigade

Unknown December 1925–1 October 1933

HHB, 226th Field Artillery Brigade (75-mm G PORT) (GHQR) **Organized Reserve Kentucky**

HQ—*Not initiated,* 1921–26; Camp Knox, KY, 1926–33

Subordinate elements—483d F.A. Regt, 1921–33; 484th F.A. Regt, 1921–33; 485th F.A. Regts., 1921–33; 397th Ord. Co., 1921–33

Constituted in the O.R. on 15 October 1921, assigned to the GHQR, and allotted to the Fifth Corps Area. Initiated in December 1926 at Camp Knox, KY. Designated mobilization station was Camp Knox, KY. Demobilized on 1 October 1933.

Commanders, 226th Field Artillery Brigade

Unknown December 1926–1 October 1933

HHB, 227th Field Artillery Brigade (75-mm G PORT) (GHQR) **Organized Reserve Michigan**

HQ—*Not initiated,* 1921–26; Detroit, MI, 1926–29; *Inactive,* 1929–33

Subordinate elements—*227th F.A. Regt.* (DNG), 1921–23; 424th F.A. Regt., 1923–27; 486th F.A. Regt., 1921–33; 487th F.A. Regt., 1921–33; 488th F.A. Regts., 1921–33; 392d Ord. Co., 1921–33

Constituted in the O.R. on 15 October 1921, assigned to the GHQR, and allotted to the Sixth Corps Area. Initiated on 9 February 1926 at Detroit, MI. Inactivated about March 1929 at Detroit by relief of personnel. Demobilized on 1 October 1933.

Commanders, 227th Field Artillery Brigade

Maj. Harold F. Pelham	9 February 1926–March 1929	*Inactive*	March 1929–1 October 1933

HHB, 228th Field Artillery Brigade (M & H) (GHQR) **Organized Reserve Ohio**

HQ—*Not initiated,* 1921–33; Dayton, OH, 1933–41

Subordinate elements—574th F.A. Regts., 1921–33; 392d Ord. Co., 1921–33

Constituted in the O.R. on 2 July 1923, assigned to the GHQR, and allotted to the Fifth Corps Area. Initiated by December 1933 at Dayton, OH. Designated mobilization station was Camp Knox, KY. Location 7 December 1941—Dayton, OH.

Status: Disbanded on 26 January 1943.

Commanders, 228th Field Artillery Brigade

Unknown	ao December 1933–7 December 1941

Chapter 20

Field Artillery Regiments

USASC Photo, NA II

Soldiers of B Battery, 2d Field Artillery prepare a 75-mm pack howitzer for an experimental airlift exercise from France Field to Rio Hato, CZ, 20 March 1931.

Field Artillery (F.A.) regiments provided indirect and direct fire support for the ground gaining arms.

Organization

As with the infantry, the field artillery regiment was considered the base artillery organization for combat, training, and administrative operations in the interwar period. For the most part, the organization and types of regiments in the postwar Army were a direct adoption of the types of units that served in World War I. The Hero Board, headed by its namesake, Brigadier General Andrew Hero Jr., found during its analysis of wartime field artillery units in 1919 that the practical utility of field artillery organizational structure was sound, but still recommended a number of changes. Though there were changes to the various artillery brigades and a few other artillery organizations, the various types of regiments were left largely intact.

There were several distinct types of field artillery regiments in this period. The organization of these units was based on the type of weapon with which they were equipped and the echelon of command to which they were assigned. At the division-level were two 75-mm G horse-drawn regiments consisting of 2 battalions and 24 guns each (12 weapons per battalion). Three truck-drawn versions of this regiment were integral to the General Headquarters Reserve (GHQR) light field artillery brigade and another three were found in the GHQR portee brigade as well. The 155-mm H regiment was part of both the corps artillery brigade (three regiments each) and in the GHQR medium and heavy (M&H) artillery brigade (two regiments each). Both regiments consisted of 3 battalions of 8 weapons in each battalion (24 total). The 155-mm G regiment was located only in the corps artillery brigade and was organized the same as the 155-mm H regiment and equipped with 24 guns versus the howitzer. The 240-mm H regiment was a part of the

Field Artillery Regiment, 75-mm Gun, Horse Drawn, 1921

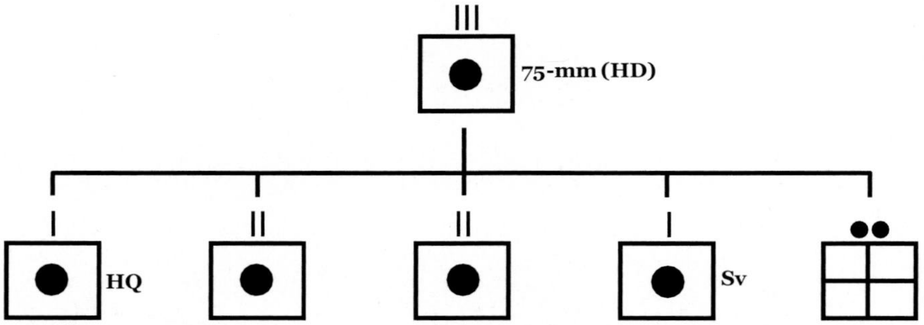

T/O:	33W
Approved:	20 January 1921
Commander:	Col.
Officers:	75
W. O.	1
Enlisted:	1495
Total:	1571

Key Equipment:	
Cars, various	2
Trucks, various	1
Horses & Mules	1,607
Wagons, various	58
Guns, 75-mm	24
Machine guns, AA	20

Field Artillery Regiment, 75-mm Gun, Motorized, GHQR, 1921

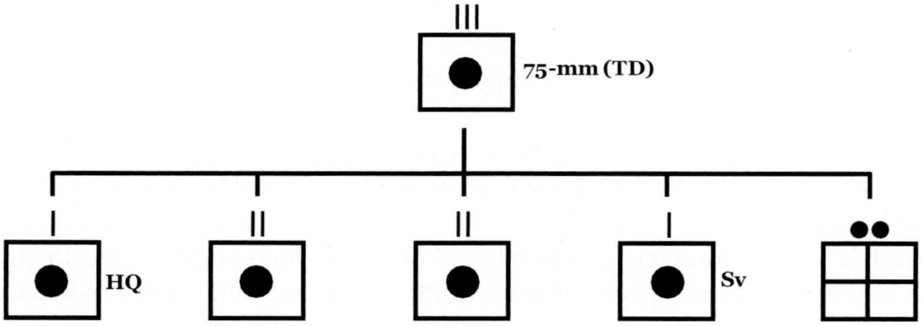

T/O:	518W
Approved:	15 December 1921
Commander:	Col.
Officers:	69
W. O.	1
Enlisted:	1,179
Total:	1,249

Key Equipment:	
Cars, various	27
Tractors, 5-Ton	78
Trucks, various	42
Guns, 75-mm	24
Machine guns, AA	12

Field artillery regiment organization, horse drawn and motorized, 1921.

Field Artillery Regiment, 75-mm Gun, Pack, 1921

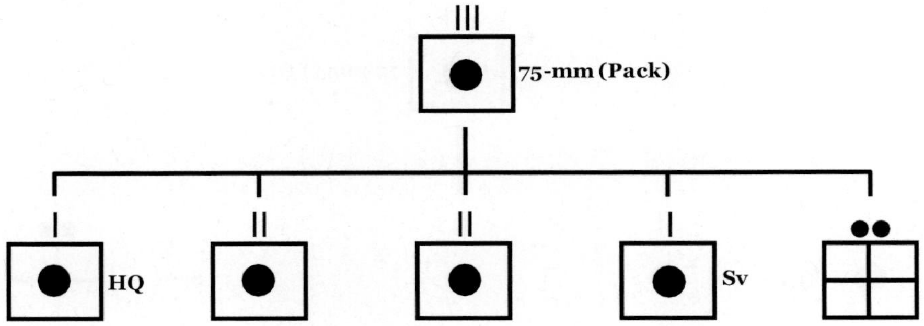

T/O:	533W
Approved:	28 February 1921
Commander:	Col.
Officers:	74
W. O.	1
Enlisted:	1,520
Total:	1,595

Key Equipment:	
Packs, Ammunition	360
Packs, Forge	16
Packs, Gun	96
Packs, various other	448
Horses & Mules	2,039
Wagons, various	28
Guns, 75-mm	24

Field Artillery Regiment, 75-mm Gun, Portée, 1921

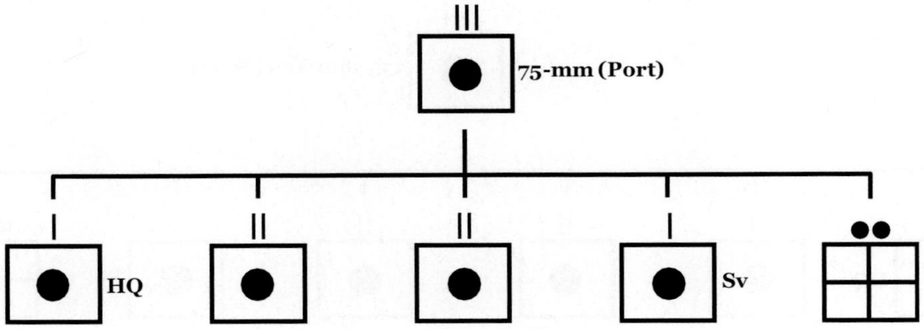

T/O:	523W
Approved:	17 June 1921
Commander:	Col.
Officers:	69
W. O.	--
Enlisted:	849
Total:	918

Key Equipment:	
Cars, various	24
Tractors, 3-Ton	6
Trucks, various	80
Guns, 75-mm	24
Machine guns, AA	12

Field artillery regiment organization, pack and portee, 1921.

Field Artillery Regiment, 75-mm Gun, Truck Drawn, 1934

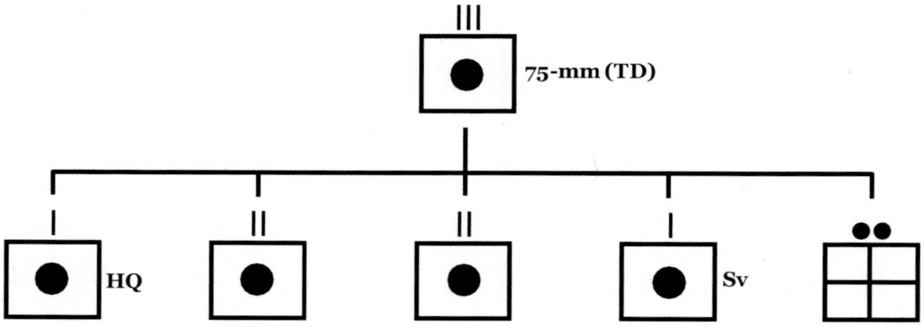

T/O:	33A
Effective:	24 October 1934
Commander:	Col.
Officers:	73
W. O.	1
Enlisted:	1,280
Total:	1,354

Key Equipment:	
Cars, various	20
Trucks, various	288
Guns, 75-mm	24
Machine guns, AA	20

Field Artillery Regiment, 155-mm Gun, Motorized, 1930

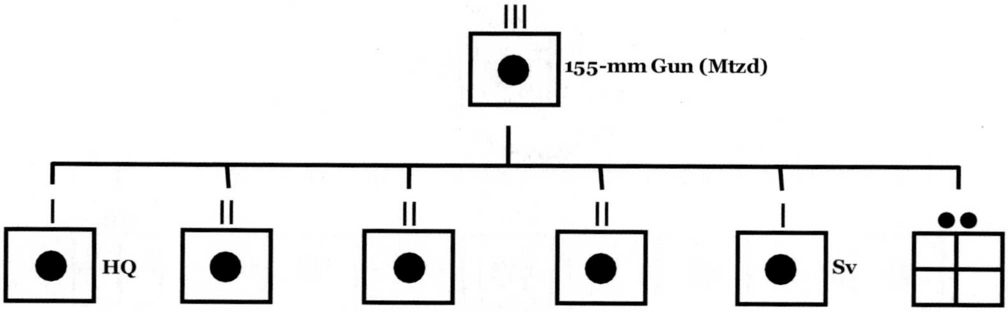

T/O:	140W
Effective	1 July 1930
Commander:	Col.
Officers:	84
W. O.	1
Enlisted:	1,743
Total:	1,828

Key Equipment:	
Cars, various	35
Tractors, 5-Ton	76
Trucks, various	145
Guns, 155-mm	24
Machine guns, AA	20

Field artillery regiment organization, truck drawn and motorized.

Field Artillery Regiment, 155-mm Howitzer, Motorized, 1921

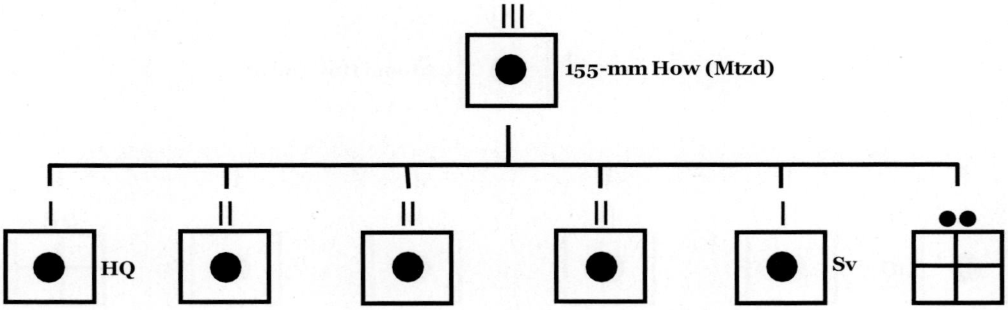

T/O:	133W
Approved:	7 March 1921
Commander:	Col.
Officers:	84
W. O.	1
Enlisted:	1,694
Total:	1,749

Key Equipment:	
Cars, various	35
Tractors, 5-Ton	88
Trucks, various	174
Howitzers, 155-mm	24
Machine guns, AA	12

Field Artillery Regiment, 155-mm Howitzer, Tractor Drawn, 1931

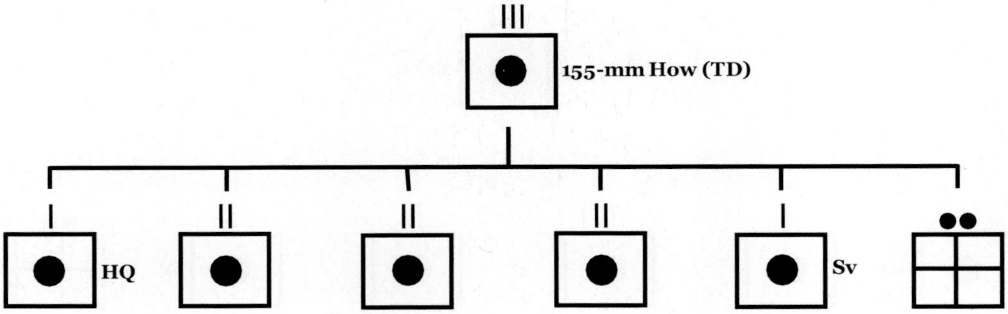

T/O:	133W
Effective:	1 July 1931
Commander:	Col.
Officers:	84
W. O.	1
Enlisted:	1,797
Total:	1,882

Key Equipment:	
Cars, various	67
Tractors, medium	88
Trucks, various	180
Howitzers, 155-mm	24
Machine guns, AA	20

Field artillery regiment organization, 155-mm Howitzer.

Field Artillery Regiment, 240-mm Howitzer, Motorized, 1921

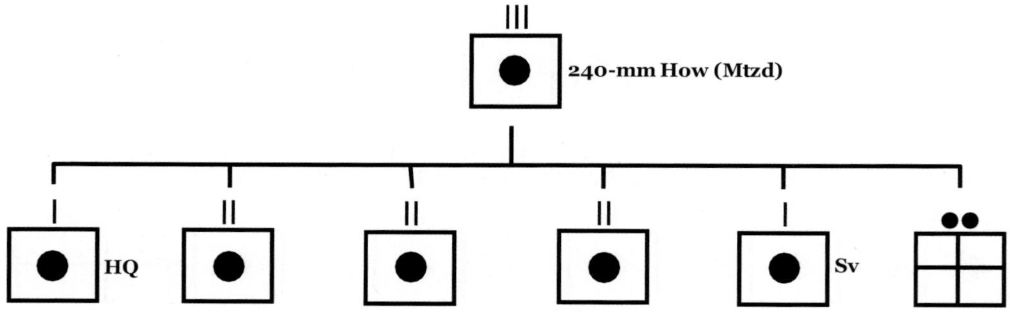

T/O:	529W
Approved:	2 November 1921
Commander:	Col.
Officers:	96
W. O.	1
Enlisted:	2,384
Total:	2,481

Key Equipment:	
Cars, various	35
Tractors, 10-Ton	148
Trucks, various	260
Howitzers, 240-mm	24
Machine guns, AA	12

Trench Mortar Regiment, 1921

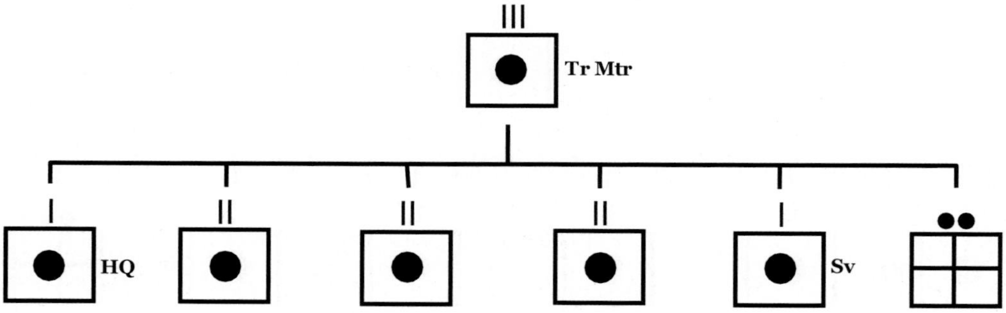

T/O:	543W
Approved:	10 May 1921
Commander:	Col.
Officers:	64
W. O.	1
Enlisted:	1,465
Total:	1,530

Key Equipment:	
Cars, various	15
Trucks, various	95
Mortars, Trench	36
Machine guns, AA	12

Field artillery organization, 240-mm Howitzer and trench motar regiment.

M&H brigade only and was organized with 3 battalions and 24 howitzers. The 6-inch G regiment was also a component of the M&H brigade and organized similarly to the 240-mm H regiment. The final type of regiment was the 75-mm pack howitzer regiment. Like other 75-mm regiments, these units also consisted of 2 battalions and 24 guns (12 weapons per battalion).

By 1921, only the regiments integral to the infantry and cavalry divisions were horse drawn, though the guns of the 75-mm pack regiments, which were generally intended for jungle or mountain terrain, were broken into component parts and carried by mules. The guns of portee regiments were carried on the bed of a portee truck or trailer. The remaining weapons were intended to be truck- or tractor-drawn, though few field artillery units were ever equipped with the latter as a prime mover.

During the interwar period, there were 87 authorized Regular Army (R.A.) field artillery regiments. Of these regiments, 27 were on the rolls as of January 1920. Between that date and October 1933, another 60 regiments would be constituted or reconstituted and added to the rolls of the Army. Of these regiments, only 12 managed to maintain an Active Duty regimental headquarters (HQ) for the entire period. Another 15 regiments were partially active with at least 1 battalion on Active Duty for all or part of that time. Nine of those regiments, less their active elements, were organized for varying lengths of time as Regular Army Inactive (RAI) regiments. Fifty-seven additional regiments were organized at some point as RAI units. Only three of the R.A. regiments remained totally inactive during the interwar period. Most of these regiments were reorganized and redesignated as divisional or nondivisional field artillery battalions during 1940–41 and activated for service in World War II. A minority remained organized as regiments and a few of those were activated as such during the same period.

Most of the RAI regiments were functional units during their period of organization as Reserve units. Generally, these regiments were organized in larger cities or affiliated with a Reserve Officers' Training Corps (ROTC) program. They also tended to have a Reserve field grade officer at the rank of major or higher in command. Typically, those that were commanded by captains or lieutenants were pool units for mobilization assignment purposes and rarely met for unit activities except for summer training camps.

The National Guard (N.G.) had 107 field artillery regiments on the rolls of the Army at some point between 1921 and 1940. Of these, 63 were active units between 1921 and 1939. There were three partially active regiments during this period, two of which were later subsumed into other regiments. There were another 28 regiments that were allotted to various states of the N.G., which were never organized. These were corps and GHQR regiments that were placed on the deferred list in 1923 and, with a few exceptions, were demobilized in 1927. Between 1939 and 1941, another 13 regiments were organized in the N.G. These were largely organized from existing Guard units that were not required by the Army's mobilization plans. The new units were formed mostly from cavalry regiments formerly belonging to the four disbanded Guard cavalry divisions. The others were former infantry regiments.

Over 220 regiments were constituted or reconstituted and allotted to the Organized Reserve (O.R.) between 1921 and 1929. The majority of these regiments were organized, but many were later inactivated with the organization of the many RAI regiments that were constituted or reconstituted and organized with Reserve personnel in the 1920s and 1930s. About 37 of the O.R. regiments were later demobilized as excess to Army needs. The majority of those organized, especially the divisional regiments, were functional units. Like most O.R. units, those regiments that were originally spread over large geographic areas in the early 1920s tended to coalesce into larger population centers, either at the battalion- or regimental-level by the late 1920s. A number of regiments, mostly GHQR and a few corps artillery regiments, remained pool units for officers who were geographically separated from larger cities and could not participate in unit training activities.

Training

The annual training cycle for R.A. field artillery regiments was similar to that for other combat arms units (see Chapter 9, Infantry Regiments, for a general description). For artillery units, the tight budgets meant that service firing with live rounds was conducted only occasionally and rarely more than twice a year. Even when live firing was conducted, rounds were used sparingly. Maneuver training was conducted, generally, in conjunction with the artillery unit's parent brigade or division, though it was not unusual for batteries to take to the field to conduct firing position occupation and battery displacement drills.

N.G. artillery units typically followed a 2-year cycle. One year the regiment, frequently as part of its parent brigade, would conduct live-firing exercises. The next year the unit would attend maneuver training. As for the R.A., when live firing, Guard artillery regiments were provided a minimal amount of ammunition for training and attempted to maximize the training value for every round. The inactive training period was conducted in a similar fashion to other Guard units (see chapter 9 for a general description).

Many O.R. field artillery regiments conducted their inactive training periods performing a lot of theoretical exercises concerning the employment of artillery. Those units lucky enough to be near an R.A. or N.G. artillery unit could often use those units' equipment, if it was available, for more basic hands-on skills. During summer camps, the training was often very elementary. Junior officers were often employed as gun crews to learn the fundamental skills of the branch. More senior officers were employed as battery commanders or instructors. If the camp was a Regular Army Training Center (R.A.T.C.)-type camp, the Reserve officers would have the opportunity to shadow an R.A. counterpart in the field. If the regimental or battalion commander felt that the Reserve unit had progressed well enough, the commander could turn over control of the unit to the Reserve officers for a few days. Live firing tended to be a more intense level of training due to the lower skill level of the Reservists and the increased possibility of a serious incident. Nevertheless, the Reserve units did get to conduct live firing about every 2 to 3 years. Given that the average Reservist attended camp only once every 3 to 4 years, however, it might be as long as 3 to 8 years between live firing events for a Reserve field artillery officer.

1st Trench Mortar Regiment (GHQR) **Organized Reserve Pennsylvania**

HQ—*Not initiated,* 1923–29; Pottstown, PA, 1926–29; *Inactive,* 1929–33

Constituted in the R.A. on 24 March 1923, assigned to the GHQR, and allotted to the Third Corps Area. Withdrawn from the R.A. on 27 February 1926 and allotted to the O.R. Initiated by September 1926 at Pottstown, PA. Withdrawn from the Coast Artillery Corps (C.A.C.) on 1 March 1928 and transferred to the F.A. Inactivated by July 1929 at Pottstown. Demobilized on 1 October 1933.

1st Trench Mortar Regiment

Unknown	ao September 1926–July 1929

1st Field Artillery Regiment (75-mm G–H) (Separate)

HQ—Fort Sill, OK, 1919–41

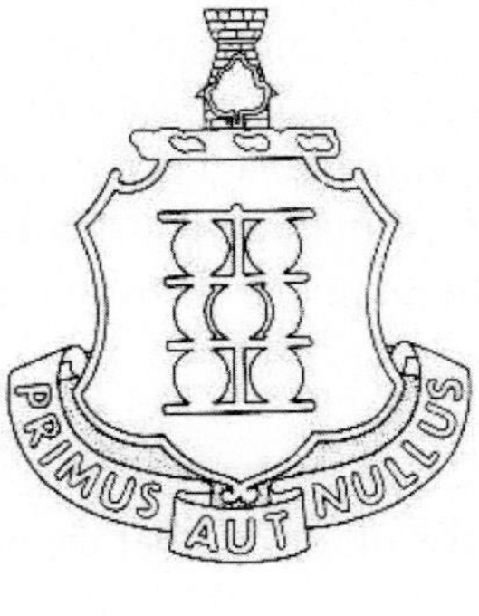

Stationed at Fort Sill, OK, as of June 1919 where it served as the demonstration and training regiment for the Field Artillery School. As the school regiment, the 1st F.A. was configured in an unusual organization, which was as follows: three horse-drawn batteries of French 75-mm guns; three motorized batteries of American 3-inch guns; one truck-drawn battery of American 75-mm guns. Additionally, the regiment had two 155-mm howitzers, two 9.2-inch howitzers, two 155-mm G.P.F. guns, four 4.7-inch guns, and one 240-mm howitzer. Assigned on 31 October 1929 to the 2d Division (Div.). Relieved from 2d Div. on 1 January 1930. Assigned on 1 October 1933 to the 4th Div. Entire regiment motorized on 26 October 1934. Relieved from the 4th Div. on 16 October 1939 and assigned to the 6th Div. Concurrently, new 3d Battalion (Bn.) constituted but not organized. Assigned Reserve officers conducted summer training with the regiment at Fort Sill. Reorganized and redesignated 1st F.A. Bn. on 1 October 1940 at Fort Sill.

Organization Day: 31 May. Adopted 31 March 1938.

Status: Assigned to the US Army Regimental System (USARS) as the 1st F.A.

Events: 65, 171, 293, 296, 303, 316, 328

Commanders, 1st Field Artillery Regiment

Col. Lucien G. Berry	6 May 191917–5 August 1917	Lt. Col. Pelham D. Glassford	20 August 1927–11 September 1927
Lt. Col. Raymond S. Pratt	5 August 1917–7 September 1917	Col. George P. Tyner	11 September 1927–23 June 1930
Col. Henry W. Butner	7 September 1917–7 December 1917	Maj. John S. Winslow	23 June 1930–9 July 1930
Lt. Col. Raymond S. Pratt	7 December 1917–June 1918	Maj. Charles Porterfield Jr.	10 July 1930–15 August 1930
Col. Rene E. De Hoyle	30 July 1918–4 March 1919	Lt. Col. Rene E. De Hoyle	15 August 1930–3 September 1930
Col. Jacob L. Devers	5 March 1919–18 May 1919	Col. Charles M. Bundel	3 September 1930–10 February 1932
Col. Ralph McT. Pennell	6 November 1919–3 August 1921	Lt. Col. George M. Peek	10 February 1932–29 June 1932
Col. Ralph S. Granger	1 September 1921–4 September 1922	Lt. Col. James L. Collins	29 June 1932–22 October 1932
Col. Fred T. Austin	4 September 1922–24 June 1924	Col. Robert C. Foy	22 October 1932–1 March 1935
Lt. Col. Raymond S. Pratt	24 June 1924–17 July 1924	Maj. John M. Carriker	20 March 1935–3 June 1935
Maj. William C. Crane	17 June 1924–18 August 1924	Lt. Col. John A. Hoag	3 June 1935–7 September 1935
Lt. Col. Edward T. Connelly	18 August 1924–8 October 1924	Col. Donald C. Cubbison	7 September 1935–31 July 1937
Col. Charles D. Herron	8 October 1924–11 May 1927	Col. Marshal G. Randol	4 August 1937–June 1940
Maj. George M. Peek	11 May 1927–20 August 1927	Col. John P. Lucas	July 1940–1 October 1940

2d Field Artillery Regiment (75-mm G) (4th Division)

HQ—Camp Zachary Taylor, KY, 1919–20; Camp Knox, KY, 1920–21; Camp Bragg, NC, 1921–22; *Inactive,* 1922–41

Stationed at Camp Zachary Taylor, KY, as of June 1919, an element of the 8th F.A. Brig. Transferred on 8 August 1920 to Camp Knox, KY. Transferred on 5 December 1921 to Camp Bragg, NC. Inactivated on 2 February 1922, less 1st Bn., at Camp Bragg. Concurrently, relieved from the 8th F.A. Brig. and 1st Bn. made Active Associate (A.A.). Regiment assigned to the 4th Div. on 1 August 1922. Concurrently, the 2d Bn. activated at Camp George G. Meade, MD. The 2d Bn. inactivated on 14 December 1922 at Fort Myer, VA, and personnel and equipment transferred to the 1st Bn., 16th F.A. Regiment relieved on 5 September 1927 from the 4th Div. The 1st Bn. concurrently inactivated at Fort Bragg and personnel and equipment transferred to the newly activated 2d Bn., 16th F.A. Regt. Assigned to the Panama Canal Division on 17 March 1930 and designated a 75-mm H (Pack) regiment. The 1st Bn. activated on 30 April 1930 at Fort Davis, CZ, by redesignation and consolidation of the 2d F.A. Bn. (Portee). Btry B participated in experimental airlift of artillery from France Field to Rio Hato, CZ, on 20 March 1931. Attached to HQ, Pacific Sector on 15 April 1932 when the Panama Canal Division was inactivated. The 1st Bn. transferred in 1934 to Fort Clayton, CZ. Regiment relieved on 1 October 1938 from the Panama Canal Division. Btry A awarded the Knox Trophy for 1939. Reorganized and redesignated 2d F.A. Bn. on 13 January 1941.

Organization Day: 6 June. Chose to commemorate the regiment's constitution and activation on 6 June 1907.

Status: Assigned to the USARS as the 2d F.A.; 2d Bn. active at Fort Sill, OK, as a training battalion.

Events: 53, 58, 69, 81, 101, 119, 140, 167, 170, 181, 223, 271, 292, 308, 333

Commanders, 2d Field Artillery Regiment

Col. George W. Van Duesen	January 1916–13 July 1918	Maj. Carl I. Rohsenberger	2 September 1919–7 February 1920
Unknown	14 July 1918–March 1919	Col. Phillip W. Booker	7 February 1920–3 July 1920
Col. Otho W.B. Farr	March 1919–10 June 1919	Maj. Stanley S. Addis	3 July 1920–6 August 1920
Col. Ernest D. Scott	19 July 1919–1 September 1919	Maj. Pierre V. Kieffer	6 August 1920–1 September 1920
	Maj. Charles P. Hollingsworth	1 September 1920–2 February 1922	

1st Battalion (active 1922–41)

Maj. Philip W. Booker	2 February 1922–1 September 1924	Maj. John B. Wogan	20 August 1930–9 July 1932
Maj. John C. Wyeth	10 September 1924–7 June 1926	Capt. Larry McHale	9 July 1932–10 September 1932
Maj. James L. Collins	7 June 1926–31 August 1927	Lt. Col. Edmund L. Gruber	10 September 1932–20 June 1935
Maj. John N. Eager	1 September 1927–14 June 1928	Lt. Col. Frederick W. Barrows	20 June 1935–10 October 1936
(Designated as 2d F.A. Bn.)	15 June 1928–30 April 1930	Maj. Ray H. Lewis	10 October 1936–11 August 1937
Lt. Col. Ned B. Rehkopf	1 May 1930–20 August 1930	Lt. Col. Gustave Franke	11 August 1937–May 1940
	Lt. Col. Horace L. McBride	May 1940–13 January 1941	

3d Field Artillery Regiment (75-mm G-H) (6th Division)

HQ—Camp Grant, IL, 1919–21; Camp Knox, KY, 1921–22; *Inactive,* 1922–27; Fort McIntosh, TX, 1927–28; Camp Knox, KY, 1928–29; Fort Sheridan, IL, 1929–30; Chicago, IL, 1930–41

Arrived at the port of New York on 19 June 1919 on the U.S.S. *Kaiserina Augusta Victoria* as an element of the 6th Div. Transferred on 20 June 1919 to Camp Mills, NY, and on 26 June 1919 to Camp Grant, IL. Transferred on 26 September 1921 to Camp Knox, KY. Inactivated on 14 September 1922, less 1st Bn., at Camp Knox and 1st Bn. made the A.A. The 1st Bn. transferred in late 1922 to Fort Benjamin Harrison, IN. Regiment was relieved from the 6th Div. on 24 March 1923 and assigned to the 5th Div. The 2d Bn. was activated on 8 September 1927 at Fort Sheridan, IL, with personnel and equipment from the inactivated 1st Bn., 14th F.A. Regimental HQ was activated on 24 October 1927 at Fort McIntosh, TX, with personnel and equipment from the inactivated 4th F.A. Regt. Regimental HQ transferred on 18 May 1928 to Camp Knox. Btry F concurrently activated at Jefferson Barracks, MO. Regimental HQ transferred on 4 June 1929 to Fort Sheridan. Relieved from 5th Div. on 1 January 1930 and assigned to the 6th Div. Regimental HQ was inactivated on 1 May 1930 at Fort Sheridan. Regiment less 1st and 2d Bns. organized in 1930 with O.R. personnel as an RAI unit at Chicago, IL. RAI elements conducted summer training with the active elements of the regiment at Camp McCoy, WI, or Fort Knox, KY. Btry D awarded the Knox Trophy for 1931. The 1st Bn. inactivated on 3 December 1934 at Fort Benjamin Harrison and personnel and equipment transferred to the newly activated 1st Bn., 19th F.A. The 3d F.A. Regt. relieved from the 6th Div. on 25 September 1939 and assigned to the 2d Cavalry (Cav.) Div. The 1st Bn. was activated on 1 October 1939 at Fort Riley, KS. Remainder of the regiment less the 2d Bn. withdrawn from the Sixth Corps Area and allotted to the Seventh Corps Area. Concurrently, reorganized from 75-mm G to 75-mm H. The 2d Bn. inactivated on 1 June 1940 at Fort Sheridan. Regiment reorganized and redesignated on 1 January 1941 as 3d F.A. Bn. at Fort Riley.

Status: Assigned to the USARS as the 3d F.A.; 2d Bn. active at Giessen, Germany, as an element of the 1st Armored (Armd.) Div., 3d Bn. active at Fort Drum, NY, as an element of the 10th Infantry (Inf.) Div. (Light), and 5th Bn. active at Fort Sill, OK, as an element of the 17th F.A. Brig.

Organization Day: 1 July. Chosen to commemorate the regiment's participation in the Battles of Gettysburg (1 July 1863) and Santiago (1 July 1898). Adopted 8 March 1926.

Events: 123, 129, 165, 172, 214, 237, 274, 285, 303, 328

Commanders, 3d Field Artillery Regiment

Col. Edward A. Millar	March 1916–17 December 1917	Col. Robert C. Foy	24 October 1927–5 December 1928
Col. Willard D. Newbill	1 January 1918–28 June 1922	Lt. Col. William S. Browning	5 December 1928–21 September 1928
Maj. William H. Shepard	28 June 1922–10 July 1922	Maj. Marshal G. Randol	21 September 1928–December 1929
Maj. Walter S. Sturgill	10 July 1922–14 September 1922	Maj. Charles D. Herron	December 1929–1 May 1930
Inactive	15 September 1922–23 October 1927	*Inactive*	2 May 1930–1 January 1941

1st Battalion (active 1922–34)

Lt. Col. Frank E. Hopkins	15 September 1922–2 October 1923	Maj. Marshal G. Randol	21 September 1928–28 February 1930
Capt. Mark A. Dawson	2 October 1923–16 March 1924	Maj. Frank Royse	28 February 1930–3 July 1930
Maj. Charles G. Helmick	16 March 1924–September 1924	Maj. Robert G. Kirkwood	3 July 1930–2 August 1932
Lt. Col. Morris E. Locke	September 1924–18 October 1926	Capt. Warren D. Davis	2 August 1932–16 September 1932
Lt. Col. George R. Greene	19 October 1926–12 July 1928	Maj. John K. Boles	16 September 1932–3 December 1934
Lt. Col. William S. Browning	12 July 1928–21 September 1928	*Inactive*	4 December 1934–30 September 1939
Lt. Col. Ralph Hospital	1 October 1939–31 December 1940		

2d Battalion (active 1927–40)

Maj. Francis A. Doniat	28 September 1927–1 July 1928	Lt. Col. Otto L. Brunzell	1 December 1931–16 January 1934
Maj. John G. Tyndall	1 July 1928–29 January 1930	Capt. Mark A. Dawson	16 January 1934–18 July 1934
Capt. Thomas B. McCormick	29 January 1930–15 September 1930	Maj. Hamilton E. McGuire	18 July 1934–21 June 1936
Maj. Arthur R. Harris	15 September 1930–29 August 1931	Maj. Calvin S. Richards	21 June 1936–17 August 1936
Maj. William E. Burr	29 August 1931–4 November 1931	Lt. Col. Carl A. Baehr	17 August 1936–8 August 1938
Capt. Thomas B. McCormick	4 November 1931–1 December 1931	Lt. Col. George A. Pollin	8 August 1938–1 June 1940

4th Field Artillery Regiment (75-mm H) (Pack) (Panama Canal Division)

HQ—Camp Stanley, TX, 1919–22; Fort Sam Houston, TX, 1922–24; Fort McIntosh, TX, 1924–27; *Inactive,* 1927–40; Fort Bragg, NC, 1940–41

Stationed at Camp Stanley, TX, as of June 1919. Ordered to the Panama Canal Zone about June 1921. The 1st Bn. transferred on 15 September 1921 to Gatun, CZ. Remainder of the regiment remained at Camp Stanley and was to be transferred when accommodations in Panama and transportation funds became available. Regiment assigned on 12 June 1922 to the Panama Canal Division. Regiment less 1st Bn. was transferred on 3 July 1922 to Fort Sam Houston, TX. Btry A conducted a difficult march cutting a trail through the jungle across the entire isthmus from Gatun to Port Chorrera, 4–17 February 1923. Regimental HQ and 2d Bn. transferred on 24 October 1924 to Fort McIntosh, TX. Btry C awarded the Knox Trophy for 1926. The 1st Bn. reorganized on 6 January 1927 as a portee unit. The 1st Bn. redesignated 2d F.A. Bn. (Portee) on 1 September 1927 at Fort Davis, CZ (hereafter separate lineage), and 2d Bn. concurrently redesignated 4th F.A. Bn. (Pack) at Fort McIntosh. Regimental HQ was inactivated on 24 October 1927 at Fort McIntosh. Concurrently the regiment was relieved from the Panama Canal Division and allotted to the Seventh Corps Area. The 4th F.A. Regt. was assigned to the 2d Cav. Div. on 17 March 1930. The 4th F.A. Bn. redesignated 2d Bn., 4th F.A. Regt. on 29 March 1930. The 2d Bn. transferred in May 1931 to Fort Bragg, NC. Regiment relieved from the 2d Cav. Div. on 23 September 1932. Relieved from the Seventh Corps Area on 1 March 1933 and allotted to the Fourth Corps Area. Assigned Reserve officers conducted summer training with the 2d Bn. at Fort Bragg. RAI elements activated on 1 June 1940, less Reserve personnel, at Fort Bragg. Regiment reorganized and redesignated 4th F.A. Bn. on 4 January 1941.

Organization Day: The 4th F.A. opted not to designate an organization day in the 1920s and 1930s giving the rational that the regiment had not yet experienced its "baptism of fire," though this was not a prerequisite for the selection of a date.

Status: Assigned to the USARS as the 4th F.A.; 2d Bn. active at Fort Sill, OK, as an element of the 214th F.A. Brig.

Events: 26, 31, 36, 40, 43, 53, 55, 58, 69, 81, 101, 119, 140, 293, 296, 323, 330

Commanders, 4th Field Artillery Regiment

Col. William J. Snow	April 1917–September 1917	Maj. Hugh P. Avent	3 April 1922–7 August 1922
Col. William H. Burke	November 1917–22 August 1918	Maj. Herbert H. White	7 August 1922–September 1922
Col. George W. Van Deusen	22 August 1918–20 January 1919	Lt. Col. Eben Swift Jr.	September 1922–5 February 1924
Lt. Col. Herman Erlenkotter	20 January 1919–18 September 1920	Col. Pierce A. Murphy	6 February 1924–10 April 1926
Lt. Col. Robert O. Mason	18 September 1920–2 February 1921	Maj. Joseph A. Rogers	10 April 1926–12 October 1926
Maj. William McCleave	2 February 1921–9 July 1921	Col. Robert C. Foy	12 October 1926–24 October 1927
Lt. Col. Daniel F. Craig	9 July 1921–10 September 1921	*Inactive*	24 October 1927–1 June 1940
Maj. William McCleave	9 September 1921–3 April 1922	Lt. Col. Ira T. Wyche	1 June 1940–August 1940
	Lt. Col. Reese M. Howell	August 1940–1 January 1941	

2d Battalion (active 1930–40)

Lt. Col. Laurin L. Lawson	29 March 1930–24 March 1931	Maj. Richard A. Gordon	5 March 1935–19 August 1936
Maj. Orville M. Moore	24 March 1931–30 June 1932	Lt. Col. John P. Lucas	19 August 1936–8 December 1937
Lt. Col. Joe R. Brabson	30 June 1932–25 July 1934	Lt. Col. Donald M. Beere	8 December 1937–1 September 1938
Lt. Col. Thomas D. Osborne	25 July 1934–5 March 1935	Lt. Col. Ira T. Wyche	1 October 1938–1 June 1940

5th Field Artillery Regiment (155-mm G) (13th Field Artillery Brigade)

HQ—Camp Zachary Taylor, KY, 1919–20; Camp Bragg, NC, 1920–31; Madison Barracks, NY, 1931–40

Arrived at the port of New York on 5 September 1919 on the U.S.S. *Zeppelin* as an element of the 1st Div. Transferred to Camp Mills, NY, on 5 September 1919 and to Camp George G. Meade, MD, on 18 September 1919. Transferred on 4 October 1919 to Camp Zachary Taylor, KY. Transferred on 22 November 1920 to Camp Bragg, NC. Relieved on 4 November 1920 from the 1st Div. Assigned on 5 March 1921 to the 13th F.A. Brig. (IV Corps). The 3d Bn. was inactivated on 1 August 1922 at Camp Bragg and allotted to the Fourth Corps Area. The 3d Bn. was organized about 1927 with O.R. personnel as an RAI unit in Mississippi. The regiment was organized under special tables of organization from 1922 to 1933. The 1st Bn. was armed with the 155-mm G.P.F. gun and the 2d Bn. was armed with the 240-mm howitzer until June 1930, when the 1st Bn. was rearmed with the 155-mm howitzer and the 2d Bn. was rearmed with one battery of 155-mm G.P.F. guns and one battery of 240-mm howitzers. Relieved from the 13th F.A. Brig. on 1 January 1930 and assigned to the 1st Div. The HQ and 1st Bn. were transferred on 27 October 1931 to Madison Barracks, NY. The 2d Bn. was inactivated on 1 October 1933 at Fort Bragg, and the entire regiment was concurrently reorganized as a 155-mm H unit. Concurrently, the 2d and 3d Bns. were withdrawn from allotment to the Fourth Corps Area and allotted to the Second Corps Area. The 2d Bn., less Btry D, was activated on 5 December 1933 at Madison Barracks. The 3d Bn. was organized by 1934 with O.R. personnel as an RAI unit in New York. Btry D (Alexander Hamilton Btry) was reactivated on 1 July 1939 at Madison Barracks. The 3d Bn. was disbanded on 26 October 1939. Assigned Reserve officers conducted summer training with the regiment at Madison Barracks. Regiment was relieved from the 1st Div. on 16 October 1939. Assigned to 18th F.A. Brig. (VIII Corps) on 1 July 1940. Regiment reorganized and redesignated 5th F.A. Bn. on 1 October 1940.

Organization Day: 28 October. Chosen to commemorate the participation of Btry D (organized in 1775 as Alexander Hamilton's Company of Artillery, the oldest unit in the R.A.) in the Battle of White Plains on 28 October 1776. Adopted 30 October 1928.

Status: Assigned to the USARS as the 5th F.A.; 1st Bn. active at Fort Riley, KS, as an element of the 1st Inf. Div. (Mecz) and 2d Bn. active at Fort Sill, OK, as an element of the 212th F.A. Brig.

Events: 153, 219, 241, 265, 280

Commanders, 5th Field Artillery Regiment

Col. Charles T. Menoher	ao June 1917–26 August 1917
Col. George V. H. Moseley	26 August 1917–6 November 1917
Col. Dwight E. Aultman	6 November 1917–12 April 1918
Col. Maxwell Murray	12 April 1918–31 July 1918
Lt. Col. John T. Kennedy	1 August 1918–16 November 1918
Col. Clifford L. Corbin	16 November 1918–1 April 1919
Col. Donald C. McDonald	2 April 1919–August 1919
Lt. Col. Newton N. Polk	August 1919–ao September 1919
Maj. David S. Baggett	ao January 1920–5 February 1920
Col. George H. Payne	5 February 1920–April 1920
Lt. Col. Harcourt Hervey	April 1920–July 1920
Maj. Sumner M. Smith	July 1920–28 September 1920
Col. Albert J. Bowley	28 September 1920–24 December 1920
Maj. Freeman W. Bowley	24 December 1920–6 August 1921
Maj. Benjamin F. Miller	6 August 1921–20 October 1921
Maj. Freeman W. Bowley	20 October 1921–7 January 1922
Maj. Benjamin F. Miller	7 January 1922–5 February 1923
Col. John C. MacArthur	5 February 1923–2 July 1924
Col. Henry W. Butner	3 July 1924–15 August 1925
Lt. Col. George P. Hawes Jr.	15 August 1925–15 September 1925
Lt. Col. James H. Bryson	15 September 1925–22 March 1926
Col. Thomas E. Merrill	22 March 1926–23 May 1928
Lt. Col. Creed F. Cox	23 May 1928–16 July 1928
Col. Albert U. Faulkner	16 July 1928–1 July 1931
Maj. Edwin R. Van Deusen	1 July 1931–26 September 1931
Col. John R. Thomas Jr.	27 September 1931–8 March 1933
Lt. Col. Walter S. Sturgill	8 March 1933–11 October 1933
Col. Raymond W. Briggs	11 October 1933–21 May 1936
Col. Harold W. Huntley	21 May 1936–4 August 1936
Col. Maxwell Murray	4 August 1936–15 August 1938
Col. Samuel R. Hopkins	15 August 1938–5 July 1939
Col. Raymond E. Lee	5 July 1939–5 March 1940
Col. Carl Baehr	April 1940–1 October 1940

6th Field Artillery Regiment (75-mm G-H) (1st Division)

HQ—Camp Zachary Taylor, KY, 1919–20; Camp Dix, NJ, 1920–22; Fort Hoyle, MD, 1922–40

Regiment, less 2d Bn., arrived at the port of New York on 5 September 1919 on the U.S.S. *Zeppelin* as an element of the 1st Div. Transferred on 4 October 1919 to Camp Zachary Taylor, KY. The 2d Bn. remained assigned to the 2d Brig., American Forces in Germany until 4 May 1922. Regiment less 2d Bn. transferred on 24 September 1920 to Camp Dix, NJ. The 2d Bn. sailed on 22 April 1922 on the US Army Transport (U.S.A.T.) *Cambrai* and arrived on 4 June 1922 at Montauk, NY, where it joined the regiment on summer training duties. Entire regiment transferred on 25 September 1922 to Fort Hoyle, MD. Participated in the inaugural parade for President Herbert Hoover on 4 March 1925. The 1st Bn. motorized in January 1928 and transferred to participate in tests of the Mechanized Force at Camp Holabird, MD, and Camp George G. Meade, MD, January–April 1928. Regiment relieved from the 1st Div. on 16 October 1939 and assigned to the GHQR. Assigned to the 8th Div. on 22 June 1940. Relieved from the 8th Div. on 20 July 1940. Assigned Reserve officers conducted summer training with the regiment at Fort Hoyle. Inactivated on 1 August 1940, less 1st Bn.; 1st Bn. concurrently redesignated 6th F.A. Bn.

Organization Day: 31 May. Chosen to commemorate the regiment's original organization on 31 May 1907 and the regiment's participation in the Battle of Cantigny, 28–31 May 1918.

Status: Assigned to the USARS as the 6th F.A.; 1st Bn. active at Bamberg, Germany, as an element of the 1st Inf. Div. (Mecz).

Events: 19, 24, 38, 60, 63, 66, 72, 89, 98, 106, 153, 155, 176, 191, 218, 240, 263, 287, 293, 296, 301, 323, 330

Commanders, 6th Field Artillery Regiment

Col. William S. McNair	ao June 1917–5 October 1917	Col. Alfred A. Starbird	11 October 1923–7 January 1925
Col. Ernest D. Scott	5 October 1917–25 February 1918	Lt. Col. Thomas P. Bernard	7 January 1925–21 April 1925
Lt. Col. Cortlandt Parker	25 February 1918–3 August 1918	Lt. Col. Augustine McIntyre	21 April 1925–11 August 1927
Col. William H. Dodds Jr.	5 August 1918–15 May 1919	Col. Harry G. Bishop	11 August 1927–20 December 1928
Lt. Col. Guy R. Maloney	16 May 1919–ao September 1919	Col. William S. McNair	20 December 1928–14 January 1931
Col. Samuel C. Harrison Jr.	ao January 1920–September 1920	Lt. Col. John W. Downer	15 January 1931–31 March 1931
Maj. Gordon H. McCoy	September 1920–29 November 1920	Col. Laurin L. Lawson	31 March 1931–13 December 1934
Maj. Richard B. Paddock	29 November 1920–7 January 1921	Col. Ned B. Rehkopf	13 December 1934–24 June 1935
Maj. Corlandt Parker	7 January 1921–15 July 1921	Col. William Bryson	24 June 1935–6 August 1935
Maj. Albert W. Waldron	15 July 1921–16 August 1921	Lt. Col. Roscoe C. Batson	6 August 1935–29 September 1935
Maj. Harold G. Fitz	16 August 1921–November 1921	Col. William P. Ennis	29 September 1935–16 May 1938
Maj. Albert W. Waldron	November 1921–5 February 1922	Maj. George S. Buerket	16 May 1938–30 June 1938
Lt. Col. Allen J. Crane	5 February 1922–25 April 1922	Col. James L. Collins	30 June 1938–23 February 1939
Col. Wright Smith	25 April 1922–10 October 1922	Lt. Col. John S. Winslow	23 February 1939–30 May 1939
Lt. Col. Albert U. Faulkner	10 October 1922–11 October 1923	Maj. Samuel D. Bedinger	30 May 1939–1 July 1939
	Col. Rene E.D. Hoyle	1 July 1939–August 1940	

7th Field Artillery Regiment (75-mm G-H) (1st Division)

HQ—Camp Zachary Taylor, KY, 1919–20; Camp Dix, NJ, 1920–22; Fort Ethan Allen, VT, 1922–40

Arrived at the port of New York on 1 September 1919 on the U.S.S. *Von Steuben* as an element of the 1st Div. Transferred on 4 October 1919 to Camp Zachary Taylor, KY. Transferred on 7 October 1920 to Camp Dix, NJ. Regiment, less 2d Bn. transferred on 29 May 1922 to Fort Ethan Allen, VT. The 2d Bn. transferred on 5 September 1922 to Madison Barracks, NY. Btry D awarded the Knox Trophy for 1924. Responsible for the support and administration of the 2d Civilian Conservation Corps (CCC) District (New Hampshire and Vermont), First Corps Area, 1933–41. Regiment motorized on 26 October 1934. The 2d Bn. inactivated on 1 December 1934 at Madison Barracks and personnel and equipment transferred to the 2d Bn., 25th F.A. The 3d Bn. constituted on 16 October 1939 and organized on 1 June 1940 at Fort Ethan Allen, VT. Regiment reorganized and redesignated 7th F.A. Bn. on 1 October 1940 at Fort Ethan Allen.

Organization Day: 15 July. Chosen to commemorate the regiment's date of original organization on 15 July 1916.

Status: Assigned to the USARS as the 7th F.A.; 1st Bn. active at Schweinfurt, Germany, as an element of the 1st Inf. Div. (Mecz), and 3d Bn. active at Schofield Barracks, HI, as an element of the 25th Inf. Div. (Light)

Events: 60, 62, 63, 64, 66, 72, 78, 89, 106, 132, 133, 153, 190, 262, 266, 280, 287, 293, 296, 301, 323, 330

Commanders, 7th Field Artillery Regiment

Col. Samuel D. Sturgis Jr.	3 July 1916–2 July 1917
Col. William L. Kenly	2 July 1917–25 August 1917
Col. Lucius R. Holbrook	25 August 1917–11 July 1918
Col. Francis A. Ruggles	11 July 1918–5 January 1920
Col. Donald M. Beere	5 January 1920–4 July 1920
Lt. Col. Robert U. Rutledge	4 July 1920–30 October 1920
Lt. Col. Howard L. Landers	30 October 1920–22 August 1921
Maj. William H. Kennedy	22 August 1921–October 1921
Col. Henry L. Newbold	October 1921–4 February 1923
Lt. Col. William S. Browning	4 February 1923–25 June 1923
Maj. Francis T. Armstrong	25 June 1923–12 September 1923
Lt. Col. T. Worthington Hollyday	12 September 1923–6 February 1924
Col. Philip E. Ward	6 February 1924–9 June 1924
Lt. Col. T. Worthington Hollyday	9 June 1924–12 January 1925
Col. Alfred A. Starbird	12 January 1925–6 June 1926
Col. Upton Birnie Jr.	6 June 1926–5 July 1927
Col. Frank E. Hopkins	5 July 1927–5 October 1929
Maj. William R. Gruber	5 October 1929–12 December 1929
Col. Daniel W. Hand	12 December 1929–18 June 1931
Col. Joseph F. Barnes	19 June 1931–1 July 1935
Col. Ned B. Rehkopf	2 July 1935–31 March 1936
Lt. Col. Cortlandt Parker	31 May 1936–8 September 1936
Col. Benjamin F. Miller	9 September 1936–13 October 1938
Lt. Col. Raymond W. Barker	13 October 1938–5 September 1939
Col. Edmund L. Gruber	5 September 1939–20 October 1939

8th Field Artillery Regiment (75-mm G Mtzd) (Hawaiian Division)

HQ—Camp Funston, KS, 1919–20; Camp George G. Meade, MD, 1920–21; Schofield Barracks, TH ,1921–41

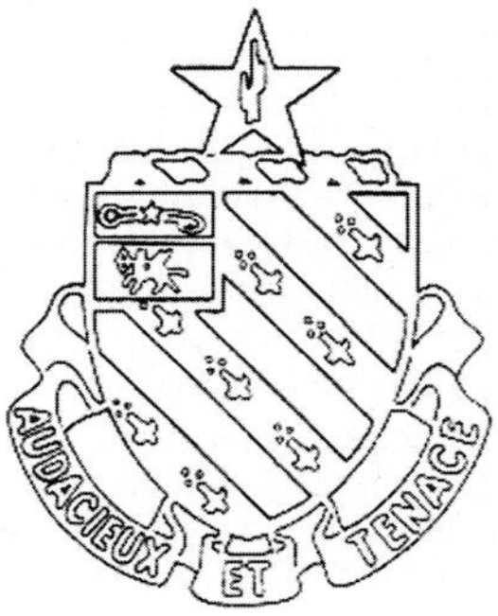

Arrived at the port of New York on 20 June 1919 on the U.S.S. *Imperator* as an element of the 7th Div. Transferred on 27 June 1919 to Camp Funston, KS. Relieved from the 7th Div. on 30 November 1920. Transferred on 15 January 1921 to the Presidio of San Francisco, CA. Embarked on 4 February 1921 on the U.S.A.T. *Sheridan* at Fort Mason, CA, for transfer to Schofield Barracks, TH, and arrived there on 12 February 1921. Assigned to the Hawaiian Division on 5 February 1921. Further assigned to the 11th F.A. Brig. on 2 March 1921. Btry A awarded the Knox Trophy for 1925. Conducted annual summer camp at Hauula, Puuiki, or Camp Waimanalo, TH, 1924–35. Reorganized and redesignated 8th F.A. Bn. on 1 October 1941 and concurrently assigned to the 24th Div.

Organization Day: 6 July. Chosen to commemorate the regiment's original organization on 6 July 1917 at Fort Bliss, TX. Adopted 4 January 1927.

Status: Assigned to the USARS as the 8th F.A.; 2d Bn. active at Schofield Barracks, HI, as an element of the 25th Inf. Div. (Light).

Events: 33, 37, 48, 75, 88, 120, 138, 141, 158, 189, 211, 225, 248, 276, 297, 312

Commanders, 8th Field Artillery Regiment

Col. Peyton C. March	25 August 1916–30 May 1917
Col. George LeR. Irwin	22 June 1917–10 November 1917
Maj. Clifford K. Corbin	10 November 1917–15 June 1918
Col. Harrison Hall	15 June 1918–27 November 1918
Lt. Col. Jason McV. Austin	27 November 1918–11 January 1919
Col. John W. B. Corey	11 January 1919–31 August 1919
Col. Edward A. Millar	1 September 1919–20 April 1920
Maj. Avery J. French	20 April 1920–26 August 1920
Col. Brook Payne	26 August 1920–13 December 1920
Maj. Hamilton Templeton	13 December 1920–24 February 1921
Lt. Col. Lewis S. Ryan	24 February 1921–19 March 1921
Maj. Hamilton Templeton	19 March 1921–6 September 1921
Lt. Col. Lewis S. Ryan	6 September 1921–7 March 1923
Col. Harold L. Newbold	7 March 1923–16 March 1926
Col. Henry B. Farrar	17 March 1926–31 August 1928
Maj. John E. Hatch	1 September 1928–3 October 1928
Lt. Col. Edmond H. DeArmond	4 October 1928–25 January 1929
Col. Harry B. Bishop	25 January 1929–10 March 1930
Lt. Col. Edward H. DeArmond	10 March 1930–9 September 1930
Col. James P. Barney	9 September 1930–4 October 1932
Col. Creed F. Cox	4 October 1932–24 May 1933
Maj. Frank B. Jordan	24 May 1933–14 September 1933
Maj. Harold G. Fitz	14 September 1933–27 November 1933
Col. William K. Moore	28 November 1933–7 December 1936
Col. Cortlandt Parker	8 December 1936–19 August 1938
Lt. Col. William Spence	19 August 1938–30 September 1938
Col. Donald C. McDonald	30 September 1938–ao October 1940
Col. John Keliher	15 June 1941–20 September 1941

9th Field Artillery Regiment (155-mm H) (7th Division)

HQ—Fort Sill, OK, 1919–21; *Inactive,* 1921–27; Seventh Corps Area at large, 1927–30; *Inactive,* 1930–40

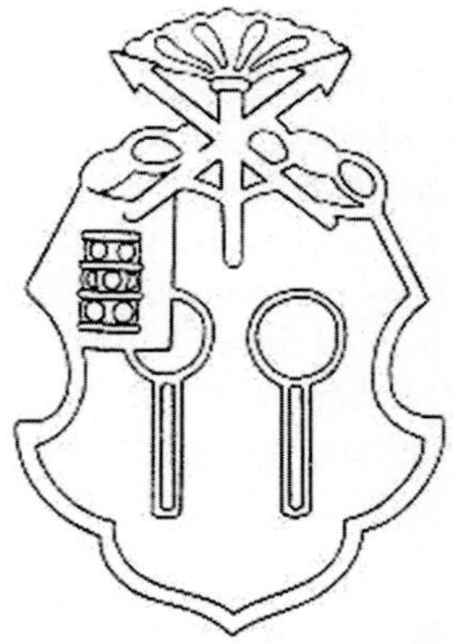

Stationed at Fort Sill, OK, as of June 1919. Inactivated on 1 September 1921 at Fort Sill. Concurrently, personnel and equipment transferred to the 1st F.A. and the Field Artillery School Detachment. Btry C activated on 5 August 1922 at Fort Snelling, MN, with personnel and assets of the 7th F.A. Training (Tng.) Btry. The 1st and 2d Bns. activated on 1 October 1922 at Fort Des Moines, IA, and Fort Sill, respectively. The 2d Bn. subsequently inactivated on 31 December 1922 at Fort Sill and 1st Bn. made the A.A. Btry A transferred in June 1923 to Fort Riley, KS. Regiment assigned to the 7th Div. on 24 March 1923 and allotted to Seventh Corps Area. Relieved from the 7th Div. on 15 August 1927 and assigned to the 9th Div. Concurrently, the 1st Bn. consolidated with 2d Bn., 18th F.A. Regt. on 15 August 1927; new 1st Bn. concurrently constituted as an inactive unit. Entire regiment organized in 1927 with O.R. personnel as an RAI unit in the Seventh Corps Area at large. RAI elements conducted summer training at Camp McCoy, WI, 1927, and Fort Riley, KS, 1928–29. Withdrawn from allotment to the Seventh Corps Area on 1 January 1930 and allotted to the Fourth Corps Area; new 3d Bn. constituted and allotted to the Fourth Corps Area. Concurrently relieved from 9th Div. and assigned to the 4th Div. Additionally, armament changed from 75-mm G to 155-mm H (Mtzd). Regiment was not reorganized in the Fourth Corps Area as an RAI unit. The 1st Bn. was withdrawn from the Fourth Corps Area on 30 April 1930 and activated at Fort Lewis, WA. Withdrawn from allotment to the Fourth Corps Area on 1 October 1933 and allotted to the Ninth Corps Area. Concurrently relieved from 4th Div. and assigned to the 3d Div. The 2d Bn. activated on 1 May 1939 at Fort Lewis. The 3d Bn. disbanded on 16 October 1939. Regiment reorganized as 9th F.A. Bn. on 1 October 1940 at Fort Lewis.

Status: Assigned to the USARS as the 9th F.A.; 1st Bn. active at Fort Stewart, GA, as an element of the 3d Inf. Div. (Mecz).

Events: 145, 161, 203, 208, 226, 238, 273, 289, 294, 304, 306, 309, 314, 326

Commanders, 9th Field Artillery Regiment

Col. John E. McMahon	3 June 1916–July 1917	Col. John R. Starkey	5 December 1919–January 1920
Col. Raymond S. Pratt	July 1917–30 July 1918	Col. Richard H. McMaster	January 1920–26 November 1920
Col. E. DeL. Smith	30 July 1918–16 November 1918	Lt. Col. Henry B. Farrar	26 November 1920–1 July 1921
Col. Jacob L. Devers	16 November 1918–5 December 1919	Maj. James H. Van Horn	17 July 1921–1 September 1921
Inactive	2 September 1921–1 October 1940		

1st Battalion (active 1922–40)

Maj. W. H. Shepherd	October 1922–5 January 1925	Maj. Bertram Frankenberger	10 July 1930–22 February 1934
Capt. John D. White	5 January 1925–6 April 1925	Capt. John R. Williams	22 February 1934–24 August 1934
Maj. Joseph M. Swing	6 April 1925–19 June 1925	Maj. William F. Maher	24 August 1934–11 September 1936
Lt. Col. George A. Taylor	19 June 1925–10 April 1926	Lt. Col. Robert G. Kirkwood	16 September 1936–1 February 1938
Capt. Guy H. Dosher	10 April 1926–1 November 1926	Lt. Col. Robert M. Milam	1 February 1938–18 July 1938
Lt. Col. Fred C. Doyle	1 November 1926–15 August 1927	Maj. Clyde Alexander	18 July 1938–1 August 1938
Inactive	15 August 1927–29 April 1930	Lt. Col. William A. Alexander	1 August 1938–8 July 1939
Capt. Howard F. Long	30 April 1930–10 July 1930	Lt. Col. Harold C. Vanderveer	8 July 1939–1 October 1940

10th Field Artillery Regiment (75-mm G-H) (3d Division)

HQ—Camp Pike, AR, 1919–21; Fort Lewis, WA, 1921–40

Arrived at the port of Hoboken on 23 August 1919 on the U.S.S. *Prinz Frederich Wilhelm* as an element of the 3d Div. Transferred on the same day to Camp Merritt, NJ. Transferred on 27 August 1919 to Camp Pike, AR. Transferred on 15 September 1921 to Camp Lewis, WA. Participated in the making of the First National Production Company movie, "The Patent Leather Kid" in March–April 1927. Per War Department instructions issued 1 January 1930, the regiment's armament was designated to be changed from 75-mm G to 155-mm H (Mtzd) on mobilization. Regiment motorized on 26 October 1935. The 3d Bn. constituted on 12 October 1939 and activated at Fort Lewis. Regiment reorganized and redesignated 10th F.A. Bn. on 1 October 1940 at Fort Lewis.

Organization Day: 14 July. Chosen to commemorate the regiment's participation in the defense of the Marne River on 14 July 1918, which blunted the last great German offensive in World War I.

Status: Assigned to the USARS as the 10th F.A.; 1st Bn. active at Fort Benning, GA, as an element of the 3d Inf. Div. (Mecz).

Events: 57, 114, 135, 145, 161, 203, 208, 221, 226, 238, 251, 273, 289, 294, 304, 306, 309, 314, 326

Commanders, 10th Field Artillery Regiment

Col. Brooke Payne	22 May 1917–25 June 1917	Col. Allen J. Greer	5 February 1928–19 February 1929
Col. Edward F. McGlachlin	25 June 1917–7 September 1917	Maj. Joseph R. Davis	19 February 1929–1 May 1929
Col. Charles R. Lloyd	7 September 1917–29 November 1919	Col. Richard H. McMaster	1 May 1929–10 May 1932
Maj. Thomas J. Johnson	29 November 1919–15 July 1921	Lt. Col. Abbot Boone	10 May 1932–23 June 1932
Col. George G. Gatley	15 July 1921–4 August 1924	Col. Francis W. Clark	23 June 1932–11 September 1935
Col. William M. Cruikshank	17 August 1924–31 August 1925	Col. Frank S. Bowen	11 September 1935–30 January 1938
Lt. Col. Francis W. Clark	1 September 1925–23 January 1926	Col. Col. Robert G. Kirkwood	1 February 1938–22 August 1939
Col. Philip R. Ward	23 January 1926–5 January 1928	Lt. Col. Sylvester D. Downs	22 August 1939–10 November 1939
Lt. Col. Francis W. Clark	5 January 1928–5 February 1928	Col. Kenneth S. Perkins	11 November 1939–1 October 1940

11th Field Artillery Regiment (155-mm H) (Hawaiian Division)

HQ—Camp Grant, IL, 1919–21; Schofield Barracks, TH, 1921–41

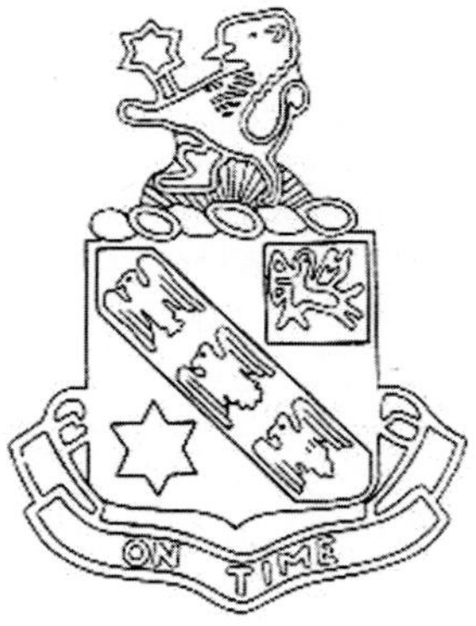

Arrived at the port of New York on 10 June 1919 on the U.S.S. *Mount Vernon* as an element of the 6th Div. Transferred to Camp Mills, NY, on 11 September 1919 and to Camp Grant, IL, on 17 June 1919. Relieved from the 6th Div. on 12 November 1920. Transferred on 27 December 1920 to the Presidio of San Francisco, CA. Embarked on the U.S.A.T. *Sheridan* for transfer to Schofield Barracks, TH, and arrived there on 13 January 1921. Reorganized on 26 January 1921 as a 155-mm H regiment. Assigned to the Hawaiian Division on 2 March 1921. The 3d Bn. inactivated on 1 May 1930 at Schofield Barracks and allotted to the Hawaiian Department. Conducted annual summer camp at Hauula, Kawaihapai, Camp Waimanalo, Puuiki, or Kawailoa, TH, 1924–35. Btry B awarded the Knox Trophy for 1932. Btry C awarded the Knox Trophy for 1940. The 3d Bn. disbanded on 1 March 1940. Reorganized and redesignated 11th F.A. Bn. on 1 October 1941 and concurrently assigned to the 24th Div.

Organization Day: 1 June. Chosen to commemorate the regiment's original organization on 1 June 1917 at Douglas, AZ.

Status: Assigned to the USARS as the 11th F.A.; 2d Bn. active at Schofield Barracks, HI, as an element of the 25th Inf. Div. (Light), and 4th Bn. active at Fort Wainright, AK, as an element of the 172d Inf. Brig. (Sep.).

Events: 33, 37, 48, 75, 88, 120, 138, 141, 158, 189, 211, 225, 248, 276, 297, 312

Commanders, 11th Field Artillery Regiment

Col. Harry G. Bishop	15 May 1917–9 July 1918	Col. Ernest D. Scott	13 February 1929–2 November 1931
Col. William F. Sharp	10 July 1918–24 October 1918	Lt. Col. George E. Nelson	2 November 1931–8 December 1931
Col. Willis G. Peace	25 October 1918–31 August 1919	Col. Eben Swift Jr.	8 December 1931–15 November 1934
Lt. Col. Joseph A. Rogers	31 August 1919–12 February 1921	Lt. Col. Edward W. Wildrick	15 November 1934–12 January 1935
Lt. Col. Beverly F. Browne	12 February 1921–20 March 1923	Col. Laurin L. Lawson	12 January 1935–23 March 1937
Col. Otho W. B. Farr	20 March 1923–12 September 1925	Col. Roger S. Parrott	24 March 1937–13 March 1939
Lt. Col. James P. Barney	12 September 1925–2 February 1926	Col. Chester B. McCormick	13 March 1939–14 September 1939
Col. Manus McCloskey	2 February 1926–13 November 1928	Col. Leonard C. Sparks	14 September 1939–November 1940
Lt. Col. Augustine McIntyre	13 November 1928–13 February 1929	Col. Robert M. Bathurst	November 1940–1 October 1941

12th Field Artillery Regiment (75-mm G-H) (2d Division)

HQ—Camp Travis, TX, 1919–20; Fort Sam Houston, TX, 1920–40

Arrived at the port of New York on 6 August 1919 on the U.S.S. *Leviathan* as an element of the 2d Div. Transferred to Camp Mills, NY, on 7 August 1919 and to Camp Travis, TX, on 16 August 1919. Transferred in 1920 to Fort Sam Houston, TX, proper. Regiment was motorized on 3 December 1938. Reorganized on 29 September 1939 as a 155-mm H regiment. Assigned Reserve officers conducted summer training with the regiment at Fort Sam Houston or Camp Bullis, TX. Reorganized and redesignated 12th F.A. Bn. on 1 October 1940 at Fort Sam Houston.

Organization Day: 7 June. Chosen to commemorate the regiment's baptism of fire near Vaux, France, 7 June 1918.

Status: Assigned to the USARS as the 12th F.A.; 1st Bn. active at Fort Sill, OK, as an element of the 17th F.A. Brig.

Events: 45, 47, 55, 70, 74, 80, 105, 125, 147, 163, 216, 242, 258, 282, 288, 295, 296, 299, 300, 317, 328

Commanders, 12th Field Artillery Regiment

Col. Manus McCloskey	7 June 1917–4 August 1918	Maj. George W. Dearmond	25 June 1925–14 September 1925
Lt. Col. James A. Holabird	4 August 1918–12 November 1918	Col. Oliver L. Spaulding Jr.	14 September 1925–9 August 1926
Col. David M. McKell	13 November 1918–9 August 1919	Col. Philip S. Golderman	10 August 1926–6 July 1929
Lt. Col. John D. Von Holtzendorff	9 August 1919–15 March 1920	Col. Charles M. Bundel	23 July 1929–31 August 1930
Col. Jacob A. Mack	15 March 1920–26 July 1920	Col. Joseph F. Herron	31 August 1930–15 June 1933
Maj. John G. Tyndall	26 July 1920–August 1921	Col. James H. Bryson	15 June 1933–1 September 1935
Maj. Bernard R. Peyton	August 1921–27 June 1922	Col. William F. Jones	21 September 1935–1 April 1937
Col. Henry B. Farrar	27 June 1922–7 July 1924	Col. Oliver A. Dickenson	1 April 1937–15 July 1937
Col. Francis Lej. Parker	7 July 1924–22 November 1924	Maj. Townsend R. Heard	15 July 1937–5 August 1937
Maj. Francis A. Doniet	22 November 1924–26 December 1924	Col. Benjamin M. Bailey	5 August 1937–1 July 1939
Lt. Col. Clifton R. Norton	26 December 1924–25 June 1925	Col. Allen C. McBride	20 July 1939–1 October 1940

13th Field Artillery Regiment (75-mm G-H) (Hawaiian Division)

HQ—Camp Dodge, IA, 1919–20; Camp Lewis, WA, 1920; Schofield Barracks, TH, 1920–41

Arrived at the port of New York on 31 July 1919 on the U.S.S. *Zeelandia* as an element of the 4th Div. Transferred to Camp Merritt, NJ, on 31 July 1919 and to Camp Dodge, IA, on 5 August 1919. Transferred on 22 August 1920 to Camp Lewis, WA. Transferred on 15 October 1920 to the Presidio of San Francisco, CA. Embarked on the U.S.A.T. *Great Northern* for transfer to Schofield Barracks, TH, and arrived there on 21 October 1920. Relieved from the 4th Div. on 28 October 1920. Assigned to the Hawaiian Division on 5 February 1921. Further assigned to the 11th F.A. Brig. on 2 March 1921. The regiment was selected to conduct experiments using portee artillery in the mid-to-late 1920s. Conducted annual summer camp at Kahuka, Camp Waimanalo, or Mokuleia, TH, 1924–35. Batteries A and B awarded the Knox Trophy for 1930 and 1934, respectively. The 2d Bn. reorganized in April 1936 from Pack artillery to 75-mm G (TD). Reorganized and redesignated 13th F.A. Bn. on 1 October 1941 and concurrently assigned to the 24th Div.

Status: Assigned to the USARS as the 13th F.A.; 3d Bn. active at Fort Sill, OK, as an element of the 214th F.A. Brig.

Events: 17, 33, 37, 48, 75, 88, 120, 138, 141, 158, 189, 211, 225, 248, 276, 297, 312

Commanders, 13th Field Artillery Regiment

Col. Wright Smith	1 June 1917–25 August 1919	Col. Augustine McIntyre	30 July 1929–17 July 1931
Lt. Col. James A. Gillespie	25 August 1919–15 June 1920	Lt. Col. Robert M. Danford	17 July 1931–20 October 1931
Col. Wright Smith	15 June 1920–1 December 1920	Col. Raymond S. Pratt	20 October 1931–29 May 1935
Lt. Col. Lewis S. Ryan	1 December 1920–24 March 1921	Maj. Marvin C. Heyser	29 May 1935–11 June 1935
Lt. Col. George M. Brooke	24 March 1921–5 November 1922	Lt. Col. Marshall Magruder	11 June 1935–28 August 1935
Col. Tiemann N. Horn	6 November 1922–5 May 1923	Col. Robert M. Danford	28 August 1935–24 June 1937
Lt. Col. George M. Brooke	5 May 1923–22 August 1923	Maj. George E. Cook	24 June 1937–1 July 1937
Lt. Col. Beverly Browne	24 August 1923–29 October 1923	Lt. Col. Dean Hudnutt	1 July 1937–4 September 1937
Col. Andrew Moses	29 October 1923–10 July 1926	Lt. Col. Karl C. Greenwald	4 September 1937–20 November 1937
Capt. Nathan E. McCluer	10 July 1926–September 1926	Lt. Col. Richard C. Burleson	20 November 1937–8 February 1939
Capt. Richard M. Wightman	September 1926–6 October 1926	Lt. Col. Isaac Spaulding	8 February 1939–14 August 1939
Col. Oliver L. Spaulding Jr.	6 October 1926–30 July 1929	Col. Edwin R. Van Deusen	15 August 1939–15 June 1941
Col. Stanley E. Reinhardt	1 July 1941–31 October 1941		

14th Field Artillery Regiment (75-mm G-H) (6th Division) **Regular Army Inactive**

HQ—Fort Sill, OK, 1919–21; *Inactive,* 1921–26; Urbana, IL, 1926–32; Champaign, IL, 1932–33; *Inactive,* 1933–36; Davenport, IA, 1936–40; Fort Benning, GA, 1940–41

Stationed at Fort Sill, OK, as of June 1919. Inactivated on 1 September 1921 at Fort Sill. Assigned to the 6th Div. on 15 December 1922; 1st Bn. concurrently activated at Fort Sheridan, IL. Regiment less 1st Bn. allotted to Sixth Corps Area and 1st Bn. made A.A. Regiment less 1st Bn. organized in May 1926 with O.R. personnel as an RAI unit with HQ at Urbana, IL. Regiment relieved from the 6th Div. on 1 April 1927 and assigned to the 7th Div. The 1st Bn. consolidated with 2d Bn., 3d F.A. on 5 September 1927; new 1st Bn. concurrently constituted and allotted to the Sixth Corps Area. Affiliated on 15 April 1929 with the University of Illinois ROTC. Relocated on 26 February 1932 to Champaign, IL. Relieved from the Sixth Corps Area on 1 October 1933 and allotted to the Seventh Corps Area. The 1st Bn. activated on 1 December 1934, less Reserve personnel, at Fort Riley, KS; 2d Bn. concurrently activated at Fort Snelling, MN. Reorganized by 1936, less 1st and 2d Bns., with O.R. personnel as an RAI unit with HQ at Davenport, IA. Batteries B and D awarded the Knox Trophy for 1935 and 1936, respectively. The 1st Bn. inactivated on 1 July 1936 at Fort Riley. RAI elements typically conducted Inactive Training Period meetings at the Pure Oil Building in Chicago, 1926–33. RAI elements conducted summer training at Camp McCoy, WI; Camp Custer, MI; Fort Riley, KS; or Fort Snelling. Conducted Citizens Military Training Camp (CMTC) training some years at Fort Snelling, MN, as an alternate form of summer training. The 2d Bn. inactivated on 1 July 1939 at Fort Snelling. Regiment relieved from the 7th Div. on 16 October 1939. Regiment assigned to the 2d Armd. Div. on 15 July 1940 and activated, less Reserve personnel, at Fort Benning, GA. Location 7 December 1941—Fort Benning, GA.

Status: Assigned to the USARS as the 14th F.A.; 1st Bn. active at Fort Sill, OK, as an element of the 214th F.A. Brig.

Events: 32, 50, 188, 233, 256

Commanders, 14th Field Artillery Regiment

Col. Adrian S. Fleming	1 July 1916–12 April 1918	Maj. Frank L. Gottschalk**	18 May 1928–ao July 1930
Col. Walter H. Smith	21 December 1919–7 October 1920	Unknown	ao July 1930–ao June 1938
Lt. Col. Ralph S. Granger	7 October 1920–29 August 1921	Lt. Col. Leland N. Jones**	ao July 1935–ao September 1935
Inactive	29 August 1921–May 1926	Unknown	ao September 1935–ao June 1938
Maj. R. C. Lehman**	May 1926–December 1927	Maj. Austin J. Kilgore**	ao June 1938–ao August 1938
Lt. Col. Joseph F. Barnes*	December 1927–16 July 1928	Unknown	ao August 1938–14 July 1940
	Lt. Col. Roland P. Shugg	15 July 1940–1 July 1940	

1st Battalion (active 1922–27; 1934–36)

Maj. Walter S. Sturgill	15 December 1922–13 December 1923	*Inactive*	5 September 1927–1 December 1934
Maj. Robert F. Hyatt	13 December 1923–30 August 1925	Maj. Ira T. Wyche	1 December 1934–24 August 1934
Maj. Casey H. Hayes	30 August 1925–14 April 1926	Maj. Sumner M. Smith	24 August 1934–3 November 1935
Maj. Francis A. Doniat	24 April 1926–5 September 1927	Maj. William H. Colbern	3 November 1935–30 June 1936

2d Battalion (active 1934–39)

Maj. Robert V. Maraist	1 December 1934–15 August 1936	Unknown	oa October 1936–1 July 1939

*RAI commanders: R.A. officers.
**RAI commanders: O.R. officers.

15th Field Artillery Regiment (75-mm G-H) (2d Division)

HQ—Camp Travis, TX, 1919–20; Fort Sam Houston, TX, 1920–29; *Inactive,* 1929–34; Fort Sam Houston, TX, 1934–40

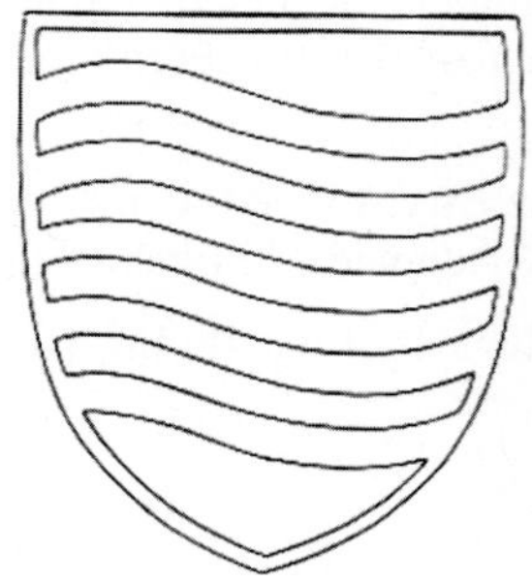

Arrived at the port of New York on 4 August 1919 on the U.S.S. *Julia Luckenbach* as an element of the 2d Div. Transferred to Camp Mills, NY, on 4 August 1919 and to Camp Travis, TX, on 16 August 1919. Transferred in 1920 to Fort Sam Houston, TX, proper. Participated in the making of Famous Players–Lasky Corporation movie "Rough Riders" and in the production of the MGM movie "Wings" at Camp Stanley, TX, 27 September–23 October 1926. Regiment inactivated on 31 October 1929, less 2d Bn., at Fort Sam Houston and allotted to the Eighth Corps Area. Concurrently, relieved from the 2d Div. and assigned to the 4th Div. Relieved from the 4th Div. on 1 January 1930 and assigned to the 2d Div. Regiment activated on 1 December 1934 at Fort Sam Houston. Btry D awarded the Knox Trophy for 1936. The 3d Bn. constituted on 27 September 1939 and activated on 7 October 1939 at Fort Sam Houston. Assigned Reserve officers conducted summer training with the regiment at Sam Houston or Camp Bullis, TX. Regiment reorganized and redesignated 15th F.A. Bn. on 1 October 1940 at Fort Sam Houston.

Organization Day: 3 October. Chosen to commemorate the regiment's participation in the battle for Mont Blanc in the Ardennes, France, 3 October 1918. Adopted 26 July 1920.

Status: Assigned to the USARS as the 15th F.A.; 1st Bn. active at Camp Casey, Korea, as an element of the 2d Inf. Div., and 2d Bn. active at Fort Drum, NY, as an element of the 10th Inf. Div. (Light).

Events: 45, 47, 55, 70, 74, 105, 125, 147, 163, 242, 258, 282, 284, 288, 295, 296, 299, 300, 317, 328

Commanders, 15th Field Artillery Regiment

Col. Thomas E. Merrill	1 June 1917–5 May 1918	Col. George G. Gatley	20 February 1929–31 October 1929
Col. William M. Cruikshank	5 May 1918–19 May 1918	*Inactive*	1 November 1929–30 November 1934
Col. Joseph R. Davis	19 May 1918–14 June 1920	Lt. Col. Ralph McT. Pennell	1 December 1934–4 June 1935
Col. Robert C. Foy	16 August 1920–26 December 1920	Maj. Douglas J. Page	4 June 1935–16 August 1935
Lt. Col. George V. H. Moseley	26 December 1920–3 July 1921	Col. Francis W. Honeycutt	31 August 1935–10 March 1937
Maj. Philip L. Thurber	3 July 1921–December 1921	Lt. Col. Faulkner Heard	10 March 1937–14 July 1937
Lt. Col. Laurin L. Lawson	December 1921–20 December 1922	Lt. Col. John N. Hauser	14 July 1937–24 August 1937

Maj. Philip L. Thurber	20 December 1922–7 February 1923	Col. John N. Greely	24 August 1937–3 May 1939
Col. Clarence R. Day	7 February 1923–16 April 1925	Lt. Col. Thomas J.J. Christian	3 May 1939–5 June 1939
Col. Harry G. Bishop	16 April 1925–3 August 1927	Lt. Col. Stanley Bacon	5 June 1939–23 June 1939
Col. Ernest D. Scott	3 August 1927–31 December 1928	Col. Ralph McT. Pennell	23 June 1939–September 1940
Lt. Col. Francia A. Ruggles	31 December 1928–20 February 1929	Col. Norman P. Morrow	September 1940–1 October 1940

2d Battalion (active 1929–34)

Maj. Louis R. Dougherty	31 October 1929–7 August 1930	Lt. Col. Richard C. Burleson	6 August 1932–22 March 1933
Maj. Bernard R. Peyton	7 August 1930–6 August 1932	Lt. Col. Ralph McT. Pennell	1 April 1933–1 December 1934

16th Field Artillery Regiment (75-mm G-H) (8th Division)

HQ—Camp Lewis, WA, 1921; *Inactive,* 1921–41: Fort Myer, VA, 1941

Arrived at the port of New York on 29 July 1919 on the U.S.S. *Zeppelin* as an element of the 4th Div. Transferred the same day to Camp Merritt, NJ. Transferred on 4 August 1919 to Camp Dodge, IA. Transferred on 18 August 1920 to Camp Lewis, WA. Inactivated on 21 September 1921 at Camp Lewis and the 10th F.A. designated as the A.A. The 1st Bn. activated on 14 December 1922 at Fort Myer, VA, with personnel and equipment from the inactivated 2d Bn., 2d F.A. Regt less 1st Bn. allotted to the Fourth Corps Area and 1st Bn. made A.A. Regiment relieved from the 4th Div. on 24 March 1923 and assigned to the 8th Div. The 2d Bn. activated on 5 September 1927 at Fort Bragg, NC, with personnel from the inactivated 1st Bn., 2d F.A. Regt. Regiment concurrently relieved from the 8th Div. and assigned to the 4th Div. Btry F awarded the Knox Trophy for 1928. The 1st Bn. participated in the inaugural parades of President Herbert Hoover on 4 March 1929 and President Franklin D. Roosevelt on 4 March 1933. Inactive elements of the regiment withdrawn from the Fourth Corps Area on 18 August 1933 and allotted to the Third Corps Area. The 2d Bn. inactivated on 1 October 1933 at Fort Bragg and personnel and equipment transferred to the newly activated 2d Bn., 83d F.A. Regt. relieved from the 4th Div. on 1 October 1933 and assigned to the 8th Div. Relieved from the 8th Div. on 16 October 1939 and assigned to the GHQR. Assigned Reserve officers conducted summer training with the regiment at Fort Myer or Fort Belvoir, VA. Regiment activated on 3 January 1941 at Fort Myer. Reorganized and redesignated 16th F.A. Bn. on 13 January 1941 at Fort Myer.

Organization Day: 6 August. Chosen to commemorate the regiment's baptism of fire when Btry A fired the first fire mission in the opening stages of the Meuse-Argonne Campaign in France, on 6 August 1918. Adopted 27 March 1925.

Status: Assigned to the USARS as the 16th F.A.; 3d Bn. active at Fort Hood, TX, as an element of the 4th Inf. Div. (Mecz).

Events: 38, 66, 94, 96, 98, 121, 137, 155, 176, 240, 281, 301

Commanders, 16th Field Artillery Regiment

Col. John E. McMahon	21 May 1917–5 August 1917	Lt. Col. Harold H. Bateman	18 October 1918–7 November 1918
Col. Henry L. Newbold	5 August 1917–8 May 1918	Col. Henning F. Colley	7 November 1918–23 November 1918
Maj. Harold H. Bateman	8 May 1918–7 June 1918	Lt. Col. William H. Rucker	23 November 1918–9 December 1918
Lt. Col. Albert T. Bishop	7 June 1918–9 June 1918	Col. Oliver P.M. Hazzard	9 December 1918–1 January 1919
Col. Henry W. Butner	9 June 1918–17 August 1918	Lt. Col. William H. Rucker	1 January 1919–22 February 1919
Maj. Harold H. Bateman	17 August 1918–27 August 1918	Col. Oliver P.M. Hazzard	22 February 1919–2 March 1919
Lt. Col. William H. Rucker	27 August 1918–18 October 1918	Lt. Col. William H. Rucker	2 March 1919–1 August 1919
Col. William C. Webb	1 August 1919–1 September 1921		

1st Battalion (active 1922–40)

Maj. Charles P. George	14 December 1922–10 July 1924	Lt. Col. Charles P. George	5 September 1930–26 June 1934
Maj. Rene E. D. Hoyle	10 July 1924–14 June 1926	Lt. Col. Jacob L. Devers	26 June 1934–21 March 1936
Maj. Maxwell Murray	19 July 1926–4 July 1928	Maj. John Nash	21 March 1936–25 June 1936
Lt. Col. Cortlandt Parker	4 July 1928–15 August 1930	Lt. Col. John A. Crane	25 June 1936–29 June 1938
Capt. George D. Shea	15 August 1930–5 September 1930	Maj. John Nash	29 June 1938–22 July 1938
Lt. Col. William C. Crane Jr.	22 July 1938–March 1940		

2d Battalion (active 1927–33)

Maj. James L. Collins	30 September 1927–30 December 1927	Lt. Col. William P. Ennis	30 August 1929–30 August 1931
Maj. John S. Wood	30 December 1927–10 June 1929	Lt. Col. Charles S. Blakeley	1 September 1931–20 June 1933
Maj. George H. Paine	10 June 1929–30 August 1929	Lt. Col. Leslie J. McNair	29 June 1933–30 September 1933

17th Field Artillery Regiment (155-mm H) (13th Field Artillery Brigade)

HQ—Camp Travis, TX, 1919–20; Fort Sam Houston, TX, 1920–21; Fort Bragg, NC, 1921–41

Arrived at the port of New York on 4 August 1919 on the U.S.S. *Rijndam* as an element of the 2d Div. Transferred the same day to Camp Mills, NY. Transferred on 11 August 1919 to Camp Travis, TX. Transferred in 1920 to Fort Sam Houston, TX, proper. Relieved on 18 December 1920 from the 2d Div. Transferred on 9 January 1921 to Camp Bragg, NC. Reorganized on 26 January 1921 from a 4.7-inch G regiment to a 155-mm H regiment. Assigned to the 13th F.A. Brig. (IV Corps) on 1 September 1921. The 3d Bn. inactivated on 1 August 1922 at Camp Bragg. The 3d Bn. allotted to the Fourth Corps Area on 28 February 1927. Regiment relieved from the 13th F.A. Brig. on 22 July 1929 and assigned to the 1st Div. Relieved from the 1st Div. on 1 January 1930 and assigned to the 2d Div. The 3d Bn. activated on 1 April 1930 at Fort Leavenworth, KS, and transferred on 9 September 1931 to Fort Des Moines, IA. The 3d Bn. inactivated 1 October 1933 at Fort Des Moines; personnel and equipment transferred to the newly activated 3d Bn., 80th F.A. The 3d Bn. concurrently allotted to the Fourth Corps Area and organized with Reserve officers as an RAI unit. Assigned Reserve officers conducted summer training with the active elements of the regiment at Fort Bragg. Reserve officers also conducted Field Artillery CMTC at Fort Bragg in 1937. The 3d Bn. activated on 15 October 1939, less Reserve personnel, at Fort Bragg. Regiment relieved from the 2d Div. on 16 October 1939 and assigned to the 13th F.A. Brig. (I Corps). Concurrently, the 3d Bn. was disbanded. Location 7 December 1941—Fort Bragg, NC.

Status: Assigned to the USARS as the 17th F.A.; 1st Bn. active at Fort Sill, OK, as an element of the 75th F.A. Brig., and 2d Bn. active at Camp Hovey, Korea, as an element of the 2d Inf. Div.

Events: 94, 96, 121, 255, 293, 296, 300, 330

Commanders, 17th Field Artillery Regiment

Col. Albert J. Bowley	11 July 1917–26 June 1918	Maj. John E. Mort	15 August 1922–26 June 1923
Lt. Col. Leonard C. Sparks	27 June 1918–25 September 1918	Lt. Col. Allen J. Greer	26 June 1923–31 October 1923
Col. Walter S. Sturgill	25 September 1918–16 October 1918	Col. Conrad H. Lanza	31 October 1923–1 November 1925
Lt. Col. Leonard C. Sparks	16 October 1918–6 November 1918	Lt. Col. Raymond W. Briggs	1 November 1925–8 February 1926
Col. Walter S. Sturgill	6 November 1918–8 October 1918	Lt. Col. Creed Fox	9 February 1926–16 May 1926
Col. Robert L. Dunlap	8 October 1918–December 1918	Lt. Col. Raymond W. Briggs	16 May 1926–10 September 1926
Col. John R. Kelly	December 1918–20 March 1919	Col. Conrad H. Lanza	10 September 1926–29 August 1929
Lt. Col. Louis A. Craig	21 March 1919–August 1920	Lt. Col. George R. Allin	29 August 1929–20 December 1929
Maj. Frank A. Turner	August 1920–October 1920	Col. Philip R. Ward	20 December 1929–28 April 1930
Maj. Charles E. Ide	October 1920–11 January 1921	Lt. Col. George R. Allin	28 August 1929–18 August 1930
Maj. William F. Maher	11 January 1921–February 1921	Col. J. Alfred Moss	18 August 1930–9 September 1933
Lt. Col. Robert C. Foy	February 1921–10 July 1921	Col. E.R.W. McCabe	16 September 1933–1 December 1936
Lt. Col. John E. Sloan	10 July 1921–20 September 1921	Col. John G. Tyndall	1 December 1936–14 December 1936
Lt. Col. Albert U. Faulkner	20 September 1921–30 October 1921	Col. George R. Allin	14 December 1936–31 July 1939
Col. Richard H. McMaster	30 October 1921–1 April 1922	Lt. Col. Archibald V. Arnold	31 July 1939–May 1941
Lt. Col. Clifton R. Norton	1 April 1922–15 August 1922	Col. Reese M. Howell	May 1941–June 1943

18th Field Artillery Regiment (75-mm G-H) (9th Division)

HQ—Camp Pike, AR, 1919–22; *Inactive,* 1922–27; Oklahoma City, OK, 1927–33; *Inactive,* 1933–35; Fort Sill, OK, 1935–41

Arrived at the port of Hoboken on 20 August 1919 on the U.S.S. *America* as an element of the 3d Div. Transferred on the same day to Camp Merritt, NJ. Transferred on 23 August 1919 to Camp Pike, AR. Inactivated on 15 February 1922 at Camp Pike, AR, and the 5th F.A. designated as the A.A. The 1st Bn. activated on 31 December 1922 at Fort Sill, OK, with personnel and equipment from the inactivated 2d Bn., 9th F.A. Regt., minus 1st Bn., allotted to Eighth Corps Area, and 1st Bn. made A.A. in lieu of the 5th F.A. The Regt. relieved from the 3d Div. on 24 March 1923 and assigned to the 9th Div. Relieved from the 9th Div. on 15 August 1927 and assigned to the 6th Div. The 2d Bn. withdrawn from the Eighth Corps Area on 15 September 1927 and allotted to the Seventh Corps Area. Concurrently activated, less Batteries E and G, at Fort Des Moines, IA, by consolidation with the 1st Bn., 9th F.A. Consolidated unit redesignated 2d Bn., 18th F.A. Regt. Btry E concurrently activated at Fort Riley, KS, and Btry G at Fort Snelling, MN. Regiment, less 1st and 2d Bns. both active, organized by September 1927 with O.R. personnel as an RAI unit with HQ at Oklahoma City, OK. Regiment relieved from the 6th Div. on 1 January 1930 and assigned to the 3d Div. Relieved from the 3d Div. on 23 September 1932 and assigned to the 2d Cav. Div. The 2d Bn. transferred in 1933 to Fort Riley. Reserve personnel in Oklahoma relieved on 29 September 1933. Regiment, less 1st and 2d Bns., withdrawn from the Eighth Corps Area on 1 October 1933 and allotted to the Seventh Corps Area. The 2d Bn. inactivated on 1 December 1934 at Fort Riley. Regiment less 1st Bn. withdrawn from the Seventh Corps Area on 31 December 1934 and allotted to the Eighth Corps Area. Regiment less 1st Bn. activated on 1 January 1935 at Fort Sill. Regiment relieved from the 2d Cav. Div. on 16 October 1939 and assigned to the GHQR. Concurrently, the 3d Bn. constituted and organized with 155-mm howitzers. Assigned to the Field Artillery Replacement and School Command as a demonstration and training regiment and reorganized under special tables of organization with 1st Bn. armed with 75-mm guns (horse drawn) and 2d Bn. armed with 155-mm howitzers (truck drawn). Assigned Reserve officers conducted summer training with the regiment at Fort Sill, 1927–33 and 1935–40. The 4th Bn. constituted on 1 March 1941 and organized at Fort Sill with 105-mm howitzers. Location 7 December 1941—Fort Sill, OK.

Organization Day: 15 July. Chosen to commemorate the regiment's participation in the 2d Battle of the Marne in France, 15 July 1918.

Status: Assigned to the USARS as the 18th F.A.; 2d Bn. active at Fort Sill, OK, as an element of the 212th F.A. Brig., and 3d Bn. active at Fort Sill, OK, as an element of the 17th F.A. Brig.

Events: 136, 150, 171, 177

Commanders, 18th Field Artillery Regiment

Col. Fred T. Austin	29 June 1917–15 December 1917	Col. Tiemann N. Horn	19 August 1920–24 March 1921
Col. Otho W. B. Farr	15 December 1917–15 August 1918	Maj. William D. Geary	24 March 1921–26 June 1921
Col. Albert S. Fuger	15 August 1918–7 December 1918	Maj. John B. W. Corey	26 June 1921–15 February 1922
Col. Raymond S. Pratt	7 December 1918–31 July 1919	*Inactive*	15 February 1922–31 December 1934
Lt. Col. Telesphon G. Gottschalk	31 July 1919–19 August 1919	Maj. Henry D. Jay	1 January 1935–13 January 1935
Maj. Edmund B. Edwards	ao January 1920–February 1920	Col. Edward H. De Armond	13 January 1935–5 August 1938
Lt. Col. Jason McV. Austin	February 1920–10 March 1920	Col. Edwin R. Van Deusen	5 August 1938–14 September 1938
Maj. George J. Downing	10 March 1920–July 1920	Col. Charles P. George	14 September 1938–July 1941
Maj. James G. Coxetter	July 1920–19 August 1920	Col. Louis A. Craig	July 1941–February 1942

1st Battalion (active 1922–34)

Lt. Col. William F. Jones	1 January 1923–2 July 1924	Maj. Lucien Taliaferro	8 September 1930–17 August 1931
Maj. Fred C. Wallace	12 July 1924–1 July 1927	Capt. W.W. Belcher	17 August 1931–7 September 1931
Maj. Francis W. Honeycutt	1 July 1927–30 August 1928	Capt. Samuel Marshall	7 September 1931–5 November 1931
Maj. Allen C. McBride	30 August 1928–15 May 1930	Lt. Col. Ralph Talbot Jr.	5 November 1931–29 June 1932
Capt. John M. Fray	15 May 1930–8 September 1930	Capt. W.W. Belcher	29 June 1932–27 July 1932
Maj. Henry D. Jay	27 July 1932–31 December 1934		

2d Battalion (active 1927–34)

Lt. Col. Fred C. Doyle	15 September 1927–30 June 1929	Lt. Col. Thomas G.M. Oliphant	22 June 1931–4 December 1933
Capt. Louis W. Hasslock	30 June 1929–12 September 1929	Capt. Sumner M. Smith	4 December 1933–19 July 1934
Maj. Clifford M. Tutuer	12 September 1929–22 June 1931	Maj. Ira T. Wyche	19 July 1934–30 November 1934

19th Field Artillery Regiment (75-mm G-H) (5th Division) **Regular Army Inactive**

HQ—Camp Bragg, NC, 1919–20; Camp Jackson, SC, 1920–21; *Inactive,* 1921–27; Columbus, OH, 1927–39; Fort Knox, KY, 1939–40

Arrived at the port of New York on 13 July 1919 on the U.S.S. *America* as an element of the 5th Div. Transferred the same day to Camp Mills, NY. Transferred on 26 August 1919 to Camp Bragg, NC. The 2d Bn. transferred in August 1920 to Fort Myer, VA. Regiment less 2d Bn. transferred on 19 November 1920 to Camp Jackson, SC. Regiment less 2d Bn. transferred on 3 September 1921 to Camp Bragg. Regiment inactivated on 6 September 1921 at Camp Bragg and the 6th F.A. designated as the A.A. Personnel and equipment from the inactivated 2d Bn. concurrently transferred to the newly activated 2d Bn., 16th F.A. at Fort Myer. The 6th F.A. relieved as A.A. on 25 March 1923 and the 1st Bn., 3d F.A. designated as A.A. Organized on 4 October 1927 with O.R. personnel as an RAI unit with HQ at Columbus, OH. Affiliated with Ohio State University ROTC on 28 April 1930 and organized as an RAI unit with personnel from the ROTC Detachment and O.R. commissioned from the program. Conducted summer training at Camp Knox, KY, 1927–39. Conducted CMTC training some years at Fort Benjamin Harrison, IN, as an alternate form of summer training. The 1st Bn. activated on 3 December 1934 at Fort Benjamin Harrison with personnel and equipment transferred from the inactivated 1st Bn., 3d F.A. The 3d Bn. constituted on 27 September 1939. Regimental HQ activated on 5 October 1939 at Fort Knox. The 2d and 3d Bns. activated on 11 October 1939, less Reserve personnel, at Fort Knox. Concurrently relieved from the 5th Div. Regiment reorganized and redesignated on 1 October 1940 as 19th F.A. Bn. at Fort Knox.

Organization Day: 26 September. Chosen to commemorate the regiment's great loss in personnel on 26 September 1918 and the numerous members of the regiment recommended for the Distinguished Service Cross that day during the Meuse-Argonne Campaign. Adopted 3 February 1920.

Status: Assigned to the USARS as the 19th F.A.; 1st Bn. active at Fort Sill, OK, as a training battalion.

Events: 185, 213, 214, 220, 293, 296, 302, 316, 328

Commanders, 19th Field Artillery Regiment

Col. Lucius R. Holbrook	June 1917–July 1917	Maj. Milton H. Taulbee	September 1920–16 October 1920
Col. Dwight E. Aultman	July 1917–18 September 1917	Maj. Marshall Magruder	16 October 1920–11 December 1920
Col. Conrad H. Lanza	19 September 1917–22 August 1918	Col. Richard H. McMaster	11 December 1920–3 September 1921
Lt. Col. Charles P. Hollingsworth	22 August 1918–19 October 1918	*Inactive*	3 September 1921–13 June 1927
Lt. Col. William E. Dunn	19 October 1918–23 October 1918	Maj. Alexander C. Sullivan*	14 June 1927–22 August 1931
Col. Louis H. McKindlay	23 October 1918–10 November 1918	Maj. Clinton I. McClure*	22 August 1931–1 October 1933
Lt. Col. William E. Dunn	11 November 1918–8 December 1918	Capt. Enno G. Fruewald**	1 October 1933–ao June 1934
Col. Robert C. Foy	9 December 1918–6 August 1919	Unknown	ao June 1934–ao June 1938
Lt. Col. Eugene T. Spencer	ao January 1920–August 1920	Capt. Raymond De H. Woods**	ao May 1938–ao June 1938
Maj. William J. Murphy	August 1920–September 1920	Unknown*	ao June 1938–4 October 1939
	Col. Cortlandt Parker	5 October 1939–1 October 1940	

1st Battalion (active 1934–40)

Maj. John K. Boles	4 December 1934–15 June 1935	Lt. Col. Philip Hayes	August 1935–11 October 1937
Capt. Charles M. Thirlkeld	15 June 1935–1 August 1935	Lt. Col. Albert W. Waldron	August 1937–1 June 1940

*RAI commanders: R.A. officers.
**RAI commanders: O.R. officers.

20th Field Artillery Regiment (75-mm G-H) (5th Division) **Regular Army Inactive**

HQ—Camp Bragg, NC, 1919–20; Camp Jackson, SC, 1920–21; *Inactive,* 1921–26; Fort Myer, VA, 1926–30; Toledo, OH, 1929–40; Fort Benning, GA, 1940

Arrived at the port of New York on 21 July 1919 on the U.S.S. *Agamemnon* as an element of the 5th Div. Transferred on the same day to Camp Merritt, NJ. Transferred on 24 July 1919 to Camp Bragg, NC. Transferred on 22 November 1920 to Camp Jackson, SC. Inactivated on 5 September 1921 at Camp Jackson and the 12th F.A. designated as the A.A. Relieved from the 5th Div. on 24 March 1923 and assigned to the 8th Div. Designated mobilization training station was Camp Bragg, 1922–33. The 12th F.A. relieved as the A.A. in 1925 and the 1st Bn., 16th F.A. designated as A.A. Organized on 13 April 1926 with O.R. personnel as an RAI unit with HQ at Fort Myer, VA. Withdrawn from allotment to the Third Corps Area on 1 January 1930 and allotted to the Fifth Corps Area. Concurrently relieved from 8th Div. and assigned to the 5th Div. Organized about March 1930 with O.R. personnel as an RAI unit with HQ at Toledo, OH. RAI elements conducted summer training at Fort Knox, KY, and some years at Fort Benjamin Harrison, IN. Relieved from the 5th Div. on 16 October 1939. Regiment activated on 1 June 1940, less Reserve personnel, at Fort Benning, GA, and concurrently assigned to the 4th Div. Reorganized and redesignated 20th F.A. Bn. on 1 October 1940 at Fort Benning.

Organization Day: 18 August. Chosen to commemorate the regiment's baptism of fire near Frapelle, Lorraine, France, on 18 August 1918. Adopted 9 February 1920.

Status: Assigned to the USARS as the 20th F.A.; 2d Bn. active at Fort Hood, TX, as an element of the 4th Inf. Div. (Mecz).

Events: 310, 330

Commanders, 20th Field Artillery Regiment

Col. Brook Payne	August 1917–8 December 1918	Maj. Richard S. Dawson*	14 August 1928–31 December 1929
Col. George R. Greene	8 December 1918–30 December 1918	*Inactive*	1 January 1930–March 1930
Col. John W. B. Corey	30 December 1918–December 1919	Capt. Thaddeus R. Geisert**	March 1930–ao August 1930
Col. Leo J. Ahern	December 1919–30 June 1920	Unknown	ao August 1930–ao August 1933
Capt. Guyler L. Clark	1 July 1920–30 September 1920	Maj. Ewing G. Wells**	ao August 1933–ao September 1933
Lt. Col. Albert U. Faulkner	20 September 1930–5 September 1921	Unknown	ao September 1933–ao June 1936
Inactive	5 September 1921–13 April 1926	Lt. Col. Frank M. Hammit**	ao June 1936–ao August 1936
2d Lt. Ernest L. Bricker**	13 April 1926–11 May 1926	Unknown	ao August 1936–ao July 1937
1st Lt. Edgar M. Carpenter**	11 May 1926–28 February 1927	Lt. Col. Eugene T. Spencer**	ao July 1937–1 June 1940
Col. Andrew Moses*	28 February 1927–14 August 1928	Lt. Col. Charles G. Helmick	1 June 1940–1 October 1940

*RAI commanders: R.A. officers.
**RAI commanders: O.R. officers.

21st Field Artillery Regiment (155-mm H) (5th Division) **Regular Army Inactive**

HQ—Camp Bragg, NC, 1919–21; *Inactive,* 1921–27; Lafayette, IN, 1927–39; Fort Knox, KY, 1939–40

Arrived at the port of New York on 14 July 1919 on the S.S. *Rotterdam* as an element of the 5th Div. Transferred in July 1919 to Camp Bragg, NC. Relieved from the 5th Div. on 4 November 1920. Assigned to the 13th F.A. Brig. (IV Corps) on 5 March 1921. Inactivated on 23 September 1921 at Camp Bragg and the 5th F.A. Regt. designated as the A.A. Designated mobilization training station was Camp Bragg, 1922–33. Relieved from the 13th F.A. Brig. on 24 March 1923 and assigned to the 9th Div. The 5th F.A. relieved as the A.A. in 1925 and the 1st Bn., 18th F.A. designated as A.A. Withdrawn from the First Corps Area on 15 August 1927 and allotted to the Fifth Corps Area. Organized by August 1927 with O.R. personnel as an RAI unit with HQ at Lafayette, IN. Affiliated with Purdue University ROTC in April 1930 and organized as an RAI unit with personnel from the ROTC Detachment and O.R. commissioned from the program. Relieved from 9th Div. on 1 January 1930 and assigned to the 5th Div. Armament concurrently changed from 75-

mm G to 155-mm H (Mtzd). RAI elements conducted summer training at Fort Knox, KY. The 3d Bn. disbanded on 26 September 1939. Regiment activated on 6 October 1939, less Reserve personnel, at Fort Knox, KY. Reorganized and redesignated 21st F.A. Bn. on 1 October 1940 at Fort Knox.

Organization Day: 17 August. Chosen to commemorate the regiment's baptism of fire near Frapelle, Lorraine, France, on 17 August 1918.

Status: Assigned to the USARS as the 21st F.A.; 1st Bn. active at Fort Hood, TX, as an element of the 1st Cav. Div.

Events: 293, 296, 302, 316, 328

Commanders, 21st Field Artillery Regiment

Col. William S. Guinard	15 May 1917–6 November 1917	Maj. Philip P. Cole**	4 October 1927–9 July 1928
Col. Richard H. McMaster	6 November 1917–22 September 1919	Maj. John E. McMahon*	7 August 1928–1 October 1933
Col. Albert U. Faulkner	ao January 1920–4 March 1920	Maj. Harris C. Mahin**	1 October 1933–ao June 1935
Maj. Milton H. Taulbee	4 March 1920–11 May 1920	Unknown	ao June 1935–ao June 1936
Maj. Schaumberg McGehee	11 May 1920–15 June 1920	Maj. Charles W. Lanning**	ao June 1936–ao July 1936
Maj. Milton H. Taulbee	15 June 1920–21 September 1920	Unknown	ao July 1936–ao July 1937
Maj. Jason McV. Austin	October 1920–5 September 1921	Maj. James A. Pickering**	ao July 1937–ao August 1937
Col. Richard H. McMaster	5 September 1921–21 September 1921	Unknown	ao August 1937–ao July 1938
Inactive	5 September 1921–August 1927	Capt. James C. Gabriel**	ao July 1938–ao August 1938
Capt. Lewis S. Ryan*	August 1927–24 September 1927	Unknown	ao August 1938–1 November 1939
	Col. David E. Cain	1 November 1939–1 May 1941	

*RAI commanders: R.A. officers, who were concurrently PMS&T at Purdue University.
**RAI commanders: O.R. officers.

22d Field Artillery Regiment (155-mm H) (13th Field Artillery Brigade) **Regular Army Inactive**

HQ—*Not organized,* 1921–27; Fort Bragg, NC, 1927–30; Chicago, IL, 1930–41

Constituted in the R.A. on 16 August 1921 and allotted to the Panama Canal Department. The 1st Bn. organized on 1 July 1921 from the Separate Battalion of Mountain Artillery at Corozal, CZ. The 1st Bn. inactivated on 15 September 1921 at Corozal and personnel and equipment transferred to the newly activated 1st Bn., 4th F.A. The 15th F.A. Regt. designated as the A.A. Regiment allotted to the Fourth Corps Area on 24 March 1923 and assigned to the 13th F.A. Brig. (IV Corps). Concurrently, the 15th F.A. relieved as the A.A. and the 5th F.A. designated as the A.A. Organized on 7 June 1927 with O.R. personnel as an RAI unit with HQ at Fort Bragg, NC. Relieved from the 13th F.A. Brig. on 22 July 1929 and assigned to the 4th Div. Withdrawn from allotment to the Fourth Corps Area on 1 January 1930 and allotted to the Sixth Corps Area. Concurrently relieved from the 4th Div. and assigned to the 6th Div. Organized by July 1930 with O.R. personnel as an RAI unit with HQ at Chicago, IL. Conducted summer training at Camp McCoy, WI. Conducted CMTC training some years at Camp McCoy as an alternate form of summer training. Relieved from the 6th Div. on 2 October 1939. Redesignated the 22d F.A. Bn. on 13 January 1941.

Status: Assigned to the USARS as the 22d F.A.; 1st Bn. active at Fort Sill, OK, as a training battalion.

Events: 162

Commanders, 22d Field Artillery Regiment

Not organized	16 August 1921–7 June 1927	Maj. Arthur V. Swedberg**	15 December 1927–ao July 1930
Col. Robert C. McMillan*	7 June 1927–15 December 1927	Unknown	ao July 1930–ao July 1938
	Maj. Andrew J. Bradley**	ao July 1938–13 January 1941	

1st Battalion

Maj. William C. Houghton	August 1921–15 September 1922

*RAI commanders: R.A. officers.
**RAI commanders: O.R. officers.

23d Field Artillery Regiment (155-mm H) (13th Field Artillery Brigade) **Regular Army Inactive**

HQ—*Not organized,* 1921–26; Fort Bragg, NC, 1926–30; *Inactive,* 1930–41

Constituted in the R.A. on 16 August 1921, assigned to the Philippine Division, and allotted to the Fourth Corps Area. The 76th F.A. Regt. designated as the A.A. Designated mobilization training station was Fort Bragg, NC, 1922–30. Relieved from the Philippine Division on 24 March 1923 and assigned to the 13th F.A. Brig. (IV Corps). Concurrently, 76th F.A. relieved as the A.A. and the 17th F.A. designated as the A.A. Organized on 18 May 1926 with O.R. personnel as an RAI unit with HQ at Fort Bragg, NC. Withdrawn from allotment to the Fourth Corps Area on 1 January 1930 and allotted to the Philippine Department. Concurrently relieved from the 13th F.A. Brig. and assigned to the Philippine Division as a Philippine Scout Regiment. Additionally, armament changed from 155-mm H to 75-mm G. Btry A activated on 1 March 1935 at Fort Stotsenberg, PI. Remainder of 1st Bn. activated on 14 March 1941. Location 7 December 1941—Fort Stotsenberg, PI (1st Bn. only).

Status: Disbanded 23 April 1946.

Commanders, 23d Field Artillery Regiment

Col. Richard H. McMaster*	18 May 1926–15 December 1927	Maj. Leslie A. Fitch**	24 May 1929–11 January 1930
Unknown	16 December 1927–24 May 1929	*Inactive*	11 January 1930–7 December 1941

*RAI commanders: R.A. officers.
**RAI commanders: O.R. officers.

1st Battalion (active 1941)

LTC Hanford R. Lockwood	14 March 1941–April 1942

24th Field Artillery Regiment (PS) (2.95 in Pack) (Philippine Division)

HQ—Fort Stotsenberg, PI, 1921–41

Constituted in the R.A. on 22 December 1920 and allotted to the Philippine Department. Organized on 15 May 1921 from the 11th and 12th Inf. Bns. (PS) and the 1st Philippine Field Artillery (Provisional) (Mountain) and redesignated as the 24th F.A. Regt. (PS) at Fort Stotsenberg, PI. Concurrently assigned to the Philippine Division. Regiment reorganized on 2 September 1931 from 2.95-inch (Pack) to 75-mm G (Mtzd). The regiment constructed Ward's Bridge over the Pinatubo River, 1924–25. During the 1920s and 1930s, the regiment also built the artillery trail from Fort Stotsenberg over the Zambales Pass to the China Sea. Location 7 December 1941—Fort Stotsenberg, PI.

Organization Day: 15 May. Chosen to commemorate the date that the organization was formed from Philippine Scout units, 15 May 1921.

Status: Disbanded 25 March 1952.

Events: 27, 35, 41, 52, 68, 82, 100, 118, 139, 169, 179, 198, 223, 245, 270

Commanders, 24th Field Artillery Regiment (Philippine Scouts)

Maj. Charles E. Ide	15 May 1921–7 March 1922	Col. Allen J. Greer	28 December 1929–25 December 1931
Lt. Col. William C. Webb	7 March 1922–10 June 1922	Col. Upton Birnie Jr.	25 December 1931–26 March 1934
Col. Richard H. McMaster	10 June 1922–24 March 1924	Lt. Col. Donald C. McDonald	26 March 1934–2 June 1934
Maj. Raymond E. Lee	24 March 1924–2 June 1924	Maj. John C. Wyeth	3 June 1934–3 October 1934
Lt. Col. James P. Robinson	2 June 1924–29 August 1924	Col. Francis A. Ruggles	3 October 1934–9 February 1937
Col. Philip R. Ward	29 August 1924–19 July 1925	Lt. Col. Frank K. Ross	9 February 1937–25 February 1937
Lt. Col. James P. Robinson	19 July 1925–15 December 1925	Col. John G. Tyndall	25 February 1937–24 March 1939
Col. Henry W. Butner	15 December 1925–5 December 1927	Col. Louis R. Dougherty	24 March 1939–December 1940
Col. Daniel W. Hand	5 December 1927–12 October 1929	Col. John M. Lentz	December 1940–June 1941
Maj. Karl C. Greenwald	12 October 1929–28 December 1929	Unknown	June 1941–7 December 1941

25th Field Artillery Regiment (PS) (75-mm G) (Philippine Division) **Regular Army Inactive**

HQ—Fort William McKinley, PI, 1921; Camp Stotsenberg, PI, 1921–22; *Inactive,* 1922–30; Seventh Corps Area, 1930–33; *Inactive,* 1933–36; New York City, NY, 1936–40

Demobilized on 8 February 1919 at Camp McClellan, AL, as an element of the 9th Div. Reconstituted in the R.A. on 22 December 1920 as the 25th F.A. Regt. (PS). Organized 26 September 1921 at Fort William McKinley, PI, and assigned to Philippine Division. Inactivated on 30 September 1922 at Camp Stotsenberg, PI, and 24th F.A. Regt. designated as the A.A. Enlisted personnel transferred to the 26th Cav.; officers transferred to the 24th F.A. (PS). Withdrawn from allotment to the Philippine Department on 1 January 1930 and allotted to the Seventh Corps Area. Concurrently relieved from the Philippine Division and assigned to the 9th Div. Additionally, designation as a Philippine Scout Regiment rescinded. Organized in 1930 with O.R. personnel as an RAI unit in the Seventh Corps Area. Conducted summer training at Fort Riley, KS, Camp McCoy, WI, or Camp Ripley, MN, 1930–33. Withdrawn from the Seventh Corps Area on 1 October 1933 and allotted to the First Corps Area. Andover, MA, designated as HQ location on organization, but the unit was never organized at that location. Relieved from the First Corps Area on 1 December 1934 and allotted to the Second Corps Area. Concurrently, the 2d Bn. activated at Madison Barracks, NY, with personnel and equipment from the inactivated 2d Bn., 7th F.A. Remainder of the regiment reorganized on 20 March 1936 with O.R. personnel as an RAI unit with HQ at New York City, NY. RAI elements conducted summer training at Pine Camp, NY, with the active elements of the 25th F.A. or with the 5th F.A. The regiment relieved from the 9th Div. on 16 October 1939. The 2d Bn. sailed from the Brooklyn Army Base on the U.S.A.T. *St. Mihiel* and arrived on 15 November 1939 at San Juan, PR. Assigned to the Puerto Rican Department and transferred to Henry Barracks, PR. The 2d Bn. reorganized and redesignated 25th F.A. Bn. on 30 December 1940 at Henry Barracks with personnel and equipment of the 2d Bn.

Status: Assigned to the USARS as the 25th F.A.

Events: 190, 219, 241, 266, 280, 329

Commanders, 25th Field Artillery Regiment

Maj. Thomas G. M. Oliphant	31 October 1921–6 April 1922	Unknown	ao December 1930–1 October 1933
Lt. Col. Daniel W. Hand	6 April 1922–30 September 1922	*Inactive*	1 October 1933–20 March 1936
Inactive	30 September 1922–ao December 1930	2d Lt. Reverdy Walsworth**	20 March 1936–ao June 1936
		1st Lt. Charles W. Raymond**	ao March 1937–30 December 1940

**RAI commanders: O.R. officers.

2d Battalion (active 1934–40)

Maj. Emer Yeager	1 December 1934–1 September 1936	Lt. Col. Carlos Brewer	15 August 1938–December 1939
Col. William H. Shepherd	1 September 1936–15 August 1938	Lt. Col. John A. Hoag	December 1939–30 December 1940

26th Field Artillery Regiment (155-mm H) (14th Field Artillery Brigade) **Regular Army Inactive**

HQ—*Inactive,* 1923–27; Indianapolis, IN, 1927–33; Andover, MA, 1933–37; Lawrence, MA, 1937–40; Fort Bragg, NC 1940

Demobilized on 9 February 1919 at Camp McClellan, AL, as an element of the 9th Div. Reconstituted in the R.A. on 24 March 1923, assigned to the 14th F.A. Brig. (VII Corps), and allotted to the Fifth Corps Area. The 5th F.A. Regt. designated as the A.A. Organized on 12 October 1927 with O.R. personnel as an RAI unit with HQ at Indianapolis, IN. Conducted summer training at Camp Knox, KY, 1928–33. Relieved from the 14th F.A. Brig. on 22 July 1929 and assigned to the 5th Div. Relieved from 5th Div. on 1 January 1930 and assigned to the 9th Div. Armament concurrently changed from 155-mm H (Mtzd) to 75-mm G. Relieved from the Fifth Corps Area on 1 October 1933 and allotted to the First Corps Area. Organized by 1934 with O.R. personnel as an RAI unit with HQ at Andover, MA. Regiment relocated in 1937 to Lawrence, MA. Conducted summer training at Fort Ethan Allen, VT, 1937–39. Conducted CMTC training some years at Fort

Ethan Allen as an alternate form of summer training. Designated mobilization station was Fort Ethan Allen, 1933–40. Activated on 1 August 1940 at Fort Bragg, NC. Reorganized and redesignated as the 26th F.A. Bn. on 1 October 1940 at Fort Bragg.

Events: 330

Commanders, 26th Field Artillery Regiment

Col. Henry S. Kilbourne	7 August 1918–5 January 1919	Maj. John J. Reinhard**	17 October 1927–25 May 1931
Maj. William C. Houghton	5 January 1919–9 February 1919	Maj. Emil W. McCoy**	25 May 1931–1 October 1933
Demobilized/Inactive	10 February 1919–11 October 1927	Unknown	1 October 1933–ao July 1936
		Maj. Paul K. Thomas**	ao July 1936–1 October 1940

*RAI commanders: R.A. officers.
**RAI commanders: O.R. officers.

27th Field Artillery Regiment (155-mm H) (14th Field Artillery Brigade) **Regular Army Inactive**

HQ—*Inactive,* 1923–27; Lafayette, IN, 1927–40

Demobilized on 9 February 1919 at Camp McClellan, AL, as an element of the 9th Div. Reconstituted in the R.A. on 24 March 1923, assigned to the 14th F.A. Brig. (VII Corps), and allotted to the Fifth Corps Area. The 17th F.A. Regt. designated as the A.A. Organized by June 1927 with O.R. personnel as an RAI unit with HQ at Lafayette, IN. Affiliated with Purdue University ROTC in April 1930 and organized as an RAI unit with personnel from the ROTC Detachment and O.R. commissioned from the program. Relieved from the 14th F.A. Brig. on 1 January 1930 and assigned to the 9th Div. Awarded the Toulmin Trophy in 1933. Relieved from the 9th Div. on 1 October 1933. Conducted summer training at Camp Knox, KY, and Camp McCoy, WI, 1927–40. Designated mobilization station was Fort Sill, OK. Redesignated 27th F.A. Bn. on 15 July 1940, assigned to the 1st Armd. Div., and activated, less Reserve personnel, at Fort Knox.

Status: Assigned to the USARS as the 27th F.A.; 3d Bn. active at Fort Bragg, NC, as an element of the 18th F.A. Brig. (Abn); 4th Bn. active at Baumholder, Germany, as an element of the 1st Armd. Div.; and 6th Bn. active at Fort Sill, OK, as an element of the 75th F.A. Brig.

Events: 328, 330

Commanders, 27th Field Artillery Regiment

Col. Walter H. Smith	8 September 1918–11 November 1918	Capt. Cornelius H. Liebert**	1 October 1933–ao January 1934
Col. John S. Hammond	12 November 1918–9 February 1919	Unknown	ao January 1934–ao June 1935
Demobilized/Inactive	9 February 1919–ao March 1926	Maj. Dudley P. Craig**	ao June 1935–ao July 1935
Lt. Col. George A. Taylor*	ao June 1927–24 September 1927	Unknown	ao July 1935–ao July 1937
Unknown	24 September 1927–24 August 1929	Maj. R. B. McBride**	ao July 1937–ao August 1937
Maj. Lawrence H. Hanley*	24 August 1929–1 October 1933	Unknown	ao August 1937–15 July 1940

*RAI commanders: R.A. officers.
**RAI commanders: O.R. officers.

28th Field Artillery Regiment (155-mm H) (14th Field Artillery Brigade) **Regular Army Inactive**

HQ—*Inactive,* 1923–27; Fifth Corps Area, 1927–30; Pittsburgh, PA, 1930–34; *Inactive,* 1934–37; Pittsburgh, PA, 1930–40; Camp Jackson, SC, 1940

Demobilized on 7 February 1919 at Camp Funston, KS, as an element of the 10th Div. Reconstituted in the R.A. on 24 March 1923, assigned to the 14th F.A. Brig. (VII Corps), and allotted to the Fifth Corps Area. The 17th F.A. Regt. designated as the A.A. Organized by August 1927 with O.R. personnel as an RAI unit in the Fifth Corps Area. Conducted summer training at Camp Knox, KY. Withdrawn from allotment to the Fifth Corps Area on 1 January 1930 and allotted to the Third Corps Area. Concurrently relieved from the 14th F.A. Brig. and assigned to the 8th Div. Organized on 10 May 1930 with O.R. personnel as an RAI unit with HQ at Pittsburgh, PA. Inactivated about June 1934 at Pittsburgh by relief of Reserve personnel. Reorganized on 18 May 1937 with O.R. personnel as an RAI unit with HQ at Pittsburgh. Conducted summer training at Fort Hoyle, MD. Designated mobilization station was the Roanoke Concentration Area, VA. Relieved from assignment to the 8th Div. on 16 October 1939. Concurrently, the 3d Bn. disbanded. Regiment activated on 1 July 1940, less Reserve personnel, at Camp Jackson, SC, and assigned to the 8th Div. Reorganized and redesignated 28th F.A. Bn. on 1 October 1940 at Camp Jackson.

Events: 330

Commanders, 28th Field Artillery Regiment

Demobilized/Inactive	7 February 1919–ao August 1927	Unknown	3 November 1932–18 October 1933
Maj. Carl C. Bank**	ao August 1927–24 September 1927	Maj. Alfred Le R. Sawyer**	18 October 1933–June 1934
Maj. Lee B. Harr**	3 July 1928–1 January 1930	*Inactive*	June 1934–18 May 1937
Inactive	1 January 1930–10 May 1930	Capt. Kenneth C. Crow**	18 May 1937–ao June 1937
Unknown	10 May 1930–25 May 1931	Unknown	ao June 1937–ao July 1938
Maj. John J. Reinhard**	25 May 1931–3 November 1932	Capt. Joseph A. Monn**	ao July 1938–6 December 1938
		Lt. Col. George S. Blair**	7 December 1938–1 July 1940

**RAI commanders: O.R. officers.

29th Field Artillery Regiment (155-mm H) (15th Field Artillery Brigade) **Regular Army Inactive**

HQ—*Inactive,* 1923–27; Fort Bragg, NC, 1927–40; Fort Benning, GA, 1940

Demobilized on 4 February 1919 at Camp Funston, KS, as an element of the 10th Div. Reconstituted in the R.A. on 24 March 1923, assigned to the 15th F.A. Brig. (II Corps), and allotted to the Fourth Corps Area. The 5th F.A. Regt. designated as the A.A. Organized on 17 June 1927 with O.R. personnel as an RAI unit with HQ at Fort Bragg, NC. Relieved from the 15th F.A. Brig. on 29 August 1929 and assigned to the 13th F.A. Brig. (IV Corps). Conducted summer training at Fort Bragg, NC. Designated mobilization station was Fort Bragg. Relieved from the 13th F.A. Brig. on 1 August 1940, assigned to the 4th Div., and activated, less Reserve personnel, at Fort Benning, GA. O.R. personnel relieved from assignment on 16 September 1940. Reorganized and redesignated 29th F.A. Bn. on 1 October 1940 at Fort Benning.

Status: Assigned to the USARS as the 29th F.A.; 3d Bn. active at Fort Carson, CO, as an element of the 4th Inf. Div. (Mecz).

Events: 310, 330

Commanders, 29th Field Artillery Regiment

Lt. Col. William N. Taylor	2 August 1918–8 November 1918	Maj. Samuel G. Harrison**	27 June 1929–14 December 1934
Col. Charles J. Daley	8 November 1918–8 December 1918	Capt. Irvin F. Kurth**	14 December 1934–19 October 1935
Col. F. Thorp Jr.	8 December 1918–4 February 1919	Capt. Delbert Heinbaugh**	19 October 1935–30 June 1936
Demobilized/Inactive	4 February 1919–16 June 1927	Col. Harold E. Marr**	1 July 1936–30 June 1937
Maj. James S. Dusenbury*	17 June 1927–15 December 1927	Maj. James P. Dodge Jr.**	1 July 1937–31 July 1940
Maj. Leslie T. Bolton**	26 January 1928–27 June 1929	Col. Julian F. Barnes	1 August 1940–1 October 1940

*RAI commanders: R.A. officers.
**RAI commanders: O.R. officers.

30th Field Artillery Regiment (155-mm H) (15th Field Artillery Brigade) **Regular Army Inactive**

HQ—*Inactive,* 1923–26; Atlanta, GA, 1926–33; Columbus, OH, 1933–40; Camp Roberts, CA, 1941

Demobilized on 5 February 1919 at Camp Funston, KS, as an element of the 10th Div. Reconstituted in the R.A. on 24 March 1923, assigned to the 15th F.A. Brig. (II Corps), and allotted to the Fourth Corps Area. The 5th F.A. Regt. designated as the A.A. Organized on 26 December 1926 with O.R. personnel as an RAI unit with HQ at Atlanta, GA. Relieved from the 15th F.A. Brig. on 1 January 1930 and assigned to the 13th F.A. Brig. (IV Corps). Relieved from the 13th F.A. Brig. on 1 October 1933. Concurrently withdrawn from the Fourth Corps Area, and allotted to the Fifth Corps Area. Organized about October 1933 with O.R. personnel as an RAI unit with HQ at Columbus, OH. Conducted summer training at Fort Bragg, NC, and at Fort Knox, KY. Designated mobilization station was Fort Bragg, 1923–33, and Fort Sill, OK, 1933–40. Assigned on 7 November 1940 to the 26th F.A. Brig. (III Corps). Regiment activated on 4 June 1941, less Reserve personnel, at Camp Roberts, CA. Location 7 December 1941—Camp Roberts, CA.

Status: Assigned to the USARS as the 30th F.A.; 1st and 3d Bns. active at Fort Sill, OK, as training battalions.

Commanders, 30th Field Artillery Regiment

Demobilized/Inactive	5 February 1919–25 December 1926	Maj. Roy S. Wood**	14 June 1932–15 November 1936
Maj. John W. Garner**	22 December 1926–5 April 1932	Capt. Edgar A. Work**	15 November 1936–ao July 1937
Maj. Enos P. Scott**	5 April 1932–14 June 1932	Unknown	ao July 1937–7 December 1941

**RAI commanders: O.R. officers.

31st Field Artillery Regiment (155-mm H) (15th Field Artillery Brigade) **Regular Army Inactive**

HQ—Fort Sill, OK, 1929–33; *Inactive,* 1933–36; Los Angeles, CA, 1936–40; Camp Ord, CA, 1940

Demobilized on 6 December 1918 at Camp George G. Meade, MD, as an element of the 11th Div. Reconstituted in the R.A. on 22 July 1929, assigned to the 2d Div., and allotted to the Eighth Corps Area. Organized on 8 October 1929 with O.R. personnel as an RAI unit with HQ at Fort Sill, OK. Relieved from the 2d Div. on 1 January 1930 and assigned to the 15th F.A. Brig. (II Corps). Inactivated on 28 September 1933 at Fort Sill by relief of Reserve personnel. Relieved from the Eighth Corps Area on 1 October 1933 and allotted to the Ninth Corps Area. Organized on 20 February 1936 with O.R. personnel as an RAI unit with HQ at Los Angeles, CA. Conducted Citizens Military Training Camp (CMTC) training at the Presidio of Monterey as an alternate form of summer training. Relieved from the 15th F.A. Brig. on 1 July 1940 and assigned to the 7th Div. Concurrently activated, less Reserve personnel, at Camp Ord, CA. Reorganized and redesignated 31st F.A. Bn. on 1 October 1940 at Camp Ord.

Events: 314, 326

Commanders, 31st Field Artillery Regiment

Col. Arthur M. Compton	30 July 1918–4 September 1918	Maj. Archie E. Lang**	June 1930–28 September 1933
Col. Henry L. Stimson	10 September 1918–7 December 1918	*Inactive*	28 September 1933–20 February 1936
Demobilized/Inactive	7 December 1918–7 October 1929	Unknown	20 February 1936–13 February 1937
Unknown	8 October 1929–23 April 1930	Capt. Ralph N. Goebel**	13 February 1937–ao June 1937
Capt. Homer S. Reese**	24 April 1930–June 1930	Unknown	ao June 1937–21 July 1940
Col. Ray W. Barker	21 July 1940–1 October 1940		

**RAI commanders: O.R. officers.

32d Field Artillery Regiment (155-mm H) (15th Field Artillery Brigade) **Regular Army Inactive**

HQ—Corvallis, OR, 1929–40

Demobilized on 10 December 1918 at Camp George G. Meade, MD, as an element of the 11th Div. Reconstituted in the R.A. on 22 July 1929, assigned to the 3d Div., and allotted to the Ninth Corps Area. Relieved from the 3d Div. on 1 January 1930 and assigned to the 15th F.A. Brig. (IX Corps). Affiliated with Oregon State Agricultural College ROTC on 23 July 1929 and organized at Corvallis, WA, as an RAI unit with personnel from the ROTC Detachment and O.R. commissioned from the program. Conducted summer training most years at Fort Lewis, WA, and some years at Fort Douglas, UT. Relieved from the 15th F.A. Brig. (IX Corps) on 23 September 1932 and assigned to the 3d Div. Relieved from the 3d Div. on 1 October 1933 and assigned to the 15th F.A. Brig. (IX Corps). Redesignated 32d F.A. Bn., assigned to the 1st Div., and concurrently activated on 1 October 1940, less Reserve personnel, at Fort Ethan Allen, VT.

Status: Assigned to the USARS as the 32d F.A.; 6th Bn. active at Fort Sill, OK, as an element of the 212th F.A. Brig.

Events: 287, 293, 296, 301, 323, 330

Commanders, 32d Field Artillery Regiment

Col. Arthur M. Compton	4 September 1918–12 December 1918	Col. Henry R. Richmond*	23 July 1929–5 August 1930
Demobilized/Inactive	12 December 1918–23 July 1929	Col. William H. Patterson*	5 August 1930–1 October 1933
Maj. James Frankland**	2 October 1933–1 October 1940		

*RAI commanders: R.A. officers who were concurrently PMS&T at Oregon State Agricultural College.
**RAI commanders: O.R. officers.

33d Field Artillery Regiment (155-mm H) (14th Field Artillery Brigade) **Regular Army Inactive**

HQ—*Inactive,* 1929–30; Fourth Corps Area, 1930–33; *Inactive,* 1933–34; Indianapolis, IN, 1934–38; Fourth Corps Area, 1938–40

Demobilized on 11 December 1918 at Camp George G. Meade, MD, as an element of the 11th Div. Reconstituted in the R.A. on 22 July 1929, assigned to the 6th Div., and allotted to the Sixth Corps Area. Chicago, IL, designated as HQ location on organization, but the unit was never organized at that location. Withdrawn from allotment to the Sixth Corps Area on 1 January 1930 and allotted to the Fourth Corps Area. Concurrently relieved from the 6th Div. and assigned to the 14th F.A. Brig. (VII Corps). Organized on 11 January 1930 with O.R. personnel as an RAI unit in the Fourth Corps Area. Relieved from the Fourth Corps Area on 1 October 1933 and allotted to the Fifth Corps Area. Organized by May 1934 with O.R. personnel as an RAI unit with HQ at Indianapolis, IN. Conducted summer training most years at Fort Knox, KY. Awarded the Toulmin Trophy in 1935. Withdrawn from the Fifth Corps Area on 1 January 1938 and allotted to the Fourth Corps Area. Organized by February 1938 with O.R. personnel as an RAI unit in the Fourth Corps Area. Redesignated 33d F.A. Bn. (105-mm TD), assigned to the 1st Div. and concurrently activated on 1 October 1940, less Reserve personnel, at Fort Ethan Allen, VT.

Status: Assigned to the USARS as the 33d F.A.; 1st Bn. active at Bamberg, Germany, as an element of the 1st Inf. Div. (Mecz).

Events: 287, 293, 296, 301, 323, 330

Commanders, 33d Field Artillery Regiment

Lt. Col. Louie A. Beard	15 October 1918–11 December 1918	Maj. Harry Burton**	May 1934–ao August 1935
Demobilized/Inactive	12 December 1918–10 January 1930	Maj. Tyner W. Myers**	ao May 1936–31 December 1937
Maj. Leslie A. Fitch**	11 January 1930–1 October 1933	Capt. Paul Van Tuyl**	31 December 1937–1 January 1938
Inactive	1 October 1933–May 1934	Unknown	ao February 1938–1 October 1940

**RAI commanders: O.R. officers.

34th Field Artillery Regiment (155-mm H) (14th Field Artillery Brigade) **Regular Army Inactive**

HQ—*Inactive,* 1929–30; Cleveland, OH, 1930–33; *Inactive,* 1933–34; Andover, MA, 1934–37; Providence, RI, 1937–40; Fort Bragg, NC, 1940–41

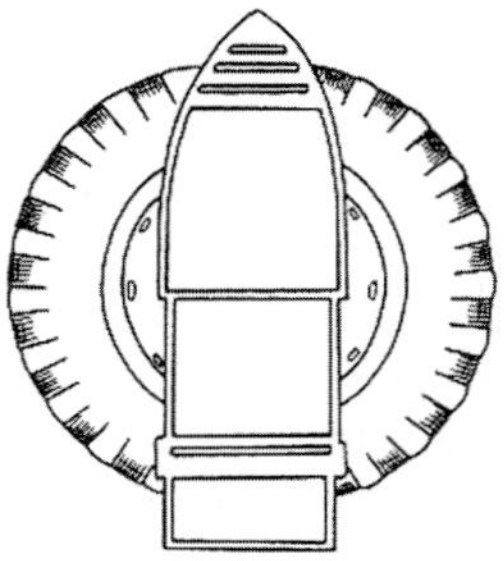

Demobilized on 6 February 1919 at Camp McClellan, AL, as an element of the 12th Div. Reconstituted in the R.A. on 22 July 1929, assigned to the 7th Div., and allotted to the Seventh Corps Area. Withdrawn from allotment to the Seventh Corps Area on 1 January 1930 and allotted to the Fifth Corps Area. Concurrently relieved from 7th Div. and assigned to the 14th F.A. Brig. (VII Corps). Organized by June 1930 with O.R. personnel as an RAI unit with HQ at Cleveland, OH. Relieved from the 14th F.A. Brig. (V Corps) and alloted to the Fifth Corps Area on 1 October 1933. Concurrently, assigned to the 9th Div. and allotted to the First Corps Area. Organized by December 1934 with O.R. personnel as an RAI unit with HQ at Andover, MA. Regiment relocated by August 1937 to Providence, RI. Conducted summer training at Camp Knox, KY, 1930–33, and at Fort Ethan Allen, VT, 1937–40. Designated mobilization station was Fort Ethan Allen, 1933–40. Activated on 1 August 1940, less Reserve personnel, at Fort Bragg, NC. Reorganized and redesignated 34th F.A. Bn. on 1 October 1940 at Fort Bragg.

Events: 330

Commanders, 34th Field Artillery Regiment

Lt. Col. James F. Edmonds	2 August 1918–13 September 1918	Unknown	19 December 1918–6 February 1919
Col. Ralph McT. Pennell	13 September 1918–13 December 1918	*Demobilized/Inactive*	6 February 1919–ao June 1930
Col. William S. Wood	13 December 1918–19 December 1918	Unknown	ao June 1930–ao March 1937
Capt. William W. Edson**	ao March 1937–1 August 1940		

**RAI commanders: O.R. officers.

35th Field Artillery Regiment (155-mm H) (14th Field Artillery Brigade) **Regular Army Inactive**

HQ—*Inactive,* 1929–30; Akron, OH, 1930–41; Camp Blanding, FL, 1941

Demobilized on 6 February 1919 at Camp McClellan, AL, as an element of the 12th Div. Reconstituted in the R.A. on 22 July 1929, assigned to the 8th Div., and allotted to the Third Corps Area. Withdrawn from allotment to the Third Corps Area on 1 January 1930 and allotted to the Fifth Corps Area. Concurrently relieved from the 8th Div. and assigned to the 14th F.A. Brig. (VII Corps). Additionally, armament changed from 155-mm H (Mtzd) to 155-mm G (Mtzd). Organized by June 1930 with O.R. personnel as an RAI unit with HQ at Akron, OH. Conducted summer training most years at Camp Knox, KY. Designated mobilization station was Fort Bragg, NC. Activated on 10 February 1941, less Reserve personnel, at Camp Blanding, FL, and assigned to the 74th F.A. Brig. (IV Corps). Location 7 December 1941—Camp Blanding, FL.

Status: Assigned to the USARS as the 35th EA; no active elements.

Commanders, 35th Field Artillery Regiment

Maj. Clift Andrus	2 August 1918–18 September 1918	Unknown	ao July 1935–ao June 1937
Col. Henry H. Pfeil	30 July 1918–12 December 1918	Capt. John H. Carpenter**	ao June 1937–ao July 1937
Unknown	12 December 1918–6 February 1919	Unknown	ao July 1937–ao April 1938
Demobilized/Inactive	6 February 1919–ao June 1930	Capt. Lawrence W. Jenkinson**	ao April 1938–ao May 1938
Unknown	ao June 1930–ao June 1934	Unknown	ao May 1938–10 February 1941
Maj. John L. Milburn**	ao June 1934–ao July 1935	Col. Julian F. Barnes	10 February 1941–September 1941
Lt. Col. Russell H. Dixon	September 1941–27 March 1942		

**RAI commanders: O.R. officers.

36th Field Artillery Regiment (155-mm G) (13th Field Artillery Brigade) **Regular Army Inactive**

HQ—*Inactive,* 1929–30; Gainesville, FL, 1930–39; Fort Bragg, NC, 1939–41

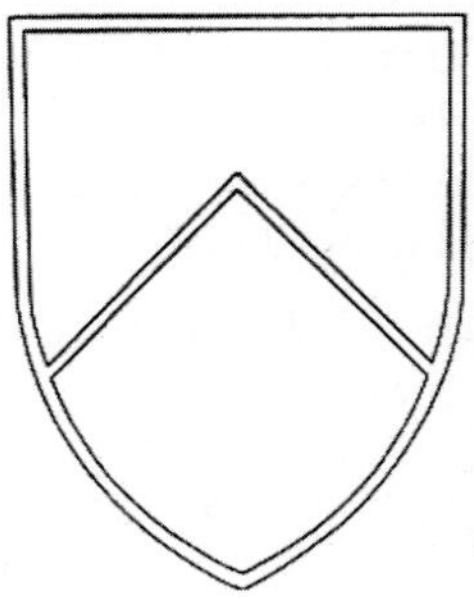

Demobilized on 8 February 1919 at Camp McClellan, AL, as an element of the 12th Div. Reconstituted in the R.A. on 22 July 1929, assigned to the 9th Div., and allotted to the Fifth Corps Area. Withdrawn from allotment to the Fifth Corps Area on 1 January 1930 and allotted to the Fourth Corps Area. Concurrently relieved from 9th Div. and assigned to the 13th F.A. Brig. (IV Corps). Additionally, armament changed from 155-mm H (Mtzd) to 155-mm G (Mtzd). Organized on 11 January 1930 with O.R. personnel as an RAI unit with HQ at Gainesville, FL. Affiliated with the University of Florida ROTC on 1 October 1933 and organized as an RAI unit with personnel from the ROTC Detachment and O.R. commissioned from the program. The 2d Bn. activated on 1 October 1933 at Fort Bragg, NC, with personnel and equipment from the inactivated 2d Bn., 5th F.A. RAI elements of the regiment conducted summer training most years at Fort Bragg, 1935–39. Assigned Reserve officers conducted field artillery CMTC in 1937 at Fort Bragg, NC. Designated mobilization station was Fort Bragg. Regimental HQ activated on 10 October 1939, less Reserve personnel, at Fort Bragg and assigned to the 13th F.A. Brig. (IV Corps). The 1st and 3d Bns. activated on 6 November 1939, less Reserve personnel, at Fort Bragg. Location 7 December 1941—Fort Bragg, NC.

Events: 293, 296, 300, 330

Commanders, 36th Field Artillery Regiment

Lt. Col. J. B. Maynard	4 September 1918–24 October 1918	Unknown	ao October 1934–1 July 1936
Col. Neil G. Finch	24 October 1918–8 February 1919	Lt. Col. William R. Gruber**	1 July 1936–30 June 1937
Demobilized/Inactive	8 February 1919–11 January 1930	Capt. Frederic T. Parker**	30 January 1937–ao June 1938
Maj. Lee F. Banks**	11 January 1930–ao October 1934	Unknown	30 June 1937–14 October 1939
Col. Walter W. Hess Jr.	10 October 1939–20 September 1943		

**RAI commanders: O.R. officers.

1st Battalion

Maj. Frank Royse	1 October 1933–15 September 1934	Maj. Orville M. Moore	10 October 1936–23 October 1937
Capt. Owen M. Marshburn	15 September 1934–23 October 1935	Lt. Col. William R. Gruber	23 October 1937–1 August 1938
Lt. Col. Charles M. Busbee	23 October 1935–10 October 1936	Capt. Winfield S. Scott	1 August 1938–1 September 1938
Lt. Col. Walter W. Hess Jr.	1 September 1938–10 October 1939		

37th Field Artillery Regiment (155-mm H) (19th Field Artillery Brigade) **Regular Army Inactive**

HQ—*Inactive,* 1933–34; Andover, MA, 1934–37; Springfield, MA, 1937–40

Demobilized on 11 February 1919 at Camp Lewis, WA, as an element of the 13th Div. Reconstituted in the R.A. on 1 October 1933, assigned to the 19th F.A. Brig. (I Corps) , and allotted to the First Corps Area. Organized by December 1934 with O.R. personnel as an RAI unit with HQ at Andover, MA. Regiment relocated in 1937 to Springfield, MA. Typically conducted Inactive Training Period meetings at the Post Office Building in Boston, MA. Conducted summer training most years at Fort Ethan Allen, VT. Reorganized and redesignated 37th F.A. Bn. (105-mm TD) on 1 October 1940, relieved from the 19th F.A. Brig., and assigned to the 2d Div.

Status: Assigned to the USARS as the 37th F.A.; 1st Bn. active at Fort Lewis, WA, and 6th Bn. active at Camp Stanley, Korea, as elements of the 2d Inf. Div.

Events: 295, 296, 299, 300, 317, 328

Commanders, 37th Field Artillery Regiment

Col. Benjamin M. Bailey	20 July 1918–2 August 1918	Unknown	ao September 1937–ao June 1938
Lt. Col. Harold E. Marr	2 August 1918–11 February 1919	Capt. Philip C. Rutledge**	ao June 1938–ao July 1938
Demobilized/Inactive	11 February 1919–ao December 1934	Unknown	ao July 1938–ao June 1939
Unknown	ao December 1934–ao August 1937	Capt. Aylmer S.N. Thompson**	ao June 1939–ao July 1939
Capt. Stephen M. Weld**	ao August 1937–ao September 1937	Unknown	ao July 1939–1 October 1940

**RAI commanders: O.R. officers.

38th Field Artillery Regiment (155-mm H) (19th Field Artillery Brigade) **Regular Army Inactive**

HQ—*Inactive,* 1933–34; Andover, MA, 1934–37; Springfield, MA, 1937–40

Demobilized on 10 February 1919 at Camp Lewis, WA, as an element of the 13th Div. Reconstituted in the R.A. on 1 October 1933, assigned to the 19th F.A. Brig. (I Corps), and allotted to the First Corps Area. Organized by December 1934 with O.R. personnel as an RAI unit with HQ at Andover, MA. Regiment relocated in 1937 to Springfield, MA. Typically conducted Inactive Training Period meetings at the Post Office Building in Boston, MA. Reorganized and redesignated 38th F.A. Bn. on 1 October 1940, relieved from the 19th F.A. Brig., and assigned to the 2d Div.

Status: Assigned to the USARS as the 38th F.A.; 1st Bn. active at Camp Stanley, Korea, as an element of the 2d Inf. Div.

Events: 295, 296, 299, 300, 317, 328

Commanders, 38th Field Artillery Regiment

Lt. Col. Julian I. Chamberlain	12 January 1918– 12 January 1918	Unknown	ao December 1934–ao October 1937
Col. Thomas E. Merrill	12 January 1919–10 February 1919	Capt. Charles F. Shugrue**	ao October 1937–ao July 1939
Demobilized/Inactive	10 February 1919–ao December 1934	Unknown	ao July 1939–1 October 1940

**RAI commanders: O.R. officers.

39th Field Artillery Regiment (155-mm H) (20th Field Artillery Brigade) **Regular Army Inactive**

HQ—*Inactive,* 1933–38; New York City, NY, 1938–40

Demobilized on 26 February 1919 at Camp Lewis, WA, as an element of the 13th Div. Reconstituted in the R.A. on 1 October 1933, assigned to the 20th F.A. Brig. (II Corps), and allotted to the Second Corps Area. Organized on 17 October 1938 with O.R. personnel as an RAI unit with HQ at New York City. Conducted monthly meetings at the offices of the Building Trades Employer Association at 2 Park Avenue in New York City, NY. Designated mobilization station was Fort Bragg, NC. Inactivated by June 1940 at New York City by relief of Reserve personnel. Reorganized and redesignated 39th F.A. Bn. on 1 October 1940, relieved from the 20th F.A. Brig., and assigned to the 3d Div.

Status: Assigned to the USARS as the 39th F.A.; 1st Bn. active at Fort Stewart, GA, as an element of the 3d Inf. Div. (Mecz).

Events: 294, 306, 309, 314, 325

Commanders, 39th Field Artillery Regiment

Col. Arthur P.S. Hyde	ao October 1918–6 November 1918	*Demobilized/Inactive*	26 February 1919–17 October 1938
Col. Harold E. Marr	6 November 1918–26 February 1919	2d Lt. Edward R. Billings	17 October 1938–ao November 1938
Unknown	ao November 1938–June 1940		

40th Field Artillery Regiment (155-mm H) (20th Field Artillery Brigade) **Regular Army Inactive**

HQ—*Inactive,* 1933–36; New York City, NY, 1936–40; *Inactive,* 1940–41; Camp Roberts, CA, 1941

Demobilized on 6 February 1919 at Camp Custer, MI, as an element of the 14th Div. Reconstituted in the R.A. on 1 October 1933, assigned to the 20th F.A. Brig. (II Corps), and allotted to the Second Corps Area. Organized by December 1936 with O.R. personnel as an RAI unit with HQ at New York City, NY. Conducted monthly meetings at the Hotel Delmonico at 59th Street and Park Avenue in New York City, NY. Designated mobilization station was Fort Bragg, NC. Inactivated by June 1940 at New York City by relief of Reserve personnel. Relieved from the 20th F.A. Brig. on 7 November 1940 and assigned to the 26th F.A. Brig. (III Corps). Activated on 4 June 1941 at Camp Roberts, CA. Location 7 December 1941—Camp Roberts, CA.

Status: Assigned to the USARS as the 40th F.A.; 1st Bn. active at Fort Sill, OK, as a training battalion.

Commanders, 40th Field Artillery Regiment

Col. William F. Morrison	10 August 1918–6 February 1919	*Demobilized/Inactive*	7 February 1919–ao December 1936
Unknown	ao December 1936–June 1940		

41st Field Artillery Regiment (155-mm H) (21st Field Artillery Brigade) **Regular Army Inactive**

HQ—*Inactive,* 1919–33; Wilkes-Barre, PA, 1933–36; Philadelphia, PA, 1936–40

Demobilized on 6 February 1919 at Camp Custer, MI, as an element of the 14th Div. Reconstituted in the R.A. on 1 October 1933, assigned to the 21st F.A. Brig. (III Corps), and allotted to the Third Corps Area. Organized about December 1933 with O.R. personnel as an RAI unit with HQ at Wilkes-Barre, PA. Relocated in 1936 to Philadelphia, PA. Inactivated on 9 August 1940 at Philadelphia by relief of personnel. Conducted summer training at Fort George G. Meade, MD, or Fort Hoyle, MD. Reorganized and redesignated 41st F.A. Bn. on 1 October 1940, relieved from the 21st F.A. Brig., and assigned to the 3d Div.

Status: Consolidated with the 1st Bn., 41st Coast Artillery (C.A.) on 28 June 1950 and consolidated unit designated 41st Artillery (Arty.) on 31 July 1959; assigned to the USARS as the 41st F.A.; 1st Bn. active at Fort Stewart, GA, as an element of the 3d Inf. Div. (Mecz).

Events: 294, 306, 309, 314, 325

Commanders, 41st Field Artillery Regiment

Lt. Col. Robert G. Kirkwood	2 August 1918–ao September 1918	Unknown	December 1933–ao December 1936
Unknown	ao September 1918–6 February 1919	Maj. Henry L. Jones II**	ao December 1936–27 January 1939
Demobilized/Inactive	6 February 1919–December 1933	Maj. Donald G. Mayer**	7 February 1939–9 August 1940

**RAI commanders: O.R. officers.

42d Field Artillery Regiment (155-mm H) (21st Field Artillery Brigade) **Regular Army Inactive**

HQ—*Inactive,* 1919–39; Pennsylvania, 1939–40; *Inactive,* 1940

Demobilized on 7 February 1919 at Camp Custer, MI, as an element of the 14th Div. Reconstituted in the R.A. on 1 October 1933, assigned to the 21st F.A. Brig. (III Corps), and allotted to the Third Corps Area. Organized on 11 July 1939 with O.R. personnel as an RAI unit with HQ in eastern Pennsylvania. Conducted summer training at Fort Hoyle, MD. Inactivated on 31 August 1940 by relief of personnel. Reorganized and redesignated 42d F.A. Bn. on 1 October 1940, relieved from the 21st F.A. Brig., and assigned to the 4th Div.

Status: Consolidated with the 1st Bn., 42d C.A. on 28 June 1950 and consolidated unit designated 42d Arty. on 1 April 1957; assigned to the USARS as the 42d F.A.; 4th Bn. active at Fort Hood, TX, as an element of the 4th Inf. Div. (Mecz).

Events: 310, 330

Commanders, 42d Field Artillery Regiment

Col. Solon J. Carter	28 September 1918–7 February 1919	Lt. Col. Willard R. Ginder**	11 July 1939–9 August 1940
Demobilized/Inactive	7 February 1919–11 July 1939	*Inactive*	9 August 1940–1 October 1940

**RAI commanders: O.R. officers.

43d Field Artillery Regiment (155-mm H) (22d Field Artillery Brigade) **Regular Army Inactive**

HQ—*Not organized,* 1933–35; Champaign, IL, 1935–41

Constituted in the R.A. on 1 October 1933, allotted to the Sixth Corps Area, and assigned to the 22d F.A. Brig. (VI Corps). Organized by April 1935 with O.R. personnel as an RAI unit with HQ at Champaign, IL. Conducted summer training most years at Camp McCoy, WI. Designated mobilization station was Fort Sill, OK. Redesignated 43d F.A. Bn. on 13 January 1941.

Commander, 43d Field Artillery Regiment

Unknown	ao April 1935–1 September 1936	Lt. Col. Walter S. Stanton**	1 September 1936–13 January 1941

**RAI commanders: O.R. officers.

44th Field Artillery Regiment (155-mm H) (17th Field Artillery Brigade) **Regular Army Inactive**

HQ—*Not organized,* 1933–34; St. Louis, MO, 1934–41; Fort Bragg, NC, 1941

Constituted in the R.A. on 1 October 1933, assigned to the 17th F.A. Brig. (VII Corps), and allotted to the Seventh Corps Area. Organized by December 1934 with O.R. personnel as an RAI unit with HQ at St. Louis, MO. Conducted summer training at Camp Ripley, MN, or Fort Riley, KS. Conducted CMTC training at Fort Snelling, MN, as an alternate form of summer training. Designated mobilization station was Fort Sill, OK. Activated on 1 June 1941, less Reserve personnel, at Fort Bragg, NC. Location 7 December 1941—Fort Bragg, NC.

Events: 310, 330

Commander, 44th Field Artillery Regiment

Unknown	ao December 1934–7 December 1941

45th Field Artillery Regiment (155-mm H) (17th Field Artillery Brigade) **Regular Army Inactive**

HQ—*Not organized,* 1933–34; St. Louis, MO, 1934–41

Constituted in the R.A. on 1 October 1933, assigned to the 17th F.A. Brig. (VII Corps), and allotted to the Seventh Corps Area. Organized by December 1934 with O.R. personnel as an RAI unit with HQ at St. Louis, MO. Conducted summer training at Camp Ripley, MN, or Fort Riley, KS. Designated mobilization station was Fort Lewis, WA. Redesignated 45th F.A. Bn. on 13 January 1941.

Commanders, 45th Field Artillery Regiment

Unknown	ao December 1934–13 January 1941

46th Field Artillery Regiment (155-mm H) (18th Field Artillery Brigade) **Regular Army Inactive**

HQ—*Not organized,* 1933–34; Oklahoma City, OK, 1934–40

Constituted in the R.A. on 1 October 1933, assigned to the 18th F.A. Brig. (VIII Corps), and allotted to the Eighth Corps Area. Organized on 22 October 1934 with O.R. personnel as an RAI unit with HQ at Oklahoma City, OK. Conducted summer training at Fort Sill, OK. Redesignated 46th F.A. Bn. on 1 October 1940 and assigned to the 5th Div.

Events: 293, 296, 302, 316, 328

Commanders, 46th Field Artillery Regiment

Capt. Max C. Farber**	22 October 1934–ao December 1934	Unknown	ao December 1934–1 October 1940

47th Field Artillery Regiment (75-mm TD) (25th Field Artillery Brigade) **Regular Army Inactive**

HQ—*Not organized,* 1933–36; Des Moines, IA, 1936–41; Fort Bragg, NC, 1941

Constituted in the R.A. on 1 October 1933, assigned to the 25th F.A. Brig. (GHQR), and allotted to the Seventh Corps Area. Organized by June 1936 with O.R. personnel as an RAI unit with HQ at Des Moines, IA. Typically conducted Inactive Training Period meetings at the New Armory or the Federal Building in Des Moines. Conducted summer training at Fort Sill, OK. Conducted CMTC training at Fort Snelling, MN, as an alternate form of summer training. Designated mobilization station was Fort Lewis, WA. Activated on 1 June 1941, less Reserve personnel, at Fort Bragg, NC, and assigned to the First Army. Concurrently, relieved from the 25th F.A. Brig., and attached to the Fort Bragg Provisional F.A. Brig. Location 7 December 1941—Fort Bragg, NC.

Events: 330

Commanders, 47th Field Artillery Regiment

Unknown	ao June 1936–ao June 1938	Maj. Roy W. Ames**	ao June 1939–ao September 1939
Capt. Glenn W. Trindel	ao June 1938–ao July 1938	Unknown	ao September 1939–1 June 1941
Unknown	ao July 1938–ao June 1939	Lt. Col. Arthur R. Harris	1 June 1941–ao December 1941

**RAI commanders: O.R. officers.

48th Field Artillery Regiment (155-mm H) (29th Field Artillery Brigade) **Regular Army Inactive**

HQ—*Not organized,* 1933–34; Andover, MA, 1934–36; New York City, NY, 1936–40; *Inactive,* 1940–41

Constituted in the R.A. on 1 October 1933, assigned to the 29th F.A. Brig. (GHQR), and allotted to the First Corps Area. Organized by 1934 with O.R. personnel as an RAI unit with HQ at Andover, MA. Withdrawn from the First Corps Area in 1936 and allotted to the Second Corps Area. Organized by late 1936 with O.R. personnel as an RAI unit with HQ at New York City. Conducted monthly meetings at the Hotel George Washington at 23d Street and Lexington Avenue in New York City, NY. Designated mobilization station was Fort Bragg, NC. Inactivated by June 1940 at New York City by relief of Reserve personnel. Redesignated 48th F.A. Bn. on 13 January 1941.

Commanders, 48th Field Artillery Regiment

Unknown	ao December 1934–13 January 1941	*Inactive*	June 1940–13 January 1941

49th Field Artillery Regiment (155-mm H) (29th Field Artillery Brigade) **Regular Army Inactive**

HQ—*Not organized,* 1933–34; Andover, MA, 1934–36; New York City, NY, 1936–40; *Inactive,* 1940–41

Constituted in the R.A. on 1 October 1933, assigned to the 29th F.A. Brig. (GHQR), and allotted to the First Corps Area. Organized by 1934 with O.R. personnel as an RAI unit with HQ at Andover, MA. Withdrawn from the First Corps Area in 1936 and allotted to the Second Corps Area. Organized by late 1936 with O.R. personnel as an RAI unit with HQ at New York City. Conducted monthly meetings at the Princeton Club at 38th Street and Park Avenue in New York City, NY. Designated mobilization station was Fort Bragg, NC. Inactivated by June 1940 at New York City by relief of Reserve personnel. Redesignated 49th F.A. Bn. on 1 June 1941, assigned to the 7th Div., and activated at Fort Ord, CA.

Commanders, 49th Field Artillery Regiment

Unknown	ao December 1934–ao March 1939	Col. John C. Bohan**	ao March 1939–June 1940
Inactive	June 1940–1 June 1941		

**RAI commanders: O.R. officers.

50th Field Artillery Regiment (155-mm H) (29th Field Artillery Brigade) **Regular Army Inactive**

HQ—*Not organized,* 1933–34; Hartford, CT, 1934–38; Ithaca, NY, 1938–40

Constituted in the R.A. on 1 October 1933, assigned to the 29th F.A. Brig. (GHQR), and allotted to the First Corps Area. Organized by 1934 with O.R. personnel as an RAI unit with HQ at Hartford, CT. Withdrawn from the First Corps Area on 1 January 1938 and allotted to the Second Corps Area. Organized on 4 January 1938 with O.R. personnel as an RAI unit with HQ at Ithaca, NY. Conducted summer training at Pine Camp, NY, with the 5th F.A. Redesignated 50th F.A. Bn. on 1 October 1940, assigned to the 5th Div., and activated, less Reserve personnel, at Fort Sheridan, IL.

Events: 293, 296, 302, 316, 328

Commanders, 50th Field Artillery Regiment

Unknown	ao December 1934–1 January 1938	*Inactive*	1 January 1938–4 January 1938
Capt. James C. Avery**	4 January 1938–30 September 1940		

**RAI commanders: O.R. officers.

51st Field Artillery Regiment (155-mm H) (18th Field Artillery Brigade) **Regular Army Inactive**

HQ—*Not organized,* 1933–34; Tulsa, OK, 1934–40

Constituted in the R.A. on 1 October 1933, assigned to the 18th F.A. Brig. (VIII Corps), and allotted to the Eighth Corps Area. Organized on 22 October 1934 with O.R. personnel as an RAI unit with HQ at Tulsa, OK. Conducted summer training at Fort Sill, OK. Designated mobilization station was Fort Sill, OK. Redesignated 51st F.A. Bn. on 1 October 1940, assigned to the 6th Div., and activated, less Reserve personnel, at Fort Sill.

Events: 293, 296, 303, 316, 328

Commanders, 51st Field Artillery Regiment

Capt. Floyd D. Mobray**	22 October 1934–ao February 1938	Unknown	ao February 1938–1 October 1940

**RAI commanders: O.R. officers.

52d Field Artillery Regiment (155-mm H) (45th Field Artillery Brigade) **Regular Army Inactive**

HQ—*Not organized,* 1933–34; Fort Sill, OK, 1934–36; *Inactive,* 1936–39; Chicago, IL, 1939–41

Constituted in the R.A. on 1 October 1933, assigned to the 45th F.A. Brig. (GHQR), and allotted to the Eighth Corps Area. Organized 22 October 1934 with O.R. personnel as an RAI unit with HQ at Fort Sill, OK. Conducted summer training at Fort Sill, 1934–35. Conducted CMTC training at Fort Sam Houston in 1935 as an alternate form of summer training. Designated mobilization station was Fort Sill, OK, 1933–36. Organized on 22 October 1934 with O.R. personnel as an RAI unit with HQ at Chicago, IL. Withdrawn from the Eighth Corps Area on 5 June 1936 and allotted to the Sixth Corps Area. Reorganized on 7 June 1939 with O.R. personnel as an RAI unit with HQ at Chicago, IL. Redesignated 52d F.A. Bn. on 26 August 1941 and assigned to the 24th Div.

Commanders, 52d Field Artillery Regiment

2d Lt. William D. Bowen**	22 October 1934–ao November 1934	Lt. Col. Casey Hayes*	ao August 1935–5 June 1936
Unknown	ao November 1934–ao August 1935	*Inactive*	5 June 1936–7 June 1939
Maj. Charles H. Leihy**	7 June 1939–26 August 1941		

*RAI commanders: R.A. officers.

**RAI commanders: O.R. officers.

53d Field Artillery Regiment (155-mm H) (45th Field Artillery Brigade) **Regular Army Inactive**

HQ—*Not organized,* 1933–34; San Antonio, TX, 1933–41

Constituted in the R.A. on 1 October 1933, assigned to the 45th F.A. Brig. (GHQR), and allotted to the Eighth Corps Area. Organized on 7 July 1934 with O.R. personnel as an RAI unit with HQ at San Antonio, TX. Typically conducted Inactive Training Period meetings at the San Antonio Vocational and Technical School and, at times, at the Smith-Young Tower in San Antonio. Conducted summer training at Camp Bullis, TX, or Fort D.A. Russell, TX, 1934–40. Conducted CMTC training at Fort Sam Houston in 1935 as an alternate form of summer training. Designated mobilization station was Fort Sill, OK, 1933–41. Location 7 December 1941—San Antonio, TX.

Events: 293, 296, 303, 316, 328

Commanders, 53d Field Artillery Regiment

Capt. John E. Caldwell**	7 July 1934–28 January 1935	Unknown	28 January 1935–7 December 1941.

**RAI commanders: O.R. officers.

54th Field Artillery Regiment (155-mm H) (46th Field Artillery Brigade) **Regular Army Inactive**

HQ—*Not organized,* 1933–36; Los Angeles, CA, 1936–41

Constituted in the R.A. on 1 October 1933, assigned to the 46th F.A. Brig. (GHQR), and allotted to the Ninth Corps Area. Organized on 27 February 1936 with O.R. personnel as an RAI unit with HQ at Los Angeles, CA. Conducted summer training at Del Monte, CA. Redesignated 54th F.A. Bn. on 13 January 1941, and assigned to the 3d Armd. Div.

Commanders, 54th Field Artillery Regiment

Capt. Carl R. Jack**	27 February 1936–May 1937	Maj. Hylan B. Tebbetts**	May 1937–14 January 1938
Unknown	14 January 1938–13 January 1941		

**RAI commanders: O.R. officers.

55th Field Artillery Regiment (155-mm H) (46th Field Artillery Brigade) **Regular Army Inactive**

HQ—*Not organized,* 1933–36; Los Angeles, CA, 1936–41

Constituted in the R.A. on 1 October 1933, assigned to the 46th F.A. Brig. (GHQR), and allotted to the Ninth Corps Area. Organized on 13 January 1936 with O.R. personnel as an RAI unit with HQ at Los Angeles, CA. Location 7 December 1941—Los Angeles, CA.

Commanders, 55th Field Artillery Regiment

Unknown	13 January 1936–7 December 1941

57th Field Artillery Regiment (155-mm G) (26th Field Artillery Brigade) **Regular Army Inactive**

HQ—*Not organized,* 1933–41

Constituted in the R.A. on 1 October 1933, assigned to the 26th F.A. Brig. (GHQR), and allotted to the Third Corps Area. Allotted to the geographical area of the state of Virginia in December 1937, but the unit was never organized. Redesignated 57th F.A. Bn. on 13 January 1941.

58th Field Artillery Regiment (155-mm G) (26th Field Artillery Brigade) **Regular Army Inactive**

HQ—*Not organized,* 1933–41

Constituted in the R.A. on 1 October 1933, assigned to the 26th F.A. Brig. (GHQR), and allotted to the Third Corps Area. Allotted to the geographical area of the state of Virginia in December 1937, but the unit was never organized. Redesignated 58th F.A. Bn., and assigned to the 5th Armd. Div. on 28 August 1941.

63d Field Artillery Regiment (155-mm G) (27th Field Artillery Brigade) **Regular Army Inactive**

HQ—*Not organized,* 1933–41

Constituted in the R.A. on 1 October 1933, assigned to the 27th F.A. Brig. (GHQR), and allotted to the Fourth Corps Area. Location 7 December 1941—*Not organized.*

66th Field Artillery Regiment (75-mm G-P) (23d Field Artillery Brigade) **Regular Army Inactive**

HQ—*Not organized,* 1933–36; New York City, NY, 1936–40; *Inactive,* 1940–41; Pine Camp, NY, 1941

Constituted in the R.A. on 1 October 1933, assigned to the 23d F.A. Brig. (GHQR), and allotted to the Second Corps Area. Organized by 1936 with O.R. personnel as an RAI unit with HQ at New York City. Conducted monthly meetings at the offices of the Building Trades Employer Association at 2 Park Avenue in New York City, NY. Inactivated by June 1940 at New York City by relief of Reserve personnel. Activated on 15 April 1941 at Pine Camp, NY, and assigned to the 4th Armd. Div. Location 7 December 1941—Pine Camp, NY.

Commanders, 66th Field Artillery Regiment

Unknown	ao December 1936–June 1940	*Inactive*	June 1940–15 April 1941

67th Field Artillery Regiment (75-mm G-P) (24th Field Artillery Brigade) **Regular Army Inactive**

HQ—Milwaukee, WI, 1933–41

Constituted in the R.A. on 1 October 1933, assigned to the 24th F.A. Brig. (GHQR), and allotted to the Sixth Corps Area. Organized about October 1933 with O.R. personnel as an RAI unit with HQ at Milwaukee, WI. Reorganized from portee to truck-drawn on 13 March 1935. Conducted summer training at Camp McCoy, WI. Designated mobilization station was Fort Sill, OK. Assigned to the 3d Armd. Div. on 13 January 1941. Activated on 15 April 1941, less Reserve personnel, at Camp Beauregard, LA. Transferred on 11 June 1941 to Camp Polk, LA. Location 7 December 1941—Camp Polk, LA.

Commanders, 67th Field Artillery Regiment

Unknown	October 1933–15 April 1941

68th Field Artillery Regiment (75-mm G-P) (24th Field Artillery Brigade) **Regular Army Inactive**

HQ—La Crosse. WI. 1933–34; *Inactive,* 1934–40; Fort Knox, KY, 1940–41

Constituted in the R.A. on 1 October 1933, assigned to the 24th F.A. Brig. (GHQR), and allotted to the Sixth Corps Area. Organized about October 1933 with O.R. personnel as an RAI unit with HQ at La Crosse, WI. The 1st Bn., less Btry C, activated on 1 December 1934 at Fort Knox, KY. Remainder of the regiment concurrently withdrawn from allotment to the Sixth Corps Area and allotted to the Fifth Corps Area. Relieved from the 24th F.A. Brig. on 13 March 1935 and assigned to the 7th Cav. Brig. (Mecz). Concurrently reorganized from 75-mm Gun, Portee (G-P) to 105-mm Howitzer (H) (Mtzd). Regiment redesignated 68th F.A. Regt. (Mecz) and activated on 1 March 1940, less 2d Bn., at Fort Knox utilizing personnel and equipment from the 1st Bn. Redesignated 68th F.A. Regt. (Armd.) and assigned to the 1st Armd. Div. on 15 July 1940. Location 7 December 1941—Fort Knox, KY.

Events: 185, 213, 214, 220, 230, 253, 269, 277, 280, 295, 296, 302, 328, 330

Commanders, 68th Field Artillery Regiment

Unknown	October 1933–1 December 1934	Col. Marshall Magruder	1 March 1940–June 1940
Inactive	1 December 1934–1 March 1940	Col. John B. Wogan	June 1940–25 August 1941
	1st Battalion (active 1934–40)		
Lt. Col. Alvan C. Sandeford	1 December 1934–8 May 1937	Maj. Basil H. Perry	8 May 1937–28 September 1937
Lt. Col. Marshall Magruder	28 September 1937–1 March 1940		

69th Field Artillery Regiment (75-mm G-P) (24th Field Artillery Brigade) **Regular Army Inactive**

HQ—Detroit, MI, 1933–41

Constituted in the R.A. on 1 October 1933, assigned to the 24th F.A. Brig. (GHQR), and allotted to the Sixth Corps Area. Organized about October 1933 with O.R. personnel as an RAI unit with HQ at Detroit, MI. Reorganized from portee to truck drawn on 13 March 1935. Conducted summer training at Camp McCoy, WI. Conducted CMTC training at Camp McCoy as an alternate form of summer training. Location 7 December 1941—Detroit, MI.

Status: Disbanded 29 November 1949.

Commanders, 69th Field Artillery Regiment

Unknown	October 1933–ao June 1939	Maj. Jack Drew**	ao June 1939–ao July 1939
Unknown	ao July 1939–7 December 1941		

**RAI commanders: O.R. officers.

70th Field Artillery Regiment (75-mm G-P) (25th Field Artillery Brigade) **Regular Army Inactive**

HQ— *Not organized,* 1933–37; Davenport, IA, 1937–41

Constituted in the R.A. on 1 October 1933, assigned to the 25th F.A. Brig. (GHQR), and allotted to the Seventh Corps Area. Organized by March 1937 with O.R. personnel as an RAI unit with HQ at Davenport, IA. Typically conducted Inactive Training Period meetings at the Post Office building in Davenport. Conducted summer training at Fort Riley, KS, or Fort Snelling, MN. Conducted CMTC training at Fort Snelling, MN, as an alternate form of summer training. Location 7 December 1941—Davenport, IA.

Commanders, 70th Field Artillery Regiment

Unknown	ao March 1937–ao June 1939	Lt. Col. Egbert D. Brown	ao June 1939–ao September 1939
Unknown	ao September 1939–7 December 1941		

72d Field Artillery Regiment (75-mm TD) (23d Field Artillery Brigade) **Regular Army Inactive**

HQ—*Not organized,* 1933–37; Englewood, NJ, 1937–39; *Inactive,* 1939–41; Fort Bragg, NC, 1941

Constituted in the R.A. on 1 October 1933, assigned to the 23d F.A. Brig. (GHQR), and allotted to the Second Corps Area. Organized on 23 December 1937 with O.R. personnel as an RAI unit with HQ at Englewood, NJ. Inactivated by January 1939 at Englewood by relief of Reserve personnel. Designated mobilization station was Fort Bragg, NC. Activated on 1 June 1941 at Fort Bragg, NC, and assigned to the First Army. Concurrently, attached to the Fort Bragg Provisional Field Artillery Brigade. Location 7 December 1941—Fort Bragg, NC.

Events: 330

Commanders, 72d Field Artillery Regiment

1st Lt. Charles L. Rings	23 December 1937–31 December 1937	Unknown	ao January 1938–January 1939
Capt. Walter H. Stubenrauch	31 December 1937–ao January 1938	*Inactive*	January 1939–1 June 1941
Col. Stafford LeR. Irwin	1 June 1941–March 1942		

73d Field Artillery Regiment (75-mm TD) (23d Field Artillery Brigade) **Regular Army Inactive**

HQ—*Not organized,* 1933–34; Newark, NJ, 1934–37; *Inactive,* 1937–41

Demobilized on 28 December 1918 at Camp Jackson, SC, as an element of the 22d F.A. Brig. (Corps). Reconstituted in the R.A. on 1 October 1933, assigned to the 23d F.A. Brig. (GHQR), and allotted to the Second Corps Area. Organized in 1934 with O.R. personnel as an RAI unit with HQ at Newark, NJ. Inactivated by March 1937 at Newark by relief of Reserve personnel. Redesignated 73d F.A. Bn. on 13 January 1941.

Commanders, 73d Field Artillery Regiment

Col. Marshall G. Randol	12 October 1918–28 December 1918	Unknown	ao December 1934–ao March 1937
Demobilized/Inactive	28 December 1918–ao December 1934	*Inactive*	ao March 1937–13 January 1941

75th Field Artillery Regiment (75-mm TD) (24th Field Artillery Brigade) **Regular Army Inactive**

HQ—*Not organized,* 1933–34; Chicago, IL, 1934–37; Decatur, IL, 1937–41

Demobilized on 11 December 1918 at Camp Sheridan, AL, as an element of the 23d F.A. Brig. (Corps). Reconstituted in the R.A. on 1 October 1933, assigned to the 24th F.A. Brig. (GHQR), and allotted to the Sixth Corps Area. Organized by December 1934 with O.R. personnel as an RAI unit with HQ at Chicago, IL. Attached to the 1st Provisional Field Artillery Brigade on 8 January 1935. Reorganized from tractor-drawn to truck-drawn on 13 March 1935. Relocated on 7 April 1937 to Decatur, IL. Conducted summer training at Camp McCoy, WI. Redesignated as the 75th F.A. Bn. on 13 January 1941.

75th Field Artillery Regiment

Col. Dawson Olmstead	5 October 1918–26 December 1918	Unknown	ao December 1934–2 May 1937
Demobilized/Inactive	26 December 1918–ao December 1934	Maj. Victor A. Elmblad**	3 May 1937–ao December 1939
Unknown	ao December 1939–13 January 1941		

**RAI commanders: O.R. officers.

76th Field Artillery Regiment (75-mm G-H) (3d Division)

HQ—Camp Pike, AR, 1919–21; Camp Lewis, WA, 1921–22; Fort D.A. Russell, WY, 1922–40; Presidio of Monterey, CA, 1940–41

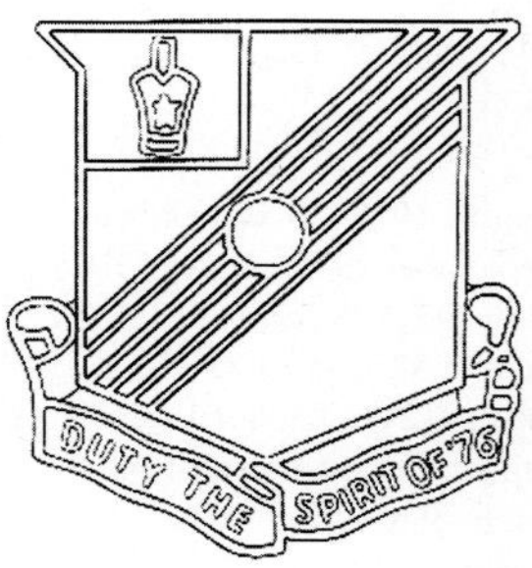

Arrived at the port of New York on 23 August 1919 on the U.S.S. *Madawaska* as an element of the 3d Div. Transferred to Camp Merritt, NJ, on 23 August 1919 and to Camp Pike, AR, on 29 August 1919. Transferred on 21 September 1921 to Camp Lewis, WA. Regiment, less 2d Bn., transferred on 28 June 1922 to Fort D.A. Russell, WY (later redesignated Fort Francis E. Warren). The 2d Bn. transferred on 21 August 1922 to the Presidio of Monterey, CA. Btry B awarded the Knox Trophy for 1937. Assigned Reserve officers conducted summer training with the 2d Bn. at Fort Francis E. Warren. Relieved from 3d Div. on 16 October 1939 and assigned to the GHQR. Transferred on 17 May 1940 to Presidio of Monterey, CA. Assigned to the 7th Div. on 1 July 1940. Concurrently, the 3d Bn. constituted and activated at Camp Ord, CA. Reorganized and redesignated as the 76th F.A. Bn. on 22 January 1941.

Organization Day: 6 June. Chosen to commemorate the regiment's original organization on 6 June 1917 at Fort Ethan Allen, VT.

Status: Assigned to the USARS as the 76th F.A.

Events: 57, 79, 112, 114, 130, 134, 141, 144, 152, 166, 212, 231, 232, 238, 273, 289, 314, 326

Commanders, 76th Field Artillery Regiment

Col. William C. Rivers	1 November 1917–13 October 1918	Lt. Col. Alden F. Brewster	22 January 1923–19 March 1924
Lt. Col. Jonathan W. Anderson	13 October 1918–26 October 1918	Col. Joseph S. Herron	19 March 1925–7 July 1926
Lt. Col. William Rodgers	26 October 1918–15 November 1918	Lt. Col. William K. Moore	7 July 1926–20 August 1927
Col. E. St. John Greble	15 November 1918–April 1919	Maj. Orlando Ward	20 August 1927–1 September 1927
Col. Charles M. Bundel	April 1919–15 July 1919	Lt. Col. William H. Peek	1 September 1927–16 December 1927
Lt. Col. William Rodgers	16 July 1919–31 August 1919	Col. Fred E. Buchan	16 December 1927–13 January 1930
Lt. Col. John J. Waterman	1 September 1919–30 June 1920	Col. Alden F. Brewster	13 January 1930–2 May 1932
Maj. James A. Force	30 June 1920–19 October 1920	Col. Clifford R. Norton	30 May 1932–11 June 1935
Maj. Albert R. Gardner	19 October 1920–22 December 1920	Lt. Col. John R. Starkey	11 June 1935–21 October 1935
Maj. Robert M. Milem	22 December 1920–1 February 921	Col. Alden F. Brewster	21 October 1935–17 September 1936
Maj. John J. Waterman	1 February 1921–14 March 1921	Col. Harvey D. Higley	17 September 1936–24 December 1936
Maj. Robert M. Milem	14 March 1921–15 September 1921	Col. John E. Mort	25 December 1936–9 July 1939
Col. Otho W.B. Farr	22 September 1921–22 January 1923	Lt. Col. Hamilton Templeton	9 July 1939–May 1940
	Col. John E. Sloan	May 1940–22 January 1941	

77th Field Artillery Regiment (75-mm G-H) (4th Division)

HQ—Camp Dodge, IA, 1919–20; Camp Lewis, WA, 1920–21; *Inactive,* 1921–27; Des Moines, IA, 1927–30; Fort Bragg, NC, 1930–35; Fort D.A. Russell, TX, 1935–41

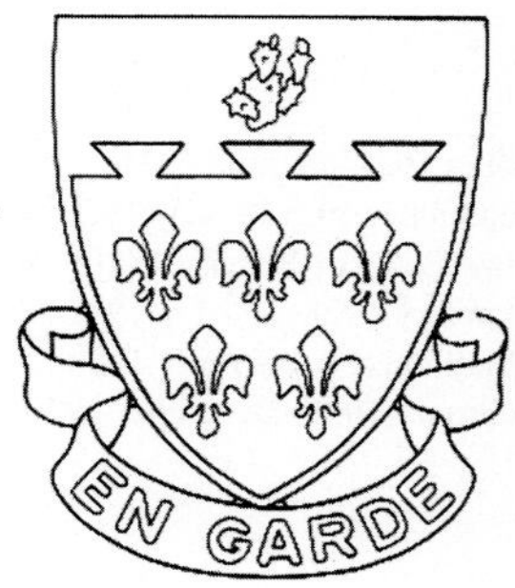

Arrived at the port of New York on 29 July 1919 on the U.S.S. *Tiger* as an element of the 4th Div. Transferred to Camp Merritt, NJ, on 29 July 1919 and to Camp Dodge, IA, on 4 August 1919. Transferred on 24 August 1920 to Camp Lewis, WA. Inactivated on 21 September 1921 at Camp Lewis. The 76th F.A. Regt. designated as the A.A. Relieved from the 4th Div. on 24 March 1923, assigned to the 7th Div., and allotted to the Seventh Corps Area. Concurrently, the 76th F.A. relieved as the A.A. and the 1st Bn., 9th F.A. designated as the A.A. Organized by May 1927 with O.R. personnel as an RAI unit at Des Moines, IA. Conducted summer training at Fort Riley, KS, 1927–29. Withdrawn from allotment to the Seventh Corps Area on 1 January 1930 and allotted to the Fourth Corps Area. Concurrently relieved from the 7th Div. and assigned to the 4th Div. Organized on 11 January 1930 with O.R. personnel as an RAI unit at Fort Bragg, NC. Armament changed on 1 October 1933 from 75-mm Gun (G) to 155-mm H (Mtzd). The 1st Bn. activated on 1 January 1935 at Fort Sill, OK. Regimental HQ and 2d Bn. activated on 1 September 1935, less Reserve personnel, at Fort D.A. Russell,

TX. Reserve officers assigned to the unit conducted summer training at Fort D.A. Russell, TX, or with the 1st Bn. at Fort Sill, 1935–40. Relieved from the 4th Div. on 16 October 1939 and assigned to the 18th F.A. Brig. (VIII Corps). Location 7 December 1941—Fort D.A. Russell, TX.

Status: Assigned to the USARS as the 77th F.A.; 1st Bn. active at Fort Sill, OK, as an element of the 75th F.A. Brig.

Events: 242, 258, 282, 288, 295, 296, 300, 317, 328

Commanders, 77th Field Artillery Regiment

Col. Guy H. Preston	1 November 1917–1 May 1918	Col. Otho W.B. Farr	25 August 1920–20 September 1921
Maj. Frederick E. Snyder	1 May 1918–8 May 1918	*Inactive*	20 September 1921–ao May 1927
Lt. Col. Archibald F. Commisky	8 May 1918–25 August 1918	Unknown	ao May 1927–28 June 1932
Col. Creed F. Cox	25 August 1918–25 September 1918	Maj. William K. McClure Jr.**	28 June 1932–ao July 1932
Col. Archibald F. Commisky	25 September 1918–6 January 1919	Unknown	ao July 1932–1 October 1935
Lt. Col. Kenneth P. Lord	6 January 1919–16 March 1919	Col. Robert H. Lewis	1 October 1935–1 March 1940
Col. Archibald F. Commisky	16 March 1919–14 February 1920	Lt. Col. Bertram Frankenberger	1 March 1940–June 1941
Maj. Leland Wadsworth Jr.	14 February 1920–27 April 1920	Lt. Col. Louis A. Craig	June 1941–3 August 1941
Lt. Col. Alpha Brumage	6 May 1920–25 August 1920	Col. Francis P. Armstrong	3 August 1941–ao January 1942

**RAI commanders: O.R. officers.

78th Field Artillery Regiment (75-mm G-H) (6th Division)

HQ—Camp Grant, IL, 1919–21; *Inactive,* 1921–26; Chicago, IL, 1926–40

Arrived at the port of New York on 19 June 1919 on the U.S.S. *Kaiserin Augusta Victoria* as an element of the 6th Div. Transferred to Camp Mills, NY, on 20 June 1919 and to Camp Grant, IL, on 26 June 1919. Inactivated on 7 September 1921 at Camp Grant and allotted to the Sixth Corps Area. The 15th F.A. Regt. designated as the A.A. The 15th F.A. relieved as the A.A. in 1925 and the 1st Bn., 14th F.A. designated as the A.A. Organized on 8 May 1926 with O.R. personnel as an RAI unit with HQ at Chicago, IL. Affiliated on 15 April 1929 with the University of Chicago ROTC. Reorganized from horse drawn to truck drawn on 13 March 1935. Typically conducted Inactive Training Period meetings at the Army and Navy Club, Post Office Building, or the Pure Oil Building in Chicago. Conducted summer training camps most years at Camp McCoy, WI. Conducted summer training at Camp Williams, WI, with the 120th F.A. in 1928. Relieved from the 6th Div. on 2 October 1939. Redesignated 78th F.A. Bn. on 15 July 1940, assigned to the 2d Armd. Div. and activated, less Reserve personnel, at Fort Benning, GA.

Organization Day: 1 June. Chosen to commemorate the regiment's original organization on 1 June 1917 at Fort Riley, KS.

Status: Assigned to the USARS as the 78th F.A.

Events: 162, 310, 328, 330

Commanders, 78th Field Artillery Regiment

Col. Tyree R. Rivers	18 November 1917–June 1918	Col. Lucien G. Berry	13 May 1921–19 June 1921
Col. Lucien G. Berry	15 June 1919–12 September 1920	*Inactive*	8 September 1921–8 May 1926
Lt. Col. Louis T. Boiseau	12 September 1920–4 December 1920	Maj. Lester L. Falk **	8 May 1926–14 January 1928
Maj. William S. Wood	4 December 1920–13 May 1921	Maj. Ralph A. Kimble**	15 January 1928–15 May 1928
Col. Henry B. Farrar	1 July 1921–7 September 1921	Col. Henry L. Newbold*	15 May 1928–5 February 1929
Maj. William S. Wood	19 June 1921–1 July 1921	Maj. Thomas J.J. Christian*	5 February 1929–December 1929
		Maj. Hiram A. Miller Jr.**	December 1929–14 July 1940

*RAI commanders: R.A. officers, who were concurrently the PMS&T at the University of Chicago.
**RAI commanders: O.R. officers.

79th Field Artillery Regiment (155-mm G) (14th Field Artillery Brigade) **Regular Army Inactive**

HQ—Camp Funston, KS, 1919–21; Camp George G. Meade, MD, 1921; *Inactive,* 1921–27; Third Corps Area at large, 1927–30; Sioux City, IA, 1930–41; Fort Bragg, NC, 1941

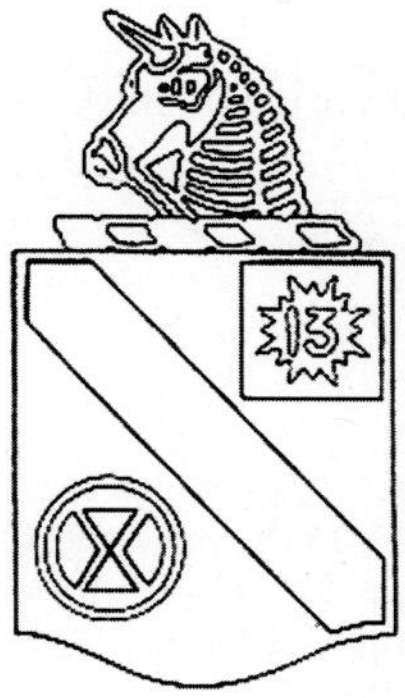

Arrived at the port of New York on 20 June 1919 on the U.S.S. *Imperator* as an element of the 7th Div. Transferred to Camp Mills, NY, on 23 June 1919 and to Camp Funston, KS, on 27 June 1919. Transferred on 8 January 1921 to Camp George G. Meade, MD. Inactivated on 14 September 1921 at Camp George G. Meade and personnel transferred to the 6th F.A. Regt. Concurrently, the 6th F.A. designated as the A.A. Allotted to the Fifth Corps Area on 24 March 1923 and assigned to the 14th F.A. Brig. (VII Corps). Concurrently the 6th F.A. relieved as A.A. and the 5th F.A. Regt. designated as the A.A. Organized on 25 October 1927 with O.R. personnel as an RAI unit in the Third Corps Area. Withdrawn from allotment to the Fifth Corps Area on 1 January 1930 and allotted to the Seventh Corps Area. Concurrently relieved from the 14th F.A. Brig. and assigned to the 7th Div. Additionally, armament changed from 155-mm G (Mtzd) to 75-mm G-H. Organized on 11 January 1930 with O.R. personnel as an RAI unit with HQ at Sioux City, IA. Affiliated on 28 April 1930 with Iowa State College ROTC. Conducted summer training camps at Fort Riley, KS, or Camp Ripley, MN. Relieved from the 7th Div. on 16 October 1939. Withdrawn from the Seventh Corps Area on 4 June 1940 and allotted to the Fourth Corps Area. Armament changed on 1 June 1940 from 75-mm G to 240-mm H. Concurrently, the 1st Bn. was activated at Fort Bragg, NC. Remainder of the regiment activated on 1 June 1941 at Fort Bragg, assigned to the First Army, and attached to the Fort Bragg Provisional Field Artillery Brigade. Location 7 December 1941—Fort Bragg, NC.

Status: Assigned to the USARS as the 79th F.A.; 1st Bn. active at Fort Sill, OK, as a training battalion.

Events: 330

Commanders, 79th Field Artillery Regiment

Col. Charles D. Rhodes	1 November 1917–4 April 1918	Maj. Ballard Lyerly	17 May 1921–August 1921
Col. Edgar A. Sirmyer	4 April 1918–27 August 1918	Maj. Clifford H. Tuteur	August 1921–14 September 1921
Col. Copley Enos	21 September 1918–12 May 1919	*Inactive*	14 September 1921–24 October 1927
Col. Edgar A. Sirmyer	20 June 1919–September 1920	Unknown	25 October 1927–5 September 1928
Maj. Joseph B. Treat	September 1920–6 December 1920	Maj. John L. Milburn**	6 September 1928–1 January 1930
Maj. Vincent P. Erwin	6 December 1920–10 January 1921	Unknown	11 January 1930–31 May 1941
Maj. Nelson E. Margetta	10 January 1921–17 May 1921	Col. Charles M. Busbee	1 June 1941–9 December 1941

**RAI commanders: O.R. officers.

80th Field Artillery Regiment (155-mm H) (15th Field Artillery Brigade) **Regular Army Inactive**

HQ—Camp Funston, KS, 1919–20; Camp George G. Meade, MD, 1920–21; *Inactive,* 1921–27; Fort Bragg, NC, 1927–30; Ames, IA, 1930–39; Fort Lewis, WA, 1939–40; Fort Des Moines, IA, 1940

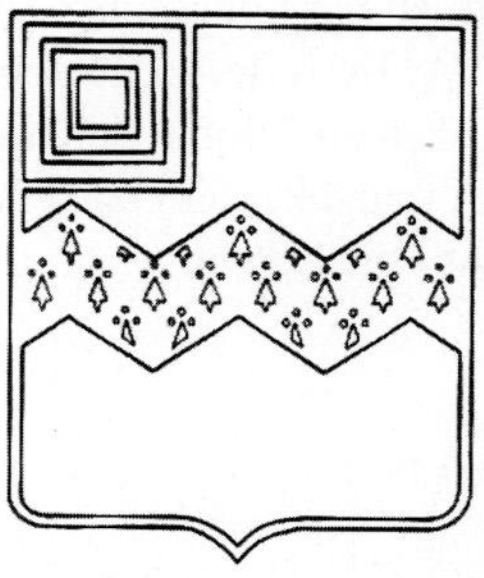

Arrived at the port of New York on 20 June 1919 on the U.S.S. *Imperator* as an element of the 7th Div. Transferred to Camp Mills, NY, on 21 June 1919 and to Camp Funston, KS, on 27 June 1919. Transferred 8 January 1921 to Camp George G. Meade, MD. Inactivated 10 September 1921 at Camp George G. Meade. The 7th F.A. Regt. was designated as the A.A. Relieved from the 7th Div. on 24 March 1923, allotted to the Fourth Corps Area, and assigned to the 15th F.A. Brig. (II Corps). Concurrently the 7th F.A. relieved as the A.A. and the 17th F.A. Regt. designated as the A.A. Organized by August 1927 with O.R. personnel as an RAI unit with HQ at Fort Bragg, NC. Withdrawn from allotment to the Fourth Corps Area on 1 January 1930 and allotted to the Seventh Corps Area. Concurrently relieved from the 15th F.A. Brig. and assigned to the 7th Div. Organized on 11 January 1930 with O.R. personnel as an RAI unit with HQ at Ames, IA. Typically conducted Inactive Training Period meetings at the Iowa State College ROTC armory or the Memorial Building in Ames. Conducted summer training camps at

Camp McCoy, WI; Fort Riley, KS; or Camp Ripley, MN. The 3d Bn. activated on 1 October 1933 at Fort Des Moines, IA, with personnel and equipment from the inactivated 2d Bn., 17th F.A. Regiment activated on 12 October 1939, less Reserve personnel, at Fort Lewis, WA. Relieved from the 7th Div. on 16 October 1939 and assigned to the 6th Div. Concurrently, the 3d Bn. disbanded. Transferred on 31 May 1940 to Fort Des Moines. Reorganized and redesignated 80th F.A. Bn. on 1 October 1940 at Fort Des Moines.

Organization Day: 1 November. Chosen to commemorate the regiment's original organization on 1 November 1917 at Fort Oglethorpe, GA.

Status: Assigned to the USARS as the 80th F.A.; 2d Bn. active at Fort Sill, OK, as a training battalion.

Events: 184, 233, 256, 269, 274, 293, 296, 303, 316, 328

Commanders, 80th Field Artillery Regiment

Col. Robert J. Fleming	16 December 1917–13 June 1918	*Inactive*	11 September 1921–16 June 1927
Col. Frederick T. Arnold	July 1918–5 November 1918	Col. Robert H. Peck*	17 June 1927–15 December 1927
Col. Frederick W. Stopford	5 November 1918–January 1919	Unknown	16 December 1927–15 August 1929
Maj. Frank Bloom	16 March 1920–5 November 1920	Maj. Lee F. Banks**	16 August 1929–11 January 1930
Lt. Col. Robert F. Woods	5 November 1920–10 February 1921	Unknown	11 January 1930–11 October 1939
Maj. Vincent A. Erwin	10 February 1921–30 March 1921	Lt. Col. David E. Cain	12 October 1939–12 November 1939
Col. Wright Smith	31 March 1921–10 September 1921	Maj. Lawrence H. Bixby	12 November 1939–1 October 1940

*RAI commanders: R.A. officers.
**RAI commanders: O.R. officers.

3d Battalion (active 1934–39)

Maj. William J. Jones	1 October 1934–1 June 1935	Maj. Lloyd S. Partridge	10 August 1937–7 September 1937
Maj. Everette G. Williams	25 June 1935–29 January 1936	Maj. Thomas R. Miller	7 September 1937–14 September 1937
Maj. William E. Corkill	29 January 1936–3 March 1936	Lt. Col. John S. Wood	14 September 1937–1 July 1939
Maj. Benjamin B. Lattimore	3 March 1936–18 July 1936	Maj. Alfred M. Goldman	1 July 1939–19 July 1939
Lt. Col. John H. Wallace	18 July 1936–9 August 1937	Maj. Lawrence H. Bixby	19 July 1939–October 1939
Lt. Col. Richard C. Burleson	October 1939–12 October 1939		

81st Field Artillery Regiment (155-mm G) (15th Field Artillery Brigade) **Regular Army Inactive**

HQ—Camp Knox, KY, 1919–22; Camp Bragg, NC, 1922; *Inactive,* 1922–27; Fort Bragg, NC, 1927–30; *Inactive,* 1930–36; Lynchburg, VA, 1936–39; *Inactive,* 1939–40; Fort Lewis, WA, 1940

Arrived at the port of New York on 18 January 1919 on the U.S.S. *President Grant* as an element of the 8th Div. Transferred to Camp Mills, NY, on 18 January 1919 and to Camp Knox, KY, on 25 January 1919. Transferred on 5 January 1922 to Camp Bragg, NC. Inactivated on 7 January 1922 at Camp Bragg. The 10th F.A. Regt. designated as the A.A. Relieved from the 8th Div. on 24 March 1923, allotted to the Fourth Corps Area, and assigned to the 15th F.A. Brig. (II Corps). Concurrently the 10th F.A. relieved as the A.A. and the 17th F.A. Regt. designated as the A.A. Organized by August 1927 with O.R. personnel as an RAI unit with HQ at Fort Bragg, NC. Withdrawn from allotment to the Fourth Corps Area on 1 January 1930 and allotted to the Third Corps Area. Concurrently relieved from the 15th F.A. Brig. and assigned to the 8th Div. Additionally, armament changed from 155-mm G (Mtzd) to 75-mm gun, horse drawn (G-H). Organized on 14 December 1936 with O.R. personnel as an RAI unit with HQ at Lynchburg, VA. Designated mobilization station was Fort Bragg. Inactivated by April 1939 at Lynchburg, VA, by relief of Reserve personnel. Relieved from the 8th Div. on 16 October 1939. Withdrawn from the Third Corps Area on 7 June 1940 and allotted to the Ninth Corps Area. Concurrently, the 1st Bn. activated at Fort Lewis, WA. Btry A transferred in late June 1940 to Anchorage, AK. Reorganized and redesignated 81st F.A. Bn. on 16 December 1940 at Fort Lewis.

Commanders, 81st Field Artillery Regiment

Col. William W. Littebrant	3 November 1917–12 July 1918	Col. Henry B. Farrar	24 October 1921–7 September 1922
Col. James N. Munro	12 July 1918–30 July 1918	*Inactive*	8 September 1922–17 June 1927
Col. William W. Littebrant	30 July 1918–1 October 1918	Col. James J. Hornbrook*	17 June 1927–15 December 1927
Unknown	1 October 1918–ao January 1920	Unknown	16 December 1927–14 December 1936
Maj. Alfred L. P. Sands	ao January 1920–2 September 1921	Maj. Hallock P. Long**	14 December 1936–9 April 1937
Unknown	10 April 1937–15 December 1940		

*RAI commanders: R.A. officers.
**RAI commanders: O.R. officers.

82d Field Artillery Regiment (75-mm G-H) (1st Cavalry Division)

HQ—Fort Bliss, TX, 1919–21; *Demobilized,* 1921–30; *Inactive,* 1930–34; Fort Bliss, TX, 1934–41

Stationed at Fort Bliss, TX, as of June 1919. Regiment less 1st and 2d Bns. demobilized on 9 September 1921 at Fort Bliss. Concurrently, the 1st Bn. redesignated 82d F.A. Bn. (Horse) and assigned to 1st Cav. Div.; the 2d Bn. inactivated, redesignated 84th F.A. Bn. (Horse), allotted to the Eighth Corps Area, and assigned to the 2d Cav. Div. Btry B awarded the Knox Trophy for 1927. Regiment reconstituted on 17 March 1930, and all elements concurrently assigned to the 1st Cav. Div. The 82d F.A. Bn. concurrently redesignated 1st Bn. and 84th F.A. Bn. redesignated 2d Bn. Regiment activated on 1 December 1934 at Fort Bliss. Regiment concurrently motorized. Assigned Reserve officers conducted summer training with the regiment at Fort Bliss. Reorganized and redesignated 82d F.A. Bn. on 3 January 1941.

Organization Day: 1 December. Chosen to commemorate the regiment's reactivation on 1 December 1934 at Fort Bliss, TX. Adopted on 7 August 1935 at Fort Bliss.

Status: Assigned to the USARS as the 82d F.A.; 1st, 2d, and 3d Bns. active at Fort Hood, TX, as elements of the 1st Cav. Div.

Events: 3, 30, 65, 83, 97, 127, 146, 206, 242, 250, 258, 259, 282, 284, 295, 296, 300, 315, 328

Commanders, 82d Field Artillery Regiment

Col. Francis C. Marshall	1 November 1917–6 February 1918	Lt. Col. Albert S. Fuger	28 August 1921–8 September 1921
Col. Harold P. Howard	8 April 1918–16 October 1918	*Inactive*	9 September 1921–30 November 1934
Unknown	17 October 1918–20 February 1919	Col. George P. Tyner	1 December 1934–7 May 1936
Col. Thomas E. Merrill	21 February 1919–1 April 1919	Col. Phillip W. Booker	7 May 1936–3 September 1936
Col. Henry L. Newbold	1 April 1919–6 October 1920	Col. William H. Dodds Jr.	3 September 1936–22 October 1938
Maj. Albert S. Fuger	6 October 1920–21 November 1920	Lt. Col. Walter F. Winton	23 October 1938–19 July 1939
Col. Ernest D. Scott	21 November 1920–28 August 1921	Col. Ernest J. Dawley	19 July 1939–October 1940
	Col. Joseph P. Swing	October 1940–3 January 1941	

1st Battalion (active 1930-1934)

Maj. John P. Lucas	17 March 1930–15 July 1931	Lt. Col. Leonard C. Sparks	18 September 1931–1 July 1934
Capt. Walter Hitzfeldt	15 July 1931–18 September 1931	Col. George P. Tyner	1 July 1934–30 November 1934

83d Field Artillery Regiment (75-mm G-TD) (8th Division) **Regular Army Inactive**

HQ—Camp Knox, KY, 1919–21; Camp Bragg, NC, 1921–22; *Inactive,* 1922–27 and 1930–40; Fort Benning, GA, 1940–41

Arrived at the port of New York on 18 January 1919 on the U.S.S. *President Grant* as an element of the 8th Div. Transferred on 18 January 1919 to Camp Mills, NY. Transferred on 23 January 1919 to Camp Knox, KY. Relieved on 5 September 1919 from the 8th Div. The 1st Bn. conducted a 623-mile march from Camp Knox to Camp Benning, GA, 15 September–30 October 1920. Assigned to the Infantry School as a school support and demonstration unit. Regiment less 1st Bn. transferred on 5 December 1921 to Camp Bragg, NC. Regiment less 1st Bn. inactivated on 7 January 1922 at Camp Bragg. Demobilized on 28 February 1927 and 1st Bn. concurrently reorganized as 83d F.A. Bn. The 83d F.A. Bn. reorganized on 1 May 1927 from tractor drawn to horse drawn. Btry A awarded the Knox Trophy for 1929. The 83d F.A. Bn. assigned on 1 January 1930 to the 8th Div. Regiment reconstituted on 17 March 1930 and assigned to the 8th Div. The 83d F.A. Bn. concurrently redesignated 1st Bn. at Fort Benning. The 2d Bn. activated on 1 October 1933 at Fort Bragg with personnel and equipment from the inactivated 2d Bn., 16th F.A. Regiment concurrently relieved from the 8th Div. and assigned to the 4th Div. Regiment motorized on 26 October 1934. Btry B awarded the Knox Trophy for 1938. Relieved from the 4th Div. on 16 October 1939 and assigned to the GHQR. Assigned Reserve officers conducted summer training with the 2d Bn. at Fort Bragg. Regiment activated on 1 June 1940, less 1st and 2d Bns. already active, at Fort Benning and assigned to the 4th Div. Relieved from the 4th Div. on 20 July 1940 and assigned to the 8th Div. Reorganized and redesignated 83d F.A. Bn. on 9 January 1941 at Fort Benning.

Events: 54, 121, 143, 209, 228, 293, 296, 330

Commanders, 83d Field Artillery Regiment

Col. Francis J. Koester	1 November 1917–10 October 1918	Lt. Col. William A. Pendleton	13 January 1921–15 September 1921
Col. William E. Larned	30 October 1918–11 April 1919	Maj. Joseph W. Rumbough	15 September 1921–7 January 1922
Col. Henry B. Farrar	12 April 1919–26 January 1920	*Inactive*	8 January 1922–31 May 1940
Lt. Col. Julian I. Chamberlain	26 January 1920–7 August 1920	Col. Julian F. Barnes	1 June 1940–30 October 1940
Col. Manus McCloskey	7 August 1920–13 January 1921	Unknown	31 October 1940–9 January 1941

1st Battalion (active 1922–40)

Maj. Joseph W. Rumbough	7 January 1922–1 August 1923	Maj. Frank K. Ross	31 July 1929–26 June 1931
Maj. Edward B. King	1 August 1923–31 December 1923	Maj. Clyde A. Selleck	27 June 1931–9 June 1934
Maj. John B. Anderson	31 December 1923–1 July 1924	Capt. Robert G. Mangum	10 June 1934–7 July 1934
Capt Roland P. Shugg	1 July 1924–15 August 1924	Lt. Col. Leroy P. Collins	7 July 1934–3 July 1936
Maj. Lloyd E. Jones	15 August 1924–23 October 1924	Maj. Frederic H. Timmerman	3 July 1936–10 July 1936
Maj. Edward B. King	23 October 1924–17 August 1925	Maj. Jay W. McKelvie	10 July 1936–31 July 1936
Maj. Robert S. Donaldson	17 August 1925–30 June 1927	Lt. Col. Orlando Ward	31 July 1936–29 January 1938
Maj. Lloyd E. Jones	1 July 1927–31 July 1929	Maj. Jay W. McKelvie	29 January 1938–10 June 1938
	Lt. Col. Charles G. Helmick	10 June 1938–1 June 1940	

2d Battalion (active 1933–40)

Lt. Col. Leslie J. McNair	30 September 1933–1 April 1935	Maj. Peyton Winlock	12 August 1936–18 August 1936
Maj. Cuyler L. Clark	1 April 1935–13 May 1935	Col. George P. Allin	18 August 1936–15 September 1936
Maj. Breckinridge A. Day	13 May 1935–20 July 1935	Col. John T. Kennedy	15 September 1936–1 July 1938
Capt. Peyton Winlock	20 July 1935–25 August 1935	Capt. Hamilton F. Seawright	20 July 1938–1 September 1938
Lt. Col. Edwin P. Parker	25 August 1935–12 August 1936	Lt. Col. Edwin A. Zundel	1 September 1938–October 1940

84th Field Artillery Regiment (75-mm G-H) (3d Cavalry Division) — Regular Army Inactive

HQ—Fort Collins, CO, 1930–34; *Inactive,* 1934–36; Seventh Corps Area 1936–40

Demobilized on 13 December 1918 at Camp Sheridan, AL, as an element of the 21st F.A. Brig. (Corps). Reconstituted in the R.A. on 17 March 1930, assigned to the 3d Cav. Div., and allotted to the Eighth Corps Area. Concurrently organized as an RAI unit at the Colorado Agricultural College, Fort Collins, CO, as an RAI unit with personnel from the ROTC Detachment and O.R. officers commissioned from the program. Affiliation with the Colorado Agricultural College ROTC program terminated on 29 October 1934 and unit inactivated by relief of Reserve personnel. Concurrently, Fort Bliss, TX, designated as HQ location on reorganization, but the unit was never organized at that location. Withdrawn from the Eighth Corps Area on 5 June 1936 and allotted to the Seventh Corps Area. The 1st Bn. activated on 1 July 1936 at Fort Riley, KS, with personnel and equipment from the inactivated 1st Bn., 14th F.A. Remainder of the regiment organized on 13 October 1936 with O.R. personnel as an RAI unit in the Seventh Corps Area. Conducted summer training at Fort Riley, KS. The 1st Bn. inactivated on 30 September 1939 at Fort Riley. Regiment relieved from the 3d Cav. Div. on 16 October 1939. Remainder of the regiment inactivated on 11 December 1939 by relief of Reserve personnel. Reserve personnel concurrently transferred to the 3d F.A. Regiment redesignated 84th F.A. Bn. on 1 October 1940, activated at Fort Bragg, NC, and assigned to the 9th Div.

Organization Day: 3 October. Chosen to commemorate the 1st Bn.'s reactivation on 1 December 1934 at Fort Bliss, TX. Adopted on 7 August 1935 at Fort Bliss.

Commanders, 84th Field Artillery Regiment

Maj. Yarrow D. Veasley*	17 March 1930–29 October 1934	Capt. James W. Holzinger**	13 October 1936–August 1939
Inactive	29 October 1934–13 October 1936	Capt. Robert B. Handley**	August 1939–11 December 1939
Inactive	11 December 1939–1 October 1940		

*RAI commanders: R.A. officers who were concurrently PMS&T at the Colorado Agricultural College.
**RAI commanders: O.R. officers.

1st Battalion (active 1936–39)

Maj. William H. Colbern	1 July 1936–2 July 1936	Maj. Winfred C. Green	2 July 1936–25 August 1938
Lt. Col. Ralph Hospital	25 August 1938–30 September 1939		

85th Field Artillery Regiment (75-mm G-H) (GHQR) — Regular Army Inactive

HQ—*Inactive,* 1923–26; Auburn, AL, 1926–36; Dayton, OH, 1936–41

Demobilized on 13 December 1918 at Camp Sheridan, AL, as an element of the 21st F.A. Brig. (Corps). Reconstituted in the R.A. on 24 March 1923, assigned to the 4th Div., and allotted to the Fourth Corps Area. The 1st Bn., 2d F.A. Regt. designated as the A.A. Organized on 26 July 1926 with O.R. personnel as an RAI unit with HQ at Auburn, AL. Affiliated with Alabama Polytechnic Institute ROTC on 25 February 1927 and organized as an RAI unit with personnel from the ROTC Detachment and O.R. officers commissioned from the program. Relieved from the 4th Div. on 31 October 1929 and assigned to the GHQR. Inactivated on 1 May 1936 at Auburn, AL, by relief of Reserve personnel. Withdrawn from the Fourth Corps Area on 5 June 1936 and allotted to the Fifth Corps Area. Organized by June 1936 with O.R. personnel as an RAI unit with HQ at Dayton, OH. Conducted summer training at Fort Bragg, NC, 1930–35, and at Fort Knox, KY, 1937–39. Designated mobilization station was Fort Bragg. Assigned to the 26th F.A. Brig. (III Corps) on 7 November 1940. Location 7 December 1941—Dayton, OH.

Status: Disbanded on 11 November 1944.

Commanders, 85th Field Artillery Regiment

1st Lt. Robert C. Robertson**	26 July 1926–31 May 1927	Maj. Gustave H. Frankes**	22 July 1931–1 November 1934
Capt. James F. Mabry**	1 June 1927–July 1927	Maj. Victor Lee**	1 November 1934–1 May 1936
Maj. Frank J. Malone**	July 1927–11 April 1929	Capt. Clarence E. Caldwell Jr.**	June 1936–3 November 1936
Maj. Harry M. Daugherty**	11 April 1929–21 July 1931	Maj. Harold R. Miller **	3 November 1936–ao April 1940
Unknown	ao April 1940–7 December 1941		
Col. Hu B. Myers†	1 June 1927–15 December 1927	Maj. John T. Kennedy†	15 December 1927–1 October 1929

**RAI commanders: O.R. officers.
†R.A. officers designated as commander for mobilization purposes only.

86th Field Artillery Regiment (75-mm G-H) (8th Division) — Regular Army Inactive

HQ—*Not organized,* 1927–28; Gainesville, FL, 1928–33; *Inactive,* 1933–34; Los Angeles, CA, 1934–41

Constituted in the R.A. on 15 August 1927, assigned to the 8th Div., and allotted to Fourth Corps Area. Fort Benning, GA, designated on 15 December 1927 as HQ location on organization, but the unit was never organized at that location. Organized on 26 January 1928 with O.R. personnel as an RAI unit with HQ at Gainesville, FL. Relieved from the 8th Div. on 1 January 1930 and assigned to the 15th F.A. Brig. (II Corps). Armament concurrently changed from 75-mm G-H to 155-mm G (Mtzd). Affiliated with the University of Florida ROTC on 21 April 1930 and reorganized as an RAI unit with personnel from the ROTC Detachment and O.R. commissioned from the program. Withdrawn from the Fourth Corps Area as a component of the 15th F.A. Brig. on 1 October 1933, allotted to the Ninth Corps Area, and assigned with the 15th F.A. Brig. to the IX Corps. Organized on 1 November 1934 with O.R. personnel as an RAI unit with HQ at Los Angeles, CA. Conducted summer training at Fort Bragg, NC. Regiment relieved from the 15th F.A. Brig. on 12 April 1941 and redesignated 86th F.A. Bn. (PS). Concurrently inactivated and allotted to the Philippine Department.

Status: Inactive as the 86th F.A. Bn. (PS).

Commands, 86th Field Artillery Regiment

Maj. William F. McMillan**	26 January 1928–11 January 1930	Maj. Howard H. Smith**	22 July 1930–5 April 1932
Inactive	11 January 1930–21 April 1930	Maj. John W. Garner**	5 April 1932–5 March 1935
Maj. James V. Blackwell**	21 April 1930–22 July 1930	Lt. Col. William F. McMillan**	5 March 1935–11 January 1939
Unknown	12 January 1939–12 April 1941		
Maj. James A. Van Fleet†	12 June 1929–19 August 1932	Maj. Daniel A. Connor†	19 August 1932–1 October 1933

**RAI commanders: O.R. officers.
†R.A. officers designated as commander for mobilization purposes only.

87th Field Artillery Regiment (75-mm G Mtzd) (Panama Canal Division) **Regular Army Inactive**

HQ—*Not organized,* 1930–40

Constituted in the R.A. on 28 May 1930, assigned to the Panama Canal Division, and allotted to the Panama Canal Department. Relieved from the Panama Canal Division on 1 October 1938. The 1st Bn. activated on 15 July 1940 at Fort William D. Davis, CZ, and assigned to the Panama Mobile Force. Reorganized and redesignated 87th F.A. Bn. on 16 December 1940 utilizing personnel and equipment from the 1st Bn.

Events: 292, 308, 333

88th Field Artillery Regiment (155-mm G) (19th Field Artillery Brigade) **Regular Army Inactive**

HQ—*Not organized,* 1933–34; Andover, MA, 1934–36; *Inactive,* 1936–37; Springfield, MA, 1937–41; Fort Stotsenberg, PI, 1941

Constituted in the R.A. on 1 October 1933, assigned to the 19th F.A. Brig. (I Corps), and allotted to the First Corps Area. Organized by December 1934 with O.R. personnel as an RAI unit with HQ at Andover, MA. Inactivated by 1936 at Andover, MA, by relief of Reserve personnel. Reorganized by May 1937 with O.R. personnel as an RAI unit with HQ at Springfield, MA. Typically conducted Inactive Training Period meetings at the Post Office Building in Boston, MA. Withdrawn from the First Corps Area on 12 April 1941 and allotted to the Philippine Department. Concurrently reorganized as 75-mm G, designated Philippine Scouts (PS), and assigned to the Philippine Division. Partially activated on 19 April 1941 at Fort Stotsenberg, PI. Location 7 December 1941—Fort Stotsenberg, PI.

Status: *Inactive* as HHB, 14th Inf. Div. Arty. (PS).

Commanders, 88th Field Artillery Regiment

Unknown	ao December 1934–December 1936	*Inactive*	December 1936–May 1937
Unknown	May 1937–7 December 1941		

89th Field Artillery Regiment (155-mm G) (21st Field Artillery Brigade) **Regular Army Inactive**

HQ—*Not organized,* 1933–36; Norfolk, VA, 1936; *Inactive,* 1936–38; Utica, NY, 1938–41

Constituted in the R.A. on 1 October 1933, assigned to the 21st F.A. Brig. (III Corps), and allotted to the Third Corps Area. Organized by March 1936 with O.R. personnel as an RAI unit with HQ at Norfolk, VA. Withdrawn from the Third Corps Area on 5 June 1936 and allotted to the Second Corps Area. Reserve personnel at Norfolk relieved in December 1936. Organized on 12 July 1938 with O.R. personnel as an RAI unit with HQ at Utica, NY. Frequently conducted Inactive Training Period meetings at the Everson Building in Syracuse, NY. Conducted summer training at Pine Camp, NY, with the 5th F.A. Designated mobilization training station was Fort Bragg, NC. Redesignated 89th F.A. Bn. on 26 August 1941 and assigned to the 25th Div.

Commanders, 89th Field Artillery Regiment

1st Lt. Hunter H. Walkup**	ao March 1936–December 1936	Capt. James P. Furlong**	13 July 1938–21 December 1939
Inactive	December 1936–13 July 1938	Lt. Col. Charles W. Jacobsen**	21 December 1939–14 July 1941
Capt. Charles E. Tegtmeyer**	16 July 1941–26 August 1941		

**RAI commanders: O.R. officers.

90th Field Artillery Regiment (155-mm G) (22d Field Artillery Brigade) **Regular Army Inactive**

HQ—*Not organized,* 1933–34; Chicago, IL, 1934–41

Constituted in the R.A. on 1 October 1933, assigned to the 22d F.A. Brig. (VI Corps), and allotted to the Sixth Corps Area. Organized by June 1934 with O.R. personnel as an RAI unit with HQ at Chicago, IL. Conducted summer training at Camp McCoy, WI. Provided a number of officers to units of the 58th F.A. Brig. at Camp Custer, MI, for the 1936 Second Army Maneuver. Designated mobilization station was Fort Sill, OK. Redesignated 90th F.A. Bn. and assigned to the 25th Div. on 26 August 1941.

Events: 214

Commanders, 90th Field Artillery Regiment

Lt. Col. James N. Hamilton**	ao June 1934–25 August 1941

**RAI commanders: O.R. officers.

91st Field Artillery Regiment (155-mm G) (17th Field Artillery Brigade) **Regular Army Inactive**

HQ—*Not organized,* 1933–34; Kansas City, MO, 1934–41

Constituted in the R.A. on 1 October 1933, assigned to the 17th F.A. Brig. (VII Corps), and allotted to the Seventh Corps Area. Organized about January 1934 with O.R. personnel as an RAI unit with HQ at Kansas City, MO. Conducted summer training at Fort Riley, KS,or Camp Ripley, MN. Conducted summer training with units of the 60th F.A. Brig. at Fort Riley in 1936. Designated mobilization station was Fort Sill, OK. Location 7 December 1941—Kansas City, MO.

Commanders, 91st Field Artillery Regiment

Unknown	ao January 1934–ao June 1938	Capt. Wayne M. Kirby**	ao June 1938–ao September 1938
Unknown	ao September 1938–7 December 1941		

**RAI commanders: O.R. officers.

92d Field Artillery Regiment (155-mm G) (18th Field Artillery Brigade) **Regular Army Inactive**

HQ—*Not organized,* 1933–34; Tulsa, OK, 1934–40; *Inactive,* 1940–41; Tulsa, OK, 1941

Constituted in the R.A. on 1 October 1933, assigned to the 18th F.A. Brig. (VIII Corps), and allotted to the Eighth Corps Area. Organized by 1934 with O.R. personnel as an RAI unit with HQ at Tulsa, OK. Conducted summer training at Fort Sill, OK. Inactivated by January 1940 at Tulsa, OK, by relief of Reserve personnel. Reorganized by February 1941 with O.R. personnel as an RAI unit with HQ at Tulsa. Location 7 December 1941—Tulsa, OK.

Commanders, 92d Field Artillery Regiment

Unknown	ao December 1934–ao February 1941	Capt. James P. Furlong**	ao February 1941–7 December 1941

94th Field Artillery Regiment (240mm H) (C) (27th Field Artillery Brigade) **Regular Army Inactive**

HQ—*Not organized,* 1933–35; Chattanooga, TN, 1935–41

Constituted in the R.A. on 1 October 1933, assigned to the 27th F.A. Brig. (GHQR), and allotted to the Fourth Corps Area. Organized on 31 July 1935 with O.R. personnel as an RAI unit with HQ at Chattanooga, TN. Conducted summer training at Fort Bragg, NC. Designated mobilization station was Fort Bragg, NC. Location 7 December 1941—Chattanooga, TN.

Status: Assigned to the USARS as the 94th F.A.; 2d Bn. active at Idar-Oberstein, Germany, as an element of the 1st Armd. Div.

Commanders, 94th Field Artillery Regiment

2d Lt. Cecil C. Clements**	24 August 1935–6 September 1935	Capt. Frederick W. Yates**	29 February 1936–5 November 1936
Capt. Leroy E. Everette**	27 September 1935–19 October 1935	Capt. George Davidson Jr.**	15 November 1936–18 March 1939
Maj. Enos P. Scott**	19 October 1935–29 February 1936	Maj. Hunter V. Herndon**	19 March 1939–December 1941

**RAI commanders: O.R. officers.

99th Field Artillery Regiment (75-mm TD) (25th Field Artillery Brigade) **Regular Army Inactive**

HQ—Omaha, NE, 1933–40

Constituted in the R.A. on 1 October 1933, assigned to the 25th F.A. Brig. (GHQR), and allotted to the Seventh Corps Area. Organized about October 1933 with O.R. personnel as an RAI unit with HQ at Omaha, NE. Conducted summer training at Fort Riley, KS. Designated mobilization station was Fort Sill, OK. The 1st Bn. activated on 1 June 1940 at Fort Hoyle, MD, and 2d Bn. concurrently activated at Fort Lewis, WA. Regimental HQ activated on 31 July 1940, less Reserve personnel, at Fort Hoyle. Reorganized and redesignated 99th F.A. Bn. 75-mm (Pack) at Fort Hoyle on 16 December 1940.

Events: 307, 323, 330

Commanders, 99th Field Artillery Regiment

Unknown	ao October 1933–12 March 1938	Capt. William H. Foxwell**	25 November 1938–ao June 1939
Capt. Milton R. Scott**	12 March 1938–25 November 1938	Capt. Paul B. Britt**	ao July 1939–ao September 1939
Unknown	ao September 1939–16 December 1940		

**RAI commanders: O.R. officers.

100th Field Artillery Regiment (75-mm TD) (25th Field Artillery Brigade) **Regular Army Inactive**

HQ—*Not organized,* 1933–34; Wichita, KS, 1934–40; *Inactive,* 1940–41

Constituted in the R.A. on 1 October 1933, assigned to the 25th F.A. Brig. (GHQR), and allotted to the Seventh Corps Area. Organized by December 1934 with O.R. personnel as an RAI unit with HQ at Wichita, KS. Conducted summer training at Fort Riley, KS. Inactivated by December 1940 at Wichita by relief of Reserve personnel. Location 7 December 1941—*Inactive.*

Status: Disbanded 11 November 1944.

Commanders, 100th Field Artillery Regiment

Unknown	ao December 1934–23 July 1938	Capt. Earl L. Waldrip**	23 July 1938–ao January 1939
Unknown	ao January 1939–December 1940		

**RAI commanders: O.R. officers.

101st Field Artillery Regiment (75-mm G-H) (26th Division) **Massachusetts National Guard**

HQ—Boston, MA, 1921–41; Camp Edwards, MA, 1941

Arrived at the port of Boston on 8 April 1919 on the U.S.S. *Agamemnon* as the 101st F.A., an element of the 26th Div. Demobilized on 29 April 1919 at Camp Devens, MA. Reconstituted in the N.G. in 1921 and allotted to the state of Massachusetts. Reorganized on 30 September 1921 by redesignation of the 1st F.A., Massachusetts N.G. (organized on 2 May 1919 at Boston, MA, as the 101st F.A., Massachusetts Volunteer Militia; federally recognized on 12 November 1920 as the 1st F.A., Massachusetts N.G.) at Boston and assigned to the 26th Div. Converted from horse drawn to truck drawn on 1 July 1933. Btry B awarded the Knox Trophy in 1936. The regiment, or elements thereof, was called up to perform the following state duties: riot control duties during a textile strike in New Bedford, MA, in July 1928; flood relief duties in the Merrimac Valley after the hurricane of September 1938. Conducted annual summer training most years at Camp Devens, MA, and some years at the Underhill Artillery Range, Fort Ethan Allen, VT, or at the Massachusetts State Reservation at Falmouth, MA. Inducted into Federal service on 16 January 1941 in Boston as an element of the 26th Div., and moved to Camp Edwards, MA, where it arrived on 23 January 1941. Location 7 December 1941—Camp Edwards, MA.

Status: Assigned to the USARS as the 101st F.A.; 1st Bn. active at New Bedford, MA, and Btry E active at Rehoboth, NJ, as elements of the 42d Inf. Div.

Events: 190, 280, 301, 330

Commanders, 101st Field Artillery Regiment

Col. John H. Sherburne	8 August 1917–25 July 1918	Col. Robert E. Goodwin	26 October 1918–29 April 1919
Lt. Col. Robert E. Goodwin	25 July 1918–4 August 1918	*Demobilized/Inactive*	29 April 1919–19 April 1921
Col. Albert T. Bishop	4 August 1918–9 September 1918	Col. Erland F. Fish	20 April 1921–10 September 1926
Lt. Col. Robert E. Goodwin	2 September 1918–16 October 1918	Col. Daniel Needham	10 September 1926–16 December 1930
Col. Creed F. Cox	16 October 1918–26 October 1918	Col. Warren S. Keith	16 December 1930–15 December 1937
Col. Charles L. Furber	15 December 1937–12 December 1941		

102d Field Artillery Regiment (75-mm G-H) (26th Division) **Massachusetts National Guard**

HQ—Salem, MA, 1921–41; Camp Edwards, MA, 1941

Arrived at the port of Boston in April 1919 on the U.S.S. *Patricia* as the 102d F.A., an element of the 26th Div. Demobilized on 29 April 1919 at Camp Devens, MA. Reconstituted in the N.G. in 1921 and allotted to the state of Massachusetts. Reorganized on 30 September 1921 by redesignation of the 2d F.A., Massachusetts N.G. (organized and federally recognized on 20 April 1921 with HQ at Salem, MA) and assigned to the 26th Div. Btry C awarded the Knox Trophy in 1931. Converted from horse drawn to truck drawn on 1 July 1933. Called up to perform flood relief duties in the Merrimac River Valley in April 1936 and again after the hurricane of September 1938. Conducted annual summer training most years at Camp Devens, MA, and some years at the Underhill Artillery Range, Fort Ethan Allen, VT, or at the Massachusetts State Reservation at Falmouth, MA. Inducted into Federal service on 16 January 1941 at Salem as an element of the 26th Div., and moved to Camp Edwards, MA, where it arrived on 23 January 1941. Location 7 December 1941—Camp Edwards, MA.

Status: Assigned to the USARS as the 102d F.A.; 1st Bn. active at Quincy, MA, as an element of the 113th F.A. Brig.

Events: 190, 280, 301, 330

Commanders, 102d Field Artillery Regiment

Lt. Col. Thorndike D. Howe	22 August 1917–30 August 1917	*Demobilized/Inactive*	*11 April 1919–23 June 1921*
Col. Morris E. Locke	30 August 1917–13 August 1918	Col. Ernest R. Redmond	24 June 1921–28 June 1928
Col. John F. J. Herbert	13 August 1918–12 October 1918	Col. Roger W. Eckfeldt	29 June 1928–16 November 1934
Col. Jacob A. Mack	12 October 1918–10 April 1919	Col. William F. Howe	4 December 1934–15 November 1939
Col. Albert T. Harrington	16 November 1939–11 February 1942		

103d Field Artillery Regiment (75-mm G-H) (43d Division) **Rhode Island National Guard**

HQ—*Not organized,* 1921–30; Providence, RI, 1930–41; Camp Blanding, FL, 1941

Arrived at the port of Boston on 6 April 1919 on the S.S. *Mongolia* as the 103d F.A., an element of the 26th Div. Demobilized on 29 April 1919 at Camp Devens, MA. Reconstituted in the N.G. in 1921 and allotted to the state of Rhode Island. The 1st Bn. organized on 17 November 1921 and federally recognized with HQ at Providence, RI. Regimental HQ organized on 8 January 1930 at Providence, RI, and assigned to the 43d Div. Concurrently, 2d Bn. organized from the 1st Squadron (Sq.), 122d Cav. and other existing units. Converted from horse drawn to truck drawn on 1 June 1933. The regiment, or elements thereof, was called up to perform the following state duties: detachment to perform strike duty at Pawtuxet, RI, 20 February–14 October 1922; 1st Bn. to perform strike duty at Manville, RI, 31 August–3 September 1926; entire regiment for riot control in the textile workers strike at Saylesville and Bristol, RI, 10–14 September 1934; entire regiment for flood relief duties along the Pawtuxet River, 19–20 March 1936; entire regiment for flood relief duties along the Pawtuxet River at Norwood, RI, 24–26 July 1938; and entire regiment for hurricane relief duty at Providence, Westerly, and Newport, RI, 21–25 September 1938. Conducted annual summer training most years at Charleston, RI, 1921–27; Camp Devens, 1928–33; and the Underhill Artillery Range, Fort Ethan Allen, VT, 1934–38. Inducted into Federal service on 24 February 1941 at Providence as an element of the 43d Div., and moved to Camp Blanding, FL, where it arrived on 17 March 1941. Location 7 December 1941—Camp Blanding, FL.

Status: Assigned to the USARS as the 103d F.A.; 1st Bn. active at Providence, RI, as an element of the 103d F.A. Brig.

Events: 190, 280, 301, 316, 324, 328

Commanders, 103d Field Artillery Regiment

Lt. Col. Richard K. Hale	22 August 1917–September 1917	Col. John A. Twachtman	20 October 1918–29 April 1919
Col. Emery T. Smith	September 1917–17 June 1918	*Demobilized/Inactive*	29 April 1919–7 January 1930
Col. Pelham D. Glassford	17 June 1918–20 October 1918	Col. Harold R. Barker	8 January 1930–5 February 1937
Col. Francis W. Rollins	5 February 1937–19 February 1942		

104th Field Artillery Regiment (75-mm G-H) (27th Division) **New York National Guard**

HQ—New York City, NY, 1921–36; Jamaica, NY, 1936–40; Fort McClellan, AL, 1940–41

Arrived at the port of New York on 3 March 1919 on the U.S.S. *America* as the 104th F.A., an element of the 27th Div. Demobilized on 3 April 1919 at Camp Upton, NY. Reconstituted in the N.G. on 30 December 1920 and allotted to the state of New York. Reorganized on 1 June 1921 by redesignation of the 1st F.A., New York N.G. (organized and federally recognized on 10 January 1921 with HQ at New York City, NY) and assigned to the 27th Div. George Herman "Babe" Ruth enlisted as a private in May 1924. Converted from horse drawn to tractor drawn on 1 February 1933 and further reorganized to truck drawn on 1 June 1933. The 1st Bn. was called up to perform flood relief work near Binghamton, NY, 18–20 March 1936. Regimental HQ relocated on 5 April 1936 to Jamaica, NY. Conducted additional week-long winter training directed by the War Department at Camp Upton, NY, 26–31 December 1939. Conducted annual summer training most years at Camp Welsh, NY, 1921–22, and Pine Camp, NY, 1923–38. Inducted into Federal service on 15 October 1940 at Jamaica as an element of the 27th Div., and moved to Fort McClellan, AL, where it arrived 25 October 1940. Location 7 December 1941—Fort McClellan, AL.

Status: Assigned to the USARS as the 104th F.A.; no active elements.

Events: 61, 190, 280, 301, 316, 324, 328

Commanders, 104th Field Artillery Regiment

Col. Merritt H. Smith	1 October 1917–18 October 1918	Col. John T. Delaney	10 January 1921–19 June 1923
Lt. Col. John T. Delaney	18 October 1918–6 November 1918	Col. James E. Austin	19 June 1923–3 June 1926
Col. Charles C. Pulis	6 November 1918–3 April 1919	Col. Charles G. Blakeslee	3 June 1926–23 October 1936
Demobilized/Inactive	3 April 1919–9 January 1921	Col. Redmond F. Kernan Jr.	23 October 1936–1 September 1942

105th Field Artillery Regiment (75-mm G-H) (27th Division) **New York National Guard**

HQ—New York City, NY, 1920–40; Fort McClellan, AL, 1940–41

Arrived at the port of New York on 3 March 1919 on the U.S.S. *America* as the 105th F.A., an element of the 27th Div. Demobilized on 3 April 1919 at Camp Upton, NY. Reconstituted in the N.G. on 30 December 1920 and allotted to the state of New York. Reorganized on 1 June 1921 by redesignation of the 2d F.A., New York N.G. (organized and federally recognized on 17 December 1920 with HQ at New York City, NY) and assigned to the 27th Div. Converted from horse drawn to truck drawn on 31 December 1934. Conducted annual summer training most years at Camp Welsh, NY, 1921–22, and Pine Camp, NY, 1923–38. Inducted into Federal service on 15 October 1940 at New York City as an element of the 27th Div., and moved to Fort McClellan, AL, where it arrived on 25 October 1940. Location 7 December 1941—Fort McClellan, AL.

Status: Assigned to the Combat Arms Regimental System (CARS) as the 105th F.A.; no active elements.

Events: 61, 190, 280, 301, 316, 324, 328

Commanders, 105th Field Artillery Regiment

Col. George A. Wingate	October 1917–1 January 1918	Col. Frank H. Hines	11 January 1926–8 May 1929
Col. DeWitt C. Weld Jr.	1 January 1918–2 April 1919	Lt. Col. Clarence H. Higginson	8 May 1929–23 May 1929
Demobilized/Inactive	3 April 1919–9 January 1921	Col. John W. Kilbreth	23 May 1929–9 April 1930
Col. DeWitt C. Weld Jr.	9 January 1920–17 December 1920	Col. Clarence W. Higginson	9 April 1930–16 September 1940
Col. Robert W. Marshall	17 December 1920–2 October 1925	Col. James Andrews	16 September 1940–1 September 1942

106th Field Artillery Regiment (155-mm H) (II Corps) **New York National Guard**

HQ—*Not organized,* 1920–22; Buffalo, NY, 1922–40; Fort McClellan, AL, 1940–41

Arrived at the port of New York on 3 March 1919 on the U.S.S. *America* as the 106th F.A., an element of the 27th Div. Demobilized on 3 April 1919 at Camp Upton, NY. Reconstituted in the N.G. on 30 December 1920 and allotted to the state of New York. Partially reorganized on 1 June 1921 by redesignation of the active elements of the 65th F.A. New York N.G. as the 106th F.A. Assigned on 29 July 1921 to the II Corps. Reorganized on 11 October 1921 from a 155-mm G to a 155-mm H regiment. Regimental HQ reorganized and federally recognized on 22 May 1922 at Buffalo, NY. Further assigned to the 15th F.A. Brig. (II Corps) on 2 July 1923. Relieved from the 15th F.A. Brig. (II Corps) on 20 November 1929 and assigned to 27th Div. Conducted annual summer training most years at Camp Pine Camp, NY, 1921–38, and some years at Tobyhanna, PA. Inducted into Federal service on 15 October 1940 at Buffalo as an element of the 27th Div., and moved to Fort McClellan, AL, where it arrived on 25 October 1940. Location 7 December 1941—Fort McClellan, AL.

Events: 61, 190, 280, 301, 316, 328

Commanders, 106th Field Artillery Regiment

Col. John D. Howland	1 October 1917–6 August 1918	*Demobilized/Inactive*	9 April 1919–22 May 1922
Lt. Col. John T. Delaney	6 August 1918–1 September 1918	Col. William F. Schohl	22 May 1922–14 May 1928
Col. Emery T. Smith	1 September 1918–November 1918	Col. Douglas P. Walker	24 July 1928–10 June 1940
Maj. Lewis H. Eller	November 1918–27 February 1919	Col. Ronald C. Brock	1 August 1940–1 September 1942
Col. Karl D. Klemm	27 February 1919–8 April 1919		

107th Field Artillery Regiment (75-mm G-H) (28th Division) **Pennsylvania National Guard**

HQ—Pittsburgh, PA, 1919–41; Indiantown Gap, PA, 1941

Arrived at the port of New York on 8 May 1919 on the S.S. *Mongolia* as the 107th F.A., an element of the 28th Div. Demobilized on 20 May 1919 at Camp Dix, NJ. Reconstituted in the N.G. in 1921 and allotted to the state of Pennsylvania. Reorganized on 1 April 1921 by redesignation of the 1st F.A., Pennsylvania N.G. (organized on 16 October 1919 with HQ at Pittsburgh, PA) and assigned to the 28th Div. Federally recognized on 22 June 1921 with HQ at Pittsburgh. Converted from horse drawn to truck drawn on 1 January 1935. Called up to perform relief duties during the massive statewide flooding in the spring of 1936. Conducted annual summer training most years at Tobyhanna, PA, and some years at Indiantown Gap, PA. Inducted into Federal service on 17 February 1941 at Pittsburgh as an element of the 28th Div., and moved to Indiantown Gap where it arrived 26 February 1941. Location 7 December 1941—Indiantown Gap, PA.

Status: Assigned to the USARS as the 107th F.A.; 1st Bn. active at New Castle, PA, as an element of the 28th Inf. Div.

Events: 191, 203, 281, 301, 330

Commanders, 107th Field Artillery Regiment

Col. William S. McKee	11 October 1917–8 May 1918	*Demobilized/Inactive*	21 May 1919–22 June 1921
Lt. Col. Albert V. Crookston	8 May 1918–10 September 1918	Col. Churchill B. Mehard	22 June 1921–23 July 1923
Col. Richard C. Burleson	10 September 1918–26 March 1919	Col. Eric F. Wood	16 November 1923–19 December 1940
Lt. Col. Albert V. Crookston	26 March 1919–21 May 1919	Lt. Col. John Nuckel	20 December 1940–7 February 1942

108th Field Artillery Regiment (155-mm H) (III Corps) **Pennsylvania National Guard**

HQ—Philadelphia, PA, 1919–41; Indiantown Gap, PA, 1941

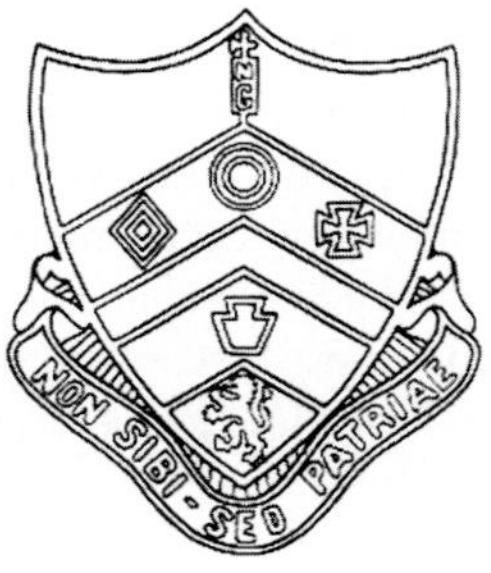

Arrived at the port of Philadelphia on 16 May 1919 on the U.S.S. *Peerless* as the 108th F.A., an element of the 28th Div. Demobilized on 24 May 1919 at Camp Dix, NJ. Reconstituted in the N.G. in 1921 and allotted to the state of Pennsylvania. Reorganized on 1 April 1921 by redesignation of active elements of the 2d F.A., Pennsylvania N.G. (organized on 16 October 1919 with HQ at Philadelphia, PA) as the 108th F.A. and assigned to the 82d F.A. Brig. (III Corps) (redesignated 190th F.A. Brig. on 2 July 1923 and allotted to the O.R.). Regimental HQ reorganized and federally recognized on 21 December 1922 at Philadelphia. Relieved from the 190th F.A. Brig. (III Corps) in December 1929 and assigned to 28th Div. Called up to perform relief duties during the massive statewide flooding in the spring of 1936. Conducted annual summer training most years at Tobyhanna, PA, and some years at Indiantown Gap, PA. Inducted into Federal service on 17 February 1941 at Philadelphia as an element of the 28th Div., and moved to Indiantown Gap where it arrived on 26 February 1941. Location 7 December 1941—Indiantown Gap, PA.

Events: 191, 203, 281, 301, 330

Commanders, 108th Field Artillery Regiment

Col. Hamilton D. Turner	11 October 1917–28 December 1917	Lt. Col. Horace Fuller	5 November 1918–13 November 1918
Maj. E. St. John Greble Jr.	28 December 1917–16 April 1918	Col. Francis Lecocq	13 November 1918–24 May 1919
Col. Hamilton D. Turner	16 April 1918–8 May 1918	*Demobilized/Inactive*	24 May 1919–21 December 1922
Col. E. St. John Greble Jr.	15 August 1917–5 November 1918	Col. William A. March	21 December 1922–6 December 1940
Col. Edward Hubbs	6 December 1940–7 February 1942		

109th Field Artillery Regiment (75-mm G-H) (28th Division) **Pennsylvania National Guard**

HQ—Wilkes-Barre, PA, 1920–41; Indiantown Gap, PA, 1941

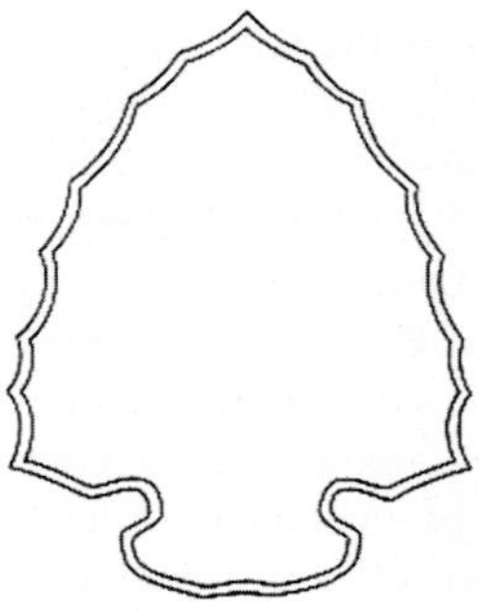

Arrived at the port of New York on 8 May 1919 on the S.S. *Mongolia* as the 109th F.A., an element of the 28th Div. Demobilized on 17 May 1919 at Camp Dix, NJ. Reconstituted in the N.G. in 1921 and allotted to the state of Pennsylvania. Reorganized on 1 April 1921 by redesignation of active elements of the 3d F.A., Pennsylvania N.G. (organized 1920–21 and federally recognized on 24 August 1920 with HQ at Wilkes-Barre, PA) as the 109th F.A. and assigned to the 28th Div. Regimental HQ reorganized and federally recognized on 29 June 1921 at Wilkes-Barre. Converted from horse drawn to truck drawn on 1 January 1935. Called up to perform relief duties during the massive statewide flooding in the spring of 1936. Conducted annual summer training most years at Tobyhanna, PA, and some years at Indiantown Gap, PA. Inducted into Federal service on 17 February 1941 at Wilkes-Barre as an element of the 28th Div., and moved to Indiantown Gap where it arrived on 26 February 1941. Location 7 December 1941—Indiantown Gap, PA.

Status: Assigned to the USARS as the 109th F.A.; 1st Bn. active at Wilkes-Barre, PA, as an element of the 28th Inf. Div.

Events: 191, 203, 281, 301, 330

Commanders, 109th Field Artillery Regiment

Col. Asher Miner	11 October 1917–4 October 1918	Col. E. St. John Greble Jr.	11 April 1919–19 May 1919
Lt. Col. William H. Zeirdt	4 October 1918–18 November 1918	*Demobilized/Inactive*	19 May 1919–21 June 1921
Lt. Col. Horace C. Fuller	18 November 1918–14 January 1919	Col. William S. McLean Jr.	29 June 1921–7 February 1927
Col. Charles M. Bundel	14 January 1919–11 April 1919	Col. Stephen Elliot	7 February 1927–1 July 1940
Col. Thomas H. Atherton	1 July 1940–January 1942		

110th Field Artillery Regiment (75-mm G-H) (29th Division) **District Of Columbia and Maryland National Guard**

HQ—*Not organized,* 1921–25; Baltimore, MD, 1925–30; Pikesville, MD, 1930–41; Fort George G. Meade, MD, 1941

Arrived at the port of Newport News on 21 May 1919 on the U.S.S. *Orizaba* as the 110th F.A., an element of the 29th Div. Demobilized on 4 June 1919 at Camp Dix, NJ. Reconstituted in the N.G. in 1921. Regiment less 2d Bn. allotted to the District of Columbia and the 2d Bn. allotted to the state of Maryland. Active elements of the regiment provided the escort to Marshal Ferdinand Foch on his visit to Baltimore, MD, in 1922. Allotted elements withdrawn from the District of Columbia on 7 July 1923 and entire regiment allotted to state of Maryland. Subordinate elements reorganized 1921–25. Regimental HQ reorganized and federally recognized on 31 March 1925 at Baltimore and assigned to the 29th Div. Regimental HQ relocated on 24 January 1930 to Pikesville, MD. Converted from horse drawn to truck drawn on 1 January 1935. Conducted annual summer training most years at Tobyhanna, PA, and some years at Mount Gretna, PA; Indiantown Gap, PA; or Camp Ritchie, MD. Inducted into Federal service on 3 February 1941 at Pikesville as an element of the 29th Div., and moved to Fort George G. Meade, MD, where it arrived on 20 February 1941. Location 7 December 1941—Fort George G. Meade, MD.

Status: Assigned to the USARS as the 110th F.A.; 2d Bn. active at Pikesville, MD, as an element of the 29th Inf. Div. (Light).

Events: 191, 281, 301, 330

Commanders, 110th Field Artillery Regiment

Col. Washington Bowie	27 November 1917–4 June 1919	Col. James C. McLanahan	31 March 1925–10 July 1931
Demobilized/Inactive	4 June 1919–31 March 1925	Col. Beverly Ober	10 July 1931–3 February 1941
Col. Henry C. Evans	3 February 1941–28 February 1942		

111th Field Artillery Regiment (75-mm G-H) (29th Division) **Virginia National Guard**

HQ—*Not organized*, 1921–23; Norfolk, VA, 1923–39; Hampton, VA, 1939–41; Fort George G. Meade, MD, 1941

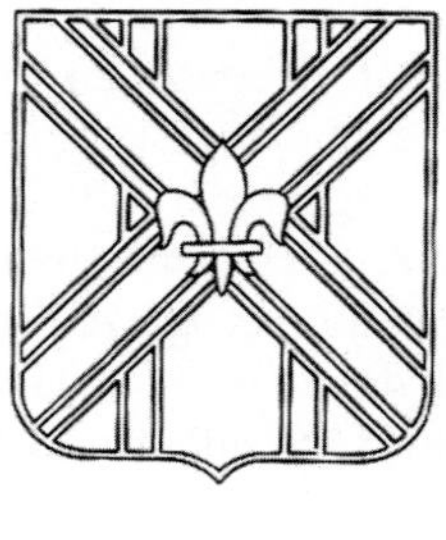

Arrived at the port of Newport News in May 1919 as the 111th F.A., an element of the 29th Div. Demobilized on 4 June 1919 at Camp Lee, VA. Reconstituted in the N.G. in 1921 and allotted to the state of Virginia. Subordinate elements reorganized 1920–23. Regimental HQ federally recognized on 26 May 1923 at Norfolk, VA, and assigned to the 29th Div. Converted from horse drawn to truck drawn on 20 November 1934. Regimental HQ relocated on 28 August 1939 to Hampton, VA. The regiment, or elements thereof, was called up to perform the following state duties: hurricane relief duties at Ocean View, VA, in August 1935; flood relief duties at Fredericksburg, VA, in April 1937. Conducted annual summer training most years at Tobyhanna, PA, and some years at Mount Gretna, PA; Indiantown Gap, PA; or Fort Bragg, NC. Inducted into Federal service on 3 February 1941 at Hampton as an element of the 29th Div., and moved to Fort George G. Meade, MD, where it arrived on 20 February 1941. Location 7 December 1941—Fort George G. Meade, MD.

Status: Assigned to the USARS as the 111th F.A.; 1st Bn. active at Norfolk, VA, and 2d Bn. active at Petersburg, VA, as elements of the 54th F.A. Brig. and Btry E active as an element of the 29th Inf. Div. (Light).

Events: 191, 281, 301, 330

Commanders, 111th Field Artillery Regiment

Col. Thomas M. Wortham	15 September 1917–1 October 1917	Lt. Col. Edward C. James	1 June 1918–25 June 1918
Maj. F. H. Couch	1 October 1917–3 January 1918	Col. William C. Jones	25 June 1918–2 June 1919
Col. Thomas M. Wortham	3 January 1918–10 January 1918	*Demobilized/Inactive*	2 June 1919–26 May 1923
Lt. Col. Elijah B. Martindale	10 January 1918–10 March 1918	Col. McChesney H. Jeffries	26 May 1923–1 October 1924
Col. Thomas M. Wortham	10 March 1918–1 June 1918	Col. William H. Sands	1 October 1924–8 August 1939
	Col. E. Slater Montague	9 August 1939–28 February 1942	

112th Field Artillery Regiment (75-mm G-H) (44th Division) **New Jersey National Guard**

HQ—*Not organized,* 1921–24; Camden, NJ, 1924–29; Trenton, NJ, 1929–41; Fort Bragg, NC, 1941

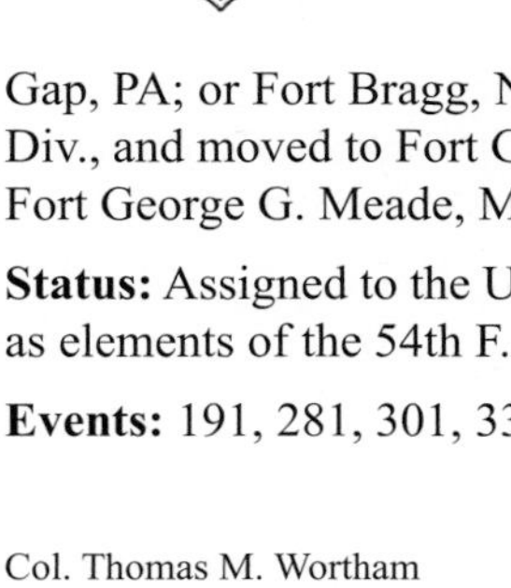

Arrived at the port of Newport News on 21 May 1919 on the U.S.S. *Orizaba* as the 112th F.A., an element of the 29th Div. Demobilized on 31 May 1919 at Camp George G. Meade, MD. Reconstituted in the N.G. in 1921 and allotted to the state of New Jersey. Subordinate elements reorganized 1920–24 as elements of the 1st F.A. Bn., New Jersey N.G. Expanded and redesignated 112th F.A. on 20 April 1922 and assigned to the 44th Div. Regimental HQ organized and federally recognized on 8 January 1924 at Camden, NJ. Regimental HQ relocated on 10 May 1929 to Trenton, NJ. Conducted annual summer training most years at Pine Camp, NY, and some years at Tobyhanna, PA; Camp Welsh, NY; or Indiantown Gap, PA. Relieved from the 44th Div. on 25 April 1940 and assigned to the 21st Cav. Div. Relieved from the 21st Cav. Div. on 1 October 1940 and assigned to the GHQR. Attached to the First Army on 30 December 1940. Inducted into Federal service on 27 January 1941 at Trenton and moved to Fort Bragg, NC, where it arrived on 8 February 1941. Attached to the Fort Bragg Provisional Field Artillery Brigade. Converted from horse drawn to truck drawn on 1 December 1941 making it the last horse-drawn field artillery regiment in the US Army. Location 7 December 1941—Fort Bragg, NC.

Status: Assigned to the USARS as the 112th F.A.; 3d Bn. active at Morristown, NJ, as an element of the 42d Inf. Div.

Events: 191, 281, 301, 330

Commanders, 112th Field Artillery Regiment

Col. Quincy A. Gillmore	17 July 1917–30 May 1919	Col. Edward C. Rose	18 March 1929–6 August 1938
Demobilized/Inactive	31 May 1919–8 January 1924	Col. Edward J. Towers	12 September 1938–31 January 1940
Col. Samuel G. Barnard	8 January 1924–19 February 1929	Col. Armand J. Salmon	1 February 1940–1 May 1943

113th Field Artillery Regiment (155-mm H) (IV Corps) — North Carolina National Guard

HQ—*Not organized,* 1921–24; Raleigh, NC, 1924–40; Fort Jackson, SC, 1940–41

Arrived at the port of Newport News on 18 March 1919 on the U.S.S. *Orizaba* as the 113th F.A., an element of the 30th Div. Demobilized 28 March 1919 at Camp Jackson, SC. Reconstituted in the N.G. in 1921 and allotted to the state of North Carolina. Subordinate elements reorganized 1921–24 as the 117th F.A. and assigned to the IV Corps. Active elements called up 2–18 December 1922 to prevent looting after the New Bern fire. Regimental HQ reorganized and federally recognized on 3 March 1924 at Raleigh, NC. Redesignated 113th F.A. on 12 January 1927. Relieved from the IV Corps on 18 December 1929 and assigned to the 30th Div. Several batteries called up 6–21 September 1934 to perform riot control during textile strikes in Gastonia and High Point, NC. Conducted annual summer training most years at Fort Bragg, NC. Inducted into Federal service on 16 September 1940 at Dunn, NC, as an element of the 30th Div. and moved to Fort Jackson, SC, where it arrived on 1 October 1940. Location 7 December 1941—Fort Jackson, SC.

Status: Assigned to the USARS as the 113th F.A.; 1st Bn. active at Charlotte, NC, as an element of the 30th Inf. Brig. (Sep.) and the 5th Bn. active at Louisburg, NC, as an element of the 113th F.A. Brig.

Events: 255, 300, 316, 330

Commanders, 113th Field Artillery Regiment

Col. Albert L. Cox	12 September 1917–31 December 1917	*Demobilized/Inactive*	29 March 1919–11 January 1927
Lt. Col. Jacob A. Mack	31 December 1917–26 March 1918	Col. William T. Joyner	12 January 1927–November 1932
Col. Albert L. Cox	26 March 1918–28 March 1919	Col. Godfrey Cheshire	2 December 1932–February 1941
Col. Albert T. Willis	February 1941–16 February 1942		

114th Field Artillery Regiment (155-mm H) (31st Division) — Mississippi National Guard

HQ—*Not organized,* 1932–33; Greeneville, MS, 1933–40; Camp Blanding, FL, 1940–41

Constituted in the N.G. on 15 November 1932, allotted to the state of Mississippi, and assigned to the 31st Div. Partially organized on 15 November 1932 by redesignation of the 1st Bn., 178th F.A. (organized and federally recognized on 20 May 1926 with HQ at Greenville, MS; assigned to the 189th F.A. Brig. (IX Corps) for mobilization assignment) as 1st Bn., 114th F.A. Regimental HQ organized and federally recognized on 20 May 1933 at Greenville. Concurrently, 2d Bn. organized and federally recognized with HQ at Columbus, MS. The 3d Bn. organized and federally recognized on 18 June 1933 with HQ at Biloxi, MS. Conducted annual summer training most years at Fort Bragg, NC, and some years at Fort Knox, KY, or Camp Shelby, MS. Inducted into Federal service on 25 November 1940 at Greenville and moved to Camp Blanding, FL, where it arrived on 21 December 1940. Location 7 December 1941—Camp Blanding, FL.

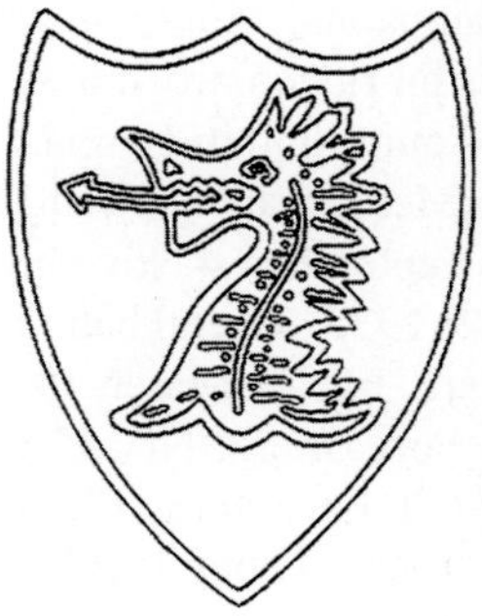

Status: Assigned to the USARS as the 114th F.A.; 1st Bn. active at Greenwood, MS, as an element of the 631st F.A. Brig.; 2d Bn. active at Starkville, MS, as an element of the 155th Armd. Brig. (Sep.).

Events: 56, 255, 300, 325, 328, 330

Commander, 114th Field Artillery Regiment

Col. Alexander G. Paxton	20 May 1933–22 February 1942

115th Field Artillery Regiment (75-mm G-H) (30th Division) **Tennessee and South Carolina National Guard**

HQ—*Not organized,* 1921–24; Memphis, TN, 1924–40; Fort Jackson, SC, 1940–41

Constituted in the N.G. in 1921, allotted to the states of Tennessee and South Carolina, and assigned to the 30th Div. Regimental HQ, HQ Battery, and 1st Bn. allotted to the state of Tennessee and the 2d Bn. allotted to the state of South Carolina. Organized on 2 April 1924, less 2d Bn., with HQ federally recognized at Memphis, TN. The 2d Bn. was organized on 25 April 1929 and federally recognized at Andrews, SC. Regiment less 2d Bn. converted from horse drawn to truck drawn on 1 July 1933; 2d Bn. converted from horse drawn to truck drawn on 10 August 1933. The 2d Bn. called up in 1934 to perform riot control during textile strikes in Spartanburg, Greenville, and Chester, SC. The 2d Bn. withdrawn from the South Carolina N.G. on 1 April 1938 and allotted to the state of Tennessee. Concurrently, the 2d Bn. was reorganized at Maryville, TN, by redesignation of the 2d Bn., 178th F.A. Conducted annual summer training most years at Camp Jackson, SC, and some years at Fort Bragg, NC. Inducted into Federal service on 16 September 1940 at Memphis and moved to Fort Jackson, SC, where it arrived on 26 September 1940. Location 7 December 1941—Fort Jackson, SC.

Status: Assigned to the USARS as the 115th F.A.; 1st Bn. active at Winchester, TN, 2d Bn. active at Henderson, TN, and 3d Bn. active at Memphis, all as elements of the 196th F.A. Brig.

Events: 255, 300, 316, 330

Commanders, 115th Field Artillery Regiment

Col. William L. Terry	2 April 1924–15 November 1940	Col. Ray C. Reeves	15 November 1940–16 February 1942

116th Field Artillery Regiment (75-mm G-H) (31st Division) **Florida National Guard**

HQ—*Not organized,* 1921–24; Tampa, FL, 1924–40; Camp Blanding, FL, 1940–41

Arrived at the port of New York in January 1919 on the U.S.S. *Manchuria* as the 116th F.A., an element of the 31st Div. Demobilized on 16 January 1919 at Camp Gordon, GA. Reconstituted on 14 December 1921 in the N.G. and allotted to the state of Florida. Reorganized 1921–24 and assigned to the 31st Div. Regimental HQ reorganized and federally recognized on 20 January 1924 at Tampa, FL. Converted from horse drawn to truck drawn on 16 July 1933. The regiment, or elements thereof, was called up to perform the following state duties: hurricane relief duties at Tampa and Moore Haven, FL, 16 September–7 November 1926; regiment less two batteries for riot control duties in connection with the protection of prisoners at the Hillsborough County Jail in Tampa, 31 May–6 June 1927; entire regiment for duties associated with the Mediterranean Fruit Fly quarantine in July 1928; 2d Bn. for hurricane relief duties at Palm Beach–Okeechobee, FL, 17 September–4 November 1928; entire regiment for riot control duties in connection with elections in Tampa in September 1935; several batteries for guard duties in connection with the visit of President Franklin D. Roosevelt to Winter Park, FL, 31 March 1936. Conducted annual summer training most years at Camp Jackson, SC, and some years at Fort Bragg, NC; Camp Beauregard, LA; or Camp Shelby, MS. Inducted into Federal service on 25 November 1940 at St. Petersburg, FL, and moved to Camp Blanding, FL, where it arrived on 19 December 1940. Location 7 December 1941—Camp Blanding, FL.

Status: Assigned to the USARS as the 116th F.A.; 2d Bn. active at Lakeland, FL, as an element of the 53d Inf. Brig. (Sep.).

Events: 56, 255, 300, 325, 328, 330

Commanders, 116th Field Artillery Regiment

Col. Samuel C. Harrison Jr.	18 September 1917–1 January 1918	Col. Samuel C. Harrison Jr.	April 1918–19 January 1919
Lt. Col. Edmund L. Gruber	1 January 1918–8 March 1918	*Demobilized/Inactive*	19 January 1919–20 January 1924
Maj. E. L. Anderson	8 March 1918–April 1918	Col. Sumpter D. Lowry Jr.	20 January 1924–4 October 1934
Col. Homer W. Hesterly	23 October 1934–26 February 1942		

117th Field Artillery Regiment (I) **(155-mm H)** (IX Corps) **North Carolina National Guard**

HQ—*Not organized,* 1921–24; Raleigh, NC, 1924–27

Arrived at the port of Newport News on 18 March 1919 on the U.S.S. *Orizaba* as the 113th F.A., an element of the 30th Div. Demobilized 28 March 1919 at Camp Jackson, SC. Reconstituted in the N.G. in 1921 as the 117th F.A. and allotted to the state of North Carolina. Washington, NC, designated as regimental HQ on organization, but the unit was never organized at that location. Subordinate elements reorganized 1921–24 as the 117th F.A. and assigned to the 189th F.A. Brig. (IX Corps). Regimental HQ reorganized and federally recognized on 3 March 1924 at Raleigh, NC. Conducted annual summer training at Fort Bragg, NC, 1924–27. Redesignated 113th F.A. on 12 January 1927.

Commander, 117th Field Artillery Regiment (I)

Col. William T. Joyner	3 March 1924–12 January 1927

117th Field Artillery Regiment (II) **(75-mm G-H)** (31st Division) **Alabama National Guard**

HQ—*Not organized,* 1921–25; Montgomery, AL, 1925–28; Florala, AL, 1928–40; Camp Blanding, FL, 1940–41

Arrived at the port of New York on 22 January 1919 on the U.S.S. *Manchuria* as the 117th F.A., an element of the 31st Div. Demobilized on 18 January 1919 at Camp Gordon, GA. Reconstituted in the N.G. in 1921 as the 141st F.A. and allotted to the states of Alabama and Louisiana. Regimental HQ, HQ Battery, and 2d Bn. allotted to Alabama and the 1st Bn. allotted to Louisiana. Partially organized in Louisiana and Alabama, 1921–22, and assigned to the 39th Div. Relieved from the 39th Div. on 1 July 1923 and assigned to 31st Div. Regimental HQ organized and federally recognized on 26 March 1925 as the 141st F.A. at Montgomery, AL. Redesignated as the 117th F.A. on 12 January 1927 (Louisiana elements concurrently withdrawn and retained the 141st F.A. designation). Regimental HQ concurrently relocated to Florala, AL. New 1st Bn. organized on 15 March 1929 by reorganization and redesignation of the 55th Machine Gun (MG) Sq. Converted from horse drawn to truck drawn on 1 August 1933. Conducted annual summer training most years at Camp Beauregard, LA, and some years at Camp Jackson, SC, or Camp Shelby, MS. Conducted additional week-long winter training directed by the War Department at Camp Shelby in December 1939. Inducted into Federal service on 25 November 1940 at Florala and moved to Camp Blanding, FL, where it arrived on 19 December 1940. Location 7 December 1941—Camp Blanding, FL.

Status: Assigned to the USARS as the 117th F.A.; 1st Bn. active at Andalusia, AL, as an element of the 31st Armd. Brig.

Events: 56, 255, 300, 325, 328, 330

Commanders, 117th Field Artillery Regiment (II)

Lt. Col. Abram Levy	4 October 1917–November 1917
Col. Bibb Graves	November 1917–8 January 1918
Lt. Col. Nelson E. Margetts	8 January 1918–March 1918
Col. Bibb Graves	March 1918–17 January 1919
Demobilized/Inactive	18 January 1919–26 March 1925
Col. Percy S. McClung	26 March 1925–31 December 1941
Col. James A. Lake	31 December 1941–26 February 1942

118th Field Artillery Regiment (75-mm G-H) (30th Division) **Georgia National Guard**

HQ—Savannah, GA, 1920–40; Fort Jackson, SC, 1940–41

Demobilized 14–18 January 1919 at Camp Gordon, GA, as an element of the 31st Div. Reconstituted in the N.G. in 1921 and allotted to the state of Georgia. Reorganized 2 November 1921 by redesignation of the 1st F.A., Georgia N.G. (organized 1920–21 with HQ at Savannah, GA) as the 118th Field Artillery and assigned to the 30th Div. Regimental HQ federally recognized on 30 December 1921 at Savannah. Converted from horse drawn to truck drawn on 1 December 1934. Conducted annual summer training most years at Camp Jackson, SC, and some years at Fort Bragg, NC. Inducted into Federal service on 16 September 1940 at Savannah and moved to Fort Jackson, where it arrived on 26 September 1940. Location 7 December 1941—Fort Jackson, SC.

Status: Assigned to the USARS as the 118th F.A.; 1st Bn. active at Savannah, GA, as an element of the 48th Inf. Brig. (Mecz).

Events: 255, 300, 316, 330

Commanders, 118th Field Artillery Regiment

Col. John G. Butler	23 September 1917–1 January 1918	Col. Robert J. Travis	30 December 1921–18 June 1923
Lt. Col. Carroll J. Goodfellow	1 January 1918–March 1918	Col. Joseph H. Thompson	5 November 1923–ao June 1928
Col. John G. Butler	March 1918–November 1918	Lt. Col. Walter R. Neal	ao June 1929–30 May 1931
Lt. Col. Robert J. Travis	November 1918–18 January 1919	Col. Sheftall B. Coleman	30 May 1931–September 1941
Demobilized/Inactive	19 January 1919–29 December 1921	Col. Albert C. Stanford (R.A.)	September 1941–16 February 1942

119th Field Artillery Regiment (75-mm G-H) (32d Division) **Michigan National Guard**

HQ—*Not organized,* 1921–22; Lansing, MI, 1922–41; Fort Knox, KY, 1941; Fort Leonard Wood, MO, 1941

Arrived at the port of New York on 3 May 1919 on the S.S. *Frederick* as the 119th F.A., an element of the 32d Div. Demobilized on 16 May 1919 at Camp Custer, MI. Reconstituted in the N.G. in 1921 and allotted to the state of Michigan. Assigned in June 1921 to the 32d Div. The 1st Bn. organized and federally recognized on 22 July 1921 at Lansing, MI. The 2d Bn. organized and federally recognized on 12 October 1921 at Jackson, MI. Regimental HQ organized and federally recognized on 10 February 1922 at Lansing. Converted from horse drawn to truck drawn on 1 August 1933. Elements called up to perform riot control duty at the auto workers strike at Flint, MI, 13 January–16 February 1937. Conducted annual summer training most years at Camp Grayling and some years at Camp Custer, MI. The regiment conducted joint summer training at Camp Grayling with the 329th F.A. in 1928, 1932, and 1937, and with the 328th F.A. in 1929 and 1936. Relieved from the 32d Div. on 18 September 1940 and assigned to the 72d F.A. Brig. (V Corps). Armament changed on 11 October 1940 from 75-mm G to 155-mm G. Inducted into Federal service on 7 April 1941 at Lansing and moved to Fort Knox, KY, where it arrived on 17 April 1941. Transferred on 2 June 1941 to Fort Leonard Wood, MO. Location 7 December 1941—Fort Leonard Wood, MO.

Status: Assigned to the USARS as the 119th F.A.; 1st Bn. active at Lansing as an element of the 38th Inf. Div.

Events: 214, 302, 324

Commanders, 119th Field Artillery Regiment

Col. Chester B. McCormick	22 September 1917–16 May 1919	Col. Joseph H. Lewis	10 February 1922–January 1939
Demobilized/Inactive	19 May 1919–9 February 1922	Col. Glenn W. Carey	January 1939–16 February 1942
Col. Lloyd M. Hanna	16 February 1942–1 March 1943		

120th Field Artillery Regiment (75-mm G-H) (32d Division) **Wisconsin National Guard**

HQ—*Not organized,* 1921–22; Milwaukee, WI, 1922–40; Camp Beauregard, LA, 1940–41; Camp Livingston, LA, 1941

Constituted in the N.G. in 1921 and allotted to the state of Wisconsin. Reorganized on 1 April 1921 by redesignation of the 2d F.A., Wisconsin N.G. (organized 1920–21 from elements of the World War I 120th F.A. Regt.) and assigned to the 32d Div. Regimental HQ organized and federally recognized on 18 May 1922 at Milwaukee, WI. The regiment, or elements thereof, called up to perform the following state duties: several elements to perform duties in connection with fighting forest fires near Superior, WI, 8–12 October 1923; two batteries to perform riot control during the "Milk Strike" at Shawano, WI, 15–20 May 1933; two batteries to perform strike duty during the labor disturbances at Kohler, WI, 28 July–20 August 1934. Converted from horse drawn to tractor drawn on 1 September 1930. Converted from tractor drawn to truck drawn on 13 March 1935. Conducted annual summer training most years at Camp Sparta/Camp McCoy, WI, and some years at Camp Custer, MI, or Camp Douglas, WI. The regiment conducted joint summer training at Camp Douglas with the 78th F.A. (RAI) in 1928. Inducted into Federal service on 15 October 1940 at Superior, WI, and moved to Camp Beauregard, LA, where it arrived on 25 October 1940. Transferred on 13 February 1941 to Camp Livingston, LA. Location 7 December 1941—Camp Livingston, LA.

Status: Assigned to the USARS as the 120th F.A.; 1st Bn. active at Wisconsin Rapids, WI, as an element of the 32d Inf. Brig. (Sep.).

Events: 214, 302, 320, 328

Commanders, 120th Field Artillery Regiment

Col. Carl Penner	28 September 1917–16 May 1919	Col. Alvin A. Kuechenmeister	18 May 1922–9 October 1940
Demobilized/Inactive	17 May 1919–19 May 1922	Col. Jim Dan Hill	9 October 1940–16 January 1942

121st Field Artillery Regiment (155-mm H) (VI Corps) **Wisconsin National Guard**

HQ—*Not organized,* 1921–27; Milwaukee, WI, 1927–28; Madison, WI, 1928–34; Racine, WI, 1934–36; Beloit, WI, 1936–40; Camp Beauregard, LA, 1940–41; Camp Livingston, LA, 1941

Arrived at the port of Boston on 12 May 1919 on the U.S.S. *Georgia* as the 121st F.A., an element of the 32d Div. Demobilized on 19 May 1919 at Camp Grant, IL. Reconstituted in the N.G. in 1921 and allotted to the state of Wisconsin. Reorganized on 1 April 1921 by redesignation of the 1st F.A., Wisconsin N.G. (organized 1920–21) and assigned to the 84th F.A. Brig. (VI Corps). Relieved from the 84th F.A. Brig. on 2 July 1923 and assigned to the 185th F.A. Brig. (VI Corps). Regimental HQ reorganized and federally recognized on 16 June 1927 at Milwaukee, WI. Regimental HQ successively relocated as follows: to Madison, WI, 27 June 1928; Racine, WI, 9 February 1934; and Beloit, WI, 2 March 1936. Relieved from the 185th F.A. Brig. (VI Corps) in December 1929 and assigned to the 32d Div. Elements called up to perform duties in connection with fighting forest fires near Superior, WI, 8–12 October 1923. Conducted annual summer training most years at Camp Sparta/Camp McCoy, WI, and some years at Camp Custer, MI, or Camp Douglas, WI. Inducted into Federal service on 15 October 1940 at Abbotsford, WI, and moved to Camp Beauregard, LA, where it arrived on 25 October 1940. Transferred on 13 February 1941 to Camp Livingston, LA. Location 7 December 1941—Camp Livingston, LA.

Status: Assigned to the USARS as the 121st F.A.; 1st Bn. active at Milwaukee, WI, as an element of the 57th F.A. Brig.

Events: 214, 302, 320, 328

Commanders, 121st Field Artillery Regiment

Col. Philip C. Westfahl	19 September 1917–23 July 1918	Col. J. Tracy Hale	16 June 1927–5 January 1928
Lt. Col. Robert Arthur	4 July 1918–29 October 1918	Col. Albert H. Smith	5 January 1928–ao July 1934
Col. James A. Thomas	30 October 1918–16 May 1919	Col. George W. Rickeman	ao August 1935–1 March 1936
Demobilized/Inactive	17 May 1919–15 June 1927	Col. William S. Wood (R.A.)	2 March 1936–14 October 1940
Col. Waldemar F. Breidster	15 October 1940–16 January 1942		

122d Field Artillery Regiment (75-mm G-H) (33d Division) **Illinois National Guard**

HQ—Chicago, IL, 1921–40; Camp Forrest, TN, 1940–41

Arrived at the port of New York on 24 May 1919 on the U.S.S. *America* as the 122d F.A., an element of the 33d Div. Demobilized on 10 June 1919 at Camp Grant, IL. Reconstituted in the N.G. in 1921 and allotted to the state of Illinois. Reorganized on 13 December 1921 by redesignation of the 1st F.A., Illinois N.G. (regimental HQ organized on 20 August 1919 at Chicago, IL; federally recognized on 11 November 1921) and assigned to the 33d Div. Converted from horse drawn to truck drawn on 9 October 1939. Conducted annual summer training most years at Camp Grant, IL, and some years at Camp Sparta/Camp McCoy, WI, or Camp Custer, MI. For at least 1 year, in 1937, the regiment also trained 15 company-grade field artillery officers of the 86th Div. at Camp McCoy. Converted from horse drawn to truck drawn on 9 October 1939. Inducted into Federal service on 5 March 1941 at Chicago and moved to Camp Forrest, TN, where it arrived on 15 March 1941. Location 7 December 1941—Camp Forrest, TN.

Status: Assigned to the USARS as the 122d F.A.; 2d Bn. active at Chicago, IL, as an element of the 35th Inf. Div. (Mecz).

Events: 214, 302, 316, 324, 328

Commanders, 122d Field Artillery Regiment

Col. Milton J. Foreman	21 September 1917–10 June 1919
Demobilized/Inactive	11 June 1919–10 November 1921
Col. Frank R. Schwengel	11 November 1921–29 May 1926
Col. Samuel T. Lawton	11 June 1926–10 February 1936
Col. Robert E. Myhrman	11 February 1936–8 December 1941

123d Field Artillery Regiment (155-mm H) (VI Corps) **Illinois National Guard**

HQ—*Not organized,* 1921–36; Monmouth, IL, 1936–41; Camp Forrest, TN, 1941

Arrived at the port of New York on 24 May 1919 on the U.S.S. *America* as the 123d F.A., an element of the 33d Div. Demobilized on 9 June 1919 at Camp Grant, IL. Reconstituted in the N.G. in 1921 and allotted to the state of Illinois. The 1st Bn. organized on 17 August 1921 at Monmouth, IL. Regiment concurrently assigned to the 84th F.A. Brig. (VI Corps). Relieved from the 84th F.A. Brig. on 2 July 1923 and assigned to the 185th F.A. Brig. (VI Corps). Relieved from the 185th F.A. Brig. (VI Corps) in December 1929 and assigned to the 33d Div. Regimental HQ organized and federally recognized on 26 July 1936 at Monmouth. The regiment, or elements thereof, was called up to perform the following state duties: 1st Bn. for strike duty in the coal fields near Monmouth–Galesburg, IL, 19–25 July 1922; 1st Bn. for riot control at a railroad workers' strike at Bloomington, IL, 25 July–9 August 1922; 1st Bn. for strike duty at a coal miners' strike at Taylorville and Springfield, IL, in March–April 1933; and 3d Bn. for tornado relief work at Belleville, IL, in March 1938. Conducted annual summer training most years at Camp Grant, IL, and some years at Camp Sparta/Camp McCoy, WI, or Camp Custer, MI. For at least 1 year, in 1937, the regiment also trained 14 company-grade field artillery officers of the 86th Div. at Camp McCoy. Inducted into Federal service on 5 March 1941 in Monmouth and moved to Camp Forrest, TN, where it arrived on 15 March 1941. Location 7 December 1941—Camp Forrest, TN.

Status: Assigned to the USARS as the 123d F.A.; 2d Bn. active at Milan, IL.

Events: 214, 302, 316, 324, 328

Commanders, 123d Field Artillery Regiment

Col. Charles G. Davis	19 September 1917–9 June 1919
Demobilized/Inactive	10 June 1919–25 July 1936
Col. Dell B. Hardin	26 July 1936–12 February 1942

124th Field Artillery Regiment (75-mm G-H) (33d Division) **Illinois National Guard**

HQ—*Not organized,* 1921–36; Chicago, IL, 1936–41; Camp Forrest, TN, 1941

Arrived at the port of New York on 24 May 1919 on the U.S.S. *America* as the 124th F.A., an element of the 33d Div. Demobilized on 10 June 1919 at Camp Grant, IL. Reconstituted in the N.G. in 1921 and allotted to the state of Illinois. Reorganized on 13 December 1921 by the redesignation of active elements of the 2d F.A., Illinois N.G. (organized as the 7th Inf., Illinois N.G. in June 1919; converted and redesignated 2d F.A., Illinois N.G. on 1 May 1921) as the 124th F.A. and assigned to the 33d Div. Regimental HQ organized and federally recognized on 20 October 1922 at Chicago, IL. Converted from horse drawn to truck drawn on 9 October 1939. Conducted annual summer training most years at Camp Grant, IL, and some years at Camp Sparta/Camp McCoy, WI, or Camp Custer, MI. For at least 1 year, in 1937, the regiment also trained 16 company-grade field artillery officers of the 86th Div. at Camp McCoy. Inducted into Federal service on 5 March 1941 at Chicago and moved to Camp Forrest, TN, where it arrived on 15 March 1941. Location 7 December 1941—Camp Forrest, TN.

Status: Assigned to the USARS as elements of the 122d F.A.

Events: 214, 302, 316, 324, 328

Commanders, 124th Field Artillery Regiment

Col. Gordon Strong	12 October 1917–12 January 1918
Col. Horatio B. Hackett	12 January 1918–28 September 1918
Maj. Frank L. Reardon	28 September 1918–4 October 1918
Col. Joseph A. Rogers	4 October 1918–January 1919
Col. Arthur L. Keesling	January 1919–9 June 1919
Demobilized/Inactive	10 June 1919–19 October 1922
Col. Thomas S. Hammond	20 October 1922–27 November 1931
Col. Charles C. Haffner	27 November 1931–17 May 1940
Col. Fred B. Skeates	17 May 1940–12 February 1942

125th Field Artillery Regiment (75-mm G-H) (34th Division) **Minnesota National Guard**

HQ—*Not organized,* 1921–24; Duluth, MN, 1924–41; Camp Claiborne, LA, 1941

Arrived at the port of Newport News on 10 January 1919 on the S.S. *Köningen der Nederlanden* as the 125th F.A., an element of the 34th Div. Demobilized on 23 January 1919 at Camp Dodge, IA. Reconstituted in the N.G. on 14 January 1921 and allotted to the state of Minnesota. Reorganized on 21 October 1921 by redesignation of the 2d F.A., Minnesota N.G. (organized 1920–24) as the 125th F.A. and assigned to the 34th Div. Regimental HQ organized and federally recognized on 24 July 1924 at Duluth, MN. Converted from horse drawn to tractor drawn on 1 September 1930 and further reorganized to truck drawn on 15 August 1933. Conducted annual summer training at numerous locations to include Lake City, MN; Fort Snelling, MN; Camp Douglas, WI; Camp Custer, MI; Camp McCoy, WI; and most years at Camp Ripley, MN. For at least 2 years, in 1938 and 1940, the regiment also trained 15 company-grade field artillery officers of the 88th Div. at Camp Ripley. Inducted into Federal service on 10 February 1941 at Duluth and moved to Camp Claiborne, LA, where it arrived on 5 March 1941. Location 7 December 1941—Camp Claiborne, LA.

Status: Assigned to the USARS as the 125th F.A.; 1st Bn. active at New Ulm, MN, as an element of the 34th Inf. Div.

Events: 233, 303, 320, 328

Commanders, 125th Field Artillery Regiment

Col. Hubert V. Eva	1 October 1917–8 May 1918
Unknown	8 May 1918–25 June 1918
Col. Thomas W. Hollyday	25 June 1918–8 November 1918
Unknown	8 November 1918–23 January 1919
Demobilized/Inactive	23 January 1919–23 July 1924
Col. Elmer W. McDevitt	24 July 1924–24 May 1940
Lt. Col. Alfred C. Ott	25 May 1940–ao July 1941

126th Field Artillery Regiment (75-mm G) (32d Division) **Wisconsin National Guard**

HQ—Milwaukee, WI, 1940–41; Camp Livingston, LA, 1941

Constituted in the N.G. in 1921 as the 105th Cav., assigned to the 22d Cav. Div., and allotted to the state of Wisconsin. Regimental HQ organized and federally recognized on 24 May 1921 at Milwaukee, WI. Relieved from the 22d Cav. Div. on 1 October 1940, converted and redesignated 126th F.A., and assigned to the 32d Div. Inducted into Federal service on 15 October 1940 at Milwaukee and moved to Camp Beauregard, LA, where it arrived on 25 October 1940. Transferred on 13 February 1941 to Camp Livingston, LA. Location 7 December 1941—Camp Livingston, LA.

Status: Assigned to the USARS as the 126th F.A.; 1st Bn. active at Kenosha, WI, as an element of the 57th F.A. Brig.

Events: 320, 328

Commanders, 126th Field Artillery Regiment

Col. Frederick C.T. John	1 October 1940–16 January 1942

127th Field Artillery Regiment (I) **(155-mm H)** (VII Corps) **Nebraska National Guard**

HQ—*Not organized,* 1921–27

Constituted in the N.G. in 1921 and assigned to the VII Corps and allotted to the state of Nebraska. Placed on the DNG list on 2 July 1923. Withdrawn from the state of Nebraska in April 1926. Withdrawn from the N.G. on 17 September 1927 and demobilized.

127th Field Artillery Regiment (II) **(155-mm H)** (35th Division) **Kansas National Guard**

HQ—Topeka, KS, 1940–41; Camp Joseph T. Robinson, AR, 1941

Constituted in the N.G. in 1921 as the 114th Cav., assigned to the 24th Cav. Div., and allotted to the state of Kansas. Regimental HQ organized and federally recognized on 10 January 1925 at Topeka, KS. Relieved from the 24th Cav. Div. on 1 October 1940, converted and redesignated 127th F.A., and assigned to the GHQR. Assigned on 21 October 1940 to the 35th Div. Inducted into Federal service on 23 December 1940 at Topeka and moved to Camp Joseph T. Robinson, AR, where it arrived on 4 January 1941. Location 7 December 1941—Camp Joseph T. Robinson, AR.

Status: Assigned to the USARS as the 127th F.A.; 1st Bn. active at Ottawa, KS, as an element of the 130th F.A. Brig.

Events: 316, 324, 328

Commanders, 127th Field Artillery Regiment

Col. Paul A. Cannady	1 October 1940–3 February 1942

128th Field Artillery Regiment (75-mm P) (GHQR) **Missouri National Guard**

HQ—*Not organized,* 1921–23; Columbia, MO, 1923–40; Fort Jackson, SC, 1940–41; Camp Blanding, FL, 1941

Arrived at the port of Boston on 22 April 1919 on the S.S. *Vedic* as the 128th F.A., an element of the 35th Div. Demobilized on 19 May 1919 at Fort Riley, KS. Reconstituted in the N.G. in 1921 and allotted to the state of Missouri. Reorganized on 1 October 1921 by redesignation of the 1st F.A., Missouri N.G. (organized as the 1st Bn., F.A., Missouri N.G. on 4 December 1920; expanded and redesignated 1st F.A. (Portee), Missouri N.G. on 29 January 1921) as the 128th F.A. and assigned to the GHQR. Regimental HQ reorganized and federally recognized on 21 April 1923 at Columbia, MO. Enlisted personnel of HQ battery composed primarily from students from the ROTC program at the University of Missouri. Enlisted personnel of Btry C composed primarily from students from the Missouri State Teachers College. Assigned on 1 October 1933 to the 25th F.A. Brig. (GHQR). Converted from portee to truck drawn on 1 January 1935. The regiment, or elements thereof, was called up to perform the following state duties: 2d Bn. for railway strike duty at Poplar Bluff, MO, 14 July–13 August 1922; Btry F acted as the salute battery for General John J. Pershing's dedication of the Liberty Memorial at Kansas City, MO, in November 1926; Btry B acted as the salute battery for President Franklin D. Roosevelt's dedication of the Mark Twain bridge at Hannibal, MO, on 2 September 1936. Conducted annual summer training most years at Fort Riley, KS, and some years at Camp Clark, MO, or Fort Sill, OK. For at least 2 years, in 1939 and 1940, the regiment also trained 29 company-grade field artillery officers of the 102d Div. at Fort Sill and Camp Ripley, MN. Inducted into Federal service on 25 November 1940 at Columbia and moved to Fort Jackson, SC, where it arrived on 10 December 1940. Assigned to the First Army and attached to the Fort Bragg Provisional Field Artillery Brigade. Transferred on 3 December 1941 to Camp Blanding, FL. Location 7 December 1941—Camp Blanding, FL.

Status: Assigned to the USARS as the 128th F.A.; 1st Bn. active at Columbia, MO, as an element of the 138th F.A. Brig.

Events: 236, 303, 330

Commanders, 128th Field Artillery Regiment

Col. Frank M. Rumbold	1 October 1917–22 January 1918	Col. George A. Taylor	16 November 1918–2 May 1919
Lt. Col. Harold W. Huntley	22 January 1918–15 April 1918	*Demobilized/Inactive*	3 May 1919–20 April 1923
Col. Frank M. Rumbold	15 April 1917–23 September 1918	Col. John F. Williams	21 April 1923–1 January 1937
Lt. Col. Walter J. Warner	23 September 1918–16 November 1918	Col. Charles E. Barkshire	1 January 1937–February 1942

129th Field Artillery Regiment (75-mm G) (GHQR) **Missouri National Guard**

HQ—*Not organized,* 1921–27

Constituted in the N.G. in 1921, allotted to the state of Missouri, and assigned to the GHQR. Placed on the Deferred National Guard (DNG) list on 2 July 1923, redesignated the 418th F.A. (DNG), and allotted to the Seventh Corps Area. Withdrawn from the N.G. on 17 September 1927 and demobilized.

130th Field Artillery Regiment (75-mm G-H) (35th Division) **Kansas National Guard**

HQ—*Not organized,* 1921–22; Topeka, KS, 1922–26; Lawrence, KS, 1926; Hutchison, KS, 1926–40; Topeka, KS, 1940; Camp Joseph T. Robinson, AR, 1941

Arrived at the port of New York on 21 April 1919 on the U.S.S. *Mobile* as the 130th F.A., an element of the 35th Div. Demobilized on 11 May 1919 at Camp Funston, KS. Reconstituted in the N.G. in 1921 and allotted to the state of Kansas. Reorganized on 4 November 1921 by redesignation of the 1st F.A., Kansas N.G. (organized as the 1st Bn., 1st F.A., Kansas N.G. on 7 August 1920; expanded and redesignated 1st F.A., Kansas N.G. in 1921) as the 130th F.A. and assigned to the 35th Div. Regimental HQ reorganized and federally recognized on 18 April 1922 at Topeka, KS. Regimental HQ successively relocated as follows: to Lawrence, KS, on 12 March 1926; Hutchison, KS, on 27 April 1926; and to Topeka, on 18 November 1940. The regiment, or elements thereof, was called up to perform the following state emergency duties: 1st Bn. for strike duty in the coal fields near Pittsburg, KS, 14 December 1921–26 February 1922; several batteries for tornado relief duties at Hutchison, 13–15 January 1923, and at Horton, KS, 18–19 June 1923; 1st Bn. for the state reformatory fire at Hutchison on 13 January 1925; 1st Bn. for tornado relief duties at Hutchison, 8–9 May 1927; 1st Bn. for flood relief duties at Hutchison, July 1929. Converted from horse drawn to truck drawn on 1 July 1933. Conducted annual summer training most years at Fort Riley, KS, and some years at Fort Sill, OK. For at least 2 years, in 1939 and 1940, the regiment also trained 36 company-grade field artillery officers of the 89th Div. at Fort Riley and Camp Ripley, MN. Inducted into Federal service on 23 December 1940 at Topeka and moved to Camp Joseph T. Robinson, AR, where it arrived on 4 January 1941. Location 7 December 1941—Camp Joseph T. Robinson, AR.

Status: Assigned to the USARS as the 130th F.A.; Headquarters and Headquarters Battery (HHB) active in the Kansas N.G. at Hutchison, KS, as HHB, 130th F.A. Brig.; 2d Bn. active at Hiawatha, KS, as an element of the 130th F.A. Brig.

Events: 236, 303, 316, 324, 328

Commanders, 130th Field Artillery Regiment

Col. Hugh Means	1 October 1917–9 May 1918	Lt. Col. William F. Thurston	7 September 1918–8 November 1918
Maj. Thomas H. Jennings	9 May 1918–30 May 1918	Col. Hugh S. Brown	8 November 1918–11 May 1919
Lt. Col. Roy F. Waring	30 May 1918–5 July 1918	*Demobilized/Inactive*	12 May 1919–17 April 1922
Maj. Thomas H. Jennings	5 July 1918–3 August 1918	Col. Leigh Hunt	18 April 1922–18 April 1928
Lt. Col. James E. Wilson	3 August 1918–7 September 1918	Col. Guy C. Rexroad	19 April 1928–3 February 1942

131st Field Artillery Regiment (75-mm G-H) (36th Division) **Texas National Guard**

HQ—*Not organized,* 1921–22; Amarillo, TX, 1922–25; Corsicana, TX, 1925–31; Lubbock, TX, 1931–36; Corpus Christi, TX, 1936–39; Austin, TX, 1939–40; Plainview, TX, 1940; Camp Bowie, TX, 1940–41

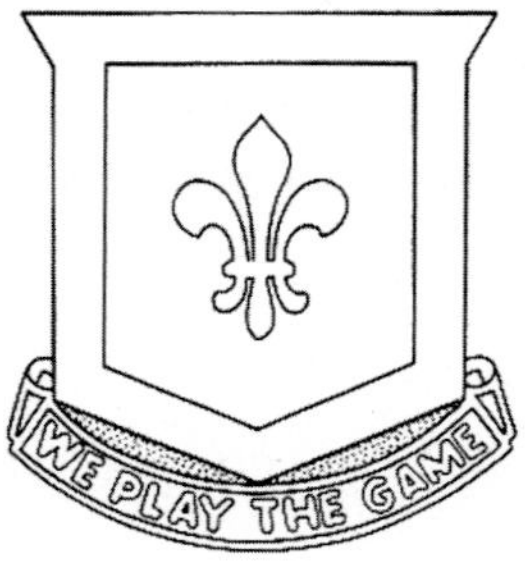

Arrived at the port of Newport News on 13 March 1919 on the U.S.S. *Aeolus* as the 131st F.A., an element of the 36th Div. Demobilized on 2 April 1919 at Camp Travis, TX. Reconstituted in the N.G. in 1921 and allotted to the state of Texas. Regimental HQ reorganized and federally recognized on 10 November 1922 at Amarillo, TX. Regimental HQ successively relocated as follows: to Corsicana, TX, on 2 December 1925; Lubbock, TX, on 22 September 1931; Corpus Christi, TX, on 1 January 1936; Austin, TX, on 1 August 1939; and Plainview, TX, on 1 September 1940. The regiment, or elements thereof, was called up to perform the following state emergency duties: relief duties during flooding at Abilene, TX, in 1933; relief duties during the Concho River flood at San Angelo, TX, in 1937; tornado relief duties at Clyde, TX, in June 1938. Converted from horse drawn to truck drawn on 30 June 1933. Conducted annual summer training at numerous locations to include Fort Sill, OK; Camp Stanley, TX; Camp Bullis, TX; and Camp Hulen, TX. Designated mobilization training station was Camp Stanley. Inducted into Federal service on 25 November 1940 at Plainview and moved to Camp Bowie, TX, where it arrived on 11 January 1941. The 1st Bn. ordered to the Southwest Pacific and departed the San Francisco Port of Embarkation on 22 November 1941 on the U.S.S. *Republic* as part of the Pensacola convoy. Location 7 December 1941—Camp Bowie, TX.

Status: Assigned to the USARS as the 131st F.A.; 2d Bn. active at San Antonio, TX, as an element of the 36th Inf. Div. (Mecz).

Events: 258, 300, 317, 328

Commanders, 131st Field Artillery Regiment

Col. Claude V. Birkhead	1 October 1917–2 April 1919	Col. Charles A. Davis	2 December 1925–16 September 1935
Demobilized/Inactive	3 April 1919–28 October 1922	Col. Harold J. Weiler	16 September 1935–11 July 1940
Col. John B. Golding	29 October 1922–1 December 1925	Col. Thomas A. Bay	11 July 1940–1 February 1942

132d Field Artillery Regiment (75-mm G-H) (36th Division) **Texas National Guard**

HQ—*Not organized,* 1921–23; Dallas, TX, 1923–40; Camp Bowie, TX, 1940–41

Arrived at the port of Newport News in March 1919 on the U.S.S. *Kroonland* as the 132d F.A., an element of the 36th Div. Demobilized on 10 April 1919 at Camp Bowie, TX. Reconstituted in the N.G. in 1921 and allotted to the state of Texas. Regimental HQ reorganized and federally recognized on 15 May 1923 at Dallas, TX. The regiment, or elements thereof, was called up to perform state emergency duties to include tornado relief at Frost, TX, in May 1930, and the New London, TX, school disaster on 18 March 1937. Converted from horse drawn to truck drawn on 30 June 1933. Conducted annual summer training at numerous locations to include Fort Sill, OK; Camp Stanley, TX; Camp Bullis, TX; and Camp Hulen, TX. Designated mobilization training station was Camp Stanley. Inducted into Federal service on 25 November 1940 at Corsicana, TX, and moved to Camp Bowie, TX, where it arrived on 10 January 1941. Location 7 December 1941—Camp Bowie, TX.

Events: 258, 300, 317, 328

Commanders, 132d Field Artillery Regiment

Col. Arthur R. Sholars	15 October 1917–10 April 1919	Col. Robert O. Whiteaker	24 May 1933–8 April 1938
Col. Archibald C. Allen	29 October 1922–May 1933	Col. Kenneth K. Bullock	8 April 1938–1 February 1942

133d Field Artillery Regiment (155-mm H) (36th Division) **Texas National Guard**

HQ—*Not organized,* 1921–36; San Antonio, TX, 1936–40; Camp Bowie, TX, 1940–41

Arrived at the port of Newport News on 21 March 1919 on the U.S.S. *Rijndam* as the 133d F.A., an element of the 36th Div. Demobilized on 2 April 1919 at Camp Bowie, TX. Reconstituted in the N.G. in 1921 and allotted to the state of Texas. Waco, TX, originally designated by the Texas N.G. Adjutant General as HQ on reorganization. Assigned in December 1929 to the 36th Div. Regimental HQ reorganized and federally recognized on 9 July 1936 at San Antonio, TX. Elements called up to perform relief duties during the flooding of the Colorado River at Brady, TX, in February 1938. Conducted annual summer training at Camp Stanley, TX; Camp Bullis, TX; and Camp Hulen, TX. Designated mobilization training station was Camp Stanley. Inducted into Federal service on 25 November 1940 at San Antonio and moved to Camp Bowie, TX, where it arrived on 10 January 1941. Location 7 December 1941—Camp Bowie, TX.

Status: Assigned to the USARS as the 133d F.A.; 1st Bn. active at Beaumont, TX, 3d Bn. active at El Paso, TX, and 4th Bn. active at New Braunfels, TX, as elements of the 36th Inf. Div. (Mecz).

Events: 258, 300, 317, 328

Commanders, 133d Field Artillery Regiment

Col. Fred A. Logan	15 October 1917–2 April 1919	*Demobilized/Inactive*	3 April 1919–31 May 1936
Col. Raymond Phelps	1 June 1936–1 February 1942		

134th Field Artillery Regiment (75-mm G-H) (37th Division) **Ohio National Guard**

HQ—*Not organized,* 1921–22; Columbus, OH, 1922–40; Camp Shelby, MS, 1940–41

Arrived at the port of Newport News on 24 March 1919 on the U.S.S. *New Hampshire* as the 134th F.A., an element of the 37th Div. Demobilized on 9 April 1919 at Camp Sherman, OH. Reconstituted in the N.G. in 1921 and allotted to the state of Ohio. Reorganized on 1 July 1921 by redesignation of the 1st F.A., Ohio N.G. (organized as the 1st F.A., Ohio N.G. on 4 August 1919) as the 134th F.A. and assigned to the 37th Div. Regimental HQ reorganized and federally recognized on 6 May 1922 at Columbus, OH. Converted from horse drawn to truck drawn on 1 January 1935. The regiment, or elements thereof, was called up to perform the following state emergency duties: President Warren G. Harding's funeral in August 1923; guard duties at the crash site of the dirigible U.S.S. *Shenandoah* in September 1925; riot control during the Ohio State Penitentiary riot and fire, 29 April–14 May 1930; strike duty in the coal fields near Cadiz, OH, 16 April–17 August 1932; strike duty and riot control at the AutoLite plant in Toledo, OH, in April–May 1934; flood relief duties along the Ohio River in January–February 1937; strike duty at the steel workers' strike in the Mahoning Valley, OH, 22 June–15 July 1937. Conducted annual summer training most years at Camp Knox, KY. Inducted into Federal service on 15 October 1940 at Columbus and moved to Camp Shelby, MS, where it arrived on 24 October 1940. Location 7 December 1941—Camp Shelby, MS.

Status: Assigned to the USARS as the 134th F.A.; 1st Bn. active at Columbus, OH, as an element of the 38th Inf. Div.

Events: 213, 220, 302, 320, 328

Commanders, 134th Field Artillery Regiment

Col. Harold M. Bush	15 September 1917–9 April 1919	Col. Thomas R. Leahy	15 September 1932–15 June 1939
Demobilized/Inactive	10 April 1919–5 May 1922	Col. Roy D. Prushing	15 June 1939–30 September 1940
Col. Edward S. Thacher	6 May 1922–15 September 1932	Col. Edward T. Kirkendall	1 October 1940–16 January 1942

135th Field Artillery Regiment (75-mm G-H) (37th Division) **Ohio National Guard**

HQ—*Not organized,* 1921–22; Cleveland, OH, 1922–40; Camp Shelby, MS, 1940–41

Arrived at the port of Newport News on 24 March 1919 on the U.S.S. *Vermont* as the 135th F.A., an element of the 37th Div. Demobilized on 9 April 1919 at Camp Sherman, OH. Reconstituted in the N.G. in 1921 and allotted to the state of Ohio. Reorganized on 1 July 1921 by redesignation of the 1st F.A., Ohio N.G. (organized as the 1st F.A., Ohio N.G. on 4 August 1919) as the 135th F.A. and assigned to the 37th Div. Regimental HQ reorganized and federally recognized on 1 February 1922 at Cleveland, OH. Converted from horse drawn to truck drawn on 1 January 1935. The regiment, or elements thereof, was called up to perform the following state emergency duties: President Warren G. Harding's funeral in August 1923; two batteries from 1st Bn. called up to perform duties in connection with public disorders in Niles, OH, 1–5 November 1923; tornado relief duties at Lorain-Sandusky, OH, 28 June–16 July 1924; riot control during the Ohio State Penitentiary riot and fire, 29 April–14 May 1930; strike duty in the coal fields near Cadiz, OH, 16 April–17 August 1932; flood relief duties along the Ohio River, January–February 1937; riot control during a workers' strike at the Mahoning Valley steel plants, 22 June–15 July 1937. Conducted annual summer training most years at Camp Knox, KY. Inducted into Federal service on 15 October 1940 at Cleveland and moved to Camp Shelby, MS, where it arrived on 25 October 1940. Location 7 December 1941—Camp Shelby, MS.

Events: 213, 220, 302, 320, 328

Commanders, 135th Field Artillery Regiment

Col. Dudley J. Hard	15 September 1917–11 April 1919	Col. Clarence F. Bluem	1 February 1922–January 1933
Demobilized/Inactive	12 April 1919–31 January 1922	Col. Carl A. Shem	15 January 1933–15 November 1937
Col. Robert D. Schmidt	15 November 1937–16 January 1942		

136th Field Artillery Regiment (155-mm H) (37th Division) **Ohio National Guard**

HQ—*Not organized,* 1929–37; Columbus, OH, 1937–40; Camp Shelby, MS, 1940–41

Constituted in the N.G. in December 1929, assigned to the 37th Div., and allotted to the state of Ohio. Regimental HQ organized and federally recognized on 1 April 1937 at Columbus. Subordinate battalion HQ organized and federally recognized as follows: 1st Bn. at Dayton, OH, on 7 July 1936; 2d Bn. at Piqua, OH, on 25 August 1936; and 3d Bn. at Columbus, OH, on 1 July 1937. Elements called up to perform flood relief duties along the Ohio River, January–February 1937. Conducted annual summer training most years at Camp Knox, KY. Inducted into Federal service on 15 October 1940 at Columbus and moved to Camp Shelby, MS, where it arrived on 25 October 1940. Location 7 December 1941—Camp Shelby, MS.

Status: Assigned to the USARS as elements of the 134th F.A.

Events: 220, 302, 320, 328

Commanders, 136th Field Artillery Regiment

Col. Leo M. Kreber	1 April 1937–14 October 1940	Col. Kenneth Cooper	14 October 1940–1 February 1942

138th Field Artillery Regiment (75-mm G-H) (38th Division) **Kentucky National Guard**

HQ—*Not organized,* 1921–22; Louisville, KY, 1922–40; Camp Shelby, MS, 1940–41

Arrived at the port of New York on 22 December 1918 on the S.S. *Mongolia* as the 138th F.A., an element of the 38th Div. Demobilized on 8 January 1919 at Camp Zachary Taylor, KY. Reconstituted in the N.G. in 1921 and allotted to the state of Kentucky. Regimental HQ organized and federally recognized on 30 June 1922 at Louisville, KY, and assigned to the 38th Div. Converted from horse drawn to truck drawn on 1 January 1935. The regiment, or elements thereof, was called up to perform the following state emergency duties: 1st Bn. for strike duty in the coal fields near Madisonville–Fronde–Central City, KY, 8 July–30 August 1922; entire regiment for flood relief duties along the Ohio River, January–February 1937. Conducted annual summer training most years at Camp Knox, KY. Inducted into Federal service on 17 January 1941 in Louisville and moved to Camp Shelby, MS, where it arrived on 29 January 1941. The 2d Bn. detached and sailed for Hawaii on 3 December 1941 on the U.S.A.T. *President Johnson*. Location 7 December 1941—Camp Shelby, MS.

Status: Assigned to the USARS as the 138th F.A.; 2d Bn. active at Lexington, KY, as an element of the 35th Inf. Div. (Mecz).

Events: 213, 220, 302, 320, 328

Commanders, 138th Field Artillery Regiment

Col. William A. Colston	9 October 1917–8 January 1919	Col. Daniel M. Carrell	20 June 1922–30 November 1933
Demobilized/Inactive	14 January 1919–19 January 1922	Col. Sidney Smith	30 November 1933–21 June 1940
	Col. George M. Chescheir	21 June 1940–1 March 1942	

139th Field Artillery Regiment (75-mm G-H) (38th Division) **Indiana National Guard**

HQ—*Not organized,* 1921–22; Indianapolis, IN, 1922–40; Camp Shelby, MS, 1940–41

Demobilized on 16 January 1919 at Fort Benjamin Harrison, IN, as various elements of the 38th Div. Regimental HQ organized and federally recognized on 13 November 1922 at Indianapolis, IN. Concurrently assigned to the 38th Div. Converted from horse drawn to truck drawn on 1 January 1935. The regiment, or elements thereof, was called up to perform the following state emergencies: tornado relief duties at Princeton, IN, 18–28 March 1925; 2d Bn. called up to perform riot control during labor troubles in Vanderburg and Warwick Counties, 22 February–23 March 1926; flood relief duties at Hazelton, IN, during the Wabash River flood, 15–21 January 1930; four batteries called up to perform riot control during a coal miners' strike at the Dixie Bee Mine, August–October 1932; entire regiment for guard and security duties in connection with the visit of President Roosevelt to Vincennes, IN, on 14 June 1936; entire regiment to perform flood relief duties along the Ohio River, January–February 1937. Conducted annual summer training most years at Camp Knox, KY. Inducted into Federal service on 17 January 1941 at Indianapolis and moved to Camp Shelby, MS, where it arrived on 1 February 1941. Location 7 December 1941—Camp Shelby, MS.

Status: Assigned to the USARS as the 139th F.A.; 1st Bn. active at Crawfordsville, IN, as an element of the 38th Inf. Div.

Events: 213, 220, 302, 320, 328

Commanders, 139th Field Artillery Regiment

Col. John S. Fishback	13 November 1922–17 September 1939	Col. Louis L. Roberts	18 September 1939–10 February 1942

141st Field Artillery Regiment (I) **(75-mm G-H)** (39th Division) **Alabama and Louisiana National Guard**

HQ—*Not organized,* 1921–25; Montgomery, AL, 1925–27

Arrived at the port of New York on 18 April 1919 on the U.S.S. *Kaiserin Auguste Victoria* as the 141st F.A., an element of the 39th Div. Demobilized on 2 May 1919 at Camp Shelby, MS. Reconstituted in the N.G. in 1921 and allotted to the states of Alabama and Louisiana. Regimental HQ, HQ Battery, and 1st Bn. were allotted to the state of Louisiana, and 2d Bn. was allotted to the state of Alabama. Dothan, AL, designated as HQ on organization, but the unit was never organized at that location. Assigned to the 39th Div. in 1921. The 1st Bn. organized and federally recognized in November 1921 with HQ in New Orleans, LA; redesignated as the 2d Bn. on 2 May 1922, and again redesignated as the 1st Bn. on 18 July 1922. The 2d Bn. organized and federally recognized on 14 September 1922 with HQ at Geneva, AL. Regiment relieved from the 39th Div. on 1 July 1923 and assigned to 31st Div. Regimental HQ withdrawn from the state of Louisiana on 26 March 1925 and allotted to the state of Alabama. Regimental HQ concurrently organized and federally recognized at Montgomery, AL. Conducted annual summer training most years at Fort Bragg, NC, and some years at Camp Beauregard, LA; Camp McClellan, AL; or Camp Jackson, SC. The 1st Bn. redesignated 167th Sep. Bn., F.A. (Horse) on 1 September 1926 and assigned to the 23d Cav. Div. Concurrently, a new 1st Bn. allotted to the state of Alabama. Alabama elements withdrawn from allotment on 17 January 1927 and redesignated as the 117th F.A.

Commanders, 141st Field Artillery Regiment (I)

Col. Owen Allison	27 September 1917–2 May 1919	*Demobilized/Inactive*	3 May 1919–25 March 1925
Col. Percy S. McClung	26 March 1925–17 January 1927		

141st Field Artillery Regiment (II) **(75-mm G-H)** (23d Cavalry Division) **Louisiana National Guard**

HQ—New Orleans, LA, 1939–41; Camp Shelby, MS, 1941

Constituted in the N.G. on 6 June 1939 as 141st F.A. Regt., assigned to the 23d Cav. Div., and allotted to the state of Louisiana. Regimental HHB concurrently organized and federally recognized at New Orleans, LA. The 1st Bn. organized on 6 June 1939 from the 141st F.A. Bn. (organized and federally recognized in November 1921 with HQ in New Orleans, LA; redesignated 2d Bn. on 2 May 1922, and again redesignated 1st Bn. on 18 July 1922; redesignated 167th Sep. Bn., F.A. (Horse) on 1 September 1926 and assigned to the 23d Cav. Div.; redesignated 141st Sep. Bn., F.A. (Horse) on 14 January 1927; reorganized and redesignated 141st F.A. Bn. (Mtzd) on 1 July 1937). The 2d Bn. organized and federally recognized on 27 September 1939 with HQ at New Orleans. Regiment relieved on 1 October 1940 from the 23d Cav. Div. Reorganized and rearmed with 155-mm howitzers in November 1940. Inducted into Federal service on 13 January 1941 at New Orleans and assigned to the 73d F.A. Brig. (V Corps). Moved to Camp Shelby, MS, where it arrived on 20 January 1941. Location 7 December 1941—Camp Shelby, MS.

Status: Assigned to the USARS as the 141st F.A.; 1st Bn. active at New Orleans, LA, as an element of the 256th Inf. Brig. (Sep.).

Events: 300

Commanders, 141st Field Artillery Regiment (II)

Col. Henry B. Curtis	6 June 1939–October 1940	Col. Waldemar F. Breidster	October 1940–15 January 1942

142d Field Artillery Regiment (I) **(75-mm G Mtzd)** (GHQR) **Arkansas National Guard**

HQ—*Not organized,* 1921–27

Constituted in the N.G. in 1921, assigned to the GHQR, and allotted to the state of Arkansas. Placed on the DNG list on 2 July 1923, redesignated the 419th F.A. (DNG), and allotted to the Seventh Corps Area. Withdrawn from the N.G. on 17 September 1927 and demobilized.

142d Field Artillery Regiment (II) **(155-mm H)** (35th Division) **Arkansas National Guard**

HQ—*Not organized,* 1928–36; Prescott, AR, 1936–37; El Dorado, AR, 1937–41; Fort Sill, OK, 1941

Arrived at the port of Newport News on 10 June 1919 on the U.S.S. *Amphion* as the 142d F.A., an element of the 39th Div. Demobilized on 26 June 1919 at Camp Pike, AR. Reconstituted in the N.G. in February 1928 as the 142d F.A. Regt. (75-mm G Mtzd), assigned to the GHQR, and allotted to the state of Arkansas. Allotment changed from 75-mm guns to 155-mm howitzers on 13 July 1931, and regiment concurrently assigned to the 35th Div. The 1st Bn. organized and federally recognized on 31 July 1931 with HQ at Fayetteville, AR. The 2d Bn. organized and federally recognized on 21 April 1936 with HQ at Mena, AR. Concurrently, regimental HQ organized and federally recognized at Prescott, AR. Regimental HQ relocated on 25 June 1937 to El Dorado, AR. The 3d Bn. organized and federally recognized on 31 May 1937 with HQ at Fayetteville, AR. The regiment, or elements thereof, was called up to perform the following state duties: regiment (-) to perform flood relief duty at Forrest City, Camp Barton, and Jonesboro, AR, January–February 1937. Conducted annual summer training at Camp Pike, AR; Fort Riley, KS; and Fort Sill, OK. For at least 1 year, in 1940, the regiment also trained 36 company-grade field artillery officers of the 89th Div. at Camp Ripley, MN. Relieved from the 35th Div. on 21 October 1940 and assigned to the GHQR. Relieved from the GHQR on 30 December 1940 and assigned to the VIII Corps. The 3d Bn. inactivated in January 1941 at Fayetteville,

AR. Remainder of the regiment inducted into Federal service on 6 January 1941 at Texarkana, AR, and assigned to the 18th F.A. Brig. (VIII Corps). Moved to Fort Sill, OK, where it arrived on 17 January 1941. Location 7 December 1941—Fort Sill, OK.

Status: Assigned to the USARS as the 142d F.A.; 1st Bn. active at Harrison, AR, and 2d Bn. active at Fort Smith, AR, as elements of the 142d F.A. Brig.

Events: 236, 303, 317, 328

Commanders, 142d Field Artillery Regiment (II)

Col. Henry Stroupe	27 September 1917–May 1918	Col. Samuel B. Scott	21 April 1936–30 May 1937
Col. William G. Ownbey	May 1918–26 June 1919	Col. Ebenezer L. Compere	31 May 1937–5 January 1941
Demobilized/Inactive	27 April 1919–20 April 1936	Col. Jerome F. Thompson (R.A.)	5 January 1941–8 February 1943

143d Field Artillery Regiment (75-mm G-H) (40th Division) **California National Guard**

HQ—*Not organized,* 1921–24; Oakland, CA, 1924–1928; Stockton, CA, 1928–41; Camp San Luis Obispo, CA, 1941

Constituted in the N.G. in 1921, assigned to the 40th Div., and allotted to the state of California. Regimental HQ organized and federally recognized on 30 July 1924 at Oakland, CA. Regimental HQ relocated on 11 October 1928 to Stockton, CA. Converted from horse drawn to truck drawn on 7 August 1933. The regiment, or elements thereof, was called up to perform the following state duties: 2d Bn. to perform riot control duty at the Folsom State Prison, 24–29 November 1927; regiment to perform riot control duty for the San Francisco street car workers' strike, 5–21 July 1934. Conducted annual summer training most years at Camp San Luis Obispo, CA, and some years at Fort Lewis, WA, or Del Monte, CA. Regiment conducted a 2,000-mile round trip road march from Stockton, CA, to Camp W.G. Williams, UT, for summer camp with the 65th F.A. Brig., 11–26 June 1938. Inducted into Federal service on 3 March 1941 at Stockton as an element of the 40th Div., and moved to Camp San Luis Obispo, CA, where it arrived on 16 March 1941. Location 7 December 1941—Camp San Luis Obispo, CA.

Status: Assigned to the USARS as the 143d F.A.; 1st Bn. active at Walnut Creek, CA, as an element of the 40th Inf. Div. (Mecz).

Events: 231, 304, 314, 326

Commanders, 143d Field Artillery Regiment

Col. Marshall G. Randol (R.A.)	30 July 1924–4 October 1928	Col. Otto E. Sandman (CA)	5 October 1928–10 April 1941
Col. Lloyd H. Duffin (UT)	10 April 1941–ao December 1941		

144th Field Artillery Regiment (155-mm G) (GHQR) **California National Guard**

HQ—*Not organized,* 1936–40; Santa Barbara, CA, 1940–41; Fort Lewis, WA, 1941

Constituted in the N.G. on 2 June 1936, assigned to the GHQR, and allotted to the state of California. The 2d Bn. organized and federally recognized on 28 May 1936 as 2d Bn., 196th F.A. with HQ at Santa Barbara, CA; redesignated 2d Bn., 144th F.A. on 1 July 1936. The 3d Bn. allotted to the state of Oregon on 3 August 1936. The 3d Bn. withdrawn from the state of Oregon in May 1940 and allotted to the state of California. Regimental HQ organized and federally recognized on 21 August 1940 at Santa Barbara, CA. Assigned on 30 December 1940 to the IX Corps. Conducted annual summer training at Camp San Luis Obispo, CA, 1936–39. Inactive elements of the regiment organized and federally recognized on 3 February 1941. Concurrently inducted into Federal service at Santa Barbara and moved to Camp San Luis Obispo, CA, where it arrived on 18 February 1941. Assigned to the 76th F.A. Brig. (IX Corps). Location 7 December 1941—Fort Lewis, WA.

Status: Assigned to the USARS as the 144th F.A.; 1st Bn. active at Burbank, CA, Btry D active at Ventura, CA, and

Btry F active at Los Angeles, CA, as elements of the 40th Inf. Div. (Mecz).

Events: 231, 326

Commanders, 144th Field Artillery Regiment

Col. Ralph W. Coane	3 February 1941–8 February 1943

145th Field Artillery Regiment (75-mm G-H) (40th Division) **Utah National Guard**

HQ—*Not organized,* 1921–23; Salt Lake City, UT, 1923–41; Camp San Luis Obispo, CA, 1941

Arrived at the port of New York on 5 January 1919 on the U.S.S. *Santa Teresa* as elements of the 40th Div. Demobilized 21–29 January 1919 at Fort Logan, CO. Reconstituted in the N.G. on 11 October 1921, assigned to the 40th Div., and allotted to the state of Utah. Partially organized on 11 October 1921 by redesignation of existing elements of the 1st F.A., Utah N.G. (organized, less HQ, 1919–21) as elements of the 145th F.A. Regimental HQ organized and federally recognized on 13 July 1923 at Salt Lake City, UT. Converted from horse drawn to truck drawn on 1 August 1933. Conducted an experimental 970-mile road march to Camp San Luis Obispo, CA, over a 4-day period in July 1938 to test the ability of a N.G. unit to rapidly reinforce the coast in the event of enemy invasion. Conducted annual summer training most years Camp W.G. Williams, UT, and some years at Fort Lewis, WA. Inducted into Federal service on 3 March 1941 at Salt Lake City and moved to Camp San Luis Obispo where it arrived on 18 March 1941. Location 7 December 1941—Camp San Luis Obispo, CA.

Status: Assigned to the USARS as the 145th F.A.; 1st Bn. active at Salt Lake City, UT, as an element of the 115th F.A. Brig.

Events: 231, 304, 314, 326

Commanders, 145th Field Artillery Regiment

Col. Richard W. Young	3 October 1917–13 October 1917	Col. Ernest L. Bourne	13 July 1923–1 January 1934
Col. William C. Webb	13 October 1917–16 October 1918	Col. Carl A. Badger	1 January 1934–10 May 1937
Col. Ernest L. Bourne	16 October 1918–January 1919	Col. Lloyd H. Duffin	10 May 1937–10 April 1941
Demobilized/Inactive	January 1919–12 July 1923	Col. Otto E. Sandman (CA)	10 April 1941–ao December 1941

146th Field Artillery Regiment (75-mm G-H) (41st Division) **Washington National Guard**

HQ—Seattle, WA, 1921–40; Camp Murray, WA, 1940–41; Fort Lewis, WA, 1941

Constituted in the N.G. in 1921, assigned to the 41st Div., and allotted to the state of Washington. Regimental HQ organized and federally recognized on 10 May 1921 at Seattle, WA. Consolidated on 20 October 1922 with the 146th F.A. Regt. (a World War I unit organized on 19 September 1917 at Camp Greene, NC; demobilized in June 1919 at Logan, UT; reconstituted on 20 October 1922). On 29 April 1925, 25 former officers of the former Imperial Russian Army, including Lt. Gen. Alexander der Elshen, commander of the Russian XX Corps, enlisted as privates in Btry C in Seattle. Converted from horse drawn to tractor drawn on 15 April 1931; further converted to truck drawn on 1 January 1935. Conducted annual summer training most years at Camp Lewis, WA, 1921–22, and Camp Murray, WA, 1923–39. Inducted into Federal service on 16 September 1940 at Seattle as an element of the 41st Div., and moved to Camp Murray, WA, where it arrived on 23 September 1940. Transferred on 20 March 1941 to Fort Lewis, WA. Location 7 December 1941—Fort Lewis, WA.

Status: Assigned to the USARS as the 146th F.A.; 2d Bn. active at Olympia, WA, as an element of the 81st Inf. Brig. (Sep.).

Events: 238, 304, 314, 326

Commanders, 146th Field Artillery Regiment

Col. William H. Edelblute	19 September 1917–5 May 1918	*Demobilized/Inactive*	18 June 1919–9 May 1921
Col. Ernest D. Scott	6 May 1918–5 June 1918	Col. Harry G. Winsor	10 May 1921–29 March 1929
Col. Leroy V. Patch	5 June 1918–16 November 1918	Col. Albert H. Beebe	30 March 1929–10 October 1934
Col. Philip H. Worcester	16 November 1918–17 June 1919	Col. Henry A. Wise	10 October 1934–19 April 1941
		Lt. Col. Charles W. Hendrickson	19 April 1941–ao December 1941

147th Field Artillery Regiment (75-mm G Portee) (GHQR) — South Dakota National Guard

HQ—*Not organized*, 1921–22; Pierre, SD, 1922–28; Vermilion, SD, 1928–38; Rapid City, SD, 1938–39; Sioux Falls, SD, 1939–40; Fort Ord, CA, 1940–41

Arrived at the port of Philadelphia on 14 May 1919 on the U.S.S. *Kansas* as the 147th F.A., an element of the 41st Div. Demobilized on 24 May 1919 at Camp Dodge, IA. Reconstituted in the N.G. in 1921, assigned to the GHQR, and allotted to the state of South Dakota. Regimental HQ reorganized and federally recognized on 11 May 1922 at Pierre, SD. Converted from truck drawn to portee in February 1927. Regimental HQ successively relocated as follows: to Vermilion, SD, on 1 January 1928; Rapid City, SD, on 8 February 1938; and Sioux Falls, SD, on 14 February 1939. Converted from portee to truck drawn on 1 January 1935. Conducted annual summer training most years at numerous locations to include Fort Meade, SD; Pierre, SD; Mitchell, SD; Camp Sparta, WI; and most years at Camp Rapid, Rapid City, SD. Inducted into Federal service on 25 November 1940 at Sioux Falls. Transferred on 8 December 1940 to Fort Ord, CA, and assigned to the 26th F.A. Brig. Reorganized in 1941 as a 105-mm howitzer regiment. Departed San Francisco Port of Embarkation on 22 November 1941 on the U.S.A.T. *Willard A. Holbrook* as part of the Pensacola convoy. Location 7 December 1941—en route to Australia.

Status: Assigned to the USARS as the 147th F.A.; 1st Bn. active at Sioux Falls, SD, and 2d Bn. active at Watertown, SD, as elements of the 147th F.A. Brig.

Events: 233, 303, 331

Commanders, 147th Field Artillery Regiment

Col. Boyd Wales	3 October 1917–June 1919	Col. Eugene I. Foster	17 June 1939–June 1941
Demobilized/Inactive	June 1919–10 May 1922	Lt. Col. Leslie Jensen	June 1941–13 August 1941
Col. Boyd Wales	11 May 1922–22 August 1937	Col. Paul V. Kane (R.A.)	13 August 1941–26 June 1942

148th Field Artillery Regiment (75-mm G-H) (41st Division) — Washington and Idaho National Guard

HQ—*Not organized,* 1921–27; Tacoma, WA, 1927–35; Coeur d' Alene, ID, 1935–40; Camp Murray, WA, 1940–41; Fort Lewis, WA, 1941

Constituted in the N.G. in 1921, assigned to the 41st Div., and allotted to the states of Washington and Idaho. Regimental HQ, HQ Battery, and 2d Bn. allotted to the state of Washington and 1st Bn. allotted to the state of Idaho. The 1st Bn. organized and federally recognized on 15 May 1926 with HQ at Coeur d' Alene, ID. Regimental HQ organized and federally recognized on 6 May 1927 at Tacoma, WA. The 2d Bn. organized and federally recognized on 5 November 1930 with HQ at Tacoma, WA. Converted from horse drawn to tractor drawn on 15 April 1931. Washington elements conducted summer training most years at Camp Murray, WA; Idaho elements at Boise Barracks, ID. HQ withdrawn from the state of Washington on 23 July 1934 and allotted to the state of Idaho. Regimental HQ concurrently organized at Coeur d' Alene. Converted from tractor drawn to truck drawn on 1 January 1935. Inducted into Federal service on 16 September 1940 at Coeur d' Alene as an element of the 41st Div., and moved to Camp Murray, WA, where it arrived on 23 September 1940. Transferred on 20 March 1941 to Fort Lewis, WA. The 1st Bn. ordered to the Southwest Pacific and departed the San Francisco Port of Embarkation on 22 November 1941 on the U.S.A.T. *Willard A. Holbrook* as part of the Pensacola convoy. Location 7 December 1941—Fort Lewis, WA.

Events: 238, 304, 314, 326

Commanders, 148th Field Artillery Regiment

Maj. Oliver C. Nelson (ID)	5 May 1927–10 April 1930	Col. Edwin T. Powell (ID)	July 1934–12 October 1940
Col. Carlos A. Penington (WA)	10 April 1930–23 July 1934	Unknown	12 October 1940–7 December 1941

150th Field Artillery Regiment (155-mm H) (V Corps) **Indiana National Guard**

HQ—Kokomo, IN, 1921–1936; Indianapolis, IN, 1936–41; Camp Shelby, MS, 1941

Arrived at the port of New York on 25 April 1919 on the U.S.S. *Leviathan* as the 150th F.A., an element of the 42d Div. Demobilized on 9 May 1919 at Camp Zachary Taylor, KY. Reorganized on 30 June 1921 as the 181st F.A. (organized as the 1st F.A., Indiana N.G. and federally recognized on 30 June 1921 with HQ at Kokomo, IN) and assigned to the 83d F.A. Brig. (V Corps). Redesignated 150th F.A. on 1 January 1922. Relieved from the 83d F.A. Brig. (V Corps) on 2 July 1923 and assigned to the 184th F.A. Brig. (V Corps). Relieved from the 184th F.A. Brig. (V Corps) in December 1929 and assigned to the 38th Div. Converted from horse drawn to truck drawn on 1 January 1935. Regimental HQ relocated on 16 March 1936 to Indianapolis, IN. The regiment, or elements thereof, was called up to perform the following state emergencies: snowstorm relief at Kokomo in December 1929; tornado relief duties in Vernon, IN, 7–10 July 1931; two batteries for guard and security duties in connection with the visit of President Roosevelt to Vincennes, IN, on 14 June 1936; entire regiment called up to perform flood relief duties along the Ohio River in January–February 1937. Conducted annual summer training most years at Camp Knox, KY. Inducted into Federal service on 17 January 1941 at Indianapolis and moved to Camp Shelby, MS, where it arrived on 29 January 1941. Location 7 December 1941—Camp Shelby, MS.

Status: Assigned to the USARS as the 150th F.A.; 2d Bn. active at Bloomington, IN, as an element of the 38th Inf. Div.

Events: 213, 220, 302, 320, 328

Commanders, 150th Field Artillery Regiment

Col. Robert H. Tyndall	14 August 1917–9 May 1919	Col. Walter W. Unvershaw	30 June 1921–31 March 1936
Demobilized/Inactive	9 May 1919–12 November 1922	Col. Elmer F. Straub	1 April 1936–1 March 1942

151st Field Artillery Regiment (75-mm G-H) (34th Division) **Minnesota National Guard**

HQ—Minneapolis, MN, 1921–41; Camp Claiborne, LA, 1941

Arrived at the port of New York on 28 April 1919 on the U.S.S. *Huntington* as the 151st F.A., an element of the 42d Div. Demobilized on 10 May 1919 at Camp Dodge, IA. Reconstituted in the N.G. on 14 January 1921 and allotted to the state of Minnesota. Reorganized on 21 November 1921 by redesignation of the 1st F.A., Minnesota N.G. (organized and federally recognized on 18 November 1919 with HQ at Minneapolis, MN) as the 151st F.A. and assigned to the 34th Div. Converted from horse drawn to tractor drawn on 1 September 1930 and further reorganized to truck drawn on 15 August 1933. The regiment, or elements thereof, was called up to perform the following state emergency duties: 2d Bn. to perform strike duty at the Swift and Armour Meat Packing Plants at St. Paul, MN, on 6 December 1921–11 February 1922; entire regiment for riot control during a commercial transit workers' strike in Minneapolis, MN, in May and 17 July–23 August 1934. Conducted annual summer training at numerous locations to include Fort Snelling, MN; Camp Douglas, WI; Camp McCoy, WI; and most years at Camp Ripley, MN. For at least 3 years, 1938–40, the regiment also trained 21 company-grade field artillery officers of the 88th Div. at Camp Ripley. Inducted into Federal service on 10 February 1941 at Minneapolis and moved to Camp Claiborne, LA, where it arrived on 5 March 1941. Location 7 December 1941—Camp Claiborne, LA.

Status: Assigned to the USARS as the 151st F.A.; 1st Bn. active at Montevideo, MN, as an element of the 34th Inf. Div.

Events: 233, 303, 320, 328

Commanders, 151st Field Artillery Regiment

Col. George A. Leach	18 August 1917–14 July 1919	Col. George A. Leach	21 November 1921–28 July 1924
Demobilized/Inactive	15 July 1919–20 November 1921	Col. Charles A. Green	25 May 1925–June 1940
Col. Stewart G. Collins	June 1940–30 January 1942		

152d Field Artillery Regiment (75-mm G-H) (43d Division) **Maine National Guard**

HQ—*Not organized,* 1921–29; Bangor, ME, 1929–41; Camp Blanding, FL, 1941

Constituted in the N.G. in 1921, assigned to the 43d Div., and allotted to the state of Maine. The 1st Bn. organized on 15 May 1922 with HQ at Houlton, ME. Regimental HQ and HQ, 2d Bn. organized and federally recognized on 3 April 1929 at Bangor, ME. Converted from horse drawn to truck drawn on 22 July 1933. Conducted annual summer training at numerous locations to include Bangor; Camp Keyes, ME; Brewer, ME; the Underhill Artillery Range, VT; Fort Ethan Allen, VT; and Camp Devens, MA. Inducted into Federal service on 24 February 1941 at Bangor as an element of the 43d Div., and moved to Camp Blanding, FL, where it arrived on 14 March 1941. Location 7 December 1941—Camp Blanding, FL.

Status: Assigned to the USARS as the 152d F.A.

Events: 190, 280, 301, 325, 328, 330

Commanders, 152d Field Artillery Regiment

Col. Herbert L. Bowen	3 April 1929–29 June 1940	Col. John F. Choate	30 June 1940–19 February 1942

153d Field Artillery Regiment (155-mm H) (I Corps) **Massachusetts National Guard**

HQ—*Not organized,* 1921

Constituted in the N.G. on 22 November 1921, assigned to the 81st F.A. Brig. (I Corps), and allotted to the state of Massachusetts. Unit designation withdrawn from the state of Massachusetts in December 1921 and the designation "171st" allotted instead.

156th Field Artillery Regiment (75-mm G-H) (44th Division) **New York National Guard**

HQ—Newburgh, NY, 1924–40; Fort Dix, NJ, 1940–41

Constituted in the N.G. in 1924, assigned to the 44th Div., and allotted to the state of New York. Organized by redesignation and reorganization of elements of the 132d Ammunition (Ammo.) Train (Tn.) as subordinate batteries. Regimental HQ organized and federally recognized on 8 July 1924 at Newburgh, NY. Converted from horse drawn to truck drawn on 1 April 1936. Conducted additional week-long winter training directed by the War Department at New Paltz, NY, 27 November–3 December 1939. Conducted annual summer training most years at Pine Camp, NY. Inducted into Federal service on

16 September 1940 at Newburgh as an element of the 44th Div., and moved to Fort Dix, NJ, where it arrived on 25 September 1940. Location 7 December 1941—Fort Dix, NJ.

Status: Assigned to the USARS as the 156th F.A.; 1st Bn. active at Kingston, NY, as an element of the 27th Inf. Brig. (Sep.).

Events: 190, 280, 301, 330

Commanders, 156th Field Artillery Regiment

Col. Raphael A. Egan	8 July 1924–14 May 1930	Col. James T. Cassedy	6 December 1930–16 January 1935
Lt. Col. John A. Korschen	14 May 1930–6 December 1930	Col. Otto Thiede	13 January 1935–14 September 1940
Col. Lansing McVickar	14 September 1940–16 February 1942		

157th Field Artillery Regiment (155-mm H) (44th Division) **New Jersey National Guard**

HQ—*Not organized,* 1930–36; Camden, NJ, 1936–40; Fort Dix, NJ, 1940–41

Constituted in the N.G. in February 1930, assigned to the 44th Div., and allotted to the state of New Jersey. Organized on 24 June 1936 from elements of the 112th F.A. Regimental HQ concurrently organized and federally recognized at Camden, NJ. Conducted annual summer training at Pine Camp, NY, and Indiantown Gap, PA. Inducted into Federal service on 16 September 1940 at Camden as an element of the 44th Div., and moved to Fort Dix, NJ, where it arrived on 25 September 1940. Location 7 December 1941—Fort Dix, NJ.

Status: 1st and 2d Battalions assigned to the USARS as elements of the 112th F.A.

Events: 280, 301, 330

Commander, 157th Field Artillery Regiment

Col. Richard P. Hartdegen 24 June 1936–17 February 1942

158th Field Artillery Regiment (75-mm G-H) (45th Division) **Oklahoma, Colorado, Arizona, and New Mexico National Guard**

HQ—*Not organized,* 1921–23; Tulsa, OK, 1923–25; Anadarko, OK, 1925–40; Fort Sill, OK, 1940–41

Constituted in the N.G. 26 February 1920 and assigned to the 45th Div. Regimental HQ, HQ Battery, and service battery allotted to the state of Oklahoma; 1st Bn. allotted to the states of Colorado and New Mexico; 2d Bn. allotted to the states of Arizona and Oklahoma. Regimental HQ organized and federally recognized on 15 May 1923 at Tulsa, OK. Elements called up to perform flood relief duties in Oklahoma City, OK, 13 September–8 October 1923. Regimental HQ relocated on 23 September 1925 to Anadarko, OK. The 1st Bn. redesignated 168th F.A. Bn. on 1 July 1926. New 1st Bn. constituted and allotted to the state of Oklahoma. The HQ, 1st Bn. organized on 20 May 1927 with HQ at Kingfisher, OK. Converted from horse drawn to truck drawn on 2 August 1933. Conducted annual summer training 1923–39 as follows: Oklahoma elements at Fort Sill, OK; Colorado elements at Camp George West, CO; New Mexico elements at Fort Bliss, TX, or Camp Maximilliano Luna, Las Vegas, NM; Arizona elements at Fort Tuthill, AZ. Inducted into Federal service on 16 September 1940 at Anadarko as an element of the 45th Div., and moved to Fort Sill, OK, where it arrived on 24 September 1940. Location 7 December 1941—Fort Sill, OK.

Status: Assigned to the USARS as the 158th F.A.; 1st Bn. active at Lawton, OK, as an element of the 45th F.A. Brig.

Events: 258, 300, 317, 328

Commanders, 158th Field Artillery Regiment

Col. Charles A. Holden	15 May 1923–5 September 1925	Col. Grover C. Walmsley	23 September 1925–11 February 1942

160th Field Artillery Regiment (75-mm G-H) (45th Division) **Oklahoma National Guard**

HQ—Wewoka, OK, 1921–29; Tulsa, OK, 1929–40; Fort Sill, OK, 1940–41; Camp Barkeley, TX, 1941

Constituted in the N.G. 10 October 1921, assigned to the 45th Div., and allotted to the state of Oklahoma. Regimental HQ organized and federally recognized on 22 November 1921 at Wewoka, OK. Converted from horse drawn to truck drawn on 2 August 1933. Regimental HQ relocated on 1 July 1929 to Tulsa, OK. Conducted annual summer training at Fort Sill, OK. Inducted into Federal service on 16 September 1940 at Tulsa as an element of the 45th Div., and moved to Fort Sill, OK, where it arrived on 24 September 1940. Transferred on 28 January 1941 to Camp Barkeley, TX. Location 7 December 1941—Camp Barkeley, OK.

Status: Assigned to the USARS as the 160th F.A.; 1st Bn. active at Chandler, OK, as an element of the 45th Inf. Brig. (Sep.).

Events: 258, 300, 317, 328

Commanders, 160th Field Artillery Regiment

Col. Stacy Knopf (R.A.)	7 March 1921–4 October 1921	Col. William S. Key	26 December 1923–1 July 1925
Col. Alva J. Niles	5 October 1921–25 December 1922	Col. Charles A. Holden	6 September 1925–11 February 1942

161st Field Artillery Regiment (75-mm G-H) (35th Division) **Kansas National Guard**

HQ—*Not organized,* 1921–23; Topeka, KS, 1923–41; Camp Joseph T. Robinson, AR, 1941

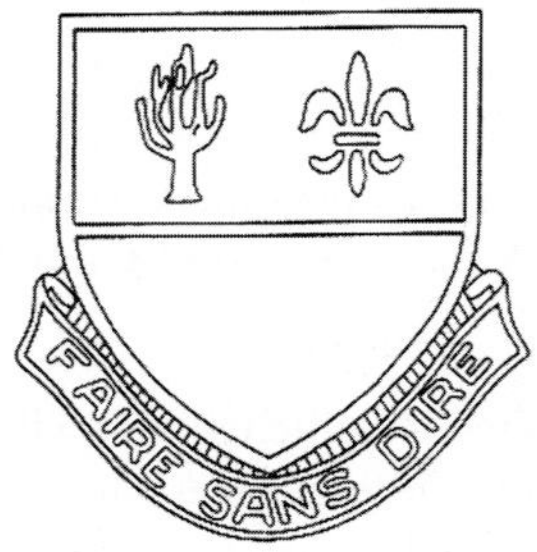

Constituted in the N.G. 1 November 1921, assigned to the 35th Div., and allotted to the state of Kansas. Regimental HQ organized and federally recognized on 25 May 1923 at Topeka, KS. Converted from horse drawn to truck drawn on 1 July 1933. The regiment, or elements thereof, was called up to perform the following state emergency duties: three batteries to perform road patrols and bridge guard duties in connection with the Kansas State Penitentiary breakout, 19–20 January 1934; 2d Bn. for strike duty in the coal fields near Columbus, KS, 17–25 June 1935; 1st Bn. for strike duty in the coal fields near Columbus, KS, 28 June–6 August 1935. Conducted annual summer training at Fort Riley, KS, and some years at Fort Sill, OK. For at least 1 year, in 1939, the regiment also trained 37 company-grade F.A. officers of the 89th Div. at Fort Riley. Inducted into Federal service on 23 December 1940 at Topeka as an element of the 35th Div., and moved to Camp Joseph T. Robinson, AR, where it arrived on 4 January 1941. Location 7 December 1941—Camp Joseph T. Robinson, AR.

Status: Assigned to the USARS as the 161st F.A.; 1st Bn. active at Wichita, KS, as an element of the 35th Inf. Div. (Mecz).

Events: 236, 303, 316, 324, 328

Commanders, 161st Field Artillery Regiment

Lt. Col. Milton R. McLean	25 May 1923–2 April 1925	Col. George H. Wark	2 April 1925–19 January 1933
Col. Nels A. Anderson	19 January 1933–1 March 1942		

162d Field Artillery Regiment (75-mm G) (Puerto Rican Department) **Puerto Rico National Guard**

HQ—*Not organized,* 1940–41

Constituted in the N.G. on 8 May 1940, assigned to the Puerto Rican Department, and allotted to the Commonwealth of Puerto Rico. The 1st Bn. organized and federally recognized on 25 August 1940 with HQ at San Juan, PR. The 1st Bn. inducted into Federal service on 15 October 1940 at Henry Barracks, PR, and assigned to the Puerto Rican Mobile Force. Location 7 December 1941—Henry Barracks, PR (1st Bn. only).

Status: Assigned to the USARS as the 162d F.A.; 1st Bn. active at Hato Rey, PR, 2d Bn. active at Hato Rey, PR, and 3d Bn. active at Ponce, PR.

Events: 329

165th Field Artillery Regiment (75-mm G-H) (21st Cavalry Division) **Virginia/New Jersey National Guard**

HQ—East Orange, NJ, 1940; Fort Dix, NJ, 1940–41

Constituted in the N.G. as the 165th Sep. Bn., F.A. (Horse) in June 1921 and assigned to the 21st Cav. Div. Allotted in April 1927 to the state of Virginia. Redesignated 165th F.A. Regt. (75-mm G Mtzd) in January 1939, withdrawn from the state of Virginia, and allotted, less 1st Bn., to the state of New Jersey. The 1st Bn. was allotted on 15 November 1939 to the state of New Jersey. The 1st Bn. was organized and federally recognized on 1 December 1939 at Morristown, NJ. The regimental HQ was organized and federally recognized on 1 February 1940 at East Orange, NJ. Relieved from the 21st Cav. Div. on 21 April 1940 and assigned to the 44th Div. The 2d Bn. was organized and federally recognized on 1 July 1940 at Englewood, NJ. Inducted into Federal service on 16 September 1940 at East Orange as an element of the 44th Div. and moved to Fort Dix, NJ, where it arrived on 24 September 1940. Location 7 December 1941—Fort Dix, NJ.

Events: 301, 330

Commander, 165th Field Artillery Regiment

Col. Edward J. Towers	1 February 1940–20 February 1942

166th Field Artillery Regiment (75-mm G-H) (22d Cavalry Division) **Pennsylvania National Guard**

HQ—Harrisburg, PA, 1939–41; Camp Shelby, MS, 1941

Constituted in the N.G. as 166th Sep. Bn., F.A. (Horse) in June 1921, assigned to the 22d Cav. Div., and allotted to the state of Wisconsin. Withdrawn from allotment to Wisconsin in February 1939 and allotted, less 1st Bn., to the state of Pennsylvania. Concurrently redesignated 166th F.A. Regt. Regimental HQ and HQ, 2d Bn. organized and federally recognized on 18 June 1939 at Harrisburg, PA. The 1st Bn. was allotted on 23 September 1940 to the state of Pennsylvania. Concurrently organized and federally recognized with HQ at Philadelphia, PA. Relieved from the 22d Cav. Div. on 1 October 1940 and rearmed with 155-mm howitzers. Inducted into Federal service on 13 January 1941 at Philadelphia and moved to Camp Shelby, MS, where it arrived on 23 January 1941. Assigned to the 73d F.A. Brig. (V Corps). Location 7 December 1941—Camp Shelby, MS.

Status: Assigned to the CARS as the 166th F.A. Regt.; all elements inactive in the Pennsylvania N.G.

Events: 301

Commanders, 166th Field Artillery Regiment

Col. Albert H. Stackpole	18 June 1939–21 March 1940	Col. Brenton G. Wallace	21 March 1940–ao April 1942

168th Field Artillery Regiment (75-mm G-H) (24th Cavalry Division) **Colorado National Guard**

HQ—Denver, CO, 1933–41; Camp Forrest, TN, 1941

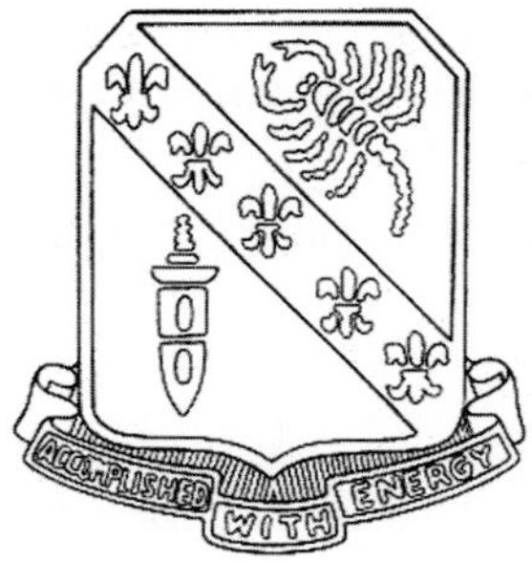

Constituted in the N.G. on 1 August 1933, allotted to the state of Colorado, and assigned to the 24th Cav. Div. Organized on 1 August 1933 by the redesignation of the 168th F.A. Bn. as the 1st Bn. and the conversion and redesignation of the 117th Sep. Cav. Sq. as the 2d Bn. Concurrently, the regimental HQ was organized and federally recognized at Denver, CO. Regiment called up to perform duties in connection with the grasshopper infestations in eastern Colorado, 28 June–26 August 1937, and for the Green Mountain Mine strike in Kremmling County, CO, 3–31 August 1939. Conducted annual summer training most years at Camp George West, CO. Relieved on 1 November 1940 from the 24th Cav. Div. Concurrently, armament changed from 75-mm G to 155-mm G. Inducted into Federal service on 24 February 1941 at Denver and moved to Camp Forrest, TN, where it arrived on 11 March 1941. Assigned to the 75th F.A. Brig. (VII Corps). Location 7 December 1941—Camp Forrest, TN.

Status: Assigned to the USARS as elements of the 157th F.A. Regt.

Events: 300, 324

Commanders, 168th Field Artillery Regiment

Col. Joseph W. Le Fever	1 August 1933–31 March 1934	Lt. Col. William Q. Howell	31 March 1934–9 December 1935
Col. John P. Donovan	9 December 1935–ao March 1941		

171st Field Artillery Regiment (155-mm G) (I Corps) **Massachusetts National Guard**

HQ—*Not organized,* 1921–27

Constituted in the N.G. in 1921, and assigned to the 81st F.A. Brig. (I Corps), and allotted to the state of Massachusetts in December 1921. Placed on the DNG list on 2 July 1923. Withdrawn from the state of Massachusetts in March 1926, but remained allotted to the First Corps Area. Withdrawn from the N.G. on 17 September 1927 and demobilized.

172d Field Artillery Regiment (155-mm H) (I Corps) **New Hampshire National Guard**

HQ—*Not organized,* 1921–36; Manchester, NH, 1936–41; Camp Blanding, FL, 1941

Constituted in the N.G. on 9 June 1921, assigned to the 81st F.A. Brig. (I Corps) for mobilization assignment, and allotted to the state of New Hampshire. The 81st F.A. Brig. redesignated the 194th F.A. Brig. on 2 July 1923 and allotted to the O.R. Subordinate elements of the regiment organized 1921–36. Attached to the 26th Div. in 1929 for mobilization purposes only until a howitzer regiment could be allotted and organized in the Massachusetts N.G. Regimental HQ organized and federally recognized on 15 May 1936 at Manchester, NH. Conducted annual summer training at numerous locations to include Tobyhanna, PA; Warner, NH; Webster, NH; Salisbury, NH; the Underhill Artillery Range at Fort Ethan Allen, VT; and Camp Devens, MA. Relieved in September 1940 from attachment to the 26th Div. Inducted into Federal service on 24 February 1941 at Manchester and moved to Camp Blanding, FL, where it arrived on 14 March 1941. Assigned to the 74th F.A. Brig. (IV Corps). Location 7 December 1941—Camp Blanding, FL.

Status: Assigned to the USARS as the 172d F.A.; 1st Bn. active at Manchester, NH, as an element of the 197th F.A. Brig.

Events: 190, 280, 301, 330

Commander, 172d Field Artillery Regiment

Col. John Jacobson Jr. 15 May 1936–27 March 1942

173d Field Artillery Regiment (155-mm G) (I Corps) **Connecticut, Rhode Island, and Vermont National Guard**

HQ—*Not organized,* 1921–27

Constituted in the N.G. in 1921 and assigned to the 81st F.A. Brig. (I Corps). Allotted to the states of Connecticut, Rhode Island, and Vermont as follows: the regimental HQ, HQ Btry, and 1st Bn. allotted to Connecticut; 2d Bn. allotted to Rhode Island; and 3d Bn. allotted to Vermont. Btry A organized on 8 July 1921 at Branford, CT. Placed on the deferred list on 2 July 1923 (less Btry A), redesignated 392d F.A. and transferred to the O.R. as a DNG unit. Concurrently relieved from assignment to the 81st F.A. Brig. (I Corps) and assigned to the 194th F.A. Brig. (I Corps). Btry A redesignated 43d Tank Company (Co.) on 28 March 1924. Withdrawn as a DNG unit on 11 January 1927 and permanently allotted to the O.R. as the 392d F.A.

175th Field Artillery Regiment (155-mm H) (III Corps) **Pennsylvania National Guard**

HQ—*Not organized,* 1921

Constituted in the N.G. on 26 May 1921, assigned to the 82d F.A. Brig. (III Corps), and allotted to the state of Pennsylvania. Unit designation withdrawn from the state of Pennsylvania about August 1921.

176th Field Artillery Regiment (155-mm H) (III Corps) **Pennsylvania National Guard**

HQ—*Not organized,* 1921–22; Pittsburgh, PA, 1922–41; Fort George G. Meade, MD, 1941

Constituted in the N.G. on 26 May 1921, assigned to the 82d F.A. Brig. (III Corps), and allotted to the state of Pennsylvania. Organized on 1 April 1921 by redesignation of the 18th Inf., Pennsylvania N.G. (organized and federally recognized on 31 July 1920 with HQ at Pittsburgh, PA) as the 176th F.A. Regimental HQ organized and federally recognized on 9 May 1922 at Pittsburgh. The 82d F.A. Brig. was placed on the deferred list on 2 July 1923, transferred to the O.R., and redesignated as the 190th F.A. Brig. (III Corps). Relieved from the 190th F.A. Brig. in February 1930 and assigned to the 29th Div. Conducted annual summer training most years at Tobyhanna, PA, and some years at Indiantown Gap, PA. Inducted into Federal service on 3 February 1941 at Pittsburgh as an element of the 29th Div., and moved to Fort George G. Meade, MD, where it arrived on 20 February 1941. Location 7 December 1941—Fort George G. Meade, MD.

Events: 191, 281, 301, 330

Commanders, 176th Field Artillery Regiment

Col. William R. Dunlap	9 May 1922–24 May 1939	Lt. Col. John Nash (R.A.)	6 March 1941–27 October 1941
Col. Arthur P. Schock	11 September 1939–6 March 1941	Lt. Col. Karl W. Curtis	27 October 1941–28 February 1942

177th Field Artillery Regiment (I) **(155-mm H)** (IV Corps) **North Carolina National Guard**

HQ—*Not organized,* 1921

Constituted in the N.G. in 1921, assigned to the IV Corps, and allotted to the state of North Carolina. Unit designation withdrawn from allotment to the state of North Carolina in late 1921 and the designation "117th" substituted instead.

177th Field Artillery Regiment (II) **(155-mm H)** (V Corps) **Michigan National Guard**

HQ—Detroit, MI, 1940–41; Fort Knox, KY, 1941; Fort Leonard Wood, MO, 1941

Constituted in the N.G. on 18 September 1940, assigned to the 72d F.A. Brig. (V Corps), and allotted to the state of Michigan. Regimental HQ organized and federally recognized on 18 September 1940 at Detroit, MI. Remainder of regiment organized from elements of the 1st Sq., 106th Cav. and 107th Quartermaster (Q.M.) Regt. The 3d Bn. inactivated on 6 February 1941 at Detroit. Inducted into Federal service on 7 April 1941 at Detroit and moved to Fort Knox, KY, where it arrived on 19 April 1941. Transferred on 12 June 1941 to Fort Leonard Wood, MO. Location 7 December 1941—Fort Leonard Wood, MO.

Events: 324

Commander, 177th Field Artillery Regiment

Col. Russell G. Simpson 18 September 1940–ao April 1941

178th Field Artillery Regiment (155-mm H) (IV Corps) **Tennessee, Mississippi and South Carolina National Guard**

HQ—*Not organized,* 1921–38; Andrews, SC, 1938–41; Fort Bragg, NC, 1941

Constituted in the N.G. in 1921, assigned to the IV Corps, and allotted to the states of Tennessee, Mississippi, and South Carolina. Regimental HQ, HQ Btry, Service Btry, and 1st Bn. were allotted to the state of Mississippi; 2d Bn. allotted to the state of Tennessee; and 3d Bn. allotted to the state of South Carolina. Greenwood, MS, designated as regimental HQ on organization, but the unit was never organized at that location. The 2d Bn. organized and federally recognized on 16 May 1925 with HQ at Maryville, TN. The 1st Bn. organized and federally recognized on 20 May 1926 with HQ at Greenville, MS. The 1st Bn. called up to perform flood relief duties at Vicksburg, MS, April–May 1927. Relieved from the IV Corps on 18 December 1929 and assigned to the 31st Div. The 1st Bn. redesignated 1st Bn., 114th F.A. on 15 November 1932. Concurrently, the 1st Bn., 178th F.A. withdrawn from the state of Mississippi and allotted to the Fourth Corps Area for mobilization responsibility. In addition, the regiment was relieved from the 31st Div. and assigned to the 13th F.A. Brig. (IV Corps). The 2d Bn. redesignated 2d Bn., 115th F.A. on 1 April 1938. Concurrently, the 2d Bn., 178th F.A. withdrawn from the state of Tennessee and allotted to the state of South Carolina. The entire regiment allotted to the state of South Carolina on the same date. Regimental HQ organized on 1 April 1938 by redesignation of HQ, 2d Bn., 115th F.A. at Andrews, SC; concurrently, the 1st Bn. organized by conversion and redesignation of the 2d Bn., 105th Engineers (Engrs.) at Spartanburg, SC; the 2d Bn. (HQ organized new) organized by redesignation of subordinate batteries of the 2d Bn., 115th F.A. at Georgetown, SC. The 3d Bn. organized new with HQ at Sumter, SC. Active battalions conducted annual summer training most years at Camp Knox, KY, and some years at Fort Bragg, NC. Assigned on 29 September 1939 to the 13th F.A. Brig. (IV Corps). As part of the 13th F.A. Brig., relieved from the IV Corps on 1 November 1940 and assigned to the I Corps. Inducted into Federal service on 27 January 1941 at Abbeville, SC, and moved to Fort Bragg, NC, where it arrived on 4 February 1941. Location 7 December 1941—Fort Bragg, NC.

Status: Assigned to the USARS as the 178th F.A.; 1st Bn. active at Greer, SC, as an element of the 218th Inf. Brig. (Sep.); 3d Bn. active at Lancaster, SC, and 4th Bn. active at Georgetown, SC, as elements of the 151st F.A. Brig.

Events: 255, 300, 330

Commander, 178th Field Artillery Regiment

Col. Vernon T. Anderson 1 April 1938–ao February 1941

179th Field Artillery Regiment (I) **(155-mm H)** (V Corps) **Ohio National Guard**

HQ—*Not organized,* 1921–27

Constituted in the N.G. in 1921, assigned to the 83d F.A. Brig. (V Corps), and allotted to the state of Ohio. Withdrawn from the N.G. on 2 July 1923 and demobilized.

179th Field Artillery Regiment (II) **(155-mm H)** (GHQR) **Georgia National Guard**

HQ—Atlanta, GA, 1939–41; Camp Blanding, FL, 1941

Constituted in the N.G. on 1 July 1939, assigned to the GHQR, and allotted to the state of Georgia. Organized by redesignation of the 122d Inf. (organized and federally recognized on 10 March 1924 with HQ at Atlanta, GA), less 3d Bn. Inducted into Federal service on 24 February 1941 at Atlanta and moved to Camp Blanding, FL, where it arrived on 3 March 1941. Assigned to the 74th F.A. Brig. (IV Corps). Location 7 December 1941—Camp Blanding, FL.

Events: 300, 330

Commander, 179th Field Artillery Regiment

Col. Thomas L. Alexander	1 July 1939–ao December 1941

180th Field Artillery Regiment (I) **(155-mm H)** (V Corps) **Kentucky and West Virginia National Guard**

HQ—*Not organized,* 1921–27

Constituted in the N.G. in 1921 and assigned to the 83d F.A. Brig. (V Corps). HQ, HQ Btry, and the 1st and 2d Bns. allotted to the state of Kentucky; 3d Bn. allotted to the state of West Virginia. Placed on the DNG list on 2 July 1923. All elements withdrawn from the states of Kentucky and West Virginia in March 1926, but remained allotted to the Fifth Corps Area. Withdrawn from the N.G. on 17 September 1927 and demobilized.

180th Field Artillery Regiment (II) **(155-mm H)** (26th Division) **Massachusetts National Guard**

HQ—Boston, MA, 1940–41; Camp Edwards, MA, 1941

Constituted in the N.G. on 9 October 1940, assigned to the 26th Div., and allotted to the state of Massachusetts. Concurrently organized by conversion and redesignation of the 110th Cav. (organized and federally recognized on 3 July 1924 with HQ at Boston, MA, as an element of the 23d Cav. Div.). Inducted into Federal service on 16 January 1941 at Boston and moved to Camp Edwards, MA, where it arrived on 28 January 1941. Location 7 December 1941—Camp Edwards, MA.

Events: 330

Commanders, 180th Field Artillery Regiment

Col. John A. Agnew	9 October 1940–ao May 1942

181st Field Artillery Regiment (I) **(155-mm H)** (V Corps) **Indiana National Guard**

HQ—Kokomo, IN, 1921–22

Constituted in the N.G. in 1921, assigned to the 83d F.A. Brig. (V Corps), and allotted to the state of Indiana. Organized by redesignation of the 1st F.A., Indiana N.G. and federally recognized on 30 June 1921 with HQ at Kokomo, IN. Redesignated 150th F.A. on 1 January 1922.

Commanders, 181st Field Artillery Regiment (I)

Col. Walter W. Unversaw	30 June 1921–1 January 1922

181st Field Artillery Regiment (II) **(155-mm H)** (VII Corps) **Tennessee National Guard**

HQ—Chattanooga, TN, 1940–41; Camp Forrest, TN, 1941

Constituted in the N.G. on 1 October 1940 and allotted to the state of Tennessee. Concurrently, organized by conversion and redesignation of the 109th Cav. (organized and federally recognized on 6 June 1923 with HQ at Chattanooga, TN, as an element of the 23d Cav. Div.). Inducted into Federal service on 24 February 1941 at Chattanooga and moved to Camp Forrest, TN, where it arrived on 4 March 1941. Assigned to the 75th F.A. Brig. (VII Corps). Location 7 December 1941—Camp Forrest, TN.

Status: Assigned to the USARS as the 181st F.A.; 1st Bn. active at Chattannoga, TN, as an element of the 196th F.A. Brig.

Events: 324

Commanders, 181st Field Artillery Regiment (II)

Col. Ira R. Summers	1 October 1940–ao December 1941

182d Field Artillery Regiment (155-mm H) (VI Corps) **Michigan National Guard**

HQ—*Not organized,* 1921–22; Detroit, MI, 1922–41; Fort Knox, KY, 1941

Constituted in the N.G. in 1921, assigned to the 84th F.A. Brig. (VI Corps), and allotted to the state of Michigan. The 1st Bn. organized and federally recognized on 1 November 1922 with HQ at Detroit, MI. Regimental HQ organized and federally recognized on 6 December 1922 at Detroit. Relieved from the 84th F.A. Brig. (VI Corps) on 2 July 1923 and assigned to the 185th F.A. Brig. (VI Corps). Relieved from the 185th F.A. Brig. (VI Corps) on 1 October 1933 and assigned to the 22d F.A. Brig. (VI Corps). The 2d Bn. organized and federally recognized on 10 April 1939 with HQ at Detroit, MI. Conducted annual summer training most years at Camp Grayling, MI, and some years at Camp Custer, MI, or Camp Ripley, MN. For annual training in the summer of 1926, the regiment, a tractor-drawn unit, conducted a 250-mile round trip road march to Camp Grayling without losing a single vehicle. The regiment was reorganized as a truck-drawn unit in 1935. Relieved from the 22d F.A. Brig. (VI Corps) on 30 December 1940 and assigned to the 72d F.A. Brig. (V Corps). Inducted into Federal service on 7 April 1941 at Detroit and moved to Fort Knox, KY, where it arrived on 14 April 1941. Location 7 December 1941—Fort Knox, KY.

Status: Assigned to the USARS as the 182d F.A.

Events: 214, 264, 302, 324

Commanders, 182d Field Artillery Regiment

Col. Heinrich A. Pickert	6 December 1922–6 July 1935	Col. George V. N. Lothrop	6 July 1935–ao November 1940
Unknown	ao November 1940–7 December 1941		

183d Field Artillery Regiment (I) **(155-mm H)** (VI Corps) **Wisconsin National Guard**

HQ—*Not organized,* 1921–27

Constituted in the N.G. in 1921, assigned to the 84th F.A. Brig. (VI Corps), and allotted to the state of Wisconsin. Placed on the DNG list on 2 July 1923 and withdrawn from the state of Wisconsin, but remained allotted to the Sixth Corps Area. Withdrawn from the N.G. on 17 September 1927 and demobilized.

183d Field Artillery Regiment (II) **(155-mm H)** (IX Corps) **Idaho National Guard**

HQ—Boise, ID, 1940–41; Fort Francis E. Warren, WY, 1941

Constituted in the N.G. on 16 September 1940 and allotted to the state of Idaho. Concurrently, organized by conversion and redesignation of the 116th Cav. Regt. (organized and federally recognized on 11 February 1922 with HQ at Boise, ID, as an element of the 24th Cav. Div.). Assigned on 30 December 1940 to the IX Corps. Inducted into Federal service on 1 April 1941 at Boise and moved to Fort Francis E. Warren, WY, where it arrived on 15 April 1941. Assigned to the 76th F.A. Brig. (IX Corps). Location 7 December 1941—Fort Francis E. Warren, WY.

Events: 326

Commander, 183d Field Artillery Regiment

Col. Samuel D. Hays 16 September 1940–January 1942

184th Field Artillery Regiment (I) **(155-mm H)** (VI Corps) **Illinois National Guard**

HQ—*Not organized,* 1921

Constituted in the N.G. in 1921, assigned to the 84th F.A. Brig. (VI Corps), and allotted to the state of Illinois. Withdrawn from the state of Illinois on 18 November 1921 and the 123d F.A. substituted and allotted to the state of Illinois instead.

184th Field Artillery Regiment (II) **(Colored) (155-mm H)** **Illinois National Guard**

HQ—Chicago, IL, 1940–41; Fort Custer, MI, 1941

Constituted in the N.G. on 6 October 1940 and allotted to the state of Illinois. Concurrently organized by conversion and redesignation of the 8th Inf., Illinois N.G. (organized and federally recognized on 25 August 1921 with HQ at Chicago, IL). Attached to the Second Army on 30 December 1940. Inducted into Federal service on 6 January 1941 at Chicago and moved to Fort Custer, MI, where it arrived on 15 January 1941. Location 7 December 1941—Fort Custer, MI.

Commanders, 184th Field Artillery Regiment

Col. William J. Warfield	6 October 1940–17 December 1940
Col. Julian Dawson	17 December 1940–5 January 1941
Lt. Col. Oscar Randall	5 January 1941–September 1942

185th Field Artillery Regiment (155-mm H) (VII Corps) **Iowa and North Dakota National Guard**

HQ—*Not organized,* 1921–24; Davenport, IA, 1924–41; Fort Knox, KY, 1941

Constituted in the N.G. in 1921, assigned to the VII Corps Arty., and allotted to the states of Iowa and North Dakota. Regimental HQ, HQ Btry, and 1st and 2d Bns. allotted to the state of Iowa; 3d Bn. allotted to the state of North Dakota. The 1st Bn. organized and federally recognized on 8 February 1922 with HQ at Davenport, IA. Assigned on 2 July 1923 to the 14th F.A. Brig. (VII Corps). Regimental HQ organized and federally recognized on 1 June 1924 at Davenport. The 2d Bn. organized and federally recognized on 19 June 1924 with HQ at Boone, IA. Relieved from the VII Corps in December 1929 and assigned to the 34th Div. The 3d Bn. organized and federally recognized on 3 April 1937 with HQ at Jamestown, ND. The 3d Bn. withdrawn from allotment to the state of North Dakota on 18 September 1940 and allotted to the state of Iowa. Conducted annual summer training at Camp Knox, KY; Camp McCoy, WI; and Camp Ripley, MN. For at least 3 years, 1938–40, the regiment also trained some 26 company-grade field artillery officers of the 88th Div. at Camp Ripley and Camp Grafton. Inducted into Federal service on 7 April 1941 at Boone, IA, and moved to Camp Claiborne, LA, where it arrived on 10 March 1941. Location 7 December 1941—Fort Knox, KY.

Status: Assigned to the CARS as the 185th F.A. Regt.; all elements inactive in the Iowa N.G.

Events: 233, 303, 320, 328

Commanders, 185th Field Artillery Regiment

Col. Harry W. Ward	1 June 1924–25 January 1941	Col. Walter L. Anderson	25 January 1941–ao December 1941

186th Field Artillery Regiment (155-mm H) (VI Corps) **New York National Guard**

HQ—Brooklyn, NY, 1940–41; Fort Ethan Allen, VT, 1941

Constituted in the N.G. on 1 September 1940, assigned to the 71st F.A. Brig. (VI Corps), and allotted to the state of New York. Concurrently, organized by conversion and redesignation of the 106th Inf. (organized and federally recognized on 31 March 1920 with HQ at Brooklyn, NY), less 3d Bn. Inducted into Federal service on 3 February 1941 at Brooklyn and moved to Fort Ethan Allen, VT, where it arrived on 19 February 1941. Location 7 December 1941—Fort Ethan Allen, VT.

Events: 330

Commander, 186th Field Artillery Regiment

Col. James M. Garrett	1 September 1940–ao February 1942

187th Field Artillery Regiment (I) **(155-mm H)** (VIII Corps) **Colorado National Guard**

HQ—*Not organized,* 1921–27

Constituted in the N.G. in 1921, assigned to the 85th F.A. Brig. (VIII Corps), and allotted to the state of Colorado. Placed on the deferred list on 2 July 1923, redesignated 393d F.A., and transferred to the O.R. as a DNG unit. Concurrently, relieved from the 85th F.A. Brig. (VIII Corps) and assigned to the 187th F.A. Brig. (VIII Corps). Withdrawn as a DNG unit on 11 January 1927 and permanently allotted to the O.R. as the 393d F.A.

187th Field Artillery Regiment (II) **(155-mm H)** (VI Corps) **New York National Guard**

HQ—Brooklyn, NY, 1940–41; Fort Ethan Allen, VT, 1941

Constituted in the N.G. on 1 September 1940, assigned to the 71st F.A. Brig. (VI Corps), and allotted to the state of New York. Concurrently organized, less 3d Bn., by conversion and redesignation of the 14th Inf., New York N.G. (organized and federally recognized on 31 March 1920 with HQ at Brooklyn, NY). Inducted into Federal service on 3 February 1941 at Brooklyn and moved to Fort Ethan Allen, VT, where it arrived on 19 February 1941. Location 7 December 1941—Fort Ethan Allen, VT.

Status: HQ active in the New York N.G. as Detachment 1, 1442d Military Police (M.P.) Co.; remaining elements assigned to the USARS as the 187th F.A.; no active elements.

Events: 330

Commanders, 187th Field Artillery Regiment

Col. James G. Conroy	1 September 1940–December 1940	Lt. Col. Oscar A. Axelson	25 February 1941–9 May 1941
Col. Chester B. McCormick	December 1940–25 February 1941	Col. Winifred C. Greene	9 May 1941–8 February 1943

188th Field Artillery Regiment (I) **(155-mm H)** (VIII Corps) **Texas National Guard**

HQ—*Not organized,* 1921–39

Constituted in the N.G. in 1921, assigned to the 85th F.A. Brig. (VIII Corps), and allotted to the state of Texas. Dallas, TX, designated as HQ on organization, but the unit was never organized at that location. Designated mobilization training station was Fort Sill, OK, 1923–39. Relieved from the 85th F.A. Brig. (VIII Corps) on 2 July 1923 and assigned to the 187th F.A. Brig. (VIII Corps). Designated mobilization training station was Fort Sill. Allotment withdrawn from the Texas N.G. on 17 September 1927, but unit remained allotted to the Eighth Corps Area until withdrawn in 1939.

188th Field Artillery Regiment (II) **(155-mm H)** (IX Corps) **North Dakota National Guard**

HQ—Bismarck, ND, 1940–41; Fort Francis E. Warren, WY, 1941

Constituted in the N.G. on 18 September 1940 and allotted to the state of North Dakota. Concurrently, organized with personnel and assets from the 3d Bn., 185th F.A. and the 3d Bn., 164th Inf. Regimental HQ organized and federally recognized at Bismarck, ND. Assigned on 30 December 1940 to the IX Corps. Inducted into Federal service on 1 April 1941 at Bismarck and moved to Fort Francis E. Warren, WY, where it arrived on 16 April 1941. Assigned to the 76th F.A. Brig. (IX Corps). Location 7 December 1941—Fort Francis E. Warren, WY.

Events: 326

Commander, 188th Field Artillery Regiment

Col. Percy Hansen	18 September 1940–8 February 1943

189th Field Artillery Regiment (155-mm H) (VIII Corps) **Oklahoma National Guard**

HQ—*Not organized,* 1921–23; Enid, OK, 1923–40; Fort Sill, OK, 1940–41; Camp Barkeley, TX, 1941

Constituted in the N.G. in 1921, assigned to the 85th F.A. Brig. (VIII Corps), and allotted to the state of Oklahoma. Organized on 14 October 1921 by redesignation of the 2d F.A., Oklahoma N.G. (subordinate elements organized 1919–20) as the 189th F.A. Relieved from the 85th F.A. Brig. (VIII Corps) on 2 July 1923 and assigned to the 187th F.A. Brig. (VIII Corps). Entire regiment, or elements thereof, called up to perform the following state duties: elements performed flood relief duties at Oklahoma City, OK, 13 Sep–8 October 1923; elements performed oil well disaster relief at Oklahoma City, 30 October–1 November 1930. Regimental HQ organized and federally recognized on 23 December 1923 at Enid, OK. Relieved from the 187th F.A. Brig. (VIII Corps) in March 1930 and assigned to the 45th Div. Conducted annual summer training at Fort Sill, OK. Designated mobilization training station was Fort Sill. Inducted into Federal service on 16 September 1940 at Enid as an element of the 45th Div., and moved to Fort Sill, where it arrived on 24 September 1940. Transferred on 12 June 1941 to Camp Barkeley, TX. Location 7 December 1941—Camp Barkeley, TX.

Status: Assigned to the CARS as the 189th F.A. Regt.; all elements inactive in the Oklahoma N.G.

Events: 258, 300, 317, 328

Commanders, 189th Field Artillery Regiment

Col. William A. Graves	9 May 1922–23 February 1938	Col. George A. Hutchinson	8 March 1938–11 February 1942

190th Field Artillery Regiment (I) **(155-mm H)** (IX Corps) **Idaho, Utah, and Montana National Guard**

HQ—*Not organized,* 1921–40

Constituted in the N.G. in 1921 and assigned to the 86th F.A. Brig. (IX Corps). HQ, HQ Btry, and 1st Bn. allotted to the state of Idaho; 2d Bn. allotted to the state of Montana; 3d Bn. allotted to the state of Utah. Relieved from assignment to the 86th F.A. Brig. (IX Corps) on 2 July 1923 and assigned to the 189th F.A. Brig. (IX Corps). Idaho elements withdrawn on 14 June 1926 and allotted to the state of Montana. Relieved from assignment to the 189th F.A. Brig. (IX Corps) on 5 September 1928 and assigned to the 195th F.A. Brig. (IX Corps). Relieved from assignment to the 195th F.A. Brig. (IX Corps) on 1 October 1933 and assigned to the 46th F.A. Brig. (GHQR). Withdrawn from the states of Montana and Utah in May 1940.

190th Field Artillery Regiment (II) **(155-mm G)** (V Corps) **Pennsylvania National Guard**

HQ—Tyrone, PA, 1940–41; Camp Shelby, MS, 1941

Constituted in the N.G. on 23 September 1940 and allotted to the state of Pennsylvania. Concurrently, organized by conversion and redesignation of the 103d Cav. (organized and federally recognized on 16 October 1919 with HQ at Philadelphia, PA). Inducted into Federal service on 13 January 1941 at Tyrone, PA, and moved to Camp Shelby, MS, where it arrived on 3 February 1941. Assigned to the 73d F.A. Brig. (V Corps). Location 7 December 1941—Camp Shelby, MS.

Commanders, 190th Field Artillery Regiment

Col. Samuel B. Wolfe	23 September 1940–March 1942

191st Field Artillery Regiment (155-mm H) (IX Corps) **California National Guard**

HQ—*Not organized,* 1921–27

Constituted in the N.G. in 1921, assigned to the 86th F.A. Brig. (IX Corps), and allotted to the state of California. Placed on the DNG list on 2 July 1923. Withdrawn from allotment to the state of California in March 1926, but remained allotted to the Ninth Corps Area. Withdrawn from the N.G. on 17 September 1927 and demobilized.

191st Field Artillery Regiment (155-mm H) (VII Corps) **Tennessee National Guard**

HQ—*Not organized,* 1939–40; Nashville, TN, 1940–41; Camp Forrest, TN, 1941

Constituted in the N.G. on 4 December 1939 and allotted to the state of Tennessee. The 2d Bn. concurrently organized by redesignation of the 2d Bn., 115th F.A. at Maryville, TN. The 3d Bn. organized on 15 February 1940 with HQ at Kingsport, TN. Regimental HQ organized and federally recognized on 20 February 1940 at Nashville, TN. The 1st Bn. organized on 28 April 1940 with HQ at Nashville. Inducted into Federal service on 24 February 1941 at Nashville and moved to Camp Forrest, TN, where it arrived on 3 March 1941. Assigned to the 75th F.A. Brig. (VII Corps). Location 7 December 1941—Camp Forrest, TN.

Events: 324

Commander, 191st Field Artillery Regiment

Col. Harry S. Berry	13 December 1939–ao December 1941

192d Field Artillery Regiment (155-mm H) (I Corps) **Connecticut National Guard**

HQ—New London, CT, 1921–41; Camp Blanding, FL, 1941

Constituted in the N.G. in 1921 as the 192d Arty., C.A.C., and allotted to the state of Connecticut. Organized on 23 May 1921 by redesignation of the 1st C.A., Connecticut N.G. (organized and federally recognized on 1 March 1921 with HQ at New London, CT) as the 192d Artillery, C.A.C. Redesignated as the 192d F.A. on 3 November 1921 and assigned to the 81st F.A. Brig. (I Corps). Relieved from assignment to the 81st F.A. Brig. (I Corps) on 2 July 1923 and assigned to the 194th F.A. Brig. (I Corps). Relieved from assignment to the 194th F.A. Brig. (I Corps) in December 1929 and assigned to the 43d Div. The regiment, or elements thereof, were called up to perform the following state duties: riot control at the textile workers strike at Putnam, CT; flood relief at Hartford, CT, 19 March–1 April 1936; hurricane relief near Rockville, CT, 22–27 September 1938. Conducted annual summer training at numerous locations to include Camp Devens, MA; Camp Welsh, NY; Fort Eustis, VA; Tobyhanna, PA; Niantic, CT; and the Underhill Artillery Range at Fort Ethan Allen, VT. Inducted into Federal service on 24 February 1941 at New London as an element of the 43d Div., and moved to Camp Blanding, FL, where it arrived on 18 March 1941. Location 7 December 1941—Camp Blanding, FL.

Status: Assigned to the USARS as the 192d F.A.; 2d Bn. active at New Haven, CT, as an element of the 29th Inf. Div. (Light).

Events: 190, 280, 301, 325, 328, 330

Commanders, 192d Field Artillery Regiment

Col. Morris B. Payne	3 November 1921–21 June 1923	Lt. Col. George J. Schoen	20 December 1934–27 December 1934
Col. Mogens J. Mogensen	21 June 1923–2 January 1933	Col. Otto H. Schroeter	27 December 1934–1 October 1940
Col. C. Hadlai Hull	2 January 1933–20 December 1934	Col. George J. Schoen	1 October 1940–19 February 1942

194th Field Artillery Regiment (155-mm G) (V Corps) **Ohio, Indiana, and Kentucky National Guard**

HQ—*Not organized,* 1921–27

Constituted in the N.G. in 1921 and assigned to the 83d F.A. Brig. (V Corps). Regimental HQ, HQ Btry, and 1st Bn. allotted to the state of Ohio; 2d Bn. allotted to the state of Indiana; and 3d Bn. allotted to the state of Kentucky. All elements withdrawn from the states of Ohio, Indiana, and Kentucky in March 1926, but remained allotted to the Fifth Corps Area. Withdrawn from the N.G. on 17 September 1927 and demobilized.

195th Field Artillery Regiment (155-mm G) (VII Corps) **Kansas and Minnesota National Guard**

HQ—*Not organized,* 1921–27

Constituted in the N.G. in 1921 and assigned to the VII Corps. Regimental HQ, HQ Btry, and 1st Bn. allotted to the state of Kansas, and 2d and 3d Bns. allotted to the state of Minnesota. Assigned on 2 July 1923 to the 14th F.A. Brig. (VII Corps). All elements withdrawn from allotment to the states of Kansas and Minnesota in March 1926. Withdrawn from the N.G. on 17 September 1927 and demobilized.

196th Field Artillery Regiment (155-mm G) (IX Corps) **California, Washington, and Oregon National Guard**

HQ—*Not organized,* 1921–36

Constituted in the N.G. in 1921 and assigned to the 86th F.A. Brig. (IX Corps). Regimental HQ, HQ Btry, and 2d Bn. allotted to the state of California; 1st Bn. allotted to the state of Washington; and 3d Bn. allotted to the state of Oregon. Relieved from assignment to the 86th F.A. Brig. (IX Corps) on 2 July 1923 and assigned to the 189th F.A. Brig. (IX Corps). Relieved from assignment to the 189th F.A. Brig. (IX Corps) on 5 September 1928 and assigned to the 195th F.A. Brig. (IX Corps). Relieved from assignment to the 195th F.A. Brig. (IX Corps) on 1 October 1933 and assigned to the 46th F.A. Brig. (GHQR). The 2d Bn. organized on 16 April 1936 at Santa Barbara, CA. Unit designation "196th" withdrawn from the respective states on 1 July 1936 and "144th" substituted. Concurrently the 2d Bn., 196th F.A. redesignated as the 2d Bn., 144th F.A.

216th Field Artillery Regiment (75-mm G) (GHQR) **Michigan National Guard**

HQ—*Not organized,* 1921–40

Constituted in the N.G. on 20 April 1921, assigned to the 221st F.A. Brig. (GHQR), and allotted to the state of Michigan. Placed on the DNG list on 2 July 1923, allotted to the O.R. as the 415th F.A. (DNG), and allotted to the Sixth Corps Area. Withdrawn from the O.R. in February 1928 and reallotted to the Michigan N.G. as the 216th F.A. Assigned on 1 October 1933 to the 24th F.A. Brig. (GHQR). Converted from tractor drawn to truck drawn on 13 March 1935. Designated mobilization training station was Camp Custer, MI. Withdrawn from the N.G. in May 1940.

217th Field Artillery Regiment (75-mm G) (GHQR) **Illinois National Guard**

HQ—*Not organized,* 1921–27

Constituted in the N.G. in 1921, assigned to the 221st F.A. Brig. (GHQR), and allotted to the state of Illinois. Placed on the DNG list on 2 July 1923, redesignated the 416th F.A. (DNG), and allotted to the Sixth Corps Area. Withdrawn from the N.G. on 17 September 1927 and demobilized.

218th Field Artillery Regiment (75-mm G-H) (GHQR) **Illinois/Oregon National Guard**

HQ—*Not organized,* 1921–30; Portland, OR, 1930–40; Camp Murray, WA, 1940–41; Fort Lewis, WA, 1941

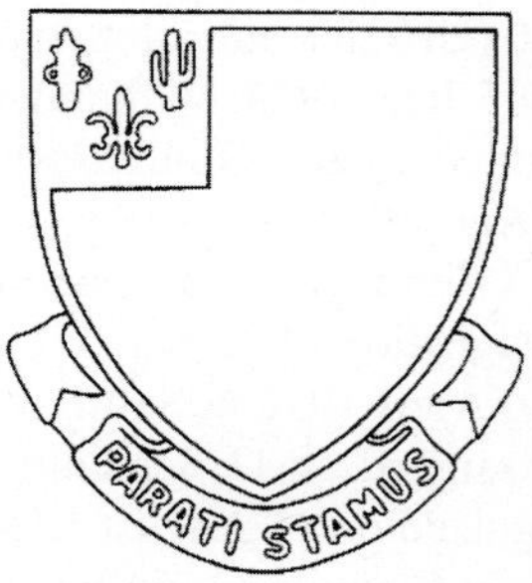

Constituted in the N.G. in 1921, assigned to the 224th F.A. Brig. (GHQR), and allotted to the state of Illinois. Placed on the DNG list on 2 July 1923, redesignated the 417th F.A. (DNG), and allotted to the Sixth Corps Area. The 1st Bn. withdrawn from the allotment to the state of Illinois on 30 September 1924 and allotted to the state of Oregon. Btry. A organized on 18 May 1925 at Portland, OR, by re-designation of Btry. A, 148th F.A. Reminder of the regiment withdrawn from the Sixth Corps Area on 17 September 1927. HQ, 1st Bn. organized and federally recognized on 5 April 1929 at Portland. Remainder of the regiment allotted to the state of Oregon on 13 November 1929 and reorganized as a 155-mm howitzer regiment. Assigned on 12 December 1929 to the 41st Div. Regimental HQ organized and federally recognized on 5 June 1930 at Portland. The 3d Bn. organized and federally recognized on 6 June 1930 at Portland. Conducted annual summer training at numerous locations to include Fort Lewis, WA; Camp Jackson, OR; Camp Clatsop, OR; Camp Murray, WA; and most years at Fort Stevens, OR. Inducted into Federal service on 16 September 1940 at Portland as an element of the 41st Div., and moved to Camp Murray, WA, where it arrived on 19 September 1940. Transferred on 20 March 1941 to Fort Lewis, WA. Location 7 December 1941—Fort Lewis, WA.

Status: Assigned to the USARS as the 218th F.A.; 2d Bn. active at Portland, OR, as an element of the 41st Inf. Brig. (Sep.).

Events: 238, 304, 309, 314, 326

Commander, 218th Field Artillery Regiment

Col. William D. Jackson 5 June 1930–14 February 1942

219th Field Artillery Regiment (75-mm G Mtzd) (GHQR) **Deferred National Guard**

HQ—*Not organized,* 1921–27

Constituted in the N.G. in 1921 and assigned to the 222d F.A. Brig. (GHQR). Placed on the DNG list on 2 July 1923. Withdrawn from the N.G. on 17 September 1927 and demobilized.

220th Field Artillery Regiment (75-mm G) (GHQR) **Deferred National Guard**

HQ—*Not organized,* 1921–27

Constituted in the N.G. in 1921 and assigned to the 222d F.A. Brig. (GHQR). Placed on the DNG list on 2 July 1923. Withdrawn from the N.G. on 17 September 1927 and demobilized.

221st Field Artillery Regiment (75-mm G) (GHQR) **Missouri National Guard**

HQ—*Not organized,* 1921–27

Constituted in the N.G. in 1921, assigned to the 224th F.A. Brig. (GHQR), and allotted to the state of Missouri. Withdrawn in September 1921 from the state of Missouri. Placed on the DNG list on 2 July 1923. Withdrawn from the N.G. on 17 September 1927 and demobilized.

222d Field Artillery Regiment (75-mm G) (GHQR) **Missouri/Utah National Guard**

HQ—*Not organized,* 1921–26; Salt Lake City, UT, 1926–41; San Luis Obispo, CA, 1941

Constituted in the N.G. in 1921, assigned to the 224th F.A. Brig. (GHQR), and allotted to the state of Missouri. Withdrawn from the state of Missouri on 5 June 1924. Withdrawn from the Seventh Corps Area on 5 February 1925 and allotted to the Ninth Corps Area. The 1st Bn. (organized and federally recognized on 27 April 1921 as 1st Sq., 1st Cav., Utah N.G.; redesignated on 11 October 1921 as 2d Sq., 116th Cav.) organized on 9 February 1925 at Brigham City, UT, by conversion and redesignation of 2d Sq., 116th Cav. Regimental HQ organized and federally recognized on 16 April 1926 at Salt Lake City, UT. Reorganized on 1 July 1930 as a 155-mm H Regt. Assigned on 11 September 1930 to the 40th Div. The 3d Bn. organized and federally recognized on 16 August 1930 at Richfield, UT. Conducted annual summer training most years at Camp W.G. Williams, UT, and some years at Camp Lewis, WA, or Camp San Luis Obispo, CA. Inducted into Federal service on 3 March 1941 at Salt Lake City as an element of the 40th Div., and moved to Camp San Luis Obispo, CA, where it arrived on 18 March 1941. Location 7 December 1941—Camp San Luis Obispo, CA.

Status: Assigned to the USARS as the 222d F.A.; 2d Bn. active at Cedar City, UT, as an element of the 45th F.A. Brig.

Events: 231, 304, 314, 326

Commanders, 222d Field Artillery Regiment

Col. Hamilton Gardner	26 April 1926–18 March 1937	Col. Albert E. Wilfong	18 March 1937–26 December 1939
Col. J. Wallace West	27 December 1939–ao January 1942		

223d Field Artillery Regiment (75-mm G-P) (GHQR) **Ohio National Guard**

HQ—*Not organized,* 1921–27

Constituted in the N.G. in 1921, assigned to the 220th F.A. Brig. (GHQR), and allotted to the state of Ohio. Placed on the DNG list on 2 July 1923, redesignated the 421st F.A. (DNG), and allotted to the Fifth Corps Area. Withdrawn from the N.G. on 17 September 1927 and demobilized.

224th Field Artillery Regiment (75-mm G-P) (GHQR) **Kentucky National Guard**

HQ—*Not organized,* 1921–27

Constituted in the N.G. in 1921, assigned to the 220th F.A. Brig. (GHQR), and allotted to the state of Kentucky. Placed on the DNG list on 2 July 1923, redesignated the 422d F.A. (DNG), and allotted to the Fifth Corps Area. Withdrawn from the N.G. on 17 September 1927 and demobilized.

225th Field Artillery Regiment (75-mm G-P) (GHQR) **Indiana National Guard**

HQ—*Not organized,* 1921–27

Constituted in the N.G. in 1921, assigned to the 223d F.A. Brig. (GHQR), and allotted to the state of Indiana. Placed on the DNG list on 2 July 1923, redesignated the 423d F.A. (DNG), and allotted to the Fifth Corps Area. Withdrawn from the N.G. on 17 September 1927 and demobilized.

226th Field Artillery Regiment (75-mm G-P) (GHQR) **National Guard**

HQ—*Not organized,* 1921–27

Constituted in the N.G. in 1921 and assigned to the 223d F.A. Brig. (GHQR). Placed on the DNG list on 2 July 1923. Withdrawn from the N.G. on 17 September 1927 and demobilized.

227th Field Artillery Regiment (155-mm G) (GHQR) **Missouri National Guard**

HQ—*Not organized,* 1921–27

Constituted in the N.G. in 1921, assigned to the 227th F.A. Brig. (GHQR), and allotted to the state of Missouri. Placed on the DNG list on 2 July 1923, redesignated the 424th F.A. (DNG), and allotted to the Seventh Corps Area. Withdrawn from the N.G. on 17 September 1927 and demobilized.

228th Field Artillery Regiment (6in G) (GHQR) **New York National Guard**

HQ—*Not organized,* 1921–27

Constituted in the N.G. in 1921, assigned to the GHQR, and allotted to the state of New York. Placed on the DNG list on 2 July 1923, redesignated the 425th F.A. (DNG), and allotted to the Second Corps Area. Withdrawn from the N.G. on 17 September 1927 and demobilized.

258th Field Artillery Regiment (155-mm G) (II Corps) **New York National Guard**

HQ—New York City, NY, 1921–41; Fort Ethan Allen, VT, 1941; Madison Barracks, NY, 1941

Constituted in the N.G. on 30 December 1920 as the 193d Artillery, C.A.C. and allotted to the state of New York. Organized by redesignation of active elements of the 8th Coast Defense Command, New York N.G. Regimental HQ was organized and federally recognized on 11 May 1921 at New York City, NY. Redesignated on 12 September 1921 as the 193d F.A. Regt. Redesignated on 11 October 1921 as the 258th F.A. and assigned to the II Corps Artillery. Further assigned to the 15th F.A. Brig. (II Corps) on 2 July 1923. The regiment sailed from New York harbor on 1 August 1925 on the U.S.S. *George Washington* to Fort Eustis, VA, to attend annual summer training. Relieved from assignment to the 15th F.A. Brig. (II Corps) in 1927, but remained assigned to the II Corps. Assigned on 1 October 1933 to the 20th F.A. Brig. (II Corps). Conducted annual summer training most years at numerous locations to include Camp Welsh, NY; Fort Eustis, VA; Fort Ontario, NY; Camp Smith, NY; Pine Camp, NY; and Fort Bragg, NC. Designated mobilization training station was Fort Bragg, NC. Relieved from assignment to the II Corps on 1 September 1940 and assigned to the 71st F.A. Brig. (VI Corps). Inducted into Federal service on 3 February 1941 at New York City and moved to Fort Ethan Allen, VT, where it arrived on 18 February 1941. Transferred on 2 June 1941 to Madison Barracks, NY. Location 7 December 1941—Camp Blanding, FL.

Status: Assigned to the USARS as the 258th F.A.; 1st Bn. active at Jamaica, NY, as an element of the 42d Inf. Div.

Events: 280, 330

Commanders, 258th Field Artillery Regiment

Col. Elmore F. Austin	28 November 1921–18 March 1927	Col. Paul Loeser	25 March 1927–18 November 1939
Col. Lewis L. Leavell	15 January 1940–ao January 1942		

301st Field Artillery Regiment (75-mm G) (94th Division) **Organized Reserve Massachusetts**

HQ—Boston, MA, 1921–41

Arrived at the port of New York on 5 January 1919 on the S.S. *Nieuw Amsterdam* as the 301st F.A., an element of the 76th Div. Demobilized on 20 January 1919 at Camp Devens, MA. Reconstituted in the O.R. on 24 June 1921, assigned to the 94th Div., and allotted to the First Corps Area. Initiated on 19 November 1921 with regimental HQ at Boston, MA. Subordinate battalion HQ concurrently organized as follows: 1st Bn. at Concord, MA, and 2d Bn. at Boston. Typically conducted Inactive Training Period meetings at the University Club in Boston. Conducted summer training most years with the 7th F.A. at Fort Ethan Allen, VT. Conducted field artillery CMTC training some years at Fort Ethan Allen as an alternate form of annual training. Primary ROTC feeder school was Harvard University. Location 7 December 1941—Boston, MA.

Status: Inactive in the US Army Reserve as the 301st F.A. Bn., a component of the 94th Inf. Div.

Commanders, 301st Field Artillery Regiment

Col. George M. Brooks	5 August 1917–20 January 1919	Unknown	ao June 1932–ao June 1934
Demobilized/Inactive	20 January 1919–18 November 1921	Lt. Col. Earl F. Bliss	ao June 1934–ao September 1935
Maj. Earl F. Bliss	19 November 1921–25 November 1922	Unknown	ao September 1935–ao June 1936
Col. Robert E. Goodwin	25 November 1922–ao June 1932	Col. Francis T. Colby	ao June 1936–ao June 1939
Unknown	ao June 1939–7 December 1941		

302d Field Artillery Regiment (75-mm G) (76th Division) **Organized Reserve Rhode Island**

HQ—Providence, RI, 1921–41

Arrived at the port of Boston on 3 May 1919 on the U.S.S. *Canandaigua* as the 302d F.A., an element of the 76th Div. Demobilized on 7 May 1919 at Camp Devens, MA. Reconstituted in the O.R. on 24 June 1921, assigned to the 76th Div., and allotted to the First Corps Area. Initiated on 30 December 1921 with regimental HQ at Providence, RI. Typically conducted Inactive Training Period meetings at the Benefit Street Arsenal until October 1929; thereafter at the Armory of Mounted Commands in Providence. The regiment established an unusually close training relationship with the 103d F.A., Rhode Island N.G. It often used the armory, weapons, horses, and equipment of the 103d F.A. during its Inactive Training Period meetings. Numerous regimental officers attended each field service firing of the 103d F.A. Conducted summer training with the 7th F.A. at Fort Ethan Allen, VT. Conducted summer training at Charleston, RI, in 1925 and 1928 with the 103d F.A. Colonel Barker became the first postwar regimental commander of the 103d F.A. in 1930 when that unit expanded to a full regiment. Several other officers from the 302d F.A. also concurrently accepted positions in the 103d F.A. Primary ROTC feeder schools were Harvard and Yale Universities. Designated mobilization station was Pine Camp, NY. Location 7 December 1941—Providence, RI.

Status: Disbanded on 1 May 1959 as the 302d F.A. Bn.

Commanders, 302d Field Artillery Regiment

Col. Daniel F. Craig	4 September 1917–15 October 1918	Maj. Jonathan H. Harwood	30 December 1921–7 July 1922
Lt. Col. Edward R.W. McCabe	15 October 1918–6 November 1918	Col. Harold R. Barker	8 July 1922–1 January 1930
Col. William P. Platt	6 November 1918–7 May 1919	Col. Jonathan H. Harwood	2 January 1930–ao January 1940
Demobilized/Inactive	7 May 1919–30 December 1921	Unknown	ao January 1940–7 December 1941

303d Field Artillery Regiment (75-mm G) (97th Division) **Organized Reserve Maine**

HQ—Auburn, ME, 1921–25; Portland, ME, 1925–41

Arrived at the port of Boston on 3 May 1919 on the U.S.S. *Canandaigua* as the 303d F.A., an element of the 76th Div. Demobilized on 1 May 1919 at Camp Devens, MA. Reconstituted in the O.R. on 24 June 1921, assigned to the 97th Div., and allotted to the First Corps Area. Initiated on 27 December 1921 with regimental HQ at Auburn, ME. Subordinate battalion HQ concurrently organized as follows: 1st Bn. at Bangor, ME, and 2d Bn. at Lewiston, ME. Regimental HQ relocated in 1925 to Portland, ME. Typically conducted Inactive Training Period meetings at City Hall in Portland. Conducted summer training with the 7th F.A. at Fort Ethan Allen, VT. Conducted summer training with the 152d F.A. at Fort Ethan Allen in 1938. Conducted field artillery CMTC training some years at Fort Ethan Allen as an alternate form of annual training. Provided officers to reinforce the 152d F.A. for the 1939 First Army Maneuver at Plattsburg, NY. Primary ROTC feeder school was the University of Maine. Location 7 December 1941—Portland, ME.

Status: Inactive in the US Army Reserve as the 303d F.A. Bn., a component of the 97th Inf. Div.

Commanders, 303d Field Artillery Regiment

Col. Arthur S. Conklin	2 September 1917–November 1918	Col. Frederick E. Gignoux	27 December 1921–ao January 1932
Col. Leroy V. Patch	16 November 1918–1 May 1919	Col. Charles A. Meserve	ao June 1932–July 1934
Demobilized/Inactive	1 May 1919–December 1921	Col. Frank E. Lowe	July 1934–May 1941
	Lt. Col. Sherman L. Kiser	May 1941–7 December 1941	

304th Field Artillery Regiment (75-mm G) (77th Division) **Organized Reserve New York**

HQ—Brooklyn, NY, 1921–41

Arrived at the port of New York on 29 April 1919 on the U.S.S. *Agamemnon* as the 304th F.A., an element of the 77th Div. Demobilized on 19 May 1919 at Camp Upton, NY. Reconstituted in the O.R. on 24 June 1921, assigned to the 77th Div., and allotted to the Second Corps Area. Initiated on 5 October 1921 with the entire regiment at Brooklyn, NY. Conducted summer training most years with the 7th F.A. at Pine Camp, NY, and some years with the 6th F.A. at Fort Hoyle, MD. Conducted field artillery CMTC training some years at Madison Barracks, NY, as an alternate form of annual training. Primary ROTC feeder school was Princeton University. Designated mobilization station was Camp Dix, NJ. Location 7 December 1941—Brooklyn, NY.

Status: Inactive in the US Army Reserve as the 304th F.A. Bn., a component of the 77th Inf. Div.

Commanders, 304th Field Artillery Regiment

Col. John R. Reilly	5 September 1917–1 April 1918	Maj. Grinnell Martin	28 September 1924–11 September 1926
Col. Raymond W. Briggs	1 April 1918–10 September 1918	Col. James E. Austin	11 September 1926–9 January 1929
Lt. Col. William McCleave	10 September 1918–20 November 1918	Col. Lewis Sanders	9 January 1929–18 June 1932
Col. Copley Enos	20 November 1918–10 May 1919	Lt. Col. Gustavus G. Reiniger	18 June 1932–15 June 1937
Demobilized/Inactive	10 May 1919–5 October 1921	Col. James E. Austin	15 June 1937–19 June 1941
Maj. Elliot C. Bacon	6 October 1921–27 September 1924	Lt. Col. Edward V. Heiskel	10 June 1941–ao December 1941

305th Field Artillery Regiment (75-mm G) (77th Division) **Organized Reserve New York**

HQ—Manhattan, NY, 1921–41

Arrived at the port of New York on 29 April 1919 on the U.S.S. *Agamemnon* as the 305th F.A., an element of the 77th Div. Demobilized on 10 May 1919 at Camp Upton, NY. Reconstituted in the O.R. on 24 June 1921, assigned to the 77th Div., and allotted to the Second Corps Area. Initiated on 11 October 1921 with regimental HQ at Manhattan, NY. Subordinate battalion HQ concurrently organized as follows: 1st Bn. at Manhattan and 2d Bn. at Bronx, NY. Conducted summer training most years with the 7th F.A. at Pine Camp, NY, and some years with the 6th F.A. at Fort Hoyle, MD. Conducted field artillery CMTC training some years at Madison Barracks, NY, as an alternate form of annual training. Primary ROTC feeder school was Princeton University. Designated mobilization station was Camp Dix, NJ. Location 7 December 1941—Manhattan, NY.

Status: Inactive in the US Army Reserve as the 305th F.A. Bn., a component of the 77th Inf. Div.

Commanders, 305th Field Artillery Regiment

Col. Fred C. Doyle	24 August 1917–10 May 1919	Col. William W. Thurston	9 November 1926–2 December 1927
Demobilized/Inactive	10 May 1919–11 October 1921	Col. George C. Haas	2 December 1927–25 July 1930
Unknown	11 October 1921–15 December 1921	Lt. Col. Eugene S. Bibb	25 July 1930–ao December 1933
Col. Henry L. Stimson	15 December 1921–26 July 1922	Maj. Howard R. Humphrey	ao July 1934–ao July 1935
Lt. Col. Robert L. Bacon	26 July 1922–11 August 1923	Unknown	ao July 1935–ao July 1936
Col. Leonard Sullivan	11 August 1923–21 December 1923	Col. Lewis Sanders	ao July 1936–2 August 1941
Maj. Eugene S. Bibb	11 December 1923–8 November 1926	Maj. William W. Owens	2 August 1941–ao December 1941

306th Field Artillery Regiment (155-mm H) (XII Corps) **Organized Reserve New York**

HQ—Bronx, NY, 1921–41

Arrived at the port of New York on 29 April 1919 on the U.S.S. *Agamemnon* as the 306th F.A., an element of the 77th Div. Demobilized on 10 May 1919 at Camp Upton, NY. Reconstituted in the O.R. on 24 June 1921, assigned to the 181st F.A. Brig. (XII Corps), and allotted to the Second Corps Area. Initiated on 23 November 1921 with regimental HQ at Bronx, NY. Subordinate battalion HQ concurrently organized as follows: 1st Bn. at Bronx, NY; 2d Bn. at New Rochelle, NY; and 3d Bn. at Newburgh, NY. Regiment relieved from the 181st F.A. Brig. on 21 December 1929 and assigned to the 77th Div. Typically conducted Inactive Training Period meetings at the armory of the 258th F.A. in New York City, NY. Conducted summer training most years with the 7th F.A. at Pine Camp, NY, and some years at Fort Hoyle, MD, or Fort Bragg, NC. Primary ROTC feeder school was Princeton University. Location 7 December 1941—Bronx, NY.

Status: Inactive in the US Army Reserve as the 306th F.A. Bn., a component of the 77th Inf. Div.

Commanders, 306th Field Artillery Regiment

Col. Lawrence S. Miller	22 August 1917–31 July 1918	Unknown	ao July 1926–22 November 1929
Lt. Col. Frederick H. Smith	31 July 1918–11 September 1918	Lt. Col. Alexander Maxwell	22 November 1929–8 April 1930
Col. Charles D. Winn	11 September 1918–10 May 1919	Col. Roger H. Williams	8 April 1930–10 May 1930
Demobilized/Inactive	10 May 1919–November 1921	Lt. Col. James O. Safford	21 May 1930–ao July 1937
Capt. Clark J. Lawrence	23 November 1921–8 April 1922	Lt. Col. Tom B. Blocker	ao June 1938–24 April 1941
Col. Holland S. Duell	8 April 1922–ao July 1926	Lt. Col. John H. Allen	24 April 1941–ao December 1941

307th Field Artillery Regiment (75-mm G) (78th Division) **Organized Reserve New Jersey**

HQ—Perth Amboy, NJ, 1921–28; Trenton, NJ, 1928–41

Arrived at the port of New York on 14 May 1919 on the S.S. *Guiseppi Verde* as the 307th F.A., an element of the 78th Div. Demobilized on 17 May 1919 at Camp Dix, NJ. Reconstituted in the O.R. on 24 June 1921, assigned to the 78th Div., and allotted to the Second Corps Area. Initiated on 23 November 1921 with regimental HQ at Perth Amboy, NJ. Subordinate battalion HQ concurrently organized as follows: 1st Bn. at Trenton, NJ, and 2d Bn. at Elizabeth, NJ. Entire regiment relocated on 27 August 1928 to Trenton. Typically conducted Inactive Training Period meetings at the Post Office Building or the Federal Building in Trenton. Conducted summer training most years with the 7th F.A. at Pine Camp, NY, and some years with the 6th F.A. at Fort Hoyle, MD. Conducted field artillery CMTC training some years at Madison Barracks, NY, as an alternate form of annual training. Primary ROTC feeder school was Princeton University. Designated mobilization station was Camp Dix, NJ. Location 7 December 1941—Trenton, NJ.

Status: Inactive in the US Army Reserve as the 307th F.A. Bn., a component of the 78th Inf. Div.

Commanders, 307th Field Artillery Regiment

Col. Edward T. Donelly	6 September 1917–30 April 1918
Col. Henry A. Howe	30 April 1918–15 May 1918
Col. James H. Bryson	15 May 1918–21 October 1918
Col. Arthur G. Fisher	21 October 1918–17 April 1919
Col. Francis G. Baldwin	17 April 1919–17 May 1919
Demobilized/Inactive	17 May 1919–23 November 1921
Capt. John K. Dunn	23 November 1921–28 December 1921
Maj. James H. Genung	29 December 1921–16 January 1922
Col. Samuel G. Bernard	17 January 1922–7 January 1924
Lt. Col. George A. Mount	7 January 1924–ao July 1926
Unknown	ao July 1926–ao June 1927
Col. Leigh K. Lydecker	ao June 1927–ao August 1940
Unknown	ao August 1940–7 December 1941

308th Field Artillery Regiment (75-mm G) (78th Division) **Organized Reserve New Jersey**

HQ—Hoboken, NJ, 1921–37; Newark, NJ, 1937–41

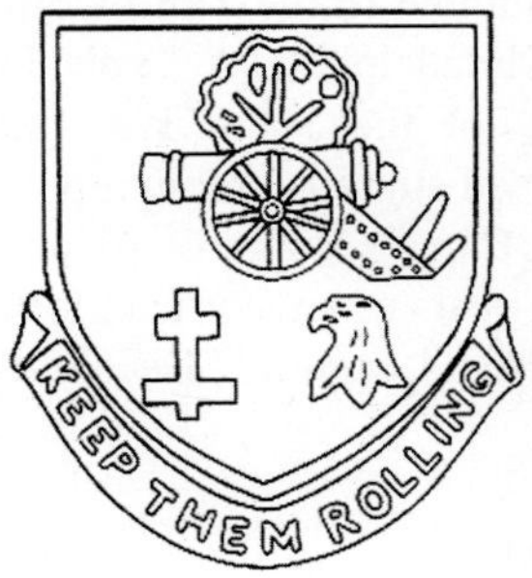

Arrived at the port of New York on 14 May 1919 on the S.S. *Pesaro* as the 308th F.A., an element of the 78th Div. Demobilized on 27 May 1919 at Camp Dix, NJ. Reconstituted in the O.R. on 24 June 1921, assigned to the 78th Div., and allotted to the Second Corps Area. Initiated on 2 November 1921 with regimental HQ at Hoboken, NJ. Subordinate battalion HQ concurrently organized as follows: 1st Bn. at Jersey City, NJ, and 2d Bn. at Newark, NJ. Entire regiment relocated in 1937 to Newark. Conducted summer training with the 2d Bn., 7th F.A. at Madison Barracks, NY, and some years with the 6th F.A. at Fort Hoyle, MD. Primary ROTC feeder school was Princeton University. Designated mobilization station was Camp Dix, NJ. Location 7 December 1941—Newark, NJ.

Status: Disbanded on 1 May 1959 as the 308th F.A. Bn.

Commanders, 308th Field Artillery Regiment

Col. Charles M. Bunker	September 1917–ao December 1918
Unknown	ao December 1918–27 May 1919
Demobilized/Inactive	27 May 1919–November 1921
Col. Samuel A. Welldon	2 November 1921–12 August 1931
Lt. Col. William H. Caldwell	12 August 1931–27 June 1937
Lt. Col. Robert N. Errington	27 June 1937–9 April 1941

309th Field Artillery Regiment (155-mm H) (XII Corps) **Organized Reserve New York**

HQ—*Not initiated,* 1921–22; Brooklyn, NY, 1922–41

Arrived at the port of New York on 7 May 1919 on the S.S. *Infanta Isebella* as the 309th F.A., an element of the 78th Div. Demobilized 14 May 1919 at Camp Dix, NJ. Reconstituted in the O.R. on 24 June 1921, assigned to the 181st F.A. Brig. (XII Corps), and allotted to the Second Corps Area. Initiated on 27 March 1922 with the entire regiment, less the 3d Bn., at Brooklyn, NY. Concurrently, the 3d Bn. organized at Oyster Bay, NY. Reorganized on 8 May 1929 as 75-mm G. Relieved from the 181st F.A. Brig. on 25 November 1929 and assigned to the 78th Div. Typically conducted Inactive Training Period meetings at the armory of the 104th F.A. in Jamaica, NY, or at 70 Pine Street in New York City. Conducted summer training with the 2d Bn., 7th F.A. at Madison Barracks, NY, and some years with the 2d Bn., 16th F.A. at Fort Bragg, NC. Conducted CMTC at Madison Barracks some years as an alternate form of training. Primary ROTC feeder school was Princeton University. Designated mobilization station was Camp Dix, NJ. Location 7 December 1941—Brooklyn, NY.

Status: Disbanded on 1 May 1959 as the 308th F.A. Bn.

Commanders, 309th Field Artillery Regiment

Col. Edward O. Sarratt	4 September 1917–14 May 1919	Col. Louis J. Campbell	24 July 1922–26 April 1926
Demobilized/Inactive	14 May 1919–March 1922	Col. Harry F. Wanvig	26 April 1926–October 1940
Maj. Elmore C. Kerr	27 March 1922–24 July 1922	Lt. Col. Thomas S. Poole	October 1940–September 1941

310th Field Artillery Regiment (75-mm G) (79th Division) **Organized Reserve Pennsylvania**

HQ—Philadelphia, PA, 1921–41

Arrived at the port of New York on 31 May 1919 on the U.S.S. *Tiger* as the 310th F.A., an element of the 79th Div. Demobilized on 29 May 1919 at Camp Dix, NJ. Reconstituted in the O.R. on 24 June 1921, assigned to the 79th Div., and allotted to the Third Corps Area. Initiated on 27 October 1921 with the entire regiment at Philadelphia, PA. Typically conducted Inactive Training Period meetings at the armory of the 108th F.A. and occasionally at the 112th F.A. armory in Camden, NJ. Conducted summer training most years with the 6th F.A. at Fort Hoyle, MD, and some years at Camp George G. Meade, MD, or Fort Eustis, VA. Conducted CMTC at Fort Hoyle some years as an alternate form of training. Primary ROTC feeder school was Duquesne University. Location 7 December 1941—Philadelphia, PA.

Status: Inactive in the US Army Reserve as the 310th F.A. Bn., a component of the 79th Inf. Div.

Commanders, 310th Field Artillery Regiment

Col. Howard L. Landers	29 August 1917–29 May 1919	Maj. Vincent A. Carroll	27 October 1921–4 November 1921
Demobilized/Inactive	29 May 1919–27 October 1921	Lt. Col. William N. Taylor	4 November 1921–17 October 1922
	Col. Joseph W. Keller	17 October 1922–June 1941	

311th Field Artillery Regiment (75-mm G) (79th Division) **Organized Reserve Pennsylvania**

HQ—Philadelphia, PA, 1921–41

Arrived at the port of New York on 27 May 1919 on the U.S.S. *Edgar F. Luckenbach* as the 310th F.A., an element of the 79th Div. Demobilized on 3 June 1919 at Camp Dix, NJ. Reconstituted in the O.R. on 24 June 1921, assigned to the 79th Div., and allotted to the Third Corps Area. Initiated on 2 November 1921 with the entire regiment at Philadelphia, PA. Conducted summer training most years with the 6th F.A. at Fort Hoyle, MD, and some years at Camp George G. Meade, MD. Conducted CMTC at Fort Hoyle some years as an alternate form of training. Primary ROTC feeder school was Duquesne University. Location 7 December 1941—Philadelphia, PA.

Status: Inactive in the US Army Reserve as the 311th F.A. Bn., a component of the 79th Inf. Div.

Commanders, 311th Field Artillery Regiment

Lt. Col. Charles G. Mortimer	30 August 1917–3 November 1917
Col. Raymond W. Briggs	3 November 1917–9 April 1918
Col. Charles G. Mortimer	9 April 1918–3 June 1919
Demobilized/Inactive	3 June 1919–2 November 1921
Maj. Charles B. Heston	4 November 1921–6 May 1922
Col. Daniel M. Bates	6 May 1922–27 December 1932
Col. Horace W. Shelmire	27 December 1932–22 September 1941

312th Field Artillery Regiment (155-mm H) (79th Division) **Organized Reserve Pennsylvania**

HQ—Philadelphia, PA, 1929–41

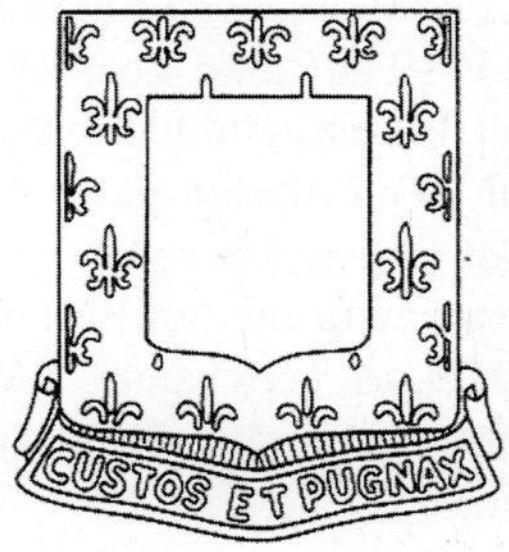

Arrived at the port of Newport News on 25 May 1919 on the U.S.S. *Virginian* as the 312th F.A., an element of the 79th Div. Demobilized on 31 May 1919 at Camp Dix, NJ. Reconstituted in the O.R. on 13 September 1929, assigned to the 79th Div., and allotted to the Third Corps Area. Initiated in November 1929 with the entire regiment at Philadelphia, PA. Conducted summer training most years with the 6th F.A. at Fort Hoyle, MD, and some years at Camp George G. Meade, MD, or Fort Bragg, NC. Conducted CMTC at Fort Hoyle some years as an alternate form of training. Primary ROTC feeder school was Duquesne University. Location 7 December 1941—Philadelphia, PA.

Status: Inactive in the US Army Reserve as the 312th F.A. Bn., a component of the 79th Inf. Div.

Commanders, 312th Field Artillery Regiment

Col. Earle d'Arcy Pearce	27 August 1917–8 September 1917
Col. James F. Brady	9 September 1917–7 July 1918
Col. Harry P. Wilber	7 July 1918–31 May 1919
Demobilized/Inactive	31 May 1919–November 1929
Maj. William K. Bonnell	November 1929–30 April 1930
Col. Vincent A. Carroll	30 April 1930–10 April 1936
Lt. Col. Colbert C. McClain	10 April 1936–7 August 1941

313th Field Artillery Regiment (75-mm G) (80th Division) **Organized Reserve District of Columbia**

HQ—Washington, DC, 1921–41

Arrived at the port of Newport News on 28 May 1919 on the U.S.S. *Zeppelin* as the 313th F.A., an element of the 80th Div. Demobilized on 10 June 1919 at Camp Lee, VA. Reconstituted in the O.R. on 24 June 1921, assigned to the 80th Div., and allotted to the Third Corps Area. Initiated on 7 November 1921 with regimental HQ at Washington, DC. Subordinate battalion HQ concurrently organized as follows: 1st Bn. at Baltimore, MD, and 2d Bn. at Washington, DC. Typically conducted Inactive Training Period meetings at the Munitions Building in Washington. Conducted summer training most years with the 6th F.A. at Fort Hoyle, MD, and some years at Camp George G. Meade, MD, or Tobyhanna, PA. Conducted CMTC at Fort Hoyle some years as an alternate form of training. Primary ROTC feeder school was the Virginia Military Institute. Location 7 December 1941—Washington, DC.

Status: Disbanded 23 March 1959 as the 313th F.A. Bn.

Commanders, 313th Field Artillery Regiment

Col. Charles D. Herron	25 August 1917–20 July 1918	Col. Otto L. Brunzell	11 November 1918–28 March 1919
Lt. Col. William Tidball	20 July 1918–27 July 1918	*Demobilized/Inactive*	29 March 1919–November 1921
Col. Charles J. Ferris	27 July 1918–11 November 1918	Maj. Edwin F. A. Morgan	7 November 1921–16 December 1921
Col. Leroy W. Herron	16 December 1921–January 1942		

314th Field Artillery Regiment (75-mm G) (80th Division) **Organized Reserve Virginia**

HQ—Richmond, VA, 1921–41

Arrived at the port of Newport News on 28 May 1919 on the U.S.S. *Zeppelin* as the 314th F.A., an element of the 80th Div. Demobilized on 7 June 1919 at Camp Lee, VA. Reconstituted in the O.R. on 24 June 1921, assigned to the 80th Div., and allotted to the Third Corps Area. Initiated on 22 October 1921 with regimental HQ at Richmond, VA. Subordinate battalion HQ concurrently organized as follows: 1st Bn. at Roanoke, VA, and 2d Bn. at Norfolk, VA. Conducted summer training most years with the 6th F.A. at Fort Hoyle, MD, and some years at Camp George G. Meade, MD, or Tobyhanna, PA. Conducted CMTC at Fort Hoyle some years as an alternate form of training. Primary ROTC feeder school was the Virginia Military Institute. Location 7 December 1941—Richmond, VA.

Status: Disbanded on 11 May 1959 as the 314th F.A. Bn.

Commanders, 314th Field Artillery Regiment

Col. Robert S. Welsh	5 August 1917–16 September 1918	Col. Elisha F. Riggs	25 January 1922–31 July 1923
Col. James F. Walker	17 September 1918–1 May 1919	Col. Edwin F.A. Morgan	21 July 1923–2 April 1930
Demobilized/Inactive	7 June 1919–22 October 1921	Col. Irving C. Moller	2 April 1930–7 January 1932
Maj. James H. Beazley	24 October 1921–25 January 1922	Lt. Col. Ernest S. Cox	7 January 1932–ao January 1940
Unknown	ao January 1940–7 December 1941		

315th Field Artillery Regiment (155-mm H) (80th Division) **Organized Reserve District of Columbia and Virginia**

HQ—Washington, DC, 1929–41

Arrived at the port of Newport News on 28 May 1919 on the U.S.S. *Zeppelin* as the 313th F.A., an element of the 80th Div. Demobilized on 10 June 1919 at Camp Lee, VA. Reconstituted in the O.R. on 13 September 1929, assigned to the 80th Div., and allotted to the Third Corps Area. Initiated in December 1929 with regimental HQ at Washington, DC. Subordinate battalion HQ concurrently organized as follows: 1st Bn. at Washington, DC; 2d Bn. at Richmond, VA; and 3d Bn. at Richmond, VA. Typically conducted Inactive Training Period meetings at the Munitions Building in Washington. Conducted summer training most years with the 6th F.A. at Fort Hoyle, MD, and some years at Camp George G. Meade, MD, or Fort Bragg, NC. Conducted CMTC at Fort Hoyle some years as an alternate form of training. Primary ROTC feeder school was the Virginia Military Institute. Location 7 December 1941—Washington, DC.

Status: Disbanded on 6 March 1959 as the 315th F.A. Bn.

Commanders, 315th Field Artillery Regiment

Lt. Col. Russell P. Reeder	5 August 1917–27 August 1917	Col. Joseph F. Barnes	6 March 1919–10 June 1919
Col. Charles J. Ferris	27 August 1917–5 January 1918	*Demobilized/Inactive*	10 June 1919–December 1929
Col. Russell P. Reeder	5 January 1918–20 May 1918	Col. Elisha F. Riggs	2 April 1930–8 February 1933
Col. Carroll J. Goodfellow	20 May 1918–28 September 1918	Lt. Col. Philip P. Cole	8 February 1933–ao September 1935
Col. William Tidball	29 September 1918–23 January 1919	Lt. Col. Frederick W. Franke	ao May 1936–23 June 1937
Col. George P. Hawes	5 February 1919–6 March 1919	Col. Fitz W. McM. Woodrow	23 June 1937–ao June 1940
	Unknown	ao June 1940–7 December 1941	

316th Field Artillery Regiment (75-mm G) (81st Division) **Organized Reserve North Carolina**

HQ—*Not initiated,* 1921–22; Raleigh, NC, 1922–41

Arrived at the port of Newport News on 10 June 1919 on the U.S.S. *Minnesota* as the 316th F.A., an element of the 81st Div. Demobilized at Camp Lee, VA, on 13 June 1919 as an element of the 81st Div. Reconstituted in the O.R. on 24 June 1921, assigned to the 81st Div., and allotted to the Fourth Corps Area. Initiated on 5 November 1921 with regimental HQ at Raleigh, NC. Subordinate battalion HQ concurrently organized as follows: 1st Bn. at Fayetteville, NC, and 2d Bn. at Charlotte, NC. Conducted summer training with the 2d Bn., 16th F.A. at Fort Bragg, NC. Conducted CMTC at Fort Bragg some years as an alternate form of training. Primary ROTC feeder school was North Carolina State College. Location 7 December 1941—Raleigh, NC.

Status: Disbanded on 1 May 1959 as the 316th F.A. Bn.

Commanders, 316th Field Artillery Regiment

Col. Andrew Moses	31 August 1917–9 July 1918	Col. Albert L. Cox	17 January 1922–10 November 1922
Col. Russell P. Reeder	9 July 1918–13 June 1919	Maj. Joseph S. Huske	10 November 1922–30 December 1923
Demobilized/Inactive	13 June 1919–5 November 1921	Lt. Col. Sidney C. Chambers	30 December 1923–17 January 1928
Maj. Joseph J. Mora	5 November 1921–17 January 1922	Col. John W. Harrelson	17 January 1928–ao May 1940
	Unknown	ao May 1940–7 December 1941	

317th Field Artillery Regiment (75-mm G) (81st Division) **Organized Reserve Tennessee**

HQ—*Not initiated,* 1921–22; Nashville, TN, 1922–41

Arrived at the port of Newport News on 9 June 1919 on the U.S.S. *South Carolina* as the 317th F.A., an element of the 81st Div. Demobilized on 13 June 1919 at Camp Morrison, VA. Reconstituted in the O.R. on 24 June 1921, assigned to the 81st Div., and allotted to the Fourth Corps Area. Initiated in February 1922 with regimental HQ at Nashville, TN. Subordinate battalion HQ concurrently organized as follows: 1st Bn. at Chattanooga, TN, and 2d Bn. at Nashville, TN. Conducted summer training with the 2d Bn., 16th F.A. at Fort Bragg, NC. Conducted CMTC at Fort Bragg some years as an alternate form of training. Primary ROTC feeder school was the University of Tennessee. Location 7 December 1941—Nashville, TN.

Status: Disbanded 1 May 1959 as the 317th F.A. Bn.

Commanders, 317th Field Artillery Regiment

Col. George M. Appel	31 August 1917–ao November 1917	*Demobilized/Inactive*	13 June 1919–February 1922
Col. Nelson E. Margetts	ao July 1918–ao November 1918	Col. Luke Lea	2 February 1922–11 April 1929
Lt. Col. Roger S. Parrott	26 March 1919–12 May 1919	Col. William J. Bacon	11 April 1929–March 1940
		Unknown	March 1940–7 December 1941

318th Field Artillery Regiment (155-mm H) (81st Division) **Organized Reserve Louisiana/ North Carolina/Florida**

HQ—*Not initiated,* 1921–22; Alexandria, LA, 1922–30; Greensboro, NC, 1930–41

Arrived at the port of Newport News on 28 May 1919 on the U.S.S. *Zeppelin* as the 318th F.A., an element of the 81st Div. Demobilized on 16 June 1919 at Fort Oglethorpe, GA. Reconstituted in the O.R. on 29 July 1921 as the 397th F.A. Regiment, assigned to the 183d F.A. Brig. (XIV Corps), and allotted to the Fourth Corps Area. Initiated on 12 December 1921 with regimental HQ at Alexandria, LA. Subordinate battalion HQ concurrently organized as follows: 1st Bn. at New Orleans, LA; 2d Bn. at Crowley, LA; and 3d Bn. at Monroe, LA. Redesignated 318th F.A. Regt. on 5 October 1929, relieved from the 183d F.A. Brig., and assigned to the 81st Div. HQ relocated in 1930 to Greensboro, NC. Conducted summer training with the 5th F.A. at Fort Bragg, NC. Conducted CMTC at Fort Bragg some years as an alternate form of training. Primary ROTC feeder school was the North Carolina State College. Location 7 December 1941—Greensboro, NC.

Status: Disbanded on 1 May 1959 as the 318th F.A. Bn.

Commanders, 318th Field Artillery Regiment

Lt. Col. Ernest R. Tilton	September 1917–10 January 1918	Maj. John A. Myers	June 1928–August 1930
Col. James P. Robinson	11 January 1918–22 April 1919	Unknown	August 1930–October 1939
Demobilized/Inactive	16 June 1919–12 December 1921	Col. James W. Love	ao October 1939–ao May 1940
Col. Thomas F. Porter Jr.	12 December 1921–June 1928	Unknown	ao May 1940–7 December 1941

319th Field Artillery Regiment (75-mm G) (82d Division) **Organized Reserve Georgia**

HQ—Decatur, GA, 1921–41

Arrived at the port of New York on 11 May 1919 on the U.S.S. *Alaskan* as the 319th F.A., an element of the 82d Div. Demobilized on 18 May 1919 at Camp Dix, NJ. Reconstituted in the O.R. on 24 June 1921, assigned to the 82d Div., and allotted to the Fourth Corps Area. Initiated on 14 December 1921 with regimental HQ at Decatur, GA. Subordinate battalion HQ concurrently organized as follows: 1st Bn. at Madison, GA, and 2d Bn. at Savannah, GA. Conducted summer training with the 2d Bn., 16th F.A. at Fort Bragg, NC. Conducted CMTC at Fort Bragg some years as an alternate form of training. Primary ROTC feeder school was the Georgia Institute of Technology. Location 7 December 1941—Decatur, GA.

Status: Assigned to the USARS as the 319th F.A.

Commanders, 319th Field Artillery Regiment

Col. James F. Brady	22 August 1917–9 September 1917
Col. Earle d'Arcy Pearce	9 September 1917–9 November 1918
Col. William P. Platt	25 October 1918–5 November 1918
Col. Earle d'Arcy Pearce	6 November 1918–18 May 1919
Demobilized/Inactive	18 May 1919–January 1922
Lt. Col. Abram Levy	14 December 1921–June 1925
Col. Frank B. Willingham	June 1925–ao March 1931
Unknown	ao March 1931–28 March 1936
Col. James H. Genung Jr.	28 March 1936–ao June 1936
Unknown	ao June 1936–ao January 1938
Col. Henry F. Meyer	ao January 1938–ao May 1940
Unknown	ao May 1940–7 December 1941

320th Field Artillery Regiment (75-mm G) (82d Division) **Organized Reserve South Carolina**

HQ—Columbia, SC, 1921–27; Spartanburg, SC, 1927–41

Arrived at the port of New York on 7 May 1919 on the U.S.S. *Kentuckian* as the 320th F.A., an element of the 82d Div. Demobilized on 12 May 1919 at Camp Dix, NJ. Reconstituted in the O.R. on 24 June 1921, assigned to the 82d Div., and allotted to the Fourth Corps Area. Initiated on 7 December 1921 with regimental HQ at Columbia, SC. Subordinate battalion HQ concurrently organized as follows: 1st Bn. at Greenville, SC, and 2d Bn. at Sumter, SC. HQ relocated on 8 July 1927 to Spartanburg, SC. Conducted summer training with the 2d Bn., 16th F.A. at Fort Bragg, NC. Conducted CMTC at Fort Bragg some years as an alternate form of training. Primary ROTC feeder school was the Citadel. Location 7 December 1941—Spartanburg, SC.

Status: Assigned to the USARS as the 320th F.A.

Commanders, 320th Field Artillery Regiment

Col. Harry C. Williams	29 August 1917–11 May 1919
Demobilized/Inactive	12 May 1919–7 December 1921
Lt. Col. Irvine F. Belser	7 December 1921–ao March 1922
Unknown	ao March 1922–12 September 1929
Col. Irvine F. Belser	12 September 1929–ao October 1941

321st Field Artillery Regiment (155-mm H) (82d Division) **Organized Reserve Georgia/Florida**

HQ—Macon, GA, 1930–36; Gainesville, FL, 1936–41

Demobilized at Camp Dix, NJ, on 26 May 1919 as an element of the 82d Div. Reconstituted in the O.R. on 5 June 1930 and consolidated with the existing 321st F.A. (constituted in the O.R. in July 1923 as the 452d F.A., allotted to the Fourth Corps Area, and organized in October 1923 with regimental HQ at Macon, GA; redesignated 321st F.A. Regt. on 5 October 1929) and consolidated unit designated as the 321st F.A. and assigned to the 82d Div. HQ relocated on 1 July 1936 to Gainesville, FL. Conducted summer training with the 5th F.A. at Fort Bragg, NC. Conducted CMTC at Fort Bragg some years as an alternate form of training. Primary ROTC feeder school was the Georgia Institute of Technology. Location 7 December 1941—Gainesville, FL.

Status: Assigned to the USARS as the 321st F.A.

Commanders, 321st Field Artillery Regiment

Col. Clarence Deems Jr.	21 August 1917–8 November 1918
Col. Thomas W. Hollyday	8 November 1918–March 1919
Lt. Col. Churchill B. Mehard	March 1919–25 May 1919
Demobilized/Inactive	26 May 1919–5 June 1930
Lt. Col. Louis H. Harper	5 June 1930–14 June 1930
Col. Louis E. Goodrich	14 June 1930–4 April 1936
Col. Louis H. Harper	4 April 1936–ao May 1940
Unknown	ao May 1940–7 December 1941

322d Field Artillery Regiment (75-mm G) (83d Division) **Organized Reserve Ohio**

HQ—Akron, OH, 1921–31; Cleveland, OH, 1931–41

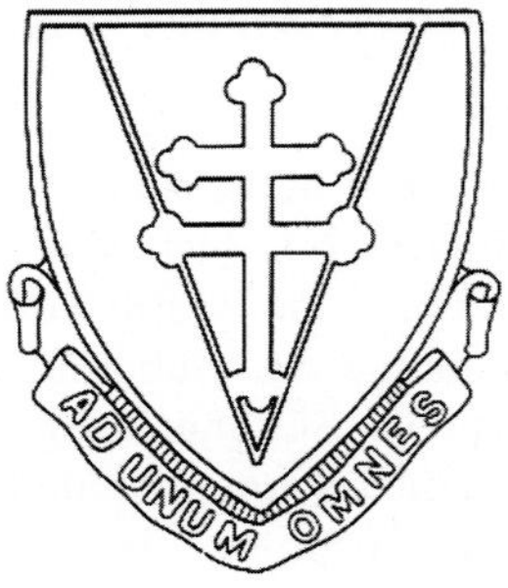

Arrived at the port of New York on 16 May 1919 on the U.S.S. *Plattsburg* as the 322d F.A., an element of the 83d Div. Demobilized on 2 June 1919 at Camp Sherman, OH. Reconstituted in the O.R. on 24 June 1921, assigned to the 83d Div., and allotted to the Fifth Corps Area. Initiated in December 1921 with regimental HQ at Akron, OH. Subordinate battalion HQ concurrently organized as follows: 1st Bn. at Akron and 2d Bn. at Cleveland, OH. Band organized at Akron about 1923; inactivated in 1933. HQ relocated on 12 December 1931 to Cleveland, OH. Typically conducted Inactive Training Period meetings at the Bulkey Building in Cleveland. Conducted summer training with the 1st Bn., 3d F.A., 1922–34, and 1st Bn., 19th F.A., 1935–40, at Camp Knox, KY, and some years at Fort Benjamin Harrison, IN. Conducted CMTC at Camp Knox some years as an alternate form of training. Primary ROTC feeder school was Ohio State University. Location 7 December 1941—Cleveland, OH.

Status: Inactive in the US Army Reserve as the 322d F.A. Bn., a component of the 83d Inf. Div.

Commanders, 322d Field Artillery Regiment

Col. Augustus B. Warfield	29 August 1917–February 1919
Lt. Col. Samuel R. Hopkins	February 1919–March 1919
Col. Thomas W. Hollyday	March 1919–April 1919
Lt. Col. Samuel R. Hopkins	April 1919–2 June 1919
Demobilized/Inactive	2 June 1919–December 1921
Col. Charles M. Piper	December 1921–3 January 1933
Col. Earnest G. Rarey	3 January 1933–ao June 1941

323d Field Artillery Regiment (75-mm G) (83d Division) **Organized Reserve Ohio**

HQ—Columbus, OH, 1921–41

Arrived at the port of Hoboken on 13 May 1919 on the U.S.S. *Von Steuben* as the 323d F.A., an element of the 83d Div. Demobilized on 21 May 1919 at Camp Dix, NJ. Reconstituted in the O.R. on 24 June 1921, assigned to the 83d Div., and allotted to the Fifth Corps Area. Initiated on 7 November 1921 with regimental HQ at Columbus, OH. Subordinate battalion HQ concurrently organized as follows: 1st Bn. at Dayton, OH, and 2d Bn. at Grovesport, OH. Conducted summer training with the 1st Bn., 3d F.A., 1922–34, and 1st Bn., 19th F.A., 1935–40, at Camp Knox, KY, and some years at Fort Benjamin Harrison, IN. Conducted CMTC at Fort Benjamin Harrison some years as an alternate form of training. Primary ROTC feeder school was Ohio State University. Location 7 December 1941—Columbus, OH.

Status: Inactive in the US Army Reserve as the 323d F.A. Bn., a component of the 83d Inf. Div.

Commanders, 323d Field Artillery Regiment

Maj. Hugh S. Brown	29 August 1917–1 September 1917	Col. Harry L. Morse	11 November 1918–December 1918
Maj. Samuel R. Hopkins	1 September 1917–6 September 1917	Lt. Col. B.O. Kennedy	December 1918–19 January 1919
Lt. Col. William F. Morrison	6 September 1917–11 October 1917	Col. Fred T. Cruse	19 January 1919–21 May 1919
Col. Louis T. Boisseau	11 October 1917–June 1918	*Demobilized/Inactive*	21 May 1919–7 November 1921
Lt. Col. Samuel R. Hopkins	June 1918–29 July 1918	Col. Simeon Nash	7 November 1921–December 1934
Col. Frederick B. Hennesey	29 July 1918–5 October 1918	Unknown	December 1934–ao June 1937
Col. Louis H. McKinlay	5 October 1918–27 October 1918	Col. Theodore S. Pattison	ao June 1937–ao June 1938
Lt. Col. Samuel R. Hopkins	27 October 1918–11 November 1918	Unknown	ao June 1938–7 December 1941

324th Field Artillery Regiment (155-mm H) (83d Division) **Organized Reserve Ohio**

HQ—Fort Hayes, OH, 1929; Akron, OH, 1929–41

Arrived at the port of New York on 31 May 1919 on the U.S.S. *Seattle* as the 324th F.A., an element of the 83d Div. Demobilized in June 1919 at Camp Sherman, OH. Reconstituted in the O.R. on 13 September 1929, assigned to the 83d Div., and allotted to the Fifth Corps Area. Initiated on 25 September 1929 with regimental HQ at Fort Hayes, OH. HQ relocated in November 1929 to Akron, OH. Conducted summer training with the 1st Bn., 3d F.A., 1930–34, and 1st Bn., 19th F.A., 1935–40, at Camp Knox, KY. Primary ROTC feeder school was Ohio State University. Location 7 December 1941—Akron, OH.

Status: Inactive in the US Army Reserve as the 324th F.A. Bn., a component of the 83d Inf. Div.

Commanders, 324th Field Artillery Regiment

Col. Thomas Q. Ashburn	22 August 1917–5 June 1919	Maj. Frederick W. Franke	25 September 1929–ao July 1930
Demobilized/Inactive	5 June 1919–25 September 1929	Col. John A. Bickel	ao May 1931–ao July 1937
Unknown	ao July 1937–7 December 1941		

325th Field Artillery Regiment (75-mm G) (84th Division) **Organized Reserve Indiana**

HQ—Indianapolis, IN, 1921–29; Fort Wayne, IN, 1929–41

Arrived at the port of New York in February 1919 on the U.S.S. *Eurane* as the 325th F.A., an element of the 84th Div. Demobilized on 1 March 1919 at Camp Sherman, OH. Reconstituted in the O.R. on 24 June 1921, assigned to the 84th Div., and allotted to the Fifth Corps Area. Initiated on 28 September 1921 with regimental HQ at Indianapolis, IN. Subordinate battalion HQ concurrently organized as follows: 1st Bn. at Goodland, IN, and 2d Bn. at Auburn, IN. Conducted summer training with the 1st Bn., 3d F.A., 1922–34, and 1st Bn., 19th F.A., 1935–40, at Camp Knox, KY, and some years at Fort Benjamin Harrison, IN. Conducted CMTC at Fort Benjamin Harrison some years as an alternate form of training. Primary ROTC feeder school was Purdue University. Location 7 December 1941—Fort Wayne, IN.

Status: Disbanded on 1 May 1959 as the 325th F.A. Bn.

Commanders, 325th Field Artillery Regiment

Col. Charles M. Bundel	22 August 1917–6 February 1918	Col. Robert L. Moorhead	July 1924–November 1927
Unknown	6 February 1918–26 November 1918	Maj. Don L. Essex	November 1927–ao July 1930
Col. John R. Starkey	26 November 1918–1 March 1919	Unknown	ao July 1930–ao June 1934
Demobilized/Inactive	1 March 1919–28 September 1921	Maj. Oliver K. Appelman	ao June 1934–31 December 1937
Col. Solon J. Carter	28 September 1921–27 April 1923	Col. George Byers	31 December 1937–May 1938
Lt. Col. Orville B. Kilmer	27 April 1923–July 1924	Maj. Oliver K. Appelman	May 1938–ao May 1940
Unknown	ao May 1940–7 December 1941		

326th Field Artillery Regiment (75-mm G) (84th Division) **Organized Reserve Indiana**

HQ—Indianapolis, IN, 1921–41

Demobilized at Camp Zachary Taylor, KY, on 8 March 1919 as an element of the 84th Div. Reconstituted in the O.R. on 24 June 1921, assigned to the 84th Div., and allotted to the Fifth Corps Area. Initiated on 28 September 1921 with regimental HQ at Indianapolis, IN. Conducted summer training with the 1st Bn., 3d F.A., 1922–34, and 1st Bn., 19th F.A., 1935–40, at Camp Knox, KY, and some years at Fort Benjamin Harrison, IN. Conducted summer training at Camp Knox with units of the 62d F.A. Brig., 1928–30. Conducted CMTC at Fort Benjamin Harrison some years as an alternate form of training. Regiment awarded the Toulmin Trophy for 1928. Primary ROTC feeder school was Purdue University. Location 7 December 1941—Indianapolis, IN.

Status: Disbanded 1 May 1959 as the 326th F.A. Bn.

Commanders, 326th Field Artillery Regiment

Col. Augustine McIntyre	12 September 1917–18 April 1918	Col. Robert L. Moorhead	28 September 1921–July 1924
Col. John B.W. Corey	19 April 1918–7 March 1919	Col. Paul V. McNutt	July 1924–10 March 1937
Demobilized/Inactive	8 March 1919–28 September 1921	Lt. Col. David H. Jennings	10 March 1937–ao July 1938
Unknown	ao July 1938–7 December 1941		

327th Field Artillery Regiment (155-mm H) (84th Division) **Organized Reserve Indiana**

HQ—Hammond, IN, 1929–41

Arrived at the port of New York on 31 January 1919 on the U.S.S. *Mallory* as the 327th F.A., an element of the 84th Div. Demobilized on 21 February 1919 at Camp Grant, IL. Reconstituted in the O.R. on 13 September 1929, assigned to the 84th Div., and allotted to the Fifth Corps Area. Initiated in December 1933 with regimental HQ at Hammond, IN. Conducted summer training with the 1st Bn., 3d F.A., 1930–34, and 1st Bn., 19th F.A., 1935–40, at Camp Knox, KY. Primary ROTC feeder school was Purdue University. Location 7 December 1941—Hammond, IN.

Status: Disbanded on 1 May 1959 as the 327th F.A. Bn.

Commanders, 327th Field Artillery Regiment

Col. Frederick E. Johnston	17 August 1917–7 November 1917	*Demobilized/Inactive*	21 February 1919–December 1933
Unknown	1 November 1917–1 October 1918	Lt. Col. Clarence C. Bassett	December 1933–June 1937
Col. Joseph F. Barnes	1 October 1918–13 December 1918	Lt. Col. Lowell F. Bowers	June 1937–ao August 1937
Unknown	14 December 1918–21 February 1919	Col. George L. Miller	ao April 1938–ao June 1939
Unknown	ao June 1939–7 December 1941		

328th Field Artillery Regiment (75-mm G) (85th Division) **Organized Reserve Michigan**

HQ—*Not initiated,* 1921–22; Detroit, MI, 1922–41

Arrived at the port of New York on 2 April 1919 on the U.S.S. *Ulua* as the 328th F.A., an element of the 85th Div. Demobilized on 25 April 1919 at Camp Custer, MI. Reconstituted in the O.R. on 24 June 1921, assigned to the 85th Div., and allotted to the Sixth Corps Area. Initiated on 10 March 1922 with the entire regiment at Detroit, MI. Reorganized from horse drawn to truck drawn on 13 March 1935. Conducted summer training most years at Camp McCoy, WI, and some years at Camp Custer, MI. Conducted summer training at Camp Grayling, MI, with the 119th F.A. in 1929 and 1936. Provided a number of officers to the 119th F.A. at Camp Custer, MI, for the 1936 Second Army Maneuver. Primary ROTC feeder school was Michigan State College. Location 7 December 1941—Detroit, MI.

Status: Disbanded 1 June 1959 as the 328th F.A. Bn.

Events: 214

Commanders, 328th Field Artillery Regiment

Maj. Louis R. Dougherty	1 September 1917–2 September 1917	Lt. Col. Harold S. Barker	21 August 1923–16 July 1931
Col. Frank E. Hopkins	2 September 1917–ao August 1918	Unknown	16 July 1931–ao June 1932
Demobilized/Inactive	21 April 1919–10 March 1922	Col. Philip K. Fletcher	ao June 1932–ao August 1933
Maj. Charles V. Crane	10 March 1922–3 March 1923	Col. Harold E. Matthys	ao June 1934–ao July 1939
Col. Lee A. McCalla	3 March 1923–21 August 1923	Unknown	ao July 1939–7 December 1941

329th Field Artillery Regiment (75-mm G) (85th Division) **Organized Reserve Michigan**

HQ—*Not initiated,* 1921–22; Escanaba, MI, 1922–25; Grand Rapids, MI, 1925–41

Arrived at the port of New York on 2 April 1919 on the U.S.S. *Leviathan* as the 329th F.A., an element of the 85th Div. Demobilized on 25 April 1919 at Camp Custer, MI. Reconstituted in the O.R. on 24 June 1921, assigned to the 85th Div., and allotted to the Sixth Corps Area. Initiated on 10 March 1922 with regimental HQ at Escanaba, MI. Subordinate battalion HQ concurrently organized as follows: 1st Bn. at Marquette, MI, and 2d Bn. at Menominee, MI. Regimental HQ relocated on 2 June 1925 to Grand Rapids, MI. Subordinate battalion HQ concurrently relocated as follows: 1st Bn. at Lansing, MI, and 2d Bn. at Muskegon, MI. Conducted summer training most years at Camp Sparta/McCoy, WI, or Camp Custer, MI. Conducted summer training at Camp Grayling, MI, with the 119th F.A. in 1928, 1932, and 1937. Primary ROTC feeder school was Michigan State College. Location 7 December 1941—Grand Rapids, MI.

Status: Inactive in the US Army Reserve as the 329th F.A. Bn., a component of the 85th Inf. Div.

Commanders, 329th Field Artillery Regiment

Col. William Bryden	August 1917–October 1917	Unknown	ao January 1923–ao July 1925
Col. Tilman Campbell	October 1917–24 April 1919	Maj. August Kroon	ao July 1925–September 1925
Demobilized/Inactive	24 April 1919–March 1922	Maj. Orla G. Miller	September 1925–17 November 1926
1st Lt. Charles A. Lindberg	10 March 1922–6 July 1922	Col. Ralph C. Huston	17 November 1926–ao January 1940
1st Lt. Charles B. Hedgecock	6 July 1922–ao January 1923	Unknown	ao January 1940–7 December 1941

330th Field Artillery Regiment (155-mm H) (85th Division) **Organized Reserve Illinois**

HQ—*Not initiated,* 1929–32; Rockford, IL, 1932–41

Arrived at the port of New York on 10 April 1919 on the S.S. *Pannonia* as the 330th F.A., an element of the 85th Div. Demobilized on 26 April 1919 at Camp Custer, MI. Reconstituted in the O.R. on 13 September 1929, assigned to the 85th Div., and allotted to the Sixth Corps Area. Relieved from the 85th Div. on 5 October 1929 and assigned to the 185th F.A. Brig. (XVI Corps). Initiated by June 1932 with regimental HQ at Rockford, IL. Subordinate battalion HQ concurrently organized as follows: 1st Bn. at Rockford, IL; 2d Bn. at Geneva, IL; and 3d Bn. at Freeport, IL. Conducted summer training most years at Camp McCoy, WI. The 3d Bn. typically conducted Inactive Training Period meetings at the N.G. armory in Monmouth, IL. Conducted summer training at Camp Grayling, MI, with the 182d F.A. in 1937. Primary ROTC feeder school was the University of Illinois. Location 7 December 1941—Rockford, IL.

Status: Disbanded on 11 November 1944 as the 330th F.A. Bn.

Commanders, 330th Field Artillery Regiment

Col. Phillip R. Ward	August 1917–20 October 1917	*Demobilized/Inactive*	April 1919–June 1932
Col. Harold E. Cloke	20 October 1917–15 December 1918	Col. Harold P. Goodnow	June 1932–March 1936
Col. Joseph F. Barnes	15 December 1918–2 March 1919	Col. William McK. Jackson	March 1936–ao January 1940
	Unknown	ao January 1940–7 December 1941	

331st Field Artillery Regiment (75-mm G) (86th Division) **Organized Reserve Illinois**

HQ—Chicago, IL, 1922–41

Arrived at the port of Hoboken on 3 January 1919 on the U.S.S. *Siboney* as the 331st F.A., an element of the 86th Div. Demobilized on 22 February 1919 at Camp Grant, IL. Reconstituted in the O.R. on 24 June 1921, assigned to the 86th Div., and allotted to the Sixth Corps Area. Initiated on 16 January 1922 with the entire regiment at Chicago, IL. Reorganized from horse drawn to truck drawn on 13 March 1935. Conducted summer training most years at Camp McCoy, WI, and some years at Camp Custer, MI. Conducted field artillery CMTC training some years at Camp McCoy, WI, as an alternate form of annual training. Primary ROTC feeder school was the University of Chicago. Location 7 December 1941—Chicago, IL.

Status: Inactive in the US Army Reserve as the 331st F.A. Bn., a component of the 86th Inf. Div.

Events: 162

Commanders, 331st Field Artillery Regiment

Col. William McK. Lambdin	29 August 1917–22 February 1919	Col. Horatio B. Hackett	16 January 1922–1 July 1929
Demobilized/Inactive	22 February 1919–16 January 1922	Col. Edward N. Wentworth	1 July 1929–ao November 1941

332d Field Artillery Regiment (75-mm G) (86th Division) **Organized Reserve Illinois**

HQ—Chicago, IL, 1921–41

Arrived at the port of Newport News on 13 February 1919 on the U.S.S. *Antigone* as the 332d F.A., an element of the 86th Div. Demobilized on 28 February 1919 at Camp Grant, IL. Reconstituted in the O.R. on 24 June 1921, assigned to the 86th Div., and allotted to the Sixth Corps Area. Initiated on 19 December 1921 with the entire regiment at Chicago, IL. Most of the officers joining in 1922 had served in the 149th F.A., 42d Div. during World War I. Typically conducted Inactive Training Period meetings at the armory of the 124th F.A. in Chicago. Conducted summer training at Camp Sparta/McCoy, WI. Primary ROTC feeder school was the University of Chicago. Regimental commander, Col. Noble B. Judah, later became Ambassador to Cuba. Location 7 December 1941—Chicago, IL.

Status: Inactive in the US Army Reserve as the 332d F.A. Bn., a component of the 86th Inf. Div.

Events: 162

Commanders, 332d Field Artillery Regiment

Col. Robert C. Foy	4 September 1917–9 December 1918	Col. Noble B. Judah	30 November 1923–September 1930
Unknown	10 December 1918–28 February 1919	Col. Laurence B. Robbins	September 1930–3 August 1937
Demobilized/Inactive	28 February 1919–19 December 1921	Lt. Col. Hugh R. Montgomery	4 August 1937–22 November 1938
Maj. W.L. Martin	19 December 1921–16 January 1922	Lt. Col. Louis E. Legner	22 November 1939–March 1939
Col. Robert R. McCormick	16 January 1922–6 August 1923	Lt. Col. Robert A.N. Baltz	March 1939–ao January 1940
Col. Edward B. Ellicott	7 August 1923–30 November 1923	Unknown	ao January 1940–7 December 1941

333d Field Artillery Regiment (155-mm H) (86th Division) **Organized Reserve Illinois**

HQ—*Not initiated,* 1929–30; Chicago, IL, 1930–37; *Inactive*, 1937–41

Arrived at the port of New York in January and February 1919 on various vessels as the 333d F.A., an element of the 86th Div. Demobilized on 23 January 1919 at Camp Grant, IL. Reconstituted in the O.R. on 13 September 1929, assigned to the 86th Div., and allotted to the Sixth Corps Area. Relieved from the 86th Div. on 5 October 1929 and assigned to the 185th F.A. Brig. (XVI Corps). Initiated in December 1930 with the entire regiment at Chicago, IL. Inactivated on 2 October 1937 at Chicago by relief of personnel. Conducted summer training at Camp McCoy, WI. Primary ROTC feeder school was the University of Chicago. Location 7 December 1941—*Inactive.*

Status: Assigned to the CARS as the 333d F.A.

Commanders, 333d Field Artillery Regiment

Col. Philip R. Ward	26 August 1917–December 1917	Maj. Charles T. Prindeville	December 1930–1 March 1935
Col. Francis N. Cooke	December 1917–May 1918	Unknown	1 March 1935–15 August 1935
Col. Philip R. Ward	May 1918–23 January 1919	Lt. Col. Ralph A. Kimball	15 August 1935–December 1936
Demobilized/Inactive	23 January 1919–December 1930	Capt. William P. Oliver	December 1936–2 October 1937
Inactive	2 October 1937–7 December 1941		

334th Field Artillery Regiment (75-mm G) (87th Division) **Organized Reserve Alabama**

HQ—Montgomery, AL, 1921–29; Birmingham, AL, 1929–41

Arrived at the port of New York on 22 February 1919 on the U.S.S. *Orizaba* as the 334th F.A., an element of the 87th Div. Demobilized on 4 March 1919 at Camp Dix, NJ. Reconstituted in the O.R. on 24 June 1921, assigned to the 87th Div., and allotted to the Fourth Corps Area. Initiated on 19 December 1921 with regimental HQ at Montgomery, AL. Subordinate battalion HQ concurrently organized as follows: 1st Bn. at Decatur, AL, and 2d Bn. at Talledega, AL. HQ relocated on 1 July 1929 to Birmingham, AL. Conducted summer training most years with the 2d Bn., 16th F.A. at Fort Bragg, NC, and many years with the 12th F.A. at Fort Sam Houston, TX; Camp Stanley, TX; or Camp Bullis, TX. Conducted field artillery CMTC training some years at Fort Bragg as an alternate form of annual training. Primary ROTC feeder school was the Alabama Polytechnic Institute. Location 7 December 1941—Birmingham, AL.

Status: Inactive in the US Army Reserve as the 334th F.A. Bn., a component of the 81st Inf. Div.

Commanders, 334th Field Artillery Regiment

Col. F. Wharton Griffin	18 August 1917–4 March 1919	Lt. Col. Edward C. Harris	25 November 1923–June 1925
Demobilized/Inactive	4 March 1919–December 1921	Col. Harry S. Berry	June 1925–25 October 1930
Maj. William L. Martin	19 December 1921–25 November 1923	Col. William S. Pritchard	25 October 1930–ao May 1940
Unknown	ao May 1940–7 December 1941		

335th Field Artillery Regiment (155-mm H) (87th Division) **Organized Reserve Mississippi**

HQ—Jackson, MS, 1921–41

Arrived at the port of New York on 5 March 1919 on the U.S.S. *Powhatan* as the 335th F.A., an element of the 87th Div. Demobilized on 17 March 1919 at Camp Dix, NJ. Reconstituted in the O.R. on 29 July 1921 as the 398th F.A. Regt., assigned to the 183d F.A. Brig. (XIV Corps), and allotted to the Fourth Corps Area. Initiated in October 1921 with regimental HQ at Jackson, MS. Redesignated the 335th F.A. Regt. on 5 October 1929, relieved from the 183d F.A. Brig., and assigned to the 87th Div. Conducted summer training with the 2d Bn., 5th F.A. at Fort Bragg, NC, and many years with the 12th F.A. at Fort Sam Houston, TX; Camp Stanley, TX; or Camp Bullis, TX. Conducted field artillery CMTC training some years at Fort Bragg as an alternate form of annual training. Primary ROTC feeder school was Mississippi State College. Location 7 December 1941—Jackson, MS.

Status: Inactive in the US Army Reserve as the 335th F.A. Bn., a component of the 87th Inf. Div.

Commanders, 335th Field Artillery Regiment

Col. Henry S. Kilbourne	25 August 1917–5 August 1918	*Demobilized/Inactive*	16 March 1919–October 1921
Unknown	5 August 1918–ao November 1918	Unknown	October 1921–ao November 1937
Col. Lewis S. Ryan	ao November 1918–December 1918	Col. Richard H. Miller	ao November 1937–ao May 1940
Unknown	December 1918–16 March 1919	Unknown	ao May 1940–7 December 1941

336th Field Artillery Regiment (75-mm G) (87th Division) **Organized Reserve Louisiana**

HQ—Baton Rouge, LA, 1921–25; New Orleans, LA, 1925–41

Arrived at the port of New York on 5 March 1919 on the U.S.S. *Powhatan* as the 336th F.A., an element of the 87th Div. Demobilized on 17 March 1919 at Camp Dix, NJ. Reconstituted in the O.R. on 24 June 1921, assigned to the 87th Div., and allotted to the Fourth Corps Area. Initiated on 28 November 1921 with regimental HQ at Baton Rouge, LA. Subordinate battalion HQ concurrently organized as follows: 1st Bn. at New Orleans and 2d Bn. at Alexandria, LA. HQ relocated by 1925 to New Orleans. Conducted summer training most years with the 2d Bn., 16th F.A. at Fort Bragg, NC; many years with the 12th F.A. at Fort Sam Houston, TX; Camp Stanley, TX; or Camp Bullis, TX; and some years at Camp Beauregard, LA. Conducted field artillery CMTC training some years at Fort Bragg as an alternate form of annual training. Primary ROTC feeder school was Louisiana State University. Location 7 December 1941— New Orleans, LA.

Status: Inactive in the US Army Reserve as the 336th F.A. Bn., a component of the 87th Inf. Div.

Commanders, 336th Field Artillery Regiment

Col. Roderick L. Carmichael	18 August 1917–3 November 1918	Col. James F. Edmonds	28 November 1921–26 February 1927
Lt. Col. Frederick H. Smith	1 January 1919–8 March 1919	Col. Thomas F. Porter Jr.	31 December 1927–ao June 1940
Demobilized/Inactive	16 March 1919–28 November 1921	Unknown	ao June 1940–7 December 1941

337th Field Artillery Regiment (75-mm G) (88th Division) **Organized Reserve Minnesota**

HQ—Minneapolis, MN, 1921–41

Arrived at the port of New York on 25 January 1919 on the U.S.S. *Rochambeau* as the 337th F.A., an element of the 88th Div. Demobilized on 31 January 1919 at Camp Dodge, IA. Reconstituted in the O.R. on 24 June 1921, assigned to the 88th Div., and allotted to the Seventh Corps Area. Initiated on 25 October 1921 with regimental HQ at Minneapolis, MN. Subordinate battalion HQ concurrently organized as follows: 1st Bn. at Minneapolis and 2d Bn. at St. Paul, MN. Typically conducted Inactive Training Period meetings at the University of Minnesota ROTC armory or the Federal Building in Minneapolis and at the N.G. armory in St. Paul. Conducted summer training at numerous locations to include Fort Des Moines, IA; Camp McCoy, WI; Camp Ripley, MN; and Fort Riley, KS. Selected personnel conducted summer training in 1936 with the 125th F.A. Regt. at Camp Ripley, MN. Provided a number of officers to the 125th F.A. for the 1937 Fourth Army Maneuver at Camp Ripley, MN. Conducted field artillery CMTC training some years at Fort Snelling, MN, as an alternate form of annual training. Primary ROTC feeder school was the University of Minnesota. Location 7 December 1941—Minneapolis, MN.

Status: Inactive in the R.A. as the 337th F.A. Bn.

Commanders, 337th Field Artillery Regiment

Col. George R. Greene	30 August 1917–December 1918	Lt. Col. Ceylon A. Lyman	25 October 1921–October 1927
Lt. Col. H.R. Freeman	December 1918–31 January 1919	Col. Franklyn W. Matson	October 1927–29 November 1938
Demobilized/Inactive	31 January 1919–25 October 1921	Col. Jerome Jackman	29 November 1938–April 1942

338th Field Artillery Regiment (75-mm G) (88th Division) **Organized Reserve Iowa**

HQ—Muscatine, IA, 1921–26; Cedar Rapids, IA, 1926–41

Arrived at the port of Newport News in January 1919 on the U.S.S. *Pocahontas* as the 338th F.A., an element of the 88th Div. Demobilized in February 1919 at Camp Dodge, IA. Reconstituted in the O.R. on 24 June 1921, assigned to the 88th Div., and allotted to the Seventh Corps Area. Initiated on 12 October 1921 with regimental HQ at Muscatine, IA. Subordinate battalion HQ concurrently organized as follows: 1st Bn. at Burlington, IA, and 2d Bn. at Sioux City, IA. HQ relocated on 26 May 1926 to Cedar Rapids, IA. Subordinate battalion HQ concurrently relocated as follows: 1st Bn. to Davenport, IA, and 2d Bn. to Waterloo, IA. Typically conducted Inactive Training Period meetings at the Federal Building in Cedar Rapids, at the Post Office building in Burlington, at the Chamber of Commerce building in Sioux City, at the Post Office building in Davenport, and at the Russell-Lamson Hotel in Waterloo. Conducted summer training at numerous locations to include Fort Des Moines, IA; Camp McCoy, WI; Camp Ripley, MN; and Fort Riley, KS. Provided a number of officers to the 151st F.A. for the 1937 Fourth Army Maneuver at Camp Ripley, MN. Conducted field artillery CMTC training some years at Fort Snelling, MN, as an alternate form of annual training. Primary ROTC feeder school was the Iowa State College of Agriculture and Mechanic Arts. Location 7 December 1941—Cedar Rapids, IA.

Status: Inactive in the US Army Reserve as the 338th F.A. Bn., a component of the 88th Inf. Div.

Commanders, 338th Field Artillery Regiment

Lt. Col. Francis W. Honeycutt	30 August 1917–7 June 1918	Lt. Col. Otto W. Mull	12 October 1921–9 May 1924
Col. Ned B. Rehkopf	7 July 1918–16 January 1919	Col. Arthur M. Compton	9 May 1924–August 1924
Demobilized/Inactive	16 January 1919–12 October 1921	Col. Otto W. Mull	August 1924–April 1942

339th Field Artillery Regiment (155-mm H) (88th Division) **Organized Reserve Iowa**

HQ—*Not initiated,* 1929–30; Sioux City, IA, 1930–41

Arrived at the port of New York on 25 January 1919 on the U.S.S. *Rochambeau* as the 339th F.A., an element of the 88th Div. Demobilized on 17 February 1919 at Camp Dodge, IA. Reconstituted in the O.R. on 12 July 1929, assigned to the 88th Div., and allotted to the Seventh Corps Area. Initiated in January 1930 with regimental HQ at Sioux City, IA. Typically conducted Inactive Training Period meetings at the Post Office building in Sioux City. Conducted summer training at numerous locations to include Fort Des Moines, IA; Camp McCoy, WI; Camp Ripley, MN; and Fort Riley, KS. Provided a number of officers to the 182d F.A. for the 1937 Fourth Army Maneuver at Camp Ripley, MN. Conducted field artillery CMTC training some years at Fort Snelling, MN, as an alternate form of annual training. Primary ROTC feeder school was the Iowa State College of Agriculture and Mechanic Arts. Location 7 December 1941—Sioux City, IA.

Status: Inactive in the US Army Reserve as the 339th F.A. Bn., a component of the 88th Inf. Div.

Commanders, 339th Field Artillery Regiment

Col. Samuel C. Vestal	30 August 1917–November 1917	1st Lt. John C.S. Fleming	January 1930–ao February 1930
Lt. Col. Harold D. Burdick	November 1918–31 January 1919	Col. Jerome Jackman	ao June 1930–29 September 1938
Demobilized/Inactive	31 January 1919–January 1930	Col. William H. Donaghue	29 September 1938–December 1940
	Unknown	December 1940–7 December 1941	

340th Field Artillery Regiment (75-mm G) (89th Division) **Organized Reserve Kansas**

HQ—Topeka, KS, 1921–24; Wichita, KS, 1924–41

Arrived at the port of New York on 24 May 1919 on the U.S.S. *Agamemnon* as the 340th F.A., an element of the 89th Div. Demobilized in June 1919 at Camp Funston, KS. Reconstituted in the O.R. on 24 June 1921, assigned to the 89th Div., and allotted to the Seventh Corps Area. Initiated on 28 November 1921 with regimental HQ at Topeka, KS. Subordinate battalion HQ concurrently organized as follows: 1st Bn. at Topeka, KS, and 2d Bn. at Iola, KS. HQ relocated on 9 February 1924 to Wichita, KS. Conducted summer training at numerous locations to include Fort Des Moines, IA; Camp McCoy, WI; Fort Robinson, NE; and Fort Riley, KS. Provided a number of officers to the 147th F.A. at Camp Ripley, MN, and to the units of the 60th F.A. Brig. at Fort Riley for the 1937 Fourth Army Maneuver. Primary ROTC feeder school was the Kansas State Agricultural College. Location 7 December 1941—Wichita, KS.

Status: Disbanded 30 September 1959 as the 340th F.A. Bn.

Commanders, 340th Field Artillery Regiment

Col. Edgar H. Yule	2 September 1917–2 June 1918	*Demobilized/Inactive*	11 June 1919–28 November 1921
Maj. Leland A. Wind	2 June 1918–8 June 1918	Maj. William P. MacLean	28 November 1921–ao January 1922
Lt. Col. Earl Biscoe	8 June 1918–2 July 1918	Unknown	ao January 1922–ao June 1927
Col. Ernest S. Wheeler	3 July 1918–16 February 1919	Lt. Col. Frederick G. Apt	ao June 1927–ao August 1931
Maj. Leland A. Wind	16 February 1919–29 March 1919	Unknown	ao August 1931–ao July 1938
Lt. Col. Joseph C. King	29 March 1919–18 April 1919	Lt. Col. John C. McArthur	ao July 1938– ao August 1938
Col. Ernest S. Wheeler	18 April 1919–11 June 1919	Unknown	ao August 1938–7 December 1941

341st Field Artillery Regiment (75-mm G) (89th Division) **Organized Reserve Nebraska**

HQ—Omaha, NE, 1921–41

Arrived at the port of New York on 24 May 1919 on the U.S.S. *Agamemnon* as the 341st F.A., an element of the 89th Div. Demobilized on 10 June 1919 at Fort D.A. Russell, WY. Reconstituted in the O.R. on 24 June 1921, assigned to the 89th Div., and allotted to the Seventh Corps Area. Initiated on 5 October 1921 with regimental HQ at Omaha, NE. Subordinate battalion HQ concurrently organized as follows: 1st Bn. at Omaha and 2d Bn. at Lincoln, NE. Band organized on 16 July 1924 at Omaha; relocated 1 December 1925 to Beatrice, NE, and still active as of April 1937. The 2d Bn. typically conducted Inactive Training Period meetings at the Lincoln and Capitol Hotels in Lincoln. Conducted summer training at numerous locations to include Fort Des Moines, IA; Camp McCoy, WI; Fort Robinson, NE; and Fort Riley, KS. In conjunction with the 3d Bn., 80th F.A., conducted a 1,480–mile motor march from Fort Des Moines to Fort Meade, SD, and return, 7–17 July 1936. Provided a number of officers to the 147th F.A. at Camp Ripley, MN, and to the units of the 60th F.A. Brig. at Fort Riley for the 1937 Fourth Army Maneuver. Conducted field artillery CMTC training some years at Des Moines as an alternate form of annual training. Primary ROTC feeder school was the University of Nebraska. Location 7 December 1941—Omaha, NE.

Status: Disbanded on 30 September 1959 as the 341st F.A. Bn.

Commanders, 341st Field Artillery Regiment

Maj. Telesphor G. Gottschalk	5 September 1917–21 October 1917	Col. Robert A. Davis	1 January 1918–10 June 1919
Lt. Col. Henry B. Clark	21 October 1917–5 November 1917	*Demobilized/Inactive*	10 June 1919–5 October 1921
Lt. Col. Ralph McCoy	5 November 1917–1 January 1918	Col. Leo J. Crosby	5 October 1921–ao August 1941

342d Field Artillery Regiment (155-mm H) (89th Division) **Organized Reserve Nebraska**

HQ—Omaha, NE, 1929–36; Lincoln, NE, 1936–41

Arrived at the port of Hoboken on 27 May 1919 on the U.S.S. *Prinz Frederick Wilhelm* as the 342d F.A., an element of the 89th Div. Demobilized on 10 June 1919 at Camp Funston, KS. Reconstituted in the O.R. on 13 September 1929, assigned to the 89th Div., and allotted to the Seventh Corps Area. Initiated in October 1929 with regimental HQ at Omaha, NE. HQ relocated by 1936 to Lincoln, NE. Typically conducted Inactive Training Period meetings at the Paxton Hotel in Omaha or the Lincoln Hotel in Lincoln. Conducted summer training at numerous locations to include Fort Des Moines, IA; Camp McCoy, WI; Fort Robinson, NE; and Fort Riley, KS. Primary ROTC feeder school was the University of Nebraska. Location 7 December 1941—Lincoln, NE.

Status: Disbanded on 30 September 1959 as the 342d F.A. Bn.

Commanders, 342d Field Artillery Regiment

Col. George A. Nugent	25 August 1917–26 August 1918	Lt. Col. Joseph C. King	19 April 1919–17 May 19
Col. Emery T. Smith	26 August 1918–5 September 1918	Col. Otto L. Brunzell	17 May 1919–9 June 1919
Col. Earl Biscoe	5 September 1918–15 February 1919	*Demobilized/Inactive*	10 June 1919–October 1929
Lt. Col. William W. Overton	15 February 1919–22 February 1919	Lt. Col. Frank Warner	October 1929–2 December 1931
Col. Earl Biscoe	22 February 1919–12 April 1919	Col. Dwight P. Griswold	2 December 1931–21 December 1939
Maj. Albert J. Watson	12 April 1919–19 April 1919	Col. Edward L. Wilbur	28 December 1939–ao August 1940
Unknown	ao August 1940–7 December 1941		

343d Field Artillery Regiment (75-mm G) (90th Division) **Organized Reserve Texas**

HQ—Fort Worth, TX, 1921–25; Bryan, TX, 1925–41

Arrived at the port of New York on 7 June 1919 on the S.S. *H.B. Farrar* as the 343d F.A., an element of the 90th Div. Demobilized on 19 June 1919 at Camp Pike, AR. Reconstituted in the O.R. on 24 June 1921, assigned to the 90th Div., and allotted to the Eighth Corps Area. Initiated in November 1921 with regimental HQ at Fort Worth, TX. Subordinate battalion HQ concurrently organized as follows: 1st Bn. at Fort Worth and 2d Bn. at Wichita Falls, TX. Regimental HQ relocated on 10 July 1925 to Bryan, TX. Typically conducted Inactive Training Period meetings at the Texas Hotel in Fort Worth, 1922–25. Conducted summer training with the 12th and 15th F.A. Regts. at Fort Sam Houston, TX; Camp Stanley, TX; or Camp Bullis, TX. Conducted field artillery CMTC training some years at Camp Bullis as an alternate form of annual training. Primary ROTC feeder school was Texas A&M. Location 7 December 1941—Fort Worth, TX.

Status: Inactive in the US Army Reserve as the 343d F.A. Bn., a component of the 90th Inf. Div.

Commanders, 343d Field Artillery Regiment

Col. Henry B. Farrar	22 August 1917–6 June 1919	Maj. Roy Stockwell	13 September 1922–22 February 1923
Demobilized/Inactive	19 June 1919–November 1921	Col. Fred A. Logan	23 February 1923–1 April 1930
Capt. Harry Brelsford	23 January 1922–18 February 1922	Col. Hap H. Hanks	1 April 1930–ao May 1933
Maj. Louis L. White	18 February 1922–13 September 1922	Unknown	ao May 1933–7 December 1941

344th Field Artillery Regiment (75-mm G) (90th Division) **Organized Reserve Texas**

HQ—Dallas, TX, 1921–25; Waco, TX, 1925–41

Arrived at the port of Newport News on 14 June 1919 on the U.S.S. *Suwanee* as the 344th F.A., an element of the 90th Div. Demobilized on 27 June 1919 at Camp Bowie, TX. Reconstituted in the O.R. on 24 June 1921, assigned to the 90th Div., and allotted to the Eighth Corps Area. Initiated on 19 October 1921 with regimental HQ at Dallas, TX. Subordinate battalion HQ concurrently organized as follows: 1st Bn. at Dallas and 2d Bn. at Sherman, TX. Regimental HQ relocated on 10 July 1925 to Waco, TX. Conducted summer training with the 12th and 15th F.A. Regts. at Fort Sam Houston, TX; Camp Stanley, TX; or Camp Bullis, TX. Conducted field artillery CMTC training some years at Camp Bullis as an alternate form of annual training. Primary ROTC feeder school was Texas A&M. Location 7 December 1941—Dallas, TX.

Status: Inactive in the US Army Reserve as the 344th F.A. Bn., a component of the 90th Inf. Div.

Events: 163, 216

Commanders, 344th Field Artillery Regiment

Col. Samuel W. Frankenberger	23 August 1917–June 1918
Col. Albert U. Faulkner	June 1918–May 1919
Unknown	May 1919–27 June 1919
Demobilized/Inactive	27 June 1919–19 October 1921
Col. Dan T. Moore	19 October 1921–April 1935
Lt. Col. Louis B. Reed	April 1935–ao August 1936
Unknown	ao August 1936–ao December 1938
Col. Martin E. Collis	ao December 1938–February 1940
Lt. Col. Arthur M. Risdon	February 1940–January 1941

345th Field Artillery Regiment (155-mm H) (90th Division) **Organized Reserve Texas**

HQ—*Not initiated,* 1929–30; Harlingen, TX, 1930–41

Arrived at the port of Newport News on 7 June 1919 on the U.S.S. *Huron* as the 345th F.A., an element of the 90th Div. Demobilized on 23 June 1919 at Camp Bowie, TX. Reconstituted in the O.R. on 12 July 1929, assigned to the 90th Div., and allotted to the Eighth Corps Area. Initiated on 24 April 1930 with regimental HQ at Harlingen, TX. Subordinate battalion HQ concurrently organized as follows: 1st Bn. at Brownsville, TX; 2d Bn. at McAllen, TX; and 3d Bn. at Corpus Christi, TX. San Antonio officers typically conducted Inactive Training Period meetings at the San Antonio Vocational and Technical School and, at times, at the Smith-Young Tower in San Antonio. Conducted summer training most years with the 12th and 15th F.A. Regts. at Camp Stanley, TX, or Camp Bullis, TX, and some years with the 77th F.A. at Fort D.A. Russell, TX. Primary ROTC feeder school was Texas A&M. Location 7 December 1941—Harlingen, TX.

Status: Inactive in the US Army Reserve as the 345th F.A. Bn., a component of the 75th Inf. Div.

Commanders, 345th Field Artillery Regiment

Lt. Col. LaVert Coleman	23 August 1917–30 September 1917
Col. Robert S. Abernethy	30 September 1917–23 October 1918
Col. George L. Wertenbaker	23 October 1918–23 June 1919
Demobilized/Inactive	23 June 1919–24 April 1930
Lt. Col. Frank M. Hicks	24 April 1930–25 February 1939
Col. Edmund H. Levy	25 March 1939–ao January 1940
Unknown	ao January 1940–7 December 1941

346th Field Artillery Regiment (75-mm G) (91st Division) **Organized Reserve California**

HQ—San Francisco, CA, 1921–41

Arrived at the port of New York on 15 January 1919 on the U.S.S. *St. Louis* as the 346th F.A., an element of the 91st Div. Demobilized on 8 February 1919 at Camp Lewis, WA. Reconstituted in the O.R. on 24 June 1921, assigned to the 91st Div., and allotted to the Ninth Corps Area. Initiated on 5 November 1921 with regimental HQ at San Francisco, CA. Subordinate battalion HQ concurrently organized as follows: 1st Bn. at San Francisco and 2d Bn. at Palo Alto, CA. The 2d Bn. was relocated about April 1930 to San Francisco. Typically conducted Inactive Training Period meetings at the Oakland City Hall in Oakland, CA, or at the Mills Building in San Francisco. Conducted summer training most years with the 2d Bn., 76th F.A. at the Presidio of Monterey, CA, and some years at Del Monte, CA. Conducted field artillery CMTC training some years at the Presidio of Monterey as an alternate form of annual training. Primary ROTC feeder school was Stanford University. Location 7 December 1941—San Francisco, CA.

Status: Disbanded 1 May 1959 as the 346th F.A. Bn.

Commanders, 346th Field Artillery Regiment

Col. Fred T. Austin	2 September 1917–30 October 1917	Col. Willam G. Devereaux	5 November 1921–6 July 1925
Col. Raymond S. Pratt	6 June 1918–30 September 1918	Lt. Col. William A. Boekel Jr.	6 July 1925–ao July 1928
Col. Samuel W. Frakenberger	14 December 1918–8 February 1919	Unknown	ao July 1928–ao December 1930
Demobilized/Inactive	8 February 1919–5 November 1921	Col. Lionel S. Schmitt	ao December 1930–ao January 1940
Unknown	ao January 1940–7 December 1941		

347th Field Artillery Regiment (75-mm G) (91st Division) **Organized Reserve California**

HQ—Los Angeles, CA, 1921–41

Arrived at the port of New York on 2 April 1919 on the U.S.S. *Leviathan* as the 347th F.A., an element of the 91st Div. Demobilized on 29 April 1919 at the Presidio of San Francisco, CA. Reconstituted in the O.R. on 24 June 1921, assigned to the 91st Div., and allotted to the Ninth Corps Area. Initiated on 5 November 1921 with regimental HQ at Los Angeles, CA. Subordinate battalion HQ concurrently organized as follows: 1st Bn. at Los Angeles and 2d Bn. at San Diego, CA. The 2d Bn. was relocated about April 1930 to Los Angeles. The regiment invested Hollywood actress Joan Bennett as "honorary colonel of the regiment" in April 1932. Many unit personnel participated in earthquake relief operations, 14–22 March 1933, in the Los Angeles area. Typically conducted Inactive Training Period meetings at the Chamber of Commerce Building or at 751 Figuroa Street in Los Angeles. Conducted summer training most years with the 2d Bn., 76th F.A. at the Presidio of Monterey, CA, and some years at Del Monte, CA. Primary ROTC feeder school was Stanford University. Location 7 December 1941—Los Angeles, CA.

Status: Disbanded 1 May 1959 as the 347th F.A. Bn.

Commanders, 347th Field Artillery Regiment

Col. Ralph S. Granger	16 August 1917–22 August 1918	Lt. Col. Thomas H. Jennings	5 November 1921–14 August 1925
Col. Lewis D. Barnett	ao March 1919–29 April 1919	Col. Jean A. Jeancon	14 August 1925–11 September 1937
Demobilized/Inactive	29 April 1919–5 November 1921	Lt. Col. Louis E. Legner	11 September 1937–26 February 1938
Unknown	26 February 1938–7 December 1941		

348th Field Artillery Regiment (155-mm H) (91st Division) **Organized Reserve California**

HQ—Los Angeles, CA, 1929–41

Arrived at the port of New York on 2 April 1919 on the U.S.S. *Leviathan* as the 348th F.A., an element of the 91st Div. Demobilized on 20 April 1919 at Fort D.A. Russell, WY. Reconstituted in the O.R. on 13 September 1929, assigned to the 91st Div., and allotted to the Ninth Corps Area. Initiated on 20 October 1929 with the entire regiment at Los Angeles, CA. Typically conducted Inactive Training Period meetings at the Chamber of Commerce Building or at 751 Figuroa Street in Los Angeles. Conducted summer training most years with the 2d Bn., 76th F.A. at the Presidio of Monterey, CA, and some years at Del Monte, CA. Primary ROTC feeder school was Stanford University. Location 7 December 1941—Los Angeles, CA.

Status: Disbanded on 1 May 1959 as the 348th F.A. Bn.

Commanders, 348th Field Artillery Regiment

Col. Sam F. Bottoms	September 1917–July 1918
Col. Rex Van Den Corput	July 1918–31 October 1918
Col. Sam F. Bottoms	1 November 1918–20 April 1919
Demobilized/Inactive	20 April 1919–20 October 1929
Col. William H. Neblett	20 October 1929–16 June 1941

349th Field Artillery Regiment (75-mm G) (GHQR) **Organized Reserve Texas**

HQ—*Not initiated,* 1930–31; El Paso, TX, 1931–40; Fort Sill, OK, 1940–41

Constituted in the O.R. on 12 July 1929 and allotted to the Sixth Corps Area. Designated to be assigned to the 92d Div. as a "Colored" unit on reorganization of that division. Constitution rescinded on 13 September 1929. Reconstituted in the O.R. on 4 September 1930, assigned to the GHQR, and allotted to the Eighth Corps Area. Concurrently consolidated with the 349th F.A. Regt. (organized in November 1917 at Camp Dix, NJ, and assigned to the 92d Div.; arrived at the port of New York on 3 March 1919 on the U.S.S. *Great Northern*; demobilized on 17 March 1919 at Camp Dix, NJ). Initiated in January 1931 with regimental HQ at El Paso, TX. Subordinate battalion HQ concurrently organized as follows: 1st Bn. at El Paso; 2d Bn. at Abilene, TX; and 3d Bn. at Amarillo, TX. Conducted summer training most years with the 12th and 15th F.A. Regts. at Camp Bullis, TX, and some years with the 77th F.A. at Fort D.A. Russell, TX. Conducted CMTC training at Fort Sam Houston in 1935 as an alternate form of summer training. Reserve personnel relieved on 1 August 1940 and regiment withdrawn from the O.R. Concurrently, allotted to the R.A. and activated at Fort Sill, OK, as the Field Artillery School support regiment. Reorganized on 15 August 1940 as (155-mm G). Relieved from the Field Artillery School on 15 December 1940 and assigned to the 18th F.A. Brig. (VIII Corps). Location 7 December 1941—Fort Sill, OK.

Status: HHB is inactive in the R.A. as HHB, 72d F.A. Brig.; 1st Bn. is inactive in the R.A. as the 96th F.A. Bn.; 2d Bn. is inactive in the R.A. as the 686th F.A. Bn.

Events: 317, 328

Commanders, 349th Field Artillery Regiment

Col. Dan T. Moore	26 October 1917–25 October 1918
Col. John O'Neill	26 October 1917–17 March 1919
Demobilized/Inactive	17 March 1919–January 1931
Col. Otto K. Seidel	January 1931–ao August 1938
Unknown	ao August 1938–14 August 1940
Col. Alfred L. P. Sands	15 August 1940–10 December 1941
Col. Charles E. Boyle	10 December 1941–ao January 1942

350th Field Artillery Regiment (155-mm H) (Colored) (46th Field Artillery Brigade)

HQ—*Not initiated,* 1940–41; Camp Livingston, LA, 1941

Constituted in the O.R. on 12 July 1929 and allotted to the Sixth Corps Area. Designated to be assigned to the 92d Div. as a "Colored" unit on reorganization of that division. Constitution rescinded on 13 September 1929. Reconstituted in the R.A. on 16 December 1940. Concurrently consolidated with the 350th F.A. Regt. (organized in November 1917 at Camp Dix, NJ, and assigned to the 92d Div.; arrived at the port of New York on 3 March 1919 on the U.S.S. *Rochambeau*; demobilized on 12 March 1919 at Camp Dix, NJ). Assigned to the 46th F.A. Brig. and activated on 10 February 1941 at Camp Livingston, LA. Location 7 December 1941—Camp Livingston, LA.

Status: HHB is inactive in the R.A. as HHB, 350th F.A. Group; 1st Bn. is inactive in the R.A. as the 98th F.A. Bn.; 2d Bn. is inactive in the US Army Reserve as the 572d F.A. Bn.

Commanders, 350th Field Artillery Regiment

Col. Fred T. Austin	30 October 1917–29 April 1918	*Demobilized/Inactive*	12 March 1919–10 February 1941
Col. Walter E. Prosser	30 April 1918–12 March 1919	Col. Thomas G.M. Oliphant	10 February 1941–ao March 1941

351st Field Artillery Regiment (155-mm H) (Colored) (46th Field Artillery Brigade)

HQ—*Not initiated,* 1940–41; Camp Livingston, LA, 1941

Constituted in the O.R. on 12 July 1929 and allotted to the Sixth Corps Area. Designated to be assigned to the 92d Div. as a "Colored" unit on reorganization of that division. Constitution rescinded on 13 September 1929. Reconstituted in the R.A. on 16 December 1940. Concurrently consolidated with the 351st F.A. Regt. (organized in November 1917 at Camp Dix, NJ, and assigned to the 92d Div.; arrived at the port of New York on 16 February 1919 on the U.S.S. *Louisville*; demobilized on 12 March 1919 at Camp Dix, NJ). Assigned to the 46th F.A. Brig. and activated on 10 February 1941 at Camp Livingston, LA. Location 7 December 1941—Camp Livingston, LA.

Status: HHB is inactive in the R.A. as HHB, 351st F.A. Group; 1st Bn. is assigned to the USARS as elements of the 12th F.A. (consolidated on 10 November 1951); the 2d Bn. is inactive in the US Army Reserve as the 508th F.A. Bn.

Commanders, 351st Field Artillery Regiment

Col. Albert E. Saxton	27 October 1917–8 November 1917	Col. Wade A. Carpenter	11 September 1918–11 March 1919
Col. William E. Cole	8 November 1917–26 August 1918	*Demobilized/Inactive*	6 March 1919–10 February 1941
Col. George H. Paine	10 February 1941–5 April 1941		

352d Field Artillery Regiment (155-mm H) (XII Corps) **Organized Reserve New York**

HQ—*Not initiated,* 1929–30; Bronx, NY, 1930–41

Constituted in the O.R. on 12 July 1929 and allotted to the Sixth Corps Area. Constitution rescinded and regiment reconstituted in the O.R. on 13 September 1929, allotted to the Second Corps Area, and assigned to the 181st F.A. Brig. (XII Corps). Further designated to be assigned to the 93d Div. as a "Colored" unit on reorganization of that division. Initiated on 30 January 1930 with regimental HQ at Bronx, NY. Subordinate battalion HQ concurrently organized as follows: 1st Bn. at Bronx; 2d Bn. at New Rochelle, NY; and 3d Bn. at Newburgh, NY. Typically conducted Inactive Training Period meetings at the Hotel Delmonico at 59th Street and Park Avenue in New York City, NY. Conducted summer training with the 7th F.A. at Pine Camp, NY. Conducted field artillery CMTC training some years at Madison Barracks, NY, as an alternate form of annual training. Primary ROTC feeder schools were Princeton University and Cornell University. Designated mobilization station was Pine Camp, NY. Location 7 December 1941—Bronx, NY.

Status: Disbanded on 26 January 1943.

Events: 267

Commanders, 352d Field Artillery Regiment

Lt. Col. Harold Lee	30 January 1930–18 June 1932	Col. Henry F. Boyce	18 June 1932–August 1941
Lt. Col. Joseph H. Bonneville	August 1941–20 November 1941		

353d Field Artillery Regiment (155-mm H) (XII Corps) **Organized Reserve New York**

HQ—*Not initiated,* 1929–30; Brooklyn, NY, 1930–37; *Inactive,* 1937–40

Constituted in the O.R. on 12 July 1929 and allotted to the Sixth Corps Area. Constitution rescinded and regiment constituted in the O.R. on 13 September 1929, allotted to the Second Corps Area, and assigned to the 181st F.A. Brig. (XII Corps). Further designated to be assigned to the 93d Div. as a "Colored" unit on reorganization of the division. Initiated in January 1930 with regimental HQ, 1st Bn., and 2d Bn. at Brooklyn, NY, and 3d Bn. at Oyster Bay, NY. Primary ROTC feeder school was Princeton University. Designated mobilization station was Pine Camp, NY. Inactivated in February 1937 at Brooklyn by relief of personnel. Disbanded 31 July 1940.

Commanders, 353d Field Artillery Regiment

Unknown	January 1930–February 1937	*Inactive*	February 1937–31 January 1940

354th Field Artillery Regiment (155-mm H) (GHQR) **Organized Reserve Michigan**

HQ—*Not initiated,* 1929–41

Constituted in the O.R. on 12 July 1929 and allotted to the Sixth Corps Area. Detroit, MI, designated as the regimental HQ on organization, but the unit was never organized. Regiment withdrawn from Sixth Corps Area on 13 September 1929. Designated to be assigned to the 93d Div. as a "Colored" unit on reorganization of that division. Location 7 December 1941—*Not initiated.*

355th Field Artillery Regiment (75-mm G) (76th Division) **Organized Reserve Connecticut**

HQ—New Haven, CT, 1921–41

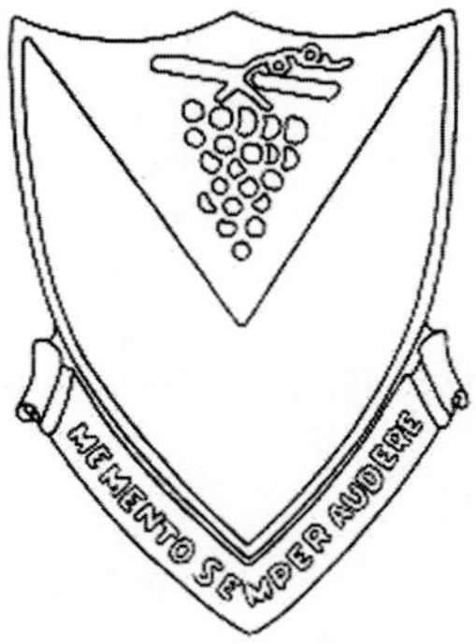

Constituted in the O.R. on 24 June 1921, assigned to the 76th Div., and allotted to the First Corps Area. Initiated on 27 December 1921 with regimental HQ at New Haven, CT. Subordinate battalion HQ concurrently organized as follows: 1st Bn. at New Haven and 2d Bn. at Bridgeport, CT. Typically conducted Inactive Training Period meetings at the armory of the Governor's Foot Guards or at Artillery Hall in New Haven. Conducted summer training with the 7th F.A. at Fort Ethan Allen, VT. Primary ROTC feeder school was Yale University. Location 7 December 1941—New Haven, CT.

Status: Disbanded on 30 April 1959 as the 355th F.A. Bn.

Commanders, 355th Field Artillery Regiment

Maj. Herbert H. Vreeland Jr.	27 December 1921–12 November 1924	Col. Herbert H. Vreeland Jr.	January 1927–August 1936
Lt. Col. James W. Gilson	12 November 1924–June 1925	Col. Theodore Crane	August 1936–ao February 1940
Lt. Col. Theodore Crane	June 1925–January 1927	Unknown	ao February 1940–7 December 1941

356th Field Artillery Regiment (75-mm G) (94th Division) **Organized Reserve Massachusetts**

HQ—Worcester, MA, 1921–41

Constituted in the O.R. on 24 June 1921, assigned to the 94th Div., and allotted to the First Corps Area. Initiated on 4 November 1921 with regimental HQ at Worcester, MA. Subordinate battalion HQ concurrently organized as follows: 1st Bn. at Fitchburg, MA, and 2d Bn. at Worcester. Typically conducted Inactive Training Period meetings at the Federal Building in Worcester. Conducted summer training with the 7th F.A. at Fort Ethan Allen, VT. Conducted field artillery CMTC training some years at Fort Ethan Allen as an alternate form of annual training. Primary ROTC feeder school was Harvard University. Location 7 December 1941—Worcester, MA.

Status: Disbanded on 1 May 1959 as the 356th F.A. Bn.

Commanders, 356th Field Artillery Regiment

Col. Robert L. Whipple	4 November 1921–ao April 1929	Col. Ralph H. Whitney	May 1931–ao January 1940
Lt. Col. Douglas Crocker	ao May 1929–May 1931	Unknown	ao January 1940–7 December 1941

357th Field Artillery Regiment (155-mm H) (94th Division) **Organized Reserve Michigan/Connecticut**

HQ—New Haven, CT, 1929–41

Constituted in the O.R. on 12 July 1929 and allotted to the Sixth Corps Area. Detroit, MI, designated as the regimental HQ on organization, but the unit was never organized. Withdrawn from Sixth Corps Area on 13 September 1929, allotted to the First Corps Area, and assigned to the 94th Div. Relieved from the 94th Div. on 5 October 1929 and assigned to the 180th F.A. Brig. (XI Corps). Initiated in October 1929 with regimental HQ and 1st Bn. at New Haven, CT; the 2d Bn. at Hartford, CT; and the 3d Bn. at Bridgeport, CT. Primary ROTC feeder school was Yale University. Location 7 December 1941—New Haven, CT.

Status: Disbanded on 26 January 1943.

Commanders, 357th Field Artillery Regiment

Unknown	October 1929–7 December 1941

358th Field Artillery Regiment (75-mm G) (95th Division) **Organized Reserve Oklahoma**

HQ—*Not initiated,* 1921–22; Muskogee, OK, 1922–25; Sapulpa, OK, 1925–41

Constituted in the O.R. on 24 June 1921, assigned to the 95th Div., and allotted to the Eighth Corps Area. Initiated on 12 January 1922 with regimental HQ at Muskogee, OK. Subordinate battalion HQ concurrently organized as follows: 1st Bn. at Tulsa, OK, and 2d Bn. at McAlester, OK. Regimental HQ relocated on 10 July 1925 to Sapulpa, OK. Conducted summer training with the 1st F.A. at Fort Sill, OK. Conducted field artillery CMTC training some years at Fort Sill as an alternate form of annual training. Primary ROTC feeder school was the University of Oklahoma. Location 7 December 1941—Sapulpa, OK.

Status: Disbanded on 1 April 1959 as the 358th F.A. Bn.

Commanders, 358th Field Artillery Regiment

Medical officers only	12 January 1922–8 February 1922	Unknown	ao February 1922–ao January 1924
Maj. William A. Green	8 February 1922–12 January 1923	Maj. Edward L. Heiser	ao January 1924–ao April 1930
Lt. Col. Walton Clark Jr.	12 January 1923–ao February 1922	Unknown	ao April 1930–7 December 1941

359th Field Artillery Regiment (75-mm G) (95th Division) **Organized Reserve Oklahoma**

HQ—*Not initiated,* 1921–22; El Reno, OK, 1922–24; Ardmore, OK, 1924–41

Constituted in the O.R. on 24 June 1921, assigned to the 95th Div., and allotted to the Eighth Corps Area. Initiated on 17 January 1922 with regimental HQ at El Reno, OK. Subordinate battalion HQ concurrently organized as follows: 1st Bn. at Enid and 2d Bn. at Lawton, OK. HQ relocated in October 1924 to Ardmore, OK. Conducted summer training with the 1st F.A. at Fort Sill, OK. Conducted field artillery CMTC training some years at Fort Sill as an alternate form of annual training. Primary ROTC feeder school was the University of Oklahoma. Location 7 December 1941—Ardmore, OK.

Status: Disbanded on 1 April 1959 as the 359th F.A. Bn.

Commanders, 359th Field Artillery Regiment

Medical officers only	17 January 1922–27 January 1922	Lt. Col. Herbert B. Peck	5 April 1922–13 September 1922
Capt. Otis E. Nelson	27 January 1922–8 February 1922	Maj. Emmet C. Choate	13 September 1922–February 1923
Maj. Rensselaer W. McClure Jr.	8 February 1922–5 April 1922	Lt. Col. Harold B. Fell	February 1923–ao June 1930
Unknown	ao June 1930–7 December 1941		

360th Field Artillery Regiment (155-mm H) (95th Division) **Organized Reserve Oklahoma**

HQ—Edmond, OK, 1929–41

Constituted in the O.R. on 13 September 1929, assigned to the 95th Div., and allotted to the Eighth Corps Area. Initiated on 17 December 1929 with regimental HQ at Edmond, OK. Subordinate battalion HQ concurrently organized as follows: 1st Bn. at Enid, OK; 2d Bn. at Ponca City, OK; and 3d Bn. at El Reno, OK. Conducted summer training with the 1st F.A. at Fort Sill, OK. Conducted field artillery CMTC training some years at Fort Sill as an alternate form of annual training. Primary ROTC feeder school was the University of Oklahoma. Location 7 December 1941—Edmond, OK.

Status: Disbanded on 1 April 1959 as the 360th F.A. Bn.

Commanders, 360th Field Artillery Regiment

Unknown	17 December 1929–26 April 1930	Maj. William O. Pratt	26 April 1930–ao May 1930
Unknown	ao May 1930–7 December 1941		

361st Field Artillery Regiment (75-mm G) (96th Division) **Organized Reserve Oregon**

HQ—Portland, OR, 1921–41

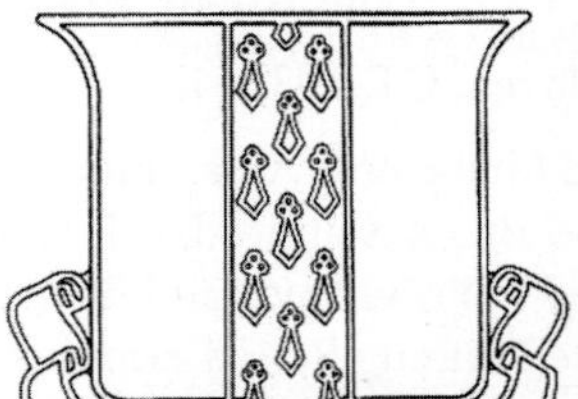

Constituted in the O.R. on 24 June 1921, assigned to the 96th Div., and allotted to the Ninth Corps Area. Initiated on 15 December 1921 with regimental HQ at Portland, OR. Subordinate battalion HQ concurrently organized as follows: 1st Bn. at Portland and 2d Bn. at Pendleton, OR. Conducted summer training with the 10th F.A. at Fort Lewis, WA. Typically conducted Inactive Training Period meetings at the Multenomah Hotel, New Post Office Building, or Thielis Restaurant in Portland. Conducted field artillery CMTC training some years at Fort Lewis as an alternate form of annual training. Primary ROTC feeder school was Oregon State Agricultural College. Location 7 December 1941—Portland, OR.

Status: Inactive in the US Army Reserve as the 361st F.A. Bn., a component of the 96th Inf. Div.

Commanders, 361st Field Artillery Regiment

Col. Henry C.R. Akin	15 December 1921–ao August 1939	Lt. Col. Quincy Scott	ao December 1940–2 April 1941
Unknown	August 1939–ao December 1940	Unknown	2 April 1941–7 December 1941

362d Field Artillery Regiment (75-mm G) (96th Division) **Organized Reserve Washington**

HQ—Seattle, WA, 1921–41

Constituted in the O.R. on 24 June 1921, assigned to the 96th Div., and allotted to the Ninth Corps Area. Initiated on 31 December 1921 with regimental HQ at Seattle, WA. Subordinate battalion HQ concurrently organized as follows: 1st Bn. at Tacoma, WA, and 2d Bn. at Ellensburg, WA. Conducted summer training with the 10th F.A. at Fort Lewis, WA. Conducted field artillery CMTC training some years at Fort Lewis as an alternate form of annual training. Primary ROTC feeder school was the University of Washington. Location 7 December 1941—Seattle, WA.

Status: Inactive in the US Army Reserve as the 362d F.A. Bn., a component of the 96th Inf. Div.

Commanders, 362d Field Artillery Regiment

Maj. Edwin K. Brown	31 December 1921–February 1922	Col. Malcolm Douglas	February 1922–ao March 1941
Unknown	ao March 1941–7 December 1941		

363d Field Artillery Regiment (155-mm H) (96th Division) **Organized Reserve Oregon**

HQ—*Not initiated,* 1929–30; Portland, OR, 1930–41

Constituted in the O.R. on 13 September 1929, assigned to the 96th Div., and allotted to the Ninth Corps Area. Initiated on 7 January 1930 with the entire regiment at Portland, OR. Conducted summer training with the 10th F.A. at Fort Lewis, WA. Typically conducted Inactive Training Period meetings at the Multenomah Hotel, New Post Office Building, or Thielis Restaurant in Portland. Conducted field artillery CMTC training some years at Fort Lewis as an alternate form of annual training. Primary ROTC feeder school was Oregon State Agricultural College. Location 7 December 1941—Portland, OR.

Status: Inactive in the US Army Reserve as the 363d F.A. Bn., a component of the 96th Inf. Div.

Commanders, 363d Field Artillery Regiment

Col. Roy K. Terry	7 January 1930–ao January 1941	Unknown	ao January 1941–7 December 1941

364th Field Artillery Regiment (155-mm H) (76th Division) **Organized Reserve Connecticut and Rhode Island**

HQ—*Not initiated,* 1929–30; Greenwich, CT, 1930–32; Providence, RI, 1932–35; New Haven, CT, 1935–42

Constituted in the O.R. on 13 September 1929, assigned to the 76th Div., and allotted to the First Corps Area. Initiated on 18 January 1930 with regimental HQ, 1st Bn., and 2d Bn. at Greenwich, CT, and the 3d Bn. at Stamford, CT. HQ relocated in November 1932 to Providence, RI. Concurrently, 1st Bn. and 2d Bn. relocated to Providence and the 3d Bn. to Newport, RI. HQ relocated in 1935 to New Haven, CT. Typically conducted Inactive Training Period meetings at the Greenwich Armory in Greenwich or at Artillery Hall in New Haven. Conducted summer training with the 7th F.A. at Fort Ethan Allen, VT. Primary ROTC feeder school was Yale University. Location 7 December 1941—New Haven, CT.

Status: Disbanded on 30 April 1959 as the 364th F.A. Bn.

Commanders, 364th Field Artillery Regiment

Col. Charles F. Tillinghast	18 January 1930–February 1931	Col. John A. Twachtman	ao July 1932–ao January 1940
Lt. Col. Robert G. Thackeray	February 1931–ao March 1932	Unknown	ao January 1940–7 December 1941

365th Field Artillery Regiment (75-mm G) (97th Division) **Organized Reserve New Hampshire and Vermont**

HQ—*Not initiated,* 1921–22; Manchester, NH, 1922–41

Constituted in the O.R. on 24 June 1921, assigned to the 97th Div., and allotted to the First Corps Area. Initiated in June 1922 with regimental HQ at Manchester, NH. Subordinate battalion HQ concurrently organized as follows: 1st Bn. at Newport, VT, and 2d Bn. at Franklin, NH. Typically conducted Inactive Training Period meetings at 855 Elm Street in Manchester. Conducted summer training with the 7th F.A. at Fort Ethan Allen, VT. Primary ROTC feeder school was the University of New Hampshire. Location 7 December 1941—Manchester, NH.

Status: Inactive in the US Army Reserve as the 365th F.A. Bn., a component of the 97th Inf. Div.

Commanders, 365th Field Artillery Regiment

Col. George L. Taylor	June 1922–ao July 1929	Unknown	ao June 1936–ao May 1937
Unknown	ao July 1929–ao June 1930	Lt. Col. Victor H. Smith	ao May 1937–26 June 1937
Col. Charles A. Meserve	ao June 1930–ao June 1936	Col. Frank Knox	26 June 1937–September 1941

366th Field Artillery Regiment (155-mm H) (XI Corps) **Organized Reserve Massachusetts/ New Jersey**

HQ—*Not initiated,* 1929–41

Constituted in the O.R. on 12 July 1929 as a 75-mm G Regt. and allotted to the Seventh Corps Area. Withdrawn from the Seventh Corps Area on 13 September 1929, allotted to the First Corps Area, and assigned to the 97th Div. Relieved from the 97th Div. on 5 October 1929 and assigned to the 180th F.A. Brig. (XI Corps). Concurrently reorganized as 155-mm H. Withdrawn from the First Corps Area on 5 June 1936 and allotted to the Second Corps Area. Elizabeth, NJ, designated in April 1937 as HQ on organization, but the unit was never organized at that location. Location 7 December 1941—*Not initiated.*

Status: Disbanded 26 January 1943.

367th Field Artillery Regiment (75-mm G) (98th Division) **Organized Reserve New York**

HQ—Troy, NY, 1921–37; Albany, NY, 1937–41

Constituted in the O.R. on 24 June 1921, assigned to the 98th Div., and allotted to the Second Corps Area. Initiated on 4 October 1921 with regimental HQ at Troy, NY. Subordinate battalion HQ concurrently organized as follows: 1st Bn. at Binghamton, NY, and 2d Bn. at Utica, NY. Entire regiment relocated in 1937 to Albany, NY. Conducted summer training with the 5th F.A. most years at Pine Camp, NY, and some years at Madison Barracks, NY. Conducted field artillery CMTC training some years at Madison Barracks as an alternate form of annual training. Primary ROTC feeder school was Cornell University. Designated mobilization station was Pine Camp. Location 7 December 1941—Albany, NY.

Status: Disbanded on 1 May 1959 as the 367th F.A. Bn.

Commanders, 367th Field Artillery Regiment

Col. Harry C. Wilder	4 October 1921–30 June 1929	Unknown	ao November 1936–ao July 1938
Col. Harold Remington	30 June 1929–ao November 1936	Lt. Col. Frank A. McNamee	ao July 1938–1 March 1939
	Lt. Col. Robert H. Cushing	1 March 1939–22 July 1941	

368th Field Artillery Regiment (75-mm G) (98th Division) **Organized Reserve New York**

HQ—Rochester, NY, 1921–32; Buffalo, NY, 1932–41

Constituted in the O.R. on 24 June 1921, assigned to the 98th Div., and allotted to the Second Corps Area. Initiated on 4 October 1921 with regimental HQ at Rochester, NY. Subordinate battalion HQ concurrently organized as follows: 1st Bn. at Rochester and 2d Bn. at Buffalo, NY. Entire regiment relocated on 8 February 1932 to Buffalo. Conducted summer training with the 5th F.A. most years at Pine Camp, NY, and some years at Madison Barracks, NY. Conducted field artillery CMTC training some years at Madison Barracks as an alternate form of annual training. Primary ROTC feeder school was Cornell University. Designated mobilization station was Pine Camp. Location 7 December 1941—Buffalo, NY.

Status: Disbanded on 1 May 1959 as the 368th F.A. Bn.

Commanders, 368th Field Artillery Regiment

Col. Guido F. Verbeck	4 October 1921–27 July 1940	Col. Charles W. Jacobsen	9 August 1940–22 July 1941
Lt. Col. Robert H. Cushing	27 July 1940–9 August 1940	Lt. Col. Robert H. Cushing	22 July 1941–ao December 1941

369th Field Artillery Regiment (155-mm H) (98th Division) **Organized Reserve New York**

HQ—Syracuse, NY, 1929–37; Buffalo, NY, 1937–41

Constituted in the O.R. on 13 September 1929, assigned to the 77th Div., and allotted to the Second Corps Area. Relieved from the 77th Div. on 26 October 1929 and assigned to the 98th Div. Initiated in February 1930 with regimental HQ at Syracuse, NY. HQ relocated in 1937 to Buffalo, NY. Conducted summer training with the 5th F.A. most years at Pine Camp, NY, and some years at Madison Barracks, NY. Primary ROTC feeder school was St. Bonaventure College. Location 7 December 1941—Buffalo, NY.

Status: Disbanded on 1 May 1959 as the 369th F.A. Bn.

Commanders, 369th Field Artillery Regiment

Col. Charles B. Sayre	February 1930–ao November 1936	Lt. Col. William W. Lewis	ao July 1937–8 April 1940
Unknown	ao November 1936–ao July 1937	Col. Charles W. Jacobsen	8 April 1940–9 August 1940
Unknown	9 August 1940–7 December 1941		

370th Field Artillery Regiment (75-mm G) (99th Division) **Organized Reserve Pennsylvania**

HQ—Pittsburgh, PA, 1921–41

Constituted in the O.R. on 24 June 1921, assigned to the 99th Div., and allotted to the Third Corps Area. Initiated on 7 December 1921 with the entire regiment at Pittsburgh, PA. Conducted summer training most years with the 6th F.A. at Fort Hoyle, MD, and some years with the 109th F.A. at Tobyhanna, PA. Conducted field artillery CMTC training some years at Fort Hoyle as an alternate form of annual training. Primary ROTC feeder school was Duquesne University. Location 7 December 1941—Pittsburgh, PA.

Status: Inactive in the US Army Reserve as the 370th F.A. Bn., a component of the 99th Inf. Div.

Commanders, 370th Field Artillery Regiment

Unknown	7 December 1921–18 April 1922	Lt. Col. Thomas Fitzgerald	9 January 1923–26 February 1925
Lt. Col. Edwin C. Carter Jr.	18 April 1922–9 January 1923	Col. Edwin C. Carter Jr.	26 February 1925–ao January 1940
Unknown	ao January 1940–7 December 1941		

371st Field Artillery Regiment (75-mm G) (99th Division) **Organized Reserve Pennsylvania**

HQ—Pittsburgh, PA, 1921–41

Constituted in the O.R. on 24 June 1921, assigned to the 99th Div., and allotted to the Third Corps Area. Initiated in November 1921 with the entire regiment at Pittsburgh, PA. Conducted summer training most years with the 6th F.A. at Fort Hoyle, MD, and some years with the 109th F.A. at Tobyhanna, PA. Conducted field artillery CMTC training some years at Fort Hoyle as an alternate form of annual training. Primary ROTC feeder school was Duquesne University. Location 7 December 1941—Pittsburgh, PA.

Status: Inactive in the US Army Reserve as the 371st F.A. Bn., a component of the 99th Inf. Div.

Commanders, 371st Field Artillery Regiment

Maj. Harry Howe	7 December 1921–10 November 1922	Lt. Col. Harry Howe	25 January 1929–11 March 1929
Col. Henry R. Freeman Jr.	10 November 1922–25 January 1929	Col. Clinton T. Bundy	11 March 1929–7 January 1938
Col. John J. Daub	7 January 1938–August 1941		

372d Field Artillery Regiment (155-mm H) (99th Division) **Organized Reserve Pennsylvania**

HQ—Pittsburgh, PA, 1921–41

Constituted in the O.R. on 13 September 1929, assigned to the 99th Div., and allotted to the Third Corps Area. Initiated in November 1929 with the entire regiment at Pittsburgh, PA. Typically conducted inactive training period meetings at the Fort Pitt Hotel in Pittsburg. Conducted summer training most years with the 6th F.A. at Fort Hoyle, MD, and some years with the 109th F.A. at Tobyhanna, PA. Conducted field artillery CMTC training some years at Fort Hoyle as an alternate form of annual training. Primary ROTC feeder school was Duquesne University. Location 7 December 1941—Pittsburgh, PA.

Status: Inactive in the US Army Reserve as the 372d F.A. Bn., a component of the 99th Inf. Div.

Events: 109

Commanders, 372d Field Artillery Regiment

Col. Leopold W. Depuy	13 January 1930–August 1941

373d Field Artillery Regiment (155-mm H) (100th Division) **Organized Reserve West Virginia, Ohio, and Kentucky**

HQ—*Not initiated,* 1929–30; Huntington, WV, 1930–32; Cincinnati, OH, 1932–34; Wheeling, WV, 1934–37; Lexington, KY, 1937–41

Constituted in the O.R. on 12 July 1929, assigned to the 100th Div., and allotted to the Fifth Corps Area. Initiated in April 1930 with regimental HQ at Huntington, WV. Regimental HQ successively relocated as follows: Cincinnati, OH, in October 1932; Wheeling, WV, in April 1934; and to Lexington, KY, in April 1937. Conducted summer training with the 1st Bn., 3d F.A., 1930–34, and the 1st Bn., 19th F.A., 1935–39, at Fort Knox, KY. Primary ROTC feeder school was West Virginia University. Location 7 December 1941—Lexington, KY.

Status: Disbanded on 17 April 1959 as the 373d F.A. Bn.

Commander, 373d Field Artillery Regiment

Unknown	April 1930–7 December 1941

374th Field Artillery Regiment (75-mm G) (100th Division) **Organized Reserve West Virginia**

HQ—Clarksburg, WV, 1921–30; Wheeling, WV, 1930–41

Constituted in the O.R. on 24 June 1921, assigned to the 100th Div., and allotted to the Fifth Corps Area. Initiated on 30 November 1921 with regimental HQ at Clarksburg, WV. Subordinate battalion HQ concurrently organized as follows: 1st Bn. at Wheeling, WV, and 2d Bn. at Grafton, WV. HQ relocated in 1930 to Wheeling, WV. Conducted summer training with the 1st Bn., 3d F.A., 1930–34, and the 1st Bn., 19th F.A., 1935–39, at Fort Knox, KY. Primary ROTC feeder school was West Virginia University. Location 7 December 1941—Wheeling, WV.

Status: Disbanded on 17 April 1959 as the 374th F.A. Bn.

Commander, 374th Field Artillery Regiment

Col. Elliot B. Hopkins	30 November 1921–ao May 1941

375th Field Artillery Regiment (75-mm G) (100th Division) **Organized Reserve West Virginia**

HQ—Charleston, WV, 1921–41

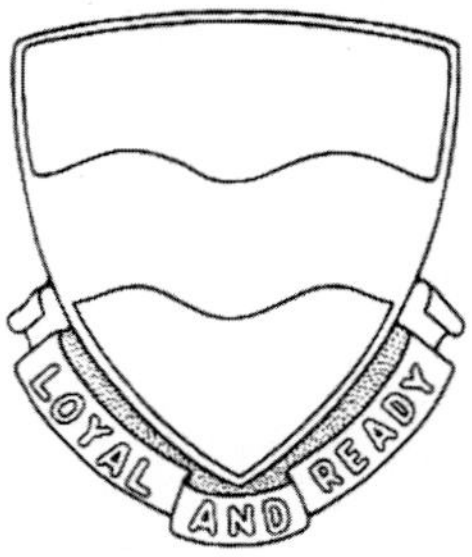

Constituted in the O.R. on 24 June 1921, assigned to the 100th Div., and allotted to the Fifth Corps Area. Initiated on 30 November 1921 with regimental HQ at Charleston, WV. Subordinate battalion HQ concurrently organized as follows: 1st Bn. at Huntington, WV, and 2d Bn. at Hinton, WV. Typically conducted Inactive Training Period meetings at the Charleston Public Library in Charleston. Conducted summer training with the 1st Bn., 3d F.A. at Fort Knox, KY. Primary ROTC feeder school was West Virginia University. Location 7 December 1941—Charleston, WV.

Status: Disbanded on 17 April 1959 as the 375th F.A. Bn.

Commanders, 375th Field Artillery Regiment

Maj. Charles W. Strickling	30 November 1921–10 March 1925
Lt. Col Abney Payne	10 March 1925–ao May 1928
Unknown	ao May 1928–ao June 1930
Maj. Charles I. Thornburgh	ao June 1930–June 1934
Unknown	June 1934–ao December 1936
Lt. Col. Earl E. Major	ao December 1936–ao March 1939
Unknown	ao March 1939–7 December 1941

376th Field Artillery Regiment (75-mm G) (101st Division) **Organized Reserve Wisconsin**

HQ—Milwaukee, WI, 1921–41

Constituted in the O.R. on 24 June 1921, assigned to the 101st Div., and allotted to the Sixth Corps Area. Initiated on 13 October 1921 with regimental HQ at Milwaukee, WI. Subordinate battalion HQ concurrently organized as follows: 1st Bn. at Racine, WI, and 2d Bn. at Milwaukee. The 1st Bn. relocated by 1924 to Madison, WI. Reorganized from horse drawn to truck drawn on 13 March 1935. Conducted summer training most years with the 2d Bn., 3d F.A. at Camp Sparta/McCoy, WI, and some years at Camp Custer, MI. Primary ROTC feeder school was the University of Wisconsin. Location 7 December 1941—Milwaukee, WI.

Status: Disbanded on 6 August 1942 as the 376th F.A. Bn.

Commanders, 376th Field Artillery Regiment

Col. Irving A. Fish	13 October 1921–January 1927	Unknown	ao June 1936–ao June 1937
Lt. Col. William Fraedrich	January 1927–ao June 1934	Maj. Walter S. Jones	ao June 1937–ao July 1939
Lt. Col. H.H. Vaughn	ao June 1935–ao June 1936	Unknown	ao July 1939–7 December 1941

377th Field Artillery Regiment (75-mm G) (101st Division) **Organized Reserve Wisconsin**

HQ—Green Bay, WI, 1921–41

Constituted in the O.R. on 24 June 1921, assigned to the 101st Div., and allotted to the Sixth Corps Area. Initiated on 27 October 1921 with regimental HQ at Green Bay, WI. Subordinate battalion HQ concurrently organized as follows: 1st Bn. at Oshkosh, WI, and 2d Bn. at Hudson, WI. The 2d Bn. relocated by 1929 to Waupaca, WI. Conducted summer training most years with the 2d Bn., 3d F.A. at Camp Sparta/McCoy, WI, and some years at Camp Knox, KY. Primary ROTC feeder school was the University of Wisconsin. Location 7 December 1941—Green Bay, WI.

Status: Assigned to the CARS as the 377th F.A.

Commanders, 377th Field Artillery Regiment

Maj. Clarence W. Straubel	27 October 1921–ao May 1925	Lt. Col. Clifford M. La Mar	ao July 1929–August 1932
Maj. Wakeman Hackett	ao July 1925–ao January 1929	Maj. Wakeman Hackett	August 1932–December 1932
Unknown	ao January 1929–ao July 1929	Lt. Col. Elbert M. Webster	December 1932–ao July 1939
Unknown	ao July 1939–7 December 1941		

378th Field Artillery Regiment (155-mm H) (101st Division) **Organized Reserve Wisconsin**

HQ—*Not initiated,* 1929–30; Milwaukee, WI, 1930–33

Constituted in the O.R. on 13 September 1929, assigned to the 101st Div., and allotted to the Sixth Corps Area. Relieved from the 101st Div. on 5 October 1929. Initiated by December 1930 with regimental HQ at Milwaukee, WI. Conducted summer training at Camp Knox, KY, in 1931. Primary ROTC feeder school was the University of Wisconsin. Demobilized on 1 October 1933 and personnel concurrently transferred to the 67th F.A. (RAI).

Status: Disbanded on 14 May 1952 as the 378th F.A. Bn.

Commander, 378th Field Artillery Regiment

Unknown	ao December 1930–1 October 1933

379th Field Artillery Regiment (75-mm G) (102d Division) **Organized Reserve Missouri**

HQ—Kansas, City, MO, 1921–41

Constituted in the O.R. on 24 June 1921, assigned to the 102d Div., and allotted to the Seventh Corps Area. Initiated on 25 October 1921 with regimental HQ at Kansas City, MO. Subordinate battalion HQ concurrently organized as follows: 1st Bn. at Kansas City; 2d Bn. at Springfield, MO. Maj. Harry S. Truman originally assigned on 5 October 1921 as Commander, 1st Bn. Conducted summer training with Btry A, 9th F.A. and Btry D, 18th F.A. at Fort Riley, KS, and some years at Camp Ripley, MN. Typically conducted Inactive Training Period meetings at the 110th Engrs. armory or the O.R. Center building at 20th and Vine Streets in Kansas City. Conducted summer training at Fort Riley with the units of the 60th F.A. Brig. in 1931 and 1932. Primary ROTC feeder school was the University of Missouri. Location 7 December 1941—Kansas City, MO.

Status: Inactive in the US Army Reserve as the 379th F.A. Bn., a component of the 102d Inf. Div.

Commanders, 379th Field Artillery Regiment

Col. Arthur J. Elliot	25 October 1921–28 November 1930	Col. Harry S. Truman	ao December 1935–ao July 1938
Lt. Col. Thomas C. Bourke	28 November 1930–28 July 1932	Unknown	ao July 1938–ao May 1941
Lt. Col. Robert D. Groves	28 July 1932–ao May 1935	Lt. Col. Hale	ao May 1941–ao August 1941

380th Field Artillery Regiment (75-mm G) (102d Division) **Organized Reserve Missouri/Arkansas**

HQ—St. Louis, MO, 1921–28; Fort Smith, AR, 1928–41

Constituted in the O.R. on 24 June 1921, assigned to the 102d Div., and allotted to the Seventh Corps Area. Initiated on 25 October 1921 with regimental HQ at St. Louis, MO. Subordinate battalion HQ concurrently organized as follows: 1st Bn. at St. Louis; 2d Bn. at Flat River, MO. Conducted summer training with Btry A, 9th F.A. Regt. and Btry D, 18th F.A. at Fort Riley, KS, and some years at Camp Ripley, MN. Typically conducted Inactive Training Period meetings at the N.G. armory at Grand and Market Streets in St. Louis. Relocated on 3 April 1928 with regimental HQ at Fort Smith, AR. Subordinate battalion HQ concurrently relocated as follows: 1st Bn. at Fayetteville, AR, and 2d Bn. at Fort Smith. Conducted summer training at Fort Riley with the units of the 60th F.A. Brig. in 1931 and 1932. Conducted field artillery CMTC training some years at Fort Des Moines, IA, as an alternate form of annual training. Primary ROTC feeder school was the University of Missouri. Location 7 December 1941—Fort Smith, AR.

Status: Inactive in the US Army Reserve as the 380th F.A. Bn., a component of the 102d Inf. Div.

Commanders, 380th Field Artillery Regiment

Lt. Col. Walter F. Seigmund	25 October 1921–ao January 1922	Unknown	ao January 1922–ao December 1930
Lt. Col. Harry H. Vaughn	ao December 1930–ao January 1941		

381st Field Artillery Regiment (155-mm H) (102d Division) **Organized Reserve Arkansas**

HQ—*Not initiated,* 1929–30; Little Rock, AR, 1930–41

Constituted in the O.R. on 13 September 1929, assigned to the 102d Div., and allotted to the Seventh Corps Area. Initiated in April 1930 with regimental HQ at Little Rock, AR. Conducted summer training most years with Btry D, 18th F.A. at Fort Riley, KS, and some years with the units of the 60th F.A. Brig. or at Camp Ripley, MN. Location 7 December 1941—Little Rock, AR.

Status: Inactive in the US Army Reserve as the 381st F.A. Bn., a component of the 102d Inf. Div.

Commanders, 381st Field Artillery Regiment

Unknown	April 1930–17 June 1932	Col. Harry S. Truman	17 June 1932–12 March 1935
Col. John W. Snyder	12 March 1935–ao November 1941		

382d Field Artillery Regiment (75-mm G) (103d Division) **Organized Reserve Arizona and New Mexico**

HQ—Prescott, AZ, 1921–27; Phoenix, AZ, 1927–41

Constituted in the O.R. on 24 June 1921, assigned to the 103d Div., and allotted to the Eighth Corps Area. Initiated on 9 November 1921 with regimental HQ at Prescott, AZ. Subordinate battalion HQ concurrently organized as follows: 1st Bn. at Mesa, AZ, and 2d Bn. at Lowell, AZ. Entire regiment, less 1st Bn., relocated on 5 December 1927 to Phoenix, AZ. Concurrently, 1st Bn. relocated to Deming, NM. Typically conducted Inactive Training Period meetings at the Federal Building in Phoenix. Conducted summer training most years with the 82d F.A. at Fort Bliss, TX, and some years with the 77th F.A. at Fort D.A. Russell, TX. Primary ROTC feeder school was the University of Arizona. Location 7 December 1941—Phoenix, AZ.

Status: Inactive in the US Army Reserve as the 382d F.A. Bn., a component of the 103d Inf. Div.

Commanders, 382d Field Artillery Regiment

Maj. Claude D. Jones	9 November 1921–ao September 1923	Unknown	ao May 1930–ao April 1931
Unknown	ao September 1923–ao March 1924	Maj. Edwin L. Glazier	ao April 1931–ao May 1931
Lt. Col. Michael J.G. Dougherty	ao March 1924–ao May 1930	Unknown	ao May 1931–7 December 1941

383d Field Artillery Regiment (75-mm G) (103d Division) **Organized Reserve Colorado**

HQ—Denver, CO, 1921–41

Constituted in the O.R. on 24 June 1921, assigned to the 103d Div., and allotted to the Eighth Corps Area. Initiated on 26 October 1921 with regimental HQ at Denver, CO. Subordinate battalion HQ concurrently organized as follows: 1st Bn. at Denver and 2d Bn. at Colorado Springs, CO. Typically conducted Inactive Training Period meetings at the Kitteridge Building or the Albany Hotel in Denver. Conducted summer training most years with the 76th F.A. at Fort Francis E. Warren, WY, and some years with the 82d F.A. at Fort Bliss, TX. Primary ROTC feeder school was Colorado State College of Agriculture and Mechanic Arts. Location 7 December 1941—Denver, CO.

Status: Inactive in the US Army Reserve as the 383d F.A. Bn., a component of the 103d Inf. Div.

Events: 232

Commanders, 383d Field Artillery Regiment

Lt. Col. Canton O'Donnell	26 October 1921–ao November 1926	Unknown	ao January 1932–ao June 1932
Unknown	ao November 1926–ao August 1929	Lt. Col. George A. Bonnet	ao June 1932–ao January 1933
Lt. Col. William L. Hogg	ao August 1929–ao January 1932	Unknown	ao May 1931–7 December 1941

384th Field Artillery Regiment (155-mm H) (103d Division) — **Organized Reserve Colorado, Arizona, and New Mexico**

HQ—Denver, CO, 1929–41

Constituted in the O.R. on 12 July 1929, assigned to the 103d Div., and allotted to the Eighth Corps Area. Initiated on 17 December 1929 with regimental HQ at Denver, CO. Subordinate battalion HQ concurrently organized as follows: 1st Bn. at Denver; 2d Bn. at Mesa, AZ; and 3d Bn. at Vaughn, NM. Typically conducted Inactive Training Period meetings at the Kitteridge Building or the Albany Hotel in Denver. Conducted summer training with the 82d F.A. at Fort Bliss, TX, and with the 76th F.A. at Fort Francis E. Warren, WY. Primary ROTC feeder school was Colorado State College of Agriculture and Mechanic Arts. Location 7 December 1941—Denver, CO.

Status: Inactive in the US Army Reserve as the 384th F.A. Bn., a component of the 103d Inf. Div.

Commanders, 384th Field Artillery Regiment

Lt. Col. Willard N. Greim	17 December 1929–ao June 1933	Unknown	ao June 1933–7 December 1941

385th Field Artillery Regiment (75-mm G) (104th Division) — **Organized Reserve Utah**

HQ—*Not initiated,* 1921–22; Salt Lake City, UT, 1922–41

Constituted in the O.R. on 24 June 1921, assigned to the 104th Div., and allotted to the Ninth Corps Area. Initiated in January 1922 with regimental HQ at Salt Lake City, UT. Subordinate battalion HQ concurrently organized as follows: 1st Bn. at Salt Lake City and 2d Bn. at Ogden, UT. Typically conducted Inactive Training Period meetings at the Federal Building in Salt Lake City and the Ogden Armory in Ogden, UT. Conducted summer training most years with the 76th F.A. at Fort Francis E. Warren, WY, and some years at Fort Douglas, UT, or Fort Lewis, WA. Primary ROTC feeder school was the University of Utah. Location 7 December 1941—Salt Lake City, UT.

Status: Disbanded on 11 June 1959 as the 385th F.A. Bn.

Commanders, 385th Field Artillery Regiment

Lt. Col. Wesley E. King	January 1922–December 1924	Lt. Col. Lawrence Clayton	ao May 1929–20 January 1931
Lt. Col. James W. Gilson	December 1924–ao September 1925	Col. Joseph W. Palmer	21 January 1931–ao July 1940
Unknown	ao September 1925–ao May 1929	Unknown	ao July 1940–7 December 1941

386th Field Artillery Regiment (75-mm G) (104th Division) — **Organized Reserve Montana and Idaho**

HQ—*Not initiated,* 1921–22; Helena, MT, 1922–41

Constituted in the O.R. on 24 June 1921, assigned to the 104th Div., and allotted to the Ninth Corps Area. Initiated in April 1922 with regimental HQ at Helena, MT. Subordinate battalion HQ concurrently organized as follows: 1st Bn. at Great Falls, MT, and 2d Bn. at Boise, ID. The 1st Bn. relocated by 1931 to Helena. Conducted summer training most years with the 76th F.A. at Fort Francis E. Warren, WY, and some years at Fort Douglas, UT, or with the 148th F.A. at Boise Barracks, ID. Primary ROTC feeder school was the University of Montana. Location 7 December 1941—Helena, MT.

Status: Disbanded on 11 June 1959 as the 386th F.A. Bn.

Commanders, 386th Field Artillery Regiment

Unknown	April 1922–ao August 1929	Col. Goulet Gallatin	ao August 1929–April 1932
Col. Ralph Poulton	April 1932–ao July 1941		

387th Field Artillery Regiment (155-mm H) (104th Division) **Organized Reserve Utah, Idaho, Montana, and Wyoming**

HQ—*Not initiated,* 1929–30; Salt Lake City, UT, 1930–41

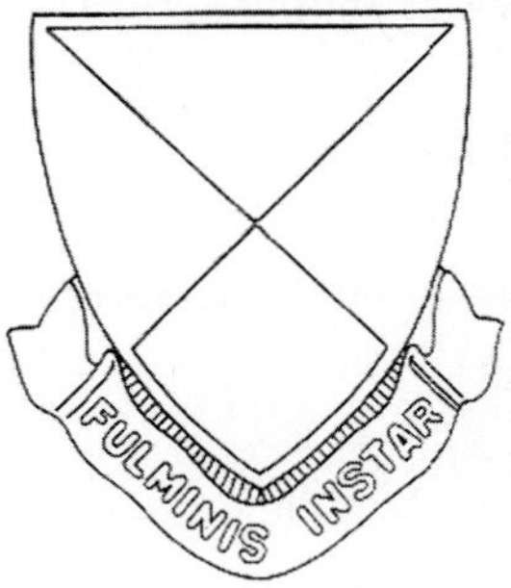

Constituted in the O.R. on 13 September 1929, assigned to the 104th Div., and allotted to the Ninth Corps Area. Initiated on 28 June 1930 with regimental HQ at Salt Lake City, UT. Subordinate battalion HQ concurrently organized as follows: 1st Bn. at Boise, ID; 2d Bn. at Billings, MT; and 3d Bn. at Cheyenne, WY. Salt Lake City area personnel typically conducted Inactive Training Period meetings at the American Legion Hall or the Ogden Armory in Ogden, UT. Conducted summer training with the 76th F.A. at Fort Francis E. Warren, and some years with the 148th F.A. at Boise Barracks, ID, and the 222d F.A. at Camp Williams, UT. Location 7 December 1941—Salt Lake City, UT.

Status: Disbanded 11 June 1959 as the 387th F.A. Bn.

Commanders, 387th Field Artillery Regiment

Lt. Col. Joseph W. Palmer	28 June 1930–20 January 1931	Unknown	ao March 1935–ao June 1937
Lt. Col. Lawrence Clayton	20 January 1931–ao March 1935	Col. Alan H. Means	ao June 1937–ao August 1940
Unknown	ao August 1940–7 December 1941		

388th Field Artillery Regiment (155-mm H) (XI Corps) **Organized Reserve Massachusetts**

HQ—Brookline, MA, 1921–23; Taunton, MA, 1923–41

Constituted in the O.R. on 29 July 1921, assigned to the 180th F.A. Brig. (XI Corps), and allotted to the First Corps Area. Initiated on 10 November 1921 with regimental HQ at Brookline, MA. Subordinate battalion HQ concurrently organized as follows: 1st Bn. at Brookline; 2d Bn. at Brockton, MA; and 3d Bn. at Fall River, MA. HQ relocated on 28 March 1923 to Taunton, MA. Typically conducted Inactive Training Period meetings at the State Armory in Taunton or the University Club in Boston. Conducted summer training with the 7th F.A. at Fort Ethan Allen, VT. Primary ROTC feeder school was Harvard University. Location 7 December 1941—Taunton, MA.

Status: Disbanded on 26 January 1943.

Commanders, 388th Field Artillery Regiment

Capt. Roger D. Hunneman	10 November 1921–ao April 1922	Unknown	ao June 1928–ao October 1929
Lt. Col. Roger D. Merrill	ao November 1922–ao April 1926	Col. Henry O. Silsbee II	ao October 1929–ao April 1939
Col. Thorndyke D. Howe	ao November 1926–ao June 1928	Lt. Col. Osborn Palmer	ao July 1939–ao January 1940
Unknown	ao January 1940–7 December 1941		

389th Field Artillery Regiment (155-mm H) (XI Corps) **Organized Reserve Massachusetts/ New Hampshire**

HQ—Haverhill, MA, 1921–23; Lowell, MA, 1923–29; Concord, NH, 1929–41

Constituted in the O.R. on 29 July 1921, assigned to the 180th F.A. Brig. (XI Corps), and allotted to the First Corps Area. Initiated on 10 November 1921 with regimental HQ at Haverhill, MA. Subordinate battalion HQ concurrently organized as follows: 1st Bn. at Waverly, MA; 2d Bn. at Andover, MA; and 3d Bn. at Lynn, MA. Initiated the first regimental band in the O.R. at Lowell in 1922; inactivated on 7 November 1927. HQ relocated on 28 March 1923 to Lowell, MA. Subordinate battalion HQ concurrently relocated as follows: 1st Bn. to Lowell; 2d Bn. to Lawrence, MA. Relieved from the 180th F.A. Brig. on 13 September 1929 and assigned to the 97th Div. HQ concurrently relocated to Concord, NH. Relieved from attachment to the 97th Div. on 17 October 1929 and attached to the 94th Div. for organization, administration, and training. Typically conducted Inactive Training Period meetings at the Federal Building in Haverhill, the Hildroth Building in Lowell, or the University Club in Boston. Conducted summer training with the 7th F.A. at Fort Ethan Allen, VT, and some years at Camp Devens, MA. Primary ROTC feeder school was Harvard University, 1921–29, and the University of New Hampshire, 1929–41. Location 7 December 1941—Concord, NH.

Status: Inactive in the US Army Reserve as the 389th F.A. Bn., a component of the 97th Inf. Div.

Commanders, 389th Field Artillery Regiment

Col. George W. Langdon Jr.	10 November 1921–ao August 1938	Lt. Col. Wayland M. Minot	ao July 1939–7 December 1941

390th Field Artillery Regiment (155-mm H) (XI Corps) **Organized Reserve Massachusetts**

HQ—Pittsfield, MA, 1921–41

Constituted in the O.R. on 24 June 1921, assigned to the 180th F.A. Brig. (XI Corps), and allotted to the First Corps Area. Initiated on 10 November 1921 with regimental HQ at Pittsfield, MA. Subordinate battalion HQ concurrently organized as follows: 1st Bn. at Williamstown, MA; 2d Bn. at Springfield, MA; and 3d Bn. at Pittsfield, MA. Band organized at Pittsfield in May 1924 from the Pittsfield American Legion Band; inactivated on 11 March 1930. Relieved from the 180th F.A. Brig. on 13 September 1929 and assigned to the 94th Div. Typically conducted Inactive Training Period meetings at the Springfield Armory, the Hotel Kimball, or the Federal Building in Pittsfield. Conducted summer training with the 7th F.A. at Fort Ethan Allen, VT, and some years at Camp Devens, MA. Primary ROTC feeder school was Harvard University. Location 7 December 1941—Pittsfield, MA.

Status: Inactive in the US Army Reserve as the 390th F.A. Bn., a component of the 94th Inf. Div.

Commanders, 390th Field Artillery Regiment

Col. William H. Eaton	10 November 1921–ao June 1939	Unknown	ao June 1939–7 December 1941

391st Field Artillery Regiment (155-mm H) (XII Corps) **Organized Reserve New York**

HQ—Manhattan, NY, 1921–41

Constituted in the O.R. on 29 July 1921, assigned to the 180th F.A. Brig. (XII Corps), and allotted to the Second Corps Area. Initiated on 22 September 1921 with the entire regiment at Manhattan, NY. Reorganized on 8 May 1928 as 75-mm Portee. Withdrawn from the O.R. on 1 October 1933 and allotted to the R.A. as an RAI unit. Typically conducted Inactive Training Period meetings at the armory of the 212th C.A. in the 1920s and later at the Hotel George Washington at 23d Street and Lexington Avenue in New York City, NY, in the 1930s. Conducted summer training with the 5th F.A. at Pine Camp, NY. Conducted CMTC at Madison Barracks, NY, as an alternate form of summer training. Primary ROTC feeder school was Princeton University. Location 7 December 1941—Manhattan, NY.

Status: Inactive in the R.A. as the 391st Armd. F.A. Bn.

Events: 267

Commanders, 391st Field Artillery Regiment

Col. William E. Shepherd Jr.	22 September 1921–25 October 1924	Col. William E. Shepherd Jr.	ao April 1926–8 September 1926
Lt. Col. Emmet C. Choate	25 October 1924–ao July 1925	Col. Robert P. Marshall	8 September 1926–16 August 1941

392d Field Artillery Regiment (155-mm H) (I Corps) **Organized Reserve Connecticut/ Indiana/Alabama**

HQ—*Not initiated,* 1923–27; Fort Wayne, IN, 1927–30; *Inactive,* 1930–33; Birmingham, AL, 1934–41

Constituted in the N.G. in 1921 as the 173d F.A. and assigned to the 81st F.A. Brig. (I Corps). Allotted to the states of Connecticut, Rhode Island, and Vermont as follows: the regimental HQ, HQ Btry, and 1st Bn. allotted to Connecticut; 2d Bn. allotted to Rhode Island; and 3d Bn. allotted to Vermont. Btry A organized on 8 July 1921 at Branford, CT. Placed on the deferred list on 2 July 1923 (less Btry A), redesignated 392d F.A. and transferred to the O.R. as a DNG unit. Concurrently relieved from assignment to the 81st F.A. Brig. (I Corps) and assigned to the 194th F.A. Brig. (I Corps). Btry A redesignated 43d Tank Co. on 28 March 1924. Reorganized in July 1924 as 155-mm G. Withdrawn as a DNG unit on 11 January 1927 and permanently allotted to the O.R. as the 392d F.A. Concurrently withdrawn from the First Corps Area and allotted to the Fifth Corps Area; regiment remained assigned to the 194th F.A. Brig. and I Corps. HQ organized in 1927 at Fort Wayne, IN. Inactivated by March 1930 at Fort Wayne by relief of personnel. Withdrawn from the Fifth Corps Area on 1 October 1933, and allotted to the Fourth Corps Area. Concurrently, assigned to the 183d F.A. Brig. (XIV Corps). Reorganized in May 1934 with the entire regiment at Birmingham, AL. Conducted summer training some years as individuals at Camp Knox, KY, 1927–33, and later with the 17th F.A. at Fort Bragg, NC, 1934–40. Primary ROTC feeder schools were Purdue University, 1927–33, and Alabama Polytechnic Institute, 1934–41. Location 7 December 1941—Birmingham, AL.

Status: Disbanded 26 January 1943.

Commanders, 392d Field Artillery Regiment

Unknown	ao December 1927–March 1930	*Inactive*	March 1930–May 1934
Unknown	May 1934–7 December 1941		

393d Field Artillery Regiment (155-mm H) (XVIII Corps) **Organized Reserve Missouri/Minnesota**

HQ—*Not initiated,* 1923–31; Minneapolis, MN, 1931–41

Constituted in the N.G. in 1921 as the 187th F.A. Regt., allotted to the state of Colorado, and assigned to the 85th F.A. Brig. (VIII Corps). Placed on the deferred list on 2 July 1923, redesignated 393d F.A., and transferred to the O.R. as a DNG unit. Concurrently, relieved from the 85th F.A. Brig. (VIII Corps) and assigned to the 193d F.A. Brig. (XVIII Corps). Withdrawn as a DNG unit on 11 January 1927 and permanently allotted to the O.R. as the 393d F.A. Concurrently withdrawn from the Eighth Corps Area and allotted to the Seventh Corps Area. Regiment remained assigned to the 193d F.A. Brig. (XVIII Corps). St. Louis, MO, designated as HQ on organization, but the unit was never organized at that location. Initiated in October 1931 with the entire regiment at Minneapolis, MN. Relieved from the 193d F.A. Brig. (XVIII Corps) on 1 October 1933 and assigned to the 187th F.A. Brig. (XVII Corps). Primary ROTC feeder school was the University of Minnesota. Location 7 December 1941—Minneapolis, MN.

Status: Disbanded on 6 January 1943.

Commander, 393d Field Artillery Regiment

Unknown October 1931–7 December 1941

394th Field Artillery Regiment (155-mm H) (XIII Corps) **Organized Reserve Pennsylvania**

HQ—Kittanning, PA, 1921–38; *Inactive,* 1938–41

Constituted in the O.R. on 29 July 1921, assigned to the 182d F.A. Brig. (XIII Corps), and allotted to the Third Corps Area. Initiated on 1 December 1921 with regimental HQ at Kittanning, PA. Subordinate battalion HQ concurrently organized as follows: 1st Bn. at New Castle, PA; 2d Bn. at Clarion, PA; and 3d Bn. at Indiana, PA. Entire regiment relocated on 11 December 1929 to Kittanning. Conducted summer training with the 6th F.A. at Fort Hoyle, MD, and some years at Fort Eustis, VA, or Tobyhanna, PA. Primary ROTC feeder school was Duquesne University. Inactivated by June 1938 at Kittanning by relief of personnel. Location 7 December 1941—*Inactive.*

Status: Disbanded 26 January 1943.

Commanders, 394th Field Artillery Regiment

Capt. William F. Thorpe	2 December 1921–ao January 1924	Col. Daniel M. Bates	27 December 1932–15 January 1935
Unknown	ao January 1924–17 April 1925	Unknown	15 January 1935–ao March 1936
Maj. John G. Sims	17 April 1925–15 May 1930	Lt. Col. Raymond A. Heffernan	ao March 1936–ao April 1936
Unknown	15 May 1930–27 December 1932	Unknown	ao April 1936–ao June 1938
	Inactive	ao June 1938–7 December 1941	

395th Field Artillery Regiment (155-mm H) (XIII Corps) **Organized Reserve Pennsylvania**

HQ—Bedford, PA, 1922–29; *Inactive,* 1929–41

Constituted in the O.R. on 29 July 1921, assigned to the 182d F.A. Brig. (XIII Corps), and allotted to the Third Corps Area. Initiated on 19 January 1922 with regimental HQ at Bedford, PA. Subordinate battalion HQ concurrently organized as follows: 1st Bn. at Brownsville, PA; 2d Bn. at Greensburg, PA; and 3d Bn. at Chambersburg, PA. Inactivated by July 1929 at Bedford by relief of personnel. DuBois, PA, designated on 11 December 1929 as HQ on reorganization, but the unit was never organized at that location. Conducted summer training with the 1st Bn., 16th F.A. at Camp George G. Meade, MD; and at Fort Eustis, VA; and Tobyhanna, PA. Primary ROTC feeder school was Duquesne University. Location 7 December 1941—*Inactive.*

Status: Disbanded on 26 January 1943.

Commanders, 395th Field Artillery Regiment

1st Lt. Clayton H. Hoffman	19 January 1922–20 March 1922	Maj. Azel W. McNeal	ao January 1924–22 September 1924
Capt. William B. Gilmore	20 March 1922–12 April 1922	Maj. Robert C. Lehman	22 September 1924–9 January 1925
Maj. Edward H. Lang	12 April 1922–ao February 1923	Lt. Col. William H. Beckner	9 January 1925–July 1929
	Inactive	July 1929–7 December 1941	

396th Field Artillery Regiment (155-mm H) (XIII Corps) **Organized Reserve Pennsylvania**

HQ—Altoona, PA, 1921–29; *Inactive,* 1929–41

Constituted in the O.R. on 29 July 1921, assigned to the 182d F.A. Brig. (XIII Corps), and allotted to the Third Corps Area. Initiated on 30 December 1921 with regimental HQ at Altoona, PA. Subordinate battalion HQ concurrently organized as follows: 1st Bn. at Ridgway, PA; 2d Bn. at Bellefonte, PA; and 3d Bn. at Huntingdon, PA. Entire regiment relocated on 11 December 1929 to Altoona. Conducted summer training with the 1st Bn., 16th F.A. at Camp George G. Meade, MD, and some years with the 109th F.A. at Tobyhanna, PA. Primary ROTC feeder school was Duquesne University. Inactivated by July 1929 at Altoona by relief of personnel. Location 7 December 1941—*Inactive.*

Status: Disbanded 26 January 1943.

Commanders, 396th Field Artillery Regiment

1st Lt. Gravin R. Wylie	30 December 1921–1 March 1922	Unknown	ao January 1926–ao June 1927
Maj. Grover C. Zimmerman	1 March 1922–ao January 1926	Lt. Col. M.C. McNeal	ao June 1927–July 1929
	Inactive	July 1929–7 December 1941	

397th Field Artillery Regiment (155-mm H) (I) (XIV Corps) **Organized Reserve Louisiana**

HQ—Alexandria, LA, 1921–29

Constituted in the O.R. on 29 July 1921, assigned to the 183d F.A. Brig. (XIV Corps), and allotted to the Fourth Corps Area. Initiated on 12 December 1921 with regimental HQ at Alexandria, LA. Subordinate battalion HQ concurrently organized as follows: 1st Bn. at New Orleans, LA; 2d Bn. at Crowley, LA; and 3d Bn. at Monroe, LA. Conducted summer training with the 5th F.A. at Fort Bragg, NC, and some years at Camp Beauregard, LA. Designated mobilization station was Camp Jackson, SC. Primary ROTC feeder school was Louisiana State University Redesignated as the 318th F.A. on 5 October 1929 and relieved from the 183d F.A. Brig.

Commanders, 397th Field Artillery Regiment

Col. Thomas F. Porter Jr.	12 December 1921–June 1928	Maj. John A. Myers	June 1928–5 October 1929

397th Field Artillery Regiment (155-mm H) (II) (XIV Corps) **Organized Reserve Florida**

HQ—*Not initiated,* 1929–30; Tampa, FL, 1930–41

Constituted in the O.R. on 5 October 1929, assigned to the 183d F.A. Brig. (XIV Corps), and allotted to the Fourth Corps Area. Initiated in August 1930 with regimental HQ at Tampa, FL. Conducted summer training with the 5th F.A. at Fort Bragg, NC. Designated mobilization station was Fort Bragg. Location 7 December 1941—Tampa, FL. (Inactivated on 16 March 1942.)

Commanders, 397th Field Artillery Regiment

Unknown	August 1930–7 December 1941

398th Field Artillery Regiment (155-mm H) (I) (XIV Corps) **Organized Reserve Mississippi**

HQ—Jackson, MS, 1921–29

Constituted in the O.R. on 29 July 1921, assigned to the 183d F.A. Brig. (XIV Corps), and allotted to the Fourth Corps Area. Initiated on 30 December 1921 with regimental HQ at Jackson, MS. Subordinate battalion HQ concurrently organized as follows: 1st Bn. at Corinth, MS; 2d Bn. at Starkville, MS; and 3d Bn. at Collins, MS. Conducted summer training most years with the 5th F.A. at Fort Bragg, NC, and some years with the 83d F.A. Bn. at Fort McClellan, AL. Primary ROTC feeder school was Mississippi State College. Designated mobilization station was Camp Jackson, SC. Redesignated as the 335th F.A. on 5 October 1929 and relieved from the 183d F.A. Brig.

Commanders, 398th Field Artillery Regiment

Maj. Leslie L. Anderson	30 December 1921–ao September 1925	Unknown	ao September 1925–5 October 1929

398th Field Artillery Regiment (155-mm H) (II) (XIV Corps) **Organized Reserve Alabama**

HQ—Montgomery, AL, 1929–33

Constituted in the O.R. on 5 October 1929, assigned to the 183d F.A. Brig. (XIV Corps), and allotted to the Fourth Corps Area. Initiated in August 1930 with regimental HQ at Montgomery, AL. Demobilized on 1 October 1933.

Commanders, 398th Field Artillery Regiment

Unknown	August 1930–1 October 1933

399th Field Artillery Regiment (155-mm H) (XIV Corps) **Organized Reserve North Carolina**

HQ—*Not initiated,* 1921–22; Charlotte, NC, 1922–28

Constituted in the O.R. on 29 July 1921, assigned to the 183d F.A. Brig. (XIV Corps), and allotted to the Fourth Corps Area. Initiated on 21 March 1922 with regimental HQ at Charlotte, NC. Subordinate battalion HQ concurrently organized as follows: 1st Bn. at Raleigh, NC; 2d Bn. at Concord, NC; and 3d Bn. at Pineville, NC. Conducted summer training with the 5th F.A. at Fort Bragg, NC. Primary ROTC feeder school was North Carolina State College. Designated mobilization station was Camp Jackson, SC. Demobilized on 6 October 1928.

Commanders, 399th Field Artillery Regiment

Maj. James H. Carson	21 March 1922–12 September 1922
Maj. John W. Gardner	12 September 1922–25 March 1925
Lt. Col. Marlin A. Prather	25 March 1925–6 October 1928

400th Field Artillery Regiment (155-mm H) (XV Corps) — Organized Reserve Ohio/Indiana

HQ—*Not initiated,* 1921–22; Dayton, OH, 1922–23; Evansville, IN, 1923–30; *Inactive,* 1930–41

Constituted in the O.R. on 29 July 1921, assigned to the 184th F.A. Brig. (XV Corps), and allotted to the Fifth Corps Area. Initiated in May 1922 with regimental HQ at Dayton, OH. Relocated by June 1923 to Evansville, IN. Relieved from the 184th F.A. Brig. (XV Corps) on 2 July 1923 and assigned to the 191st F.A. Brig. (XV Corps). Inactivated by March 1930 at Evansville by relief of personnel. Relieved on 1 October 1933 from the 191st F.A. Brig. (XV Corps). Conducted summer training most years with the 14th and 19th F.A. Regts. at Camp Knox, KY, and some years at Fort Benjamin Harrison, IN. Primary ROTC feeder school was Purdue University. Location 7 December 1941—*Inactive.*

Status: Disbanded on 26 January 1943.

Commanders, 400th Field Artillery Regiment

Maj. W.M. Brenner	May 1922–18 October 1923
Maj. Guy S. Poling	18 October 1923–ao December 1923
Capt. Abram E. Aub	ao September 1924–ao May 1925
Unknown	ao May 1925–ao February 1930
Col. Robert L. Moorhead	ao February 1930–March 1930
Inactive	March 1930–7 December 1941

401st Field Artillery Regiment (155-mm H) (XV Corps) — Organized Reserve Kentucky/Ohio

HQ—*Not initiated,* 1921–25; Louisville, KY, 1925–30; *Inactive,* 1930–37; Toledo, OH, 1937–41

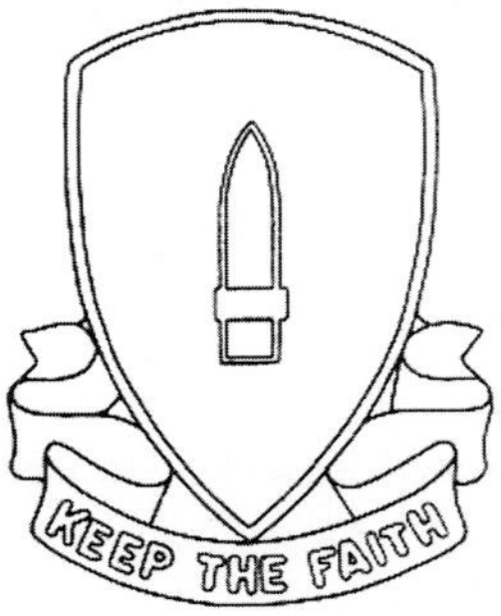

Constituted in the O.R. on 29 July 1921, assigned to the 184th F.A. Brig. (XV Corps), and allotted to the Fifth Corps Area. Relieved from the 184th F.A. Brig. (XV Corps) on 2 July 1923 and assigned to the 191st F.A. Brig. (XV Corps). Initiated in May 1925 with regimental HQ at Louisville, KY. Inactivated by March 1930 at Louisville by relief of personnel. Relieved from the 191st F.A. Brig. (XV Corps) on 1 October 1933 and assigned to the 184th F.A. Brig. (XV Corps). Reorganized on 5 April 1937 at Toledo, OH. Conducted summer training with the 1st Bn., 3d F.A. and 1st Bn., 19th F.A. at Fort Knox, KY. Primary ROTC feeder schools were the University of Kentucky, 1925–37, and Ohio State University, 1937–41. Location 7 December 1941—Toledo, OH.

Status: Disbanded 26 January 1943.

Commanders, 401st Field Artillery Regiment

Unknown	May 1925–March 1930
Inactive	March 1930–5 April 1937
Maj. Clifford E. Shank	5 April 1937–June 1938
Col. Edward P. Felker	June 1938–ao July 1938
Unknown	ao July 1938–ao March 1940
Maj. Ewing G. Wells	ao March 1940–ao April 1940
Unknown	ao April 1940–7 December 1941

402d Field Artillery Regiment (155-mm H) (XV Corps) — Organized Reserve Indiana/Ohio

HQ—*Not initiated,* 1921–22; Fort Wayne, IN, 1922–29; *Inactive,* 1929–41

Constituted in the O.R. on 29 July 1921, assigned to the 184th F.A. Brig. (XV Corps), and allotted to the Fifth Corps Area. Relieved from the 184th F.A. Brig. (XV Corps) on 2 July 1923 and assigned to the 191st F.A. Brig. (XV Corps). Initiated in May 1925 with regimental HQ at Fort Wayne, IN. Inactivated by December 1929 at Fort Wayne by relief of personnel. Relieved on 1 October 1933 from the 191st F.A. Brig. (XV Corps). Conducted summer training with the

1st Bn., 3d F.A., 1925–29, at Fort Knox, KY, and some years at Fort Benjamin Harrison, IN. Primary ROTC feeder school was Purdue University. Location 7 December 1941— Fort Wayne, IN.

Status: Disbanded 26 January 1943.

Commanders, 402d Field Artillery Regiment

Unknown	May 1925–ao October 1926	Maj. Howard N. Randall	ao October 1926–December 1929
Unknown	ao November 1926–7 December 1941		

403d Field Artillery Regiment (155-mm H) (XVI Corps) **Organized Reserve Illinois/Michigan**

HQ—*Not initiated*,1921–22; Moline, IL, 1922–24; Genesco, IL, 1924–25; Peoria, IL, 1925–30; Detroit, MI, 1930–41

Constituted in the O.R. on 29 July 1921, assigned to the 185th F.A. Brig. (XVI Corps), and allotted to the Sixth Corps Area. Initiated on 6 June 1922 with regimental HQ at Moline, IL. Subordinate battalion HQ concurrently organized as follows: 1st Bn. at Moline; 2d Bn. at Joliet, IL; and 3d Bn. at La Salle, IL. Relieved from the 185th F.A. Brig. (XVI Corps) on 2 July 1923 and assigned to the 192d F.A. Brig. (VI Corps). HQ relocated as follows: to Genesco, IL, 18 April 1924; and to Peoria, IL, 28 July 1925. Relieved from the 192d F.A. Brig. on 5 October 1929 and assigned to the 85th Div. Entire regiment relocated on 3 December 1930 to Detroit, MI. Conducted summer training most years at Camp McCoy, WI, and some years at Camp Knox, KY. Primary ROTC feeder schools were the University of Illinois, 1922–30, and Michigan State College, 1930–41. Location 7 December 1941—Detroit, MI.

Status: Disbanded on 1 June 1959.

Commanders, 403d Field Artillery Regiment

Capt. Charles D. Wiman	6 June 1922–5 January 1923	Lt. Col. Walter S. Stanton	4 December 1930–ao August 1932
Col. Charles G. Davis	6 January 1923–ao June 1929	Unknown	ao August 1932–ao August 1933
Unknown	ao June 1929–ao May 1930	Lt. Col. Charles A. Liebst	ao August 1933–ao July 1939
Lt. Col. Harold P. Goodnow	ao May 1930–3 December 1930	Unknown	ao July 1939–7 December 1941

404th Field Artillery Regiment (155-mm H) (XVI Corps) **Organized Reserve Illinois**

HQ—*Not initiated,* 1921–22; Chicago, IL, 1922–41

Constituted in the O.R. on 29 July 1921, assigned to the 185th F.A. Brig. (XVI Corps), and allotted to the Sixth Corps Area. Initiated on 6 March 1922 with the entire regiment at Chicago, IL. Relieved from the 185th F.A. Brig. (XVI Corps) on 2 July 1923 and assigned to the 192d F.A. Brig. (VI Corps). Relieved from the 192d F.A. Brig. on 5 October 1929 and assigned to the 86th Div. Conducted summer training most years at Camp McCoy, WI, and some years at Camp Custer, MI. Conducted summer training at Camp Grant, IL, with the 58th F.A. Brig. in 1931. Primary ROTC feeder school was the University of Illinois. Location 7 December 1941—Chicago, IL.

Status: Inactive in the US Army Reserve as the 404th F.A. Bn.

Events: 162

Commanders, 404th Field Artillery Regiment

Lt. Col. Harold P. Goodnow	6 March 1922–ao July 1927	Maj. Milton B. Parsons	ao December 1933–27 February 1936
Lt. Col. Charles C. Haffner Jr.	ao June 1929–26 November 1931	Maj. Donald H. Miller	27 February 1936–4 February 1937
Unknown	26 November 1931–ao December 1933	Col. Clifford L. Burnham	4 February 1937–ao January 1940
Unknown	ao January 1940–7 December 1941		

405th Field Artillery Regiment (155-mm H) (XVI Corps) **Organized Reserve Wisconsin**

HQ—*Not initiated,* 1921–22; Milwaukee, WI, 1922–27; *Inactive,* 1927–28

Constituted in the O.R. on 29 July 1921, assigned to the 185th F.A. Brig. (XVI Corps), and allotted to the Sixth Corps Area. Initiated by October 1922 with the entire regiment at Milwaukee, WI. Relieved from the 185th F.A. Brig. (XVI Corps) on 2 July 1923 and assigned to the 192d F.A. Brig. (VI Corps). Withdrawn from the Sixth Corps Area on 11 January 1927 and allotted to the Fourth Corps Area as a "Colored" unit. Conducted summer training at Camp McCoy, WI. Primary ROTC feeder school was the University of Wisconsin, 1922–27. Demobilized on 6 October 1928.

Commanders, 405th Field Artillery Regiment

Unknown	ao October 1922–11 January 1927	*Inactive*	11 January 1927–6 October 1928

406th Field Artillery Regiment (155-mm H) (XVII Corps) **Organized Reserve Missouri/Kansas**

HQ—*Not initiated,* 1921–22; St. Louis, MO, 1922–26; Wichita, KS, 1926–41

Constituted in the O.R. on 29 July 1921, assigned to the 186th F.A. Brig. (XVII Corps), and allotted to the Seventh Corps Area. Initiated on 11 March 1922 with regimental HQ at St. Louis, MO. Subordinate battalion HQ concurrently organized as follows: 1st Bn. at Hannibal, MO; 2d Bn. at St. Louis; and 3d Bn. at Flat River, MO. Entire regiment relocated on 26 May 1926 to Wichita, KS. Relieved from the 186th F.A. Brig. (XVII Corps) on 1 October 1933 and assigned to the 187th F.A. Brig. (XVII Corps). Conducted summer training at Camp McCoy, WI, or Fort Riley, KS. Primary ROTC feeder school was Washington University, 1922–31, and Kansas State College, 1931–41. Location 7 December 1941—Wichita, KS.

Status: Disbanded on 26 January 1943.

Commanders, 406th Field Artillery Regiment

2d Lt. Enos Compton	11 March 1922–ao April 1922	Lt. Col. Newell I. Patterson	ao April 1925–June 1927
Unknown	ao April 1922–ao April 1925	Unknown	June 1927–7 December 1941

407th Field Artillery Regiment (155-mm H) (XVII Corps) **Organized Reserve Iowa**

HQ—*Not initiated,* 1921–22; Des Moines, IA, 1922–29; *Inactive,* 1929–31; Sioux City, IA, 1931–41

Constituted in the O.R. on 29 July 1921, assigned to the 186th F.A. Brig. (XVII Corps), and allotted to the Seventh Corps Area. Initiated in June 1922 with regimental HQ at Des Moines, IA. Subordinate battalion HQ concurrently organized as follows: 1st Bn. at Des Moines; 2d Bn. at Council Bluffs, IA; and 3d Bn. at Sioux City, IA. Inactivated on 18 October 1929 at Des Moines by relief of personnel. Entire regiment reorganized in October 1931 at Sioux City, IA. Relieved on 1 October 1933 from the 186th F.A. Brig. (XVII Corps). Conducted summer training at Camp McCoy, WI, or Fort Des Moines, IA, and with the 185th F.A. in 1925 at Camp Knox, KY. Primary ROTC feeder school was Iowa State College. Location 7 December 1941—Sioux City, IA.

Status: Disbanded on 26 January 1943.

Commanders, 407th Field Artillery Regiment

2d Lt. Aumack Bruner	June 1922–13 September 1922	Col. Arthur M. Compton	August 1924–ao June 1927
1st Lt. Howard J. Bashford	13 September 1922–ao October 1922	Unknown	ao June 1927–18 October 1929
Unknown	ao October 1922–August 1924	*Inactive*	18 October 1929–October 1931
Unknown	October 1931–7 December 1941		

408th Field Artillery Regiment (155-mm H) (XVII Corps) **Organized Reserve Kansas and Arkansas**

HQ—*Not initiated,* 1921–22; Kansas City, KS, 1922–26; Little Rock, AR, 1926–28

Constituted in the O.R. on 29 July 1921, assigned to the 186th F.A. Brig. (XVII Corps), and allotted to the Seventh Corps Area. Initiated in March 1922 with regimental HQ at Kansas City, KS. Subordinate battalion HQ concurrently organized as follows: 1st Bn. at Caldwell, KS; 2d Bn. at Jonesboro, AR; and 3d Bn. at Helena, AR. Regimental HQ relocated on 26 May 1926 to Little Rock, AR. Subordinate battalion HQ concurrently relocated as follows: 1st Bn. at Helena, AR; 2d Bn. at Pine Bluff, AR; and 3d Bn. at Arkansas City, AR. Conducted summer training at Camp McCoy, WI, or Fort Riley, KS. Primary ROTC feeder schools were Kansas State College, 1922–26, and Arkansas State College, 1922–28. Withdrawn from the Seventh Corps Area on 15 December 1928.

Commanders, 408th Field Artillery Regiment

Unknown	March 1922–15 December 1928

409th Field Artillery Regiment (155-mm H) (XVIII Corps) **Organized Reserve Oklahoma**

HQ—*Not initiated,* 1921–22; Tulsa, OK, 1922–41

Constituted in the O.R. on 29 July 1921, assigned to the 187th F.A. Brig. (XVIII Corps), and allotted to the Eighth Corps Area. Initiated on 12 August 1922 with regimental HQ at Tulsa, OK. Subordinate battalion HQ concurrently organized as follows: 1st Bn. at Ada, OK; 2d Bn. at Ardmore, OK; and 3d Bn. at Chickasha, OK. The 3d Bn. relocated by March 1925 to El Reno, OK. Relieved from the 187th F.A. Brig. (XVIII Corps) on 2 July 1923 and assigned to the 193d F.A. Brig. (XVIII Corps). Relieved from the 193d F.A. Brig. (XVIII Corps) on 1 October 1933 and assigned to the 188th F.A. Brig. (XVIII Corps). Conducted summer training with the 1st F.A. at Fort Sill, OK. Primary ROTC feeder school was the University of Oklahoma. Designated mobilization training station was Fort Sill. Location 7 December 1941—Tulsa, OK.

Status: Disbanded on 26 January 1943.

Commanders, 409th Field Artillery Regiment

Capt. Marvin S. McMurtrey	12 August 1922–5 September 1922	Unknown	ao April 1930–2 January 1935
Maj. Rensselaer W. McClure Jr.	5 September 1922–December 1924	Maj. Norman E. Holden	2 January 1935–5 October 1935
Maj. Marmaduke J. Harrison	December 1924–ao April 1925	Maj. Reuben G. Lewis	5 October 1935–ao June 1937
Maj. Robert L. Lewis	ao September 1925–ao April 1930	Unknown	ao June 1937–7 December 1941

410th Field Artillery Regiment (155-mm H) (XVIII Corps) **Organized Reserve Texas/Iowa/Michigan**

HQ—*Not initiated,* 1921–22; Fort Worth, TX, 1922–27; Des Moines, IA, 1927–33; *Inactive,* 1933–34; Kalamazoo, MI, 1934–41

Constituted in the O.R. on 29 July 1921, assigned to the 187th F.A. Brig. (XVIII Corps), and allotted to the Eighth Corps Area. Initiated on 26 July 1922 with the entire regiment at Fort Worth, TX. Relieved on 2 July 1923 from the 187th F.A. Brig. (XVIII Corps). Withdrawn from the Eighth Corps Area on 13 January 1927 and allotted to the Seventh Corps Area. Reorganized by December 1927 at Des Moines, IA. Subordinate battalion HQ concurrently organized as follows: 1st Bn. at Des Moines; 2d Bn. at Fort Dodge, IA; and 3d Bn. at Waterloo, IA. Withdrawn from the Seventh Corps Area on 1 October 1933 and allotted to the Sixth Corps Area. Reorganized by June 1934 with the entire regiment at Kalamazoo, MI. Conducted summer training most years, 1922–26, with the 1st F.A. at Fort Sill, OK, and some years with the 15th F.A. at Fort Sam Houston, TX. Conducted summer training at Camp McCoy, WI, 1927–39. Primary ROTC feeder school was Texas A&M, 1922–27, and Michigan State College, 1934–41. Location 7 December 1941—Kalamazoo, MI.

Status: Disbanded on 26 January 1943.

Commanders, 410th Field Artillery Regiment

Lt. Col. Ralph B. Fairchild	26 July 1922–17 September 1926	Unknown	December 1927–1 October 1933
Col. Frank J. Hobbs	ao August 1926–13 January 1927	*Inactive*	1 October 1933–June 1934
Inactive	13 January 1927–December 1927	Lt. Col. Leland N. Jones	ao June 1934–ao July 1941

411th Field Artillery Regiment (155-mm H) (XVIII Corps) **Organized Reserve Texas**

HQ—*Not initiated,* 1921–22; Dallas, TX, 1922–41

Constituted in the O.R. on 29 July 1921, assigned to the 187th F.A. Brig. (XVIII Corps), and allotted to the Eighth Corps Area. Initiated about April 1922 with the entire regiment at Dallas, TX. Relieved from the 187th F.A. Brig. (XVIII Corps) on 2 July 1923 and assigned to the 193d F.A. Brig. (XVIII Corps). The regiment invested Hollywood actress Helen Kane on 9 April 1931 as the honorary colonel of the regiment. Relieved from the 193d F.A. Brig. (XVIII Corps) on 1 October 1933 and assigned to the 188th F.A. Brig. (XVIII Corps). Typically conducted Inactive Training Period meetings at the Liggett Building, the Federal Building, or the US Terminal Annex building in Dallas. Conducted summer training most years with the 12th F.A. at Fort Sam Houston, TX; Camp Stanley, TX; or Camp Bullis, TX; and some years with the 77th F.A. at Fort D.A. Russell, TX. Primary ROTC feeder school was Texas A&M. Designated mobilization training station was Fort Sill, OK. Location 7 December 1941—Dallas, TX.

Status: Disbanded 26 January 1943.

Commanders, 411th Field Artillery Regiment

1st Lt. Sterling R. Cunningham	ao April 1922–ao August 1922	Col. Frank G. Anderson	14 January 1927–ao January 1939
Lt. Col. William A. Obenchain	ao March 1923–14 January 1927	Unknown	ao January 1939–7 December 1941

412th Field Artillery Regiment (155-mm H) (Colored) (XIX Corps) **Organized Reserve Oregon and Washington**

HQ—*Not initiated,* 1921–22; Portland, OR,1922–33

Constituted in the O.R. on 29 July 1921, assigned to the 188th F.A. Brig. (XIX Corps), and allotted to the Ninth Corps Area. Initiated on 31 October 1922 with regimental HQ at Portland, OR. Subordinate battalion HQ concurrently organized as follows: 1st Bn. at Portland; 2d Bn. at Medford, OR; and 3d Bn. at Eugene, OR. Designation changed from "Colored" to white in 1926. Relieved from the 188th F.A. Brig. (XIX Corps) on 5 September 1928 and assigned to the 189th F.A. Brig. (IX Corps). The 2d and 3d Bns. relocated on 1 November 1929 to Tacoma, WA. Inactivated on 7 January 1930 at Portland, and all personnel transferred to the 363d F.A. Typically conducted Inactive Training Period meetings at the Porter Building in Portland. Conducted summer training with the 10th F.A. at Fort Lewis, WA. Primary ROTC feeder school was Oregon State Agricultural College. Demobilized on 1 October 1933.

Commanders, 412th Field Artillery Regiment

2d Lt. Herbert A. Davis	31 October 1922–ao November 1922	Unknown	ao November 1926–ao June 1927
Unknown	ao November 1922–ao August 1924	Maj. Roy K. Terry	ao June 1927–January 1930
Col. Frank N. Brooks	ao August 1924–ao November 1926	*Inactive*	7 January 1930-1 October 1933

413th Field Artillery Regiment (155-mm H) (XIX Corps) **Organized Reserve Washington/California**

HQ—*Not initiated,* 1921–22; Seattle, WA, 1922–37; San Francisco, CA, 1937–41

Constituted in the O.R. on 29 July 1921, assigned to the 188th F.A. Brig. (XIX Corps), and allotted to the Ninth Corps Area. Initiated on 18 October 1922 with regimental HQ at Seattle, WA. Subordinate battalion HQ concurrently organized as follows: 1st Bn. at Tacoma, WA; 2d Bn. at Everette, WA; and 3d Bn. at Spokane, WA. Relieved from the 188th F.A. Brig. (XIX Corps) on 5 September 1928 and assigned to the 189th F.A. Brig. (IX Corps). Entire regiment relocated about April 1930 to Seattle. Relieved from the 189th F.A. Brig. (IX Corps) on 1 October 1933 and assigned to the 195th F.A. Brig. (XIX Corps). Inactivated on 2 March 1937 at Seattle by relief of personnel. Reorganized on 14 May 1937 with the entire regiment at San Francisco. Conducted summer training with the 10th F.A. at Fort Lewis, WA. Primary ROTC feeder schools were the University of Washington, 1922–37, and Stanford University, 1937–41. Location 7 December 1941—San Francisco, CA.

Status: Disbanded 26 January 1943.

Commanders, 413th Field Artillery Regiment

Col. Paul H. Weyrauch	18 October 1922–6 June 1926	Unknown	ao June 1929–ao June 1931
Lt. Col. Paul Edwards	6 June 1926–ao June 1929	Lt. Col. William M. Day	ao June 1931–2 March 1937
Unknown	2 March 1937–7 December 1941		

414th Field Artillery Regiment (155-mm H) (XIX Corps) — Organized Reserve California

HQ—*Not initiated,* 1921–22; Los Angeles, CA, 1922–41

Constituted in the O.R. on 29 July 1921, assigned to the 188th F.A. Brig. (XIX Corps), and allotted to the Ninth Corps Area. Initiated on 8 May 1922 with regimental HQ at Los Angeles, CA. Subordinate battalion HQ concurrently organized as follows: 1st Bn. at Los Angeles; 2d Bn. at Long Beach, CA; and 3d Bn. at San Diego, CA. Relieved from the 188th F.A. Brig. (XIX Corps) on 5 September 1928 and assigned to the 189th F.A. Brig. (IX Corps). Entire regiment relocated about April 1930 to Los Angeles. Relieved on 1 October 1933 from the 189th F.A. Brig. (IX Corps). Typically conducted Inactive Training Period meetings at the Chamber of Commerce Building or at 751 Figuroa Street in Los Angeles. Conducted summer training most years with the 76th F.A. at the Presidio of Monterey, CA; or Del Monte, CA; and some years at Fort Lewis, WA. Primary ROTC feeder school was the University of California. Location 7 December 1941—Los Angeles, CA. (Inactivated on 21 January 1942.)

Status: Disbanded on 26 January 1943; HHB reconstituted and consolidated on 7 December 1949 with HHB, 408th F.A. Gp. Inactive in the US Army Reserve as HHB, 408th F.A. Gp. Concurrenly, 1st Bn. consolidated with the 496th Armd. F.A. Bn. and 2d Bn. consolidated with the 497th Armd. F.A. Bn.

Commanders, 414th Field Artillery Regiment

Col. Benjamin F. Whittaker	8 May 1922–ao September 1924	Col. Arthur L. Keesling	11 November 1935–9 September 1937
Col. George S. Brinckley	ao June 1925–ao January 1934	Lt. Col. George C. Ferch	9 September 1937–17 December 1938
Col. William C. Vest	ao September 1934–11 November 1935	Col. Lamar M. McKinley	17 December 1938–ao July 1939
Unknown	ao July 1939–7 December 1941		

415th Field Artillery Regiment (75-mm G Mtzd) (I) (GHQR) — Organized Reserve Michigan

HQ—*Not initiated,* 1921–27

Constituted in the N.G. on 29 July 1921 as the 216th F.A., assigned to the 221st F.A. Brig. (GHQR), and allotted to the state of Michigan. Placed on the deferred list on 2 July 1923, allotted to the O.R. as a DNG unit, and redesignated as the 415th F.A. Designated mobilization training station was Camp Custer, MI. Reallotted to the Michigan N.G. on 17 September 1927 as the 216th F.A.

415th Field Artillery Regiment (75-mm G Mtzd) (II) (GHQR) — Organized Reserve New Jersey

HQ—*Not initiated,* 1928–41

Constituted in the O.R. on 5 September 1928, assigned to the GHQR, and allotted to the Second Corps Area. On 5 April 1937, Englewood, NJ, designated as HQ on organization, but the unit was never organized at that location. Designated mobilization training station was Pine Camp, NY. Location 7 December 1941—*Not initiated.*

Status: Disbanded 26 January 1943.

416th Field Artillery Regiment (75-mm G Mtzd) (I) (GHQR) **Organized Reserve Illinois**

HQ—*Not initiated,* 1921–27

Constituted in the N.G. on 29 July 1921 as the 217th F.A., assigned to the 221st F.A. Brig. (GHQR), and allotted to the state of Illinois. Placed on the deferred list on 2 July 1923, allotted to the O.R. as a DNG unit and redesignated the 416th F.A. Designated mobilization training station was Camp Sparta, WI. Withdrawn from the N.G. on 17 September 1927 and demobilized.

416th Field Artillery Regiment (75-mm G Mtzd) (II) (GHQR) **Organized Reserve New York/New Jersey**

HQ—*Not initiated,* 1928–41

Constituted in the O.R. on 5 September 1928 and assigned to the GHQR. Regiment allotted to be organized in the state of New York on 2 July 1929. Withdrawn and allotted to the New Jersey Reserve Area on 5 April 1937. Englewood, NJ, designated as HQ on organization, but the unit was never organized at that location. Designated mobilization training station was Pine Camp, NY. Location 7 December 1941—*Not initiated.*

Status: Disbanded 26 January 1943.

417th Field Artillery Regiment (I) (75-mm G Mtzd) (GHQR) **Organized Reserve Illinois**

HQ—*Not initiated,* 1921–27

Constituted in the N.G. on 29 July 1921 as the 218th F.A., assigned to the 224th F.A. Brig. (GHQR), and allotted to the state of Illinois. Placed on the deferred list on 2 July 1923, less 1st Bn., allotted to the O.R. as a DNG unit and redesignated as the 417th F.A. Designated mobilization training station was Camp Sparta, WI. The 1st Bn. was withdrawn from the state of Illinois and allotted to the state of Oregon. Remainder of the regiment redesignated as the 218th F.A. on 17 September 1927, withdrawn from allotment to the state of Illinois, and allotted to the state of Oregon.

417th Field Artillery Regiment (II) (75-mm G Mtzd) (GHQR) **Organized Reserve**

HQ—*Not initiated,* 1928–41

Constituted in the O.R. on 5 September 1928 and assigned to the GHQR. The unit was never allotted or organized. Location 7 December 1941—*Not initiated.*

418th Field Artillery Regiment (75-mm G Mtzd) (I) (GHQR) **Organized Reserve South Dakota**

HQ—*Not initiated,* 1921–24; Madison, SD, 1924–26; Pierre, SD, 1926–27

Constituted in the N.G. on 29 July 1921 as the 129th F.A., assigned to the GHQR, and allotted to the Seventh Corps Area. Placed on the deferred list on 2 July 1923, allotted to the O.R. as a DNG unit and redesignated as the 418th F.A. Initiated on 29 August 1924 with regimental HQ at Madison, SD. Subordinate battalion HQ concurrently organized as follows: 1st Bn. at Salem, SD, and 2d Bn. at De Smet, SD. HQ relocated on 26 May 1926 to Pierre, SD. Subordinate battalion HQ concurrently relocated as follows: 1st Bn. at Chamberlain, SD, and 2d Bn. at Rapid City, SD. Withdrawn from the N.G. on 17 September 1927 and demobilized.

Commander, 418th Field Artillery Regiment

Unknown	29 August 1924–17 September 1927

418th Field Artillery Regiment (75-mm G Mtzd) (II) (GHQR) **Organized Reserve Minnesota**

HQ—*Not initiated,* 1928–41

Constituted in the O.R. on 5 September 1928 and allotted to the Seventh Corps Area. Minneapolis, MN, designated on 12 October 1931 as the regiment's HQ on organization, but the unit was never organized. Location 7 December 1941—*Not initiated.*

Status: Disbanded 26 January 1943.

419th Field Artillery Regiment (75-mm G Mtzd) (GHQR) (I) **Organized Reserve North Dakota**

HQ—*Not initiated,* 1923–26; Fargo, ND, 1926–27

Constituted in the N.G. on 29 July 1921 as the 142d F.A., assigned to the GHQR, and allotted to the Seventh Corps Area. Placed on the deferred list on 2 July 1923, allotted to the O.R. as a DNG unit and redesignated the 419th F.A. Initiated on 26 May 1926 with regimental HQ at Fargo, ND. Subordinate battalion HQ concurrently organized as follows: 1st Bn. at Jamestown, ND, and 2d Bn. at Devil's Lake, ND. Withdrawn from the N.G. on 17 September 1927 and demobilized.

Commander, 418th Field Artillery Regiment

Unknown	26 May 1926–17 September 1927

419th Field Artillery Regiment (75-mm G Mtzd) (GHQR) (II) **Organized Reserve North Dakota**

HQ—*Not initiated,* 1928–41

Constituted in the O.R. on 5 September 1928, assigned to the GHQR, and allotted to the Seventh Corps Area. Unit never organized. Location 7 December 1941—*Not initiated.*

420th Field Artillery Regiment (75-mm G Mtzd) (GHQR) **Organized Reserve Arkansas**

HQ—*Not initiated,* 1923–24; Little Rock, AR 1924–25

Constituted in the N.G. on 29 July 1921 as the 222d F.A., assigned to the GHQR, and allotted to the state of Missouri. Placed on the deferred list on 2 July 1923, allotted to the O.R. as a DNG unit and redesignated the 420th F.A. On 5 June 1924, N.G. allotment withdrawn from the state of Missouri and allotted to the state of Arkansas. Initiated in August 1924 as the 420th F.A. with regimental HQ at Little Rock, AR. Subordinate battalion HQ concurrently organized as follows: 1st Bn. at De Vall's Bluff, AR, and 2d Bn. at Conway, AR. Inactivated on 5 February 1925 at Little Rock and withdrawn as a DNG unit. Concurrently withdrawn from the Seventh Corps Area and allotted to the Ninth Corps Area. Additionally allotted to the Utah N.G. as the 222d F.A.

Commander, 420th Field Artillery Regiment

Unknown	5 June 1924–5 February 1925

421st Field Artillery Regiment (75-mm G-P) (GHQR) (I) **Organized Reserve**

HQ—*Not initiated,* 1921–27

Constituted in the N.G. on 29 July 1921 as the 223d F.A., assigned to the GHQR, and allotted to the Seventh Corps Area. Placed on the deferred list on 2 July 1923, allotted to the O.R. as a DNG unit and redesignated the 421st F.A. Withdrawn from the N.G. on 17 September 1927 and demobilized.

421st Field Artillery Regiment (75-mm G-P) (GHQR) (II) **Organized Reserve Arkansas**

HQ—*Not initiated,* 1928–41

Constituted in the O.R. on 5 September 1928, assigned to the GHQR, and allotted to the Seventh Corps Area. Little Rock, AR, designated on 12 October 1931 as the regiment's HQ on organization, but the unit was never organized at that location. Location 7 December 1941—*Not initiated.*

422d Field Artillery Regiment (I) (75-mm G-P) (GHQR) **Organized Reserve**

HQ—*Not initiated,* 1923–27

Constituted in the N.G. on 29 July 1921 as the 224th F.A., assigned to the GHQR, and allotted to the Seventh Corps Area. Placed on the deferred list on 2 July 1923, allotted to the O.R. as a DNG unit and redesignated the 422d F.A. Withdrawn from the N.G. on 17 September 1927.

422d Field Artillery Regiment (II) (75-mm G-P) (GHQR) **Organized Reserve Arkansas**

HQ—*Not initiated,* 1928–31; Little Rock, AR, 1931–41

Constituted in the O.R. on 5 September 1928, assigned to the GHQR, and allotted to the Seventh Corps Area. Initiated in October 1931 with regimental HQ at Little Rock, AR. Primary ROTC feeder school was Arkansas State College. Location 7 December 1941—Little Rock, AR.

Status: HHB is inactive in the US Army Reserve as HHB, 422d F.A. Gp.; 1st Bn. is inactive in the US Army Reserve as the 422d F.A. Bn.; 2d Bn. is inactive in the R.A. as the 692d F.A. Bn.

Commanders, 422d Field Artillery Regiment

Unknown	October 1931–7 December 1941

423d Field Artillery Regiment (75-mm G-P) (GHQR) **Organized Reserve Ohio**

HQ—*Not initiated,* 1923–26; Cincinnati, OH, 1926–27

Constituted in the N.G. on 29 July 1921 as the 225th F.A., assigned to the GHQR, and allotted to the Fifth Corps Area. Placed on the deferred list on 2 July 1923, allotted to the O.R. as a DNG unit and redesignated the 423d F.A. Initiated by December 1926 with regimental HQ at Cincinnati, OH. Primary ROTC feeder school was the University of Cincinnati. Withdrawn from the N.G. on 17 September 1927 and demobilized.

Commander, 422d Field Artillery Regiment

Unknown	ao December 1926–17 September 1927

424th Field Artillery Regiment (155-mm G) (GHQR) **Organized Reserve Arkansas**

HQ—*Not initiated,* 1923–24; Pine Bluff, AR, 1924–26; Little Rock, AR, 1926–27

Constituted in the N.G. on 29 July 1921 as the 227th F.A., assigned to the 227th F.A. Brig. (GHQR), and allotted to the Seventh Corps Area. Placed on the deferred list on 2 July 1923, allotted to the O.R. as a DNG unit and redesignated the 424th F.A. Initiated by December 1924 with regimental HQ at Pine Bluff, AR. Subordinate battalion HQ concurrently organized as follows: 1st Bn. at Fordyce, AR; 2d Bn. at Prescott, AR; and 3d Bn. at Texarkana, AR. HQ relocated on 26 May 1926 to Little Rock, AR. Subordinate battalion HQ concurrently relocated as follows: 1st Bn. at Pine Bluff, AR; 2d Bn. at Prescott, AR; and 3d Bn. at Fort Smith, AR. Primary ROTC feeder school was Arkansas State College. Withdrawn from the N.G. on 17 September 1927 and demobilized.

Commanders, 424th Field Artillery Regiment

Unknown	ao December 1924–17 September 1927

425th Field Artillery Regiment (6-inch G) (GHQR) **Organized Reserve New York**

HQ—*Not initiated,* 1923–27; Manhattan, NY, 1927

Constituted in the N.G. on 29 July 1921 as the 217th F.A., assigned to the 221st F.A. Brig. (GHQR), and allotted to the Second Corps Area. Placed on the deferred list on 2 July 1923, redesignated as the 425th F.A., and allotted to the O.R. as a DNG unit. Initiated on 6 January 1927 with regimental HQ at Manhattan, NY. Primary ROTC feeder school was Princeton University. Withdrawn from the N.G. on 17 September 1927.

Commander, 425th Field Artillery Regiment

Maj. Henry T. Chickoring	6 January 1927–17 September 1927

426th Field Artillery Regiment (155-mm G) (GHQR) **Organized Reserve California**

HQ—*Not initiated,* 1923–26; Los Angeles, CA, 1926–41

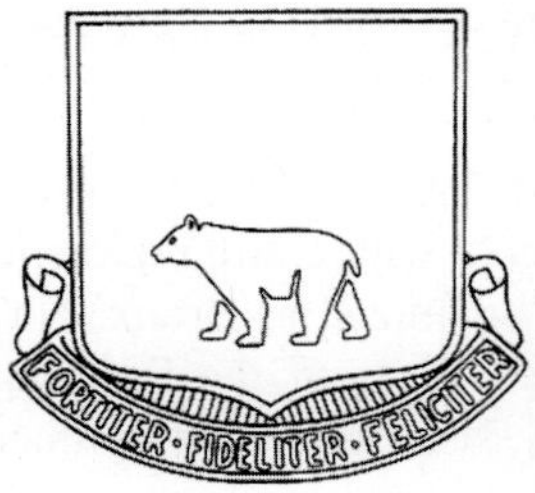

Constituted in the O.R. on 2 July 1923, assigned to the GHQR, and allotted to the Ninth Corps Area. Initiated in April 1926 with the entire regiment at Los Angeles, CA. Assigned to the 195th F.A. Brig. (XIX Corps) on 5 September 1928. Col. Wyman and a volunteer detail of 117 Reserve officers, many from the 426th F.A., participated in earthquake relief operations, 14–22 March 1933, by organizing and conducting food distribution operations in the Long Beach–Los Angeles area. Reorganized on 21 October 1933 as 155-mm H. Typically conducted Inactive Training Period meetings at the Chamber of Commerce Building or at 751 Figuroa Street in Los Angeles. Conducted summer training with the 76th F.A. at the Presidio of Monterey, CA, or Del Monte, CA, and some years at Fort Lewis, WA. Conducted field artillery CMTC training some years at the Presidio of Monterey as an alternate form of annual training. Primary ROTC feeder school was the University of California. Location 7 December 1941—Los Angeles, CA. (Inactivated on 21 January 1942.)

Status: Disbanded on 26 January 1943. Reconstituted and consolidated on 17 May 1949 as follows: HHB consolidated with HHB, 443d F.A. Gp.; 1st Bn. with the 481st F.A. Bn.; and 2d Bn. with the 829th F.A. Bn. Inactive in the US Army Reserve.

Commanders, 426th Field Artillery Regiment

Col. Benjamin Whittaker	April 1926–ao July 1928	Unknown	ao June 1938–ao June 1939
Col. Oliver C. Wyman	ao June 1929–ao June 1938	Lt. Col. Walter H. Long	ao June 1939–ao January 1941
Unknown	ao January 1941–7 December 1941		

427th Field Artillery Regiment (155-mm G) (GHQR) **Organized Reserve Louisiana/North Carolina**

HQ—*Not initiated,* 1923–24; Shreveport, LA, 1924–29; *Inactive,* 1929–41

Constituted in the O.R. on 2 July 1923, assigned to the 207th F.A. Brig. (GHQR), and allotted to the Fourth Corps Area. Initiated on 23 December 1924 with regimental HQ at Shreveport, LA. Subordinate battalion HQ concurrently organized as follows: 1st Bn. at Monroe, LA; 2d Bn. at Coushatta, LA; and 3d Bn. at Natchez, LA. Inactivated by September 1929 at Shreveport by relief of personnel. Charlotte, NC, designated on 22 October 1929 as HQ on reorganization, but the unit was never organized at that location. Assigned to the XIV Corps by 1936. Conducted summer training with the 5th F.A. at Fort Bragg, NC, and some years at Camp Beauregard, LA. Designated mobilization station was Camp Jackson, SC. Location 7 December 1941—Charlotte, NC.

Status: Disbanded 26 January 1943.

Commanders, 427th Field Artillery Regiment

Unknown	23 December 1924–September 1929	*Inactive*	September 1929–7 December 1941

431st Field Artillery Regiment (155-mm G) (XI Corps) **Organized Reserve Massachusetts**

HQ—*Not initiated,* 1921–22; Boston, MA 1922–30; *Inactive,* 1930–41

Constituted in the O.R. on 29 July 1921, assigned to the 180th F.A. Brig. (XI Corps), and allotted to the First Corps Area. Initiated on 10 March 1922 with regimental HQ at Boston, MA. Subordinate battalion HQ concurrently organized as follows: 1st and 3d Bns. at Boston and 2d Bn. at Cambridge, MA. Band organized in April 1923 at Boston. Attached to the 76th Div. on 17 October 1929 for organization, administration, and training. Conducted summer training at Fort Ethan Allen, VT, and some years with the 258th F.A. at Fort Terry, NY. Primary ROTC feeder school was Harvard University. Inactivated on 17 January 1930 by relief of personnel. Location 7 December 1941—*Inactive.*

Status: Disbanded on 26 January 1943.

Commanders, 431st Field Artillery Regiment

Maj. Alexander Wheeler	10 March 1922–12 January 1924
Lt. Col. Julian I. Chamberlain	12 January 1924–17 January 1930
Inactive	17 January 1930–7 December 1941

432d Field Artillery Regiment (155-mm G) (XII Corps) **Organized Reserve New York**

HQ—*Not initiated,* 1921–22; Manhattan, NY, 1922–41

Constituted in the O.R. on 29 July 1921, assigned to the 181st F.A. Brig. (XII Corps), and allotted to the Second Corps Area. Initiated on 15 March 1922 with entire regiment, less the 3d Bn., at Manhattan, NY. The 3d Bn. concurrently organized at Bronx, NY. Typically conducted Inactive Training Period meetings at the offices of the Building Trades Employer Association at 2 Park Avenue in New York City, NY. Conducted summer training most years with the 2d Bn., 7th F.A. at Pine Camp, NY, and some years with the 5th F.A. at Fort Bragg, NC. Primary ROTC feeder school was Princeton University. Designated mobilization training station was Pine Camp, NY. Location 7 December 1941—Manhattan, NY.

Status: Disbanded on 26 January 1943.

Events: 267

Commanders, 432d Field Artillery Regiment

Maj. Habeeb L. Saidy	15 March 1922–5 September 1922
Lt. Col. Brinton Bradford	5 September 1922–15 March 1924
Col. Robert L. Bacon	15 March 1924–16 April 1924
Lt. Col. Brinton Bradford	16 April 1924–13 June 1924
Col. Newbold Morris	13 June 1924–ao August 1929
Unknown	ao August 1929–ao June 1930
Col. Silas McBee Jr.	ao June 1930–ao June 1941

433d Field Artillery Regiment (155-mm G) (XIII Corps) **Organized Reserve Pennsylvania/ West Virginia**

HQ—*Not initiated,* 1921–22; Tyrone, PA, 1922–27; *Inactive,* 1927–41

Constituted in the O.R. on 29 July 1921, assigned to the 182d F.A. Brig. (XIII Corps), and allotted to the Third Corps Area. Initiated on 1 March 1922 with regimental HQ at Tyrone, PA. Subordinate battalion HQ concurrently organized as follows: 1st Bn. at Butler, PA; 2d Bn. at Connellsville, PA; and 3d Bn. at Lock Haven, PA. Withdrawn from the Third Corps Area on 11 January 1927 and allotted to the Fifth Corps Area. Huntington, WV, designated as HQ on reorganization, but the unit was never organized at that location. Conducted summer training with the 5th F.A. at Fort Bragg, NC. Primary ROTC feeder schools was Duquesne University, 1922–27. Location 7 December 1941—*Inactive.*

Commanders, 433d Field Artillery Regiment

2d Lt. Thomas A. Allen	1 March 1922–20 March 1922
Capt. Edward S. Dawson	20 March 1922–27 April 1922
Maj. Harris N. Summer	27 April 1922–ao May 1922
Maj. Fred S. McClintock	ao August 1922–11 January 1927
Inactive	11 January 1927–7 December 1941

434th Field Artillery Regiment (155-mm G) (XIV Corps) **Organized Reserve Tennessee/Alabama/Indiana**

HQ—*Not initiated,* 1921–22; Hendersonville, TN, 1922–29; Birmingham, AL, 1929–36; Fort Wayne, IN, 1936–41

Constituted in the O.R. on 29 July 1921, assigned to the 183d F.A. Brig. (XIV Corps), and allotted to the Fourth Corps Area. Initiated on 10 March 1922 with regimental HQ at Hendersonville, TN. Subordinate battalion HQ concurrently organized as follows: 1st Bn. at Louisville, TN; 2d Bn. at Cookeville, TN; and 3d Bn. at Memphis, TN. Entire regiment relocated on 22 October 1929 to Birmingham, AL. Withdrawn from the O.R. on 1 October 1933 and allotted to the R.A. as an RAI unit. Concurrently relieved from the 183d F.A. Brig. (XIV Corps) and assigned to the 27th F.A. Brig. (GHQR). Withdrawn from the Fourth Corps Area on 5 July 1936 and allotted to the Fifth Corps Area. Reorganized in July 1936 at Fort Wayne, IN. Conducted summer training most years with the 5th F.A. at Fort Bragg, NC, and at Fort Knox, KY, 1938–40. Designated mobilization station was Camp Jackson, SC, 1922–31, and Fort Bragg, NC, 1931–41. Primary ROTC feeder schools were University of Tennessee, 1922–29; Alabama Polytechnic Institute, 1929–36; and Purdue University, 1936–41. Location 7 December 1941—Fort Wayne, IN.

Status: Inactive in the US Army Reserve as the 434th Armd. F.A. Bn., a component of the 7th Armd. Div.

Commanders, 434th Field Artillery Regiment

Col. Harry S. Berry	10 March 1922–June 1925	Col. Louis H. Harper	ao June 1932–28 March 1936
Unknown	June 1925–25 October 1930	Col. Louis E. Goodrich	4 April 1936–15 November 1936
Lt. Col. Robert L. Pittman	25 October 1930–ao January 1931	Maj. Victor Lee	15 November 1936–29 January 1939
Unknown	ao January 1931–ao June 1932	Maj. T. Tschannen	29 January 1939–ao May 1940
Unknown	ao May 1940–7 December 1941		

435th Field Artillery Regiment (155-mm G) (XV Corps) **Organized Reserve Ohio**

HQ—*Not initiated,* 1921–22; Cleveland, OH, 1922–30; *Inactive,* 1930–34; Cleveland, OH, 1934–41

Constituted in the O.R. on 29 July 1921, assigned to the 184th F.A. Brig. (XV Corps), and allotted to the Fifth Corps Area. Initiated on 11 July 1922 with regimental HQ at Cleveland, OH. Relieved from the 184th F.A. Brig. (XV Corps) on 2 July 1923 and assigned to the 191st F.A. Brig. (XV Corps) . Inactivated by March 1930 at Cleveland by relief of personnel. Relieved on 1 October 1933 from the 191st F.A. Brig. (XV Corps). Reorganized by June 1934 at Cleveland. Typically conducted Inactive Training Period meetings at the Bulkey Building in Cleveland. Conducted summer training most years at Fort Knox, KY, and some years at Fort Benjamin Harrison, IN. Primary ROTC feeder school was Ohio State University. Location 7 December 1941—Cleveland, OH.

Status: Disbanded on 26 January 1943.

Commanders, 435th Field Artillery Regiment

Capt. Leonard S. Hole	11 July 1922–27 April 1923	Unknown	August 1927–27 May 1928
Col. Dudley J. Hard	27 April 1923–18 November 1924	Maj. Harold F. Matthys	27 May 1928–March 1930
Unknown	18 November 1924–21 February 1926	*Inactive*	March 1930–ao June 1934
Maj. Benjamin P. Bole	21 February 1926–August 1927	Maj. Howard L. Brown	ao June 1934–ao June 1937
Unknown	ao June 1937–7 December 1941		

436th Field Artillery Regiment (155-mm G) (XVI Corps) **Organized Reserve Michigan**

HQ—Adrian, MI, 1921–25; Marquette, MI, 1925–37; Grand Rapids, MI, 1937–41

Constituted in the O.R. on 29 July 1921, assigned to the 185th F.A. Brig. (XVI Corps), and allotted to the Sixth Corps Area. Initiated on 11 November 1921 with regimental HQ at Adrian, MI. Subordinate battalion HQ concurrently organized as follows: 1st Bn. at Ann Arbor, MI; 2d Bn. at Adrian; and 3d Bn. at Battle Creek, MI. Relieved from the 185th F.A. Brig. (XVI Corps) on 2 July 1923 and assigned to the 192d F.A. Brig. (VI Corps). Regimental HQ relocated on 2 June 1925 to Marquette, MI. Subordinate battalion HQ concurrently relocated as follows: 1st Bn. at Ishpeming, MI; 2d Bn. at Escanaba, MI; and 3d Bn. at Calumet, MI. Relieved from the 192d F.A. Brig. (VI Corps) on 1 October 1933 and assigned to the 185th F.A. Brig. (XVI Corps). Entire regiment reorganized on 28 July 1937 to Grand Rapids, MI. Conducted summer training at Camp McCoy, WI. Primary ROTC feeder school was Michigan State College. Location 7 December 1941—Grand Rapids, MI.

Status: Disbanded on 26 January 1943.

Commanders, 436th Field Artillery Regiment

Maj. Oscar Brady	29 November 1921–16 December 1921	Lt. Col. Ralph C. Huston	21 October 1925–17 November 1926
Maj. J. S. Ralph Gray	16 December 1921–1 November 1922	Lt. Col. Leland N. Jones	17 November 1926–ao August 1933
Lt. Col. Leland N. Jones	1 November 1922–21 October 1925	Unknown	ao August 1933–7 December 1941

437th Field Artillery Regiment (155-mm G) (XVII Corps)

Organized Reserve Minnesota, North Dakota, and South Dakota

HQ—*Not initiated,* 1921–22; St. Paul, MN, 1922–41

Constituted in the O.R. on 29 July 1921, assigned to the 186th F.A. Brig. (XVII Corps), and allotted to the Seventh Corps Area. Initiated in February 1922 with regimental HQ at St. Paul, MN. Subordinate battalion HQ concurrently organized as follows: 1st Bn. at St. Paul; 2d Bn. at Fargo, ND; and 3d Bn. at Sioux Falls, SD. Relieved from the 186th F.A. Brig. (XVII Corps) on 1 October 1933 and assigned to the 187th F.A. Brig. (XVII Corps) . Typically conducted Inactive Training Period meetings at the N.G. armory in St. Paul and at the Gardner Hotel in Fargo. Conducted summer training at Camp McCoy, WI. Primary ROTC feeder school was the University of Minnesota. Location 7 December 1941—St. Paul, MN.

Status: Disbanded on 26 January 1943.

Commanders, 437th Field Artillery Regiment

Unknown	February 1922–23 March 1923	Col. Jerome Jackman	October 1927–June 1930
Col. Franklyn W. Matson	23 March 1923–October 1927	Unknown	June 1930–7 December 1941

438th Field Artillery Regiment (155-mm G) (XVIII Corps)

Organized Reserve Texas/Minnesota

HQ—*Not initiated,* 1921–22; Houston, TX, 1922–27; *Inactive,* 1927–36; Fort Worth, TX, 1936–41

Constituted in the O.R. on 29 July 1921, assigned to the 187th F.A. Brig. (XVIII Corps), and allotted to the Eighth Corps Area. Initiated on 26 July 1922 with the entire regiment at Houston, TX. Withdrawn from the Eighth Corps Area on 13 January 1927 and allotted to the Seventh Corps Area. Minneapolis, MN, designated as HQ on organization, but the unit was never organized at that location. Withdrawn from the Seventh Corps Area on 1 October 1933, reallotted to the Eighth Corps Area, and assigned to the 188th F.A. Brig. (XVIII Corps). Regiment reorganized on 9 March 1936 with the regimental HQ at Fort Worth, TX. Houston elements typically conducted Inactive Training Period meetings at the Houston Light Guard armory. Conducted summer training most years with the 15th F.A. at Fort Sam Houston, TX, or Camp Bullis, TX, and some years with the 77th F.A. at Fort D.A. Russell, TX. Primary ROTC feeder school was Texas A&M. Location 7 December 1941—Fort Worth, TX.

Status: Disbanded 26 January 1943.

Commanders, 438th Field Artillery Regiment

Lt. Col. Frank G. Anderson	26 July 1922–13 January 1927	*Inactive*	13 January 1927–9 March 1936
Unknown	9 March 1936–7 December 1941		

439th Field Artillery Regiment (155-mm G) (XIX Corps) **Organized Reserve California**

HQ—*Not initiated,* 1921–22; San Francisco, CA, 1922–41

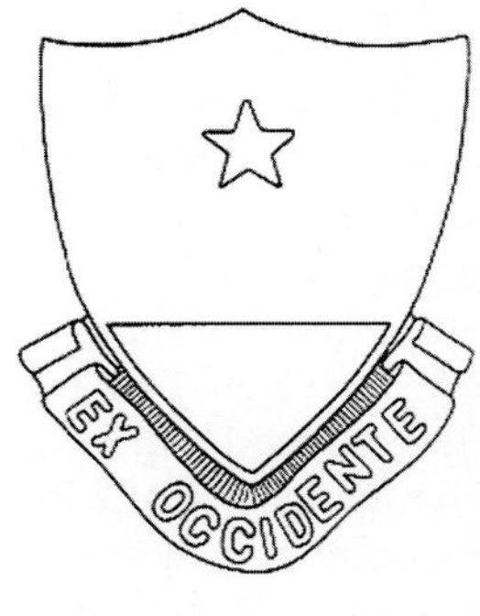

Constituted in the O.R. on 29 July 1921, assigned to the 188th F.A. Brig. (XIX Corps), and allotted to the Ninth Corps Area. Initiated on 10 January 1922 with regimental HQ at San Francisco, CA. Subordinate battalion HQ concurrently organized as follows: 1st Bn. at Oakland, CA; 2d Bn. at Berkeley, CA; and 3d Bn. at San Jose, CA. Relieved from the 188th F.A. Brig. (XIX Corps) on 5 September 1928 and assigned to the 189th F.A. Brig. (IX Corps). Entire regiment relocated about April 1930 to San Francisco. Relieved from the 189th F.A. Brig. (XIX Corps) on 1 October 1933 and assigned to the 195th F.A. Brig. (IX Corps). Typically conducted Inactive Training Period meetings at the Oakland City Hall in Oakland, CA. Conducted summer training most years with the 76th F.A. at the Presidio of Monterey, CA, and some years at Del Monte, CA; Fort Winfield Scott, CA; Fort Funston, CA; and Camp San Luis Obispo with the 144th F.A. Conducted field artillery CMTC training some years at the Presidio of Monterey as an alternate form of annual training. Primary ROTC feeder school was Stanford University. Location 7 December 1941—San Francisco, CA. (Inactivated 21 January 1942.)

Status: Components inactive in the US Army Reserve as follows: Headquarters and Headquarters Company (HHC) as HHC 427th F.A. Gp.; 1st Bn. as the 757th F.A. Bn.; 2d Bn. as the 931st F.A. Bn.

Commanders, 439th Field Artillery Regiment

Maj. Charles I. Anderson	10 January 1922–26 July 1922	Col. Arthur L. Keesling	July 1925–11 September 1933
Lt. Col. Jefferson J. Graves	1 May 1922–ao October 1922	Col. Ralph J. Faneuf	11 September 1933–5 December 1936
Unknown	ao October 1922–ao June 1925	Col. William C. Vest	5 December 1936–ao August 1939
Maj. Charles I. Anderson	ao June 1925–July 1925	Unknown	ao August 1939–7 December 1941

440th Field Artillery Regiment (155-mm G) (III Corps) **Organized Reserve Pennsylvania/Ohio**

HQ—Pottstown, PA, 1921–27; Cleveland, OH, 1927–41

Constituted in the O.R. on 29 July 1921, assigned to the 82d F.A. Brig. (III Corps), and allotted to the Third Corps Area. Initiated on 2 November 1921 with regimental HQ at Pottstown, PA. Subordinate battalion HQ concurrently organized as follows: 1st Bn. at Pottstown; 2d Bn. at Norristown, PC; and 3d Bn. at Media, PA. The 82d F.A. Brig. (III Corps) redesignated on 2 July 1923 as the 190th F.A. Brig. (III Corps) and allotted to the O.R. as a DNG unit. The 1st Bn. relocated on 10 December 1925 to Royersford, PA. Regiment withdrawn from the Third Corps Area on 11 January 1927 and allotted to the Fifth Corps Area but remained assigned to the 190th F.A. Brig. (III Corps). Reorganized on 20 November 1927 with the entire regiment at Cleveland, OH. Withdrawn from the O.R. on 1 October 1933 and allotted to the R.A. as an RAI unit. Concurrently relieved from the 190th F.A. Brig. (III Corps) and assigned to the 28th F.A. Brig. (GHQR). Typically conducted Inactive Training Period meetings at the Bulkey Building in Cleveland. Conducted summer training with the 1st Bn., 3d F.A., 1931–34, and the 1st Bn., 19th F.A., 1935–41, at Fort Knox, KY. Primary ROTC feeder school was Duquesne University, 1921–27, and Ohio State University, 1931–41. Location 7 December 1941—Cleveland, OH.

Status: Inactive in the US Army Reserve as the 440th Armd. F.A. Bn., a component of the 7th Armd. Div.

Commanders, 440th Field Artillery Regiment

Maj. Edwin A. Ziegler	2 November 1921–16 March 1922	Maj. Thomas W. McCaw	9 July 1930–ao August 1930
Capt. William B. Wise	16 March 1922–June 1923	Unknown	ao August 1930–ao July 1934
Maj. Leonard D. Frescola	June 1923–11 January 1927	Maj. Robert H. Jamison	ao July 1934–ao July 1936
Inactive	11 January 1927–20 November 1927	Unknown	ao July 1936–ao July 1937
Maj. Benjamin P. Bole	20 November 1927–9 July 1930	Lt. Col. A.B. Poole	ao July 1937–ao August 1937
Unknown	ao August 1937–7 December 1941		

441st Field Artillery Regiment (155-mm G) (IV Corps) **Organized Reserve New Jersey/New York**

HQ—*Not initiated,* 1921–22; Atlantic City, NJ, 1922–37; New York City, NY, 1937–41

Constituted in the O.R. on 29 July 1921, assigned to the IV Corps, and allotted to the Second Corps Area. Initiated on 15 March 1922 with regimental HQ at Atlantic City, NJ. Subordinate battalion HQ concurrently organized as follows: 1st Bn. at Princeton, NJ; 2d Bn. at Irvington, NJ; and 3d Bn. at Harrison, NJ. Relieved from the IV Corps on 23 April 1924 and assigned to the 15th F.A. Brig. (II Corps). Concurrently armament changed from 155-mm G to 155-mm H. Armament changed on 8 May 1929 from 155-mm HG to 75-mm G (Mtzd). Entire regiment relocated on 20 November 1937 to New York City. Typically conducted Inactive Training Period meetings at the armory of the 112th F.A. at East Orange, NJ, and at the offices of the Building Trades Employer Association at 2 Park Avenue in New York City, NY, in the late 1930s. Conducted summer training most years with the 7th F.A. at Pine Camp, NY, and some years at Camp Blauvelt, NY, or Fort Hoyle. Primary ROTC feeder schools were Princeton University and Cornell University. Designated mobilization training station was Pine Camp, NY. Location 7 December 1941—New York City, NY.

Status: Disbanded on 26 January 1943.

Events: 267

Commanders, 441st Field Artillery Regiment

1st Lt. Ray M. Miller	15 March 1922–22 April 1922	Col. Charles R. Lloyd	21 February 1924–ao February 1925
Capt. William E. Shellgrove	22 April 1922–17 May 1922	Unknown	ao February 1925–ao April 1926
Maj. Jacob E. Ridgeway	17 May 1922–21 February 1924	Maj. Paul Williams	ao April 1926–6 August 1930
Col. Alfred C.B. McNevin	6 August 1930–ao June 1941		

442d Field Artillery Regiment (155-mm G) (VI Corps) **Organized Reserve New York**

HQ—*Not initiated,* 1921–22; Brooklyn, NY, 1922–41

Constituted in the O.R. on 29 July 1921, assigned to the 84th F.A. Brig. (VI Corps), and allotted to the Second Corps Area. Initiated on 15 March 1922 with the entire regiment at Brooklyn, NY. Relieved from the 84th F.A. Brig. on 24 April 1924 and assigned to the 184th F.A. Brig. (V Corps). Concurrently attached to the II Corps for administrative control. Designated armament changed on 8 May 1929 to 6-inch Gun. Typically conducted Inactive Training Period meetings at the armory of the 105th F.A. at Brooklyn, NY, in the 1920s and later at the Hotel George Washington at 23d Street and Lexington Avenue in New York City, NY, in the 1930s. Conducted summer training most years with the 5th F.A. at Fort Bragg, NC, or the 7th F.A. at Pine Camp, NY. Conducted field artillery CMTC training some years at Madison Barracks, NY, as an alternate form of annual training. Primary ROTC feeder school was Princeton University. Designated mobilization training station was Pine Camp, NY. Location 7 December 1941—Brooklyn, NY.

Status: Disbanded on 26 January 1943.

Events: 267

Commanders, 442d Field Artillery Regiment

Maj. Jacob R. Martin	15 March 1922–21 April 1922	Maj. William H. Caldwell	24 October 1924–1 May 1925
Maj. William H. Caldwell	21 April 1922–16 February 1924	Col. Cleveland C. Lansing	1 May 1925–18 February 1930
Col. Wade H. Carpenter	16 February 1924–24 October 1924	Col. Edward C.O. Thomas	18 February 1930–ao July 1941

443d Field Artillery Regiment (155-mm G) (VII Corps) **Organized Reserve Missouri, Arkansas, and Kansas/Illinois**

HQ—*Not initiated,* 1921–22; Kansas City, MO, 1922–33; *Inactive,* 1933–35; Eighth Corps Area, 1935–36; *Inactive,* 1936–37; Chicago, IL, 1937–41

Constituted in the O.R. on 9 July 1921, assigned to the VII Corps, and allotted to the Seventh Corps Area. Initiated in 1922 with regimental HQ at Kansas City, MO. Subordinate battalion HQ concurrently organized as follows: 1st Bn. at Kansas City; 2d Bn. at Little Rock, AR; and 3d Bn. at Junction City, KS. Assigned to the 14th F.A. Brig. (VII Corps) on 2 July 1923. Relieved from the 14th F.A. Brig. on 5 September 1928. Withdrawn from the Seventh Corps Area on 1 October 1933 and allotted to the Eighth Corps Area. Reorganized on 9 March 1935 with HQ in the Eighth Corps Area. Withdrawn from the Eighth Corps Area on 5 June 1936 and allotted to the Sixth Corps Area. Personnel in Eighth Corps Area relieved on 12 May 1937 and unit inactivated. Initiated on 28 July 1937 with the entire regiment at Chicago, IL. Typically conducted Inactive Training Period meetings, 1922–33, at the 110th Engrs. armory or the O.R. Center building at 20th and Vine Streets in Kansas City. Conducted summer training at Fort Riley, KS, 1926–33, and at Fort D.A. Russell, TX, in 1936. Primary ROTC feeder schools were the University of Missouri, 1922–33, and the University of Illinois, 1937–41. Location 7 December 1941—Chicago, IL.

Status: Disbanded on 26 January 1943.

Commanders, 443d Field Artillery Regiment

Unknown	ao December 1922–7 December 1941

444th Field Artillery Regiment (75-mm G-H) (ZI) **Organized Reserve Tennessee**

HQ—*Not initiated,* 1923–24; Memphis, TN, 1924–28

Constituted in the O.R. on 2 July 1923, assigned to the Zone of the Interior, and allotted to the Fourth Corps Area. Initiated on 16 April 1924 with regimental HQ at Memphis, TN. Subordinate battalion HQ concurrently organized as follows: 1st Bn. at Jackson, TN, and 2d Bn. at Clarksville, TN. Conducted summer training with the 5th F.A. at Fort Bragg, NC. Designated mobilization station was Fort Bragg, NC. Primary ROTC feeder school was University of Tennessee. Withdrawn from the Fourth Corps Area on 5 September 1928.

Status: Disbanded 1952.

Commanders, 444th Field Artillery Regiment

Col. William J. Bacon	16 April 1924–5 September 1928

445th Field Artillery Regiment (75-mm G-H) (ZI) **Organized Reserve Kentucky**

HQ—*Not initiated,* 1923–26; NE Kentucky, 1926–28

Constituted in the O.R. on 2 July 1923, assigned to the Zone of the Interior, and allotted to the Fifth Corps Area. Initiated in January 1926 with HQ in northeastern Kentucky. Conducted summer training with the 1st Bn., 3d F.A. at Fort Knox, KY. Primary ROTC feeder school was Eastern Kentucky State Teachers College. Demobilized on 5 September 1928.

Commanders, 445th Field Artillery Regiment

Unknown	January 1926–5 September 1928

446th Field Artillery Regiment (75-mm G) (ZI) **Organized Reserve California**

HQ—*Not initiated,* 1923–25; San Francisco, CA, 1925–28

Constituted in the O.R. on 2 July 1923, assigned to the Zone of the Interior, and allotted to the Ninth Corps Area. Initiated on 10 October 1925 with the entire regiment at San Francisco, CA. Conducted summer training with the 76th F.A. at the Presidio of Monterey, CA. Primary ROTC feeder school was Stanford University. Demobilized on 5 September 1928.

Commanders, 446th Field Artillery Regiment

Maj. Robert S. La Motte	10 October 1925–January 1926	Maj. William C. Vest	January 1926–5 September 1928

447th Field Artillery Regiment (75-mm G) (ZI) **Organized Reserve California**

HQ—*Not initiated,* 1923–25; Los Angeles, CA 1925–28

Constituted in the O.R. on 2 July 1923, assigned to the Zone of the Interior, and allotted to the Ninth Corps Area. Initiated on 14 October 1925 with the entire regiment at Los Angeles, CA. Conducted summer training with the 76th F.A. at the Presidio of Monterey, CA. Primary ROTC feeder school was University of California. Demobilized on 5 September 1928.

Commanders, 447th Field Artillery Regiment

Maj. Walter H. Long	14 October 1925–ao June 1927	Maj. William H. Neblett	ao December 1927–5 September 1928

448th Field Artillery Regiment (75-mm G-H) (ZI) **Organized Reserve North Carolina**

HQ—*Not initiated,* 1923–24; Wilmington, NC, 1924–28

Constituted in the O.R. on 2 July 1923, assigned to the Zone of the Interior, and allotted to the Fourth Corps Area. Initiated in April 1924 with regimental HQ at Wilmington, NC. Subordinate battalion HQ concurrently organized as follows: 1st Bn. at Fayetteville, NC, and 2d Bn. at Raleigh, NC. Conducted summer training with the 5th F.A. at Fort Bragg, NC. Designated mobilization station was Fort Bragg, NC. Primary ROTC feeder school was North Carolina State College. Demobilized on 5 September 1928.

Commanders, 448th Field Artillery Regiment

Unknown	April 1924–5 September 1928

449th Field Artillery Regiment (75-mm G) (ZI) **Organized Reserve Indiana**

HQ—*Not initiated,* 1923–24; Fort Wayne, IN, 1924–28

Constituted in the O.R. on 2 July 1923, assigned to the Zone of the Interior, and allotted to the Fifth Corps Area. Initiated in September 1924 with regimental HQ at Fort Wayne, IN. Conducted summer training with the 1st Bn., 3d F.A. at Fort Knox, KY. Primary ROTC feeder school was Purdue University. Demobilized on 5 September 1928.

Commanders, 449th Field Artillery Regiment

Unknown	September 1924–5 September 1928

450th Field Artillery Regiment (75-mm G) (ZI) **Organized Reserve Oklahoma**

HQ—*Not initiated,* 1923–27; Fort Sill, OK, 1927–28

Constituted in the O.R. on 2 July 1923, assigned to the Zone of the Interior, and allotted to the Eighth Corps Area. Initiated by August 1927 with the entire regiment at Fort Sill, OK. Mobilization assignment was to support the F.A. school. Designated mobilization station was Fort Sill, OK. Demobilized on 5 September 1928.

Commanders, 450th Field Artillery Regiment

Unknown	ao August 1927–5 September 1928

452d Field Artillery Regiment (155-mm H) (I) (ZI) — Organized Reserve Georgia and Florida

HQ—Macon, GA, 1923–29

Constituted in the O.R. on 2 July 1923, assigned to the Zone of the Interior, and allotted to the Fourth Corps Area. Initiated in October 1923 with regimental HQ at Macon, GA. Subordinate battalion HQ concurrently organized as follows: 1st Bn. at La Grange, GA; 2d Bn. at Dublin, GA; and 3d Bn. at Athens, GA. Assigned to the 82d Div. on 18 July 1928. Entire regiment relocated on 22 October 1929 to Macon. Conducted summer training with the 5th F.A. at Fort Bragg, NC. Primary ROTC feeder school was Georgia School of Technology. Designated mobilization station was Fort Bragg, NC. Redesignated as the 321st F.A. Regiment on 5 October 1929.

Commanders, 452d Field Artillery Regiment (I)

Lt. Col. Marlin A. Prather	October 1923–25 March 1925	Lt. Col. Louis H. Harper	25 March 1925–5 October 1929

452d Field Artillery Regiment (155-mm H) (II) (ZI) — Organized Reserve Georgia

HQ—*Not initiated,* 1929–30; Augusta, GA, 1930–33

Constituted in the O.R. on 5 October 1929, assigned to the Zone of the Interior, and allotted to the Fourth Corps Area. Initiated by August 1930 with regimental HQ at Augusta, GA. Conducted summer training with the 5th F.A. at Fort Bragg, NC. Primary ROTC feeder school was Georgia School of Technology. Demobilized on 1 October 1933.

Commanders, 452d Field Artillery Regiment (II)

Unknown	ao August 1930–1 October 1933

453d Field Artillery Regiment (155-mm H) (ZI) — Organized Reserve California/Indiana

HQ—*Not initiated,* 1923–26; San Francisco, CA, 1926–29; *Inactive,* 1929–37; Lafayette, IN, 1937–41

Constituted in the O.R. on 2 July 1923, assigned to the Zone of the Interior, and allotted to the Ninth Corps Area. Initiated in March 1926 with the entire regiment at San Francisco, CA. Conducted summer training with the 76th F.A. at the Presidio of Monterey. Inactivated on 15 October 1929 at San Francisco by relief of personnel. Withdrawn from the Ninth Corps Area on 5 June 1936, and allotted to the Fifth Corps Area. Reorganized in April 1937 with regimental HQ at Lafayette, IN. Primary ROTC feeder school was Stanford University, 1926–36, and Purdue University, 1936–41. Location 7 December 1941—Lafayette, IN.

Status: Disbanded on 26 January 1943.

Commanders, 453d Field Artillery Regiment

Lt. Col. Thomas H. Jennings	March 1926–15 October 1929	Maj. James C. Gabriel	April 1937–ao March 1940
Inactive	15 October 1929–April 1937	Unknown	ao March 1940–7 December 1941

454th Field Artillery Regiment (155-mm H) (ZI) — Organized Reserve South Carolina

HQ—*Not initiated,* 1923–24; Columbia, SC, 1924

Constituted in the O.R. on 2 July 1923, assigned to the Zone of the Interior, and allotted to the Fourth Corps Area. Initiated in April 1924 with regimental HQ at Columbia, SC. Subordinate battalion HQ concurrently organized as follows: 1st Bn. at Sumter SC; 2d Bn. at Denmark, SC; and 3d Bn. at Spartanburg, SC. Designated mobilization station was Fort Bragg, NC. Demobilized on 13 June 1924.

Commanders, 454th Field Artillery Regiment

Unknown	April 1924–13 June 1924

455th Field Artillery Regiment (155-mm H) (ZI) **Organized Reserve Ohio**

HQ—*Not initiated,* 1923–24; Cincinnati, OH, 1924–40; Dayton, OH, 1940–41

Constituted in the O.R. on 2 July 1923, assigned to the Zone of the Interior, and allotted to the Fifth Corps Area. Initiated in September 1924 with regimental HQ at Cincinnati, OH. Regiment awarded the Toulmin Trophy for 1929. Relieved from the Zone of the Interior on 1 October 1933 and assigned to the 184th F.A. Brig. (XV Corps). Regimental HQ relocated on 23 February 1940 to Dayton, OH. Conducted summer training with the 1st Bn., 3d F.A. at Fort Knox, KY. Primary ROTC feeder school was Xavier University. Location 7 December 1941—Dayton, OH.

Status: Inactive in the US Army Reserve as the 455th F.A. Bn.

Commanders, 455th Field Artillery Regiment

Unknown	September 1924–ao September 1929
Maj. M.V. Loewenstein	ao September 1929–ao February 1930
Unknown	ao February 1930–ao July 1932
Capt. Roland M. Kehr	ao July 1932–July 1934
Maj. James C. Van Dancke	July 1934–ao June 1936
Unknown	ao June 1936–7 December 1941

456th Field Artillery Regiment (155-mm H) (ZI) **Organized Reserve Oklahoma**

HQ—*Not initiated,* 1923–27; Fort Sill, OK, 1927–28

Constituted in the O.R. on 2 July 1923, assigned to the Zone of the Interior, and allotted to the Eighth Corps Area. Initiated by August 1927 with the entire regiment at Fort Sill, OK. Conducted summer training with the 1st F.A. at Fort Sill, OK. Primary ROTC feeder school was the University of Oklahoma. Mobilization assignment was to support the Field Artillery School. Designated mobilization station was Fort Sill. Demobilized on 5 September 1928.

Commanders, 456th Field Artillery Regiment

Unknown	ao August 1927–5 September 1928

457th Field Artillery Regiment (155-mm G) (ZI) **Organized Reserve Alabama**

HQ—*Not initiated,* 1923–24; Birmingham, AL, 1924

Constituted in the O.R. on 2 July 1923, assigned to the Zone of the Interior, and allotted to the Fourth Corps Area. Initiated on 30 April 1924 with regimental HQ at Birmingham, AL. Subordinate battalion HQ concurrently organized as follows: 1st Bn. at Tuscaloosa, AL; 2d Bn. at Talledega, AL; and 3d Bn. at Montgomery, AL. Designated mobilization station was Fort Bragg, NC. Demobilized on 13 June 1924.

Commanders, 457th Field Artillery Regiment

Unknown	30 April 1924–13 June 1924

458th Field Artillery Regiment (155-mm G) (ZI) **Organized Reserve**

HQ—*Not initiated,* 1923–24

Constituted in the O.R. on 2 July 1923, assigned to the Zone of the Interior, and allotted to the Fifth Corps Area. Demobilized on 13 June 1924.

459th Field Artillery Regiment (240-mm H) (ZI) **Organized Reserve Florida**

HQ—*Not initiated,* 1923–24; Jacksonville, FL, 1924–28

Constituted in the O.R. on 2 July 1923 as the 459th F.A. Regt., assigned to the Zone of the Interior, and allotted to the Fourth Corps Area. Initiated in April 1924 with regimental HQ at Jacksonville, FL. Subordinate battalion HQ concurrently organized as follows: 1st Bn. at Jasper, FL; 2d Bn. at Sanford, FL; and 3d Bn. at Tallahassee, FL. Reorganized and redesignated on 13 June 1924 as the 459th F.A. Bn. Conducted summer training with the 5th F.A. at Fort Bragg, NC. Designated mobilization station was Fort Bragg, NC. Primary ROTC feeder school was University of Florida. Demobilized on 5 September 1928.

Commanders, 459th Field Artillery Regiment

Unknown	April 1924–31 March 1925	Maj. Robert C. Bailey	31 March 1925–5 September 1928

460th Field Artillery Regiment (240-mm H) (ZI) **Organized Reserve Ohio**

HQ—*Not initiated,* 1923–26; Cincinnati, OH, 1926–28

Constituted in the O.R. on 2 July 1923 as the 460th F.A. Regt., assigned to the Zone of the Interior, and allotted to the Fifth Corps Area. Reorganized and redesignated on 13 June 1924 as the 460th F.A. Bn. Initiated in February 1926 with HQ at Cincinnati, OH. Primary ROTC feeder school was Xavier University. Demobilized on 5 September 1928.

Commanders, 460th Field Artillery Regiment

Unknown	February 1926–5 September 1928

467th Field Artillery Regiment (75-mm G-H) (ZI) **Organized Reserve North Dakota**

HQ—*Not initiated,* 1923–28

Constituted in the O.R. on 2 July 1923, assigned to the Zone of the Interior, and allotted to the Seventh Corps Area. Btry A (only component authorized) organized in August 1924 at Grand Forks, ND. Btry A relocated on 26 May 1926 to Beach, ND. Btry A inactivated on 1 December 1926. Demobilized on 5 September 1928.

471st Field Artillery Regiment (75-mm G Mtzd) (GHQR) **Organized Reserve New Jersey**

HQ—*Not initiated,* 1921–22; Paterson, NJ 1922–27; *Inactive,* 1927–33

Constituted in the O.R. on 15 October 1921, assigned to the 213th F.A. Brig. (GHQR), and allotted to the Second Corps Area. Initiated on 17 March 1922 with regimental HQ at Paterson, NJ. Subordinate battalion HQ concurrently organized as follows: 1st Bn. at East Orange, NJ, and 2d Bn. at West Hoboken, NJ. Inactivated by December 1927 at Paterson by relief of personnel. Relieved from the 213th F.A. Brig. on 2 July 1929 and assigned to the 78th Div. Concurrently, 3d Bn. constituted, and Hoboken, NJ, designated as the battalion's home station. Additionally, armament changed from 75-mm G (Mtzd) to 155-mm H. Relieved from the 78th Div. on 26 October 1929. Typically conducted Inactive Training Period meetings at the armory of the 112th F.A. at East Orange, NJ. Conducted summer training with the 7th F.A. at Pine Camp, NY. Primary ROTC feeder school was Princeton University. Demobilized on 1 October 1933.

Commanders, 471st Field Artillery Regiment

1st Lt. Robert L. Logan	17 March 1922–9 May 1922	Unknown	ao December 1924–ao May 1927
Capt. Frank S. Jones	9 May 1922–ao June 1922	Maj. Paul Williams	ao May 1927–ao August 1927
Unknown	ao June 1922–13 November 1924	Unknown	ao August 1927–December 1927
Capt. Victor A. Lord	13 November 1924–ao December 1924	*Inactive*	December 1927–1 October 1933

472d Field Artillery Regiment (75-mm G Mtzd) (GHQR) **Organized Reserve New York**

HQ—*Not initiated,* 1921–22; Buffalo, NY 1922–27; *Inactive,* 1927–41

Constituted in the O.R. on 15 October 1921, assigned to the 213th F.A. Brig. (GHQR), and allotted to the Second Corps Area. Initiated on 29 March 1922 with regimental HQ at Buffalo, NY. Subordinate battalion HQ concurrently organized as follows: 1st Bn. at Buffalo, NY, and 2d Bn. at Elmira, NY. Inactivated on 5 December 1927 at Buffalo by relief of personnel. Relieved from the 213th F.A. Brig. on 12 July 1929 and assigned to the 98th Div. Concurrently 3d Bn. constituted and Rochester, NY, designated as the battalion's home station. Additionally, the regiment was reorganized as 155-mm H. Relieved on 26 October 1929 from the 98th Div. Concurrently armament changed from 75-mm G (Mtzd) to 75-mm G-P. On 5 April 1937, Syracuse, NY, designated as HQ on reorganization, but the unit was never organized at that location. Conducted summer training with the 7th F.A. at Pine Camp, NY, or Madison Barracks, NY. Primary ROTC feeder school was Cornell University. Designated mobilization training station was Pine Camp, NY. Location 7 December 1941—*Inactive*.

Status: HHB is inactive in the US Army Reserve as HHB, 472d F.A. Gp.; 1st Bn. is inactive in the US Army Reserve as the 472d Glider F.A. Bn.; 2d Bn. is inactive in the US Army Reserve as the 694th F.A. Bn.

Commanders, 472d Field Artillery Regiment

2d Lt. Elmer C. Baker	29 March 1922–ao May 1922	Unknown	ao May 1923–15 July 1924
Unknown	ao May 1922–23 January 1923	Capt. James A. Webster	15 July 1924–ao August 1924
Lt. Col. Lee A. McCalla	23 January 1923–3 March 1923	Maj. Hinton F. Longino	ao May 1925–22 August 1925
2d Lt. Harrison M. Barker	3 March 1923–ao May 1923	Col. Charles B. Sayre	22 August 1925–5 December 1927
Inactive	5 December 1927–7 December 1941		

473d Field Artillery Regiment (75-mm G Mtzd) (GHQR) **Organized Reserve Pennsylvania**

HQ—Pittston, PA, 1921–29; *Inactive,* 1929–33

Constituted in the O.R. on 15 October 1921, assigned to the 213th F.A. Brig. (GHQR), and allotted to the Third Corps Area. Initiated on 2 November 1921 with regimental HQ at Pittston, PA. Subordinate battalion HQ concurrently organized as follows: 1st Bn. at Scranton, PA, and 2d Bn. at Wilkes-Barre, PA. Inactivated on 11 December 1929 at Pittston by relief of personnel. Conducted summer training at Tobyhanna, PA, or Fort Eustis, VA. Primary ROTC feeder school was Duquesne University. Demobilized on 1 October 1933.

Commanders, 473d Field Artillery Regiment

2d Lt. Stewart C. Marple	2 November 1921–12 November 1921	Maj. Charles S. Yeomans	21 September 1924–June 1927
1st Lt. Louis A. Eaton	12 November 1921–21 November 1921	Lt. Col. James H. Genung Jr.	June 1927–11 December 1929
Capt. William K. Russell	21 November 1921–21 September 1924	*Inactive*	11 December 1929–1 October 1933

474th Field Artillery Regiment (75-mm G Mtzd) (GHQR) **Organized Reserve Ohio/Indiana**

HQ—*Not initiated,* 1921–22; Toledo, OH, 1922–30; *Inactive,* 1930–33

Constituted in the O.R. on 15 October 1921, assigned to the 214th F.A. Brig. (GHQR), and allotted to the Fifth Corps Area. Initiated in June 1922 with regimental HQ at Toledo, OH. Inactivated by March 1930 at Toledo by relief of personnel. Lafayette, IN, designated on 9 July 1931 as HQ on reorganization, but the unit was never organized at that location. Conducted summer training with the 1st Bn., 3d F.A. at Fort Knox, KY. Primary ROTC feeder school was Ohio State University, 1922–29. Demobilized on 1 October 1933.

Commanders, 474th Field Artillery Regiment

Capt. Martin S. Dodd	June 1922–ao January 1923	Unknown	ao January 1923–March 1930
Inactive	March 1930–1 October 1933		

475th Field Artillery Regiment (75-mm G Mtzd) (GHQR) **Organized Reserve Ohio**

HQ—*Not initiated,* 1921–24; Dayton, OH, 1924–41

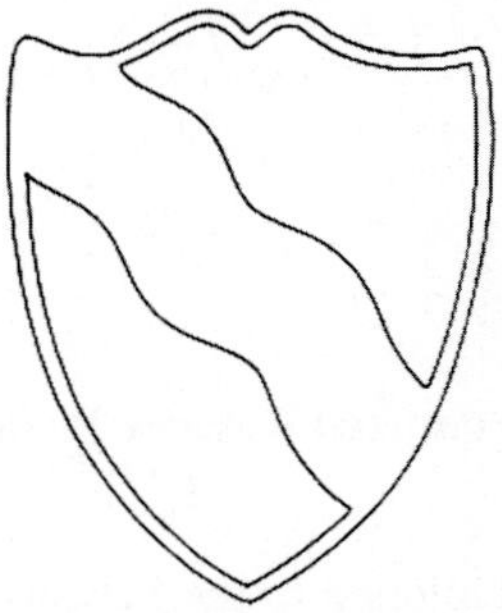

Constituted in the O.R. on 15 October 1921, assigned to the 214th F.A. Brig. (GHQR), and allotted to the Fifth Corps Area. Initiated in September 1924 with regimental HQ at Dayton, OH. Conducted summer training with the 1st Bn., 3d F.A. at Fort Knox, KY. Primary ROTC feeder school was Ohio State University. Location 7 December 1941—Dayton, OH.

Status: Disbanded 26 January 1943.

Commanders, 475th Field Artillery Regiment

Unknown	September 1924–ao July 1930	Maj. William M. Vance	ao June 1934–ao January 1935
Maj. Claude J. Edwards	ao July 1930–ao August 1930	Maj. Clifford E. Shank	ao June 1935–ao June 1937
Unknown	ao August 1930–ao June 1934	Unknown	ao June 1937–7 December 1941

476th Field Artillery Regiment (75-mm G Mtzd) (GHQR) **Organized Reserve Kentucky and Ohio**

HQ—*Not initiated,* 1921–24; Harrodsburg, KY, 1924–41

Constituted in the O.R. on 15 October 1921, assigned to the 214th F.A. Brig. (GHQR), and allotted to the Fifth Corps Area. Initiated in October 1924 with regimental HQ at Harrodsburg, KY. Relieved on 1 October 1933 from the 214th F.A. Brig. Typically conducted Inactive Training Period meetings at the Watterson Hotel in Louisville. Conducted summer training with the 1st Bn., 3d F.A., 1924–34, and 1st Bn., 19th F.A., 1935–41, at Fort Knox, KY. Regiment awarded the Toulmin Trophy for 1934. Primary ROTC feeder school was Eastern Kentucky State Teachers College. Location 7 December 1941—Harrodsburg, KY.

Status: Disbanded on 26 January 1943.

Commanders, 476th Field Artillery Regiment

Unknown	October 1924–5 January 1927	Lt. Col. Joseph R. Gray	January 1932–ao June 1937
Lt. Col. James B. Shea	5 January 1927–January 1932	Unknown	ao June 1937–7 December 1941

477th Field Artillery Regiment (75-mm G Mtzd) (GHQR) **Organized Reserve Illinois**

HQ—*Not initiated,* 1921–22; Rockford, IL, 1922–25; La Salle, IL, 1925–29; *Inactive,* 1929–34 La Salle, IL, 1934–41

Constituted in the O.R. on 15 October 1921, assigned to the 217th F.A. Brig. (GHQR), and allotted to the Sixth Corps Area. Initiated on 6 June 1922 with regimental HQ at Rockford, IL. Subordinate battalion HQ concurrently organized as follows: 1st Bn. at Belvidere, IL, and 2d Bn. at Oregon, IL. Regimental HQ relocated on 28 July 1925 to La Salle, IL. Subordinate battalion HQ concurrently relocated as follows: 1st Bn. to Kewanee, IL, and 2d Bn. to Kankakee, IL. Inactivated about July 1929 at La Salle by relief of personnel. Reorganized from tractor drawn to truck drawn on 13 March 1935. Entire regiment reorganized by June 1934 at La Salle. Inactivated on 18 May 1938 at La Salle by relief of personnel. Conducted summer training most years at Camp McCoy, WI, and some years with the 5th F.A. at Fort Bragg, NC. Primary ROTC feeder school was the University of Illinois. Location 7 December 1941—*Inactive.*

Status: Disbanded 26 January 1943.

Commanders, 477th Field Artillery Regiment

Lt. Col. Bradford Brinton	6 June 1922–15 November 1923	*Inactive*	July 1929–ao June 1934
Lt. Col. George J. Bugbee	15 November 1923–ao June 1928	Unknown	ao June 1934–ao September 1936
Unknown	ao June 1928–July 1929	Lt. Col. Roscoe R. Snapp	ao September 1936–18 May 1938
Inactive	18 May 1938–7 December 1941		

478th Field Artillery Regiment (75-mm G Mtzd) (GHQR) **Organized Reserve Iowa**

HQ—*Not initiated,* 1921–24; Des Moines, IA, 1924–28; Ottumwa, IA, 1928–41

Constituted in the O.R. on 15 October 1921, assigned to the 217th F.A. Brig. (GHQR), and allotted to the Seventh Corps Area. Initiated in November 1924 with regimental HQ at Des Moines, IA. Subordinate battalion HQ concurrently organized as follows: 1st Bn. at Fort Dodge, IA, and 2d Bn. at Ottumwa, IA. Regimental HQ relocated on 3 April 1928 to Ottumwa. Conducted summer training with the 1st Bn., 9th F.A. at Fort Riley, KS, and some years with the 5th F.A. at Fort Bragg, NC. Primary ROTC feeder school was Iowa State College. Location 7 December 1941—Ottumwa, IA.

Status: Disbanded on 26 January 1943.

Commanders, 478th Field Artillery Regiment

Unknown	November 1924–7 December 1941

479th Field Artillery Regiment (75-mm G Mtzd) (GHQR) **Organized Reserve Iowa**

HQ—*Not initiated,* 1921–22; Des Moines, IA, 1922–26; Waterloo, IA, 1926–41

Constituted in the O.R. on 15 October 1921, assigned to the 217th F.A. Brig. (GHQR), and allotted to the Seventh Corps Area. Initiated in June 1922 with regimental HQ at Des Moines, IA. Subordinate battalion HQ concurrently organized as follows: 1st Bn. at Des Moines and 2d Bn. at Sioux City, IA. Entire regiment relocated on 26 May 1926 to Waterloo, IA. Conducted summer training with the 14th F.A. at Camp Sparta/McCoy, WI. Primary ROTC feeder school was Iowa State College. Location 7 December 1941—Waterloo, IA.

Commanders, 479th Field Artillery Regiment

Unknown	June 1922–26 May 1926	Col. Jerome Jackman	26 May 1926–October 1927
Unknown	October 1927–7 December 1941		

480th Field Artillery Regiment (75-mm G-P) (GHQR) **Organized Reserve New Jersey/New York**

HQ—*Not initiated,* 1921–22; Elizabeth, NJ, 1922–27; *Inactive,* 1927–41

Constituted in the O.R. on 15 October 1921, assigned to the 225th F.A. Brig. (GHQR), and allotted to the Second Corps Area. Initiated on 27 March 1922 with regimental HQ at Elizabeth, NJ. Subordinate battalion HQ concurrently organized as follows: 1st Bn. at Englewood, NJ, and 2d Bn. at Camden, NJ. Inactivated on 6 December 1927 at Elizabeth by relief of personnel. Reorganized on 8 May 1929 as 155-mm H. Concurrently, 3d Bn. constituted and Camden designated as the battalion's home station. Relieved on 1 October 1933 from the 225th F.A. Brig. Rochester, NY, designated on 5 April 1937 as HQ on reorganization, but the unit was never organized at that location. Conducted summer training with the 7th F.A. at Pine Camp, NY. Primary ROTC feeder school was Princeton University. Designated mobilization training station was Pine Camp, NY. Location 7 December 1941—*Inactive.*

Status: Disbanded 26 January 1943.

Commanders, 480th Field Artillery Regiment

Capt. Noble S. Warren	27 March 1922–10 March 1923	Unknown	21 February 1924–13 January 1925
Maj. James H. Genung Jr.	12 March 1923–7 June 1923	Maj. Albert C. Demarest	13 January 1925–6 December 1927
Col. Charles R. Lloyd	7 June 1923–21 February 1924	*Inactive*	6 December 1927–7 December 1941

481st Field Artillery Regiment (75-mm G-P) (GHQR) **Organized Reserve New York**

HQ—*Not initiated,* 1921–22; Schenectady, NY, 1922–27; *Inactive,* 1927–33

Constituted in the O.R. on 15 October 1921, assigned to the 225th F.A. Brig. (GHQR), and allotted to the Second Corps Area. Initiated on 10 February 1922 with regimental HQ at Schenectady, NY. Subordinate battalion HQ concurrently organized as follows: 1st Bn. at Utica, NY, and 2d Bn. at Syracuse, NY. Inactivated on 6 December 1927 at Schenectady by relief of personnel. Reorganized on 8 May 1929 as 155-mm H. Concurrently, 3d Bn. constituted and Syracuse designated as the battalion's home station. Conducted summer training with the 7th F.A. at Pine Camp, NY. Primary ROTC feeder school was Cornell University. Demobilized on 1 October 1933.

Commanders, 481st Field Artillery Regiment

Maj. Theodore R. Murphy	10 February 1922–17 March 1922	Lt. Col. Harold Remington	17 March 1922–6 December 1927
Inactive	6 December 1927–1 October 1933		

482d Field Artillery Regiment (75-mm G-P) (GHQR) **Organized Reserve Pennsylvania**

HQ—Sunbury, PA, 1921–29; *Inactive,* 1929–33

Constituted in the O.R. on 15 October 1921, assigned to the 225th F.A. Brig. (GHQR), and allotted to the Third Corps Area. Initiated on 7 November 1921 with regimental HQ at Sunbury, PA. Subordinate battalion HQ concurrently organized as follows: 1st Bn. at Sunbury and 2d Bn. at Shenandoah, PA. Inactivated on 31 July 1929 at Sunbury by relief of personnel. Conducted summer training at Tobyhanna, PA, or Fort Eustis, VA. Conducted summer training at Tobyhanna in 1928 with the 110th F.A. Primary ROTC feeder school was Duquesne University. Demobilized on 1 October 1933.

Commanders, 482d Field Artillery Regiment

1st Lt. Donald W. Simler	7 November 1921–11 February 1922	Unknown	ao January 1924–ao December 1925
Lt. Col. Arthur L. Zulick	11 February 1922–1 March 1922	Maj. Romanus Fellman	ao December 1925–31 July 1929
1st Lt. William E. Montgomery	ao August 1922–ao January 1924	*Inactive*	31 July 1929–1 October 1933

483d Field Artillery Regiment (C) (75-mm G-P) (GHQR) **Organized Reserve Kentucky**

HQ—*Not initiated,* 1921–22; Louisville, KY, 1922–30; *Inactive,* 1930–41

Constituted in the O.R. on 15 October 1921, assigned to the 226th F.A. Brig. (GHQR), and allotted to the Fifth Corps Area. Initiated in 1922 with regimental HQ at Louisville, KY. Inactivated by March 1930 at Louisville by relief of personnel. Lexington, KY, designated as HQ on reorganization, but the unit was never organized at that location. Relieved on 1 October 1933 from the 226th F.A. Brig. Conducted summer training with the 1st Bn., 3d F.A. at Fort Knox, KY. Primary ROTC feeder school was Eastern Kentucky State Teachers College. Location 7 December 1941—*Inactive*.

Status: Disbanded on 6 January 1943.

Commanders, 483d Field Artillery Regiment

Unknown	ao December 1922– March 1930	*Inactive*	March 1930–7 December 1941

484th Field Artillery Regiment (C) (75-mm G-P) (GHQR) **Organized Reserve Ohio**

HQ—*Not initiated,* 1921–22; Xenia, OH, 1922–30; *Inactive,* 1930–33

Constituted in the O.R. on 15 October 1921, assigned to the 226th F.A. Brig. (GHQR), and allotted to the Fifth Corps Area. Initiated in 1922 with regimental HQ at Xenia, OH. Inactivated by March 1930 at Xenia by relief of personnel. Conducted summer training with the 1st Bn., 3d F.A. at Fort Knox, KY. Primary ROTC feeder school was Ohio State University. Demobilized on 1 October 1933.

Commanders, 484th Field Artillery Regiment

Unknown	ao December 1922– March 1930	*Inactive*	March 1930–1 October 1933

485th Field Artillery Regiment (C) (75-mm G-P) (GHQR) **Organized Reserve Ohio/Alabama**

HQ—*Not initiated,* 1921–22; Cincinnati, OH, 1922–27; *Inactive,* 1927–33

Constituted in the O.R. on 15 October 1921, assigned to the 226th F.A. Brig. (GHQR), and allotted to the Fifth Corps Area. Initiated in 1922 with regimental HQ at Cincinnati, OH. Withdrawn from the Fifth Corps Area on 11 January 1927 and allotted to the Fourth Corps Area. Tuskegee, AL, designated on 22 October 1929 as HQ on reorganization, but the unit was never organized at that location. Conducted summer training with the 1st Bn., 3d F.A. at Fort Knox, KY, 1922–26. Primary ROTC feeder school was Xavier University, 1922–27. Demobilized on 1 October 1933.

Commanders, 485th Field Artillery Regiment

Unknown	ao December 1922–11 January 1927	*Inactive*	11 January 1927–1 October 1933

486th Field Artillery Regiment (75-mm G-P) (GHQR) **Organized Reserve Michigan**

HQ—Alpena, MI, 1921–25; Flint, MI, 1925–29; *Inactive,* 1929–41

Constituted in the O.R. on 15 October 1921, assigned to the 227th F.A. Brig. (GHQR), and allotted to the Sixth Corps Area. Initiated on 28 December 1921 with regimental HQ at Alpena, MI. Subordinate battalion HQ concurrently organized as follows: 1st Bn. at Saginaw, MI,and 2d Bn. at Owosso, MI. Regimental HQ relocated on 2 June 1925 to Flint, MI. Concurrently the 2d Bn. relocated to Pontiac, MI. Inactivated about September 1929 at Flint by relief of personnel. Relieved on 1 October 1933 from the 227th F.A. Brig. Reorganized on 13 March 1935 as 105-mm H (TD). Conducted summer training with the 14th F.A. and with the 2d Bn., 3d F.A. at Camp Sparta/McCoy, WI. Primary ROTC feeder school was Michigan State College. Location 7 December 1941—*Inactive.*

Status: Disbanded on 26 January 1943.

Commanders, 486th Field Artillery Regiment

Capt. Frederick H. Loud	28 December 1921–5 April 1922	Lt. Col. Philip K. Fletcher	22 June 1922–September 1929
Maj. Harvey C. Beeson	5 April 1922–22 June 1922	*Inactive*	September 1929–7 December 1941

487th Field Artillery Regiment (75-mm G-P) (GHQR) **Organized Reserve Illinois**

HQ—*Not initiated,* 1921–24; Quincy, IL, 1924–29; *Inactive,* 1929–34; Quincy, IL, 1934–37; Belleville, IL, 1937–41

Constituted in the O.R. on 15 October 1921, assigned to the 227th F.A. Brig. (GHQR), and allotted to the Sixth Corps Area. Initiated on 11 March 1924 with regimental HQ at Quincy, IL. Subordinate battalion HQ concurrently organized as follows: 1st Bn. at Princeton, IL, and 2d Bn. at Joliet, IL. The 1st and 2d Bns. relocated on 28 July 1925 to Macomb and Jacksonville, IL, respectively. Inactivated about December 1929 at Quincy, IL, by relief of personnel. Relieved on 1 October 1933 from the 227th F.A. Brig. Reorganized by June 1934 at Quincy, IL. Reorganized on 13 March 1935 as 105-mm H (TD). Entire regiment relocated on 28 July 1937 to Belleville, IL. Conducted summer training most years with the 2d Bn., 3d F.A. Conducted summer training at Camp McCoy, WI, in 1928 with the units of the 58th F.A. Brig. Primary ROTC feeder school was the University of Illinois. Designated mobilization training station was Camp Sparta, WI. Location 7 December 1941—Belleville, IL.

Status: Disbanded on 26 January 1943.

Commanders, 487th Field Artillery Regiment

Capt. J.C. Reddington	11 March 1924–29 March 1924	*Inactive*	December 1929–ao April 1934
Maj. F.W. Bowles	29 March 1924–4 September 1925	Lt. Col. Walter S. Stanton	ao April 1934–1 September 1936
Lt. Col. Frank L. Rearden	4 September 1925–ao June 1929	Unknown	1 September 1936–7 December 1941

488th Field Artillery Regiment (75-mm G-P) (GHQR) — Organized Reserve Missouri and Kansas/South Dakota

HQ—*Not initiated,* 1921–22; Springfield, MO, 1922–27; *Inactive,* 1927–28; Sioux Falls, SD, 1928–41

Constituted in the O.R. on 15 October 1921, assigned to the 227th F.A. Brig. (GHQR), and allotted to the Seventh Corps Area. Initiated in April 1922 with regimental HQ at Springfield, MO. Subordinate battalion HQ concurrently organized as follows: 1st Bn. at Springfield and 2d Bn. at Clinton, MO. Inactivated on 28 May 1927. Reorganized on 3 April 1928 with the entire regiment at Sioux Falls, SD. Relieved on 1 October 1933 from the 227th F.A. Brig. Reorganized on 5 March 1935 as 105-mm Mtzd (TD). Conducted summer training with the 1st Bn., 9th F.A. at Fort Des Moines, IA. Primary ROTC feeder school was the University of Missouri, 1922–31, and South Dakota State College, 1931–41. Location 7 December 1941—Sioux Falls, SD.

Status: Disbanded on 26 January 1943.

Commanders, 488th Field Artillery Regiment

Unknown	April 1922–7 December 1941

489th Field Artillery Regiment (155-mm G Mtzd) (GHQR) — Organized Reserve Rhode Island/Indiana

HQ—*Not initiated,* 1921–22; Providence, RI, 1922–27; *Inactive*, 1927–30; Gary, IN, 1930–41

Constituted in the O.R. on 15 October 1921, assigned to the 211th F.A. Brig. (GHQR), and allotted to the First Corps Area. Initiated on 10 March 1922 with regimental HQ at Providence, RI. Subordinate battalion HQ concurrently organized as follows: 1st Bn. at Providence; 2d Bn. at Pawtucket, RI; and 3d Bn. at Bristol, RI. Withdrawn from the First Corps Area on 11 January 1927 and allotted to the Fifth Corps Area. Personnel concurrently transferred to the 431st F.A. Reorganized by June 1930 with the entire regiment at Gary, IN. Withdrawn from the O.R. on 1 October 1933, and allotted to the R.A. as an RAI unit. Concurrently relieved from the 211th F.A. Brig. and assigned to the 28th F.A. Brig. (RAI). Conducted summer training with the 258th F.A. at Fort Terry, NY, and at Camp Devens, MA, 1925–26. Conducted summer training at Fort Knox, KY, 1931–40. Primary ROTC feeder schools were Yale University, 1922–27, and Purdue University, 1928–41. Location 7 December 1941—Gary, IN.

Status: Inactive in the US Army Reserve as the 489th Armd. F.A. Bn., a component of the 7th Armd. Div.

Commanders, 489th Field Artillery Regiment

Col. Charles F. Tillinghast	10 March 1922–11 January 1927	Unknown	ao July 1930–ao June 1933
Inactive	11 January 1927–ao June 1930	Lt. Col. Clarence C. Bassett	ao June 1933–December 1933
Lt. Col. George J. Bugbee	ao June 1930–ao July 1930	Lt. Col. Lowell F. Bowers	December 1933–June 1937
Unknown	ao June 1937–7 December 1941		

490th Field Artillery Regiment (155-mm G) (GHQR) **Organized Reserve New York**

HQ—*Not initiated,* 1921–22; Bronx, NY, 1922–28; *Inactive,* 1928–41

Constituted in the O.R. on 15 October 1921, assigned to the 211th F.A. Brig. (GHQR), and allotted to the Second Corps Area. Initiated on 2 November 1922 with regimental HQ at Bronx, NY. Subordinate battalion HQ concurrently organized as follows: 1st Bn. at Manhattan, NY; 2d Bn. at Mount Vernon, NY; and 3d Bn. at Brooklyn, NY. Inactivated on 14 May 1928 at Bronx by relief of personnel. Reorganized on 8 May 1929 as 155-mm H. Syracuse, NY, designated on 5 April 1937 as HQ on reorganization, but the unit was never organized at that location. Conducted summer training with the 2d Bn., 7th F.A. at Pine Camp, NY. Primary ROTC feeder school was Princeton University. Designated mobilization training station was Pine Camp, NY. Location 7 December 1941—*Inactive.*

Status: Disbanded on 26 January 1943.

Commanders, 490th Field Artillery Regiment

Col. George C. Haas	2 November 1922–2 December 1927	Col. William W. Thurston	2 December 1927–14 May 1928
Inactive	14 May 1928–7 December 1941		

491st Field Artillery Regiment (155-mm G) (GHQR) **Organized Reserve Pennsylvania**

HQ—Williamsport, PA, 1921–29; *Inactive,* 1929–41

Constituted in the O.R. on 15 October 1921, assigned to the 215th F.A. Brig. (GHQR), and allotted to the Third Corps Area. Initiated on 12 November 1921 with regimental HQ at Williamsport, PA. Relieved from the 215th F.A. Brig. on 1 July 1927, and assigned to the 182d F.A. Brig. Conducted summer training at Fort Eustis, VA. Primary ROTC feeder school was Duquesne University. Inactivated about 10 May 1929 at Williamsport by relief of personnel. Location 7 December 1941—*Inactive.*

Status: Disbanded 26 January 1943.

Commanders, 491st Field Artillery Regiment

1st Lt. William R. Young	12 November 1921–18 April 1922	Unknown	ao January 1924–26 March 1926
Capt. David R. Brobst	18 April 1922–11 July 1923	Lt. Col. Wilbur S. Barker	26 March 1926–10 May 1929
Capt. Robert S. Lambert	11 July 1923–ao January 1924	*Inactive*	10 May 1929–7 December 1941

492d Field Artillery Regiment (155-mm G) (GHQR) **Organized Reserve Ohio/Indiana**

HQ—*Not initiated,* 1921–22; Toledo, OH, 1922–31; Lafayette, IN, 1931–38; *Inactive,* 1938–41

Constituted in the O.R. on 15 October 1921, assigned to the 215th F.A. Brig. (GHQR), and allotted to the Fifth Corps Area. Initiated on 2 May 1922 with regimental HQ at Toledo, OH. Entire regiment relocated on 9 July 1931 to Lafayette, IN. Regiment awarded the Toulmin Trophy for 1931. Relieved from the 215th F.A. Brig. on 1 October 1933 and assigned to the 28th F.A. Brig. (RAI). Primary ROTC feeder school was Ohio State University, 1922–31, and Purdue University, 1931–38. Conducted summer training at Camp Knox, KY. Withdrawn from the Fifth Corps Area on 1 January 1938 and allotted to the Fourth Corps Area. Location 7 December 1941—*Inactive.*

Status: Disbanded on 26 January 1943.

Commanders, 492d Field Artillery Regiment

Capt. Clifford A. Rowley	2 May 1922–ao September 1924	Col. George Byers	ao June 1929–31 December 1937
Unknown	ao September 1924–ao June 1929	*Inactive*	1 January 1938–7 December 1941

493d Field Artillery Regiment (C) (155-mm G) (GHQR) **Organized Reserve Michigan/Illinois**

HQ—*Not initiated,* 1921–22; Saginaw, MI, 1922–28; Chicago, IL, 1928–33

Constituted in the O.R. on 15 October 1921, assigned to the 216th F.A. Brig. (GHQR), and allotted to the Sixth Corps Area. Initiated in October 1922 with regimental HQ at Saginaw, MI. Subordinate battalion HQ concurrently organized as follows: 1st Bn. at Saginaw; 2d Bn. at Flint, MI; and 3d Bn. at Port Huron, MI. Entire regiment, less 3d Bn., relocated about January 1928 to Chicago, IL. Concurrently 3d Bn. relocated to Detroit, MI. Primary ROTC feeder school was Michigan State College, 1922–30. Designated mobilization training station was Fort Sill, OK. Demobilized on 1 October 1933 and personnel transferred to the 90th F.A. (RAI).

Commanders, 493d Field Artillery Regiment

Unknown	October 1922–1 October 1933

494th Field Artillery Regiment (155-mm G) (GHQR) **Organized Reserve Missouri, Arkansas, and Kansas/Texas/Illinois**

HQ—*Not initiated,* 1921–22; St. Louis, MO, 1922–33; *Inactive,* 1933–36; Waco, TX, 1935–36; Chicago, IL, 1936–37; *Inactive,* 1937–41

Constituted in the O.R. on 15 October 1921, assigned to the 216th F.A. Brig. (GHQR), and allotted to the Seventh Corps Area. Initiated in March 1922 with regimental HQ at St. Louis, MO. Subordinate battalion HQ concurrently organized as follows: 1st Bn. at St. Louis; 2d Bn. at Fort Smith, AR; and 3d Bn. at Salina, KS. Withdrawn from the Seventh Corps Area on 1 October 1933 and allotted to the Eighth Corps Area. Reorganized by December 1935 with regimental HQ at Waco, TX. Withdrawn from the Eighth Corps Area on 5 June 1936 and allotted to the Sixth Corps Area. Entire regiment organized by October 1936 at Chicago, IL. Inactivated on 12 May 1937 at Chicago by relief of personnel. Conducted summer training at Camp Sparta/McCoy, WI, in 1926. Conducted summer training with the 77th F.A. at Fort D.A. Russell, TX, in 1936. Primary ROTC feeder schools were Washington University, 1922–33, and the University of Illinois, 1936–41. Location 7 December 1941—*Inactive.*

Commanders, 494th Field Artillery Regiment

Unknown	March 1922–1 October 1933	Unknown	ao December 1935–12 May 1937
Inactive	1 October 1933–ao December 1935	*Inactive*	12 May 1937–7 December 1941

495th Field Artillery Regiment (C) (240-mm H) (GHQR) **Organized Reserve New York**

HQ—*Not initiated,* 1921–22; Manhattan, NY, 1922–33

Constituted in the O.R. on 15 October 1921, assigned to the 211th F.A. Brig. (GHQR), and allotted to the Second Corps Area. Initiated on 10 February 1922 with entire regiment, less 3d Bn., at Manhattan, NY. The 3d Bn. concurrently organized at Bronx, NY. Conducted summer training in 1925 at Fort Eustis, VA. Primary ROTC feeder school was Princeton University. Demobilized on 1 October 1933.

Commanders, 495th Field Artillery Regiment

Maj. Logan W. Serles	10 February 1922–24 October 1924	Col. Wade A. Carpenter	24 October 1924–1 October 1933

496th Field Artillery Regiment (240-mm H) (GHQR) **Organized Reserve Maryland/District of Columbia**

HQ—*Not initiated,* 1921–22; Easton, MD, 1922–29; *Inactive,* 1929–41

Constituted in the O.R. on 15 October 1921, assigned to the 211th F.A. Brig. (GHQR), and allotted to the Third Corps Area. Initiated on 1 March 1922 with regimental HQ at Easton, MD. Inactivated about August 1929 at Easton by relief of personnel. Washington, DC, designated on 11 December 1929 as HQ on reorganization, but the unit was never organized at that location. Typically conducted Inactive Training Period meetings at the Munitions Building in Washington. Conducted summer training at Tobyhanna, PA, or Fort Eustis, VA. Primary ROTC feeder school was the Virginia Military Institute. Location 7 December 1941—Washington, DC.

Status: Disbanded on 26 January 1943.

Commanders, 496th Field Artillery Regiment

Maj. George W. Small	1 March 1922–27 February 1923	Col. Elisha F. Riggs	27 August 1923–August 1929
Capt. Horace C. Funk	27 February 1923–27 August 1923	*Inactive*	August 1929–7 December 1941

497th Field Artillery Regiment (240-mm H) (GHQR) **Organized Reserve Illinois**

HQ—*Not initiated,* 1921–23; East St. Louis, IL, 1923–25; Chicago, IL, 1925–41

Constituted in the O.R. on 15 October 1921, assigned to the 216th F.A. Brig. (GHQR), and allotted to the Sixth Corps Area. Initiated on 11 March 1923 with the entire regiment at East St. Louis, IL. Relocated on 28 July 1925 to Chicago, IL. Attached to the 1st Provisional Field Artillery Brigade on 8 January 1935. Typically conducted Inactive Training Period meetings at the Federal Building in Edwardsville, IL, 1923–25, and at the Swedish Club in Chicago. Conducted summer training with the 14th F.A. at Camp McCoy, WI. Conducted field artillery CMTC training some years at Camp McCoy as an alternate form of annual training. Primary ROTC feeder school was the University of Illinois. Location 7 December 1941—Chicago, IL.

Status: Disbanded on 26 January 1943.

Commanders, 497th Field Artillery Regiment

Capt. Leslie G. George	14 March 1923–2 April 1923	Lt. Col. Frank L. Reardon	21 March 1923–4 September 1925
	Col. John C. Bohan	4 September 1925–7 December 1941	

498th Field Artillery Regiment (240-mm H) (GHQR) **Organized Reserve Texas/Missouri**

HQ—*Not initiated,* 1921–23; Austin, TX, 1923–24; *Inactive*, 1924–25; Kansas City, MO, 1925–28; *Inactive,* 1928–41

Constituted in the O.R. on 15 October 1921, assigned to the 216th F.A. Brig. (GHQR), and allotted to the Eighth Corps Area. Initiated on 5 March 1923 with regimental HQ at Austin, TX. Withdrawn from the Eighth Corps Area in 1924 and allotted to the Seventh Corps Area. Reorganized by December 1925 with HQ at Kansas City, MO. Subordinate battalion HQ concurrently organized as follows: 1st Bn. at St. Joseph, MO; 2d Bn. at Joplin, MO; and 3d Bn. at Sedalia, MO. Inactivated by April 1928 at Kansas City by relief of personnel. Springfield, MO, designated on 3 April 1928 as HQ on reorganization, but the unit was never organized at that location. Conducted summer training at Fort Riley, KS. Primary ROTC feeder school was the University of Missouri. Location 7 December 1941—*Inactive*.

Status: Disbanded on 26 January 1943.

Commanders, 498th Field Artillery Regiment

2d Lt. R.H. Scales	5 March 1923–December 1924	Unknown	ao December 1925–April 1928
Inactive	December 1924–ao December 1925	*Inactive*	April 1928–7 December 1941

499th Field Artillery Regiment (240-mm H) (GHQR) **Organized Reserve Texas/Iowa/Kansas**

HQ—*Not initiated,* 1921–23; College Station, TX,1923–25; Sioux City, IA, 1925–28; *Inactive,* 1928–41

Constituted in the O.R. on 15 October 1921, assigned to the 215th F.A. Brig. (GHQR), and allotted to the Eighth Corps Area. Initiated on 5 March 1923 with regimental HQ at College Station, TX. Withdrawn from the Eighth Corps Area about January 1925 and allotted to the Seventh Corps Area. Reorganized in 1925 with regimental HQ at Sioux City, IA. Subordinate battalion HQ concurrently organized as follows: 1st Bn. at Sioux City; 2d Bn. at Council Bluffs, IA; and 3d Bn. at Des Moines, IA. Inactivated by April 1928 at Sioux City by relief of personnel. Des Moines designated on 3 April 1928 as HQ on reorganization, but the unit was never organized at that location. Designated HQ changed on 12 October 1931 to Kansas City, KS, but the unit was never organized at that location. Conducted summer training at Fort Riley, KS. Primary ROTC feeder school was Iowa State College, 1923–28. Location 7 December 1941—*Inactive.*

Status: Disbanded on 26 January 1943.

Commanders, 499th Field Artillery Regiment

Unknown	5 March 1923–April 1928	*Inactive*	April 1928–7 December 1941

500th Field Artillery Regiment (240-mm H) (GHQR) **Organized Reserve California, Oregon, and Washington/Ohio**

HQ—*Not initiated,* 1921–22; San Francisco, CA, 1922–25; Spokane, WA, 1925–36; *Inactive,* 1936–37; Cleveland, OH, 1937–41

Constituted in the O.R. on 15 October 1921, assigned to the 215th F.A. Brig. (GHQR), and allotted to the Ninth Corps Area. Initiated on 20 October 1922 with regimental HQ at San Francisco, CA. Subordinate battalion HQ concurrently organized as follows: 1st Bn. at Oakland, CA; 2d Bn. at Portland, OR; and 3d Bn. at Seattle, WA. Regimental HQ and 1st Bn. relocated on 25 September 1925 to Spokane, WA. Withdrawn from the Ninth Corps Area on 5 June 1936 and allotted to the Fifth Corps Area. Reorganized on 5 April 1937 with regimental HQ at Cleveland, OH. Conducted summer training with the 10th F.A. at Fort Lewis, WA, 1922–35. Primary ROTC feeder school was Stanford University, 1922–25; University of Washington, 1925–36; and Ohio State University, 1937–41. Location 7 December 1941—Cleveland, OH.

Status: Disbanded on 26 January 1943.

Commanders, 500th Field Artillery Regiment

2d Lt. Raymond H. Skinner	20 October 1922–ao November 1922	Unknown	ao June 1931–5 June 1936
Unknown	ao November 1922–ao April 1929	*Inactive*	5 June 1936–5 April 1937
Maj. Robert S. LaMotte	ao April 1929–ao June 1931	Unknown	5 April 1937–7 December 1941

560th Field Artillery Regiment (240-mm H) (GHQR) **Organized Reserve Mississippi/Florida/Tennessee**

HQ—*Not initiated,* 1923–24; Jackson, MS, 1924–29; Memphis, TN, 1929–36; Tampa, FL, 1936–41

Constituted in the O.R. on 2 July 1923, assigned to the 207th F.A. Brig. (GHQR), and allotted to the Fourth Corps Area. Initiated on 23 December 1924 with regimental HQ at Jackson, MS. Subordinate battalion HQ concurrently organized as follows: 1st Bn. at Greenwood, MS; 2d Bn. at West Point, MS; and 3d Bn. at Hattiesburg, MS. Entire regiment relocated on 22 October 1929 to Memphis, TN. Entire regiment relocated on 1 July 1936 to Tampa, FL. Conducted summer training with the 5th F.A. at Fort Bragg, NC. Primary ROTC feeder school was the University of Florida. Designated mobilization station was Camp Jackson, SC. Location 7 December 1941—Tampa, FL.

Status: Disbanded on 26 January 1943.

Commanders, 560th Field Artillery Regiment

Unknown	23 December 1924–ao October 1930	Unknown	ao November 1930–ao June 1932
Lt. Col. Richard H. Miller	ao October 1930–15 November 1930	Col. Emmet C. Choate	ao June 1932–15 November 1936
Lt. Col. Ira C. Hopper	15 November 1930–ao November 1930	Col. Lewis E. Goodrich	15 November 1936–ao May 1940
Unknown	ao May 1940–7 December 1941		

561st Field Artillery Regiment (6-inch G) (GHQR) **Organized Reserve New York**

HQ—*Not initiated,* 1921–22; Manhattan, NY, 1922–33

Constituted in the O.R. on 15 October 1921, assigned to the 211th F.A. Brig. (GHQR), and allotted to the Second Corps Area. Initiated on 10 February 1922 with regimental HQ at Manhattan, NY. Subordinate battalion HQ concurrently organized as follows: 1st Bn. at Manhattan; 2d Bn. at Bronx, NY; and 3d Bn. at Ossening, NY. Primary ROTC feeder school was Princeton University. Demobilized on 1 October 1933.

Commanders, 561st Field Artillery Regiment

Maj. Frank E. Emery	10 February 1922–15 May 1922	Maj. Walton Clark Jr.	18 July 1924–3 October 1924
Maj. Nat D. Jackson	15 May 1922–1 July 1922	Capt. Edward L. Jenkins	27 October 1924–ao November 1924
Col. Roger H. Williams	24 July 1922–18 July 1924	Unknown	ao November 1924–1 October 1933

562d Field Artillery Regiment (6-inch G) (GHQR) **Organized Reserve New York**

HQ—*Not initiated,* 1921–22; Brooklyn, NY, 1922–30; *Inactive,* 1930–33

Constituted in the O.R. on 15 October 1921, assigned to the 215th F.A. Brig. (GHQR), and allotted to the Second Corps Area. Initiated on 2 May 1922 with regimental HQ at Brooklyn, NY. Subordinate battalion HQ concurrently organized as follows: 1st Bn. at Manhattan, NY; 2d and 3d Bns. at Brooklyn, NY. Reorganized on 8 May 1929 as 155-mm G. Inactivated on 17 February 1930 at Brooklyn by relief of personnel. Conducted summer training with the 5th F.A. at Fort Bragg, NC. Primary ROTC feeder school was Princeton University. Demobilized on 1 October 1933.

Commanders, 562d Field Artillery Regiment

Unknown	2 May 1922–11 May 1926	Col. Edward C.O. Thomas	11 May 1926–17 February 1930
Inactive	17 February 1930–1 October 1933		

563d Field Artillery Regiment (6-inch G) (GHQR) **Organized Reserve Ohio**

HQ—*Not initiated,* 1921–22; Cincinnati, OH, 1922–33

Constituted in the O.R. on 15 October 1921, assigned to the 216th F.A. Brig. (GHQR), and allotted to the Fifth Corps Area. Initiated in July 1922 with regimental HQ at Cincinnati, OH. Primary ROTC feeder school was Xavier University. Conducted summer training at Fort Knox, KY. Demobilized on 1 October 1933.

Commanders, 563d Field Artillery Regiment

Maj. John H. Burlingame	July 1922–ao September 1924	Unknown	ao September 1924–1 October 1933

564th Field Artillery Regiment (75-mm G-P) (Porto Rican Division) **Organized Reserve Puerto Rico**

HQ—*Not initiated,* 1921–22; San Juan, PR, 1922–27; *Inactive,* 1927–33

Constituted in the O.R. on 15 October 1921 and allotted to the Second Corps Area. Initiated in December 1922 with regimental HQ at San Juan, PR. Subordinate battalion HQ concurrently organized as follows: 1st Bn. at Aguadilla, PR, and 2d Bn. at Humacao, PR. Attached to the 211th Inf. Brig. for control purposes until such time that the Puerto Rican Division would be organized. Withdrawn from allotment to Puerto Rico on 16 March 1927. Primary ROTC feeder school was the University of Puerto Rico. Demobilized on 1 October 1933.

Commanders, 564th Field Artillery Regiment

Unknown	December 1922–16 March 1927	*Inactive*	16 March 1927–1 October 1933

565th Field Artillery Regiment (240-mm H) (GHQR) **Organized Reserve Indiana**

HQ—*Not initiated,* 1923–26; Muncie, IN, 1926–41

Constituted in the O.R. on 2 July 1923, assigned to the GHQR, and allotted to the Fifth Corps Area. Initiated in February 1926 with regimental HQ at Muncie, IN. Regiment awarded the Toulmin Trophy for 1932. Conducted summer training at Fort Knox, KY. Primary ROTC feeder school was Purdue University. Location 7 December 1941—Muncie, IN.

Status: Disbanded 26 January 1943.

Commanders, 565th Field Artillery Regiment

Maj. Russell F. Albert	February 1926–ao July 1930	Col. George J. Bugbee	ao January 1933–ao July 1939
Unknown	ao July 1930–ao January 1933	Unknown	ao July 1939–7 December 1941

566th Field Artillery Regiment (75-mm G Mtzd) (GHQR) **Organized Reserve New York**

HQ—Brooklyn, NY, 1921–41

Constituted in the O.R. on 15 October 1921, assigned to the 222d F.A. Brig. (GHQR), and allotted to the Second Corps Area. Initiated in November 1921 with regimental HQ at Brooklyn, NY. Subordinate battalion HQ concurrently organized as follows: 1st Bn. at Brooklyn and 2d Bn. at Islip, Long Island, NY. Withdrawn from the O.R. on 1 October 1933 and allotted to the R.A. as an RAI unit. Concurrently relieved from the 222d F.A. Brig. (GHQR) and assigned to the 23d F.A. Brig. (GHQR). Typically conducted Inactive Training Period meetings in the 1930s at the Blue Ribbon Restaurant at 145 West 44th Street in New York City, NY. Conducted summer training with the 7th F.A. at Pine Camp, NY, and some years at Fort Hoyle, MD. Primary ROTC feeder school was Princeton University. Location 7 December 1941—Brooklyn, NY.

Commanders, 566th Field Artillery Regiment

Unknown	November 1921–29 March 1922	Maj. Harry C. Miller	16 February 19245–17 June 1924
Capt. Roger B.T. Anderson	29 March 1922–29 April 1922	Lt. Col. Jack D. Rainer	17 June 1924–25 October 1924
Lt. Col. Jack D. Rainer	29 April 1922–16 February 1924	Lt. Col. Robert L. Gray	25 October 1924–17 December 1929
Col. Roger Merrill	17 December 1929–ao June 1941		

567th Field Artillery Regiment (75-mm G Mtzd) (GHQR) **Organized Reserve Illinois**

HQ—*Not initiated,* 1921–22; Taylorville, IL, 1922–41

Constituted in the O.R. on 15 October 1921, assigned to the 221st F.A. Brig. (GHQR), and allotted to the Second Corps Area. Initiated on 4 February 1922 with regimental HQ at Taylorville, IL. Subordinate battalion HQ concurrently organized as follows: 1st Bn. at Macomb, IL, and 2d Bn. at Peoria, IL. The 1st and 2d Bns. relocated on 28 July 1925 to Decatur and Effingham, IL, respectively. Withdrawn from the O.R. on 1 October 1933 and allotted to the R.A. as an RAI unit. Concurrently relieved from the 221st F.A. Brig. (GHQR) and assigned to the 24th F.A. Brig. (GHQR). Attached to the 1st Provisional Field Artillery Brigade on 8 January 1935. Reorganized on 13 March 1935 as 105-mm H (TD). Conducted summer training most years at Camp McCoy, WI. Conducted an experimental camp at the estate of the regimental commander, Col. George E. Seamans, in Taylorville, IL, during the summer of 1924. The camp included the 567th F.A., the 1st Bn. 14th F.A., and F.A. cadets from the ROTC program at the

University of Illinois. Conducted field artillery CMTC training some years at Camp McCoy as an alternate form of annual training. Primary ROTC feeder school was the University of Illinois. Location 7 December 1941—Taylorville, IL.

Commanders, 567th Field Artillery Regiment

Col. George G. Seaman	4 February 1922–8 February 1932	Lt. Col. Leal W. Reese	8 February 1932–1 June 1941

568th Field Artillery Regiment (75-mm G-P) (GHQR) **Organized Reserve Massachusetts/ Missouri/Nebraska**

HQ—*Not initiated,* 1921–23; Boston, MA, 1923; Cambridge, MA, 1923–24; Jefferson City, MO, 1924–26; North Platte, NE, 1926–33

Constituted in the O.R. on 15 October 1921, assigned to the 218th F.A. Brig. (GHQR), and allotted to the First Corps Area. Initiated in January 1923 with the entire regiment at Boston, MA. Regimental HQ relocated on 28 March 1923 to Cambridge, MA. Subordinate battalion HQ concurrently relocated as follows: 1st Bn. at Cambridge and 2d Bn. at Roxbury, MA. Withdrawn from the First Corps Area on 13 June 1924 and allotted to the Seventh Corps Area. Initiated in November 1924 with regimental HQ at Jefferson City, MO. Subordinate battalion HQ concurrently organized as follows: 1st Bn. at Jefferson City and 2d Bn. at St. Louis, MO. Regimental HQ relocated on 26 May 1926 to North Platte, NE. Subordinate battalion HQ concurrently relocated as follows: 1st Bn. to Scottsbluff, NE, and 2d Bn. to North Platte, NE. Entire regiment relocated on 12 October 1931 to North Platte. Primary ROTC feeder school was the University of Missouri. Demobilized on 1 October 1933.

Commanders, 568th Field Artillery Regiment

Lt. Col. Julian I. Chamberlain	January 1923–13 June 1924	*Inactive*	13 June 1924–November 1924
Unknown	November 1924–1 October 1933		

569th Field Artillery Regiment (75-mm G-P) (GHQR) **Organized Reserve New York**

HQ—Manhattan, NY, 1921–29; *Inactive,* 1929–41

Constituted in the O.R. on 15 October 1921, assigned to the 218th F.A. Brig. (GHQR), and allotted to the Second Corps Area. Initiated on 10 December 1921 with regimental HQ at Manhattan. Subordinate battalion HQ concurrently organized as follows: 1st Bn. at Queens, NY, and 2d Bn. at Manhattan. Inactivated by December 1929 at Manhattan by relief of personnel. Reorganized on 5 March 1935 as 105-mm H Mtzd (TD). Buffalo, NY, designated on 5 April 1937 as HQ on organization, but the unit was never organized at that location. Conducted summer training with the 7th F.A. at Pine Camp, NY. Primary ROTC feeder school was Cornell University. Designated mobilization training station was Pine Camp, NY. Location 7 December 1941—*Inactive*.

Status: Disbanded on 26 January 1943.

Commanders, 569th Field Artillery Regiment

Lt. Col. Silas McBee	10 December 1921–ao August 1929	*Inactive*	December 1929–7 December 1941

570th Field Artillery Regiment (75-mm G-P) (GHQR) **Organized Reserve New York**

HQ—*Not initiated,* 1921–22; Bronx, NY, 1922–41

Constituted in the O.R. on 15 October 1921, assigned to the 218th F.A. Brig. (GHQR), and allotted to the Second Corps Area. Initiated on 17 March 1922 with regimental HQ at Bronx, NY. Subordinate battalion HQ concurrently organized as follows: 1st Bn. at White Plains, NY, and 2d Bn. Middletown, NY. Withdrawn from the O.R. on 1 October 1933 and allotted to the R.A. as an RAI unit. Concurrently relieved from the 218th F.A. Brig. (GHQR) and assigned to the 23d F.A. Brig. (GHQR). Participated in an amphibious training exercise at Fire Island in August 1939 with the 3d Bn., United States Marine Corps (U.S.M.C.) Reserve. Withdrawn from the R.A. on 31 July 1940 and allotted to the O.R. Concurrently reorganized as 155-mm H (TD). Typically conducted Inactive Training Period meetings at the Army Building at 39 Whitehall Street in New York City, NY. Conducted summer training with the 7th F.A. at Pine Camp, NY, and some years at Fort Hoyle, MD. Conducted field artillery CMTC training some years at Madison Barracks, NY, as an alternate form of annual training. Primary ROTC feeder schools were Princeton University and Cornell University. Location 7 December 1941—Bronx, NY.

Commanders, 570th Field Artillery Regiment

1st Lt. James P. Kelly	17 March 1922–29 April 1922	Lt. Col James H. Genung Jr.	2 October 1925–July 1927
Lt. Col. Jean A. Jeancon	29 April 1922–5 March 1923	Unknown	July 1927–10 February 1930
Col. Wade H. Carpenter	5 March 1923–16 February 1924	Lt. Col. John D. Groves	10 February 1930–8 January 1932
Col. Roger H. Williams	18 July 1924–2 October 1925	Col. Irving C. Moller	8 January 1932–31 March 1933
Col. Edward J. W. Proffitt	31 March 1933–ao June 1941		

571st Field Artillery Regiment (75-mm G-P) (GHQR) **Organized Reserve Pennsylvania**

HQ—Reading, PA, 1921–31; Pittsburgh, PA, 1931–41

Constituted in the O.R. on 15 October 1921, assigned to the 220th F.A. Brig. (GHQR), and allotted to the Third Corps Area. Initiated on 12 November 1921 with regimental HQ at Reading, PA. Subordinate battalion HQ concurrently organized as follows: 1st Bn. at Reading and 2d Bn. at Coatsville, PA. HQ relocated on 27 February 1931 to Pittsburgh, PA. Conducted summer training most years at Fort Hoyle, MD, and some years at Tobyhanna, PA, or Fort Bragg, NC. Primary ROTC feeder school was Duquesne University. Location 7 December 1941—Pittsburgh, PA.

Status: Disbanded on 26 January 1943.

Commanders, 571st Field Artillery Regiment

Capt. Frank A. Tiffany	12 November 1921–18 November 1921	Maj. George S. Wallace	19 September 1930–18 January 1932
Capt. Philip E. Jackson	18 November 1921–3 November 1922	Lt. Col. Thomas Fitzgerald	21 January 1932–21 April 1934
Maj. Edward S. Gow	3 November 1922–11 June 1926	Lt. Col. Frank F. Hennaman	21 April 1934–July 1935
Col. Edward J.W. Proffitt	11 June 1926–19 September 1930	Lt. Col. William K. McKnight	July 1935–ao June 1940
Unknown	ao June 1940–7 December 1941		

572d Field Artillery Regiment (75-mm G-P) (GHQR) **Organized Reserve Wisconsin**

HQ—*Not initiated,* 1921–25; Wausau, WI, 1925–41

Constituted in the O.R. on 15 October 1921, assigned to the 223d F.A. Brig. (GHQR), and allotted to the Sixth Corps Area. Initiated in September 1925 with regimental HQ at Wausau, WI. Subordinate battalion HQ concurrently organized as follows: 1st Bn. at Wisconsin Rapids, WI, and 2d Bn. at Chippewa Falls, WI. Relieved from the 223d F.A. Brig. on 5 October 1929 and assigned to the 101st Div. Concurrently reorganized as 155-mm H. The newly constituted 3d Bn. was organized at Hudson, WI. Typically conducted Inactive Training Period meetings at the Central Hotel in Wausau. Conducted summer training at Camp McCoy, WI. Conducted field artillery CMTC training some years at Camp McCoy and Fort Sheridan, IL, as an alternate form of annual training. Primary ROTC feeder school was the University of Wisconsin. Designated mobilization training station was Camp Sparta, WI. Location 7 December 1941—Wausau, WI.

Status: Disbanded on 6 August 1942 as the 572d F.A. Bn.

Commanders, 572d Field Artillery Regiment

Unknown	September 1925–11 November 1925	Unknown	ao June 1935–ao November 1936
Lt. Col. Elbert M. Webster	11 November 1925–ao July 1930	Lt. Col. Olin G. Dryer	ao November 1936–June 1939
Unknown	ao July 1930–ao June 1932	Col. Arthur E. Woody	June 1939–June 1940
Lt. Col. Arthur E. Woody	ao June 1932–ao June 1935	Lt. Col. Olin G. Dryer	June 1940–7 December 1941

573d Field Artillery Regiment (155-mm G) (GHQR) **Organized Reserve Pennsylvania**

HQ—York, PA, 1921–29; *Inactive,* 1929–41

Constituted in the O.R. on 15 October 1921, assigned to the 219th F.A. Brig. (GHQR), and allotted to the Third Corps Area. Initiated on 2 November 1921 with regimental HQ at York, PA. Inactivated about August 1929 at York by relief of personnel. Carlisle, PA, designated on 11 December 1929 as HQ on reorganization, but the unit was never organized at that location. Conducted summer training at Fort Eustis, VA. Primary ROTC feeder school was Duquesne University. Location 7 December 1941—*Inactive.*

Status: Disbanded on 26 January 1943.

Commanders, 573d Field Artillery Regiment

Maj. Harris N. Summer	2 November 1921–27 April 1922	Unknown	ao January 1924–April 1925
Unknown	27 April 1922–21 February 1923	Lt. Col. William H. Beckner	ao April 1925–August 1929
Capt. Henry H. Hall	21 February 1923–ao January 1924	*Inactive*	August 1929–7 December 1941

574th Field Artillery Regiment (155-mm G) (GHQR) **Organized Reserve Kentucky**

HQ—*Not initiated,* 1921–24; Louisville, KY, 1924–30; *Inactive,* 1930–37; Paris, KY, 1937–41

Constituted in the O.R. on 15 October 1921, assigned to the 228th F.A. Brig. (GHQR), and allotted to the Fifth Corps Area. Initiated in September 1924 with regimental HQ at Louisville, KY. Inactivated by March 1930 at Louisville by relief of personnel. Relieved from the 228th F.A. Brig. (GHQR) on 1 October 1933 and assigned to the 184th F.A. Brig. (XV Corps). Reorganized on 5 April 1937 at Paris, KY. Conducted summer training with the 1st Bn., 3d F.A., 1925–34, and the 1st Bn., 19th F.A.,1935–40, at Fort Knox, KY. Primary ROTC feeder school was the University of Kentucky. Location 7 December 1941—Paris, KY.

Status: Disbanded on 26 January 1943.

Commanders, 574th Field Artillery Regiment

Unknown	September 1924–March 1930	Maj. Philip Wilson	5 April 1937–ao August 1938
Inactive	March 1930–5 April 1937	Unknown	ao August 1938–7 December 1941

575th Field Artillery Regiment (155-mm G) (GHQR) — Organized Reserve Wisconsin

HQ—*Not initiated,* 1921–25; Sheboygan, WI, 1925–30; *Inactive,* 1930–34; Sheboygan, WI, 1934–37; *Inactive,* 1937–41

Constituted in the O.R. on 15 October 1921, assigned to the GHQR, and allotted to the Sixth Corps Area. Initiated on 29 October 1925 with regimental HQ at Sheboygan, WI. Subordinate battalion HQ concurrently organized as follows: 1st Bn. at Rhinelander, WI; 2d Bn. at Ladysmith, WI; and 3d Bn. at Manitowoc, WI. Inactivated about October 1930 at Sheboygan by relief of personnel. Reorganized by May 1934 at Sheboygan. Inactivated by June 1937 at Sheboygan by relief of personnel. Conducted summer training at Camp McCoy, WI. Primary ROTC feeder school was University of Wisconsin. Location 7 December 1941—*Inactive.*

Status: Disbanded on 26 January 1943.

Commanders, 575th Field Artillery Regiment

Capt. H.C. Runge	29 October 1925–27 March 1926
Maj. Frank L. Gottschalk	27 March 1926–19 March 1928
Maj. James B. Bereth	19 May 1928–October 1930
Inactive	October 1930–ao May 1934
Lt. Col. Otto A. Miller	ao May 1934–ao July 1934
Unknown	ao July 1934–ao June 1937
Inactive	ao June 1937–7 December 1941

576th Field Artillery Regiment (240-mm H) (GHQR) — Organized Reserve New York/New Jersey

HQ—*Not initiated,* 1921–22; Manhattan, NY, 1922–27; *Inactive,* 1927–41

Constituted in the O.R. on 15 October 1921, assigned to the GHQR, and allotted to the Second Corps Area. Initiated on 2 May 1922 with the entire regiment at Manhattan, NY. Inactivated by December 1927 at Manhattan by relief of personnel. Newark, NJ, designated on 5 April 1937 as HQ on organization, but the unit was never organized at that location. Conducted summer training with the 5th F.A. at Fort Bragg, NC. Primary ROTC feeder school was Princeton University. Designated mobilization training station was Pine Camp, NY. Location 7 December 1941—*Inactive.*

Status: Disbanded 26 January 1943.

Commanders, 576th Field Artillery Regiment

Unknown	2 May 1922–26 October 1922
Col. Robert P. Marshall	26 October 1922–8 September 1926
Maj. Samuel G. Rea	ao July 1927–December 1927

577th Field Artillery Regiment (240-mm H) (GHQR) — Organized Reserve New York

HQ—*Not initiated,* 1921–22; Brooklyn, NY, 1922–41

Constituted in the O.R. on 15 October 1921, assigned to the GHQR, and allotted to the Second Corps Area. Initiated on 10 February 1922 with entire regiment, less 3d Bn., at Brooklyn, NY. The 3d Bn. concurrently organized at Manhattan, NY. Typically conducted Inactive Training Period meetings at the armory of the 245th C.A. in the 1920s and later at the Princeton Club at 38th Street and Park Avenue in New York City, NY, in the 1930s. Conducted summer training with the 5th F.A. at Fort Bragg, NC, and some years at Pine Camp, NY. Designated mobilization training station was Pine Camp, NY. Primary ROTC feeder school was Princeton University. Location 7 December 1941—Brooklyn, NY.

Status: Disbanded on 26 January 1943.

Commanders, 577th Field Artillery Regiment

Maj. S.W. Perry	10 February 1922–9 June 1922
Maj. Paul Williams	9 June 1922–10 November 1922
Col. Noel B. Fox	11 November 1922–ao June 1941

578th Field Artillery Regiment (240-mm H) (GHQR) **Organized Reserve Pennsylvania**

HQ—*Not initiated,* 1921–22; Easton, PA, 1922–29; Philadelphia, PA, 1929–36; Harrisburg, PA, 1936–41

Constituted in the O.R. on 15 October 1921, assigned to the 219th F.A. Brig. (GHQR), and allotted to the Third Corps Area. Initiated on 8 November 1921 with regimental HQ at Easton, PA. Subordinate battalion HQ concurrently organized as follows: 1st Bn. at Chataquah, PA; 2d Bn. at Doylestown, PA; and 3d Bn. at Stroudsburg, PA. Regimental HQ and 1st Bn. relocated on 11 December 1929 to Philadelphia, PA. Withdrawn from the O.R. on 1 October 1933, and allotted to the R.A. as an RAI unit. Concurrently relieved from the 219th F.A. Brig. (GHQR) and assigned to the 26th F.A. Brig. (GHQR). HQ relocated in 1936 to Harrisburg, PA. Typically conducted Inactive Training Period meetings at the N.G. armory or Central High School in York, and at the Keystone Building in Harrisburg. Conducted summer training most years with the 5th F.A. at Fort Bragg, NC, and some years at Fort Eustis, VA, or Fort Hoyle, MD. Conducted field artillery CMTC training some years at Fort Hoyle as an alternate form of annual training. Primary ROTC feeder school was Duquesne University. Location 7 December 1941—Harrisburg, PA.

Status: HHB is inactive in the R.A. as HHB, 578th F.A. Gp.; 1st Bn. was disbanded on 10 June 1952 as the 578th F.A. Bn.; 2d Bn. is inactive in the R.A. as the 999th F.A. Bn.

Commanders, 578th Field Artillery Regiment

1st Lt. Albert A. Simpler	8 November 1921–22 February 1922	Lt. Col. Azel W. McNeal	18 November 1930–16 July 1931
Maj. William R. Maull	22 February 1922–27 March 1924	Lt. Col. Wilbur S. Barker	16 July 1931–May 1934
Maj. James H. Genung Jr.	27 March 1924–2 October 1925	Unknown	May 1934–ao May 1936
Unknown	2 October 1925–18 November 1930	Lt. Col. Henry E. Smith	ao May 1936–ao August 1941

579th Field Artillery Regiment (240-mm H) (GHQR) **Organized Reserve Michigan**

HQ—Detroit, MI, 1921–41

Constituted in the O.R. on 15 October 1921, assigned to the GHQR, and allotted to the Sixth Corps Area. Initiated on 9 November 1921 with the entire regiment at Detroit, MI. Withdrawn from the O.R. on 1 October 1933, and allotted to the R.A. as an RAI unit. Conducted summer training most years at Camp McCoy, WI, and some years at Camp Custer, MI. Conducted summer training at Camp Grayling, MI, with the 182d F.A. in 1931 and 1939. Primary ROTC feeder school was Michigan State College. Location 7 December 1941—Detroit, MI.

Status: Inactive in the US Army Reserve as the 579th F.A. Bn.

Commanders, 579th Field Artillery Regiment

Col. William B. Rosevear Jr.	9 November 1921–July 1939	Lt. Col. Aaron C. Moore	July 1939–7 December 1941

580th Field Artillery Regiment (6-inch G) (GHQR) **Organized Reserve Pennsylvania**

HQ—Bethlehem, PA, 1921–31; Philadelphia, PA, 1931–41

Constituted in the O.R. on 15 October 1921, assigned to the 219th F.A. Brig. (GHQR), and allotted to the Third Corps Area. Initiated on 12 November 1921 with regimental HQ at Bethlehem, PA. Subordinate battalion HQ concurrently organized as follows: 1st Bn. at Bethlehem; 2d Bn. at Muach Chunk, PA; and 3d Bn. at Allentown, PA. HQ relocated on 27 February 1931 to Philadelphia, PA. Withdrawn from the O.R. on 1 October 1933, and allotted to the R.A. as an RAI unit. Concurrently relieved from the 219th F.A. Brig. (GHQR) and assigned to the 26th F.A. Brig. (GHQR). Conducted summer training with the 109th F.A. at Tobyhanna, PA; the 5th F.A. at Fort Bragg, NC; or the 6th F.A. at Fort Hoyle, MD. Conducted field artillery CMTC training some years at Fort Hoyle as an alternate form of annual training. Primary ROTC feeder school was Duquesne University. Location 7 December 1941—Philadelphia, PA.

Commanders, 580th Field Artillery Regiment

2d Lt. Harry O. Sugden	12 November 1921–ao October 1922	Col. James H. Genung Jr.	5 May 1933–9 April 1935
1st Lt. John J. McGinley	ao January 1924–ao February 1924	Lt. Col. Willard R. Ginder	9 April 1935–2 January 1936
Unknown	ao February 1924–10 January 1928	Col. Philip P. Cole	2 January 1936–24 July 1939
Col. Edward J.W. Proffitt	10 January 1928–27 March 1933	Lt. Col. Brenton G. Wallace	24 July 1939–21 March 1940
Col. Philip P. Cole	21 March 1940–ao January 1941		

581st Field Artillery Regiment (6-inch G) (GHQR) **Organized Reserve Illinois**

HQ—*Not initiated,* 1921–22; Peoria, IL, 1922–24; Champaign, IL, 1924–25; Chicago, IL, 1925–33

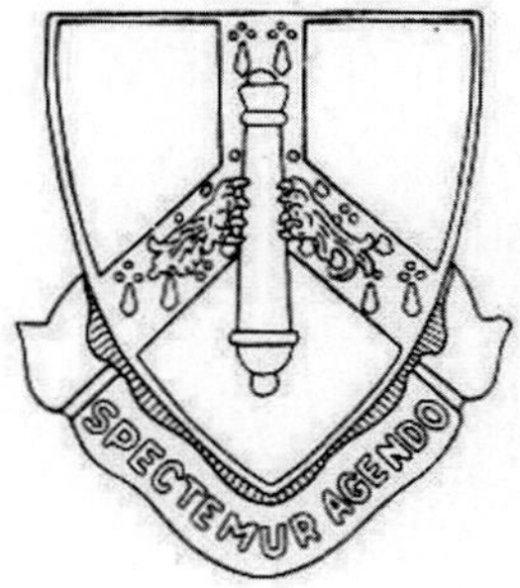

Constituted in the O.R. on 15 October 1921, assigned to the GHQR, and allotted to the Sixth Corps Area. Initiated on 4 December 1922 with regimental HQ at Peoria, IL. Entire regiment relocated on 4 May 1923 to Peoria. Regimental HQ relocated on 18 April 1924 to Champaign, IL. Subordinate battalion HQ concurrently relocated as follows: 1st and 2d Bn. remained at Peoria; 3d Bn. relocated to Bloomington, IL. Entire regiment relocated on 28 July 1925 to Chicago, IL. Conducted summer training at Camp McCoy, WI. Designated mobilization training station was Fort Sill, OK. Primary ROTC feeder school was the University of Chicago. Demobilized on 1 October 1933.

Commanders, 581st Field Artillery Regiment

Lt. Col. George B. Sayre	4 December 1922–9 February 1926	Lt. Col. Harold T. Pease	9 February 1926–16 December 1929
Col. Irving Odell	16 December 1929–1 October 1933		

600th Field Artillery Regiment (6-inch G) (GHQR) **Organized Reserve Minnesota**

HQ—*Not initiated,* 1928–33

Constituted in the O.R. on 5 September 1928, assigned to the GHQR, and allotted to the Seventh Corps Area. Minneapolis, MN, designated on 12 October 1931 as the regimental HQ on organization, but the unit was never organized. Demobilized on 1 October 1933.

601st Field Artillery Regiment (155-mm G) (GHQR) **Organized Reserve Washington**

HQ—*Not initiated,* 1928–30; Seattle, WA, 1930–33

Constituted in the O.R. on 5 September 1928, assigned to the GHQR, and allotted to the Ninth Corps Area. Initiated in April 1930 with the entire regiment at Seattle, WA. Conducted summer training with the 10th F.A. at Camp Lewis, WA. Demobilized on 1 October 1933.

Commanders, 601st Field Artillery Regiment

Unknown	April 1930–1 October 1933

861st Field Artillery Regiment (75-mm G-H) (61st Cavalry Division) **Organized Reserve New York**

HQ—New York City, NY, 1921–41

Constituted in the O.R. on 15 October 1921 as the 461st F.A. Bn. (75-mm G-H), assigned to the 61st Cav. Div., and allotted to the Second Corps Area. Initiated on 13 September 1921 with the entire battalion at New York City, NY. Reorganized and redesignated on 1 July 1929 as the 861st F.A. Regt. Conducted summer training with the 2d Bn., 7th F.A. and 2d Bn., 25th F.A. at Pine Camp, NY. Primary ROTC feeder school was Princeton University. Designated mobilization training station was Pine Camp, NY. Location 7 December 1941—New York City, NY.

Status: Disbanded on 26 January 1943.

Events: 267

Commanders, 861st Field Artillery Regiment

Maj. Axel F. Hatch	1 July 1929–7 January 1930	Lt. Col. Axel F. Hatch	17 March 1934–14 November 1935
Col. Arthur H. Carter	7 January 1930–3 August 1934	Col. Charles M. Piper	14 November 1935–16 August 1941
Col. Michael J. Fibich	16 August 1941–ao December 1941		

862d Field Artillery Regiment (75-mm G-H) (62d Cavalry Division) **Organized Reserve Maryland**

HQ—*Not initiated,* 1921–22; Baltimore, MD, 1922–36; Towson, MD, 1936–41

Constituted in the O.R. on 15 October 1921 as the 462d F.A. Bn. (75-mm G-H), assigned to the 62d Cav. Div., and allotted to the Third Corps Area. Initiated in January 1922 with regimental HQ at Baltimore, MD. Reorganized and redesignated on 1 July 1929 as the 862d F.A. Regt. HQ relocated in 1936 to Towson, MD. Typically conducted Inactive Training Period meetings at the Post Office Building in Baltimore. Conducted summer training most years with the 6th F.A. at Fort Hoyle, MD, and some years with the 16th F.A. at Camp George G. Meade, MD. Conducted field artillery CMTC training some years at Fort Hoyle as an alternate form of annual training. Primary ROTC feeder school was Duquesne University. Location 7 December 1941—Towson, MD.

Status: Disbanded on 26 January 1943.

Commanders, 862d Field Artillery Regiment

Col. Roger S.B. Hartz	1 July 1929–December 1937	Maj. Frank Gosnell Jr.	March 1938–ao January 1940
Lt. Col. Ralph C. Bishop	December 1937–March 1938	Unknown	ao January 1940–7 December 1941

863d Field Artillery Regiment (75-mm G-H) (63d Cavalry Division) **Organized Reserve North Carolina**

HQ—*Not initiated,* 1921–22; Charlotte, NC, 1922–41

Constituted in the O.R. on 15 October 1921 as the 463d F.A. Bn. (75-mm G-H), assigned to the 63d Cav. Div., and allotted to the Fourth Corps Area. Initiated on 24 May 1922 with regimental HQ at Charlotte, NC. Reorganized and redesignated on 1 July 1929 as the 863d F.A. Regt. Conducted summer training with the 5th F.A. at Fort Bragg, NC. Provided a number of officers to the 113th F.A. for the 1938 Third Army Maneuver in the DeSoto National Forest. Primary ROTC feeder school was North Carolina State College. Location 7 December 1941—Charlotte, NC.

Status: Disbanded on 26 January 1943.

Commanders, 863d Field Artillery Regiment

Capt. Charles S. Manning	1 July 1929–25 October 1930	Col. Robert L. Pittman	16 May 1937–ao May 1940
Col. Harry S. Berry	25 October 1930–16 May 1937	Unknown	ao May 1940–7 December 1941

864th Field Artillery Regiment (75-mm G-H) (64th Cavalry Division) **Organized Reserve Kentucky/Ohio**

HQ—*Not initiated,* 1921–22; Lexington, KY, 1922–30; Louisville, KY, 1930–37; Columbus, OH, 1937–41

Constituted in the O.R. on 15 October 1921 as the 464th F.A. Bn. (75-mm G-H), assigned to the 64th Cav. Div., and allotted to the Fifth Corps Area. Initiated on 13 February 1922 with regimental HQ at Lexington, KY. Reorganized and redesignated on 1 July 1929 as the 864th F.A. Regt. HQ successively relocated as follows: to Louisville, KY, in 1930; and to Columbus, OH, on 5 April 1937. Conducted summer training with the 1st Bn., 3d F.A., 1929–34, and the 1st Bn., 19th F.A., 1935–41, at Fort Knox, KY. Primary ROTC feeder school was the University of Kentucky. Location 7 December 1941—Columbus, OH.

Status: Disbanded on 26 January 1943.

Commanders, 864th Field Artillery Regiment

Maj. Charles Dobbs	1 July 1929–ao August 1929	Lt. Col. Hart G. Foster	ao August 1933–ao June 1937
Unknown	ao August 1929–ao August 1933	Unknown	ao June 1937–7 December 1941

865th Field Artillery Regiment (75-mm G-H) (65th Cavalry Division) **Organized Reserve Illinois**

HQ—*Not initiated,* 1921–22; Chicago, IL, 1922–41

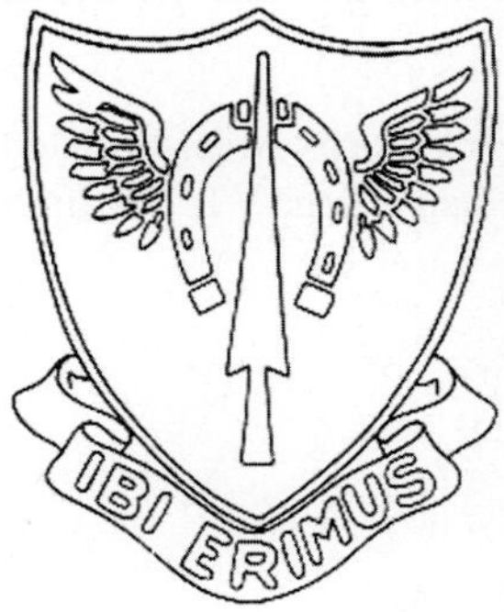

Constituted in the O.R. on 15 October 1921 as the 465th F.A. Bn. (75-mm G-H), assigned to the 65th Cav. Div., and allotted to the Sixth Corps Area. Initiated on 4 May 1922 with the entire battalion at Chicago, IL. Reorganized and redesignated on 1 July 1929 as the 865th F.A. Regt. Newly constituted elements (2d and 3d Bns.) organized at Chicago. Reorganized on 27 July 1935 as 75-mm H. Typically conducted Inactive Training Period meetings at the 122d F.A. armory, the Army-Navy Club, or the 65th Cav. Div. HQ in Chicago. Conducted regular equestrian training with the horses of the 1st Sq., 14th Cav. at Fort Sheridan, IL. Conducted summer training with the 1st Bn., 14th F.A., 1921–27, and the 2d Bn., 3d F.A., 1927–39, at Camp McCoy, WI, or Fort Sheridan, IL. Conducted summer training in June 1935 with the 58th F.A. Brig. at Camp McCoy, WI. Conducted field artillery CMTC training some years at Camp McCoy as an alternate form of annual training. Primary ROTC feeder school was the University of Chicago. Location 7 December 1941—Chicago, IL.

Status: Disbanded on 26 January 1943.

Commanders, 865th Field Artillery Regiment

Col. George Richardson	1 July 1929–May 1931	Lt. Col. Louis E. Legner	ao June 1932–ao April 1934
Maj. Earl W. Harkness	May 1931–ao June 1931	Col. Irving Odell	ao January 1935–7 December 1941

866th Field Artillery Regiment (75-mm G-H) (66th Cavalry Division) — Organized Reserve Missouri/Kansas

HQ—*Not initiated,* 1921–22; Kansas City, MO, 1922–26; Topeka, KS, 1926–41

Constituted in the O.R. on 15 October 1921 as the 466th F.A. Bn. (75-mm G-H), assigned to the 66th Cav. Div., and allotted to the Seventh Corps Area. Initiated in January 1922 in western Missouri with regimental HQ at Kansas City, MO. HQ relocated on 26 May 1926 to Topeka, KS, and reorganized in eastern Kansas. Reorganized and redesignated on 1 July 1929 as the 866th F.A. Regt. Entire regiment relocated on 12 October 1931 to Topeka, KS. Typically conducted Inactive Training Period meetings, 1922–26, at the 110th Engrs. armory or the O.R. Center building at 20th and Vine Streets in Kansas City. Conducted summer training with the 9th F.A. at Fort Riley, KS, and some years with the units of the 60th F.A. Brig. Primary ROTC feeder school was the University of Nebraska, 1922–31, and the University of Kansas, 1931–41. Location 7 December 1941—Topeka, KS.

Status: Disbanded 26 January 1943.

Commanders, 866th Field Artillery Regiment

Col. William H. Donahue	1 July 1929–October 1931	Col. Joe W. Leedom	October 1931–ao January 1940
	Unknown	ao January 1940–7 December 1941	

1101st Field Artillery Training Regiment (ZI) — Organized Reserve Connecticut

HQ—Willamantic, CT, 1929–41

Constituted in the O.R. in 1929, assigned to the Zone of the Interior, and allotted to the First Corps Area. Initiated on 1 November 1929 with regimental HQ at Willamantic, CT. Conducted summer training at Fort Ethan Allen, VT. Location 7 December 1941—Willamantic, CT.

Commanders, 1101st Field Artillery Training Regiment

Unknown	1 November 1929–7 December 1941

1102d Field Artillery Training Regiment (ZI) — Organized Reserve Massachusetts

HQ—Andover, MA, 1929–41

Constituted in the O.R. in 1929, assigned to the Zone of the Interior, and allotted to the First Corps Area. Initiated on 1 November 1929 with regimental HQ at Andover, MA. Conducted summer at Fort Ethan Allen, VT. Location 7 December 1941—Andover, MA.

Commanders, 1102d Field Artillery Training Regiment

Unknown	1 November 1929–7 December 1941

Chapter 21

Field Artillery Battalions

1st Cav. Div. Web site

The 82d Field Artillery Battalion on parade at Fort Bliss, TX.

Field Artillery battalions provided indirect and direct fire support for the ground gaining arms.

Organization

As with the field artillery regiments, the separate battalions were armed with several distinct types of weapons in this period. These consisted of 75-mm Gun (G), 75-mm Howitzer (H), 2.95-in Vickers-Maxim (VM), 155-mm H, 155 G, and 240-mm H weapons. The prime mover for each type of weapon depended on the mission and echelon of command to which they were assigned. With the exception of the 83d Field Artillery (F.A.) Battalion (Bn.), which was tractor drawn until 1927, the 75-mm G battalions were horse drawn. The two 75-mm H battalions were designated as pack units, though the 2d F.A. Bn. was actually organized as a portee unit during its brief existence. The other pack unit, the 4th F.A. Bn., was the only battalion armed with the 2.95-in VM, a British-made mountain gun, though the 24th F.A. Regiment (Regt.) in the Philippines was also equipped with the same weapon. The remaining battalions were truck-drawn organizations. In general, those battalions assigned to support divisions were horse drawn, pack, or portee units; and those assigned to corps and General Headquarters Reserve (GHQR) field artillery brigades were truck drawn.

There were 30 separate field artillery battalions in the Regular Army (R.A.) in the interwar period. Only six of those served on Active Duty and most had only a brief existence. All but one of the active service battalions were organized from preexisting regiments and all of them had disappeared by April 1930 after being reabsorbed by a reorganized regiment. The other 24 R.A. battalions were Regular Army Inactive (RAI) units and only 1 of those was organized with reservists.

There were only four separate field artillery battalions authorized in the National Guard (N.G.) (the 141st and 167th Bns. were the same organization) during this period. Those battalions were assigned to the four Guard cavalry divisions. They were active as separate battalions. The two active units (the 141st and 168th F.A. Bns.) were absorbed by new regiments between 1932 and 1939. The remaining two battalions were reorganized and redesignated as regiments in a “not organized” status in 1939.

A total of 19 field artillery battalions were constituted and allotted to the Organized Reserve (O.R.) between 1921 and 1923. Of these, six were horse-drawn 75-mm G battalions assigned to the O.R. cavalry divisions. All six of these battalions were functional units and were later expanded and redesignated as field artillery regiments in 1929. The remaining 13 battalions were a mixture of 75-mm G, 155-mm G, 155-mm H, and 240-mm H units. Only five of these were known to have been initiated. Since these organizations were assigned to the Zone of the Interior, it appears that most of these battalions were to be assigned to various training centers as training support units. Two were assigned to Fort Sill, OK, for mobilization purposes, and Fort Bragg, a major artillery training post, was designated as the mobilization station for several others. All 13 were demobilized in 1928 and replaced by RAI units in the mobilization plans. It is unlikely that any of the five initiated Zone of the Interior battalions were functional units.

Training

Training opportunities and activities for field artillery battalions were generally the same as that for field artillery regiments of the same component (i.e., R.A., N.G., or O.R.).

Separate Battalion of Mountain Artillery (75-mm H) (Pack) (Panama Canal Department)

HQ—Gatun, CZ, 1919–21; Corozal, CZ, 1921

Active in the R.A. at Gatun, CZ, as of January 1919 and assigned to the Panama Canal Department. Transferred on 1 June 1921 to Corozal, CZ. Concurrently demobilized and personnel and equipment transferred to the newly activated 1st Bn., 22d F.A.

Commanders, Separate Battalion of Mountain Artillery

Maj. William C. Houghton	ao January 1921–1 June 1921

2d Field Artillery Battalion (75-mm H) (Portee) (Panama Canal Division)

HQ—Fort Davis, CZ, 1927–30

Organized on 1 September 1927 by redesignation of 1st Bn., 4th F.A. Regt. (Pack) at Fort Davis, CZ, as the 2d F.A. Bn. Reorganized as a portee unit, and concurrently assigned to the Panama Canal Division. Attached to the 19th Infantry (Inf.) Brigade (Brig.) on 1 July 1928. Consolidated with the inactive 1st Bn., 2d F.A. on 30 April 1930 and redesignated as 1st Bn., 2d F.A. at Fort Davis. Concurrently reorganized as a pack artillery unit.

Events: 53, 58, 69, 81, 101

Commanders, 2d Field Artillery Battalion

Maj. John N. Eager	1 September 1927–14 June 1928	Lt. Col. Ned B. Rehkopf	20 July 1928–1 May 1930

4th Field Artillery Battalion (2.95 VM) (Pack) (2d Cavalry Division)

HQ—Fort McIntosh, TX, 1927–28; Fort Robinson, NE, 1928–30

Organized on 24 October 1927 by redesignation of 2d Bn., 4th F.A. Regt. at Fort McIntosh, TX, as the 4th F.A. Bn. Concurrently assigned to the 2d Cavalry (Cav.) Division (Div.). Assigned reserve personnel from Texas relieved on 27 April 1928 pending transfer of the battalion. Battalion marched 500 miles overland on a change of station from Fort McIntosh to Fort Robinson, NE, during May–June 1928. Its mission at Fort Robinson was to provide support to the newly revived Pack Field Artillery Board. Conducted a 500-mile march from Fort Robinson to Fort Meade, SD, and return during July–August 1928. Redesignated 2d Bn., 4th F.A. Regt. on 29 March 1930.

Organization Day: 24 October. Chosen to commemorate the battalion's redesignation on 24 October 1927. Adopted 25 March 1929.

Commanders, 4th Field Artillery Battalion

Maj. Joseph J. Rogers 1 September 1927–24 October 1927
Lt. Col. William F. Morrison 24 October 1927–22 December 1928
Lt. Col. Laurin L. Lawson 22 December 1928–29 March 1930

31st Field Artillery Battalion (75-mm G-H) (ZI) **Regular Army Inactive**

HQ—*Not organized,* 1928–41

Constituted in the R.A. on 5 September 1928, allotted to the First Corps Area, and assigned to the Zone of the Interior. Unit further allotted to the area of Massachusetts for mobilization purposes. Assigned to the First Army on 1 October 1933. Withdrawn from allotment to the First Corps Area on 5 June 1936 and allotted to the Second Corps Area. New York City, NY, designated as headquarters (HQ) on organization, but the unit was never organized at that location. Location 7 December 1941—*Not organized.*

32d Field Artillery Battalion (75-mm G-H) (ZI) **Regular Army Inactive**

HQ—*Not organized,* 1928–41

Constituted in the R.A. on 5 September 1928, allotted to the First Corps Area, and assigned to the Zone of the Interior. Unit further allotted to the area of Massachusetts for mobilization purposes. Assigned to the First Army on 1 October 1933. Withdrawn from allotment to the First Corps Area on 5 June 1936 and allotted to the Second Corps Area. New York City, NY, designated as HQ on organization, but the unit was never organized at that location. Location 7 December 1941—*Not organized.*

33d Field Artillery Battalion (75-mm G-H) (ZI) **Regular Army Inactive**

HQ—*Not organized,* 1928–41

Constituted in the R.A. on 5 September 1928, allotted to the Third Corps Area, and assigned to the Zone of the Interior. Assigned to the Third Army on 1 October 1933. Location 7 December 1941—*Not organized.*

34th Field Artillery Battalion (75-mm G-H) (ZI) **Regular Army Inactive**

HQ—*Not organized,* 1928–41

Constituted in the R.A. on 5 September 1928, allotted to the Third Corps Area, and assigned to the Zone of the Interior. Assigned to the Third Army on 1 October 1933. Location 7 December 1941—*Not organized.*

35th Field Artillery Battalion (75-mm G-H) (ZI) **Regular Army Inactive**

HQ—*Not organized,* 1928–41

Constituted in the R.A. on 5 September 1928, allotted to the Third Corps Area, and assigned to the Zone of the Interior. Assigned to the Third Army on 1 October 1933. Location 7 December 1941—*Not organized.*

36th Field Artillery Battalion (75-mm G-H) (ZI) **Regular Army Inactive**

HQ—*Not organized,* 1928–41

Constituted in the R.A. on 5 September 1928, allotted to the Fourth Corps Area, and assigned to the Zone of the Interior. Assigned to the Third Army on 1 October 1933. Location 7 December 1941—*Not organized.*

37th Field Artillery Battalion (75-mm G-H) (ZI) **Regular Army Inactive**

HQ—*Not organized,* 1928–41

Constituted in the R.A. on 5 September 1928, allotted to the Fourth Corps Area, and assigned to the Zone of the Interior. Assigned to the Third Army on 1 October 1933. Location 7 December 1941—*Not organized.*

38th Field Artillery Battalion (75-mm G-H) (ZI) **Regular Army Inactive**

HQ—*Not organized,* 1928–41

Constituted in the R.A. on 5 September 1928, allotted to the Fourth Corps Area, and assigned to the Zone of the Interior. Assigned to the Third Army on 1 October 1933. Location 7 December 1941—*Not organized.*

39th Field Artillery Battalion (75-mm G-H) (ZI) **Regular Army Inactive**

HQ—*Not organized,* 1928–41

Constituted in the R.A. on 5 September 1928, allotted to the Fourth Corps Area, and assigned to the Zone of the Interior. Assigned to the Third Army on 1 October 1933. Location 7 December 1941—*Not organized.*

40th Field Artillery Battalion (75-mm G-H) (ZI) **Regular Army Inactive**

HQ—*Not organized,* 1928–41

Constituted in the R.A. on 5 September 1928, allotted to the Fourth Corps Area, and assigned to the Zone of the Interior. Assigned to the Third Army on 1 October 1933. Location 7 December 1941—*Not organized.*

41st Field Artillery Battalion (75-mm G-H) (ZI) **Regular Army Inactive**

HQ—*Not organized,* 1928–41

Constituted in the R.A. on 5 September 1928, allotted to the Fourth Corps Area, and assigned to the Zone of the Interior. Assigned to the Third Army on 1 October 1933. Location 7 December 1941—*Not organized.*

42d Field Artillery Battalion (75-mm G-H) (ZI) **Regular Army Inactive**

HQ—*Not organized,* 1928–35; Chicago, IL, 1934–41

Constituted in the R.A. on 5 September 1928, allotted to the Sixth Corps Area, and assigned to the Zone of the Interior. Assigned to the Second Army on 1 October 1933. Organized by April 1934 with O.R. personnel as an RAI unit with HQ at Chicago, IL. Designated mobilization station was Camp McCoy, WI. Location 7 December 1941—Chicago, IL.

43d Field Artillery Battalion (75-mm G-H) (ZI) **Regular Army Inactive**

HQ—*Not organized,* 1928–41

Constituted in the R.A. on 5 September 1928, allotted to the Seventh Corps Area, and assigned to the Zone of the Interior. Fort Meade, SD, designated as HQ location on organization, but the unit was never organized at that location. Assigned to the Fourth Army on 1 October 1933. Location 7 December 1941—*Not organized.*

44th Field Artillery Battalion (75-mm G-H) (ZI) **Regular Army Inactive**

HQ—*Not organized,* 1928–41

Constituted in the R.A. on 5 September 1928, allotted to the Seventh Corps Area, and assigned to the Zone of the Interior. Fort Meade, SD, designated as HQ location on organization, but the unit was never organized at that location. Assigned to the Fourth Army on 1 October 1933. Location 7 December 1941—*Not organized.*

45th Field Artillery Battalion (75-mm G-H) (ZI) **Regular Army Inactive**

HQ—*Not organized,* 1928–41

Constituted in the R.A. on 5 September 1928, allotted to the Seventh Corps Area, and assigned to the Zone of the Interior. Fort Meade, SD, designated as HQ location on organization, but the unit was never organized at that location. Assigned to the Fourth Army on 1 October 1933. Location 7 December 1941—*Not organized.*

46th Field Artillery Battalion (75-mm G-H) (ZI) **Regular Army Inactive**

HQ—*Not organized,* 1928–41

Constituted in the R.A. on 5 September 1928, allotted to the Ninth Corps Area, and assigned to the Zone of the Interior. Assigned to the Fourth Army on 1 October 1933. San Francisco, CA, designated as HQ location on organization, but the unit was never organized at that location. Demobilized on 12 September 1935.

47th Field Artillery Battalion (75-mm G-H) (ZI) **Regular Army Inactive**

HQ—*Not organized,* 1928–41

Constituted in the R.A. on 5 September 1928, allotted to the Ninth Corps Area, and assigned to the Zone of the Interior. Assigned to the Fourth Army on 1 October 1933. San Francisco, CA, designated as HQ location on organization, but the unit was never organized at that location. Demobilized on 12 September 1935.

48th Field Artillery Battalion (75-mm G-H) (ZI) **Regular Army Inactive**

HQ—*Not organized,* 1928–41

Constituted in the R.A. on 5 September 1928, allotted to the Ninth Corps Area, and assigned to the Zone of the Interior. Assigned to the Fourth Army on 1 October 1933. Seattle, WA, designated as HQ location on organization, but the unit was never organized at that location. Demobilized on 12 September 1935.

49th Field Artillery Battalion (75-mm G-H) (ZI) **Regular Army Inactive**

HQ—*Not organized,* 1928–41

Constituted in the R.A. on 5 September 1928, allotted to the Fourth Corps Area, and assigned to the Zone of the Interior. Assigned to the Third Army on 1 October 1933. Location 7 December 1941—*Not organized.*

50th Field Artillery Battalion (75-mm G-H) (ZI) **Regular Army Inactive**

HQ—*Not organized,* 1928–41

Constituted in the R.A. on 5 September 1928, allotted to the Fourth Corps Area, and assigned to the Zone of the Interior. Assigned to the Third Army on 1 October 1933. Location 7 December 1941—*Not organized.*

51st Field Artillery Battalion (75-mm G-H) (ZI) **Regular Army Inactive**

HQ—*Not organized,* 1928–41

Constituted in the R.A. on 5 September 1928, allotted to the Fourth Corps Area, and assigned to the Zone of the Interior. Assigned to the Third Army on 1 October 1933. Location 7 December 1941—*Not organized.*

52d Field Artillery Battalion (75-mm G-H) (ZI) **Regular Army Inactive**

HQ—*Not organized,* 1928–41

Constituted in the R.A. on 5 September 1928, allotted to the Fifth Corps Area, and assigned to the Zone of the Interior. Assigned to the Third Army on 1 October 1933. Indianapolis, IN, designated as HQ location on organization, but the unit was never organized at that location. Location 7 December 1941—*Not organized.*

53d Field Artillery Battalion (75-mm G-H) (ZI) **Regular Army Inactive**

HQ—*Not organized,* 1928–41

Constituted in the R.A. on 5 September 1928, allotted to the Fifth Corps Area, and assigned to the Zone of the Interior. Assigned to the Third Army on 1 October 1933. Owensboro, KY, designated as HQ location on organization, but the unit was never organized at that location. Location 7 December 1941—*Not organized.*

54th Field Artillery Battalion (75-mm G-H) (ZI) **Regular Army Inactive**

HQ—*Not organized,* 1928–41

Constituted in the R.A. on 5 September 1928, allotted to the Fifth Corps Area, and assigned to the Zone of the Interior. Assigned to the Third Army on 1 October 1933. Cincinnati, OH, designated as HQ location on organization, but the unit was never organized at that location. Location 7 December 1941—*Not organized.*

82d Field Artillery Battalion (75-mm G-H) (1st Cavalry Division)

HQ—Fort Bliss, TX, 1921–30

Stationed at Fort Bliss, TX, as of June 1919 as the 1st Bn., 82d F.A. Redesignated 82d F.A. Bn. (Horse) on 9 September 1921 and assigned to the 1st Cav. Div. Redesignated 1st Bn., 82d F.A. on 17 March 1930.

Organization Day: 16 June. Chosen to commemorate the regiment's baptism of fire on 16 June 1919 when Battery (Btry) A fired into Juarez, Mexico, during the Battle of Juarez.

Events: 3, 30, 65, 83, 97

Commanders, 82d Field Artillery Battalion

Lt. Col. Albert S. Fuger	9 September 1921–30 September 1921	Capt. John M. Jenkins	16 June 1926–4 August 1926
Maj. Henry L.C. Jones	30 September 1921–21 July 1923	Maj. Alfred P. Sands	4 August 1926–10 July 1929
Maj. William H. Rucker	21 July 1923–16 June 1926	Maj. John P. Lucas	10 July 1929–17 March 1930

83d Field Artillery Battalion (75-mm G) (8th Division)

HQ—Fort Benning, GA, 1927–30

Arrived at the port of New York on 18 January 1919 on the U.S. Army Transport (U.S.A.T.) *President Grant* as the 1st Bn., 83d F.A. an element of the 8th Div. Transferred to Camp Mills, NY, on 18 January 1919 and to Camp Knox, KY, on 23 January 1919. Regiment relieved from the 8th Div. on 5 September 1919. The 1st Bn. conducted a 623-mile march from Camp Knox to Camp Benning, GA, 15 September–30 October 1920. Assigned to the Infantry School as a school support and demonstration unit. Regiment transferred to Camp Bragg, NC, on 5 December 1921. Regiment less 1st Bn. inactivated on 7 January 1922 at Camp Bragg. Regiment demobilized on 28 February 1927 and 1st Bn. concurrently reorganized as 83d F.A. Bn. The 83d F.A. Bn. reorganized on 1 May 1927 from tractor drawn to horse drawn. Btry A awarded the Knox Trophy for 1929. The 83d F.A. Bn. assigned on 1 January 1930 to the 8th Div. Regiment reconstituted on 17 March 1930 and assigned to the 8th Div. The 83d F.A. Bn. concurrently redesignated 1st Bn. at Fort Benning.

Commanders, 83d Field Artillery Battalion

Maj. Robert S. Donaldson	28 February 1927–30 June 1927	Maj. Lloyd E. Jones	1 July 1927–31 July 1929
Maj. Frank K. Ross	31 July 1929–17 March 1930		

84th Field Artillery Battalion (75-mm G-H) (2d Cavalry Division) **Regular Army Inactive**

HQ—*Inactive,* 1921–27; Fort Collins, CO, 1927–30

Stationed at Fort Bliss, TX, as of June 1919 as the 2d Bn., 82d F.A. The 2d Bn. inactivated on 9 September 1921, redesignated 84th F.A. Bn. (Horse), assigned to the 2d Cav. Div. and allotted to the Eighth Corps Area. Organized on 31 July 1926 with O.R. personnel as an RAI unit with HQ at Fort Collins, CO. Affiliated with the Colorado Agricultural College on 10 June 1927 and reorganized at Fort Collins as an RAI unit with personnel from the Reserve Officers' Training Corps (ROTC) detachment and O.R. officers commissioned from the program. Relieved from the 2d Cav. Div. on 15 August 1927 and assigned to the 3d Cav. Div. Conducted summer training most years at Fort Riley, KS, and some years at Fort Bliss with the 82d F.A. Bn. Redesignated 2d Bn., 82d F.A. and relieved from the 3d Cav. Div. on 17 March 1930.

Events: 54, 121, 143

Commanders, 84th Field Artillery Battalion

Unknown	31 July 1926–10 June 1927
Maj. John P. Lucas*	10 June 1927–28 June 1929
Maj. Yarrow D. Veasley*	28 June 1929–17 March 1930

*RAI commanders: R.A. officers who were concurrently PMS&T at the Colorado Agricultural College.

141st Separate Battalion, Field Artillery (Horse) (75-mm G) (23d Cavalry Division) **Louisiana National Guard**

HQ—New Orleans, LA, 1927–39

Constituted as the 167th Separate (Sep.) Bn., F.A. (Horse) in June 1921 and assigned to the 23d Cav. Div. Allotted to the state of Louisiana in December 1925. Organized on 1 September 1926 by the redesignation of the 1st Bn., 141st F.A. Regt. (organized as 2d Bn., 141st F.A. Regt. in New Orleans, LA, and federally recognized on 2 May 1922; redesignated 1st Bn., 141st F.A. Regt. on 18 July 1922). Redesignated 141st Sep. Bn., F.A. (Horse) on 14 January 1927. Called up to perform flood relief duties at New Orleans, 26 April–4 June 1927. Reorganized and redesignated 141st F.A. Bn. (Mtz) on 5 June 1937. Conducted annual summer training at Camp Beauregard, LA, 1926–39. Reorganized and redesignated 1st Bn., 141st F.A. on 6 June 1939.

Events: 255, 300

Commander, 141st Field Artillery Battalion (Horse)

Lt. Col. Henry B. Curtis	14 January 1927–6 June 1939

165th Separate Battalion, Field Artillery (Horse) (75-mm G) (21st Cavalry Division) **Virginia National Guard**

HQ—*Not organized,* 1921–40

Constituted in the N.G. as the 165th Sep. Bn., F.A. (Horse) in June 1921 and assigned to the 21st Cav. Div. Allotted to the state of Virginia in April 1927. Reorganized and redesignated 165th F.A. Regt. (75-mm G Mtz) in January 1939.

166th Separate Battalion, Field Artillery (Horse) (75-mm G) (22d Cavalry Division) **Wisconsin/ Pennsylvania National Guard**

HQ—*Not organized,* 1921–39

Constituted in the N.G. as 166th Sep. Bn., F.A. (Horse) in June 1921, assigned to the 22d Cav. Div., and allotted to the state of Wisconsin. Medical Department Detachment organized and federally recognized on 7 April 1922 at Superior, WI; inactivated by June 1923. Milwaukee designated in January 1935 as HQ on organization, but the unit was never organized at that location. Converted from 75-mm G to 75-mm H on 27 July 1935. Withdrawn from allotment to the state of Wisconsin in February 1939 and allotted to the state of Pennsylvania. Concurrently redesignated 166th F.A. Regt.

167th Separate Battalion, Field Artillery (Horse) (75-mm G) (23d Cavalry Division) **Louisiana National Guard**

HQ—*Not organized,* 1921–26; New Orleans, LA, 1926–27

Constituted in the N.G. as the 167th Sep. Bn., F.A. (Horse) in June 1921 and assigned to the 23d Cav. Div. Allotted in December 1925 to Alabama. Withdrawn from the state of Alabama on 31 August 1926 and allotted to the state of Louisiana. Organized on 1 September 1926 by the redesignation of the 1st Bn., 141st F.A. Regt. (organized as 2d Bn., 141st F.A. Regt. in New Orleans, LA, and federally recognized on 2 May 1922; redesignated 1st Bn., 141st F.A. Regt. on 18 July 1922) as the 167th Sep. Bn., F.A. (Horse). Redesignated 141st Sep. Bn., F.A. (Horse) on 14 January 1927.

Commander, 167th Separate Battalion, Field Artillery (Horse)

Lt. Col. Henry B. Curtis	1 September 1926–14 January 1927

168th Separate Battalion, Field Artillery (Horse) (75-mm G) (24th Cavalry Division) **North Dakota/ Colorado National Guard**

HQ—*Not organized,* 1921–26; Denver, CO, 1926–33

Constituted in the N.G. in June 1921 as the 168th Sep. Bn., F.A. (Horse) and assigned to the 24th Cav. Div. On 14 September 1921, allotted to the state of North Dakota. Withdrawn from the state of North Dakota in March 1926 and allotted to the state of Colorado. Organized by the redesignation of the 1st Bn., 158th F.A. on 1 July 1926 as the 168th Sep. Bn., F.A. (Horse). HQ Btry and combat train called up to perform strike duty at the Columbine Mine near Boulder, CO, 21 November 1927–6 April 1928. Conducted annual summer training at Camp George West, CO. Reorganized and redesignated 1st Bn., 168th F.A. Regt. on 1 August 1933.

Commander, 168th Separate Battalion, Field Artillery (Horse)

Maj. William Q. Howell	1 July 1926–1 August 1933

461st Field Artillery Battalion (75-mm G-H) (61st Cavalry Division) **Organized Reserve New York**

HQ—New York City, NY, 1921–29

Constituted in the O.R. on 15 October 1921, assigned to the 61st Cav. Div., and allotted to the Second Corps Area. Initiated on 13 September 1921 with battalion HQ at New York City, NY. Conducted summer training with the 7th F.A. at Pine Camp, NY. Primary ROTC feeder school was Princeton University. Reorganized and redesignated on 1 July 1929 as the 861st F.A. Regt.

Commanders, 461st Field Artillery Battalion

Maj. Paul H.M. Converse	13 September 1921–4 April 1923	Capt. Duncan McD. Little	March 1928–5 April 1929
Maj. George W.L. Prettyman	4 April 1923–March 1928	Maj. George W.L. Prettyman	5 April 1929–30 June 1929

462d Field Artillery Battalion (75-mm G-H) (62d Cavalry Division) **Organized Reserve Maryland**

HQ—*Not initiated,* 1921–22; Baltimore, MD, 1922–29

Constituted in the O.R. on 15 October 1921, assigned to the 62d Cav. Div., and allotted to the Third Corps Area. Initiated in January 1922 with battalion HQ at Baltimore, MD. Typically conducted Inactive Training Period meetings at the Post Office Building in Baltimore. Conducted summer training with the 16th F.A. at Fort George G. Meade, MD, and with the 6th F.A. at Fort Hoyle, MD. Primary ROTC feeder school was Duquesne University. Reorganized and redesignated on 1 July 1929 as the 862d F.A. Regt.

Commanders, 462d Field Artillery Battalion

Maj. Joseph A.W. Inglehart	January 1922–8 January 1925	Maj. Roger S.B. Hartz	19 October 1926–13 February 1928
Capt. Frank Gosnell Jr.	8 January 1925–4 February 1925	Maj. Frank Gosnell Jr.	13 February 1928–1 October 1928
Maj. Frank B. Ober	4 February 1925–19 October 1926	Lt. Col. Roger S.B. Hartz	1 October 1928–1 July 1929

463d Field Artillery Battalion (75-mm G-H) (63d Cavalry Division) **Organized Reserve North Carolina**

HQ—*Not initiated,* 1921–22; Charlotte, NC, 1922–29

Constituted in the O.R. on 15 October 1921, assigned to the 63d Cav. Div., and allotted to the Fourth Corps Area. Initiated on 24 May 1922 with battalion HQ at Charlotte, NC. Conducted summer training with the 2d Bn., 16th F.A. at Fort Bragg, NC. Primary ROTC feeder school was North Carolina State College. Designated mobilization training station was Fort Oglethorpe, GA. Reorganized and redesignated on 1 July 1929 as the 863d F.A. Regt.

Commanders, 463d Field Artillery Battalion

Maj. James H. Carson	29 May 1922–18 December 1922	Unknown	ao September 1925–ao May 1929
Maj. John W. Moore	18 December 1922–ao September 1925	Capt. Charles S. Manning	ao May 1929–30 June 1929

464th Field Artillery Battalion (75-mm G-H) (64th Cavalry Division) **Organized Reserve Kentucky**

HQ—*Not initiated,* 1921–22; Lexington, KY, 1922–29

Constituted in the O.R. on 15 October 1921, assigned to the 64th Cav. Div., and allotted to the Fifth Corps Area. Initiated on 13 February 1922 with battalion HQ at Lexington, KY. Conducted summer training with the 1st Bn., 3d

F.A. at Fort Knox, KY. Primary ROTC feeder school was Eastern Kentucky State Teachers College. Reorganized and redesignated on 1 July 1929 as the 864th F.A. Regt.

Commanders, 464th Field Artillery Battalion

Maj. William S. Webb	13 February 1922–ao September 1924	Unknown	ao September 1924–ao August 1925
Maj. Charles Dobbs	ao August 1925–30 June 1929		

465th Field Artillery Battalion (75-mm G-H) (65th Cavalry Division) **Organized Reserve Illinois**

HQ—*Not initiated,* 1921–22; Galesburg, IL, 1922–25; Chicago, IL, 1925–29

Constituted in the O.R. on 15 October 1921, assigned to the 65th Cav. Div., and allotted to the Sixth Corps Area. Initiated on 4 May 1922 with battalion HQ at Galesburg, IL. HQ relocated on 28 July 1925 to Chicago, IL. Typically conducted Inactive Training Period meetings at the 122d F.A. armory, the Army-Navy Club, or the 65th Cav. Div. HQ in Chicago. Conducted summer training with the 2d Bn., 3d F.A. at Fort Sheridan, IL, and some years at Camp McCoy, WI. Primary ROTC feeder school was the University of Illinois. Reorganized and redesignated on 1 July 1929 as the 865th F.A. Regt.

Commanders, 465th Field Artillery Battalion

Capt. Carter Jenkins	4 May 1922–20 April 1923	Maj. Earl W. Harkness	22 June 1926–14 December 1928
Maj. Robert W. Fernwald	20 April 1923–22 June 1926	Lt. Col. George Richardson	14 December 1928–30 June 1929

466th Field Artillery Battalion (75-mm G-H) (66th Cavalry Division) **Organized Reserve Missouri/Kansas**

HQ—*Not initiated,* 1921–22; Kansas City, MO, 1922–26; Topeka, KS, 1926–29

Constituted in the O.R. on 15 October 1921, assigned to the 66th Cav. Div., and allotted to the Seventh Corps Area. Initiated in January 1922 with battalion HQ at Kansas City, MO. HQ relocated on 26 May 1926 to Topeka, KS. Conducted regular equestrian training the horses of the 114th Cav. at the cavalry armory in Topeka. Conducted summer training with the 9th F.A. at Fort Riley, KS. Primary ROTC feeder school was the University of Missouri, 1922–26, and Kansas State Agricultural College, 1927–29. Reorganized and redesignated on 1 July 1929 as the 866th F.A. Regt.

Commanders, 466th Field Artillery Battalion

Unknown	January 1922–15 May 1924	Maj. R.G. Bryant	15 May 1924–30 June 1929

559th Field Artillery Battalion (240-mm H) (GHQR) **Organized Reserve Florida**

HQ—*Not initiated,* 1923–24; Miami, FL, 1924–41

Constituted in the O.R. on 2 July 1923 as the 559th F.A. Regt., assigned to the 207th F.A. Brig. (GHQR), and allotted to the Fourth Corps Area. Reorganized and redesignated on 5 May 1924 as the 559th F.A. Bn. Initiated in October 1924 with HQ at Miami, FL. Conducted summer training with the 5th F.A. at Fort Bragg, NC. Primary ROTC feeder school was the University of Florida. Location 7 December 1941—Tampa, FL.

Commanders, 559th Field Artillery Battalion

Unknown	October 1924–7 December 1941

582d Field Artillery Battalion (75-mm G-H) (ZI) **Organized Reserve Mississippi**

HQ—*Not initiated,* 1923–24

Constituted in the O.R. on 2 July 1923, assigned to the Zone of the Interior, and allotted to the Fourth Corps Area. Columbus, MS, designated as HQ on organization, but the unit was never organized at that location. Designated mobilization station was Fort Bragg, NC. Demobilized on 13 June 1924.

583d Field Artillery Battalion (75-mm G-H) (ZI) **Organized Reserve**

HQ—*Not initiated,* 1923–24

Constituted in the O.R. on 2 July 1923, assigned to the Zone of the Interior, and allotted to the Fifth Corps Area. Demobilized on 13 June 1924.

584th Field Artillery Battalion (75-mm G-H) (ZI) **Organized Reserve**

HQ—*Not initiated,* 1923–24

Constituted in the O.R. on 2 July 1923, assigned to the Zone of the Interior, and allotted to the Ninth Corps Area. Demobilized on 13 June 1924.

585th Field Artillery Battalion (75-mm G-H) (ZI) **Organized Reserve**

HQ—*Not initiated,* 1923–24

Constituted in the O.R. on 2 July 1923, assigned to the Zone of the Interior, and allotted to the Eighth Corps Area. Demobilized on 13 June 1924.

586th Field Artillery Battalion (155-mm H) (ZI) **Organized Reserve Florida**

HQ—*Not initiated,* 1923–24

Constituted in the O.R. on 2 July 1923, assigned to the Zone of the Interior, and allotted to the Fourth Corps Area. Pensacola, FL, designated as HQ on organization, but the unit was never organized at that location. Designated mobilization station was Fort Bragg, NC. Demobilized on 13 June 1924.

587th Field Artillery Battalion (155-mm H) (ZI) **Organized Reserve**

HQ—*Not initiated,* 1923–28

Constituted in the O.R. on 2 July 1923, assigned to the Zone of the Interior, and allotted to the Fifth Corps Area. Demobilized on 5 September 1928.

588th Field Artillery Battalion (240-mm H) (ZI) **Organized Reserve Oklahoma**

HQ—*Not initiated,* 1923–28

Constituted in the O.R. on 2 July 1923, assigned to the Zone of the Interior, and allotted to the Eighth Corps Area. Fort Sill, OK, designated on 10 July 1925 as the HQ on organization, but the unit was never organized at that location. Mobilization assignment was to support the Field Artillery School. Designated mobilization station was Fort Sill. Demobilized on 5 September 1928.

589th Field Artillery Battalion (240-mm H) (ZI) **Organized Reserve California**

HQ—*Not initiated,* 1923–26; Los Angeles, CA, 1926–28

Constituted in the O.R. on 2 July 1923, assigned to the Zone of the Interior, and allotted to the Ninth Corps Area. Initiated in March 1926 with HQ at Los Angeles, CA. Demobilized on 5 September 1928.

Commanders, 593d Field Artillery Battalion

Maj. William M. Montgomery	March 1926–5 September 1928

590th Field Artillery Battalion (155-mm G) (ZI) **Organized Reserve Florida**

HQ—*Not initiated,* 1923–24; Palatka, FL, 1924–28

Constituted in the O.R. on 2 July 1923, assigned to the Zone of the Interior, and allotted to the Fourth Corps Area. Initiated on 30 April 1924 with HQ at Palatka, FL. Conducted summer training with the 17th F.A. at Fort Bragg, NC. Designated mobilization station was Fort Bragg, NC. Demobilized on 5 September 1928.

Commanders, 590th Field Artillery Battalion

Unknown	30 April 1924–27 January 1925	Maj. Frank J. Malone	27 January 1925–5 September 1928

591st Field Artillery Battalion (155-mm G) (ZI) **Organized Reserve Ohio**

HQ—*Not initiated,* 1923–24; Cleveland, OH, 1924–28

Constituted in the O.R. on 2 July 1923, assigned to the Zone of the Interior, and allotted to the Fifth Corps Area. Initiated in September 1924 with HQ at Cleveland, OH. Typically conducted Inactive Training Period meetings at the Bulkey Building in Cleveland. Demobilized on 5 September 1928.

Commanders, 591st Field Artillery Battalion

Unknown	September 1924–5 September 1928

592d Field Artillery Battalion (155-mm G) (ZI) **Organized Reserve Oklahoma**

HQ—*Not initiated,* 1923–28

Constituted in the O.R. on 2 July 1923, assigned to the Zone of the Interior, and allotted to the Eighth Corps Area. Fort Sill, OK, designated on 10 July 1925 as the HQ on organization, but the unit was never organized at that location. Mobilization assignment was to support the Field Artillery School. Designated mobilization station was Fort Sill. Demobilized on 5 September 1928.

593d Field Artillery Battalion (155-mm G) (ZI) **Organized Reserve California**

HQ—*Not initiated,* 1923–26; San Francisco, CA, 1926–28

Constituted in the O.R. on 2 July 1923, assigned to the Zone of the Interior, and allotted to the Ninth Corps Area. Initiated in March 1926 with HQ at San Francisco, CA. Demobilized on 5 September 1928.

Commanders, 593d Field Artillery Battalion

Maj. Russell P. Tyler	March 1926–5 September 1928

Chapter 22

Observation Battalions (Sound and Flash)

USASC Photo, NA II

Soldiers conduct training on a sound detection system, circa 1925.

Field Artillery observation battalions provided the detection and spotting capabilities for General Headquarters Reserve (GHQR) and corps field artillery brigades to perform counterbattery fires against enemy artillery positions.

Organization

Field Artillery observation battalions consisted of a headquarters (HQ) battery (btry) and two line batteries composed of two sound and flash detection platoons. The batteries were generally deployed on or near the front lines in a series of sound and flash teams. The teams attempted to determine the location of enemy artillery by individual observation (flash) and sound detection with sensitive microphones. The intent was to have two or more teams detect an enemy gun position and pinpoint the location through the triangularization process. The enemy location could then be sent to an artillery fire direction center, which would plot the position and provide firing data to a supporting battery.

There were 38 sound and flash battalions constituted during the interwar period—10 in the Regular Army (R.A.), 3 in the National Guard (N.G.), and the remainder in the Organized Reserve (O.R.). Only the

Observation Battalion (Sound & Flash), Corps Artillery, 1930

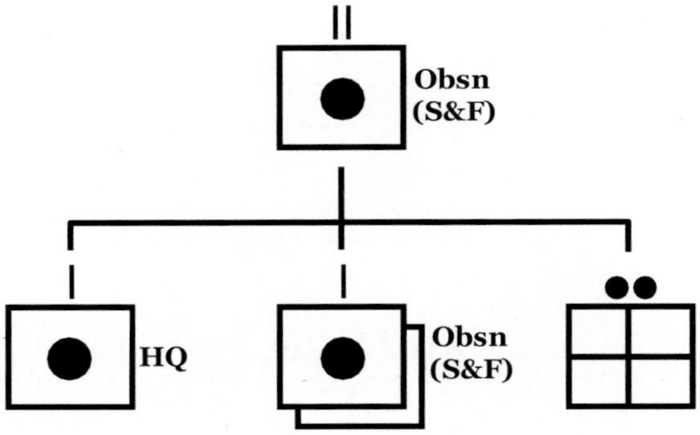

T/O:	153W
Effective:	1 July 1930
Commander:	Maj.
Officers:	22
W. O.	--
Enlisted:	408
Total:	430

Key Equipment:	
Cars, various	33
Tractors, various	5
Trucks, various	25
Machine guns, AA	6
Sound Ranging Sets	2

Observation battalion organization.

1st Observation (Obsn.) Battalion (Bn.) was in active service before 1940, but all of the remaining R.A. battalions were active as Regular Army Inactive (RAI) units.

There were only three battalions authorized in the N.G. during this period. None of the three were ever organized and all were placed on the deferred list in 1923 as Deferred National Guard (DNG) units. All three were withdrawn in 1927 and presumably demobilized.

Not including the 3 DNG battalions, 22 sound and flash battalions were constituted and allotted to the O.R. With the exception of two of the deferred battalions, all of these battalions were initiated at some point during the period. Many were later demobilized due to the constitution of the RAI battalions in 1933.

Training

The majority of the RAI and O.R. battalions appear to have been pool units and, therefore, held no meetings during the Inactive Training Period. Training opportunities for the personnel of these units was rather limited given the small number of units and until 1934, only one sound and flash battery was active in the R.A. Consequently, these organizations were sent to summer camp as units on an infrequent basis. The personnel were more often sent as individuals and formed into provisional units at the camp. Generally, the units and personnel trained with the 1st Obsn. Bn. at Fort Bragg and with the sound and flash section of the Field Artillery School at Fort Sill. These two installations were also the designated mobilization training station for the majority of the sound and flash battalions. Additionally, the units had the opportunity to send personnel to attend the sound and flash course periodically conducted for the Army at the University of Pennsylvania in the 1930s and early 1940s.

1st Observation Battalion (Sound and Flash) (IV Corps)

HQ—*Not organized,* 1929–34; Fort Bragg, NC, 1934–41

Constituted in the R.A. on 29 April 1929, assigned to the 13th Field Artillery (F.A.) Brigade (Brig.) (IV Corps), and allotted to the Fourth Corps Area. Activated on 1 December 1934 (Btry A, constituted on 18 July 1922 as the 1st Obsn. Btry (Flash) and activated on 7 August 1922 at Fort Bragg, NC, already active), less Btry B, at Fort Bragg, NC. Btry B activated on 1 May 1939 at Fort Bragg. Relieved with the 13th F.A. Brig. from the IV Corps on 1 November 1940 and assigned to the I Corps. Redesignated on 4 November 1940 as the 1st F.A. Obsn. Bn. Location 7 December 1941—Fort Bragg, NC.

Events: 94, 96, 121, 255, 281, 293, 296, 300, 330

2d Observation Battalion (Sound and Flash) (II Corps) **Regular Army Inactive**

HQ—*Not organized,* 1933–37; Syracuse, NY, 1937–40; Fort Sill, OK, 1940–41

Constituted in the R.A. on 1 October 1933, assigned to the 20th F.A. Brig. (II Corps), and allotted to the Second Corps Area. Organized on 23 April 1937 with O.R. personnel as an RAI unit at Syracuse, NY. Designated mobilization training station was Fort Bragg, NC, 1933–40. Activated on 1 June 1940, less Reserve personnel, at Fort Sill, OK. Concurrently relieved from the 20th F.A. Brig. (II Corps) and assigned to the 18th F.A. Brig. (VIII Corps). Location 7 December 1941—Fort Sill, OK.

Events: 317, 328

3d Observation Battalion (Sound and Flash) (III Corps) **Regular Army Inactive**

HQ—Philadelphia, PA, 1933–40; *Inactive,* 1940–41; Fort Bragg, NC, 1941

Constituted in the R.A. on 1 October 1933, assigned to the 21st F.A. Brig. (III Corps), and allotted to the Third Corps Area. Organized in late 1933 with O.R. personnel as an RAI unit at Philadelphia, PA. Inactivated on 9 July 1940 at Philadelphia by relief of personnel. Designated mobilization training station was Fort Bragg, NC, 1933–40. Activated on 1 June 1941 at Fort Bragg, and assigned to the First Army. Concurrently attached to the Fort Bragg Provisional Field Artillery Brigade. Location 7 December 1941—Fort Bragg, NC.

Events: 330

7th Observation Battalion (Sound and Flash) (VII Corps) **Regular Army Inactive**

HQ—*Not organized,* 1933–38; Montgomery, AL, 1938–41; Fort Bragg, NC, 1941

Constituted in the R.A. on 1 October 1933, assigned to the 17th F.A. Brig. (VII Corps), and allotted to the Seventh Corps Area. Kansas City, MO, designated as HQ on organization, but the unit was never organized at that location. Withdrawn from the Seventh Corps Area on 1 June 1936 and allotted to the Fourth Corps Area. Organized on 12 June 1938 with O.R. personnel as an RAI unit at Montgomery, AL. Designated mobilization training station was Fort Bragg, NC, 1933–40. Activated on 1 June 1941, less Reserve personnel, at Fort Bragg, NC. Location 7 December 1941—Fort Bragg, NC.

Events: 330

8th Observation Battalion (Sound and Flash) (VIII Corps) **Regular Army Inactive**

HQ—*Not organized,* 1933–34; Tulsa, OK, 1934–41; Fort Sill, OK, 1941

Constituted in the R.A. on 1 October 1933, assigned to the 18th F.A. Brig. (VIII Corps), and allotted to the Eighth Corps Area. Organized by 1934 with O.R. personnel as an RAI unit at Tulsa, OK. Relieved on 1 June 1940 from the 18th F.A. Brig. (VIII Corps). On 24 January 1941, attached to the Third Army. Activated on 1 June 1941, less Reserve personnel, at Fort Sill, OK. Location 7 December 1941—Fort Sill, OK.

12th Observation Battalion (Sound and Flash) (GHQR) **Regular Army Inactive**

HQ—*Not organized,* 1933–38; Baton Rouge, LA, 1938–41

Constituted in the R.A. on 1 October 1933, assigned to the 23d F.A. Brig. (GHQR), and allotted to the Second Corps Area. Jamestown, NY, designated as HQ on organization, but the unit was never organized at that location. Withdrawn from the Second Corps Area on 1 January 1938 and allotted to the Fourth Corps Area. Organized on 4 January 1938 with O.R. personnel as an RAI unit at Baton Rouge, LA. Location 7 December 1941—Baton Rouge, LA.

13th Observation Battalion (Sound and Flash) (GHQR) **Regular Army Inactive**

HQ—*Not organized,* 1933–34; Grand Rapids, MI, 1934–41

Constituted in the R.A. on 1 October 1933, assigned to the 24th F.A. Brig. (GHQR), and allotted to the Sixth Corps Area. Organized by June 1934 with O.R. personnel as an RAI unit at Grand Rapids, MI. Location 7 December 1941—Grand Rapids, MI.

14th Observation Battalion (Sound and Flash) (VII Corps) **Regular Army Inactive**

HQ—*Not organized,* 1923–32; Lafayette, IN, 1932–41; Fort Sill, OK, 1941

Constituted in the R.A. on 24 March 1923, assigned to the 14th F.A. Brig. (VII Corps), and allotted to the Eighth Corps Area. Withdrawn from the Eighth Corps Area on 28 February 1927 and allotted to the Fifth Corps Area. Concurrently relieved from the VII Corps and assigned to the V Corps as part of the 14th F.A. Brig. Organized by September 1932 with O.R. personnel as an RAI unit at Lafayette, IN. Designated mobilization training station was Fort Bragg, NC, 1923–40. Attached to the Third Army on 24 January 1941. Activated on 1 June 1941, less Reserve personnel, at Fort Sill, OK. Location 7 December 1941—Fort Sill, OK.

15th Observation Battalion (Sound and Flash) (VI Corps) **Regular Army Inactive**

HQ—*Not organized,* 1923–30; Fourth Corps Area at large, 1927–33; *Inactive,* 1933–36; Los Angeles, CA, 1936–41

Constituted in the R.A. on 24 March 1923, assigned to the 185th F.A. Brig. (VI Corps), and allotted to the Fourth Corps Area. Relieved from the 185th F.A. Brig. (VI Corps) in September 1927 and assigned to the 15th F.A. Brig. (II Corps). Organized by August 1927 with O.R. personnel as an RAI unit in the Fourth Corps Area. Withdrawn from the Fourth Corps Area on 1 October 1933 and allotted to the Ninth Corps Area. Concurrently relieved from the II Corps and assigned to the IX Corps as part of the 15th F.A. Brig. Organized on 9 July 1936 with O.R. personnel as an RAI unit at Los Angeles, CA. Designated mobilization training station was Fort Bragg, NC, 1923–40. Location 7 December 1941—Los Angeles, CA.

17th Observation Battalion (Sound and Flash) (GHQR) **Regular Army Inactive**

HQ—*Not organized,* 1933–34; Sioux Falls, SD, 1934–36; *Inactive*, 1936–38; Atlanta, GA, 1938–41

Constituted in the R.A. on 1 October 1933, assigned to the 25th F.A. Brig. (GHQR), and allotted to the Seventh Corps Area. Organized in 1934 with O.R. personnel as an RAI unit at Sioux Falls, SD. Withdrawn from the Seventh Corps on 1 June 1936 and allotted to the Fourth Corps Area. Organized on 12 June 1938 with O.R. personnel as an RAI unit at Atlanta, GA. Location 7 December 1941—Atlanta, GA.

101st Observation Battalion (Sound and Flash) (I Corps) **Massachusetts National Guard**

HQ—*Not organized,* 1921–27

Constituted in the N.G. in 1921, assigned to the 81st F.A. Brig. (I Corps), and allotted to the state of Massachusetts. Placed on the deferred list on 2 July 1923, redesignated 313th Obsn. Bn. (Sound and Flash), and transferred to the O.R. as a DNG unit. Concurrently relieved from assignment to the 81st F.A. Brig. (I Corps) and assigned to the 194th F.A. Brig. (I Corps). Withdrawn as a DNG unit on 11 January 1927 and permanently allotted to the O.R. as the 313th Obsn. Bn. (Sound and Flash). Concurrently withdrawn from the First Corps Area and allotted to the Fifth Corps Area. Battalion remained assigned to the 194th F.A. Brig. and I Corps.

102d Observation Battalion (Sound and Flash) (II Corps) **New York National Guard**

HQ—*Not organized,* 1921–27

Constituted in the N.G. in 1921, assigned to the II Corps Artillery, and allotted to the state of New York. Placed on the deferred list on 2 July 1923, redesignated 314th Obsn. Bn. (Sound and Flash), and transferred to the O.R. as a DNG unit. Withdrawn from the N.G. on 17 September 1927.

103d Observation Battalion (Sound and Flash) (V Corps) **Indiana National Guard**

HQ—*Not organized,* 1921–27

Constituted in the N.G. in 1921, assigned to the 83d F.A. Brig. (V Corps), and allotted to the state of Indiana. Placed on the deferred list on 2 July 1923, redesignated 315th Obsn. Bn. (Sound and Flash), and transferred to the O.R. as a DNG unit. Concurrently, relieved from the 83d F.A. Brig. (V Corps) assigned to the 184th F.A. Brig. (V Corps). Withdrawn from the N.G. on 17 September 1927.

301st Observation Battalion (Sound and Flash) (XI Corps) **Organized Reserve Connecticut/Indiana**

HQ—*Not initiated,* 1921–24; Hartford, CT, 1924–27; *Inactive,* 1927–33; Lafayette, IN, 1933–41; Indianapolis, IN, 1941

Constituted in the O.R. on 29 July 1921, assigned to the 180th F.A. Brig. (XI Corps), and allotted to the First Corps Area. Initiated in October 1924 at Hartford, CT. Conducted annual summer training with the 1st Obsn. Btry (later with the 1st Obsn. Bn.) at Fort Bragg, NC, 1924–26. Withdrawn from the First Corps Area on 11 January 1927, allotted to the Fifth Corps Area, and relieved from the 180th F.A. Brig. (XI Corps). Concurrently assigned to the GHQR. Reorganized by December 1933 at Lafayette, IN. Designated mobilization training station was Fort Bragg, 1924–26, and Fort Sill, OK, 1926–41. Location 7 December 1941—Indianapolis, IN.

302d Observation Battalion (Sound and Flash) (XII Corps) **Organized Reserve New York**

HQ—*Not initiated,* 1921–22; Manhattan, NY, 1922–37; *Inactive,* 1937–39; Manhattan, NY, 1939–41

Constituted in the O.R. on 29 July 1921, assigned to the 181st F.A. Brig. (XII Corps), and allotted to the Second Corps Area. Initiated on 11 March 1922 at Manhattan, NY. Relieved from the XII Corps on 1 October 1933 and assigned to the II Corps. Conducted annual summer training most years with the 1st Obsn. Btry (later with the 1st Obsn. Bn.) at Fort Bragg, NC, 1924–41. Designated mobilization training station was Pine Camp, NY. Inactivated by February 1937 at Manhattan by relief of personnel. Reorganized by November 1939 at Manhattan. Location 7 December 1941—Manhattan, NY.

303d Observation Battalion (Sound and Flash) (XIII Corps) **Organized Reserve Pennsylvania**

HQ—*Not initiated,* 1921–22; Johnstown, PA, 1922–39; *Inactive,* 1939–41

Constituted in the O.R. on 29 July 1921, assigned to the 182d F.A. Brig. (XIII Corps), and allotted to the Third Corps Area. Initiated on 20 March 1922 at Johnstown, PA. Conducted annual summer training most years with the 1st Obsn. Btry (later with the 1st Obsn. Bn.) at Fort Bragg, NC, 1924–38. Designated mobilization training station was Fort Sill, OK, 1926–41. Inactivated by April 1939 at Johnstown by relief of personnel. Location 7 December 1941—*Inactive.*

304th Observation Battalion (Sound and Flash) (XIV Corps) **Organized Reserve Louisiana/Florida**

HQ—*Not initiated,* 1921–22; New Orleans, LA, 1922–29; Jacksonville, FL, 1929–41

Constituted in the O.R. on 29 July 1921, assigned to the 183d F.A. Brig. (XIV Corps), and allotted to the Fourth Corps Area. Initiated in May 1922 at New Orleans, LA. Relocated 22 October 1929 to Jacksonville, FL. Conducted annual summer training most years with the 1st Obsn. Btry (later with the 1st Obsn. Bn.) at Fort Bragg, NC, 1922–41. Designated mobilization training station was Camp Jackson, SC, 1922–24; Fort Bragg, NC, 1924–26; and Fort Sill, OK, 1926–41. Location 7 December 1941—Jacksonville, FL.

305th Observation Battalion (Sound and Flash) (XV Corps) **Organized Reserve Ohio**

HQ—*Not initiated,* 1921–24; Columbus, OH, 1924–30; *Inactive,* 1930–41

Constituted in the O.R. on 29 July 1921, assigned to the 184th F.A. Brig. (XV Corps), and allotted to the Fifth Corps Area. Relieved from the 184th F.A. Brig. (XV Corps) on 2 July 1923 and assigned to the 191st F.A. Brig. (XV Corps). Initiated in 1924 at Columbus, OH. Relieved from the 191st F.A. Brig. (XV Corps) on 17 September 1927 and assigned to the 184th F.A. Brig.(XV Corps). Inactivated by March 1930 at Columbus by relief of personnel. Conducted annual summer training most years with the 1st Obsn. Btry (later with the 1st Obsn. Bn.) at Fort Bragg, NC, 1924–29. Designated mobilization training station was Camp Knox, KY. Location 7 December 1941—*Inactive.*

306th Observation Battalion (Sound and Flash) (XVI Corps) **Organized Reserve Illinois**

HQ—*Not initiated,* 1921–22; Evanston, IL, 1922–41

Constituted in the O.R. on 29 July 1921, assigned to the 185th F.A. Brig. (XVI Corps), and allotted to the Sixth Corps Area. Initiated in January 1922 at Evanston, IL. Relieved from the 185th F.A. Brig. (XVI Corps) on 2 July 1923 and assigned to the 192d F.A. Brig. (XVI Corps). Withdrawn from the O.R. on 1 October 1933 and allotted to the R.A. Concurrently relieved from the 192d F.A. Brig. (XVI Corps) and assigned to the 22d F.A. Brig. (VI Corps). Typically conducted Inactive Training Period meetings at the Post Office Building in Chicago. Conducted annual summer training most years with the 1st Obsn. Btry (later with the 1st Obsn. Bn.) at Fort Bragg, NC, 1924–41. Designated mobilization training station was Camp Konx, KY, 1922–26, and Fort Sill, OK, 1926–41. Location 7 December 1941—Evanston, IL.

307th Observation Battalion (Sound and Flash) (XVII Corps) **Organized Reserve Minnesota**

HQ—*Not initiated,* 1921–22; St. Paul, MN, 1922–41

Constituted in the O.R. on 29 July 1921, assigned to the 186th F.A. Brig. (XVII Corps), and allotted to the Seventh Corps Area. Initiated in December 1922 at St. Paul, MN. Relieved from the 186th F.A. Brig. (XVII Corps) on 1 October 1933 and assigned to the 187th F.A. Brig. (XVII Corps). Conducted annual summer training most years with the 1st Obsn. Btry (later with the 1st Obsn. Bn.) at Fort Bragg, NC, 1924–41. Designated mobilization training station was Fort Sill, OK, 1926–41. Location 7 December 1941—St. Paul, MN.

308th Observation Battalion (Sound and Flash) (XVIII Corps) **Organized Reserve Arizona/Nebraska**

HQ—*Not initiated,* 1921–23; Tucson, AZ, 1923–27; Norfolk, NE, 1927–33

Constituted in the O.R. on 29 July 1921, assigned to the 187th F.A. Brig. (XVIII Corps), and allotted to the Eighth Corps Area. Initiated on 13 April 1923 at Tucson, AZ. As an element of the 187th F.A. Brig., the battalion was relieved from the XVIII Corps on 2 July 1923 and assigned to the VIII Corps. Withdrawn from the Eighth Corps Area on 11 January 1927 and allotted to the Seventh Corps Area. The battalion remained assigned to the 187th F.A. Brig. and XVIII Corps. Reorganized on 3 August 1927 with HQ at Norfolk, NE. Conducted annual summer training most years with the 1st Obsn. Btry (later with the 1st Obsn. Bn.) at Fort Bragg, NC, 1924–26. Designated mobilization training station was Fort Sill, OK, 1926–41. Demobilized 1 October 1933.

309th Observation Battalion (Sound and Flash) (XIX Corps) **Organized Reserve California**

HQ—*Not initiated,* 1921–22; San Francisco, CA, 1922–25; Los Angeles, CA, 1925–37; San Francisco, CA, 1937–41

Constituted in the O.R. on 29 July 1921, assigned to the 188th F.A. Brig. (XIX Corps), and allotted to the Ninth Corps Area. Initiated in October 1922 at San Francisco, CA. Relocated in 1925 to Los Angeles. Relieved from the 188th F.A. Brig. (XIX Corps) on 5 September 1928 and assigned to the 195th F.A. Brig. (XIX Corps). Relocated on 11 February 1937 to San Francisco. Typically conducted Inactive Training Period meetings, 1925–37, at the Chamber of Commerce Building or at 751 Figuroa Street in Los Angeles. Conducted annual summer training most years with the 76th F.A. at the Presidio of Monterrey, CA, 1924–33. Designated mobilization training station was Fort Sill, OK, 1926–41. Location 7 December 1941—San Francisco, CA.

310th Observation Battalion (Sound and Flash) (III Corps) **Organized Reserve Pennsylvania**

HQ—*Not initiated,* 1921–22; Media, PA, 1922–33

Constituted in the O.R. on 29 July 1921, assigned to the 82d F.A. Brig. (III Corps) (redesignated 190th F.A. Brig. on 2 July 1923), and allotted to the Third Corps Area. Organized in October 1922 at Media, PA. Conducted annual summer training most years with the 1st Obsn. Btry (later with the 1st Obsn. Bn.) at Fort Bragg, NC, 1924–33, and at Fort Sill, OK, 1931. Designated mobilization training station was Pine Camp, NY. Demobilized on 1 October 1933.

311th Observation Battalion (Sound and Flash) (IX Corps) **Organized Reserve New Jersey/Delaware**

HQ—*Not initiated,* 1921–22; Kearney, NJ, 1922–29; Wilmington, DE, 1929–40; *Inactive,* 1940–41

Constituted in the O.R. on 29 July 1921, assigned to the 86th F.A. Brig. (IX Corps) (redesignated 189th F.A. Brig. on 2 July 1923), and allotted to the Second Corps Area. Initiated on 17 March 1922 at Kearney, NJ. Relocated on 22 October 1929 to Wilmington, DE. Relieved from the189th F.A. Brig. (IX Corps) on 1 October 1933 and assigned to the GHQR. Inactivated by 1940 at Wilmington by relief of personnel. Conducted annual summer training most years with the 1st Obsn. Btry (later with the 1st Obsn. Bn.) at Fort Bragg, NC, 1925–41. Designated mobilization training station was Pine Camp, NY. Location 7 December 1941—Wilmington, DE.

312th Observation Battalion (Sound and Flash) (VIII Corps) **Organized Reserve Colorado/Texas**

HQ—*Not initiated,* 1921–22; Boulder, CO, 1922–37; Houston, TX, 1937–41

Constituted in the O.R. on 29 July 1921, assigned to the 85th F.A. Brig. (VIII Corps) (redesignated 193d F.A. Brig. on 2 July 1923), and allotted to the Eighth Corps Area. Initiated on 12 September 1922 at Boulder, CO. Relocated by August 1937 to Houston, TX. Conducted annual summer training most years with the 1st Obsn. Btry (later with the 1st Obsn. Bn.) at Fort Bragg, NC, 1924–28, and at Fort Sill, OK, 1928–30, and Fort Francis E. Warren, WY, 1931–39. Designated mobilization training station was Fort Sill, OK, 1926–41. Location 7 December 1941—Houston, TX.

313th Observation Battalion (Sound and Flash) (XV Corps) **Organized Reserve Ohio**

HQ—*Not initiated,* 1921–33

Constituted in the N.G. on 29 July 1921 as the 101st Obsn. Bn., assigned to the 81st F.A. Brig. (I Corps), and allotted to the state of Massachusetts. Placed on the deferred list on 2 July 1923, redesignated 313th Obsn. Bn. (Sound and Flash), and transferred to the O.R. as a DNG unit. The 81st F.A. Brig. (I Corps) concurrently redesignated 194th F.A. Brig. (I Corps). Withdrawn as a DNG unit on 11 January 1927 and permanently allotted to the O.R. as the 313th Obsn. Bn. (Sound and Flash). Concurrently withdrawn from the First Corps Area and allotted to the Fifth Corps Area. The battalion remained assigned to the 194th F.A. Brig. (I Corps). Cincinnati, OH, designated as HQ on organization, but the unit was never organized at that location. Designated mobilization training station was Pine Camp, NY, 1921–27, and Camp Knox, KY, 1927–33. Demobilized on 1 October 1933.

314th Observation Battalion (Sound and Flash) (I) (II Corps) **Organized Reserve New York**

HQ—*Not initiated,* 1921–23; Manhattan, NY, 1923–27

Constituted in the N.G. on 29 July 1921 as the 102d Obsn. Bn., assigned to the II Corps Artillery, and allotted to the state of New York. Placed on the deferred list on 2 July 1923, redesignated 314th Obsn. Bn. (Sound and Flash) and transferred to the O.R. as a DNG unit. Initiated in 1923 at Manhattan, NY. Withdrawn from the N.G. on 17 September 1927.

314th Observation Battalion (Sound and Flash) (II) (GHQR) **Organized Reserve Massachusetts**

HQ—Haverhill, MA, 1930–41

Constituted in the O.R. on 5 March 1930, assigned to the GHQR, and allotted to the First Corps Area. Initiated on 25 April 1930 at Haverhill, MA. Relieved from the GHQR on 1 October 1933 and assigned to the 19th F.A. Brig. (I Corps). Concurrently withdrawn from the O.R. and allotted to the R.A. Typically conducted Inactive Training Period meetings at the Post Office Building in Boston, MA. Conducted annual summer training most years with the 1st Obsn. Btry (later with the 1st Obsn. Bn.) at Fort Bragg, NC, 1930–41. Designated mobilization training station was Fort Sill, OK, 1930–41. Location 7 December 1941—Haverhill, MA.

315th Observation Battalion (Sound and Flash) (I) (II Corps) **Organized Reserve Ohio**

HQ—*Not initiated,* 1923–27

Constituted in the N.G. on 29 July 1921 as the 103d Obsn. Bn., assigned to the 83d F.A. Brig. (V Corps), and allotted to the state of Indiana. Placed on the deferred list on 2 July 1923, redesignated 315th Obsn. Bn. (Sound and Flash), and transferred to the O.R. as a DNG unit. Concurrently relieved from the 83d F.A. Brig. (V Corps) and assigned to the 184th F.A. Brig. (V Corps). Cincinnati, OH, designated as HQ on organization, but the unit was never organized at that location. Withdrawn from the N.G. on 17 September 1927.

315th Observation Battalion (Sound and Flash) (II) (XI Corps) **Organized Reserve Massachusetts**

HQ—Boston, MA, 1930–41

Constituted in the O.R. on 5 March 1930, assigned to the 180th F.A. Brig. (XI Corps), and allotted to the First Corps Area. Initiated on 25 April 1930 at Boston, MA. Conducted annual summer training most years with the 1st Obsn. Btry (later with the 1st Obsn Bn.) at Fort Bragg, NC, 1930–41. Designated mobilization training station was Pine Camp, NY. Location 7 December 1941—Boston, MA.

316th Observation Battalion (Sound and Flash) (I) (ZI) **Organized Reserve Florida**

HQ—*Not initiated,* 1921–24; Tampa, FL, 1924–28

Constituted in the O.R. on 29 July 1921, assigned to the Zone of the Interior, and allotted to the Fourth Corps Area. Initiated in November 1924 at Tampa, FL. Conducted annual summer training most years with the 1st Obsn. Btry (later with the 1st Obsn. Bn.) at Fort Bragg, NC, 1925–28. Designated mobilization training station was Fort Bragg, NC. Withdrawn from the Fourth Corps Area on 28 November 1928 and demobilized.

316th Observation Battalion (Sound and Flash) (II) (ZI) **Organized Reserve Florida**

HQ—Tampa, FL, 1930–41

Constituted in the O.R. on 5 March 1930, assigned to the Zone of the Interior, and allotted to the Fourth Corps Area. Initiated on 19 August 1930 at Tampa, FL. Conducted annual summer training most years with the 1st Obsn. Btry (later with the 1st Obsn. Bn.) at Fort Bragg, NC, 1931–41. Designated mobilization training station was Fort Bragg, NC. Location 7 December 1941—Tampa, FL.

317th Observation Battalion (Sound and Flash) (ZI) **Organized Reserve Ohio**

HQ—*Not initiated,* 1923–24; Cincinnati, OH, 1924–30; *Inactive,* 1930–33

Constituted in the O.R. on 2 July 1923, assigned to the Zone of the Interior, and allotted to the Fifth Corps Area. Initiated in September 1924 at Cincinnati, OH. Assigned to the 184th F.A. Brig. (V Corps) on 17 September 1927. Inactivated by March 1930 at Cincinnati by relief of personnel. Conducted annual summer training most years with the 1st Obsn. Btry (later with the 1st Obsn. Bn.) at Fort Bragg, NC, and some years at Camp Knox, KY. Designated mobilization training station was Fort Bragg. Demobilized on 1 October 1933.

318th Observation Battalion (Sound and Flash) (I) (ZI) **Organized Reserve California**

HQ—*Not initiated,* 1923–26; Los Angeles, CA, 1926–28

Constituted in the O.R. on 2 July 1923, assigned to the Zone of the Interior, and allotted to the Ninth Corps Area. Initiated in 1926 at Los Angeles, CA. Conducted annual summer training most years at the Presidio of Monterrey, CA, 1926–28. Designated mobilization training station was Fort Bragg, NC. Withdrawn on 28 November 1928.

318th Observation Battalion (Sound and Flash) (II) (ZI) **Organized Reserve Illinois**

HQ—*Not initiated,* 1930–34; Quincy, IL, 1934–37; Chicago, IL, 1937–41

Constituted in the O.R. on 5 March 1930, assigned to the Zone of the Interior, and allotted to the Sixth Corps Area. Assigned to the 185th F.A. Brig. (XVI Corps) on 1 October 1933. Initiated by June 1934 at Quincy, IL. Relocated on 7 April 1937 to Chicago, IL. Conducted annual summer training most years with the 1st Obsn. Btry (later with the 1st Obsn. Bn.) at Fort Bragg, NC, 1930–41. Designated mobilization station was Fort Bragg. Location 7 December 1941—Chicago, IL.

319th Observation Battalion (Sound and Flash) (ZI) **Organized Reserve Oklahoma/Illinois**

HQ—*Not initiated,* 1923–29; Lawton, OK, 1929–36; *Inactive,* 1936–37; Chicago, IL, 1937–41

Constituted in the O.R. on 2 July 1923, assigned to the Zone of the Interior, and allotted to the Eighth Corps Area. Initiated on 17 December 1929 at Lawton, OK. Conducted annual summer training most years at Fort Sill, OK, 1930–36. Withdrawn from the Eighth Corps Area on 5 June 1936 and allotted to the Sixth Corps Area. Reorganized by December 1937 at Chicago, IL. Designated mobilization training station was Fort Sill, OK, 1923–41. Location 7 December 1941—Chicago, IL.

320th Observation Battalion (Sound and Flash) (GHQR) **Organized Reserve Michigan**

HQ—*Not initiated,* 1930–32; Grand Rapids, MI, 1932–33

Constituted in the O.R. on 5 March 1930, assigned to the GHQR, and allotted to the Sixth Corps Area. Initiated in January 1932 at Grand Rapids, MI. Demobilized on 1 October 1933.

321st Observation Battalion (Sound and Flash) (GHQR) **Organized Reserve Oregon**

HQ—Portland, OR, 1930–33

Constituted in the O.R. on 5 March 1930, assigned to the GHQR, and allotted to the Ninth Corps Area. Initiated in April 1930 at Portland, OR. Demobilized on 1 October 1933.

Chapter 23

Ammunition Trains

Trading Post Magazine

Headquarters, Second Ammunition Train.

Ammunition trains provided the ammunition haul and delivery capability for General Headquarters Reserve (GHQR), corps, and division field artillery brigades and GHQR and army coast artillery brigades.

Organization

There were three types of ammunition train in the postwar period. The army-level trains consisted of a headquarters battery and six motorized ammunition resupply batteries. The corps train was composed of essentially the same organization as that of the army train, less one ammunition resupply battery. This table of organization (T/O) was also used for those trains assigned or attached to GHQR brigades. The division ammunition train was significantly different from the other two trains. It consisted of a headquarters battery, one horse-drawn ammunition transportation battery, and one motorized ammunition resupply battery. The divisional train underwent a major reorganization in 1931 when it expanded to consist of a headquarters battery, one horse-drawn ammunition resupply battery, and two motorized ammunition resupply batteries, one motorized transportation section, and one horse-drawn transportation section. Concurrently, the train's personnel strength tripled in size.

There was a total of 109 ammunition trains constituted during the interwar period—22 in the Regular Army (R.A.), 27 in the National Guard (N.G.), and 60 in the Organized Reserve (O.R.). Of these, 13 were army trains, 33 were corps trains, 6 were allocated to the GHQR, and 57 were assigned to infantry divisions. All of the R.A. trains except one were active or organized as Regular Army Inactive (RAI) units. Most of the active trains were inactivated in 1930 and only the 2d Ammunition (Ammo.) Train (Tn.) survived on Active Duty into the late 1930s as a Field Artillery School support and training unit. Most of the inactivated trains were reorganized as RAI units.

Only 11 of the 27 N.G. trains were active at some point in the interwar period—10 divisional trains and one army-level train. Most of the active trains were reorganized at some point into other organizations, mostly field artillery units. Only three trains survived into the late 1930s and all three were converted into other organizations during the major reorganizations of the N.G. during 1939–40.

Ammunition Train, Army Artillery, 1931

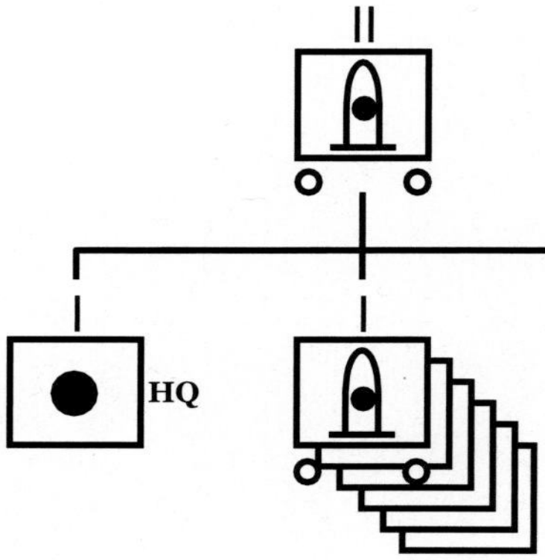

T/O:	256
Effective:	1 July 1931
Commander:	Maj.
Officers:	27
W. O.	--
Enlisted:	792
Total:	819

Key Equipment:	
Cars, various	7
Trucks, various	189
Machine-guns, AA	20

Ammunition Train, Corps Artillery Brigade, 1930

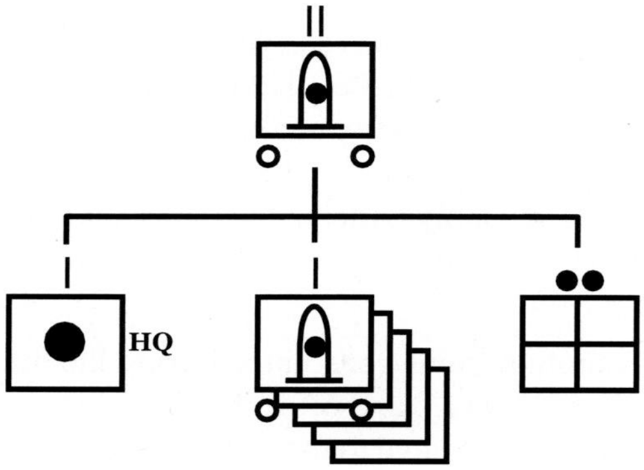

T/O:	156W
Effective:	1 July 1930
Commander:	Maj.
Officers:	21
W. O.	--
Enlisted:	667
Total:	688

Key Equipment:	
Cars, various	??
Trucks, various	??
Machine-gun, AA	17

Ammunition train organization.

Ammunition Train, Division Artillery Brigade, 1921

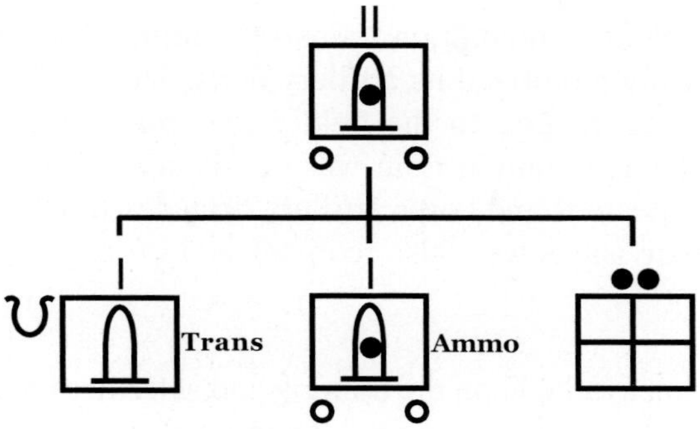

T/O:	56W
Approved:	20 January 1921
Commander:	Maj.
Officers:	7
W. O.	--
Enlisted:	162
Total:	169

Key Equipment:	
Car, various	2
Horses & Mules	131
Trucks, various	33
Wagons	28
Machine-guns, AA	2

Ammunition Train, Division Artillery Brigade, 1931

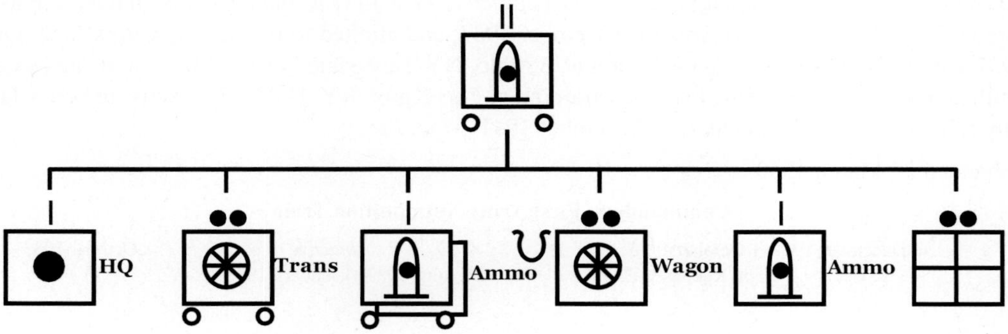

T/O:	56W
Effective:	1 July 1931
Commander:	Maj.
Officers:	16
W. O.	--
Enlisted:	424
Total:	440

Key Equipment:	
Cars, various	2
Horses & Mules	147
Trucks, various	68
Wagons	28
Machine-guns, AA	11

Ammunition train, division artillery brigade organization.

The vast majority of the O.R. ammunition trains were initiated during the interwar period. Most of those that were not, were Deferred National Guard (DNG) units. A number of the GHQR trains were demobilized in 1923 when the War Plans Division (WPD) determined that they would not be needed. Additional trains were demobilized in 1933 due to the constitution of new RAI ammunition trains needed for the nine lower numbered corps and the four field armies in accordance with the four-army plan.

The requirement to have separate ammunition trains for hauling and delivering ammunition became less acute in the 1930s as the Army motorized its artillery units. The combat trains, ordnance companies, and quartermaster truck regiments integral to the field forces made the ammunition train superfluous to the needs of those forces. The ammunition train was eliminated from the triangular division in 1939 and eliminated from all Guard divisions and corps artillery brigades in 1940. Trains survived in the O.R. divisions until 1942 when those divisions were also reorganized as triangular divisions.

Training

There is not much information available on the training and activities of ammunition trains. While they were in service, the Active Duty R.A. trains supported the training of divisional field artillery units during field training and live-fire exercises. Of course, the 2d Ammo. Tn. lived on a while longer in the 1930s supporting the training at the Field Artillery School. RAI trains were almost all pool units and only attended summer training as units. Only the 6th Ammo. Tn. appears to have held unit training during the Inactive Training Period. N.G. trains held normal drills during the Inactive Training Period and attended summer training with their respective brigades. The majority of the O.R. division ammunition trains were likely functional units, though not much evidence has been found either way. The remaining trains were mostly pool units and only one corps train was determined to have held activities as a unit during the Inactive Training Period.

First Army Ammunition Train (First Army) **Regular Army Inactive**

HQ—Cincinnati, OH, 1927–33; *Inactive,* 1933–37; Buffalo, NY, 1937–38; *Inactive,* 1938–41

Constituted in the R.A. on 18 October 1927, assigned to the 31st Coast Artillery (C.A.) Brigade (Brig.) (First Army), and allotted to the Fifth Corps Area. Organized by December 1927 with O.R. personnel as an RAI unit at Cincinnati, OH. Withdrawn from the Fifth Corps Area on 1 October 1933, and allotted to the Second Corps Area. Organized on 28 April 1937 with O.R. personnel as an RAI unit at Buffalo, NY. Designated in 1939 to be activated as a "Colored" unit on mobilization. Conducted annual summer training at Fort Knox, KY, 1928–33. Inactivated on 4 January 1938 at Buffalo by relief of personnel. Location 7 December 1941—*Inactive.*

Status: Disbanded 27 March 1953.

Commanders, First Army Ammunition Train

Unknown	ao December 1927–1 October 1933	*Inactive*	1 October 1933–28 April 1937
Capt. Rueben E.F. Ott	28 April 1937–4 January 1938		

Second Army Ammunition Train (Second Army) **Regular Army Inactive**

HQ—Cincinnati, OH, 1933–40; *Inactive,* 1940–41

Constituted in the R.A. on 1 October 1933, assigned to the 33d C.A. Brig. (Second Army), and allotted to the Fifth Corps Area. Concurrently organized as an RAI unit with O.R. personnel previously assigned to the First Army Ammunition Train at Cincinnati, OH. Inactivated about June 1940 at Cincinnati by relief of personnel. Conducted annual summer training at Fort Knox, KY. Designated mobilization training station was Fort Bragg, NC. Location 7 December 1941—*Inactive.*

Status: Disbanded 27 March 1953.

Commanders, Second Army Ammunition Train

Unknown	1 October 1933–ao June 1937	Capt. M.K. Kurtz	ao July 1937–ao September 1937
Unknown	ao September 1937–June 1940		

Third Army Ammunition Train (Third Army) **Regular Army Inactive**

HQ—*Not organized,* 1933–34; Ardmore, OK, 1934–40; *Inactive,* 1940–41; Ardmore, OK, 1941

Constituted in the R.A. on 1 October 1933, assigned to the 34th C.A. Brig. (Third Army), and allotted to the Eighth Corps Area. Organized on 30 November 1934 with O.R. personnel as an RAI unit at Ardmore, OK. Designated in 1939 to activated as a "Colored" unit on mobilization. Inactivated in 1940 at Ardmore by relief of personnel. Conducted annual summer training at Fort Sill, OK. Designated mobilization training station was Fort Sill, OK. Reorganized by February 1941 with O.R. personnel as an RAI unit with HQ at Ardmore. Location 7 December 1941—Ardmore, OK.

Status: Disbanded 27 March 1953.

Commanders, Third Army Ammunition Train

Unknown	30 November 1934–7 December 1941

Fourth Army Ammunition Train (Fourth Army) **Regular Army Inactive**

HQ—*Not organized,* 1933–35; Little Rock, AR, 1935–40; *Inactive,* 1940–41

Constituted in the R.A. on 1 October 1933, assigned to the 35th C.A. Brig. (Fourth Army), and allotted to the Seventh Corps Area. Organized on 18 January 1935 with O.R. personnel as an RAI unit at Little Rock, AR. Inactivated about June 1940 at Little Rock by relief of personnel. Location 7 December 1941—*Inactive.*

Status: Disbanded 27 March 1953.

Commanders, Fourth Army Ammunition Train

Unknown	18 January 1935–ao January 1938	1st Lt. Edward P. Arnold	ao January 1938–ao March 1938
Unknown	ao March 1938–June 1940		

1st Ammunition Train (1st Division)

HQ—Camp Zachary Taylor, KY, 1919–20; Camp Dix, NJ, 1920–22; Fort Hoyle, MD, 1922–30; *Inactive,* 1930–36; New York City, NY, 1936–39

Arrived at the port of New York on 1 September 1919 on the U.S.S. *Von Steuben* after 9 months of occupation duty in Coblenz, Germany, as an element of the 1st Division (Div.). Transferred to Camp Zachary Taylor, KY, and arrived there in late September 1919. Transferred to Camp Dix, NJ, and arrived there on 20 September 1920. Transferred on 18 October 1922 to Fort Hoyle, MD. Inactivated on 30 April 1930 at Fort Hoyle and allotted to the Third Corps Area. Organized about September 1932 with O.R. personnel as an RAI unit with HQ in the Third Corps Area at large. Withdrawn from the Third Corps Area on 1 October 1933, and allotted to the Second Corps Area. Organized on 12 March 1936 with O.R. personnel as an RAI unit at New York City, NY. Designated mobilization training station was Fort Bragg, NC. Disbanded on 16 October 1939.

Organization Day: 23 July. Chosen to commemorate the date of organization of the Horsed Section of the 1st Ammo. Tn. on 23 July 1917 at Fort Bliss, TX, and the train's participation in the Aisne-Marne Offensive on 23 July 1918.

Events: 63, 98, 106

Commanders, 1st Ammunition Train

Lt. Col. Pierce A. Murphy	6 August 1917–14 January 1918
Lt. Col. William H. Monroe	14 January 1918–July 1918
Lt. Col. Avery J. Cooper	July 1918–25 July 1918
Lt. Col. Harcourt Hervey	25 July 1918–25 October 1919
Lt. Col. Frederick F. Black	25 October 1919–14 October 1920
Capt. George A. Ivanick	14 October 1920–12 December 1920
1st Lt. Bennie C. Hampton	12 December 1920–16 January 1921
Maj. Albert W. Waldron	16 January 1921–13 July 1921
1st Lt. Robert R. Montague	13 July 1921–7 February 1922
Capt. Rex B. Shaw	7 February 1922–May 1922
1st Lt. Robert R. Montague	May 1922–11 December 1922
1st Lt. Edmund W. Sorby	11 December 1922–February 1923
1st Lt. Irvin B. Warner	February 1923–17 March 1924
1st Lt. Harry Crawford	17 March 1924–12 August 1926
1st Lt. Homer W. Kiefer	12 August 1926–14 September 1926
Capt. Ray C. Montgomery	14 September 1926–14 June 1929
Capt. Howard C. Brenizer	14 June 1929–30 April 1930
Capt. William E. Barkman**	30 April 1930–12 October 1931
1st Lt. Frederick F. Stephen**	12 October 1931–1 November 1933
Inactive	1 November 1933–13 March 1936
Unknown**	12 March 1936–16 October 1939

**RAI commanders: O.R. officers.

2d Ammunition Train (2d Division)

HQ—Fort Sam Houston, TX, 1919–30; San Antonio, TX, 1930–33; Fort Sill, OK, 1933–38; *Inactive,* 1938–39

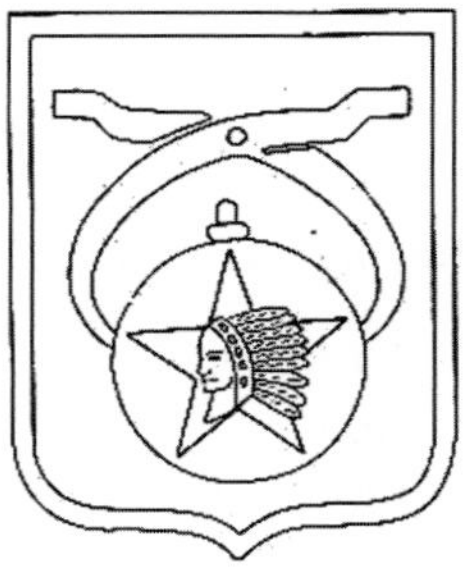

Arrived at the port of New York on 8 August 1919 on the S.S. *Finland* after 7 months of occupation duty near Coblenz and Heddesdorf, Germany, as an element of the 2d Div. Transferred to Camp Travis, TX, and arrived there on 11 August 1919. Transferred in 1922 with 2d Div. to Fort Sam Houston proper. Participated in the production of the MGM movie "Wings" at Camp Stanley, TX, 20 September–2 November 1926. Inactivated on 31 May 1930 at Fort Sam Houston, TX, and allotted to the Eighth Corps Area. Organized by August 1930 with O.R. personnel as an RAI unit at San Antonio, TX. Activated, less Reserve personnel, on 1 October 1933 at Fort Sill, OK, with personnel and equipment from the inactivated 3d Ammo. Tn. Inactivated on 1 December 1938 at Fort Sill, OK, and allotted to the Eighth Corps Area. Assigned Reserve officers conducted summer training with the train at Fort Sill and Fort Sam Houston. Disbanded on 16 October 1939.

Organization Day: 11 October. Chosen to commemorate the date of organization of the 2d Ammo. Tn. on 11 October 1917 at Chickamauga Park, GA.

Events: 45, 47, 55, 70, 74, 105, 125, 147

Commanders, 2d Ammunition Train

Capt. Paul W. Mapes	ao January 1920–4 March 1920
Lt. Col. John B. Corbly	4 March 1920–2 August 1920
Lt. Col. Charles O. Thomas Jr.	27 September 1920–15 November 1920
Capt. Paul W. Mapes	15 November 1920–January 1921
Capt. Andrew R. Reeves	January 1921–October 1921
Capt. James L. McIlhenny	October 1921–20 August 1923
Capt. Derrill deS. Trenholm	20 August 1923–1 March 1924
Capt. Leo F. Crane	1 March 1924–November 1924
Capt. Stanley Richardson	November 1924–February 1925
Capt. Norbert C. Manley	February 1925–4 December 1926
Capt. Robert H. Crosby	4 December 1926–11 July 1927
1st Lt. Charles H. Brammell	11 July 1927–16 August 1927
1st Lt. John A. Smith Jr.	16 August 1927–26 May 1928
1st Lt. John C. Howard	26 May 1928–28 September 1928
1st Lt. John A. Smith Jr.	28 September 1928–31 May 1930
Inactive	1 June 1930–August 1930
Capt. Roy E. Adair**	December 1930–30 September 1933
Capt. Murray C. Wilson	1 October 1933–1 April 1934
Capt. James F. Brittingham	1 April 1934–14 May 1935
Maj. Leonard H. Frasier	14 May 1935–8 November 1936
Capt. Rochester F. McEldowney	8 November 1936–15 August 1937
Capt. Frank J. Hierholzer	15 August 1937–1 July 1938
Maj. John A. Chase	1 July 1938–1 December 1938

**RAI commanders: O.R. officers.

3d Ammunition Train (3d Division)

HQ—Camp Pike, AR, 1919–21; Camp Lewis, WA, 1921–25; Fort Sill, OK, 1925–33; *Inactive,* 1933–34; Anaconda, MT, 1934–36; Fort Lewis, WA, 1936–39

Arrived at the port of New York on 26 August 1919 on the U.S.S. *Canandaigua* after 8 months of occupation duty in Mayen, Germany, as an element of the 3d Div. Transferred to Camp Pike, AR, and arrived there on 1 September 1919. Transferred to Camp Lewis, WA, and arrived there on 21 September 1921. Transferred to Fort Sill, OK, and arrived there on 24 May 1925. Mission at Fort Sill was to provide training support to the Field Artillery School. Inactivated at Fort Sill on 1 October 1933 and allotted to the Ninth Corps Area. Organized by December 1934 with O.R. personnel as an RAI unit at Anaconda, MT. Relocated on 3 July 1936 to Fort Lewis. Disbanded on 16 October 1939.

Events: 57, 114

Commanders, 3d Ammunition Train

Lt. Col. George E. Lovell	15 December 1917–17 November 1920	Capt. Edgar A. O'Hair	27 March 1926–7 July 1926
Capt. George A. Hadd	17 November 1920–15 November 1921	Capt. Edward F. Hart	7 July 1926–ao April 1927
Capt. Albert C. Searle	15 November 1921–21 July 1922	1st Lt. Lawrence E. Heyduck	ao August 1928–12 June 1929
Capt. Lloyd S. Partridge	21 July 1922–17 March 1923	Capt. John M. Devine	12 June 1929–October 1931
Capt. John McDowell	17 March 1923–28 May 1923	Capt. Murray C. Wilson	October 1931–1 October 1933
1st Lt. Lonnie O. Field	28 May 1923–27 March 1926	*Inactive*	1 October 1933–ao December 1934
Unknown**	ao December 1934–16 October 1939		

**RAI commanders: O.R. officers.

4th Ammunition Train (4th Division) **Regular Army Inactive**

HQ—Camp Dodge, IA, 1919–20; Camp Lewis, WA, 1920–21; *Inactive,* 1921–30; Fourth Corps Area at large, 1927–38; *Inactive,* 1938–41

Arrived at Newport News, VA, on 31 July 1919 on the U.S.S. *Antigone* after 7 months of occupation duty in Adenau and Ahrweiler, Germany, as an element of the 4th Div. Transferred to Camp Dodge, IA, and arrived there on 8 August 1919. Transferred to Camp Lewis, WA, and arrived there on 2 July 1920. Inactivated on 21 September 1921 at Camp Lewis. The 3d Ammo. Tn. made Active Associate (A.A.), 1921–23. The 1st Bn., 2d F.A. made A.A., 1923–27. Allotted to the Fourth Corps Area on 28 February 1927. Organized on 26 August 1927 with O.R. personnel as an RAI unit in the Fourth Corps Area at large. Withdrawn from the Fourth Corps Area on 14 March 1938 and allotted to the Eighth Corps Area. Inactivated on 10 April 1938 in the Fourth Corps Area by relief of personnel. Location 7 December 1941—*Inactive.*

Status: Disbanded 27 March 1953.

Commanders, 4th Ammunition Train

Maj. Joseph G. Bye	ao December 1919–25 August 1920	Unknown	6 June 1929–21 June 1932
Capt. Charles E. Pell	25 August 1920–November 1920	2d Lt. Walter C. Phillips Jr.**	21 June 1932–22 December 1934
Capt. Derrill deS. Trenholm	November 1920–1 September 1921	2d Lt. Frank E. Grubbs**	22 December 1934–29 February 1936
Inactive	2 September 1921–25 August 1927	1st Lt. James M. Herren**	29 February 1936–14 November 1936
Capt. Robert D. Furguson**	26 August 1927–6 June 1929	Capt. Clarence E. Caldwell Jr.**	15 November 1936–10 April 1938
Inactive	10 April 1938–16 October 1939		

**RAI commanders: O.R. officers.

5th Ammunition Train (5th Division) **Regular Army Inactive**

HQ—Camp Gordon, GA, 1919–20; Camp Jackson, SC, 1920–21; *Inactive,* 1921–28; Lima, OH, 1928–39

Arrived at Hoboken, NJ, on 21 July 1919 on the U.S.S. *Agamemnon* after 6 months of occupation duty in Luxembourg, as an element of the 5th Div. Transferred to Camp Gordon, GA, and arrived there on 27 July 1919. Transferred to Camp Jackson, SC, and arrived there on 13 October 1920. Transferred to Camp Bragg, NC, and arrived there on 5 September 1921. Inactivated on 6 September 1921 at Camp Bragg. Train personnel and equipment concurrently transferred to the 13th Ammo. Tn. The 1st Ammo. Tn. made A.A., 1921–23. The 1st Bn., 3d F.A. made A.A., 1923–27. Allotted to the Fifth Corps Area on 28 February 1927. Organized on 13 January 1928 with O.R. personnel as an RAI unit at Lima, OH. Conducted annual summer training at Fort Knox, KY. Designated mobilization training station was Fort Benjamin Harrison, IN, 1923–27, and Fort Knox, 1927–38. Disbanded on 16 October 1939.

Commanders, 5th Ammunition Train

Capt. Harry E. Menezes	ao January 1920–16 September 1920
Capt. James V. Ware	16 September 1920–11 February 1921
Capt. Louis W. Hasslock	12 February 1921–2 September 1921
Inactive	2 September 1921–13 January 1928
Unknown	13 January 1928–10 August 1928
2d Lt. Frederick R. Ryan**	10 August 1928–ao September 1928
Unknown	ao September 1928–ao July 1930
2d Lt. Kenneth J. Rupp**	ao July 1930–ao September 1930
Unknown	ao September 1930–ao July 1937
Capt. Frank Camm**	ao July 1937–ao September 1937
Capt. M. King**	ao July 1938–16 October 1939

**RAI commanders: O.R. officers.

6th Ammunition Train (6th Division) **Regular Army Inactive**

HQ—Camp Grant, IL, 1919–21; Camp Knox, KY, 1921; *Inactive,* 1921–26; Chicago, IL, 1926–39

Arrived at Newport News, VA, on 11 July 1919 on the U.S.S. *Siboney* after 6 months of occupation duty in the vicinity of Aignay-le-Duc, France, and Bad Bertrich, Germany, as an element of the 6th Div. Transferred to Camp Grant, IL, and arrived there on 18 June 1919. Transferred to Camp Knox, KY, and arrived there on 25 October 1921. Inactivated on 17 November 1921 at Camp Knox. Train personnel concurrently transferred to the 83d F.A. The 2d Ammo. Tn. made A.A., 1921–23. The 1st Bn., 14th F.A. made A.A., 1923–27. Organized on 10 September 1926 with O.R. personnel as an RAI unit at Chicago. Typically conducted Inactive Training Period meetings at the Pure Oil Building in Chicago. Conducted annual summer training most years at Camp McCoy, WI. Conducted summer training in 1928 with Headquarters and Headquarters Battery (HHB), 57th F.A. Brig. at Camp Williams, WI. Designated mobilization training station was Camp Grant. Disbanded on 16 October 1939.

Commanders, 6th Ammunition Train

Maj. Frank J. Laraway	ao December 1919–4 February 1920
Maj. Rush Clinton	4 February 1920–21 February 1921
1st Lt. Zim E. Lawhon	21 February 1921–16 March 1921
Capt. Armand S. Miller	16 March 1921–17 November 1921
Inactive	18 November 1921–9 September 1926
Capt. Charles H. Welles**	10 September 1926–January 1927
Maj. Horace R. Denton**	January 1927–30 June 1927
Capt. Charles H. Welles**	30 June 1927–ao June 1928
Unknown	ao June 1928–ao June 1930
Capt. Leland S. Jennings**	ao June 1930–ao June 1933
Unknown	ao June 1933–16 February 1937
Capt. Max T. Terrill**	16 February 1937–ao June 1937
1st Lt. Gilbert H. Erb**	ao June 1938–16 October 1939

**RAI commanders: O.R. officers.

7th Ammunition Train (7th Division) **Regular Army Inactive**

HQ—Camp Funston, KS, 1919–20; Camp George G. Meade, MD, 1920–21; *Inactive,* 1921–26; Sioux City, IA, 1926–39

Arrived at the port of New York on 22 June 1919 on the S.S. *H. R. Mallory* after 6 months of occupation duty in the vicinity of the Puvenelle Sector, and the Colombey-les-Belles Training Area, France, as an element of the 7th Div. Transferred to Camp Funston, KS, and arrived there on 30 June 1919. Transferred to Camp George G. Meade, MD, and arrived there on 8 January 1921. Inactivated on 30 September 1921 at Camp Dix, NJ. Train personnel concurrently transferred to the 1st Ammo. Tn. The 1st Ammo. Tn. made A.A., 1921–23. The 1st Bn., 9th F.A. made A.A., 1923–27. Organized on 27 October 1926 with O.R. personnel as an RAI unit at Sioux City, IA. Conducted annual summer training at Fort Riley, KS. Designated mobilization training station was Camp McCoy, WI, 1927–38. Disbanded 16 October 1939.

Commanders, 7th Ammunition Train

Lt. Col. LeRoy Bartlett	16 February 1919–1 February 1920	Capt. Harry L. Powell Jr.	November 1920–30 September 1921
Capt. William H. Sweet	1 February 1920–13 April 1920	1st Lt. James R. Whitaker**	27 October 1926–ao June 1927
Maj. William R. McCleary	13 April 1920–November 1920	Unknown	ao June 1927–16 October 1939

**RAI commanders: O.R. officers.

8th Ammunition Train (8th Division) **Regular Army Inactive**

HQ—Camp Knox, KY, 1919; *Demobilized,* 1921–22; *Inactive,* 1922–27; Roanoke, VA, 1927–32; *Inactive,* 1932–39

Arrived at Camp Mills, NY, in January 1919 after 2 months of duty at Ploermel, France, as an element of the 8th Div. Transferred to Camp Knox, KY, and arrived there on 22 January 1919. Relieved from the 8th Div. Demobilized on 24 February 1919 at Camp Knox. Reconstituted in the R.A. on 8 February 1921. Concurrently activated at Camp Knox as an element of the 8th F.A. Brig. Transferred on 11 November 1921 to Camp Bragg, NC. Inactivated on 7 January 1922 at Camp Bragg. Train personnel concurrently transferred to the 13th Ammo. Tn. The 13th Ammo Tn. made A.A., 1922–23. The 1st Bn., 16th F.A. made A.A., 1923–27. Assigned to the 8th Div. on 24 March 1923. Allotted to the Third Corps Area on 28 February 1927. Organized on 29 June 1927 with O.R. personnel as an RAI unit at Roanoke, VA. Inactivated by July 1932 at Roanoke by relief of personnel. Designated mobilization training station was Fort Myer, VA, 1923–27, and Camp George G. Meade, MD, 1927–38. Disbanded on 16 October 1939.

Commanders, 8th Ammunition Train

1st Lt. Paul G. Bell	10 March 1921–7 January 1922	1st Lt. Water C. Ames**	29 June 1927–2 December 1929
Inactive	8 January 1922–29 June 1927	1st Lt. Morrell W. Talbot**	2 December 1929–ao January 1930
		Inactive	July 1932–16 October 1939

**RAI commanders: O.R. officers.

9th Ammunition Train (9th Division) **Regular Army Inactive**

HQ—*Inactive,* 1923–28; Wheeling, WV, 1928–33; *Inactive*, 1933–37; Pittsfield, MA, 1937–40

Stationed at Camp McClellan, AL, as an element of the 9th Div. Demobilized on 8 February 1919 at Camp McClellan. Reconstituted in the R.A. on 24 March 1923 as an element of the 9th Div. The 1st Bn., 18th F.A. made A.A., 1923–27. Allotted to the Fifth Corps Area on 15 August 1927. Organized on 7 November 1928 with O.R. personnel as an RAI unit at Wheeling, WV. Inactivated at Wheeling on 1 October 1933, withdrawn from the Fifth Corps Area, and allotted to the First Corps Area. Reorganized 13 February 1937 with O.R. personnel as an RAI unit at Pittsfield, MA. Typically held Inactive Training Period meetings at the Hotel Kimball or the Federal Building in Springfield, MA. Designated mobilization training stations were Fort Sill, OK, 1923–33; Andover, MA, 1933–36; and Lawrence, MA, 1936–40. Disbanded on 1 July 1940.

Commanders, 9th Ammunition Train

Capt. Roy C. Bobbitt**	7 November 1928–1 October 1933	Capt. Woodward J. May**	13 February 1937–28 November 1937
Inactive	1 October 1933–13 February 1937	Capt. Albert C. Cushman**	28 November 1937–1 July 1940

**RAI commanders: O.R. officers.

11th Ammunition Train (Hawaiian Division)

HQ—Schofield Barracks, TH, 1921–30; *Inactive,* 1930–41

Constituted in the R.A. on 28 February 1921, assigned to the Hawaiian Div., and allotted to the Hawaiian Department. Organized on 14 April 1921 at Schofield Barracks, TH. Typically conducted training camps at Kawaihapai, Camp Kahuku, and Kawailoa, TH. Inactivated on 30 November 1930 at Schofield Barracks, TH, and train personnel transferred to units of the 11th F.A. Brig. Location 7 December 1941—*Inactive.*

Status: Disbanded on 27 March 1953.

Events: 33, 37, 75, 88, 120

Commanders, 11th Ammunition Train

Unknown	14 April 1921–ao April 1923	Capt. William D. Alexander	31 August 1927–23 March 1928
Capt. Clarence C. Park	ao April 1923–October 1923	1st Lt. Hugh Cort	23 March 1928–1 September 1929
Unknown	October 1923–ao April 1925	1st Lt. Eugene McGinley	1 September 1929–29 December 1929
Capt. Douglas L. Crane	ao April 1925–31 August 1927	1st Lt. Bjarne Furuholmen	29 December 1929–30 November 1930

12th Ammunition Train (Philippine Division) **Regular Army Inactive**

HQ—*Not organized,* 1921–41

Constituted in the R.A. on 22 October 1921, assigned to the Philippine Div., and allotted to the Philippine Department. The 1st Bn., 24th F.A. made A.A., 1922–27. Location 7 December 1941—*Inactive.*

Status: Disbanded on 27 March 1953.

13th Ammunition Train (Corps)

HQ—Fort Bragg, NC, 1921–30; *Inactive,* 1930–34; North Carolina at large, 1934–40

Constituted in the R.A. on 13 May 1921 and assigned to the 13th F.A. Brig. Organized on 8 June 1921 at Fort Bragg, NC, with personnel from the 5th, 17th, and 21st F.A. Regts. Assigned as an element of the 13th F.A. Brig. to the IV Corps on 2 July 1923. Inactivated on 30 April 1930 at Fort Bragg and allotted to the Fourth Corps Area. Organized on 11 September 1934 with O.R. personnel as an RAI unit in North Carolina. Conducted summer training with the regiment at Fort Bragg. Designated mobilization training station was Fort Bragg, 1930–40. Designated in 1939 to be activated as a "Colored" unit on mobilization. Disbanded on 1 July 1940.

Organization Day: 13 May. Chosen to commemorate the date of constitution of the 13th Ammo. Tn., 13 May 1921.

Commanders, 13th Ammunition Train

Capt. Josiah Wallace	8 June 1921–13 July 1921	1st Lt. Louis E. Snell	17 February 1928–24 July 1929
1st Lt. William B. Leitch	13 July 1921–September 1921	1st Lt. William L. Carr	24 July 1929–14 November 1929
Capt. William D. Hays	September 1921–January 1922	Capt. Lloyd S. Partridge	14 November 1929–30 April 1930
Capt. Robert H. Crosby	January 1922–August 1922	*Inactive*	30 April 1930–11 September 1934
Capt. Schaumburg McGehee	August 1922–5 September 1923	1st Lt. Walter L Morrow**	11 September 1934–1 November 1934
Capt. John D. Key	5 September 1923–January 1925	1st Lt. Wade Wood Jr.**	1 November 1934–ao December 1934
1st Lt. Edward H. Barr	January 1925–January 1927	Unknown	ao December 1934–29 February 1936
1st Lt. Thomas McGregor	January 1927–17 February 1928	Lt. Col. John H. Gerber**	29 February 1936–ao March 1936
		Unknown	ao March 1936–1 July 1940

**RAI commanders: O.R. officers.

14th Ammunition Train (Corps) **Regular Army Inactive**

HQ—*Not organized,* 1921–28; Vincennes, IN, 1928–40

Stationed at Camp Custer, MI, as an element of the 14th Div. Demobilized on 6 February 1919 at Camp Custer. Reconstituted in the R.A. on 24 March 1923, assigned to the 190th F.A. Brig. (III Corps) and allotted to the Fifth Corps Area. The 13th Ammo. Tn. made A.A., 1923–27. Organized on 13 January 1928 with O.R. personnel as an RAI unit at Vincennes, IN. Relieved from the 190th F.A. Brig. (III Corps) on 17 September 1927 and assigned to the 14th F.A. Brig. (VII Corps). Relieved with the 14th F.A. Brig. from the VII Corps on 1 October 1933 and assigned to the V Corps. Designated mobilization training station was Fort Bragg, NC, 1927–40. Designated in 1939 to be activated as a "Colored" unit on mobilization. Disbanded on 1 July 1940.

Commanders, 14th Ammunition Train

Unknown	13 January 1928–5 March 1928	Unknown	ao October 1928–ao August 1933
2d Lt. Roland B. Vandegrift**	5 March 1928–27 September 1928	Maj. Virgil L. Eikenberry**	ao August 1933–ao July 1937
1st Lt. Claude A. Robinson**	27 September 1928–ao October 1928	Unknown	ao July 1937–1 July 1940

**RAI commanders: O.R. officers.

15th Ammunition Train (Corps) **Regular Army Inactive**

HQ—*Not organized,* 1921–27; St. Petersburg, FL, 1927–33; *Inactive,* 1933–36; Los Angeles, CA, 1936–40

Stationed at Camp Stanley, TX, as an element of the 15th Div. Demobilized on 17 February 1919 at Camp Stanley. Reconstituted in the R.A. on 24 March 1923, assigned to the 187th F.A. Brig. (VIII Corps), and allotted to the Fourth Corps Area. The 13th Ammo. Tn. made A.A., 1923–27. Organized on 12 May 1927 with O.R. personnel as an RAI unit at St. Petersburg, FL. Relieved from the 187th F.A. Brig. (VIII Corps) on 5 September 1928 and assigned to the 15th F.A. Brig. (II Corps). Withdrawn from the Fourth Corps Area on 1 October 1933 and allotted to the Ninth Corps Area. Concurrently, relieved with the 15th F.A. Brig. from the II Corps on 1 October 1933 and assigned to the IX Corps. Reorganized on 27 May 1936 with O.R. personnel as an RAI unit at Los Angeles, CA. Designated mobilization training station was Fort Bragg, NC, 1927–33. Disbanded 1 July 1940.

Commanders, 15th Ammunition Train

Capt. John D. Grady**	12 May 1927–17 June 1927	Maj. Roy S. Wood**	30 April 1929–14 June 1932
Capt. Asa N. Skinner**	17 June 1927–15 December 1927	Capt. Herman J. Bankston Jr.**	15 June 1932–1 October 1933
Maj. Howard B. Shofner**	15 December 1927–14 November 1928	*Inactive*	1 October 1933–27 May 1936
Unknown	15 November 1928–29 April 1929	2d Lt. John H. Greene**	27 May 1936–12 December 1936
Unknown	12 December 1936–1 July 1940		

17th Ammunition Train (Corps) **Regular Army Inactive**

HQ—*Not organized,* 1933–35; Kansas City, KS, 1935–40

Constituted in the R.A. on 1 October 1933, assigned to the 17th F.A. Brig. (VII Corps), and allotted to the Seventh Corps Area. Organized on 19 January 1935 with O.R. personnel as an RAI unit at Kansas City, KS. Consolidated on 30 October 1936 with the 17th Ammo. Tn. (a World War I unit organized in September 1918 at Camp Bowie, TX, and assigned to the 17th Div.; demobilized in February 1919 at Fort Sill, OK). Designated in 1939 to be activated as a "Colored" unit on mobilization. Disbanded 1 July 1940.

Commanders, 17th Ammunition Train

Unknown	19 January 1935–ao January 1938	Capt. Warner J. Bishop	ao January 1938–ao March 1938
Unknown	ao January 1938–1 July 1940		

18th Ammunition Train (Corps) **Regular Army Inactive**

HQ—*Not organized,* 1933–34; Chickasha, OK, 1934–40

Constituted in the R.A. on 1 October 1933, assigned to the 18th F.A. Brig. (VIII Corps), and allotted to the Eighth Corps Area. Organized on 20 November 1934 with O.R. personnel as an RAI unit at Chickasha, OK. Consolidated on

20 October 1936 with the 18th Ammo. Tn. (a World War I unit organized in September 1918 at Camp Travis, TX, and assigned to the 18th Div.; demobilized in February 1919 at Camp Travis). Disbanded on 1 July 1940.

Commanders, 18th Ammunition Train

Unknown	20 November 1934–ao July 1938	2d Lt. Robert H. Mitchell	ao July 1938–ao August 1938
Unknown	ao August 1938–1 July 1940		

19th Ammunition Train (Corps) **Regular Army Inactive**

HQ—*Not organized,* 1933–34; Boston, MA, 1934–40

Constituted in the R.A. on 1 October 1933, assigned to the 19th F.A. Brig. (I Corps), and allotted to the First Corps Area. Organized on 26 April 1934 with O.R. personnel as an RAI unit at Boston, MA. Consolidated on 30 October 1936 with the 19th Ammo. Tn. (a World War I unit organized in September 1918 at Camp Bowie, TX, and assigned to the 19th Div.; demobilized in February 1919 at Fort Sill, OK). Typically conducted Inactive Training Period meetings at the Post Office Building in Boston. Disbanded on 1 July 1940.

Commanders, 19th Ammunition Train

Unknown	26 April 1934–1 July 1940

22d Ammunition Train (Corps) **Regular Army Inactive**

HQ—*Not organized,* 1933–34; Chicago, IL, 1934–40

Constituted in the R.A. on 1 October 1933, assigned to the 22d F.A. Brig. (VI Corps), and allotted to the Sixth Corps Area. Organized on 29 March 1934 with O.R. personnel as an RAI unit at Chicago, IL. Designated in 1939 to be activated as a "Colored" unit on mobilization. Disbanded on 1 July 1940.

Commanders, 22d Ammunition Train

Maj. Endocen H. Hillman	29 March 1934–16 February 1937	Capt. Leo B. Briethaupt	16 February 1937–ao January 1940

101st Ammunition Train (26th Division) **Massachusetts National Guard**

HQ—Allston, MA, 1921–39

Constituted in the N.G. in 1921, assigned to the 26th Div., and allotted to the state of Massachusetts. Organized on 10 March 1921 as the 1st Artillery (Arty.) Brig. Ammo. Tn. at Allston, MA, and federally recognized on 23 March 1921. Redesignated 101st Ammo. Tn. on 13 September 1921. Consolidated on 31 May 1930 with the 101st Ammo. Tn. (a World War I unit organized in August 1917 at Camp Bartlett, MA, and assigned to the 26th Div.; demobilized in April 1919 at Camp Devens, MA). Conducted annual summer training most years at Camp Devens, MA, 1922–38. Subordinate batteries reorganized and redesignated Troops A and F, 121st Quartermaster (Q.M.) Squadron (Sq.) on 1 April 1939. HQ disbanded on 1 July 1940.

Events: 190, 280

Commanders, 101st Ammunition Train

Capt. Harry R. Williams	30 July 1921–8 December 1924	Capt. Wolcott E. Chesley	9 December 1924–22 June 1936
1st Lt. Harold F. Drew	23 June 1936–1 April 1939		

102d Ammunition Train (27th Division) **New York National Guard**

HQ—White Plains, NY, 1921–28; *Inactive,* 1928–40

Reconstituted in the N.G. on 30 December 1920, assigned to the 27th Div., and allotted to the state of New York. Organized and federally recognized on 14 November 1921 at White Plains, NY, with personnel from Company A, 1st Infantry (Inf.), New York N.G. Conducted annual summer training most years at Pine Camp, NY, 1922–28. Inactivated on 2 April 1928 at White Plains. Unit requirement remained allotted to the state of New York. Designated mobilization training station was Fort Bragg, NC, 1928–40. Disbanded on 1 July 1940.

Commanders, 102d Ammunition Train

Capt. John A. Lubs	14 November 1921–17 September 1925	1st Lt. Shelton P. Hubbard	17 September 1925–20 January 1927
Capt. William MacRossie	20 January 1927–2 April 1928		

103d Ammunition Train (28th Division) **Pennsylvania National Guard**

HQ—Tamaqua, PA, 1921–40

Reconstituted in the N.G. in 1921, assigned to the 28th Div., and allotted to the state of Pennsylvania. Organized on 6 August 1921 and federally recognized at Tamaqua, PA. Conducted annual summer training most years at Tobyhanna, PA, 1922–40. Converted and redesignated on 1 March 1940 as Troop C, 122d Q.M. Sq. Unit requirement remained allotted to the state of Pennsylvania. Disbanded on 1 July 1940.

Events: 191, 203, 281

Commanders, 103d Ammunition Train

Capt. Frank C. Martel	6 August 1921–24 May 1927	Capt. Edward C. Houser	25 May 1927–1 March 1940

104th Ammunition Train (29th Division) **District Of Columbia/Maryland/Virginia National Guard**

HQ—*Not organized,* 1921–40

Reconstituted in the N.G. in 1921, assigned to the 29th Div., and allotted to the District of Columbia. Withdrawn from the District of Columbia on 7 July 1923 and allotted to state of Maryland. Withdrawn from the state of Maryland on 10 July 1931 and allotted to the state of Virginia. Disbanded on 1 July 1940.

105th Ammunition Train (30th Division) **Georgia National Guard**

HQ—*Inactive,* 1921–24; Waynesboro, GA, 1924–25; *Inactive,* 1925–40

Reconstituted in the N.G. in 1921, assigned to the 30th Div., and allotted to the state of Georgia. Organized on 18 June 1924 and federally recognized at Waynesboro, GA. Conducted annual summer training at Fort Bragg, NC, in 1924. Redesignated A Btry, 118th F.A. on 17 April 1925. Unit requirement remained allotted to the state of Georgia. Atlanta, GA, designated as HQ on reorganization, but the unit was never organized at that location. Designated mobilization training station was Fort Bragg, NC. Disbanded on 1 July 1940.

Commanders, 105th Ammunition Train

Capt. Evan H. McElmurray	18 June 1924–17 April 1925

106th Ammunition Train (31st Division) **Alabama National Guard**

HQ—*Inactive,* 1921–22; Elba, AL, 1922–32; Luverne, AL, 1932–39; *Inactive,* 1939–40

Reconstituted in the N.G. in 1921 as the 114th Ammo. Tn., an element of the 39th Div., and allotted to the state of Alabama. Organized on 16 September 1922 and federally recognized at Elba, AL. Relieved from the 39th Div. on 2 July 1923 and assigned to the 31st Div. Redesignated 106th Ammo. Tn. on 16 January 1924. Conducted annual summer training at Fort Bragg, NC, 1922–25, and Camp Beauregard, LA, 1926–32. Called up in March 1929 for flood relief duty at Elba, AL. Reorganized and redesignated Btry D, 117th F.A. on 1 April 1932. Concurrently, 106th Ammo. Tn. reorganized at Luverne, AL, by redesignation of Btry D, 117th F.A. (organized and federally recognized in 1921 as Btry A, F.A.; redesignated Btry A, 141st F.A. on 1 July 1922; redesignated Btry D, 117th F.A. on 17 June 1927). Train reorganized and redesignated Service (Sv) Company (Co.), 106th Medical (Med.) Regt. on 1 October 1939. Disbanded on 30 September 1939.

Events: 56, 255

Commanders, 106th Ammunition Train

Capt. Charles L. Rowe	16 September 1922–7 July 1932	Capt. James D. Finlay	8 July 1932–1 October 1939

107th Ammunition Train (32d Division) **Wisconsin National Guard**

HQ—River Falls, WI, 1921–27; *Inactive,* 1927–40

Reconstituted in the N.G. in 1921, assigned to the 32d Div., and allotted to the state of Wisconsin. Organized on 7 April 1921 and federally recognized at River Falls, WI. Conducted annual summer training most years at Camp Sparta, WI, 1921–27; Camp Custer, MI, 1922; and Camp Douglas, WI, 1923. Redesignated HQ Btry and Combat Train, 2d Bn., 121st F.A. on 1 June 1927. Unit requirement remained allotted to the state of Wisconsin. Milwaukee, WI, designated in January 1935 as HQ on reorganization, but the unit was never organized at that location. Designated HQ changed by 1938 to Whitefish Bay, WI, but the unit was never organized at that location. Disbanded on 1 July 1940.

Commanders, 107th Ammunition Train

Capt. Charles A. Dawson	7 April 1921–6 April 1923	Capt. Kenneth S. White	6 April 1923–1 June 1927

108th Ammunition Train (33d Division) **Illinois National Guard**

HQ—*Inactive,* 1921–40

Reconstituted in the N.G. in 1921, assigned to the 33d Div., and allotted to the state of Illinois. Chicago, IL, designated as HQ on organization, but the unit was never organized at that location. Designated mobilization station was Camp Grant, IL. Disbanded on 1 July 1940.

109th Ammunition Train (34th Division) **Minnesota National Guard**

HQ—*Inactive,* 1921–40

Reconstituted in the N.G. in 1921, assigned to the 34th Div., and allotted to the state of Minnesota. Disbanded on 1 July 1940.

110th Ammunition Train (35th Division) **Kansas National Guard**

HQ—*Inactive,* 1921–40

Reconstituted in the N.G. in 1921, assigned to the 35th Div., and allotted to the state of Kansas. Disbanded on 1 July 1940.

111th Ammunition Train (36th Division) **Texas National Guard**

HQ—*Inactive,* 1921–40

Reconstituted in the N.G. in 1921, assigned to the 36th Div., and allotted to the state of Texas. El Paso, TX, designated as HQ on organization, but the unit was never organized at that location. HQ location changed in 1930 to San Antonio, TX, but the unit was never organized at that location. Disbanded on 1 July 1940.

112th Ammunition Train (37th Division) **Ohio National Guard**

HQ—Akron, OH, 1921–22; *Inactive,* 1922–40

Reconstituted in the N.G. in 1921, assigned to the 37th Div., and allotted to the state of Ohio. Organized on 13 September 1921 and federally recognized at Akron, OH. Conducted annual summer training in 1922 at Camp Knox, KY. Inactivated on 31 October 1922. Unit requirement remained allotted to the state of Ohio. Designated mobilization training station was Fort Bragg, NC. Disbanded on 1 July 1940.

Commanders, 112th Ammunition Train

Capt. Daniel O. Webster 13 September 1921–31 October 1922

113th Ammunition Train (38th Division) **Kentucky National Guard**

HQ—Stanford, KY, 1921; Louisville, KY, 1921–22; Beattyville, KY, 1922–23; *Inactive,* 1923–40

Reconstituted in the N.G. in 1921, assigned to the 38th Div., and allotted to the state of Kentucky. Organized on 14 May 1921 and federally recognized at Stanford, KY. Unit reorganized and redesignated Co. I, 149th Inf. on 1 July 1921. New 113th Ammo. Tn. concurrently organized and federally recognized from Co. E, 1st Kentucky Inf. at Louisville, KY. Train relocated on 30 March 1922 to Beattyville, KY. Conducted annual summer training in 1922 and 1923 at Camp Knox, KY. Inactivated about September 1923. Unit requirement remained allotted to the state of Kentucky. Designated mobilization training station was Fort Bragg, NC. Disbanded on 1 July 1940.

Commanders, 113th Ammunition Train

Capt. John O. Reid 14 May 1921–1 July 1921
Capt. Robert Cain 1 July 1921–March 1922
Capt. Edward B. Saxton 30 March 1922–September 1923

114th Ammunition Train (39th Division) **Alabama National Guard**

HQ—*Inactive,* 1921–22; Elba, AL, 1922–24

Reconstituted in the N.G. in 1921, assigned to the 39th Div., and allotted to the state of Alabama. Organized on 16 September 1922 and federally recognized at Elba, AL. Conducted annual summer training in 1923 at Camp McClellan, AL. Relieved from the 39th Div. on 2 July 1923 and assigned to the 31st Div. Designated mobilization station was Camp McClellan, AL. Redesignated 106th Ammo. Tn. on 16 January 1924.

Commanders, 114th Ammunition Train

Capt. Charles L. Rowe 16 September 1922–16 January 1924

115th Ammunition Train (40th Division) **Utah National Guard**

HQ—*Inactive,* 1921–40

Reconstituted in the N.G. in 1921, assigned to the 40th Div., and allotted to the state of Utah. Disbanded on 1 July 1940.

116th Ammunition Train (41st Division) **Washington National Guard**

HQ—*Inactive,* 1921–40

Reconstituted in the N.G. in 1921, assigned to the 41st Div., and allotted to the state of Washington. Disbanded on 1 July 1940.

118th Ammunition Train (43d Division) **Vermont National Guard**

HQ—*Not organized,* 1921–40

Constituted in the N.G. in 1921, assigned to the 43d Div., and allotted to the state of Vermont. Disbanded on 1 July 1940.

119th Ammunition Train (44th Division) **New Jersey National Guard**

HQ—*Not organized,* 1921–40

Constituted in the N.G. in 1921, assigned to the 44th Div., and allotted to the state of New Jersey. Designated mobilization training station was Fort Bragg, NC. Disbanded on 1 July 1940.

120th Ammunition Train (45th Division) **Oklahoma National Guard**

HQ—*Not organized,* 1921–23; Bristow, OK, 1923–24; Sperry, OK, 1923–26; Haskell, OK, 1926–27; *Inactive,* 1926–40

Constituted in the N.G. in 1921, assigned to the 45th Div., and allotted to the state of Oklahoma. Organized on 17 May 1923 and federally recognized at Bristow, OK. Demobilized on 31 May 1924 at Bristow. New 120th Ammo. Tn. organized on 16 June 1924 and federally recognized at Sperry, OK. Conducted annual summer training at Fort Sill, OK, 1923–25. Reorganized on 16 June 1926 as HQ Btry, 160th F.A. Concurrently, a new 120th Ammo. Tn. organized and federally recognized at Haskell, OK. Reorganized on 1 January 1927 as Btry B, 160th F.A. Unit requirement remained allotted to the state of Oklahoma. Designated mobilization training station was Fort Sill. Disbanded on 1 July 1940.

Commanders, 120th Ammunition Train

Unknown	17 May 1923–31 May 1924	Capt. Charles R. Taylor	31 May 1924–16 June 1926
Unknown	16 June 1926–1 January 1927		

131st Ammunition Train (I Corps) **Massachusetts National Guard**

HQ—*Not organized,* 1921–23

Constituted in the N.G. in 1921, assigned to the 81st F.A. Brig. (I Corps), and allotted to the state of Massachusetts. Placed on the deferred list on 2 July 1923, redesignated 330th Ammo. Tn., and transferred to the O.R. as a DNG unit. Concurrently relieved from assignment to the 81st F.A. Brig. (I Corps) and assigned to the 194th F.A. Brig. (I Corps). Withdrawn as a DNG unit on 11 January 1927 and allotted permanently to the O.R. as the 330th Ammo. Tn.

132d Ammunition Train (II Corps) **New York National Guard**

HQ—*Not organized,* 1921–22; Middletown, NY, 1922–24; *Inactive,* 1924–27

Constituted in the N.G. on 18 October 1921, assigned to the II Corps Artillery, and allotted to the state of New York. Organized and federally recognized on 25 May 1922 at Middletown, NY, with personnel from the 1st Inf., New York N.G. Assigned to the 15th F.A. Brig. (II Corps) on 2 July 1923. Conducted annual summer training in 1923 at Fort Eustis, VA. HHB inactivated on 24 May 1924, and subordinate batteries reorganized and redesignated as batteries of the 156th F.A. Regt. Concurrently, unit placed on the deferred list, redesignated 331st Ammo. Tn., and transferred to the O.R. as a DNG unit. Withdrawn from allotment to the N.G. on 17 September 1927.

Commanders, 132d Ammunition Train

Maj. John A. Korschen	25 May 1922–24 May 1924

133d Ammunition Train (IV Corps) **Georgia, Alabama, and Tennessee National Guard**

HQ—*Not organized,* 1921–23

Constituted in the N.G. in 1921, assigned to the IV Corps Artillery, and allotted to the states of Georgia, Alabama, and Tennessee. HHB and Batteries E, F, and G allotted to Georgia; Batteries A, B, and I allotted to Tennessee; and Batteries C, D, and H allotted to Alabama. Savannah, GA, designated as HQ on organization, but the unit was never organized at that location. Placed on the deferred list on 2 July 1923, redesignated 332d Ammo. Tn., and transferred to the O.R. as a DNG unit. Withdrawn from allotment to the N.G. on 17 September 1927.

134th Ammunition Train (V Corps) **Indiana National Guard**

HQ—*Not organized,* 1921–23

Constituted in the N.G. in 1921, assigned to the 84th F.A. Brig. (V Corps), and allotted to the state of Indiana. Placed on the deferred list on 2 July 1923, redesignated 333d Ammo. Tn., and transferred to the O.R. as a DNG unit. Concurrently relieved from assignment to the 84th F.A. Brig. (V Corps), and assigned to the 191st F.A.Brig. (V Corps). Demobilized on 5 September 1928.

135th Ammunition Train (VI Corps) **Michigan National Guard**

HQ—*Not organized,* 1921–23

Constituted in the N.G. in 1921, assigned to the 85th F.A. Brig. (VI Corps), and allotted to the state of Michigan on 20 April 1921. Placed on the deferred list on 2 July 1923, redesignated 334th Ammo. Tn., and transferred to the O.R. as a DNG unit. Concurrently, relieved from assignment to the 85th F.A. Brig. (VI Corps) and assigned to the 192d F.A. Brig. (XVI Corps). Designated mobilization training station was Camp Custer, MI. Demobilized on 5 September 1928.

136th Ammunition Train (VII Corps) **Minnesota, Missouri, and North Dakota National Guard**

HQ—*Not organized,* 1921–23

Constituted in the N.G. in 1921, assigned to the VII Corps Artillery, and allotted to the states of Minnesota, Missouri, and North Dakota. HHB and Batteries E, F, and I allotted to Minnesota; Batteries A, B, and G allotted to Missouri; and Batteries C, D, and H allotted to North Dakota. Placed on the deferred list on 2 July 1923, redesignated 335th Ammo. Tn., and transferred to the O.R. as a DNG unit. Concurrently assigned to the 14th F.A. Brig. Demobilized on 5 September 1928.

141st Ammunition Train (First Army) **Pennsylvania National Guard**

HQ—*Not organized,* 1921–23

Constituted in the N.G. in 1921, assigned to the First Army Artillery, and allotted to the state of Pennsylvania. Placed on the deferred list on 2 July 1923, redesignated 336th Ammo. Tn., and transferred to the O.R. as a DNG unit. Withdrawn from allotment to the N.G. on 17 September 1927.

142d Ammunition Train (Third Army) **Nebraska National Guard**

HQ—*Not organized,* 1921–23

Constituted in the N.G. in 1921, assigned to the Third Army Artillery, and allotted to the state of Nebraska. Placed on the deferred list on 2 July 1923, redesignated 337th Ammo. Tn., and transferred to the O.R. as a DNG unit. Initiated as an O.R. unit in 1924 at Davenport, IA. Demobilized on 5 September 1928.

301st Ammunition Train (76th Division) **Organized Reserve Connecticut**

HQ—*Not initiated,* 1921–22; Hartford, CT, 1922–41

Constituted in the O.R. on 24 June 1921, assigned to the 76th Div., and allotted to the First Corps Area. Initiated on 27 April 1922 at Hartford, CT. Consolidated on 28 October 1936 with the 301st Ammo. Tn. (a World War I unit organized in September 1917 at Camp Devens, MA; demobilized on 20 January 1919 at Camp Devens; reconstituted on 28 October 1936). Typically conducted Inactive Training Period meetings at the armory of the Governor's Foot Guards or at Artillery Hall in New Haven. Conducted annual summer training most years with the 7th F.A. at Camp Devens, MA, 1922–40. Designated mobilization training station was Camp Devens, MA. Location 7 December 1941—Hartford, CT.

Status: Inactive in the US Army Reserve as HHD, 2d Brig., 76th Div. (Tng.).

Commanders, 301st Ammunition Train

2d Lt. Donald B. Swett	27 April 1922–May 1922
Maj. Percival F. Sneed	May 1922–5 January 1923
Maj. Theodore Crane	5 January 1923–June 1925
Maj. Charles H. Shons	June 1925–September 1927
Unknown	September 1927–October 1928
Maj. Burgoyne Hamilton	October 1928–ao September 1930
Maj. Allan E. MacNichol	ao May 1931–ao July 1934
Capt. Benjamin D. Kornfield	ao May 1935–ao September 1938
Maj. Sigmund Fischer	ao May 1939–ao July 1939
Capt. James S. Thompson	29 May 1940–ao June 1940
Unknown	ao June 1940–7 December 1941

302d Ammunition Train (77th Division) **Organized Reserve New York**

HQ—Manhattan, NY, 1921–41

Constituted in the O.R. on 24 June 1921, assigned to the 77th Div., and allotted to the Second Corps Area. Initiated on 15 October 1921 at Manhattan, NY. Consolidated on 28 October 1936 with the 302d Ammo. Tn. (a World War I unit organized in September 1917 at Camp Upton, NY; arrived at the port of New York on 27 March 1919 on the U.S.S. *Great Northern*; transferred to Camp Upton where it was demobilized on 15 May 1919; reconstituted on 28 October 1936). Conducted annual summer training most years at Pine Camp, NY, 1922–40. Designated mobilization training station was Camp Dix, NJ. Location 7 December 1941—Manhattan, NY.

Status: Inactive in the US Army Reserve as the 902d F.A. Bn.

Commanders, 302d Ammunition Train

Capt. Albert V. Rockwell	15 October 1921–16 February 1922
Maj. James M. Mayes	16 February 1922–16 February 1927
Unknown	17 February 1927–11 June 1930
Maj. Henry J. Amy	12 June 1930–3 May 1940
Capt. Frank C. Smith	3 May 1940–23 May 1940
Unknown	23 May 1940–7 December 1941

303d Ammunition Train (78th Division) **Organized Reserve New Jersey and Delaware**

HQ—Jersey City, NJ, 1921–37; Trenton, NJ, 1937–41

Constituted in the O.R. on 24 June 1921, assigned to the 78th Div., and allotted to the Second Corps Area. Initiated on 15 October 1921 at Jersey City, NJ. Consolidated on 28 October 1936 with the 303d Ammo. Tn. (a World War I unit organized in December 1917 at Camp Dix, NY; arrived at the port of Newport News on 21 May 1919 on the S.S. *President Wilson*; transferred to Camp Dix where it was demobilized on 23 May 1919; reconstituted on 28 October 1936). Relocated by 1937 to Trenton, NJ. Typically held Inactive Training Period meetings at the Federal Building in Trenton or the Federal Building in Wilmington, DE. Conducted annual summer training most years with the 1st Ammo. Tn. or 6th F.A. at Camp Dix, NJ, or Fort Hoyle, MD, 1922–40. Designated mobilization training station was Camp Dix, NJ. Primary Reserve Officers' Training Corps (ROTC) feeder school was Princeton University. Location 7 December 1941—Trenton, NJ.

Status: Currently active in the R.A. at Fort Dix, NJ, as HHD, 2d Brig., 78th Div. (Tng. Support).

Commanders, 303d Ammunition Train

Maj. Wellstood White	15 October 1921–3 January 1930	Maj. Walton B. Butterworth	28 February 1939–1 July 1940
Unknown	3 January 1930–28 February 1939	1st Lt. Stephen Halsey	12 January 1941–22 February 1941
Maj. Charles W. Lippett	22 February 1941–ao April 1941		

304th Ammunition Train (79th Division) **Organized Reserve Pennsylvania**

HQ—Philadelphia, PA, 1921–41

Constituted in the O.R. on 24 June 1921, assigned to the 79th Div., and allotted to the Third Corps Area. Initiated on 9 December 1921 at Philadelphia, PA. Consolidated on 28 October 1936 with the 304th Ammo. Tn. (a World War I unit organized in September 1917 at Camp George G. Meade, MD; arrived at the port of New York on 27 May 1919 on the U.S.S. *Princess Matoika*; transferred to Camp Dix where it was demobilized, 3–6 June 1919; reconstituted on 28 October 1936). Conducted annual summer training most years with the 1st Ammo. Tn. or 6th F.A. at Fort Hoyle, MD, 1922–40. Designated mobilization training station was Camp Dix, NJ. Location 7 December 1941—Philadelphia, PA.

Status: Inactive in the US Army Reserve as the 904th F.A. Bn.

Commanders, 304th Ammunition Train

2d Lt. W.F. Brinkmann	9 December 1921–ao January 1922	Maj. Horace W. Shelmire	ao August 1922–July 1924
Unknown	July 1924–7 December 1941		

305th Ammunition Train (80th Division) **Organized Reserve District of Columbia**

HQ—Washington, DC, 1921–41

Constituted in the O.R. on 24 June 1921, assigned to the 80th Div., and allotted to the Third Corps Area. Initiated on 5 December 1921 at Washington, DC. Consolidated on 28 October 1936 with the 305th Ammo. Tn. (a World War I unit organized in September 1917 at Camp Lee, VA; arrived at the port of Philadelphia on 1 June 1919 on the U.S.S. *Canandaigua*; transferred to Camp Dix where it was demobilized on 9 June 1919; reconstituted on 28 October 1936). Typically conducted Inactive Training Period meetings at the Munitions Building in Washington. Conducted annual summer training most years with the 1st Ammo. Tn. or 6th F.A. at Fort Hoyle, MD, 1922–40. Location 7 December 1941—Washington, DC.

Status: Currently active in the US Army Reserve at Salem, VA, as HHD, 2d Brig., 80th Div. (Institutional Training).

Commanders, 305th Ammunition Train

1st Lt. J.C. Walker	5 December 1921–16 January 1922	Maj. Henry H. Chapman	ao June 1928–29 September 1935
Maj. Fred A. Carter	16 January 1922–ao October 1922	Capt. William Hayes	29 September 1935–12 January 1936
Maj. Edward M. Nevils	ao August 1923–ao January 1924	Maj. Henry H. Chapman	12 January 1936–ao July 1937
Unknown	ao January 1924–ao June 1928	Maj. Basil P. Cooper	ao July 1938–ao September 1938
Unknown	ao September 1938–7 December 1941		

306th Ammunition Train (81st Division) **Organized Reserve North Carolina**

HQ—*Not initiated,* 1921–22; Greensboro, NC, 1922–40; *Inactive,* 1940–41

Constituted in the O.R. on 24 June 1921, assigned to the 81st Div., and allotted to the Fourth Corps Area. Initiated in April 1922 at Greensboro, NC. Consolidated on 28 October 1936 with the 306th Ammo. Tn. (a World War I unit organized in October 1917 at Camp Jackson, SC; arrived at the port of New York on 7 June 1919 on the U.S.S. *Missouri*; transferred to Camp Jackson where it was demobilized on 28 June 1919; reconstituted on 28 October 1936). Conducted annual summer training most years with the 13th Ammo. Tn. at Fort Bragg, NC, 1922–40. Designated mobilization training station was Camp Jackson, SC. Inactivated on 29 August 1940 at Greensboro by relief of personnel. Location 7 December 1941—*Inactive.*

Status: Inactive in the US Army Reserve as the 906th F.A. Bn.

Commanders, 306th Ammunition Train

Maj. Samuel R. Dighton	ao December 1923–ao February 1924	Unknown	ao August 1925–ao October 1939
Unknown	ao February 1924–ao July 1925	Maj. Louis D. Bejach	ao October 1939–ao November 1939
Maj. William D. Harris	ao July 1925–ao August 1925	Unknown	ao November 1939–29 August 1940
Inactive	29 August 1940–7 December 1941		

307th Ammunition Train (82d Division) **Organized Reserve South Carolina**

HQ—*Not initiated,* 1921–22; Newberry, SC, 1922–41

Constituted in the O.R. on 24 June 1921, assigned to the 82d Div., and allotted to the Fourth Corps Area. Initiated on 14 January 1922 at Newberry, SC. Consolidated on 28 October 1936 with the 307th Ammo. Tn. (a World War I unit organized in October 1917 at Camp Gordon, GA; arrived at the port of New York on 12 May 1919 on the U.S.S. *Arcadia*; transferred to Camp Upton, NY, where it was demobilized on 23 May 1919; reconstituted on 28 October 1936). Conducted annual summer training most years with the 13th Ammo. Tn. at Fort Bragg, NC, 1922–40. Location 7 December 1941—Newberry, SC.

Status: Inactive in the US Army Reserve as the 907th F.A. Bn.

Commanders, 307th Ammunition Train

Maj. Charles E. Littlejohn	14 January 1922–ao February 1922	Unknown	ao April 1936–ao October 1939
Unknown	ao February 1922–28 March 1936	Maj. John W. LeCraw	ao October 1939–ao May 1940
Capt. William J. Horsley Jr.	28 March 1936–ao April 1936	Unknown	ao May 1940–7 December 1941

308th Ammunition Train (83d Division) **Organized Reserve Ohio**

HQ—*Not initiated,* 1921–22; Cleveland, OH, 1922–31; Columbus, OH, 1931–41

Constituted in the O.R. on 24 June 1921, assigned to the 83d Div., and allotted to the Fifth Corps Area. Initiated in March 1922 at Cleveland, OH. Consolidated on 7 March 1927 with the 308th Ammo. Tn. (a World War I unit organized in October 1917 at Camp Sherman, OH; demobilized on 14 May 1919; reconstituted on 7 March 1927). Relocated on 9 July 1931 to Columbus, OH. Conducted annual summer training most years at Camp Knox, KY, 1922–40. Location 7 December 1941—Columbus, OH.

Status: Inactive in the US Army Reserve as the 908th F.A. Bn.

Commanders, 308th Ammunition Train

Maj. John A. Bickel	March 1922–16 January 1923	Maj. Robert H. Jamison	ao April 1926–ao August 1926
Capt. Daniel O. Webster	16 January 1923–ao September 1924	Unknown	ao August 1926–ao May 1934
Unknown	ao September 1924–ao April 1926	Maj. Earl C. Duncan	ao May 1934–ao June 1937
Unknown	ao May 1934–7 December 1941		

309th Ammunition Train (84th Division) **Organized Reserve Indiana**

HQ—Fort Wayne, IN, 1921–41

Constituted in the O.R. on 24 June 1921, assigned to the 84th Div., and allotted to the Fifth Corps Area. Initiated on 28 September 1921 at Fort Wayne, IN. Conducted annual summer training most years at Camp Knox, KY, 1922–40. Consolidated on 20 October 1936 with the 309th Ammo. Tn. (a World War I unit organized in September 1917 at Camp Zachary Taylor, KY; arrived at the port of New York on 3 February 1919 on the U.S.S. *Siboney*; transferred to Camp Sherman, OH, where it was demobilized on 17 February 1919; reconstituted on 20 October 1936). Designated mobilization training station was Fort Knox, KY. Location 7 December 1941—Fort Wayne, IN.

Status: Currently active in the US Army Reserve at Beaver Dam, WI, as HHD, 2d Brig., 84th Div. (Institutional Tng.).

Commanders, 309th Ammunition Train

Maj. Jay T. Shafer	28 September 1921–ao January 1923	Capt. Allen M. Emerson	ao June 1937–ao July 1937
Unknown	ao January 1923–ao June 1937	Unknown	ao July 1937–7 December 1941

310th Ammunition Train (85th Division) **Organized Reserve Michigan**

HQ—*Not initiated,* 1921–22; Sault Ste. Marie, MI, 1922–23; Amasa, MI, 1923–25; Manistee, MI, 1925–37, Detroit, MI, 1937–41

Constituted in the O.R. on 24 June 1921, assigned to the 85th Div., and allotted to the Sixth Corps Area. Initiated on 10 January 1922 at Sault Ste. Marie, MI. Successively relocated as follows: to Amasa, MI, in late 1923; to Manistee, MI, on 2 June 1925; and to Detroit, MI, in July 1937. Consolidated on 28 October 1936 with the 310th Ammo. Tn. (a World War I unit organized in September 1917 at Camp Custer, MI; demobilized on 29 April 1919; reconstituted on 28 October 1936). Conducted annual summer training most years at Camp Custer, MI, and Camp McCoy, WI, 1922–40. Designated mobilization training station was Camp Custer, MI. Location 7 December 1941—Detroit, MI.

Status: Currently active in the R.A. at Fort McCoy, WI, as HHD, 2d Brig., 85th Div. (Tng. Support).

Commanders, 310th Ammunition Train

1st Lt. Charles B. Giles	10 January 1922–ao January 1923	Unknown	ao August 1927–ao June 1929
Unknown	ao January 1923–ao September 1925	Maj. Orla G. Miller	ao June 1929–ao August 1929
Capt. Charles H. Schutz	ao September 1925–ao October 1925	Unknown	ao August 1929–ao July 1938
Maj. August Klein	ao May 1926–June 1926	1st Lt. Henry X. Haas	ao July 1938–ao June 1939
Maj. Stephen W. Collins	June 1926–ao August 1927	Unknown	ao June 1939–7 December 1941

311th Ammunition Train (86th Division) **Organized Reserve Illinois**

HQ—*Not initiated,* 1921–22; Centralia, IL, 1922–25; Chicago, IL, 1925–41

Constituted in the O.R. on 24 June 1921, assigned to the 86th Div., and allotted to the Sixth Corps Area. Initiated on 1 April 1922 at Centralia, IL. Relocated on 28 July 1925 to Chicago, IL. Consolidated on 28 October 1936 with the 311th Ammo. Tn. (a World War I unit organized in September 1917 at Camp Grant, IL; arrived at the port of Newport News on 29 January 1919 on the U.S.S. *Zeelandia*; transferred to Camp Grant, where it was demobilized on 11 February 1919; reconstituted on 28 October 1936). Conducted annual summer training most years at Camp Custer, MI, and Camp McCoy, WI, 1922–40. Designated mobilization training station was Camp Grant. Location 7 December 1941—Chicago, IL.

Status: Inactive in the US Army Reserve as the 911th F.A. Bn.

Commanders, 311th Ammunition Train

Capt. George I. Moseley	1 April 1922–17 February 1926	Maj. Ray Harrison	5 November 1928–12 January 1929
Maj. Egbert Robertson	18 February 1926–ao September 1927	Maj. George C. Hager	12 January 1929–ao June 1932
Maj. Milton B. Parsons	ao May 1928–5 November 1928	Unknown	ao June 1932–7 December 1941

312th Ammunition Train (87th Division) **Organized Reserve Mississippi**

HQ—Greenville, MS, 1921–41

Constituted in the O.R. on 24 June 1921, assigned to the 87th Div., and allotted to the Fourth Corps Area. Initiated on 19 December 1921 at Greenville, MS. Consolidated on 28 October 1936 with the 312th Ammo. Tn. (a World War I unit organized in September 1917 at Fort Logan H. Roots, AR; arrived at the port of Newport News on 3 March 1919 on the U.S.S. *Sierra*; transferred to Camp Dix, NJ, where it was demobilized in March 1919; reconstituted on 28 October 1936). Conducted annual summer training most years at Fort Bragg, NC, 1922–40. Location 7 December 1941—Greenville, MS

Status: Currently active in the R.A. at Patrick Air Force Base, FL, as HHD, 2d Brig., 87th Div. (Tng. Support).

Commanders, 312th Ammunition Train

Maj. W.H. Dubard	19 December 1921–ao January 1922	Unknown	ao June 1938–ao October 1939
Unknown	ao January 1922–ao September 1936	Lt. Col. Leslie A. Fitch	ao October 1939–ao May 1940
Capt. Abram D. Somerville	ao September 1936–ao June 1938	Unknown	ao May 1940–7 December 1941

313th Ammunition Train (88th Division) **Organized Reserve Iowa**

HQ—Des Moines, IA, 1921–26; Council Bluffs, IA, 1926–41

Constituted in the O.R. on 24 June 1921, assigned to the 88th Div., and allotted to the Seventh Corps Area. Initiated on 12 October 1921 at Des Moines, IA. Relocated on 26 May 1926 to Council Bluffs, IA. Consolidated on 9 November 1936 with the 313th Ammo. Tn. (a World War I unit organized in November 1917 at Camp Dodge, IA; arrived at the port of New York on 25 May 1919 on the U.S.S. *Pastoren* and transferred to Camp Dodge where it was demobilized on 12 June 1919; reconstituted on 9 November 1936). Conducted annual summer training most years at Fort Des Moines or Fort Riley, KS, and some years at Camp McCoy, WI, 1922–40. Location 7 December 1941—Council Bluffs, IA.

Status: Inactive in the US Army Reserve as the 913th F.A. Bn.

Commanders, 313th Ammunition Train

Lt. Col. Henry G. Geiger	12 October 1921–ao January 1922	Unknown	ao June 1927–ao July 1928
Unknown	ao January 1922–August 1924	Maj. John H. MacMillan	ao July 1928–ao April 1929
Maj. Willard J. Stanton	August 1924–April 1926	Unknown	ao April 1929–ao May 1931
Capt. W.R. Philip	April 1926–ao June 1927	Maj. Earle C. Duncan	ao May 1931–ao August 1931
Unknown	ao August 1931–7 December 1941		

314th Ammunition Train (89th Division) **Organized Reserve Kansas/Nebraska**

HQ—*Not initiated,* 1921–22; Topeka, KS, 1922–24; Atchison, KS, 1924–26; O'Neill, NE, 1926–41

Constituted in the O.R. on 24 June 1921, assigned to the 89th Div., and allotted to the Seventh Corps Area. Initiated in March 1922 at Topeka, KS. Successively relocated to Atchison, KS, on 9 February 1924 and to O'Neill, NE, on 26 May 1926. Consolidated on 26 October 1936 with the 314th Ammo. Tn. (a World War I unit organized in October 1917 at Camp Funston, KS; arrived at the port of New York on 24 May 1919 on the U.S.S. *Agamemnon* and transferred to Camp Dodge, IA, where it was demobilized on 4 June 1919; reconstituted on 26 October 1936). Conducted annual summer training most years at Fort Riley, KS, or Fort Des Moines, IA, 1922–40. Designated mobilization training station was Fort Riley, KS. Location 7 December 1941—O'Neill, NE.

Status: Currently inactive in the US Army Reserve as HHD, 2d Brig., 89th Div. (Tng.).

Commanders, 314th Ammunition Train

Unknown	March 1922–ao February 1938	Maj. Dwight L. Williams	17 March 1938–ao June 1938
Maj. Robert D. Flory	ao February 1938–17 March 1938	Unknown	ao June 1938–7 December 1941

315th Ammunition Train (90th Division) **Organized Reserve Texas**

HQ—Dallas, TX, 1921–25; Waco, TX, 1925–41

Constituted in the O.R. on 24 June 1921, assigned to the 90th Div., and allotted to the Eighth Corps Area. Initiated on 26 November 1921 at Dallas, TX. Relocated on 15 April 1925 to Waco, TX. Consolidated on 28 October 1936 with the 315th Ammo. Tn. (a World War I unit organized in September 1917 at Camp Travis, TX; arrived at the port of Boston on 8 June 1919 on the U.S.S. *Edgar Luckenbach* and transferred to Camp Devens, MA, where it was demobilized on 14 June 1919; reconstituted on 28 October 1936). Conducted annual summer training most years with the 2d Ammo. Tn. or other units of the 2d F.A. Brig. at Fort Sam Houston, TX, 1922–40. Designated mobilization training station was Fort Sill, OK. Location 7 December 1941—Waco, TX.

Status: Currently inactive in the US Army Reserve as HHC, 3d Brig., 90th Inf. Div.

Commanders, 315th Ammunition Train

1st Lt. Frank A. Nice	26 November 1921–20 January 1922	Unknown	ao November 1926–ao March 1928
Maj. Eldred B. LaRue	20 January 1922–ao January 1925	Capt. Leon Goodman	ao March 1928–ao April 1928
Capt. George E. Dewees	ao March 1925–ao September 1925	Unknown	ao April 1928–ao September 1933
Capt. Douglas McKenzie	ao December 1925–January 1926	Capt. Francis W. Kephart	ao September 1933–ao October 1933
Maj. Edward J. Roe	January 1926–ao November 1926	Unknown	ao October 1933–7 December 1941

316th Ammunition Train (91st Division) **Organized Reserve California**

HQ—San Francisco, CA, 1921–41

Constituted in the O.R. on 24 June 1921, assigned to the 91st Div., and allotted to the Ninth Corps Area. Initiated on 23 November 1921 at San Francisco, CA. Consolidated on 28 October 1936 with the 316th Ammo. Tn. (a World War I unit organized in September 1917 at Camp Lewis, WA; arrived at the port of New York on 20 April 1919 on the U.S.S. *Virginian* and transferred to the Presidio of San Francisco, CA, where it was demobilized on 15 May 1919; reconstituted on 28 October 1936). Conducted annual summer training most years at the Presidio of Monterrey, CA, 1922–40. Location 7 December 1941—San Francisco, CA.

Status: Currently active in the R.A. at Fort Carson, CO, as HHD, 2d Brig., 91st Div. (Tng. Support).

Commanders, 316th Ammunition Train

Maj. Joseph J. Mora	23 November 1921–ao November 1924	Capt. Harold P. Ballf	20 August 1934–ao May 1935
Unknown	ao November 1924–ao July 1934	Unknown	ao May 1935–ao June 1936
Capt. Charles W. Leihy	ao July 1934–20 August 1934	Maj. Allen J. Stampa	ao June 1936–ao January 1940
Unknown	ao January 1940–7 December 1941		

319th Ammunition Train (94th Division) **Organized Reserve Massachusetts**

HQ—Worcester, MA, 1921–41

Constituted in the O.R. on 24 June 1921, assigned to the 94th Div., and allotted to the First Corps Area. Initiated in November 1921 at Worcester, MA. Typically conducted Inactive Training Period meetings at the State Armory in Worcester or the University Club in Boston. Conducted annual summer training most years at Camp Devens, MA, 1922–40. Designated mobilization training station was Fort Devens, MA. Location 7 December 1941—Worcester, MA.

Status: Inactive in the US Army Reserve as the 919th F.A. Bn.

Commanders, 319th Ammunition Train

Capt. Thomas L. Logie	November 1921–6 February 1923	Maj. Charles R. Crosset	ao April 1938–May 1938
Maj. Patrick L. Lynch	6 February 1923–ao September 1926	Maj. Isaac A. Crapo	May 1938–ao January 1940
Unknown	ao September 1926–ao April 1938	Unknown	ao January 1940–7 December 1941

320th Ammunition Train (95th Division) **Organized Reserve Oklahoma**

HQ—*Not initiated,* 1921–22; Lawton, OK, 1922–25; Norman, OK, 1925–31; Ardmore, OK, 1931–39; Oklahoma City, OK, 1939–41

Constituted in the O.R. on 24 June 1921, assigned to the 95th Div., and allotted to the Eighth Corps Area. Initiated on 9 January 1922 at Lawton, OK. Successively relocated as follows: to Norman, OK, on 10 July 1925; Ardmore, OK, on 29 April 1931; and to Oklahoma City, OK, on 15 June 1939. Consolidated on 23 October 1936 with the 320th Ammo. Tn. (a World War I unit constituted in the National Army on 30 August 1918; organized on 24 October 1918 at Camp Knox, KY; demobilized on 21 December 1918 at Camp Knox; reconstituted on 23 October 1936). Conducted annual summer training most years with the 2d and 3d Ammo. Tns. at Fort Sill, OK, 1922–40. Designated mobilization training station was Fort Sill. Location 7 December 1941—Oklahoma City, OK.

Status: Currently active in the US Army Reserve at Norman, OK, as HHD, 2d Brig., 95th Div. (Institutional Tng.).

Commanders, 320th Ammunition Train

Capt. Lang A. Mitchell	9 January 1922–11 August 1922	Maj. Reuben G. Lewis	ao February 1926–30 August 1932
Capt. Clarence L. Tylee	11 August 1922–ao April 1925	Unknown	30 August 1932–7 December 1941

321st Ammunition Train (96th Division) **Organized Reserve Washington**

HQ—Seattle, WA, 1921–41

Constituted in the O.R. on 24 June 1921, assigned to the 96th Div., and allotted to the Ninth Corps Area. Initiated on 17 April 1922 at Seattle, WA. Consolidated on 28 October 1936 with the 321st Ammo. Tn. (a World War I unit constituted in the National Army on 25 July 1918; organized on 21 September 1918 at Camp Kearny, CA; demobilized on 21 December 1918). Conducted annual summer training most years at Fort Lewis, WA, 1922–40. Location 7 December 1941—Seattle, WA.

Status: Inactive in the US Army Reserve as the 921st F.A. Bn.

Commanders, 321st Ammunition Train

Maj. James C. Exline	3 May 1922–ao June 1922	Unknown	ao June 1922–7 December 1941

322d Ammunition Train (97th Division) **Organized Reserve New Hampshire/Maine**

HQ—*Not initiated,* 1921–22; Derry, NH, 1922–25; Portland, ME, 1925–41

Constituted in the O.R. on 24 June 1921, assigned to the 97th Div., and allotted to the First Corps Area. Initiated in December 1922 at Derry, NH. Relocated on 10 November 1925 to Portland, ME. Conducted annual summer training most years at Fort Ethan Allen, VT. Location 7 December 1941—Portland, ME.

Status: Inactive in the US Army Reserve as the 922d F.A. Bn.

Commanders, 322d Ammunition Train

Maj. Ralph E. Sawyer	December 1922–ao August 1933	Unknown	ao August 1933–7 December 1941

323d Ammunition Train (98th Division) **Organized Reserve New York**

HQ—Schenectady, NY, 1921–37; Rochester, NY, 1937–41

Constituted in the O.R. on 24 June 1921, assigned to the 98th Div., and allotted to the Second Corps Area. Initiated on 3 December 1921 at Schenectady, NY. Relocated by 1937 to Rochester, NY. Conducted annual summer training most years at Madison Barracks, NY, 1922–40. Designated mobilization training station was Pine Camp, NY. Location 7 December 1941—Rochester, NY.

Status: Currently active in the US Army Reserve at Buffalo, NY, as HHD, 2d Brig., 98th Div. (Institutional Tng.).

Commanders, 323d Ammunition Train

Maj. D. E. McMath	3 December 1921–ao January 1922	2d Lt. Laurence P. Fridley	ao June 1934–ao August 1934
Unknown	ao January 1922–ao May 1927	Unknown	ao August 1934–6 April 1937
Maj. Walter J. Tennant	ao May 1927–ao June 1927	Maj. Thomas J. Shea	6 April 1937–7 June 1940
Unknown	ao June 1927–ao June 1934	Unknown	7 June 1940–7 December 1941

324th Ammunition Train (99th Division) **Organized Reserve Pennsylvania**

HQ—*Not initiated,* 1921–22; Pittsburgh, PA, 1922–41

Constituted in the O.R. on 24 June 1921, assigned to the 99th Div., and allotted to the Third Corps Area. Initiated in May 1922 at Pittsburgh, PA. Conducted annual summer training most years at Fort Hoyle, MD, 1922–40, with the 1st Ammo. Tn. and the 6th F.A. Location 7 December 1941—Pittsburgh, PA.

Status: Inactive in the US Army Reserve as the 924th F.A. Bn.

Commanders, 324th Ammunition Train

1st Lt. Samuel W. Pringle	May 1922–21 November 1922	Unknown	ao September 1925–ao May 1935
Maj. Henry C. Armstrong	21 November 1922–ao September 1925	Maj. Elisha K. Kane	ao May 1935–ao June 1935
Unknown	ao June 1935–7 December 1941		

325th Ammunition Train (100th Division) **Organized Reserve West Virginia**

HQ—Shepherdstown, WV, 1921–31; Parkersburg, WV, 1931–41

Constituted in the O.R. on 24 June 1921, assigned to the 100th Div., and allotted to the Fifth Corps Area. Initiated on 30 November 1921 at Shepherdstown, WV. Relocated on 9 July 1931 to Parkersburg, WV. Conducted annual summer training most years at Fort Knox, KY, 1922–40. Location 7 December 1941—Parkersburg, WV.

Status: Currently active in the US Army Reserve at Owensboro, KY, as HHD, 2d Brig., 100th Div. (Institutional Tng.).

Commanders, 325th Ammunition Train

2d Lt. Samuel G. Williamson	30 November 1921–ao January 1923	Unknown	ao January 1923–7 December 1941

326th Ammunition Train (101st Division) **Organized Reserve Wisconsin**

HQ—*Not initiated,* 1921–22; Kenosha, WI, 1922–37; Milwaukee, WI, 1937–41

Constituted in the O.R. on 24 June 1921, assigned to the 101st Div., and allotted to the Sixth Corps Area. Initiated on 20 October 1922 at Kenosha, WI. Relocated on 28 July 1937 to Milwaukee, WI. Conducted annual summer training most years at Camp McCoy, WI, 1922–40. Location 7 December 1941—Milwaukee, WI.

Status: Disbanded on 6 August 1942.

Commanders, 326th Ammunition Train

Maj. Martin D. Imhoff	20 October 1922–14 March 1923	Maj. Ralph B. Ritter	ao June 1930–ao September 1930
Capt. Palle P.M. Jorgensen	14 March 1923–16 May 1924	Unknown	ao September 1930–ao July 1932
Maj. George W. Rickeman	16 May 1924–ao June 1928	Maj. Edward C. Millstead	ao July 1932–ao September 1938
Unknown	ao June 1928–ao June 1930	Unknown	ao September 1938–7 December 1941

327th Ammunition Train (102d Division) **Organized Reserve Missouri**

HQ—Kansas City, MO, 1921–26; Joplin, MO, 1926–41

Constituted in the O.R. on 24 June 1921, assigned to the 102d Div., and allotted to the Seventh Corps Area. Initiated on 25 October 1921 at Kansas City, MO. Relocated on 26 May 1926 to Joplin, MO. Conducted annual summer training most years at Fort Riley, KS, 1921–40. Location 7 December 1941—Joplin, MO.

Status: Inactive in the US Army Reserve as the 927th F.A. Bn.

Commanders, 327th Ammunition Train

Maj. William H. Knight	25 October 1921–ao May 1922	Unknown	ao May 1922–7 December 1941

328th Ammunition Train (103d Division) **Organized Reserve Colorado**

HQ—*Not initiated,* 1921–22; Denver, CO, 1922–41

Constituted in the O.R. on 24 June 1921, assigned to the 103d Div., and allotted to the Eighth Corps Area. Initiated on 9 January 1922 at Denver, CO. Conducted annual summer training most years at Fort Bliss, TX, or Fort Francis E. Warren, WY, 1922–37. Location 7 December 1941—*Inactive.*

Status: Inactive in the US Army Reserve as the 928th F.A. Bn.

Commanders, 328th Ammunition Train

Maj. Ezra W. Koontz	9 January 1922–8 March 1922	Unknown	ao November 1926–ao January 1929
Capt. Archie A. McFarland	8 March 1922–ao April 1924	Capt. D. M. Sinseng	ao January 1929–September 1930
Maj. Percy D. Whittaker	ao December 1924–ao November 1926	Unknown	September 1930–7 December 1941

329th Ammunition Train (104th Division) **Organized Reserve Wyoming**

HQ—*Not initiated,* 1921–23; Casper, WY, 1923–41; *Inactive,* 1941

Constituted in the O.R. on 24 June 1921, assigned to the 104th Div., and allotted to the Ninth Corps Area. Initiated in May 1923 at Casper, WY. Conducted annual summer training most years at Fort Francis E. Warren, WY, 1921–40. Inactivated on 21 January 1941 at Casper by relief of personnel. Location 7 December 1941—*Inactive.*

Status: Currently active in the US Army Reserve as HHD, 2d Brig., 104th Div. (Institutional Tng.).

Commanders, 329th Ammunition Train

Maj. Bayard C. Wilson	May 1923–ao September 1925	Maj. Leroy O. Moss	ao May 1929–ao September 1929
Unknown	ao September 1925–ao May 1929	Unknown	ao September 1929–21 January 1941
Inactive	21 January 1941–7 December 1941		

330th Ammunition Train (Corps) **Organized Reserve Massachusetts/Ohio/Connecticut**

HQ—*Not initiated,* 1923–27; Dayton, OH, 1927–33; *Inactive,* 1933–34; New Haven, CT, 1934–40

Constituted in the N.G. in 1921 as the 131st Ammo. Tn., assigned to the 81st F.A. Brig. (I Corps), and allotted to the state of Massachusetts. Placed on the deferred list on 2 July 1923, redesignated 330th Ammo. Tn., and transferred to the O.R. as a DNG unit. Concurrently relieved from assignment to the 81st F.A. Brig. (I Corps) and assigned to the 194th F.A. Brig. (I Corps). Withdrawn as a DNG unit on 11 January 1927 and permanently allotted to the O.R. as the 330th Ammo. Tn. Concurrently withdrawn from the First Corps Area and allotted to the Fifth Corps Area. Train remained assigned to the 194th F.A. Brig. and I Corps. Initiated in 1927 at Dayton, OH. Withdrawn from the Fifth Corps Area on 1 October 1933, allotted to the First Corps Area, and concurrently assigned to the 180th F.A. Brig. (XI Corps). Reorganized by August 1934 at New Haven, CT. Conducted annual summer training in 1934 at Fort Sill, OK. Designated mobilization training station was Fort Devens, MA. Disbanded on 1 July 1940.

Commanders, 330th Ammunition Train

Unknown	ao December 1927–1 October 1933	Unknown	ao August 1934–ao January 1940
Inactive	1 October 1933–ao August 1934	Capt. James S. Thompson	ao January 1940–29 May 1940
Unknown	29 May 1940–7 December 1941		

331st Ammunition Train (Corps) (I) **Organized Reserve New York**

HQ—*Not organized,* 1921–22; Middletown, NY, 1922–24; *Inactive,* 1924–26; New York City, NY, 1926–27

Constituted in the N.G. in 1921 as the 132d Ammo. Tn., assigned to the II Corps Artillery, and allotted to the state of New York. Organized on 25 May 1922 and federally recognized at Middletown, NY. Assigned to the 15th F.A. Brig. (II Corps) on 2 July 1923. Conducted annual summer training at Fort Eustis, VA, in 1923. HHB inactivated on 24 May 1924, and subordinate batteries reorganized and redesignated as batteries of the 156th F.A. Regt. Concurrently, unit placed on the deferred list, redesignated 331st Ammo. Tn., and transferred to the O.R. as a DNG unit. Initiated on 19 October 1926 at New York City, NY. Withdrawn from allotment to the N.G. on 17 September 1927 and demobilized.

Commander, 331st Ammunition Train (I)

1st Lt. Ralph J. Bowman	19 October 1926–17 September 1927

331st Ammunition Train (Corps) (II) **Organized Reserve Washington**

HQ—*Not initiated,* 1928–30; Seattle, WA, 1930–33

Constituted in the O.R. on 5 September 1928, assigned to the 189th F.A. Brig. (IX Corps), and allotted to the Ninth Corps Area. Initiated in July 1930 at Seattle, WA. Conducted annual summer training at Fort Lewis, WA. Demobilized on 1 October 1933.

Commanders, 331st Ammunition Train (II)

Unknown	July 1930–1 October 1933

332d Ammunition Train (Corps) (I) **Organized Reserve North Carolina**

HQ—*Not initiated,* 1923–27

Constituted in the N.G. in 1921 as the 133d Ammo. Tn., assigned to the IV Corps Artillery, and allotted to the states of Georgia, Alabama, and Tennessee. HHB and Batteries E, F, and G allotted to Georgia; Batteries A, B, and I allotted to Tennessee; and Batteries C, D, and H allotted to Alabama. Goldsboro, NC, designated as HQ on organization, but the unit was never organized at that location. Placed on the deferred list on 2 July 1923, redesignated 332d Ammo. Tn., and transferred to the O.R. as a DNG unit. Concurrently, relieved from the IV Corps Artillery and assigned to the 189th F.A. Brig. (IX Corps). Designated mobilization training station was Camp Jackson, SC, 1923–27. Withdrawn from allotment to the N.G. on 17 September 1927 and demobilized.

332d Ammunition Train (Corps) (II) **Organized Reserve New York**

HQ—*Not initiated,* 1928–29; Manhattan, NY, 1929–37; *Inactive,* 1937–40

Constituted in the O.R. on 5 September 1928 and allotted to the Second Corps Area. Initiated in July 1929 with HQ at Manhattan, NY. Assigned to the 181st F.A. Brig. (XII Corps) on 1 October 1933. Conducted annual summer training at Fort Hoyle, MD. Designated mobilization training station was Pine Camp, NY, 1928–40. Inactivated in February 1937 at Manhattan by relief of personnel. Disbanded on 1 July 1940.

Commanders, 332d Ammunition Train (II)

Unknown	July 1929–February 1937

333d Ammunition Train (Corps) (I) **Organized Reserve**

HQ—*Not initiated,* 1923–28

Constituted in the N.G. in 1921 as the 134th Ammo. Tn., assigned to the 84th F.A. Brig. (V Corps), and allotted to the state of Indiana. Placed on the deferred list on 2 July 1923, redesignated 333d Ammo. Tn., and transferred to the O.R. as a DNG unit. Concurrently relieved from assignment to the 84th F.A. Brig. (V Corps), and assigned to the 191st F.A. Brig. (V Corps). Demobilized on 5 September 1928.

333d Ammunition Train (Corps) (II) **Organized Reserve Pennsylvania**

HQ—*Not initiated,* 1928–29; Johnstown, PA, 1929–39; *Inactive,* 1939–40

Constituted in the O.R. on 5 September 1928 and allotted to the Third Corps Area. Initiated in December 1929 with HQ at Johnstown, PA. Assigned to the 182d F.A. Brig. (XIII) Corps on 1 October 1933. Inactivated by April 1939 at Johnstown by relief of personnel. Disbanded on 1 July 1940.

Commanders, 333d Ammunition Train (II)

Unknown	December 1929–April 1939

334th Ammunition Train (Corps) (I) **Organized Reserve Florida**

HQ—*Not initiated,* 1923–28

Constituted in the N.G. in 1921 as the 135th Ammo. Tn., assigned to the 85th F.A. Brig. (VI Corps), and allotted to the state of Michigan. Placed on the deferred list on 2 July 1923, redesignated 334th Ammo. Tn., and transferred to the O.R. as a DNG unit. Concurrently, relieved from assignment to the 85th F.A. Brig. (VI Corps) and assigned to the 192d F.A. Brig. (XVI Corps). Designated mobilization training station was Camp Custer, MI. Demobilized on 5 September 1928.

334th Ammunition Train (Corps) (II) **Organized Reserve Florida**

HQ—*Not initiated,* 1928–29; Miami, FL, 1929–33

Constituted in the O.R. on 5 September 1928, attached to the 183d F.A. Brig. (XIV Corps), and allotted to the Fourth Corps Area. Initiated in October 1929 with HQ at Miami, FL. Conducted annual summer training at Fort Bragg, NC. Demobilized on 1 October 1933.

Commanders, 334th Ammunition Train (II)

Unknown	October 1929–1 October 1933

335th Ammunition Train (Corps) (I) **Organized Reserve Minnesota**

HQ—*Not initiated,* 1923–28

Constituted in the N.G. in 1921 as the 136th Ammo. Tn., assigned to the VII Corps Artillery, and allotted to the states of Minnesota, Missouri, and North Dakota. HHB and Batteries E, F, and I allotted to Minnesota; Batteries A, B, and G allotted to Missouri; and Batteries C, D, and H allotted to North Dakota. Placed on the deferred list on 2 July 1923, redesignated 335th Ammo. Tn., and transferred to the O.R. as a DNG unit. Concurrently allotted entirely to the state of Minnesota and assigned to the 14th F.A. Brig. St. Paul, MN, designated as HQ on organization, but the unit was never organized at that location. Demobilized on 5 September 1928.

335th Ammunition Train (Corps) (II) **Organized Reserve Texas**

HQ—*Not initiated,* 1928–29; Fort Worth, TX, 1929–40

Constituted in the O.R. on 5 September 1928, assigned to the 187th F.A. Brig. (XVIII Corps), and allotted to the Eighth Corps Area. Initiated on 11 June 1929 with HQ at Fort Worth, TX. Conducted annual summer training at Fort Sam Houston, TX. Relieved from the 187th F.A. Brig. (XVIII Corps) on 1 October 1933 and assigned to the 188th F.A. Brig. (XVIII Corps). Designated mobilization training station was Fort Sill, OK. Disbanded on 1 July 1940.

Commanders, 335th Ammunition Train (II)

Unknown	11 June 1929–1 July 1940

336th Ammunition Train (First Army) (I) **Organized Reserve**

HQ—*Not initiated,* 1923–27

Constituted in the N.G. in 1921 as the 141st Ammo. Tn., assigned to the First Army Artillery, and allotted to the state of Delaware. Placed on the deferred list on 2 July 1923, redesignated 336th Ammo. Tn., and transferred to the O.R. as a DNG unit. Withdrawn from allotment to the N.G. on 17 September 1927 and demobilized.

336th Ammunition Train (First Army) (II) **Organized Reserve New York**

HQ—*Not initiated,* 1928–29; New York at large, 1929–33

Constituted in the O.R. on 5 September 1928, assigned to the First Army, and allotted to the Second Corps Area. Initiated in July 1929 in New York. Demobilized on 1 October 1933.

Commanders, 336th Ammunition Train (II)

Unknown	July 1929–1 October 1933

337th Ammunition Train (Third Army) **Organized Reserve Iowa**

HQ—*Not initiated,* 1923–24; Davenport, IA, 1924–28

Constituted in the N.G. in 1921 as the 142d Ammo. Tn., assigned to the Third Army Artillery, and allotted to the state of Nebraska. Placed on the deferred list on 2 July 1923, redesignated 337th Ammo. Tn., and transferred to the O.R. as a DNG unit. Initiated by December 1924 at Davenport, IA. Demobilized on 5 September 1928.

Commanders, 337th Ammunition Train

Unknown	ao December 1924–5 September 1928

341st Ammunition Train (Corps) **Organized Reserve Massachusetts/Indiana/Ohio**

HQ—Boston, MA, 1921–27; Bloomington, IN, 1927–37; Columbus, OH, 1937–40

Constituted in the O.R. on 29 July 1921, assigned to the 180th F.A. Brig. (XI Corps), and allotted to the First Corps Area. Initiated on 5 October 1921 with HQ at Boston, MA. Withdrawn from the First Corps Area on 11 January 1927, relieved from the 180th F.A. Brig. (XI Corps), and allotted to the Fifth Corps Area. Concurrently attached to the XV Corps. Reorganized about July 1927 at Bloomington, IN. Assigned to the 184th F.A. Brig. (XV Corps) on 1 October 1933. Relocated on 5 April 1937 to Columbus, OH. Designated mobilization training station was Camp Devens, MA, 1921–27, and Fort Knox, KY, 1927–40. Disbanded on 1 July 1940.

Commanders, 341st Ammunition Train

Lt. Col. Walter L. Bell	5 October 1921–ao January 1922	Lt. Col. R. M. Ames	15 June 1924–ao September 1924
1st Lt. Herman Brody	ao December 1922–ao January 1923	Unknown	ao September 1924–ao June 1937
Maj. Frank B. Cawley	ao August 1923–15 June 1924	Maj. Tyner W. Myers	ao June 1937–ao July 1938
Unknown	ao July 1938–1 July 1940		

342d Ammunition Train (Corps) **Organized Reserve New York/New Jersey**

HQ—Manhattan, NY, 1921–37; *Inactive,* 1937–38; Newark, NJ, 1938–40

Constituted in the O.R. on 29 July 1921, assigned to the 181st F.A. Brig. (XII Corps), and allotted to the Second Corps Area. Initiated on 15 December 1921 with HQ at Manhattan, NY. Withdrawn from the O.R. on 1 October 1933, allotted to the R.A., and assigned to the 20th F.A. Brig. (II Corps). Inactivated by March 1937 at Manhattan by relief of personnel. Reorganized on 7 January 1938 at Newark, NJ. Conducted annual summer training at Madison Barracks or Pine Camp, NY. Disbanded on 1 July 1940.

Commanders, 342d Ammunition Train

Capt. John H. Wiepert	15 December 1921–4 April 1924	Unknown	ao June 1934–7 January 1938
Unknown	4 April 1924–16 June 1931	2d Lt. Richard E. Barter	7 January 1938–11 October 1938
Maj. William C. McEndoe	16 June 1931–ao June 1934	Capt. Willard Potter	11 October 1938–17 April 1939
Capt. Henry F. Branstatter	17 April 1939–25 May 1940		

343d Ammunition Train (Corps) **Organized Reserve Pennsylvania**

HQ—*Not initiated,* 1921–22; Huntington, PA, 1922–29; Altoona, PA, 1929–40

Constituted in the O.R. on 29 July 1921, assigned to the 182d F.A. Brig. (XIII Corps), and allotted to the Third Corps Area. Initiated on 30 March 1922 with HQ at Huntington, PA. Relocated on 11 December 1929 to Altoona, PA. Withdrawn from the O.R. on 1 October 1933, allotted to the R.A., and assigned to the 21st F.A. Brig. (III Corps). Conducted annual summer training at Fort Hoyle, MD. Disbanded on 1 July 1940.

Commanders, 343d Ammunition Train

2d Lt. Davied E. Kessler	30 March 1922–25 April 1922	Maj. Frank F. Henneman	12 March 1929–22 February 1933
Maj. Albert D. Neal	25 April 1922–27 February 1923	Capt. John C. Peightel	23 February 1933–2 March 1933
1st Lt. William C. Campbell	27 February 1923–ao January 1924	Maj. Frank F. Henneman	2 March 1933–21 April 1934
Unknown	ao January 1924–12 March 1929	Maj. John C. Peightel	21 April 1934–29 August 1939
Unknown	29 August 1939–1 July 1940		

344th Ammunition Train (Corps) **Organized Reserve Georgia/Alabama**

HQ—*Not initiated,* 1921–22; Macon, GA, 1922–29; Montgomery, AL, 1929–40

Constituted in the O.R. on 29 July 1921, assigned to the 183d F.A. Brig. (XIV Corps), and allotted to the Fourth Corps Area. Initiated on 23 March 1922 with HQ at Macon, GA. Relocated on 22 October 1929 to Montgomery, AL. Conducted annual summer training at Fort Bragg, NC. Disbanded on 1 July 1940.

Commanders, 344th Ammunition Train

Lt. Col. Stuart Coleman	23 March 1922–7 December 1929
Maj. Thomas H. Nicholson	ao November 1930–ao June 1932
Unknown	ao June 1932–ao January 1936
Capt. Clarence E. Caldwell Jr.	ao January 1936–29 February 1936
Capt. William J. Horsley Jr.	29 February 1936–28 March 1936
Unknown	28 March 1936–2 May 1927
Maj. Victor Lee	2 May 1937–29 January 1939
Unknown	29 January 1939–1 July 1940

345th Ammunition Train (Corps) **Organized Reserve Ohio/West Virginia**

HQ—*Not initiated,* 1921–22; Cleveland, OH, 1922–31; Huntington, WV, 1931–33

Constituted in the O.R. on 29 July 1921, assigned to the 184th F.A. Brig. (XV Corps), and allotted to the Fifth Corps Area. Initiated in April 1922 with HQ at Cleveland, OH. Relieved with the 184th F.A. Brig. from assignment to the XV Corps on 2 July 1923 and assigned to the V Corps. Relocated on 9 July 1931 to Huntington, WV. Conducted annual summer training at Fort Knox, KY. Demobilized on 1 October 1933.

Commanders, 345th Ammunition Train

1st Lt. Nelson D. Foster	April 1922–ao January 1923
Unknown	ao January 1923–1 October 1933

346th Ammunition Train (Corps) Organized **Reserve Illinois**

HQ—*Not initiated,* 1921–22; Woodstock, IL, 1922–25; Oregon, IL, 1925–29; *Inactive,* 1929–35; Oregon, IL, 1935–37; Chicago, IL, 1937–40

Constituted in the O.R. on 29 July 1921, assigned to the 185th F.A. Brig. (XVI Corps), and allotted to the Sixth Corps Area. Initiated in February 1922 with HQ at Woodstock, IL. Relocated on 28 July 1925 to Oregon, IL. Relieved with the 185th F.A. Brig. from assignment to the XVI Corps on 2 July 1923 and assigned to the VI Corps. Inactivated by December 1929 at Oregon by relief of personnel. Relieved with the 185th F.A. Brig. from the VI Corps on 1 October 1933 and assigned to the XVI Corps. Reorganized on 12 September 1935 at Oregon. Relocated on 28 July 1937 to Chicago, IL. Designated mobilization training station was Camp Grant, IL. Disbanded on 1 July 1940.

Commanders, 346th Ammunition Train

Unknown	February 1922–11 July 1922
Lt. Col. Clyde C. Miner	11 July 1922–ao June 1929
Inactive	ao December 1929–12 September 1935
Lt. Col. Louis E. Legner	12 September 1935–4 February 1937
Unknown	4 February 1937–1 July 1940

347th Ammunition Train (Corps) **Organized Reserve Nebraska/Iowa**

HQ—*Not initiated,* 1921–22; Lincoln, NE, 1922–31; Waterloo, IA, 1931–40

Constituted in the O.R. on 29 July 1921, assigned to the 186th F.A. Brig. (XVII Corps), and allotted to the Seventh Corps Area. Initiated in June 1922 with HQ at Lincoln, NE. Relocated on 28 October 1931 to Waterloo, IA. Relieved from the 186th F.A. Brig. (XVII Corps) on 1 October 1933 and assigned to the 187th F.A. Brig. (XVII Corps). Conducted annual summer training at Fort Riley, KS. Disbanded on 1 July 1940.

Commanders, 347th Ammunition Train

Capt. Stephen D. Day	June 1922–13 September 1922
2d Lt. Lee H. Ager	13 September 1922–ao October 1922
Unknown	ao October 1922–1 July 1940

348th Ammunition Train (Corps) **Organized Reserve Texas/Alabama**

HQ—*Not initiated,* 1921–22; Waco, TX, 1922–27; *Inactive,* 1927–29; Tuskegee, AL, 1929–33

Constituted in the O.R. on 29 July 1921, assigned to the 187th F.A. Brig. (XVIII Corps), and allotted to the Eighth Corps Area. Initiated on 5 October 1922 with HQ at Waco, TX. Relieved from the 187th F.A. Brig. on 2 July 1923 and assigned to the 193d F.A. Brig. (XVIII Corps). Conducted annual summer training at Fort Sam Houston, TX, 1922–27. Withdrawn from the Eighth Corps Area on 11 January 1927 and allotted to the Fourth Corps Area as a "Colored" unit, but remained assigned to the XVIII Corps. Initiated on 22 October 1929 at Tuskegee, AL. Designated mobilization training station was Fort Sill, OK, 1922–33. Demobilized on 1 October 1933.

Commanders, 348th Ammunition Train

1st Lt. Frank J. Brophy	5 October 1922–ao April 1924	Lt. Col. William S.T. Holcomb	ao July 1926–11 January 1927
Maj. Edward J. Roe	ao December 1924–ao December 1925	*Inactive*	11 January 1927–22 October 1929
Unknown	ao December 1925–ao July 1926	Unknown	22 October 1929–1 October 1933

349th Ammunition Train (Corps) **Organized Reserve Washington/California**

HQ—*Not initiated,* 1921–22; Seattle, WA, 1922–30; Los Angeles, CA, 1930–37; *Inactive,* 1937–40

Constituted in the O.R. on 29 July 1921, assigned to the 188th F.A. Brig. (XIX Corps), and allotted to the Ninth Corps Area. Initiated on 20 October 1922 with HQ at Seattle, WA. Relieved from assignment to the 188th F.A. Brig. on 5 September 1928 and assigned to the 195th F.A. Brig. (XIX Corps). Relocated on 28 January 1930 to Los Angeles, CA. Typically conducted Inactive Training Period meetings at the Chamber of Commerce Building or at 751 Figuroa Street in Los Angeles, 1930–37. Conducted annual summer training at the Presidio of Monterrey, CA. Inactivated on 11 February 1937 at Los Angeles by relief of personnel. Disbanded on 1 July 1940.

Commanders, 349th Ammunition Train

Maj. Louis L. White	20 October 1922–ao January 1923	Unknown	ao June 1934–ao May 1936
Unknown	ao January 1923–ao June 1932	Maj. William L. Roach	ao May 1936–11 February 1937
Maj. Clarence H. Vose	ao June 1932–ao June 1934	*Inactive*	11 February 1937–1 July 1940

361st Ammunition Train (Fourth Army) **Organized Reserve Pennsylvania**

HQ—*Not initiated,* 1921–22; Erie, PA, 1922–33

Constituted in the O.R. on 15 October 1921, assigned to the 198th C.A. Brig. (Fourth Army), and allotted to the Third Corps Area. Initiated on 25 April 1922 with HQ at Erie, PA. Demobilized on 1 October 1933.

Commanders, 361st Ammunition Train

2d Lt. Rollin A. Sherman	25 April 1922–27 February 1923	1st Lt. Atreus H. Kratzke	ao June 1924–ao July 1924
1st Lt. Thomas M. Boyle	27 February 1923–ao January 1924	Unknown	ao July 1924–1 October 1933

362d Ammunition Train (Fifth Army) **Organized Reserve Indiana**

HQ—*Not initiated,* 1921–24; South Bend, IN, 1924–33

Constituted in the O.R. on 15 October 1921, assigned to the 199th C.A. Brig. (Fifth Army), and allotted to the Fifth Corps Area. Initiated by December 1924 with HQ at South Bend, IN. Conducted annual summer training at Fort Knox, KY. Demobilized on 1 October 1933.

Commanders, 362d Ammunition Train

Unknown	ao December 1924–ao December 1927	2d Lt. Ray D. Jones	19 May 1928–ao June 1928
2d Lt. Horace D. Weigle	ao December 1927–19 May 1928	Unknown	ao June 1928–1 October 1933

363d Ammunition Train (Sixth Army) **Organized Reserve North Dakota**

HQ—*Not initiated,* 1921–22; Bismarck, ND, 1922–33

Constituted in the O.R. on 15 October 1921, assigned to the 200th C.A. Brig. (Sixth Army), and allotted to the Seventh Corps Area. Initiated on 13 October 1922 with HQ at Bismarck, ND. Conducted annual summer training at Camp Sparta, WI. Demobilized on 1 October 1933.

Commanders, 363d Ammunition Train

Unknown	13 October 1922–1 October 1933

364th Ammunition Train (GHQR) **Organized Reserve New York**

HQ—*Not initiated,* 1921–22; Queens, NY, 1922–23

Constituted in the O.R. on 15 October 1921, assigned to the GHQR, and allotted to the Second Corps Area. Initiated on 2 May 1922 with HQ at Queens, NY. Demobilized on 2 July 1923.

Commanders, 364th Ammunition Train

Capt. William Neuss	2 May 1922–2 July 1923

365th Ammunition Train (GHQR) **Organized Reserve Pennsylvania**

HQ—Shamokin, PA, 1921–23

Constituted in the O.R. on 15 October 1921, assigned to the 213th F.A. Brig. (GHQR), and allotted to the Third Corps Area. Initiated on 22 November 1921 with HQ at Shamokin, PA. Demobilized on 2 July 1923.

Commanders, 365th Ammunition Train

2d Lt. M.W. Wilson	22 November 1921–2 July 1923

370th Ammunition Train (Second Army) **Organized Reserve Kentucky/Indiana**

HQ—*Not initiated,* 1921–22; Shelbyville, KY, 1922–25; Paducah, KY, 1925–31; New Albany, IN, 1931–33

Constituted in the O.R. on 15 October 1921, assigned to the 202d C.A. Brig. (Second Army), and allotted to the Fifth Corps Area. Initiated in April 1922 with HQ at Shelbyville, KY. Successively relocated as follows: to Paducah, KY, in April 1925; to New Albany, IN, on 1 July 1931. Conducted annual summer training at Fort Knox, KY. Demobilized on 1 October 1933.

Commanders, 370th Ammunition Train

Maj. Herbert B. Kinsolving	April 1922–24 November 1922	Unknown	ao January 1923–ao May 1933
Maj. Thompson B. Short	24 November 1922–ao January 1923	2d Lt. Maurice G. Knoy	ao May 1933–1 October 1933

371st Ammunition Train (GHQR) **Organized Reserve New York**

HQ—*Not initiated,* 1921–23

Constituted in the O.R. on 15 October 1921, assigned to the 218th F.A. Brig. (GHQR), and allotted to the Second Corps Area. Albany, NY, designated as HQ on organization, but the unit was never organized at that location. Demobilized on 2 July 1923.

372d Ammunition Train (GHQR) **Organized Reserve Pennsylvania**

HQ—*Not initiated,* 1921–22; York, PA, 1922–23

Constituted in the O.R. on 15 October 1921, assigned to the 219th F.A. Brig. (GHQR), and allotted to the Third Corps Area. Initiated on 12 April 1922 with HQ at York, PA. Demobilized on 2 July 1923.

Commanders, 372d Ammunition Train

Capt. Charles P. Hetrick	12 April 1922–2 July 1923

373d Ammunition Train (GHQR) **Organized Reserve Michigan**

HQ—Detroit, MI, 1921–23

Constituted in the O.R. on 15 October 1921, assigned to the 220th F.A. Brig. (GHQR), and allotted to the Sixth Corps Area. Initiated on 8 November 1921 at Detroit, MI. Demobilized on 2 July 1923.

Commanders, 373d Ammunition Train

Capt. Harold F. Matthys	8 November 1921–2 July 1923

374th Ammunition Train (GHQR) **Organized Reserve**

HQ—*Not initiated,* 1921–23

Constituted in the O.R. on 15 October 1921, assigned to the 221st F.A. Brig. (GHQR), and allotted to the Sixth Corps Area. Demobilized on 2 July 1923.

Part V

Coast Artillery Organizations

1919–41

Specific C.A. Abbreviations

Weapon Type/Type of Mount:

AA	Antiaircraft
A/C/BC	British Armstrong weapon/Casemated/Barbette Carriage
A/DC	British Armstrong weapon/Disappearing Carriage
A/P	British Armstrong weapon/Pedestal mount
AGL	Altered Gun Lift
ARF	All around fire (i.e., 360 degrees)
BC	Barbette Carriage
BP	Balanced Piller mount
C/A/P	Casemated/Armstrong weapon/Pedestal mount
C/BC	Casemated/Barbette Carriage
C/P	Casemated/Pedestal mount
Composite	Composite AA battery (usually three 3" AA guns and 3 to 12 .50-cal MGs)
DC	Disappearing Carriage
FM	Field Mount
GPF	Grande Puissance Filloux (a French-designed mobile heavy artillery piece)
P	Pedestal mount
PM	Panama mount
LR	Long Range
LRA	Long Range, Army
LRH	Long Range, Howitzer
LRN	Long Range, Navy
mm	millimeter
MG	Machine Gun
MP	Masking Pedestal mount
MR	Medium Range
NP	Navy gun, Pedestal mount
RY	Railway mount, Gun
RM	Railway mount, Mortar
SL	Searchlight
TM	Turret Mount

Status:

a/c	battery armament type changed
comp.	battery completed
d/a	battery disarmed; weapons removed; position still functional
r/d	battery reduced; number of weapons reduced

Chapter 24

Coast Artillery Major Commands

George H. Ruhlen collection, Ival Lawhon, St. Joseph, MO.

Troops of the 59th Coast Artillery conduct life firing at Battery Hearn, Corregidor, PI, 1938.

There were five types of major coast artillery (C.A.) commands during the interwar years. These commands consisted of C.A. districts, harbor defenses, coast defense commands, coastal frontiers, and sectors. These headquarters (HQ) provided command and control of C.A. organizations assigned or attached to the various coast defenses located along the bays and harbors of the continental United States or in one of the overseas departments.

The five numbered C.A. districts (First, Second, Third, Fourth, and Ninth) were organized in August 1920 from five previously existing geographically named districts. The new districts were numbered and geographically reorganized to align with the corresponding corps areas to which they were subordinated. The new commands did not necessarily mirror the older command's areas of responsibility. Additionally, there were two overseas districts: one in the Hawaiian Department and one in the Panama Canal Department. The Coast Defenses of Manila and Subic Bays essentially functioned as a district for the Philippine Department, and though it never attained that status, it was typically commanded by a brigadier general in peacetime. C.A. districts provided command and control of the various fixed C.A. commands within the department or corps area. They also exercised command and control over attached mobile forces, C.A. and otherwise, for training exercises and wartime defense of harbors and shores. The districts were charged with the coastal defense of harbors, shores, and operationally significant maritime areas within their respective areas of responsibility. The districts' responsibilities included antiaircraft defense as well as planning and coordination requirements with aerial defense commands and naval districts. In peacetime, each C.A. district consisted of two or more fixed defense commands designated as "coast defenses" (later redesignated as "harbor defenses"). For operations, additional mobile assets could be attached to the districts from a department, field army, or General Headquarters Reserve (GHQR).

The stateside C.A. districts also had several peacetime requirements concerning the Reserve Components. Each district was responsible for coordinating and assisting the annual training of National Guard (N.G.) harbor defense regiments and battalions assigned to one of the harbor defense commands in the corps area.

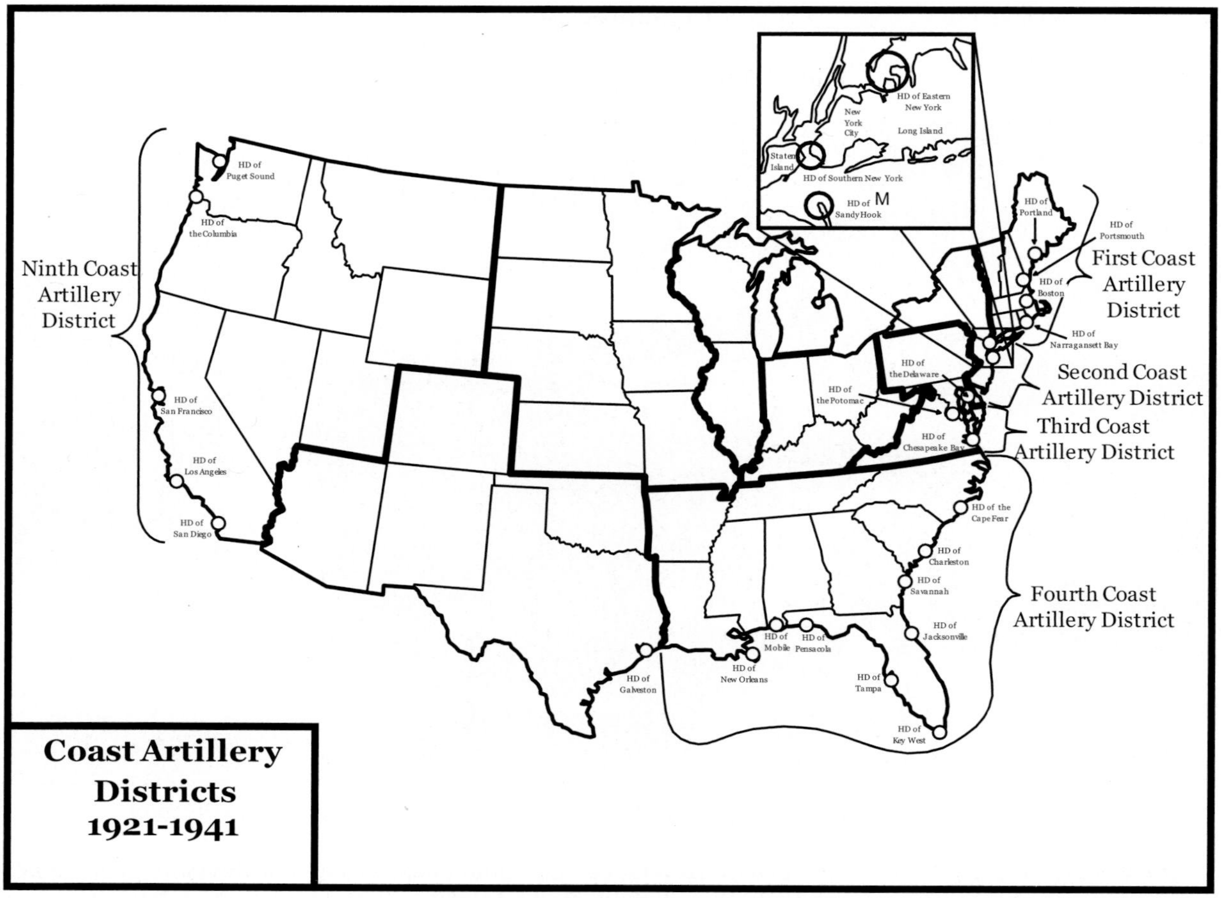

Map, Coast Artillery Districts, 1921–41.

The districts also oversaw preparation of those units' mobilization plans and typically provided the annual inspection teams that verified the readiness of the Guard unit in accordance with Federal requirements. Moreover, the districts assisted the coordination between the Guard unit and its harbor defense command on issues such as integration of the units into the harbor defenses and logistical support on mobilization.

The districts performed essentially the same functions for Organized Reserve (O.R.) C.A. units as those for the N.G.; however, their responsibilities for the former were even greater. In addition, the districts managed the Reserve C.A. units in generally the same manner as the Regular Army (R.A.) staffs did for the Reserve divisions. The district's staff managed the administration of the Reserve personnel assigned to the units, issued general orders and special orders in regard to the units, and determined which units would attend camp in a given year and when and where those camps would be conducted.

As of January 1919, there were 27 R.A. coast defense commands in the continental United States, two in the Canal Zone, and one each in the Philippine and Hawaiian Departments. By 1921, the stateside commands had been significantly reduced in manpower. Many had only a skeletal force to man the batteries and none were maintained at war strength. One coast defense command was placed in caretaker status each year from 1921 to 1924. During the latter year, to maximize use of available manpower and scarce budget dollars, five coast defense commands were placed in caretaker status. Between 1924 and 1930, seven of those commands had all remaining weapons removed and were totally inactivated, though they were retained in mobilization plans for possible reactivation.

Harbor Defenses Continental United States T/O: 302W Approved: 14 July 1926	Coast Artillery Districts	HD of Portland	HD of Portsmouth	HD of Boston	HD of New Bedford	HD of Narragansett Bay	HD of Long Island Sound	HD of Southern New York	HD of Sandy Hook	HD of The Delaware
Corps Area		First	First	First	First	First	First	Second	Second	Second
Regiments & Battalions		8th 240th 613th	8th 614th	9th 241st 615th	10th 616th	10th 243d 616th	11th 242d 618th	5th 619th	7th 245th 262d 620th	7th 261st 621st
Total Batteries in HD		27	7	30	5	20	24	21	29	14
Brigadiers Generals	5	1	--	1	--	1	1	1	1	--
Colonels	5	3	1	3	1	2	2	2	3	1
Lieutenant Colonels	5	3	1	3	--	3	2	2	3	1
Majors	--	16	3	20	1	11	14	16	12	5
Captains	10	46	10	40	7	39	36	35	25	22
1st Lieutenants	--	43	9	45	6	29	30	24	35	19
2d Lieutenants	--	46	10	47	7	22	35	30	45	25
Total Commissioned	25	158	34	167	22	117	120	110	134	73
Warrant Officers	--	3	1	3	1	2	2	2	3	1
Master/Technical/Staff Sergeants	15	105	25	128	80	88	71	81	48	125
First Sergeants	--	27	7	30	5	20	24	21	29	14
Sergeants	10	352	81	406	53	265	267	189	253	176
Corporals	5	458	112	470	64	324	356	267	350	202
Privates First Class	10	936	205	1086	136	689	819	740	851	527
Privates	10	1884	415	2184	288	1385	1637	1490	1788	1074
Total Enlisted	50	3762	846	4304	566	2763	3191	2778	3382	2041
Aggregate	75	3923	881	4474	589	2882	3313	2890	3519	2115

Continental United States Harbor Defense manning chart.

During the same period, the remaining commands suffered cuts as well, but each of them maintained at best two or more active batteries of troops to service key positions determined to be necessary for immediate defense. The remaining battery positions at those commands were also placed in caretaker status. In January 1930, as a further economic measure, 13 more commands were placed in caretaker status and their troops redistributed among the remaining active coast defenses.

In June 1935, the War Department revised the status of various coast defense commands based on classes of readiness. The revised system consisted of the following:

Harbor Defense Classifications
June 1935

Class I — (Full Training) Harbor defense training will consist of all phases and types of C.A. exercises to include firing of harbor defense guns, submarine mine training, and antiaircraft training.

Class II — (Limited Training) Harbor defense training will consist of all phases and types of C.A. exercises except as they are limited by maintenance duties. At harbor defenses having a submarine mine project, special emphasis will be placed on submarine mine training.

T/O: 302W Approved: 14 July 1926	HD of Chesapeake Bay	HD of Charleston	HD of Key West	HD of Pensacola	HD of Galveston	HD of San Diego	HD of Los Angeles	HD of The Columbia	HD of San Francisco	HD of Puget Sound
Corps Area	Third	Fourth	Fourth	Fourth	Eighth	Ninth	Ninth	Ninth	Ninth	Ninth
Regiments & Battalions	12th 246th 260th 622d	13th 252d 263d	13th 264th 265th	13th 266h 267th 623d	13th 268th 624th	3d 251st 625th	3d 251st 626th	3rd 249th 629th	6th 627th 628th	14th 248th 630th
Total Batteries in HD	29	10	6	10	9	7	11	14	33	33
Brigadiers Generals	1		--	--	--	--	--	--	1	1
Colonels	4	1	1	1	--	1	2	1	3	3
Lieutenant Colonels	4	--	1	--	1	1	2	1	3	3
Majors	19	4	6	5	3	4	7	13	13	13
Captains	48	14	12	14	14	20	20	35	55	60
1st Lieutenants	45	16	14	19	16	14	14	27	58	60
2d Lieutenants	50	17	16	19	15	14	16	26	60	59
Total Commissioned	171	52	47	58	49	54	61	103	193	199
Warrant Officers	4	1	--	1	--	1	2	1	3	3
Master/Technical/Staff Sergeants	44	27	39	39	34	30	49	72	124	104
First Sergeants	29	10	8	10	9	7	11	14	33	33
Sergeants	304	94	66	89	73	78	107	156	335	349
Corporals	378	125	91	115	102	106	147	199	400	482
Privates First Class	1068	343	243	353	292	243	376	450	1132	1136
Privates	2137	688	499	714	594	499	756	902	2278	2295
Total Enlisted	4041	1304	934	1320	1104	963	1446	1793	4302	4399
Aggregate	4216	1357	987	1379	1153	1018	1509	1897	4498	4601

Harbor Defense Manning Chart, T/O: 302W.

Class III (Maintenance) Harbor defense training will primarily consist of maintenance of harbor defense armament and accessories. Firing of harbor defense guns will be conducted only on special authorization from the War Department.

These classifications remained in use until the beginning of World War II.

The various fixed defense commands designated as coast defenses were redesignated as harbor defenses in 1925 to provide a title that more accurately reflected the actual mission of the units. The entire coastline of the United States was impossible to defend everywhere, so the system of coast defense comprised both harbor defenses and mobile defenses. In short, the harbor defenses were primarily of a fixed nature and included dispositions and operations for the defense of a limited portion of the seacoast, ordinarily defined as important harbors. The mission of harbor defenses was to deny an enemy the possession, use, or destruction of harbors and facilities. The mission of mobile defenses (i.e., infantry, artillery, and engineer units) in the scheme of coast defense was to prevent the enemy from landing and securing a lodgment on the shore adjacent to, and usually out of the range of, the fixed harbor defenses.

In peacetime, harbor defense commands provided the direct command and control for the harbor defense batteries within the command and ensured the readiness of the defenses for war. The commands also provided the structure around which assigned Regular Army Inactive (RAI), N.G., and O.R. units could assemble and mobilize. The commands also provided various types of training for these Reserve

Component units. Perhaps more so than for most units in the Army, the Reserve Component training provided by the harbor defense commands was extremely relevant as it often took place on the very guns the units would be expected to man in wartime.

Organizationally, these harbor defense commands consisted of a number of separately numbered R.A., N.G., and O.R. C.A. companies until 1924. The number of companies varied with the command, as the manning requirements were not the same for any two commands. In 1924, most of the companies in all three components were redesignated as batteries and integrated into several different types of C.A. units, most of which were fixed harbor defense regiments and separate battalions. The remaining companies were demobilized.

In wartime, the harbor defense commands were responsible for the integration of all harbor defense activities including fixed defenses, mobile defenses, antiaircraft defenses, and mine planting. Many of the commands were large enough to require temporary subordinate commands called groups and groupments. These levels of command were wartime groupings of various battalions, batteries, positions, and minefields within the harbor defense command. The group or groupment provided command and control for a sector of the harbor defenses. Typically, the commanders and staffs of mobilized Guard or Reserve regiments were to form these temporary commands until such time that they were no longer needed.

Harbor Defenses Overseas Garrisons T/O: 854W Approved: 20 May 1921	**HD of Manila & Subic Bays**	**Headquarters, Hawaiian Coast Artillery District**	**HD of Honolulu & HD of Pearl Harbor**	**Total Hawaiian Coast Artillery District**	**Headquarters, Panama Coast Artillery District**	**HD of Balboa HD of Cristobal**	**Total Panama Coast Artillery District**	**Total Overseas Garrisons**
Regiments & Battalions	**59th 60th 91st 92d**		**15th 16th 41st 55th**			**1st 2d 4th 12th 17th 65th**		
Brigadiers Generals	**1**	**1**	**--**	**1**	**1**	**--**	**1**	**3**
Colonels	**3**	**1**	**3**	**4**	**1**	**6**	**7**	**14**
Lieutenant Colonels	**3**	**--**	**3**	**3**	**--**	**6**	**6**	**12**
Majors	**11**	**1**	**11**	**12**	**1**	**20**	**21**	**44**
Captains	**34**	**--**	**37**	**37**	**--**	**83**	**83**	**154**
1st Lieutenants	**33**	**2**	**32**	**34**	**2**	**108**	**110**	**154**
2d Lieutenants	**30**	**--**	**29**	**29**	**--**	**107**	**107**	**343**
Total Commissioned	**115**	**5**	**115**	**120**	**5**	**330**	**335**	**570**
Warrant Officers	**2**	**--**	**2**	**2**	**--**	**2**	**2**	**6**
Master/Technical/Staff Sergeants	**17**	**--**	**15**	**15**	**--**	**40**	**40**	**72**
First Sergeants	**29**	**--**	**29**	**29**	**--**	**58**	**58**	**116**
Sergeants	**335**	**2**	**296**	**298**	**2**	**635**	**637**	**1270**
Corporals	**439**	**--**	**355**	**355**	**--**	**828**	**828**	**1822**
Privates First Class	**1007**	**1**	**832**	**833**	**1**	**3751**	**3752**	**7618**
Privates	**2117**	**1**	**1748**	**1749**	**1**	**3751**	**3752**	**7618**
Total Enlisted	**4000**	**5**	**3320**	**3325**	**5**	**7239**	**7244**	**14,569**
Aggregate	**4117**	**10**	**3437**	**3447**	**10**	**7571**	**7581**	**15,145**

*Note: Assigned regiments are as of 1924-1939.

Harbor Defenses Overseas Garrisons.

Compared to the stateside commands, the overseas harbor defense commands were maintained at much higher levels of readiness. Though not all elements remained active in all units, some regiments were maintained at or near peace strength, and others would have a minimum of at least one full peace-strength battalion.

The eight N.G. coast defense commands organized in the early 1920s were, in effect, regimental HQ for the fixed defense C.A. companies allotted to the commands' respective states. These command HQ and companies were allotted based on mobilization requirements to support fixed defenses in the harbor defense command where the units were intended to serve in wartime. The companies were provided mobilization assignments to the various named batteries in the harbor defenses. It was not clear as to the role of the command HQ however; most likely, the HQ would have been integrated into the HQ for the harbor defense or perhaps formed the command and control element for a fort, group, or groupment. By 1924, all of these commands were reorganized and redesignated as numbered C.A. regiments or battalions.

In 1936, 12 new wartime command HQ were constituted in the R.A. These were three coastal frontiers and nine sectors. The coastal frontiers were intended to supersede the five C.A. districts on activation. The North Atlantic Coastal Frontier would assume command and control for all assigned assets of the First, Second, and Third C.A. Districts. The South Atlantic Frontier would assume command and control for all assigned assets of the Fourth C.A. District, plus the Harbor Defenses of Galveston in Texas. The Pacific Frontier would assume command and control for all assigned assets of the Ninth C.A. District. Each of these frontiers was further divided into three sectors. The sectors would command and control two or more harbor defense commands. As World War II approached in 1941, however, War Department planners determined that the five C.A. districts should convert from peacetime administrative and coordination HQ to wartime frontier command HQ responsible for the integration of coast defense assets for the purposes of frontier defense. This change was instituted right after Pearl Harbor and the districts were redesignated as "Frontier Defense Sectors" in December 1941.

First Coast Artillery District (First Corps Area)

HQ—Boston, MA, 1920–41

Established in the R.A. on 15 November 1920 with HQ at the Textile Building, 99 Chauncey Street, Boston, MA. Organized with personnel and assets from the North Atlantic C.A. District. The district HQ was transferred in 1921 to the Army Base in Boston, MA. The area of the district was identical to that of the First Corps Area. Subordinate commands consisted of the Coast (later redesignated Harbor) Defenses of Boston, Long Island Sound, Narragansett Bay, New Bedford, Portland, and Portsmouth. Responsible for the coastal defense of harbors and operationally significant maritime areas of the North Atlantic seaboard.

Status: Discontinued in February 1944 at Boston as the New England Defense Sector.

Events: 77, 313

Commanders, First Coast Artillery District

Brig. Gen. John W. Ruckman	15 November 1920–7 June 1921	Brig. Gen. Alston Hamilton	7 October 1930–30 July 1935
Col. George F. Landers	7 June 1921–14 December 1921	Lt. Col. Robert E. Guthrie	30 July 1935–1 November 1935
Brig. Gen. Mark L. Hersey	14 December 1921–8 November 1924	Brig. Gen. Arthur S. Conklin	1 November 1935–1 August 1936
Brig. Gen. John D. Barrette	8 November 1924–26 April 1926	Col. Robert W. Collins	1 August 1936–10 August 1936
Col. Frank E. Harris	26 April 1926–19 November 1926	Brig. Gen. Sherwood Cheney	10 August 1936–15 June 1937
Brig. Gen. William P. Jackson	19 November 1926–12 November 1929	Col. Robert W. Collins	15 June 1937–26 May 1938
Col. Homer B. Grant	1 December 1929–22 February 1930	Col. Lloyd P. Horsfall	26 May 1938–June 1938
Col. George H. McManus	22 February 1930–8 May 1930	Brig. Gen. William H. Wilson	June 1938–1 October 1938
Brig. Gen. William E. Cole	8 May 1930–12 September 1930	Brig. Gen. Edmund L. Daley	1 October 1938–15 June 1939
Col. George H. McManus	12 September 1930–6 October 1930	Col. Rodney H. Smith	15 June 1939–20 October 1940
Maj. Gen. Thomas A. Terry	20 October 1940–17 December 1941		

Second Coast Artillery District (Second Corps Area)

HQ—Fort Totten, NY, 1920–31; Manhattan, NY, 1931–41; Fort Hamilton, NY, 1941

Established in the R.A. on 15 November 1920 with HQ at Fort Totten, NY. The district HQ was successively transferred as follows: to 39 Whitehall St., Manhattan, NY, on 11 June 1931; 641 Washington Street in Manhattan on 6 July 1933; 90 Church Street in Manhattan on 3 May 1939; and finally to Fort Hamilton, NY, on 5 March 1941. Organized with personnel and assets from the New York and Delaware portions of the old Middle Atlantic C.A. District. The area of the district was identical to that of the Second Corps Area. Subordinate commands consisted of the Coast (later redesignated Harbor) Defenses of the Delaware, Eastern New York, Sandy Hook, and Southern New York. Also under the command of the Second C.A. District was the Harbor Defense Group, O.R., which was redesignated on 9 April 1923 as HQ, C.A. Reserves, Second C.A. District. Responsible for the coastal defense of harbors and operationally significant maritime areas of New York, New Jersey, and Delaware.

Status: Discontinued on 24 February 1944 at Fort Hamilton as the New York–Philadelphia Defense Sector.

Events: 87, 321

Commanders, Second Coast Artillery District

Brig. Gen. Charles J. Bailey	15 November 1920–18 July 1921
Brig. Gen. Robert E. Callan	21 July 1921–23 November 1921
Brig. Gen. Willoughby Walke	23 November 1921–14 February 1922
Brig. Gen. Andre W. Brewster	14 February 1922–31 December 1922
Brig. Gen. Willoughby Walke	31 December 1922–28 January 1923
Col. James F. Brady	28 January 1923–4 March 1923
Brig. Gen. Hugh A. Drum	4 March 1923–3 December 1923
Col. Gordon G. Heiner	3 December 1923–1 August 1924
Brig. Gen. Johnson Hagood	1 August 1924–10 October 1925
Brig. Gen. William M. Cruikshank	10 October 1925–28 January 1927
Col. Marcellus G. Sparks	28 January 1927–17 April 1927
Brig. Gen. Alston Hamilton	17 April 1927–9 September 1927
Brig. Gen. Stuart Heintzelman	24 October 1927–7 July 1929
Col. Frank K. Fergusson	8 July 1929–22 November 1929
Brig. Gen. Andrew Moses	24 November 1929–24 February 1930
Brig. Gen. Henry J. Hatch	24 February 1930–31 December 1931
Col. Frank K. Fergusson	31 December 1931–4 November 1932
Brig. Gen. William E. Cole	4 November 1932–20 January 1936
Col. Frank K. Fergusson	20 January 1936–31 May 1937
Brig. Gen. Walter K. Wilson	31 May 1937–6 December 1937
Col. Earl Biscoe	6 December 1937–23 August 1938
Col. Avery J. Cooper	23 August 1938–17 November 1940
Brig. Gen. Forrest E. Williford	17 November 1940–29 November 1941
Brig. Gen. Arthur G. Campbell	29 November 1941–17 December 1941

Third Coast Artillery District (Third Corps Area)

HQ—Fort Howard, MD, 1920–22; Baltimore, MD, 1922–23; Fort Monroe, VA, 1923–41

Established in the R.A. on 15 November 1920 with HQ at Fort Howard, MD. The district HQ was successively transferred as follows: to St. Paul Place and Franklin Street in Baltimore, MD, on 12 May 1922; and to Fort Monroe, VA, on 15 May 1923. Organized with personnel and assets from those portions of the old Middle Atlantic C.A. District not incorporated into the Second C.A. District. The area of the district was identical to that of the Third Corps Area. Subordinate commands consisted of the Coast (later redesignated Harbor) Defenses of Baltimore, Chesapeake Bay, and the Potomac. Responsible for the coastal defense of harbors and operationally significant maritime areas of Maryland and Virginia.

Status: Discontinued in February 1944 at Fort Monroe as the Chesapeake Defense Sector.

Events: 128

Commanders, Third Coast Artillery District

Brig. Gen. Harry F. Hodges	15 November 1920–22 December 1921
Unknown	23 December 1921–1 July 1922
Col. John P. Hains	1 July 1922–4 January 1923
Brig. Gen. William R. Smith	4 January 1923–21 December 1924
Brig. Gen. Robert E. Callan	21 December 1924–3 June 1929
Brig. Gen. Charles D. Roberts	4 June 1929–24 August 1929
Maj. Gen. Henry D. Todd Jr.	24 August 1929–31 August 1930
Brig. Gen. Stanley D. Embick	1 September 1930–25 April 1932
Col. Harold E. Cloke	25 April 1932–2 August 1932
Brig. Gen. Joseph P. Tracy	2 August 1932–24 November 1936
Col. Fulton Q.C. Gardner	24 November 1936–3 January 1937
Brig. Gen. John W. Gulick	3 January 1937–12 October 1938
Col. William E. Shedd	12 October 1938–22 November 1938
Maj. Gen. Frederick H. Smith	22 November 1938–8 November 1940
Brig. Gen. Rollin L. Tilton	8 November 1940–17 December 1941

Fourth Coast Artillery District (Fourth Corps Area)

HQ—Fort McPherson, GA, 1920–26; Atlanta, GA, 1926–27; Fort McPherson, GA, 1927–41

Established in the R.A. on 15 November 1920 with HQ at Fort McPherson, GA. The district HQ was successively transferred as follows: to Atlanta, GA, on 1 October 1926; and back to Fort McPherson on 30 June 1927. Organized with personnel and assets from the old South Atlantic C.A. District. The area of the district was identical to that of the Fourth Corps Area. Subordinate commands consisted of the Coast (later redesignated Harbor) Defenses of Cape Fear, Charleston, Key West, Mobile, New Orleans, Pensacola, Savannah, and Pensacola. Responsible for the coastal defense of harbors and operationally significant maritime areas of the South Atlantic seaboard and the Gulf of Mexico, not including the Texas coast.

Status: Discontinued in February 1944 at Fort McPherson as the Gulf Coast Frontier Defense Sector.

Commanders, Fourth Coast Artillery District

Brig. Gen. Johnson Hagood	15 November 1920–1 September 1921	Brig. Gen. Harold B. Fiske	27 November 1928–17 March 1931
Unknown	2 September 1921–27 January 1922	Brig. Gen. William S. McNair	24 March 1931–20 September 1932
Brig. Gen. Frank L. Winn	28 January 1922–5 December 1922	Brig. Gen. James H. Reeves	20 September 1932–30 September 1934
Col. Frederick E. Johnston	5 December 1922–16 July 1923	Brig. Gen. Percy B. Bishop	30 September 1934–15 July 1936
Brig. Gen. William H. Johnson	16 July 1923–6 November 1924	Col. Robert Arthur	16 July 1936–6 January 1937
Col. Alston Hamilton	6 November 1924–16 June 1925	Col. William M. Colvin	7 January 1937–1 April 1938
Col. Andrew Hero Jr.	16 June 1925–12 January 1926	Brig. Gen. Fulton Q.C. Gardner	6 June 1938–1 November 1938
Col. Clint C. Hearn	12 January 1926–31 May 1927	Col. Robert W. Collins	1 November 1938–1 December 1938
Col. Edward Carpenter	31 May 1927–4 January 1928	Brig. Gen. William E. Shedd Jr.	1 December 1938–30 September 1939
Brig. Gen. Frank S. Cocheu	4 January 1928–20 November 1928	Col. Ralph M. Mitchell	30 September 1939–4 December 1941
Brig. Gen. Richard F. Cox	4 December 1941–24 March 1942		

Ninth Coast Artillery District (Ninth Corps Area)

HQ—San Francisco, CA, 1920–21; Presidio of San Francisco, CA, 1921–41

Established in the R.A. on 15 November 1920 with HQ at the Monadnock Building in San Francisco, CA. The HQ was transferred in June 1921 to the Presidio of San Francisco. Organized with personnel and assets from the old North and South Pacific C.A. Districts. The area of the district was identical to that of the Ninth Corps Area. Subordinate commands consisted of the Coast (later redesignated Harbor) Defenses of Columbia, Los Angeles, Puget Sound, San Diego, and San Francisco. Responsible for the coastal defense of harbors and operationally significant maritime areas of the Pacific seaboard.

Status: Discontinued in February 1944 at the Presidio of San Francisco as the Pacific Defense Sector.

Events: 108, 142, 235, 289, 335

Commanders, Ninth Coast Artillery District

Brig. Gen. John D. Barrette	15 November 1920–10 August 1921	Brig. Gen. James H. Reeves	31 July 1931–3 August 1932
Col. Ira A. Haynes	10 August 1921–31 October 1921	Col. Earle D'A. Pearce	3 August 1932–27 May 1933
Brig. Gen. Chase W. Kennedy	31 October 1921–30 November 1922	Brig. Gen. Sherwood A. Cheney	27 May 1933–1 August 1936
Brig. Gen. Ira A. Haynes	30 November 1922–10 September 1923	Brig. Gen. James A. Woodruff	August 1936–1 January 1937
Brig. Gen. Henry D. Todd	11 September 1923–19 August 1926	Brig. Gen. Joseph P. Tracy	1 January 1937–18 June 1938
Brig. Gen. Richmond P. Davis	19 August 1926–25 June 1927	Col. Richard H. Williams	18 June 1938–1 July 1938
Col. Lawrence C. Brown	25 June 1927–13 February 1928	Col. Francis H. Lincoln	1 July 1938–1 October 1938
Brig. Gen. Frank M. Caldwell	13 February 1928–30 November 1930	Brig. Gen. Henry T. Burgin	1 October 1938–29 July 1941
Brig. Gen. James K. Parsons	30 November 1930–31 July 1931	Maj. Gen. Walter K. Wilson	3 August 1941–23 December 1941

Hawaiian Coast Artillery District (Hawaiian Department)

HQ—Honolulu, TH, 1921; Fort Shafter, TH, 1921–25; *Inactive,* 1925–35

Established in the R.A. on 15 November 1920. Organized on 5 April 1921 with HQ at the Young Hotel in Honolulu, TH. HQ transferred on 21 June 1921 to Fort Shafter, TH. Subordinate commands consisted of the Coast (later redesignated Harbor) Defenses of Honolulu and Pearl Harbor. Responsible for the coastal defense of harbors and operationally significant maritime areas of the Hawaiian Islands. Inactivated on 1 March 1925 when the district's subordinate elements were integrated into the Hawaiian Separate (Sep.) C.A. Brigade (Brig.). HQ nominally transferred to Fort DeRussey in October 1929. The district was permanently discontinued on 1 April 1935.

Commanders, Hawaiian Coast Artillery District

Col. Willoughby Walke	November 1919–5 April 1921	Brig. Gen. Richmond P. Davis	12 August 1924–1 March 1925
Brig. Gen. John D. Barrette	5 April 1921–12 August 1924	*Inactive*	2 March 1925–1 April 1935

Panama Coast Artillery District (Panama Department)

HQ—Fort Amador, CZ, 1919–26; Quarry Heights, CZ, 1926–32

Active as of June 1919 with HQ at Fort Amador, CZ. HQ transferred on 29 November 1926 to Quarry Heights, CZ. Subordinate commands consisted of the Coast (later redesignated Harbor) Defenses of Balboa and Cristobal. Responsible for the coastal defense of harbors and operationally significant maritime areas of the Canal Zone. The district was discontinued on 15 April 1932 when its subordinate elements were integrated into the newly organized Atlantic and Pacific Sectors.

Events: 26, 31, 36, 40, 43, 58, 69, 81, 101, 102, 119, 140, 167, 170, 181, 223, 271

Commanders, Panama Coast Artillery District

Col. Alston Hamilton	9 May 1919–4 August 1921	Col. Frank C. Jewell	3 November 1926–3 February 1927
Col. Andrew Hero Jr.	4 August 1921–2 December 1921	Brig. Gen. William M. Cruikshank	3 February 1927–7 January 1930
Brig. Gen. Robert E. Callan	2 December 1921–22 September 1924	Col. Frank K. Fergusson	8 January 1930–8 March 1930
Col. John C. Gilmore Jr.	15 September 1924–12 January 1925	Brig. Gen. Andrew Moses	8 March 1930–7 October 1931
Brig. Gen. William W. Harts	12 January 1925–3 November 1926	Col. Percy M. Kessler	7 October 1931–15 April 1932

Coast Defenses of Balboa (Panama Coast Artillery District)

HQ—Fort Amador, CZ, 1919–41

Subordinate elements—8th, 40th, 45th, 73d, 81st, 87th, 116th, 144th, and *195th* C.A. Companies (Cos.), 1922–24; 4th C.A., 1924–39; *17th C.A.* (RAI), 1926–33; *12th C.A.* (RAI), 1932–40; 65th C.A., 1924–32; U.S.A.M.P. *Col. George F.E. Harrison,* 1921–22; U.S.A.M.P. *Gen. J. Franklin Bell,* 1940–41

Active as of June 1919 with HQ at Fort Amador, CZ. Responsible for the coastal defense of the Pacific approaches to the Panama Canal. Subordinate coast defense installations included batteries at Forts Amador, Kobbe, and Grant. Redesignated Harbor Defenses of Balboa on 9 June 1925. Assigned on 15 April 1932 to HQ, Pacific Sector. Harbor defenses organized as follows:

Harbor Defense Headquarters Fort Amador

Batteries	No. Guns	Weapon/Mount	Location	Remarks:
Battery Haan	2	16" BC LRN	Fort Kobbe, Batele Point	comp. 1926
Battery Murray	2	16" BC LRN	Fort Kobbe, Bruja Point	comp. 1929
Battery Newton	1	16" DC	Fort Grant, Perico Is.	
Battery Warren	2	14" DC	Fort Grant, Flamenco Is.	
Battery #8	2	14" RY	Fort Grant, Culebra Is.	comp. 1928 note 1
Battery Burnside	2	14" DC	Fort Grant, Naos Is.	
Battery Buell	2	14" DC	Fort Grant, Naos Is.	
Battery Carr	4	12" M	Fort Grant, Flamenco Is.	
Battery Merritt	4	12" M	Fort Grant, Flamenco Is.	
Battery Prince	4	12" M	Fort Grant, Flamenco Is.	
Battery Smith	2	6" DC	Fort Amador	
Battery Birney	2	6" DC	Fort Amador	
Battery Parke	2	6" DC	Fort Grant, Naos Is.	
Battery T	2	155-mm GPF PM	Fort Grant, Flamenco Is.	
Battery U	2	155-mm GPF PM	Fort Grant, Flamenco Is.	
Battery V	2	155-mm GPF PM	Fort Grant, Culebra Is.	
Battery W	4	155-mm GPF PM	Taboquilla Is.	
Battery X	2	155-mm GPF PM	Urara Is.	
Battery Y	4	155-mm GPF PM	Taboga Is.	
Battery Z	4	155-mm GPF PM	Fort Kobbe	
Battery 2B	2	155-mm GPF PM	Taboquilla Is.	
Battery (unnamed)	4	155-mm GPF PM	Paitilla Is.	
Battery (unnamed)	2	155-mm GPF PM	Fort Grant, Naos Is.	
75-mm Battery	2	75-mm Gun	Fort Grant, Culebra Is.	
75-mm Battery	4	75-mm Gun	Fort Kobbe	
AA Battery No. 23	3	3" AA	Fort Grant, Naos Is.	
SL Battery	1	60" SL	Fort Grant, Perico Is.	
SL Battery	1	60" SL	Fort Kobbe	

Note 1: The 14" RY guns for this battery could be used in the railway battery at Fort Randolph on the Atlantic side of the Panama Canal as well.

Events: 26, 31, 36, 40, 43, 58, 69, 81, 101, 102, 119, 140, 167, 170, 180, 181, 202, 223, 271

Commanders, Coast Defenses of Balboa

Col. Harry L. Steele	ao January 1920–7 October 1922
Maj. Rollin L. Tilton	7 October 1922–3 November 1922
Col. John T. Geary	3 November 1922–4 December 1923
Col. Jacob E. Johnson	4 December 1923–12 January 1925
Col. Frank E. Harris	13 January 1925–30 July 1925
Maj. Fulton Q.C. Gardner	30 July 1925–20 August 1925
Maj. La Rhett L. Stuart	20 August 1925–9 October 1925
Col. Frank C. Jewell	9 October 1925–21 August 1928
Lt. Col. William M. Colvin	21 August 1928–24 September 1928
Col. James B. Mitchell	24 September 1928–3 December 1929
Col. Robert E. Wyllie	3 December 1929–6 June 1930
Maj. Robert C. Garrett	6 June 1930–25 June 1930
Maj. Otto H. Schrader	25 June 1930–10 September 1930
Col. Laurence C. Brown	10 September 1930–7 June 1932
Lt. Col. George Ruhlen Jr.	7 June 1932–10 September 1932
Col. Russell P. Reeder	10 September 1932–8 September 1934
Lt. Col. James S. Dusenbury	8 September 1934–16 November 1934
Col. Earle D'A. Pearce	16 November 1934–6 May 1937
Col. Francis E. Williford	7 May 1937–28 October 1938
Col. Charles B. Meyer	28 October 1938–21 November 1938
Col. Edward W. Putney	21 November 1938–4 December 1939
Col. William R. Nichols	4 December 1939–21 January 1941
Col. Frederick A. Mountford	21 January 1941–5 November 1944

Coast Defenses of Baltimore (Third Coast Artillery District)

HQ—Fort Howard, MD, 1919–27; *Inactive,* 1927–32; Baltimore, MD, 1932–35; *Inactive,* 1935–41

Subordinate elements—164th C.A. Co., 1922–24; 12th C.A., 1924–32; 2d Battalion (Bn.) and Battery (Btry) D, 622d C.A., 1924–41; *632d C.A.* (Organized Reserve Inactive [ORI]), 1929–41

Active as of June 1919 with HQ at Fort Howard, MD. Responsible for the coastal defense of the approaches to Baltimore Harbor and the northern reaches of Chesapeake Bay. Subordinate coast defense batteries located at Forts Howard, Carroll, Armistead, and Smallwood. Reduced to caretaker status about January 1922. Redesignated Harbor Defenses of Baltimore on 9 June 1925. In accordance with Third Corps Area General Order #3, the Coast Defenses of Baltimore were discontinued on 5 November 1927. All remaining weapons and armament, less Batteries Stricker and Towson, were removed by Ordnance Corps personnel in 1927. However, war plans called for the reactivation of the Harbor Defenses of Baltimore in the event of war. HQ and Medical Department Detachment (Med. Dept. Det.) organized by June 1932 as an RAI unit with O.R. personnel at Baltimore, MD. Inactivated by June 1935 at Baltimore by relief of personnel. Harbor defenses organized as follows:

Harbor Defense Headquarters — Fort Howard

Batteries	**No. Guns**	**Weapon/Mount**	**Location**	**Remarks:**
Battery Key	8	12” M	Fort Howard	d/a 1927
Battery Stricker	2	12” DC	Fort Howard	
Battery Towson	2	12” BC	Fort Carroll	
Battery Hartshorn	2	6” DC	Fort Smallwood	d/a 1927
Battery Nicholson	2	6” DC	Fort Howard	d/a 1927
Battery Augustin	2	3” MP	Fort Carroll	d/a 1920
Battery Clagett	2	3” MP	Fort Howard	d/a 1920
Battery Lazear	2	3” MP	Fort Howard	d/a 1920
Battery Mudge	2	3” MP	Fort Armistead	d/a 1920
Battery Sykes	2	3” P	Fort Smallwood	d/a 1927

Commanders, Harbor Defenses of Baltimore

Col. George W. Gatchell	30 June 1919–6 December 1919	Capt. Charles S. Harris	31 August 1921–7 September 1923
Col. Ellison L. Gilmer	26 December 1919–17 November 1920	1st Lt. Joseph S. Robinson	7 September 1923–May 1925
Capt. August Muehlhouse	17 November 1920–1 December 1920	Capt. Albert Mossman	May 1925–25 July 1927
Maj. Philip B. Connelly	1 December 1920–31 May 1922	1st Lt. William J. Burke	25 July 1927–5 November 1927

Coast Defenses of Boston (First Coast Artillery District)

HQ—Fort Warren, MA, 1919–21; Fort Strong, MA, 1921–22; Fort Banks, MA, 1922; Fort Warren, MA, 1927–41

Subordinate elements—59th, 120th, and 172d C.A. Cos., 1922–24; 9th C.A., 1924–41; 241st C.A., 1922–33, 1939–41; 601st C.A., 1923–41; 606th C.A., 1923–41; 615th C.A., 1924–41; U.S.A.M.P. *Gen. Royal T. Frank,* 1920–22; U.S.A.M.P. *Gen. Absalom Baird,* 1937–41; U.S.A.C.S. *Joseph Henry* 1941

Active as of June 1919 with HQ at Fort Warren, MA. HQ successively transferred as follows: to Fort Strong, MA, in December 1921; Fort Warren on 18 March 1922; Fort Banks, MA, in August 1922; Fort Warren by 1927. Responsible for the coastal defense of the approaches to Boston Harbor. Subordinate coast defense installations included batteries at Forts Warren, Andrews, Banks, Duvall, Heath, Revere, Rodman, Ruckman, Standish, and Strong. Reduced to caretaker status by June 1924. Redesignated Harbor Defenses of Boston on 9 June 1925. Caretaker status reconfirmed on 6 January 1930. Reclassified in June 1935 as a Class II (Limited Training) harbor defense. Defenses upgraded during 1939–41 to Class I (Full Training) with the activation of additional batteries of the 9th C.A. Hosted the visit of President Roosevelt to the Harbor Defenses of Boston on 10 August 1940. The 241st C.A. arrived at Fort Andrews on 23 September 1940 and shortly thereafter assumed the mission of manning batteries in the Harbor Defenses of Boston. Harbor defenses organized as follows:

Harbor Defense Headquarters	Fort Warren
Harbor Entrance Control Post	Fort Dawes
1 Groupment	
6 Groups	

Batteries	**No. Guns**	**Weapon/Mount**	**Location**	**Remarks:**
Mine Battery 1	4 Groups	–		
Mine Battery 2	5 Groups	–		
Battery Long	2	16" BC LR	Fort Duvall	comp. 1927
Battery Gardner	2	12" BC LR	Fort Ruckman	comp. 1924
Battery Winthrop	3	12" DC MR	Fort Heath	
Battery Stevenson	2	12" DC MR	Fort Warren	
Battery Ripley	2	12" BC MR	Fort Revere	
Battery Lincoln	6	12" M	Fort Banks	
Battery Kellog	6	12" M	Fort Banks	
Battery Cushing	4	12" M	Fort Andrews	
Battery Whitman	6	12" M	Fort Andrews	
Battery Burbeck	2	10" DC	Fort Standish	
Battery Bartlett	4	10" DC	Fort Warren	
Battery Hitchcock	3	10" DC	Fort Strong	d/a 1939
Battery Morris	2	10" DC	Fort Standish	
Battery Ward	2	10" DC	Fort Strong	d/a 1939
Battery McCook	2	6" P	Fort Andrews	
Battery Sanders	3	6" BC	Fort Revere	
Battery Terrill	3	6" DC	Fort Standish	
Battery Whipple	2	6" P	Fort Standish	
Battery Plunkett	2	4" P	Fort Warren	d/a 1925
155-mm Battery	4	155-mm GPF PM	East Point	
Battery Stevens	2	3" P	Fort Strong	
Battery Smyth	2	3" P	Fort Strong	d/a 1921 note 1
Battery Taylor	3	3" P	Fort Strong	
Battery Bassinger	2	3" MP	Fort Strong	a/c 1921 note 1
Battery Lowell	3	3" MP	Fort Warren	d/a 1920
Battery Vincent	4	3" MP	Fort Standish	d/a 1920
Battery Bumpus	2	3" P	Fort Andrews	
Battery Weir	2	3" P	Fort Standish	d/a 1926
Battery Williams	2	3" P	Fort Standish	
AA Battery No. 1	Composite			
AA Battery No. 2	Composite			
AA Battery No. 3	Composite			
AA Battery No. 4	Composite			
AA Battery No. 5	Composite			

Note 1: The 3" MP guns from Battery Bassinger were replaced in 1921 with the 3" P guns from Battery Smyth.

Events: 77, 174

Commanders, Coast Defenses of Boston

Col. Morris K. Barroll	20 March 1918–22 February 1919
Col. Stephen M. Foote	15 May 1919–30 October 1919
Col. James F. Howell	1 November 1919–4 August 1921
Col. John T. Geary	4 August 1921–22 October 1922
Lt. Col. George A. Wieczorek	22 October 1922–1 September 1924
Col. Charles E. Kilbourne Jr.	2 September 1924–1 September 1925
Maj. Edgar H. Thompson	6 September 1925–2 November 1925
Col. Frank E. Harris	2 November 1925–30 March 1927
Maj. Edgar H. Thompson	30 March 1927–1 July 1927
Col. Robert F. McMillan	1 July 1927–28 June 1928
Maj. George D. Holland	3 July 1928–1 July 1929
Col. Alexander Greig Jr.	1 July 1929–16 December 1931
Capt. Edward B. McCarthy	16 December 1931–6 February 1932
Capt. Manly B. Gibson	6 February 1932–29 April 1932
Lt. Col. Paul D. Bunker	29 April 1932–22 October 1934
Capt. Manly B. Gibson	22 October 1934–3 January 1935
Capt. Charles S. Denney	3 January 1935–8 March 1935
Capt. Joseph H. Gilbreth	8 March 1935–28 June 1935
Lt. Col. Rollin L. Tilton	28 June 1935–14 July 1937
Capt. Joseph H. Gilbreth	14 July 1937–24 July 1937
Col. Monte J. Hickok	24 July 1937–9 May 1941
Brig. Gen. Kenneth T. Blood	9 May 1941–23 December 1941

Coast Defenses of the Cape Fear (Fourth Coast Artillery District)

HQ—Fort Caswell, NC, 1919–24; *Inactive,* 1924–41

Subordinate elements—19th Coast Defense Co., 1923–24; 252d C.A., 1924–33 and 1938–41; *634th C.A.* (ORI), 1929–41

Active as of June 1919 with HQ at Fort Caswell, NC. Responsible for the coastal defense of the approaches to Wilmington Harbor, NC. Subordinate coast defense batteries at Fort Caswell. Coast Defenses (CD) of the Cape Fear inactivated on 1 July 1924 and placed in caretaker status. Redesignated Harbor Defenses of Cape Fear on 9 June 1925. Although all remaining weapons and armament were removed by Ordnance Corps personnel in 1925, war plans called for the reactivation of the Harbor Defenses of the Cape Fear in the event of war. Harbor defenses organized as follows:

Harbor Defense Headquarters — Fort Caswell

Batteries	No. Guns	Weapon/Mount	Location	Remarks:
Battery Caswell	2	12" BC MR	Fort Caswell	d/a 1925
Battery Bagley	8	12" M	Fort Caswell	d/a 1925
Battery Swift	4	8" DC	Fort Caswell	d/a 1920
Battery Shipp	2	5" BP	Fort Caswell	d/a 1919
Battery McKavett	2	3" MP	Fort Caswell	d/a 1920
Battery McDonough	2	3" P	Fort Caswell	d/a 1925

Commanders, Coast Defenses of the Cape Fear

Col. Arthur Chase	2 September 1917–7 January 1919
Maj. LeRoy Bartlett	20 November 1920–12 December 1920
Capt. Harold B. Bliss	12 December 1920–10 April 1923
1st Lt. Howard H. Newman Jr.	10 April 1923–1 April 1924

Coast Defenses of Charleston (Fourth Coast Artillery District)

HQ—Fort Moultrie, SC, 1919–41

Subordinate elements—*145th*, 170th, and *180th* C.A. Cos., 1922–24; 13th C.A., 1924–41; 263d C.A. Bn., 1924–30; 263d C.A. Regiment (Regt.), 1930–33 and 1938–41; U.S.A.M.P. *Gen. John M. Schofield,* 1921

Active as of June 1919 with HQ at Fort Moultrie, SC. Responsible for the coastal defense of the approaches to Charleston Harbor. Subordinate coast defense installations included batteries at Fort Moultrie and Sumter. Redesignated Harbor Defenses of Charleston on 9 June 1925. Reduced to caretaker status on 6 January 1930. Reclassified in June 1935 as a Class III (Maintenance) harbor defense. Defenses upgraded during 1940–41 to Class I (Full Training) with the activation of additional batteries of the 2d Bn., 13th C.A. The 263d C.A. arrived at Fort Moultrie on 13 January 1941 and shortly thereafter assumed the mission of manning batteries in the Harbor Defenses of Charleston. Harbor defenses organized as follows:

Harbor Defense Headquarters — Fort Moultrie
Harbor Entrance Control Post — Fort Moultrie
3 Groups

Batteries	No. Guns	Weapon/Mount	Location	Remarks:
Battery Huger	1	12" DC MR	Fort Sumter	
" "	1	12" BC MR	Fort Sumter	
Battery Capron	8	12" M	Fort Moultrie	
Battery Butler	8	12" M	Fort Moultrie	
Battery Jasper	4	10" DC	Fort Moultrie	
Battery Thompson	2	10" DC	Fort Moultrie	
Battery Logan	4	6" A/DC	Fort Moultrie	
155-mm Battery	4	155-mm GPF	Fort Moultrie	
Battery McCorkle	3	3" MP	Fort Moultrie	
Battery Lord	2	3" P	Fort Moultrie	
AA Battery No. 1	Composite			
AA Battery No. 2	Composite			
AA Battery No. 3	Composite			

Events: 334

Commanders, Coast Defenses of Charleston

Col. Charles A. Bennet	August 1918–10 May 1920	No officer assigned	3 August 1924–1 December 1924
Capt. John T. Bowe	10 May 1920–19 August 1920	Capt. Harold S. Johnson	2 December 1934–2 June 1927
Col. Samuel C. Vestal	19 August 1920–15 October 1920	Maj. Edwin C. Mead	2 June 1927–28 July 1930
Maj. John H. Birdsall	15 October 1920–December 1920	Maj. Richmond T. Gibson	28 July 1930–5 July 1932
Lt. Col. Frank S. Long	December 1920–21 September 1921	1st Lt. Frederick R. Keeler	5 July 1932–29 September 1932
Capt. Rolla V. Ladd	21 September 1921–5 July 1922	Maj. Octave DeCarre	29 September 1932–September 1934
Capt. Arthur W. Burton	5 July 1922–21 August 1923	Lt. Col. Walter K. Dunn	September 1934–19 July 1937
1st Lt. Edwin C. Calicutt	21 August 1923–2 August 1924	Col. Philip S. Gage	19 July 1937–11 September 1939

Coast Defenses of Chesapeake Bay (Third Coast Artillery District)

HQ—Fort Monroe, VA, 1919–41

Subordinate elements—35th, 41st, 58th, 69th, *103d*, *166th*, and *169th* C.A. Cos., 1922–24; 2d C.A., 1932–41; 61st C.A., 1921–30; 12th C.A., 1924–32; 57th C.A., 1941; 246th C.A., 1922–33 and 1939–41; 609th C.A. Bn., 1923–28; 622d C.A., less 2d Bn., 1924–41; U.S.A.M.P. *Gen. Samuel M. Mills,* 1920–22; U.S.A.M.P. *Gen. Wallace F. Randolph,* 1920–21; U.S.A.M.P. *Gen. John M. Schofield,* 1921–41; U.S.A.C.S. *Joseph Henry,* 1940–41

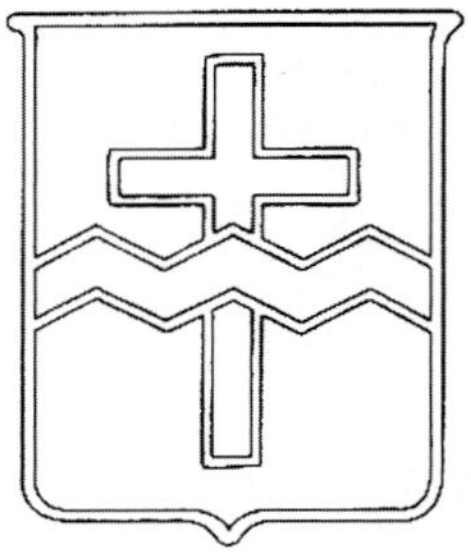

Active as of June 1919 with HQ at Fort Monroe, VA. Responsible for the coastal defense of the approaches to Chesapeake Bay. Subordinate coast defense installations included batteries at Forts Monroe, Story, Wool, and John Custis. Redesignated Harbor Defenses of Chesapeake Bay on 9 June 1925. Classified in June 1935 as a Class I (Full Training) harbor defense. Hosted the visit of President Roosevelt to Fort Monroe on 29 July 1940. The 246th C.A. arrived at Fort Monroe on 23 September 1940 and shortly thereafter assumed the mission of manning batteries in the Harbor Defenses of Chesapeake Bay. Headquarters and Headquarters Battery (HHB), Harbor Defenses of Chesapeake Bay activated on 17 March 1941 at Fort Monroe. Harbor defenses organized as follows:

Harbor Defense Headquarters	Fort Monroe
Harbor Entrance Control Post	Fort Story
3 Groupments	
9 Groups	

Batteries	**No. Guns**	**Weapon/Mount**	**Location**	**Remarks:**
Mine Battery 1	6 Groups	–		
Mine Battery 2	22 Groups	–		
Battery Pennington	2	16" LRH	Fort Story	note 1
Battery Walke	2	16" LRH	Fort Story	note 1
Battery Parrott	2	12" DC MR	Fort Monroe	
Battery Bomford	2	10" DC	Fort Monroe	d/a 1940
Battery Church	2	10" DC	Fort Monroe	
Battery Eustis	2	10" DC	Fort Monroe	
Battery DeRussy	3	12" DC	Fort Monroe	
Battery Anderson	8	12" M	Fort Monroe	
Battery Ruggles	8	12" M	Fort Monroe	
Railway Battery	2	8" RY	Fort Monroe	
Battery Gates	2	6" DC	Fort Wool	
Battery Montgomery	2	6" P	Fort Monroe	note 2
Battery (unnamed)	2	6" P	Fort Story	d/a 1919
Battery (unnamed)	2	5" P	Fort Story	d/a 1919
Battery (unnamed)	4	5" P	Fort John Custis	d/a 1919

Batteries	No. Guns	Weapon/Mount	Location	Remarks:
Battery Irwin	4	3" MP	Fort Monroe	d/a @ 1924
Battery Lee	4	3" P	Fort Wool	
Battery Hindman	2	3" P		Fort Wool
155-mm Battery	4	155-mm GPF PM	Fort John Custis	
155-mm Battery	4	155-mm GPF PM	Fort Story	
155-mm Battery	4	155-mm GPF PM	Fort Story	
AA Battery No. 1	3	3" AA	–	
AA Battery No. 2	3	3" AA	–	
AA Battery No. 3	3	3" AA	–	
AA Battery No. 4	3	3" AA	–	
AA Battery No. 5	3	3" AA	–	
AA MG Battery No. 1	12	.50-cal MG	–	
AA MG Battery No. 2	12	.50-cal MG	–	
AA MG Battery No. 3	12	.50-cal MG	–	
AA MG Battery No. 4	12	.50-cal MG	–	
AA MG Battery No. 5	12	.50-cal MG	–	
AA MG Battery No. 6	12	.50-cal MG	–	
AA MG Battery No. 7	12	.50-cal MG	–	
AA MG Battery No. 8	12	.50-cal MG	–	

Notes:

1. Batteries Pennington and Walke were originally designated Battery Pennington only; Battery Walke was designated as such in 1941.
2. The two 6" P guns from Battery Montgomery were removed in 1920 and reinstalled in 1941.

Status: Disbanded on 19April 1944.

Events: 25, 73, 86, 128

Commanders, Coast Defenses of Chesapeake Bay

Col. Adelbert Cronkhite	1 October 1919–January 1920	Col. Harold E. Cloke	11 June 1931–15 September 1934
Col. Alexander Grieg Jr.	January 1920–24 February 1920	Col. Percy P. Bishop	15 September 1934–2 October 1934
Col. James B. Mitchell	24 February 1920–15 August 1922	Lt. Col. Joseph F. Cottrell	2 October 1934–21 November 1934
Maj. Edward Montgomery	15 August 1922–10 September 1922	Col. Russell P. Reeder	21 November 1934–1 April 1936
Col. James F. Howell	10 September 1922–1 June 1924	Col. Horace F. Spurgin	1 April 1936–1 September 1937
Col. Edward Carpenter	21 June 1924–1 July 1926	Col. Eugene B. Walker	2 September 1937–30 September 1937
Col. Arthur S. Conklin	1 July 1926–1 July 1928	Col. William E. Shedd Jr.	1 October 1937–30 November 1938
Col. George A. Nugent	3 July 1928–1 November 1930	Col. Eugene B. Walker	1 December 1938–25 April 1939
Maj. Charles D. Y. Ostrum	1 November 1930–30 November 1930	Col. Francis P. Hardaway	25 April 1939–8 November 1940
Lt. Col. Franc Leccoq	30 November 1930–11 July 1931	Brig. Gen. Rollin L. Tilton	8 November 1940–December 1941

Coast Defenses of the Columbia (Ninth Coast Artillery District)

HQ—Fort Stevens, OR, 1919–41

Subordinate elements—34th, *93d*, and *160th* C.A. Cos., 1922–24; 3d Bn., 3d C.A., 1924–41; 18th C.A., less 2d Bn., 1940–41; 249th C.A., 1922–30, 1940–41; 3d Bn., 604th C.A., 1923–41; 628th C.A., 1924–41; 629th C.A. Bn., 1924–41

Active as of June 1919 with HQ at Fort Stevens, OR. Responsible for the coastal defense of the approaches to the Columbia River. Subordinate coast defense installations included batteries at Forts Stevens, Canby, and Columbia, and Camp Clatsop. Redesignated Harbor Defenses of the Columbia on 9 June 1925. Reduced to caretaker status on 6 January 1930. Reclassified in June 1935 as a Class II (Limited Training) harbor defense. Defenses upgraded during 1939–41 to Class I (Full Training) with the activation of additional batteries of the 3d Bn., 3d C.A. and the 18th C.A. (less the 2d Bn.). The 249th C.A. arrived at Camp Clatsop, OR, on 23 September 1940 and shortly thereafter assumed the mission of manning batteries in the Harbor Defenses of the Columbia. Harbor defenses organized as follows:

Harbor Defense Headquarters	Fort Stevens
Harbor Entrance Control Post	Fort Canby
2 Groupments	
5 Groups	

Batteries	No. Guns	Weapon/Mount	Location	Remarks:
Mine Battery 1	4 Groups	–		
Mine Battery 2	3 Groups	–		
Battery Clark	8	12" M	Fort Stevens	r/d 1918 note 1
Battery Guenther	4	12" M	Fort Canby	comp. 1921 note 1
Battery Lewis	2	10" DC	Fort Stevens	d/a 1920
Battery Mishler	2	10" DC	Fort Stevens	
Battery Russell	2	10" DC	Fort Stevens	
Battery Walker	2	10" DC	Fort Stevens	
Battery Pratt	2	6" DC	Fort Stevens	d/a 1920
Battery Allen	2	6" DC	Fort Canby	
Battery Murphy	2	6" DC	Fort Columbia	
Battery Freeman	2	6" P	Fort Stevens	d/a 1920 note 2
" "	1	3" MP	Fort Stevens	d/a 1920
Battery (unnamed)	2	6" P	Willapa Bay	comp. 1920 note 2
Battery Crenshaw	2	3" MP	Fort Columbia	d/a 1920
Battery Smur	2	3" MP	Fort Stevens	d/a 1920
AA Battery No. 1	Composite			
AA Battery No. 2	Composite			
AA Battery No. 3	Composite			

Notes:

1. Originally an eight-gun position, four 12" M were removed from Battery Clark to establish the new Battery Guenther at Fort Canby in 1921.
2. The two 6" P guns from Battery Freeman were used to arm the battery at Willapa Bay; Willapa Bay battery disarmed in 1932.

Commanders, Coast Defenses of the Columbia

Lt. Col. William S. Dowd	1 November 1919–5 February 1920
Lt. Col. Albert C. Thompson	5 February 1920–23 December 1920
Capt. William R. Carlson	23 December 1920–18 March 1921
Maj. Charles K. Wing	18 March 1921–26 October 1921
Capt. William R. Carlson	26 October 1921–20 February 1923
Capt. Fenton G. Epling	29 February 1923–June 1924
1st Lt. Sargent P. Huff	June 1924–27 July 1926
Capt. Ernest R. Percy	27 July 1926–30 June 1927
Capt. George R. Owens	30 June 1927–21 November 1930
Maj. Reinold Melberg	21 November 1930–22 July 1934
Maj. William R. Stewart	22 July 1934–10 February 1937
Maj. Allison W. Jones	10 February 1937–29 August 1937
Maj. Edgar H. Thompson	29 August 1937–1 February 1940
Col. Kelley B. Lemmon	1 February 1940–January 1941
Col. Robert P. Glassburn	January 1941–May 1941
Col. Kelley B. Lemmon	May 1941–October 1941
Col. Clifton M. Irwin	October 1941–ao January 1942

Coast Defenses of Cristobal (Panama Coast Artillery District)

HQ—Fort De Lesseps, CZ, 1919–31; Fort Sherman, CZ, 1931–41

Subordinate elements—15th, 16th, 21st, 44th, 119th, 124th, 192d, *193d*, and 194th C.A. Cos., 1922–24; 1st C.A., 1924–41; 2d C.A., 1924–32; 72d C.A., 1940–41; 73d C.A., 1940–41; U.S.A.M.P. *Cyrus W. Field,* 1919–21; U.S.A.M.P. *Gen. William M. Graham,* 1919–41

Established in the R.A. on 2 December 1913 as the Coast Defenses of Cristobal with HQ at Fort Randolph, CZ. Active as of June 1919 with HQ at Fort De Lesseps, CZ. Redesignated Harbor Defenses of Cristobal on 9 June 1925. HQ relocated on 26 February 1931 to Fort Sherman, CZ. Responsible for the coastal defense of the Atlantic approaches to the Panama Canal. Subordinate coast defense installations included batteries at Forts De Lesseps, Sherman, and Randolph. Assigned on 15 April 1932 to HQ, Atlantic Sector. Hosted the visit of President Roosevelt to the Harbor Defenses of Cristobal on 16 February 1940. Harbor defenses organized as follows:

Harbor Defense Headquarters Fort De Lesseps

Batteries	No. Guns	Weapon/Mount	Location	Remarks:
Battery Stanley	1	14" DC	Fort Sherman	
Battery Mower	1	14" DC	Fort Sherman	
Battery Webb	2	14" DC	Fort Randolph, Margarita	
Railway Battery #1	2	14" RY	Fort Randolph, Margarita	comp. 1928 note 1
Battery Pratt	2	12" BC LR	Fort Sherman, Iglesia Pt.	comp. 1924
Battery Mackenzie	2	12" BC LR	Fort Sherman, Iglesia Pt.	comp. 1924
Battery Baird	4	12" M	Fort Sherman	
Battery Howard	4	12" M	Fort Sherman	
Battery Tidball	4	12" M	Fort Randolph, Margarita	
Battery Zalinski	4	12" M	Fort Randolph, Margarita	
Battery Morgan	2	6" P	Fort De Lesseps	
Battery Weed	2	6" DC	Fort Randolph, Margarita	
Battery Kilpatrick	2	6" DC	Fort Sherman	
Battery 1B	4	155-mm GPF PM	Galetta Is.	comp. 1940
Battery 2C	4	155-mm GPF PM	Fort Randolph, Margarita	comp. 1940
Battery 5A	4	155-mm GPF PM	Fort Randolph, Margarita	comp. 1940
Battery U	4	155-mm GPF PM	Tortuguilla Pt.	
Battery V	4	155-mm GPF PM	Naranjitos Pt.	comp. 1940
Battery W	4	155-mm GPF PM	Fort Sherman	comp. 1940
Battery X	4	155-mm GPF PM	Fort Randolph, Margarita	comp. 1940
Battery Y	4	155-mm GPF PM	Palma Media Is.	comp. 1940
Battery Z	4	155-mm GPF PM	Galetta Is.	comp. 1940
75-mm Battery	4	75-mm Gun	Fort Randolph, Margarita	
75-mm Battery	4	75-mm Gun	Fort Randolph, Toro Pt.	
AA Battery No. 1	3	3" AA	Fort Sherman	
AA Battery No. 2	3	3" AA	Fort Sherman	

Note 1: The 14" RY guns for this battery could be moved by rail to similarly prepared positions at Fort Grant to defend the Pacific side of the Panama Canal as well.

Events: 26, 31, 36, 40, 43, 58, 69, 81, 101, 102, 119, 140, 167, 170, 181, 223, 271

Commanders, Coast Defenses of Cristobal

Col. Thomas B. Lamoreaux	4 June 1917–20 March 1919
Col. Harold E. Cloke	September 1919–18 August 1922
Col. William F. Stewart	18 August 1922–12 September 1922
Maj. Lawrence Watts	12 September 1922–3 November 1922
Col. John C. Gillmore	3 November 1922–30 July 1925
Col. Godwin Ordway	30 July 1925–28 February 1926
Col. Alexander Greig, Jr.	28 February 1926–28 November 1928
Lt. Col. Walter Singles	28 November 1928–9 December 1928
Col. Robert E. Wyllie	9 December 1928–30 November 1929
Col. Frank K. Fergusson	30 November 1929–4 November 1931
Col. Percy M. Kessler	4 November 1931–12 April 1932
Col. Ralph M. Mitchell	12 April 1932–25 October 1932
Col. Clarence G. Bunker	26 October 1932–4 August 1934
Maj. Daniel N. Swan	4 August 1934–September 1934
Col. Richard I. McKenney	September 1934–10 October 1934
Col. William M. Colvin	14 October 1934–15 September 1936
Col. William T. Carpenter	15 September 1936–8 July 1939
Lt. Col. Avery J. French	8 July 1939–8 August 1939
Col. Rufus F. Maddux	8 August 1939–April 1940
Col. Avery J. French	April 1940–ao September 1940

Coast Defenses of the Delaware (Second Coast Artillery District)

HQ—Fort Du Pont, DE, 1919–41

Subordinate elements—112th, *139th*, and *179th* C.A. Cos., 1922–24; 3d Bn., 7th C.A., 1924–40; 21st C.A., 1940–41; *261st C.A. Bn.* (NGI), 1924–30; 261st C.A. Regt., 1940–41; 621st C.A., 1924–41

Active as of June 1919 with HQ at Fort DuPont, DE. Responsible for the coastal defense of the approaches to the Delaware River. Subordinate coast defense installations included batteries at Forts DuPont, Delaware, Saulsbury, and Mott. Redesignated Harbor Defenses of the Delaware on 9 June 1925. Reduced to caretaker status on 6 January 1930. Reclassified in June 1935 as a Class III (Maintenance) harbor defense. Defenses upgraded during 1940–41 to

Class I (Full Training) with the activation of the 21st C.A. HHB, Coast Defenses of the Delaware fully activated on 1 April 1941. The 261st C.A. Bn. arrived at Fort DuPont in January 1941 and shortly thereafter assumed the mission of manning batteries in the Harbor Defenses of the Delaware. Harbor defenses organized as follows:

Harbor Defense Headquarters	Fort DuPont
Harbor Entrance Control Post	Fort Miles
2 Groupments	
7 Groups	

Batteries	**No. Guns**	**Weapon/Mount**	**Location**	**Remarks:**
Mine Battery 1	11 Groups	–		
Mine Battery 2	14 Groups	–		
Battery Hall	2	12" BC LR	Fort Saulsbury	comp. 1924
Battery Haslet	2	12" BC LR	Fort Saulsbury	comp. 1924
Battery Arnold	3	12" DC MR	Fort Mott	
Battery Torbert	3	12" DC MR	Fort Delaware	
Battery Rodney	8	12" M	Fort DuPont	
Battery Best	8	12" M	Fort DuPont	
Battery Harker	3	10" DC	Fort Mott	d/a 1941 note 1
Railway Battery	4	8" RY	Fort Miles	
Railway Battery	4	8" RY	Fort Miles	
155-mm Battery	4	155-mm GPF PM	Cape May	
155-mm Battery	4	155-mm GPF PM	Fort Miles	
Battery Hentig	2	3" BC	Fort Delaware	
Battery Edwards	2	3" C/BC	Fort Mott	d/a 1920
Battery Albertus	2	3" MP	Fort Delaware	d/a 1920
Battery Allen	2	3" MP	Fort Delaware	d/a 1920
Battery Elder	2	3" P	Fort DuPont	d/a 1922 note 2
AA Battery No. 1	3	3" AA	–	
AA Battery No. 2	3	3" AA	–	
AA Battery No. 3	3	3" AA	–	
AA Battery No. 4	3	3" AA	–	
AA MG Battery No. 1	12	.50-cal MG	–	
AA MG Battery No. 2	12	.50-cal MG	–	
AA MG Battery No. 3	12	.50-cal MG	–	
AA MG Battery No. 4	12	.50-cal MG	–	
AA SL Battery No. 1				
AA SL Battery No. 2				

Notes:
1. The three 10" DC guns from Battery Harker were removed and sent to a coast defense site in Canada in 1941.
2. The two 3" P guns from Battery Elder were removed in 1922 and installed at Delaware Beach, DE.

Events: 87, 174

Commanders, Coast Defenses of the Delaware

Col. Frank G. Mauldin	October 1918–June 1919
Col. Alfred M Hasbrouck	June 1919–5 September 1919
Col. Archibald Campbell	5 September 1919–3 July 1920
Lt. Col. Elijah B. Martindale	3 July 1920–3 August 1920
Col. Frank K. Fergusson	3 August 1920–27 August 1920
Maj. Charles L. Williams	27 August 1920–27 September 1920
Lt. Col. John P. Spurr	27 September 1920–11 June 1922
Capt. Valentine P. Foster	11 June 1922–31 August 1922
1st Lt. William J. Burke	1 September 1922–31 July 1923
Capt. Evan C. Seaman	31 July 1923–20 August 1925
Capt. William R. Maris	20 August 1925–15 September 1930
Capt. Frederic W. Cooke	15 September 1930–2 March 1932
Capt. F. Webster Cook	3 March 1932–26 May 1933
Capt. John H. Harrington	26 May 1933–29 July 1933
Maj. Donald M. Ashbridge	29 July 1933–5 August 1933
Capt. Ephraim P. Jolls	5 August 1933–21 December 1933
Capt. F. Webster Cook	21 December 1933–11 December 1934
Capt. Ephraim P. Jolls	11 December 1934–15 February 1935
Capt. George F. Nichols	15 February 1935–23 December 1938
Capt. Paul A. Harris	23 December 1938–5 June 1939
Lt. Col. James C. Hutson	5 June 1939–January 1941
Lt. Col. Ephraim P. Jolls	January 1941–5 December 1941
Lt. Col. Henry K. Roscoe (DE)	5 December 1941–ao January 1942

Coast Defenses of Eastern New York (Second Coast Artillery District)

HQ—Fort Totten, NY, 1919–41

Subordinate elements—135th Coast Defense Co., 1923–24; 62d C.A., 1924–41; 607th C.A., 1923–41; *631st C.A.* (ORI), 1929–41; U.S.A.M.P. *Gen. John M. Schofield,* 1920–22; U.S.A.C.S. *Joseph Henry,* 1920–21; U.S.A.M.P. *Gen. Edward O. C. Ord,* 1920–23

Active as of June 1919 with HQ at Fort Totten, NY. Responsible for the coastal defense of the western reaches of Long Island Sound and the East River. Subordinate coast defense installations included batteries at Fort Totten, Slocum, and Schuyler. Redesignated Harbor Defenses of Eastern New York on 9 June 1925. Considered for inactivation in 1927 for being uneconomically feasible to maintain and being "considerably withdrawn from the seashore" and the harbor of New York. Reduced to caretaker status on 6 January 1930. Nevertheless, the Harbor Defenses of Eastern New York was one of the few harbor defense HQ commanded by general officers and full colonels in the interwar period. Harbor defenses organized as follows:

Harbor Defense Headquarters — Fort Totten

Batteries	**No. Guns**	**Weapon/Mount**	**Location**	**Remarks:**
Battery Gansevoort	2	12" DC	Fort Schuyler	d/a 1935
Battery Mahan	2	12" DC	Fort Totten	d/a 1919
Battery Haskin	8	12" M	Fort Slocum	d/a 1919
Battery King	8	12" M	Fort Totten	
Battery Overton	8	12" M	Fort Slocum	d/a 1919
Battery Graham	2	10" DC	Fort Totten	d/a 1918
Battery Hazzard	2	10" DC	Fort Schuyler	
Battery Sumner	2	8" DC	Fort Totten	d/a 1918
Battery Beecher	2	3" MP	Fort Schuyler	
Battery Baker	4	3" MP	Fort Totten	note 1
Battery Burnes	2	3" P	Fort Totten	

Note 1: Two 3" P guns replaced by two 3" MP guns in the 1920s.

Status: Inactivated 9 May 1942 and consolidated with the Harbor Defenses of New York; disbanded 22 May 1944.

Events: 87

Commanders, Coast Defenses of Eastern New York

Col. Willoughby Walke	February 1919–November 1919	Brig. Gen. Stuart Heintzelman	24 October 1927–7 July 1929
Col. Howard K. Loughry	November 1919–30 August 1920	Col. Frank K. Fergusson	7 July 1929–24 November 1929
Col. William R. Doores	30 August 1920–15 August 1921	Col. Andrew Hero Jr.	24 November 1929–February 1930
Maj. Theodore M. Chase	15 August 1921–September 1921	Brig. Gen. Henry J. Hatch	February 1930–10 June 1931
Col. Willoughby Walke	September 1921–1 January 1923	Col. Edward Kimmel	10 June 1931–29 April 1932
Col. Charles H. Hilton	1 January 1923–3 July 1924	Col. Arthur S. Conklin	30 April 1932–22 August 1934
Maj. Mannin M. Kimmel	3 July 1924–28 July 1924	Lt. Col. Clair W. Baird	22 August 1934–1 September 1934
Maj. Karl F. Baldwin	28 July 1924–28 August 1924	Col. Frank K. Fergusson	1 September 1934–18 July 1937
Col. Marcellus G. Spinks	28 August 1924–10 April 1925	Lt. Col. Eli E. Bennett	18 July 1937–6 October 1937
Brig. Gen. Johnson Hagood	10 April 1925–30 September 1925	Col. Henry W.T. Eglin	6 October 1937–8 April 1937
Brig. Gen. William M. Cruikshank	1 October 1925–28 January 1927	Lt. Col. Charles R. Finley	9 April 1939–15 September 1939
Col. Marcellus G. Spinks	28 January 1927–16 April 1927	Col. Oliver L. Spiller	15 September 1939–30 September 1940
Brig. Gen. Alston Hamilton	16 April 1927–9 September 1927	Col. Rodney H. Smith	1 November 1940–6 April 1941
Col. William R. Doores	9 September 1927–24 October 1927	Brig. Gen. Philip S. Gage	6 April 1941–9 May 1942

Coast Defenses of Galveston (Eighth Corps Area)

HQ—Fort Crockett, TX, 1919–41

Subordinate elements—183d C.A. Co., 1922–24; 60th Artillery (Arty.) Bn. (AA), C.A.C., 1922–23; *3d Bn., 13th C.A.,* 1924–36; 69th C.A., 1935–41; 20th C.A., 1940–41; 264th C.A. Bn., 1938–39; 265th C.A. Regt, 1941; *268th C.A. Bn.* (NGI), 1924–36; 624th C.A., 1924–41

Active as of June 1919 with HQ at Fort Crockett, TX. Responsible for the coastal defense of the approaches to Galveston Bay. Subordinate coast defense installations included batteries at Forts Crockett, San Jacinto, and Travis. Reduced to caretaker status in October 1921. Redesignated Harbor Defenses of Galveston on 9 June 1925. Reclassified in June 1935 as a Class III (Maintenance) harbor defense. Defenses upgraded during 1940–41 to Class I (Full Training) with the activation of the 20th C.A. The 265th C.A. arrived at Fort Crockett on 15 January 1941 and shortly thereafter assumed the mission of manning batteries in the Harbor Defenses of Galveston. Harbor defenses organized as follows:

Harbor Defense Headquarters	Fort Crockett
Harbor Entrance Control Post	Fort San Jacinto
4 Groups	

Batteries	**No. Guns**	**Weapon/Mount**	**Location**	**Remarks:**
Battery Hoskins	2	12" BC LR	Fort Crockett	comp. 1924
Battery Kimble	1	12" BC LR	Fort Travis	comp. 1922
Battery Mercer	8	12" M	Fort San Jacinto	
Battery Izard	8	12" M	Fort Crockett	note 1
Battery Heilman	1	10" DC ARF	Fort San Jacinto	
" "	1	10" DC	Fort San Jacinto	
Battery Hampton	2	10" BC	Fort Crockett	
155-mm Battery	4	155-mm GPF PM	Freeport, TX	
Battery Ernst	3	3" MP	Fort Travis	note 2
Battery Croghan	2	3" MP	Fort San Jacinto	note 2
Battery Laval	2	3" MP	Fort Crockett	note 2
AA Battery No. 1	Composite		–	
AA Battery No. 2	Composite		–	
AA Battery No. 3	Composite		–	

Notes:
1. Originally an eight gun position, four 12" M were removed from Battery Izard in the early 1920s.
2. Batteries Ernst, Croghan, and Laval were converted from 3" MP to 3" P sometime after World War I.

Commanders, Coast Defenses of Galveston

Col. Ernest L. Tilton	September 1918–16 March 1920
Capt. Herbert E. Ellis	16 March 1920–5 June 1920
Capt. Furman E. McCammon	5 June 1920–9 August 1920
Maj. Rollo F. Anderson	9 August 1920–8 September 1920
Lt. Col. William A. Covington	8 September 1920–22 August 1921
Maj. Frederick R. Garcin	22 August 1921–3 January 1922
Maj. Stewart O. Elting	3 January 1922–8 April 1923
2d Lt. Oland T. Green	8 April 1923–15 October 1923
Capt. William F. Lafranz	15 October 1923–25 June 1927
1st Lt. Thomas W. Munford	25 June 1927–28 August 1930
Maj. Glenn P. Anderson	28 August 1930–5 September 1932
Capt. Walter H. Carlisle	5 September 1932–2 June 1933
Maj. John B. Martin	2 June 1933–23 March 1935
Col. Richard Donovan	23 March 1935–2 May 1937
Col. Allen Kimberly	2 May 1937–10 June 1938
Lt. Col. Otto G. Pitz	10 June 1938–8 August 1938
Lt. Col. Cyril A.W. Dawson	30 August 1938–2 November 1938
Col. Olin H. Longino	2 November 1938–11 February 1941
Col. Robert E. Guthrie	3 March 1941–26 June 1942

Coast Defenses of Honolulu (Hawaiian Coast Artillery District)

HQ—Fort Ruger, TH, 1921; Fort Armstrong, TH, 1921–24; Fort DeRussey, TH, 1924–41

Subordinate elements—*2d*, 10th, *55th*, 104th, 105th, *159th*, and *186th* C.A. Cos., 1922–24; 16th C.A., 1924–41; 2d Bn., 55th C.A., 1922–41; 3d Balloon (Bln.) Co., 1921–22

Established in the R.A. on 13 December 1920 as the Coast Defenses of Honolulu. Organized on 5 April 1921 from the Coast Defenses of Oahu with HQ at Fort Ruger, TH. HQ was successively transferred as follows: to Fort Armstrong, TH, on 15 August 1921 and to Fort DeRussey, TH, on 1 July 1924. Redesignated Harbor Defenses of Honolulu on 9 June 1925. Responsible for the coastal defense of the approaches to Honolulu harbor. Subordinate coast defense installations included batteries at Forts Armstrong, Ruger, and DeRussey. Harbor defenses organized as follows:

Harbor Defense Headquarters — Fort DeRussey

Batteries	**No. Guns**	**Weapon/Mount**	**Location**	**Remarks:**
Battery Randolph	2	14" DC	Fort DeRussey	
Battery Harlow	8	12" M	Fort Ruger	
Battery Birkhimer	4	12" M	Fort Ruger	
Battery Granger Adams	2	8" BC	Fort Fuger, Black Point	comp. 1935
Battery Dudley	2	6" DC	Fort DeRussey	
Battery S.C. Mills	2	5" BP	Fort Ruger, Black Point	d/a 1925
Battery Hulings	2	4.7" A	Fort Ruger	d/a 1925
Battery Dodge	2	4.7" A	Fort Ruger	d/a 1925
Battery Tiernon	2	3" P	Fort Armstrong	
Battery B	12	2.4" P	Fort Ruger	
240-mm Battery	2	240-mm	Waimanalo	comp. 1929
240-mm Battery	2	240-mm	Kaawa	comp. 1927
240-mm Battery	2	240-mm	Ulupao	comp. 1927
155-mm Battery	4	155-mm GPF PM	Sand Is.	comp. 1937
Battery Koko Head	2	155-mm GPF PM	Koko Head	comp. 1941
AA Battery	4	3" AA	Fort DeRussey	
AA Battery	6	3" AA	Fort Ruger	
AA Battery	2	3" AA	Sand Is.	

Events: 33, 37, 160

Status: Disbanded on 25 May 1944.

Commanders, Coast Defenses of Honolulu

Col. Gordon G. Heiner	12 February 1921–1 November 1923
Col. Lawrence C. Brown	1 November 1923–4 August 1926
Maj. Harry W. Stark	4 August 1926–14 December 1926
Col. Percy B. Bishop	14 December 1926–30 July 1929
Lt. Col. Walter H. Merrill	30 July 1929–25 October 1929
Col. Harold E. Cloke	25 October 1929–9 June 1931
Maj. Monte J. Hickok	9 June 1931–8 December 1931
Col. Harry L. Steele	8 December 1931–16 August 1934
Lt. Col. William E. Shedd Jr.	17 August 1934–23 October 19 34
Col. George L. Wertenbaker	23 October 1934–17 September 1936
Col. George A. Wildrick	17 September 1936–6 October 1938
Lt. Col. Felix E. Cross	6 October 1938–16 November 1938
Col. William D. Frazer	16 November 1938–14 July 1940
Lt. Col. Adam E. Potts	14 July 1940–3 October 1940
Lt. Col. Shuey E. Wolfe	3 October 1940–December 1940
Col. Paul H. Herman	December 1940–ao January 1941

Coast Defenses of Jacksonville (Fourth Coast Artillery District)

HQ—*Inactive,* 1924–41

Subordinate elements—Btry A, 625th C.A., 1924–41; *636th C.A.* (ORI), 1929–41

Active as of June 1919 with HQ at Jacksonville, FL. Responsible for the coastal defense of the approaches to the harbor of Jacksonville, FL. This command was apparently discontinued shortly after World War I, however, reference to its planned reestablishment appears in several documents in the pre–World War II O.R. unit card files at the Center of Military History. Units were designated to man its defenses on mobilization. Harbor defenses organized as follows:

Harbor Defense Headquarters

Batteries	No. Guns	Weapon/Mount	Location	Remarks:
Battery (unnamed)	2	3.2" FM	Cape May	
155-mm Battery	4	155-mm GPF PM	Mayport	

Coast Defenses of Key West (Fourth Coast Artillery District)

HQ—Key West Barracks, FL, 1919–41

Subordinate elements—182d C.A. Co., 1922–24; Btry E, 13th C.A., 1924–41

Active as of June 1919 with HQ at Key West Barracks, FL. Responsible for the coastal defense of the approaches to the Florida Keys. Subordinate coast defense installations included batteries at Key West Barracks and Fort Taylor. Redesignated Harbor Defenses of Key West on 9 June 1925. Reduced to caretaker status on 6 January 1930. Reclassified in June 1935 as a Class III (Maintenance) harbor defense. Harbor defenses organized as follows:

Harbor Defense Headquarters	Key West Barracks
Harbor Entrance Control Post	Fort Taylor
3 Groups	

Batteries	No. Guns	Weapon/Mount	Location	Remarks:
Battery Oseola	2	12" BC MR	Fort Taylor	
Battery Seminole	4	12" M	Fort Taylor	
Battery DeLeon	4	10" DC	Fort Taylor	d/a 1940
155-mm Battery	4	155-mm GPF PM	Fort Taylor	comp. 1940
Battery Adair	4	3" MP	Fort Taylor	
Battery Dilworth	2	3" MP	Fort Taylor	d/a 1920
Battery Ford	2	3" P	Fort Taylor	
Battery Inman	2	3" P	West Martello Tower	
AA Battery No. 1	3	3" AA		
AA MG Battery No. 2	12	.50-cal MG		

Commanders, Coast Defenses of Key West

Maj. Ralph D. Bates	20 March 1918–21 February 1919
Col. Oscar I. Straub	May 1919–24 June 1920
Maj. Lawrence B. Ross	24 June 1920–26 August 1920
Lt. Col. James D. Watson	26 August 1920–31 January 1922
Lt. Col. James B. Taylor	31 January 1922–11 August 1922
Maj. Robert W. Clark	11 August 1922–16 September 1922
Capt. Edward B. Wharton	16 September 1922–5 April 1924
1st Lt. Austin M. Wilson Jr.	5 April 1924–12 November 1924
Capt. John J. Maher	November 1924–27 June 19 26
2d Lt. Ernest B. Thompson	27 June 1926–22 September 1926
Capt. Joseph B. Varela	22 September 1926–24 October 1927
2d Lt. Ernest B. Thompson	24 October 1927–14 November 1927
Capt George T. Rice	14 November 1927–26 October 1931
1st Lt. Michael H. Zwicker	26 October 1931–8 January 1932
Maj. Wade W. Rhein	8 January 1932–31 October 1936
Capt. Granger Anderson	31 October 1936–3 November 1936
Lt. Col. James D. McMillan	3 November 1936–July 1940
Col. Louis L. Pendleton	July 1940–31 October 1941

Coast Defenses of Long Island Sound (First Coast Artillery District)

HQ—Fort H.G. Wright, NY, 1919–41

Subordinate elements—43d, *50th*, *79th*, 100th, 131st, 132d, 133d, *141st*, *146th*, *157th*, and *175th* C.A. Cos., 1922–24; 11th C.A., 1924–41; 242d C.A., 1922–33, 1939–41; 618th C.A. Bn., 1924–41; 18th Sound Ranging Btry; U.S.A.M.P. *Gen. Absalom Baird,* 1920–37

Active as of June 1919 with HQ at Fort H.G. Wright, NY. Responsible for the coastal defense of the approaches to the eastern reaches of Long Island Sound. Subordinate coast defense installations included batteries at Forts H.G. Wright, Michie, and Terry. Redesignated Harbor Defenses of Long Island Sound on 9 June 1925. In April 1933, the HQ assumed command and control of the Fifth Civilian Conservation Corps (CCC) District, Second Corps Area. Subordinate units supported CCC activities on eastern Long Island. Classified in June 1935 as a Class I (Full Training) harbor defense. The 242d C.A. arrived at Fort H.G. Wright on 23 September 1940 and shortly thereafter assumed the mission of manning batteries in the Harbor Defenses of Long Island Sound. Harbor defenses organized as follows:

Harbor Defense Headquarters	Fort H.G. Wright
Harbor Entrance Control Post	Fort H.G. Wright
3 Groupments (Fort Wright, Fort Terry, Antiaircraft)	
7 Groups	

Batteries	No. Guns	Weapon/Mount	Location	Remarks:
Battery Davis	1	16" DC ARF	Fort Michie	comp. 1923
Battery Palmer	2	12" DC MR	Fort Michie	
Battery Butterfield	2	12" DC MR	Fort H. G. Wright	
Battery Clinton	4	12" M	Fort H. G. Wright	
Battery Stoneman	4	12" M	Fort Terry	
Battery Steele	2	10" DC	Fort Terry	
Battery Barlow	2	10" DC	Fort H. G. Wright	d/a 1938
Railway Battery	2	8" RY	Fort H. G. Wright	
Battery Dutton	3	6" DC	Fort H. G. Wright	
Battery Bradford	2	6" DC	Fort Terry	
Battery Benjamin	2	6" P	Fort Michie	
Battery Maitland	2	6" P	Fort Michie	
155-mm Battery	4	155-mm GPF	Fort Terry	
Battery Campbell	2	3" P	Fort Terry	d/a 1934
Battery Eldridge	2	3" P	Fort Terry	
Battery Dalliba	2	3" P	Fort Terry	
Battery Greble	2	3" P	Fort Terry	d/a 1932
Battery Hagner	2	3" P	Fort Terry	d/a 1932
Battery Hoffman	2	3" P	Fort H.G. Wright	
Battery Hoppock	2	3" P	Fort H.G. Wright	
Battery Pasco	2	3" P	Fort Michie	d/a 1934
AA Battery No. 1	Composite		–	
AA Battery No. 2	Composite		–	
AA Battery No. 3	Composite		–	
AA Battery No. 4	Composite		–	
AA MG Battery No. 1				

Status: Inactivated on 4 May 1942 and consolidated with the Harbor Defenses of New York; disbanded on 22 May 1944.

Events: 59, 77, 107, 174, 313

Commanders, Coast Defenses of Long Island Sound

Col. James L. Long	ao December 1919–19 January 1920	Col. George A. Nugent	1 December 1930–20 May 1933
Col. John P. Hains	19 January 1920–14 August 1921	Maj. Hollis LeR. Muller	20 May 1933–10 June 1933
Col. John C. Goodfellow	14 August 1921–12 October 1921	Col. William H. Wilson	10 June 1933–10 June 1935
Col. Robert S. Abernethy	12 October 1921–30 June 1924	Lt. Col. Monte J. Hickok	10 June 1935–1 August 1935
Lt. Col. John R. Musgrave	1 July 1924–14 November 1924	Col. Edward J. Cullen	1 August 1935–5 May 1936
Col. Frank K. Fergusson	14 November 1924–8 January 1928	Lt. Col. Monte J. Hickok	5 May 1936–10 June 1936
Lt. Col. Edward D. Powers	8 January 1928–1 April 1928	Col. Robert W. Collins	12 June 1936–26 May 1938
Col. Charles H. Hilton	1 April 1928–25 October 1930	Lt. Col. William C. Foote	26 May 1938–12 September 1939
Lt. Col. Richard I. McKenney	25 October 1930–1 December 1930	Brig. Gen. Thomas H. Jones	12 September 1939–December 1941

Coast Defenses of Los Angeles (Ninth Coast Artillery District)

HQ—Fort MacArthur, CA, 1919–41

Subordinate elements—27th, 38th, and 158th C.A. Co., 1922–24; 3d C.A., less 2d and 3d Bns., 1924–41; 63d C.A., 1930–41; 605th C.A. Bn., 1930–41; 608th C.A., 1929–41; Btry A, 610th C.A., 1923–28; 626th C.A., 1924–41

Active as of June 1919 with HQ at Fort MacArthur, CA. Responsible for the coastal defense of the approaches to San Pedro Bay. Subordinate coast defense batteries all located on the upper reservation, Fort MacArthur, less those at Deadman's Island, and several antiaircraft positions and railway firing positions. Redesignated Harbor Defenses of Los Angeles on 9 June 1925. Reduced to caretaker status on 6 January 1930. In April 1933, the HQ assumed command and control of the Fort MacArthur CCC District. Subordinate units supported CCC activities near Los Angeles, CA. Reclassified in June 1935 as a Class II (Limited Training) harbor defense. Defenses upgraded during 1939–41 to Class I (Full Training) with the activation of additional batteries of the 3d C.A. Harbor defenses organized as follows:

Harbor Defense Headquarters — Fort McArthur
4 Groups

Batteries	No. Guns	Weapon/Mount	Location	Remarks:
Battery Erwin	2	14" RY	Fort McArthur	comp. 1926 note 1
Battery Farley	1	14" DC MR	Fort McArthur	
Battery Osgood	1	14" DC MR	Fort McArthur	
Battery Leary	1	14" DC MR	Fort McArthur	
Battery Merriam	1	12" DC MR	Fort McArthur	
Battery Barlow	4	12" M	Fort McArthur	
Battery Saxton	4	12" M	Fort McArthur	
Battery Eubanks	2	8" RY	Manhattan Beach	comp. 1940
155-mm Battery	4	155-mm GPF PM	Fort McArthur	
155-mm Battery	4	155-mm GPF PM	Fort McArthur	
Battery Lodor	4	3" P	Deadman's Is.	comp. 1919;d/a 1927
AA Battery No. 1	Composite		–	
AA Battery No. 2	Composite		–	
AA Battery No. 3	Composite		–	
AA MG Battery No. 1	16	.50-cal MG	–	
AA MG Battery No. 2	16	.50-cal MG	–	
AA MG Battery No. 3	8	.50-cal MG	–	
AA SL Battery No. 1	1	60" SL		

Note 1. Battery Erwin consisted of two 14" /50 railway guns. The first gun arrived in 1925 and the first firing platform and the initial rail lines were completed in February 1926. The second gun arrived in 1929. Two new emplacements with supporting rail lines were completed on the mud flats below the Lower Reservation in June 1937.

Events: 116, 142, 319, 335

Commanders, Coast Defenses of Los Angeles

Col. George Blakeley	3 July 1919–6 September 1920
Maj. William Tidball	6 September 1920–20 November 1920
Col. Henry J. Hatch	20 November 1920–8 April 1922
Mal. Phillip L. Milnor	8 April 1922–2 June 1922
Maj. Isaac E. Titus	2 June 1922–1 August 1922
Lt. Col. Ernest E. Tilton	1 August 1922–12 November 1922
Lt. Col. William H. Raymond	20 November 1922–13 December 1922
Maj. George Ruhlen Jr.	13 December 1922–6 July 1925
Maj. Lincoln B. Chambers	6 July 1925–11 September 1926
Capt. George D. Davidson	11 September 1926–25 October 1926
Lt. Col. Willis G. Peace	25 October 19 26–19 January 1929
Col. Robert F. Woods	19 January 1929–20 February 1930
Maj. Kelley B. Lemmon	20 February 1930–15 March 1930
Lt. Col. Carr W. Waller	15 March 1930–28 August 1930
Maj. Kelley B. Lemmon	28 August 1930–4 February 1931
Lt. Col. Matthew A. Cross	4 February 1931–1 July 1931
Lt. Col. Howard S. Miller	1 July 1931–14 December 1932
Maj. Myron S. Crissy	14 December 1932–7 January 1933
Col. Charles H. Hilton	7 January 1933–20 July 1934
Lt. Col. Homer R. Oldfield	20 July 1934–22 July 1936
Lt. Col. Robert D. Brown	22 July 1936–29 August 1936
Lt. Col. Claude M. Theile	29 August 1936–6 September 1938
Maj. Harold P. Detwiler	6 September 1938–2 February 1939
Col. Edward A. Stockton Jr.	2 February 1939–17 October 1940
Lt. Col. Edwin C. Mead	17 October 1940–10 November 1940
Col. Allen Kimberly	10 November 1940–25 March 1941
Col. H. Leroy Muller	25 March 1941–29 May 1941
Lt. Col. Edwin C. Mead	29 May 1941–9 June 1941
Col. Arthur E. Rowland	9 June 1941–18 June 1941
Col. William W. Hicks	18 June 1941–29 September 1945

Coast Defenses of Manila and Subic Bays (Philippine Department)

HQ—Fort Mills, PI, 1919–41

Subordinate elements—4th, *11th*, *18th*, 23d, 36th, 42d, *70th*, *86th*, *90th*, 95th, 111th, *138th*, *142d*, *187th–191st*, 275th–286th, and 289th C.A. Cos., 1922–24; 59th C.A. Regt., 1921–41, 60th C.A. Regt., 1923–41, 91st and 92d C.A. Regts., 1924–41; U.S.A.M.P. *Gen. Henry J. Hunt,* 1919–23; U.S.A.M.P. *Gen. Henry Knox,* 1919–23; U.S.A.M.P. *Gen. George F.E. Harrison,* 1923–41

Active as of June 1919 with HQ at Fort Mills, PI. Responsible for the coastal defense of the approaches to Manila and Subic Bays. Subordinate coast defense installations included batteries at Forts Mills, Drum, Wint, Hughes, and Frank. Redesignated Harbor Defenses of Manila and Subic Bays on 9 June 1925. Reorganized and redesignated as the Philippine Coast Artillery Command on 1 August 1941. Harbor defenses organized as follows:

Harbor Defense Headquarters — Fort Mills

Batteries	No. Guns	Weapon/Mount	Location	Remarks:
Battery Marshall	2	14" TM	Fort Drum, El Fraile Is.	
Battery Wilson	2	14" TM	Fort Drum, El Fraile Is.	
Battery Crofton	1	14" DC	Fort Frank, Carabao Is.	
Battery Greer	1	14" DC	Fort Frank, Carabao Is.	
Battery Woodruff	1	14" DC	Fort Hughes, Caballo Is.	
Battery Gillespie	1	14" DC	Fort Hughes, Caballo Is.	
Battery Wheeler	2	12" DC	Fort Mills, Corregidor Is.	
Battery Crockett	2	12" DC	Fort Mills, Corregidor Is.	
Battery Cheney	2	12" DC	Fort Mills, Corregidor Is.	
Battery Smith	1	12" BC LR	Fort Mills, Corregidor Is.	comp. 1921
Battery Hearn	1	12" BC LR	Fort Mills, Corregidor Is.	comp. 1921
Battery Koehler	8	12" M	Fort Frank, Carabao Is.	
Battery Craighill	4	12" M	Fort Hughes, Caballo Is.	comp. 1919
Battery Geary	8	12" M	Fort Mills, Corregidor Is.	
Battery Way	4	12" M	Fort Mills, Corregidor Is.	
Battery Grubbs	2	10" DC	Fort Mills, Corregidor Is.	
Battery Warwick	2	10" DC	Fort Wint, Subic Bay	
Battery McCrea	2	6" C/BC	Fort Drum, El Fraile Is.	
Battery Roberts	2	6" C/BC	Fort Drum, El Fraile Is.	
Battery Leach	2	6" DC	Fort Hughes, Caballo Is.	
Battery Hall	2	6" DC	Fort Wint, Subic Bay	

Batteries	No. Guns	Weapon/Mount	Location	Remarks:
Battery Woodruff	2	6" DC	Fort Wint, Subic Bay	
Battery Ramsay	3	6" DC	Fort Mills, Corregidor Is.	
Battery Morrison	2	6" DC	Fort Mills, Corregidor Is.	
Battery Conception	3	155-mm GPF PM	Fort Mills, Corregidor Is.	
Battery Frank	4	155-mm GPF PM	Fort Frank, Carabao Is.	
Battery Hamilton	3	155-mm GPF PM	Fort Mills, Corregidor Is.	
Battery Hooker	1	155-mm GPF PM	Fort Hughes, Caballo Is.	
Battery Kysor	2	155-mm GPF PM	Fort Mills, Corregidor Is.	
Battery Leavegood	2	155-mm GPF PM	Fort Mills, Corregidor Is.	
Battery Martin	2	155-mm GPF PM	Fort Mills, Corregidor Is.	
Battery Monja	2	155-mm GPF PM	Fort Mills, Corregidor Is.	
Battery Rock Point	2	155-mm GPF PM	Fort Mills, Corregidor Is.	
Battery Stockade	2	155-mm GPF PM	Fort Mills, Corregidor Is.	
Battery Sunset	4	155-mm GPF PM	Fort Mills, Corregidor Is.	
Battery Williams	2	155-mm GPF PM	Fort Hughes, Caballo Is.	
Battery (unnamed)	4	155-mm GPF PM	Ogonbol	
75-mm Battery	2	75-mm Gun	Corregidor, Infantry Point	
Battery Cushing	2	3" P	Fort Mills, Corregidor Is.	comp. 1919
Battery Flake	4	3" P	Fort Wint, Subic Bay	
Battery Hanna	2	3" P	Fort Mills, Corregidor Is.	comp. 1919
Battery Hoyle	2	3" P	Fort Frank, Carabao Is.	note 1
Battery Hoyle (new)	2	3" P	Fort Drum, El Fraile Is.	comp. 1941 note 1
Battery Fuger	4	3" P	Fort Hughes, Caballo Is.	
Battery James	4	3" P	Fort Mills, Corregidor Is.	
Battery Jewell	4	3" P	Fort Wint, Subic Bay	
Battery Keys	2	3" P	Fort Mills, Corregidor Is.	
AA Battery	5	3" AA	Fort Mills, Corregidor Is.	
AA Battery	2	3" AA	Fort Mills, Corregidor Is.	

Note 1: The two 3" P guns from Battery Hoyle were removed to arm the new Battery Hoyle in 1941.

Events: 44, 51, 68, 122, 223, 245, 270

Commanders, Coast Defenses of Manila and Subic Bay

Col. Samuel E. Allen	16 February 1919–16 May 1919
Col. Richmond P. Davis	16 May 1919–14 March 1921
Lt. Col. Ernest R. Tilton	14 March 1921–3 April 1921
Col. Charles H. Barth	3 April 1921–13 August 1921
Brig Gen. Henry D. Todd	13 August 1921–2 July 1923
Col. Andrew Hero Jr.	2 July 1923–18 November 1923
Brig. Gen. Malin Craig	18 November 1923–10 July 1924
Col. Andrew Hero Jr.	10 July 1924–4 October 1924
Col. Earle D'A. Pearce	4 October 1924–26 August 1924
Brig. Gen. Campbell King	26 August 1924–24 April 1925
Col. William R. Doores	24 April 1925–16 July 1925
Brig. Gen. Frank M. Caldwell	16 July 1925–18 November 1927
Lt. Col. Avery J. Cooper	18 November 1927–1 December 1927
Brig. Gen. Henry J. Hatch	1 December 1927–14 September 1929
Col. William H. Monroe	14 September 1929–4 October 1929
Brig. Gen. Charles E. Kilbourne Jr.	28 October 1929–17 June 1932
Brig. Gen. Stanley D. Embick	18 June 1932–20 February 1935
Col. William S. Bowen	20 February 1935–19 March 1935
Brig. Gen. Charles E. Kilbourne Jr.	19 March 1935–14 November 1935
Brig. Gen. John W. Gulick	14 November 1935–6 November 1936
Brig. Gen. Percy P. Bishop	6 November 1936–25 February 1937
Brig. Gen. Walter K. Wilson	26 February 1937–November 1940
Brig. Gen. George S. Moore	November 1940–13 May 1942

Coast Defenses of Mobile Bay (Fourth Coast Artillery District)

HQ—Fort Morgan, AL, 1920–24; *Inactive,* 1924–32; Fourth Corps Area, 1932–41

Subordinate elements—39th C.A. Co., 1922–24; *266th C.A. Bn.* (NGI), 1925–36; *638th C.A.* (ORI), 1929–41

Active as of June 1919 with HQ at Fort Morgan, AL. Responsible for the coastal defense of the approaches to Mobile Bay. Subordinate coast defense installations included batteries at Bogalusa, AL, Fort Gaines, and Fort Morgan. Coast Defenses of Mobile inactivated on 1 July 1924 and designated as a subordinate command of the Coast Defenses of Pensacola. Concurrently reduced to caretaker status. Redesignated Harbor Defenses of Mobile on 9 June 1925. Though all remaining weapons and armament were removed by Ordnance Corps personnel in 1928, war plans called for the reactivation of the Harbor Defenses of Mobile in the event of war. HQ, HQ Btry, and the Med. Dept. Det. organized by September 1932 as an RAI unit with O.R. personnel from the Fourth Corps Area at large. Harbor defenses organized as follows:

Harbor Defense Headquarters — Fort Morgan

Batteries	**No. Guns**	**Weapon/Mount**	**Location**	**Remarks:**
Battery Duportail	2	12" DC	Fort Morgan	d/a 1928
Battery Dearborn	2	12" M	Fort Morgan	d/a 1928
Battery Stanton	3	6" DC	Fort Gaines	d/a 1928
Battery Schenk	2	3" MP	Fort Morgan	d/a 1923
" "	1	3" P	Fort Morgan	d/a 1923
Battery Terrett	3	3" MP	Fort Gaines	d/a 1923

Commanders, Coast Defenses of Mobile Bay

Col. James A. Shipton	15 October 1919–21 February 1920
Lt. Col. Louis D. Pepin	21 February 1920–July 1920
Maj. Hugh J.B. McElgin	July 1920–August 1920
Lt. Col. Robert F. McMillan	August 1920–14 February 1921
Lt. Col. George A. Wieczorek	14 February 1921–September 1921
Capt. James R. Townsend	September 1921–1 December 1921
1st Lt. Roy D. Paterson	1 December 1921–23 March 1922
Capt. Robert Chaplin	23 March 1922–31 March 1924

Coast Defenses of Narragansett Bay (First Coast Artillery District)

HQ—Fort Adams, RI, 1919–41

Subordinate elements—*14th*, *97th*, 102d, 110th, *129th*, 173d, and 174th C.A. Cos., 1922–24; 10th C.A., 1924–41; 243d C.A., 1922–33, 1939–41; 2d Bn., 616th C.A., 1926–36; U.S.A.M.P. *Col. John V. White,* 1920–21

Active as of June 1919 with HQ at Fort Adams, RI. Responsible for the coastal defense of the approaches to Rhode Island Sound and Narragansett Bay. Subordinate coast defense installations included batteries at Forts Adams, Greble, Kearny, and Wetherill. Redesignated Harbor Defenses of Narragansett Bay on 9 June 1925. Reduced to caretaker status on 6 January 1930. Reclassified in June 1935 as a Class II (Limited Training) harbor defense. Defenses upgraded during 1940–41 to Class I (Full Training) with the activation of additional batteries of the 10th C.A. The 243d C.A. arrived at Fort Adams on 22 September 1940 and shortly thereafter assumed the mission of manning batteries in the Harbor Defenses of Narragansett Bay. Harbor defenses organized as follows:

Harbor Defense Headquarters	Fort Adams
Harbor Entrance Control Post	Fort Burnside
1 Groupment	
6 Groups	

Batteries	**No. Guns**	**Weapon/Mount**	**Location**	**Remarks:**
Mine Battery 1	4 Groups	–		
Mine Battery 2	8 Groups	–		
Battery Varnum	2	12" BC MR	Fort Wetherill	
Battery Wheaton	2	12" DC MR	Fort Wetherill	
Battery Tousard	3	12" DC MR	Fort Getty	
Battery Greene	4	12" M	Fort Adams	
Battery Edgerton	4	12" M	Fort Adams	
Battery Sedgwick	8	12" M	Fort Greble	
Battery Walbach	3	10" DC	Fort Wetherill	
Battery Hale	3	10" DC	Fort Greble	
Railway Battery	2	8" RY	Various	
Battery Cram	2	6" DC	Fort Kearny	
Battery Dickenson	2	6" P	Fort Wetherill	
Battery House	2	6" P	Fort Getty	
Battery Sakonnet	4	155-mm GPF		
Point Judith Battery	4	155-mm GPF	Point Judith	
Battery (unnamed)	2	4.7" A/P	Sachuest Point	d/a 1919
Battery Armistead	2	3" BC	Fort Kearny	
Battery Belton	2	3" P	Fort Adams	d/a 1925
Battery Cooke	2	3" MP	Fort Wetherill	d/a 1920
Battery Ogden	2	3" MP	Fort Greble	d/a 1920
Battery Crittenden	2	3" P	Fort Wetherill	
Battery Whiting	2	3" P	Fort Getty	
AA Battery No. 1	Composite		–	
AA Battery No. 2	Composite		–	
AA Battery No. 3	Composite		–	
AA Battery No. 4	Composite		–	
AA Battery No. 5	Composite		–	
AA Battery No. 6	Composite		–	
AA MG Battery No. 1				

Events: 59, 77, 107, 174, 272, 313

Commanders, Coast Defenses of Narragansett Bay

Col. Oscar I. Straub	9 September 1917–28 June 1919
Col. George F. Landers	28 June 1919–6 July 1921
Col. William R. Doores	6 July 1921–28 October 1923
Lt. Col. Samuel G. Shartle	28 October 1923–15 October 1926
Capt. Ernest R. Barrows	15 October 1926–3 February 1927
Col. Thomas F. Dwyer	3 February 1927–10 August 1927
Col. James F. Brady	10 August 1927–27 January 1928
Lt. Col. William H. Raymond	27 January 1928–13 March 1928
Col. Hugh K. Taylor	13 March 1928–18 July 1928
Capt. Ernest R. Barrows	18 July 1928–20 July 1931
Maj. John P. Smith	20 July 1931–1 November 1930
Maj. Edward B. Dennis	1 November 1930–1 November 1933
Maj. John P. McCaskey	5 November 1933–19 June 1934
Maj. Carl R. Adams	20 June 1934–10 September 1936
Col. Paul H. Herman	10 September 1936–26 August 1938
Maj. Edward L. Supple	26 August 1938–November 1939
Maj. Ephraim P. Jolls	November 1939–April 1940
Maj. George W. Brent	April 1940–23 September 1940
Col. Earl C. Webster	23 September 1940–7 March 1941
Brig. Gen. Ralph B. Haines	7 March 1941–8 September 1941
Col. Martin J. O'Brien	8 September 1941–23 January 1942

Coast Defenses of New Bedford (First Coast Artillery District)

HQ—Fort Rodman, MA, 1919–41

Subordinate elements—52d C.A. Co., 1921–24; Btry E, 10th C.A., 1924–40; 23d C.A., 1940–41; 616th C.A. Bn., 1924–26; 616th C.A. Regt., less 2d Bn., 1926–40

Active as of June 1919 with HQ at Fort Rodman, MA. Responsible for the coastal defense of the approaches to Apponagansett and Buzzards Bays. Subordinate coast defense batteries at Fort Rodman. Redesignated Army Stations, New Bedford Harbor on 1 November 1922. Redesignated Coast Defenses of New Bedford on 1 December 1923. Redesignated Harbor Defenses of New Bedford on 9 June 1925. Reduced to caretaker status on 6 January 1930. Placed under the command of the commanding officer, Harbor Defenses of Narragansett Bay on 26 January 1931. Reclassified in June 1935 as a Class III (Maintenance) harbor defense. Defenses upgraded on 1 February 1940 to Class I (Full Training) with the activation of the 23d C.A. Concurrently released from command of the commanding officer, Harbor Defenses of Narragansett Bay. Harbor defenses organized as follows:

Harbor Defense Headquarters — Fort Rodman
2 Groups

Batteries	**No. Guns**	**Weapon/Mount**	**Location**	**Remarks:**
Battery Millikin	2	12" BC LR	Fort Rodman	comp. 1924
Battery Walcott–Barton	2	8" DC MR	Fort Rodman	
Battery Cross	2	5" P	Fort Rodman	d/a 1920
Battery Craig	2	3" MP	Fort Rodman	d/a 1920
Battery Gaston	2	3" MP	Fort Rodman	d/a 1920
155-mm Battery	4	155-mm GPF PM	Fort Rodman	
AA Battery No. 1	Composite		–	

Events: 59, 313

Commanders, Coast Defenses of New Bedford

Col. William W. Rose	26 November 1918–17 January 1919
Maj. H.W. Smith	17 January 1919–28 June 1919
Col. George F. Landers	28 June 1919–6 July 1921
Capt. Arthur J. Lacouture	6 July 1921–24 January 1922
1st Lt. George B. Anderson	24 January 1922–April 1925
Col. Edward P. O'Hern	April 1925–20 December 1926
Capt. B. Reynolds	20 December 1926–25 June 1927
1st Lt. William H. Speidel	25 June 1927–5 August 1927
Maj. Stewart O. Elting	5 August 1927–12 December 1928
1st Lt. Nevins D. Young	12 December 1928–February 1931
2d Lt. William F. Neithamer	February 1931–May 1931
Capt. John J. Johnson	May 1931–9 October 1937
1st Lt. Harrison A. Gerhardt	9 October 1937–11 November 1937
Capt. Charles N. Branham	11 November 1937–September 1940
Capt. John H. Kochevar	September 1940–December 1940
Lt. Col. Charles J. Herzer	December 1940–December 1941

Coast Defenses of New Orleans (Ninth Coast Artillery District)

HQ—Jackson Barracks, LA, 1920–24; *Inactive,* 1924–35; New Orleans, LA, 1935–36; *Inactive,* 1936–41

Subordinate elements—Two C.A. companies, 1919–23; *267th C.A. Bn.* (NGI), 1925–33; *639th C.A.* (ORI), 1929–41

Active as of June 1919 with HQ at Jackson Barracks, LA. Responsible for the coastal defense of the entrances to the Mississippi River. Subordinate coast defense installations included batteries at Forts St. Philip and Jackson. Coast Defenses of New Orleans inactivated on 1 July 1924. Redesignated Harbor Defenses of New Orleans on 9 June 1925. Though all remaining weapons and armament were removed by Ordnance Corps personnel in 1920, war plans called for the reactivation of the Harbor Defenses of New Orleans in the event of war. HQ, HQ Btry, and the Med. Dept. Det. organized on 4 January 1935 as an RAI unit with O.R. personnel with HQ at New Orleans. Inactivated on 6 June 1936 at New Orleans by relief of personnel. Harbor defenses organized as follows:

Harbor Defense Headquarters				Jackson Barracks
Batteries	**No. Guns**	**Weapon/Mount**	**Location**	**Remarks:**
Battery Pike	2	10" DC	Fort St. Philip	d/a 1919
Battery Merrill	2	8" DC	Fort St. Philip	d/a 1920
Battery Brooke	2	3" MP	Fort St. Philip	d/a 1920
Battery Millar	2	3" MP	Fort Jackson	d/a 1920
Battery Scott	2	3" MP	Fort St. Philip	d/a 1920

Commanders, Coast Defenses of New Orleans

Col. Earle D'A. Pearce	10 July 1919–2 August 1920	1st Lt. Frank A. Hollingshead	25 August 1921–6 October 1921
Lt. Col. George L. Wertenbaker	2 August 1920–30 December 1920	Maj. Ralph D. Bates	6 October 1921–1 July 1924
Maj. Cherebusco Newton	30 December 1920–29 January 1921	*Inactive*	1 July 1924–3 January 1935
1st Lt. Louis H. Thompson	29 January 1921–13 March 1921	Capt. Nolan Pyroux**	4 January 1935–6 June 1936
Maj. Jacob A. Mack	13 March 1921–25 August 1921	*Inactive*	6 June 1936–7 December 1941

**RAI commanders: O.R. officers.

Coast Defenses of Oahu (Hawaiian Coast Artillery District)

HQ—Fort Kamehameha, TH, 1919–21

Subordinate elements—1st –14th Cos., CD of Oahu, 1920–21; U.S.A.M.P. *Col. Garland N. Whistler,* 1920–21

Established in the R.A. on 1 January 1914. Active as of June 1919 with HQ at Fort Kamehameha, TH. Responsible for the coastal defense of the approaches to Pearl Harbor. Subordinate coast defense installations included batteries at Forts Kamehameha, Armstrong, Ruger, and DeRussey. Reorganized into two commands which were designated as the Coast Defenses of Pearl Harbor and Coast Defenses of Honolulu on 5 April 1921.

Commanders, Coast Defenses of Oahu

Col. Thomas Ridgway	March 1919–27 September 1919	Lt. Col. Joseph Matson	6 October 1920–14 January 1921
Col. Willougby Walke	27 September 1919–6 October 1920	Lt. Col. Ellison L. Gilmer	14 January 1921–12 February 1921

Coast Defenses of Pearl Harbor (Hawaiian Coast Artillery District)

HQ—Fort Kamehameha, TH, 1921–41

Subordinate elements—68th, 75th, *91st*, 125th, *143d*, *184th*, and 185th C.A. Cos., 1922–24; 55th C.A. Regt. (less 2d Bn.), 1921–41; 15th and 41st C.A. Regts., 1924–41; 21st Bln. Co., 1921–22

Established in the R.A. on 13 December 1920 as the Coast Defenses of Pearl Harbor. Organized on 5 April 1921 from the Coast Defenses of Oahu with HQ at Fort Kamehameha, TH. Redesignated Harbor Defenses of Pearl Harbor on 9 June 1925. Responsible for the coastal defense of the approaches to Pearl Harbor. Subordinate coast defense installations included batteries at Forts Kamehameha, Weaver, and Barrette. Harbor defenses organized as follows:

Harbor Defense Headquarters — Fort Kamehameha

Batteries	No. Guns	Weapon/Mount	Location	Remarks:
Battery Hatch	2	16" BC LRN	Fort Barrette	comp. 1934
Battery Williston	2	16" BC LRA	Fort Weaver	comp. 1924
Battery Hasbrouck	8	12" M	Fort Kamehameha	
Battery Selfridge	2	12" DC	Fort Kamehameha	
Battery Clossen	2	12" BC LR	Fort Kamehameha	comp. 1924
Battery Jackson	2	6" DC	Fort Kamehameha	
Brown's Camp Battery	4	8" RY	Kahe Point	comp. 1937
Battery Adair	2	6" A/C/BC	Ford Is.	comp. 1925
Battery Boyd	2	6" A/C/BC	Ford Is.	comp. 1925
Battery Barri	2	4.7" A/C/BC	Fort Kamehameha	d/a 1924
Battery Chandler	2	3" C/P	Fort Kamehameha	
Battery Hawkins	2	3" P	Fort Kamehameha	
240-mm Battery	2	240-mm	Laie	comp. 1931
240-mm Battery	3	240-mm	Makua	comp. 1930
240-mm Battery	1	240-mm	Pupukea	comp. 1927
Battery Kam	4	155-mm GPF PM	Fort Kamehameha	
Battery Weaver	4	155-mm GPF PM	Fort Weaver	
Barber's Point Battery	4	155-mm GPF PM	Barber's Point	comp. 1937
AA Battery	4	3" AA	Fort Kamehameha	
AA Battery	4	3" AA	Ford Is.	
AA Battery	4	3" AA	Fort Barrette	comp. 1936

Status: Inactivated on 10 April 1945.

Events: 33, 37, 160

Commanders, Coast Defenses of Pearl Harbor

Lt. Col. Ellison L. Gilmer	12 February 1921–15 May 1921
Lt. Col. Joseph Matson	15 May 1921–19 January 1922
Col. Louis R. Burgess	19 January 1922–17 April 1924
Col. Henry M. Merriam	17 April 1924–14 May 1925
Col. William E. Cole	15 May 1925–31 August 1927
Lt. Col. Lewis Turtle	31 August 1927–18 June 1928
Col. Robert S. Abernethy	18 January 1928–20 August 1930
Lt. Col. John R. Musgrave	20 August 1930–10 November 1930
Col. Homer B. Grant	10 November 1930–2 December 1933
Col. Avery J. Cooper	2 December 1933–22 August 1935
Lt. Col. Peter H. Ottosen	22 August 1935–14 October 1935
Col. Earl Biscoe	14 October 1935–11 October 1937
Col. Henry M. Merriam	12 October 1937–September 1939
Lt. Col. Robert H. Volkenburgh	September 1939–October 1939
Col. Eugene B. Walker	October 1939–ao February 1941
Unknown	ao February 1941–7 December 1941

Coast Defenses of Pensacola (Fourth Coast Artillery District)

HQ—Fort Barrancas, FL, 1919–41

Subordinate elements—20th, *22d*, and *163d* C.A. Cos., 1922–24; 13th C.A., 1924–41; 265th C.A. Bn., 1923–30; 265th C.A. Regt., 1930–33 and 1938–41; 623d C.A., 1924–41; U.S.A.M.P. *Gen. John P. Story,* 1920–21

Active as of June 1919 with HQ at Fort Barrancas, FL. Responsible for the coastal defense of the approaches to Pensacola Bay. Subordinate coast defense installations included batteries at Forts Pickens and McRee. Redesignated Harbor Defenses of Pensacola on 9 June 1925. In April 1933, the HQ assumed command and control of CCC District G, Fourth Corps Area. Subordinate units supported CCC activities in western Florida. Classified in June 1935 as a Class I (Full Training) harbor defense. Harbor defenses organized as follows:

Harbor Defense Headquarters	Fort Barrancas
Harbor Entrance Control Post	Fort Pickens
3 Groups	

Batteries	No. Guns	Weapon/Mount	Location	Remarks:
Battery Langdon	2	12" BC LR	Fort Pickens	comp. 1923
Battery Pensacola	2	12" DC	Fort Pickens	d/a 1935
Battery Worth	4	12" M	Fort Pickens	note 1
Battery Sevier	2	10" DC	Fort Pickens	d/a 1934
155-mm Battery	4	155-mm GPF PM	Fort Pickens	comp. 1937
Battery Van Swearingen	2	4.7" A	Fort Pickens	d/a 1921
Battery Truman	2	3" BC	Fort Pickens	
Battery Payne	2	3" BC	Fort Pickens	
Battery Center	4	3" MP	Fort McRee	d/a 1920
AA Battery No. 1	Composite		–	
AA Battery No. 2	Composite		–	

Note 1: Originally an eight-gun position, four 12" M were removed from Battery Worth about 1918. Battery Worth eventually would serve as the Harbor Entrance Control Post.

Commanders, Coast Defenses of Pensacola

Col. Frank G. Mauldin	September 1919–4 June 1920
Maj. Philip S. Golderman	4 June 1920–5 July 1920
Capt. C. L. Cooke	5 July 1920–19 August 1920
Col. James F. Brady	19 August 1920–5 September 1920
Maj. Austin McC. McDonnell	5 September 1920–5 December 1920
Capt. John J. Maher	5 December 1920–11 January 1921
Maj. Rollin L. Tilton	11 January 1921–27 August 1924
Maj. Walter K. Dunn	27 August 1924–23 September 1924
Lt. Col. Richard H. Williams	23 September 1924–22 September 1926
Maj. Walter Singles	22 September 1926–1 March 1927
Lt. Col. Robert W. Collins	14 March 1927–7 March 1928
Lt. Col. Walter Singles	7 March 1928–25 June 1928
Lt. Col. Hartman L. Butler	25 June 1928–28 July 1930
Maj. Charles K. Wing	28 July 1930–11 November 1930
Col. Francis H. Lincoln	11 November 1930–24 June 1933
Lt. Col. Clifford R. Jones	25 June 1933–27 December 1933
Col. Arthur L. Fuller	27 December 1933–12 October 1935
Col. Robert Arthur	12 October 1935–28 February 1937
Lt. Col. George F. Humbert	1 March 1937–14 September 1937
Col. Benjamin H. L. Williams	14 September 1937–9 September 1939
Col. Harvey C. Allen	9 September 1939–30 September 1940
Col. Louis L. Pendleton	30 September 1940–April 1941
Col. Lloyd B. Magruder	April 1941–1 October 1941
Maj. George W. Palmer	1 October 1941–12 December 1941

Coast Defenses of Portland (First Coast Artillery District)

HQ—Fort Williams, ME, 1919–41

Subordinate elements—24th, *51st*, *154th*, *155th*, and *171st* C.A. Cos., 1922–24; 8th C.A., 1924–41; 240th C.A., 1922–33 and 1939–41; 613th C.A. Bn., 1923–36; U.S.A.M.P. *Gen. Edmund Kirby,* 1920–21

Active as of June 1919 with HQ at Fort Williams, ME. Responsible for the coastal defense of the approaches to Casco Bay. Subordinate coast defense installations included batteries at Forts Williams, McKinley, Levett, Preble, and Lyon. Redesignated Harbor Defenses of Portland on 9 June 1925. Reduced to caretaker status on 6 January 1930. Reclassified in June 1935 as a Class II (Limited Training) harbor defense. Defenses upgraded during 1940–41 to Class I (Full Training) with the activation of additional batteries of the 8th C.A. The 240th C.A. arrived at Fort McKinley on 23 September 1940 and shortly thereafter assumed the mission of manning batteries in the Harbor Defenses of Portland. Harbor defenses organized as follows:

Harbor Defense Headquarters	Fort Williams
Harbor Entrance Control Post	Fort Williams
1 Groupment	
6 Groups	

Batteries	**No. Guns**	**Weapon/Mount**	**Location**	**Remarks:**
Mine Battery 1	7 Groups	–		
Mine Battery 2	3 Groups	–		
Battery Foote	2	12" BC LR	Fort Levett	
Battery Bowdoin	3	12" DC MR	Fort Levett	
Battery Blair	2	12" DC MR	Fort Williams	
Battery Berry	2	12" DC MR	Fort McKinley	
Battery Chase	4	12" M	Fort Preble	
Battery Kearney	4	12" M	Fort Preble	
Battery Ingalls	4	12" M	Fort McKinley	
Battery Kendrick	2	10" DC	Fort Levett	
Battery Sullivan	3	10" DC	Fort Williams	d/a 1938
Battery DeHart	2	10" DC	Fort Williams	d/a 1934
Battery Thompson	3	8" DC	Fort McKinley	
Battery Weymouth	3	8" DC	Fort McKinley	
Battery Honeycutt	2	8" DC	Fort McKinley	
Battery Ferguson	2	6" P	Fort Levett	
Battery Acker	2	6" DC	Fort McKinley	
Battery Carpenter	2	6" BC	Fort McKinley	
Battery Keyes	2	3" BC	Fort Williams	
Battery Mason	1	3" BC	Fort Preble	
Battery Abbott	3	3" BC		
Battery Farry	2	3" MP	Fort McKinley	d/a 1920
Battery Ramsey	2	3" MP	Fort McKinley	d/a 1920
Battery Daniels	3	3" MP	Fort Levett	d/a 1920
AA Battery No. 1	Composite			
AA Battery No. 2	Composite			
AA Battery No. 3	Composite			
AA MG Battery No. 1				

Events: 174

Commanders, Coast Defenses of Portland

Col. Edward E. Farnsworth	1 January 1919–19 June 1919
Col. William Forse	July 1919–4 February 1920
Col. James A. Ruggles	4 February 1920–March 1920
Col. John B. Christian	March 1920–20 July 1920
Col. Clint C. Hearn	20 July 1920–3 March 1922
Lt. Col. Charles E. N. Howard	3 March 1922–14 July 1922
Capt. Harry R. Pierce	14 July 1922–August 1922
Lt. Col. Henry C. Merriam	August 1922–9 May 1923
Capt. Harry R. Pierce	9 May 1923–29 January 1923
Maj. Edward E. Farnsworth	29 January 1923–25 July 1925
Lt. Col. Charles E. Wheatley	25 July 1925–4 November 1925
Capt. Earl R. Reynolds	4 November 1925–20 June 1926
Capt. Douglas M. Griggs	20 June 1926–2 July 1926
Lt. Col. Edward E. Farnsworth	2 July 1926–7 May 1929
Capt. Harry R. Pierce	7 May 1929–18 January 1930
Lt. Col. Francis J. Behr	18 January 1930–10 April 1930
Capt. Harry R. Pierce	10 April 1930–20 November 1930
Lt. Col. Walter Singles	20 November 1930–6 June 1933
Maj. Thomas O. Humphreys	7 June 1933–26 September 1934
Capt. William Hasketh	26 September 1934–12 November 1934
Lt. Col. Charles A. French	12 November 1934–5 September 1937
Maj. Arthur W. Waldron	5 September 1937–15 July 1937
Maj. Harry W. Lims	15 July 1937–14 September 1937
Lt. Col. Otto H. Schrader	15 September 1937–5 December 1939
Col. Robert C. Garrett	5 December 1939–26 September 1940
Col. Charles B. Meyer	26 September 1940–13 December 1940
Brig. Gen. Robert C. Garrett	13 December 1940–14 October 1941
Brig. Gen. Harold F. Loomis	14 October 1941–17 May 1942

Coast Defenses of Portsmouth (First Coast Artillery District)

HQ—Fort Constitution, NH, 1920–21; *Inactive,* 1921–22; Fort Constitution, NH, 1922–41

Subordinate elements—156th C.A. Co., 1922–24; Btry E, 8th C.A., 1924–41; 22d C.A., 1940–41; 614th C.A. Bn., 1924–41

Active as of June 1919 with HQ at Fort Constitution, NH. Responsible for the coastal defense of the approaches to Portsmouth, NH. Subordinate coast defense batteries at Forts Constitution, Foster, and Stark. Inactivated on 13 September 1921. Activated on 1 June 1922. Redesignated on 21 October 1922 as Army Stations, Portsmouth Harbor. Redesignated Coast Defenses of Portsmouth on 1 January 1924. Redesignated Harbor Defenses of Portsmouth on 9 June 1925. Beginning in November 1927, the commanding officer of the Harbor Defenses of Portland also served as the commanding officer of the Harbor Defenses of Portsmouth until 1 February 1940. Concurrently, Harbor Defenses of Portsmouth designated a subcommand of the Harbor Defenses of Portland. Reduced to caretaker status on 6 January 1930. The Harbor Defenses of Portsmouth were selected in June 1930 by the War Department to perform a mobilization exercise. The command successfully tested how quickly and effectively a C.A. unit could get a battery that was in caretaker status back into operation. Reclassified in June 1935 as a Class III (Maintenance) harbor defense. Harbor Defenses of Portsmouth were upgraded to Class I (Field Training) harbor defense with the activation of the 22d C.A. Regt. on 1 February 1940 at Fort Constitution. Relieved as a subcommand of the Harbor Defenses of Portland on 27 September 1940 and resumed operations as a separate harbor defense command. Harbor defenses organized as follows:

Harbor Defense Headquarters — Fort Constitution
2 Groups

Batteries	No. Guns	Weapon/Mount	Location	Remarks:
Mine Battery 1	6 Groups	–		
Battery Hunter	2	12" DC MR	Fort Stark	
Battery Bohlen	3	10" DC MR	Fort Foster	
Battery Hackleman	2	3" P	Fort Constitution	
Battery Chapin	2	3" P	Fort Foster	
Battery Hayes	2	3" BC	Fort Stark	
Battery Lytle	2	3" BC	Fort Stark	
AA Battery No. 1				

Commanders, Coast Defenses of Portsmouth

Col. Thomas Ridgway	6 August 1918–February 1919
Col. Frederick L. Buck	February 1919–28 December 1920
Maj. Clark A. Thomas	28 December 1920–1 February 1921
Maj. Theodore M. Chase	1 February 1921–15 August 1921
1st Lt. Ephraim P. Jolls	15 August 1921–10 September 1923
Capt. Douglas M. Griggs	10 September 1923–26 June 1924
WO Johannes Hoebee	ao November 1925–November 1927
Lt. Col. Edward E. Farnsworth	November 1927–7 May 1929
Capt. Harry R. Pierce	7 May 1929–18 January 1930
Lt. Col. Francis J. Behr	18 January 1930–10 April 1930
Capt. Harry R. Pierce	10 April 1930–20 November 1930
Lt. Col. Walter Singles	20 November 1930–6 June 1933
Maj. Thomas O. Humphreys	7 June 1933–26 September 1934
Capt. William Hasketh	26 September 1934–12 November 1934
Lt. Col. Charles A. French	12 November 1934–5 September 1937
Maj. Arthur W. Waldron	5 September 1937–15 July 1937
Maj. Harry W. Lims	15 July 1937–14 September 1937
Lt. Col. Otto H. Schrader	15 September 1937–5 December 1939
Col. Robert C. Garrett	5 December 1939–16 September 1940
Col. George E. Fogg	16 September 1940–December 1940
Lt. Col. Edward G. Gowen	December 1940–5 January 1941
Col. Walter K. Dunn	5 January 1941–7 January 1942

Coast Defenses of the Potomac (Third Coast Artillery District)

HQ—Fort Washington, MD, 1920–23; *Inactive,* 1923–32; Third Corps Area at large, 1932–35; *Inactive,* 1935–41

Subordinate elements—47th C.A. Co., 1922–24; Btry E, 12th C.A., 1924–29; 260th C.A., 1924–29; 622d C.A., 1924–40; *633d C.A.* (ORI), 1929–40

Active as of June 1919 with HQ at Fort Washington, MD. Responsible for the coastal defense of the approaches to the Potomac River. Reduced to caretaker status in August 1923. Commanding officers from March 1924 to July 1939 were officers from the 12th Infantry (Inf.) assigned to the position as an additional duty. Redesignated Harbor Defenses of the Potomac on 1 July 1924 and, concurrently, command and control transferred to the District of Washington. Subordinate coast defense batteries were located at Fort Washington and Fort Hunt, VA. HQ and Med. Dept. Det. organized by June 1932 as an RAI unit with O.R. personnel from the Third Corps Area at large. Inactivated by June 1935 by relief of personnel. All remaining weapons and armament removed by Ordnance Corps personnel from Fort Monroe in 1939 and the Harbor Defenses of the Potomac permanently disbanded soon thereafter. Harbor defenses organized as follows:

Harbor Defense Headquarters — Fort Washington, MD

Batteries	**No. Guns**	**Weapon/Mount**	**Location**	**Remarks:**
Mine Battery	6 Groups	–	Fort Washington	d/a 1939
Battery Meigs	8	12" M	Fort Washington	
Battery Decatur	2	10" DC	Fort Washington	d/a 1918
Battery Emory	2	10" DC	Fort Washington	d/a 1929
Battery Humphreys	2	10" DC	Fort Washington	d/a 1929
Battery Wilkin	2	6" DC	Fort Washington	d/a 1928
Battery White	2	4" P	Fort Washington	d/a 1921
Battery Smith	2	3" MP	Fort Washington	d/a 1920
Battery Sater	2	3" MP	Fort Hunt	d/a 1920
Battery Many	2	3" P	Fort Washington	d/a 1928

Commanders, Coast Defenses of the Potomac

Col. Wilmot E. Ellis	31 August 1918–30 June 1920	1st Lt. Fred B. Waters	2 July 1923–12 March 1924
Maj. Frederic A. Price	30 June 1920–9 September 1920	1st Lt. Earle T. Loucks (Inf.)*	12 March 1924–August 1925
Col. William F. Stewart Jr.	9 September 1920–July 1921	Capt. Thomas L. Lamoreux (Inf.)*	August 1925–12 September 1928
Maj. Gooding Packard	July 1921–31 August 1921	Capt. John V. Stark (Inf.)*	12 September 1928–1 July 1929
Capt. Vernon W. Hall	31 August 1921–21 September 1921	1st Lt. John D. Armstrong (Inf.)*	1 July 1929–1 April 1930
Capt. Parry W. Lewis	21 September 1921–15 October 1921	Lt. Col. Alexander M. Patch, Jr. (Inf.)*	1 April 1930–26 June 1931
Lt. Col. James Prentice	15 October 1921–7 December 1921	Lt. Col. Louis A. Kunzig (Inf.)*	26 June 1931–21 August 1934
Capt. Parry W. Lewis	7 December 1921–16 October 1922	Lt. Col. James G. Ord (Inf.)*	17 September 1934–1 September 1936
1st Lt. Fred B. Waters	16 October 1922–17 November 1922	Lt. Col. Harland F. Seeley (Inf.)*	1 September 1936–30 September 1936
Capt. Robert M. Connell	17 November 1922–2 July 1923	Lt. Col. Gilbert R. Cook (Inf.)*	30 September 1936–1 September 1938
		Lt. Col. William F. Lee (Inf.)*	21 September 1938–1 July 1939

*These officers, assigned to the 12th Infantry at Fort Washington, were assigned as commanders of the Harbor Defense of the Potomac as an additional duty, 1924–39.

Coast Defenses of Puget Sound (Ninth Coast Artillery District)

HQ—Fort Worden, WA, 1919–41

Subordinate elements—*26th*, *49th*, *62d*, *63d*, *71st*, 85th, *92d*, *94th*, 106th, 108th, 126th, *149th*, and 150th C.A. Cos., 1922–24; 14th C.A., 1924–41; 248th C.A., 1923–33, 1939–41; 605th C.A. Bn., 1923–30; 630th C.A., 1924–41; U.S.A.M.P. *Maj. Samuel Ringgold,* 1920–22; U.S.A.M.P. *Col. Albert Todd,* 1920–21; U.S.A.M.P. *Gen. J. Franklin Bell,* 1922–40

Active as of June 1919 with HQ at Fort Worden, WA. Responsible for the coastal defense of the approaches to Puget Sound. Subordinate coast defense installations included batteries at Forts Worden, Casey, Flagler, Whitman, and Ward. Redesignated Harbor Defenses of Puget Sound on 9 June 1925. Classified in June 1935 as a Class I (Full Training) harbor defense. The 248th C.A. arrived at Fort Worden on 23 September 1940 and shortly thereafter assumed the mission of manning batteries in the Harbor Defenses of Puget Sound. Harbor defenses organized as follows:

Harbor Defense Headquarters	Fort Worden
Harbor Entrance Control Post	Fort Worden
3 Groupments	
8 Groups	

Batteries	No. Guns	Weapon/Mount	Location	Remarks:
Battery Ash	2	12" BC MR	Fort Worden	
Battery Wilhelm	2	12" AGL	Fort Flagler	
Battery Kinzie	2	12" DC MR	Fort Worden	
Battery Brannan	8	12" M	Fort Worden	
Battery Powell	8	12" M	Fort Worden	
Battery Schenck	8	12" M	Fort Casey	
Battery Seymour	8	12" M	Fort Casey	
Battery Bankhead	8	12" M	Fort Flagler	
Railway Battery	4	12" RM	Cape George	comp. 1920s
Battery Revere	2	10" BC	Fort Flagler	d/a 1941 note 1
Battery Benson	2	10" DC	Fort Worden	
Battery Kingsbury	2	10" DC	Fort Casey	
Battery Moore	3	10" DC	Fort Casey	
Battery Worth	2	10" DC	Fort Casey	
Railway Battery	2	8" RY	Cape George	comp. 1920s
Battery Tolles A	2	6" DC	Fort Worden	
Battery Tolles B	2	6" P	Fort Worden	comp. 1937 note 2
Battery Harrison	4	6" DC	Fort Whitman	
155-mm Battery	4	155-mm GPF		
Battery Warner	2	5" P	Fort Ward	d/a 1925
Battery Downes	2	3" P	Fort Flagler	
North & South Batteries	4	3" P	Deception Pass	note 3
Battery Putnam	2	3" P	Fort Worden	
Battery Trevor	2	3" P	Fort Casey	d/a 1933
Battery Van Horn	2	3" P	Fort Casey	
Battery Walker	2	3" P	Fort Worden	
Battery Waynesboro	2	3" P	Fort Flagler	
Battery Thornburgh	4	3" MP	Fort Ward	d/a 1920
Battery Vinton	2	3" MP	Fort Ward	d/a 1920

Notes:
1. Battery Revere's two 10" BC weapons were transferred to coast defense positions in Canada in 1941; battery modified for 3" AA weapons.
2. The two 6" P guns at Battery Tolles B came from the disarmed battery at Willapa Bay.
3. The guns for the Deception Pass batteries were never mounted but kept in storage for rapid mounting in the event of war.

Events: 90, 113, 199, 204

Commanders, Coast Defenses of Puget Sound

Col. Charles I. Phillips	March 1918–20 June 1919
Col. John L. Hayden	20 June 1919–31 March 1922
Col. Henry C. Merriam	31 March 1922–2 August 1923
Lt. Col. Ralph M. Mitchell	2 August 1923–5 September 1923
Col. Percy M. Kessler	5 September 1923–15 August 1927
Col. Henry M. Merriam	22 August 1927–1 February 1929
Maj. Raymond H. Fenner	1 February 1929–18 May 1929
Col. Archibald H. Sunderland	18 May 1929–1 July 1930
Maj. George R. Meyer	1 July 1930–15 November 1930
Col. Frederick W. Phisterer	15 November 1930–23 February 1933
Col. Alexander Grieg Jr.	23 February 1933–31 August 1933
Lt. Col. William R. McCleary	31 August 1933–10 February 1934
Col. Ralph M. Mitchell	10 February 1934–4 November 1936
Lt. Col. William D. Frazer	4 November 1936–16 January 1937
Col. Willis G. Peace	16 January 1937–2 May 1939
Brig. Gen. James H. Cunningham	2 May 1939–30 April 1946

Coast Defenses of San Diego (Ninth Coast Artillery District)

HQ—Fort Rosecrans, CA, 1919–41

Subordinate elements—28th, *89th*, and *115th* C.A. Cos., 1922–24; 2d Bn., 3d C.A., 1924–41; 19th C.A., 1940–41; 251st C.A., 1924–30; Btry A, 625th C.A., 1924–41

Active as of June 1919 with HQ at Fort Rosecrans, CA. Responsible for the coastal defense of the approaches to San Diego Bay. Subordinate coast defense installations included batteries at Forts Rosecrans, Emory, and Pio Pico. Redesignated Harbor Defenses of San Diego on 9 June 1925. Reduced to caretaker status on 6 January 1930. Reclassified in June 1935 as a Class II (Limited Training) harbor defense. Defenses upgraded during 1940–41 to Class I (Full Training) with the activation of additional batteries of the 2d Bn., 3d C.A. and the 19th C.A. Harbor defenses organized as follows:

Harbor Defense Headquarters — Fort Rosecrans
4 Groups

Batteries	**No. Guns**	**Weapon/Mount**	**Location**	**Remarks:**
Battery Whistler	4	12" M	Fort Rosecrans	
Battery White	4	12" M	Fort Rosecrans	
Battery Calef	2	10" DC	Fort Rosecrans	
Battery Wilkeson	2	10" DC	Fort Rosecrans	
Battery Strong	2	8" BC LRN	Fort Rosecrans	comp. 1941
Railway Battery	2	8" RY	Fort Rosecrans	
Battery Zeilin	2	7" NP	Fort Rosecrans	comp. 1937
Battery Gillespie	3	5" NP	Fort Rosecrans	comp. 1937
Battery Imperial	4	155-mm GPF PM	Fort Emory	
155mm Battery	4	155-mm GPF PM	Point Loma	
Battery McGrath	2	3" BC	Fort Rosecrans	note 1
Battery Fetterman	2	3" MP	Fort Rosecrans	d/a 1940
Battery Meed	2	3" P	Fort Pio Pico	d/a 1919 note 1
AA Battery No. 1	3	Composite	–	
AA Battery No. 2	3	Composite	–	
AA Battery No. 1	3	Composite	–	

Note 1: The two 3" P guns from Battery Meed were removed to Battery McGrath in 1919.

Events: 84, 92, 311, 332

Commanders, Coast Defenses of San Diego

Col. Louis R. Burgess	6 January 1919–19 June 1919
Col. Edwin Landon	19 June 1919–10 July 1922
Capt. John P. O'Neill	10 July 1922–14 August 1922
Maj. Edgar B. Colladay	14 August 1922–14 February 1923
Capt. William H. Sweet	14 February 1923–July 1923
1st Lt. Bernard C. Dailey	July 1923–12 July 1924
2d Lt. Robert H. Kreuger	12 July 1924–2 August 1924
Maj. Ward E. Duvall	2 August 1924–28 May 1928
Maj. William H. Kendall	28 May 1928–12 September 1928
Lt. Col. Jacob A. Mack	12 September 1928–4 August 1930
1st Lt. William E. Griffin	4 August 1930–30 November 1931
Maj. Joseph F. Cottrell	30 November 1931–24 July 1933
Lt. Col. George Ruhlen Jr.	24 July 1933–10 October 1934
Capt. William E. Griffin	10 October 1934–4 November 1934
Maj. Philip W. Hardie	4 November 1934–28 October 1935
Lt. Col. Edward L. Kelly	28 October 1935–1 June 1938
Maj. James P. Jacobs	1 June 1938–23 July 1938
Col. Robert E. Guthrie	23 July 1938–May 1940
Maj. V. R. Woodruff	May 1940–21 July 1940
Col. Peter H. Ottosen	21 July 1940–31 July 1945

Coast Defenses of Sandy Hook (Second Coast Artillery District)

HQ—Fort Hancock, NJ, 1919–41

Subordinate elements—*48th*, 56th, 76th, *113th*, 136th, 137th, and *178th* C.A. Cos., 1922–24; 7th C.A., 1924–41; 245th C.A., 1922–33, 1939–41; *262d C.A. Bn.* (NGI), 1924–30; 602d C.A., 1923–41; U.S.A.M.P. *Gen. Edward O.C. Ord,* 1923–41; U.S.A.M.P. *Joseph Henry,* 1921–41

Active as of June 1919 with HQ at Fort Hancock, NJ. Responsible for the coastal defense of the approaches to Sandy Hook and Raritan Bays. Subordinate coast defense batteries at Fort Hancock. Redesignated Harbor Defenses of Sandy Hook on 9 June 1925. Reduced to caretaker status on 6 January 1930. Reclassified in June 1935 as a Class II (Limited Training) harbor defense. Defenses upgraded during 1939–41 to Class I (Full Training) with the activation of additional batteries of the 7th C.A. The 245th C.A. arrived at Fort Hancock on 24 September 1940 and shortly thereafter assumed the mission of manning batteries in the Harbor Defenses of Sandy Hook. Harbor defenses organized as follows:

Harbor Defense Headquarters	Fort Hancock
2 Groupments	
6 Groups	

Batteries	**No. Guns**	**Weapon/Mount**	**Location**	**Remarks:**
Mine Battery 1	12 Groups	–		
Mine Battery 2	11 Groups	–		
Battery Harris	2	16" BC	Fort Hancock	
Battery Mills	2	12" BC LR	Fort Hancock	comp. 1922
Battery Kingman	2	12" BC LR	Fort Hancock	comp. 1922
Battery Alexander	2	12" DC	Fort Hancock	
Battery Bloomfield	2	12" DC MR	Fort Hancock	
Battery Richardson	2	12" DC MR	Fort Hancock	
Battery McCook	8	12" M	Fort Hancock	d/a 1923
Battery (unnamed)	4	12" M	Fort Hancock	d/a 1920 note 1
Battery Granger	2	10" DC	Fort Hancock	
Battery Halleck	2	10" DC	Fort Hancock	
Battery Arrowsmith	2	8" DC	Fort Hancock	d/a 1921
Battery Peck	2	6" BC	Fort Hancock	
Battery Gunnison	2	6" DC	Fort Hancock	
West Battery	2	6" BC	Fort Hancock	
East Battery	2	2" BC	Fort Hancock	
Battery Urmston	3	3" MP	Fort Hancock	note 2
Battery Morris	3	3" P	Fort Hancock	
Battery Burns	2	3" BC	Fort Hancock	
Battery Baker	2	3" BC	Fort Hancock	
AA Battery No. 1	3	Composite	Fort Hancock	
AA Battery No. 2	3	Composite	Fort Hancock	
AA Battery No. 3	3	Composite	Fort Hancock	
AA MG Battery No. 1	16	.50-cal MG	Fort Hancock	
AA MG Battery No. 2	12	.50-cal MG	Fort Hancock	
AA MG Battery No. 3	8	.50-cal MG	Fort Hancock	
AA SL Battery No. 1			Fort Hancock	
AA SL Battery No. 2			Fort Hancock	

Notes:
1. This battery was located at Highlands Military Reservation at Navesink, NJ.
2. Two 3" MP guns from Battery Urmston were replaced with 3" P guns in the early 1920s.

Status: Inactivated on 9 May 1942 and consolidated with the Harbor Defenses of New York.

Events: 77, 87, 93, 115, 174, 321

Commanders, Coast Defenses of Sandy Hook

Col. James F. Brady	12 August 1918–4 August 1920
Col. Frederick W. Stopford	4 August 1920–23 October 1920
Maj. John S. Williams	23 October 1920–18 November 1920
Lt. Col. Ellison L. Gilmer	18 November 1920–8 December 1920
Lt. Col. George F. Connolly	14 December 1920–4 February 1921
Col. Joseph B. Douglas	4 February 1921–25 March 1922
Lt. Col. Robert P. Woods	25 March 1922–23 December 1922
Col. James F. Brady	23 December 1922–12 September 1923
Lt. Col. Lynn S. Edwards	12 September 1923–October 1923
Col. Elijah B. Martindale Jr.	October 1923–12 October 1925
Col. John W. Gulick	12 October 1925–13 March 1926
Col. Godwin Ordway	13 March 1926–24 February 1929
Col. Jacob C. Johnson	24 February 1929–27 July 1932
Lt. Col. George W. Cocheu	27 July 1932–30 June 1934
Capt. Victor Schmidt	30 June 1934–20 September 1934
Col. Percy M. Kessler	20 September 1934–15 September 1935
Lt. Col. Richard S. Dawson	16 September 1935–25 October 1935
Lt. Col. Edward B. Dennis	25 October 1935–1 November 1935
Col. Lloyd H. Magruder	1 November 1935–2 November 1937
Col. Fulton Q. C. Gardner	3 November 1937–4 May 1938
Lt. Col. Edward W. Turner	5 May 1938–10 November 1938
Col. Francis E. Williford	10 November 1938–16 November 1940
Col. Philip S. Gage	16 November 1940–6 April 1941
Brig. Gen. Philip S. Gage	6 April 1941–9 May 1942

Coast Defenses of San Francisco (Ninth Coast Artillery District)

HQ—Fort Winfield Scott, CA, 1919–41

Subordinate elements—13th, *25th*, *57th*, 60th, *61st*, 64th, *65th*, *66th*, 67th, *147th*, *148th*, and *161st* C.A. Cos., 1922–24; 6th C.A., 1924–41; 63d C.A., 1924–30; 2d Bn., 18th C.A. 1940–41; 56th C.A., 1941; 65th C.A., 1938–41; 250th C.A., 1921–30 and 1940–41; 604th C.A., less 3d Bn., 1923–41; 608th C.A., 1923–29; 627th C.A., 1924–41; 14th Bln. Co., 1920–21; 24th Bln. Co., 1920–21; U.S.A.M.P. *Col. George Armistead,* 1920–37; U.S.A.M.P. *Gen. J. Franklin Bell,* 1920–22; U.S.A.M.P. *Col. Ellery W. Niles,* 1937–41

Active as of June 1919 with HQ at Fort Winfield Scott, CA. Responsible for the coastal defense of the approaches to San Francisco Bay. Subordinate coast defense installations included batteries at Forts Winfield Scott, Barry, Baker, Cronkhite, Funston, and Miley. Redesignated Harbor Defenses of San Francisco on 9 June 1925. Classified in June 1935 as a Class I (Full Training) harbor defense. In 1937, the Harbor Defenses of San Francisco were selected for a model upgrade program to improve harbor defenses throughout the United States, the Panama Canal, the Hawaiian Islands, and the Philippines. The program began with the construction of a 16-inch gun emplacement at Battery Davis at Fort Funston and continued into World War II. Harbor defenses organized as follows:

Harbor Defense Headquarters	Fort Winfield Scott
Harbor Entrance Control Post	Fort Winfield Scott
4 Groupments (Barry, Miley, Funston, and Antiaircraft)	
9 Groups	

Batteries	**No. Guns**	**Weapon/Mount**	**Location**	**Remarks:**
Mine Battery 1	8 Groups	–	Fort Winfield Scott	
Mine Battery 2	6 Groups	–	Fort Barry	
Battery Davis & 2	2	16" C/BC LRN	Fort Funston	comp. 1939 note 1
Battery Townsley	2	16" C/BC LRN	Fort Cronkhite	comp. 1940 note 1
Battery Wallace	2	12" BC LR	Fort Barry	comp. 1919
Battery Saffold	2	12" BC MR	Fort Winfield Scott	
Battery Godfrey	3	12" BC MR	Fort Winfield Scott	
Battery Lancaster	3	12" DC MR	Fort Winfield Scott	d/a 1918
Battery Mendell	2	12" DC MR	Fort Baker	
Battery Spencer	3	12" BC MR	Fort Baker	note 3
Battery Chester	2	12" DC MR	Fort Miley	
" "	1	12" BC MR	Fort Miley	
Battery Kirby	2	12" DC MR	Fort Baker	d/a 1933/41 note 4
Battery Alexander	8	12" M	Fort Barry	r/d 1920 note 5
Battery Livingston	8	12" M	Fort Miley	r/d 1920 note 5

Batteries	No. Guns	Weapon/Mount	Location	Remarks:
Battery Springer	8	12" M	Fort Miley	r/d 1920 note 5
Battery Stotsenburg	8	12" M	Fort Winfield Scott	note 6
Battery McKinnon	8	12" M	Fort Winfield Scott	r/d 1920 note 5
Battery Howe	8	12" M	Fort Winfield Scott	d/a 1920
Battery Howe	4	12" M	Fort Funston	comp. 1919 note 6
Battery Wagner	8	12" M	Fort Winfield Scott	d/a 1920
Battery Miller	3	10" DC	Fort Winfield Scott	d/a 1920
Battery Cranston	2	10" DC	Fort Winfield Scott	
Battery Crosby	2	6" DC	Fort Winfield Scott	
Battery Chamberlain	4	6" DC	Fort Winfield Scott	a/c 2 x 6" BC 1920
Battery Guthrie	2	6" BC	Fort Barry	
Battery Smith	2	6" BC	Fort Barry	
Battery Rathbone	2	6" BC	Fort Barry	
Battery McIndoe	2	6" BC	Fort Barry	
155-mm Battery	4	155-mm GPF PM	Fort Funston	
Battery Bruff	2	5" P	Fort Funston	d/a 1919
Battery Call	4	5" P	Fort Miley	d/a 1921
Battery O'Rorke	4	3" BC	Fort Barry	
Battery Yates	6	3" BC	Fort Baker	r/d 1941 note 7
Battery Baldwin	2	3" MP	Fort Winfield Scott	d/a 1920
Battery Blaney	4	3" MP	Fort Winfield Scott	d/a 1920
AA Battery No. 1	3	Composite	Fort Cronkhite	comp. 1940
AA Battery No. 2	3	Composite	Fort Barry	comp. 1925
AA Battery No. 3	3	Composite	Fort Funston	comp. 1925
AA Battery	3	Composite	Fort Winfield Scott	comp. 1920

Notes:

1. The 16" guns for these batteries were originally manufactured for mounting on the battle cruisers U.S.S. *Lexington* and the U.S.S. *Saratoga* before they were converted to aircraft carriers.
2. Battery Davis was the prototype for all casemated 16" batteries at stateside harbor defenses. Constructed as part of the 1937 model program, which was begun in the Harbor Defenses of San Francisco.
3. Originally a battery of three 12" BC weapons; one gun removed in 1918.
4. One gun from Battery Kirby was sent to the Philippines and remounted in the Harbor Defenses of Manila and Subic Bay in 1933; the other was removed and sent to the Philippines in 1941.
5. Originally an eight-gun position; four 12" M were removed from Batteries Alexander, Livingston, McKinnon, and Springer in 1920.
6. Originally an eight-gun position; four 12" M were removed from Battery Stotsenburg to establish the new Battery Howe at Fort Funston in 1919.
7. Battery Yates reduced from six 3" P weapons to two in 1941.

Events: 76, 108, 111, 235, 331, 335

Commanders, Coast Defenses of San Francisco

Col. Ira P. Haynes	25 June 1919–19 December 1919
Col. Robert F. McMillan	19 December 1919–30 June 1920
Maj. William A. Covington	30 June 1920–8 July 1920
Col. Percy M. Kessler	8 July 1920–6 September 1920
Col. Ira P. Haynes	6 September 1920–16 October 1922
Lt. Col. John P. Spurr	16 October 1922–7 February 1924
Col. Percy P. Bishop	7 February 1924–3 June 1925
Lt. Col. John P. Spurr	3 June 1925–8 September 1925
Col. William F. Hase	8 September 1925–1 December 1928
Col. Elijah B. Martindale Jr.	1 December 1928–20 June 1929
Lt. Col. Frank Geere	20 June 1929–5 July 1929
Col. John T. Geary	5 July 1929–24 January 1932
Col. Earle D'A. Pearce	24 January 1932–17 September 1934
Lt. Col. Allen Kimberly	17 September 1934–13 October 1934
Col. Harold E. Cloke	13 October 1934–15 May 1937
Lt. Col. La Rhett L. Stuart	16 May 1937–17 June 1937
Col. Henry T. Burgin	17 June 1937–30 September 1938
Lt. Col. John T. O'Rear	30 September 1938–20 April 1939
Col. Thomas A. Terry	21 April 1939–17 September 1940
Col. Rollin L. Tilton	18 September 1940–17 October 1940
Brig. Gen. Edward A. Stockton Jr.	17 October 1940–13 July 1942

Coast Defenses of Savannah (Fourth Coast Artillery District)

HQ—Fort Screven, GA, 1920–24; *Inactive,* 1924–35; Savannah, GA, 1935–36; *Inactive,* 1936–41

Subordinate elements—*72d*, 121st, and *181st* C.A. Cos., 1922–24; 264th C.A. Bn., 1924–36; *635th C.A.* (ORI), 1929–41

Active as of June 1919 with HQ at Fort Screven, GA. Responsible for the coastal defense of the approaches to Savannah Harbor. Subordinate coast defense installations included batteries at Forts Screven, Pulaski, and Fremont. Coast Defenses of Savannah inactivated on 24 November 1924 and reduced to caretaker status. Redesignated Harbor Defenses of Savannah on 9 June 1925. Caretaker status reconfirmed on 6 January 1930 and Harbor Defenses of Savannah concurrently designated a subordinate command of the Harbor Defenses of Charleston. Though all remaining weapons and armament were removed by Ordnance Corps personnel in 1928, war plans called for the reactivation of the Harbor Defenses of Savannah in the event of war. HQ, HQ Btry, and the Med. Dept. Det. were organized on 9 November 1935 as an RAI unit with O.R. personnel with HQ at Savannah. Inactivated on 4 July 1936 at Savannah by relief of personnel. Though the 252d C.A. (155-mm G.P.F.) (Truck Drawn) arrived at Fort Screven in January 1941, and shortly thereafter assumed the mission of manning mobile batteries in the vicinity of the Harbor Defenses of Savannah, the harbor defense HQ was not officially reactivated. Harbor defenses organized as follows:

Harbor Defense Headquarters — Fort Screven

Batteries	**No. Guns**	**Weapon/Mount**	**Location**	**Remarks:**
Battery Garland	1	12" BC	Fort Screven	d/a 1920
Battery Fenwick	1	12" BC	Fort Screven	d/a 1920
Battery Habersham	8	12" M	Fort Screven	d/a 1928
Battery Backus	2	4.7" A	Fort Screven	d/a 1920
Battery Gantt	2	3" MP	Fort Screven	d/a 1920
Battery Hambright	2	3" MP	Fort Pulaski	d/a unknown

Organization Day: 2 August. Chosen to commemorate the command's organization on 2 August 1898.

Commanders, Coast Defenses of Savannah

Col. Archibald Campbell	5 October 1916–21 May 1919	Lt. Col. Hugh K. Taylor	May 1921–3 September 1921
Col. Gordon G. Heiner	27 November 1919–1 December 1920	Lt. Col. Jacob E. Wyke	3 September 1921–30 November 1922
Lt. Col. Jacob E. Wyke	1 December 1920–May 1921	Capt. Paul S. Roper	30 November 1922–24 November 1924

Coast Defenses of Southern New York (Second Coast Artillery District)

HQ—Fort Hamilton, NY, 1919–41

Subordinate elements—*3d*, *53d*, *54th*, 98th, *123d*, *176th*, and *177th* C.A. Cos., 1922–24; 5th C.A., 1924–41; 245th C.A., 1922–33, 1939–41; 619th C.A., 1924–41; 620th C.A., 1924–41

Active as of June 1919 with HQ at Fort Hamilton, NY. Responsible for the coastal defense of the approaches to the Lower Bay and New York Harbor. Subordinate coast defense installations included batteries at Forts Hamilton, Wadsworth, and Tilden. Redesignated Harbor Defenses of Southern New York on 9 June 1925. Reduced to caretaker status on 6 January 1930. Reclassified in June 1935 as a Class III (Maintenance) harbor defense. Defenses upgraded during 1940–41 to Class I (Full Training) with the activation of additional batteries of the 5th C.A. Harbor defenses organized as follows:

Harbor Defense Headquarters	Fort Hamilton
Harbor Entrance Control Post	Fort Tilden
Harbor Entrance Control Post	Fort Wadsworth
4 Groups	

Batteries	No. Guns	Weapon/Mount	Location	Remarks:
Mine Battery 1	4 Groups	–		
Battery Harris	2	16" BC LRA	Fort Tilden	comp. 1924
Battery Neary	2	12" BC	Fort Hamilton	d/a 1935
Battery Ayres	2	12" DC MR	Fort Wadsworth	
Battery Brown	2	12" DC MR	Fort Hamilton	
Battery Dix	2	12" DC MR	Fort Wadsworth	
Battery Doubleday	2	12" DC MR	Fort Hamilton	
Battery Hudson	2	12" DC MR	Fort Wadsworth	
Battery Richmond	2	12" DC MR	Fort Wadsworth	
Battery Piper	8	12" M	Fort Tilden	
Battery (unnamed)	4	12" M	Fort Hamilton	d/a 1919
Battery Upton	2	10" DC	Fort Wadsworth	d/a 1925
Battery Gillmore	4	10" M	Fort Hamilton	
Battery Barbour	2	6" A/P	Fort Wadsworth	d/a 1920
" "	2	4.7" A/P	Fort Wadsworth	d/a 1920
Battery Livingston	2	6" DC	Fort Hamilton	
Battery Johnston	2	6" DC	Fort Hamilton	
Battery Mills	2	6" DC	Fort Wadsworth	
Battery Kessler	2	6" P	Fort Tilden	
Battery Ferguson	2	6" P	Fort Tilden	
Battery Griffin	2	3" P	Fort Hamilton	note 1
Battery Catlin	6	3" BC	Fort Wadsworth	
Battery Turnbull	6	3" P	Fort Wadsworth	
AA Battery No. 1	3	3" AA	–	
AA Battery No. 2	3	3" AA	–	
AA MG Battery No. 1	12	.50-cal MG	–	
AA MG Battery No. 2	12	.50-cal MG	–	

Note 1. Two 3" MP guns removed in 1920, leaving only two 3" P guns.

Status: Inactivated on 9 May 1942 and consolidated with the Harbor Defenses of New York; disbanded on 22 May 1944.

Events: 84, 174, 321

Commanders, Coast Defenses of Southern New York

Col. Louis R. Burgess	6 January 1919–15 August 1919
Col. Alfred M. Hunter	15 August 1919–27 January 1921
Col. Louis R. Burgess	15 March 1921–17 December 1921
Lt. Col. James L. Long	17 December 1921–15 July 1922
Capt. Thomas L. Cleaver	15 July 1922–23 May 1923
Capt. Arthur W. Waldron	23 May 1923–28 May 1925
Capt. Walter Hart	28 May 1925–16 May 1928
Capt. Lawrence Iverson	16 May 1928–30 July 1929
Lt. Col. Gilbert Marshall	30 July 1929–21 June 1934
Lt. Col. Lloyd P. Horsfall	21 June 1934–3 December 1934
Capt. Carroll G. Riggs	3 December 1934–31 March 1935
Maj. Walter J. Gilbert	31 March 1935–10 February 1938
Maj. Ernest R. Barrows	10 February 1938–1 December 1939
Col. Manning M. Kimmel	1 December 1939–22 July 1942

Coast Defenses of Tampa (Fourth Coast Artillery District)

HQ—Fort Dade, FL, 1920–24; *Inactive,* 1924–41

Subordinate elements—Two C.A. companies, 1919–23; *637th C.A.* (ORI), 1929–41

Active as of June 1919 with HQ at Fort Dade, FL. Responsible for the coastal defense of the approaches to Tampa Bay. Subordinate coast defense installations included batteries at Forts Dade and De Soto. Coast Defenses of Tampa inactivated on 1 July 1924 and designated as a subordinate command of the Harbor Defenses of Pensacola. Concurrently reduced to caretaker status. Redesignated Harbor Defenses of Tampa on 9 June 1925. Though all remaining weapons and armament were removed by Ordnance Corps personnel in 1926, war plans called for the reactivation of the Harbor Defenses of Tampa in the event of war. HQ, HQ Btry, and the Med. Dept. Det. organized on 16 November 1935 as an RAI unit with O.R. personnel from the Fourth Corps Area at large. Harbor defenses organized as follows:

Harbor Defense Headquarters — Fort Dade

Batteries	**No. Guns**	**Weapon/Mount**	**Location**	**Remarks:**
Battery Laidley	8	12" M	Fort De Soto	d/a 1921 note 1
Battery McIntosh	2	8" DC	Fort Dade	d/a 1923
Battery Howard	2	6" DC	Fort Dade	d/a 1926
Battery Burchsted	2	6" A/P	Fort Dade	d/a 1919
" "	1	3" MP	Fort Dade	d/a 1920
Battery Bigelow	2	3" MP	Fort De Soto	d/a 1920
Battery Mellon	3	3" MP	Fort Dade	d/a 1920
Battery Page	2	3" P	Fort Dade	d/a 1919

Note: Four 12" M were removed from Battery Laidley about 1921. The other four remained in position in caretaker status.

Commanders, Coast Defenses of Tampa

Lt. Col. Ralph M. Mitchell	ao February 1921–Unknown
1st Lt. R.A. Knapp	ao November 1922–1 July 1924
Inactive	1 July 1924–16 November 1935
Unknown	16 November 1935–15 February 1936
2d Lt. Orville A. Korf**	16 February 1936–Unknown

**RAI commanders: O.R. officers.

HHC, North Atlantic Coastal Frontier

HQ—*Not organized,* 1936–38; New York City, NY, 1938–41

Subordinate elements—HHC, New England Sector; HHC, New York Sector; HHC Delaware–Chesapeake Sector

Constituted in the R.A. on 20 September 1936 and allotted to the Second Corps Area. When activated, the North Atlantic Coastal Frontier would assume command and control of those Harbor Defenses in the First, Second, and Third Corps Areas. HQ organized by 1938 as an RAI unit with O.R. personnel at New York City, NY. Inactivated in August 1941 at New York City by relief of personnel. Location 7 December 1941—*Inactive.*

Commanders, North Atlantic Coastal Frontier

Col. Frank H. Phipps**	21 January 1939–8 November 1940
Maj. John S. Mayer**	12 June 1941–August 1941

**RAI commanders: O.R. officers.

HHC, Southern Coastal Frontier

HQ—*Not organized,* 1936–37; Atlanta, GA, 1937–41

Subordinate elements—HHC, Carolina Sector; HHC, Florida Sector; HHC, Gulf Sector

Constituted in the R.A. on 20 September 1936 and allotted to the Fourth Corps Area. When activated, the Southern Coastal Frontier would assume command and control of those Harbor Defenses in the Fourth and Eighth Corps Areas. HQ organized on 15 January 1937 as an RAI unit with O.R. personnel at Atlanta, GA. Designated mobilization training station was the Fourth C.A. District HQ, Atlanta, GA. Conducted summer training at Fort Barrancas, FL. Location 7 December 1941—Atlanta, GA.

Commanders, Southern Coastal Frontier

Capt. John A. Worfred**	15 January 1937–ao March 1937	Unknown	ao March 1937–7 December 1941

**RAI commanders: O.R. officers.

HHC, Pacific Coastal Frontier

HQ—*Not organized,* 1936–38; San Francisco, CA, 1938–40; *Inactive,* 1940–41

Subordinate elements—HHC, Southern California Sector; HHC, Northern California Sector; HHC, Northwestern Sector

Constituted in the R.A. on 20 September 1936 and allotted to the Ninth Corps Area. San Francisco, CA, designated as the unit's HQ on organization. HHC organized on 15 September 1938 at San Francisco as an RAI unit by the assignment of O.R. personnel. When activated, the Pacific Coastal Frontier would assume command and control of those Harbor Defenses in the Ninth Corps Area. Designated mobilization training station and HQ was Fort Winfield Scott, CA. Inactivated on 1 October 1940 at San Francisco by relief of personnel. Location 7 December 1941—*Inactive.*

Commanders, Pacific Coastal Frontier

Unknown	15 September 1938–1 October 1940

HHC, Atlantic Sector (Panama Canal Department)

HQ—Fort DeLesseps, CZ, 1932–40

Subordinate elements—Harbor Defenses of San Cristobal, 1st C.A., 14th Inf. Regt., 61st Quartermaster (Q.M.) Pack Troop, Det., Panama Signal Co., and U.S.A.M.P. *Gen. William M. Graham,* 1932–40

Constituted in the R.A. on 15 April 1932 and assigned to the Panama Canal Department. Concurrently organized at Fort DeLesseps, CZ. The units of the Atlantic Sector had the responsibility for the defense of the Atlantic side of the Panama Canal Zone from the Gamboa Bridge north and east to the Atlantic Ocean. Assumed control of units previously assigned to the 19th Inf. Brig., the Harbor Defenses of San Cristobal, and certain support elements previously assigned to the inactivated Panama Canal Division. Inactivated on 16 February 1940 and all subordinate units reassigned to the Panama Mobile Force or the Panama Sep. C.A. Brig.

Events: 167, 170

Commanders, Atlantic Sector

Brig. Gen. Harold B. Fiske	15 April 1932–5 September 1933	Brig. Gen. Frank W. Rowell	20 March 1936–16 March 1938
Col. James V. Heidt	5 September 1933–24 January 1934	Col. William T. Carpenter	16 March 1938–12 April 1938
Brig. Gen. Lytle Brown	24 January 1934–10 November 1935	Brig. Gen. Richard C. Moore	12 April 1938–23 October 1939
Col. William R. Pope	10 November 1935–20 March 1936	Brig. Gen. Joseph M. Cummins*	23 October 1939–16 February 1940

*Concurrently commanding the 18th Inf. Brig., December 1939–February 1940.

HHC, Pacific Sector (Panama Canal Department)

HQ—Balboa, CZ, 1932–40

Subordinate elements—Harbor Defenses of Balboa, 4th C.A., 33d Inf. Regt., 1st Bn., 2d Field Artillery (F.A.), Det., Panama Signal Co., and U.S.A.M.P. *Col. Ellery W. Niles,* 1932–40

Constituted in the R.A. on 15 April 1932 and assigned to the Panama Canal Department. Concurrently organized at Balboa, CZ. The units of the Pacific Sector had the responsibility for the defense of the Pacific side of the Panama Canal Zone from the Gamboa Bridge south and west to the Pacific Ocean. Assumed control of units previously assigned to the 20th Inf. Brig., the Harbor Defenses of Balboa, and certain support elements previously assigned to the inactivated Panama Canal Division. Inactivated on 16 February 1940 and all subordinate units reassigned to the Panama Mobile Force or the Panama Sep. C.A. Brig.

Events: 167, 170

Commanders, Pacific Sector

Brig. Gen. Thomas W. Darrah	15 April 1932–8 September 1934	Brig. Gen. Lawrence Halstead	9 November 1935–5 October 1937
Col. George Williams	8 September 1934–3 October 1934	Col. John D. Long	5 October 1937–26 October 1937
Brig. Gen. John W. Gulick	3 October 1934–24 September 1935	Brig. Gen. Frederic H. Smith	26 October 1937–29 October 1938
Col. Earle d'A. Pearce	24 September 1935–9 November 1935	Col. John D. Long	29 October 1938–9 December 1938
Maj. Gen. Ben Lear	9 December 1938–16 February 1940		

HHC, Carolina Sector (Southern Coastal Frontier)

HQ—*Not organized,* 1936–37; Columbia, SC, 1937–41

Subordinate elements—Harbor Defenses of Charleston; Harbor Defenses of Savannah; Harbor Defenses of Cape Fear

Constituted in the R.A. on 20 September 1936 and allotted to the Fourth Corps Area. HQ organized on 15 January 1937 as an RAI unit with O.R. personnel at Columbia, SC. Designated mobilization station was Fort Moultrie, SC. Conducted summer training at Fort Barrancas, FL. Location 7 December 1941—Columbia, SC.

Commanders, Carolina Sector, Southern Coastal Frontier

Capt. William A. Cauthen**	15 January 1937–ao March 1937	Unknown	ao March 1937–7 December 1941

**RAI commanders: O.R. officers.

HHC, Delaware—Chesapeake Sector (North Atlantic Coastal Frontier)

HQ—*Not organized,* 1936–37; Third Corps Area, 1937–41

Subordinate elements—Harbor Defenses of Chesapeake Bay; Harbor Defenses of Baltimore; Harbor Defenses of the Potomac

Constituted in the R.A. on 20 September 1936 and allotted to the Third Corps Area. HQ organized by January 1937 as an RAI unit with O.R. personnel in the Third Corps Area. Designated mobilization station was Fort Monroe, VA. Location 7 December 1941—Third Corps Area.

Commanders, Delaware—Chesapeake Sector, North Atlantic Coastal Frontier

Unknown	ao January 1937–7 December 1941

HHC, Florida Sector (Southern Coastal Frontier)

HQ—*Not organized,* 1936–37; Lakeland, FL, 1937–41

Subordinate elements—Harbor Defenses of Jacksonville; Harbor Defenses of Key West; Harbor Defenses of Tampa; Harbor Defenses of Pensacola

Constituted in the R.A. on 20 September 1936 and allotted to the Fourth Corps Area. HQ organized on 15 January 1937 as an RAI unit with O.R. personnel at Lakeland, FL. Designated mobilization station was Fort Barrancas, FL. Conducted summer training at Fort Barrancas, FL. Location 7 December 1941—Lakeland, FL.

Commanders, Florida Sector, Southern Coastal Frontier

Capt. Leon W. Pickett**	15 January 1937–20 August 1938	Capt. Oscar H. Thompson**	30 April 1939–ao January 1940
Capt. William R. Galt**	21 August 1938–29 April 1939	Unknown	ao January 1941–7 December 1941

**RAI commanders: O.R. officers.

HHC, Gulf Sector (Southern Coastal Frontier)

HQ—*Not organized,* 1936–37; Baton Rouge, LA 1937–41

Subordinate elements—Harbor Defenses of Mobile; Harbor Defenses of New Orleans; Harbor Defenses of Galveston

Constituted in the R.A. on 20 September 1936 and allotted to the Fourth Corps Area. HQ organized on 15 January 1937 as an RAI unit with O.R. personnel at Baton Rouge, LA. Designated mobilization station was Fort Crockett, TX. Conducted summer training at Fort Barrancas, FL. Location 7 December 1941—Baton Rouge, LA.

Commanders, Gulf Sector

Capt. Cornelius W. O'Leary**	15 January 1937–ao March 1937	Unknown	ao March 1937–7 December 1941

**RAI commanders: O.R. officers.

HHC, New England Sector (North Atlantic Coastal Frontier)

HQ—*Not organized,* 1936–39; First Corps Area, 1939–41

Subordinate elements—Harbor Defenses of Portland; Harbor Defenses of Portsmouth; Harbor Defenses of Boston; Harbor Defenses of Narragansett Bay; Harbor Defenses of New Bedford

Constituted in the R.A. on 20 September 1936 and allotted to the First Corps Area. HQ organized by May 1939 as an RAI unit with O.R. personnel in the First Corps Area. Location 7 December 1941—First Corps Area.

Commanders, New England Sector

Unknown	ao May 1939–7 December 1941

HHC, New York Sector (North Atlantic Coastal Frontier)

HQ—*Not organized,* 1936–39; New York City, NY, 1939–41

Subordinate elements—Harbor Defenses of Eastern New York; Harbor Defenses of Southern New York; Harbor Defenses of Sandy Hook; Harbor Defenses of the Delaware; Harbor Defenses of Long Island Sound

Constituted in the R.A. on 20 September 1936 and allotted to the Second Corps Area. HQ organized on 21 January 1939 as an RAI unit with O.R. personnel at New York City, NY. Inactivated in July 1941 at New York City by relief of personnel. Location 7 December 1941—*Inactive.*

Commanders, New York Sector

Maj. Albert J. Engleberg**	21 January 1939–July 1941

**RAI commanders: O.R. officers.

HHC, Northern California Sector (Pacific Coastal Frontier)

HQ—*Not organized,* 1936–38; San Francisco, CA, 1938–40; *Inactive,* 1940–41

Subordinate elements—Harbor Defenses of San Francisco

Constituted in the R.A. on 20 September 1936 and allotted to the Ninth Corps Area. HHC organized on 15 September 1938 at San Francisco, CA, as an RAI unit by the assignment of O.R. personnel. Designated mobilization training station and HQ was Fort Winfield Scott, CA. Inactivated on 1 October 1940 at San Francisco by relief of personnel. Location 7 December 1941—*Inactive.*

Commanders, Northern California Sector

Unknown	15 September 1938–1 October 1940

HHC, Northwestern Sector (Pacific Coastal Frontier)

HQ—*Not organized,* 1936–38; Fort Worden, WA, 1938–41

Subordinate elements—Harbor Defenses of Puget Sound; Harbor Defenses of the Columbia

Constituted in the R.A. on 20 September 1936 and allotted to the Ninth Corps Area. HHC organized on 15 September 1938 at Fort Worden, WA, as an RAI unit by the assignment of O.R. personnel. Designated mobilization training station and HQ was Fort Worden. Location 7 December 1941—Fort Worden, WA.

Commanders, Northwestern Sector

Unknown	15 September 1938–7 December 1941

HHC, Southern California Sector (Pacific Coastal Frontier)

HQ—*Not organized,* 1936–38; San Diego, CA, 1938–40; *Inactive,* 1940–41

Subordinate elements—Harbor Defenses of Los Angeles; Harbor Defenses of San Diego

Constituted in the R.A. on 20 September 1936 and allotted to the Ninth Corps Area. Los Angeles, CA, designated as the unit's HQ on organization. HHC organized on 15 September 1938 at San Diego, CA, as an RAI unit by the assignment of O.R. personnel. Designated mobilization training station and HQ was Fort MacArthur, CA. Inactivated on 1 October 1940 at San Diego by relief of personnel. Location 7 December 1941—*Inactive.*

Commanders, Southern California Sector

Unknown	15 September 1938–1 October 1940

1st Coast Defense Command, C.A.C., California National Guard

HQ—San Francisco, CA, 1921–23

Subordinate elements—459th–473d C.A. Cos., 1921–23

Organized in the California N.G., 1921–22, as separate C.A. companies. Companies organized into the 1st Coast Defense Command, C.A.C. and HQ federally recognized on 9 November 1921 at San Francisco, CA. Redesignated on 6 October 1923 as the 250th Arty. Regt. (Harbor Defense), C.A.C.

Commanders, 1st Coast Defense Command, C.A.C., California National Guard

Col. Richard E. Mittelsteadt	9 November 1921–6 October 1923

1st Coast Defense Command, C.A.C., Maine National Guard

HQ—Portland, ME, 1922–23

Subordinate elements—301st–312th C.A. Cos., 1921–23

Demobilized on 13 March 1919 as elements of the 54th Arty. Regt., C.A.C. Reorganized in the Maine N.G., 1920–21, with old and new companies as the 1st Coast Defense Command, C.A.C. Assigned to the Harbor Defenses of Portland. HQ federally recognized on 11 July 1922 at Portland, ME. Redesignated on 17 September 1923 as the 240th Arty. Regt. (Harbor Defense), C.A.C.

Commanders, 1st Coast Defense Command, C.A.C., Maine National Guard

Col. George E. Fogg	15 May 1922–17 September 1923

1st Coast Defense Command, C.A.C., Massachusetts National Guard

HQ—Boston, MA, 1919–23

Subordinate elements—319th–330th C.A. Cos., 1921–23

Demobilized March–May 1919 as elements of the 26th Division (Div.), 55th Arty. Regt., C.A.C., and Coast Defenses of Boston. Reorganized in the Massachusetts N.G. on 19 May 1919 as the 1st Coast Defense Command, C.A.C. and assigned to the Harbor Defenses of Boston. HQ federally recognized on 14 March 1921 at Boston, MA. Redesignated on 1 October 1923 as the 241st Arty. Regt. (Harbor Defense), C.A.C.

Commanders, 1st Coast Defense Command, C.A.C., Massachusetts National Guard

Col. Benjamin B. Shedd	14 March 1921–1 October 1923

1st Coast Defense Command, C.A.C., Rhode Island National Guard

HQ—Providence, RI, 1920–23

Subordinate elements—345th–352d C.A. Cos., 1921–23

Constituted in the Rhode Island N.G. on 19 May 1920 as the 1st Coast Defense Command, C.A.C. and assigned to the Harbor Defenses of Arty. Regt. (Harbor Defense), C.A.C.

Commanders, 1st Coast Defense Command, C.A.C., Rhode Island National Guard

Col. Cyril L.D. Wells	19 May 1920–1 October 1923

1st Coast Defense Command, C.A.C., South Carolina National Guard

HQ—Beaufort, SC, 1923–24

Subordinate elements—427th–429th C.A. Cos., 1922–24

Organized and federally recognized on 21 July 1923 in the South Carolina N.G. as the 1st Coast Defense Command, C.A.C. with HQ at Beaufort, SC. Assigned to the Harbor Defenses of Charleston. Redesignated on 25 March 1924 as the 1st Sep. Bn., C.A. (Harbor Defense), South Carolina N.G.

Commanders, 1st Coast Defense Command, C.A.C., South Carolina National Guard

Maj. Claud C. Smith	21 July 1923–25 March 1924

1st Coast Defense Command, C.A.C., Virginia National Guard

HQ—Richmond, VA, 1922–23

Subordinate elements—409th–416th C.A. Co., 1922–24

Constituted in the Virginia N.G. on 8 March 1922 as the 1st Coast Defense Command, C.A.C. and assigned to the Harbor Defenses of Chesapeake Bay. Concurrently, HQ federally recognized at Richmond, VA. Redesignated on 5 November 1923 as the 246th Arty. Regt. (Harbor Defense), C.A.C. to be organized as an eight-battery regiment. Redesignated on 19 August 1924 as the 246th C.A. Regt. (Harbor Defense).

Commanders, 1st Coast Defense Command, C.A.C., Virginia National Guard

Col. Marshall M. Milton	8 March 1922–5 November 1923

9th Coast Defense Command, C.A.C., New York National Guard

HQ—New York City, NY, 1921–24

Subordinate elements—369th–380th C.A. Cos., 1922–24

Active in the New York N.G. as of June 1919 as the 9th C.A.C. Redesignated on 13 June 1921 as the 9th Coast Defense Command, C.A.C and concurrently federally recognized with HQ at New York City, NY. Redesignated on 1 February 1924 as the 244th Arty. (Harbor Defense), C.A.C.

Commanders, 9th Coast Defense Command, C.A.C., New York National Guard

Col. John J. Byrne	13 June 1921–31 January 1924

13th Coast Defense Command, C.A.C., New York National Guard

HQ—New York City, NY, 1920–24

Subordinate elements—357th–368th C.A. Cos., 1922–24

Organized and federally recognized in the New York N.G. on 18 June 1920 as the 13th Coast Defense Command, C.A.C., with HQ at Brooklyn, NY. Assigned to the Harbor Defenses of Sandy Hook. Redesignated on 1 January 1924 as the 245th Arty. Regt. (Harbor Defense), C.A.C.

Commanders, 13th Coast Defense Command, C.A.C., New York National Guard

Col. Sydney Grant	18 June 1920–1 January 1924

Chapter 25

Coast Artillery Brigades

CAJ (now Air Defense Magazine)

The 41st Coast Artillery (Railway), Hawaiian Separate Coast Artillery Brigade passes in review at Schofield Barracks, TH, 1935.

Coast artillery (C.A.) brigades provided command and control for assigned or attached C.A. regiments, battalions, and other elements attached for operations. The brigades' primary mission was to plan, coordinate, and conduct indirect and direct fire and antiaircraft artillery support in defense of mobile units, harbor defenses, airfields, and other key installations.

Organization

There were three distinct types of C.A. brigade tables of organization (T/Os) in the interwar period. These were the antiaircraft artillery brigade, railway artillery brigade, and tractor-drawn artillery brigade. Each type of brigade consisted of a HQ, a HQ battery, and three C.A. regiments. Each type of brigade had different missions. The antiaircraft brigade provided antiaircraft defense for the Army's mobile units in the theater of operations. These brigades could also be used for fixed installations such as harbor defenses, airfield, important industrial facilities, key government centers, and communications facilities, either in the Zone of the Interior or the theater of operations. The railway brigades were intended to be devoted to harbor and coast defense, but could be employed as heavy artillery in a theater of operations. The tractor-drawn brigades were to be used as mobile batteries for harbor and coast defense as well, but could also be used in the medium or heavy artillery mode.

Additionally, there was also three other brigades in existence during the interwar period that were not organized in accordance with a standard T/O, but were formed to meet the defensive needs of a specific geographical area. These were the Hawaiian Separate (Sep.) C.A. Brigade (Brig.), the Panama Sep. C.A.

Coast Artillery Brigade, Tractor Drawn (155-mm Guns), 1927

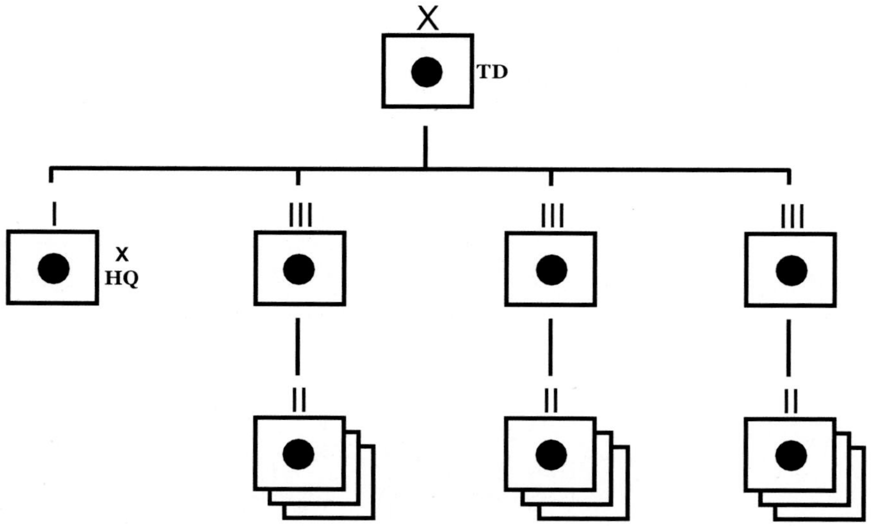

T/O:	331W
Approved:	24 February 1927
Commander:	Brig. Gen.
Officers:	260
W. O.	3
Enlisted:	6092
Total:	6375

Key Equipment:	
Cars, Reconnaissance	48
Tractors, 10-ton	129
Trucks, various	572
Guns, 155-mm or 6-in	72
Machine guns, AA	144

Coast Artillery Brigade, Antiaircraft, 1927

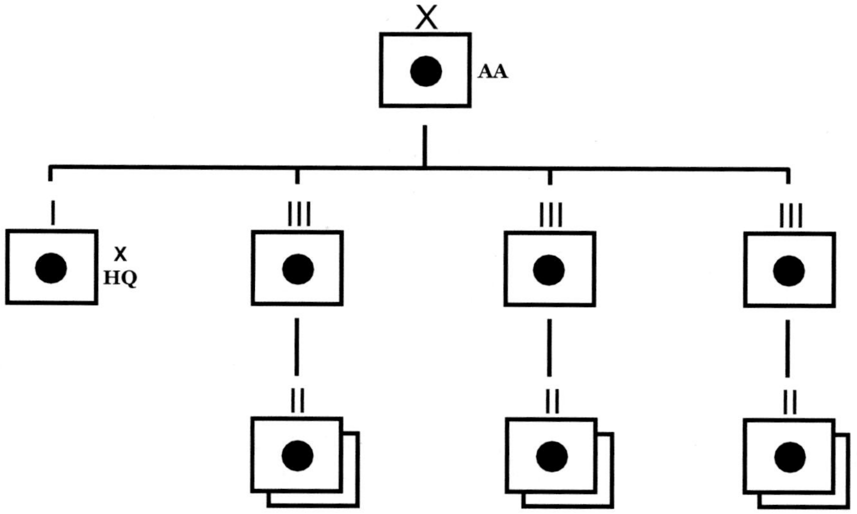

T/O:	221W
Approved:	24 February 1927
Commander:	Brig. Gen.
Officers:	220
W. O.	3
Enlisted:	5450
Total:	5673

Key Equipment:	
Cars, various	78
Tractors, 5-ton	9
Trucks, various	599
Searchlights	36
Guns, AA	36
Machine guns, AA	258

Coast artillery brigade organization.

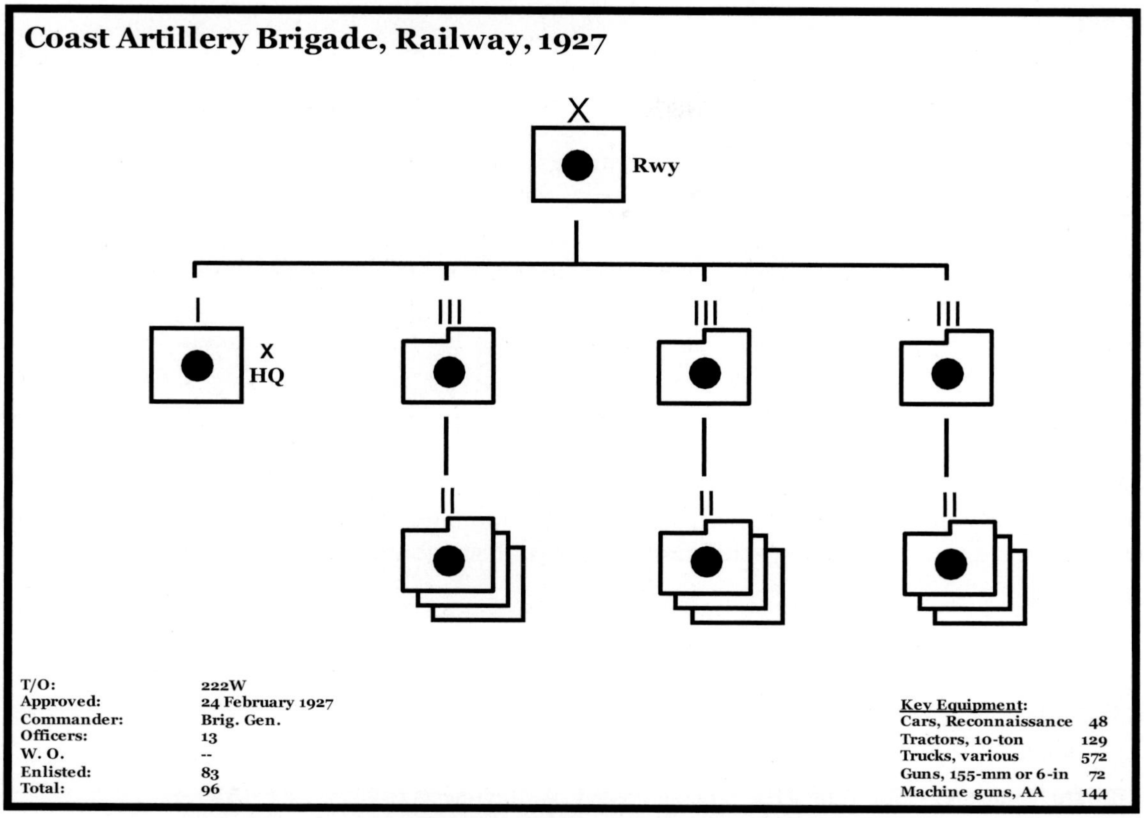

Coast artillery brigade organization.

Brig., and the New York C.A. Brig. All three were organized primarily for harbor defense missions, though the latter two included antiaircraft artillery and railway units, and all three controlled mobile C.A. units (tractor drawn) in addition to fixed-gun harbor defense regiments.

There were 15 brigades in the Regular Army (R.A.), of which 2 were railway brigades, 3 were tractor-drawn brigades, and 10 were antiaircraft artillery brigades. The remaining two were the nonstandard Hawaiian and Panama Sep. C.A. Brig. Only the Hawaiian Sep. C.A. Brig. and the 30th C.A. Brig. (RY) were in active service for more than 2 years before World War II. Several of the antiaircraft brigades were activated during the 1940–41 buildup. Each of the inactive RA brigades were organized as Regular Army Inactive (RAI) units at various times after 1929. Like almost all brigade and higher RAI commands, these units did not function as actual HQ and only a few were functional units. Most were pool units.

There were only two National Guard (N.G.) brigades. One was the already mentioned New York C.A. Brig., which was reorganized and redesignated as the 102d C.A. Brig. (AA) in 1940. An additional Guard brigade, 101st C.A. Brig. (AA) was also created in 1940 by the reorganization and redesignation of Minnesota's 92d Infantry (Inf.) Brig. as part of the mobilization for World War II.

There were 14 C.A. brigades constituted in the Organized Reserve (O.R.) between 1921 and 1928, and one brigade, the 239th, was transferred to the O.R. from the R.A. in 1927. All but one of these brigades were initiated at some point during the interwar years. Of these commands, 14 were antiaircraft artillery brigades. The remaining unit, again the 239th, was a tractor-drawn brigade. Six of the brigades were demobilized in 1933 and replaced in the Army's mobilization plans by RAI brigades. As with the RAI brigades, most of the O.R. commands were pool units, though at least one was functional.

Training

The training of the few active R.A. C.A. brigades was generally conducted in the coast defense areas where they would actually perform their wartime missions. The one stateside brigade, the 30th, was often called on to support the summer training of O.R. brigades and regiments at Fort Eustis. Since few, if any, of the RAI brigades were functional, they apparently held no training activities as units during the Inactive Training Period. Additionally, only four appear to have attended a summer training camp as a unit.

The New York C.A. Brig. typically performed its drills during the Inactive Training Period at its home armory in New York City. The HQ and staff usually focused on staff skills while the various HQ battery sections concentrated on support tasks. Occasionally the brigade HQ participated in command post exercises (CPXs) as part of their inactive training. The brigade typically attended summer training at Fort Ontario or Camp Smith, NY.

Since they were generally pool units, the personnel of most O.R. C.A. brigade headquarters and headquarters batteries (HHB) attended Inactive Training Period training activities with one of the brigade's subordinate regiments or with another local unit. Additionally, there is no evidence that any of these brigades functioned as command and control HQ during summer training camps either. Most likely, the brigades' personnel attended summer training activities with one of their subordinate regiments.

HHB, Hawaiian Separate Coast Artillery Brigade

HQ—Fort Shafter, TH, 1925–29; Fort DeRussey, TH, 1929–41

Subordinate elements—15th, 16th, 41st, 55th, and 64th C.A. Regiments (Regts.), 1925–41

Constituted in the R.A. on 28 February 1925 and assigned to the Hawaiian Department. Organized on 1 March 1925 at Fort Shafter, TH, with personnel and assets from the concurrently inactivated Hawaiian C.A. District. Transferred in October 1929 to Fort DeRussey, TH. Redesignated Hawaiian C.A. Command (Cmd) on 1 August 1941. Location 7 December 1941—Fort DeRussey, TH.

Events: 75, 88, 120, 138, 141, 158, 160, 189, 211, 225, 248, 276, 291, 297, 312

Commanders, Hawaiian Separate Coast Artillery Brigade

Maj. Gen. Henry D. Todd Jr.	25 August 1926–28 August 1929	Brig. Gen. Robert S. Abernethy	3 October 1932–15 January 1937
Brig. Gen. Robert E. Callan	28 August 1929–6 January 1931	Brig. Gen. James A. Woodruff	19 January 1937–16 March 1938
Brig. Gen. William E. Cole	7 April 1931–3 October 1932	Brig. Gen. Philip B. Peyton	April 1938–7 December 1938
Brig. Gen. Fulton Q.C. Gardner	16 December 1938–1 August 1941		

HHB, Panama Separate Coast Artillery Brigade

HQ—*Not organized,* 1936–39; Quarry Heights, CZ, 1939–41

Subordinate elements—72d and 73d C.A. Regts., 1939–41; 1st and 4th C.A. Regts., 1940–41

Constituted in the R.A. in 1936 and allotted to the First Corps Area. Organized at Quarry Heights on 1 November 1939 as the Provisional (Prov.) C.A. Brig. Redesignated Panama Sep. C.A. Brig. on 16 February 1940. Redesignated HHB, Panama C.A. Cmd on 1 September 1941. Subordinate elements transferred to the newly activated Atlantic and Pacific C.A. Brigades. Location 7 December 1941—Quarry Heights, CZ.

Events: 292, 308

Commander, Panama Separate Coast Artillery Brigade

Brig. Gen. Sanderford Jarman	6 December 1939–30 June 1942

HHB, 30th Coast Artillery Brigade (RY) **Regular Army Inactive**

HQ—Fort Eustis, VA, 1919–21; *Inactive,* 1921–26; Fort Eustis, VA, 1926–30; *Inactive,* 1930–37; Third Corps Area, 1937–40; *Inactive,* 1940–41

Subordinate elements—42d and 43d C.A. Regts. (RAI), 1919–41; 51st C.A. Regt., 1926–29; 52d C.A. Regt., 1919–40; 53d C.A. Regt. (RAI), 1919–30

Arrived at the port of Newport News on 1 January 1919 on the U.S.S. *Princess Matoika* as the 30th Artillery (Arty.) Brig., Coast Artillery Corps (C.A.C.) (Railway). Transferred in January 1919 to Fort Eustis, VA. Inactivated on 17 August 1921 at Fort Eustis. Activated on 17 June 1926 at Fort Eustis with a cadre from the 51st C.A. Inactivated on 31 March 1930 at Fort Eustis and allotted to the Third Corps Area. Reorganized about June 1937 with O.R. personnel as an RAI unit in the Third Corps Area. Inactivated by June 1940 by relief of personnel. Location 7 December 1941—*Inactive*.

Status: Inactive in the R.A. as HHB, 30th Antiaircraft (AA) Arty. Brig.

Commanders, 30th Coast Artillery Brigade

Brig. Gen. Johnson Hagood	17 November 1918–7 September 1920	Brig. Gen. Charles D. Roberts	4 June 1929–11 December 1929
Col. William E. Cole	7 September 1920–30 June 1921	Brig. Gen. William E. Cole	15 January 1929–31 March 1930
Col. John C. Gilmore	30 June 21–17 August 1921	*Inactive*	1 April 1930–June 1937
Inactive	17 August 1921–17 June 1926	Unknown	June 1937–ao August 1938
Col. Joseph P. Tracy	17 July 1926–8 August 1928	2d Lt. Harry M. Meyers Jr.**	ao August 1938–ao June 1939
Col. Gordon G. Heiner	15 September 1928–29 May 1929	Unknown	ao June 1939–ao June 1940
Inactive	ao June 1940–7 December 1941		

**RAI commanders: O.R. officers.

HHB, 31st Coast Artillery Brigade (AA) (First Army) **Regular Army Inactive**

HQ—Fort Winfield Scott, CA, 1919; Camp Lewis, WA, 1919–21; *Inactive,* 1921–37; Philadelphia, PA, 1937–41

Subordinate elements—55th, 57th, and 59th C.A. Regts. (HT), 1919–21; 44th C.A. Regt. (HT) (RAI), 1926–41; 907th, 910th, and 917th C.A. Regts. (RAI), First Army Ammunition (Ammo.) Train (RAI), 1933–41

Arrived at the port of New York on 12 March 1919 on the U.S.S. *Calamares* as the 31st Heavy (Hv) Arty. Brig., C.A.C. Transferred to Fort Winfield Scott, CA. Transferred in October 1919 to Camp Lewis, WA. Inactivated on 30 June 1921 at Camp Lewis. Concurrently, allotted to the Third Corps Area and the 30th C.A. Brig. and made the Active Associate (A.A.). Assigned to the First Army on 1 October 1933 and redesignated as an antiaircraft brigade. Reorganized about June 1937 with O.R. personnel as an RAI unit with HQ at Philadelphia, PA. Location 7 December 1941—Philadelphia, PA.

Status: Active in the R.A. at Fort Bliss, TX, as HHB, 31st Air Defense Arty. Brig.

Commanders, 31st Coast Artillery Brigade

Brig. Gen. William C. Davis	September 1918–1 February 1919	Col. Earle d'A. Pearce	28 August 1920–7 December 1920
Col. John L. Hayden	12 March 1919–27 May 1919	Brig. Gen. Henry D. Todd Jr.	7 December 1920–3 June 1921
Brig. Gen. William C. Davis	27 May 1919–28 August 1920	*Inactive*	3 June 1921–June 1937
Unknown	June 1937–7 December 1941		

HHB, 32d Coast Artillery Brigade (TD) (Harbor Defense) **Regular Army Inactive**

HQ—*Not organized,* 1927–30; New York City, NY, 1930–41

Subordinate elements—62d, 197th, and 198th C.A. Regts., 1927–41; 361st Ammo. Train, 1927–33; 21st Ordnance (Ord.) Company (Co.) (RAI), 1927–33

Constituted in the R.A. on 15 August 1927 and allotted to the Second Corps Area. Designated mobilization station was Fort Totten, NY, 1927–33, and Fort Eustis, VA, 1933–41. Reorganized on 16 March 1929 with O.R. personnel as an RAI unit with HQ at New York City, NY. Location 7 December 1941—New York City, NY.

Status: Active in the R.A. at Fort Bliss, TX, as HHB, 32d Air and Missile Defense Cmd.

Commanders, 32d Coast Artillery Brigade

Maj. Granville B. Smith**	16 March 1929–July 1941

**RAI commanders: O.R. officers.

HHB, 33d Coast Artillery Brigade (AA) (Second Army) **Regular Army Inactive**

HQ—*Not organized,* 1933–34; Indianapolis, IN, 1934–41; Camp Hulen, TX, 1941

Subordinate elements—932d C.A. Regt., 1933–41; 938th and 951st C.A. Regts. (RAI), 1933–41; Second Army Ammo. Train (RAI), 1933–41; 69th C.A. Regt., 1941; 197th C.A. Regt., 1941; 203d C.A. Regt., 1941

Constituted in the R.A. on 1 October 1933, assigned to the Second Army, and allotted to the Fifth Corps Area. Organized by June 1934 with O.R. personnel as an RAI unit with HQ at Indianapolis, IN. Designated mobilization station was Fort Crockett, TX. Relieved from the Second Army on 24 January 1941 and assigned to the Third Army. Activated on 10 February 1941 less Reserve personnel at Camp Hulen, TX. Location 7 December 1941—Camp Hulen, TX.

Status: Disbanded on 12 April 1944.

Events: 325, 328, 330

Commanders, 33d Coast Artillery Brigade

Unknown	June 1934–10 February 1941	Brig. Gen. Harvey C. Allen	10 February 1941–1 December 1941
Brig. Gen. Charles C. Curtis	6 December 1941–July 1943		

HHB, 34th Coast Artillery Brigade (AA) (Third Army) **Regular Army Inactive**

HQ—*Not organized,* 1933–35; Columbia, SC, 1935–39; Augusta, GA, 1939–41; Fort Bragg, NC, 1941

Subordinate elements—67th C.A. Regt. (RAI), 1933–41; Third Army Ammo. Train (RAI), 1933–41; 76th C.A. Regt. 1941; 77th C.A. Regt., 1941

Constituted in the R.A. on 1 October 1933, assigned to the Third Army, and allotted to the Fourth Corps Area. Organized on 9 November 1935 with O.R. personnel as an RAI unit with HQ at Columbia, SC. Designated mobilization training station was the DeSoto National Forest (Camp Shelby), MS. Conducted summer training at Fort Barrancas, FL. Relocated in 1939 to Augusta, GA. Attached to the First Army on 24 January 1941. Activated on 10 February 1941 less Reserve personnel at Fort Bragg, NC. Location 7 December 1941—Fort Bragg, NC.

Status: Inactive in the R.A. as HHB, 34th AA Arty. Brig.

Events: 327, 330, 334

Commanders, 34th Coast Artillery Brigade

Capt. Ollie L. Ashcraft**	9 November 1935–ao January 1936	Capt. Stanley B. Deltart**	27 March 1938–9 February 1941
Unknown	ao January 1936–27 March 1938	Brig. Gen. Claude M. Thiele	10 February 1941–June 1942

**RAI commanders: O.R. officers.

HHB, 35th Coast Artillery Brigade (AA) (Fourth Army) **Regular Army Inactive**

HQ—*Not organized,* 1933–34; Ventura, CA, 1934–40; *Inactive,* 1940–41

Subordinate elements—515th C.A. Regt., 960th C.A. Regt. (RAI), 979th C.A. Regt., Fourth Army Ammo. Train (RAI) and *45th Ordnance Company,* 1933–41

Constituted in the R.A. on 1 October 1933, assigned to the Fourth Army, and allotted to the Ninth Corps Area. Organized by December 1934 with O.R. personnel as an RAI unit with HQ at Ventura, CA. Inactivated on 30 July 1940 at Ventura by relief of personnel. Location 7 December 1941—*Inactive.*

Status: Active in the R.A. at Osan Air Base, South Korea as HHB, 35th Air Defense Arty. Brig.

Commanders, 35th Coast Artillery Brigade

Unknown	December 1934–30 July 1940	*Inactive*	30 July 1940–7 December 1941

HHB, 36th Coast Artillery Brigade (AA) (GHQR) **Regular Army Inactive**

HQ—*Not organized,* 1933–38; Englewood, NJ, 1938–41; Camp Edwards, MA, 1941

Subordinate elements—68th C.A. Regt., 1941; 198th C.A. Regt., 1941; 208th C.A. Regt., 1941; 102d C.A. Battalion (Bn.), 1941

Constituted in the R.A. on 1 October 1933, assigned to the General Headquarters Reserve (GHQR), and allotted to the Second Corps Area. Consolidated on 14 October 1936 with the 36th Arty. Brig., C.A.C. (a World War I unit organized in June 1918 at Fort DuPont, DE, as the 36th Brig., C.A.C.; arrived at the port of New York on 2 March 1919 on the U.S.S. *America*; demobilized in March 1919 at Fort Totten, NY, reconstituted on 14 October 1936). Organized on 1 February 1938 at Englewood, NJ. Designated mobilization station was Fort DuPont, DE, 1933–39, and Camp Shelby, MS, 1939–41. Primary ROTC feeder school was Fordham University. Attached to the First Army on 24 January 1941. Activated on 10 February 1941, less Reserve personnel, at Camp Edwards, MA. Location 7 December 1941—Camp Edwards, MA.

Status: Disbanded on 25 March 1944.

Commanders, 36th Coast Artillery Brigade

2d Lt. Thaddeus H. Keilch**	1 February 1938–3 May 1938	Col. Charles D. Meyer	10 February 1941–11 February 1941
Capt. Clarence J. Lundblad**	3 May 1938–9 February 1941	Brig. Gen. Olin H. Longino	11 February 1941–February 1943

**RAI commanders: O.R. officers.

HHB, 37th Coast Artillery Brigade (AA) (GHQR) **Regular Army Inactive**

HQ—*Not organized,* 1933–37; Third Corps Area, 1937–40; *Inactive,* 1940–41; Camp Haan, CA, 1941

Subordinate elements—65th C.A. Regt., 1938–41; 78th C.A. Regt., 1940–41

Constituted in the R.A. on 1 October 1933, assigned to the GHQR, and allotted to the Third Corps Area. Organized about June 1937 with O.R. personnel as an RAI unit in the Third Corps Area. Inactivated by December 1940 by relief of personnel. Attached to the Fourth Army on 24 January 1941. Activated on 10 February 1941 at Camp Haan, CA. Location 7 December 1941—Camp Haan, CA.

Status: Inactive in the R.A. as HHB, 37th AA Arty. Brig.

Events: 335

Commanders, 37th Coast Artillery Brigade

Unknown	June 1937–December 1940	Brig. Gen. Edgar B. Colladay	10 February 1941–September 1941
Inactive	December 1940–10 February 1941	Brig. Gen. Leroy Lutes	7 November 1941–15 February 1942

HHB, 38th Coast Artillery Brigade (AA) (GHQR) **Regular Army Inactive**

HQ—*Not organized,* 1933–35; Jackson, MS, 1935–39; Pensacola, FL, 1939–40; *Inactive,* 1940–41; Camp Stewart, GA, 1940–41

Arrived at the Port of Newport News on 17 February 1919 on the U.S.S. *Kroonland* as the 38th Arty. Brig., C.A.C. Transferred in late February 1919 to Fort Monroe, VA. Demobilized on 28 February 1919 at Fort Monroe. Reconstituted in the R.A. on 1 October 1933, assigned to the GHQR, and allotted to the Fourth Corps Area. Reorganized on 9 November 1935 with O.R. personnel as an RAI unit with HQ at Jackson, MS. Relocated in 1939 to Pensacola, FL. Designated mobilization training station was the DeSoto National Forest (Camp Shelby), MS. Conducted summer training at Fort Barrancas, FL. Inactivated on 19 August 1940 at Pensacola by relief of personnel. Attached to the First Army on 24 January 1941. Activated on 10 February 1941 at Camp Stewart, GA. Location 7 December 1941—Camp Stewart, GA.

Status: Inactive in the R.A. as HHB, 38th Air Defense Arty. Brig.

Events: 330

Commanders, 38th Coast Artillery Brigade

Capt. Burford A. Spencer**	9 November 1935–6 June 1936
Capt. Moxley L. Beck**	6 June 1936–19 August 1940
Inactive	19 August 1940–10 February 1941
Brig. Gen. Richard F. Cox	10 February 1941–3 December 1941
Brig. Gen. Dale D. Hinman	3 December 1941–February 1942

**RAI commanders: O.R. officers.

HHB, 39th Coast Artillery Brigade (HT) (I) (GHQR) **Regular Army Inactive**

HQ—Fort Hamilton, NY 1919; Camp Jackson, SC 1919–21; *Inactive,* 1921–27

Subordinate elements—*44th, 51st,* and *56th C.A. Regts.,* 1921–26

Arrived at the Port of Hoboken on 14 January 1919 on the U.S.S. *Huntington* as the 39th Hv Arty. Brig., C.A.C. (HT). Transferred in February 1919 to Fort Hamilton, NY. Transferred in October 1919 to Camp Jackson, SC. Inactivated on 31 August 1921 at Camp Jackson. Withdrawn from allotment to the R.A. on 26 January 1926. Redesignated on 25 August 1927 as the 239th C.A. Brig. (TD) and allotted to the O.R. Concurrently allotted to the Third Corps Area.

Status: Inactive in the R.A. as HHB, 39th AA Arty. Brig.

Commanders, 39th Coast Artillery Brigade

Brig. Gen. William C. Davis	March 1919–26 May 1919
Brig. Gen. Andrew Hero Jr.	27 May 1919–31 August 1921

HHB, 39th Coast Artillery Brigade (AA) (II) (GHQR) **Regular Army Inactive**

HQ—*Not organized,* 1933–34; Cincinnati, OH, 1934–41; Fort Bliss, TX, 1941

Subordinate elements—933d and 938th C.A. Regts. (RAI), 1933–41; 62d C.A. Regt., 1941; 202d C.A. Regt., 1941; 206th C.A. Regt., 1941

Constituted in the R.A. on 1 October 1933, assigned to the GHQR, and allotted to the Fifth Corps Area. Organized in March 1934 with O.R. personnel as an RAI unit with HQ at Cincinnati, OH. Designated mobilization station was Fort Bliss, TX. Attached to the Third Army on 24 January 1941. Activated on 25 February 1941, less Reserve personnel, at Fort Bliss, TX. Location 7 December 1941—Fort Bliss, TX.

Status: Inactive in the R.A. as HHB, 39th AA Arty. Brig.

Commanders, 39th Coast Artillery Brigade

Maj. Everard H. Boeckh**	March 1934–ao June 1937
Unknown	ao June 1937–25 February 1941
Brig. Gen. Oliver L. Spiller	25 February 1941–April 1942

**RAI commanders: O.R. officers.

HHB, 40th Coast Artillery Brigade (AA) (GHQR) **Regular Army Inactive**

HQ—*Not organized,* 1933–37; Detroit, MI, 1937–41; Fort Sheridan, IL, 1941

Subordinate elements—526th C.A. Regt., 951st C.A. Regt. (RAI), and 973d C.A. Regt. (RAI), 1933–41; 61st C.A. Regt., 1941; 210th C.A. Regt., 1941; 103d C.A. Bn., 1941

Constituted in the R.A. on 1 October 1933, assigned to the GHQR, and allotted to the Sixth Corps Area. Organized by June 1937 with O.R. personnel as an RAI unit with HQ at Detroit, MI. Conducted summer training at Fort Sheridan,

IL. Activated on 23 January 1941, less Reserve personnel, at Fort Sheridan. Assigned to the Second Army on 24 January 1941. Location 7 December 1941—Fort Sheridan, IL.

Status: Inactive in the R.A. as HHB, 40th AA Arty. Brig.

Commanders, 40th Coast Artillery Brigade

Unknown	ao June 1937–23 January 1941
Brig. Gen. John L. Homer	23 January 1941–14 November 1941
Brig. Gen. Robert H. Van Volkenburgh	14 November 1941–2 May 1944

HHB, 41st Coast Artillery Brigade (AA) (GHQR) **Regular Army Inactive**

HQ—*Not organized,* 1933–34; St. Louis, MO, 1934–41

Constituted in the R.A. on 1 October 1933, assigned to the GHQR, and allotted to the Seventh Corps Area. Organized by December 1934 with O.R. personnel as an RAI unit with HQ at St. Louis, MO. Conducted summer training at Fort Sheridan, IL. Location 7 December 1941—St. Louis, MO.

Status: Inactive in the R.A. as HHB, 41st AA Arty. Brig.

Commanders, 41st Coast Artillery Brigade

Unknown	ao December 1934–7 December 1941

HHB, 101st Coast Artillery Brigade (AA) **Minnesota National Guard**

HQ—St. Paul, MN, 1940–41; Camp Haan, CA, 1941

Subordinate elements—215th, 216th, and 217th C.A. Regts., 1940–41

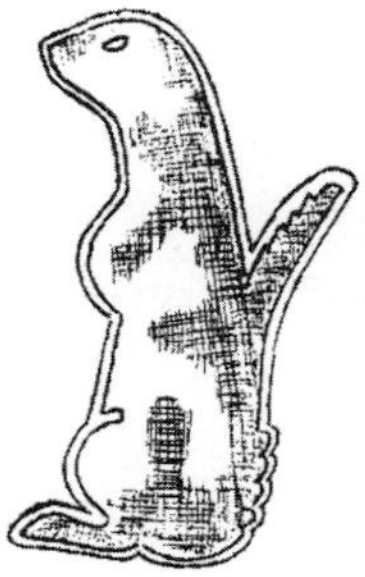

Constituted in the N.G. in April 1926 as Headquarters and Headquarters Company (HHC), 92d Inf. Brig. and allotted to the state of Minnesota. HQ organized and federally recognized on 22 April 1927 at St. Paul, MN. Reorganized and redesignated on 1 July 1940 as HHB, 101st C.A. Brig. Assigned on 30 December 1940 to the Fourth Army. Inducted into active Federal service on 6 January 1941 at White Bear Lake, MN. Transferred on 19 January 1941 to Camp Haan, CA. Location 7 December 1941—Camp Haan, CA.

Events: 335

Commanders, 101st Coast Artillery Brigade

Col. Ivan Bowen	1 July 1940–August 1940
Brig. Gen. Donald B. Robinson	August 1940–ao December 1941

HHD, 102d (New York) Coast Artillery Brigade (HD) **New York National Guard**

HQ—New York City, NY, 1929–41

Subordinate elements—212th, 244th, and 245th C.A. Regts., 1929–41; 207 and 209th C.A. Regts., 1941

Constituted in the N.G. on 16 March 1929 as the New York C.A. Brig. and allotted to the state of New York. HQ organized on 19 April 1929 as the New York C.A. Brig. and federally recognized on 22 April 1929 at New York City, NY. HQ detachment organized and federally recognized on 8 May 1929 at New York City. Typically conducted annual summer training at Fort Ontario, NY, 1929–40. Reorganized and redesignated on 1 September 1940 as HHB, 102d C.A. Brig. (AA). HQ battery disbanded on 30 September 1940. New HQ battery organized and federally recognized on 21 October 1940 at West New Brighton, NY. Assigned on 30 December 1940 to the First Army. Inducted into active Federal service on 16 February 1941 at New York City, NY. Transferred on 20 February 1941 to Camp Stewart, GA. Location 7 December 1941—Camp Stewart, GA.

Status: Inactive in the New York N.G. as HHB, XVII Corps Arty.

Events: 61, 301, 330

Commanders, 102d (New York) Coast Artillery Brigade

Brig. Gen. John J. Byrne	22 April 1929–12 September 1935	Brig. Gen. William Ottman	24 September 1935–4 September 1940
Brig. Gen. Nathanial H. Egleston	1 October 1940–1 January 1946		

HHB, 198th Coast Artillery Brigade (AA) (Fourth Army) **Organized Reserve Pennsylvania**

HQ—*Not initiated,* 1921–22; Erie, PA, 1922–32; Pittsburgh, PA, 1932–41

Subordinate elements—521st, 522d, and 523d C.A. Regts., 361st Ammo. Train, and 384th Ord. Co., 1921–41

Constituted in the O.R. on 15 October 1921, assigned to the Fourth Army, and allotted to the Third Corps Area. Initiated on 1 October 1922 at Erie, PA. Inactivated about June 1929 at Erie by relief of personnel. Pittsburgh, PA, designated on 7 April 1932 as HQ on reorganization. Relieved from assignment to the Fourth Army on 1 October 1933 and assigned to the GHQR. Reorganized about June 1939 at Pittsburgh. Location 7 December 1941—Pittsburgh, PA.

Status: Disbanded on 2 April 1943.

Commanders, 198th Coast Artillery Brigade

Maj. Augustus Norton	1 October 1922–ao March 1927	*Inactive*	June 1929–ao June 1939
Unknown	ao March 1927–June 1929	Lt. Col. Joseph A. Kelly	ao June 1939–6 November 1941

HHB, 199th Coast Artillery Brigade (AA) (Fifth Army) **Organized Reserve Indiana/Ohio/Kentucky**

HQ—*Not initiated,* 1921–22; Indianapolis, IN, 1922–26; Cincinnati, OH, 1926–30; *Inactive,* 1930–37; Indianapolis, IN, 1937–41

Subordinate elements—524th, 525th, and 526th C.A. Regts., 362d Ammo. Train, and 380th Ord. Co., 1921–33; 525th, 535th, and 541st C.A. Regts., 1933–41

Constituted in the O.R. on 15 October 1921, assigned to the Fifth Army, and allotted to the Fifth Corps Area. Initiated in March 1922 at Indianapolis, IN. Relocated in July 1926 to Cincinnati, OH. Relieved from assignment to the Fifth Army on 1 October 1933 and assigned to the GHQR. Inactivated by March 1930 at Cincinnati by relief of personnel. Indianapolis designated on 24 February 1936 as HQ on reorganization. Reorganized in July 1937 at Indianapolis. Location 7 December 1941—Indianapolis, IN.

Status: Disbanded on 2 April 1943.

Commanders, 199th Coast Artillery Brigade

Lt. Col. Bowman Elder	March 1922–July 1926	*Inactive*	ao March 1930–July 1938
Unknown	July 1926–ao March 1930	Lt. Col. Collis P. Hudson	July 1937–ao July 1938
Unknown	ao July 1938–7 December 1941		

HHB, 200th Coast Artillery Brigade (AA) (Sixth Army) **Organized Reserve Iowa**

HQ—*Not initiated,* 1921–22; Des Moines, IA, 1922–41

Subordinate elements—527th, 528th, and 529th C.A. Regts., 363d Ammo Train, and 387th Ord. Co., 1921–41

Constituted in the O.R. on 15 October 1921, assigned to the Sixth Army, and allotted to the Seventh Corps Area. Initiated in August 1922 at Des Moines, IA. Relieved from assignment to the Sixth Army on 1 October 1933 and assigned to the GHQR. Location 7 December 1941—Des Moines. IA.

Status: Disbanded on 2 April 1943.

Commanders, 200th Coast Artillery Brigade

Unknown	August 1922–16 May 1939	Capt. Julian S. Albergotti	16 May 1939–ao June 1939
Unknown	June 1939–7 December 1941		

HHB, 201st Coast Artillery Brigade (AA) (First Army) **Organized Reserve New York**

HQ—*Not initiated,* 1921–23; New York City, NY, 1923–41

Subordinate elements—212th, 213th, and 533d C.A. Regts., 336th Ammo. Train, and 382d Ord. Co., 1921–41

Constituted in the O.R. on 15 October 1921, assigned to the First Army, and allotted to the Second Corps Area. Initiated on 27 August 1923 at New York City, NY. Relieved from assignment to the First Army on 1 October 1933 and assigned to the GHQR. Designated mobilization station was Camp Upton, NY. Location 7 December 1941—New York City, NY.

Status: Disbanded on 2 April 1943.

Commanders, 201st Coast Artillery Brigade

Maj. Chandler Smith	27 August 1923–11 January 1931	Maj. James T. Catlett	4 June 1937–23 September 1937
Unknown	11 January 1931–18 May 1937	Lt. Col. Millard E. Kurtz	23 September 1937–9 May 1941
Capt. William E. Sutherland	18 May 1937–4 June 1937	Maj. James T. Catlett	9 May 1941–29 November 1941

HHB, 202d Coast Artillery Brigade (AA) (Second Army) **Organized Reserve North Carolina**

HQ—*Not initiated,* 1921–22; Raleigh, NC, 1922–37; Charlotte, NC, 1937–41

Subordinate elements—*520th* (DNG), 534th, and 535th C.A. Regts., 370th Ammo. Train, and 386th Ord. Co., 1921–41

Constituted in the O.R. on 15 October 1921, assigned to the Second Army, and allotted to the Fourth Corps Area. Initiated on 12 September 1922 at Raleigh, NC. Relieved from assignment to the Second Army on 1 October 1933 and assigned to the GHQR. Relocated on 22 March 1937 to Charlotte, NC. Conducted annual summer training at Fort Barrancas, FL. Designated mobilization training station was Camp Jackson, SC. Location 7 December 1941—Charlotte, NC.

Status: Disbanded on 2 April 1943.

Commanders, 202d Coast Artillery Brigade

Lt. Col. Andrew Bramlett	12 September 1922–19 June 1924	Maj. James M. Mozley	22 March 1937–ao September 1938
Unknown	19 June 1924–22 March 1937	Capt. Rolland S. Abrahams	30 April 1939–ao September 1940
Unknown	ao September 1940–7 December 1941		

HHB, 203d Coast Artillery Brigade (AA) (Third Army) **Organized Reserve Michigan/California**

HQ—*Not initiated,* 1921–22; Detroit, MI, 1922–30; *Inactive,* 1929–34; Ventura, CA, 1934–41

Subordinate elements—536th, 537th, and 538th C.A. Regts., 337th Ammo. Train (DNG), and 388th Ord. Co., 1921–41

Constituted in the O.R. on 15 October 1921, assigned to the Third Army, and allotted to the Sixth Corps Area. Initiated in October 1922 at Detroit, MI. Inactivated by June 1929 at Detroit by relief of personnel. Withdrawn from the Sixth Corps Area on 1 October 1933 and allotted to the Ninth Corps Area. Concurrently relieved from assignment to the Third Army and assigned to the GHQR. Reorganized in April 1934 at Ventura, CA. Location 7 December 1941—Ventura, CA.

Commanders, 203d Coast Artillery Brigade

Maj. Reinold Melberg	October 1922–20 April 1923	*Inactive*	ao June 1929–April 1934
Maj. Charles J. Collins	20 April 1923–16 December 1924	Unknown	April 1934–20 December 1937
Maj. James R. Milton	16 December 1924–ao January 1927	Capt. James W. Magee	20 December 1937–ao January 1938
Unknown	ao January 1927–ao June 1929	Unknown	ao January 1938–7 December 1941

HHB, 208th Coast Artillery Brigade (AA) (GHQR) **Organized Reserve New York**

HQ—*Not initiated,* 1921–23; Syracuse, NY, 1923–24; Buffalo, NY, 1924–33

Subordinate elements—513th and 514th C.A. Regts., 1921–33

Constituted in the O.R. on 15 October 1921, assigned to the GHQR, and allotted to the Second Corps Area. Initiated on 4 December 1923 at Syracuse, NY. Relocated in 1924 to Buffalo, NY. Demobilized on 1 October 1933.

Commanders, 208th Coast Artillery Brigade

Maj. William Warfield	4 December 1923–3 January 1924	Col. Charles E. Warren	3 January 1924–7 April 1928
Unknown	7 April 1928–1 October 1933		

HHB, 209th Coast Artillery Brigade (AA) (GHQR) **Organized Reserve Massachusetts**

HQ—*Not initiated,* 1921–24; Boston, MA, 1924–33

Subordinate elements—542d, 543d, and 544th C.A. Regts., 1921–33

Constituted in the O.R. on 15 October 1921, assigned to the GHQR, and allotted to the First Corps Area. Initiated in August 1924 at Boston, MA. Inactivated by July 1928 at Boston by relief of personnel. Demobilized on 1 October 1933.

Commanders, 209th Coast Artillery Brigade

Maj. Oramel E. Haney	August 1924–ao August 1927	Unknown	ao August 1927–ao July 1928
Inactive	ao July 1928–1 October 1933		

HHB, 210th Coast Artillery Brigade (AA) (GHQR) **Organized Reserve California**

HQ—*Not initiated,* 1921–26; San Francisco, CA, 1926–33

Subordinate elements—517th, 518th, and 519th C.A. Regts., 1921–33

Constituted in the O.R. on 15 October 1921, assigned to the GHQR, and allotted to the Ninth Corps Area. Initiated in October 1926 at San Francisco, CA. Typically conducted Inactive Training Period meetings at Building 171 at the Presidio of San Francisco. Inactivated by July 1929 at San Francisco by relief of personnel. Demobilized on 1 October 1933.

Commanders, 210th Coast Artillery Brigade

Unknown	October 1926–ao July 1929	*Inactive*	ao July 1929–1 October 1933

HHB, 212th Coast Artillery Brigade (AA) (GHQR) **Organized Reserve New York**

HQ—*Not initiated,* 1921–23; Queens, NY, 1923–33

Subordinate elements—530th and 539th C.A. Regts., 1921–33

Constituted in the O.R. on 15 October 1921, assigned to the GHQR, and allotted to the Second Corps Area. Initiated on 12 March 1923 at New York City, NY. Demobilized on 1 October 1933.

Commanders, 212th Coast Artillery Brigade

Brig. Gen. Howard S. Borden	12 March 1923–12 June 1931	Unknown	12 June 1931–1 October 1933

HHB, 239th Coast Artillery Brigade (TD) (GHQR) **Organized Reserve Virginia**

HQ—Camp Jackson, SC, 1919–21; *Inactive,* 1921–29; Richmond, VA, 1929–37; *Inactive,* 1937–41

Subordinate elements—606th and 607th C.A. Regts., 1927–41; 608th C.A. Regt., 1927–33

Arrived at the Port of Hoboken, NJ, in January 1919 as the 39th Arty. Brig., C.A.C. and transferred in February 1919 to Fort Hamilton, NY. Transferred in October 1919 to Camp Jackson, SC. Inactivated on 31 August 1921 at Camp Jackson, SC. Withdrawn from the R.A. on 26 January 1926. Redesignated on 25 August 1927 as the 239th C.A. Brig. (TD) and allotted to the O.R. Concurrently allotted to the Third Corps Area. Reorganized by December 1929 at Richmond, VA. Inactivated by June 1937 at Richmond by relief of personnel. Location 7 December 1941—*Inactive.*

Status: Disbanded on 2 April 1943. Reconstituted and consolidated with the 39th AA Arty Brig. on 1 October 1952.

Commanders, 239th Coast Artillery Brigade

Unknown	ao December 1929–ao June 1937	*Inactive*	ao June 1937–7 December 1941

HHB, 401st Coast Artillery Brigade (AA) (GHQR) **Organized Reserve Pennsylvania**

HQ—*Not initiated,* 1928–29; Philadelphia, PA, 1929–33

Subordinate elements—913th and 916th C.A. Regts., 1928–33

Constituted in the O.R. on 5 September 1928 as the 213th C.A. Brig. (AA), assigned to the GHQR, and allotted to the Third Corps Area. Redesignated 401st C.A. Brig. (AA) on 30 November 1928. Initiated in December 1929 at Philadelphia, PA. Conducted summer training most years at Fort Monroe, VA, 1930–33. Demobilized on 1 October 1933.

Commanders, 401st Coast Artillery Brigade

Unknown	December 1929–1 October 1933

HHB, 402d Coast Artillery Brigade (AA) (GHQR) **Organized Reserve Pennsylvania**

HQ—*Not initiated,* 1928–29; Pittsburgh, PA, 1929–33

Subordinate elements—917th and 920th C.A. Regts., 1928–33

Constituted in the O.R. on 5 September 1928 as the 214th C.A. Brig. (AA), assigned to the GHQR, and allotted to the Third Corps Area. Redesignated 402d C.A. Brig. (AA) on 30 November 1928. Initiated in December 1929 at Pittsburgh, PA. Conducted summer training most years at Fort Monroe, VA, 1930–33. Demobilized on 1 October 1933.

Commanders, 402d Coast Artillery Brigade

Unknown	December 1929–1 October 1933

HHB, 403d Coast Artillery Brigade (AA) (GHQR) **Organized Reserve Ohio**

HQ—*Not initiated,* 1928–33

Subordinate elements—932d, 933d, and 941st C.A. Regts., 1928–33

Constituted in the O.R. on 5 September 1928 as the 215th C.A. Brig. (AA), assigned to the GHQR, and allotted to the Fifth Corps Area. Redesignated 403d C.A. Brig. (AA) on 30 November 1928. Camp Perry, OH, designated on 9 July 1931 as HQ on organization, but the unit was never organized at that location. Demobilized on 1 October 1933.

Commanders, 403d Coast Artillery Brigade

Unknown	ao December 1931–1 October 1933

HHB, 404th Coast Artillery Brigade (AA) (GHQR) **Organized Reserve Texas**

HQ—San Antonio, TX, 1928–33

Subordinate elements—969th, 970th, 972nd, and 974th C.A. Regts., 1928–33.

Constituted in the O.R. on 5 September 1928 as the 216th C.A. Brig. (AA), assigned to the GHQR, and allotted to the Eighth Corps Area. Redesignated 404th C.A. Brig. (AA) on 30 November 1928. Initiated on 12 October 1928 at San Antonio, TX. Conducted summer training most years at Fort Crockett, TX, 1929–33. Designated mobilization training station was the Houston Antiaircraft Training Camp near Houston, TX. Demobilized on 1 October 1933.

Commanders, 404th Coast Artillery Brigade

Unknown	12 October 1928–1 October 1933

Chapter 26

Coast Artillery Regiments and Battalions

USASC photo, NA II

A gun crew from the 61st C. A. practices its gunnery skills on the shores of Lake Michigan, Fort Sheridan, IL, 1925.

Coast artillery (C.A.) regiments and battalions provided indirect and direct fire and antiaircraft artillery support in defense of mobile units, harbor defenses, airfields, and other key installations.

Organization

For the most part, the organization and types of C.A. regiments and battalions in the post-war Army were an adoption of the types of units that served in World War I. The advent of the aircraft as a weapon of war prompted the Army to add antiaircraft units to its structure and these units were formed from largely inert and not needed fixed C.A. units as a stopgap measure during the war. The 1920 National Defense Act formally assigned the antiaircraft mission to the C.A. Five distinct types of C.A. regiments and battalions were retained for the post-war Army. These units were organized based on their mission and type of weapon with which they were equipped. They included harbor defense, railway, tractor drawn, antiaircraft, and trench mortar regiments and battalions. The table on the next page illustrates the allotment of those types of units to the various components through 1940.

Fixed harbor defense units were the traditional mainstay of the C.A. Prior to 1923, each harbor defense was allotted a number of Regular Army (R.A.), National Guard (N.G.), and Organized Reserve (O.R.) C.A. companies to man its fixed defenses. That year, in coordination with War Department plans, the N.G. and O.R. began to reorganize existing harbor defense commands and separate C.A. batteries into regiments and battalions. The R.A. batteries were similarly reorganized in June and July of the following year. These regiments and battalions were organized into one of four type units (Type A, B, C, or D) each with varying numbers of batteries. Because these units were tailored organizationally to more properly fit the harbor defense command to which they were assigned for wartime, there was no standard number of

Unit allotments.

Regiments	HD	Rwy	AA	TD	TM
R.A.	24	2	16	4	1
RAI	0	3	3	2	0
N.G.	14	0	26	2	0
O.R.	22	4	136	3	0
Totals	60	7	181	11	1
Battalions	**HD**	**Rwy**	**AA**	**TD**	
R.A.	1	0	4	0	0
RAI	0	0	0	0	0
N.G.	8	0	2	0	0
O.R.	3	2	1	1	0
Totals	12	2	7	1	0

batteries. During the interwar period, most of the active R.A. units were woefully undermanned. Some regiments only had one battery on Active Duty for the majority of the period. Others had two or three. With the exception of the defenses in the three overseas departments, none was fully active. As World War II neared, however, the R.A. regiments began to reactivate many of their battalions and batteries that had been dormant. These units were bolstered in 1940 and 1941 by those of the N.G., which had been, for the most part, fully organized but at peace strength. By the time of Pearl Harbor, there were 23 R.A. and 11 N.G. fixed harbor defense regiments on Active Duty.

Railway regiments and battalions were assigned to a specific harbor defense command; but due to their mobility, they could be used in the broader coast defense missions or easily transferred to support and

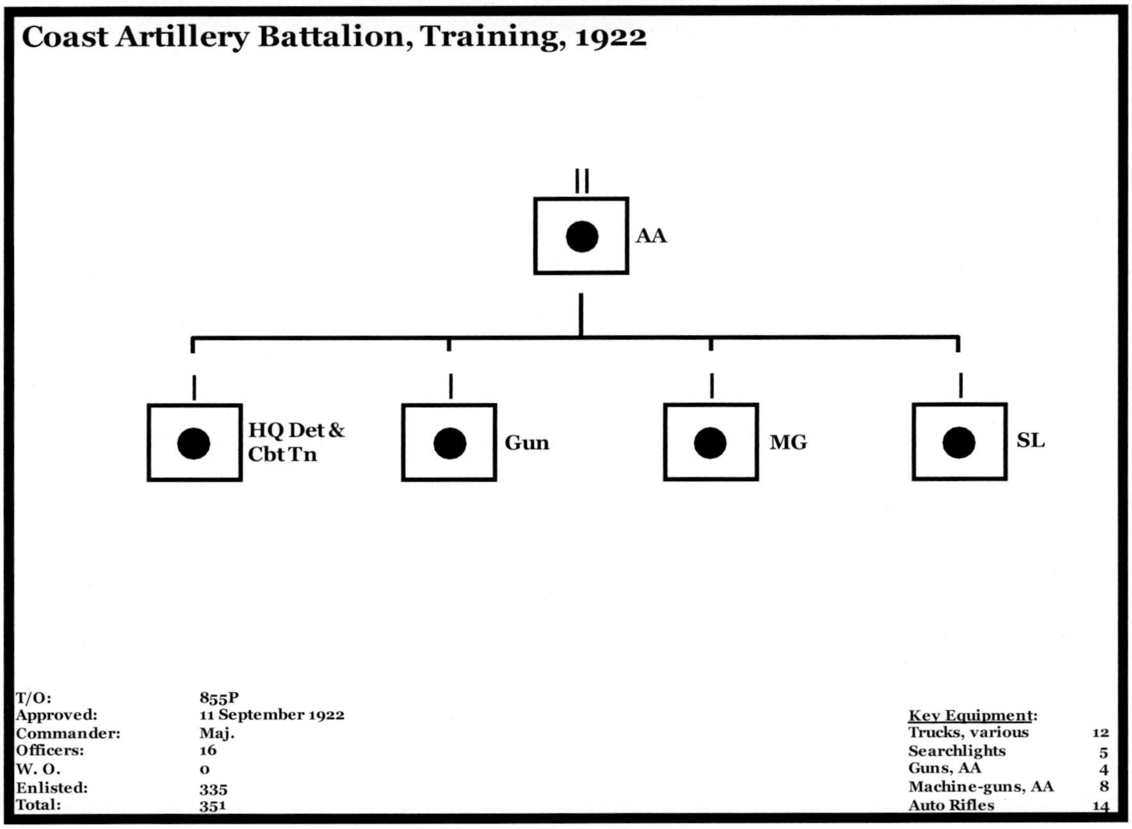

Coast artillery organization.

Coast Artillery Regiment, Railway, 12", 14" or 16" Guns, 1921

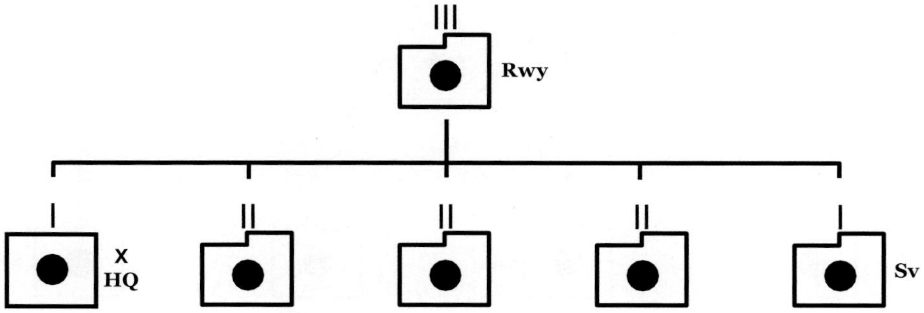

T/O:	553W
Approved:	10 May 1921
Commander:	Col.
Officers:	75
W. O.	1
Enlisted:	1349
Total:	1425

Key Equipment:	
Cars, various	10
Cars, railway	95
Locomotives	4
Machine-guns, AA	24
Guns 12", 14", or 16"	12

Coast Artillery Regiment, Railway, 1928

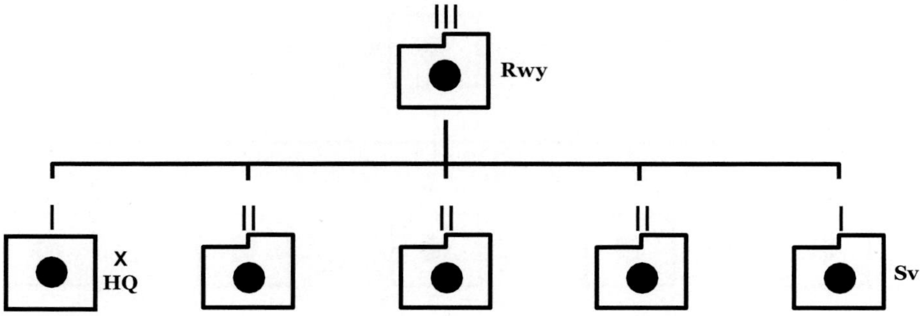

T/O:	323W
Approved:	28 February 1928
Commander:	Col.
Officers:	87
W. O.	1
Enlisted:	1862
Total:	1950

Key Equipment:	
Cars, various	21
Cars, railway	90
Locomotives	3
Machine-guns, AA	36
Guns, 8" & 10" & 12" mortar	24
or	
Guns 12" & 14"	12

Coast artillery organization.

Coast Artillery Regiment, Antiaircraft, 1930

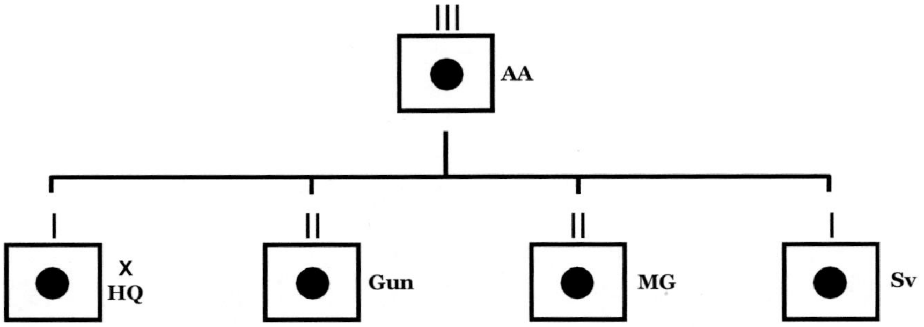

T/O:	120W
Approved:	17 March 1930
Commander:	Col.
Officers:	60
W. O.	1
Enlisted:	1871
Total:	1942

Key Equipment:	
Cars, various	16
Tractors, 5-ton	6
Trucks, various	196
Searchlights	15
Guns, AA	12
Machine guns, AA	60

Coast Artillery Regiment, Tractor Drawn (155-mm Guns), 1927

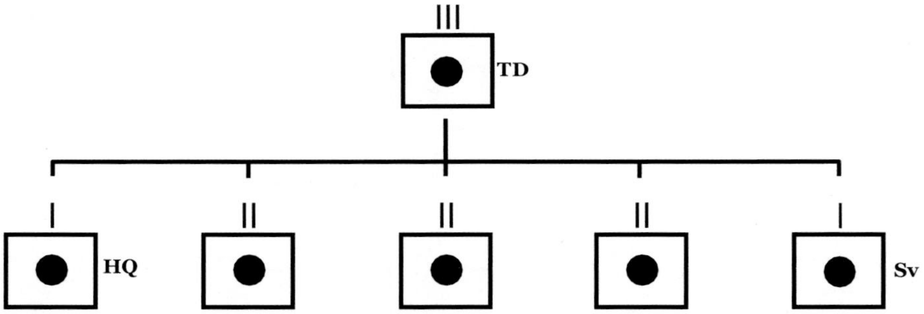

T/O:	333W
Approved:	24 February 1927
Commander:	Col.
Officers:	69
W. O.	1
Enlisted:	2003
Total:	2093

Key Equipment:	
Cars, Reconnaissance	15
Tractors, 10-ton	43
Trucks, various	189
Guns, 155-mm or 6-in	24
Machine guns, AA	48

Coast artillery regiment organization.

supplement other harbor defenses as the need arose. As in World War I, the units could also be deployed to a theater of operations to be employed in harbor/coast defense roles overseas or as heavy artillery in support of mobile forces. These organizations could be equipped with varying types and sizes of weapons including 6-, 8-, 10-, 12-, 14- or 16-inch guns or 8-, 10-, or 12-inch mortars. Only two of these units were active, or at least partially active, in the interwar period, and none of the remaining three were activated as railway organizations for World War II service. Nor were any of the O.R. railway units activated for World War II service, at least as railway units, as the War Plans Division (WPD) apparently determined that such organizations would not be needed.

The largest category of C.A. units in terms of the number of organizations was the antiaircraft regiments and battalions. These units were intended to provide antiaircraft defense for mobile units, harbor defenses, key industrial facilities, command and communications centers, and similarly important fixed locations. The units were typically brigaded three or four regiments to a brigade, especially those slated for operations with field armies. As the airplane took on added importance in the world's military forces, the US Army expanded its antiaircraft defense structure and in 1928 constituted a large number of O.R. antiaircraft regiments. In 1933, a large number of those regiments were demobilized and replaced in the Army's force structure by Regular Army Inactive (RAI) regiments, or were withdrawn from the O.R. and reallotted as RAI antiaircraft units. The number of N.G. antiaircraft regiments also increased during 1939–40 when several excess infantry and cavalry regiments were converted to C.A. antiaircraft regiments. By the time of Pearl Harbor, 29 R.A. (some of which were former O.R. units) and 23 N.G. antiaircraft regiments were on Active Duty. Only a handful of the O.R. regiments were later activated for service during the war.

The tractor-drawn C.A. unit was organized similarly to a standard field artillery regiment. It was equipped with the 155-mm G.P.F. (Grande Puissance Filloux) gun, a French-made artillery piece that won great favor with American gun crews in World War I. The United States manufactured a large number of these guns during and after the war, and they became the mainstay of tractor-drawn C.A. organizations from 1918 until well into World War II. The rugged reliability, mobility, and range of these guns made them particularly well suited for use in coast defense work. The accuracy of these guns was enhanced when they were installed on what became known as a "Panama Mount." The mount was a leveled, circular concrete base with a centered pintle post and a steel circular rail that allowed the rapid traverse of the gun left and right. The mount enabled the gun crew to rapidly engage several ships or to target fast moving destroyers or mine sweepers. The added benefit of the 155-mm G.P.F. tractor-drawn unit was that it could be deployed to defend harbors overseas or used as heavy artillery in the combat zone, just as they were in World War I. At the time of Pearl Harbor, there were a total of eight of these regiments on Active Duty—four R.A. and four N.G. None of the O.R. regiments were activated for World War II service.

The remaining category of C.A. units was the trench mortar regiment and there was only one of its kind constituted in the Army's force structure. This unit was equipped with heavy, but mobile, 12-inch trench mortars that had great range and destructive power. The regiment was intended to be used in coast defense work or for the reduction of heavy field fortifications in the combat zone. Given its mobility and that it would most likely be used in the latter role more than the former, it was transferred to the field artillery in 1928.

Training

The annual training cycle for R.A. C.A. regiments was similar to that for other combat arms units (see Chapter 9, Infantry Regiments, for a general description). As with field artillery units, the tight budgets meant that service firing with live rounds was conducted only occasionally and rarely more than twice a year. In the case of railway and fixed defense units, the larger the caliber, the rarer the opportunities for live firing. For the few 16-inch pieces in either category, firing was conducted on only a handful of occasions for the entire interwar period. For the 155-mm G.P.F. units, maneuver and live-fire training was conducted, generally, in conjunction with the occasional exercises conducted by the harbor defense command to which they were assigned. Antiaircraft units, on the other hand, conducted relatively frequent maneuver training with ground mobile forces and during various air corps exercises conducted in many locations across the United States. Like their sister organizations, however, AA units only engaged in live fire exercises on an infrequent basis.

The information regarding most RAI units seems to indicate that all or most of those that were organized (three were not) were functional units. These units usually conducted their summer training with similarly organized and equipped active units.

During the Inactive Training Period, N.G. regiments and battalions participated in the general drill program followed by most Guard units. For summer training, harbor defense units typically trained on the guns of the harbor defense command to which they were assigned for wartime mobilization. Some tractor-drawn regiments, because they were not tied to fixed harbor defenses, trained at a variety of locations, but, in general, trained at locations where they could conduct realistic live-fire exercises. These units conducted live-fire training almost every year during summer camp. The same was true for Guard antiaircraft units. For some of the antiaircraft units, however, finding a location for live firing was a problem. The firing of antiaircraft (AA) weapons was usually conducted over water so that the rounds could fall harmlessly to earth. Therefore, AA units in the interior United States, such as Missouri's 203d C.A., often had to travel out of state to conduct their training. In addition, all of these types of units engaged the services of the various N.G. observation squadrons to provide spotter and tow-target aircraft to improve the realism of their training exercises.

Most of the O.R. C.A. regiments were functional units and many were some of the most active and well-trained Reserve organizations in the Army, especially those that were fixed harbor defense units. These units conducted their Inactive Training Periods performing exercises, demonstrations, and lectures covering theoretical employment and operations of the various kinds of C.A. guns and organizations. Those outfits lucky enough to be situated near a harbor defense installation or a R.A. or N.G. C.A. unit could often use those units' equipment, if it was available, for more basic hands-on skills. For fixed defense organizations, the summer training was usually conducted on the very guns these units were expected to man in wartime. As with the field artillery, junior officers and enlisted reservists were often employed as gun crews, in the fire control center, or ammunition handling to learn the fundamental skills of the branch. More senior officers were employed as battery commanders or instructors. For mobile units (tractor drawn and AA), if the camp was at a Regular Army Training Camp (R.A.T.C.) or during a maneuver, the Reserve officers would often have the opportunity to shadow a R.A. counterpart in the field. C.A. mobile units were able to conduct some live firing most years when they were ordered to camp. Railway units usually trained with harbor defense units and only rarely trained on actual railway guns. Only once, apparently, did any Reserve units have the opportunity to live fire with a railway artillery piece during the interwar period.

1st Trench Mortar Regiment (GHQR)

HQ—*Not organized,* 1923–26; Pottstown, PA, 1926–28

Constituted in the R.A. on 24 March 1923, assigned to the General Headquarters Reserve (GHQR), and allotted to the Third Corps Area. Withdrawn from the R.A. on 27 February 1926 and allotted to the O.R. Initiated by September 1926 at Pottstown, PA. Withdrawn from the Coast Artillery Corps (C.A.C.) on 1 March 1928 and transferred to the field artillery (F.A.).

1st Trench Mortar Regiment

Unknown	ao September 1926–1 March 1928

1st Coast Artillery Regiment (Harbor Defense) (Type C)

HQ—Fort De Lesseps, CZ, 1924–32; Fort Sherman, CZ, 1932–41

Reconstituted in the R.A. on 1 July 1924 and assigned to the Harbor Defenses of Cristobal. Concurrently, regimental headquarters (HQ) activated at Fort De Lesseps, CZ. Subordinate elements constituted, organized, or redesignated as follows:

HQ Battery (Btry) organized by redesignation of 7th Company (Co.), C.A.C.; active at Fort De Lesseps.

HQ, 1st Battalion (Bn.) constituted on 1 July 1924 (inactive); activated on 1 June 1926 at Fort Randolph; inactivated on 31 July 1926; activated on 15 April 1932 at Fort Randolph; inactivated on 30 March 1941.

Btry A organized on 1 July 1924 by redesignation of 8th Co., C.A.C. and concurrently inactivated at Fort Grant; activated on 15 April 1932 at Fort Randolph.

Btry B organized on 1 July 1924 by redesignation of 2d Co., C.A.C. (inactive); activated on 15 April 1932 at Fort Randolph.

HQ, 2d Bn. constituted on 1 July 1924 (inactive); activated on 15 April 1932 at Fort Sherman; inactivated on 30 March 1941.

Btry C organized on 1 July 1924 by redesignation of 3d Co., C.A.C. (inactive); activated on 15 April 1932 at Fort Sherman.

Btry D organized on 1 July 1924 by redesignation of 4th Co., C.A.C. (inactive); activated on 15 April 1932 at Fort Randolph.

HQ, 3d Bn. constituted and activated on 1 July 1924 at Fort Randolph; inactivated on 15 April 1932 at Fort Randolph; activated on 15 March 1940 at Fort Randolph.

Btry E (Mine) organized on 1 July 1924 by redesignation of 10th Co., C.A.C., and activated at Fort Randolph; inactivated on 30 March 1941 at Fort Sherman.

Btry F organized on 1 July 1924 by redesignation of 5th Co., C.A.C. (inactive); activated on 15 April 1932 at Fort Sherman; inactivated on 30 March 1941.

Btry G organized on 1 July 1924 by redesignation of 11th Co., C.A.C. and activated at Fort Randolph; inactivated on 31 May 1926 at Fort Randolph; activated on 1 November 1938 at Fort Sherman.

Btry H constituted on 22 April 1929 (inactive); activated on 15 April 1932 at Fort Sherman.

Btry I constituted on 22 April 1929 (inactive).

The crew of the U.S.A.M.P. *William M. Graham* was assigned to HQ Btry from 30 June 1924 to 12 March 1927. Regiment reorganized on 15 April 1932 under special tables of organization and redesignated (AA and Harbor Defense). The 1st Bn. was reorganized as the AA element of the regiment. Concurrently regimental HQ transferred to Fort Sherman, CZ. Reorganized entirely as a Harbor Defense regiment on 26 October 1939 and all AA personnel and assets transferred to the 72d C.A. (AA). Relieved from assignment to the Harbor Defenses of Cristobal on 1 February 1940 and assigned to the Panama Separate C.A. Brigade (Brig.). Provided the honor guard and security for the visit of the Honorable Patrick J. Hurley, Secretary of War, on his visit to Fort Randolph on 6 November 1930 to review activities of the Harbor Defenses of Cristobal. Provided the honor guard and security for the visit of President Roosevelt to Fort Randolph on 16 February 1940. Location 7 December 1941—Fort Sherman, CZ.

Organization Day: 20 August. Chosen to commemorate the Battle of Churubusco in which elements of the regiment participated on 20 August 1847. Adopted on 5 July 1929.

Status: Assigned to the US Army Regimental System (USARS) as the 1st Air Defense Artillery (Arty.).

Events: 36, 40, 43, 58, 69, 81, 101, 102, 119, 140, 167, 170, 180, 181, 202, 223, 271, 292, 308

Commanders, 1st Coast Artillery Regiment

Col. John C. Gilmore	1 July 1924–30 July 1925	Col. Clarence G. Bunker	26 October 1932–4 August 1934
Col. Godwin Ordway	30 July 1925–28 February 1926	Col. Richard I. McKenney	4 August 1934–10 October 1934
Col. Alexander Greig Jr.	28 February 1926–25 November 1928	Col. William M. Colvin	14 October 1934–15 September 1936
Lt. Col. Walter Singles	25 November 1928–9 December 1928	Col. William T. Carpenter	15 September 1936–8 July 1939
Col. Robert E. Wyllie	9 December 1928–30 November 1929	Lt. Col. Avery J. French	8 July 1939–8 August 1939
Col. Frank K. Fergusson	30 November 1929–17 March 1931	Col. Rufus F. Maddux	8 August 1939–April 1940
Maj. Francis P. Hardaway	17 March 1931–15 April 1932	Lt. Col. Avery J. French	April 1940–October 1940
Col. Ralph M. Mitchell	15 April 1932–25 October 1932	Col. Eli E. Bennett	October 1940–ao September 1941

2d Coast Artillery Regiment (Harbor Defense) (Type B)

HQ—Fort Sherman, CZ, 1924–32; Fort Monroe, VA, 1932–41

Reconstituted in the R.A. on 1 July 1924 and assigned to the Harbor Defenses of Cristobal. Concurrently, regimental HQ activated at Fort Sherman, CZ. Subordinate elements constituted, organized, or redesignated as follows:

HQ Btry organized by redesignation of 21st Co., C.A.C.; active at Fort Sherman.

HQ, 1st Bn. constituted and activated on 1 July 1924 at Fort Sherman; inactivated on 15 April 1932 at Fort Sherman; reorganized and redesignated Headquarters and Headquarters Battery (HHB), 1st Bn. on 15 August 1935; activated in November 1940 at Fort Monroe.

Btry A (12-inch DC gun) organized by redesignation of 22d Co., C.A.C. (inactive); activated on 1 September 1935 at Fort Monroe.

Btry B (AA) organized by redesignation of 13th C., C.A.C. (inactive); activated on 1 November 1938 at Fort Monroe; reorganized as a 155-mm gun battery in November 1939.

Btry C organized by redesignation of 14th Co., C.A.C. (inactive); activated on 30 April 1926 at Fort Sherman; inactivated on 15 April 1932 at Fort Sherman; activated on 30 April 1932 at Fort Monroe.

HQ, 2d Bn. constituted and activated on 1 July 1924 at Fort Sherman; inactivated on 15 April 1932 at Fort Sherman; activated on 1 August 1940 at Fort Monroe.

Btry D organized by redesignation of 15th Co., C.A.C. (inactive); activated on 1 November 1938 at Fort Monroe as an AA battery.

Btry E organized by redesignation of 16th Co., C.A.C. and activated at Fort Sherman; inactivated on 15 April 1932 at Fort Sherman; activated on 30 April 1932 at Fort Story.

Btry F (8-inch railway gun) organized by redesignation of 23d Co., C.A.C. (inactive); activated on 1 February 1940 at Fort Monroe.

HQ, 3d Bn. constituted and activated on 1 July 1924 at Fort Randolph; inactivated on 15 April 1932 at Fort Sherman; demobilized on 15 August 1935.

Btry G organized by redesignation of 24th Co., C.A.C. and activated at Fort Randolph; inactivated on 15 April 1932 at Fort Sherman; demobilized on 15 August 1935; activated on 1 March 1941 at Fort Monroe.

Btry H organized by redesignation of 18th Co., C.A.C. and activated at Fort Sherman; inactivated on 15 April 1932 at Fort Sherman; activated on 30 April 1932 at Fort Monroe; inactivated on 1 September 1935 at Fort Monroe and demobilized.

Btry I organized by redesignation of 19th Co., C.A.C. (inactive); demobilized on 15 August 1935.

HQ, 4th Bn. constituted on 22 April 1929 (inactive); demobilized on 15 August 1935.

Btry K organized by redesignation of 20th Co., C.A.C. (inactive); demobilized on 15 August 1935.

Btry L constituted on 22 April 1929 (inactive); demobilized on 15 August 1935.

Relieved from assignment to the Harbor Defenses of Cristobal on 15 April 1932 and inactivated at Fort Sherman. Regimental HHB activated on 30 April 1932 at Fort Monroe, VA, and assigned to the Harbor Defenses of Chesapeake Bay. Provided training support for the Coast Artillery School, 1932–41. Habitually trained the O.R. harbor defense units assigned to the Harbor Defenses of the Chesapeake Bay, 1932–41. Reserve officers assigned to the regiment conducted summer training with the regiment at Fort Monroe. Responsible for the support and administration of the Civilian Conservation Corps (CCC) District 4, Third Corps Area, 1933–39. Provided the honor guard and security for the visit of President Roosevelt to Fort Monroe on 29 July 1940. Location 7 December 1941—Fort Monroe, VA.

Organization Day: 13 September. Chosen to commemorate the artillery duel at Fort McHenry, Baltimore, MD, in 1814 in which C Btry battled against the British fleet. Adopted on 5 July 1929.

Status: Assigned to the USARS as the 2d Air Defense Arty.

Events: 36, 40, 43, 102, 268, 283

Commanders, 2d Coast Artillery Regiment

Col. Godwin Ordway	1 July 1924–2 June 1925	Lt. Col. Joseph F. Cottrell	15 September 1934–21 November 1934
Lt. Col. George L. Wertenbaker	2 June 1925–27 October 1927	Col. Russell P. Reeder	21 November 1934–1 April 1936
Col. Lynn S. Edwards	27 October 1927–28 November 1928	Lt. Col. Frank S. Clark	1 April 1936–9 May 1936
Maj. Frank Drake	28 November 1928–14 May 1930	Col. Horace F. Spurgin	9 May 1936–1 September 1937
Maj. Harold E. Small	14 May 1930–15 August 1930	Maj. Paul H. French	2 September 1937–1 October 1937
Lt. Col. Malcolm P. Andruss	15 August 1930–17 March 1931	Col. William E. Shedd Jr.	1 October 1937–30 November 1938
Col. Frank K. Fergusson	17 March 1931–4 November 1931	Maj. Paul H. French	1 December 1938–27 December 1938
Lt. Col. Malcolm P. Andruss	4 November 1931–14 November 1931	Col. Eugene B. Walker	27 December 1938–25 April 1939
Col. Percy M. Kessler	14 November 1931–12 April 1932	Lt. Col. Paul H. French	25 April 1939–October 1939
No commander assigned	12 April 1932–30 April 1932	Col. Francis P. Hardaway	October 1939–15 November 1940
Col. Harold E. Cloke	1 May 1932–15 September 1934	Lt. Col. Francis B. Christian	10 December 1940–March 1942

3d Coast Artillery Regiment (Harbor Defense) (Type B)

HQ—Fort MacArthur, CA, 1924–41

Reconstituted in the R.A. on 1 July 1924 and assigned to the Harbor Defenses of Los Angeles, San Diego, and the Columbia. Concurrently, regimental HQ activated at Fort MacArthur, CA. Subordinate elements constituted, organized, or redesignated as follows:

HQ Btry organized by redesignation of 36th Co., C.A.C., active at Fort MacArthur.

HQ, 1st Bn. constituted and activated on 1 July 1924 at Fort MacArthur, CA.

Btry A organized by redesignation of 25th Co., C.A.C., active at Fort MacArthur; inactivated on 1 March 1930 at Fort MacArthur; activated on 1 July 1939 at Fort MacArthur.

Btry B organized by redesignation of 26th Co., C.A.C., active at Fort MacArthur; inactivated on 1 March 1930 at Fort MacArthur.

HQ, 2d Bn. constituted and activated on 1 July 1924 at Fort Rosecrans, CA; HQ Btry constituted on 12 September 1935 (inactive).

Btry C organized by redesignation of 31st Co., C.A.C. (inactive); activated on 2 December 1940 at Fort Rosecrans.

Btry D organized by redesignation of 27th Co., C.A.C., active at Fort Rosecrans; inactivated on 1 February 1940 at Fort Rosecrans; activated on 2 December 1940 at Fort Rosecrans.

HQ, 3d Bn. constituted and activated on 1 July 1924 at Fort Stevens, O.R.; demobilized on 15 August 1935.

Btry E organized by redesignation of 28th Co., C.A.C., active at Fort Stevens.

Btry F organized by redesignation of 34th Co., C.A.C. (inactive); activated on 1 July 1939 at Fort Stevens; inactivated on 1 February 1940 at Fort Stevens; activated on 2 December 1940 at Fort Stevens.

Btry G organized by redesignation of 35th Co., C.A.C. (inactive); demobilized on 15 August 1935; reconstituted and activated on 1 June 1941 at Los Angeles; inactivated on 29 August 1941 at Fort MacArthur.

Habitually trained the O.R. harbor defense units assigned to the Harbor Defenses of Los Angeles, San Diego, and the Columbia, 1924–41. Reserve officers assigned to the regiment conducted summer training with the regiment at Fort MacArthur and Fort Rosecrans, CA. Location 7 December 1941—Fort MacArthur, CA.

Organization Day: 23 February. Chosen to commemorate the Battle of Buena Vista in which elements of the regiment participated on 23 February 1847. Adopted on 1 July 1924.

Status: Assigned to the USARS as the 3d Air Defense Arty.

Events: 84, 92, 142, 311, 318, 319, 335

Commanders, 3d Coast Artillery Regiment

Maj. George Ruhlen Jr.	1 July 1924–6 July 1925
Maj. Lincoln B. Chambers	6 July 1925–14 September 1926
Maj. Ward E. Duvall	14 September 1926–25 October 1926
Lt. Col. Willis G. Peace	25 October 19 26–19 January 1929
Col. Robert F. Woods	19 January 1929–6 February 1930
Lt. Col. Jacob A. Mack	6 February 1930–4 August 1930
Maj. Kelley B. Lemmon	4 August 1930–1 July 1931
Lt. Col. Howard S. Miller	1 July 1931–14 December 1932
Maj. Joseph F. Cottrell	14 December 1932–7 January 1933
Col. Charles H. Hilton	7 January 1933–20 July 1934
Lt. Col. George Ruhlen Jr.	20 July 1934–10 October 1934
Maj. William R. Stewart	10 October 1934–29 October 1935
Lt. Col. Edward L. Kelly	29 October 1935–28 August 1937
Col. Edward H. Thompson	28 August 1937–September 1939
Lt. Col. Edwin C. Mead	October 1939–10 November 1940
Col. Allen Kimberly	10 November 1940–29 May 1941
Lt. Col. Edwin C. Mead	29 May 1941–9 June 1941
Col. Arthur E. Rowland	9 June 1941–18 June 1941
Col. William W. Hicks	18 June 1941–29 September 1945

4th Coast Artillery Regiment (Harbor Defense) (Type C)

HQ—Fort Amador, CZ, 1924–41

Reconstituted in the R.A. on 1 July 1924 and assigned to the Harbor Defenses of Balboa. Regimental HQ activated on 18 August 1924 at Fort Amador, CZ. Subordinate elements constituted, organized, or redesignated as follows:

HQ Btry organized by redesignation of 44th Co., C.A.C., active at Fort Amador.

HQ, 1st Bn. constituted on 1 July 1924 (inactive); activated on 18 August 1924 at Fort Amador, CZ.

Btry A (AA) organized by redesignation of 45th Co., C.A.C. (inactive); activated on 18 August 1924 at Fort Amador.

Btry B (AA) organized by redesignation of 46th Co., C.A.C. (inactive); activated on 15 April 1932 at Fort Amador.

Btry C (Searchlight) organized by redesignation of 38th Co., C.A.C. (inactive); activated on 18 August 1924 at Fort Amador; inactivated on 31 July 1926 at Fort Amador; activated on 15 April 1932 at Fort Amador.

HQ, 2d Bn. constituted on 1 July 1924 (inactive); activated on 18 August 1924 at Fort Amador, CZ.

Btry D (Mine/6-inch DC gun) organized by redesignation of 39th Co., C.A.C. (inactive); activated on 18 August 1924 at Fort Amador.

Btry E (Antiaircraft) organized by redesignation of 40th Co., C.A.C. (inactive); activated on 1 February 1938 at Fort Amador.

Btry F (Antiaircraft) organized by redesignation of 47th Co., C.A.C. (inactive); activated on 15 April 1932 at Fort Amador.

HQ, 3d Bn. constituted on 1 July 1924 (inactive); activated on 18 August 1924 at Fort Amador, CZ; inactivated on 15 April 1932 at Fort Amador, CZ; activated on 15 March 1940 at Fort Kobbe, CZ.

Btry G (14-inch Railway Gun) organized by redesignation of 41st Co., C.A.C.; activated on 18 August 1924 at Fort Amador.

Btry H organized by redesignation of 42d Co., C.A.C.; activated on 18 August 1924 at Fort Amador.

Btry I (16-inch Gun) organized by redesignation of 43d Co., C.A.C.; activated on 18 August 1924 at Fort Amador.

Btry K organized by redesignation of 48th Co., C.A.C. (inactive).

Btrys I and D awarded the Knox Trophy for C.A. in 1930 and 1938, respectively. Reorganized entirely as a Harbor Defense regiment on 1 November 1939 and all AA personnel and assets transferred to the 73d C.A. (AA). Relieved from assignment to the Harbor Defenses of Balboa and assigned to the Panama Separate C.A. Brig. on 1 February 1940. Location 7 December 1941—Fort Amador, CZ.

Organization Day: 20 August. Chosen to commemorate the regiment's participation in the battle of Contreras, 20 August 1846.

Status: Assigned to the USARS as the 4th Air Defense Arty.

Events: 36, 40, 43, 58, 69, 81, 101, 102, 119, 140, 167, 170, 180, 181, 202, 223, 271, 292, 308

Commanders, 4th Coast Artillery Regiment

Col. Jacob E. Johnson	1 July 1924–13 January 1925	Col. Laurence C. Brown	10 September 1930–7 June 1932
Col. Frank E. Harris	13 January 1925–30 July 1925	Lt. Col. George Ruhlen Jr.	7 June 1932–10 September 1932
Maj. Fulton Q.C. Gardner	30 July 1925–20 August 1925	Col. Russell P. Reeder	10 September 1932–8 September 1934
Maj. La Rhett L. Stuart	20 August 1925–9 October 1925	Lt. Col. James S. Dusenbury	8 September 1934–16 November 1934
Col. Frank C. Jewell	9 October 1925–21 August 1928	Col. Earle D'A. Pearce	16 November 1934–6 May 1937
Lt. Col. William M. Colvin	21 August 1928–24 September 1928	Col. Francis E. Williford	7 May 1937–28 October 1938
Col. James B. Mitchell	24 September 1928–3 December 1929	Col. Charles B. Meyer	28 October 1938–21 November 1938
Col. Robert E. Wyllie	3 December 1929–6 June 1930	Col. Edward W. Putney	21 November 1938–4 December 1939
Maj. Robert C. Garrett	6 June 1930–25 June 1930	Col. William R. Nichols	4 December 1939–21 January 1941
Maj. Otto H. Schrader	25 June 1930–10 September 1930	Col. Frederick A. Mountford	21 January 1941–3 November 1944

5th Coast Artillery Regiment (Harbor Defense) (Type A)

HQ—Fort Hamilton, NY, 1924–41

Reconstituted in the R.A. on 1 July 1924 and assigned to the Harbor Defenses of Southern New York. Concurrently, regimental HQ activated at Fort Hamilton, NY. Subordinate elements constituted, organized, or redesignated as follows:

HQ Btry organized by redesignation of 57th Co., C.A.C., active at Fort Hamilton.

HQ, 1st Bn. constituted on 1 July 1924 (inactive).

Btry A organized by redesignation of 48th Co., C.A.C. (inactive); activated on 1 August 1940 at Fort Wadsworth.

Btry B organized by redesignation of 50th Co., C.A.C. (inactive); activated on 15 January 1941 at Fort Wadsworth.

HQ, 2d Bn. constituted on 1 July 1924 (inactive).

Btry C organized by redesignation of 51st Co., C.A.C. (inactive).

Btry D organized by redesignation of 56th Co., C.A.C. (inactive); activated on 15 January 1941 at Fort Hamilton.

HQ, 3d Bn. constituted on 1 July 1924 (inactive).

Btry E organized by redesignation of 54th Co., C.A.C. (inactive).

Btry F organized by redesignation of 55th Co., C.A.C. (inactive).

Btry G organized by redesignation of 53d Co., C.A.C. (inactive).

Regiment, less active elements, allotted to the Second Corps Area on 28 February 1927 for mobilization purposes. Only the regimental HHB were active in caretaker status at Fort Hamilton until 1 August 1940; remainder of regiment was inactive, 1924–40. Habitually trained the O.R. harbor defense units assigned to the Harbor Defenses of Southern New York, 1924–41. Location 7 December 1941—Fort Hamilton, NY.

Organization Day: 1 July. Chosen to commemorate the regiment's reconstitution and activation, 1 July 1924.

Status: Assigned to the USARS as the 5th Air Defense Arty.

Events: 87, 174, 321

Commanders, 5th Coast Artillery Regiment

Capt. Arthur W. Waldron	1 July 1924–28 May 1925	Lt. Col. Lloyd P. Horsfall	21 June 1934–3 December 1934
Capt. Walter Hart	28 May 1925–16 May 1928	Capt. Carroll G. Riggs	3 December 1934–31 March 1935
Capt. Lawrence Iverson	16 May 1928–30 July 1929	Maj. Walter J. Gilbert	31 March 1935–10 February 1938
Lt. Col. Gilbert Marshall	30 July 1929–21 June 1934	Lt. Col. Ernest R. Barrows	10 February 1938–21 May 1941
Col. Clarence Lininger	21 May 1941–April 1944		

6th Coast Artillery Regiment (Harbor Defense) (Type C)

HQ—Fort Winfield Scott, CA, 1924–41

Reconstituted in the R.A. on 1 July 1924 and assigned to the Harbor Defenses of San Francisco. Concurrently, regimental HQ activated at Fort Winfield Scott, CA. Subordinate elements constituted, organized, or redesignated as follows:

HQ Btry organized by redesignation of 71st Co., C.A.C., active at Fort Winfield Scott.

HQ, 1st Bn. constituted on 1 July 1924 (inactive); reorganized and redesignated HHB, 1st Bn. on 15 August 1935; activated on 1 July 1939 at Fort Winfield Scott, CA.

Btry A organized by redesignation of 60th Co., C.A.C., active at Fort Winfield Scott.

Btry B organized by redesignation of 61st Co., C.A.C. (inactive).

Btry C organized by redesignation of 62d Co., C.A.C. (inactive).

HQ, 2d Bn. constituted on 1 July 1924 (inactive); reorganized and redesignated HHB, 2d Bn. on 15 August 1935; activated on 1 July 1939 at Fort Winfield Scott.

Btry D organized by redesignation of 68th Co., C.A.C. (inactive); activated on 15 January 1941 at Fort Barry.

Btry E organized by redesignation of 63d Co., C.A.C., active at Fort Winfield Scott.

Btry F organized by redesignation of 64th Co., C.A.C. (inactive).

HQ, 3d Bn. constituted on 1 July 1924 (inactive); reorganized and redesignated HHB, 3d Bn. on 15 August 1935; activated on 2 June 1941 at Fort Winfield Scott.

Btry G organized by redesignation of 69th Co., C.A.C. (inactive).

Btry H organized by redesignation of 65th Co., C.A.C. (inactive); activated on 2 June 1941 at Fort Barry.

Btry I organized by redesignation of 66th Co., C.A.C. (inactive); activated on 2 June 1941 at Fort Baker.

Btry K organized by redesignation of 67th Co., C.A.C., active at Fort Baker; inactivated on 30 September 1930 at Fort Baker; activated on 1 January 1931 at Fort Baker.

HHB, 4th Bn. constituted on 15 August 1935 (inactive); activated on 15 June 1941 at Fort Funston.

Btry L constituted on 15 August 1935 (inactive); activated on 15 January 1941 at Fort Baker.

Btry M constituted on 15 August 1935 (inactive); activated on 15 January 1941 at Fort Baker.

Btry N constituted on 15 August 1935 (inactive); activated on 15 January 1941 at Fort Winfield Scott.

Btry O constituted on 15 August 1935 (inactive).

The crew of the U.S.A.M.P. *George Armistead* assigned to HQ Btry from 30 June 1924 to July 1927. Regiment, less active elements, allotted to the Ninth Corps Area on 28 February 1927 for mobilization purposes. Participated in the opening ceremonies for the Golden Gate Bridge in June 1937. Habitually trained the O.R. harbor defense units assigned to the Harbor Defenses of San Francisco, 1924–40. Reserve officers assigned to the regiment conducted summer training with the regiment at Fort Winfield Scott. Location 7 December 1941—Fort Winfield Scott, CA.

Organization Day: 6 January. Adopted on 29 September 1924.

Status: Assigned to the USARS as the 6th Air Defense Arty.

Events: 34, 76, 108, 111, 116, 231, 235, 331, 335

Commanders, 6th Coast Artillery Regiment

Col. Percy P. Bishop	1 July 1924–3 June 1925	Lt. Col. Allen Kimberly	18 September 1934–13 October 1934
Lt. Col. John P. Spurr	3 June 1925–8 September 1925	Col. Harold E. Cloke	13 October 1934–15 May 1937
Col. William F. Hase	8 September 1925–1 December 1928	Lt. Col. La Rhett L. Stuart	16 May 1937–17 June 1937
Col. Elijah B. Martindale Jr.	1 December 1928–20 June 1929	Col. Henry T. Burgin	17 June 1937–30 September 1938
Lt. Col. Frank Geere	20 June 1929–5 July 1929	Lt. Col. Henry C. Davis	30 September 1938–20 April 1939
Col. John T. Geary	5 July 1929–24 January 1932	Col. Thomas L. Terry	21 April 1939–31 August 1940
Col. Earle D'A. Pearce	24 January 1932–18 September 1934	Col. Rollin L. Tilton	31 August 1940–8 November 1940
Col. Karl F. Baldwin	8 November 1940–January 1942		

7th Coast Artillery Regiment (Harbor Defense) (Type B)

HQ—Fort Hancock, NJ, 1924–41

Reconstituted in the R.A. on 1 July 1924 and assigned to the Harbor Defenses of the Delaware and Sandy Hook. Concurrently, regimental HQ activated at Fort Hancock, NJ. Subordinate elements constituted, organized, or redesignated as follows:

HQ Btry organized by redesignation of 78th Co., C.A.C., active at Fort Hancock.

HQ, 1st Bn. constituted and activated on 1 July 1924 at Fort Hancock, NJ; inactivated on 7 April 1930; activated on 11 January 1941 at Fort Hancock.

Btry A organized by redesignation of 72d Co., C.A.C., active at Fort Hancock; inactivated at Fort Hancock on 7 April 1930; activated at Fort Hancock on 1 July 1939.

Btry B organized by redesignation of 73d Co., C.A.C., active at Fort Hancock; inactivated at Fort Hancock on 7 April 1930; activated at Fort Hancock on 1 July 1939.

HQ, 2d Bn. constituted and activated on 1 July 1924 at Fort Hancock, NJ; inactivated on 28 February 1930; activated on 11 January 1941 at Fort Hancock.

Btry C organized by redesignation of 79th Co., C.A.C. (inactive); activated on 1 August 1940 at Fort Tilden; transferred on 11 January 1941 to Fort Hancock.

Btry D organized by redesignation of 74th Co., C.A.C., active at Fort Hancock; inactivated at Fort Hancock on 7 April 1930; activated on 11 January 1941 at Fort Tilden.

HQ, 3d Bn. constituted and activated on 1 July 1924 at Fort Du Pont, DE.

Btry E organized by redesignation of 75th Co., C.A.C., active at Fort Du Pont; inactivated on 1 February 1940 at Fort Du Pont; activated on 13 January 1941 at Fort Hancock; transferred on 17 March 1941 to Fort Tilden.

Btry F organized by redesignation of 76th Co., C.A.C. (inactive); activated on 13 January 1941 at Fort Hancock; transferred on 17 March 1941 to Fort Tilden.

Btry G organized by redesignation of 81st Co., C.A.C. (inactive); activated on 1 June 1941 at Fort Tilden.

Habitually trained the O.R. harbor defense units assigned to the Harbor Defenses of the Delaware and Sandy Hook, 1924–41. Location 7 December 1941—Fort Hancock, NJ.

Organization Day: 1 July. Chosen to commemorate the regiment's date of constitution, 1 July 1924. Adopted on 6 March 1926.

Status: Assigned to the USARS as the 7th Air Defense Arty.

Events: 77, 87, 93, 115, 174, 321

Commanders, 7th Coast Artillery Regiment

Col. Elijah B. Martindale Jr.	1 July 1924–12 October 1925
Col. John W. Gulick	12 October 1925–13 March 1926
Col. Godwin Ordway	13 March 1926–23 February 1929
Col. Jacob C. Johnson	24 February 1929–27 July 1932
Lt. Col. George W. Cocheu	27 July 1932–11 July 1934
Capt. Victor Schmidt	11 July 1934–20 September 1934
Col. Percy M. Kessler	20 September 1934–15 September 1935
Lt. Col. Edward B. Dennis	11 September 1935–1 November 1935
Col. Lloyd H. Magruder	1 November 1935–2 November 1937
Col. Fulton Q. C. Gardner	3 November 1937–4 May 1938
Lt. Col. Edward W. Turner	4 May 1938–10 November 1938
Col. Francis E. Williford	10 November 1938–16 November 1940
Col. Philip S. Gage	16 November 1940–6 April 1941
Lt. Col. Thomas E. Jeffords	6 April 1941–10 June 1941
Col. Ralph W. Wilson	10 June 1941–December 1941

8th Coast Artillery Regiment (Harbor Defense) (Type B)

HQ—Fort Preble, ME, 1924–41

Constituted in the R.A. on 1 July 1924 and assigned to the Harbor Defenses of Portland and Portsmouth. Concurrently, regimental HQ activated at Fort Preble, ME. Subordinate elements constituted, organized, or redesignated as follows:

HQ Btry organized by redesignation of 123d Co., C.A.C., active at Fort Preble.

HQ, 1st Bn. constituted on 1 July 1924 (inactive), activated on 10 February 1941 at Fort Preble.

Btry A organized by redesignation of 154th Co., C.A.C. (inactive); activated on 1 August 1940 at Fort Preble.

Btry B organized by redesignation of 155th Co., C.A.C. (inactive); activated on 1 August 1940 at Fort Preble.

HQ, 2d Bn. constituted on 1 July 1924 (inactive), activated on 10 February 1941 at Fort Preble.

Btry C organized by redesignation of 171st Co., C.A.C. (inactive); activated on 10 February 1941 at Fort Preble.

Btry D organized by redesignation of 196th Co., C.A.C. (inactive); activated on 10 February 1941 at Fort Preble.

HQ, 3d Bn. constituted 1 July 1924 (inactive); activated on 10 February 1941.

Btry E organized by redesignation of 156th Co., C.A.C.; active at Fort Constitution; inactivated on 1 August 1940 at Fort Constitution.

Btry F organized by redesignation of 246th Co., C.A.C. (inactive); activated on 10 February 1941 at Fort Strong.

Btry G (Searchlight) organized by redesignation of 251st Co., C.A.C. (inactive); activated on 10 February 1941 at Fort McKinley.

Regiment, less active elements, allotted to the First Corps Area on 28 February 1927 for mobilization purposes. Btry E selected by the War Department to perform a mobilization exercise in June 1930 that tested how quickly and effectively a C.A. unit could get a battery that was in caretaker status back into operation. Organized four provisional batteries of the Panama Coast Artillery Detachment on 22 December 1939; batteries trained and transferred in 1940 to reinforce Panama harbor defenses. Habitually trained the O.R. harbor defense units assigned to the Harbor Defenses of Portland and Portsmouth, 1924–41. Location 7 December 1941—Fort Preble, ME.

Organization Day: 20 August. Chosen to commemorate the fact that three of the regiment's batteries (154th, 155th, and 156th C.A. Cos.) were originally organized on 20 August 1907. Adopted on 3 September 1924.

Events: 59, 95, 174, 313, 330

Commanders, 8th Coast Artillery Regiment

Maj. Edward E. Farnsworth	1 July 1924–25 July 1925
Lt. Col. Charles E. Wheatley	25 July 1925–4 November 1925
Capt. Earl R. Reynolds	4 November 1925–20 June 1926
Capt. Douglas M. Griggs	20 June 1926–2 July 1926
Lt. Col. Edward E. Farnsworth	2 July 1926–7 May 1929
Capt. Harry R. Pierce	7 May 1929–18 January 1930
Lt. Col. Francis J. Behr	18 January 1930–10 April 1930
Capt. Harry R. Pierce	10 April 1930–20 November 1930
Lt. Col. Walter Singles	20 November 1930–6 June 1933
Maj. Thomas O. Humphreys	7 June 1933–26 September 1934
Capt. William Hasketh	26 September 1934–12 November 1934
Lt. Col. Charles A. French	12 November 1934–5 September 1937
Maj. Arthur W. Waldron	5 September 1937–15 July 1937
Maj. Harry W. Lims	15 July 1937–14 September 1937
Lt. Col. Otto H. Schrader	15 September 1937–28 June 1940
Col. Franklin Kemble	29 June 1940–1 October 1941
Col. Charles R. Finley	1 October 1941–12 December 1941

9th Coast Artillery Regiment (Harbor Defense) (Type A)

HQ—Fort Banks, MA, 1924–41

Constituted in the R.A. on 1 July 1924 and assigned to the Harbor Defenses of Boston. Concurrently, regimental HQ activated at Fort Banks, MA. Subordinate elements constituted, organized, or redesignated as follows:

HQ Btry organized by redesignation of 172d Co., C.A.C.; active at Fort Banks.

HQ, 1st Bn. constituted on 1 July 1924 (inactive); activated on 10 February 1941 at Fort Strong, MA.

Btry A organized by redesignation of 59th Co., C.A.C.; active at Fort Banks; inactivated on 20 February 1930 at Fort Banks; activated on 1 July 1939 at Fort Banks; transferred on 1 August 1940 to Fort Strong.

Btry B organized by redesignation of 113th Co., C.A.C. (inactive); activated on 1 July 1940 at Fort Warren.

HQ, 2d Bn. constituted on 1 July 1924 (inactive); activated on 19 February 1941 at Fort Dawes, MA.

Btry C organized by redesignation of 120th Co., C.A.C.; active at Fort Revere; inactivated on 20 February 1930 at Fort Banks; activated on 1 July 1939 at Fort Warren.

Btry D organized by redesignation of 136th Co., C.A.C. (inactive); activated on 10 February 1940 at Fort Banks, MA.

HQ, 3d Bn. constituted on 1 July 1924 (inactive); activated on 1 June 1941 at Fort Banks.

Btry E organized by redesignation of 137th Co., C.A.C.; active at Fort Revere.

Btry F organized by redesignation of 177th Co., C.A.C. (inactive); activated on 10 February 1941 at Fort Strong.

Btry G organized by redesignation of 178th Co., C.A.C. (inactive).

Regiment, less active elements, allotted to the First Corps Area on 28 February 1927 for mobilization purposes. HHB were active in caretaker status at Fort Banks until 1940. Provided the honor guard and security for the visit of President Roosevelt to the Harbor Defenses of Boston on 10 August 1940. Habitually trained the O.R. harbor defense units assigned to the Harbor Defenses of Boston, 1924–41. Location 7 December 1941—Fort Banks, MA.

Organization Day: 1 July. Chosen to commemorate the regiment's constitution and activation on 1 July 1924. Adopted on 3 September 1924.

Status: Disbanded on 26 June 1944.

Events: 59, 77, 93, 95, 174, 313

Commanders, 9th Coast Artillery Regiment

Lt. Col. George A. Wieczorek	1 July 1924–18 August 1924	Capt Edward B. McCarthy	16 December 1931–5 February 1932
Capt. Henry Linsert	18 August 1924–2 September 1924	Capt. Manly B. Gibson	5 February 1932–29 April 1932
Col. Charles E. Kilbourne Jr.	2 September 1924–1 September 1925	Lt. Col. Paul D. Bunker	29 April 1932–22 October 1934
Maj. Edgar H. Thompson	6 September 1925–2 November 1925	Capt. Manly B. Gibson	22 October 1934–2 January 1935
Col. Frank E. Harris	2 November 1925–29 April 1927	Capt. Charles S. Denney	4 January 1935–7 March 1935
Maj. Edgar H. Thompson	30 April 1927–1 July 1927	Capt. Joseph H. Gilbreth	7 March 1935–27 June 1935
Col. Robert F. McMillan	1 July 1927–28 June 1928	Lt. Col. Rollin L. Tilton	28 June 1935–14 July 1937
Maj. George D. Holland	3 July 1928–1 July 1929	Capt. Joseph H. Gilbreth	14 July 1937–25 July 1937
Col. Alexander Greig Jr.	1 July 1929–16 December 1931	Col. Monte J. Hickok	25 July 1937–9 May 1941

10th Coast Artillery Regiment (Harbor Defense) (Type B)

HQ—Fort Adams, RI, 1924–41

Constituted in the R.A. on 1 July 1924 and assigned to the Harbor Defenses of Narragansett Bay and New Bedford. Concurrently, regimental HQ activated at Fort Adams, RI. Subordinate elements constituted, organized, or redesignated as follows:

HQ Btry organized by redesignation of 173d Co., C.A.C. active at Fort Adams.

HQ, 1st Bn. constituted on 1 July 1924 (inactive); activated on 10 April 1941 at Fort Adams.

Btry A organized by redesignation of 97th Co., C.A.C. (inactive); activated on 1 August 1940 at Fort Adams.

Btry B organized by redesignation of 102d Co., C.A.C. (inactive); activated on 1 August 1940 at Fort Adams.

HQ, 2d Bn. constituted on 1 July 1924 (inactive); activated on 10 April 1941 at Fort Adams.

Btry C organized by redesignation of 110th Co., C.A.C. (inactive); activated on 10 April 1941 at Fort Adams.

Btry D organized by redesignation of 129th Co., C.A.C. (inactive); activated on 10 April 1941 at Fort Adams.

HQ, 3d Bn. constituted on 1 July 1924 (inactive).

Btry E organized by redesignation of 52d Co., C.A.C. active at Fort Rodman; inactivated on 1 August 1940 at Fort Rodman.

Btry F organized by redesignation of 147th Co., C.A.C. (inactive).

Btry G organized by redesignation of 174th Co., C.A.C. (inactive).

Regiment, less active elements, allotted to the First Corps Area on 28 February 1927 for mobilization purposes. Organized five provisional batteries of the Panama Coast Artillery Detachment on 22 December 1939; batteries trained and transferred in 1940 to reinforce Panama harbor defenses. Habitually trained the O.R. harbor defense units assigned to the Harbor Defenses of Narragansett Bay and New Bedford, 1924–41. Location 7 December 1941—Fort Adams, MA.

Organization Day: 1 July. Chosen to commemorate the regiment's constitution and activation on 1 July 1924. Adopted on 3 September 1924.

Events: 59, 77, 95, 174, 272, 280, 313

Commanders, 10th Coast Artillery Regiment

Lt. Col. Samuel G. Shartle	1 July 1924–15 October 1926	Maj. Edward B. Dennis	1 November 1930–1 November 1933
Capt. Ernest R. Barrows	15 October 1926–3 February 1927	Maj. John P. McCaskey	5 November 1933–19 June 1934
Col. Thomas F. Dwyer	3 February 1927–15 August 1927	Maj. Carl R. Adams	19 June 1934–10 September 1936
Col. James F. Brady	15 August 1927–27 January 1928	Col. Paul H. Herman	10 September 1936–26 August 1938
Lt. Col. William H. Raymond	27 January 1928–13 March 1928	Maj. Edward L. Supple	26 August 1938–April 1940
Col. Hugh K. Taylor	13 March 1928–18 July 1928	Maj. George W. Brent	April 1940–June 1940
Capt. Ernest R. Barrows	18 July 1928–20 July 1931	Col. Allen Kimberly	June 1940–23 September 1940
Maj. John P. Smith	20 July 1931–1 November 1930	Col. Randolph T. Pendleton	23 September 1940–8 September 1941
Col. Martin J. O'Brien	8 September 1941–23 January 1942		

11th Coast Artillery Regiment (Harbor Defense) (Type B)

HQ—Fort H.G. Wright, NY, 1924–41

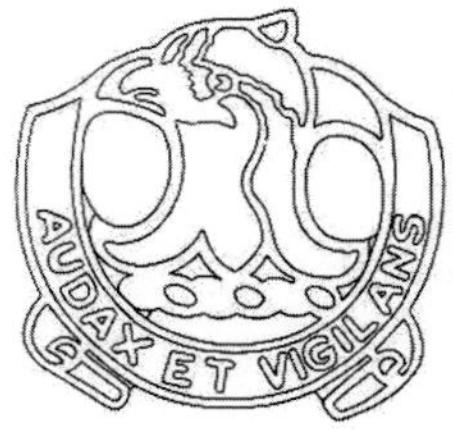

Constituted in the R.A. on 1 July 1924 and assigned to the Harbor Defenses of Long Island Sound. Concurrently, regimental HQ activated at Fort H.G. Wright, NY. Subordinate elements constituted, organized, or redesignated as follows:

HQ Btry organized by redesignation of 133d Co., C.A.C., active at Fort H. G. Wright.

HQ, 1st Bn. constituted on 1 July 1924 (inactive); activated in 1936 at Fort H.G. Wright, NY.

Btry A organized by redesignation of 135th Co., C.A.C. (inactive); activated in 1936 at Fort H.G. Wright.

Btry B organized by redesignation of 141st Co., C.A.C. (inactive); activated in 1936 at Fort H.G. Wright.

Btry C organized by redesignation of 148th Co., C.A.C. (inactive); activated in 1936 at Fort H.G. Wright.

HQ, 2d Bn. constituted on 1 July 1924 (inactive); activated on 1 July 1939 at Fort H.G. Wright.

Btry D organized by redesignation of 157th Co., C.A.C. (inactive); activated on 1 July 1939 at Fort H.G. Wright.

Btry E organized by redesignation of 161st Co., C.A.C. (inactive); activated on 1 July 1939 at Fort H.G. Wright.

Btry F organized by redesignation of 175th Co., C.A.C. (inactive).

HQ, 3d Bn. constituted and activated on 1 July 1924 at Fort H.G. Wright; inactivated in 1936.

Btry G organized by redesignation of 100th Co., C.A.C. at Fort H.G. Wright; inactivated in 1936 at Fort H.G. Wright.

Btry H organized by redesignation of 131st Co., C.A.C. at Fort H.G. Wright; inactivated in 1936 at Fort H.G. Wright.

Btry I organized by redesignation of 132d Co., C.A.C. at Fort H.G. Wright; inactivated on 1 March 1928 at Fort H.G. Wright.

Btry K organized by redesignation of 146th Co., C.A.C. at Fort H.G. Wright; inactivated in 1936 at Fort H.G. Wright.

Regiment, less active elements, allotted to the First Corps Area on 28 February 1927 for mobilization purposes. Habitually trained the O.R. harbor defense units assigned to the Harbor Defenses of Long Island Sound, 1924–41. Reserve officers assigned to the regiment conducted summer training with the regiment at Fort H.G. Wright. Reserve officers conducted Citizens Military Training Camp (CMTC) training at Fort Adams, RI, in 1940. Responsible for the support and administration of CCC District 5 (Connecticut), First Corps Area, 1933–39. Location 7 December 1941—Fort H.G. Wright, NY.

Organization Day: 28 March.

Status: HHB active in the Regular Army at Fort Bliss, TX as HHB, 11th Air Defense Arty. Brig.

Events: 59, 77, 93, 95, 174, 280, 301, 313

Commanders, 11th Coast Artillery Regiment

Lt. Col. John R. Musgrave	1 July 1924–14 November 1924
Col. Frank K. Fergusson	14 November 1924–8 January 1928
Lt. Col. Edward D. Powers	8 January 1928–1 April 1928
Col. Charles H. Hilton	1 April 1928–25 October 1930
Lt. Col. Richard I. McKenney	25 October 1930–1 December 1930
Col. George A. Nugent	1 December 1930–20 May 1933
Maj. Hollis LeR. Muller	20 May 1933–10 June 1933
Col. William H. Wilson	10 June 1933–10 June 1935
Lt. Col. Monte J. Hickok	10 June 1935–1 August 1935
Col. Edward J. Cullen	1 August 1935–5 May 1936
Lt. Col. Monte J. Hickok	5 May 1936–12 June 1936
Col. Robert W. Collins	12 June 1936–26 May 1938
Lt. Col. William C. Foote	26 May 1938–12 September 1939
Col. Thomas H. Jones	12 September 1939–10 July 1941
Lt. Col. Mark Mark A. Dawson	10 July 1941-4 December 1941

12th Coast Artillery Regiment (Harbor Defense) (Type A)

HQ—Fort Monroe, VA, 1924–32

Constituted in the R.A. on 1 July 1924 and assigned to the Harbor Defenses of the Potomac and Chesapeake Bay. Concurrently, regimental HQ activated at Fort Monroe, VA. Subordinate elements constituted, organized, or redesignated as follows:

HQ Btry organized by redesignation of 112th Co., C.A.C., active at Fort Monroe.

HQ, 1st Bn. constituted on 1 July 1924 (inactive).

Btry A (Mine) organized by redesignation of 58th Co., C.A.C. at Fort Monroe, VA; inactivated on 15 April 1932.

Btry B organized by redesignation of 139th Co., C.A.C. at Fort Monroe, VA; inactivated on 14 March 1930.

HQ, 2d Bn. constituted on 1 July 1924 (inactive).

Btry C (AA) organized by redesignation of 158th Co., C.A.C. at Fort Monroe, VA; inactivated in March 1930.

Btry D organized by redesignation of 164th Co., C.A.C. at Fort Howard, MD; inactivated on 15 April 1932.

HQ, 3d Bn. constituted on 1 July 1924 (inactive).

Btry E organized by redesignation of 103d Co., C.A.C. at Fort Washington, MD; inactivated on 14 March 1930.

Btry F organized by redesignation of 166th Co., C.A.C. (inactive).

Btry G organized by redesignation of 169th Co., C.A.C. (inactive).

The crew of the U.S.A.M.P. *Gen. John M. Schofield* was assigned to HQ Btry from 30 June 1924 to 21 July 1926. Inactive elements allotted to the Third Corps Area on 28 February 1927 for mobilization purposes. Habitually trained the O.R. harbor defense units assigned to the Harbor Defenses of the Potomac and Chesapeake Bay, 1924–31. On departure of the 61st C.A. from Fort Monroe in May 1930, the regiment was reorganized with two active antiaircraft batteries to perform duties as the Coast Artillery School's training and demonstration regiment. Inactivated on 15 April 1932 and allotted to the Panama Canal Department. Location 7 December 1941—*Inactive.*

Status: Disbanded on 14 June 1944.

Events: 73, 86, 128, 137

Commanders, 12th Coast Artillery Regiment

Col. Edward Carpenter	1 July 1924–1 July 1926	Maj. Charles D. Y. Ostrum	1 November 1930–30 November 1930
Col. Arthur S. Conklin	1 July 1926–26 May 1928	Lt. Col. Franc Leccoq	30 November 1930–11 July 1931
Col. George A. Nugent	26 May 1928–1 November 1930	Col. Harold E. Cloke	11 June 1931–30 April 1932

13th Coast Artillery Regiment (Harbor Defense) (Type A)

HQ—Fort Barrancas, FL, 1924–41

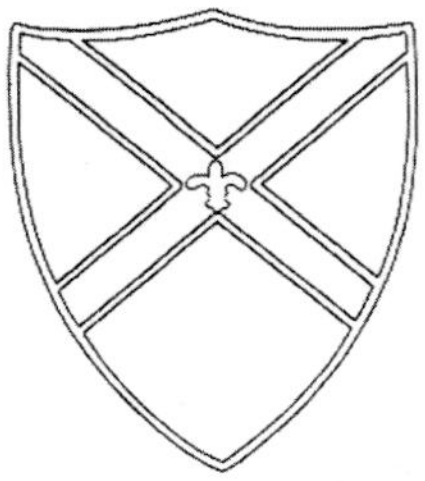

Constituted in the R.A. on 1 July 1924 and assigned, less 3d Bn., to the Harbor Defenses of Charleston, Key West, and Pensacola. Concurrently, regimental HQ activated at Fort Barrancas, FL. The 3d Bn. was allotted to the Eighth Corps Area and assigned to Coast Defenses of Galveston. Subordinate elements constituted, organized, or redesignated as follows:

HQ Btry organized by redesignation of 121st Co., C.A.C., active at Fort Barrancas.

HQ, 1st Bn. constituted on 1 July 1924 (inactive); reorganized and redesignated HHB, 1st Bn. on 15 August 1935; activated on 1 August 1940 at Fort Barrancas.

Btry A organized by redesignation of 162d Co., C.A.C., active at Fort Barrancas.

Btry B organized by redesignation of 163d Co., C.A.C., active at Fort Pickens; transferred on 4 November 1924 to Fort Barrancas.

Btry C organized by redesignation of 145th Co., C.A.C. (inactive); activated on 1 July 1939 at Fort Barrancas.

HQ, 2d Bn. constituted on 1 July 1924 (inactive); reorganized and redesignated HHB, 2d Bn. on 15 August 1935; activated on 1 August 1940 at Fort Moultrie.

Btry D organized by redesignation of 170th Co., C.A.C., active at Fort Moultrie.

Btry E organized by redesignation of 182d Co., C.A.C., active at Key West Barracks.

Btry F organized by redesignation of 181st Co., C.A.C. (inactive); activated on 1 June 1941 at Fort Barrancas.

HQ, 3d Bn. constituted on 1 July 1924 (inactive); reorganized and redesignated HHB, 1st Bn. on 15 August 1935.

Btry G organized by redesignation of 183d Co., C.A.C., active at Fort Crockett, TX; inactivated on 1 February 1940 at Fort Crockett.

Btry H organized by redesignation of 179th Co., C.A.C. (inactive).

Btry I organized by redesignation of 188th Co., C.A.C. (inactive).

Btry K organized by redesignation of 180th Co., C.A.C. (inactive); demobilized on 15 August 1935.

Habitually trained the O.R. harbor defense units assigned to the Harbor Defenses of Charleston, Key West, Pensacola, and Galveston, 1924–41. Responsible for the support and administration of CCC District G, Fourth Corps Area, 1933–39. The 3d Bn., less Btry G, was withdrawn from allotment to the Eighth Corps Area on 15 January 1936 and allotted to the Fourth Corps Area. Reserve officers assigned to the regiment conducted summer training with the regiment at Fort Barrancas. Location 7 December 1941—Fort Barrancas, FL.

Organization Day: 21 October. Chosen to commemorate the regiment's garrisoning of Fort Pickens, FL, on 21 October 1834.

Events: 334

Commanders, 13th Coast Artillery Regiment

Maj. Rollin L. Tilton	1 July 1924–27 August 1924	Lt. Col. Clifford R. Jones	25 June 1933–27 December 1933
Maj. Walter K. Dunn	27 August 1924–23 September 1924	Col. Arthur L. Fuller	27 December 1933–12 October 1935
Lt. Col. Richard H. Williams	23 September 1924–22 September 1926	Col. Robert Arthur	12 October 1935–28 February 1937
Maj. Walter Singles	22 September 1926–1 March 1927	Lt. Col. George F. Humbert	1 March 1937–14 September 1937
Lt. Col. Robert W. Collins	14 March 1927–7 March 1928	Col. Benjamin H.L. Williams	14 September 1937–9 September 1939
Lt. Col. Walter Singles	7 March 1928–25 June 1928	Col. Harvey C. Allen	9 September 1939–30 September 1940
Lt. Col. Hartman L. Butler	25 June 1928–28 July 1930	Col. Louis L. Pendleton	30 September 1940–April 1941
Maj. Charles K. Wing	28 July 1930–11 November 1930	Col. Lloyd B. Magruder	April 1941–1 October 1941
Col. Francis H. Lincoln	11 November 1930–24 June 1933	Maj. George W. Palmer	1 October 1941–12 December 1941

14th Coast Artillery Regiment (Harbor Defense) (Type A)

HQ—Fort Worden, WA, 1924–41

Constituted in the R.A. on 1 July 1924 and assigned to the Harbor Defenses of Puget Sound. Concurrently, regimental HQ activated at Fort Worden, WA. Subordinate elements constituted, organized, or redesignated as follows:

HQ Btry organized by redesignation of 106th Co., C.A.C., active Fort Worden.

HQ, 1st Bn. constituted and activated on 1 July 1924 at Fort Worden; reorganized and redesignated HHB, 1st Bn. on 15 August 1935 and inactivated at Fort Worden; activated on 1 July 1939 at Fort Worden.

Btry A organized by redesignation of 108th Co., C.A.C., active at Fort Worden.

Btry B organized by redesignation of 94th Co., C.A.C. (inactive); activated on 1 July 1941 at Fort Worden.

Btry C organized by redesignation of 92d Co., C.A.C. (inactive); activated on 1 July 1941 at Fort Worden.

HQ, 2d Bn. constituted and activated on 1 July 1924 at Fort Casey; transferred about June 1930 to Fort Worden; reorganized and redesignated HHB, 2d Bn. on 15 August 1935 and inactivated at Fort Worden; activated on 3 January 1941 at Camp Hayden, WA.

Btry D organized by redesignation of 85th Co., C.A.C., active at Fort Casey; inactivated on 30 September 1930 at Fort Casey; activated on 1 January 1931 at Fort Worden.

Btry E organized by redesignation of 93d Co., C.A.C. (inactive); activated on 1 July 1941 at Fort Worden.

Btry F organized by redesignation of 149th Co., C.A.C. C.A.C. (inactive); activated on 1 July 1941 at Fort Worden.

HQ, 3d Bn. constituted and activated on 1 July 1924 at Fort Worden; reorganized and redesignated HHB, 3d Bn. on 15 August 1935 and inactivated at Fort Worden; activated on 4 June 1941 at Fort Worden, WA.

Btry G organized by redesignation of 150th Co., C.A.C., active at Fort Worden.

Btry H organized by redesignation of 126th Co., C.A.C. (inactive); activated on 1 July 1941 at Fort Worden.

Btry I organized by redesignation of 115th Co., C.A.C. (inactive); activated on 1 July 1941 at Fort Worden.

Btry K organized by redesignation of 160th Co., C.A.C. (inactive); demobilized on 15 August 1935; reconstituted and activated on 1 July 1941 at Fort Worden.

The crew of the U.S.A.M.P. *J. Franklin Bell* was assigned to Btry G from 30 June 1924 to July 1927. Habitually trained the O.R. harbor defense units assigned to the Harbor Defenses of Puget Sound, 1924–41. Location 7 December 1941—Fort Worden, WA.

Events: 90, 113, 199, 203, 238, 328

Commanders, 14th Coast Artillery Regiment

Col. Percy M. Kessler	1 July 1924–15 August 1927	Col. Alexander Grieg Jr.	23 February 1933–31 August 1933
Col. Henry M. Merriam	22 August 1927–1 February 1929	Lt. Col. William R. McCleary	31 August 1933–10 February 1934
Maj. Raymond H. Fenner	1 February 1929–18 May 1929	Col. Ralph M. Mitchell	10 February 1934–4 November 1936
Col. Archibald H. Sunderland	18 May 1929–4 July 1930	Lt. Col. William D. Frazer	4 November 1936–16 January 1937
Maj. George R. Meyer	4 July 1930–15 November 1930	Col. Willis G. Peace	16 January 1937–2 May 1939
Col. Frederick W. Phisterer	15 November 1930–23 February 1933	Col. James H. Cunningham	2 May 1939–19 July 1941
Col. John H. Lindt	October 1941–28 February 1942		

15th Coast Artillery Regiment (Harbor Defense) (Type A)

HQ—Fort Kamehameha, TH, 1924–41

Constituted in the R.A. on 1 July 1924 and assigned to the Harbor Defenses of Pearl Harbor. Concurrently, regimental HQ activated at Fort Kamehameha, TH. Subordinate elements constituted, organized, or redesignated as follows:

HQ Btry organized by redesignation of 185th Co., C.A.C., active at Fort Kamehameha.

HQ, 1st Bn. constituted and activated 1 July 1924 at Fort Kamehameha, TH; inactivated on 15 April 1932.

Btry A organized by redesignation of 125th Co., C.A.C., active at Fort Kamehameha, TH.

Btry B organized by redesignation of 91st Co., C.A.C., active at Fort Kamehameha, TH.

HQ, 2d Bn. constituted on 1 July 1924 (inactive).

Btry C organized by redesignation of 143d Co., C.A.C., active at Fort Kamehameha, TH.

Btry D organized by redesignation of 184th Co., C.A.C. (inactive).

HQ, 3d Bn. constituted on 1 July 1924 (inactive).

Btry E organized by redesignation of 86th Co., C.A.C. (inactive).

Btry F organized by redesignation of 95th Co., C.A.C. (inactive).

Btrys G, H, and I constituted on 4 February 1932 as inactive units. Concurrently, each battalion was reorganized as follows: 1st Bn. to consist of Btrys A, B, and C; 2d Bn. to consist of Btrys D, E, and F; 3d Bn. to consist of Btrys G, H, and I. Awarded the US Coast Artillery Association Trophy for R.A. C.A. regiments for 1932. Relieved from the Harbor Defenses of Pearl Harbor in April 1935 and assigned to the Hawaiian Separate C.A. Brig. Location 7 December 1941—Fort Kamehameha, TH.

Organization Day: 1 July. Chosen to commemorate the regiment's reconstitution and activation on 1 July 1924. Adopted on 17 December 1924.

Status: HHB inactive in the Regular Army as HHB, 15th Arty. Group (Air Defense).

Events: 33, 37, 75, 88, 120, 138, 141, 158, 160, 189, 211, 225, 248, 276, 291, 297, 312

Commanders, 15th Coast Artillery Regiment

Col. Louis R. Burgess	1 July 1924–21 August 1924	Col. Avery J. Cooper	1 December 1933–22 August 1935
Lt. Col. Ralph M. Mitchell	21 August 1924–10 May 1935	Lt. Col. Peter H. Ottosen	22 August 1935–14 October 1935
Maj. John H. Hood	10 May 1925–1 July 1927	Col. Earl Biscoe	14 October 1935–11 October 1937
Lt. Col. Lewis Turtle	1 July 1927–17 February 1931	Col. Henry M. Merriam	12 October 1937–18 September 1939
Maj. Frederic A. Price	7 February 19 31–30 June 1931	Lt. Col. Robert H. Volkenburgh	18 September 1939–6 October 1939
Col. Homer B. Grant	30 June 1931–1 December 1933	Col. Eugene B. Walker	6 October 1939–April 1942

16th Coast Artillery Regiment (Harbor Defense) (Type A)

HQ—Fort DeRussey, TH, 1924–27; Fort Ruger, TH, 1927–41

Constituted in the R.A. on 1 July 1924 and assigned to the Harbor Defenses of Honolulu. Concurrently, regimental HQ activated at Fort DeRussey, TH. Btry C activated at Fort Ruger, TH. Subordinate elements constituted, organized, or redesignated as follows:

HQ Btry organized by redesignation of 104th Co., C.A.C., active Fort DeRussey; transferred in 1927 to Fort Ruger.

HQ, 1st Bn. constituted and activated on 1 July 1924 at Fort Ruger, TH; inactivated on 19 November 1931; reorganized and redesignated HHD, 1st Bn. on 4 February 1932.

Btry A organized by redesignation of 90th Co., C.A.C., active at Fort DeRussey.

Btry B organized by redesignation of 99th Co., C.A.C. (inactive).

HQ, 2d Bn. constituted and activated on 1 July 1924 at Fort DeRussey, TH; inactivated on 30 June 1931.

Btry C organized by redesignation of 105th Co., C.A.C. (inactive); activated at Fort Ruger on 1 November 1925.

Btry D organized by redesignation of 111th Co., C.A.C. (inactive); activated at Fort DeRussey on 1 November 1925.

HQ, 3d Bn. constituted on 1 July 1924 (inactive).

Btry E organized by redesignation of 159th Co., C.A.C. (inactive).

Btry F organized by redesignation of 186th Co., C.A.C. (inactive).

HQ relocated in 1927 to Fort Ruger. Relieved from the Harbor Defenses of Honolulu in 1937 and assigned to the Hawaiian Separate C.A. Brig. Location 7 December 1941—Fort Ruger, TH.

Organization Day: 3 October. Adopted on 18 December 1924.

Events: 33, 37, 75, 88, 120, 138, 141, 158, 160, 189, 211, 225, 248, 276, 291, 297, 312

Commanders, 16th Coast Artillery Regiment

Col. Lawrence C. Brown	1 July 1924–4 August 1926	Lt. Col. William E. Shedd Jr.	16 August 1934–23 October 1934
Maj. Harry W. Stark	4 August 1926–14 December 1926	Col. George L. Wertenbaker	23 October 1934–17 September 1936
Col. Percy B. Bishop	14 December 1926–30 July 1929	Col. George A. Wildrick	17 September 1936–6 October 1938
Lt. Col. Walter H. Merrill	30 July 1929–25 October 1929	Lt. Col. Felix E. Cross	6 October 1938–16 November 1938
Col. Harold E. Cloke	25 October 1929–9 June 1931	Col. William D. Frazer	16 November 1938–August 1940
Maj. Frank L. Hoskins	9 June 1931–1 July 1931	Lt. Col. Adam E. Potts	August 1940–November 1940
Maj. Monte J. Hickok	1 July 1931–8 December 1931	Lt. Col. Shuey E. Wolfe	November 1940–December 1940
Col. Harry L. Steele	8 December 1931–16 August 1934	Col. Paul H. Herman	December 1940–ao December 1941

17th Coast Artillery Regiment (Harbor Defense) (Type C) — Regular Army Inactive

HQ—*Not organized,* 1926–41

Constituted in the R.A. on 22 February 1926, assigned to the Panama Coast Artillery District, and allotted to the Panama Canal Department. The 4th C.A. designated as Active Associate, 1926–27. Withdrawn from the Panama Canal Department on 1 October 1933 and allotted to the Hawaiian Department. Location 7 December 1941—*Inactive.*

Status: Disbanded on 14 June 1944.

18th Coast Artillery Regiment (Harbor Defense) (Type B)

HQ—Fort Stevens, OR, 1940–41

Constituted in the R.A. on 19 January 1940 and assigned to the Harbor Defenses of the Columbia and San Francisco. Regimental HHB activated on 1 February 1940 at Fort Stevens, OR. Subordinate elements constituted, organized, or redesignated as follows:

HQ, 1st Bn. activated on 19 January 1940 at Fort Stevens, OR, and assigned to the Harbor Defenses of the Columbia.

HQ, 2d Bn. activated on 19 January 1940 at Fort Winfield Scott, CA, and assigned to the Harbor Defenses of San Francisco; transferred on 28 November 1941 to Fort Funston, CA.

HQ, 3d Bn. activated on 19 January 1940 at Fort Stevens and assigned to the Harbor Defenses of the Columbia.

The regiment was originally engaged in training organized batteries of replacement personnel for transfer to the harbor defenses in Panama from January of 1940–March 1941. The regiment's own subordinate batteries were organized with draftees during March-May 1941 and began training in accordance with the coast artillery mobilization training plan. The regiment assumed responsibility for fixed batteries in the harbor defenses of San Francisco and the Columbia in late 1941.

Location 7 December 1941—Fort Stevens, OR.

Status: Disbanded on 14 June 1944.

Events: 331, 335

Commanders, 18th Coast Artillery Regiment

Col. Kelley B. Lemmon	1 February 1940–September 1941	Col. Frank H. Holden (O.R.)	September 1941–ao December 1941

19th Coast Artillery Regiment (Harbor Defense) (Type A)

HQ—Fort Rosecrans, CA, 1940–41

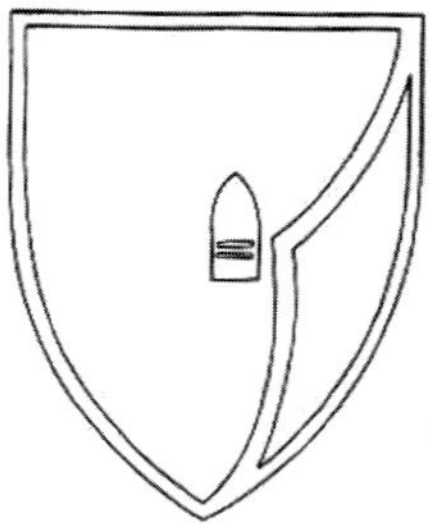

Constituted in the R.A. on 1 July 1924 as the 625th C.A. Regiment (Regt.) (Harbor Defense) (see 625th C.A.). Redesignated the 19th C.A. on 1 February 1940 and assigned to the Harbor Defenses of San Diego. Concurrently, regimental HQ activated at Fort Rosecrans, CA. Subordinate elements organized as follows:

HQ, 1st Bn. inactive, 1940–41; activated on 1 June 1941 at Fort Rosecrans.

Btry A activated on 1 February 1940 at Fort Rosecrans.

Btry B activated on 1 February 1940 at Fort Rosecrans.

HQ, 2d Bn. inactive 1940–41; activated on 1 June 1941 at Fort Rosecrans.

Btry C activated on 3 January 1941 at Fort Rosecrans.

Btry D activated on 3 January 1941 at Fort Rosecrans.

HQ, 3d Bn. inactive, 1940–41; activated on 1 June 1941 at Fort Rosecrans.

Btry E activated on 1 June 1941 at Fort Rosecrans.

Btry F activated on 1 June 1941 at Fort Rosecrans.

Location 7 December 1941—Fort Rosecrans, CA.

Status: HHB inactive Regular Army as HHB, 19th Air Defense Arty. Group.

Events: 311, 332

Commanders, 19th Coast Artillery Regiment

Col. Robert E. Guthrie	1 February 1940–1 March 1940	Col. Peter H. Ottosen	21 July 1940–31 July 1945

20th Coast Artillery Regiment (Harbor Defense) (Type A)

HQ—Fort Crockett, TX, 1940–41

Constituted in the R.A. on 19 January 1940 and assigned to the Harbor Defenses of Galveston. Regimental HQ activated on 1 February 1940 at Fort Crockett, TX. HQ Btry concurrently activated with assets and personnel from the inactivated Btry G, 13th C.A. Subordinate elements organized as follows:

HQ, 1st Bn. inactive, 1940–41; activated in February 1941 at Fort Crockett

Btry A activated in February 1941 at Fort Crockett

Btry B activated in February 1941 at Fort Crockett

HQ, 2d Bn. inactive, 1940–41.

HQ, 3d Bn. inactive, 1940–41.

HQ Btry. functioned as a caretaker unit until November 1940 when the regiment was increased by 550 men. The regiment was increased again by over 500 additional selective servicemen in February 1941 and the 1st Bn. was organized.

Location 7 December 1941—Fort Crockett, TX.

Commanders, 20th Coast Artillery Regiment

Lt. Col. Berthold Vogel	1 February 1940–2 November 1940	Lt. Col. Barnard Dailey	11 February 1941-18 September 1941
Col. Olin H. Longino	2 November 1940–11 February 1941	Col. Robert E. Guthrie	3 September 1941–26 June 1942

21st Coast Artillery Regiment (Harbor Defense) (Type B)

HQ—Fort DuPont, DE, 1940–41

Constituted in the R.A. on 19 January 1940 and assigned to the Harbor Defenses of the Delaware. Regimental HHB activated on 1 February 1940 at Fort DuPont, DE, with personnel and assets from E Btry, 7th C.A. Subordinate elements organized as follows:

HQ, 1st Bn. inactive, 1940–41; activated on 1 April 1941 at Fort DuPont.

Btry A activated on 1 August 1940 at Fort DuPont.

Btry B activated on 13 January 1941 at Fort DuPont.

Btry C activated on 13 January 1941 at Fort DuPont.

HQ, 2d Bn. inactive, 1940–41.

HQ, 3d Bn. inactive, 1940–41.

Location 7 December 1941—Fort DuPont, DE.

Organization Day: 21 February. Chosen to commemorate the regiment's first formal assembly and formation as the 21st C.A. on 21 February 1941.

Commanders, 21st Coast Artillery Regiment

Lt. Col. James C. Hutson	1 February 1940–January 1941	Lt. Col. Ephraim P. Jolls	January 1941–5 December 1941
Maj. Herbert Ryan	5 December 1941–ao January 1942		

22d Coast Artillery Regiment (Harbor Defense) (Type B)

HQ—Fort Constitution, NH, 1940–41

Constituted in the O.R. on 1 July 1924 as the 614th C.A. Regt. (Harbor Defense) (see 614th C.A.). Redesignated the 22d C.A. on 1 February 1940 and assigned to the Harbor Defenses of Portsmouth. Concurrently, regimental HHB activated on 1 February 1940 at Fort Constitution, NH. Reserve officers assigned to the regiment conducted CMTC training at Fort McKinley, ME, in 1940. Subordinate elements organized as follows:

HQ, 1st Bn. inactive, 1940–41; activated on 30 June 1941 at Camp Langdon, NH.

Btry A activated on 1 February 1941 at Fort Constitution.

Btry B activated on 30 June 1941 at Camp Langdon.

HQ, 2d Bn. inactive, 1940–41; activated on 1 June 1941 at Fort Stark, NH.

Btry C activated on 30 June 1941 at Fort Stark.

Btry D activated on 30 June 1941 at Fort Stark.

HQ, 3d Bn. inactive, 1940–41.

Location 7 December 1941—Fort Constitution, NH.

Status: Disbanded on 7 October 1944. Reconstituted and consolidated on 28 June 1950 as follows: HHB consolidated with HHB, 22d AA Arty. Group; 1st Bn. with the 22d AA Arty. Bn.; and 2d Bn. with the 37th AA Arty. Bn., all inactive in the R.A.

Events: 313

Commanders, 22d Coast Artillery Regiment

Capt. Lawrence M. Guyer	1 February 1940–9 August 1940	Maj. Edward G. Cowan	1 October 1940–5 January 1941
Maj. John D. Mitchell	9 August 1940–1 October 1940	Col. Walter K. Dunn	5 January 1941–7 January 1942

23d Coast Artillery Regiment (Harbor Defense) (Type D)

HQ—Fort Rodman, MA, 1940–41

Constituted in the R.A. on 1 July 1924 as the 616th C.A. Regt. (Harbor Defense) (see 616th C.A.). Redesignated the 23d C.A. on 1 February 1940 and assigned to the Harbor Defenses of New Bedford. Concurrently, Regimental HQ, HQ Btry, and Btry A activated on 1 February 1940 at Fort Rodman, MA. Subordinate elements organized as follows:

HQ, 1st Bn. inactive, 1940; disbanded on 27 December 1940.

Btry A activated on 1 February 1940 at Fort Rodman.

Btry B activated on 15 July 1941 at Fort Rodman.

HQ, 2d Bn. inactive, 1940; disbanded on 27 December 1940.

Btry C activated on 15 July 1941 at Fort Rodman.

Btry D activated on 15 July 1941 at Fort Rodman.

HQ, 3d Bn. inactive, 1940; disbanded on 27 December 1940.

Reorganized and redesignated on 27 December 1940 as 23d C.A. Bn. (Harbor Defense).

Location 7 December 1941—Fort Rodman, NH.

Organization Day: 1 August.

Events: 313

Commanders, 23d Coast Artillery Regiment

Maj. Charles N. Branham	1 February 1940–ao August 1940	Lt. Col. Charles J. Herzer	ao July 1941–14 August 1941

41st Coast Artillery Regiment (Railway)

HQ—Fort Kamehameha, TH, 1921–31; *Inactive,* 1931–41

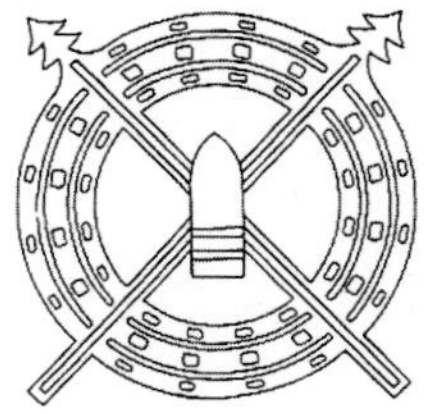

Constituted in the R.A. on 15 January 1921 as the Hawaiian Railway Bn. and assigned to the Harbor Defenses of Pearl Harbor. Regimental HQ, HQ Btry, and Btrys A and B activated on 22 December 1921 at Fort Kamehameha, TH, with personnel from the 199th and 200th C.A. Cos. Redesignated on 1 June 1922 as the 41st Arty. Bn. (Railway), C.A.C. Expanded and redesignated on 1 July 1924 as the 41st C.A. Regt. (Railway). Relieved from the Harbor Defenses of Pearl Harbor on 1 March 1925 and assigned to the Hawaiian Separate C.A. Brig. Regimental HQ inactivated on 30 June 1931 at Fort Kamehameha. Concurrently, Headquarters and Headquarters Detachment (HHD), 1st Bn. activated and all active elements attached to the 15th C.A. for command and control purposes, 1931–41. The 2d Bn. remained inactive, 1924–41. Consolidated on 5 October 1936 with the 41st Arty. Regt., C.A.C. (a World War I unit organized on 1 October 1918 at Fort Monroe, VA; demobilized in December 1918 at Fort Monroe; reconstituted on 5 October 1936). Reserve officers assigned to the regiment conducted summer training at Fort Sheridan, IL, with the 61st C.A. Btry B awarded the Knox Trophy for C.A. in 1940. Location 7 December 1941—Fort Kamehameha, TH (1st Bn.).

Status: Active at Babenhausen, Germany, as HHB, 41st F.A. Brig.

Events: 33, 37, 75, 88, 120, 138, 141, 158, 160, 189, 211, 225, 248, 276, 291, 297, 312

Commanders, 41st Coast Artillery Regiment

Maj. Joseph Matson	22 December 1921–7 July 1922	Maj. Lawrence B. Weeks	25 August 1926–3 November 1926
Maj. Kelly B. Lemmon	7 July 1922–7 July 1924	Lt. Col. John L. Holcombe	3 November 1926–24 August 1929
Maj. Lawrence B. Weeks	7 July 1924–15 May 1925	Maj. Fred M. Green	24 August 1929–1 June 1930
Maj. Frank E. Emery	15 May 1925–20 October 1925	Capt. Howard B. MacKirdy	1 June 1930–25 June 1930
Maj. Phillip S. Gage	20 October 1925–6 March 1926	Maj. George D. Holland	25 June 1930–19 November 1930
Maj. Frank E. Emery	6 March 1926–25 August 1926	Maj. Berthold Vogel	19 November 1930–30 June 1931
	Inactive	31 June 1931–7 December 1941	

(1st Battalion)

Maj. Berthold Vogel	1 July 1931–October 1931	Maj. William M. Cravens	25 May 1937–13 March 1939
Maj. Ira B. Hill	October 1931–14 August 1934	Maj. Abraham M. Lawrence	13 March 1939–December 1940
Maj. Gerald B. Robison	14 August 1934–25 May 1937	Maj. Watson L. McMorris	December 1940–September 1941

42d Coast Artillery Regiment (Railway) (30th Coast Artillery Brigade) **Regular Army Inactive**

HQ—Camp Eustis, VA, 1919–21; *Inactive,* 1921–26; Fort Eustis, VA, 1926–41

Arrived at the port of Newport News on 17 February 1919 on the U.S.S. *Kroonland* as the 42d Arty., C.A.C., an element of the 30th Arty. Brig., C.A.C. (Railway). Transferred to Camp Stuart, VA. Transferred in late February 1919 to Camp Eustis, VA. Participated in maneuvers and testing of railway artillery near Rockport—Provincetown, MA, during August–November 1920. Inactivated on 17 August 1921 at Camp Eustis, allotted to the Third Corps Area, and 52d C.A. designated as Active Associate, 1921–27. Redesignated on 20 February 1924 as the 42d C.A. Regt. (Railway). Regiment organized on 11 May 1926 as an RAI unit with O.R. personnel at Fort Eustis, VA. Concurrently attached to the 52d C.A. for training and administration. Conducted summer training at Fort Monroe. Designated mobilization training station was Fort Eustis, VA, 1922–30, and Fort Monroe, VA, 1930–41. Location 7 December 1941—Fort Eustis, VA.

Status: Inactive as HHB, 42d F.A. Brig.

Commanders, 42d Coast Artillery Regiment

Col. Harry J. Watson	ao January 1920–23 December 1920
Lt. Col. Granville Sevier	29 December 1920–18 August 1921
Maj. Otto G. Pitz	18 August 1921–1 September 1921
Inactive	1 September 1921–11 May 1926
Unknown	11 May 1926–28 February 1927
Maj. William R. Nichols*	28 February 1927–15 August 1929
Lt. Col. Allison F. H. Scott**	15 August 1929–August 1934
Maj. William J. Darmody**	August 1934–July 1940
Unknown	July 1940–7 December 1941

*RAI commanders: R.A. officers.
**RAI commanders: O.R. officers.

43d Coast Artillery Regiment (Railway) (30th Coast Artillery Brigade) **Regular Army Inactive**

HQ—Camp Eustis, VA, 1919–21; *Inactive,* 1921–26; Fort Eustis, VA, 1926–29; Pittsburgh, PA, 1929–41

Arrived at the port of Newport News on 2 January 1919 on the U.S.S. *Princess Matoika* as the 43d Arty., C.A.C., an element of the 30th Arty. Brig., C.A.C. (Railway). Transferred on 3 January 1919 to Camp Eustis, VA. Inactivated on 17 August 1921 at Camp Eustis and allotted to the Third Corps Area. The 52d C.A. designated as Active Associate, 1921–27. Redesignated on 20 February 1924 as the 43d C.A. Regt. (Railway). Regiment organized in September 1926 as an RAI unit with O.R. personnel at Fort Eustis, VA. Concurrently attached to the 52d C.A. for training and administration. HQ relocated on 21 August 1929 to Pittsburgh, PA. Conducted summer training at Fort Monroe, VA, 1938–40. Designated mobilization training station was Fort Eustis, VA, 1922–30, and Fort Monroe, VA, 1930–41. Location 7 December 1941—Pittsburgh, PA.

Status: Assigned to the USARS as the 43d Air Defense Arty.

Commanders, 43d Coast Artillery Regiment

Col. Harrison S. Kerrick	August 1918–14 November 1918
Lt. Col. Herbert R. Odell	15 November 1918–4 March 1919
Col. Harold E. Cloke	4 March 1919–September 1919
Lt. Col. John Mather	September 1919–July 1920
Maj. Philip D. Terry	July 1920–9 September 1920
Maj. Olin H. Longino	9 September 1920–20 November 1920
Lt. Col. Henry C. Merriam	20 November 1920–6 April 1921
Maj. E.B. Gray	6 April 1921–18 May 1921
Col. William E. Cole	18 May 1921–1 July 1921
Maj. E.B. Gray	1 July 1921–17 August 1921
Capt. Edgar H. Underwood	17 August 1921–9 September 1921
Inactive	1 September 1921–September 1926
Unknown	September 1926–28 February 1927
Maj. Lloyd P. Horsfall*	28 February 1927–15 August 1929
Unknown	15 August 1929–ao May 1934
Maj. Leonard J. Rose**	ao May 1934–ao December 1937
Unknown	ao December 1937–ao July 1938
Capt. Charles W. Skeele**	ao July 1938–27 September 1939
Maj. Alfred A. Gunter**	27 September 1939–December 1941

*RAI commanders: R.A. officers.
**RAI commanders: O.R. officers.

44th Coast Artillery Regiment (Heavy Tractor) (39th Coast Artillery Brigade) **Regular Army Inactive**

HQ—Fort Totten, NY, 1919–20; Camp Jackson, SC, 1920–21; *Inactive,* 1921–26; Fort Eustis, VA, 1926–30; Philadelphia, PA, 1930–1940

Arrived at the port of New York on 4 February 1919 on the S.S. *Cedric* as the 44th Arty., C.A.C., an element of the 39th Arty. Brig., C.A.C (Heavy Tractor). Transferred on 4 February 1919 to Camp Mills, NY. Transferred on 8 February 1919 to Fort Totten, NY. Transferred on 16 October 1919 to Camp Jackson, SC. Inactivated on 31 August 1921 at Camp Jackson and allotted to the Third Corps Area. The 51st C.A. designated as Active Associate, 1921–27. Redesignated on 20 February 1924 as the 44th C.A. Regt. (Heavy Tractor). Relieved from assignment to the 39th C.A. Brig. in 1926 and assigned to the 31st C.A. Brig. Redesignated on 28 April 1926 as the 44th C.A. Regt. (Tractor Drawn). Regiment organized in November 1926 as an RAI unit with O.R. personnel at Fort Eustis, VA. Attached to the 51st C.A. for training and administration on 21 January 1928. HQ relocated in November 1930 to Philadelphia, PA. Designated as a "Colored" unit in the 1939 Protective Mobilization Plan. Inactivated on 31 August 1940 at Philadelphia by relief of personnel. Redesignated as the 54th C.A. Regt. (155-mm Gun) (Colored) on 16 December 1940. Conducted summer training at Fort Monroe, VA, 1927–40. Designated mobilization training station was Fort Eustis, VA, 1922–30, and Fort Monroe, VA, 1930–40.

Status: Assigned to the USARS as the 44th Air Defense Arty.

Commanders, 44th Coast Artillery Regiment

Col. Albert L. Rhodes	October 1918–29 August 1920	*Inactive*	1 September 1921–November 1926
Col. Joseph P. Tracy	29 August 1920–28 November 1920	Maj. George H. Collins**	November 1926–ao June 1934
Maj. John P. McCaskey	28 November 1920–16 December 1920	Unknown	ao June 1934–ao April 1935
Maj. James A. Green	16 December 1920–23 August 1921	Maj. Allen M. Murphy**	ao April 1935–10 January 1940
Maj. John P. McCaskey	23 August 1921–1 September 1921	Lt. Col. John C. Henderson**	10 January 1940–30 August 1940

**RAI commanders: O.R. officers.

51st Coast Artillery Regiment (Heavy Tractor) (39th Coast Artillery Brigade) **Regular Army Inactive**

HQ—Fort Hamilton, NY, 1919–20; Camp Jackson, SC, 1920–21; Fort Eustis, VA, 1921–30; *Inactive,* 1930–41

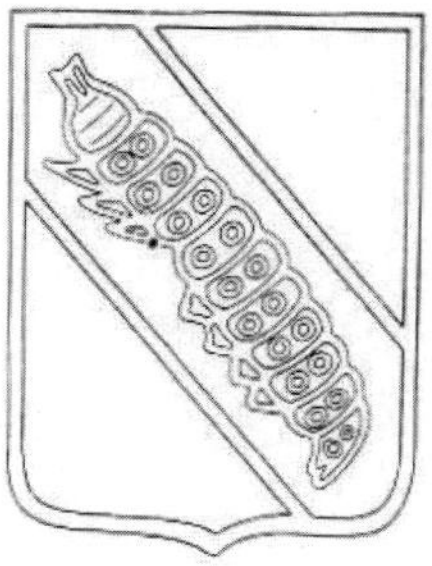

Arrived at the port of New York on 3 February 1919 on the U.S.S. *Agamemnon* as the 51st Arty., C.A.C., an element o the 39th Arty. Brig., C.A.C., (Heavy Tractor). Transferred on 3 February 1919 to Camp Mills, NY. Transferred on 9 February 1919 to Fort Hamilton, NY. Further transferred on 18 October 1920 to Camp Jackson, SC. Transferred on 22 September 1921 to Camp Eustis, VA. The 3d Bn. inactivated on 13 August 1921 at Camp Eustis. The 2d Bn. inactivated on 1 August 1922 at Camp Eustis. Pioneered the use of the 155-mm G.P.F. gun in the indirect fire mode against moving naval targets at Fort Eustis, 1921–23. Regiment redesignated on 20 February 1924 as the 51st C.A. Regt. (Heavy Tractor). Relieved from assignment to the 39th C.A. Brig. on 26 January 1926 and assigned to the 30th C.A. Brig. Redesignated on 28 April 1926 as the 51st C.A. Regt. (Tractor Drawn). Relieved from assignment to the 30th C.A. Brig. on 25 June 1929 and concurrently attached to the brigade. Regiment, less 1st Bn. and elements already inactive, inactivated on 11 March 1930 at Fort Eustis and allotted to the Third Corps Area. Concurrently, the 1st Bn. transferred to Fort Monroe, VA. Awarded the U.S. Coast Artillery Association Trophy for R.A. regiments for 1933. Provided the honor guard and security for the visit of the Honorable George H. Dern, Secretary of War, on his visit to Fort Monroe on 7 January 1935. Reserve officers assigned to the regiment conducted summer training with the 1st Bn. at Fort Monroe. Designated mobilization training station for inactive elements was Fort Monroe. The 1st Bn. transferred to Camp Buchanan, PR, on 16 October 1939 and assigned to the Harbor Defenses of San Juan. Transferred on 28 October 1940 to the Post of San Juan, PR. Location 7 December 1941—*Inactive* (less 1st Bn.).

Events: 66, 86, 128, 137, 242, 329

Commanders, 51st Coast Artillery Regiment

Col. Clarence G. Bunker	ao September 1918–29 December 1920	Lt. Col. Robert B. McBride	20 November 1925–29 June 1928
Maj. H.K. Loughry	29 December 1920–4 April 1921	Maj. Edwin K. Smith	29 June 1928–14 September 1928
Col. Charles H. Hilton	4 April 1921–4 November 1922	Lt. Col. Archibald H. Sunderland	14 September 1928–16 April 1929
Maj. Rodney H. Smith	4 November 1922–January 1923	Maj. Edwin K. Smith	16 April 1929–3 August 1929
Maj. George R. Meyer	January 1923–12 December 1923	Lt. Col. John C. Ohnsted	3 August 1929–24 January 1930
Lt. Col. James B. Taylor	12 December 1923–20 November 1925	Maj. Edwin K. Smith	24 January 1930–11 March 1930

(1st Battalion)

Maj. Edwin K. Smith	11 March 1930–7 September 1930	Capt. Ralph E. Hill	3 April 1935–31 July 1935
Maj. Delmer S. Lenzner	7 September 1930–8 August 1931	Col. Horace F. Spurgin	31 July 1935–9 March 1936
Lt. Col. Albert Gilmor	8 August 1931–14 November 1932	Maj. Oliver B. Bucher	9 March 1936–1 July 1936
Lt. Col. Robert P. Glassburn	14 November 1932–23 July 1934	Lt. Col. Eugene B. Walker	31 July 1936–27 December 1938
Col. George L. Wertenberger	23 July 1934–1 September 1934	Col. Francis P. Hardaway	27 December 1938–September 1939
Maj. Cedric F. Maguire	1 September 1934–3 October 1934	Lt. Col. Barrington L. Flanagen	September 1939–3 September 1941
Maj. Joshua D. Powers	3 October 1934–3 April 1935	Lt. Col. James de B. Walbach	3 September 1941–25 May 1942

52d Coast Artillery Regiment (Railway) (30th Coast Artillery Brigade)

HQ—Fort Eustis, VA, 1921–30; Fort Hancock, NJ, 1930–41

Arrived at the port of Newport News on 3 January 1919 on the U.S.S. *Antigone* as the 52d Arty., C.A.C. (Railway), an element of the 30th Arty. Brig., C.A.C. (Railway). Transferred on 3 January 1919 to Camp Stuart, VA. Transferred on 7 January 1919 to Camp Eustis, VA. The 3d Bn. inactivated on 16 May 1921 at Camp Eustis. The 3d Bn. reactivated on 18 August 1921 at Camp Eustis. The 1st Bn. inactivated on 1 August 1922 at Camp Eustis and the 2d Bn. designated as Active Associate. Regiment redesignated on 20 February 1924 as the 52d C.A. Regt. (Railway). A crew from the 52d C.A. manned a 14-inch railway gun for its cross-country transfer from Aberdeen Proving Ground to Fort MacArthur, CA, 12 October–14 December 1925. Btry E awarded the Knox Trophy for C.A. in 1926. The 1st Bn. allotted to the Third Corps Area on 28 February 1927 for mobilization purposes. Service Btry inactivated on 28 February 1930 at Fort Eustis. Regiment, less 1st and 2d Bns., transferred on 1 April 1930 to Fort Hancock, NJ. The 2d Bn. transferred in July 1930 to Fort Monroe, VA. The 1st Bn. remained allotted to the Third Corps Area. Active battalions reorganized in July 1930 to man one 8-inch railway gun battery and one 12-inch railway mortar battery. The 2d Bn. conducted a unique quick-reaction exercise on 11 June 1932 by railing its 8-inch railway gun and 12-inch railway mortar batteries 190 miles from Fort Hancock to Wildwood, NJ, to live fire at targets in Delaware Bay off Cape May. Regimental HQ and 2d Bn. assisted the US Navy with traffic control and site security at Lakehurst, NJ, after the *Hindenburg* disaster, 7–10 May 1937. HHB, 2d Bn., and Btry D inactivated on 31 October 1938 at Fort Monroe. Reserve officers assigned to the regiment conducted summer training with the 2d Bn. elements at Fort Monroe. Reserve officers relieved from the regiment on 18 November 1939. Relieved from the 30th C.A. Brig. in 1940 and assigned to the Harbor Defenses of Sandy Hook. Btry F inactivated on 1 February 1940 at Fort Monroe. The following units were activated on 8 January 1941 at Fort Hancock: HHB, 2d Bn.; HHB, 3d Bn.; Btry D; and Btry F. The entire 1st Bn. activated on 1 June 1941 at Fort Hancock, NJ. Location 7 December 1941—Fort Hancock, NJ.

Organization Day: 26 September. Chosen to commemorate the regiment's baptism of fire during the Meuse-Argonne campaign on 26 September 1918.

Status: Assigned to the USARS as the 52d Air Defense Arty.

Events: 73, 86, 137, 321

Commanders, 52d Coast Artillery Regiment

Col. Johnson Hagood	22 July 1917–1 November 1917	Lt. Col. James B. Taylor	20 November 1924–26 January 1925
Lt. Col. Frank B. Edwards	1 November 1917–April 1918	Col. Joseph P. Tracy	26 January 1925–15 August 1926
Col. Edward Kimmel	April 1918–July 1918	Maj. Peter H. Ottosen	15 August 1926–1 December 1926
Col. Malcolm Young	July 1918–30 November 1918	Col. Edward Kimmel	1 December 1926–1 November 1927
Col. Samuel McP. Rutherford	7 December 1918–18 February 1919	Maj. Peter H. Ottosen	1 November 1927–2 February 1928
Lt. Col. Walter W. Merrill	ao January 1920–16 August 1920	Lt. Col. George L. Wertenbaker	2 February 1928–1 July 1928
Col. William E. Cole	16 August 1920–31 May 1921	Maj. Peter Ottosen	1 July 1928–15 August 1928

Maj. Paul H. Herman	31 May 1921–July 1921	Lt. Col. James B. Taylor	15 August 1928–30 January 1930
Maj. Olin H. Longino	July 1921–18 August 1921	Maj. Eugene B. Walker	1 February 1930–27 March 1930
Lt. Col. Granville Sevier	18 August 1921–5 September 1921	Maj. Frederick A. Holmer	27 March 1930–18 July 1931
Lt. Col. John B. Murphy	5 September 1921–13 February 1922	Lt. Col. Lewis Turtle	18 July 1931–20 February 1933
Lt. Col. Francis J. Behr	13 February 1922–20 July 1922	Maj. Richard S. Dodson	20 February 1933–1 August 1933
Maj. James B. Taylor	20 July 1922–1 October 1923	Lt. Col. Thomas C. Cook	1 August 1933–30 March 1935
Maj. Lloyd P. Horsfall	1 October 1923–3 January 1924	Lt. Col. Richard S. Dodson	30 March 1935–12 October 1936
Maj. Donald M. Ashbridge	3 January 1924–6 July 1924	Lt. Col. Samuel F. Hawkins	12 October 1936–15 September 1938
Maj. William W. Hicks	6 July 1924–5 September 1924	Lt. Col. Jesse L. Sinclair	15 September 1938–August 1940
Maj. John F. Kahle	5 September 1924–20 November 1924	Lt. Col. Wade W. Rhein	August 1940–11 June 1941
		Col. Joseph C. Haw	11 June 1941–25 August 1943

53d Coast Artillery Regiment (Railway) (30th Coast Artillery Brigade) **Regular Army Inactive**

HQ—Camp Eustis, VA, 1919–21; *Inactive,* 1921–27; Fort Eustis, VA, 1927–30; *Demobilized/Inactive,* 1930–41

Arrived at the port of Newport News on11 March 1919 on the U.S.S. *Nansemond* as the 53d Arty., C.A.C., an element of the 30th Arty. Brig., C.A.C. (Railway). Transferred on 10 March 1919 to Camp Stuart, VA. Transferred on 17 March 1919 to Camp Eustis, VA. Inactivated on 17 August 1921 at Camp Eustis and allotted to the Third Corps Area. The 52d C.A. designated as Active Associate, 1921–27. Redesignated on 20 February 1924 as the 53d C.A. Regt. (Heavy Tractor). Designated mobilization training station was Fort Monroe, VA. Regiment organized on 28 February 1927 as an RAI unit with O.R. personnel at Fort Eustis, VA. Concurrently attached to the 52d C.A. for training and administration. Conducted summer training at Fort Monroe, VA. Demobilized on 22 March 1930 at Fort Eustis, VA. Reconstituted on 9 July 1941 as the 53d C.A. Regt. (155-mm Gun) (Mobile). Concurrently, 1st Bn. activated at Camp Pendleton, VA. The 2d Bn. activated on 29 August 1941. Location 7 December 1941—*Inactive* (less 1st and 2d Bns.).

Organization Day: 24 July. Chosen to commemorate the date of the regiment's original activation on 24 July 1917.

Commanders, 53d Coast Artillery Regiment

Col. Frank K. Fergusson	7 July 1917–8 October 1917	Maj. Herbert H. Atcheson	8 February 1921–2 June 1921
Unknown	8 October 1917–ao January 1920	Maj. Olin H. Longino	2 June 1921–29 July 1921
Maj. Benjamin E. Booth	ao January 1920–5 August 1920	Maj. Herbert H. Atcheson	29 July 1921–28 August 1921
Lt. Col. Francis H. Lincoln	5 August 1920–24 December 1920	*Inactive*	17 August 1921–27 February 1927
Maj. Benjamin E. Booth	24 December 1920–8 February 1921	Maj. Eli E. Bennett*	28 February 1927–22 March 1930

*RAI commanders: R.A. officers.

54th Coast Artillery Regiment (155mm Gun) (Mobile) (C)

HQ—Fort Totten, NY, 1919–20; Camp Jackson, SC, 1920–21; *Inactive,* 1921–27; Philadelphia, PA, 1927–41; Camp Wallace, TX, 1941; Camp Davis, NC, 1941

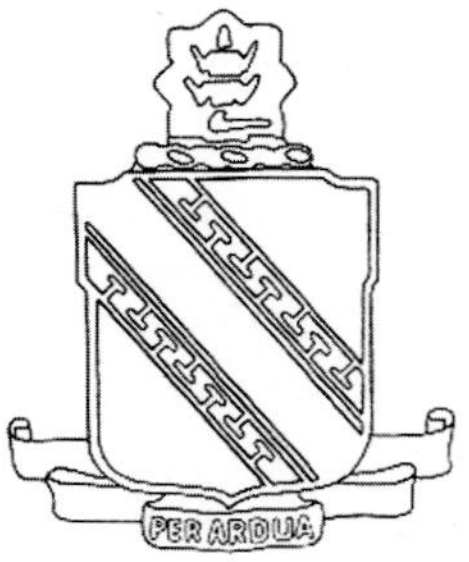

Arrived at the port of New York on 4 February 1919 on the S.S. *Cedric* as the 44th Arty., C.A.C., an element of the 39th Arty. Brig., C.A.C. (Heavy Tractor). Transferred on 4 February 1919 to Camp Mills, NY. Transferred on 8 February 1919 to Fort Totten, NY. Transferred on 16 October 1919 to Camp Jackson, SC. Inactivated on 31 August 1921 at Camp Jackson and allotted to the Third Corps Area. The 51st C.A. designated as Active Associate, 1921–27. Redesignated on 20 February 1924 as the 44th C.A. Regt. (Heavy Tractor). Relieved from assignment to the 39th C.A. Brig. in 1926 and assigned to the 31st C.A. Brig. Regiment organized on 28 February 1927 as an RAI unit with O.R. personnel at Philadelphia, PA. Designated as a "Colored" unit in the 1939 Protective Mobilization Plan. Inactivated on 31 August 1940 at Philadelphia by relief of personnel. Redesignated as the 54th C.A. Regt. (155-mm Gun) (Colored) on 16 December 1940. Conducted summer training at Fort Monroe, VA, 1927–40. Designated mobilization training station was Fort Eustis, VA, 1922–30, and Fort Monroe, VA, 1930–41. Activated on 10 February 1941 at Camp Wallace, TX, and attached to the First Army. Transferred on 22 May 1941 to Camp Davis, NC. Location 7 December 1941—Camp Davis, NC.

Status: Inactive in the US Army Reserve as follows: HHB as HHB, 153d F.A. Group; 1st, 2d and 3d Bns. as the 778th, 779th, and 780th F.A. Bns., respectively.

Commanders, 54th Coast Artillery Regiment

Col. Oscar C. Warner	10 February 1941–31 October 1941	Col. Robert M. Carswell	31 October 1941–January 1942

55th Coast Artillery Regiment (Heavy Tractor) (31st Coast Artillery Brigade)

HQ—Fort Terry, NY, 1919; Fort Winfield Scott, CA, 1919; Camp Lewis, WA, 1919–21; Fort Kamehameha, TH, 1921–31; *Inactive,* 1931–41

Arrived at the port of New York on 22 January 1919 on the S.S. *Cretic* as the 55th Arty., C.A.C., an element of the 31st Arty. Brig., C.A.C., (Heavy Tractor). Transferred on 22 January 1919 to Camp Mills, NY. Transferred on 26 January 1919 to Fort H.G. Wright, NY. Transferred to Fort Winfield Scott, CA, on 23 February 1919. Transferred on 4 October 1919 to Camp Lewis, WA. Relieved on 23 March 1921 from the 31st C.A. Brig. Transferred to the Hawaiian Department and embarked on 9 May 1921 on the U.S.A.T. *Buford* at Tacoma, WA. Arrived on 20 May 1921 at Fort Kamehameha, TH. Regiment reorganized on 22 December 1921 into three battalions of three firing batteries each. Pioneered the use of the 155-mm G.P.F. gun in the indirect fire mode against moving naval targets, 1921–23. The 2d Bn. transferred on 8 January 1922 to Fort Ruger. The 1st Bn. transferred on 11 June 1922 to Fort Shafter. Effective 12 September 1922 the regiment, less 2d Bn., was assigned to the Harbor Defenses of Pearl Harbor. The 2d Bn. was assigned to the Harbor Defenses of Honolulu. Regiment redesignated on 20 February 1924 as the 55th C.A. Regt. (Heavy Tractor). The 1st Bn. transferred on 31 March 1924 to Fort Shafter, TH. The 3d Bn. inactivated on 31 October 1925 at Fort Kamehameha. Concurrently 1st Bn. transferred to Fort Kamehameha. Relieved from assignment to the Harbor Defenses of Pearl Harbor on 1 March 1925 and assigned to the Hawaiian Separate C.A. Brig. Redesignated on 28 April 1926 as the 55th C.A. Regt. (Tractor Drawn). Btry C awarded the Knox Trophy for C.A. for 1931. Regimental HQ inactivated on 30 June 1931. Concurrently, the 1st Bn. attached to the 15th C.A. and the 2d Bn. attached to the 16th C.A. The 2d Bn. transferred in 1935 to Fort DeRussey, TH. Location 7 December 1941—*Inactive* (less 1st and 2d Battalions).

Organization Day: 17 March. Chosen to commemorate the regiment's arrival at the New York port of embarkation for shipment to France on 17 March 1918. Adopted on 5 July 1929.

Status: Disbanded on 14 June 1944.

Events: 33, 37, 75, 88, 120, 138, 141, 158, 160, 189, 211, 225, 248, 276, 291, 297, 312

Commanders, 55th Coast Artillery Regiment

Col. James F. Howell	1 December 1917–9 February 1918	Col. Robert S. Abernethy	18 January 1928–20 August 1930
Col. Granville Sevier	9 February 1918–19 October 1918	Col. Homer B. Grant	10 November 1930–30 June 1931
Col. John L. Roberts	19 October 1918–February 1919	Maj. Austin G. Frick	30 June 1931–10 November 1933
Col. James C. Dusenbury	February 1919–15 April 1920	Maj. Roy S. Atwood	10 November 1933–29 May 1935
Maj. Edgar H. Thompson	15 April 1920–2 November 1920	Capt. Arthur K. Chambers	29 May 1935–27 August 1935
Lt. Col. Frank B. Edwards	2 November 1920–18 February 1924	Maj. Wilmer S. Phillips	27 August 1935–10 September 1937
Col. Henry M. Merriam	19 February 1924–15 May 1925	Maj. Rolla V. Ladd	10 September 1937–30 June 1939
Col. William E. Cole	15 May 1925–31 August 1927	Maj. James C. Bates	30 June 1939–ao January 1940
Maj. Herbert H. Acheson	31 August 1927–18 January 1928	Lt. Col. Henry H. Slicer	ao August 1940–ao September 1940
Lt. Col. John R. Musgrave	20 August 1930–10 November 1930	Unknown	ao September 1940–7 December 1941

56th Artillery Regiment, Coast Artillery Corps (Heavy Tractor) (39th Coast Artillery Brigade)

HQ—Camp Jackson, SC, 1919–21

Arrived at the port of Hoboken on 5 January 1919 on the U.S.S. *South Dakota* as the 56th Arty., C.A.C., an element of the 31st Arty. Brig., C.A.C., (Heavy Tractor). Transferred on 5 January 1919 to Fort Schuyler, NY. Transferred in October 1919 to Camp Jackson, SC, relieved from the 31st Arty. Brig., and assigned to the 39th Arty. Brig., C.A.C. (Heavy Tractor). Disbanded on 31 July 1921 at Camp Jackson and personnel transferred to the 44th and 51st Arty. Regts., C.A.C.

Organization Day: 11 August. Chosen to commemorate the regiment's baptism of fire near Chery Chartrevue during the Oise-Aisne campaign on 11 August 1918.

Commanders, 56th Artillery Regiment, Coast Artillery Corps (Heavy Tractor)

Col. Louis R. Burgess	20 November 1917–August 1918	Maj. Robert N. Mackin	27 October 1920–November 1920
Col. James L. Long	August 1918–ao November 1918	Maj. Hugh E. Pitz	November 1920–10 December 1920
Col. Joseph S. Hardin	26 January 1920–27 October 1920	Lt. Col. John L. Roberts	10 December 1920–1 July 1921
Maj. Hugh E. Pitz	1 July 1921–1 August 1921		

56th Coast Artillery Regiment (155-mm Gun)

HQ—Fort Cronkhite, CA, 1941

Constituted in the O.R. on 29 July 1921 as the 506th Arty. (AA), C.A.C. (see 506th C.A.). Redesignated on 30 June 1924 as the 506th C.A. Regt. (AA). Withdrawn from the O.R. on 1 October 1933 and allotted to the R.A. as an RAI unit. Reorganized as a 155-mm Gun unit, redesignated as the 56th C.A. on 16 December 1940, and assigned to the Harbor Defenses of San Francisco. Attached to the Fourth Army on 24 January 1941. Regiment activated on 2 June 1941 with HQ at Fort Cronkhite, CA. Location 7 December 1941—Fort Cronkhite, CA.

Status: Assigned to the USARS as the 56th Air Defense Arty.

Events: 331, 335

Commanders, 56th Coast Artillery Regiment

Col. Frank Drake	2 June 1941–ao December 1941

57th Coast Artillery Regiment (Heavy Tractor) (31st Coast Artillery Brigade) — Regular Army Inactive

HQ—Fort Winfield Scott, CA, 1919; Camp Lewis, WA, 1919–21; *Inactive,* 1921–27; San Francisco, CA, 1927–41; Fort Monroe, VA, 1941

Arrived at the port of Hoboken on 15 January 1919 on the U.S.S. *Huntington* as the 57th Arty., C.A.C., an element of the 31st Arty. Brig., C.A.C. (Heavy Tractor). Transferred on 15 January 1919 to Fort Hancock, NJ. Transferred to Fort Winfield Scott, CA, and arrived there on 14 February 1919. Transferred to Camp Lewis, WA, and arrived there on 4 October 1919. Relieved on 3 May 1921 from the 31st Arty. Brig. Demobilized on 30 June 1921 at Camp Lewis, WA. Reconstituted in the R.A. on 22 January 1926 and allotted to the Third Corps Area. The 51st C.A. designated as Active Associate, 1926–27. Withdrawn from the Third Corps Area on 28 February 1927 and allotted to the Ninth Corps Area. Concurrently assigned to the Harbor Defenses of San Francisco. Regiment organized on 20 June 1927 with HQ at San Francisco as an RAI unit by assignment of all R.A. personnel assigned to C.A. Reserve Officers' Training Corps (ROTC) programs in the Ninth Corps Area. Reorganized at San Francisco, CA, as an RAI unit on 20 October 1930 by transfer of O.R. personnel formerly assigned to the 608th C.A. Other personnel drawn from the states of Utah and Idaho. Awarded the US Coast Artillery Association Trophy for O.R. regiments for 1936. Conducted summer training most years at Fort Winfield Scott, CA, and some years at Fort Funston, CA; Fort MacArthur, CA; or Fort Monroe, VA. Withdrawn from allotment to the Ninth Corps Area on 1 June 1940 and allotted to the Third Corps Area. Concurrently the 1st Bn. activated at Fort Story, VA. The 1st Bn. provided an honor guard for the visit of President Roosevelt to Fort Monroe on 29 July 1940. Remainder of the regiment, less 3d Bn., activated on 3 January 1941, less Reserve personnel, at Fort Monroe, VA. Concurrently assigned to the Harbor Defenses of Chesapeake Bay. Reserve personnel in the Ninth Corps Area concurrently relieved. The 3d Bn. activated on 15 June 1941 at Fort Monroe. Location 7 December 1941—Fort Monroe, VA.

Status: Assigned to the Combat Arms Regimental System (CARS) as the 57th Air Defense Arty.

Events: 330

Commanders, 57th Coast Artillery Regiment

Lt. Col. Granville Sevier	11 January 1918–4 March 1918	Col. Frank S. Long*	13 October 1927–30 January 1928
Col. Elmore F. Austin	4 March 1918–16 October 1918	Maj. Royal K. Greene**	30 January 1928–18 April 1928
Col. Louis R. Burgess	16 October 1918–12 November 1918	Col. Elijah B. Martindale*	18 April 1928–1 December 1928
Col. Lawrence C. Brown	ao January 1920–2 August 1920	Maj. Royal K. Greene**	1 December 1928–15 March 1929
Lt. Col. Philip S. Golderman	2 August 1920–17 June 1921	Maj. Robert D. Brown**	15 March 1929–25 October 1930
Inactive	30 June 1921–19 June 1927	Lt. Col. William W. Breite**	25 October 1930–15 June 1940
Col. James F. Brady*	20 June 1927–13 October 1927	Col. Manning M. Kimmel	15 June 1940–22 July 1942

*RAI commanders: R.A. officers.
**RAI commanders: O.R. officers.

59th Coast Artillery Regiment (Heavy Tractor) (31st Coast Artillery Brigade)

HQ—Fort Winfield Scott, CA, 1919; Camp Lewis, WA, 1919–21; Fort Mills, PI, 1921–41

Arrived at the port of Hoboken on 24 January 1919 on the U.S.S. *Louisiana* as the 59th Arty., C.A.C., an element of the 31st Arty. Brig., C.A.C. (Heavy Tractor). Transferred the same day to Camp Upton, NY. Transferred on 16 February 1919 to Fort Winfield Scott, CA. Transferred on 4 October 1919 to Camp Lewis, WA. Reorganized on 1 August 1921 as a 155-mm G regiment. Transferred to the Philippine Department on 13 July 1921 and embarked on the U.S.A.T. *Sherman* at Tacoma, WA. Arrived on 13 August 1921 at Manila, PI. Concurrently, transferred to "Middleside" at Fort Mills, PI, and assigned to the Harbor Defenses of Manila and Subic Bays. Relieved in September 1921 from the 31st C.A. Brig. All elements of the regiment except HHB and Btrys A and B inactivated on 30 September 1922 at Fort Mills. Btrys G and H organized on 11 October 1922 with Philippine Scout personnel at Fort Mills. Redesignated on 30 June 1924 as the 59th C.A. Regt. (Heavy Tractor), and concurrently Btrys C, D, E, and F organized at Fort Mills. Concurrently Philippine Scout personnel transferred to the 92d C.A. and Btrys G and H inactivated. The crew of the U.S.A.M.P. *George F.E. Harrison* was assigned to HQ Btry from 30 June 1924 to 31 August 1927. Redesignated on 28 April 1926 as the 59th C.A. Regt. (Tractor Drawn). Though the 59th C.A. was a tractor-drawn regiment, its subordinate batteries manned fixed Harbor Defense positions at Forts Mills, Hughes, Frank, and Drum in Manila Harbor and at Fort Wint in Subic Bay, 1927–41. Awarded the US Coast Artillery Association Trophy for R.A. regiments for 1935, 1936, and 1937. The HHBs of the subordinate battalions activated on 20 May 1941 at Fort Mills. Location 7 December 1941—Fort Mills, PI.

Organization Day: 12 September.

Status: Assigned to the CARS as the 59th Air Defense Arty.

Events: 44, 51, 68, 122, 224, 245, 270

Commanders, 59th Coast Artillery Regiment

Col. Sydney Grant	29 December 1917–8 June 1918	Maj. Raymond E. Fenner	26 August 1927–20 September 1927
Col. James M. Wheeler	8 June 1918–ao July 1918	Lt. Col. Clarence G. Bunker	20 September 1927–2 May 1928
Col. Richard K. Cravens	ao December 1918–ao January 1919	Maj. John P. McCaskey Jr.	10 May 1928–15 June 1928
Col. Harry P. Wilbur	ao January 1920–30 July 1920	Maj. Harry L. King	15 June 1928–2 July 1928
Maj. Arthur H. Doig	30 July 1920–3 October 1920	Lt. Col. Earl Biscoe	2 July 1928– 4 October 1929
Lt. Col. Harry P. Wilbur	3 October 1920–15 December 1920	Col. Earle D'A. Pearce	4 October 1929–13 November 1931
Col. Earle D'A. Pearce	15 December 1920–13 July 1921	Lt. Col. James B. Taylor	13 November 1931–6 September 1933
Maj. Edgar H. Thompson	13 July 1921–26 September 1921	Lt. Col. Matthew A. Cross	6 September 1933–10 October 1934
Lt. Col. John L. Roberts	26 September 1921–November 1922	Maj. La Rhett L. Stuart	10 October 1934–1 December 1934
Maj. Edgar H. Thompson	November 1922–14 January 1923	Col. Allen Kimberly	1 December 1934–15 April 1935
Lt. Col. Frank S. Long	14 January 1923–14 July 1923	Col. Paul D. Bunker	15 April 1935–5 April 1937
Col. Percy P. Bishop	14 July 1923–1 January 1924	Lt. Col. Edward W. Turner	5 April 1937–3 July 1937
Lt. Col. Frank S. Long	1 January 1924–30 June 1924	Col. George Ruhlen	3 July 1937–19 July 1939
Col. Stanley Embick	30 June 1924–27 February 1926	Col. Robert P. Glassburn	19 July 1939–20 June 1940
Col. Samuel C. Vestal	27 February 1926–1 October 1926	Lt. Col. Napoleon Boudreau	20 June 1940–28 February 1941
Col. Harry C. Barnes	1 October 1926–26 August 1927	Col. Paul D. Bunker	28 February 1941–13 May 1942

60th Coast Artillery Regiment (Antiaircraft)

HQ—Fort Crockett, TX, 1922–23; Fort William McKinley, PI, 1923–1929; Fort Mills, PI, 1929–41.

Constituted in the R.A. on 26 October 1922 as the 60th Arty. Bn. (AA), C.A.C., assigned to the Harbor Defenses of Galveston, and concurrently activated at Fort Crockett, TX. Relieved from the Harbor Defenses of Galveston in April 1923 and assigned to the Philippine Department. Departed Galveston on 8 April 1923 on the U.S.A.T. *St. Mihiel* and arrived on 17 April 1923 at the Army Base Brooklyn. Departed Army Base Brooklyn on 27 April 1923 on the U.S.A.T. *Grant* and arrived on 24 May 1923 at Fort Winfield Scott, CA. Departed Fort Winfield Scott on 29 May 1923 on the U.S.A.T. *Thomas* and arrived on 24 June 1923 at Manila, PI. Transferred on 24 June 1923 to Fort William McKinley, PI. Expanded and redesignated on 1 July 1924 as the 60th C.A. Regt (AA). Subordinate elements constituted, organized, or redesignated as follows:

HQ Btry constituted on 1 July 1924 and concurrently activated at Fort William McKinley.

Service Btry constituted on 1 July 1924 (inactive).

HQ Detachment (Det.) and Combat Train, 1st Bn. organized on 26 October 1922 by redesignation of 127th Co., C.A.C. as HQ Det. and Combat Train, 60th Arty. Bn. (AA), C.A.C.; redesignated HQ Det. and Combat Train, 1st Bn. at Fort William McKinley; inactivated on 31 August 1925 at Fort William McKinley; activated on 1 April 1929 at Fort Mills.

Btry A organized on 1 July 1924 by redesignation of 128th Co., C.A.C. at Fort William McKinley; transferred on 1 April 1929 to Fort Mills.

Btry B organized on 1 July 1924 by redesignation of 77th Co., C.A.C. at Fort William McKinley; transferred on 1 April 1929 to Fort Mills.

Btry C organized on 1 July 1924 by redesignation of 80th Co., C.A.C. at Fort William McKinley; inactivated on 31 August 1925 at Fort William McKinley; activated on 1 April 1929 at Fort Mills.

Btry D constituted on 1 July 1924 (inactive); activated on 1 April 1929 at Fort Mills.

HQ Det., 2d Bn. constituted on 1 July 1924 (inactive).

Btry E constituted on 1 July 1924 (inactive); activated on 31 August 1925 at Fort William McKinley; transferred on 1 April 1929 to Fort Mills.

Btry F constituted on 1 July 1924 (inactive); activated on 1 April 1929 at Fort Mills.

Btry G constituted on 1 July 1924 (inactive); activated on 1 April 1929 at Fort Mills.

Btry H constituted on 1 July 1924 (inactive); activated on 1 April 1929 at Fort Mills.

Regimental HHB activated on 31 August 1925 at Fort McKinley, PI. Regiment transferred to Fort Mills on 1 April 1929 and further assigned to the Harbor Defenses of Manila and Subic Bays. The regiment was billeted at "Topside" on Corregidor. Consolidated on 21 November 1936 with the 60th Arty., C.A.C. (a World War I unit organized in the R.A. on 19 December 1917 at Fort Monroe, VA; arrived at the port of New York, NY, on 4 February 1919 on the S.S. *Cedric*; demobilized on 24 February 1919 at Fort Washington, MD; reconstituted on 21 November 1936). Location 7 December 1941—Fort Mills, PI.

Organization Day: 26 October. Chosen to commemorate the regiment's reactivation at Fort Crockett, TX, on 26 October 1922.

Status: Assigned to the CARS as the 60th Air Defense Arty.

Events: 44, 51, 68, 122, 224, 245, 270

Commanders, 60th Coast Artillery Regiment

Maj. Stewart O. Elting	31 October 1922–1 June 1924
Maj. John T.H. O'Rear	30 June 1924–14 July 1925
Maj. Charles B. Meyer	14 July 1925–7 July 1928
Capt. Donald L. Dutton	7 July 1928–21 October 1928
Lt. Col. Franc Lecocoq	21 October 1928–4 March 1930
Col. George T. Perkins	4 March 1930–27 April 1932
Maj. Robert M. Perkins	27 April 1932–17 June 1932
Lt. Col. Benjamin Booth	17 June 1932–15 October 1932
Col. Frederick L. Dengler	15 October 1932–31 July 1933
Lt. Col. Benjamin Booth	31 July 1933–29 September 1933
Lt. Col. Howard K. Loughry	29 September 1933–15 April 1935
Col. Allen Kimberly	15 April 1935–2 December 1936
Lt. Col. Franklin Kemble	2 December 1936–15 April 1937
Capt. William L. Richardson	15 April 1937–1 May 1937
Col. James H. Cunningham	1 May 1937–19 September 1938
Maj. John H. Harrington	19 September 1938–4 November 1938
Col. William C. Koenig	4 November 1938–November 1940
Col. John L. Holcombe	November 1940–1 March 1941
Col. Theodore M. Chase	1 March 1941–6 May 1942

61st Coast Artillery Regiment (Antiaircraft)

HQ—Fort Monroe, VA, 1921–1930; Fort Sheridan, IL, 1930–41

Reconstituted in the R.A. on 1 July 1921 as the 1st AA Arty. Bn., C.A.C., assigned to the Harbor Defenses of Chesapeake Bay, and concurrently activated with Btrys A, B, and E at Fort Monroe, VA. Redesignated as the 61st Arty. Bn. (AA), C.A.C. on 1 June 1922. Expanded, reorganized, and redesignated 61st Arty. Regt. (AA), C.A.C. on 14 September 1922. Redesignated on 1 July 1924 as the 61st C.A. Regt. (AA). Subordinate elements constituted, organized, or redesignated as follows:

HQ Btry organized on 1 July 1921 by reorganization and redesignation of 9th Co., Coast Defenses of Chesapeake Bay as HQ Det. and Combat Train, 1st Arty. Bn. (AA), C.A.C.; redesignated on 1 June 1922 as HQ Det. and Combat Train, 61st Arty. Bn. (AA), C.A.C. (additional designation as 140th Co., C.A.C.); redesignated HQ Btry, 61st C.A. Regt. (AA) at Fort Monroe.

Service Btry constituted new on 1 July 1924 (inactive); activated on 18 November 1939 at Fort Sheridan.

HQ Det. and Combat Train, 1st Bn. constituted new on 14 September 1922 (inactive); activated on 18 November 1939 at Fort Sheridan.

Btry A organized on 1 July 1921 by redesignation of 6th Co., Coast Defenses of Chesapeake Bay as Searchlight Btry, 1st Arty. Bn. (AA), C.A.C. active at Fort Monroe; redesignated on 1 June 1922 as Btry A, 61st Arty. Bn. (AA), C.A.C. (additional designation as 6th Co., C.A.C.); redesignated on 1 July 1924 as Btry A, 61st C.A. Regt. (AA); transferred on 14 May 1930 to Fort Sheridan.

Btry B organized on 1 July 1921 by redesignation of 5th Co., Coast Defenses of Chesapeake Bay as Gun Btry, 1st Arty. Bn. (AA), C.A.C. active at Fort Monroe; redesignated on 1 June 1922 as Btry B, 61st Arty. Bn. (AA), C.A.C. (additional designation as 257th Co., C.A.C.); redesignated on 1 July 1924 as Btry B, 61st C.A. Regt. (AA); transferred on 14 May 1930 to Fort Sheridan.

Btry C constituted new on 1 July 1924 (inactive); activated on 18 November 1939 at Fort Sheridan.

Btry D constituted new on 1 July 1924 (inactive); activated on 18 November 1939 at Fort Sheridan.

HQ Det., 2d Bn. constituted new on 14 September 1922 (inactive); activated on 28 November 1939 at Fort Sheridan.

Btry E organized on 1 July 1921 by redesignation of 8th Co., Coast Defenses of Chesapeake Bay as Machine Gun (MG) Btry, 1st Arty. Bn. (AA), C.A.C. active at Fort Monroe; redesignated on 1 June 1922 as Btry C, 61st Arty. Bn. (AA), C.A.C. (additional designation as 257th Co., C.A.C.); redesignated on 1 July 1924 as Btry E, 61st C.A. Regt. (AA); transferred on 14 May 1930 to Fort Sheridan.

Btry F constituted new on 1 July 1924 (inactive); activated on 28 November 1939 at Fort Sheridan.

Btry G constituted new on 1 July 1924 (inactive); activated on 28 November 1939 at Fort Sheridan.

Btry H constituted new on 1 July 1924 (inactive); activated on 28 November 1939 at Fort Sheridan.

Regiment, less active elements, allotted to the Third Corps Area on 28 February 1927 for mobilization purposes. Relieved from the Harbor Defenses of Chesapeake Bay on 14 May 1930, and assigned to the Sixth Corps Area. Concurrently inactive elements withdrawn from the Third Corps Area and allotted to the Sixth Corps Area for mobilization purposes. The regiment conducted a 1,125-mile motor march from Fort Monroe to Fort Sheridan, 28 May–13 June 1930. Assigned to the 41st C.A. Brig. (Second Army) on 1 October 1933. Consolidated on 16 October 1936 with the 61st Arty., C.A.C. (organized in the R.A. in May 1918 at Fort Moultrie, SC; arrived at the port of New York on 17 February 1919 on the S.S. *Dante Alighieri*; demobilized in late February 1919 at Camp Upton, NY; reconstituted on 16 October 1936). Habitually trained the O.R. antiaircraft units assigned to the Third Corps Area, 1921–29, and those of the Fifth and Sixth Corps Areas, 1930–40. Reserve officers assigned to the regiment conducted summer training with the regiment at Fort Sheridan. Regiment, less 1st Bn., transferred on 16 October 1939 to Fort Williams, ME. Concurrently 1st Bn. transferred to the Panama Canal Zone. Entire regiment returned to Fort Sheridan by October 1940. Location 7 December 1941—Fort Sheridan, IL.

Organization Day: 1 July. Chosen to commemorate the regiment's reconstitution and activation on 1 July 1924. Adopted on 4 June 1928.

Status: Assigned to the CARS as the 61st Air Defense Arty.

Events: 25, 59, 73, 86, 128, 165, 186, 214, 255, 258, 264, 268, 274, 283, 295, 296, 302, 316, 323, 324, 330

Commanders, 61st Coast Artillery Regiment

Maj. Oliver L. Spiller	1 July 1921–3 January 1924	Maj. Evan C. Seaman	1 November 1933–31 January 1934
Maj. John S. Smylie	3 January 1924–21 February 1924	Lt. Col. Charles B. Meyer	1 February 1934–15 October 1936
Maj. William E. Shedd Jr.	21 February 1924–11 September 1925	Maj. Marvil G. Armstrong	15 October 1936–10 March 1937
Maj. Alden G. Strong	11 September 1925–5 June 1928	Col. Arthur G. Campbell	10 March 1937–4 January 1939
Maj. Robert E. Guthrie	16 June 1928–15 August 1929	Maj. Marvil G. Armstrong	4 January 1939–22 June 1939
Maj. James H. Cunningham	15 August 1929–2 July 1931	Col. John L. Homer	22 June 1939–16 April 1941
Lt. Col. Joseph A. Green	2 July 1931–1 November 1933	Col. Carl E. Hocker	16 April 1941–6 January 1942

62d Coast Artillery Regiment (Antiaircraft)

HQ—Fort Totten, NY, 1921–41

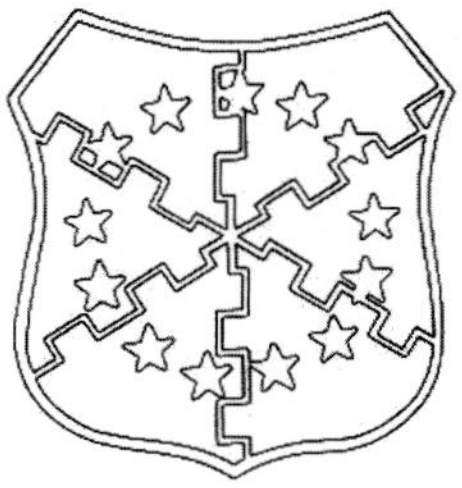

Constituted in the R.A. on 1 August 1921 as the 2d AA Arty. Bn., C.A.C., assigned to the Harbor Defenses of Eastern New York. Redesignated as the 62d Arty. Bn. (AA), C.A.C. on 1 June 1922. Expanded, reorganized, and redesignated 62d Arty. Regt. (AA), C.A.C. on 14 September 1922. Subordinate elements constituted, organized, or redesignated as follows:

HQ Btry organized by redesignation of 9th Co., C.A.C. and concurrently activated at Fort Totten.

Service Btry organized by redesignation of 37th Co., C.A.C. and concurrently activated at Fort Totten.

HQ Det. and Combat Train, 1st Bn. constituted on 1 August 1921 as HQ Det. and Combat Train, 2d Arty. Bn. (AA), C.A.C.; organized on 4 September 1921 at Fort Totten; redesignated on 1 June 1922 as HQ Det. and Combat Train, 62d Arty. Bn. (AA), C.A.C.; redesignated on 1 July 1924 as HQ Det. and Combat Train, 1st Bn., 62d C.A. Regt. (AA).

Btry A organized on 14 September 1922 by redesignation of 82d Co., C.A.C. and concurrently activated at Fort Totten.

Btry B organized on 14 September 1922 by redesignation of 17th Co., C.A.C. and concurrently activated at Fort Totten.

Btry C organized on 14 September 1922 by redesignation of 29th Co., C.A.C. and concurrently activated at Fort Totten.

Btry D organized on 14 September 1922 by redesignation of 32d Co., C.A.C. (inactive); activated on 1 July 1939 at Fort Totten.

HQ Det., 2d Bn. constituted on 14 September 1922 and concurrently activated at Fort Totten, NY.

Btry E organized on 14 September 1922 by redesignation of 30th Co., C.A.C. and concurrently activated at Fort Totten.

Btry F organized on 14 September 1922 by redesignation of 32d Co., C.A.C. and concurrently activated at Fort Totten.

Btry G organized on 14 September 1922 by redesignation of 165th Co., C.A.C. (inactive); activated on 1 July 1939 at Fort Totten.

Btry H organized on 14 September 1922 by redesignation of 167th Co., C.A.C. (inactive); activated on 1 July 1939 at Fort Totten.

Redesignated on 1 July 1924 as the 62d C.A. Regt. (AA). Assigned to the 32d C.A. Brig. (First Army) on 1 October 1933. Awarded the US Coast Artillery Association Trophy for R.A. regiments for 1936. Btry F awarded the Knox Trophy for C.A. in 1936. Habitually trained the O.R. antiaircraft units assigned to the Second Corps Area, 1921–41. Reserve officers assigned to the regiment conducted summer training with the regiment at Fort Tilden. Reserve officers also conducted C.A. CMTC training at Fort Hancock, NJ, in 1939. Relieved from the 32d C.A. Brig. and assigned to the 39th C.A. Brig. on 10 February 1941. Location 7 December 1941—Fort Totten, NY.

Organization Day: 28 October. Chosen to commemorate the regiment's participation in the battle of White Plains, NY, on 28 October 1776.

Status: Assigned to the USARS as the 62d Air Defense Arty.

Events: 49, 87, 93, 103, 149, 165, 187, 190, 252, 255, 268, 280, 283, 293, 296, 301

Commanders, 62d Coast Artillery Regiment

Maj. Theodore M. Chase	1 August 1921–10 February 1922	Col. Edward Kimmel	20 July 1930–29 April 1932
Capt. William M. Cravens	10 February 1922–5 April 1922	Col. Arthur S. Conklin	30 April 1932–22 August 1934
Maj. John B. Maynard	5 April 1922–4 November 1922	Lt. Col. Clair W. Baird	22 August 1934–1 September 1934
Col. Charles H. Hilton	4 November 1922–July 1924	Col. Frank K. Fergusson	1 September 1934–18 July 1937
Col. Marcellus G. Spinks	July 1924–1 December 1927	Lt. Col. Eli E. Bennett	18 July 1937–5 October 1937
Maj. Paul D. Bunker	1 December 1927–25 January 1929	Col. Henry W.T. Eglin	6 October 1937–9 April 1937
Col. Harry C. Barnes	25 January 1929–21 November 1929	Lt. Col. Charles R. Finley	9 April 1939–15 September 1939
Lt. Col. John M. Dunn	21 November 1929–20 July 1930	Col. Oliver L. Spiller	15 September 1939–30 September 1940
Col. Rodney H. Smith	1 November 1940–11 December 1941		

63d Coast Artillery Regiment (Antiaircraft)

HQ—Fort Winfield Scott, CA, 1921–30; Fort MacArthur, CA, 1930–41

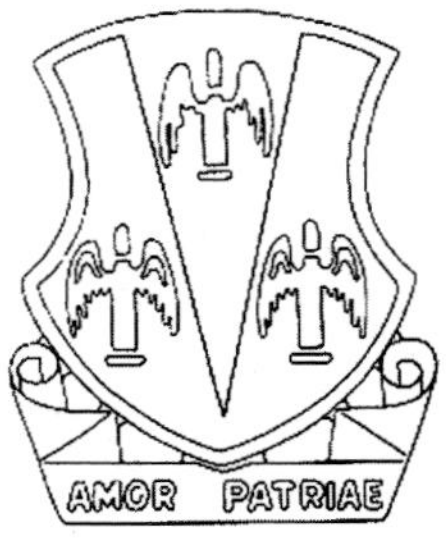

Constituted in the R.A. on 16 September 1921 as the 3d AA Arty. Bn., C.A.C., assigned to the Harbor Defenses of Los Angeles, and activated at Fort Winfield Scott, CA. Redesignated as the 63d Arty. Bn. (AA), C.A.C. on 1 June 1922. Expanded, reorganized, and redesignated on 14 September 1922 as the 63d Arty. Regt. (AA), C.A.C. Redesignated on 1 July 1924 as the 63d C.A. Regt. (AA). Subordinate elements constituted, organized, or redesignated as follows:

HQ Btry constituted new on 14 September 1922 (inactive); organized on 1 July 1924 at Fort Winfield Scott; transferred on 3 March 1930 to Fort MacArthur, CA.

Service Btry constituted new on 1 July 1924 (inactive); activated on 12 October 1939 at Fort MacArthur.

HQ Det. and Combat Train, 1st Bn. reconstituted on 16 September 1921 as HQ Det. and Combat Train, 3d Arty. Bn. (AA), C.A.C.; redesignated on 1 June 1922 as HQ Det. and Combat Train, 63d Arty. Bn. (AA), C.A.C. (additional designation as 259th Co., C.A.C.); redesignated on 1 July 1924 as HQ Det. and Combat Train, 1st Bn., 63d C.A. Regt. (AA) and inactivated at Fort Winfield Scott; activated on 12 October 1939 at Fort MacArthur.

Btry A constituted on 16 September 1921 as Searchlight Btry, 3d Arty. Bn. (AA), C.A.C. and activated at Fort Winfield Scott; redesignated on 1 June 1922 as Btry A, 63d Arty. Bn. (AA), C.A.C. (additional designation as 260th Co., C.A.C.); redesignated on 1 July 1924 as Btry A, 63d C.A. Regt. (AA); transferred on 3 March 1930 to Fort MacArthur.

Btry B constituted on 16 September 1921 as Gun Btry, 3d Arty. Bn. (AA), C.A.C. and activated at Fort Winfield Scott; redesignated on 1 June 1922 as Btry B, 63d Arty. Bn. (AA), C.A.C. (additional designation as 262d Co., C.A.C.); redesignated on 1 July 1924 as Btry B, 63d C.A. Regt. (AA); transferred on 3 March 1930 to Fort MacArthur.

Btry C constituted on 16 September 1921 as MG Btry, 3d Arty. Bn. (AA), C.A.C. and activated at Fort Winfield Scott; redesignated on 1 June 1922 as Btry B, 63d Arty. Bn. (AA), C.A.C. (additional designation as 262d Co., C.A.C.); redesignated on 1 July 1924 as Btry B, 63d C.A. Regt. (AA); transferred on 3 March 1930 to Fort MacArthur.

Btry D constituted new on 1 July 1924 (inactive).

HQ Det., 2d Bn. reconstituted on 1 July 1924 (inactive); activated on 12 October 1939 at Fort MacArthur.

Btry E constituted new on 1 July 1924 and activated at Fort Winfield Scott; transferred on 3 March 1930 to Fort MacArthur.

Btry F constituted new on 1 July 1924 (inactive); activated on 12 October 1939 at Fort MacArthur.

Btry G constituted new on 1 July 1924 (inactive); activated on 12 October 1939 at Fort MacArthur.

Btry H constituted new on 1 July 1924 (inactive); activated on 12 October 1939 at Fort MacArthur.

Relieved from the Harbor Defenses of San Francisco on 3 March 1930, assigned to the Harbor Defenses of Los Angeles, and transferred to Fort MacArthur. The regiment conducted a 500-mile motor march from Fort Winfield Scott to Fort MacArthur, 3–15 March 1930. Responsible for the support and administration of the Fort MacArthur CCC District, 1933–39. Provided the honor guard and security for the visit of the Honorable George H. Dern, Secretary of War, on his visit to Fort MacArthur on 29 July 1933 to review activities of the CCC. Habitually trained the O.R. antiaircraft units assigned to the Ninth Corps Area, 1921–41. Btrys E, A, and B awarded the Knox Trophy for C.A. in 1928, 1936, and 1939, respectively. Regiment awarded the US Coast Artillery Association Trophy for R.A. regiments for 1939. Location 7 December 1941—Fort MacArthur, CA.

Events: 34, 76, 116, 142, 154, 195, 227, 231, 238, 289, 319, 335

Commanders, 63d Coast Artillery Regiment

Maj. John S. Pratt	2 July 1924–15 May 1925
Maj. Robert R. Welshmer	15 May 1925–23 October 1926
Capt. Horace L. Whittaker	23 October 1926–8 January 1927
Lt. Col. Frederick L. Dengler	8 January 1927–8 August 1928
Lt. Col. Carr W. Waller	8 August 1928–18 August 1930
Maj. Felix E. Gross	18 August 1930–4 February 1931
Lt. Col. Matthew A. Cross	4 February 1931–1 September 1932
Maj. Avery J. French	1 September 1932–9 September 1932
Lt. Col. Myron S. Crissy	9 September 1932–20 March 1933
Maj. Avery J. French	20 March 1933–17 June 1933
Lt. Col. Homer Oldfield	17 June 1933–22 July 1936
Lt. Col. Robert D. Brown	22 July 1936–29 August 1936
Lt. Col. Claude M. Thiele	29 August 1936–6 September 1938
Maj. Harold P. Detwiler	6 September 1938–2 February 1939
Col. Edward A. Stockton Jr.	2 February 1939–7 November 1940
Lt. Col. Martin J. O'Brien	7 November 1940–January 1941
Col. Cedric M.S. Skene	January 1941– ao August 1943

64th Coast Artillery Regiment (Antiaircraft)

HQ—Fort Shafter, TH, 1921–41

Constituted in the R.A. on 2 May 1921 as the Hawaiian Antiaircraft Regiment and assigned to the Hawaiian Coast Artillery District. Regiment activated on 3 June 1921 at Fort Shafter, TH. Reorganized and redesignated on 2 June 1922 as the 64th Arty. Regt. (AA), C.A.C. Subordinate batteries given additional designations as the 263d—273d C.A. Cos., C.A.C. Redesignated on 1 July 1924 as the 64th C.A. Regt. (AA). Assigned to the Hawaiian Separate C.A. Brig. on 1 March 1925. HQ Det. and Combat Train, 3d Bn. and Btry I constituted on 31 October 1925 and activated at Fort Shafter, TH. Btrys K and L constituted and activated on 1 July 1928 at Fort Shafter. Assisted the rescue of civilians from Mauna Loa Gardens and the Kahili District from lava flows after a volcanic eruption, 18–19 November 1930. Btry B awarded the Knox Trophy for Coast Artillery in 1935. Consolidated on 5 October 1936 with the 64th Arty. Regt., C.A.C. (a World War I unit organized in January 1918 at Tampa, FL; arrived at the port of Newport News in March 1919; demobilized in April 1919 at Camp Eustis, VA; reconstituted on 5 October 1936). Regiment awarded the US Coast Artillery Association Trophy for R.A. regiments for 1938. Location 7 December 1941—Fort Shafter, TH.

Organization Day: 3 June. Chosen to commemorate the regiment's activation at Fort Shafter on 3 June 1921.

Events: 33, 37, 75, 88, 120, 138, 141, 158, 160, 189, 211, 225, 248, 276, 291, 297, 312

Commanders, 64th Coast Artillery Regiment

Lt. Col. Robert F. Woods	3 June 1921–September 1922	Lt. Col. William W. Hicks	4 September 1933–29 November 1933
Col. Robert E. Wyllie	September 1922–17 June 1924	Col. Willis G. Peace	29 November 1933–7 December 1936
Maj. Harry W. Stark	17 June 1924–16 September 1924	Col. Ralph M. Mitchell	8 December 1936–6 October 1938
Col. Charles H. Hilton	16 September 1924–20 May 1927	Col. Francis P. Hardaway	6 October 1938–12 November 1938
Maj. Edward P. Noyes	20 May 1927–24 August 1927	Lt. Col. Ferdinand F. Gallagher	12 November 1938–16 December 1938
Lt. Col. William A. Covington	24 August 1927–7 October 1927	Col. Sanderford Jarman	16 December 1938–18 March 1939
Col. Granville Sevier	7 October 1927–29 October 1930	Lt. Col. Ferdinand F. Gallagher	18 March 1939–30 June 1939
Col. Richard H. Williams	29 October 1930–4 September 1933	Col. Charles K. Wing	30 June 1939–August 1941
	Col. Hollis LeR. Muller	August 1941–ao April 1942	

65th Coast Artillery Regiment (Antiaircraft)

HQ—Fort Amador, CZ, 1924–32; *Inactive,* 1932–38; Fort Winfield Scott, CA, 1938–41; Camp Haan, CA, 1941

Arrived at the port of Philadelphia on 30 January 1919 on the S.S. *Haverford* as the 65th Arty., C.A.C., an element of the 32d Arty. Brig., C.A.C. Demobilized on 28 February 1919 at Camp Lewis, WA. Reconstituted in the R.A. on 1 July 1924 as the 65th C.A. Regt. (AA) and assigned to the Harbor Defenses of Balboa. HQ concurrently organized at Fort Amador, CZ. Subordinate elements constituted, organized, or redesignated as follows:

HQ Btry organized on 1 July 1924 by redesignation of 144th Co., C.A.C. and concurrently activated at Fort Amador; inactivated on 15 April 1932 at Fort Amador; activated on 1 June 1938 at Fort Winfield Scott.

Service Btry organized on 1 July 1924 by redesignation of 70th Co., C.A.C. (inactive); activated on 11 October 1939 at Fort Winfield Scott.

HQ Det. and Combat Train, 1st Bn. organized on 1 July 1924 by redesignation of 119th Co., C.A.C. (inactive); activated on 1 May 1930 at Fort Amador; inactivated on 15 April 1932 at Fort Amador; activated on 1 June 1938 at Fort Winfield Scott.

Btry A organized on 1 July 1924 by redesignation of 116th Co., C.A.C. and concurrently activated at Fort Amador; inactivated on 15 April 1932 at Fort Amador; activated on 1 June 1938 at Fort Winfield Scott.

Btry B organized on 1 July 1924 by redesignation of 87th Co., C.A.C. and concurrently activated at Fort Amador; inactivated on 15 April 1932 at Fort Amador; activated on 1 June 1938 at Fort Winfield Scott.

Btry C organized on 1 July 1924 by redesignation of 195th Co., C.A.C. and concurrently activated at Fort Randolph; inactivated on 15 April 1932 at Fort Randolph; activated on 11 October 1939 at Fort Winfield Scott.

Btry D organized on 1 July 1924 by redesignation of 124th Co., C.A.C. and concurrently activated at Fort Sherman.

HQ Det., 2d Bn. constituted on 1 July 1924 (inactive); activated on 1 May 1930 at Fort Randolph; inactivated on 15 April 1932 at Fort Randolph; activated on 11 October 1939 at Fort Winfield Scott.

Btry E organized on 1 July 1924 by redesignation of 194th Co., C.A.C. (inactive); activated on 31 July 1926 at Fort Randolph; inactivated on 15 April 1932 at Fort Randolph; activated on 1 June 1938 at Fort Winfield Scott.

Btry F organized on 1 July 1924 by redesignation of 89th Co., C.A.C. (inactive); activated on 31 July 1926 at Fort Amador; inactivated on 15 April 1932 at Fort Amador; activated on 11 October 1939 at Fort Winfield Scott.

Btry G organized by redesignation of 193d Co., C.A.C. (inactive); activated on 11 October 1939 at Fort Winfield Scott.

Btry H organized on 1 July 1924 by redesignation of 192d Co., C.A.C. (inactive); activated on 11 October 1939 at Fort Winfield Scott.

Btry I constituted on 1 May 1930 (inactive).

Btry C awarded the Knox Trophy for C.A. in 1927. Regiment inactivated on 15 April 1932 in the Canal Zone and personnel transferred to the 1st and 4th C.A. Regts. Withdrawn from the Panama Canal Department on 1 June 1938 and allotted to the Ninth Corps Area. Concurrently regimental HHB, 1st Bn. HHB, and Btrys A, B, and E activated at Fort Winfield Scott, CA. Assigned to the 37th C.A. Brig., but attached to the Harbor Defenses of San Francisco for command and control during peacetime. Reserve officers assigned to the regiment conducted summer training with the regiment's active elements at Fort Winfield Scott. Remainder of the regiment activated on 11 October 1939 at Fort Winfield Scott. Attached to the Fourth Army on 30 December 1940. Regiment transferred on 16 January 1941 to Camp Haan, CA. Transferred on 5 December 1941 to Los Angeles, CA. Location 7 December 1941—Los Angeles, CA.

Status: Assigned to the CARS as the 65th Air Defense Arty.

Events: 36, 40, 43, 102, 289, 304, 335

Commanders, 65th Coast Artillery Regiment

Col. John T. Geary	1 July 1924–18 July 1925	Col. Ralph M. Mitchell	31 October 1930–15 April 1932
Col. Wilmer S. Phillips	18 July 1925–9 October 1925	*Inactive*	15 April 1932–31 May 1938
Maj. Homer R. Oldfield	9 October 1925–23 September 1928	Col. Henry T. Burgin	1 June 1938–18 June 1938
Maj. Otto H. Schrader	23 September 1928–15 October 1928	Col. John T. H. O'Rear	29 June 1938–12 March 1940
Lt. Col. Louis C. Brinton	15 October 1928–31 October 1930	Col. James B. Crawford	12 March 1940–2 January 1941
	Col. Henry C. Davis	2 January 1941–ao December 1941	

66th Coast Artillery Regiment (Antiaircraft) — Regular Army Inactive

HQ—Camp Upton, NY, 1919; *Inactive,* 1926–41

Arrived at the port of New York on 5 March 1919 on the U.S.S. *Powhatan* as the 66th Arty., C.A.C., an element of the 35th Arty. Brig., C.A.C. Transferred on 5 March 1919 to Camp Mills, NY. Transferred about 10 March 1919 to Camp Upton, NY. Demobilized on 20 March 1919 at Camp Upton. Reconstituted in the R.A. on 22 January 1926 as the 66th C.A. Regt. (AA) and allotted to the Panama Canal Department. The 65th C.A. designated as Active Associate,

1926–27. Withdrawn from the Panama Canal Department in 1940 and allotted to the Puerto Rican Department. The 1st Bn. was activated on 1 February 1940 at Camp Buchanan, PR, with personnel and equipment from the inactivated 1st Bn., 69th C.A. Location 7 December 1941—*Inactive*, less 1st Bn.

Events: 329

Commanders, 66th Coast Artillery Regiment

1st Battalion

Lt. Col. Otto G. Pitz	10 February 1940–ao December 1941

67th Coast Artillery Regiment (Antiaircraft) — Regular Army Inactive

HQ—Presidio of San Francisco, CA, 1919; *Inactive,* 1926–27; Atlanta, GA, 1927–41; Fort Bragg, NC, 1941

Arrived at the port of New York on 2 March 1919 on the U.S.S. *America* as the 67th Artillery, C.A.C., an element of the 35th Arty. Brig., C.A.C. Transferred on 2 March 1919 to Camp Mills, NY. Transferred about 10 March 1919 to the Presidio of San Francisco, CA. Demobilized on 23 April 1919 at the Presidio of San Francisco. Reconstituted in the R.A. on 22 January 1926 as the 67th C.A. Regt. (AA) and allotted to the Second Corps Area. The 61st C.A. designated as Active Associate, 1926–27. Withdrawn from the Second Corps Area on 19 February 1927 and allotted to the Fourth Corps Area. Regiment, less the 2d Bn. (MG), affiliated with the Georgia Institute of Technology ROTC and organized on 2 June 1927 as an RAI unit with R.A. personnel assigned to the ROTC Det. and Reserve officers commissioned from the program. Concurrently, the 2d Bn. affiliated with and organized at The Citadel in Charleston, SC. Designated mobilization station was Camp Shelby, MS. Conducted summer training at Fort Barrancas, FL. Also conducted C.A. CMTC training some years at Fort Barrancas as an alternate form of annual training. The 1st Bn. was activated on 1 July 1940 at Fort Bragg, NC. Remainder of the regiment activated, less Reserve personnel, at Fort Bragg on 10 February 1941. Assigned to the 34th C.A. Brig. (AA) on 10 February 1941. Location 7 December 1941—Fort Bragg, NC.

Status: Assigned to the CARS as the 67th Air Defense Arty.

Events: 327, 330, 334

Commanders, 67th Coast Artillery Regiment

Col. Earle D'A. Pearce*	17 June 1927–31 December 1929
Lt. Col. Olin H. Longino*	31 December 1929–24 June 1932
Col. Marcellus G. Spinks*	24 June 1932–18 January 1933
Lt. Col. Olin H. Longino*	19 January 1933–June 1934
Maj. Samuel Lapham Jr.**	June 1934–2 August 1934
Unknown	2 August 1934–2 May 1935
Capt. Raiford F. Watkins**	25 May 1935–ao June 1935
Unknown	ao June 1935–ao January 1937
Lt. Col. Thomas H. Jones**	ao January 1937–6 March 1938
Lt. Col. Clarence N. Touart**	6 March 1938–30 October 1938
Lt. Col. Felix E. Gross**	30 October 1938–10 February 1941
Lt. Col. Robert E. Turley Jr.	10 February 1941–May 1941
Lt. Col. James P. Hogan	May 1941–9 December 1941

*RAI commanders: R.A. officers who were concurrently PMS&T at the Georgia Institute of Technology.
**RAI commanders: O.R. officers.

68th Coast Artillery Regiment (Antiaircraft) **Regular Army Inactive**

HQ—Fort Wadsworth, NY, 1919; *Not organized,* 1926–28; Cambridge, MA, 1928–39; Fort Williams, ME, 1939–40; Camp Edwards, MA, 1940–41

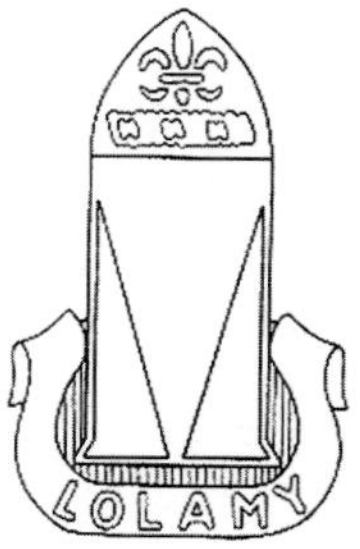

Arrived at the port of Hoboken on the U.S.S. *Matsonia* on 3 February 1919 as the 68th Arty., C.A.C., an element of the 36th Arty. Brig., C.A.C. Transferred on 3 February 1919 to Camp Mills, NY. Transferred to Fort Wadsworth, NY. Demobilized on 1 March 1919 at Fort Wadsworth. Reconstituted in the R.A. on 22 January 1926 as the 68th C.A. (AA) and allotted to the Second Corps Area. The 62d C.A. designated as Active Associate, 1926–27. Withdrawn from the Second Corps Area on 28 February 1927 and allotted to the First Corps Area for mobilization purposes. Organized on 29 June 1927 as an RAI unit with O.R. personnel at Cambridge, MA. Affiliated with the Massachusetts Institute of Technology ROTC and organized as an RAI unit in 1930 with R.A. personnel assigned to the ROTC Det. and Reserve officers commissioned from the program. Assigned on 1 October 1933 to the I Corps. Conducted summer training most years at Fort H.G. Wright, NY, and some years at Fort Andrews, MA. Also conducted C.A. CMTC training some years at Fort H.G. Wright, NY, or Fort Adams, RI, as an alternate form of annual training. Relieved from the I Corps in 1939 and assigned to the 36th C.A. Brig. (AA) (GHQR). The regiment, less 1st Bn., activated on 4 November 1939 at Fort Williams, ME, and attached to First Army. The 1st Bn. activated on 15 November 1939 at Fort Williams. Regiment transferred in October 1940 to Camp Edwards, MA. Location 7 December 1941—Camp Edwards, MA.

Status: Assigned to the CARS as the 68th Air Defense Arty.

Events: 301, 323, 330

Commanders, 68th Coast Artillery Regiment

Lt. Col. Robert C. Eddy*	29 June 1927–ao July 1927	Maj. Augustus J. Beaupre**	1 July 1937–4 November 1939
Col. Hunter C. White**	ao July 1928–August 1933	Lt. Col. Paul H. French	4 November 1939–5 December 1939
Maj. Arthur J. Maxfield**	August 1933–1 July 1937	Col. Robert C. Garrett	5 December 1939–26 September 1940
Col. Charles B. Meyer	26 September 1940–14 October 1941		

*RAI commanders: R.A. officers who were concurrently PMS&T at the Massachusetts Institute of Technology.
**RAI commanders: O.R. officers.

69th Coast Artillery Regiment (Antiaircraft)

HQ—Camp Eustis, VA, 1919; *Inactive,* 1926–27; Fort Eustis, VA, 1927–30; Aberdeen Proving Ground, MD, 1930; Fort McClellan, AL, 1930–35; Fort Crockett, TX, 1935–41; Camp Hulen, TX, 1941

Arrived at the port of Newport News on 16 February 1919 on the U.S.S. *Mercury* as the 69th Arty., C.A.C., an element of the 36th Arty. Brig., C.A.C. Transferred to Camp Eustis, VA, where it was demobilized in March 1919. Reconstituted in the R.A. on 22 January 1926 as the 69th C.A. (AA) and allotted to the Ninth Corps Area. The 63d C.A. designated as Active Associate, 1926–27. Withdrawn from the Ninth Corps Area on 28 February 1927 and allotted to the Third Corps Area for mobilization purposes. Regiment organized by June 1927 as an RAI unit with O.R. personnel at Fort Eustis, VA. Regimental HHB and Btrys A, B, and E activated on 1 February 1930 at Aberdeen Proving Ground, MD. Transferred to Fort McClellan, AL, on 13 November 1930 and assigned to the Fourth Coast Artillery District. Regiment conducted a 1,025-mile motorized march, 13 November–2 December 1930, from Aberdeen to Fort McClellan. In April 1933, the regiment assumed command and control of CCC District D, Fourth Corps Area and relinquished responsibility to the 22d Infantry (Inf.) in March 1935. Transferred to Fort Crockett, TX, on 25 March 1935 and assigned to the Harbor Defenses of Galveston. Regiment conducted an unusual 1,400-mile motorized march, 28 June–7 July 1937, along the route: Galveston–Camp Bullis–Fort Clark–Austin–Dallas–College Station–Fort Crockett. Habitually trained the O.R. AA units of the Fourth Corps Area, 1930–34, and of the Eighth Corps Area, 1935–39. Reserve officers assigned to the regiment conducted summer training with the regiment at Camp Knox, KY, in 1930 and at Fort Crockett beginning in 1935. Btrys E and B awarded the Knox Trophy for Coast Artillery in 1933 and 1937, respectively. The 1st and 2d Bn. HHBs activated on

9 September 1939 and 4 October 1939, respectively, at Fort Crockett. Concurrently, inactive subordinate batteries activated. The 1st Bn. sailed from Galveston on the U.S.A.T. *St. Mihiel* to San Juan, PR, and arrived there on 9 October 1939. The battalion was attached to the Puerto Rican Department on arrival. The 1st Bn. was inactivated at Camp Buchanan, PR, on 1 February 1940 and personnel and equipment transferred to activate the 1st Bn., 66th C.A. The 1st Bn. concurrently reactivated at Fort Crockett on 1 February 1940 with the personnel and equipment of the 2d Bn. Concurrently, the 2d Bn. was inactivated. The 2d Bn. reactivated on 1 June 1940 at Fort Story, VA. Personnel and equipment from the 2d Bn. transferred on 28 June 1940 to the 1st Bn., 74th C.A. The 2d Bn. transferred, less personnel and equipment, to Fort Crockett and reorganized on 29 June 1940 with cadres from the 1st Bn. Regiment transferred on 12 January 1941 to Camp Hulen, TX. Assigned to the 32d C.A. Brig. on 10 February 1941. Location 7 December 1941—Camp Hulen, TX.

Status: Active at Giebelstadt, Germany, as HHB, 69th Air Defense Arty. Brig.

Events: 103, 121, 143, 165, 242, 258, 268, 282, 283, 295, 300, 325, 328

Commanders, 69th Coast Artillery Regiment

Lt. Col. John R. Musgrave**	ao June 1927–24 September 1927	Col. Arthur E. Rowland	28 November 1940–23 April 1941
Unknown	24 September 1927–9 August 1928	Col. Allen Kimberly	2 May 1937–10 June 1938
Capt. George M. Lieber**	9 August 1928–1 February 1930	Lt. Col. Otto G. Pitz	10 June 1938–11 July 1938
Lt. Col. James E. Taylor	1 February 1930–21 March 1931	Col. Olin H. Longino	11 July 1938–15 October 1940
Lt. Col. Frederic H. Smith	21 March 1931–15 May 1934	Lt. Col. Joshua D. Powers	15 October 1940–28 November 1940
Maj. Kenneth McCatty	15 May 1934–8 August 1934	Col. Arthur E. Rowland	28 November 1940–23 April 1941
Col. Richard Donovan	8 August 1934–1 May 1937	Lt. Col. Joshua D. Powers	23 April 1941–27 February 1942

70th Coast Artillery Regiment (Antiaircraft)

HQ—Fort Monroe, VA, 1939–40; Fort Moultrie, SC, 1940–41

Constituted in the O.R. on 5 September 1928 as the 562d C.A. Regt. (AA). Redesignated as the 917th C.A. Regt. (AA) (see 917th C.A.) on 30 November 1928. Withdrawn from the O.R. on 1 October 1933 and allotted to the R.A. as an inactive regiment. Redesignated the 70th C.A. on 4 November 1939 and activated at Fort Monroe, VA. Regiment, less 2d Bn., transferred to Fort Moultrie, SC, on 26 June 1940 and assigned to the 38th C.A. Brig. (AA). Concurrently 2d Bn. transferred to Fort Screven, GA. Regiment transferred on 16 December 1940 to Camp Stewart, GA. Location 7 December 1941—Camp Stewart, GA.

Status: Assigned to the CARS as the 562d Air Defense Arty.

Events: 330

Commanders, 70th Coast Artillery Regiment

Col. Richard F. Cox	4 November 1939–16 December 1940	Col. Bird S. DuBois	16 December 1940–3 November 1941

71st Coast Artillery Regiment (Antiaircraft)

HQ—Fort Story, VA, 1941

Arrived at the port of New York on 7 March 1919 on the U.S.S. *Mexican* as the 71st Arty., C.A.C., an element of the 34th Arty. Brig. C.A.C. Transferred on 7 March 1919 to Camp Merritt, NJ. Transferred about 12 March 1919 to Camp Devens, MA. Demobilized in late March 1919 at Camp Devens, MA. Reconstituted in the R.A. on 1 July 1940. Concurrently, the 1st Bn. was activated at Fort Story, VA. Attached to the First Army on 30 December 1940. Remainder of regiment activated on 3 January 1941 at Fort Story. Location 7 December 1941—Fort Story, VA.

Status: Assigned to the CARS as the 71st Air Defense Arty.

Events: 330

Commanders, 71st Coast Artillery Regiment

Maj. Edward W. Timberlake 1 July 1940–August 1940
Lt. Col. Dale D. Hinman August 1940–8 May 1941
Col. Edward W. Timberlake 8 May 1941–12 October 1942

72d Coast Artillery Regiment (Antiaircraft)

HQ—Fort Randolph, CZ, 1939–41

Constituted in the R.A. on 1 November 1939, assigned to the Panama Separate C.A. Brig., and organized at Fort Randolph, CZ. Concurrently regimental elements organized from personnel transferred from the 1st Bn., 1st C.A. and the 62d C.A. Regt. Subordinate elements were organized as follows:

HQ Btry organized on 1 March 1940 at Fort Randolph.
Service Btry organized on 1 March 1940 at Fort Randolph.
HHB, 1st Bn. organized on 1 March 1940 at Fort Sherman.
- Btry A organized on 1 November 1939 at Fort Sherman.
- Btry B organized on 1 November 1939 at Fort Sherman.
- Btry C organized on 1 November 1939 at Fort Sherman.
- Btry E organized on 1 March 1940 at Fort Sherman.

HHB, 2d Bn. organized on 1 November 1939 at Fort Randolph.
- Btry G organized on 1 November 1939 at Fort Randolph.
- Btry H organized on 1 November 1939 at Fort Randolph.
- Btry I organized on 1 November 1939 at Fort Randolph.
- Btry K organized on 1 November 1939 at Fort Randolph.
- Btry L organized on 1 November 1939 at Fort Randolph.
- Btry M organized on 1 November 1939 at Fort Randolph.

HHB, 3d Bn. organized on 1 November 1939 at Fort Randolph.
- Btry N organized on 1 November 1939 at Fort Randolph.
- Btry O organized on 1 November 1939 at Fort Randolph.
- Btry P organized on 1 November 1939 at Fort Randolph.
- Btry Q organized on 1 November 1939 at Fort Randolph.
- Btry R organized on 1 November 1939 at Fort Randolph.

HHB, 4th Bn. organized on 1 November 1939 at Fort Randolph.
- Btry S organized in 1940 at Fort William C. Davis.
- Btry U organized on 1 March 1940 at Fort Randolph.
- Btry V organized on 1 November 1939 at Fort Randolph.
- Btry W organized on 1 November 1939 at Fort Randolph.
- Btry X organized in 1940 at Fort William C. Davis.

The mission of the regiment was to provide the AA defenses of the Atlantic Sector of the Canal Zone. Location 7 December 1941—Fort Randolph, CZ.

Status: Disbanded on 14 June 1944.

Events: 292, 308

Commanders, 72d Coast Artillery Regiment

Lt. Col. Charles R. Finley	1 November 1939–9 February 1940	Col. Homer R. Oldfield	9 February 1940–4 August 1941
Lt. Col. Ward E. Duvall	5 August 1941–ao December 1941		

73d Coast Artillery Regiment (Antiaircraft)

HQ—Fort Amador, CZ, 1939–41

Constituted in the R.A. on 1 November 1939 and assigned to the Panama Separate C.A. Brig. Concurrently regimental elements organized from personnel transferred from the 1st Bn., 4th C.A. and the 61st and 63d C.A. Regts. Subordinate elements were organized as follows: Regimental HHB, Service Btry, and Btrys B, C, D, E, F, G, I, K, L, and O organized at Fort Amador, CZ; 3d Bn. HHB and Btrys N, Q, R, S and T organized at Fort Amador and moved to Corozal; Btry A organized at Fort Amador and moved to Fort Kobbe, CZ. The mission of the regiment was to provide the AA defenses of the Pacific Sector of the Canal Zone. Location 7 December 1941—Fort Amador, CZ.

Status: Disbanded on 10 December 1943.

Events: 292, 308

Commanders, 73d Coast Artillery Regiment

Lt. Col. Willis McD. Chapin	1 November 1939–20 June 1942

74th Coast Artillery Regiment (Antiaircraft)

HQ—Fort Monroe, VA, 1941; Camp Pendleton, VA, 1941

Constituted in the O.R. on 29 July 1921 as the 503d Arty. Regt. (AA), C.A.C. Redesignated on 30 June 1924 as the 503d C.A. Regt. (AA) (see 503d C.A.). Withdrawn from the O.R. on 1 October 1933 and allotted to the R.A. as an inactive regiment. Redesignated the 74th C.A. on 1 July 1940. Concurrently, 1st Bn. activated at Fort Monroe, VA. The 1st Bn. provided an honor guard for the visit of President Roosevelt to Fort Monroe on 29 July 1940. Attached on 30 December 1940 to the First Army. Remainder of regiment activated on 3 January 1941 at Fort Monroe. Regiment transferred on 18 July 1941 to Camp Pendleton, VA. Location 7 December 1941—Camp Pendleton, VA.

Events: 330

Commanders, 74th Coast Artillery Regiment

Lt. Col. William Hasketh	1 July 1940–3 January 1941	Col. Samuel F. Hawkins	3 January 1941–31 January 1942

75th Coast Artillery Regiment (Antiaircraft)

HQ—Fort Lewis, WA, 1940; Fort Richardson, TA, 1940–41

Constituted in the O.R. on 29 July 1921 as the 509th Arty. Regt. (AA), C.A.C. Redesignated on 30 June 1924 as the 509th C.A. Regt. (AA) (see 509th C.A.). Withdrawn from the O.R. on 1 October 1933 and allotted to the R.A. as an inactive regiment. Redesignated the 75th C.A. on 1 July 1940 and activated at Fort Lewis, WA. Regiment transferred to Fort Richardson, TA, on 26 November 1940 and assigned to Alaskan Defense Force. Location 7 December 1941—Fort Richardson, TA.

Status: Active in the R.A. as HHB, 75th F.A. Brig.

Events: 304

Commanders, 75th Coast Artillery Regiment

Col. Edgar B. Colladay	1 July 1940–October 1940
Col. John H. Hood	October 1940–13 March 1941
Col. William D. Frazer	13 March 1941–2 October 1943

76th Coast Artillery Regiment (Antiaircraft) (C)

HQ—Fort Bragg, NC, 1941

Constituted in the O.R. on 29 July 1921 as the 502d Arty. Regt. (AA), C.A.C. Redesignated on 30 June 1924 as the 502d C.A. Regt. (AA) (see 502d C.A.). Withdrawn from the O.R. on 1 October 1933 and allotted to the R.A. as an inactive regiment. Redesignated the 76th C.A. (AA) (Colored) on 1 July 1940. The 1st Bn. activated on 1 August 1940 at Fort Bragg, NC. Remainder of regiment activated on 10 February 1941 at Fort Bragg, NC. Concurrently assigned to the 34th C.A. Brig. (AA). Location 7 December 1941—Fort Bragg, NC.

Events: 327, 330, 334

Commanders, 76th Coast Artillery Regiment

Lt. Col. Harry R. Pierce	1 August 1940–July 1941
Col. Charles A. French	July 1941–ao January 1942

77th Coast Artillery Regiment (Antiaircraft) (Colored)

HQ—Fort Bragg, NC, 1941

Constituted in the O.R. on 29 July 1921 as the 505th Arty. Regt. (AA), C.A.C. Redesignated on 30 June 1924 as the 505th C.A. Regt. (AA) (see 505th C.A.). Withdrawn from the O.R. on 1 October 1933 and allotted to the R.A. as an inactive regiment. Redesignated the 77th C.A. (AA) (Colored) on 1 July 1940. The 1st Bn. activated on 1 August 1940 at Fort Bragg, NC. Remainder of regiment activated on 10 February 1941 at Fort Bragg, NC. Concurrently assigned to the 34th C.A. Brig. (AA). Location 7 December 1941—Fort Bragg, NC.

Events: 323, 327, 330, 334

Commanders, 77th Coast Artillery Regiment

Col. Claude M. Thiele	1 August 1940–10 February 1941	Lt. Col. Riley E. McGarraugh	10 February 1941–ao January 1942

78th Coast Artillery Regiment (Antiaircraft)

HQ—Camp Haan, CA, 1941; Fort MacArthur, CA, 1941

Constituted in the O.R. on 2 July 1923 as the 517th Arty. Regt. (AA), C.A.C. Redesignated on 30 June 1924 as the 517th C.A. Regt. (AA) (see 517th C.A.). Withdrawn from the O.R. on 1 January 1938 and allotted to the R.A. as an inactive regiment. Redesignated the 78th C.A. on 1 August 1940 and assigned to the 37th C.A. Brig. (AA). Concurrently the 1st Bn. activated at Camp Haan, CA. Attached to the Fourth Army on 30 December 1940. Remainder of regiment, less 2d Bn., activated on 10 February 1941 at Camp Haan. Concurrently the 2d Bn. activated at Fort Lewis, WA. Regiment transferred on 5 December 1941 to Fort MacArthur, CA. Location 7 December 1941—Fort MacArthur, CA.

Events: 335

Commanders, 78th Coast Artillery Regiment

Col. Robert H. Van Volkenburgh	1 August 1940–15 November 1940	Col. Harry W. Starke	15 November 1940–ao January 1942

87th Coast Artillery Regiment (Antiaircraft)

HQ—*Not organized,* 1933–41

Constituted in the R.A. on 1 October 1933 and allotted to the Seventh Corps Area. The 1st Bn. assigned to the VII Corps. Location 7 December 1941—*Not organized.*

91st Coast Artillery Regiment (PS) (Harbor Defense)

HQ—Fort Mills, PI, 1924–41

Constituted in the R.A. on 30 June 1924 and assigned to the Harbor Defenses of Manila and Subic Bays. Regimental HQ organized on 1 July 1924 at Fort Mills, PI. Subordinate elements constituted, organized, or redesignated as follows:

- HQ Btry organized by redesignation of 281st Co., C.A.C., active at Fort Mills.
- HQ, 1st Bn. organized at Fort Mills.
  - Btry A organized by redesignation of 282d Co., C.A.C., active at Fort Mills.
  - Btry B organized by redesignation of 284th Co., C.A.C., active at Fort Mills.
- HQ, 2d Bn. organized at Fort Mills.
  - Btry C organized by redesignation of 277th Co., C.A.C., active at Fort Mills.
  - Btry D organized by redesignation of 279th Co., C.A.C., active at Fort Mills.
- HQ, 3d Bn. organized at Fort Mills.
  - Btry E organized by redesignation of 286th Co., C.A.C., active at Fort Hughes.

Btry F organized by redesignation of 276th Co., C.A.C., active at Fort Frank.

Btry G organized by redesignation of 285th Co., C.A.C., active at Fort Wint.

Billeted at "Bottomside" on Corregidor. Btry C awarded the Knox Trophy for C.A. in 1932. Location 7 December 1941—Fort Mills, PI.

Events: 35, 41, 44, 51, 68, 122, 224, 245, 270

Commanders, 91st Coast Artillery Regiment (PS)

Col. Andrew Hero Jr.	1 July 1924–2 March 1925	Lt. Col. Clair W. Baird	26 January 1935–6 November 1936
Lt. Col. James L. Long	2 March 1925–2 April 1925	Col. James H. Cunningham	6 November 1936–30 April 1937
Col. William R. Doores	2 April 1925–2 December 1925	Lt. Col. Richard S. Dodson	1 May 1937–5 October 1937
Lt. Col. William H. Raymond	2 December 1925–23 November 1926	Capt. Arthur L. Lavery	5 October 1937–13 October 1937
Col. Frederick W. Stopford	23 November 1926–26 October 1928	Maj. Benjamin Bowering	13 October 1937–29 October 1937
Col. William H. Monroe	26 October 1928–27 June 1930	Col. William C. Koenig	29 October 1937–4 November 1938
Lt. Col. Franc Leccoq	27 June 1930–9 October 1930	Col. Frederic A. Price	4 November 1938–23 March 1939
Lt. Col. Forrest E. Williford	9 October 1930–8 September 1932	Col. Willis Shippam	23 March 1939–28 February 1941
Col. Clarence B. Ross	8 September 1932–5 October 1934	Col. John L. Holcombe	1 March 1941–31 October 1941
Lt. Col. Hollis L. Muller	7 October 1934–26 January 1935	Col. Joseph P. Kohn	1 November 1941–13 May 1942

92d Coast Artillery Regiment (PS) (Harbor Defense) (155-mm G.P.F.)

HQ—Fort Mills, PI, 1924–41

Constituted in the R.A. on 30 June 1924 and assigned to the Harbor Defenses of Manila and Subic Bays. Regimental HQ organized on 1 July 1924 at Fort Mills, PI, with a cadre of officers and Philippine Scout personnel from the 59th C.A. Subordinate elements constituted, organized, or redesignated as follows:

HQ Btry organized by redesignation of 278th Co., C.A.C., active at Fort Mills.

HQ, 1st Bn. organized at Fort Mills.

Btry A organized by redesignation of 280th Co., C.A.C., active at Fort Mills.

Btry B organized by redesignation of 283d Co., C.A.C., active at Fort Mills.

HQ, 2d Bn. organized at Fort Mills.

Btry C organized by redesignation of 287th Co., C.A.C., active at Fort Mills.

Btry D organized by redesignation of 288th Co., C.A.C., active at Fort Mills.

HQ, 3d Bn. organized at Fort Mills.

Btry E organized by redesignation of 275th Co., C.A.C., active at Fort Mills.

Btry F organized by redesignation of 289th Co., C.A.C., active at Fort Mills.

Billeted at "Bottomside" on Corregidor. Though the 92d C.A. was designated a Harbor Defense regiment, it functioned as a tractor-drawn 155-mm howitzer regiment, 1924–41. It was officially redesignated (Tractor Drawn) on 16 July 1935 and permanently assigned the 59th C.A.'s equipment. The 3d Bn. was reorganized in September 1928 to provide the guard detail for Bilibid Prison, an extra duty the battalion continued to perform until 1941. Awarded the US Coast Artillery Association Trophy for R.A. regiments for 1940. Location 7 December 1941—Fort Mills, PI.

Organization Day: 15 November.

Events: 35, 41, 44, 51, 68, 122, 224, 245, 270

Commanders, 92d Coast Artillery Regiment (PS)

Col. William R. Doores	1 July 1924–9 November 1924	Maj. Eli E. Bennett	2 October 1930–5 July 1932
Col. Samuel C. Vestal	9 November 1924–26 February 1926	Lt. Col. Albert L. Loustalot	5 July 1932–2 October 1934
Col. Harrison S. Kerrick	26 February 1926–13 September 1927	Lt. Col. Reinold Melberg	2 October 1934–25 February 1937
Col. George O. Hubbard	14 September 1927–20 October 1928	Lt. Col. Albert H. Warren	25 February 1937–30 March 1939
Maj. Edward W. Turner	20 October 1928–11 March 1930	Lt. Col. James B. Crawford	30 March 1939–27 January 1940
Maj. Robert E. Phillips	11 March 1930–30 August 1930	Col. Joseph F. Cottrell	27 January 1940–July 1940
Maj. Estaban B. Dalao	30 August 1930–2 October 1930	Col. Octave DeCarre	July 1940–6 May 1942

141st Artillery Regiment (Antiaircraft), Coast Artillery Corps — Arkansas National Guard

HQ—Marianna, AR, 1923–24

Constituted in the N.G. in 1921, allotted to the state of Arkansas, and assigned to the Third Army. The 2d Bn. organized and federally recognized on 21 June 1921 at Nashville, AR. Regimental HQ organized and federally recognized on 24 November 1923 at Marianna, AR. Conducted annual summer training at Fort Sill, OK, in 1924. Regiment redesignated 206th Arty. Regt. (AA), C.A.C. on 1 December 1924.

Commanders, 141st Artillery Regiment (C.A.C.)

Col. Elgan C. Robertson — 24 November 1923–1 December 1924

162d Artillery Regiment (Antiaircraft), Coast Artillery Corps — Pennsylvania National Guard

HQ—*Not organized,* 1921–22

Constituted in the N.G. in 1921 as the 162d Arty. Regt. (AA), C.A.C.; allotted to the state of Pennsylvania; and assigned to the First Army. Unit designation withdrawn from the state of Pennsylvania in 1922 and the designation "213th" allotted instead.

192d Artillery Regiment (Heavy Tractor), Coast Artillery Corps — Connecticut National Guard

HQ—New London, CT, 1921

Reconstituted on 2 April 1921 as the 1st C.A., Connecticut N.G. Organized and federally recognized on 2 April 1921 with HQ at New London, CT. Redesignated on 23 May 1921 as the 192d Arty. Regt. (Heavy Tractor), C.A.C. Redesignated on 3 November 1921 as the 192d F.A. Regt.

Status: Assigned to the USARS as the 192d F.A.

193d Artillery Regiment (Heavy Tractor), Coast Artillery Corps — New York National Guard

HQ—New York City, NY, 1921

Constituted in the N.G. on 30 December 1920 as the 193d Arty., C.A.C., and allotted to the state of New York. Organized by redesignation of active elements of the 8th Coast Defense Command, New York N.G. Regimental HQ federally recognized on 2 May 1921 at New York City, NY, as the 193d Arty. Regt. (Heavy Tractor), C.A.C. Redesignated on 12 September 1921 as the 193d F.A. Regt. Redesignated on 28 November 1921 as the 258th F.A. Regt.

Status: Assigned to the USARS as the 258th F.A.

Commanders, 193d Artillery Regiment (C.A.C.)

Col. Elmore F. Austin — 11 May 1921–28 November 1921

197th Coast Artillery Regiment (Antiaircraft) (I Corps) **New Hampshire National Guard**

HQ—Concord, NH, 1922–40; Camp Hulen, TX, 1940–41

Constituted in the N.G. in 1921, allotted to the state of Connecticut, and assigned to the I Corps. Regimental HQ organized and federally recognized on 30 June 1922 at Concord, NH. Concurrently regiment redesignated 197th C.A. Regt. (AA). Relieved from the I Corps on 1 October 1933 and assigned to the 32d C.A. Brig. (AA) (GHQR). Conducted annual summer training most years at Rye Beach, NH, and some years at Fort Greble, ME; Warner, NH; or Fort Adams, RI. Inducted into Federal service on 16 September 1940 at Concord, NH, and transferred to Camp Hulen, TX, arriving there on 30 September 1940. Assigned to the 33d C.A. Brig. (AA) (GHQR) on 10 February 1941. Location 7 December 1941—Camp Hulen, TX.

Status: Assigned to the USARS as the 197th F.A.; 1st Bn. active at Berlin, NH, as an element of the 197th F.A. Brig.

Events: 280, 301, 325, 328

Commanders, 197th Coast Artillery Regiment

Col. Clarence E. Rexford 30 June 1922–15 December 1939
Col. Albert E. Colburn 15 December 1939–ao January 1942

198th Coast Artillery Regiment (Antiaircraft) (II Corps) **Delaware National Guard**

HQ—Wilmington, DE, 1921–40; Camp Upton, NY, 1940–41; Camp Edwards, MA, 1941

Constituted in the N.G. in 1921 as the 198th Arty. Regt. (AA), C.A.C., allotted to the state of Delaware, and assigned to the II Corps. Regimental HQ organized and federally recognized on 15 September 1921 at Wilmington, DE. Redesignated 198th C.A. Regt. (AA) on 16 August 1924. The 2d Bn. called up, 7–8 February 1926, to perform security duties in connection with a trial in Georgetown, DE. Relieved from the II Corps on 1 October 1933 and assigned to the 32d C.A. Brig. (AA) (GHQR). Awarded the US Coast Artillery Association Trophy for N.G. regiments for 1934 and 1939. Conducted annual summer training most years at Bethany Beach, DE, and some years at Camp Upton, NY; Fort Greble, ME; or New Castle, DE. Designated mobilization training station was Camp Upton, NY. Inducted into Federal service on 16 September 1940 at Wilmington, DE, and transferred to Camp Upton, NY, arriving there on 22 September 1940. Assigned to the 36th C.A. Brig. (AA). Transferred on 26 March 1941 to Camp Edwards, MA. Location 7 December 1941—Camp Edwards, MA.

Status: Active at Wilmington, DE, as the 198th Signal Bn.

Events: 301

Commanders, 198th Coast Artillery Regiment

Col. Harry W. Stark 14 July 1921–31 July 1923
Col. John P. LeFevre 31 July 1923–6 February 1932
Col. George J. Schulz 6 February 1932–18 February 1943

199th Artillery Regiment (Antiaircraft), Coast Artillery Corps (III Corps) **Pennsylvania National Guard**

HQ—*Not organized,* 1921–22

Constituted in the N.G. in 1921 as the 199th Arty. Regt. (AA), C.A.C.; allotted to the state of Pennsylvania; and assigned to the III Corps. Withdrawn from the state of Pennsylvania in March 1926. Withdrawn from the N.G. on 5 September 1927 and demobilized.

200th Coast Artillery Regiment (Antiaircraft) (I) (IV Corps) **Louisiana, Alabama, North Carolina, and Florida National Guard**

HQ—*Not organized,* 1921–27

Constituted in the N.G. in 1921 as the 200th Arty. Regt. (AA), C.A.C.; allotted to the states of Louisiana, Alabama, North Carolina, and Florida; and assigned to the IV Corps. Regimental HHB and Btrys B, C, D, E, F, I, K, and L allotted to the state of Louisiana; Btry A allotted to Alabama; Btry G allotted to North Carolina; and Btry M allotted to Florida. New Orleans, LA, designated as HQ location on organization, but the unit was never organized at that location. Btry G, the only active element, was organized on 5 August 1921 at Raeford, NC. Regiment redesignated 200th C.A. Regt. (AA) on 27 September 1924. Btry G conducted annual summer training at Fort Monroe, VA, 1922–25, and Fort Bragg, NC, in 1926. Btry G redesignated F Btry, 252d C.A. on 1 December 191926. Concurrently, all elements withdrawn from their respective states of allotment and transferred to the deferred list. Regiment withdrawn from the N.G. on 5 September 1927 and demobilized.

200th Coast Artillery Regiment (Antiaircraft) (II) **New Mexico National Guard**

HQ—Deming, NM, 1940–41; Fort Bliss, TX, 1941; Fort Stotsenburg, PI, 1941

Constituted in the N.G. in 1921 as the 111th Cavalry (Cav.) Regt., assigned to the 23d Cav. Division (Div.) and allotted to the states of New Mexico and Colorado (see the 111th Cav.). Converted and redesignated on 26 April 1940 as the 207th C.A. Regt. (AA) and assigned to the GHQR. Redesignated on 1 July 1940 as the 200th C.A. (AA). Conducted annual summer training in 1940 at Camp Maximiliano Luna, NM. Designated mobilization training station was Fort Bliss, TX. Attached to the Third Army on 30 December 1940. Inducted into Federal service on 6 January 1941 at Deming, NM, and transferred to Fort Bliss, TX, arriving there on 15 January 1941. Regiment received selective service replacements and brought up to wartime strength. Conducted the Mobilization Training Plan and declared ready for overseas service. Departed the San Francisco port of embarkation on 8 September 1941 on the U.S.A.T. *President Coolidge* and arrived on 26 September 1941 at Manila, PI. Transferred to Fort Stotsenburg, PI, and assigned to the Philippine C.A. Command. Assigned the mission to provide AA defenses for Clark Field. Location 7 December 1941—Fort Stotsenburg, PI.

Status: HHB active in the New Mexico N.G. as HHB, 111th Air Defense Arty. Brig. and the remainder of the regiment assigned to the USARS as elements of the 200th Air Defense Arty.; 1st Bn. active at Roswell, NM; 2d Bn. active at Rio Rancho, NM; 3d Bn. active at Belen, NM; and 4th Bn. active at Rio Rancho, NM.

Commanders, 200th Coast Artillery Regiment

Col. Charles G. Sage	26 April 1940–6 May 1942

201st Artillery Regiment (Antiaircraft), Coast Artillery Corps (V Corps) **Ohio and West Virginia National Guard**

HQ—*Not organized,* 1921–27

Constituted in the N.G. in 1921 as the 201st Arty. Regt. (AA), C.A.C., allotted to the states of Ohio and West Virginia, and assigned to the V Corps. Regiment, less the MG battalion, allotted to Ohio; the MG battalion allotted to West Virginia. Regiment relieved from the V Corps on 2 July 1923 and placed on the deferred list. All elements withdrawn from the states of Ohio and West Virginia in March 1926. Withdrawn from the N.G. on 5 September 1927 and demobilized.

201st Coast Artillery Regiment (Antiaircraft) **Puerto Rico National Guard**

HQ—*Not organized,* 1940–41

Constituted in the N.G. on 8 May 1940 as the 201st C.A. Regt. (AA) and allotted to the commonwealth of Puerto Rico. The 1st Bn. organized and federally recognized on 1 September 1940 at Mayaguez, PR. Inducted into Federal service on 15 October 1940 at Borinquen Field, PR, and assigned to the Puerto Rican Department. Redesignated the 123d C.A. Bn. on 2 April 1941.

Events: 329

Commanders, 201st Coast Artillery Regiment

1st Battalion

Maj. Rafael Charneco	15 October 1940–2 April 1941

202d Coast Artillery Regiment (Antiaircraft) (VI Corps) **Illinois National Guard**

HQ—Chicago, IL, 1923–40; Fort Bliss, TX, 1940–41

Organized on 1 October 1920 as 6th Inf. Regt., Illinois N.G. Reorganized and redesignated on 19 March 1921 as the 1st Arty. Regt. (AA), C.A.C., Illinois N.G. Redesignated on 7 December 1923 as the 202d Arty. Regt. (AA), C.A.C. and assigned to the VI Corps. Concurrently, regimental HQ organized and federally recognized at Chicago, IL. The regiment was called up to perform riot control at a coal miners' strike at Rockford, IL, 9 July–30 August 1922. Redesignated on 26 August 1924 as the 202d C.A. Regt. (AA). Conducted a regimental parade through Norfolk, VA, on 12 September 1924 during summer camp at Fort Monroe that year. Relieved from the VI Corps on 1 October 1933 and assigned to the GHQR. Conducted annual summer training at numerous locations to include Camp Grant, IL; Camp Custer, MI; Fort Monroe, VA; Camp Sparta, WI; Camp Grayling, MI; Fort Ontario, NY; Fort Barrancas, FL; Fort Sheridan, IL; and Camp Logan, IL. Conducted joint summer training with the 555th C.A. Bn. at Camp Grant in 1928. For at least 1 year, in 1937, the regiment also trained some seven company-grade Reserve officers at Camp Logan. Designated mobilization training station was Fort Crockett, TX. Inducted into Federal service on 16 September 1940 at Chicago, IL, and transferred to Fort Bliss, TX, arriving there on 27 September 1940. Assigned to the 39th C.A. Brig. (AA) on 10 February 1941. Location 7 December 1941—Fort Bliss, TX.

Status: Assigned to the USARS as the 202d Air Defense Arty.; 1st Bn. active at Kewanee, IL, as an element of the 42d Inf. Div.; Btry E active at Dixon, IL, as an element of the 45th Inf. Brig.; and Btry F active at Galva, IL, as an element of the 39th Inf. Brig.

Events: 214, 264, 302

Commanders, 202d Coast Artillery Regiment

Col. Charles K. Kraft	7 December 1923–23 October 1930	Col. Charles C. Dawes	23 October 1930–10 September 1943

203d Coast Artillery Regiment (Antiaircraft) (VII Corps) **Missouri National Guard**

HQ—Aurora, MO, 1921–33; Webb City, MO, 1933–40; Camp Hulen, TX, 1940–41

Organized in April 1921 as the 2d Arty. Regt. (AA), C.A.C., Missouri N:G. Regimental HQ organized and federally recognized on 2 June 1921 at Aurora, MO. Redesignated on 1 October 1921 as the 203d Arty. Regt .(AA), C.A.C. and assigned to the VII Corps. Redesignated on 19 April 1924 as the 203d C.A. Regt. (AA). HQ relocated on 18 March 1933 to Webb City, MO. Relieved from the VII Corps on 1 October 1933 and assigned to the GHQR. The regiment, or elements thereof, called up to perform the following state duties: 1st and 2d Bns. for riot control at a railroad workers' strike at Moberly and Macon, MO, 9 July–5 August 1922; 2d Bn. for riot control at a coal miners' strike at Mindenmines,

MO, 30 April–4 May 1934; and entire regiment for flood relief work in southern Illinois, 21 January–5 April 1937. Conducted annual summer training at numerous locations to include Camp Clark, MO; Camp Custer, MI; Fort Sill, OK; Fort Sheridan, IL; Camp Hulen, TX; Fort Riley, KS; Camp Ripley, MN; and Fort Barrancas, FL, 1921–40. For at least 2 years, 1939 and 1940, the regiment also trained some 40 company-grade Reserve officers at Fort Barrancas and Camp Ripley. Inducted into Federal service on 16 September 1940 at Webb City, MO, and transferred to Camp Hulen, TX, arriving there on 26 September 1940. Assigned to the 33d C.A. Brig. (AA) on 10 February 1941. Location 7 December 1941—Camp Hulen, TX.

Status: Active in the Missouri N.G. as the 203d Engr. Bn.

Events: 236, 303, 325, 328

Commanders, 203d Coast Artillery Regiment

Col. William A. Raupp	22 April 1921–2 June 1921	Col. Ray E. Watson	18 March 1933–October 1941
Col. Thomas H. Loy	2 June 1921–23 February 1933	Col. Berthold Vogel (R.A.)	October 1941–January 1942

204th Coast Artillery Regiment (Antiaircraft) (I) (VIII Corps) — Texas National Guard

HQ—*Not organized,* 1921–27

Constituted in the N.G. in 1921 as the 204th Arty. Regt. (AA), C.A.C., allotted to the state of Texas, and assigned to the VIII Corps. Waco, TX, designated as HQ location on organization, but the unit was never organized at that location. Redesignated on 1 June 1924 as the 204th C.A. Regt. (AA). Withdrawn from the state of Texas in March 1926. Regiment relieved from the VIII Corps on 5 September 1927 and concurrently withdrawn from the N.G.

204th Coast Artillery Regiment (Antiaircraft) (II) (GHQR) — Louisiana National Guard

HQ—Shreveport, LA, 1939–41; Camp Hulen, TX, 1941

Constituted in the N.G. on 15 December 1939, allotted to the state of Louisiana, and assigned to the GHQR. Concurrently, regimental HQ organized and federally recognized at Shreveport, LA. The 1st Bn. organized new with HQ at Shreveport and 2d Bn. organized from the 2d Bn., 156th Inf. with HQ also at Shreveport. Conducted annual summer training at Camp Beauregard, LA, in 1940. Attached to the Third Army on 30 December 1940. Inducted into Federal service on 6 January 1941 at Shreveport, LA, and transferred to Camp Hulen, TX, arriving there on 11 January 1941. Assigned to the Southern Defense Command. Location 7 December 1941—Camp Hulen, TX.

Events: 322, 325, 328

Commanders, 204th Coast Artillery Regiment

Col. James Fair Hardin	15 December 1939–30 October 1940	Col. Joseph A. Redding	30 October 1940–10 September 1943

205th Coast Artillery Regiment (Antiaircraft) (IX Corps) — Washington, California, and Oregon National Guard

HQ—*Not organized,* 1921–39; Olympia, WA, 1939–41; Fort Lewis, WA, 1941

Constituted in the N.G. in 1921 as the 205th Arty. Regt. (AA), C.A.C., allotted to the states of California, Washington, and Oregon. Concurrently assigned to the IX Corps. Regiment, less Btrys B and C, allotted to California; Btry B allotted to Washington, and Btry C allotted to Oregon. Redesignated on 1 June 1924 as the 205th C.A. Regt. (AA). All elements withdrawn from allotment to their respective states in March 1926. Regiment relieved from the IX Corps on 5 September 1927 and concurrently withdrawn from the N.G. Reallotted to the N.G. in November 1939 and entire regiment further allotted to the state of Washington. Regimental HQ organized and federally recognized on 20

November 1939 at Olympia, WA. Conducted annual summer training at Fort Worden, WA, in 1940. Attached to the Fourth Army on 30 December 1940. Inducted into Federal service on 3 February 1941 at Olympia, WA; transferred to Fort Lewis, WA, arriving there on 14 February 1941; and assigned to the Western Defense Command. Location 7 December 1941—Fort Lewis, WA.

Events: 304

Commanders, 205th Coast Artillery Regiment

Col. Edward C. Dohm	23 November 1939–April 1941	Lt. Col. William R. Carroll	April 1941–ao January 1942

206th Coast Artillery Regiment (Antiaircraft) (Third Army) **Arkansas National Guard**

HO—Marianna. AR. 1923–41; Fort Bliss, TX, 1941; Camp Murray, WA, 1941

Constituted in the N.G. in 1921, allotted to the state of Arkansas, and assigned to the Third Army. The 2d Bn. organized and federally recognized on 21 June 1921 at Nashville, AR. Regimental HQ organized and federally recognized on 24 November 1923 at Marianna, AR. Regiment redesignated 206th Arty. Regt. (AA), C.A.C. on 1 December 1923. Redesignated 206th C.A. on 22 April 1924. The regiment, or elements thereof, were called up to perform the following state duties: provisional battalion (two companies) to perform flood relief duty along the White River, 18 April–21 May 1927; provisional battalion (two companies) to perform flood relief duty at Manila, AR, June–July 1927; regiment (-) to perform flood relief duty at Camp Barton and Jonesboro, AR, January–February 1937. Relieved from the Third Army on 1 October 1933 and assigned to the GHQR. Conducted annual summer training at numerous locations to include Fort Sill, OK; Camp Pike, AR; Fort Barrancas, FL; Fort Sheridan, IL; Camp Hulen, TX; and Camp Ripley, MN. For at least 1 year, 1938, the regiment also trained some 25 company-grade Reserve officers at Joseph T. Robinson, AR. Attached to the Third Army on 30 December 1940. Inducted into Federal service on 6 January 1941 at Marianna, AR, and transferred to Fort Bliss, TX, arriving there on 18 January 1941. Assigned to the 39th C.A. Brig. (AA) on 10 February 1941. Transferred to Camp Murray, WA, on 5 August 1941 and assigned to the Western Defense Command. Location 7 December 1941—Camp Murray, WA.

Status: Assigned to the USARS as the 206th F.A.; 1st Bn. active at Russellville, AR, as an element of the 39th Inf. Brig. (Sep.).

Events: 303, 315

Commanders, 206th Coast Artillery Regiment

Col. Elgan C. Robertson	1 December 1923–31 March 1944

207th Coast Artillery Regiment (Antiaircraft) (102d Coast Artillery Brigade) **New York National Guard**

HQ—New York City, NY, 1940–41; Camp Stewart, GA, 1941

Constituted in the N.G. in 1921 as the 107th Inf. Regt., assigned to the 27th Div., and allotted to the state of New York (see the 107th Inf.). Converted and redesignated on 1 August 1940 as the 207th C.A. Regt. (AA) and assigned to the New York C.A. Brig. (later redesignated 102d C.A. Brig.). Inducted into Federal service on 10 February 1941 at New York City, NY, and transferred to Camp Stewart, GA, arriving there on 20 February 1941. Location 7 December 1941—Camp Stewart, GA.

Events: 330

Commanders, 207th Coast Artillery Regiment

Col. Ralph C. Tobin	1 August 1940–11 August 1942	Col. Charles W. Gettys	11 August 1942–21 April 1943

208th Coast Artillery Regiment (Antiaircraft) **Connecticut National Guard**

HQ—West Hartford, CT, 1940–41; Camp Edwards, MA, 1941

Constituted in the N.G. on 9 May 1940, allotted to the state of Connecticut, and assigned to the 36th C.A. Brig. Regimental HQ organized and federally recognized on 16 May 1940 at West Hartford, CT. The 1st Bn. organized on 23 May 1940 from the 1st Squadron (Sq.), 110th Cav. at New Haven, CT; and 2d Bn. organized on 13 November 1940 from elements of the 110th Cav. and 21st Reconnaissance (Rcn.) Sq. with HQ at Wethersfield, CT. Attached to the First Army on 30 December 1940. Inducted into Federal service on 6 January 1941 at West Hartford, CT, and transferred to Camp Edwards, MA, arriving there on 14 January 1941. Assigned to the 36th C.A. Brig. Location 7 December 1941—Camp Edwards, MA.

Commanders, 208th Coast Artillery Regiment

Lt. Col. Louis S. Tracy	16 May 1940–2 July 1940	Col. Francis J. Shearer	2 July 1940–March 1942

209th Coast Artillery Regiment (Antiaircraft) (102d Coast Artillery Brigade) **New York National Guard**

HQ—Rochester, NY, 1940–41; Camp Stewart, GA, 1941

Constituted in the N.G. on 23 July 1940, allotted to the state of New York, and assigned to the New York C.A. Brig. (later redesignated 102d C.A. Brig.). Organized in northwestern New York on 23 July–16 October 1940. Regimental HQ federally recognized on 6 October 1940 at Rochester, NY. Inducted into Federal service on 10 February 1941 at Rochester and transferred to Camp Stewart, GA, arriving there on 21 February 1941. Location 7 December 1941—Camp Stewart, GA.

Events: 330

Commanders, 209th Coast Artillery Regiment

Col. Kenneth C. Townson	15 October 1940–14 March 1944

210th Coast Artillery Regiment (Antiaircraft) **Michigan National Guard**

HQ—Detroit, MI, 1940–41; Fort Sheridan, IL, 1941

Constituted in the N.G. on 18 September 1940, allotted to the state of Michigan, and assigned to the 41st C.A. Brig. Regimental HQ organized and federally recognized on 20 September 1940 at Detroit, MI. The 1st Bn. organized on 11 October 1940 from new units with HQ at Detroit and 2d Bn. organized on 20 September 1940 from the 2d Sq., 106th Cav. with HQ also at Detroit. Relieved from the 41st C.A. Brig. on 30 December 1940 and assigned to the Second Army. Inducted into Federal service on 24 February 1941 at Detroit and transferred to Fort Sheridan, IL, arriving there on 5 March 1941. Further assigned to the 40th C.A. Brig. Location 7 December 1941—Fort Sheridan, IL.

Events: 328

Commanders, 210th Coast Artillery Regiment

Col. Robert F. Gleim	18 September 1940–ao December 1942

211th Coast Artillery Regiment (Antiaircraft) (201st Coast Artillery Brigade) **Massachusetts National Guard**

HQ—Boston, MA, 1927–40; Camp Edwards, MA, 1940; Camp Hulen, TX, 1940–41

Arrived at the port of New York on 4 April 1919 on the U.S.S. *Mount Vernon* as the 101st Engr. Regt., an element of the 26th Div. Demobilized on 29 April 1919 at Camp Devens, MA. Concurrently reorganized in the Massachusetts N.G. with regimental HQ federally recognized at Boston, MA. Reorganized and redesignated on 27 July 1921 as the 1st Separate (Sep.) Inf. Bn., Massachusetts N.G. Reorganized and redesignated as the 211th MG Bn. (AA), C.A.C. and assigned to the 201st C.A. Brig. (First Army). Expanded and redesignated as the 211th Arty. Regt. (AA), C.A.C. on 14 March 1922. Redesignated on 20 April 1924 as the 211th C.A. Regt. (AA). Relieved from the 201st C.A. Brig. on 1 October 1933 and assigned to the GHQR. Conducted annual summer training at numerous locations to include Camp Devens, MA; Fort Terry, NY; Fort H.G. Wright, NY; South Sandwich, MA; and the Massachusetts Military Reservation at Falmouth. Inducted into Federal service on 16 September 1940 at Boston, MA, and transferred to Camp Edwards, MA, arriving there on 21 September 1940. Transferred to Camp Hulen, TX, on 25 October 1940 and assigned to the Southern Defense Command. Location 7 December 1941—Camp Hulen, TX.

Status: Assigned to the USARS as the 211th F.A.; 1st Bn. active as an element of the 42d Inf. Div.

Events: 301, 325, 328

Commanders, 211th Coast Artillery Regiment

Lt. Col. Horace Z. Landon	1 January 1927–24 October 1930	Lt. Col. Harry L. Spencer	24 October 1930–20 October 1937
Col. Stuart G. Hall	20 October 1937–ao May 1941		

212th Coast Artillery Regiment (Antiaircraft) (201st Coast Artillery Brigade) **New York National Guard**

HQ—New York City, NY, 1921–41; Camp Hulen, TX, 1941

Demobilized on 16 April 1919 at Camp Dix, NJ, as the 52d Pioneer Inf. Reorganized by consolidation with, and redesignation as, the 12th Inf., New York N.G. Converted and redesignated on 9 July 1921 as the 212th Arty. Regt. (AA), C.A.C. Regimental HQ federally recognized on 4 August 1921 at New York City, NY. Assigned on 15 October 1921 to the 201st C.A. Brig. (First Army). Redesignated on 14 May 1924 as the 212th C.A. Regt. (AA). Attached to the New York C.A. Brig. (later redesignated 102d C.A. Brig.) on 22 April 1929 for command and control during peacetime. Relieved from the First Army (as an element of the 201st C.A. Brig.) on 1 October 1933 and assigned to the GHQR. Conducted annual summer training at numerous locations to include Fort Totten, NY; Camp Upton, NY; Fort Ontario, NY; and Camp Smith, NY. Designated mobilization training station was Camp Upton. Relieved from the 201st C.A. Brig. on 30 December 1940 and assigned to the 102d C.A. Brig. (AA). Inducted into Federal service on 10 February 1941 at New York City, NY, and transferred to Camp Stewart, GA, arriving there on 20 February 1941. Relieved from the 102d C.A. Brig. (AA) in March 1941 and assigned to the 33d C.A. Brig. (AA). Location 7 December 1941—Camp Hulen, TX.

Events: 61, 280, 301, 330

Commanders, 212th Coast Artillery Regiment

Col. Nelson B. Burr	9 December 1921–13 January 1925	Col. Edward E. Gauche	4 October 1935–29 July 1940
Col. William Ottman	13 January 1925–24 September 1935	Lt. Col. Robert V. Lee	29 July 1940–22 February 1941
Col. Francis A. Hause (R.A.)	22 February 1941–ao December 1941		

213th Coast Artillery Regiment (Antiaircraft) (201st Coast Artillery Brigade) **Pennsylvania National Guard**

HQ—Allentown, PA, 1922–40; Camp Pendleton, VA, 1940–41; Camp Stewart, GA, 1941

Demobilized 4–18 May 1919 as machine gun elements of the 28th Div. Reorganized in the Pennsylvania N.G. on 23 July 1920–6 August 1921 and designated as the Provisional (Prov.) Inf. Regt. Reorganized and redesignated on 13 November 1922 as the 213th Arty. Regt. (AA), C.A.C. Regimental HQ concurrently organized and federally recognized at Allentown, PA. Assigned to the 201st C.A. Brig. (First Army). Redesignated on 1 August 1924 as the 213th C.A. Regt. (AA). For annual summer training, the regiment sailed from Philadelphia, PA, to Fort Monroe, VA, on the U.S.A.T. *Chateau Thierry* in July 1925 and on the U.S.A.T. *St. Mihiel* in August 1926. Relieved from the First Army on 1 October 1933 and assigned to the GHQR. Entire regiment called up to perform relief duties in connection with the flooding of the Schuylkill and Susquehanna Rivers in April 1936. Conducted annual summer training at numerous locations to include Mount Gretna, PA; Indiantown Gap, PA; Bethany Beach, DE; Fort Monroe, VA; Virginia Beach, VA; and Fort Story, VA. Inducted into Federal service on 16 September 1940 at Allentown, PA, and transferred to Camp Pendleton, VA, arriving there on 24 September 1940. Regiment marched in the fourth inaugural parade of President Roosevelt on 20 January 1941. Transferred to Camp Stewart, GA, on 22 February 1941 and assigned to the 38th C.A. Brig. Location 7 December 1941—Camp Stewart, GA.

Status: Assigned to the USARS as the 213th Air Defense Arty.; 1st Bn. active at Spring City, PA, as an element of the 28th Inf. Div.

Events: 281, 301, 330

Commanders, 213th Coast Artillery Regiment

Col. Clarence J. Smith	13 November 1922–29 July 1939	Col. Charles C. Curtis	30 July 1939–5 December 1941

214th Coast Artillery Regiment (Antiaircraft) (I) **Kentucky National Guard**

HQ—*Not organized,* 1921–27

Constituted in the N.G. in 1921 as the 214th Arty. Regt. (AA), C.A.C. and allotted to the state of Kentucky. Redesignated on 1 June 1924 as the 214th C.A. Regt. (AA). Regiment withdrawn from the state of Kentucky in March 1926. Withdrawn from allotment to the N.G. on 17 September 1927 and demobilized.

214th Coast Artillery Regiment (Antiaircraft) (II) **Georgia National Guard**

HQ—Washington, GA, 1939–40; Camp Stewart, GA, 1940–41

Constituted in the N.G. on 1 May 1939 and allotted to the state of Georgia. Regimental HQ organized and federally recognized on 29 October 1939 at Washington, GA. The 1st Bn. organized on 20 October 1939 from elements of the 264th C.A. Bn. (Harbor Defense) with HQ at Thomson, GA. The 2d Bn. organized on 29 October 1939 by conversion and redesignation of the 2d Bn., 122d Inf. with HQ at Elberton, GA. Conducted annual summer training at Fort Barrancas in 1940. Inducted into Federal service on 25 November 1940 at Washington, GA, and transferred to Camp Stewart, GA, arriving there on 3 December 1940. Assigned to the 38th C.A. Brig. Location 7 December 1941—Camp Stewart, GA.

Status: Assigned to the USARS as the 214th F.A.; 1st Bn. active at Elberton, GA, as an element of the 138th F.A. Brig.

Events: 330

Commanders, 214th Coast Artillery Regiment

Col. John E. Stoddard	29 October 1939–11 November 1943

215th Coast Artillery Regiment (Antiaircraft) **Minnesota National Guard**

HQ—Mankato, MN, 1940–41; Camp Haan, CA, 1941; Fort Greely, TA, 1941

Constituted in the N.G. on 1 July 1940 and allotted to the state of Minnesota. Concurrently organized with regimental HQ at Mankato, MN, from the 205th Inf. Regt. and some elements of the 206th Inf. Assigned to the 101st C.A. Brig. Inducted into Federal service on 6 January 1941 at Mankato, MN, and transferred to Camp Haan, CA, arriving there on 19 January 1941. Transferred on 7 August 1941 to Camp Murray, WA. Concurrently relieved from the 101st C.A. Brig. Departed Seattle Port of Embarkation on 29 August 1941 on the U.S.A.T. *U.S. Grant* and transferred to Fort Greely, TA, arriving there on 3 September 1941. Assigned to the Alaskan Defense Command. Location 7 December 1941—Fort Greely, TA.

Commanders, 215th Coast Artillery Regiment

Col. Ivan Bowen	1 July 1940–13 March 1941	Col. William D. Frazer (R.A.)	13 March 1941–2 October 1943

216th Coast Artillery Regiment (Antiaircraft) **Minnesota National Guard**

HO—St. Paul. MN. 1940–41; Camp Haan, CA, 1941

Constituted in the N.G. on 1 July 1940 and allotted to the state of Minnesota. Concurrently organized from the 206th Inf. Regt. with regimental HQ at St. Paul, MN. Assigned to the 101st C.A. Brig. Inducted into Federal service on 6 January 1941 at St. Paul, MN, and transferred to Camp Haan, CA, arriving there on 19 January 1941. Temporarily transferred on 2 December 1941 to San Francisco, CA. Location 7 December 1941—San Francisco, CA.

Events: 335

Commanders, 216th Coast Artillery Regiment

Col. Donald B. Robinson	1 July 1940–August 1940	Lt. Col. Paul F. Schlick	August 1940–ao January 1941
Unknown	ao January 1941–7 December 1941		

217th Coast Artillery Regiment (Antiaircraft) **Minnesota National Guard**

HQ—St. Cloud, MN, 1940–41; Camp Haan, CA, 1941

Constituted in the N.G. on 1 July 1940 and allotted to the state of Minnesota. Concurrently organized from elements of the 205th and 206th Inf. Regts. with regimental HQ organized and federally recognized at St. Cloud, MN. Assigned to the 101st C.A. Brig. Inducted into Federal service on 10 February 1941 at St. Cloud, MN, and transferred to Camp Haan, CA, arriving there on 24 February 1941. Deployed to Oakland-Berkeley, CA, on 4 December 1941. Location 7 December 1941—Oakland-Berkeley, CA.

Events: 335

Commanders, 217th Coast Artillery Regiment

Col. John W. Carter	1 July 1940–November 1941	Lt. Col. W.J. Bergquist	November 1941–ao December 1941

240th Coast Artillery Regiment (Harbor Defense) (Type A) **Maine National Guard**

HQ—Portland, ME, 1922–40; Fort McKinley, ME, 1940–41

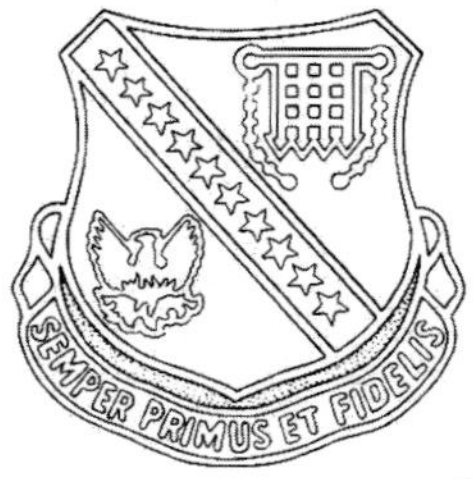

Demobilized on 13 March 1919 as elements of the 54th Arty. Regt., C.A.C. Reorganized in the Maine N.G., 1920–21, with old and new coast defense companies. Designated as the 1st Coast Defense Command, C.A.C. on 15 May 1922. Assigned to the Harbor Defenses of Portland. Regimental HQ organized and federally recognized on 11 July 1922 at Portland, ME. Redesignated on 17 September 1923 as the 240th Arty. Regt. (Harbor Defense), C.A.C. to be organized as a 12-battery regiment. Redesignated on 14 May 1924 as the 240th C.A. Regt. (Harbor Defense). The regiment, or elements thereof, called up to perform the following state duties: two batteries for relief duties in connection with a major fire in Thurston, ME, 15–17 September 1924; Btrys C and H for fighting a forest fire near Sagadahoc, ME, 3–13 September 1926. Reorganized in 1931 from 12 to 9 batteries and organized as follows; 1st Bn. as harbor defense; 2d Bn. as 155-mm G, tractor drawn; 3d Bn. as antiaircraft. Relieved from the Harbor Defenses of Portland on 1 October 1933 and assigned to the GHQR. Reassigned to the Harbor Defenses of Portland in 1938. Conducted annual summer training at Fort Williams, ME, 1921–40. Inducted into Federal service on 16 September 1940 at Portland, ME, and transferred to Fort McKinley, ME, arriving there on 23 September 1940. Assumed the mission of manning batteries in the Harbor Defenses of Portland. Location 7 December 1941—Fort McKinley, ME.

Events: 313

Commanders, 240th Coast Artillery Regiment

Col. George E. Fogg	15 May 1922–ao December 1941

241st Coast Artillery Regiment (Harbor Defense) (Type C) **Massachusetts National Guard**

HQ—Boston, MA, 1921–40; Fort Andrews, ME, 1940–41

Demobilized during March–May 1919 as elements of the 26th Div.; the 55th Arty. Regt., C.A.C.; and the Coast Defenses of Boston. Reorganized in the Massachusetts N.G. as the 1st Coast Defense Command, C.A.C. on 19 May 1919 and assigned to the Harbor Defenses of Boston. Regimental HQ organized and federally recognized on 14 March 1921 at Boston, MA. Redesignated on 1 October 1923 as the 240th Arty. Regt. (Harbor Defense), C.A.C. to be organized as a 12-battery regiment. Redesignated on 30 April 1924 as the 241st C.A. Regt. (Harbor Defense). The regiment, or elements thereof, called up to perform the following state duties: relief duties in connection with a major fire in Fall River, MA, in 1928; hurricane relief duties at Fall River in September 1938. Relieved from the Harbor Defenses of Boston on 1 October 1933 and assigned to the GHQR. Reassigned to the Harbor Defenses of Boston in 1938. The 1st Bn. reorganized as an antiaircraft unit in 1938. Btrys M, H, and G awarded the Knox Trophy for C.A. in 1931, 1936, and 1938, respectively. Conducted annual summer training at Fort H.G. Wright, NY, 1921–40. Inducted into Federal service on 16 September 1940 at Boston, MA, and transferred to Fort Andrews, MA, arriving there on 23 September 1940. Assumed the mission of manning batteries in the Harbor Defenses of Boston. Location 7 December 1941—Fort Andrews, MA.

Events: 59, 313

Commanders, 241st Coast Artillery Regiment

Col. Benjamin B. Shedd	14 March 1921–21 March 1927	Col. Harry A. Skinner	21 March 1934–October 1940
Col. George M. King	22 March 1927–20 March 1934	Col. William D. Cottam	October 1940–20 March 1942

242d Coast Artillery Regiment (Harbor Defense) (Type A) **Connecticut National Guard**

HQ—Bridgeport, CT, 1927–40; Fort H.G. Wright, NY, 1940–41

Constituted in the N.G. in 1923 as the 242d Arty. Regt. (Harbor Defense), C.A.C., to be organized as a seven-battery regiment. Allotted to the state of Connecticut and assigned to the Harbor Defenses of Long Island Sound. Separate C.A. companies in the Harbor Defenses of Long Island Sound at Bridgeport, CT, reorganized on 2 October 1923 as the 1st Bn. Regiment redesignated on 29 May 1924 as the 242d C.A. Regt. (Harbor Defense). The remainder of the regiment organized in 1927 as a five-battery regiment. Regimental HQ organized and federally recognized on 1 April 1927 at Bridgeport, CT. Relieved from the Harbor Defenses of Long Island Sound on 1 October 1933 and assigned to the GHQR. Reassigned to the Harbor Defenses of Long Island Sound in 1938. Conducted annual summer training most years at Fort Terry, NY, and many years at Fort H.G. Wright, NY, 1921–40. Inducted into Federal service on 16 September 1940 at Bridgeport, CT, and transferred to Fort H.G. Wright arriving there on 23 September 1940. Assumed the mission of manning batteries at Forts H.G. Wright and Terry in the Harbor Defenses of Long Island Sound. Location 7 December 1941—Fort H.G. Wright, NY.

Events: 59, 313

Commanders, 242d Coast Artillery Regiment

Lt. Col. L. E. Evans 1 April 1927–1 July 1929
Lt. Col. Philip Hurley 19 July 1929–10 December 1932
Col. Russell Y. Moore 10 December 1932–ao July 1942

243d Coast Artillery Regiment (Harbor Defense) (Type A) **Rhode Island National Guard**

HQ—Providence, RI, 1920–40; Fort Adams, RI, 1940–41; Fort Getty, RI, 1941

Constituted in the Rhode Island N.G. on 19 May 1920 as the 1st Coast Defense Command, C.A.C., and assigned to the Harbor Defenses of Narragansett Bay. Concurrently regimental HQ organized and federally recognized at Providence, RI. Redesignated on 1 October 1923 as the 243d Arty. Regt. (Harbor Defense), C.A.C. to be organized as a nine-battery regiment organized into three battalions. Redesignated on 11 July 1924 as the 243d C.A. Regt. (Harbor Defense). The regiment, or elements thereof, called up to perform the following state duties: entire regiment for riot control in the textile workers strike at Bristol, Pawtucket, and Warwick, RI, 20 February–14 October 1922; Btry I for fighting a forest fire near East Greenwich, RI, 12–13 May 1926; Btry H for crowd control duties in connection with the Mackinac Bridge disaster at Pawtucket, RI, 18 August 1926; entire regiment for riot control in the textile workers strike at Saylesville and Bristol, RI, 10–14 September 1934; entire regiment for flood relief duties along the Pawtuxet River, 19–20 March 1936; riot control at the Narragansett Race Track, 16–19 October 1937; entire regiment for flood relief duties along the Pawtuxet River at Norwood, RI, 24–26 July 1938; entire regiment for hurricane relief duty at Providence, Westerly, and Newport, RI, 21–25 September 1938. Awarded the US Coast Artillery Association Trophy for N.G. regiments for 1932, 1936, and 1937. Relieved from the Harbor Defenses of Narragansett Bay on 1 October 1933 and assigned to the GHQR. Reassigned to the Harbor Defenses of Narragansett Bay in 1938. Conducted annual summer training at Fort H.G. Wright, NY, 1921–40. Inducted into Federal service on 16 September 1940 at Providence, RI, and transferred to Fort Adams, RI, arriving there on 22 September 1940. Assumed the mission of manning batteries in the Harbor Defenses of Narragansett Bay. HQ relocated on 14 March 1941 to Fort Getty, RI. Location 7 December 1941—Fort Getty, RI.

Events: 59, 313

Commanders, 243d Coast Artillery Regiment

Col. Cyril L.D. Wells 3 June 1921–ao January 1932
Col. John J. Collins ao August 1933–11 April 1935
Col. Earl C. Webster 12 April 1935–12 December 1941

244th Coast Artillery Regiment (Tractor Drawn) **New York National Guard**

HQ—New York City, NY, 1921–40; Camp Pendleton, VA, 1940–41

Active in the New York N.G. as the 9th C.A.C. Redesignated as the 9th Coast Defense Command, C.A.C. on 13 June 1921 and federally recognized with HQ at New York City, NY. Redesignated on 1 February 1924 as the 244th Arty. (Harbor Defense), C.A.C. Reorganized and redesignated on 14 May 1924 as the 244th C.A. Regt. (Tractor Drawn), armed with 155-mm Guns, and assigned to the Second Coast Artillery District. Further assigned on 22 April 1929 to the New York C.A. Brig. (later redesignated 102d C.A. Brig.) for command and control during peacetime. Regiment was reviewed on 30 July 1932 at Fort Ontario, NY, by Grand Duchess Marie of the Russian Imperial Family. Regiment was reviewed on 14 July 1933 by Maj. Gen. Friedrich von Böetticher, German Military Attaché to Washington, DC. Reorganized and redesignated on 15 March 1940 as the 244th C.A. Regt. (155-mm Gun). Awarded the US Coast Artillery Association Trophy for N.G. regiments for 1940. Conducted annual summer training at various locations to include Fort Ontario, NY; Fort H.G. Wright, NY; Camp Smith, NY; and Fort Eustis, VA, 1922–40. Inducted into Federal service on 16 September 1940 at New York City, NY, and transferred to Camp Pendleton, VA, arriving there on 23 September 1940. Assigned to the Southern Defense Command. Location 7 December 1941—Camp Pendleton, VA.

Events: 61, 301, 330

Commanders, 244th Coast Artillery Regiment

Col. John J. Byrne	1 February 1924–18 April 1929
Col. Lewis M. Thiery	19 April 1929–23 November 1934
Col. Mills Miller	20 December 1934–11 July 1938
Col. Charles H. Ellard	11 July 1938–14 August 1939
Col. Malcolm W. Force	21 September 1939–1 March 1942

245th Coast Artillery Regiment (Harbor Defense) (Type C) **New York National Guard**

HQ—Brooklyn, NY, 1920–40; Fort Hancock, NJ, 1940–41

Organized in the New York N.G. as the 13th Coast Defense Command, C.A.C.; federally recognized on 18 June 1920 with HQ at Brooklyn, NY; and assigned to the Harbor Defenses of Sandy Hook. Redesignated on 26 December 1923 as the 245th Arty. Regt. (Harbor Defense), C.A.C. to be organized as a 12-battery regiment. Redesignated on 14 May 1924 as the 245th C.A. Regt. (Harbor Defense). Attached to the New York C.A. Brig. (later redesignated 102d C.A. Brig.) on 22 April 1929 for command and control during peacetime. Relieved from the Harbor Defenses of Sandy Hook on 1 October 1933 and assigned to the GHQR. Reassigned to the Harbor Defenses of Sandy Hook in 1938. Conducted annual summer training most years at Fort H.G. Wright, 1921–40, and some years at Camp Smith, NY, or Fort Hancock, NJ. Inducted into Federal service on 16 September 1940 at Brooklyn, NY, and transferred to Fort Hancock, NJ, arriving there on 24 September 1940. Assumed the mission of manning batteries in the Harbor Defenses of Sandy Hook. Location 7 December 1941—Fort Hancock, NJ.

Events: 61, 87, 93

Commanders, 245th Coast Artillery Regiment

Col. Sydney Grant	18 June 1920–30 October 1926
Col. Bryer H. Pendry	30 October 1926–7 December 1937
Col. Charles S. Gleim	29 December 1937–August 1943

246th Coast Artillery Regiment (Harbor Defense) (Type A) **Virginia National Guard**

HQ—Richmond, VA, 1922–29; Lynchburg, VA, 1929–41; Fort Monroe, VA, 1940–41

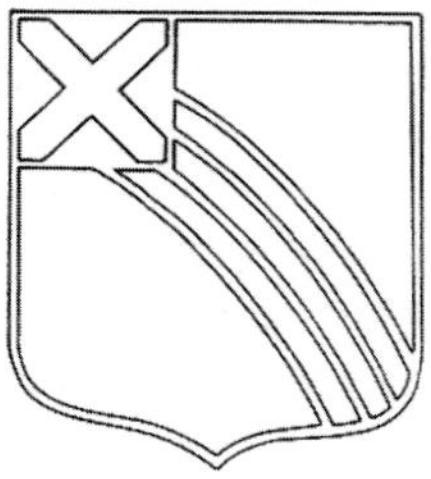

Constituted in the Virginia N.G. on 8 March 1922 as the 1st Coast Defense Command, C.A.C., and assigned to the Harbor Defenses of Chesapeake Bay. Concurrently regimental HQ organized and federally recognized at Richmond, VA. Redesignated on 5 November 1923 as the 246th Arty. Regt. (Harbor Defense), C.A.C. to be organized as an eight-battery regiment. Redesignated on 19 August 1924 as the 246th C.A. Regt. (Harbor Defense). HQ relocated on 26 August 1929 to Lynchburg, VA. Relieved from the Harbor Defenses of Chesapeake Bay on 1 October 1933 and assigned to the GHQR. Reassigned to the Harbor Defenses of Chesapeake Bay in 1938. The regiment, or elements thereof, called up to perform the following state duties: batteries to fight forest fires in the mountains of western Virginia, 1921–26; strike duty at the Dan River Cotton Mills, Schoolfield, VA, 23 January–11 February 1931; hurricane relief in the Chesapeake Bay area, 22–23 August 1933. Conducted annual summer training at Fort Monroe, VA, 1922–36, and at Fort Story, VA, 1937–40. Inducted into Federal service on 16 September 1940 at Lynchburg, VA, and transferred to Fort Monroe, VA, arriving there on 23 September 1940. Assumed the mission of manning batteries at Forts Monroe and Story in the Harbor Defenses of Chesapeake Bay. Location 7 December 1941—Fort Monroe, VA.

Status: Assigned to the USARS as the 246th F.A.; 1st Bn. active at Danville, VA, as an element of the 29th Inf. Div. (Light).

Commanders, 246th Coast Artillery Regiment

Col. Marshall M. Milton	8 March 1922–15 March 1926	Col. Alonzo E. Wood	1 July 1929–October 1941
Col. Frank B. Varney	15 March 1926–1 July 1929	Col. Richard T. Arrington	October 1941–ao December 1941

248th Coast Artillery Regiment (Harbor Defense) (Type A) **Washington National Guard**

HQ—Olympia, WA, 1923–40; Fort Worden, WA, 1940–41

Demobilized during January–March 1919 as elements of the 63d and 65th Arty. Regts., C.A.C., and Coast Defenses of Puget Sound. Reorganized on 13 November 1923 in the Washington N.G. as the 1st Bn., C.A.C. (three companies) and assigned to the Harbor Defenses of Puget Sound. Concurrently battalion HQ organized and federally recognized at Olympia, MA. Redesignated on 1 March 1924 as the 1st Bn. (Prov.), 248th Arty. Regt., C.A.C. Further redesignated on 1 May 1924 as the 1st Bn. (Prov.), 248th C.A. Regt. (Harbor Defense). Relieved from the Harbor Defenses of Puget Sound on 1 October 1933 and assigned to the GHQR. Concurrently, reorganized and redesignated as the 248th C.A. Bn. Expanded and redesignated on 1 September 1935 as the 248th C.A. Regt. (Harbor Defense) (Type B). Regiment consisted only of regimental HHB and Btrys A, B, and C; HHB, 1st Bn. and entire 2d Bn. inactive. Reassigned to the Harbor Defenses of Puget Sound in 1938. The regiment, or elements thereof, called up to perform the following state duties: riot control at an International Workers of the World strike at Aberdeen, WA, in May 1922; riot control during the "hunger marches" at Olympia, WA, 1–3 March 1933; riot control at a lumber workers strike at Aberdeen and Tacoma, WA, 24 June–9 August 1935. Conducted annual summer training at Fort Worden, WA, 1922–40. Reorganized on 1 January 1940 as a Type A regiment. Remainder of regiment organized on 1 September 1940 by activation of HHB, 1st Bn. and conversion and redesignation of the 2d Bn., 148th F.A. as the 2d Bn. Inducted into Federal service on 16 September 1940 at Olympia, MA, and transferred to Fort Worden, MA, arriving there on 23 September 1940. Assumed the mission of manning batteries in the Harbor Defenses of Puget Sound. Location 7 December 1941—Fort Worden, WA.

Status: Disbanded on 14 June 1944.

Commanders, 248th Coast Artillery Regiment

Maj. Edward C. Dohm	1 September 1935–28 November 1939	Maj. Robert W. Forbes	29 November 1939–August 1940
Col. Alfred W. McMorris	August 1940–ao December 1941		

249th Coast Artillery Regiment (Harbor Defense) (Type A) **Oregon National Guard**

HQ—Marshfield, OR, 1926–30; Salem, 1930; Portland, OR, 1930–32; Salem, 1932–40; Camp Clatsop, OR, 1940–41; Fort Stevens, OR, 1941

Organized in the Oregon N.G., 1919–21, as separate C.A. companies. Companies consolidated and redesignated on 12 December 1923 as elements of the 249th Arty. Regt. (Harbor Defense), C.A.C., to be organized as an eight-battery regiment, and assigned to the Harbor Defenses of the Columbia. Redesignated on 18 April 1924 as the 249th C.A. Regt. (Harbor Defense). Regimental HQ organized and federally recognized on 17 April 1926 at Marshfield, OR. HQ successively relocated as follows: to Salem, OR, on 21 February 1930; to Portland, OR, on 23 July 1930; and back to Salem on 1 July 1932. Relieved from the Harbor Defenses of the Columbia on 1 October 1933 and assigned to the GHQR. Reassigned to the Harbor Defenses of the Columbia in 1938. Awarded the US Coast Artillery Association Trophy for N.G. regiments for 1933 and 1938. Conducted annual summer training at numerous locations to include Fort Worden, WA; Fort Stevens, WA; Fort Casey, WA; Fort Barry, CA; and Camp Clatsop, OR. Inducted into Federal service on 16 September 1940 at Salem and transferred to Camp Clatsop, OR, arriving there on 23 September 1940. Assumed the mission of manning batteries in the Harbor Defenses of the Columbia. Transferred on 6 February 1941 to Fort Stevens, OR. Location 7 December 1941—Fort Stevens, OR.

Commanders, 249th Coast Artillery Regiment

Lt. Col. Duncan Ferguson Jr.	17 April 1926–6 February 1930	Col. Clifton M. Irwin	6 February 1930–October 1941
Lt. Col. Clyde G. Young	October 1941–ao January 1942		

250th Coast Artillery Regiment (Tractor Drawn) **California National Guard**

HQ—San Francisco, CA, 1921–40; Camp McQuaide, CA, 1940–41; Fort Greely, TA, 1941

Organized in the California N.G., 1921–22, as separate C.A. companies. Companies assigned on 9 November 1921 as elements of the 1st Coast Defense Command, C.A.C. Concurrently HQ organized and federally recognized at San Francisco, CA. The 1st Coast Defense Command redesignated on 6 October 1923 as the 250th Arty. Regt. (Harbor Defense), C.A.C. Assigned to the Ninth Coast Artillery District. Reorganized and redesignated on 1 November 1924 as the 250th C.A. Regt. (Tractor Drawn). Relieved from the Ninth Coast Artillery District on 1 October 1933 and assigned to the GHQR. Called up to perform riot duty in connection with the San Francisco Longshoreman's strike in May 1934. Assigned to the Harbor Defenses of San Francisco in 1938. Reorganized on 15 March 1940 and redesignated 250th C.A. Regt. (155-mm Gun). Conducted annual summer training most years at Camp McQuaide, CA, and some years at Fort MacArthur, CA; Fort Barry, CA; or Camp San Luis Obispo, CA. Inducted into Federal service on 16 September 1940 at San Francisco, CA, and transferred to Camp McQuaide, arriving there on 23 September 1940. Transferred on the U.S.A.T. *St. Mihiel* to Fort Greely, TA, on 19 September 1941 and assigned to the Alaskan Defense Command. Location 7 December 1941—Fort Greely, TA.

Status: 1st Bn. active in the California N.G. as the 579th Engr. Bn.

Events: 231, 289

Commanders, 250th Coast Artillery Regiment

Col. Richard E. Mittelsteadt	9 November 1921–7 October 1938	Col David P. Hardy	8 October 1938–4 November 1941

251st Coast Artillery Regiment (Harbor Defense) **California National Guard**

HQ—San Diego, CA, 1924–40; Ventura, CA, 1940; Fort Shafter, TH, 1940–41; Camp Malakole, TH, 1941

Constituted in the N.G. in 1924, allotted to the state of California, and assigned to the Harbor Defenses of San Diego. Regimental HQ organized and federally recognized on 7 November 1924 at San Diego, CA. Reorganized and redesignated on 1 January 1930 as the 251st C.A. Regt. (AA). Relieved from the Harbor Defenses of San Diego on 1 October 1933 and assigned to the GHQR. Reassigned to the Harbor Defenses of San Diego in 1938. The 2d Bn. was called up to conduct earthquake relief operations, 10–22 March 1933, in the Los Angeles area. Awarded the US Coast Artillery Association Trophy for N.G. regiments for 1935. Conducted annual summer training most years at Fort MacArthur, CA, and some years at Camp San Luis Obispo, CA, or Ventura, CA. Inducted into Federal service on 16 September 1940 at San Diego and transferred to Ventura arriving there on 22 September 1940. Ordered by the War Department on 10 October 1940 to transfer to the Hawaiian Department. The first contingent sailed from San Pedro, CA, on 30 October 1940 and arrived on 4 November 1940 at Honolulu, TH, on the U.S.S. *George Washington.* This movement made the 251st C.A. Regt. the first N.G. unit to deploy overseas after the call up for World War II. The remainder of the regiment arrived on 23 November 1940 on the U.S.A.T. *Leonard Wood* and transferred to Fort Shafter. Entire regiment transferred on 27 January 1941 to Camp Malakole, TH. Assigned in March 1941 to the Hawaiian Sep. C.A. Brig. Location 7 December 1941—Camp Malakole, TH.

Events: 231, 289, 304, 312

Commanders, 251st Coast Artillery Regiment

Col. Walter G. Gastil 7 November 1924–11 December 1927
Lt. Col. Harry H. Morehead 11 December 1927–December 1935
Col. John H. Sherman December 1935–ao January 1942

252d Coast Artillery Regiment (Harbor Defense) **North Carolina National Guard**

HQ—Wilmington, NC, 1924–40; Fort Moultrie, SC, 1940–41; Fort Screven, GA, 1941

Constituted in the N.G. in 1924, allotted to the state of North Carolina, and assigned to the Harbor Defenses of the Cape Fear. Regimental HQ organized and federally recognized on 9 June 1924 at Wilmington, NC. Reorganized and redesignated on 25 November 1929 as the 252d C.A. Regt. (Tractor Drawn). Concurrently reequipped with 155-mm G.P.F. guns. Relieved from the Harbor Defenses of the Cape Fear on 1 October 1933 and assigned to the GHQR. Reorganized and redesignated in 1937 as the 252d C.A. Regt. (Truck Drawn). Assigned to the Harbor Defenses of Charleston in 1938. Entire regiment called up to perform riot control for textile workers' strike at Greensboro and High Point, NC, 6–25 September 1934. Reorganized and redesignated on 15 March 1940 as the 252d C.A. Regt. (155-mm Gun). Conducted annual summer training most years at Fort Moultrie, SC, and some years at Fort Monroe, VA; Fort Bragg, NC; and Fort McPherson, GA. Inducted into Federal service on 16 September 1940 at Wilmington, NC. Transferred to Fort Moultrie, SC, arriving there on 23 September 1940, and assigned to the Southern Defense Command. Transferred in January 1941 to Fort Screven, GA. Location 7 December 1941—Fort Screven, GA.

Commanders, 252d Coast Artillery Regiment

Col. Royce S. McClelland 9 June 1924–ao January 1941
Unknown ao January 1941–7 December 1941

253d Coast Artillery Regiment (155-mm Gun) **Puerto Rico National Guard**

HQ—*Not organized,* 1940–41

Constituted in the N.G. on 8 May 1940, allotted to the Commonwealth of Puerto Rico, and assigned to the Puerto Rican Department. The HQ, 1st Bn. organized and federally recognized on 1 September 1940 at San Juan. The 1st

Bn. inducted into Federal service on 15 October 1940 at San Juan and assigned to the Harbor Defenses of San Juan. Location 7 December 1941—San Juan, PR (1st Bn. only).

Status: Assigned to the USARS as the 162d Field Artillery (consolidated with the 162d F.A. on 15 February 1959); 1st Bn. active at Hato Rey, PR; 2d Bn. active at Hato Rey, PR; and 3d Bn. active at Ponce, PR.

Events: 329

260th Coast Artillery Regiment (Harbor Defense) — District of Columbia National Guard

HQ—Washington, DC, 1935–41; Fort Bliss, TX, 1941

Constituted in the N.G. on 17 June 1924, allotted to the District of Columbia to be organized as a five-battery regiment, and assigned to the Harbor Defenses of the Potomac. The HQ, 1st Bn. organized and federally recognized on 3 September 1924 at Washington, DC. President Calvin Coolidge presented the unit's initial set of regimental colors to the commander at a ceremony at the White House on 19 January 1926. Reorganized and redesignated on 1 August 1929 as the 260th C.A. Regt. (AA), relieved from the Harbor Defenses of the Potomac, and assigned to the Fourth Coast Artillery District. Relieved from the Fourth Coast Artillery District on 1 October 1933 and assigned to the GHQR. Regimental HQ organized and federally recognized on 20 December 1935 at Washington, DC. Reassigned to the Fourth Coast Artillery District in 1938. The 2d Bn. organized on 1 April 1939 (subordinate batteries already active) with HQ federally recognized at Washington. Conducted annual summer training most years at Fort Monroe, VA, and some years at Fort Story, VA, or Camp Ritchie, MD. Conducted the War Department-directed week of winter training at Fort Meade, MD, 25 November–2 December 1939. Attached to the Third Army on 30 December 1940. Inducted into Federal service on 6 January 1941 at Washington, transferred to Fort Bliss, TX, arriving there on 29 January 1941, and assigned to the Southern Defense Command. Location 7 December 1941—Fort Bliss, TX.

Status: HHB is active in the District of Columbia N.G. as HHC, 260th Military Police (M.P.) Brig. at Washington, DC.

Events: 151, 281, 301

Commanders, 260th Coast Artillery Regiment

Col. Walter J. Burns	2 December 1935–2 April 1941	Col. Leroy S. Mann	2 April 1941–ao January 1942

261st Coast Artillery Battalion (Harbor Defense) (Type D) — Delaware National Guard

HQ—*Not organized,* 1924–36; Dover, DE, 1936–41; Fort DuPont, DE, 1941

Constituted in the N.G. in 1924 as the 1st Sep. Bn., C.A. (Harbor Defense), allotted to the state of Delaware to be organized as a two-battery battalion, and assigned to the Harbor Defenses of the Delaware. Designated mobilization training station was Fort DuPont, DE. Btry A organized on 24 March 1924 at Laurel, DE. Redesignated on 3 August 1925 as the 261st Bn., C.A. (Harbor Defense). Remaining batteries of the battalion were organized in 8-9 July 1936. The battalion HQ organized and federally recognized on 9 July 1936 at Dover, DE. Conducted annual summer training most years at Fort Hancock, NJ, 1924–40. The battalion was redesignated on 15 April 1940 as the 1st Bn., 261st C.A. Regt. (Harbor Defense). The 1st Bn. was redesignated 261st C.A. Bn. (Harbor Defense) on 27 January 1941, inducted into Federal service at Dover, DE, and transferred to Fort DuPont, DE. Location 7 December 1941—Fort DuPont, DE.

Commanders, 261st Coast Artillery Battalion

Lt. Col. Henry K. Roscoe	9 July 1936–5 December 1941	Maj. Ralph S. Baker	5 December 1941–ao January 1942

261st Coast Artillery Regiment (Harbor Defense) (Type B) **Delaware and New Jersey National Guard**

HQ—*Not organized,* 1940–41

Constituted in the N.G. on 15 April 1940, allotted to the states of Delaware and New Jersey, and assigned to the Harbor Defenses of the Delaware. Concurrently, the 1st Bn. organized from the 261st C.A. Bn. (Harbor Defense) at Dover. The 2d Bn. was constituted in the New Jersey N.G. on 20 July 1940 and organized and federally recognized on 25 November 1940 at Jersey City, NJ. The 2d Bn. was redesignated 122d C.A. Bn. (AA) on 15 January 1941 and inducted into Federal service on 27 January 1941 at Jersey City, NJ. The 1st Bn. redesignated 261st C.A. Bn. (Harbor Defense) on 27 January 1941, inducted into Federal service at Dover, DE, and transferred to Fort DuPont, DE.

262d Coast Artillery Battalion (Harbor Defense) (Type D) **New Jersey National Guard**

HQ—*Not organized,* 1924–35

Constituted in the N.G. in 1924, allotted to the state of New Jersey as a two-battery battalion, and assigned to the Harbor Defenses of Sandy Hook. Mission was to reinforce coast defenses at the Harbor Defenses of Sandy Hook. Designated mobilization training station was Fort Hancock, NJ. Withdrawn from the N.G. in August 1935 and demobilized.

263d Coast Artillery Battalion (Harbor Defense) (Type D) **South Carolina National Guard**

HQ—Beaufort, SC, 1923–30

Constituted in the N.G. in 1924, allotted to the state of South Carolina as a three-battery battalion, and assigned to the Harbor Defenses of Charleston. Organized from the 1st Coast Defense Command, C.A.C., on 31 July 1925 (HQ organized and federally recognized on 21 July 1923 at Beaufort, SC; redesignated on 25 March 1924 as the 1st Sep. Bn., C.A. (Harbor Defense), South Carolina N.G.; redesignated on 31 July 1925 as the 263d C.A. Bn. [Harbor Defense]). Detail from HQ Btry called up, 26–30 June 1927, to perform guard duty of state prisoners in Beaufort. Designated mobilization training station was Fort Moultrie, SC. Conducted annual summer training most years at Fort Moultrie, 1923–29, and some years at Fort Monroe, VA. Redesignated as the 1st Bn., 263d C.A. Regt. (Harbor Defense) on 10 June 1930.

Commanders, 263d Coast Artillery Battalion

Maj. Claud C. Smith	31 July 1925–10 June 1930

263d Coast Artillery Regiment (Harbor Defense) (Type B) **South Carolina National Guard**

HQ—Beaufort, SC, 1930–35; Greenwood, SC, 1935–41; Fort Moultrie, SC, 1941

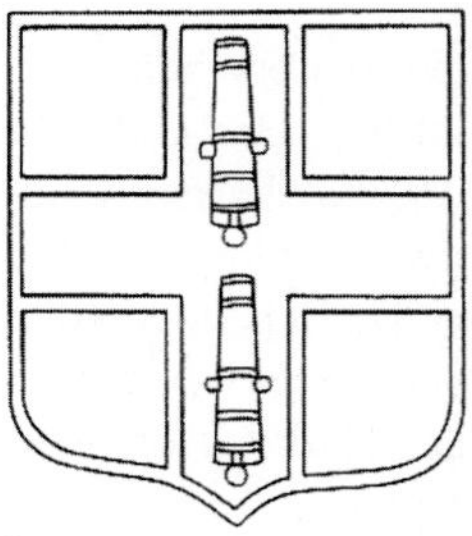

Constituted in the N.G. on 10 June 1930 as a Type B regiment to consist of 3 battalions of 9 batteries. Allotted to the state of South Carolina and assigned to the Harbor Defenses of Charleston. The 1st Bn. concurrently organized from the 263d C.A. Bn. at Beaufort. Regimental HQ organized and federally recognized on 14 June 1930 at Beaufort, SC. The 2d Bn. organized and federally recognized on 15 June 1930 at Florence, SC. Relieved from the Harbor Defenses of Charleston on 1 October 1933 and assigned to the GHQR. HQ relocated on 6 June 1935 to Greenwood, SC. Reassigned to the Harbor Defenses of Charleston in 1938. Conducted annual summer training at Fort Moultrie, SC, 1930–40, and some years at Fort Monroe, VA. Inducted into Federal service on 13 January 1941 at Greenwood and transferred to Fort Moultrie arriving there on 21 January 1941. Assumed the mission of manning batteries in the Harbor Defenses of Charleston. Location 7 December 1941—Fort Moultrie, SC.

Status: Assigned to the USARS as the 263d Air Defense Arty.; 1st Bn. active at Columbia, SC, and 2d Bn. active at Anderson, SC, as elements of the 263d Air Defense Arty. Brig.

Events: 334

Commanders, 263d Coast Artillery Regiment

Col. Claud C. Smith	14 June 1930–ao March 1942

264th Coast Artillery Battalion (Harbor Defense) (Type D) **Georgia National Guard**

HQ—Statesboro, GA, 1930–39

Constituted in the N.G. in 1924, allotted to the state of Georgia as a two-battery battalion, and assigned to the Harbor Defenses of Savannah. HQ organized and federally recognized on 16 May 1930 at Statesboro, GA. Reorganized and redesignated 1st Bn., 264th C.A. Regt. on 1 September 1935, relieved from the harbor defenses of Savannah and assigned to the GHQR. Designated mobilization training station was Fort Screven, GA. Conducted annual summer training most years at Fort Moultrie, SC, and some years at Fort Barrancas, FL.

Commanders, 264th Coast Artillery Battalion

Maj. Leroy Cowart	16 May 1930–1 September 1935

264th Coast Artillery Regiment (Harbor Defense) (Type A) **Georgia National Guard**

HQ—*Not organized,* 1935–39

Constituted in the N.G. on 1 September 1935, allotted to the state of Georgia as a nine-battery regiment, and assigned to the GHQR. The 1st Bn. organized on 1 September 1935 from the 264th C.A. Bn. (organized and federally recognized on 16 May 1930 with HQ at Statesboro, GA). Reassigned to the Harbor Defenses of Galveston in the 1938 Protective Mobilization Plan. Designated mobilization training station was Fort Screven, GA. Conducted annual summer training most years at Fort Moultrie, SC, and some years at Fort Barrancas, FL. Subordinate batteries of the 1st Bn. redesignated as batteries of the 214th C.A. (AA) on 1 October 1939. Concurrently remainder of the regiment disbanded.

Commanders, 264th Coast Artillery Regiment
(1st Battalion)

Maj. Leroy Cowart	1 September 1935-1 October 1939

265th Coast Artillery Regiment (Harbor Defense) (Type B) **Florida National Guard**

HQ—Jacksonville, FL, 1924–41; Fort Crockett, TX, 1941

Constituted in the N.G. in 1924, allotted to the state of Florida as a three-battery battalion, and assigned to the Harbor Defenses of Pensacola. Organized from the 1st Sep. Bn., C.A., on 22 July 1925 (HQ organized and federally recognized on 14 November 1923 at Jacksonville, FL; redesignated on 4 April 1924 as the 1st Sep. Bn., C.A. (Harbor Defense), Florida N.G.; redesignated on 22 July 1925 as the 265th C.A. Bn. [Harbor Defense]). Expanded to a four-battery battalion in February 1928. Battalion expanded to a five-battery, two-battalion regiment on 20 November 1929 and redesignated as the 265th C.A. Regt. (Harbor Defense). New 1st Bn. HHB concurrently organized at Jacksonville with existing batteries, and HQ, 2d Bn. organized and federally recognized at Miami, FL. Designated mobilization training station was Fort Barrancas, FL. The regiment, or elements thereof, called up to perform the following state duties: hurricane relief duties in South Florida, 20–25 September 1926, and for the Palm Beach-Okeechobee Area, 17 September–4 November 1928; guard duties in connection with the Mediterranean Fruit Fly quarantine in South Florida, July 1928–June 1930; 2d Bn. called up to perform riot control duties in connection with the Veteran's Works Project, 28 February–13 May 1935; elements called up to perform guard and security duties in connection with the visit of

President Franklin D. Roosevelt at Winter Park, FL, in March 1935. Relieved from the Harbor Defenses of Pensacola on 1 October 1933 and assigned to the GHQR. Reassigned to the Harbor Defenses of Pensacola and Key West in 1938. Reorganized on 1 May 1939 as a Type A regiment. Concurrently 3d Bn. constituted and organized in south Florida. Conducted annual summer training most years at Key West Barracks, FL; many years at Fort Barrancas, FL; and some years at Fort Monroe, VA. Inducted into Federal service on 6 January 1941 at Jacksonville and transferred to Fort Crockett, TX, arriving there on 15 January 1941. Assumed the mission of manning batteries in the Harbor Defenses of Galveston. Location 7 December 1941—Fort Crockett, TX.

Status: Assigned to the USARS as the 265th Air Defense Arty.

Commanders, 265th Coast Artillery Regiment

Lt. Col. Mayre R. Woodward	14 November 1923–1 March 1937	Col. Percy L. Wall	1 March 1937–ao January 1942

266th Coast Artillery Battalion (Harbor Defense) (Type D) — Alabama National Guard

HQ—*Not organized,* 1924–33

Constituted in the N.G. in 1924, allotted to the state of Alabama as a two-battery battalion, and assigned to the Harbor Defenses of Mobile. Mission was to reactivate coast defenses at Forts Morgan and Gaines. Designated mobilization training station was Fort Morgan, AL. Withdrawn from the state of Alabama in August 1927. Withdrawn from the N.G. on 1 October 1933 and demobilized.

267th Coast Artillery Battalion (Harbor Defense) (Type D) — Louisiana National Guard

HQ—*Not organized,* 1924–33

Constituted in the N.G. in 1924, allotted to the state of Louisiana as a two-battery battalion, and assigned to the Harbor Defenses of New Orleans. Mission was to reactivate coast defenses at Fort Jackson and Fort St. Philip. Designated mobilization training station was Jackson Barracks, LA. Withdrawn from the state of Louisiana in August 1927. Withdrawn from the N.G. on 1 October 1933 and demobilized.

268th Coast Artillery Battalion (Harbor Defense) (Type D) — Texas National Guard

HQ—*Not organized,* 1924–35

Constituted in the N.G. in 1924, allotted to the state of Texas as a two-battery battalion, and assigned to the Harbor Defenses of Galveston. Mission was to reactivate coast defenses at Forts Travis and San Jacinto. Galveston, TX, designated as HQ location on organization, but the unit was never organized at that location. Designated mobilization training station was Fort Crockett, TX. Withdrawn from the N.G. on 21 September 1935 and demobilized.

369th Coast Artillery Regiment (Antiaircraft) (C) — New York National Guard

HO—Harlem. NY. 1924–41; Fort Ontario, NY, 1941; Camp Edwards, MA, 1941

Demobilized on 28 February 1919 at Camp Upton, NY, as the 369th Inf. Regt., an element of the 93d Div. Reconstituted in the N.G. on 19 October 1920 and allotted to the state of New York as a separate regiment. Regimental HQ organized and federally recognized on 6 September 1924 at Harlem, NY. Reorganized and redesignated on 30 August 1940 as the 369th C.A. Regt. Attached to the First Army on 30 December 1940. Inducted into Federal service on 13 January 1941 at Harlem, NY. Transferred to Fort Ontario, NY, arrived there on 15 January 1941, and assigned to the Northeast Defense Command. Transferred on 5 September 1941 to Camp Edwards, MA. Location 7 December 1941—Camp Edwards, MA.

Commanders, 369th Coast Artillery Regiment

Col. Benjamin O. Davis Sr. (R.A.)	30 August 1940–25 October 1940	Col. Chauncey M. Hooper	25 October 1940–December 1943

501st Coast Artillery Regiment (Antiaircraft) (XI Corps) **Organized Reserve Massachusetts**

HQ—Boston, MA, 1921–28; *Inactive,* 1928–33

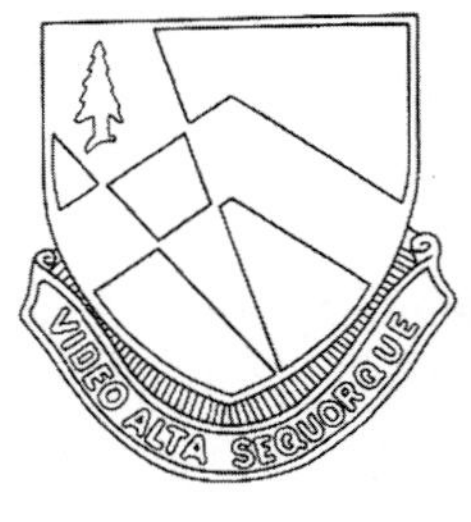

Constituted in the O.R. on 29 July 1921 as the 501st Arty. Regt. (AA), C.A.C., assigned to the XI Corps, and allotted to the First Corps Area. Initiated in November 1921 with the entire regiment at Boston, MA. Redesignated on 30 June 1924 as the 501st C.A. Regt. (AA). Inactivated about June 1928 at Boston by relief of personnel. Typically conducted Inactive Training Period meetings at the Army and Navy Club in Boston. Conducted summer training most years at Fort Adams, RI, and some years at Fort Hancock, NJ. Also conducted C.A. CMTC training some years at Camp Devens as an alternate form of annual training. Primary ROTC feeder school was the Massachusetts Institute of Technology. Designated mobilization station was Camp Devens, MA. Demobilized on 1 October 1933.

Commanders, 501st Coast Artillery Regiment

Capt. Ralph T. Kendall	November 1921–24 January 1923	Lt. Col. Stephen T. Smith	ao June 1924–ao July 1926
Capt. Frank A. Hovey	25 January 1923–April 1923	Unknown	ao July 1926–ao May 1927
Maj. Henry C. Bacon	April 1923–ao May 1923	Lt. Col. George B. Sawyer	ao May 1927–ao January 1928
Unknown	ao May 1923–ao June 1924	*Inactive*	ao July 1928–1 October 1933

502d Coast Artillery Regiment (Antiaircraft) (XII Corps) **Organized Reserve New York**

HQ—Manhattan, NY, 1921–40

Constituted in the O.R. on 29 July 1921 as the 502d Arty. Regt. (AA), C.A.C., assigned to the XII Corps, and allotted to the Second Corps Area. Initiated on 5 October 1921 with regimental HQ at Manhattan, NY. Subordinate battalion HQ concurrently organized as follows: HQ and Combat Train, 1st Bn. at Queens, NY; and HHD, 2d Bn. at Manhattan, NY. Redesignated on 30 June 1924 as the 502d C.A. Regt. (AA). Withdrawn from the O.R. on 1 October 1933 and allotted to the R.A. as an RAI unit. Concurrently relieved from assignment to the XII Corps and assigned to the II Corps. Typically conducted Inactive Training Period meetings at the armory of the 212th C.A. or the Engineer Society Building on 39th Street in New York City. Conducted summer training with the 62d C.A. most years at Fort Tilden, NY, and some years at Camp Upton, NY, or Fort Totten, NY. Also conducted C.A. CMTC training some years at Fort Hancock, NJ, as an alternate form of annual training. Primary ROTC feeder school was Fordham University. Designated mobilization station was Fort Totten, NY, for the regiment minus 1st Bn., and Camp Upton, NY, for the 1st Bn. Redesignated 76th C.A. (AA) (Colored) on 1 July 1940 and assigned to the 33d C.A. Brig. (AA).

Commanders, 502d Coast Artillery Regiment

Maj. Fred E. Stockwell	5 October 1921–10 February 1922	Col. Charles E. Warren	17 July 1923–3 January 1924
Lt. Col. Granville Sevier	10 February 1922–17 July 1923	Col. John M. Thompson	3 January 1924–14 June 1928
Col. Charles H.E. Scheer	14 June 1928–1 July 1940		

503d Coast Artillery Regiment (Antiaircraft) (XIII Corps) **Organized Reserve Pennsylvania**

HQ—*Not initiated,* 1921–22; Tyrone, PA, 1922–32; Pittsburgh, PA, 1932–40

Constituted in the O.R. on 29 July 1921 as the 503d Arty. Regt. (AA), C.A.C., assigned to the XIII Corps, and allotted to the Third Corps Area. Initiated on 1 March 1922 with regimental HQ at Tyrone, PA. Subordinate battalion HQ concurrently organized as follows: HQ and Combat Train, 1st Bn. at Washington, PA; and HHD, 2d Bn. at Lock Haven, PA. Redesignated on 30 June 1924 as the 503d C.A. Regt. (AA). Relieved from the XIII Corps in January 1927 and assigned to the III Corps. Entire regiment relocated on 14 December 1932 to Pittsburgh, PA. Withdrawn from the O.R. on 1 October 1933 and allotted to the R.A. as an RAI unit. Awarded the US Coast Artillery Association Trophy for O.R. regiments for 1940. Conducted summer training with the 61st C.A. at Fort Monroe, VA. Also conducted C.A. CMTC training some years at Fort Monroe as an alternate form of annual training. Primary ROTC feeder school was the University of Pittsburgh. Personnel relieved on 1 July 1940 and assigned to the 1st Bn., 911th C.A. and the 1321st Corps Area Service Unit. Concurrently redesignated 74th C.A. Regt. (AA) on 1 July 1940 activated at Fort Monroe, VA.

Commanders, 503d Coast Artillery Regiment

2d Lt. Herbert A. Mahaffey	1 March 1922–17 March 1922
Col. Edwin A. Ziegler	17 March 1922–1 July 1940

504th Coast Artillery Regiment (Antiaircraft) (XIV Corps) — Organized Reserve Tennessee

HQ—*Not initiated,* 1921–22; Chattanooga, TN, 1922–29; Memphis, TN, 1929–40

Constituted in the O.R. on 29 July 1921 as the 504th Arty. Regt. (AA), C.A.C., assigned to the XIV Corps, and allotted to the Fourth Corps Area. Initiated on 15 March 1922 with regimental HQ at Chattanooga, TN. Subordinate battalion HQ concurrently organized as follows: HQ and Combat Train, 1st Bn. at Knoxville, TN; and HHD, 2d Bn. at Nashville, TN. Redesignated on 30 June 1924 as the 504th C.A. Regt. (AA). Entire regiment relocated on 22 October 1929 to Memphis, TN. Withdrawn from the O.R. on 1 October 1933 and allotted to the R.A. as an RAI unit. Conducted summer training most years at Fort Barrancas, FL. Also conducted C.A. CMTC training some years at Fort Barrancas as an alternate form of annual training. Designated mobilization training station was Camp Jackson, SC. Disbanded on 1 July 1940.

Commanders, 504th Coast Artillery Regiment

Capt. Clifford A. Betts	15 March 1922–ao June 1922
Unknown	ao June 1922–16 July 1923
Col. Robert W. Clark Jr.	16 July 1923–ao June 1932
Unknown	ao June 1932–ao August 1936
Lt. Col. Francis M. Ellerbe	ao August 1936–ao August 1937
Unknown	ao August 1937–19 May 1939
Lt. Col. Fordyce L. Perego	19 March 1939–ao May 1939
Unknown	ao May 1939–ao April 1940
Col. Caldwell Dumas	ao April 1940–1 July 1940

505th Coast Artillery Regiment (Antiaircraft) (XV Corps) — Organized Reserve Ohio

HQ—Cincinnati, OH, 1921–40

Constituted in the O.R. on 29 July 1921 as the 505th Arty. Regt. (AA), C.A.C., assigned to the XV Corps, and allotted to the Fifth Corps Area. Initiated on 21 December 1921 with regimental HQ at Cincinnati, OH. Redesignated on 30 June 1924 as the 505th C.A. Regt. (AA). Withdrawn from the O.R. on 1 October 1933 and allotted to the R.A. as an RAI unit. Concurrently relieved from the XV Corps and assigned to the V Corps. Conducted summer training with the 61st C.A. most years at Fort Sheridan, IL, and some years at Camp Knox, KY, or Fort Monroe, VA. Awarded the Toulmin Trophy for 1930. Primary ROTC feeder school was the University of Cincinnati. Redesignated on 1 July 1940 as the 77th C.A. Regt. (AA).

Commanders, 505th Coast Artillery Regiment

Maj. James C. Shafer	21 December 1921–ao January 1923
Unknown	ao January 1923–ao May 1925
Col. Sidney H. Guthrie	ao May 1925–ao June 1925
Unknown	ao June 1925–ao June 1930
Lt. Col. Frank R. Miller	ao June 1930–1 July 1940

506th Coast Artillery Regiment (Antiaircraft) (XVI Corps) **Organized Reserve Wisconsin**

HQ—*Not initiated,* 1921–22; La Crosse, WI, 1922–25; Madison, WI, 1925–40

Constituted in the O.R. on 29 July 1921 as the 506th Arty. Regt. (AA), C.A.C., assigned to the XVI Corps, and allotted to the Sixth Corps Area. Initiated on 24 August 1922 with regimental HQ at La Cross, WI. Subordinate battalion HQ concurrently organized as follows: HQ and Combat Train, 1st Bn. at Milwaukee, WI; and HHD, 2d Bn. at Delafield, WI. Relieved from the XVI Corps on 2 July 1923 and assigned to the VI Corps. Redesignated on 30 June 1924 as the 506th C.A. Regt. (AA). Regimental HQ relocated on 2 June 1925 to Madison, WI. Withdrawn from the O.R. on 1 October 1933 and allotted to the R.A. as an RAI unit. Conducted summer training with the 61st C.A. most years at Fort Sheridan, IL, and some years at Camp Knox, KY. Redesignated on 1 July 1940 as the 56th C.A. Regt. (155-mm Gun).

Status: Assigned to the USARS as the 56th Air Defense Arty.

Commanders, 506th Coast Artillery Regiment

Maj. Lincoln K. Adkins	24 August 1922–22 September 1922
Col. Lincoln K. Adkins	22 September 1922–ao June 1933
Col. John C. Davis	ao November 1933–1 July 1940

507th Coast Artillery Regiment (Antiaircraft) (XVII Corps) **Organized Reserve Iowa/Minnesota**

HQ—*Not initiated,* 1921–22; Des Moines, IA, 1922–26; Minneapolis, MN, 1926–31; Des Moines, IA, 1931–41

Constituted in the O.R. on 29 July 1921 as the 507th Arty. Regt. (AA), C.A.C., assigned to the XVII Corps, and allotted to the Seventh Corps Area. Initiated in March 1922 with regimental HQ at Des Moines, IA. Subordinate battalion HQ concurrently organized as follows: HQ and Combat Train, 1st Bn. at Cedar Rapids, IA; and HHD, 2d Bn. at Council Bluffs, IA. Redesignated on 30 June 1924 as the 507th C.A. Regt. (AA). Entire regiment relocated on 26 May 1926 to Minneapolis, MN. Relocated on 12 October 1931 back to Des Moines. Relieved from the XVII Corps on 1 October 1933 and assigned to the VII Corps. Withdrawn from the O.R. on 1 October 1933 and allotted to the R.A. as an RAI unit. Awarded the US Coast Artillery Association Trophy for O.R. regiments for 1934. Typically conducted Inactive Training Period meetings at the Federal Building or the New Armory in Des Moines and at the Union Building, University of Minnesota in Minneapolis. Conducted summer training with the 61st C.A. most years at Fort Sheridan, IL, and some years at Camp Knox, KY. Primary ROTC feeder school was the Iowa State College of Agriculture and Mechanic Arts and the University of Minnesota. Location 7 December 1941—Minneapolis, MN (inactivated 22 January 1942).

Status: Disbanded on 2 April 1943.

Commanders, 507th Coast Artillery Regiment

1st Lt. Anthony P. Nugent	March 1922–14 June 1922	Unknown	ao April 1925–ao June 1927
Capt. William E. Liggett	14 June 1922–13 September 1922	Lt. Col. Roy L. Cochran	ao June 1927–October 1933
Capt. Harold E. Pride	13 September 1922–ao April 1925	Col. Harold E. Pride	October 1933–22 January 1942

508th Coast Artillery Regiment (Antiaircraft) (XVIII Corps) **Organized Reserve Texas/Pennsylvania**

HQ—*Not initiated,* 1921–22; El Paso, TX, 1922–27; *Inactive,* 1927–30; Philadelphia, PA, 1930–41

Constituted in the O.R. on 29 July 1921 as the 508th Arty. Regt. (AA), C.A.C., assigned to the XVIII Corps, and allotted to the Eighth Corps Area. Initiated in March 1922 with the entire regiment at El Paso, TX. Redesignated on 30 June 1924 as the 508th C.A. Regt. (AA). Personnel relieved in January 1927 and reassigned to the 624th C.A. Bn. Withdrawn from the Eighth Corps Area on 11 January 1927 and allotted to the Third Corps Area. Assigned to the XIII Corps about January 1927. Pittsburgh, PA, designated as HQ on organization, but the unit was never organized at that location. Entire regiment relocated on 7 February 1930 to Philadelphia, PA, and concurrently organized at that location. Withdrawn from the O.R. on 1 October 1933 and allotted to the R.A. as an RAI unit. Conducted summer training at Fort Bliss, TX, or Fort Sill, OK, 1922–26, and with the 61st C.A. at Fort Monroe, VA, 1931–40. Also conducted C.A. CMTC training some years at Fort Monroe as an alternate form of annual training. Primary ROTC feeder school was Texas A&M College, 1922–26, and Temple University, 1930–41. Location 7 December 1941—Pittsburgh, PA.

Commanders, 508th Coast Artillery Regiment

Unknown	March 1922–26 July 1922	*Inactive*	12 January 1927–7 February 1930
Lt. Col. John Perkins	26 July 1922–11 January 1927	Col. James S. Ervin	7 February 1930–December 1941

509th Coast Artillery Regiment (Antiaircraft) (XIX Corps) **Organized Reserve Washington**

HQ—*Not initiated,* 1921–22; Seattle, WA, 1922–40

Constituted in the O.R. on 29 July 1921 as the 509th Arty. Regt. (AA), C.A.C., assigned to the XIX Corps, and allotted to the Ninth Corps Area. Initiated in March 1922 with regimental HQ at Seattle, WA. Redesignated on 30 June 1924 as the 509th C.A. Regt. (AA). Withdrawn from the O.R. on 1 October 1933, allotted to the R.A. as an RAI unit, and assigned to the IX Corps. Typically conducted Inactive Training Period meetings at the Times Building in Seattle. Conducted summer training most years at Fort Worden, WA. Primary ROTC feeder school was the University of Washington. Redesignated on 1 July 1940 as the 75th C.A. Regt. (AA).

Status: HHB active at Fort Sill, OK, as HHB, 75th F.A. Brig.

Commanders, 509th Coast Artillery Regiment

Unknown	March 1922–31 October 1922	Unknown	ao November 1922–12 July 1926
Maj. James A. Durrant	31 October 1922–ao November 1922	Col. Walter S. Pollitz	12 July 1926–1 July 1940

510th Coast Artillery Regiment (Antiaircraft) (III Corps) **Organized Reserve Pennsylvania**

HQ—Chester, PA, 1921–32; Philadelphia, PA, 1932–41

Constituted in the O.R. on 29 July 1921 as the 510th Arty. Regt. (AA), C.A.C., assigned to the III Corps, and allotted to the Third Corps Area. Initiated on 10 December 1921 with regimental HQ at Chester, PA. Redesignated on 30 June 1924 as the 510th C.A. Regt. (AA). Regimental HQ relocated on 14 December 1932 to Philadelphia, PA. Conducted summer training with the 61st C.A. at Fort Monroe, VA. Also conducted C.A. CMTC training some years at Fort Monroe as an alternate form of annual training. Primary ROTC feeder school was the University of Pittsburgh. Location 7 December 1941—Philadelphia, PA.

Commanders, 510th Coast Artillery Regiment

1st Lt. Joseph M. Sullivan	30 December 1921–15 February 1922	Maj. Joseph F. Bromley Jr.	ao August 1925–June 1927
Lt. Col. George W. Small	15 February 1922–9 March 1924	Lt. Col Samuel T. Phillips	June 1927–June 1932
Maj. Cary R. Wilson	9 March 1924–ao February 1925	Lt. Col. Ulric J. Mengert	June 1932–1 October 1933
Col. Jess B. Bennett	1 October 1933–7 August 1941		

511th Coast Artillery Regiment (Antiaircraft) (V Corps) **Organized Reserve Indiana/Ohio**

HQ—*Not initiated,* 1921–22; Laconia, IN, 1922–31; Cleveland, OH, 1931–41

Constituted in the O.R. on 29 July 1921 as the 511th Arty. Regt. (AA), C.A.C., assigned to the V Corps, and allotted to the Fifth Corps Area. Initiated in May 1922 with regimental HQ at Laconia, IN. Redesignated on 30 June 1924 as the 511th C.A. Regt. (AA). Entire regiment relocated on 9 July 1931 to Cleveland, OH. Relieved from the V Corps on 1 October 1933 and assigned to the XV Corps. Typically conducted inactive training period meeting at the Cleveland Grays armory in Cleveland. Conducted summer training with the 61st C.A. most years at Fort Sheridan, IL, and some years at Camp Knox, KY. Primary ROTC feeder school was the University of Cincinnati. Location 7 December 1941—Cleveland, OH.

Commanders, 511th Coast Artillery Regiment

1st Lt. Guy H. Wayne	ao June 1922–22 January 1923	Maj. Cary R. Wilson	ao July 1924–ao February 1925
Capt. John W. Callahan	22 January 1923–ao February 1923	Unknown	ao February 1925–ao June 1930
Unknown	ao February 1923–ao August 1927	Maj. Floyd G. Brightbill	ao August 1927–ao September 1933
Col. Timothy A. Ryan	ao June 1934–December 1941		

512th Coast Artillery Regiment (Antiaircraft) (IV Corps) **Organized Reserve Louisiana**

HQ—*Not initiated,* 1921–24

Constituted in the O.R. on 29 July 1921 as the 512th Arty. Regt. (AA), C.A.C., assigned to the IV Corps, allotted to the Fourth Corps Area. New Orleans, LA, designated as HQ on organization, but the unit was never organized at that location. Designated mobilization station was Camp Jackson, SC. Withdrawn from the O.R. on 2 July 1923 and demobilized.

513th Coast Artillery Regiment (Antiaircraft) **Organized Reserve New York**

HQ—Ithaca, NY, 1923–30; Buffalo, NY, 1930–41

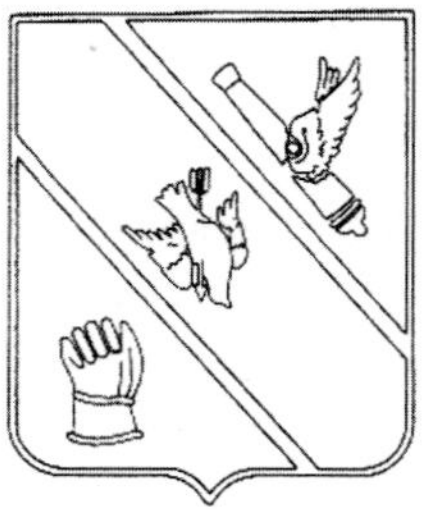

Constituted in the O.R. on 2 July 1923 as the 513th Arty. Regt. (AA), C.A.C., assigned to the 208th C.A. Brig. (GHQR), and allotted to the Second Corps Area. Initiated in August 1923 with regimental HQ at Ithaca, NY. Subordinate battalion HQ concurrently organized as follows: HQ and Combat Train, 1st Bn. at Canandygua, NY, and HHD, 2d Bn. at Utica, NY. Redesignated on 30 June 1924 as the 513th C.A. Regt. (AA). Regimental HQ relocated by 1930 to Buffalo, NY. Relieved from the 208th C.A. Brig. (AA) (GHQR) on 1 October 1933 and assigned to the XII Corps. This regiment's personnel was scattered throughout much of western New York so much of its Inactive Training Period was focused on the completion of correspondence courses and meetings with other units. Conducted summer training with the 62d C.A. at Fort Totten, NY, or Fort Tilden, NY, and some years at Camp Upton, NY. Also conducted C.A. CMTC training some years at Fort Hancock, NJ, as an alternate form of annual training. Primary ROTC feeder schools were Cornell University and Fordham University. Location 7 December 1941—Buffalo, NY.

Events: 87

Commanders, 513th Coast Artillery Regiment

Unknown	August 1923–6 November 1923	Col. John P. Young	3 July 1924–1 October 1933
Lt. Col. Frederick L. Buck	6 November 1923–3 January 1924	Lt. Col. Frederick W. Gilchrist	1 October 1933–December 1941

514th Coast Artillery Regiment (Antiaircraft) — Organized Reserve New York

HQ—Albany, NY, 1923–41

Constituted in the O.R. on 2 July 1923 as the 514th Arty. Regt. (AA), C.A.C., assigned to the 208th C.A. Brig. (GHQR), and allotted to the Second Corps Area. Initiated on 30 October 1923 with regimental HQ at Albany, NY. Subordinate battalion HQ concurrently organized as follows: HQ and Combat Train, 1st Bn. at Saratoga Springs, NY; and HHD, 2d Bn. at Bronx, NY. Redesignated on 30 June 1924 as the 514th C.A. Regt. (AA). Relieved from the 208th C.A. Brig. (AA) (GHQR) on 1 October 1933. Withdrawn from the O.R. on 1 January 1938 and allotted to the R.A. as an RAI unit. Typically conducted Inactive Training Period meetings at the General Electric Building or the National Guard armory in Schenectady, NY. Conducted summer training with the 62d C.A. most years at Fort Totten, NY, or Fort Tilden, NY, and some years at Camp Upton, NY, or Aberdeen Proving Ground, MD. Also conducted C.A. CMTC training some years at Fort Hancock, NJ, as an alternate form of annual training. Primary ROTC feeder school was Fordham University. Location 7 December 1941—Albany, NY.

Status: HHB active at Fort Bliss, TX, as HHB, 108th Air Defense Arty. Brig.

Commanders, 514th Coast Artillery Regiment

Maj. William D. Finke	30 October 1923–3 January 1924	Lt. Col. Nicholas E. Devereux Jr.	7 April 1928–15 May 1941
Col. Charles E. Warren	3 January 1924–7 April 1928	Maj. Horace S. Van Voast	31 May 1941–December 1941

515th Coast Artillery Regiment (Antiaircraft) — Organized Reserve Nebraska

HQ—*Not initiated,* 1923–24; Lincoln, NE, 1924–41

Constituted in the O.R. on 2 July 1923 as the 515th Arty. Regt. (AA), C.A.C., assigned to the GHQR, and allotted to the Seventh Corps Area. Redesignated on 30 June 1924 as the 515th C.A. Regt. (AA). Initiated in November 1924 with regimental HQ at Lincoln, NE. Subordinate battalion HQ concurrently organized as follows: HQ and Combat Train, 1st Bn. at Nebraska City, NE; and HHD, 2d Bn. at Fairbury, NE. Relieved from the GHQR on 1 October 1933 and assigned to the 35th C.A. Brig. (Fourth Army). Conducted summer training with the 61st C.A. at Fort Sheridan, IL. Primary ROTC feeder school was the University of Nebraska. Location 7 December 1941—Lincoln, NE.

Commanders, 515th Coast Artillery Regiment

Unknown	November 1924–ao August 1933	Col. Robert L. Cochran	ao August 1933–December 1941

516th Coast Artillery Regiment (Antiaircraft) **Organized Reserve Pennsylvania**

HQ—Harrisburg, PA, 1923–29; Philadelphia, PA, 1929–33

Constituted in the O.R. on 2 July 1923 as the 516th Arty .Regt. (AA), C.A.C., assigned to the GHQR, and allotted to the Third Corps Area. Organized in December 1923 with regimental HQ at Harrisburg, PA. Subordinate battalion HQ concurrently organized as follows: HQ and Combat Train, 1st Bn. at Steelton, PA; and HHD, 2d Bn. at Lancaster, PA. Redesignated on 30 June 1924 as the 516th C.A. Regt. (AA). Regimental HQ relocated on 11 December 1929 to Philadelphia, PA. Subordinate battalions concurrently relocated as follows: HQ and Combat Train, 1st Bn. at Lancaster; and HHD, 2d Bn. at York, PA. Conducted summer training at Fort Monroe, VA. Also conducted C.A. CMTC training some years at Fort Monroe as an alternate form of annual training. Primary ROTC feeder school was Drexel University. Demobilized on 1 October 1933.

Commanders, 516th Coast Artillery Regiment

Capt. Robert H. Woods	December 1923–ao February 1924	Lt. Col. Cary R. Wilson	ao August 1925–ao June 1926
Unknown	ao February 1924–ao August 1925	Lt. Col. Allison F. H. Scott	ao September 1926–May 1931
	Lt. Col. Jess B. Bennett	May 1931–1 October 1933	

517th Coast Artillery Regiment (Antiaircraft) **Organized Reserve California**

HQ—*Not initiated,* 1923–24; Presidio of San Francisco, CA, 1925–40

Constituted in the O.R. on 2 July 1923 as the 517th Arty. Regt. (AA), C.A.C., assigned to the 210th C.A. Brig. (GHQR), and allotted to the Ninth Corps Area. Redesignated on 30 June 1924 as the 517th C.A. Regt. (AA). Initiated in August 1925 with the entire regiment at San Francisco, CA. Relieved from the 210th C.A. Brig. (AA) (GHQR) on 1 October 1933 and assigned to the 203d C.A. Brig. (AA). Withdrawn from the O.R. on 1 January 1938 and allotted to the R.A. as an RAI unit. Typically conducted Inactive Training Period meetings at Building 171 at the Presidio of San Francisco. Conducted summer training with the 63d C.A. most years at Fort Winfield Scott, CA, and some years at Fort McArthur, CA, or Camp McQuaide, CA, with the 250th C.A. Primary ROTC feeder school was the University of California at Berkeley. Redesignated on 1 July 1940 as the 78th C.A. Regt. (AA).

Events: 108

Commanders, 517th Coast Artillery Regiment

Col. A.G. Wright	August 1925–ao June 1933	Unknown	ao January 1936-ao August 1937
Unknown	ao June 1933–ao November 1935	Lt. Col. James G. Scrugham	ao August 1937–ao September 1937
Lt. Col. Willis Shippen	ao November 1935-ao January 1936	Lt. Col. Albert B. Cox	ao April 1938–1 July 1940

518th Coast Artillery Regiment (Antiaircraft) **Organized Reserve California**

HQ—*Not initiated,* 1923–25; Presidio of San Francisco, CA, 1925–29; *Inactive,* 1929–30; San Francisco, CA, 1930–41

Constituted in the O.R. on 2 July 1923 as the 518th Arty. Regt. (AA), C.A.C., assigned to the 210th C.A. Brig. (GHQR), and allotted to the Ninth Corps Area. Redesignated on 30 June 1924 as the 518th C.A. Regt. (AA). Initiated in August 1925 with the entire regiment at San Francisco, CA. Typically conducted Inactive Training Period meetings at Building 171 at the Presidio of San Francisco. Conducted summer training with the 63d C.A. most years at Fort Winfield Scott, CA. Inactivated on 20 September 1929 at San Francisco by relief of personnel. Reorganized on 28 August 1930 at San Francisco. Relieved from the 210th C.A. Brig. (AA) (GHQR) on 1 October 1933. Location 7 December 1941—San Francisco, CA.

Status: Disbanded on 2 April 1943.

Commanders, 518th Coast Artillery Regiment

Unknown	August 1925–20 September 1929	*Inactive*	20 September 1929–28 August 1930
Unknown	28 August 1930–7 December 1941		

519th Coast Artillery Regiment (Antiaircraft) — Organized Reserve California

HQ—*Not initiated,* 1923–25; Los Angeles, CA, 1925–41

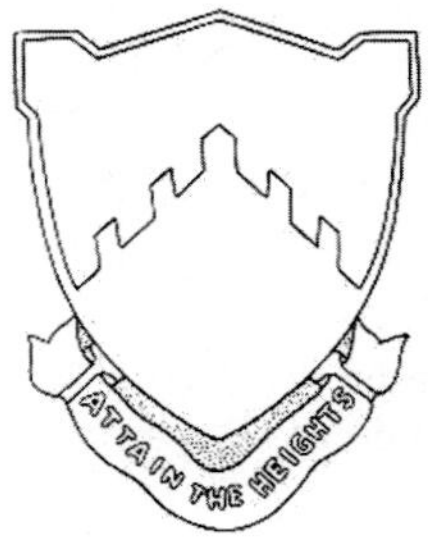

Constituted in the O.R. on 2 July 1923 as the 519th Arty. Regt. (AA), C.A.C., assigned to the 210th C.A. Brig. (GHQR), and allotted to the Ninth Corps Area. Redesignated on 30 June 1924 as the 519th C.A. Regt. (AA). Initiated in March 1925 with regimental HQ at Los Angeles, CA. Relieved from the 210th C.A. Brig. (AA) (GHQR) on 1 October 1933 and assigned to the XIX Corps. Many unit personnel participated in earthquake relief operations, 14–22 March 1933, in the Los Angeles area. Awarded the US Coast Artillery Association Trophy for O.R. regiments for 1935. As part of its Inactive Training Period, the regiment participated in a "School of Fire" on the 3-inch antiaircraft gun conducted by the 3d C.A. at Fort MacArthur, 14 and 21 December 1935. Typically conducted Inactive Training Period meetings at the Chamber of Commerce Building or the Detwiler Building in Los Angeles. Conducted summer training with the 63d C.A. most years at Fort MacArthur, CA, or some years at Camp McQuaide, CA, with the 250th C.A. Primary ROTC feeder school was the University of California at Berkeley. Location 7 December 1941—Los Angeles, CA (Inactivated 21 January 1942).

Status: Disbanded on 2 April 1943.

Events: 93

Commanders, 519th Coast Artillery Regiment

Lt. Col. C.M. Frost	March 1925–ao September 1926	Lt. Col. Frank J. Baum	ao March 1934–ao June 1939
Unknown	ao September 1926–ao June 1929	Unknown	ao June 1939–ao August 1940
Lt. Col. D.K. Smith	ao June 1929–ao December 1933	Col. Forrest E. Baker	ao August 1940–21 January 1942

520th Coast Artillery Regiment (Antiaircraft) — Organized Reserve

HQ—*Not initiated,* 1923–24

Constituted in the O.R. on 2 July 1923 as the 520th Arty. Regt. (AA), C.A.C. (DNG), assigned to the 210th C.A. Brig. (GHQR), and allotted to the Fifth Corps Area. Withdrawn from the O.R. on 13 June 1924 and demobilized.

521st Coast Artillery Regiment (Antiaircraft) — Organized Reserve New Jersey

HQ—Montclair, NJ, 1921–37; East Orange, NJ, 1937–41

Constituted in the O.R. on 15 October 1921 as the 521st Arty. Regt. (AA), C.A.C., assigned to the 198th C.A. Brig. (Fourth Army), and allotted to the Second Corps Area. Initiated on 27 October 1921 with regimental HQ at Montclair, NJ. Subordinate battalion HQ concurrently organized as follows: HQ and Combat Train, 1st Bn. at Montclair, NJ; and HHD, 2d Bn. at Morristown, NJ. Redesignated on 30 June 1924 as the 521st C.A. Regt. (AA). Relieved from the 198th C.A. Brig. (AA) (GHQR) on 1 October 1933. Typically conducted Inactive Training Period meetings at the Post Office Building in Montclair, as well as in Elizabeth and Newark. Conducted summer training with the 62d C.A. most years at Camp Upton, NY; Fort Totten, NY; or Fort Tilden, NY. Also conducted C.A. CMTC training some years at Fort Hancock, NJ, as an alternate form of annual training. Primary ROTC feeder school was Princeton University. Location 7 December 1941—East Orange, NJ.

Status: Disbanded on 2 April 1943.

Events: 93

Commanders, 521st Coast Artillery Regiment

Lt. Col. Cyril A. Coons	28 October 1921–1 June 1926	Col. James E. Nestor	1 June 1926–December 1941

522d Coast Artillery Regiment (Antiaircraft) — Organized Reserve New York

HQ—Buffalo, NY, 1921–33

Constituted in the O.R. on 15 October 1921 as the 522d Arty. Regt. (AA), C.A.C., assigned to the 198th C.A. Brig. (Fourth Army), and allotted to the Second Corps Area. Initiated on 27 October 1921 with regimental HQ at Buffalo, NY. Subordinate battalion HQ concurrently organized as follows: HQ and Combat Train, 1st Bn. at Rochester, NY; and HHD, 2d Bn. at Oneonta, NY. Redesignated on 30 June 1924 as the 522d C.A. Regt. (AA). Typically conducted Inactive Training Period meetings in Buffalo, Rochester, and Lockport, NY. Conducted summer training with the 62d C.A. most years at Camp Upton, NY; Fort Totten, NY; or Fort Tilden, NY. Primary ROTC feeder school was Fordham University. Demobilized on 1 October 1933.

Status: Disbanded on 2 April 1943.

Commanders, 522d Coast Artillery Regiment

Capt. Herbert A. Dyer	27 October 1921–31 January 1922	Maj. James W. Lyon	18 September 1922–11 May 1923
Maj. Deo O. Robinson	31 January 1922–18 September 1922	Lt. Col. Harold H. Bullis	11 May 1923–3 January 1924
Col. Frederick W. Gilchrist	3 January 1924–1 October 1933		

523d Coast Artillery Regiment (Antiaircraft) — Organized Reserve Pennsylvania

HQ—Franklin, PA, 1921–32; Pittsburgh, PA, 1932–41

Constituted in the O.R. on 15 October 1921 as the 523d Arty. Regt. (AA), C.A.C., assigned to the 198th C.A. Brig. (Fourth Army), and allotted to the Third Corps Area. Initiated on 28 November 1921 with regimental HQ at Franklin, PA. Subordinate battalion HQ concurrently organized as follows: HQ and Combat Train, 1st Bn. at Mercer, PA; and HHD, 2d Bn. at Erie, PA. Redesignated on 30 June 1924 as the 523d C.A. Regt. (AA). Entire regiment relocated on 14 December 1932 to Pittsburgh, PA. Conducted summer training with the 61st C.A. at Fort Monroe, VA. Also conducted C.A. CMTC training some years at Fort Monroe as an alternate form of annual training. Primary ROTC feeder school was the University of Pittsburgh. Location 7 December 1941—Pittsburgh, PA.

Commanders, 523d Coast Artillery Regiment

1st Lt. Thomas M. Boyle	28 November 1921–1 March 1922	Maj. Frank S. McClintock	27 August 1923–10 September 1927
2d Lt. Benjamin H. Pardee	1 March 1922–27 February 1923	Lt. Col. Albert D. Neal	17 September 1927–June 1929
2d Lt. Charles G. Clark	27 February 1923–26 August 1923	Lt. Col. James B. Bentley	June 1929–1 October 1932
Col. Carl M. Deakin	1 October 1932–December 1941		

524th Coast Artillery Regiment (Antiaircraft) — Organized Reserve Georgia

HQ—*Not initiated,* 1921–22; Decatur, GA, 1922–29; Atlanta, GA, 1929–41

Constituted in the O.R. on 15 October 1921 as the 524th Arty. Regt. (AA), C.A.C., assigned to the 199th C.A. Brig. (Fifth Army), and allotted to the Fourth Corps Area. Initiated on 27 February 1922 with regimental HQ at Decatur,

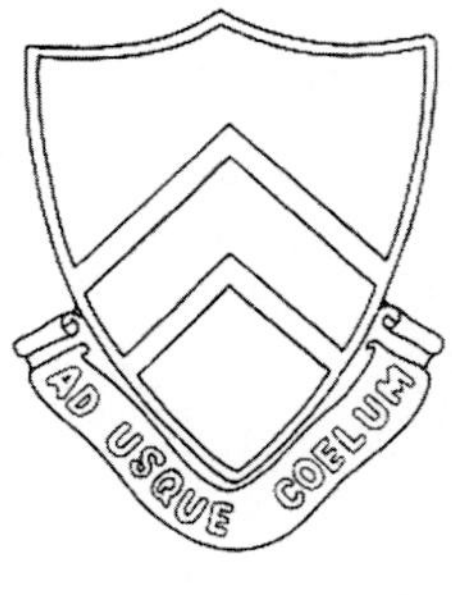

GA. Redesignated on 30 June 1924 as the 524th C.A. Regt. (AA). Entire regiment relocated on 22 October 1929 to Atlanta, GA. Relieved from the 199th C.A. Brig. (AA) (Fifth Army) on 1 October 1933 and assigned to the XIV Corps. Typically conducted Inactive Training Period at the Georgia School of Technology (Georgia Tech) or the Atlanta Elks Club. Conducted summer training at Fort Barrancas, FL. Also conducted C.A. CMTC training some years at Fort Barrancas as an alternate form of annual training. Primary ROTC feeder school was the Georgia School of Technology. Designated mobilization training station was Camp Jackson, SC. Location 7 December 1941—Atlanta, GA.

Status: Disbanded on 2 April 1943.

Commanders, 524th Coast Artillery Regiment

Lt. Col. Arthur W. Merkel	27 February 1922–19 June 1924	Lt. Col. James K. Jordan	ao October 1927–December 1932
Unknown	19 June 1924–ao May 1931	Lt. Col. Charles M. Boyer	December 1932–12 March 1941
	Col. Harry W. Porter	12 March 1941–December 1941	

525th Coast Artillery Regiment (Antiaircraft) **Organized Reserve Indiana/Kentucky/West Virginia**

HQ—*Not initiated,* 1921–22; Fort Wayne, IN, 1922–31; Louisville, KY, 1931–33; Henderson, KY, 1933–37; Huntington, WV, 1937–41

Constituted in the O.R. on 15 October 1921 as the 525th Arty. Regt. (AA), C.A.C., assigned to the 199th C.A. Brig. (Fifth Army), and allotted to the Fifth Corps Area. Initiated in May 1922 with regimental HQ at Fort Wayne, IN. Band organized at Fort Wayne in April 1923. Redesignated on 30 June 1924 as the 525th C.A. Regt. (AA). Relieved from the 199th C.A. Brig. (AA) (Fifth Army) in August 1925 and assigned to the 202d C.A. Brig. (AA) (Second Army). Regiment relocated on 9 July 1931 to Louisville, KY. Relocated on 21 December 1933 to Henderson, KY. Relocated on 5 April 1937 to Huntington, WV. Conducted summer training at Fort Sheridan, IL; Camp Knox, KY; Fort Barrancas, FL; or Fort Monroe, VA. Location 7 December 1941—Huntington, WV.

Status: Disbanded on 2 April 1943.

Commanders, 525th Coast Artillery Regiment

Capt. T.F. Carroll	May 1922–ao September 1924	Unknown	ao July 1932–ao June 1934
Unknown	ao September 1924–ao August 1930	Maj. Hubbard W. Shawhan	ao June 1934–ao July 1938
Maj. J.P. Whittinghill	ao August 1930–ao July 1932	Maj. Robert E. O'Conner	ao September 1938–December 1941

526th Coast Artillery Regiment (Antiaircraft) **Organized Reserve Illinois/Michigan**

HQ—*Not initiated,* 1921–22; Elgin, IL, 1922–24; Rockford, IL, 1924–34; Detroit, MI, 1934–41

Constituted in the O.R. on 15 October 1921 as the 526th Arty. Regt. (AA), C.A.C., assigned to the 199th C.A. Brig. (Fifth Army), and allotted to the Sixth Corps Area. Initiated in April 1922 with regimental HQ at Elgin, IL. Entire regiment relocated on 18 April 1924 to Rockford, IL. Redesignated on 30 June 1924 as the 526th C.A. Regt. (AA). HQ and Combat Train, 1st Bn. relocated on 27 January 1927 to Elgin, IL. Relieved from the 199th C.A. Brig. (AA) (Fifth Army) on 1 October 1933 and assigned to the 40th C.A. Brig. (AA) (GHQR). Entire regiment relocated on 1 February 1934 to Detroit, MI. Conducted summer training with the 61st C.A. most years at Fort Sheridan, IL, and some years at Camp Knox, KY, or Fort Monroe, VA. Primary ROTC feeder school was the University of Illinois, 1924–34. Location 7 December 1941—Detroit, MI.

Status: Disbanded on 2 April 1943.

Commanders, 526th Coast Artillery Regiment

Capt. Roscoe E. Brightup	April 1922–4 May 1922	Unknown	ao June 1933–ao June 1936
Maj. Carl M. Deakin	4 May 1922–2 March 1923	Lt. Col. Haldeman Finnie	ao June 1936–ao July 1936
Unknown	2 March 1923–24 July 1926	Unknown	ao July 1936–ao May 1938
Lt. Col. Marshall M. Milton	24 July 1926–7 March 1927	Lt. Col. John L. Niesse	ao May 1938–ao September 1938
Lt. Col. Clarence C. Tracy	8 March 1927–ao June 1933	Unknown	ao September 1938–ao August 1940
Lt. Col. John W. Fletcher	ao August 1940–December 1941		

527th Coast Artillery Regiment (Antiaircraft) — Organized Reserve Missouri/Minnesota

HQ—*Not initiated,* 1921–22; Kansas City, MO, 1922–26; Duluth, MN, 1926–31; St. Louis, MO, 1931–41

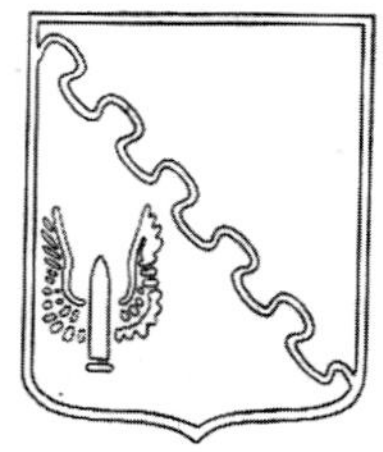

Constituted in the O.R. on 15 October 1921 as the 527th Arty. Regt. (AA), C.A.C., assigned to the 200th C.A. Brig. (Sixth Army), and allotted to the Seventh Corps Area. Initiated on 27 February 1922 with regimental HQ at Kansas City, MO. Subordinate battalion HQ concurrently organized as follows: HQ and Combat Train, 1st Bn. at Sedalia, MO; and HHD, 2d Bn. at St. Joseph, MO. Redesignated on 30 June 1924 as the 527th C.A. Regt. (AA). Regimental HQ relocated on 26 May 1926 to Duluth, MN; HQ and Combat Train, 1st Bn. to Duluth; and HHD, 2d Bn. to St. Paul, MN. Entire regiment relocated on 12 October 1931 to St. Louis, MO. Relieved from the 200th C.A. Brig. (AA) on 1 October 1933 and assigned to the XVII Corps. Conducted summer training most years with the 61st C.A. at Fort Sheridan, IL, and some years at Camp Knox, KY, or with the 206th C.A. at Fort Sill, OK. Conducted joint summer training with the 110th Observation (Obsn.) Sq. in 1934. Primary ROTC feeder school was St. Louis University, 1931–41. Location 7 December 1941—St. Louis, MO.

Status: Disbanded on 2 April 1943.

Commanders, 527th Coast Artillery Regiment

Maj. James K. Jordan	27 February 1922–ao March 1922	Lt. Col. Harold E. Pride	ao September 1933–October 1933
Unknown	ao March 1922–ao May 1931	Maj. Walter H. Ogden	October 1933–10 October 1935
Maj. Allen Hoblitzell	ao May 1931–ao June 1931	Maj. A.S. Turner	10 October 1935–ao August 1936
Unknown	ao June 1931–ao September 1933	Unknown	ao August 1936–ao August 1940
Maj. James M. Mozley	ao August 1940–December 1941		

528th Coast Artillery Regiment (Antiaircraft) — Organized Reserve Minnesota

HQ—*Not initiated,* 1921–22; St. Paul, MN, 1922–33

Constituted in the O.R. on 15 October 1921 as the 528th Arty. Regt. (AA), C.A.C., assigned to the 200th C.A. Brig. (Sixth Army), and allotted to the Seventh Corps Area. Initiated in May 1922 with regimental HQ at St. Paul, MN. Subordinate battalion HQ concurrently organized as follows: HQ and Combat Train, 1st Bn. at St. Paul, MN; and HHD, 2d Bn. at St. Cloud, MN. Redesignated on 30 June 1924 as the 528th C.A. Regt. (AA). Subordinate battalions relocated on 26 May 1926 as follows: HQ and Combat Train, 1st Bn. to Minneapolis, MN; and HHD, 2d Bn. to Rochester, MN. Conducted summer training most years at Camp Knox, KY, and some years at Fort Sheridan, IL. Primary ROTC feeder school was the University of Minnesota. Demobilized on 1 October 1933.

Commanders, 528th Coast Artillery Regiment

Unknown	May 1922–1 October 1933

529th Coast Artillery Regiment (Antiaircraft) **Organized Reserve Oklahoma/Oregon**

HQ—*Not initiated,* 1921–23; Enid, OK, 1923–24; *Inactive,* 1924–25; Portland, OR, 1925–29; *Inactive,* 1929–32; Portland, OR, 1932–39; *Inactive,* 1939–41

Constituted in the O.R. on 15 October 1921 as the 529th Arty. Regt. (AA), C.A.C., assigned to the 200th C.A. Brig. (Sixth Army), and allotted to the Eighth Corps Area. Initiated on 26 February 1923 with regimental HQ at Enid, OK. Subordinate battalion HQ concurrently organized as follows: HQ and Combat Train, 1st Bn. at Enid, OK; and HHD, 2d Bn. at Hugo, OK. Withdrawn from the Eighth Corps Area on 13 June 1924 and allotted to the Ninth Corps Area. Redesignated on 30 June 1924 as the 529th C.A. Regt. (AA). Reorganized on 16 January 1925 with regimental HQ at Portland, OR. Subordinate battalion HQ concurrently organized as follows: HQ and Combat Train, 1st Bn. at Portland; and HHD, 2d Bn. at Marshfield, OR. Inactivated on 10 September 1929 at Portland by relief of personnel. Entire regiment relocated on 20 September 1929 to Portland, OR. Regiment reorganized on 1 June 1932 entirely at Portland. Withdrawn from the O.R. on 1 October 1933, allotted to the R.A. as an RAI unit. Concurrently relieved from the 200th C.A. Brig. (Sixth Army) and assigned to the 35th C.A. Brig. (Fourth Army). Awarded the US Coast Artillery Association Trophy for O.R. regiments for 1933. Typically conducted Inactive Training Period meetings at the Post Office Building in Portland. Conducted summer training in 1924 at Fort Sill, OK, and most years at Fort Worden, WA, 1935–39. Inactivated on 10 September 1939 at Portland by relief of personnel. Location 7 December 1941—*Inactive.*

Status: Disbanded on 2 April 1943.

Commanders, 529th Coast Artillery Regiment

Unknown	26 February 1923–13 June 1924	Lt. Col. Burton K. Lawson	16 January 1925–10 September 1929
Inactive	13 June 1924–16 January 1925	*Inactive*	10 September 1929–1 June 1932
Lt. Col. Martin W. Hawkins	1 June 1932–10 September 1939		

530th Coast Artillery Regiment (Antiaircraft) **Organized Reserve New York**

HQ—Brooklyn, NY, 1921–41

Constituted in the O.R. on 15 October 1921 as the 530th Arty. Regt. (AA), C.A.C., assigned to the 212th C.A. Brig. (GHQR), and allotted to the Second Corps Area. Initiated on 25 October 1921 with regimental HQ at Brooklyn, NY. Subordinate battalion HQ concurrently organized as follows: HQ and Combat Train, 1st Bn. at Brooklyn; and HHD, 2d Bn. at Manhattan, NY. Redesignated on 30 June 1924 as the 530th C.A. Regt. (AA). Relieved from the 212th C.A. Brig. (GHQR) on 1 October 1933. Designated mobilization station was Camp Upton, NY. Typically conducted Inactive Training Period meetings at the Engineer Society Building on 39th Street in New York City. Conducted summer training with the 62d C.A. most years at Fort Totten, NY, and some years at Fort Tilden or Aberdeen Proving Ground, MD. Also conducted C.A. CMTC training some years at Fort Hancock, NJ, as an alternate form of annual training. Location 7 December 1941—Brooklyn, NY.

Status: Disbanded on 2 April 1943.

Commanders, 530th Coast Artillery Regiment

Maj. Alphonzo Pelham	25 October 1921–3 January 1924	Lt. Col. Joseph W. Barker	18 September 1931–8 August 1934
Maj. Pierce Travis	3 January 1924–ao February 1924	Lt. Col. Hazen L. Hoyt	8 August 1934–ao December 1936
Lt. Col. N. B. Jackson	ao November 1924–ao January 1925	Unknown	ao December 1936–ao May 1938
Unknown	ao January 1925–ao January 1927	Lt. Col. Will I. Levy	ao May 1938–July 1938
Lt. Col. Ernest J. Oglesby	ao January 1927–17 September 1931	Lt. Col. Charles I. Clark	July 1938–December 1941

531st Coast Artillery Regiment (Antiaircraft) **Organized Reserve Illinois**

HQ—*Not initiated,* 1921–22; Chicago, IL, 1922–41

Constituted in the O.R. on 15 October 1921 as the 531st Arty. Regt. (AA), C.A.C., assigned to the 212th C.A. Brig. (GHQR), and allotted to the Sixth Corps Area. Initiated on 4 May 1922 with the entire regiment at Chicago, IL. Redesignated on 30 June 1924 as the 531st C.A. Regt. (AA). Relieved from the 212th C.A. Brig. (GHQR) on 1 October 1933. Typically conducted Inactive Training Period meetings at the armory of the 202d C.A. or the Army and Navy Club in Chicago. Conducted summer training with the 61st C.A. most years at Fort Sheridan, IL, and some years at Camp Knox, KY, or Camp Sparta, WI. Conducted summer training with the 202d C.A. at Camp McCoy, WI, in 1925. Primary ROTC feeder school was the University of Chicago. Location 7 December 1941—Chicago, IL.

Status: Disbanded on 2 April 1943.

Commanders, 531st Coast Artillery Regiment

Lt. Col. Carl L. Barnes	4 May 1922–3 January 1925	Col. Howard W. Hodgkins	3 January 1925–December 1941

532d Coast Artillery Regiment (Antiaircraft) **Organized Reserve Illinois**

HQ—*Not initiated,* 1921–22; Decatur, IL, 1922–25; East St. Louis, IL, 1925–37; Champaign, IL, 1937–41

Constituted in the O.R. on 15 October 1921 as the 532d Arty. Regt. (AA), C.A.C., assigned to the 212th C.A. Brig. (GHQR), and allotted to the Sixth Corps Area. Initiated on 4 May 1922 with regimental HQ at Decatur, IL. Subordinate battalion HQ concurrently organized as follows: HQ and Combat Train, 1st Bn. at Alton, IL; HHD, 2d Bn. at Centralia, IL. Redesignated on 30 June 1924 as the 532d C.A. Regt. (AA). Regimental HQ relocated on 28 July 1925 to East St. Louis, IL. Relieved from the 212th C.A. Brig. (GHQR) on 1 October 1933. Entire regiment relocated on 28 July 1937 to Champaign, IL. Conducted summer training with the 61st C.A. most years at Fort Sheridan, IL, and some years at Camp Knox, KY, or Jefferson Barracks, MO. Primary ROTC feeder school was the University of Illinois. Location 7 December 1941—Champaign, IL.

Status: Disbanded on 2 April 1943.

Commanders, 532d Coast Artillery Regiment

Maj. Howard W. Hodgkins	4 May 1922–3 January 1925	Unknown	ao June 1929–ao June 1930
Maj. Kenneth G. Ives	25 November 1925–ao June 1929	Lt. Col. Ivan A. Elliott	ao June 1930–10 October 1935
Lt. Col. Walter H. Ogden	10 October 1935–December 1941		

533d Coast Artillery Regiment (Antiaircraft) **Organized Reserve New York**

HQ—Manhattan, NY, 1921–41

Constituted in the O.R. on 15 October 1921 as the 533d Arty. Regt. (AA), C.A.C., assigned to the 201st C.A. Brig. (First Army), and allotted to the Second Corps Area. Initiated on 27 October 1921 with regimental HQ at Manhattan, NY. Subordinate battalion HQ concurrently organized as follows: HQ and Combat Train, 1st Bn. at Manhattan; and HHD, 2d Bn. at Brooklyn, NY. Redesignated on 30 June 1924 as the 533d C.A. Regt. (AA). Typically conducted Inactive Training Period meetings at the Engineer Society Building on 39th Street in New York City. Conducted summer training with the 62d C.A. most years at Fort Totten, NY, and some years at Fort Tilden; Camp Upton, NY; or Aberdeen Proving Ground, MD. Also conducted C.A. CMTC training some years at Fort Hancock, NJ, or Camp Upton as an alternate form of annual training. Location 7 December 1941—Manhattan, NY.

Status: Disbanded on 2 April 1943.

Commanders, 533d Coast Artillery Regiment

Maj. Ernest J. Oglesby	27 October 1921–12 October 1922	Lt. Col. Ernest J. Oglesby	20 April 1923–8 November 1923
Maj. Eugene S. Taliaferro	12 October 1922–20 April 1923	Col. Francis R. Stoddard Jr.	8 November 1923–6 November 1935
Lt. Col. George A. Burden	6 November 1935–December 1941		

534th Coast Artillery Regiment (Antiaircraft) — Organized Reserve North Carolina/South Carolina

HQ—*Not initiated,* 1921–22; Raleigh, NC, 1922–29; Columbia, SC, 1929–41

Constituted in the O.R. on 15 October 1921 as the 534th Arty. Regt. (AA), C.A.C., assigned to the 202d C.A. Brig. (Second Army), and allotted to the Fourth Corps Area. Initiated on 15 March 1922 with regimental HQ at Raleigh, NC. Subordinate battalion HQ concurrently organized as follows: HQ and Combat Train, 1st Bn. at Wilson, NC; and HHD, 2d Bn. at Kinston, NC. Redesignated on 30 June 1924 as the 534th C.A. Regt. (AA). Entire regiment relocated on 22 October 1929 to Columbia, SC. Some elements typically conducted Inactive Training Period meetings at the Duke Power Company building in Spartanburg, SC. Conducted summer training at Fort Barrancas, FL. Also conducted C.A. CMTC training some years at Fort Barrancas as an alternate form of annual training. Primary ROTC feeder school was The Citadel, 1929–41. Designated mobilization training station was Camp Jackson, SC. Location 7 December 1941—Columbia, SC.

Status: Disbanded on 2 April 1943.

Commanders, 534th Coast Artillery Regiment

Capt. James R. Buchanan	15 March 1922–30 April 1922	Lt. Col. W.F. Robertson	ao May 1931–ao June 1931
Maj. Daniel E. Murphy	30 April 1922–25 September 1922	Unknown	ao June 1931–ao January 1936
Col. John W. Harrelson	25 September 1922–ao September 1925	Lt. Col. Fred H. All	January 1936–15 February 1936
Unknown	ao September 1925–ao May 1931	Col. Henry I. Ellerbe	15 February 1936–December 1941

535th Coast Artillery Regiment (Antiaircraft) — Organized Reserve Kentucky/Indiana

HQ—*Not initiated,* 1921–22; Georgetown, KY, 1922–25; Louisville, KY, 1925–31; Indianapolis, IN, 1931–41

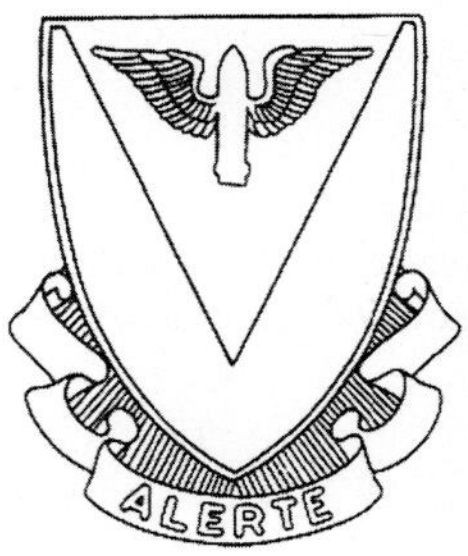

Constituted in the O.R. on 15 October 1921 as the 535th Arty. Regt. (AA), C.A.C., assigned to the 202d C.A. Brig. (Second Army), and allotted to the Fifth Corps Area. Initiated in January 1922 with regimental HQ at Georgetown, KY. Band organized about March 1923 at Louisville, KY; inactivated by August 1927. Redesignated on 30 June 1924 as the 535th C.A. Regt. (AA). Regimental HQ relocated on 15 April 1925 to Louisville. Subordinate battalion HQ concurrently relocated as follows: HQ and Combat Train, 1st Bn. to Covington, KY; and HHD, 2d Bn. at Glasgow, KY. Entire regiment relocated on 9 July 1931 to Indianapolis, IN. Relieved from the 202d C.A. Brig. on 1 October 1933 and assigned to the 199th C.A. Brig. (GHQR). Reassigned to the 202d C.A. Brig. (GHQR) in 1936. Awarded the US Coast Artillery Association Trophy for O.R. regiments for 1937. Awarded the Toulmin Trophy for 1936 and 1937. Typically conducted Inactive Training Period meetings at the Indianapolis Athletic Club. Conducted summer training with the 61st C.A. most years at Fort Sheridan, IL, and some years at Camp Knox, KY. Location 7 December 1941—Indianapolis, IN.

Status: Disbanded on 2 April 1943.

Commanders, 535th Coast Artillery Regiment

Col. Thompson Short	January 1922–July 1926	Col. Bowman Elder	July 1926–December 1941

536th Coast Artillery Regiment (Antiaircraft) **Organized Reserve Michigan**

HQ—Detroit, MI, 1921–41

Constituted in the O.R. on 15 October 1921 as the 536th Arty. Regt. (AA), C.A.C., assigned to the 203d C.A. Brig. (Third Army), and allotted to the Sixth Corps Area. Initiated on 15 November 1921 with the entire regiment at Detroit, MI. Redesignated on 30 June 1924 as the 536th C.A. Regt. (AA). Conducted summer training with the 61st C.A. most years at Fort Sheridan, IL, and some years at Camp Knox, KY, or Camp Custer, MI. Primary ROTC feeder school was the Michigan State College of Agriculture and Applied Science. Location 7 December 1941—Detroit, MI.

Commanders, 536th Coast Artillery Regiment

Lt. Col. Lee A. McCalla	15 November 1921–3 March 1923	Lt. Col. Edward M. Howell	ao July 1937–ao July 1939
Col. Carl M. Deakin	3 March 1923–1 October 1932	Unknown	ao July 1939–ao August 1940
Unknown	1 October 1932–ao July 1937	Lt. Col. Stanley D. Wiggins	ao August 1940–December 1941

537th Coast Artillery Regiment (Antiaircraft) **Organized Reserve Minnesota**

HQ—Duluth, MN, 1921–24; Minneapolis, MN, 1924–41

Constituted in the O.R. on 15 October 1921 as the 537th Arty. Regt. (AA), C.A.C., assigned to the 203d C.A. Brig. (Third Army), and allotted to the Seventh Corps Area. Initiated on 20 October 1921 with regimental HQ at Duluth, MN. Subordinate battalion HQ concurrently organized as follows: HQ and Combat Train, 1st Bn. at Minneapolis, MN; and HHD, 2d Bn. at Duluth. Redesignated on 30 June 1924 as the 537th C.A. Regt. (AA). Entire regiment relocated on 17 January 1924 to Minneapolis. Designated mobilization station was Camp Dodge, IA. Typically conducted Inactive Training Period meetings at the Federal Building or the N.G. armory in Duluth and at the Elks Club or the Union Building, University of Minnesota in Minneapolis. Conducted summer training most years with the 61st C.A. at Fort Sheridan, IL, and some years at Camp Knox, KY; Fort Snelling, MN; or with the 206th C.A. at Fort Sill, OK. Primary ROTC feeder school was the University of Minnesota. Location 7 December 1941—Minneapolis, MN (inactivated on 21 January 1942).

Status: Disbanded on 2 April 1943.

Commanders, 537th Coast Artillery Regiment

Maj. John R. Sweitzer	20 October 1921–ao January 1922	Lt. Col. Anthony Underhill	August 1937–November 1937
Unknown	ao January 1922–ao March 1923	Col. Earl E. Howard	November 1937–August 1941
Col. Arthur H. Conary	ao March 1923–August 1937	Lt. Col. Lloyd W. Walters	August 1941–21 January 1942

538th Coast Artillery Regiment (Antiaircraft) **Organized Reserve Kansas and Nebraska/Iowa**

HQ—Lawrence, KS, 1921–26; Davenport, IA, 1926–31; Topeka, KS, 1931–41

Constituted in the O.R. on 15 October 1921 as the 538th Arty. Regt. (AA), C.A.C., assigned to the 203d C.A. Brig. (Third Army), and allotted to the Seventh Corps Area. Initiated on 4 October 1921 with regimental HQ at Lawrence, KS. Subordinate battalion HQ concurrently organized as follows: HQ and Combat Train, 1st Bn. at Omaha, NE; and HHD, 2d Bn. at Lawrence, KS. Redesignated on 30 June 1924 as the 538th C.A. Regt. (AA). Entire regiment relocated on 26 May 1926 with regimental HQ at Davenport, IA. Subordinate battalion HQ concurrently relocated as follows: HQ and Combat Train, 1st Bn. to Clinton, IA; and HHD, 2d Bn. to Cedar Rapids, IA. Entire regiment relocated on 12 October 1931 to Topeka, KS. Designated mobilization station was Camp Funston, KS. Conducted summer training with the 61st C.A. most years at Fort Sheridan, IL, and some years at Camp Knox, KY, or Fort Sill, OK. Conducted summer training in 1927 at the University of Kansas at Lawrence, KS. Primary ROTC feeder school was Kansas State Agricultural College. Location 7 December 1941—Topeka, KS.

Status: Disbanded on 2 April 1943.

Commanders, 538th Coast Artillery Regiment

Maj. Raymond L. Cross	4 October 1921–ao January 1922	Lt. Col. Dinsmore Alter	ao June 1925–ao September 1933
Unknown	ao January 1922–ao June 1925	Unknown	ao September 1933–ao June 1935
Lt. Col. Gwynne G. McCaustland	ao June 1935–December 1941		

539th Coast Artillery Regiment (Antiaircraft) — Organized Reserve New York

HQ—*Not initiated,* 1921–22; Manhattan, NY, 1922–39; *Inactive,* 1939–41

Constituted in the O.R. on 15 October 1921 as the 539th Arty. Regt. (AA), C.A.C., assigned to the 212th C.A. Brig. (GHQR), and allotted to the Second Corps Area. Initiated on 24 April 1922 with regimental HQ at Manhattan, NY. Subordinate battalion HQ concurrently organized as follows: HQ and Combat Train, 1st Bn. at Brooklyn, NY; and HHD, 2d Bn. at Manhattan. Redesignated on 30 June 1924 as the 539th C.A. Regt. (AA). Relieved from the 212th C.A. Brig. (GHQR) on 1 October 1933. Designated mobilization station was Camp Upton, NY. Typically conducted Inactive Training Period meetings at the Engineer Society Building on 39th Street in New York City. Conducted summer training with the 62d C.A. most years at Camp Upton, NY, and some years at Fort Tilden, Fort Totten, NY, or Aberdeen Proving Ground, MD. Also conducted C.A. CMTC training some years at Fort Hancock, NJ, as an alternate form of annual training. Inactivated about December 1939 at Manhattan by relief of personnel. Location 7 December 1941—*Inactive.*

Status: Disbanded on 2 April 1943.

Commanders, 539th Coast Artillery Regiment

1st Lt. Charles Melter	24 April 1922–14 March 1923	Col. Henry D. Cushing	18 May 1923–2 March 1938
Capt. Arthur F. Messner	14 March 1923–18 May 1923	Lt. Col. Anastasio C. M. Azoy	2 March 1938–December 1939
Inactive	December 1939–December 1941		

540th Coast Artillery Regiment (Antiaircraft) — Organized Reserve Alabama

HQ—*Not initiated,* 1921–22; Anniston, AL, 1922–29; Birmingham, AL, 1929–41

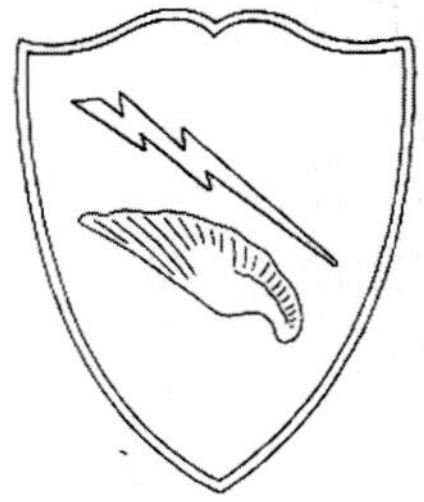

Constituted in the O.R. on 15 October 1921 as the 540th Arty. Regt. (AA), C.A.C., assigned to the 212th C.A. Brig. (GHQR), and allotted to the Fourth Corps Area. Initiated on 21 March 1922 with regimental HQ at Anniston, AL. Subordinate battalion HQ concurrently organized as follows: HQ and Combat Train, 1st Bn. at Cordova, AL; and HHD, 2d Bn. at Bessemer, AL. Redesignated on 30 June 1924 as the 540th C.A. Regt. (AA). Entire regiment relocated on 22 October 1929 to Birmingham, AL. Relieved from the 212th C.A. Brig. (GHQR) on 1 October 1933. Conducted summer training at Fort Barrancas, FL. Also conducted C.A. CMTC training some years at Fort Barrancas as an alternate form of annual training. Regiment was deleted from units to attend camp in 1936 due to an infantile paralysis epidemic that broke out in northeast Alabama that summer. Primary ROTC feeder school was the University of Alabama. Designated mobilization training station was Camp Jackson, SC. Location 7 December 1941—Birmingham, AL.

Status: Disbanded on April 1943.

Commanders, 540th Coast Artillery Regiment

Lt. Col. Robert O. Edwards	21 March 1922–19 June 1924	Unknown	ao March 1938–ao April 1939
Col. Andrew Bramlett	19 June 1924–June 1932	Col. Arthur W. Merkel	ao April 1939–28 May 1939
Lt. Col. Richard W. Coward	June 1932–ao March 1938	Unknown	28 May 1939–7 December 1941

541st Coast Artillery Regiment (Antiaircraft) — Organized Reserve Ohio/Kentucky/West Virginia

HQ—*Not initiated,* 1921–22; Hamilton, OH, 1922–23; Louisville, KY, 1923–31; Huntington, WV, 1931–40; Lexington, KY, 1940–41

Constituted in the O.R. on 15 October 1921 as the 541st Arty. Regt. (AA), C.A.C., and allotted to the Fifth Corps Area. Initiated in March 1922 with regimental HQ at Hamilton, OH. Relocated by June 1923 to Louisville, KY. Redesignated on 30 June 1924 as the 541st C.A. Regt. (AA). Entire regiment relocated on 9 July 1931 to Huntington, WV. Assigned to the 199th C.A. Brig. (GHQR) on 1 October 1933. Entire regiment relocated in April 1940 to Lexington, KY. Conducted summer training with the 61st C.A. most years at Fort Sheridan, IL, and some years at Camp Knox, KY. Location 7 December 1941—Lexington, KY.

Status: Disbanded on 2 April 1943.

Commanders, 541st Coast Artillery Regiment

Maj. Will P. Watson	March 1922–27 October 1922	Unknown	ao September 1930–ao June 1933
Maj. Vincent H. Druffner	27 October 1922–22 January 1923	Col. Pat M. Stevens	ao June 1933–ao July 1933
Col. Sidney H. Guthrie	22 January 1923–ao September 1924	Unknown	ao July 1933–ao May 1936
Lt. Col. Waldemar P. Adams	ao June 1925–ao July 1926	Maj. Robert E. O'Conner	ao May 1936–ao June 1936
Unknown	ao July 1926–ao August 1930	Unknown	ao June 1936–ao July 1940
Maj. Robert E. O'Conner	ao August 1930–ao September 1930	Lt. Col. Collis P. Hudson	ao July 1940–December 1941

542d Coast Artillery Regiment (Antiaircraft) — Organized Reserve Maine/New Hampshire

HQ—*Not initiated,* 1923–24; Portland, ME, 1924–27; *Inactive,* 1927–29; Manchester, NH, 1929–41

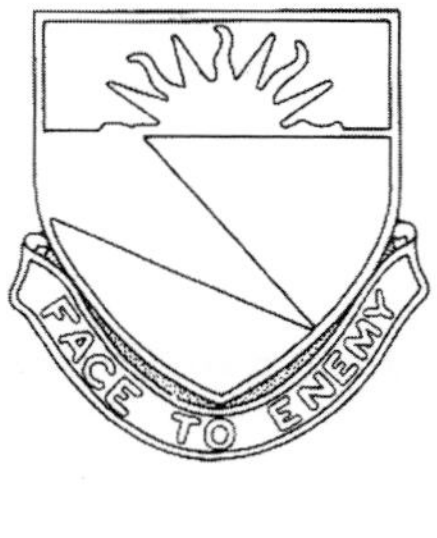

Constituted in the O.R. on 2 July 1923 as the 542d Arty. Regt. (AA), C.A.C., assigned to the 209th C.A. Brig. (GHQR), and allotted to the First Corps Area. Initiated on 2 June 1924 with regimental HQ at Portland, ME. Redesignated on 30 June 1924 as the 542d C.A. Regt. (AA). Inactivated about June 1927 at Portland by relief of personnel. Reorganized on 6 March 1929 at Manchester, NH. Subordinate battalion HQ concurrently reorganized as follows: HQ and Combat Train, 1st Bn. at Portsmouth, NH; and HHD, 2d Bn. at Nashua, NH. Relieved from the 209th C.A. Brig. (AA) (GHQR) on 1 October 1933 and assigned to the XI Corps. Conducted summer training at Fort Terry, NY, and Fort H.G. Wright, NY. Also conducted C.A. CMTC training some years at Fort Adams, RI, as an alternate form of annual training. Primary ROTC feeder school was the University of New Hampshire. Location 7 December 1941—Manchester, NH.

Status: Disbanded on 2 April 1943.

Commanders, 542d Coast Artillery Regiment

Lt. Col. Frank Geer (R.A.)	2 June 1924–31 October 1924	Col. George W. Small	May 1932–ao July 1936
Lt. Col. Wildemar P. Adams	31 October 1924–June 1927	Unknown	ao July 1936–ao May 1937
Inactive	June 1927–6 March 1929	Maj. Curtis P. O' Donnell	ao May 1937–ao July 1939
Unknown	6 March 1929–7 January 1930	Unknown	ao July 1939–ao August 1940
Col. Beryl W. Randall	7 January 1930–May 1932	Col. Gordon L. Carter	ao August 1940–December 1941

543d Coast Artillery Regiment (Antiaircraft) — **Organized Reserve Connecticut**

HQ—New London, CT, 1923–29; Hartford, CT, 1929–41

Constituted in the O.R. on 2 July 1923 as the 543d Arty. Regt. (AA), C.A.C., assigned to the 209th C.A. Brig. (GHQR), and allotted to the First Corps Area. Initiated in July 1923 with regimental HQ at New London, CT. Subordinate battalion HQ concurrently organized as follows: HQ and Combat Train, 1st Bn. at Hartford, CT; and HHD, 2d Bn. at Bridgeport, CT. Redesignated on 30 June 1924 as the 543d C.A. Regt. (AA). Regimental HQ relocated on 13 February 1929 to Hartford, CT. Typically conducted Inactive Training Period meetings at the State Capitol or the Federal Building in Hartford. Conducted summer training at Fort Terry, NY, and Fort H.G. Wright, NY. Also conducted C.A. CMTC training some years at Fort Adams, RI, as an alternate form of annual training. Primary ROTC feeder school was Yale University. Location 7 December 1941—Hartford, CT.

Status: Disbanded on 2 April 1943.

Commanders, 543d Coast Artillery Regiment

Maj. George H.G. Campbell	July 1923–ao September 1925	Lt. Col. Allyn D. Stoddard	ao September 1926–December 1941

544th Coast Artillery Regiment (Antiaircraft) — **Organized Reserve Rhode Island and Massachusetts**

HQ—Providence, RI, 1923–41

Constituted in the O.R. on 2 July 1923 as the 544th Arty. Regt. (AA), C.A.C., assigned to the 209th C.A. Brig. (GHQR), and allotted to the First Corps Area. Initiated in September 1923 with regimental HQ at Providence, RI. Subordinate battalion HQ concurrently organized as follows: HQ and Combat Train, 1st Bn. at Providence, RI; and HHD, 2d Bn. at Fall River, MA. Redesignated on 30 June 1924 as the 544th C.A. Regt. (AA). Attached to the 76th Div. on 17 October 1929 for organization, administrative, and training. Typically conducted Inactive Training Period meetings at 100 Fountain Street in Providence. Conducted summer training at Fort Terry, NY, Fort H.G. Wright, NY, and Fort Adams, RI. Primary ROTC feeder school was Rhode Island State College. Location 7 December 1941—Providence, RI.

Status: Disbanded on 2 April 1943.

Commanders, 544th Coast Artillery Regiment

Maj. Hunter C. White	September 1923–July 1925	Maj. Howard C. Arnold	ao June 1930–ao November 1937
Lt. Col. Walter B. Smith	July 1925–ao July 1927	Maj. Bernt G.V. Zetterstrom	ao July 1938–ao September 1939
Unknown	ao July 1927–ao June 1930	Col. Hunter C. White	ao June 1940–December 1941

545th Coast Artillery Regiment (Antiaircraft) — **Organized Reserve Louisiana/Mississippi**

HQ—New Orleans, LA, 1923–34; Jackson, MS, 1934–41

Constituted in the O.R. on 2 July 1923 as the 545th Arty. Regt. (AA), C.A.C., assigned to the 209th C.A. Brig. (GHQR), and allotted to the Fourth Corps Area. Initiated in November 1923 with regimental HQ at New Orleans, LA. Redesignated on 30 June 1924 as the 545th C.A. Regt. (AA). Entire regiment relocated on 25 September 1934 to Jackson, MS. Conducted summer training most years at Fort Barrancas, FL. For summer training in 1924, the regiment was composed of five batteries of CMTC candidates and one battery of ROTC cadets to conduct live firing of 12-inch guns, 12-inch mortars, and 3-inch guns. Also conducted C.A. CMTC training some years at Fort Barrancas or Camp Beauregard, LA, as an alternate form of annual training. Primary ROTC feeder school was the Mississippi Agricultural and Mechanical College. Designated mobilization station was Camp Jackson, SC. Location 7 December 1941—Jackson, MS.

Status: Disbanded on 2 April 1943.

Commanders, 545th Coast Artillery Regiment

Lt. Col. W.F. Robertson	November 1923–ao July 1924
Unknown	ao July 1924–ao May 1931
Maj. R.W. Reily	ao May 1931–ao June 1932
Unknown	ao June 1932–17 October 1933
Lt. Col. Robert L. Indest	17 October 1933–ao October 1941

546th Coast Artillery Battalion (Antiaircraft) (ZI) **Organized Reserve**

HQ—*Not initiated,* 1923–24

Constituted in the O.R. on 2 July 1923, assigned to the Zone of the Interior, and allotted to the Second Corps Area. Demobilized on 13 June 1924.

547th Coast Artillery Battalion (Antiaircraft) (ZI) **Organized Reserve Virginia**

HQ—*Not initiated,* 1923–25; Norfolk, VA, 1925–28

Constituted in the O.R. on 2 July 1923, assigned to the Zone of the Interior, and allotted to the Third Corps Area. Initiated about October 1925 at Norfolk, VA. Conducted summer training at Fort Monroe, VA. Demobilized on 5 September 1928.

Commanders, 547th Coast Artillery Battalion

Maj. Ulrich J. Mengert	October 1925–5 September 1928

548th Coast Artillery Battalion (Antiaircraft) (ZI) **Organized Reserve South Carolina**

HQ—Greenville, SC, 1923–25; Columbia, SC, 1925–28

Constituted in the O.R. on 2 July 1923, assigned to the Zone of the Interior, and allotted to the Fourth Corps Area. Initiated in December 1923 with HQ at Greenville, SC. HQ relocated on 14 January 1925 to Columbia, SC. Designated mobilization station was Camp Jackson, SC. Conducted summer training at Fort Barrancas, FL, or Fort Moultrie, SC. Demobilized on 5 September 1928.

Commanders, 548th Coast Artillery Battalion

Lt. Col. Paul N. Pittenger	December 1923–5 September 1928

549th Coast Artillery Battalion (Antiaircraft) (ZI) **Organized Reserve**

HQ—*Not initiated,* 1923–28

Constituted in the O.R. on 2 July 1923, assigned to the Zone of the Interior, and allotted to the Fifth Corps Area. Demobilized on 5 September 1928.

550th Coast Artillery Battalion (Antiaircraft) (ZI) **Organized Reserve Illinois**

HQ—*Not initiated,* 1923–24; Chicago, IL, 1924–28

Constituted in the O.R. on 2 July 1923, assigned to the Zone of the Interior, and allotted to the Sixth Corps Area. Initiated on 9 April 1924 with HQ at Chicago, IL. Designated mobilization station was Camp Logan, IL. Demobilized on 5 September 1928.

Commanders, 550th Coast Artillery Battalion

Capt. Roger D. Hunneman	9 April 1924–ao May 1924	Unknown	ao May 1924–5 September 1928

551st Coast Artillery Battalion (Antiaircraft) (ZI) **Organized Reserve**

HQ—*Not initiated,* 1923–28

Constituted in the O.R. on 2 July 1923, assigned to the Zone of the Interior, and allotted to the Seventh Corps Area. Demobilized on 5 September 1928.

552d Coast Artillery Battalion (Antiaircraft) (ZI) **Organized Reserve California**

HQ—*Not initiated,* 1923–26; San Diego, CA, 1926–28

Constituted in the O.R. on 2 July 1923, assigned to the Zone of the Interior, and allotted to the Ninth Corps Area. Initiated in April 1926 with HQ at San Diego, CA. Conducted summer training with the 63d C.A. most years at Camp McQuaide, CA. Demobilized on 5 September 1928. Personnel transferred to 976th C.A.

Commanders, 552d Coast Artillery Battalion

Unknown	April 1924–5 September 1928

553d Coast Artillery Battalion (Antiaircraft) (ZI) **Organized Reserve Massachusetts and Rhode Island/New York**

HQ—*Not initiated,* 1923–24; Boston, MA, 1924–25; *Inactive,* 1925–28

Constituted in the O.R. on 2 July 1923, assigned to the Zone of the Interior, and allotted to the First Corps Area. Initiated in November 1924 with battalion HQ at Boston, MA. Unit's original mobilization assignment was as school support troops for the First Corps Area antiaircraft training center to be established at Camp Devens, MA. Withdrawn from the First Corps Area in January 1925 and allotted to the Second Corps Area. Unit was inactivated and transferred to the Second Corps Area due to the War Department decision to train antiaircraft units from the First and Second Corps Areas at Camp Upton, NY. Fort Wadsworth, NY, designated as HQ on reorganization, but the unit was never organized at that location. Demobilized on 5 September 1928.

Commanders, 553d Coast Artillery Battalion

Unknown	November 1924–January 1925

554th Coast Artillery Battalion (Antiaircraft) (ZI) **Organized Reserve**

HQ—*Not initiated,* 1923–24

Constituted in the O.R. on 2 July 1923, assigned to the Zone of the Interior, and allotted to the Ninth Corps Area. Withdrawn from the O.R. on 13 June 1924 and demobilized.

555th Coast Artillery Battalion (Antiaircraft) (ZI) **Organized Reserve Michigan**

HQ—*Not initiated,* 1923–27; Detroit, MI, 1927–28

Constituted in the O.R. on 2 July 1923, assigned to the Zone of the Interior, and allotted to the Sixth Corps Area. Initiated on 7 January 1927 with battalion HQ at Detroit, MI. Conducted summer training in 1927 at Camp Custer, MI. Conducted summer training with the 202d C.A. at Camp Grant, IL, in 1928. Disbanded on 5 September 1928. Reconstituted on 11 April 1930 and consolidated with the 945th C.A. Regt.

Commanders, 555th Coast Artillery Battalion

Maj. John W. Callahan	7 January 1927–5 September 1928

601st Coast Artillery Regiment (Railway) **Organized Reserve Massachusetts and Connecticut**

HQ—Boston, MA, 1923–41; Bridgeport, CT, 1941

Constituted in the O.R. on 2 July 1923 as the 601st Arty. Regt. (Railway), C.A.C., assigned to the Harbor Defenses of Boston, and allotted to the First Corps Area. Initiated in May 1923 with regimental HQ at Boston, MA. Subordinate battalion HQ concurrently organized as follows: HHD, 1st Bn. at Bridgeport, CT; HHD, 2d Bn. at Newton, MA; and HHD, 3d Bn. at Waltham, MA. Regiment was designated to be transferred to the Third Corps Area after mobilization to reinforce the Harbor Defenses of Chesapeake Bay. Redesignated on 30 June 1924 as the 601st C.A. Regt. (Railway). Attached to the 94th Div. on 17 October 1929 for organization, administrative, and training. HQ relocated in April 1941 to Bridgeport, CT. Massachusetts elements typically conducted Inactive Training Period meetings at the Army and Navy Club in Boston and Connecticut elements at the State Capitol or the Federal Building in Hartford. Conducted summer training at numerous locations to include Fort Hancock, NJ; Fort Andrews, MA; Fort Adams, RI; and Fort H.G. Wright, NY. Also conducted C.A. CMTC training some years at Fort Adams or Fort H.G. Wright as an alternate form of annual training. Primary ROTC feeder school was the Massachusetts Institute of Technology. Designated mobilization station was Fort Monroe, VA. Location 7 December 1941—Bridgeport, CT.

Status: Disbanded on 22 August 1942.

Commanders, 601st Coast Artillery Regiment

Maj. Clarence C. Tracy	May 1923–June 1923
Lt. Col. Horatio Alden	June 1923–June 1929
Lt. Col. George B. Sawyer	June 1929–ao November 1929
Lt. Col. Camille Mazeau	December 1929–June 1932
Maj. Leon F. Foss	June 1932–ao July 1932
Unknown	ao July 1932–ao July 1937
Maj. Eugene M. Vigneron	ao July 1937–December 1941

602d Coast Artillery Regiment (Railway) **Organized Reserve New York and New Jersey**

HQ—Queens, NY, 1923–41

Constituted in the O.R. on 2 July 1923 as the 602d Arty. Regt. (Railway), C.A.C., assigned to the Harbor Defenses of Sandy Hook and allotted to the Second Corps Area. Initiated on 1 November 1923 with regimental HQ at Queens, NY. Subordinate battalion HQ concurrently organized as follows: HHD, 1st Bn. at Brooklyn, NY; HHD, 2d Bn. at Manhattan, NY; and HHD, 3d Bn. at Jersey City, NJ. Redesignated on 30 June 1924 as the 602d C.A. Regt. (Railway). The regiment conducted a unique quick reaction exercise with the 2d Bn., 52d C.A. by railing an 8-inch railway gun and 12-inch railway mortar to Wildwood, NJ, to live fire at targets off Cape May, 11 June 1932. Typically conducted Inactive Training Period meetings at the Engineer Society Building on 39th Street in New York City. Conducted summer training most years at Fort Hancock, NJ, with the 52d C.A., and some years at Camp Upton, NY. Also conducted C.A. CMTC training some years at Fort Hancock as an alternate form of annual training. Primary ROTC feeder schools were Cornell University and Fordham University. Designated mobilization station was Fort Hancock, NJ. The majority of the regiment's officers ordered to Active Duty during 1940–41 were assigned to duty with the 52d C.A. at Fort Hancock. Location 7 December 1941—Queens, NY.

Status: Disbanded on 22 August 1942.

Commanders, 602d Coast Artillery Regiment

Col. Azel Ames	1 November 1923–17 October 1935	Col. Charles Houston	17 October 1935–December 1941

603d Coast Artillery Regiment (Railway) **Organized Reserve Pennsylvania**

HQ—Philadelphia, PA, 1923–41

Constituted in the O.R. on 2 July 1923 as the 603d Arty. Regt. (Railway), C.A.C., assigned to the Third Coast Artillery District, and allotted to the Third Corps Area. Initiated on 3 November 1923 with regimental HQ at Philadelphia, PA. Subordinate battalion HQ concurrently organized as follows: HHD, 1st Bn. at Allentown, PA; HHD, 2d Bn. at Wilkes Barre, PA; and HHD, 3d Bn. at Scranton, PA. Redesignated on 30 June 1924 as the 603d C.A. Regt. (Railway). Conducted summer training most years at Fort Monroe, VA, and some years at Fort Eustis, VA. Also conducted C.A. CMTC training some years at Fort Monroe as an alternate form of annual training. Primary ROTC feeder school was the Drexel Institute. Designated mobilization station was Fort Monroe, VA. Location 7 December 1941—Philadelphia, PA.

Status: Disbanded on 22 August 1942.

Commanders, 603d Coast Artillery Regiment

Capt. Robert M. Zacharias	3 November 1923–ao January 1924	Lt. Col. Paul N. Pittenger	5 September 1928–12 September 1929
Maj. Richard F. Bern	ao July 1924–ao September 1924	Lt. Col. Thomas A.S. Thropp	12 September 1929–ao September 1934
Unknown	ao September 1924–ao June 1926	Col. William L. Dennen	ao June 1935–ao September 1940
Maj. Thomas A. S. Thropp	ao June 1926–5 September 1928	Col. Frederick H. Bachmann	ao December 1940–7 August 1941

604th Coast Artillery Regiment (Railway) **Organized Reserve California and Oregon/Utah**

HQ—Oakland, CA, 1923–29; San Francisco, CA, 1929–40; Salt Lake City, UT, 1940–41

Constituted in the O.R. on 2 July 1923 as the 604th Arty. Regt. (Railway), C.A.C., assigned to the Harbor Defenses of San Francisco and the Columbia, and allotted to the Ninth Corps Area. Initiated on 3 November 1923, less 3d Bn., with regimental HQ at Oakland, CA. Subordinate battalion HQ concurrently organized as follows: HHD, 1st Bn. at Oakland; and HHD, 2d Bn. at Berkeley, CA. HHD, 3d Bn. organized on 15 December 1923 at Portland, OR. Redesignated on 30 June 1924 as the 604th C.A. Regt. (Railway). Entire regiment relocated on 28 January 1930 to San Francisco. Regiment assisted the 3d C.A. with the test firing of railway guns at Carlsbad, CA, in June 1936. Regiment relocated in April 1940 to Salt Lake City, UT. Conducted summer training most years at Fort Winfield Scott, CA, and some years at Fort MacArthur, CA, or Fort Funston, CA. Primary ROTC feeder school was the University of California at Berkeley. Location 7 December 1941—Salt Lake City, UT.

Status: Disbanded on 22 August 1942.

Events: 108

Commanders, 604th Coast Artillery Regiment

Unknown	2 November 1923–ao September 1925	Unknown	ao June 1934–ao June 1936
Col. Henry G. Mathewson	ao September 1925–ao June 1934	Col. Washington B. Mel	ao June 1936–December 1941

605th Coast Artillery Battalion (Railway) **Organized Reserve Washington/California**

HQ—Seattle, WA, 1923–29; Los Angeles, CA, 1929–33

Constituted in the O.R. on 2 July 1923 as the 605th Arty. Bn. (Railway), C.A.C., assigned to the Harbor Defenses of Puget Sound and allotted to the Ninth Corps Area. Initiated on 15 November 1923 with regimental HQ at Seattle, WA. Redesignated on 30 June 1924 as the 605th C.A. Bn. (Railway). Entire battalion relocated on 10 September 1929 to Los Angeles, CA, and assigned to the Harbor Defenses of Los Angeles. Conducted an unusual (for an O.R. unit) live-fire exercise at Fort Funston in 1932 when planes from the 91st Obsn. Sq. provided aerial spotting assistance for target acquisition and fire adjustment. Many unit personnel participated in earthquake relief operations, 14–22 March 1933, in the Los Angeles area. Typically conducted Inactive Training Period meetings at the Times Building in Seattle in the 1920s and at the Chamber of Commerce Building or the Detwiler Building in Los Angeles in the 1930s. Conducted summer training most years at Fort Winfield Scott, CA, and some years at Fort MacArthur, CA, or Fort Funston, CA. Primary ROTC feeder school was the University of California at Berkeley. Demobilized on 1 October 1933.

Commanders, 605th Coast Artillery Regiment

Unknown	15 November 1923–ao September 1925	Maj. Frank J. Baum	ao September 1925–1 October 1933

606th Coast Artillery Regiment (155-mm G-Tractor) (Harbor Defense) **Organized Reserve Maine, New Hampshire, and Massachusetts**

HQ—Hallowell, ME, 1923–29; Boston, MA, 1929–41

Constituted in the O.R. on 2 July 1923 as the 606th Arty. Regt. (155-mm G-Tractor) (Harbor Defense), C.A.C., assigned to the Harbor Defenses of Boston, and allotted to the First Corps Area. Initiated provisionally in June 1923 with regimental HQ at Hallowell, ME. Subordinate battalion HQ concurrently organized as follows: HHD, 1st Bn. at Concord, NH; HHD, 2d Bn. at Walpole, MA; and HHD, 3d Bn. at Gardiner, ME. The unit was originally almost entirely composed of personnel who had served in the 303d F.A. in World War I. Redesignated on 30 June 1924 as the 606th C.A. Regt. (155-mm G-Tractor) (Harbor Defense). Relieved from the Harbor Defenses of Boston in 1927 and assigned to the 239th C.A. Brig. (GHQR). Entire regiment relocated on 10 September 1929 to Boston, MA. Conducted summer training at Fort Winfield Scott, CA; Fort Andrews, MA; and Fort H.G. Wright, NY. Also conducted C.A. CMTC training some years at Fort Adams, RI, as an alternate form of annual training. Primary ROTC feeder schools were the Massachusetts Institute of Technology and the University of New Hampshire. Location 7 December 1941—Boston, MA.

Status: Disbanded on 22 August 1942.

Commanders, 606th Coast Artillery Regiment

Col. Charles D. Winn	June 1923–15 September 1927	Unknown	ao June 1931–ao July 1934
Lt. Col. Waldemar P. Adams	15 September 1927–ao July 1929	Maj. Paul D. Harrower	ao July 1934–1 July 1935
Lt. Col. Fred E. Stockwell	ao November 1929–ao June 1931	Col. Horace J. Baum	1 July 1935–1 July 1937
Lt. Col. Arthur J. Maxfield	1 July 1937–December 1941		

607th Coast Artillery Regiment (155-mm G-Tractor) (Harbor Defense) — Organized Reserve New York

HQ—Bronx, NY, 1923–41

Constituted in the O.R. on 2 July 1923 as the 607th Arty. Regt. (155-mm G-Tractor) (Harbor Defense), C.A.C., assigned to the Harbor Defenses of Eastern New York and allotted to the Second Corps Area. Initiated on 6 November 1923 with regimental HQ at Bronx, NY. Subordinate battalion HQ concurrently organized as follows: HHD, 1st Bn. at Bronx; HHD, 2d Bn. at Bronx; and HHD, 3d Bn. at Manhattan, NY. Redesignated on 30 June 1924 as the 607th C.A. Regt. (155-mm G-Tractor) (Harbor Defense). Relieved from the Harbor Defenses of Eastern New York in 1927 and assigned to the 239th C.A. Brig. (GHQR). Regiment adopted the nickname "Seahawks" in the early 1920s in honor of the Osprey, an admirable bird of prey that was prevalent in the New York harbor area. Typically conducted Inactive Training Period meetings at the armory of the 245th C.A. or at the Engineer Society Building on 39th Street in New York City. Conducted summer training most years at Fort Hancock, NJ. Also conducted C.A. CMTC training some years at Fort Hancock as an alternate form of annual training. For the 1924 CMTC training, the regiment sailed from Brooklyn on the U.S.A.M.P. *Gen. Edward O.C. Ord* to get to Fort Hancock. Designated mobilization station was Fort Hancock, NJ. Primary ROTC feeder school was Fordham University. Location 7 December 1941—Bronx, NY.

Status: Disbanded on 22 August 1942.

Commanders, 607th Coast Artillery Regiment

Col. Robert S. Allyn	6 November 1923–8 December 1939	Col. Vergne Chappelle	8 December 1939–ao June 1941

608th Coast Artillery Regiment (155mm G-Tractor) (Harbor Defense) — Organized Reserve California

HQ—San Francisco, CA, 1923–29; Los Angeles, CA, 1929–33

Constituted in the O.R. on 2 July 1923 as the 608th Arty. Regt. (155-mm G-Tractor) (Harbor Defense), C.A.C., assigned to the Harbor Defenses of San Francisco, and allotted to the Ninth Corps Area. Initiated on 15 November 1923 with regimental HQ and all subordinate elements, less 3d Bn., located at San Francisco, CA. The 3d Bn. organized on 15 December 1923 at Los Angeles. Redesignated on 30 June 1924 as the 608th C.A. Regt. (155-mm G-Tractor) (Harbor Defense). Relieved from the Harbor Defenses of San Francisco in 1927 and assigned to the 239th C.A. Brig. (GHQR). Entire regiment relocated by February 1929 to Los Angeles and assigned to the Harbor Defenses of Los Angeles. Many unit personnel participated in earthquake relief operations, 14–22 March 1933, in the Los Angeles area. Typically conducted Inactive Training Period meetings at the Chamber of Commerce Building or the Detwiler Building in Los Angeles, 1929–33. Conducted summer training most years at Fort Winfield Scott, CA, and some years at Fort MacArthur, CA. Demobilized on 1 October 1933.

Events: 108

Commanders, 608th Coast Artillery Regiment

Maj. Arleigh C. Griffin	15 November 1923–ao January 1924	Col. David McC. McKell	ao July 1925–20 December 1927
Unknown	ao January 1924–ao July 1925	Unknown	20 December 1927–ao June 1931
Col. Forrest E. Baker	ao June 1931–1 October 1933		

609th Coast Artillery Battalion (Railway) — Organized Reserve Virginia

HQ—Roanoke, VA, 1924–25; Fort Monroe, VA, 1925–28

Constituted in the O.R. on 31 March 1924, assigned to the Harbor Defenses of Chesapeake Bay, and allotted to the Third Corps Area. Initiated in August 1925 with regimental HQ at Roanoke, VA. Relocated in late 1925 to Fort Monroe, VA. Conducted summer training at Fort Monroe, VA, or Fort Eustis, VA. Demobilized on 5 September 1928.

Commanders, 609th Coast Artillery Battalion

Capt. William K. Barnett	October 1925–ao August 1927	Maj. Granville B. Smith	ao May 1928–5 September 1928

610th Coast Artillery Battalion (Heavy Mobile Artillery) **Organized Reserve California**

HQ—*Not initiated,* 1924–28

Constituted in the O.R. on 31 March 1924, assigned to the Zone of the Interior, and allotted to the Ninth Corps Area. Btry A only organized at Los Angeles, CA. Conducted summer training at Fort MacArthur, CA. Demobilized on 5 September 1928.

613th Coast Artillery Regiment (Harbor Defense) (Type B) **Organized Reserve Maine/New York**

HQ—Portland, ME, 1924–36; *Inactive,* 1936–41

Constituted in the O.R. on 31 March 1924 as the 613th Arty. Bn. (Fixed Defenses), C.A.C., a four-battery battalion assigned to the Harbor Defenses of Portland and allotted to the First Corps Area. Redesignated on 30 June 1924 as the 613th C.A. Bn. (Harbor Defense). Initiated in November 1924 with regimental HQ at Portland, ME. Expanded to a two-battalion, six-battery regiment and redesignated on 19 March 1926 as the 613th C.A. Regt. (Harbor Defense). Expanded to a three-battalion, nine-battery regiment on 19 February 1930. Withdrawn from the First Corps Area on 5 June 1936 and allotted to the Second Corps Area. Concurrently relieved from the Harbor Defenses of Portland. New York City, designated on 5 April 1937 as HQ on organization, but the unit was never organized at that location. Reassigned to the Harbor Defenses of Portland in 1938 although the regiment remained allotted to the Second Corps Area. Conducted C.A. CMTC training some years at Fort Adams, RI, as an alternate form of annual training. Location 7 December 1941—*Inactive.*

Commanders, 613th Coast Artillery Regiment

Maj. Francis E. Cummings	November 1924–ao April 1926	Maj. Gordon L. Carter	ao June 1931–ao July 1931
Unknown	ao April 1926–ao July 1927	Unknown	ao July 1931–2 October 1933
Col. Harry Goodier	ao July 1927–ao June 1930	Col. Hunter C. White	2 October 1933–5 June 1936
Unknown	ao June 1930–June 1931	*Inactive*	6 June 1936–December 1941

614th Coast Artillery Regiment (Harbor Defense) (Type D) **Organized Reserve New Hampshire and Massachusetts**

HQ—Portsmouth, NH, 1924–40

Constituted in the O.R. on 31 March 1924 as the 614th Arty. Bn. (Fixed Defenses), C.A.C., a four-battery battalion assigned to the Harbor Defenses of Portsmouth and allotted to the First Corps Area. Redesignated on 30 June 1924 as the 614th C.A. Bn. (Harbor Defense). Initiated in November 1924 with battalion HQ and Btrys A and B at Portsmouth, NH, and Btrys C, D, and E in Massachusetts. Expanded to a two-battalion, six-battery regiment and redesignated on 19 March 1926 as the 614th C.A. Regt. (Harbor Defense). Withdrawn from the O.R. on 1 September 1935 and allotted to the R.A. as an RAI unit. Conducted summer training at Fort Andrews, MA, or Fort H.G. Wright, NY, or Fort Williams, ME. Also conducted C.A. CMTC training some years at Fort Adams, RI, as an alternate form of annual training. Primary ROTC feeder school was the University of New Hampshire, 1924–35. Redesignated on 1 February 1940 as the 22d C.A.

Commanders, 614th Coast Artillery Regiment

Maj. Gordon L. Carter	November 1924–ao April 1926	Col. George B. Sawyer	ao June 1928–ao June 1936
Unknown	ao April 1926–ao June 1928	Unknown	ao June 1936–ao June 1937
Maj. Edward B. Pratt	ao June 1937–1 February 1940		

615th Coast Artillery Regiment (Harbor Defense) (Type B) — Organized Reserve Massachusetts/Delaware

HQ—Boston, MA, 1924–36; *Inactive* 1936-1937 Wilmington, DE, 1937–41

Constituted in the O.R. on 31 March 1924 as the 615th Arty. Regt. (Harbor Defense), C.A.C., a two-battalion regiment assigned to the Harbor Defenses of Boston and allotted to the First Corps Area. Redesignated on 30 June 1924 as the 615th C.A. Regt. (Harbor Defense). Initiated in November 1924 with regimental HQ at Boston, MA, HHB. Subordinate battalion HQ concurrently organized as follows: 1st Bn. at Malden, MA, and HHB, 2d Bn. at Fitchburg, MA. Withdrawn from the First Corps Area on 5 June 1936 and allotted to the Second Corps Area. Reorganized on 15 April 1937 with regimental HQ at Wilmington, DE. Conducted summer training at Fort Andrews, MA; Fort H.G. Wright, NY; or Fort Hancock, NJ. Also conducted C.A. CMTC training some years at Fort Adams, RI, as an alternate form of annual training. Primary ROTC feeder school was the Massachusetts Institute of Technology, 1924–36, and the University of Delaware, 1936–41. Designated mobilization station was Fort Hancock, NJ, 1936–41. Location 7 December 1941—Wilmington, DE.

Status: Disbanded on 22 August 1942.

Commanders, 615th Coast Artillery Regiment

Col. Horace J. Baum	November 1924–1 July 1935	Maj. Harry C. Bailey	3 May 1938–31 October 1938
Maj. Benjamin B. D' Ewart	1 July 1935–5 June 1936	Maj. Leon B. Stayton	31 October 1938–ao April 1939
Inactive	5 June 1936–15 April 1937	Maj. Robert B. Kelton	April 1939–December 1941

616th Coast Artillery Regiment (Harbor Defense) (Type D) — Organized Reserve Massachusetts and Rhode Island

HQ—New Bedford, MA, 1924–40

Constituted in the O.R. on 31 March 1924 as the 616th Arty. Bn. (Fixed Defenses), C.A.C., a four-battery battalion assigned to the Harbor Defenses of New Bedford and allotted to the First Corps Area. Redesignated on 30 June 1924 as the 616th C.A. Bn. (Harbor Defense). Initiated in November 1924 with regimental HQ at New Bedford, MA. Expanded to a two-battalion, six-battery regiment and redesignated on 19 March 1926 as the 616th C.A. Regt. (Harbor Defense). HHD, 1st Bn. was organized at New Bedford, MA. HHD, 2d Bn. was organized at Providence, RI, and the battalion was assigned to the Harbor Defenses of Narragansett Bay. Withdrawn from the O.R. on 1 September 1935 and allotted to the R.A. as an RAI unit Conducted summer training at Fort Adams, RI; Fort Andrews, MA; or Fort H.G. Wright, NY. Also conducted C.A. CMTC training some years at Fort Adams as an alternate form of annual training. Primary ROTC feeder school was the Massachusetts Institute of Technology, 1924–35. Reorganized and redesignated as the 616th C.A. Bn. (Harbor Defense). Redesignated on 1 February 1940 as the 23d C.A.

Status: Disbanded on 22 August 1942.

Commanders, 616th Coast Artillery Regiment

Unknown	November 1924–ao September 1925	Lt. Col. J.B. Littlefield	ao June 1930–September 1931
Capt. Fred G. Haney	ao September 1925–ao October 1925	Maj. Harold A. Fasick	September 1931–July 1933
Unknown	ao October 1925–ao June 1930	Lt. Col. Ralph C. Allen	July 1933–1 February 1940

618th Coast Artillery Battalion (Harbor Defense) (Type D) — **Organized Reserve Connecticut/ New Jersey**

HQ—Hartford, CT, 1924–36; *Inactive,* 1936–37; Elizabeth, NJ, 1937–41

Constituted in the O.R. on 31 March 1924 as the 618th Arty. Bn. (Fixed Defenses), C.A.C., a three-battery battalion assigned to the Harbor Defenses of Long Island Sound and allotted to the First Corps Area. Initiated in December 1924 with regimental HQ at Hartford, CT. Redesignated on 30 June 1924 as the 618th C.A. Bn. (Harbor Defense). Btry D constituted on 1 November 1927 and organized at New Haven, CT. Battalion withdrawn from the First Corps Area on 5 June 1936 and allotted to the Second Corps Area. Reorganized in April 1937 with regimental HQ at Elizabeth, NJ. Typically conducted Inactive Training Period meetings at the Post Office Building in Elizabeth. Conducted summer training at Fort Adams, RI, or Fort Hancock, NJ. Also conducted C.A. CMTC training some years at Fort Adams as an alternate form of annual training. Primary ROTC feeder school was the Massachusetts Institute of Technology, 1924–36. Designated mobilization station was Fort Hancock, NJ. Location 7 December 1941—Elizabeth, NJ.

Status: Disbanded on 22 August 1942.

Commanders, 618th Coast Artillery Regiment

Maj. Arthur C. Bennett	December 1924–1 May 1930
Maj. Guy G. Allen	1 May 1930–ao June 1931
Unknown	ao June 1931–ao July 1933
Maj. Ira T. Hook	ao July 1933–ao June 1934
Unknown	ao June 1934–5 June 1936
Inactive	5 June 1936–April 1937
Maj. Leon B. Stayton	April 1937–31 October 1938
Maj. John F. Drake	15 February 1939–15 March 1939
Maj. Arthur L. Selby	15 March 1939–December 1941

619th Coast Artillery Regiment (Harbor Defense) (Type B) — **Organized Reserve New York**

HQ—Brooklyn, NY, 1924–41

Constituted in the O.R. on 31 March 1924 as the 619th Arty. Regt. (Fixed Defenses), C.A.C., a 12-battery regiment assigned to the Harbor Defenses of Southern New York and allotted to the Second Corps Area. Redesignated on 30 June 1924 as the 619th C.A. Regt. (Harbor Defense). Initiated in August 1924 with regimental HQ at Brooklyn, NY. Typically conducted Inactive Training Period meetings at the Engineer Society Building on 39th Street in New York City. Conducted summer training most years at Fort Hancock, NJ, and some years at Camp Upton, NY. Also conducted C.A. CMTC training some years at Fort Hancock as an alternate form of annual training. Conducted the first live firing of a "major caliber" coast defense weapon exclusively by an O.R. unit. The regiment performed the feat at Battery Bloomfield (two 12-inch medium range rifles) at Fort Hancock, NJ, on 24 June 1925. For summer training in 1936, the regiment participated in laying an inert training minefield by the U.S.A.M.P. *General E.O.C. Ord* off New York Harbor. Primary ROTC feeder school was Fordham University. Designated mobilization station was Fort Hamilton, NY. Location 7 December 1941—Brooklyn, NY.

Status: Disbanded on 22 August 1942.

Events: 87, 93

Commanders, 619th Coast Artillery Regiment

Col. Robert H. Hazeltine	August 1924–24 February 1931
Maj. Emanuel L. Meyer	24 February 1931–December 1931
Col. George W. Johnston	December 1931–25 May 1937
Col. Frank H. Phipps	25 May 1937–20 January 1939
Lt. Col. Allison F.H. Scott	20 January 1939–December 1941

620th Coast Artillery Regiment (Harbor Defense) (Type B) **Organized Reserve New York**

HQ—Manhattan, NY, 1924–41

Constituted in the O.R. on 31 March 1924 as the 620th Arty. Bn. (Fixed Defenses), C.A.C., a four-battery battalion assigned to the Harbor Defenses of Southern New York and allotted to the Second Corps Area. Redesignated on 30 June 1924 as the 620th C.A. Bn. (Harbor Defense). Initiated on 31 March 1924 by transfer of personnel from the Sandy Hook C.A. Regt. (Prov.). Regimental HQ and all subordinate elements organized at Manhattan, NY. Expanded to a two-battalion, eight-battery regiment and redesignated on 19 March 1926 as the 620th C.A. Regt. (Harbor Defense). Typically conducted Inactive Training Period meetings at the Engineer Society Building on 39th Street in New York City. Conducted summer training most years at Fort Hancock, NJ, and some years at Camp Upton, NY. Primary ROTC feeder school was Fordham University. Designated mobilization station was Fort Hancock, NJ. Location 7 December 1941—Manhattan, NY.

Status: Disbanded on 22 August 1942.

Events: 87, 93

Commanders, 620th Coast Artillery Regiment

Lt. Col. Percy S. Lyon	31 March 1924–ao May 1925	Lt. Col. Hyland R. Johns	ao June 1931–15 June 1939
Unknown	ao May 1925–ao June 1931	Lt. Col. Allan B. Campfield	15 June 1939–December 1941

621st Coast Artillery Regiment (Harbor Defense) (Type A) **Organized Reserve Delaware**

HQ—Wilmington, DE, 1924–41

Constituted in the O.R. on 31 March 1924 as the 621st Arty. Regt. (Fixed Defenses), C.A.C., a seven-battery regiment assigned to the Harbor Defenses of the Delaware and allotted to the Second Corps Area. Initiated on 31 March 1924 by transfer of personnel from the Delaware C.A. Regt. (Prov.). Regimental HQ and all subordinate elements organized at Wilmington, DE. Redesignated on 30 June 1924 as the 621st C.A. Regt. (Harbor Defense). Withdrawn from the O.R. on 1 September 1935 and allotted to the R.A. as an RAI unit. Awarded the US Coast Artillery Association Trophy for O.R. regiments for 1939. Typically conducted Inactive Training Period meetings at the Engineer Society Building on 39th Street in New York City and later at the State Armory in Wilmington. Conducted summer training at Fort Hancock, NJ. Also conducted C.A. CMTC training some years at Fort Hancock as an alternate form of annual training. Designated mobilization station was Fort DuPont, DE. Primary ROTC feeder school was the University of Delaware, 1935–41. Location 7 December 1941—Wilmington, DE.

Status: Disbanded on 22 August 1942.

Events: 87, 93

Commanders, 621st Coast Artillery Regiment

Col. Archibald E. Tanner	31 March 1924–2 December 1941

622d Coast Artillery Regiment (Harbor Defense) (Type B) — **Organized Reserve Virginia/ District of Columbia**

HQ—Norfolk, VA, 1924–33; Washington, DC, 1933–41

Constituted in the O.R. on 31 March 1924 as the 622d Arty. Regt. (Fixed Defenses), C.A.C., a two-battalion, seven-battery regiment and allotted to the Third Corps Area. Regiment, less HHD, 2d Bn. and Btry D, assigned to the Harbor Defenses of Chesapeake Bay. The HHD, 2d Bn. and Btry D assigned to the Harbor Defenses of Baltimore. Redesignated on 30 June 1924 as the 622d C.A. Regt. (Harbor Defense). Initiated in July 1924 with regimental HQ at Norfolk, VA. Subordinate battalion HQ concurrently organized as follows: HHD, 1st Bn. at Norfolk; and HHD, 2d Bn. at Baltimore, MD. HQ relocated on 3 February 1933 to Washington, DC. Withdrawn from the O.R. on 1 September 1935 and allotted to the R.A. as an RAI unit. Typically conducted Inactive Training Period meetings at the 260th C.A. armory or the Munitions Building in Washington. Conducted summer training most years at Fort Monroe, VA, and some years at Fort Eustis, VA. Also conducted C.A. CMTC training some years at Fort Monroe as an alternate form of annual training. Designated mobilization station was Fort Monroe, VA. Primary ROTC feeder school was the Virginia Polytechnic Institute. Location 7 December 1941—Washington, DC.

Status: Disbanded on 22 August 1942.

Commanders, 622d Coast Artillery Regiment

Unknown	July 1924–2 February 1925	Maj. John E. Kessler	1 February 1928–1 July 1932
Lt. Col. George W. Small	2 February 1925–1 February 1928	Col. James B. Bentley	1 July 1932–17 September 1941

623d Coast Artillery Regiment (Harbor Defense) (Type D) — **Organized Reserve Florida**

HQ—*Not initiated,* 1924–36; Jacksonville, FL, 1936–41

Constituted in the O.R. on 31 March 1924 as the 623d Arty. Regt. (Fixed Defenses), C.A.C., assigned to the Harbor Defenses of Jacksonville, and allotted to the Fourth Corps Area. Redesignated on 30 June 1924 as the 623d C.A. Regt. (Harbor Defense). Btry A only organized in August 1924 at Jacksonville, FL. Reorganized and redesignated 623d C.A. Bn. (Harbor Defense) on 25 January 1936 and remainder of battalion concurrently organized at Jacksonville. Primary ROTC feeder school was the University of Florida. Conducted summer training most years at Fort Barrancas, FL, and some years at Fort MacArthur, CA. Designated mobilization station was Fort Barrancas, FL. Location 7 December 1941—Jacksonville, FL.

Status: Disbanded on 22 August 1942.

Commanders, 623d Coast Artillery Battalion

Lt. Col. Harry W. Porter	25 January 1936–29 January 1939	Lt. Col. James R. Waltman	20 January 1939–December 1941

624th Coast Artillery Battalion (Harbor Defense) (Type D) — **Organized Reserve Texas and Oklahoma**

HQ—*Not initiated,* 1924–25; Galveston, TX, 1925–37; San Antonio, TX, 1937–40; Oklahoma City, OK, 1940–41

Constituted in the O.R. on 31 March 1924 as the 624th Arty. Bn. (Fixed Defenses), C.A.C., a three-battery battalion assigned to the Harbor Defenses of Galveston and allotted to the Eighth Corps Area. Redesignated on 30 June 1924 as the 624th C.A. Bn. (Harbor Defense). Initiated by December 1924 from new and existing units as follows: HHB at Galveston, TX; 845th Co. C.A.C. at Galveston as Btry A; 846th Co. C.A.C. at Galveston as Btry B; 849th Co. C.A.C. at Houston as Btry C. Personnel from the inactivated 508th C.A. at El Paso, TX, were assigned to the battalion in January 1927. Conducted summer training most years with Btry G, 13th C.A. at Fort Crockett, TX. Those years when the battalion did not attend camp as a unit, individual officers attended training at Fort MacArthur, CA; Fort Winfield Scott, CA; Fort Barrancas, FL; and Fort Monroe, VA. For summer training in 1936, the battalion was integrated with the HQ Btry, 3d C.A. at Fort MacArthur. The integrated unit conducted a rail movement with a 14-inch railway gun to a position near Carlsbad, CA, and conducted live-fire operations from that location. Primary ROTC feeder school was the A&M College of Texas. Designated mobilization station was Fort Crockett, TX. Location 7 December 1941—Oklahoma City, OK.

Status: Disbanded on 22 August 1942.

Commanders, 624th Coast Artillery Battalion

Maj. Allen Wright	ao December 1924–ao June 1927	Unknown	ao August 1932–ao July 1935
Unknown	ao June 1927-ao July 1931	Maj. Ray A. Larner	ao July 1935–ao September 1935
Lt. Col. William W. Holden	ao July 1931–ao August 1931	Maj. Robert F. Spottswood	ao December 1935–25 January 1936
Maj. Allen Wight	ao May 1932–ao August 1932	Unknown	25 January 1936–ao June 1940
Lt. Col. Albert N. Murphy	ao June 1940–December 1941		

625th Coast Artillery Regiment (Harbor Defense) (Type A) — Organized Reserve California

HQ—*Not initiated,* 1924–41

Constituted in the O.R. on 31 March 1924 as the 625th Arty. Regt. (Fixed Defenses), C.A.C., assigned to the Harbor Defenses of San Diego, and allotted to the Ninth Corps Area. Redesignated on 30 June 1924 as the 625th C.A. Regt. (Harbor Defense). Btry A only organized in July 1924 at San Diego, CA. Withdrawn from the O.R. on 1 September 1935 and allotted to the R.A. as an RAI unit. Btry A conducted summer training most years at Fort MacArthur, CA, and some years at Fort Winfield Scott, CA. Designated mobilization station was Fort Rosecrans, CA. Location 7 December 1941—*Not initiated.*

Commanders, 625th Coast Artillery Regiment

Battery A

Unknown	July 1924–ao June 1929	Unknown	ao May 1931–ao December 1936
Capt. J. Kammer	ao June 1929–ao May 1931	Maj. Glen I. Miller	ao December 1936–ao July 1938
Unknown	ao July 1938–7 December 1941		

626th Coast Artillery Regiment (Harbor Defense) (Type B) — Organized Reserve California

HQ—*Not initiated,*1924–25; Los Angeles, CA, 1925–41; *Inactive,* 1941

Constituted in the O.R. on 31 March 1924 as the 626th Arty. Regt. (Fixed Defenses), C.A.C., assigned to the Harbor Defenses of Los Angeles, and allotted to the Ninth Corps Area. Redesignated on 30 June 1924 as the 626th C.A. Regt. (Harbor Defense). Initiated on 4 August 1924 with regimental HQ at Los Angeles, CA. Withdrawn from the O.R. on 1 September 1935 and allotted to the R.A. as an RAI unit. As part of its Inactive Training Period, the regiment participated in a "School of Fire" on the 155-mm G.P.F. gun conducted by the 3d C.A. at Fort MacArthur on 14 and 21 December 1935. Typically conducted Inactive Training Period meetings at the Chamber of Commerce Building or the Detwiler Building in Los Angeles. Conducted summer training most years at Fort MacArthur, CA, and some years at Fort Winfield Scott, CA. Primary ROTC feeder school was the University of California at Berkeley. Inactivated on 5 February 1941 at Los Angeles by relief of personnel. Location 7 December 1941—*Inactive.*

Status: Disbanded on 22 August 1942.

Commanders, 626th Coast Artillery Regiment

Lt. Col. Junius Pierce	4 August 1924–ao September 1925	Lt. Col. Frank R. McReynolds	1 October 1933–ao August 1939
Unknown	ao September 1925–ao May 1932	Unknown	ao August 1939–ao August 1940
Lt. Col. J.P. MacNeill	ao May 1932–1 October 1933	Col. Dinsmore Alter	ao February 1940–5 February 1941

627th Coast Artillery Regiment (Harbor Defense) (Type A) **Organized Reserve California**

HQ—San Francisco, CA, 1924–41; *Inactive,* 1941

Constituted in the O.R. on 31 March 1924 as the 627th Arty. Bn. (Fixed Defenses), C.A.C., assigned to the Harbor Defenses of San Francisco, and allotted to the Ninth Corps Area. Expanded and redesignated on 30 June 1924 as the 627th C.A. Regt. (Harbor Defense) (action approved for implementation on 19 March 1926). Initiated on 10 July 1924 with regimental HQ at San Francisco, CA. The 1st and 2d Bns. organized at San Francisco, CA, and the 3d Bn. organized at Los Angeles. The 3d Bn. relocated on 28 January 1930 to San Francisco. Withdrawn from the O.R. on 1 September 1935 and allotted to the R.A. as an RAI unit. Primary ROTC feeders schools were the University of California at Berkeley and the Utah State Agricultural College. Conducted summer training most years at Fort Winfield Scott, CA, and some years at Fort Funston, CA. Inactivated on 5 February 1941 at San Francisco by relief of personnel. Location 7 December 1941—*Inactive.*

Events: 108

Commanders, 627th Coast Artillery Regiment

Col. George F. Connolly	10 July 1924–8 June 1925	Col. Charles J. Mund	10 July 1925–28 February 1937
Lt. Col. Lyle D. Wise	28 February 1937–5 February 1941		

628th Coast Artillery Regiment (Harbor Defense) (Type B) **Organized Reserve Oregon/California**

HQ—Albany, OR, 1924–29; San Francisco, 1929–34; Los Angeles, CA, 1934–41; *Inactive,* 1941

Constituted in the O.R. on 31 March 1924 as the 628th Arty. Bn. (Fixed Defenses), C.A.C., assigned to the Harbor Defenses of the Columbia, and allotted to the Ninth Corps Area. Expanded and redesignated on 30 June 1924 as the 628th C.A. Regt. (Harbor Defense) (action approved for implementation on 19 March 1926). Initiated in July 1924 with regimental HQ at Albany, OR. Personnel relieved on 20 September 1929 and regiment relocated to San Francisco, CA. Relocated on 5 April 1934 to Los Angeles, CA. Withdrawn from the O.R. on 1 September 1935 and allotted to the R.A. as an RAI unit. As part of its Inactive Training Period, the regiment participated in a "School of Fire" on the 155-mm G.P.F. gun conducted by the 3d C.A. at Fort MacArthur on 14 and 21 December 1935. Typically conducted Inactive Training Period meetings at the Chamber of Commerce Building or the Detwiler Building in Los Angeles, 1934–41. Conducted summer training most years at Fort Winfield Scott, CA, or Fort MacArthur, CA, and some years at Fort Worden, WA, or Fort Crockett, TX. Primary ROTC feeder schools were the Oregon State Agricultural College, 1924–29, and the University of California at Berkeley, 1929–41. Inactivated on 5 February 1941 at Los Angeles by relief of personnel. Location 7 December 1941—*Inactive.*

Status: Disbanded on 22 August 1942.

Events: 108

Commanders, 628th Coast Artillery Regiment

Unknown	July 1924–ao July 1929	Unknown	ao May 1931–ao June 1934
Maj. W.J. Brady	ao July 1929–ao May 1931	Col. Forrest E. Baker	ao June 1934–ao August 1936
Lt. Col. Felix M. Usis	ao May 1937–5 February 1941		

629th Coast Artillery Battalion (Harbor Defense) (Type D) **Organized Reserve Oregon**

HQ—*Not initiated,* 1924–30; Portland, OR, 1930–41

Constituted in the O.R. on 31 March 1924 as the 629th Arty. Bn. (Fixed Defenses), C.A.C., assigned to the Harbor Defenses of the Columbia and allotted to the Ninth Corps Area. Redesignated on 30 June 1924 as the 629th C.A. Bn. (Harbor Defense), a two-battery battalion (action approved for implementation on 19 March 1926). Btry A only organized on 25 July 1924 at Astoria, OR. Remainder of the battalion organized on 28 January 1930 with HQ at Portland, OR. Typically conducted Inactive Training Period meetings at the Post Office Building in Portland. Conducted summer training most years at Fort Worden, WA, and some years at Fort Stevens, OR. Primary ROTC feeder school was the Oregon State Agricultural College. Location 7 December 1941—Portland, OR (inactivated on 30 January 1942).

Status: Disbanded on 22 August 1942.

Commanders, 629th Coast Artillery Battalion

Unknown	25 July 1924–28 January 1930	Lt. Col. B.K. Lawson	28 January 1930–ao June 1938
Maj. Russell C. Dunham	ao June 1939–30 January 1942		

630th Coast Artillery Regiment (Harbor Defense) (Type A) **Organized Reserve Washington**

HQ—Seattle, WA, 1924–41

Constituted in the O.R. on 31 March 1924 as the 630th Arty. Bn. (Fixed Defenses), C.A.C., assigned to the Harbor Defenses of Puget Sound and allotted to the Ninth Corps Area. Expanded and redesignated on 30 June 1924 as the 630th C.A. Regt. (Harbor Defense) (action approved for implementation on 19 March 1926). Initiated in July 1924 with regimental HQ at Seattle, WA. Withdrawn from the O.R. on 1 September 1935 and allotted to the R.A. as an RAI unit. Typically conducted Inactive Training Period meetings at the Times Building in Seattle. Conducted summer training at Fort Worden, WA. Also conducted C.A. CMTC training some years at Fort Worden as an alternate form of annual training. Primary ROTC feeder school was the University of Washington. Location 7 December 1941—Seattle, WA.

Status: Disbanded on 22 August 1942.

Commanders, 630th Coast Artillery Regiment

Unknown	July 1924–ao July 1926	Col. Willis C. Bickford	ao July 1926–December 1941

631st Coast Artillery Regiment (Harbor Defense) **Organized Reserve New York**

HQ—*Not initiated,* 1929–41

Constituted in the O.R. on 23 July 1929 as the 631st C.A. Regt. (Harbor Defense), assigned to the Harbor Defenses of Eastern New York, and allotted to the Second Corps Area. To be organized as a three-battery regiment as follows: one Btry of 12-inch mortars, one Btry of 3-inch guns, and one Btry of 10-inch D.G. Southampton, NY, designated as HQ on organization, but the unit was never organized at that location. Location 7 December 1941—*Not initiated.*

Status: Disbanded on 22 August 1942.

632d Coast Artillery Regiment (Harbor Defense) **Organized Reserve Maryland**

HQ—*Not initiated,* 1929–41

Constituted in the O.R. on 23 July 1929 as the 632d C.A. Regt. (Harbor Defense), assigned to the Harbor Defenses of Baltimore, and allotted to the Third Corps Area. To be organized as a four-battery regiment as follows: one Btry of 10-inch railway guns, one battery of 7-inch railway guns, and two batteries of 75-mm guns. Location 7 December 1941—*Not initiated.*

Status: Disbanded on 22 August 1942.

633d Coast Artillery Regiment (Harbor Defense) **Organized Reserve Virginia**

HQ—*Not initiated,* 1929–41

Constituted in the O.R. on 23 July 1929 as the 633d C.A. Regt. (Harbor Defense), assigned to the Harbor Defenses of the Potomac, and allotted to the Third Corps Area. To be organized as an eight-battery regiment as follows: two batteries of 240-mm howitzers, one battalion (three batteries) of 75-mm guns, and one battalion consisting of a battery of 155-mm howitzers and two batteries of 75-mm guns.

Status: Disbanded on 22 August 1942.

634th Coast Artillery Regiment (Harbor Defense) **Organized Reserve North Carolina**

HQ—*Not initiated,* 1929–41

Constituted in the O.R. on 23 July 1929 as the 634th C.A. Regt. (Harbor Defense), assigned to the Harbor Defenses of the Cape Fear, and allotted to the Fourth Corps Area. To be organized as a six-battery regiment as follows: one battery of 10-inch railway guns, one battery of 7-inch railway guns, one battery of 240-mm howitzers, and one battalion (three batteries) of 75-mm guns.

Status: Disbanded on 22 August 1942.

635th Coast Artillery Regiment (Harbor Defense) **Organized Reserve Georgia**

HQ—*Not initiated,* 1929–41

Constituted in the O.R. on 23 July 1929 as the 635th C.A. Regt. (Harbor Defense), assigned to the Harbor Defenses of Savannah, and allotted to the Fourth Corps Area. To be organized as a three-battalion regiment with one battalion of 75-mm guns.

Status: Disbanded on 22 August 1942.

636th Coast Artillery Regiment (Harbor Defense) **Organized Reserve Florida**

HQ—*Not initiated,* 1929–41

Constituted in the O.R. on 23 July 1929 as the 636th C.A. Regt. (Harbor Defense), assigned to the Harbor Defenses of Jacksonville, and allotted to the Fourth Corps Area. To be organized as a six-battery regiment as follows: one battery of 10-inch railway guns, one battery of 240-mm howitzers, one battalion (three batteries) of 75-mm guns, and one battery consisting of 5 mobile searchlights.

Status: Disbanded on 22 August 1942.

637th Coast Artillery Regiment (Harbor Defense) **Organized Reserve Florida**

HQ—*Not initiated,* 1929–41

Constituted in the O.R. on 23 July 1929 as the 637th C.A. Regt. (Harbor Defense), assigned to the Harbor Defenses of Tampa, and allotted to the Fourth Corps Area. To be organized as a seven-battery regiment as follows: one battery of 10-inch railway guns, three batteries of 240-mm howitzers, and one battalion (three batteries) of 75-mm guns.

Status: Disbanded on 22 August 1942.

638th Coast Artillery Regiment (Harbor Defense) — Organized Reserve Alabama

HQ—*Not initiated,* 1929–41

Constituted in the O.R. on 3 July 1929 as the 638th C.A. Regt. (Harbor Defense), assigned to the Harbor Defenses of Mobile, and allotted to the Fourth Corps Area. To be organized as a five-battery regiment as follows: one battery of 12-inch mortars, one battery of 240-mm howitzers, and one battalion (three batteries) of 75-mm guns.

Status: Disbanded on 22 August 1942.

639th Coast Artillery Regiment (Harbor Defense) — Organized Reserve Louisiana

HQ—*Not initiated,* 1929–41

Constituted in the O.R. on 23 July 1929 as the 639th C.A. Regt. (Harbor Defense), assigned to the Harbor Defenses of New Orleans, and allotted to the Fourth Corps Area. To be organized as an eight-battery regiment as follows: one battery of 10-inch railway guns, one battery of 7-inch railway guns, three batteries of 240-mm howitzers, and one battalion (three batteries) of 75-mm guns.

Status: Disbanded on 22 August 1942.

653d Coast Artillery Battalion (Antiaircraft) — Organized Reserve New York

HQ—New York City, NY, 1925–28

Constituted in the O.R. in 1924 and allotted to the Second Corps Area. Initiated by November 1925 at New York City, NY. Demobilized on 5 September 1928.

Commanders, 653d Coast Artillery Battalion

Unknown	ao November 1925–5 September 1928

901st Coast Artillery Regiment (Antiaircraft) — Organized Reserve Massachusetts

HQ—*Not initiated,* 1928–29; Brockton, MA, 1929–39; Worcester, MA, 1939–41

Constituted in the O.R. on 5 September 1928 as the 546th C.A. Regt. (AA) and allotted to the First Corps Area. Redesignated on 4 December 1928 as the 901st C.A. Regt. (AA). Initiated on 19 August 1929 with regimental HQ at Brockton, MA. Subordinate battalion HQ concurrently organized as follows: HQ and Combat Train, 1st Bn. at Framingham, MA; and HHD, 2d Bn. at Walpole, MA. Withdrawn from the O.R. on 1 October 1933 and allotted to the R.A. as an RAI unit. Typically conducted Inactive Training Period meetings at the Army and Navy Club in Boston. Conducted summer training at Fort H.G. Wright, NY. Also conducted C.A. CMTC training some years at Fort Adams, RI, as an alternate form of annual training. Primary ROTC feeder school was the Massachusetts Institute of Technology, 1929–41. Regimental HQ relocated in 1939 to Worcester, MA. Location 7 December 1941—Worcester, MA.

Status: Disbanded on 2 April 1943.

Commanders, 901st Coast Artillery Regiment

Maj. Harold T. Howe	19 August 1929–ao October 1931	Unknown	ao October 1931–ao June 1936
Lt. Col. Stanley G. Barker	ao June 1936–December 1941		

902d Coast Artillery Regiment (Antiaircraft) — Organized Reserve Massachusetts

HQ—*Not initiated,* 1928–29; Boston, MA, 1929–41

Constituted in the O.R. on 5 September 1928 as the 547th C.A. Regt. (AA) and allotted to the First Corps Area. Redesignated on 4 December 1928 as the 902d C.A. Regt. (AA). Initiated on 5 September 1929 with regimental HQ at Boston, MA. Subordinate battalion HQ concurrently organized as follows: HQ and Combat Train, 1st Bn. at East Boston, MA; and HHD, 2d Bn. at Boston, MA. Typically conducted Inactive Training Period meetings at the Army and Navy Club in Boston. Conducted summer training at Fort H.G. Wright, NY. Also conducted C.A. CMTC training some years at Fort Adams, RI, and Fort McKinley, ME, as an alternate form of annual training. Primary ROTC feeder school was the Massachusetts Institute of Technology, 1929–41. Location 7 December 1941—Boston, MA.

Status: Disbanded on 2 April 1943.

Commanders, 902d Coast Artillery Regiment

Lt. Col. Samuel G. Shartle (R.A.)	5 September 1929–ao July 1930	Unknown	ao August 1938–ao July 1939
Lt. Col. Irving C. Whittemore	ao June 1931–ao June 1935	Lt. Col. George H. Collins	ao July 1939–ao September 1939
Unknown	ao June 1935–ao June 1936	Unknown	ao September 1939–ao July 1941
Maj. Benjamin B. D'Ewart	ao June 1936–ao August 1938	Lt. Col. Herbert K. Bear	ao July 1941–7 August 1941

903d Coast Artillery Regiment (Antiaircraft) — Organized Reserve Massachusetts/Connecticut

HQ—*Not initiated,* 1928–29; Lowell, MA, 1929–37; Hartford, CT, 1937–41

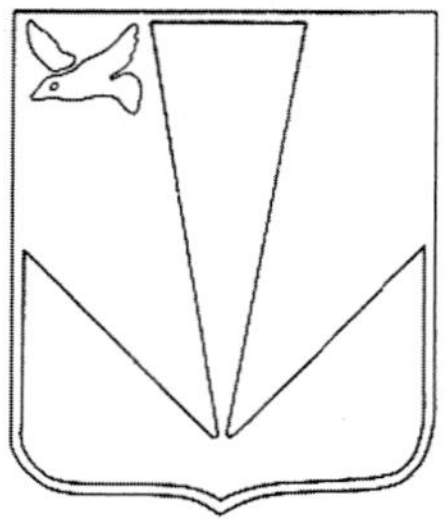

Constituted in the O.R. on 5 September 1928 as the 548th C.A. Regt. (AA) and allotted to the First Corps Area. Redesignated on 4 December 1928 as the 903d C.A. Regt. (AA). Initiated on 5 September 1929 with regimental HQ at Lowell, MA. Subordinate battalion HQ concurrently organized as follows: HQ and Combat Train, 1st Bn. at Haverhill, MA; and HHD, 2d Bn. at Gloucester, MA. Regimental HQ relocated on 10 May 1937 to Hartford, CT. Typically conducted Inactive Training Period meetings at the Army and Navy Club in Boston and the Federal Building in Springfield, MA. Conducted summer training at Fort H.G. Wright, NY. Also conducted C.A. CMTC training some years at Fort Adams, RI, as an alternate form of annual training. Primary ROTC feeder school was the Massachusetts Institute of Technology, 1929–41. Location 7 December 1941—Hartford, CT.

Status: Disbanded on 2 April 1943.

Commanders, 903d Coast Artillery Regiment

Maj. Raymond N. Symonds	5 September 1929–ao October 1931	Lt. Col. Herbert A. Dyer	2 October 1933–14 November 1935
Unknown	ao October 1931–2 October 1933	Maj. Ralph A. Armstrong	14 November 1935–December 1941

904th Coast Artillery Regiment (Antiaircraft) — Organized Reserve Massachusetts

HQ—*Not initiated,* 1928–29; Worcester, MA, 1929–33

Constituted in the O.R. on 5 September 1928 as the 549th C.A. Regt. (AA) and allotted to the First Corps Area. Redesignated on 4 December 1928 as the 904th C.A. Regt. (AA). Initiated on 10 August 1929 with regimental HQ at Worcester, MA. Subordinate battalion HQ concurrently organized as follows: HQ and Combat Train, 1st Bn. at Springfield, MA; and HHD, 2d Bn. at Pittsfield, MA. Conducted summer training at Fort H.G. Wright, NY. Primary ROTC feeder school was the Massachusetts Institute of Technology, 1929–33. Demobilized on 1 October 1933.

Commanders, 904th Coast Artillery Regiment

Lt. Col. Herbert A. Dyer	10 August 1929–1 October 1933

905th Coast Artillery Regiment (Antiaircraft) — Organized Reserve Vermont

HQ—*Not initiated,* 1928–29; Burlington, VT, 1929–33

Constituted in the O.R. on 5 September 1928 as the 550th C.A. Regt. (AA) and allotted to the First Corps Area. Redesignated on 4 December 1928 as the 905th C.A. Regt. (AA). Initiated on 5 September 1929 with regimental HQ at Burlington, VT. Subordinate battalion HQ concurrently organized as follows: HQ and Combat Train, 1st Bn. at Montpelier, VT; and HHD, 2d Bn. at Bennington, VT. Demobilized on 1 October 1933.

Commanders, 905th Coast Artillery Regiment

Col. Hunter C. White	5 September 1929–1 October 1933

906th Coast Artillery Regiment (Antiaircraft) — Organized Reserve Maine

HQ—*Not initiated,* 1928–29; Portland, ME, 1929–41

Constituted in the O.R. on 5 September 1928 as the 551st C.A. Regt. (AA) and allotted to the First Corps Area. Redesignated on 4 December 1928 as the 906th C.A. Regt. (AA). Initiated on 5 September 1929 with regimental HQ at Portland, ME. Subordinate battalion HQ concurrently organized as follows: HQ and Combat Train, 1st Bn. at Lewiston, ME; and HHD, 2d Bn. at Portland. Typically conducted Inactive Training Period meetings at the Post Office Building or the Federal Courthouse in Portland. Conducted summer training at Fort H.G. Wright, NY, or Fort Adams, RI. Location 7 December 1941—Portland, ME.

Status: Disbanded on 2 April 1943.

Commanders, 906th Coast Artillery Regiment

Col. Gordon L. Carter	5 September 1929–ao September 1939	Maj. Albert W. Waterman	ao June 1940–December 1941

907th Coast Artillery Regiment (Antiaircraft) — Organized Reserve Maine

HQ—*Not initiated,* 1928–29; Augusta, ME, 1929–41

Constituted in the O.R. on 5 September 1928 as the 552d C.A. Regt. (AA) and allotted to the First Corps Area. Redesignated on 4 December 1928 as the 907th C.A. Regt. (AA). Initiated on 5 September 1929 with regimental HQ at Augusta, ME. Subordinate battalion HQ concurrently organized as follows: HQ and Combat Train, 1st Bn. at Bangor, ME; and HHD, 2d Bn. at Skowhegan, ME. Withdrawn from the O.R. on 1 October 1933 and allotted to the R.A. as an RAI unit. Concurrently assigned to the 31st C.A. Brig. (GHQR). Conducted summer training at Fort H.G. Wright, NY. Primary ROTC feeder school was the University of Maine, 1929–41. Location 7 December 1941—Augusta, ME.

Status: Disbanded on 2 April 1943.

Commanders, 907th Coast Artillery Regiment

Unknown	5 September 1929–ao October 1930	Lt. Col. George B. Sawyer	ao October 1930–ao July 1931
Unknown	ao July 1931–7 December 1941		

908th Coast Artillery Regiment (Antiaircraft) **Organized Reserve New York**

HQ—*Not initiated,* 1928–29; Manhattan, NY, 1929–33

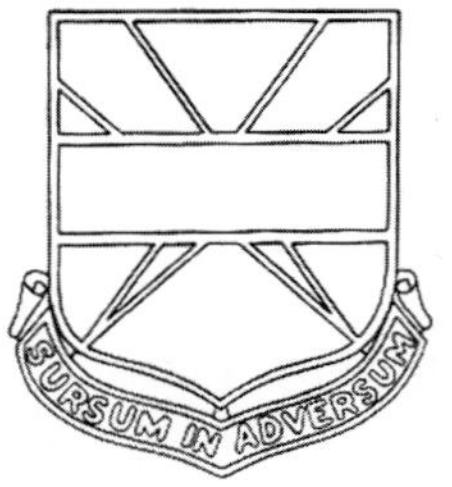

Constituted in the O.R. on 5 September 1928 as the 553d C.A. Regt. (AA) and allotted to the Second Corps Area. Redesignated on 4 December 1928 as the 908th C.A. Regt. (AA). Initiated on 2 July 1929 with the entire regiment at Manhattan, NY. Conducted summer training at Fort Hancock, NJ, and Fort Tilden, NY. Also conducted C.A. CMTC training some years at Fort Hancock as an alternate form of annual training. Demobilized on 1 October 1933.

Commanders, 908th Coast Artillery Regiment

Lt. Col. Anastasio C. M. Azoy	2 July 1929–1 October 1933

909th Coast Artillery Regiment (Antiaircraft) **Organized Reserve New York**

HQ—*Not initiated,* 1928–29; Brooklyn, NY, 1929–33

Constituted in the O.R. on 5 September 1928 as the 554th C.A. Regt. (AA) and allotted to the Second Corps Area. Redesignated on 4 December 1928 as the 909th C.A. Regt. (AA). Initiated on 2 July 1929 with the entire regiment at Brooklyn, NY. Conducted summer training at Camp Dix, NJ, and Fort Tilden, NY. Demobilized on 1 October 1933.

Commanders, 909th Coast Artillery Regiment

Col. Harry V. Van Auken	2 July 1929–1 October 1933

910th Coast Artillery Regiment (Antiaircraft) **Organized Reserve New York**

HQ—*Not initiated,* 1928–29; Garden City, NY, 1929–41

Constituted in the O.R. on 5 September 1928 as the 555th C.A. Regt. (AA) and allotted to the Second Corps Area. Redesignated on 1 December 1928 as the 910th C.A. Regt. (AA). Initiated on 2 July 1929 with the entire regiment at Garden City, NY. Withdrawn from the O.R. on 1 October 1933 and allotted to the R.A. as an RAI unit. Concurrently assigned to the 31st C.A. Brig. (GHQR). Conducted summer training at Fort Tilden, NY; Camp Dix, NJ; or Fort Totten, NY. Also conducted C.A. CMTC training some years at Fort Hancock as an alternate form of annual training. Designated mobilization training station was Camp Upton, NY. Primary ROTC feeder school was Fordham University, 1929–41. Location 7 December 1941—Garden City, NY.

Status: Disbanded on 2 April 1943.

Commanders, 910th Coast Artillery Regiment

Maj. George W. Farnham	2 July 1929–ao June 1932	Col. Clarence E. Doll	ao November 1932–December 1941

911th Coast Artillery Regiment (Antiaircraft) **Organized Reserve New York**

HQ—*Not initiated,* 1928–33

Constituted in the O.R. on 5 September 1928 as the 556th C.A. Regt. (AA) and allotted to the Second Corps Area. Redesignated on 1 December 1928 as the 911th C.A. Regt. (AA). Rochester, NY, designated on 2 July 1929 as HQ on organization, but the unit was never organized at that location. Demobilized on 1 October 1933.

912th Coast Artillery Regiment (Antiaircraft) **Organized Reserve Delaware**

HQ—*Not initiated,* 1928–33

Constituted in the O.R. on 5 September 1928 as the 557th C.A. Regt. (AA) and allotted to the Second Corps Area. Redesignated on 1 December 1928 as the 912th C.A. Regt. (AA). Wilmington, DE, designated on 2 July 1929 as HQ on organization, but the unit was never organized at that location. Demobilized on 1 October 1933.

913th Coast Artillery Regiment (Antiaircraft) **Organized Reserve District of Columbia and Virginia**

HQ—*Not initiated,* 1928–29; Washington, DC, 1929–41

Constituted in the O.R. on 5 September 1928 as the 558th C.A. Regt. (AA) and allotted to the Third Corps Area. Concurrently assigned to the 213th C.A. Brig. (redesignated on 30 November 1928 as the 401st C.A. Brig.). Redesignated on 30 November 1928 as the 913th C.A. Regt. (AA). Initiated on 27 June 1929 with the entire regiment at Washington, DC, less the Band and Btry B, which were located in Virginia. Typically conducted Inactive Training Period meetings at the Munitions Building in Washington. Conducted summer training at Fort Monroe, VA. Also conducted C.A. CMTC training some years at Fort Monroe as an alternate form of annual training. Primary ROTC feeder school was the Virginia A&M College and Polytechnic Institute, 1929–41. Location 7 December 1941—Washington, DC.

Status: Disbanded on 2 April 1943.

Commanders, 913th Coast Artillery Regiment

Lt. Col. Robert R. Hendon Jr.	27 June 1929–April 1936	Col. Thompson Short	April 1936–21 March 1937
Lt. Col. Robert R. Hendon Jr.	21 March 1937–December 1941		

914th Coast Artillery Regiment (Antiaircraft) **Organized Reserve Pennsylvania and Maryland**

HQ—*Not initiated,* 1928–32; Baltimore, MD, 1932–33

Constituted in the O.R. on 5 September 1928 as the 559th C.A. Regt. (AA) and allotted to the Third Corps Area. Concurrently assigned to the 213th C.A. Brig. (redesignated on 30 November 1928 as the 401st C.A. Brig.). Redesignated on 30 November 1928 as the 914th C.A. Regt. (AA). Initiated on 1 October 1932 with the entire regiment at Baltimore, MD. Typically conducted Inactive Training Period meetings at the Post Office Building or the US Court House in Baltimore. Demobilized on 1 October 1933.

Commanders, 914th Coast Artillery Regiment

Lt. Col. James B. Bentley	1 October 1932–1 October 1933

915th Coast Artillery Regiment (Antiaircraft) **Organized Reserve Virginia**

HQ—*Not initiated,* 1928–33

Constituted in the O.R. on 5 September 1928 as the 560th C.A. Regt. (AA) and allotted to the Third Corps Area. Concurrently assigned to the 213th C.A. Brig. (redesignated on 30 November 1928 as the 401st C.A. Brig.). Redesignated on 30 November 1928 as the 915th C.A. Regt. (AA). Norfolk, VA, designated on 11 December 1929 as HQ on organization, but the unit was never organized at that location. Demobilized on 1 October 1933.

916th Coast Artillery Regiment (Antiaircraft) **Organized Reserve Virginia**

HQ—*Not initiated,* 1928–29; Richmond, VA, 1929–41

Constituted in the O.R. on 5 September 1928 as the 561st C.A. Regt. (AA) and allotted to the Third Corps Area. Concurrently assigned to the 213th C.A. Brig. (redesignated on 30 November 1928 as the 401st C.A. Brig.). Redesignated on 30 November 1928 as the 916th C.A. Regt. (AA). Initiated on 29 June 1929 with the entire regiment at Richmond, VA. Relieved from the 401st C.A. Brig. on 1 October 1933. Provided a part of the honor guard for the visit of President Roosevelt to Fort Monroe on 29 July 1940. Typically conducted Inactive Training Period meetings at the Parcel Post Building in Richmond. Conducted summer training at Fort Monroe, VA. Also conducted C.A. CMTC training some years at Fort Monroe as an alternate form of annual training. Primary ROTC feeder school was the Virginia A&M College and Polytechnic Institute, 1929–41. Location 7 December 1941—Richmond, VA.

Status: Disbanded on 2 April 1943.

Commanders, 916th Coast Artillery Regiment

Maj. Charles R. Beaumont	29 June 1929–February 1931	Lt. Col. James L.B. Buck	8 January 1932–ao February 1933
Lt. Col. William W. Nairn Jr.	February 1931–8 January 1932	Col. Earl W. Thomson	ao June 1934–December 1941

917th Coast Artillery Regiment (Antiaircraft) **Organized Reserve Virginia**

HQ—*Not initiated,* 1928–29; Roanoke, VA, 1929–39

Constituted in the O.R. on 5 September 1928 as the 562d C.A. Regt. (AA) and allotted to the Third Corps Area. Concurrently assigned to the 214th C.A. Brig. (redesignated on 30 November 1928 as the 402d C.A. Brig.). Redesignated on 30 November 1928 as the 917th C.A. Regt. (AA). Initiated on 27 June 1929 with the entire regiment at Roanoke, VA. Withdrawn from the O.R. on 1 October 1933 and allotted to the R.A. as an RAI unit. Concurrently, relieved from the 402d C.A. Brig. and assigned to the 31st C.A. Brig. (GHQR). Typically conducted Inactive Training Period meetings at Roanoke, Lynchburg, Charlottesville, and Staunton. Conducted summer training at Fort Monroe, VA. Also conducted C.A. CMTC training some years at Fort Monroe as an alternate form of annual training. Primary ROTC feeder school was the Virginia A&M College and Polytechnic Institute, 1929–41. Redesignated the 70th C.A. on 4 November 1939 and activated at Fort Monroe, VA.

Status: Assigned to the CARS as the 562d Air Defense Arty.

Commanders, 917th Coast Artillery Regiment

Maj. Gregory J. Kessenich	27 June 1929–5 August 1929	Col. Harry P. Newton	5 August 1929–3 November 1939

918th Coast Artillery Regiment (Antiaircraft) **Organized Reserve Virginia**

HQ—*Not initiated,* 1928–33

Constituted in the O.R. on 5 September 1928 as the 563d C.A. Regt. (AA) and allotted to the Third Corps Area. Concurrently assigned to the 214th C.A. Brig. (redesignated on 30 November 1928 as the 402d C.A. Brig.). Redesignated on 30 November 1928 as the 918th C.A. Regt. (AA). Richmond, VA, designated on 11 December 1929 as HQ on organization, but the unit was never organized at that location. Demobilized on 1 October 1933.

919th Coast Artillery Regiment (Antiaircraft) **Organized Reserve Pennsylvania**

HQ—*Not initiated,* 1928–29; Pittsburgh, PA, 1929–30; Philadelphia, PA, 1930–33

Constituted in the O.R. on 5 September 1928 as the 564th C.A. Regt. (AA) and allotted to the Third Corps Area. Concurrently assigned to the 214th C.A. Brig. (redesignated on 30 November 1928 as the 402d C.A. Brig.). Redesignated on 30 November 1928 as the 919th C.A. Regt. (AA). Initiated on 11 December 1929 with the entire regiment at Pittsburgh, PA. Entire regiment relocated on 27 February 1930 to Philadelphia. Demobilized on 1 October 1933.

920th Coast Artillery Regiment (Antiaircraft) **Organized Reserve District of Columbia**

HQ—*Not initiated,* 1928–33

Constituted in the O.R. on 5 September 1928 as the 565th C.A. Regt. (AA) and allotted to the Third Corps Area. Concurrently assigned to the 214th C.A. Brig. (redesignated on 30 November 1928 as the 402d C.A. Brig.). Redesignated on 30 November 1928 as the 920th C.A. Regt. (AA). Washington, DC, designated on 11 December 1929 as HQ on organization, but the unit was never organized at that location. Demobilized on 1 October 1933.

921st Coast Artillery Regiment (Antiaircraft) **Organized Reserve South Carolina**

HQ—*Not initiated,* 1928–29; Charleston, SC 1929–33

Constituted in the O.R. on 5 September 1928 as the 566th C.A. Regt. (AA) and allotted to the Fourth Corps Area. Redesignated on 30 November 1928 as the 921st C.A. Regt. (AA). Initiated on 22 October 1929 with the entire regiment at Charleston, SC. Conducted summer training at Fort Barrancas, FL. Demobilized on 1 October 1933.

Commanders, 921st Coast Artillery Regiment

Unknown	22 October 1929–ao May 1932	Lt. Col. Francis M. Ellerbe	ao May 1932–1 October 1933

922d Coast Artillery Regiment (Antiaircraft) **Organized Reserve Florida**

HQ—*Not initiated,* 1928–29; Jacksonville, FL, 1929–33

Constituted in the O.R. on 5 September 1928 as the 567th C.A. Regt. (AA) and allotted to the Fourth Corps Area. Redesignated on 30 November 1928 as the 922d C.A. Regt. (AA). Initiated on 22 October 1929 with the entire regiment at Jacksonville, FL. Conducted summer training at Fort Barrancas, FL. Demobilized on 1 October 1933.

Commanders, 922d Coast Artillery Regiment

Maj. Harry W. Porter	22 October 1929–June 1931	Lt. Col. Benjamin H. Tolbert	June 1931–1 October 1933

923d Coast Artillery Regiment (Antiaircraft) **Organized Reserve South Carolina**

HQ—*Not initiated,* 1928–29; Spartanburg, SC, 1929–33

Constituted in the O.R. on 5 September 1928 as the 568th C.A. Regt. (AA) and allotted to the Fourth Corps Area. Redesignated on 30 November 1928 as the 923d C.A. Regt. (AA). Initiated on 12 September 1929 with the entire regiment at Spartanburg, SC. Conducted summer training at Fort Barrancas, FL. Demobilized on 1 October 1933.

Commanders, 923d Coast Artillery Regiment

Lt. Col. Paul W. Pittenger	12 September 1929–1 October 1933

924th Coast Artillery Regiment (Antiaircraft) **Organized Reserve Georgia**

HQ—*Not initiated,* 1928–29; Savannah, GA, 1929–33

Constituted in the O.R. on 5 September 1928 as the 569th C.A. Regt. (AA) and allotted to the Fourth Corps Area. Redesignated on 30 November 1928 as the 924th C.A. Regt. (AA). Initiated on 22 October 1929 with the entire regiment at Savannah, GA. Conducted summer training at Fort Barrancas, FL. Demobilized on 1 October 1933.

Commanders, 924th Coast Artillery Regiment

Lt. Col. Jefferson L. Newbern	22 October 1929–1 October 1933

925th Coast Artillery Regiment (Antiaircraft) **Organized Reserve Alabama/Florida**

HQ—*Not initiated,* 1928–29; Montgomery, AL, 1929–34; Jacksonville, FL, 1934–41

Constituted in the O.R. on 5 September 1928 as the 570th C.A. Regt. (AA) and allotted to the Fourth Corps Area. Redesignated on 30 November 1928 as the 925th C.A. Regt. (AA). Initiated on 22 October 1929 with the entire regiment at Montgomery, AL. Entire regiment relocated on 4 October 1934 to Jacksonville, FL. Conducted summer training at Fort Barrancas, FL. Also conducted C.A. CMTC training some years at Fort Barrancas as an alternate form of annual training. For the training camp in 1935, the regiment conducted the first "winter camp" at Fort Barrancas by a non-R.A. unit since 1918. Primary ROTC feeder school was the University of Alabama, 1929–34, and the University of Florida, 1934–41. Location 7 December 1941—Jacksonville, FL (inactivated on 16 March 1942).

Status: Disbanded on 2 April 1943.

Commanders, 925th Coast Artillery Regiment

Lt. Col. William N. Spencer Jr.	22 October 1929–1 October 1933	Lt. Col. William N. Spencer Jr.	23 October 1934–15 November 1936
Lt. Col. Jefferson L. Newbern	1 October 1933–23 October 1934	Lt. Col. Fred H. All	15 November 1936–16 March 1942

926th Coast Artillery Regiment (Antiaircraft) **Organized Reserve Florida**

HQ—*Not initiated,* 1928–33

Constituted in the O.R. on 5 September 1928 as the 571st C.A. Regt. (AA) and allotted to the Fourth Corps Area. Redesignated on 4 December 1928 as the 926th C.A. Regt. (AA). Miami, FL, designated on 22 October 1929 as HQ on organization, but the unit was never organized at that location. Demobilized on 1 October 1933.

927th Coast Artillery Regiment (Antiaircraft) **Organized Reserve Florida**

HQ—*Not initiated,* 1928–33

Constituted in the O.R. on 5 September 1928 as the 572d C.A. Regt. (AA) and allotted to the Fourth Corps Area. Redesignated on 4 December 1928 as the 927th C.A. Regt. (AA). Tampa, FL, designated on 22 October 1929 as HQ on organization, but the unit was never organized at that location. Demobilized on 1 October 1933.

928th Coast Artillery Regiment (Antiaircraft) **Organized Reserve North Carolina**

HQ—*Not initiated,* 1928–33

Constituted in the O.R. on 5 September 1928 as the 573d C.A. Regt. (AA) and allotted to the Fourth Corps Area. Redesignated on 4 December 1928 as the 928th C.A. Regt. (AA). Charlotte, NC, designated on 22 October 1929 as HQ on organization, but the unit was never organized at that location. Demobilized on 1 October 1933.

929th Coast Artillery Regiment (Antiaircraft) **Organized Reserve Mississippi**

HQ—*Not initiated,* 1928–33

Constituted in the O.R. on 5 September 1928 as the 574th C.A. Regt. (AA) and allotted to the Fourth Corps Area. Redesignated on 4 December 1928 as the 929th C.A. Regt. (AA). Jackson, MS, designated on 22 October 1929 as HQ on organization, but the unit was never organized at that location. Demobilized on 1 October 1933.

930th Coast Artillery Regiment (Antiaircraft) **Organized Reserve Tennessee**

HQ—*Not initiated,* 1928–33

Constituted in the O.R. on 5 September 1928 as the 575th C.A. Regt. (AA) and allotted to the Fourth Corps Area. Redesignated on 4 December 1928 as the 930th C.A. Regt. (AA). Nashville, TN, designated on 22 October 1929 as HQ on organization, but the unit was never organized at that location. Demobilized on 1 October 1933.

931st Coast Artillery Regiment (Antiaircraft) **Organized Reserve Indiana**

HQ—*Not initiated,* 1928–33

Constituted in the O.R. on 5 September 1928 as the 576th C.A. Regt. (AA) and allotted to the Fifth Corps Area. Redesignated on 1 December 1928 as the 931st C.A. Regt. (AA). Fort Wayne, IN, designated on 9 July 1931 as HQ on organization, but the unit was never organized at that location. Demobilized on 1 October 1933.

932d Coast Artillery Regiment (Antiaircraft) **Organized Reserve Ohio**

HQ—*Not initiated,* 1928–29; Columbus, OH, 1929–41

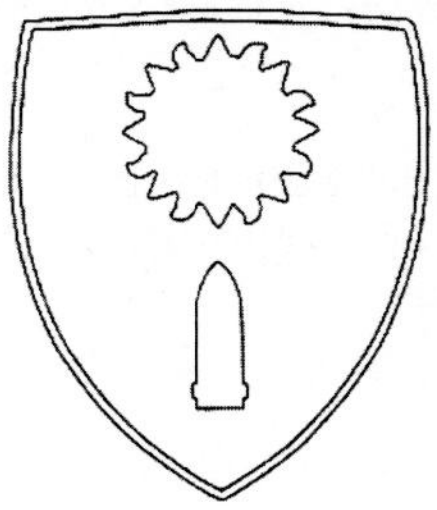

Constituted in the O.R. on 5 September 1928 as the 577th C.A. Regt. (AA) and allotted to the Fifth Corps Area. Concurrently assigned to the 215th C.A. Brig. (redesignated on 30 November 1928 as the 403d C.A. Brig.). Redesignated on 1 December 1928 as the 932d C.A. Regt. (AA). Initiated in October 1929 with the entire regiment at Columbus, OH. Relieved from the 403d C.A. Brig. on 1 October 1933 and assigned to the 33d C.A. Brig. (Second Army). Designated mobilization station was Fort Bliss, TX. Conducted summer training at Fort Sheridan, IL. Primary ROTC feeder school was the University of Cincinnati, 1929–41. Location 7 December 1941—Columbus, OH.

Status: Disbanded on 2 April 1943.

Commanders, 932d Coast Artillery Regiment

Unknown	October 1929–ao June 1930	Unknown	ao August 1931–ao April 1933
Maj. Ernest C. Ehrensberger	ao June 1930–ao August 1931	Col. Robert L. Cole	ao April 1933–December 1941

933d Coast Artillery Regiment (Antiaircraft) **Organized Reserve Ohio**

HQ—*Not initiated,* 1928–30; Toledo, OH, 1930–39; Cincinnati, OH, 1939–41

Constituted in the O.R. on 5 September 1928 as the 578th C.A. Regt. (AA) and allotted to the Fifth Corps Area. Concurrently assigned to the 215th C.A. Brig. (redesignated on 30 November 1928 as the 403d C.A. Brig.). Redesignated on 1 December 1928 as the 933d C.A. Regt. (AA). Initiated by August 1930 with the entire regiment at Toledo, OH. Withdrawn from the O.R. on 1 October 1933 and allotted to the R.A. as an RAI unit. Concurrently relieved from the 403d C.A. Brig. and assigned to the 39th C.A. Brig. (GHQR). Designated mobilization station was Fort Bliss, TX. Entire regiment relocated by 1939 to Cincinnati, OH. Conducted summer training at Fort Sheridan, IL. Primary ROTC feeder school was the University of Cincinnati, 1929–41. Location 7 December 1941—Toledo, OH.

Status: Disbanded on 2 April 1943.

Commanders, 933d Coast Artillery Regiment

Lt. Col. Earle H. Forster	ao August 1930–ao June 1937
Unknown	ao June 1937–ao August 1940
Maj. Everard H. Boeckh	ao August 1940–December 1941

934th Coast Artillery Regiment (Antiaircraft) **Organized Reserve Indiana**

HQ—*Not initiated,* 1928–33

Constituted in the O.R. on 5 September 1928 as the 579th C.A. Regt. (AA) and allotted to the Fifth Corps Area. Redesignated on 1 December 1928 as the 934th C.A. Regt. (AA). South Bend, IN, designated on 9 July 1931 as HQ on organization, but the unit was never organized at that location. Demobilized on 1 October 1933.

935th Coast Artillery Regiment (Antiaircraft) **Organized Reserve Kentucky**

HQ—*Not initiated,* 1928–33

Constituted in the O.R. on 5 September 1928 as the 580th C.A. Regt. (AA) and allotted to the Fifth Corps Area. Redesignated on 1 December 1928 as the 935th C.A. Regt. (AA). Covington, KY, designated on 9 July 1931 as HQ on organization, but the unit was never organized at that location. Demobilized on 1 October 1933.

936th Coast Artillery Regiment (Antiaircraft) **Organized Reserve West Virginia**

HQ—*Not initiated,* 1928–33

Constituted in the O.R. on 5 September 1928 as the 581st C.A. Regt. (AA) and allotted to the Fifth Corps Area. Redesignated on 1 December 1928 as the 936th C.A. Regt. (AA). Charleston, WV, designated on 9 July 1931 as HQ on organization, but the unit was never organized at that location. Demobilized on 1 October 1933.

937th Coast Artillery Regiment (Antiaircraft) **Organized Reserve Kentucky**

HQ—*Not initiated,* 1928–33

Constituted in the O.R. on 5 September 1928 as the 582d C.A. Regt. (AA) and allotted to the Fifth Corps Area. Redesignated on 1 December 1928 as the 937th C.A. Regt. (AA). Louisville, KY, designated on 9 July 1931 as HQ on organization, but the unit was never organized at that location. Demobilized on 1 October 1933.

938th Coast Artillery Regiment (Antiaircraft) **Organized Reserve Ohio**

HQ—*Not initiated,* 1928–29; Cincinnati, OH 1929–41

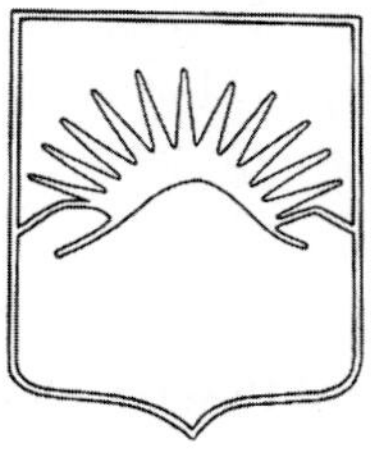

Constituted in the O.R. on 5 September 1928 as the 583d C.A. Regt. (AA) and allotted to the Fifth Corps Area. Redesignated on 1 December 1928 as the 938th C.A. Regt. (AA). Initiated on 5 September 1929 at Cincinnati, OH. Withdrawn from the O.R. on 1 October 1933 and allotted to the R.A. as an RAI unit. Concurrently assigned to the 33d C.A. Brig. (Second Army). Relieved from the 33d C.A. Brig. (Second Army) in 1940 and assigned to the 39th C.A. Brig. Designated mobilization station was Fort Bliss, TX. Conducted summer training at Fort Sheridan, IL. Primary ROTC feeder school was the University of Cincinnati, 1929–41. Location 7 December 1941—Cincinnati, OH.

Status: Disbanded on 2 April 1943.

Commanders, 938th Coast Artillery Regiment

Maj. Everard H. Boeckh	5 September 1929–ao August 1931	Unknown	ao August 1932–ao May 1934
Lt. Col. W.P. Watson	ao May 1932–ao August 1932	Lt. Col. Rupert A. Anderegg	ao May 1934–December 1941

939th Coast Artillery Regiment (Antiaircraft) **Organized Reserve Indiana**

HQ—*Not initiated,* 1928–33

Constituted in the O.R. on 5 September 1928 as the 584th C.A. Regt. (AA) and allotted to the Fifth Corps Area. Redesignated on 1 December 1928 as the 939th C.A. Regt. (AA). Indianapolis, IN, designated on 9 July 1931 as HQ on organization, but the unit was never organized at that location. Demobilized on 1 October 1933.

940th Coast Artillery Regiment (Antiaircraft) **Organized Reserve Ohio**

HQ—*Not initiated,* 1928–33

Constituted in the O.R. on 5 September 1928 as the 585th C.A. Regt. (AA) and allotted to the Fifth Corps Area. Concurrently assigned to the 215th C.A. Brig. (redesignated on 30 November 1928 as the 403d C.A. Brig.). Redesignated on 1 December 1928 as the 940th C.A. Regt. (AA). Cincinnati, OH, designated on 9 July 1931 as HQ on organization, but the unit was never organized at that location. Demobilized on 1 October 1933.

941st Coast Artillery Regiment (Antiaircraft) **Organized Reserve Ohio**

HQ—*Not initiated,* 1928–33

Constituted in the O.R. on 5 September 1928 as the 586th C.A. Regt. (AA) and allotted to the Fifth Corps Area. Concurrently assigned to the 215th C.A. Brig. (redesignated on 30 November 1928 as the 403d C.A. Brig.). Redesignated on 1 December 1928 as the 941st C.A. Regt. (AA). Toledo, OH, designated on 9 July 1931 as HQ on organization, but the unit was never organized at that location. Demobilized on 1 October 1933.

942d Coast Artillery Regiment (Antiaircraft) **Organized Reserve Kentucky**

HQ—*Not initiated,* 1928–33

Constituted in the O.R. on 5 September 1928 as the 587th C.A. Regt. (AA) and allotted to the Fifth Corps Area. Redesignated on 1 December 1928 as the 942d C.A. Regt. (AA). Louisville, KY, designated on 9 July 1931 as HQ on organization, but the unit was never organized at that location. Demobilized on 1 October 1933.

943d Coast Artillery Regiment (Antiaircraft) **Organized Reserve Indiana**

HQ—*Not initiated,* 1928–33

Constituted in the O.R. on 5 September 1928 as the 588th C.A. Regt. (AA) and allotted to the Fifth Corps Area. Redesignated on 1 December 1928 as the 943d C.A. Regt. (AA). Kokomo, IN, designated on 9 July 1931 as HQ on organization, but the unit was never organized at that location. Demobilized on 1 October 1933.

944th Coast Artillery Regiment (Antiaircraft) **Organized Reserve Ohio**

HQ—*Not initiated,* 1928–33

Constituted in the O.R. on 5 September 1928 as the 590th C.A. Regt. (AA) and allotted to the Fifth Corps Area. Redesignated on 1 December 1928 as the 944th C.A. Regt. (AA). Lima, OH, designated on 9 July 1931 as HQ on organization, but the unit was never organized at that location. Demobilized on 1 October 1933.

945th Coast Artillery Regiment (Antiaircraft) **Organized Reserve Michigan**

HQ—*Not initiated,* 1928–30; Detroit, MI, 1930–41

Constituted in the O.R. on 5 September 1928 as the 591st C.A. Regt. (AA) and allotted to the Sixth Corps Area. Redesignated on 1 December 1928 as the 945th C.A. Regt. (AA). Consolidated on 11 April 1930 with the 555th C.A. Bn. (constituted in the O.R. on 2 July 1923 and organized on 7 January 1927 with HQ at Detroit, MI; demobilized on 5 September 1928; reconstituted on 11 April 1930). Initiated in June 1930 at Detroit, MI. Conducted summer training with the 61st C.A. at Fort Sheridan, IL, 1930–41. Primary ROTC feeder school was the Michigan State College of Agriculture and Applied Science, 1930–41. Location 7 December 1941—Detroit, MI.

Status: Disbanded on 2 April 1943.

Commanders, 945th Coast Artillery Regiment

Lt. Col. Edward M. Howell	June 1930–December 1941

946th Coast Artillery Regiment (Antiaircraft) **Organized Reserve Michigan**

HQ—*Not initiated,* 1928–30; Detroit, MI, 1930–32; Grand Rapids, MI, 1932–33

Constituted in the O.R. on 5 September 1928 as the 592d C.A. Regt. (AA) and allotted to the Sixth Corps Area. Redesignated on 1 December 1928 as the 946th C.A. Regt. (AA). Initiated in June 1930 at Detroit, MI. Regimental HQ relocated on 27 September 1932 to Grand Rapids, MI. Subordinate battalions concurrently relocated as follows: 1st Bn. to Allegan, MI, and 2d Bn. to Lansing, MI. Conducted summer training at Camp Knox, KY. Demobilized on 1 October 1933.

Commanders, 946th Coast Artillery Regiment

Capt. Norman W. Whited	June 1930–August 1930	Maj. John W. Callahan	August 1930–ao November 1930
Lt. Col. Waldemar P. Adams	ao April 1931–1 October 1933		

947th Coast Artillery Regiment (Antiaircraft) **Organized Reserve Michigan**

HQ—*Not initiated,* 1928–30; Lansing, MI, 1929–41

Constituted in the O.R. on 5 September 1928 as the 593d C.A. Regt. (AA) and allotted to the Sixth Corps Area. Redesignated on 1 December 1928 as the 947th C.A. Regt. (AA). Initiated on 5 September 1929 with regimental

HQ at Lansing, MI. Subordinate battalion HQ concurrently organized as follows: HQ and Combat Train, 1st Bn. at Jackson, MI; and HHD, 2d Bn. at Lansing. Conducted summer training with the 61st C.A. at Fort Sheridan, IL, or Camp Knox, KY. Primary ROTC feeder school was the Michigan State College of Agriculture and Applied Science, 1930–33. Demobilized on 1 October 1933.

Status: Disbanded on 2 April 1943.

Commanders, 947th Coast Artillery Regiment

Capt. Dan W. Mather	5 September 1929–ao September 1931	Lt. Col. Adolph Bleki	ao May 1932–1 October 1933

948th Coast Artillery Regiment (Antiaircraft) — Organized Reserve Michigan

HQ—*Not initiated,* 1928–30; Saginaw, MI, 1929–41

Constituted in the O.R. on 5 September 1928 as the 594th C.A. Regt. (AA) and allotted to the Sixth Corps Area. Redesignated on 1 December 1928 as the 948th C.A. Regt. (AA). Initiated on 5 September 1929 with regimental HQ at Saginaw, MI. Subordinate battalion HQ concurrently organized as follows: HQ and Combat Train, 1st Bn. at Flint, MI; and HHD, 2d Bn. at Saginaw. Conducted summer training with the 61st C.A. at Fort Sheridan, IL, or Camp Knox, KY. Primary ROTC feeder school was the Michigan State College of Agriculture and Applied Science, 1930–33. Demobilized on 1 October 1933.

Status: Disbanded on 2 April 1943.

Commanders, 948th Coast Artillery Regiment

Maj. Clarence N. Winston	5 September 1929–July 1931	Lt. Col. Ralph G. Chamberlain	July 1931–1 October 1933

949th Coast Artillery Regiment (Antiaircraft) — Organized Reserve Illinois

HQ—*Not initiated,* 1928–29; Chicago, IL, 1929–41

Constituted in the O.R. on 5 September 1928 as the 595th C.A. Regt. (AA) and allotted to the Sixth Corps Area. Redesignated on 1 December 1928 as the 949th C.A. Regt. (AA). Initiated on 5 September 1929 with regimental HQ at Chicago, IL. Typically conducted Inactive Training Period meetings at the armory of the 202d C.A. or the Army and Navy Club in Chicago. Conducted summer training with the 61st C.A. at Fort Sheridan, IL, or Camp Knox, KY. Primary ROTC feeder school was the University of Illinois, 1930–33. Demobilized on 1 October 1933.

Status: Disbanded on 2 April 1943.

Commanders, 949th Coast Artillery Regiment

Lt. Col. Robert M. Zacharias	5 September 1929–1 October 1933

950th Coast Artillery Regiment (Antiaircraft) — Organized Reserve Illinois/Michigan

HQ—*Not initiated,* 1928–29; Chicago, IL, 1929–37; Lansing, MI, 1937–41

Constituted in the O.R. on 5 September 1928 as the 596th C.A. Regt. (AA) and allotted to the Sixth Corps Area. Redesignated on 1 December 1928 as the 950th C.A. Regt. (AA). Initiated on 5 September 1929 with the entire regiment at Chicago, IL. Assigned to the XVI Corps on 1 October 1933. Entire regiment relocated on 28 July 1937 to Lansing, MI. Typically conducted Inactive Training Period meetings at the armory of the 202d C.A. or the Army and Navy Club in Chicago. Conducted summer training with the 61st C.A. most years at Fort Sheridan, IL, and some years at Camp Knox, KY. Primary ROTC feeder school was the University of Illinois, 1929–41. Location 7 December 1941—Lansing, MI.

Status: Disbanded on 2 April 1943.

Commanders, 950th Coast Artillery Regiment

Lt. Col. Fordya L. Perego	5 September 1929–ao June 1931	Unknown	ao June 1931-24 February 1939
Lt. Col. Claude M. Cade	24 February 1939–December 1941		

951st Coast Artillery Regiment (Antiaircraft) **Organized Reserve Illinois**

HQ—*Not initiated,* 1928–29; Chicago, IL, 1929–41

Constituted in the O.R. on 5 September 1928 as the 597th C.A. Regt. (AA) and allotted to the Sixth Corps Area. Redesignated on 1 December 1928 as the 951st C.A. Regt. (AA). Initiated on 5 September 1929 with the entire regiment at Chicago, IL. Withdrawn from the O.R. on 1 October 1933 and allotted to the R.A. as an RAI unit. Concurrently assigned to the 33d C.A. Brig. (Second Army). Typically conducted Inactive Training Period meetings at the armory of the 202d C.A. or the Army and Navy Club in Chicago. Conducted summer training with the 61st C.A. at Fort Sheridan, IL. Primary ROTC feeder school was the University of Illinois, 1929–41. Location 7 December 1941—Chicago, IL.

Status: Disbanded on 2 April 1943.

Commanders, 951st Coast Artillery Regiment

Unknown	5 September 1929–ao June 1934	Lt. Col. Charles E. Howard.	1 October 1937–28 January 1938
Lt. Col. Fordyce L. Perego	ao June 1934–1 October 1937	Lt. Col. Fordyce L. Perego	28 January 1938–24 February 1939
Lt. Col. Sanford E. Church	24 February 1939–December 1941		

952d Coast Artillery Regiment (Antiaircraft) **Organized Reserve Wisconsin**

HQ—*Not initiated,* 1928–33

Constituted in the O.R. on 5 September 1928 as the 598th C.A. Regt. (AA) and allotted to the Sixth Corps Area. Redesignated on 1 December 1928 as the 952d C.A. Regt. (AA). Milwaukee, WI, designated on 6 December 1930 as HQ on organization, but the unit was never organized at that location. Demobilized on 1 October 1933.

953d Coast Artillery Regiment (Antiaircraft) **Organized Reserve Illinois**

HQ—*Not initiated,* 1928–33

Constituted in the O.R. on 5 September 1928 as the 599th C.A. Regt. (AA) and allotted to the Sixth Corps Area. Redesignated on 1 December 1928 as the 953d C.A. Regt. (AA). Chicago, IL, designated on 30 December 1930 as HQ on organization, but the unit was never organized at that location. Demobilized on 1 October 1933.

954th Coast Artillery Regiment (Antiaircraft) **Organized Reserve Iowa**

HQ—*Not initiated,* 1928–33

Constituted in the O.R. on 5 September 1928 as the 600th C.A. Regt. (AA) and allotted to the Seventh Corps Area. Redesignated on 1 December 1928 as the 954th C.A. Regt. (AA). Davenport, IA designated on 30 December 1930 as HQ on organization, but the unit was never organized at that location. Demobilized on 1 October 1933.

955th Coast Artillery Regiment (Antiaircraft) **Organized Reserve Minnesota**

HQ—*Not initiated,* 1928–29; Duluth, MN, 1929–41

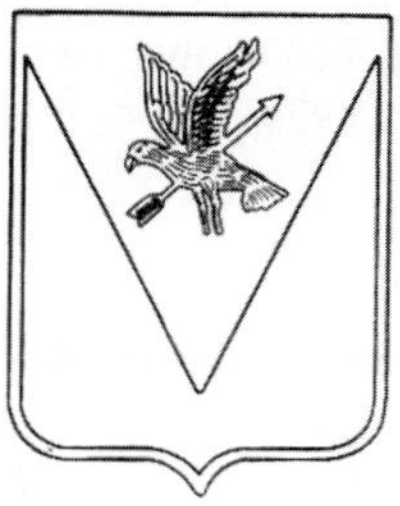

Constituted in the O.R. on 5 September 1928 as the 601st C.A. Regt. (AA) and allotted to the Seventh Corps Area. Redesignated on 1 December 1928 as the 955th C.A. Regt. (AA). Initiated on 15 June 1929 with regimental HQ at Duluth, MN. Awarded the US Coast Artillery Association Trophy for O.R. regiments for 1932. Typically conducted Inactive Training Period meetings at the Hotel Duluth, the Federal Building, or the N.G. armory in Duluth. Conducted summer training most years with the 61st C.A. at Fort Sheridan, IL, and some years at Camp Knox, KY. Primary ROTC feeder school was the University of Minnesota, 1929–41. Location 7 December 1941—Duluth, MN.

Status: Disbanded on 2 April 1943.

Commanders, 955th Coast Artillery Regiment

Unknown	15 June 1929–ao May 1932	Lt. Col. Frank C. Tenney	ao February 1933–May 1937
Lt. Col. James R. Sweitzer	ao May 1932–ao August 1932	Col. Earl E. Howard	May 1937–November 1937
	Col. Frank C. Tenney	November 1937–April 1942	

956th Coast Artillery Regiment (Antiaircraft) **Organized Reserve North Dakota**

HQ—*Not initiated,* 1928–33

Constituted in the O.R. on 5 September 1928 as the 602d C.A. Regt. (AA) and allotted to the Seventh Corps Area. Redesignated on 1 December 1928 as the 956th C.A. Regt. (AA). Fargo, ND, designated on 12 October 1931 as HQ on organization, but the unit was never organized at that location. Demobilized on 1 October 1933.

957th Coast Artillery Regiment (Antiaircraft) **Organized Reserve Nebraska**

HQ—*Not initiated,* 1928–33

Constituted in the O.R. on 5 September 1928 as the 603d C.A. Regt. (AA) and allotted to the Seventh Corps Area. Redesignated on 1 December 1928 as the 957th C.A. Regt. (AA). Omaha, NE, designated on 12 October 1931 as HQ on organization, but the unit was never organized at that location. Demobilized on 1 October 1933.

958th Coast Artillery Regiment (Antiaircraft) **Organized Reserve Missouri**

HQ—*Not initiated,* 1928–29; Kansas City, MO, 1929–31; St. Louis, MO, 1931–41

Constituted in the O.R. on 5 September 1928 as the 604th C.A. Regt. (AA) and allotted to the Seventh Corps Area. Redesignated on 1 December 1928 as the 958th C.A. Regt. (AA). Initiated on 5 September 1929 with the entire regiment at Kansas City, MO. Entire regiment relocated on 12 October 1931 to St. Louis, MO. Conducted summer training most years with the 61st C.A. at Fort Sheridan, IL, and some years at Camp Knox, KY. Primary ROTC feeder school was Washington University, 1929–41. Location 7 December 1941—St. Louis, MO.

Status: Disbanded on 2 April 1943.

Commanders, 958th Coast Artillery Regiment

Unknown	5 September 1929–ao May 1932	Col. Floyd C. Carl	ao May 1932–December 1941

959th Coast Artillery Regiment (Antiaircraft) **Organized Reserve South Dakota**

HQ—*Not initiated,* 1928–33

Constituted in the O.R. on 5 September 1928 as the 605th C.A. Regt. (AA) and allotted to the Seventh Corps Area. Redesignated on 1 December 1928 as the 959th C.A. Regt. (AA). Sioux Falls, SD, designated on 12 October 1931 as HQ on organization, but the unit was never organized at that location. Demobilized on 1 October 1933.

960th Coast Artillery Regiment (Antiaircraft) **Organized Reserve Kansas**

HQ—*Not initiated,* 1928–29; Topeka, KS, 1929–41

Constituted in the O.R. on 5 September 1928 as the 606th C.A. Regt. (AA) and allotted to the Seventh Corps Area. Redesignated on 1 December 1928 as the 960th C.A. Regt. (AA). Initiated on 5 September 1929 with regimental HQ at Topeka, KS. Withdrawn from the O.R. on 1 October 1933 and allotted to the R.A. as an RAI unit. Concurrently assigned to the 35th C.A. Brig. (GHQR). Conducted summer training most years with the 61st C.A. at Fort Sheridan, IL, and some years at Camp Knox, KY. Primary ROTC feeder school was the University of Kansas, 1929–41. Location 7 December 1941—Topeka, KS.

Status: Disbanded on 2 April 1943.

Commanders, 960th Coast Artillery Regiment

Unknown	5 September 1929-ao May 1932	Unknown	ao August 1932–ao July 1939
Maj. Dugald C. Jackson Jr.	ao May 1932–ao August 1932	Maj. George E. Rose	ao July 1939–December 1941

961st Coast Artillery Regiment (Antiaircraft) **Organized Reserve Arkansas**

HQ—*Not initiated,* 1928–33

Constituted in the O.R. on 5 September 1928 as the 607th C.A. Regt. (AA) and allotted to the Seventh Corps Area. Redesignated on 1 December 1928 as the 961st C.A. Regt. (AA). Little Rock, AR, designated on 12 October 1931 as HQ on organization, but the unit was never organized at that location. Demobilized on 1 October 1933.

962d Coast Artillery Regiment (Antiaircraft) **Organized Reserve Nebraska**

HQ—*Not initiated,* 1928–33

Constituted in the O.R. on 5 September 1928 as the 608th C.A. Regt. (AA) and allotted to the Seventh Corps Area. Redesignated on 1 December 1928 as the 962d C.A. Regt. (AA). Beatrice, NE, designated on 12 October 1931 as HQ on organization, but the unit was never organized at that location. Demobilized on 1 October 1933.

963d Coast Artillery Regiment (Antiaircraft) **Organized Reserve Arkansas**

HQ—*Not initiated,* 1928–33

Constituted in the O.R. on 5 September 1928 as the 609th C.A. Regt. (AA) and allotted to the Seventh Corps Area. Redesignated on 1 December 1928 as the 963d C.A. Regt. (AA). Little Rock, AR, designated on 12 October 1931 as HQ on organization, but the unit was never organized at that location. Demobilized on 1 October 1933.

964th Coast Artillery Regiment (Antiaircraft) **Organized Reserve Kansas**

HQ—*Not initiated,* 1928–33

Constituted in the O.R. on 5 September 1928 as the 610th C.A. Regt. (AA) and allotted to the Seventh Corps Area. Redesignated on 1 December 1928 as the 964th C.A. Regt. (AA). Topeka, KS, designated on 12 October 1931 as HQ on organization, but the unit was never organized at that location. Demobilized on 1 October 1933.

965th Coast Artillery Regiment (Antiaircraft) **Organized Reserve Iowa**

HQ—*Not initiated,* 1928–33

Constituted in the O.R. on 5 September 1928 as the 611th C.A. Regt. (AA) and allotted to the Seventh Corps Area. Redesignated on 1 December 1928 as the 965th C.A. Regt. (AA). Davenport, IA, designated on 12 October 1931 as HQ on organization, but the unit was never organized at that location. Demobilized on 1 October 1933.

966th Coast Artillery Regiment (Antiaircraft) **Organized Reserve North Dakota**

HQ—*Not initiated,* 1928–33

Constituted in the O.R. on 5 September 1928 as the 612th C.A. Regt. (AA) and allotted to the Seventh Corps Area. Redesignated on 1 December 1928 as the 966th C.A. Regt. (AA). Mandan, ND, designated on 12 October 1931 as HQ on organization, but the unit was never organized at that location. Demobilized on 1 October 1933.

967th Coast Artillery Regiment (Antiaircraft) **Organized Reserve Minnesota**

HQ—*Not initiated,* 1928–33

Constituted in the O.R. on 5 September 1928 as the 613th C.A. Regt. (AA) and allotted to the Seventh Corps Area. Redesignated on 1 December 1928 as the 967th C.A. Regt. (AA). St. Paul, MN, designated on 12 October 1931 as HQ on organization, but the unit was never organized at that location. Demobilized on 1 October 1933.

968th Coast Artillery Regiment (Antiaircraft) **Organized Reserve Minnesota**

HQ—*Not initiated,* 1928–33

Constituted in the O.R. on 5 September 1928 as the 614th C.A. Regt. (AA) and allotted to the Seventh Corps Area. Redesignated on 1 December 1928 as the 968th C.A. Regt. (AA). Albert Lea, MN, designated on 12 October 1931 as HQ on organization, but the unit was never organized at that location. Demobilized on 1 October 1933.

969th Coast Artillery Regiment (Antiaircraft) **Organized Reserve Texas**

HO—*Not initiated.* 1928–29; San Antonio, TX, 1929–41

Constituted in the O.R. on 5 September 1928 as the 615th C.A. Regt. (AA) and allotted to the Eighth Corps Area. Redesignated on 1 December 1928 as the 969th C.A. Regt. (AA). Initiated on 10 May 1929 with regimental HQ at San Antonio, TX. Subordinate battalion HQ concurrently organized as follows: HQ and Combat Train, 1st Bn. at San Antonio; and HHD, 2d Bn. at Corpus Christi, TX. Assigned to the 404th C.A. Brig. (GHQR) on 30 November 1928. Relieved from the 404th C.A. Brig. on 10 October 1933 and assigned to the XVIII Corps. Conducted summer training with the 69th C.A. at Fort Crockett, TX, and some years at Fort Barrancas, FL. Designated mobilization training station was the Houston Antiaircraft Training Camp near Houston, TX. Primary ROTC feeder school was the Agricultural and Mechanical College of Texas, 1929–41. Location 7 December 1941—San Antonio, TX.

Status: Disbanded on 2 April 1943.

Commanders, 969th Coast Artillery Regiment

Unknown	10 May 1929–May 1932	Maj. Julian B. Thomas	ao June 1938–ao July 1938
Lt. Col. William W. Holden	May 1932–ao August 1936	Unknown	ao July 1938–ao May 1940
Unknown	ao August 1936–ao June 1938	Col. John Perkins	ao May 1940–December 1941

970th Coast Artillery Regiment (Antiaircraft) — Organized Reserve Texas/New York

HQ—*Not initiated,* 1928–29; Houston, TX 1929–37; *Inactive,* 1937–41

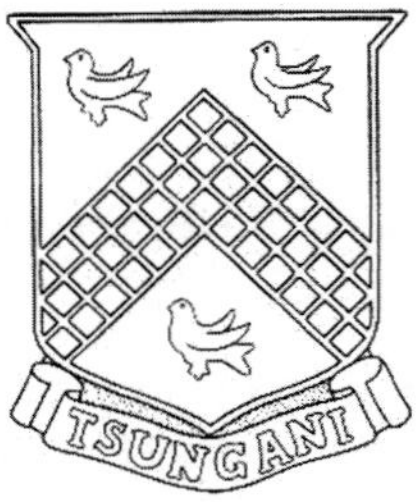

Constituted in the O.R. on 5 September 1928 as the 616th C.A. Regt. (AA) and allotted to the Eighth Corps Area. Redesignated on 1 December 1928 as the 970th C.A. Regt. (AA). Initiated on 10 May 1929 with regimental HQ at Houston, TX. Subordinate battalion HQ concurrently organized as follows: HQ and Combat Train, 1st Bn. at Houston; and HHD, 2d Bn. at Beaumont, TX. Assigned on 30 November 1928 to the 404th C.A. Brig. (GHQR). Relieved from the 404th C.A. Brig. on 1 October 1933. Withdrawn from the Eighth Corps Area on 5 June 1936 and allotted to the Second Corps Area. Inactivated on 12 May 1937 at Houston by relief of personnel. Rochester, NY, designated as HQ on reorganization, but the unit was never organized at that location. Conducted summer training with the 69th C.A. at Fort Crockett, TX, and some years at Fort Barrancas, FL. Designated mobilization training station was the Houston Antiaircraft Training Camp near Houston, TX. Primary ROTC feeder school was the Agricultural and Mechanical College of Texas, 1929–36. Location 7 December 1941—*Inactive.*

Status: Disbanded on 2 April 1943.

Commanders, 970th Coast Artillery Regiment

Unknown	10 May 1929–ao May 1931	Lt. Col. Samuel C. Lackey Jr.	May 1932–ao January 1935
Maj. Julian B. Thomas	ao May 1931–ao June 1931	Col. Jay A. Rossiter	ao May 1935–5 June 1936
Unknown	ao June 1931–ao April 1932	Lt. Col. Samuel C. Lackey Jr.	5 June 1936–12 May 1937
Lt. Col. William W. Holden	ao April 1932–May 1932	*Inactive*	12 May 1937–December 1941

971st Coast Artillery Regiment (Antiaircraft) — Organized Reserve Texas

HQ—El Paso, TX, 1928–33

Constituted in the O.R. on 5 September 1928 as the 617th C.A. Regt. (AA), and allotted to the Eighth Corps Area. Initiated on 12 October 1928 with regimental HQ at El Paso, TX. Subordinate battalion HQ concurrently organized as follows: HQ and Combat Train, 1st Bn. at El Paso; and HHD, 2d Bn. at Amarillo, TX. Redesignated on 1 December 1928 as the 971st C.A. Regt. (AA). Conducted summer training at Fort Crockett, TX. Designated mobilization training station was the Houston Antiaircraft Training Camp near Houston, TX. Primary ROTC feeder school was the Agricultural and Mechanical College of Texas, 1929–33. Demobilized on 1 October 1933.

Commanders, 971st Coast Artillery Regiment

Col. John Perkins	12 October 1928–1 October 1933

972d Coast Artillery Regiment (Antiaircraft) **Organized Reserve Texas**

HQ—Dallas, TX, 1928–41

Constituted in the O.R. on 5 September 1928 as the 618th C.A. Regt. (AA) and allotted to the Eighth Corps Area. Initiated on 12 October 1928 with regimental HQ at Dallas, TX. Subordinate battalion HQ concurrently organized as follows: HQ and Combat Train, 1st Bn. at Dallas; and HHD, 2d Bn. at Waco, TX. Redesignated on 1 December 1928 as the 972d C.A. Regt. (AA). Withdrawn from the O.R. on 1 October 1933 and allotted to the R.A. as an RAI unit. Typically conducted Inactive Training Period meetings at the Federal Building, the Post Office Building, or the Hotel Adolphus in Dallas. Conducted summer training with the 69th C.A. at Fort Crockett, TX, and some years at Fort Barrancas, FL. Designated mobilization training station was the Houston Antiaircraft Training Camp near Houston, TX. Primary ROTC feeder school was the Agricultural and Mechanical College of Texas, 1929–41. Location 7 December 1941—Dallas, TX.

Status: Disbanded on 2 April 1943.

Commanders, 972d Coast Artillery Regiment

Unknown	12 October 1928–ao May 1931	Col. John Perkins	1 October 1933–ao July 1938
Maj. Vernon G. Cox	ao May 1931–ao July 1932	Unknown	ao July 1938–ao July 1939
Unknown	ao June 1932–1 October 1933	Lt. Col. Frank F. Bell	ao July 1939–December 1941

973d Coast Artillery Regiment (Antiaircraft) **Organized Reserve Texas/Illinois**

HQ—Austin, TX, 1928–36; *Inactive,* 1936–41

Constituted in the O.R. on 5 September 1928 as the 619th C.A. Regt. (AA) and allotted to the Eighth Corps Area. Initiated on 12 October 1928 with regimental HQ at Austin, TX. Assigned on 30 November 1928 to the 404th C.A. Brig. (GHQR). Redesignated on 1 December 1928 as the 973d C.A. Regt. (AA). Withdrawn from the O.R. on 1 October 1933, allotted to the R.A. as an RAI unit, and assigned to the 40th C.A. Brig. Withdrawn from the Eighth Corps Area on 5 June 1936 and allotted to the Sixth Corps Area. Chicago, IL, designated as HQ on organization, but the unit was never organized at that location. Conducted summer training with the 69th C.A. at Fort Crockett, TX, and some years at Fort Barrancas, FL. Designated mobilization training station was the Houston Antiaircraft Training Camp near Houston, TX. Primary ROTC feeder school was the Agricultural and Mechanical College of Texas, 1929–41. Location 7 December 1941—*Inactive*.

Status: Disbanded on 2 April 1943.

Commanders, 973d Coast Artillery Regiment

Unknown	12 October 1928–ao May 1931	Col. Andrew Bramlett	ao July 1932–5 June 1936
Maj. O.M. Drake	ao May 1931–ao July 1932	*Inactive*	5 June 1936–December 1941

974th Coast Artillery Regiment (Antiaircraft) **Organized Reserve Colorado/Texas**

HO—Denver. CO. 1929–36; Port Arthur, TX, 1936–41

Constituted in the O.R. on 5 September 1928 as the 620th C.A. Regt. (AA) and allotted to the Eighth Corps Area. Redesignated on 1 December 1928 as the 974th C.A. Regt. (AA). Assigned on 30 November 1928 to the 404th C.A. Brig. (GHQR). Initiated on 10 May 1929 with regimental HQ at Denver, CO. Conducted summer training with the 69th C.A. at Fort Crockett, TX, and some years at Fort Barrancas, FL. Withdrawn from the O.R. on 1 October 1933 and allotted to the R.A. as an RAI unit. For summer training in 1935, the regiment assumed control of the personnel, vehicles, and equipment of the 69th C.A. and conducted a 40-mile motorized march to the Houston Antiaircraft Training Camp. On arrival, the regiment's officers supervised the set up of tentage and unit equipment to begin the training camp. Entire regiment relocated by November 1936 to Port Arthur, TX. Designated mobilization training station was the Houston Antiaircraft Training Camp near Houston, TX. Primary ROTC feeder school was the Colorado Agricultural College, 1929–41. Location 7 December 1941—Port Arthur, TX.

Status: Disbanded on 2 April 1943.

Commanders, 974th Coast Artillery Regiment

Unknown	10 May 1929–ao May 1931	Lt. Col. John T. Lonsdale	June 1936–ao July 1937
Maj. Ellsworth L. Guy	ao May 1931–June 1936	Unknown	ao July 1937–ao August 1940
Maj. Earl L. Mickelson	ao August 1940–December 1941		

975th Coast Artillery Regiment (Antiaircraft) **Organized Reserve California**

HQ—Los Angeles, CA, 1929–41

Constituted in the O.R. on 5 September 1928 as the 621st C.A. Regt. (AA) and allotted to the Ninth Corps Area. Redesignated on 1 December 1928 as the 975th C.A. Regt. (AA). Initiated on 10 September 1929 with the entire regiment at Los Angeles, CA. Many unit personnel participated in earthquake relief operations, 14–22 March 1933, in the Los Angeles area. As part of its Inactive Training Period, the regiment participated on 14 and 21 December 1935 in a "School of Fire" on the 3-inch antiaircraft gun conducted by the 3d C.A. at Fort MacArthur. In early 1936, the regiment also participated in a motorized night march with the 63d C.A. to March Field, CA. Typically conducted Inactive Training Period meetings at the Chamber of Commerce Building or the Detwiler Building in Los Angeles. Conducted summer training with the 63d C.A. at Fort MacArthur, CA. Primary ROTC feeder school was the University of California, 1929–41. Location 7 December 1941—Los Angeles, CA (inactivated on 12 January 1942).

Status: Disbanded on 2 April 1943.

Events: 154

Commanders, 975th Coast Artillery Regiment

Lt. Col. Frank H. Holden	10 September 1929–June 1941

976th Coast Artillery Regiment (Antiaircraft) **Organized Reserve California**

HQ—*Not initiated,* 1928–29; Los Angeles, CA, 1929–41

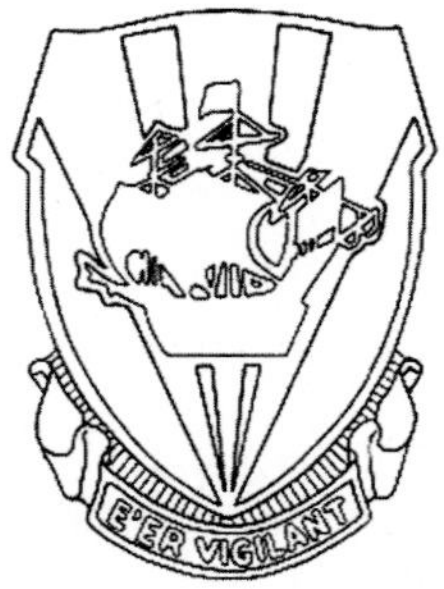

Constituted in the O.R. on 5 September 1928 as the 622d C.A. Regt. (AA) and allotted to the Ninth Corps Area. Redesignated on 1 December 1928 as the 976th C.A. Regt. (AA). Initiated on 10 September 1929 with the entire regiment at Los Angeles, CA. Typically conducted Inactive Training Period meetings at the armory of the 251st C.A. in Los Angeles. As part of its Inactive Training Period, the regiment participated on 14 and 21 December 1935 in a "School of Fire" on the 3-inch antiaircraft gun conducted by the 3d C.A. at Fort MacArthur. In early 1936, the regiment also participated in a motorized night march with the 63d C.A. to San Clemente, CA. Typically conducted Inactive Training Period meetings at the Chamber of Commerce Building or the Detwiler Building in Los Angeles. Conducted summer training with the 63d C.A. at Fort MacArthur, CA. Also conducted C.A. CMTC training some years at Fort MacArthur as an alternate form of annual training. Primary ROTC feeder school was the University of California, 1929–41. Location 7 December 1941—Los Angeles, CA (inactivated on 12 January 1942).

Status: Disbanded on 2 April 1943.

Commanders, 976th Coast Artillery Regiment

Col. George W. Fisher	10 September 1929–June 1939	Lt. Col. Lloyd E. Rolfe	June 1939–12 January 1942

977th Coast Artillery Regiment (Antiaircraft) **Organized Reserve California**

HQ—*Not initiated,* 1928–29; Los Angeles, CA, 1929–41

Constituted in the O.R. on 5 September 1928 as the 623d C.A. Regt. (AA) and allotted to the Ninth Corps Area. Redesignated on 1 December 1928 as the 977th C.A. Regt. (AA). Initiated on 10 September 1929 with the entire regiment at Los Angeles, CA. Many unit personnel participated in earthquake relief operations, 14–22 March 1933, in the Los Angeles area. As part of its Inactive Training Period, the regiment participated on 14 and 21 December 1935 in a "School of Fire" on the 3-inch antiaircraft gun conducted by the 3d C.A. at Fort MacArthur. Awarded the US Coast Artillery Association Trophy for O.R. regiments for 1938. Typically conducted Inactive Training Period meetings at the Chamber of Commerce Building or the Detwiler Building in Los Angeles. Conducted summer training with the 63d C.A. at Fort MacArthur, CA. Also conducted C.A. CMTC training some years at Fort MacArthur as an alternate form of annual training. Primary ROTC feeder school was the University of California, 1929–41. Location 7 December 1941—Los Angeles, CA (inactivated on 12 January 1942).

Status: Disbanded on 2 April 1943.

Events: 154

Commanders, 977th Coast Artillery Regiment

Col. Edward A. Evans	10 September 1929–June 1941	Unknown	June 1941–7 December 1941

978th Coast Artillery Regiment (Antiaircraft) **Organized Reserve Utah**

HQ—*Not initiated,* 1928–33

Constituted in the O.R. on 5 September 1928 as the 624th C.A. Regt. (AA) and allotted to the Ninth Corps Area. Redesignated on 1 December 1928 as the 978th C.A. Regt. (AA). Salt Lake City, UT, designated on 12 October 1931 as HQ on organization, but the unit was never organized at that location. Demobilized on 1 October 1933.

979th Coast Artillery Regiment (Antiaircraft) **Organized Reserve Washington**

HQ—*Not initiated,* 1928–29; Seattle, WA, 1929–33

Constituted in the O.R. on 5 September 1928 as the 625th C.A. Regt. (AA) and allotted to the Ninth Corps Area. Redesignated on 1 December 1928 as the 979th C.A. Regt. (AA). Initiated on 10 September 1929 with regimental HQ at Seattle, WA. Conducted summer training at Fort Worden, WA. Demobilized on 1 October 1933.

Commanders, 979th Coast Artillery Regiment

Lt. Col. Frank R. Reynolds	10 September 1929–1 October 1933

980th Coast Artillery Regiment (Antiaircraft) **Organized Reserve California**

HQ—*Not initiated,* 1928–33

Constituted in the O.R. on 5 September 1928 as the 626th C.A. Regt. (AA) and allotted to the Ninth Corps Area. Redesignated on 1 December 1928 as the 980th C.A. Regt. (AA). Oakland, CA, designated on 28 January 1930 as HQ on organization, but the unit was never organized at that location. Demobilized on 1 October 1933.

981st Coast Artillery Regiment (Antiaircraft) **Organized Reserve California**

HQ—*Not initiated,* 1928–33

Constituted in the O.R. on 5 September 1928 as the 627th C.A. Regt. (AA) and allotted to the Ninth Corps Area. Redesignated on 1 December 1928 as the 981st C.A. Regt. (AA). Los Angeles, CA, designated on 28 January 1930 as HQ on organization, but the unit was never organized at that location. Demobilized on 1 October 1933.

1101st Coast Artillery Training Battalion (ZI) **Organized Reserve New Hampshire**

HQ—*Not initiated,* 1929–30; Portsmouth, NH, 1930–41

Constituted in the O.R. in 1929, assigned to the Zone of the Interior, and allotted to the First Corps Area. Initiated on 4 February 1930 with regimental HQ at Portsmouth, NH. Location 7 December 1941—Portsmouth, NH.

Commanders, 1101st Coast Artillery Training Battalion

Unknown	4 February 1930–7 December 1941

1102d Coast Artillery Training Battalion (ZI) **Organized Reserve New Hampshire**

HQ—*Not initiated,* 1929–30; Portsmouth, NH, 1930–41

Constituted in the O.R. in 1929, assigned to the Zone of the Interior, and allotted to the First Corps Area. Initiated on 4 February 1930 with regimental HQ at Portsmouth, NH. Location 7 December 1941—Portsmouth, NH.

Commanders, 1102d Coast Artillery Training Battalion

Unknown	4 February 1930–7 December 1941

Sandy Hook Coast Artillery Regiment (Provisional) **Organized Reserve Delaware**

HQ—Manhattan, NY, 1923–24

Organized provisionally in the O.R. in December 1923 at Wilmington, DE, as the Sandy Hook C.A. Regt. Organized to provide a regimental organization for O.R. personnel in the state of Delaware who were assigned to the Harbor Defenses of Southern New York. Discontinued on 31 March 1924, and personnel transferred to the newly constituted 620th C.A. Regt. (Harbor Defense).

Commanders, Sandy Hook Coast Artillery Regiment

Lt. Col. Percy S. Lyon	December 1923–31 March 1924

Delaware Coast Artillery Regiment (Provisional) **Organized Reserve Delaware**

HQ—Wilmington, DE, 1923–24

Organized provisionally in the O.R. in December 1923 at Wilmington, DE, as the Delaware C.A. Regt. Organized to provide a regimental organization for O.R. personnel in the state of Delaware who were assigned to the Harbor Defenses of the Delaware. Discontinued on 31 March 1924 and personnel transferred to the newly constituted 621st C.A. Regt. (Fixed Defenses).

Commanders, Delaware Coast Artillery Regiment

Col. Archibald E. Tanner	December 1923–31 March 1924

Chapter 27

Army Mine Planters and Cable Ships

US National Park Service, Gulf Islands National Seashore

U.S.A.M.P. Royal T. Frank conducting mine planting operations near Fort Pickens, FL.

Before World War I, the Army possessed a fleet of mine planters, mine yawls, and distribution box boats to support its large number of coast defense commands. These boats had the wartime mission of installing and maintaining underwater mine fields and antisubmarine nets at the various harbor defenses in the continental United States and the 3 overseas departments. When war came in 1917, the number of planters was inadequate to meet the needs of these commands so the Army placed orders for at least 24 new mine planters and junior mine planters during the war. However, the new classes of boats, consisting of 8 primary and 16 junior planters were completed too late to participate in the war. In the early 1920s 5 of the 8 new primary planters were transferred to the US Coast Guard or to the US Lighthouse Service. The remaining 3, along with the 6 other older mine planters formed the backbone of the Army's mine planting service in the interwar period. Six of these boats were located at various commands in the United States. Two were located on the west coast, and the other four, one of which was a cable ship that generally performed duties as a mine planter, were stationed at defense commands on the east coast. Three of the primary planters were assigned to the Philippine (2) and Panama Canal (1) Departments. Hawaii possessed no primary planter, but did have 2, later 3, Harbor Boat Service vessels that were used to support the training of coast artillery batteries and planting sections from time to time. Occasionally, the primary planters from San Francisco or Puget Sound would travel to Hawaii to also support those activities.

Organization and Training

Though primary planters were typically assigned to a specific command, they frequently steamed to other harbor defense locations to service those commands. With over 20 active harbor defense commands to service, the primary planters were kept busy in terms of training of harbor defense planting sections, maintenance of mining equipment, and minor repairs to mine cable systems located within the harbors.

Until 1918, the Army mine planters actually served under a dual allegiance of sorts. The boats themselves were the property of the Quartermaster Corps. With the exception of the boat's commander, the personnel assigned to each boat's Operations Section (i.e., the permanent crew), including the boat's master, were civilian crews hired by the Quartermaster Corps. The Operations Section, which included the boat's commander, was responsible only for the operation of the boat. The boat's commander was a coast artillery officer from the harbor defense command to which the boat was permanently assigned. In April 1918, this changed when Congress established the Army Mine Planter Service and all crews were militarized. At that point both the Operations and Planting Sections were composed of Army personnel.

Though the Operations Section was the boat's permanent crew, mine planters did not maintain a permanent Planting Section. During training exercises or mining operations, the harbor defense command for which the boat was operating at the time provided the coast artillery personnel who composed the Planting Section. These crews were the men who actually did the work of preparing and planting each of the large antishipping mines that composed the harbor's mine field defenses and tended the antisubmarine nets.

In addition to the primary mine planters, by 1919 the Army also possessed over 30 junior mine planters. A number of these vessels, however, were sold to private businesses or transferred to other government agencies during 1920-23 and several more between 1929 and 1932. These boats were only infrequently employed in mine planting operations during peacetime. Most of the junior mine planters were used in various other capacities but mostly as freight and passenger craft supporting the Army's Harbor Boat Service, or occasionally as artillery tugs to tow target sleds on those relatively rare occasions when harbor defense crews fired the big guns during training. Even when employed in the latter capacity, these boats were far more frequently used as freight and passenger craft during this period than as vessels to support harbor defense duties. In 1941, all of these boats still in service were reconditioned and reequipped as junior mine planters and served as such during World War II.

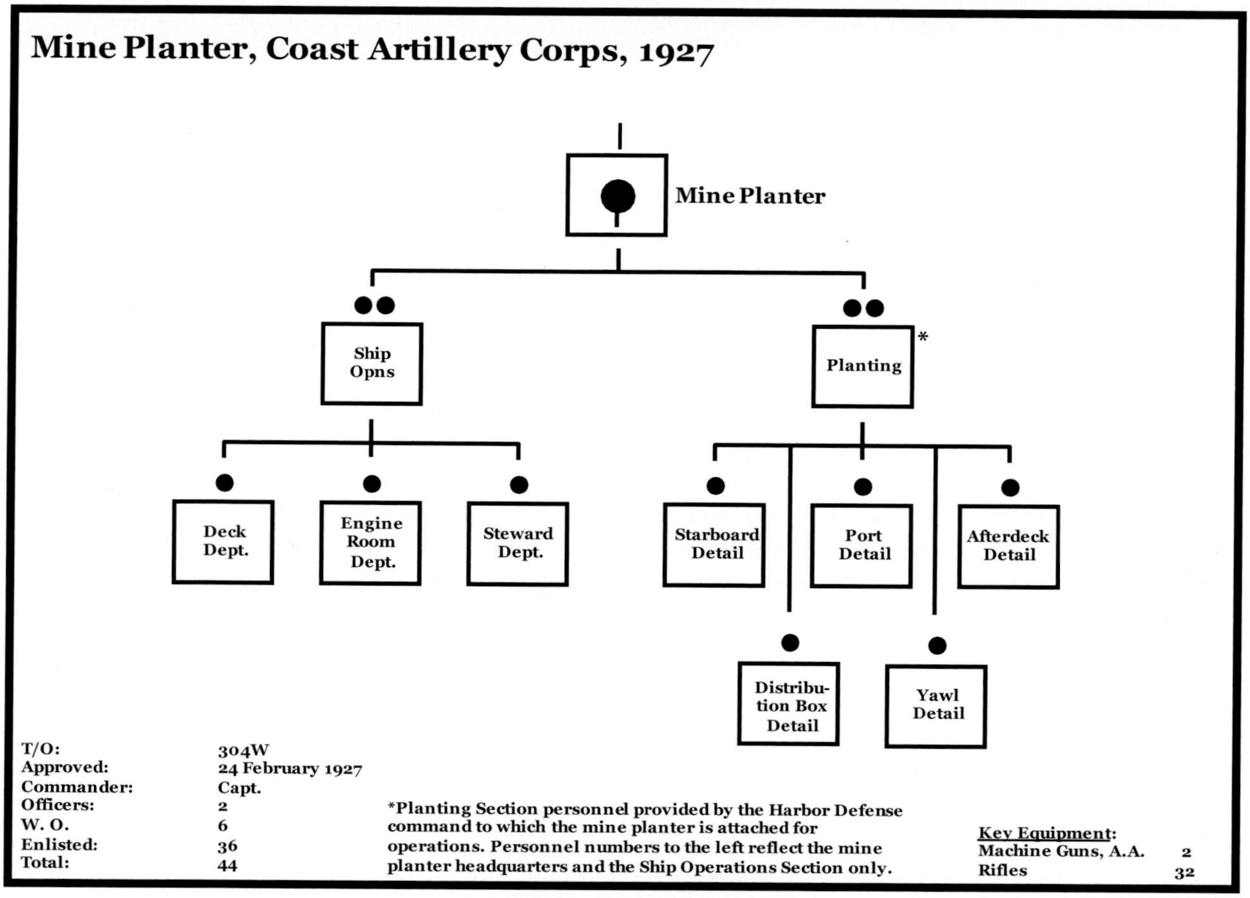

Mine Planter Crew Organization

Primary Mine Planters

Courtesy of Martin Dwyer, Scranton, PA

U.S.A.M.P. *Col. George Armistead* (Coast Defenses of San Francisco)

Station—Fort Mason, CA, 1919–23; Fort Winfield Scott, CA, 1923–37

Built by Neafie and Levy Shipyard and launched on 5 March 1904 at Philadelphia, PA. Named in honor of brevet Lt. Col. George Armistead, commanding officer of Fort McHenry when that garrison successfully defended Baltimore from attack by the British fleet in 1814. Accepted for service by the Quartermaster Department about June 1904. Assigned to the Coast Defenses of San Francisco as of January 1920. Typically docked at the piers at Fort Mason or at the mine wharf at Fort Winfield Scott, CA. On detached service to Fort Armstrong, TH, 5 April to 31 July 1920 to conduct training with the Coast Defenses of Oahu. On detached service to Fort Rosecrans, CA, 26 August to 17 September 1920 and 1 September to 30 September 1921 to conduct training with the Coast Defenses of San Diego. Personnel assigned to the *Armistead* were concurrently assigned to Headquarters Battery, 6th Coast Artillery Regiment on 30 June 1924. Personnel relieved from Headquarters Battery, 6th Coast Artillery about July 1927. Decommissioned and sold on 10 April 1937. Concurrently, personnel transferred to U.S.A.M.P. *Lt. Col. Ellery W. Niles.*

Status: Served with the U.S. Navy as the tug U.S.S. *Dekanaweda* in World War II; later worked in the Philippines as the *Celtic*; dropped off the ABS Record in 1984.

Events: 76, 92, 108, 111

Length: 150 ft. Beam: 30.5 ft. Draft: 10 ft. Displacement: 447 tons

Commanders, U.S.A.M.P. *Col. George Armistead*

Maj. Oscar A. Eastwold	3 March 1919–24 February 1920	1st Lt. John S. Crawford	17 March 1927–25 August 1927
Maj. Stewart W. Stanley	24 February 1920–16 February 1922	2d Lt. Charles W. McGeehan	26 August 1927–15 October 1927
Capt. Frank J. McSherry	16 February 1922–12 July 1922	2d Lt. Howard O. Douglas	16 October 1927–February 1929
Capt. James G. Devine	12 July 1922–9 May 1923	1st Lt. Harold W. Smith	February 1929–7 February 1930
Capt. Milton Heilfron	9 May 1923–19 November 1923	1st Lt. William B. Hawthorne	7 February 1930–1 April 1932
1st Lt. Arthur J. Weeks	19 November 1923–22 May 1924	Capt. Clare H. Armstrong	1 April 1932–14 May 1933
2d Lt. Howard O. Douglas	22 May 1924–20 October 1924	2d Lt. Lawrence E. Shaw	15 May 1933–24 July 1934
2d Lt. William G. Holder	20 October 1924–13 June 1925	Capt. William A. Weddell	24 July 1924–26 September 1934
1st Lt. William L. Richardson	13 June 1925–20 July 1925	1st Lt. George F. Heaney Jr.	26 September 1934–31 October 1934
2d Lt. Harold G. Laub	18 August 1925–9 November 1925	1st Lt. Raleigh R. Hendrix	31 October 1934–1 December 1934
1st Lt. Charles F. Wilson	9 November 1925–1 July 1926	Capt. Laurence H. Brownlee	1 December 1934–21 May 1935
2d Lt. Harold G. Laub	1 July 1926–1 August 1926	2d Lt. Deane A. Gough	21 May 1935–31 March 1936
2d Lt. Robert C. Padley	1 August 1926–3 March 1927	Capt. Rodney C. Jones	1 April 1937–10 April 1937

US Army Signal Corps, National Archives II

U.S.A.M.P. ***Gen. Absalom Baird*** (Coast Defenses of Long Island Sound)

Station—Milwaukee, WI, 1920; Hoboken, NJ, 1920; New London, CT, 1920–37; Fort Banks, MA, 1937–41

Built by Fabricated Shipbuilding Company and launched in 1920 at Milwaukee, WI. Named in honor of Maj. Gen. Absalom Baird, commanding officer of the 1st Division, XIV Corps during the Chickamauga and Atlanta Campaigns, July 1863–September 1864. Assigned to the South Pacific Coast Artillery District on 4 May 1920. Accepted for service by the Quartermaster Corps in August 1920. Departed Milwaukee in September 1920 and arrived at Hoboken, NJ, in October 1920. Relieved from the South Pacific Coast Artillery District on 9 November 1920 and assigned to the Coast Defenses of Long Island Sound. Typically docked at Pier #6 in Hoboken. Transferred in December 1920 to Fort H.G. Wright, NY. On detached service to Fort Adams, RI, 23 April 1932 to 27 May 1932 to conduct training with the Coast Defenses of Narragansett Bay. Transferred on 15 April 1937 to Fort Banks, MA. Concurrently relieved from the Harbor Defenses of Long Island Sound and assigned to the Harbor Defenses of Boston. Location 7 December 1941—Fort Banks, MA.

Status: Sold to a harbor boat service at New York Harbor; later registered in Canada; dropped off the list of US Merchant Vessels after World War II.

Events: 77, 93

Length: 172 ft. Beam: 32 ft. Draft: 17 ft. Displacement: 704 tons

Commanders, U.S.A.M.P. ***Gen. Absalom Baird***

Capt. LeRoy H. Lohmann	16 June 1920–10 September 1923
Capt. Herbert F. E. Bultman	13 September 1923–October 1928
1st Lt. Lee A. Denson Jr.	October 1928–16 June 1929
1st Lt. James F. Pichel	17 June 1929–8 August 1930
1st Lt. George F. Nichols	9 August 1930–14 April 1932
1st Lt. Frank F. Miter	23 April 1932–1 September 1932
1st Lt. Girvelle L. Field	2 September 1932–January 1933
1st Lt. William H. Burns	January 1933–5 December 1933
Maj. Percy S. Lowe	5 December 1933–30 April 1938
Maj. Albert C. Cheseldon	27 May 1938–4 August 1938
Capt. Nathan A. McLamb	4 August 1938–ao January 1942

Courtesy of Martin Dwyer, Scranton, PA

U.S.A.M.P. ***Gen. J. Franklin Bell*** (Coast Defenses of Puget Sound)

Station—Milwaukee, WI, 1920; Army Supply Base, Brooklyn, NY, 1920–21; Fort Winfield Scott, CA, 1921–22; Fort Worden, WA, 1922–40; Fort Randolph, CZ, 1940–41

Built by Fabricated Shipbuilding Company and launched in 1920 at Milwaukee, WI. Named in honor of Maj. Gen. J. Franklin Bell, Chief of Staff, US Army 1906 to 1910. Assigned to the South Pacific Coast Artillery District on 4 May 1920. Accepted for service by the Quartermaster Corps in June 1920. Transferred in October 1920 to Army Supply Base, Brooklyn, NY. Further assigned to the Coast Defenses of San Francisco on 9 November 1920. Departed the Army Supply Base, Brooklyn in October 1921 en route to Fort Winfield Scott, CA, via Cienfuegos, Cuba, and the Panama Canal. Arrived at Fort Winfield Scott in mid-November 1921. Typically docked at the piers at Fort Mason or at the mine wharf at Fort Winfield Scott, CA. Departed Fort Winfield Scott on 23 June 1922 and transferred to Fort Worden, WA, arriving there about 30 June 1922. Concurrently relieved from the Coast Defenses of San Francisco and assigned to the Coast Defenses of Puget Sound. Personnel assigned to the *Bell* were concurrently assigned to Battery G, 14th Coast Artillery on 30 June 1924. Personnel relieved from Battery G, 14th Coast Artillery about July 1927. Relieved from the Harbor Defenses of Puget Sound in May 1940 and assigned to the Harbor Defenses of Balboa. Departed Fort Worden in May 1940 and arrived at Fort Randolph, CZ, in June 1940. Redesignated as U.S.A.M.P. *Brig. Gen. John J. Hayden* in 1941. Location 7 December 1941—Fort Randolph, CZ.

Status: Sold after World War II.

Events: 90, 204, 292, 331

Length: 172 ft. Beam: 32 ft. Draft: 17 ft. Displacement: 704 tons

Commanders, U.S.A.M.P. ***Gen. J. Franklin Bell***

1st Lt. Ernest C. Bomar	24 August 1920–28 November 1920	2d Lt. John S. Henn	7 July 1928–19 December 1929
Capt. Carl S. Dorey	28 November 1928–24 September 1921	2d Lt. Oscar J. Levin	20 December 1929–1 May 1932
Capt. Edward E. Murphy	24 September 1921–3 August 1922	Capt. James R. Lowder	1 May 1932–1 March 1934
1st Lt. Dean R. Dickey	3 August 1922–17 May 1923	1st Lt. John H. Kochevar	1 March 1934–17 December 1934
1st Lt. Harold L. Stiebel	17 May 1923–19 December 1923	1st Lt. Paul A. Jaccard	17 December 1934–1 February 1936
Capt. Raymond B. Bottom	19 December 1923–1 July 1924	1st Lt. Harry F. Townsend	1 February 1936–2 July 1937
1st Lt. Frederick B. Dodge Jr.	1 July 1924–25 November 1924	1st Lt. John A. Sawyer	2 July 1937–10 August 1938
1st Lt. James R. Lowder	25 November 1924–20 July 1925	1st Lt. Robert J. Lawlor	10 August 1938–31 October 1938
Capt. Joseph F. Stiley	20 July 1925–24 March 1928	Capt. George B. Anderson	31 October 1938–6 September 1939
Capt. James R. Lowder	24 March 1928–6 July 1928	1st Lt. Lamar C. Ratcliffe	7 September 1939–1 February 1942

US Army Signal Corps, National Archives II, RG92

U.S.A.M.P. *Cyrus W. Field* (Coast Defenses of Cristobal)

Station—Fort Sherman, CZ, 1919–21

Built and launched in 1901 at Hartford, CT, as the steam lighter *Margaret*. Purchased for service by the Quartermaster Department on 6 May 1904 and converted to perform duties as a cable ship for the Signal Corps. Renamed in honor of Cyrus W. Field, renowned capitalist and entrepreneur who was responsible for laying the first Trans-Atlantic telegraph cable from the United States to Great Britain in 1866. Stationed at Fort Sherman, CZ, as of January 1919 and serving as a mine planter with the Coast Artillery. Assigned to the Panama Coast Artillery District on 4 May 1920. Further assigned to the Coast Defenses of Cristobal on 9 November 1920. Typically docked at the mine wharf at Fort Sherman, CZ. Though officially designated a mine planter by 1919, the *Field* still maintained a dual capability as a cable ship. It was also unique among the primary mine planters of this period in that it was constructed primarily of wood. The *Field* ran aground near Fort Sherman on 31 March 1921 and was severely damaged. All enlisted personnel were relieved from assignment in April 1921 and assigned to the 5th Coast Artillery Company. The boat was salvaged by the crew of the U.S.A.M.P. *Gen. William M. Graham* and stricken from the list of army mine planters on 31 July 1921.

Length: 132.1 ft. Beam: 32.2 ft. Draft: 10 ft. Displacement: 348 tons

Commanders, U.S.A.M.P. *Col. Cyrus W. Field*

Capt. William R. Deeble	18 March 1920–27 April 1921	Capt. William D. Evans	27 April 1921–31 July 1921

US Army Signal Corps, National Archives II, RG92

U.S.A.M.P. *Gen. Royal T. Frank* (Coast Defenses of Boston)

Station—Boston, MA, 1920–22; *Inactive* 1922–29; Honolulu, TH, 1929–41

Built by New York Shipbuilding Company and launched on 20 October 1908 at Camden, NJ. Named in honor of Brig. Gen. Royal Thaxter Frank, Civil War veteran and commandant of the Artillery School 1888–1898. Accepted for service by the Quartermaster Department on 3 June 1909 and assigned to the North Atlantic Coast Artillery District. Stationed at Boston, MA, as of January 1919. Further assigned to the Coast Defenses of Boston on 9 November 1920. Though assigned to the Coast Defenses of Boston, the *Frank* also serviced the Coast Defenses of Portsmouth and Narragansett Bay. Decommissioned on 30 September 1922 and placed in reserve at the R. T. Greene Shipyard, Chelsea, MA. Recommissioned on 22 April 1929 in the Harbor Boat Service. Reconditioned at Brooklyn, NY, and ordered to report to the Quartermaster for the Hawaiian Department. Arrived at Honolulu, TH, on 7 June 1929. Used by the Hawaiian Department as an inter-island transport in the Hawaiian Islands. Location 7 December 1941—Honolulu, TH.

Status: Torpedoed by a Japanese submarine off the coast of Maui 28 January 1942.

Length: 165 ft. Beam: 32 ft. Draft: 12 ft. Displacement: 621 tons

Commanders, U.S.A.M.P. *Gen. Royal T. Frank*

Maj. James H. Johnson 6 December 1919–26 February 1922
Capt. Joseph W. Barker 26 February 1922–22 April 1922
Capt. Ernest C. Bomar 22 April 1922–30 September 1922

US Army Signal Corps, National Archives II

U.S.A.M.P. *Gen. William M. Graham* (Coast Defenses of Cristobal)

Station—Fort Sherman, CZ, 1919–41

Built by New York Shipbuilding Company and launched on 29 August 1917 at Camden, NJ. Named in honor of Brig. Gen. William M. Graham, who served as a general officer in the United States Army in both the American Civil War and the Spanish-American War. Accepted for service by the Quartermaster Corps on 3 January 1918 and assigned to the Panama Coast Artillery District. The *Graham* was the first US Army boat designed to be a combined mine planter and cable ship. Stationed at Fort Sherman, CZ, as of January 1919. Further assigned to the Coast Defenses of Cristobal on 9 November 1920. Typically docked at the mine wharf at Fort Sherman. Personnel assigned to the *Graham* were concurrently assigned to Headquarters Battery, 1st Coast Artillery on 30 June 1924. Personnel relieved from Headquarters Battery, 1st Coast Artillery about August 1926. Awarded "E" for mine planting efficiency in 1937. In coordination with the U.S.A.M.P. *Lt. Col. Ellery W. Niles*, in June-August 1940 the *Graham* installed the wartime minefields that protected the Panama Canal Zone. Location 7 December 1941—Fort Sherman, CZ.

Status: Sold to Panama in 1945 as the *Panama City*; dropped off the list of US Merchant Vessels after 1949.

Events: 102, 292

Length: 170 ft. Beam: 32 ft. Draft: 17 ft. Displacement: 611 tons

Commanders, U.S.A.M.P. *Gen. William M. Graham*

Capt. William R. Deeble	1 May 1919–25 January 1920	1st Lt. Raymond M. Arthur	30 May 1930–28 April 1930
Maj. Edwin B. Spiller	25 January 1920–6 September 1920	2d Lt. John J. Holst	28 April 1930–15 August 1930
1st Lt. Evans R. Crowell	6 September 1920–8 April 1921	Capt. Willis L. Claxton	15 August 1930–25 July 1932
Capt. William D. Evans	8 April 1921–22 October 1922	Capt. Harry E. Pendleton	25 July 1932–4 August 1934
Capt. Frederic W. Cook	27 October 1922–30 June 1924	1st Lt. Virgil Kimm	4 August 1934–11 July 1936
1st Lt. Joseph Harris	30 June 1924–12 September 1924	1st Lt. Ira W. Cory	11 July 1936–21 August 1936
Capt. LeRoy H. Lohmann	12 September 1924–24 May 1927	Capt. George A. Ford	21 August 1936–9 June 1938
1st Lt. David B. Latimer	24 May 1927–11 July 1927	Capt. Gerald G. Gibbs	10 June 1938–19 September 1939
1st Lt. Charles F. Wilson	12 July 1927–29 May 1929	Capt. John J. Holst	20 September 1939–16 September 1941

US Army Signal Corps, National Archives II

U.S.A.M.P. ***Col. George F.E. Harrison*** (Coast Defenses of Manila and Subic Bay)

Station—Milwaukee, WI, 1920; Army Supply Base, Brooklyn, NY, 1920–21; Fort Sherman, CZ, 1921–22; Fort Mason, CA, 1922–23; Manila, PI, 1923–35; Fort Mills, Corregidor, PI, 1935–41

Built by Fabricated Shipbuilding Company and launched in 1920 at Milwaukee, WI. Named in honor of Col. George Francis Edward Harrison, the first American military governor of the Philippines and commandant of the Coast Artillery School 1906–09. Assigned to the Panama Coast Artillery District on 4 May 1920. Accepted for service by the Quartermaster Corps about 31 October 1920. Departed Milwaukee on 2 November 1920 and arrived at the Army Supply Base, Brooklyn, NY, on 16 December 1920. Further assigned to the Coast Defenses of Balboa on 9 November 1920. Stationed at the Army Supply Base, Brooklyn, until October 1921. Departed the Army Supply Base, Brooklyn on 19 October 1921 en route to Fort Sherman, CZ, via Charleston, SC, and Cienfuegos, Cuba. Arrived at Fort Sherman on 7 November 1921. Relieved from the Coast Defenses of Balboa on 9 August 1922 and ordered to the Philippines to replace the U.S.A.M.P.s *Hunt* and *Knox* in the Coast Defenses of Manila and Subic Bay. Departed Fort Sherman on 24 September 1922 en route for Fort Mason, CA. Arrived at Fort Mason on 29 October 1922. Departed Fort Mason on 12 February 1923 en route to Manila, PI, via Pearl Harbor, TH. Arrived at Manila on 11 March 1923 and assigned to the Coast Defenses of Manila and Subic Bay. Personnel assigned to the Harrison were concurrently assigned to the 59th Coast Artillery on 30 June 1924. Personnel were relieved from the 59th Coast Artillery on 31 August 1927. Transferred on 21 November 1935 to Fort Mills, PI. Typically docked at the ATS Dock in Manila and later at the North Dock at Fort Mills on Corregidor. Planted the Manila Bay harbor entrance/exit minefields in July-August 1941. Responsible for maintaining the harbor entrance/exit minefields in the North Channel (the US Navy was responsible for the South Channel). Location 7 December 1941—Fort Mills, Corregidor, PI.

Status: Partially sunk in the South Bay of Manila Bay on 4 or 5 May 1942 by Japanese dive bombers; subsequently raised by the Japanese and commissioned as the *Harushima Maru*; sunk by US Navy aircraft at Yokosuka harbor in 1945.

Length: 172 ft. Beam: 32 ft. Draft: 17 ft. Displacement: 704 tons

Commanders, U.S.A.M.P. *Col. George F. E. Harrison*

Maj. Belton O. Kennedy	31 October 1920–November 1920	2d Lt. Glenn Newman	February 1928–June 1928
Lt. Col. Harrison F. Kerrick	November 1920–4 December 1920	1st Lt. Victor Schmidt	June 1928–October 1928
1st Lt. Phillip S. Day	4 December 1920–17 December 1920	1st Lt. William S. Griffin	October 1928–14 June 1929
Maj. Logan W. Serles	17 December 1920–2 June 1921	1st Lt. Joseph Harris	15 June 1929–March 1930
1st. Lt. Frederick R. Chamberlain	2 June 1921–30 April 1923	1st Lt. Samuel Rubin	April 1930–May 1932
2d Lt. John L. Goff	30 April 1923–1 August 1923	Maj. Henry E. Behrens	June 1932–October 1932
2d Lt. John D. Mitchell	1 August 1923–18 October 1923	2d Lt. Peter Schmick	October 1932–May 1934
Capt. Carl S. Doney	18 October 1923–23 March 1925	Capt. Samuel Rubin	ao March 1935–1 February 1937
2d Lt. Lee A. Denson Jr.	23 March 1925–2 October 1925	Capt. Russell E. Bates	1 February 1937–11 June 1937
1st Lt. Joe D. Moss	2 October 1925–4 November 1925	1st Lt. Peter S. Peca	11 June 1937–20 May 1938
2d Lt. Samuel Rubin	4 November 1925–22 May 1926	1st Lt. Harry J. Harrison	20 May 1938–1 April 1940
2d Lt. Clark C. Witman	22 May 1926–12 September 1927	1st Lt. John McM. Gulick	2 April 1940–November 1941
Unknown	12 September 1927–February 1928	Capt. Edgar Rosenstock	November 1941–1 May 1942

Courtesy of Martin Dwyer, Scranton, PA

U.S.A.M.P. *Joseph Henry* (Coast Defenses of Sandy Hook)

Station—Fort Totten, NY, 1919–21; Fort Wood, NY, 1921–22; Governors Island, NY, 1923–28; Fort Hancock, NJ, 1928–41; Army Base, Boston, MA, 1941

Built by Newport News Shipbuilding Company and launched on 30 December 1908 at Newport News, VA. Accepted for service by the Quartermaster Department on 31 March 1909 originally as a Signal Corps cable ship. Designated as the U.S. Army Cable Ship *Joseph Henry* in honor of Dr. Joseph Henry, renowned scientist who invented the magnetic relay for electrical cables and performed experiments with new forms of casting large artillery pieces. Stationed at Fort Totten, NY, as of January 1919. Assigned to the Middle Atlantic Coast Artillery District on 4 May 1920. Further assigned to the Coast Defenses of Eastern New York on 8 November 1920. Redesignated U.S.A.M.P. *Joseph Henry* on 10 February 1921. Transferred on 16 November 1921 to Fort Wood, NY. Relieved from the Coast Defenses of Eastern New York on 25 November 1921 and assigned to the Coast Defenses of Sandy Hook. Conducted six separate voyages to perform mining and cable operations at each of the Coast Defense commands on the Atlantic seaboard and the Gulf Coast between November 1920 and September 1923. Transferred 29 June 1923 to Governors Island, NY. Personnel assigned to Headquarters Battery, 7th Coast Artillery Regiment on 30 June 1924. On detached service June to October 1926 to conduct training with the Harbor Defenses of Galveston, Pensacola, and Chesapeake Bay. Personnel relieved from Headquarters Battery, 7th Coast Artillery on 20 August 1926. On detached service February to November 1928 to conduct training with the Harbor Defenses of Eastern New York, Pensacola, Galveston, Portland, Boston, and Long Island Sound. On detached service March 1930 to June 1930 and September 1930 to April 1931 to conduct training with the Harbor Defenses of the Delaware, Chesapeake Bay, Boston, Pensacola, Charleston, and Narragansett Bay. On detached service from March 1936 to October 1936 to conduct training with the Harbor Defenses of Portland, Boston, and Narragansett Bay. On detached service from February to May 1937 to conduct training with the Harbor Defenses of Chesapeake Bay, Eastern New York, and Portland. On detached service from July 1937 to September 1937 to conduct training with the Harbor Defenses of Boston, Narragansett Bay, and Long Island Sound. Redesignated U.S. Army Cable Ship *Joseph Henry* on 31 December 1937. Returned to the Mine Planter Service as the U.S.A.M.P. *Joseph Henry* by June 1940. On detached service in September 1940 to Fort Monroe, VA. Permanently transferred on 17 September 1941 to Army Base, Boston, MA, and assigned to the Harbor Defenses of Boston. Location 7 December 1941—Army Base, Boston, MA.

Status: Inactivated and departed U. S. Army service 11 August 1945; owned by the Faliro Maritime Museum, Athens, Greece as of 2002.

Events: 87

Length: 160 ft. Beam: 32 ft. Draft: 17ft. Displacement: 601 tons

Commanders, U.S.A.M.P. *Joseph Henry*

Capt. H. E. West	23 August 1917-24 October 1919
Capt. Willard M. Hall	24 October 1919–13 November 1920
1st Lt. Ernest C. Bomar	23 November 1920–19 January 1922
Maj. Belton O. Kennedy	19 January 1921–22 February 1922
1st Lt. Joseph Harris	22 February 1922–20 October 1923
Unknown	21 October 1923–10 July 1924
Capt. Thomas R. Parker	10 July 1924–4 September 1927
Capt. LeRoy H. Lohmann	5 September 1927–30 June 1931
1st Lt. Charles F. Wilson	1 July 1931–15 October 1934
1st Lt. John D. Robertson	15 October 1934–2 March 1935
2d Lt. Richard S. Spangler	2 March 1935–9 August 1935
1st Lt. Paul A. Roy	9 August 1935–5 October 1935
Capt. D. Burgo Gill	5 October 1935–7 March 1937
Capt. William B. Hawthorne	7 March 1937–4 September 1937
Maj. James B. Carroll	2 September 1937-30 June 1941
Lt. Col. Gerald Gibbs	30 June 1941-January 1942

US Army Signal Corps, National Archives II, RG92

U.S.A.M.P. *Gen. Henry J. Hunt* (Coast Defenses of Manila and Subic Bay)

Station—Fort Mills, PI, 1919–23

Built by Neafie and Levy Shipyard and launched 5 February 1904 at Philadelphia, PA. Named in honor of Maj. Gen. Henry Jackson Hunt, chief of artillery for the Army of the Potomac. Accepted for service by the Quartermaster Department about June 1904 Stationed at Fort Mills, Corregidor, PI, as of January 1919 and assigned to the Coast Defenses of Manila and Subic Bay. Typically docked at the North Dock at Corregidor. Decommissioned on 31 March 1923 and personnel transferred to the U.S.A.M.P. *Gen. George F. E. Harrison*. Sold in 1924.

Status: Sunk off the Florida Keys.

Length: 150 ft. Beam: 30.5 ft. Draft: 10 ft. Displacement: 447 tons

Commanders, U.S.A.M.P. *Gen. Henry J. Hunt*

1st Lt. Henry T. Morrison	ao January 1920–1 June 1920	1st Lt. John D. Mitchell	15 February 1922–18 August 1922
1st Lt. B. F. Manning	1 June 1920–December 1920	1st Lt. Lawrence W. Bartlett	18 August 1922–8 November 1922
1st Lt. Edwin P. Hart	1 January 1921–15 February 1922	1st Lt. John L. Goff	8 November 1922–31 March 1923

Great Lakes Marine Collection, Milwaukee Public Library

U.S.A.M.P. *Gen. Edmund Kirby* (Coast Defenses of Portland)

Station—Milwaukee, WI, 1919–20; Fort Totten, NY, 1920–21; Army Supply Base, Brooklyn, NY, 1921; Fort Wood, NY, 1921

Built by Fabricated Shipbuilding Company and launched in 1919 at Milwaukee, WI. Named in honor of Brig. Gen. Edmund Kirby, U.S. Volunteers, who was mortally wounded at the Battle of Chancellorsville in May 1863. Assigned to the Middle Atlantic Coast Artillery District on 4 May 1920. Accepted for service by the Quartermaster Department on 22 June 1920. Departed Milwaukee on 5 September 1920 and arrived at Fort Totten, NY, on 11 October 1920. Caught fire the next day and suffered extensive damage to her superstructure. Typically docked at the 125th Street dock, New York City, NY. Further assigned to the Coast Defenses of Portland on 9 November 1920 but the *Kirby* never actually served at that location. Transferred on 26 January 1921 to the Army Supply Base, Brooklyn, NY. Transferred on 2 August 1921 to Fort Wood, NY. Decommissioned on 6 October 1921 at Fort Wood and transferred to the Lighthouse Service, Department of Commerce (and later to the U. S. Coast Guard as the U.S.C.G.T. *Ilex*, WAGL-222).

Status: Decommissioned from U.S.C.G. service; sold on 14 October 1947 to W.B. Fountain, Norfolk, VA; beached and burned in 1948.

Length: 172 ft. Beam: 32 ft. Draft: 17 ft. Displacement: 704 tons

Commanders, U.S.A.M.P. *Gen. Edmund Kirby*

1st Lt. Arthur F. Gilmore 22 June 1920–29 July 1920
Capt. Geoffrey Marshall 29 July 1920–April 1921
Capt. Ernest C. Bomar April 1921–6 October 1921

Military History Institute, Dunston Collection, Carlisle Barracks, PA

U.S.A.M.P. ***Gen. Henry Knox*** (Coast Defenses of Manila and Subic Bay)

Station—Fort Mills, PI, 1920–23

Built by Neafie and Levy Shipyard and launched on 5 March 1904 at Philadelphia, PA. Named in honor of Brigadier General Henry Knox, Revolutionary War hero and first U.S. Secretary of War. Accepted for service by the Quartermaster Department about June 1904. Stationed at Fort Mills, Corregidor, PI as of January 1920 and assigned to the Coast Defenses of Manila and Subic Bay. Typically docked at the North Dock at Corregidor. Decommissioned in March 1923 and personnel transferred to the U.S.A.M.P. *Gen. George F.E. Harrison*. Sold in 1924.

Status: Redesignated as the civilian *Vincent-Davin* in the 1920s and worked in French Indochina; dropped off the list of US Merchant Vessels in the late 1930s.

Length: 150 ft. Beam: 30.5 ft. Draft: 10 ft. Displacement: 447 tons

Commanders, U.S.A.M.P. ***Gen. Henry Knox***

Capt. Charles E. Loucks	ao January 1920–March 1921	1st Lt. Edwin P. Harts	April 1921–1 September 1921
Capt. G. D. Davidson	March 1921–April 1921	1st Lt. James E. Troupe	1 September 1921–6 December 1921
1st Lt. Lawrence W. Bartlett	6 December 1921–30 September 1922		

US Army Signal Corps, Casemate Museum, Fort Monroe, VA

U.S.A.M.P. *Gen. Samuel M. Mills* (Coast Defenses of Chesapeake Bay)

Station—Fort Monroe, VA, 1919–22

Built by New York Shipbuilding Company and launched on 13 February 1908 at Camden, NJ. Named in honor of Brigadier General Samuel Myers Mills, Chief of Artillery, 1905–06. Accepted for service by the Quartermaster Department on 19 May 1909 and assigned to the Coast Defenses of Chesapeake Bay. Stationed at Fort Monroe, VA, as of January 1919. Typically docked at the mine wharf at Fort Monroe. Decommissioned on 22 May 1922 and transferred to the US Coast Guard as the U.S.C.G. Cable Ship *Pequot*, WARC-58.

Status: Decommissioned from U.S.C.G. service and scrapped in 1947.

Length: 165 ft.	Beam: 32 ft.	Draft: 12 ft.	Displacement: 621 tons

Commanders, U.S.A.M.P. *Gen. Samuel M. Mills*

Maj. Edward S. Harrison	ao January 1920–13 September 1920	Maj. Edward N. Woodbury	13 September 1920–5 August 1921
Capt. Evans R. Crowell	15 August 1921–22 May 1922		

US Army Signal Corps, National Archives II

U.S.A.M.P. ***Lt. Col. Ellery W. Niles*** (Coast Defenses of San Francisco)

Station—Wilmington, DE, 1937–38**;** Fort Winfield Scott, CA, 1938–39; Fort Baker, CA, 1939–41

Built by Pusey and Jones Shipbuilding Company and launched on 22 July 1937 at Wilmington, DE. Named in honor of Lt. Col. Ellery W. Niles, a former mine planter commander and the chief of war plans in the Office of the Chief of Coast Artillery when he passed away in 1929. Accepted for service by the Quartermaster Corps in July 1937 and assigned to the Coast Defenses of San Francisco. Stationed at Fort Du Pont, DE, during outfitting and initial shakedown period. Departed Fort Du Pont in January 1938 en route for Fort Monroe, VA. Arrived back at Fort Du Pont via the Army Supply Base, Brooklyn, in March 1938. Departed Fort Du Pont in May 1938 en route for Fort Baker, CA, via the Panama Canal. Arrived at Fort Winfield Scott, CA, in June 1938. On arrival, additional personnel were transferred to the *Niles* from the decommissioned U.S.A.M.P. *Col. George Armistead*. Typically docked at the mine wharf at Fort Winfield Scott until 1939 when the *Niles* was moved to a new mine wharf built at Fort Baker across San Francisco Bay. On detached service to Fort Rosecrans, CA, in January 1939 to conduct training with the Harbor Defenses of San Diego and to Fort Amador, CZ, in June 1940 for mining operations with the Harbor Defenses of Balboa. In coordination with the U.S.A.M.P. Gen. *William M. Graham*, in June-August 1940 the *Niles* installed the wartime minefields that protected the Panama Canal Zone during World War II. Location 7 December 1941—Fort Baker, CA.

Status: Sold after World War II; redesignated as the civilian *F. V. Hunt* and served as an acoustical research ship in the Bahamas; operating as the *Cayman Salvage Master* in the Cayman Islands as of the mid-1980s.

Events: 235, 332

Length: 185 ft.	Beam: 35 ft.	Draft: 15 ft.	Displacement: 840 tons

Commanders, U.S.A.M.P. ***Lt. Col. Ellery W. Niles***

Capt. Rodney C. Jones	1 May 1937–7 July 1937	Maj. Samuel Rubin	31 August 1937–ao August 1940

US Army Signal Corps, National Archives II

U.S.A.M.P. ***Gen. Edward O. C. Ord*** (Coast Defenses of Sandy Hook)

Station—Fort Totten, NY, 1919–22; Army Supply Base, Brooklyn, NY, 1922–27; Fort Hancock, NJ, 1927–41

Built by Pusey and Jones Shipbuilding Company and launched on 13 February 1909 at Wilmington, DE. Named in honor of Maj. Gen. Edward Otho Cresap Ord, commanding officer of the XIII, VIII, and XVIII Corps during the Civil War. Accepted for service by the Quartermaster Department in June 1909. Stationed at Fort Totten, NY, as of January 1919. Assigned to the Coast Defenses of Eastern New York on 9 November 1920. Relieved from the Coast Defenses of Eastern New York in March 1922 and assigned to the Coast Defenses of Sandy Hook. Typically docked at the Army Supply Base in Brooklyn, NY. Transferred in July 1927 to Fort Hancock, NJ. On detached service to Fort Monroe, VA, from December 1936 to 13 March 1937 to conduct training with the Harbor Defenses of Chesapeake Bay. Awarded "E" for mine planting efficiency in 1937. Location 7 December 1941—Fort Hancock, NJ.

Status: Sold after World War II and scrapped in 1946.

Events: 77, 87, 115, 321

Length: 165 ft.	Beam: 32 ft.	Draft: 17 ft.	Displacement: 590 tons

Commanders, U.S.A.M.P. ***Gen. Edward O. C. Ord***

1st Lt. Arthur F. Gilmore	ao January 1920–May 1920
Capt. Lawrence Iverson	May 1920–24 August 1922
Capt. Alexander H. Campbell	24 August 1922–28 October 1922
Capt. Albert C. Cleveland	28 October 1922–1 December 1922
Capt. Alexander H. Campbell	1 December 1922–23 April 1924
2d Lt. Albert C. Kleinman	23 April 1924–1 July 1924
1st Lt. James F. Pichel	1July 1924–October 1925
Capt. Geoffrey C. Bunting	October 1925–September 1926
Capt. Coleman F. Driver	September 1926–June 1927
2d Lt. Richard E. O'Conner	June 1927–7 March 1929
1st Lt. John H. Fonvielle	8 March 1929–24 August 1929
1st Lt. Sanford J. Goodman	25 August 1929–10 September 1931
1st Lt. James B. Carroll	10 September 1931–8 March 1933
1st Lt. Samuel Rubin	8 March 1933–22 May 1934
Capt. William C. McFadden	22 May 1934–15 August 1934
Capt. Charles M. Wolff	16 August 1934–30 June 1938
Capt. Harold P. Tasker	30 June 1938–8 May 1939
Capt. Ernest F. Heidland	8 May 1939–10 October 1941

US Coast Guard Historian's Office, Washington, DC

U.S.A.M.P. ***Gen. Wallace F. Randolph*** (Coast Defenses of Chesapeake Bay)

Station—Milwaukee, WI, 1919–20; Fort Totten, NY, 1920–21; Fort Monroe, VA, 1920–21

Built by Fabricated Shipbuilding Company and launched in 1919 at Milwaukee, WI. Named in honor of Brig. Gen. Wallace F. Randolph, veteran of the Civil War and the Chief of Artillery, 1903–04. Assigned to the Coast Artillery Training Center on 4 May 1920. Accepted for service by the Quartermaster Corps in June 1920. Departed Milwaukee in September 1920 and arrived at Fort Totten, NY, in October 1920. Further assigned to the Coast Defenses of Chesapeake Bay on 9 November 1920. Departed the Army Supply Base, Brooklyn, NY, on 24 February 1921 and arrived at Fort Monroe, VA, on 25 February 1921. Typically docked at the mine wharf at Fort Monroe. Made numerous voyages to Fort Howard, MD, Fort Washington, MD, and Newport News, VA, between April and August 1921. Decommissioned on 16 October 1921 and transferred to the Lighthouse Service, Department of Commerce (and later to the US Coast Guard as the U.S.C.G.T. *Lupine*, WAGL-230 in January 1942).

Status: Decommissioned from U.S.C.G. service; sold 8 December 1947 to the Oakland Manufacturing Company, Oakland, CA; serving as a survey vessel in the Philippines as of the 1980s.

Length: 172 ft.	Beam: 32 ft.	Draft: 17 ft.	Displacement: 704 tons

Commanders, U.S.A.M.P. ***Gen. Wallace F. Randolph***

1st Lt. Arthur F. Gilmore	June 1920–15 June 1921	Capt. Evans R. Crowell	15 June 1921–16 October 1921

Courtesy of Steve Kobylk, Coupeville, WA

U.S.A.M.P. *Maj. Samuel Ringgold* (Coast Defenses of Puget Sound)

Station—Fort Worden, WA, 1919–22

Built by Neafie and Levy Shipyard and launched on 30 April 1904 at Philadelphia, PA. Named in honor of Maj. Samuel Ringgold, 3d U.S. Artillery, who was mortally wounded at the Battle of Palo Alto on 11 May 1846. Accepted for service by the Quartermaster Department about July 1904. Stationed at Fort Worden, WA, as of January 1919 and assigned to the Coast Defenses of Puget Sound. Decommissioned on 3 August 1922.

Status: Sold 16 May 1923 at Port Townsend, WA, to Shipowners and Merchants Tugboat Company of San Francisco and renamed the *Sea Salvor*; dropped off the list of US Merchant Vessels after 1947.

Length: 150 ft. Beam: 30.5 ft. Draft: 10 ft. Displacement: 447 tons

Commanders, U.S.A.M.P. *Maj. Samuel Ringgold*

Capt. Joseph F. Stiley	ao January 1920–15 May 1922	1st Lt. Dean R. Dickey	15 May 1922–3 August 1922

US Army Signal Corps-National Archives II, RG 92

U.S.A.M.P. ***Gen. John M. Schofield*** (Coast Defenses of Chesapeake Bay)

Station—Fort Monroe, VA, 1920–21; Fort Moultrie, SC, 1921; Fort Monroe, VA, 1921–41

Built by New York Shipbuilding Company and launched on 20 February 1909 at Camden, NJ. Named in honor of Lt. Gen. John M. Schofield, commanding general, U.S. Army 1888–95. Accepted for service by the Quartermaster Department on 2 June 1909. Stationed at Fort Monroe, VA, as of January 1919 and attached to the Coast Artillery School. Assigned to the South Atlantic Coast Artillery District on 4 May 1920. On detached service at Portsmouth, NH, and Jersey City, NJ, in May and June 1920. Further assigned to the Coast Defenses of Charleston on 9 November 1920. Departed for station at Fort Moultrie, SC, on 16 March 1921 and arrived there later that month. On detached service to Key West Barracks, FL, and Fort Barrancas, FL, in July 1921. Relieved from assignment to the Coast Defenses of Charleston on 13 August 1921 and assigned to the Coast Defenses of Chesapeake Bay. Departed Fort Barrancas on 28 August 1921 and arrived at Fort Monroe on 15 September 1921. Personnel assigned to Headquarters Battery, 12th Coast Artillery Regiment on 30 June 1924. Personnel relieved from Headquarters Battery, 12th Coast Artillery on 21 July 1926. Awarded "E" for mine planting efficiency in 1937. Supported activities associated with the visit of President Roosevelt to Fort Monroe on 29 July 1940. The *Schofield* supported the training of the Coast Artillery School and the Coast Defenses of Chesapeake Bay from 1921 until the beginning of World War II. Location 7 December 1941—Fort Monroe, VA.

Status: Inactivated and departed U. S. Army service 18 May 1949.

Events: 25, 73

Length: 165 ft.	Beam: 32 ft.	Draft: 15 ft.	Displacement: 621 tons

Commanders, U.S.A.M.P. ***Gen. John M. Schofield***

Capt. Henry F. Grimm	ao January 1920–February 1920	1st Lt. John O. Kelly	17 June 1926–21 July 1927
Capt. Clarence W. Putnam	February 1920–17 April 1920	1st Lt. Robert H. Kreuter	22 July 1927–1 August 1929
Maj. Roy S. Atwood	17 April 1920–ao November 1921	1st Lt. Charles M. Wolff	2 August 1929–5 September 1930
Capt. Evans R. Crowell	May 1922–31 August 1922	1st Lt. Will K. Stennis	6 September 1931–4 November 1931
1st Lt. Lee A. Denson Jr.	31 August 1922–June 1923	2d Lt. John H. Kochevar	5 November 1931–23 August 1932
2d Lt. Harold J. Conway	July 1923–7 November 1923	2d Lt. August W. Schermacher	24 August 1932–5 January 1934
Capt. William Sackville	7 November 1923–12 September 1924	Capt. Arthur L. Fuller	5 January 1934–30 June 1935
2d Lt. John D. Mitchell	12 September 1924–30 June 1925	1st Lt. Allison R. Hartman	1 July 1935–1 March 1937
1st Lt. William E. Griffin	30 June 1925–4 May 1926	1st Lt. William F. Spurgin	1 March 1937–31 July 1937
2d Lt. Herbert T. Benz	4 May 1926–17 June 1926	Capt. William B. Hawthorne	31 July 1937–September 1940

Great Lakes Marine Collection, Milwaukee Public Library

U.S.A.M.P. ***Gen. John P. Story*** (Coast Defenses of Pensacola)

Station—Milwaukee, WI, 1919–20; Army Supply Base, Brooklyn, NY, 1920–21; Fort Totten, NY, 1921; Fort Monroe, VA, 1921

Built by Fabricated Shipbuilding Company and launched 15 September 1919 at Milwaukee, WI. Named in honor of Maj. Gen. John Patten Story, Chief of Artillery, 1904–05. Accepted for service by the Quartermaster Corps in early 1920 and assigned to the Coast Defenses of Pensacola, but the *Story* never actually served at that location. Stationed at Milwaukee, WI, as of January 1920. Transferred in November 1920 to the Army Supply Base, Brooklyn, NY. Transferred in April 1921 to Fort Totten, NY. Transferred in August 1921 to Fort Monroe, VA. Decommissioned on 10 November 1921. Transferred on 14 April 1927 to the Lighthouse Service, Department of Commerce (and later to the US Coast Guard as the U.S.C.G.T *Acacia*, WAGL-200).

Status: Sunk by the U-*161* in the Caribbean Sea 15 March 1942.

Length: 172 ft. Beam: 32 ft. Draft: 17 ft. Displacement: 704 tons

Commanders, U.S.A.M.P. ***Gen. John P. Story***

Capt. John R. Ellis	ao January 1920–19 June 1920
Capt. Carl S. Dorey	30 June 1920–8 August 1920
Maj. Belton O. Kennedy	8 August 1920–October 1920
Capt. Carl S. Dorey	October 1920–8 December 1920
Capt. Coburn L. Berry	8 December 1920–10 November 1921

US Army Signal Corps, National Archives II

U.S.A.M.P. *Col. Albert Todd* (Coast Defenses of Puget Sound)

Station—Milwaukee, WI, 1920; Army Supply Base, Brooklyn, NY, 1920–21; Fort Totten, NY, 1921; Fort Wood, NY, 1921

Built by Fabricated Shipbuilding Company and launched in 1920 at Milwaukee, WI. Named in honor of Col. Albert Todd, a distinguished artilleryman and commander of the Eastern Artillery District 1910–11. Assigned to the North Pacific Coast Artillery District on 4 May 1920. Accepted for service by the Quartermaster Corps on 20 September 1920. Departed Milwaukee in October 1920 and arrived at the Army Supply Base, Brooklyn, NY, in November 1920. Further assigned to the Coast Defenses of Puget Sound on 9 November 1920 but the *Todd* never actually served at that location. Typically docked at Pier #6 at Hoboken, NJ. Transferred in April 1921 to Fort Totten, NY. Transferred in September 1921 to Fort Wood, NY. Decommissioned on 6 October 1921 at Fort Wood, NY, and transferred to the Lighthouse Service, Department of Commerce (and later to the U. S. Coast Guard as the U.S.C.G.T. *Lotus*, WAGL-229 in July 1941).

Status: Decommissioned from U.S.C.G. service; sold 11 June 1947 to A.F. Peavy, Minneapolis, MN; subsequently scrapped.

Length: 172 ft. Beam: 32 ft. Draft: 17 ft. Displacement: 704 tons

Commanders, U.S.A.M.P. *Col. Albert Todd*

Capt. Edward E. Murphy	20 September 1920–8 October 1921

US Army Signal Corps, National Archives II

U.S.A.M.P. *Col. Garland N. Whistler* (Coast Defenses of Oahu)

Station—Milwaukee, WI, 1920; Fort Totten, NY, 1920; Army Supply Base, Brooklyn, NY, 1920–21; Fort Hancock, NJ, 1921; Fort Wood, NY, 1921

Built by Fabricated Shipbuilding Company and launched in 1920 at Milwaukee, WI. Named in honor of Col. Garland Nelson Whistler, a distinguished artilleryman who served forty years on active duty. Assigned to the South Pacific Coast Artillery District on 4 May 1920. Accepted for service by the Quartermaster Corps on 7 September 1920. Departed Milwaukee in mid-October 1920 and arrived Fort Totten, NY, on 14 November 1920. Further assigned to the Coast Defenses of Oahu on 9 November 1920 but the *Whistler* never actually served at that location. Transferred on 20 November 1920 to the Army Supply Base, Brooklyn, NY. Typically docked at Pier #5 at Hoboken, NJ. Transferred on 11 May 1921 to Fort Hancock, NJ. Decommissioned on 22 September 1921 at Fort Wood, NY, and transferred to the Lighthouse Service, Department of Commerce (and later to the U. S. Coast Guard as the U.S.C.G.T. *Spruce*, WAGL-246).

Status: Decommissioned from U.S.C.G. service and listed as surplus 2 July 1946; transferred to the U. S. Coast and Geodetic Survey in 1947; no further record.

Length: 172 ft. Beam: 32 ft. Draft: 17 ft. Displacement: 704 tons

Commanders, U.S.A.M.P. *Col. Garland N. Whistler*

Capt. Carl S. Doney 7 September 1920–20 November 1920 Capt. Phillip S. Day 20 December 1920–22 September 1921

US Coast Guard Historian's Office, Washington, DC

U.S.A.M.P. *Col. John V. White* (Coast Defenses of Narragansett Bay)

Station—Milwaukee, WI, 1920; Army Supply Base, Brooklyn, NY, 1920–21; Fort Adams, RI, 1921

Built by Fabricated Shipbuilding Company and launched in 1920 at Milwaukee, WI. Named in honor of Col. John V. White, a distinguished artilleryman and commander of multiple coast artillery districts. Assigned to the North Atlantic Coast Artillery District on 4 May 1920. Accepted for service by the Quartermaster Corps on 22 October 1920. The crew was composed of personnel transferred from the U.S.A.M.P. *Col. George F. E. Harrison*. Departed Milwaukee on 3 November 1920 and arrived at the Army Supply Base, Brooklyn, NY, on 26 November 1920. Further assigned to the Coast Defenses of Narragansett Bay on 9 November 1920. Transferred on 2 January 1921 to Fort Adams, RI. Decommissioned on 19 October 1921 at Fort Adams and transferred to the Lighthouse Service, Department of Commerce on 23 April 1923 (and later to the US Coast Guard as the U.S.C.G.T. *Speedwell*, WAGL-245).

Status: Decommissioned from U.S.C.G. service and transferred to the U. S. Maritime Commission; sold on 30 December 1947 to the Caribbean Fruit and Steamship Company, Jacksonville, FL; no further record.

Length: 172 ft. Beam: 32 ft. Draft: 17 ft. Displacement: 704 tons

Commanders, U.S.A.M.P. *Col. John V. White*

Lt. Col. Harrison S. Kerrick	November 1920–3 December 1920	2d Lt. Ola A. Nelson	6 February 1921–18 April 1921
1st Lt. Lewis A. Hudgins	6 December 1920–16 February 1921	Unknown	19 April 1921–19 October 1921.

Mariner's Museum, Newport News, VA

U.S.A.J.M.P. *Gen. Robert Anderson* (Coast Defenses of Boston)

Station—Boston, MA, 1919-30; Fort Barrancas, FL, 1930-41

Built by Fore River Shipbuilding Company and launched in 1908 at Quincy, MA. Accepted for service by the Quartermaster Department on 25 January 1909. Named in honor of Maj. Gen. Robert Anderson, commanding officer during the defense of Fort Sumter, SC, on 12 April 1861. Stationed at Fort Banks, MA, as of January 1919 and assigned to the Coast Defenses of Boston. Functioned in the Harbor Boat Service as a freight and passenger craft 1919-30 at Boston Harbor. Reconditioned in 1930 to function as a junior mine planter and transferred to Fort Barrancas, FL. Concurrently relieved from the Harbor Defenses of Boston and assigned to the Harbor Defenses of Pensacola. Location 7 Dec 41—Fort Barrancas, FL.

Events: 59

Status: Unknown

Length: 98 ft. Beam: 22 ft. Draft: 11 ft. Displacement: 153 tons

Courtesy of Walter K. Schroeder and Arcadia Publishing, Mount Pleasant, SC

U.S.A.J.M.P. *Gen. Richard Arnold* (Coast Defenses of Narragansett Bay)

Station—Fort Adams, RI, 1919-29; Fort H.G. Wright, NY, 1929-41; Fort Constitution, NH, 1941

Built by Fore River Shipbuilding Company and launched in 1908 at Quincy, MA. Accepted for service by the Quartermaster Department on 9 February 1909. Named in honor of Maj. Gen. Richard Arnold, Chief of Artillery for the Military Division of the West Mississippi during the siege of Fort Morgan, AL, in August 1864. Stationed at Fort Adams, RI, as of January 1919 and assigned to the Coast Defenses of Narragansett Bay. Transferred to Fort H.G. Wright, NY, in 1929 and assigned to the Harbor Defenses of Long Island Sound. Transferred to Fort Constitution, NH, in 1931 and assigned to the Harbor Defenses of Portsmouth. Functioned in the Harbor Boat Service as a freight and passenger craft 1919-41. Reconditioned in 1941 to function as a junior mine planter in the Harbor Defenses of Portsmouth. Location 7 Dec 41—Portsmouth, NH.

Status: Capsized in a gale on 8 January 1942 off the Isle of Shoals, near Portsmouth, NH.

Length: 98 ft. Beam: 22 ft. Draft: 11 ft. Displacement: 153 tons

Quartermaster Review

U.S.A.J.M.P. *Gen. Romeyn B. Ayres* (Coast Defenses of Long Island Sound)

Station—Fort Trumbull, CT, 1908-22

Built by Fore River Shipbuilding Company and launched in 1908 at Quincy, MA. Accepted for service by the Quartermaster Department on 9 February 1909. Named in honor of Maj. Gen. Romeyn B. Ayres, commanding officer of the Regular Division, V Corps during the Civil War. Stationed at Fort Trumbull, CT, as of January 1919 and assigned to the Harbor Defenses of Long Island Sound. Transferred in January 1922 to the Lighthouse Service, Department of Commerce, as the U.S.L.H.T. *Pyxie*. The *Ayres* was determined to be unsuitable for the lighthouse service and returned to Army control in 1923. The boat was presumably sold shortly thereafter.

Status: Unknown

Length: 98 ft. Beam: 22 ft. Draft: 11 ft. Displacement: 153 tons

US Army Signal Corps, Corps of Engineers History Office

U.S.A.J.M.P. *Capt. Gregory Barrett* (Coast Defenses of San Francisco)

Station—Fort Winfield Scott, CA, 1919-31

Built by Willamette Iron and Steele Works and launched 22 May 1909 at Portland, OR. Accepted for service by the Quartermaster Department 15 August 1909. Named in honor of Capt. Gregory Barrett. Stationed at Fort Winfield Scott, CA, as of January 1919 and assigned to the Harbor Defenses of San Francisco. Functioned as a mine planter service training ship at Fort Winfield Scott 1919-31. Sold in 1931

Status: Unknown

Length: 87 ft. Beam: 22 ft. Draft: 10 ft. Displacement: 159 tons

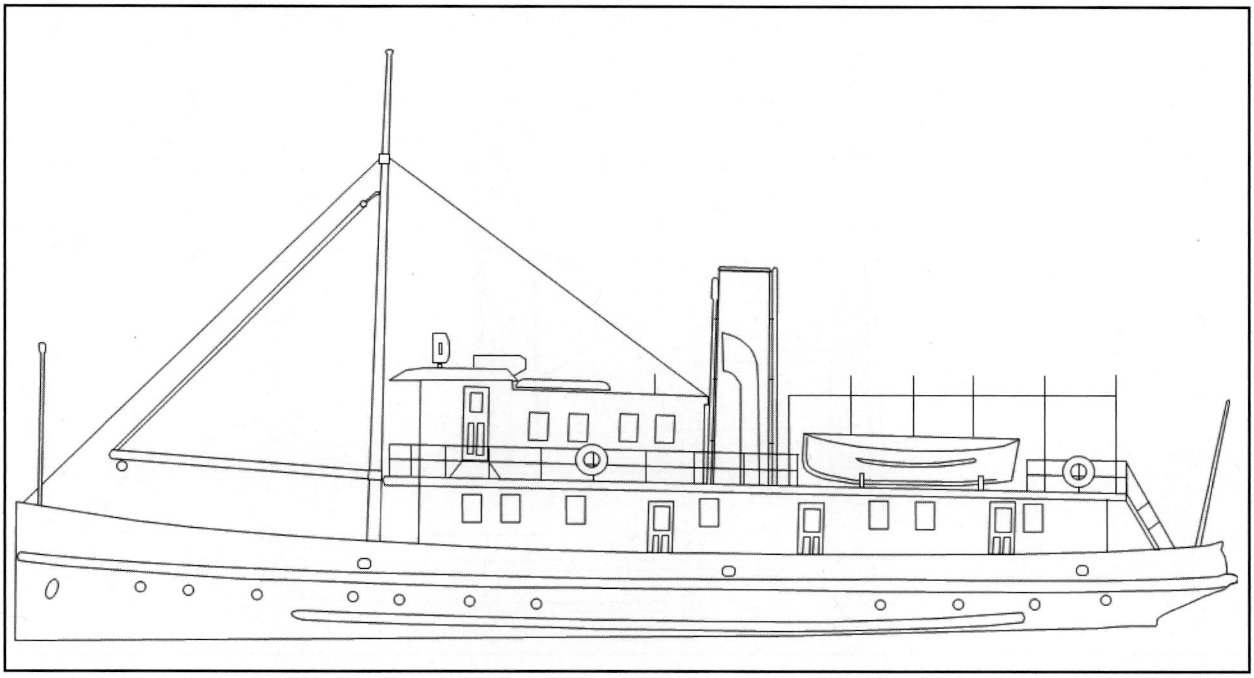

U.S.A.J.M.P. ***Gen. John M. Brannan*** (Coast Defenses of Charleston)

Station—Fort Moultrie, SC, 1909-22

Built by Fore River Shipbuilding Company and launched on 20 November 1908 at Quincy, MA. Accepted for service by the Quartermaster Department on 13 February 1909. Named in honor of Maj. Gen. John M. Brannan, commanding officer of 3rd Division, XIV Corps during the battle of Chickamauga, 1863. Stationed at Fort Moultrie, SC, as of January 1919 and assigned to the Coast Defenses of Charleston. Transferred in 1922 to the Corps of Engineers at Savannah Harbor where it functioned as a harbor tug in the Savannah Engineer District.

Status: Sank at pierside in Baltimore, MD, in 1979 as the tug *Charles H. Harper*; towed to Curtis Creek and abandoned.

Length: 98 ft. Beam: 22 ft. Draft: 11 ft. Displacement: 153 tons

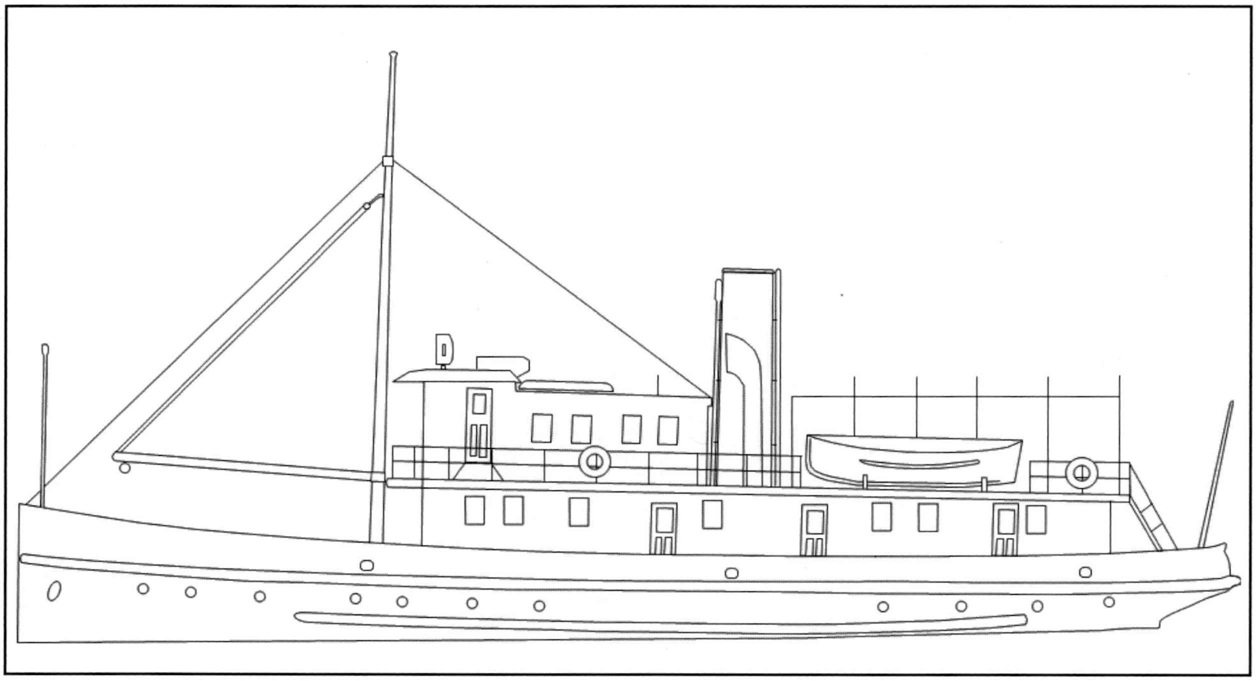

U.S.A.J.M.P. ***Gen. Harvey Brown*** (Coast Defenses of Sandy Hook)

Station—Fort Hancock, NJ, 1919-22

Built by Fore River Shipbuilding Company and launched on 24 December 1908 at Quincy, MA. Accepted for service by the Quartermaster Department on 20 February 1909. Named in honor of Maj. Gen. Harvey Brown, commanding officer of troops during the New York draft riots in 1863. Stationed at Fort Hancock, NJ, as of January 1919 and assigned to the Coast Defenses of Sandy Hook. Sold on 15 February 1922 at Port Newark, NJ, to the city of Norfolk, VA, and renamed as the S.S. *Vulcan*.

Status: Acquired by the Mathew Lewis Maritime Company about 1943 and renamed *Vivian Powell*; still in operation as of 1965.

Length: 98 ft.	Beam: 22 ft.	Draft: 11 ft.	Displacement: 153 tons

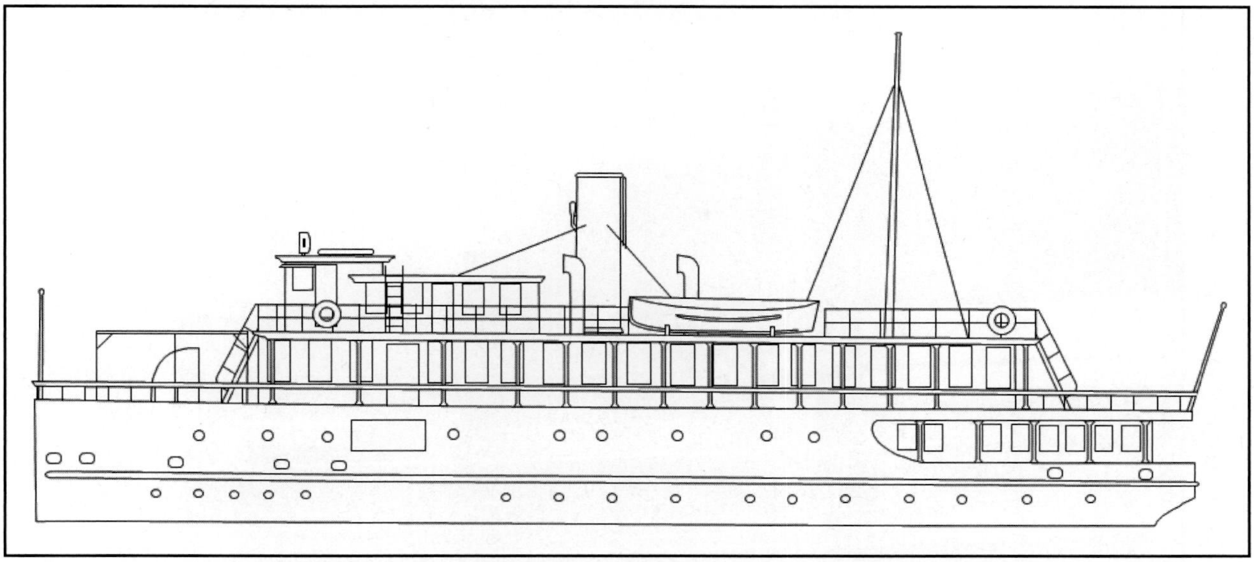

U.S.A.J.M.P. *Col. Card* (Coast Defenses of Portland)

Station—Milwaukee, WI, 1920; Quebec, Canada, 1920-21; Portland, ME, 1921-23; Fort Sherman, CZ, 1940-41

Built by Fabricated Shipbuilding Company and launched on 15 July 1920 at Milwaukee, WI. Accepted for service by the Quartermaster Corps about September 1920 and assigned to the Coast Defenses of Portland. Named in honor of Col. Benjamin C. Card, Q.M.C., brevet brigadier general, for service during the Civil War. Moored at the Louise Docks, Quebec, Canada, from November 1920 to July 1921 while en route to the east coast. Functioned in the Harbor Boat Service as a freight and passenger craft at Portland, ME. Typically docked at Fort Williams, ME. Sold to the state of Michigan in October 1923 at Fort Williams and renamed the *Mackinaw City*. Reacquired by the US Army in 1940 and renamed as the *Brig. Gen. William E. Horton*. Stationed at Fort Sherman, CZ, and assigned to the Harbor Defenses of Cristobal. Location 7 Dec 41—Fort Sherman, CZ.

Status: Wrecked 25 November 1950 at Raritan Bay, Keyport, NJ; scrapped in June 1952.

Length: 123 ft. Beam: 28 ft. Draft: 12 ft. Displacement: 535 tons

Bowling Green State University, Historical Collection Of The Great Lakes

U.S.A.J.M.P. ***Capt. Samuel C. Cardwell*** (Coast Defenses of Boston)

Station—Boston, MA, 1919-23

Built by Rocky River Dry Dock Company and launched in 1919 at Rocky River, OH. Accepted for service by the U.S. Army Quartermaster Corps in 1920 and assigned to the Coast Defenses of Boston. Named in honor of Capt. Samuel C. Cardwell, C.A.C. Functioned in the Harbor Boat Service as a freight and passenger craft at Boston Harbor. Transferred in 1923 to the Public Health Service, US Treasury Department at Boston, MA, and converted into a boarding and fumigation vessel.

Status: Scrapped in 1934.

Length: 98 ft. Beam: 23 ft. Draft: 11 ft. Displacement: 177 tons

Great Lakes Marine Collection, Milwaukee Public Library

U.S.A.J.M.P. ***Col. Clayton*** (Coast Defenses of Southern New York)

Station—Milwaukee, WI, 1920; Quebec, Canada 1920-21; Army Supply Base Brooklyn, NY, 1921-23

Built by Fabricated Shipbuilding Company and launched in 1919 at Milwaukee, WI. Accepted for service by the U.S. Army Quartermaster Corps about September 1920 and assigned to the Coast Defenses of Southern New York. Named in honor of Col. Bertram B. Clayton, Q.M.C., who was killed in action in France in May 1918. Moored at the Louise Docks, Quebec, Canada, from November 1920 to July 1921 en route to the east coast. Arrived in September 1921 at Army Supply Base Brooklyn, NY. Served as a junior mine planter and in the Harbor Boat Service at Army Base Brooklyn, NY. Sold to the city of New York in 1923 to be used as ferryboat in New York Harbor.

Status: Scrapped in 1954.

Length: 123 ft. Beam: 28 ft. Draft: 12 ft. Displacement: 535 tons

US National Park Service, Gulf Islands National Seashore

U.S.A.J.M.P. *Maj. Clarence M. Condon* (Coast Defenses of Narragansett Bay)

Station—Fort Adams, RI, 1921-29; Fort H.G. Wright, NY, 1929-31; Fort Barrancas, FL, 1931-41; Fort Amador, CZ, 1941

Built by Defoe Shipbuilding Company and launched in 1919 at Bay City MI. Accepted for service by the Quartermaster Corps on 30 June 1921. Named in honor of Maj. Clarence M. Condon, who was awarded the Medal of Honor for gallantry in action in the Philippines in 1899. Stationed at Fort Adams, RI, and assigned to the Coast Defenses of Narragansett Bay. Transferred to Fort H.G. Wright, NY, in 1929 and assigned to the Harbor Defenses of Long Island Sound. Transferred to Fort Barrancas, FL, in 1931 and assigned to the Harbor Defenses of Pensacola. Functioned in the Harbor Boat Service as a freight and passenger craft 1931-41 at Pensacola Harbor. Reconditioned as a junior mine planter in 1941, transferred to the Panama Canal Department, and assigned to the Panama Coast Artillery Command. Location 7 Dec 41—Fort Amador, CZ.
Status: Unknown

Length: 98 ft. Beam: 22 ft. Draft: 12 ft. Displacement: 170 tons

Bowling Green State University, OH, Historical Collection Of The Great Lakes

U.S.A.J.M.P. ***Lt. Harold B. Douglas*** (Coast Defenses of Puget Sound)

Station—Fort Casey, WA, 1921-24

Built by Defoe Shipbuilding Company and launched in 1920 at Bay City MI. Accepted for service by the Quartermaster Corps on 30 June 1921. Named in honor of Lt. Harold B. Douglas. Stationed at Fort Casey, WA, and assigned to the Coast Defenses of Puget Sound. Functioned in the Harbor Boat Service as a freight and passenger craft in Seattle Harbor. Sold in 1924 to the Cary-Davis Tug and Barge Company of Seattle, WA.

Status: Abandoned in 1956 and presumed scrapped; still functioning as the tug *Douglas* in San Francisco as of 1966.

Length: 101ft. Beam: 22 ft. Draft: 12 ft. Displacement: 177 tons

US Army Signal Corps, Military History Institute, Carlisle Barracks, PA

U.S.A.J.M.P. ***Capt. Joseph Fornance***

Station—Fort Seward, TA, 1919-30; Chilkoot Barracks, TA, 1930-41

Built by Willamette Iron and Steele Works and launched 22 May 1909 at Portland, OR. Accepted for service by the Quartermaster Department in June 1909. Named in honor of Capt. Joseph Fornance, 13th Infantry, who was killed in action in the charge up San Juan Hill, 1 July 1898. Stationed at Fort Seward, TA, as of January 1919. Functioned in the Harbor Boat Service as a tug and as a freight and passenger craft in Alaskan waters 1919-41. Location 7 Dec 41—Chilkoot Barracks, TA.

Status: Unknown.

Length: 98 ft. Beam: 22 ft. Draft: 11.3 ft. Displacement: 164 tons

Mariner's Museum, Newport News, VA

U.S.A.J.M.P. ***Major Albert G. Forse*** (Coast Defenses of Cristobal)

Station—Fort Sherman, CZ, 1919-22

Built by Pusey and Jones Shipbuilding Company and launched in March 1907 at Wilmington, DE. Named in honor of Maj. Albert G. Forse, 1st Cavalry, who was killed 1 July 1898 at San Juan Hill, Cuba. Accepted by the Quartermaster Department in April 1907. Stationed at Fort Sherman, CZ, as of January 1919 and assigned to the Coast Defenses of Cristobal. Functioned in the Harbor Boat Service as an artillery tug and passenger craft 1919–22. Sold in 1922.

Status: Unknown.

Length: 80 ft.	Beam: 20 ft.	Draft: 10 ft.	Displacement: 128 tons

US Army Signal Corps, Military Institute, Carlisle Barracks, PA

U.S.A.J.M.P. *Gen. G. W. Getty* (Coast Defenses of Cristobal)

Station—Fort Sherman, CZ, 1919-36

Built by Fore River Shipbuilding Company and launched in 1908 at Quincy, MA. Accepted for service by the Quartermaster Department 1 March 1909. Named in honor of Maj. Gen. George Washington Getty, commanding officer of the 2nd Division, VI Corps during the Battle of the Wilderness in 1864. Stationed at Fort Sherman, CZ, as of January 1919 and assigned to the Coast Defenses of Cristobal. Functioned in the Harbor Boat Service as a freight and passenger craft 1919-36 in the Canal Zone.

Status: Unknown.

Length: 89 ft.	Beam: 22 ft.	Draft: 11 ft.	Displacement: 163 tons

U.S.A.J.M.P. ***Lt. Col. Robert C. Gildart***

Station—Unknown 1920-22

Built by Defoe Shipbuilding Company and launched in 1920 at Bay City MI. Accepted for service by the U.S. Army Quartermaster Corps on 30 June 1921. Named in honor of Lt. Col. Robert C. Gildart. Functioned in the Harbor Boat Service as a freight and passenger craft 1921–22. Sold in 1922.

Status: Unknown.

Length: 101 ft. Beam: 22 ft. Draft: 12 ft. Displacement: 177 tons

US Army Signal Corps, Casemate Museum, Fort Monroe, VA

U.S.A.J.M.P. ***Lt. George M. Harris*** (Coast Defenses of San Diego)

Station—Fort Rosecrans, CA, 1919-23

Built by Puget Sound Engineering Works and launched in July 1905 at Seattle, WA. Accepted for service by the U.S. Army Quartermaster Corps 22 September 1905. Named in honor of Lt. George M. Harris, 4th Artillery, who mortally wounded in a battle with Modoc Indians on 26 Apr 1873 at the Lava Beds, CA.. Stationed at Fort Rosecrans, CA, as of January 1919 and assigned to the Coast Defenses of San Diego. Functioned in the Harbor Boat Service primarily as a tug, but also as a freight and passenger craft at San Diego harbor. Sold in March 1923 to the Foss Maritime Company of Seattle, WA, and renamed as the tug *Andrew Foss*.

Status: Collided with the tug *Macloufay* on 4 August 1951 and sank.

Length: 105 ft. Beam: 22 ft. Draft: 10 ft. Displacement: 120 tons

US Army Signal Corps, Military History Institute, Carlisle Barracks, PA

U.S.A.J.M.P. ***Maj. Albert G. Jenkins*** (Harbor Defenses of Pensacola)

Station—Fort Barrancas, FL, 1920-41

Built by Defoe Shipbuilding Company and launched in 1920 at Bay City MI. Accepted for service by the Quartermaster Corps on 30 June 1921. Named in honor of Maj. Albert G. Jenkins. Stationed at Fort Barrancas, FL, and assigned to the Coast Defenses of Pensacola. Functioned in the Harbor Boat Service as a freight and passenger craft at Pensacola 1919-41. Damaged in a hurricane at Fort Barrancas, FL, in 1927. Underwent an extensive overhaul in 1932. Location 7 Dec 41—Fort Barrancas, FL.

Status: Decommissioned from U.S. Army service in 1951 and sold to the Oil Transport Company, New Orleans, LA. Foundered off Staten Island, NY, in 1972.

Length: 98.5 ft. Beam: 22 ft. Draft: 12 ft. Displacement: 170 tons

U.S.A.J.M.P. ***Maj. Carl A. Lohr***

Station—Army Base, Brooklyn, NY, 1921-22

Built by Defoe Shipbuilding Company and launched in 1920 at Bay City MI. Accepted for service by the U.S. Army Quartermaster Corps on 30 June 1921. Named in honor of Maj. Carl A. Lohr. Arrived at New York Harbor about August 1921. Assigned to the Coast Defenses of New Orleans. Transferred to New Orleans, LA, in April 1922 Functioned in the Harbor Boat Service as a freight and passenger craft 1921–22. Sold in late 1922 at New Orleans.

Status: Unknown.

Length: 101 ft.	Beam: 22 ft.	Draft: 12 ft.	Displacement: 177 tons

Bowling Green State University, OH, Historical Collection Of The Great Lakes

U.S.A.J.M.P. *Capt. Edwin C. Long* (Coast Defenses of Key West)

Station—Fort Taylor, FL, 1919-22

Built by Rocky River Dry Dock Company and launched in 1919 at Rocky River, OH. Accepted for service by the U.S. Army Quartermaster Corps in 1919. Named in honor of Capt. Edwin C. Long. Stationed at Fort Taylor, FL, and assigned to the Coast Defenses of Key West. Functioned in the Harbor Boat Service as a freight and passenger craft at Key West, FL, 1919–22. Transferred in January 1922 to the Lighthouse Service, Department of Commerce, as the U.S.L.H.T. *Sundew*.

Status: Decommissioned from the U.S.C.G. in 1939 and sold in 1941; scrapped in 1959.

Length: 101 ft. Beam: 22 ft. Draft: 12 ft. Displacement: 177 tons

Bowling Green State University, OH, Historical Collection Of The Great Lakes

U.S.A.J.M.P. ***Capt. John W. McKie*** (Coast Defenses of Mobile)

Station—Fort Morgan, AL, 1921–32

Built by Defoe Shipbuilding Company and launched in 1920 at Bay City MI. Accepted for service by the U.S. Army Quartermaster Corps on 30 June 1921. Named in honor of Capt. John W. McKie, Assistant to the Superintendent, Army Transport Service. Stationed at Fort Morgan, AL, and assigned to the Coast Defenses of Mobile. Functioned in the Harbor Boat Service as a freight and passenger craft at Mobile Bay 1921–32. Sold in 1932 to the Inland Waterways Corporation of Mobile, AL

Status: Abandoned in near Mobile in 1940 and presumed scrapped.

Length: 98.5 ft. Beam: 22 ft. Draft: 12 ft. Displacement: 170 tons

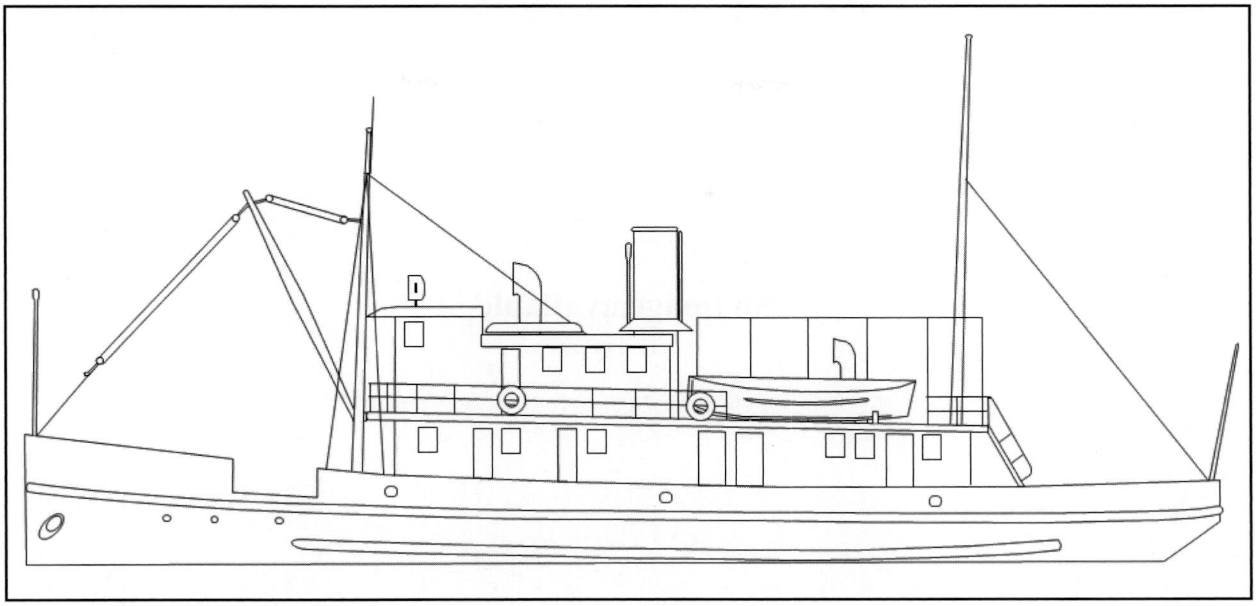

U.S.A.J.M.P. ***Maj. Lester M. Moreton***

Station—Army Base, Brooklyn, NY, 1921-22

Built by Defoe Shipbuilding Company and launched in 1919 at Bay City MI. Accepted for service by the U.S. Army Quartermaster Corps on 30 June 1921. Named in honor of Maj. Lester M. Moreton. Functioned in the Harbor Boat Service as a freight and passenger craft 1921–22. Transferred in 1922 to the USPHS and converted into a boarding and fumigation steamer operated in New York Harbor.

Status: Renamed in 1929 as the *Joseph J. Kinyoun*; dropped of the list of US Merchant Vessels in 1935 and presumed scrapped.

Length: 101 ft. Beam: 22 ft. Draft: 12 ft. Displacement: 177 tons

No image available

U.S.A.J.M.P. ***Captain T.W. Morrison*** (Coast Defenses of the Cape Fear)

Station—Fort Caswell, NC, 1919-24

Built by Pusey and Jones Shipbuilding Company and launched 18 April 1907 at Wilmington, DE. Named in honor of Captain Theophilus W. Morrison, 16th Infantry, who was killed in action on 1 July 1898 during the charge up San Juan Hill. Accepted by the Quartermaster Department in May 1907. Stationed at Fort Caswell, NC, as of January 1919 and assigned to the Coast Defenses of the Cape Fear. Functioned in the Harbor Boat Service as an artillery tug and passenger craft 1919–24. Sold 11 July 1924 to Quebec Preserving Company of Montreal, Canada.

Status: Owned by National Dock & Dredging Co., 1925-45; Marine Industries Ltd. 1945-72; Richelieu Dredging Inc. 1972-96; apparently scrapped in Montreal in 1996.

Length: 80 ft. Beam: 20 ft. Draft: 10 ft. Displacement: 128 tons

No image available

U.S.A.J.M.P. ***Neptune*** (Harbor Defenses of Manila and Subic Bays)

Station—Fort Mills, Corregidor, PI, 1941-42

Built by Hong Kong & Whampoa Dock Company and launched in 1930 at Hong Kong, China. Purchased by the Quartermaster Corps in 1941 and assigned to the Inter-Island Service at Manila Harbor. Stationed at Fort Mills and typically docked at the mine wharf at Corregidor. Reconditioned about June 1941 as a junior mine planter. In coordination with the U.S.A.M.P. *George F.E. Harrison*, planted the Army mine field in the North Channel in 1941. Location 7 December 1941—Manila Harbor, PI.

Status: Sunk by artillery fire the night of 20 February 1942 while discharging cargo at Fort Frank.

Length: 96 ft. Beam: 24 ft. Draft: 9 ft. Displacement: 164 tons

Bowling Green State University, OH, Historical Collection Of The Great Lakes

U.S.A.J.M.P. *Capt. Edward P. Nones* (Coast Defenses of Cristobal)

Station—Fort Sherman, CZ, 1921-32

Built by Rocky River Dry Dock Company and launched in 1919 at Rocky River, OH. Accepted for service by the U.S. Army Quartermaster Corps on 30 June 1921. Named in honor of Capt. Edward P. Nones, C.A.C., who drowned at Galveston, TX, in 1916. Stationed at Fort Sherman, CZ, and assigned to the Coast Defenses of Cristobal. Served as a junior mine planter and in the Harbor Boat Service at Fort Sherman, CZ, 1921-32. Sold 2 February 1932 to Ferdinand Geiben and C. A. Wilson at Colon, Panama.

Status: Scrapped in 1934.

Length: 101 ft. Beam: 22 ft. Draft: 12 ft. Displacement: 177 tons

U.S.A.J.M.P. ***Maj. William P. Pence*** (Coast Defenses of the Delaware)

Station—Fort Delaware, DE, 1921-25; Governors Island, NY, 1925-30; Fort Monroe, VA, 1930-33

Built by Defoe Shipbuilding Company and launched in 1919 at Bay City MI. Accepted for service by the Quartermaster Corps on 30 June 1921. Named in honor of Maj. William P. Pence. Stationed at Fort Delaware, DE, and assigned to the Coast Defenses of the Delaware. Transferred to Governors Island, NY, in 1925 and assigned to the Harbor Defenses of Southern New York. Transferred to Fort Monroe, VA, in 1930 and assigned to the Harbor Defenses of Chesapeake Bay. Functioned in the Harbor Boat Service as a freight and passenger craft 1921-33. Transferred to the U. S. Coast Guard in 1933.

Status: Sold by the Coast Guard in 1938 and renamed as the S.S. *Helen Miller*; renamed in 1963 as the towboat *Jane Frank*.

Length: 98.5 ft. Beam: 22 ft. Draft: 13 ft. Displacement: 170 tons

Bowling Green State University, OH, Historical Collection Of The Great Lakes

U.S.A.J.M.P. ***Capt. Fred L. Perry*** (Coast Defenses of Southern New York)

Station—Governor's Island, NY, 1919-29; Fort Hancock, NJ, 1929-34; Army Supply Base, Brooklyn, NY, 1934
Built by Rocky River Dry Dock Company and launched in 1919 at Rocky River, OH. Accepted for service by the Quartermaster Corps in 1919. Named in honor of Capt. Fred L. Perry. Stationed at Governor's Island, NY, and assigned to the Coast Defenses of Southern New York. Transferred to Fort Hancock, NJ, in 1929 and assigned to the Harbor Defenses of Sandy Hook. Transferred to the Army Supply Base, Brooklyn, NY, in 1934. Functioned in the Harbor Boat Service as a freight and passenger craft 1919-34 in New York Harbor. Sold to the Reinauer Yacht Corporation on 14 December 1934 and renamed as the S. S. *Consort*.
Status: Scrapped in 1947.

Length: 101 ft. Beam: 22 ft. Draft: 12 ft. Displacement: 177 tons

Michigan State Archive, East Lansing, MI

U.S.A.J.M.P. *Col. Pond*

Station—Milwaukee, WI, 1920; Quebec, Canada, 1920-21; Fort Banks, MA, 1921-23; Fort Hancock, NJ, 1940-41

Built by Fabricated Shipbuilding Company and launched in 1919 at Milwaukee, WI. Accepted for service by the U.S. Army Quartermaster Corps about September 1920 and assigned to the Coast Defenses of Boston. Named in honor of Col. George E. Pond, Q.M.C., Assistant Quartermaster General of the US Army. Moored at the Louise Docks, Quebec, Canada, from November 1920 to July 1921 while en route to the east coast. Arrived 2 August 1921 at Fort Banks, MA. Functioned in the Harbor Boat Service as a freight and passenger craft in Boston Harbor. Sold at Boston to the Michigan State Department of Highways in October 1923 and renamed the *Sainte Ignace*. Reacquired by the US Army in 1940 and renamed as the *Brig. Gen. Arthur W. Yates*. Stationed at Fort Hancock, NJ, and assigned to the Harbor Defenses of Sandy Hook. Location 7 Dec 41—Fort Hancock, NJ.

Status: Wrecked 25 November 1950 at Raritan Bay, Keyport, NJ; scrapped in June 1952.

Length: 123 ft. Beam: 28 ft. Draft: 12 ft. Displacement: 535 tons

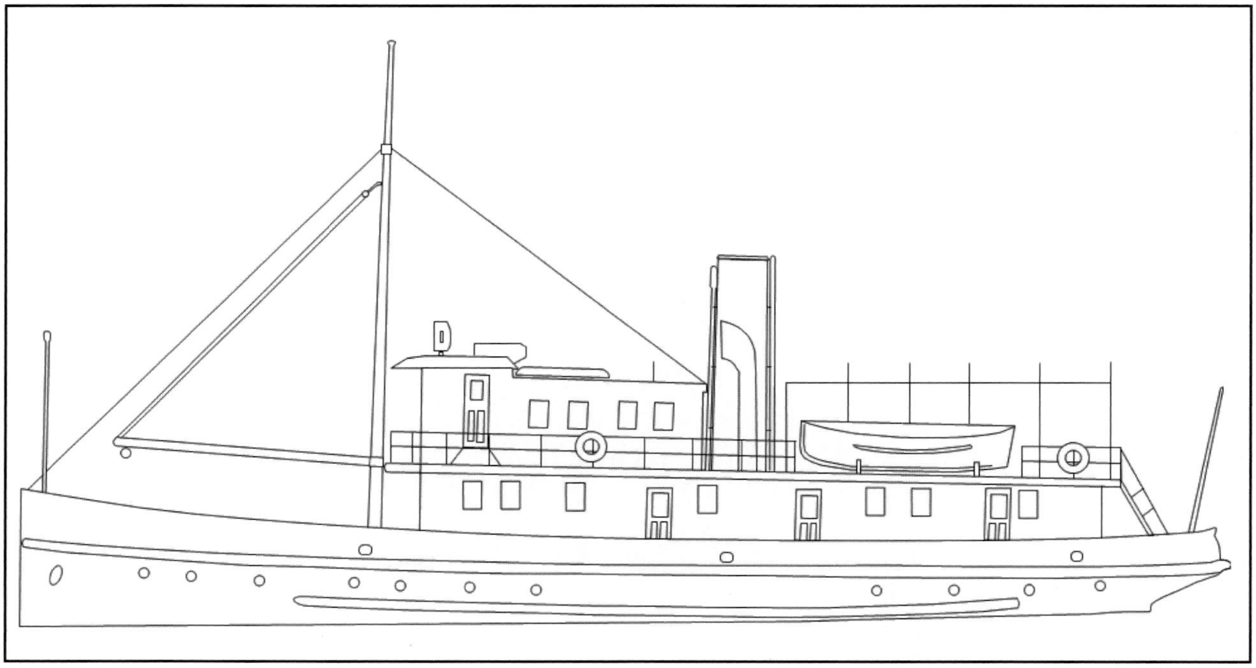

U.S.A.J.M.P. ***Gen. A.M. Randol*** (Coast Defenses of Portland)

Station—Fort Preble, ME, 1909–41

Built by Fore River Shipbuilding Company and launched 21 January 1909 at Quincy, MA. Accepted for service by the Quartermaster Department on 19 March 1909. Named in honor of Brig. Gen. Alanson M. Randol, U.S.V., who served as commander of the 2nd New York Cavalry 1862-65. Stationed at Fort Preble, ME, as of January 1919 and assigned to the Coast Defenses of Portland. Functioned in the Harbor Boat Service as a freight and passenger craft 1919–41 in Portland Harbor. Reconditioned in 1941 to function as a junior mine planter in the Coast Defenses of Portland. Location 7 December 1941—Fort Preble, ME.

Status: Unknown.

Length: 98 ft. Beam: 22 ft. Draft: 11 ft. Displacement: 153 tons

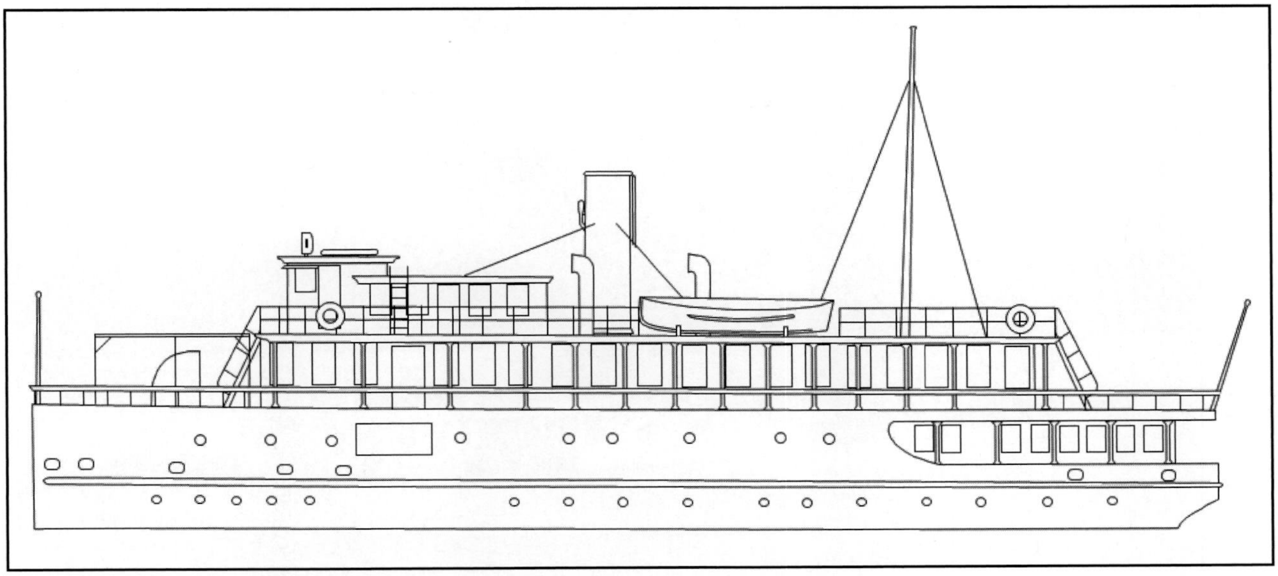

U.S.A.J.M.P. ***Gen. Rochester***

Station—Milwaukee, WI, 1920; Quebec, Canada, 1920-21; Fort Banks, MA, 1921-23

Built by Fabricated Shipbuilding Company and launched in 1919 at Milwaukee, WI. Accepted by the Quartermaster Corps about September 1920 and assigned to the Harbor Boat Service at Boston Harbor. Named in honor of Brigadier General William B. Rochester, Paymaster General of the US Army 1882-1890. Moored at the Louise Docks, Quebec, Canada, from November 1920 to July 1921 while en route to the east coast. Arrived 2 August 1921 at Fort Banks, MA. Functioned in the Harbor Boat Service as a freight and passenger craft in Boston Harbor. Sold in 1923 to the city of Boston, MA, and renamed as the *Michael J. Perkins*.

Status: Scrapped in 1950.

Length: 123 ft. Beam: 28 ft. Draft: 12 ft. Displacement: 535 tons

Pulsey and Jones Collection, Hagley Museum, Wilmington, DE

U.S.A.J.M.P. *Capt. Charles W. Rowell* (Coast Defenses of Long Island Sound)

Station—Fort H.G. Wright, NY, 1919-22

Built by Pusey and Jones Shipbuilding Company and launched 12 May 1907 at Wilmington, DE. Named in honor of Capt. Charles W. Rowell, 2nd Infantry, who was killed 16 July 1898 at Santiago, Cuba. Accepted by the Quartermaster Department in May 1907. Stationed at Fort H.G. Wright, NY, as of January 1919 and assigned to the Coast Defenses of Long Island Sound. Functioned in the Harbor Boat Service as an artillery tug and passenger craft 1919–22. Sold in 1922.

Status: Unknown.

Length: 80 ft. Beam: 20 ft. Draft: 10 ft. Displacement: 128 tons

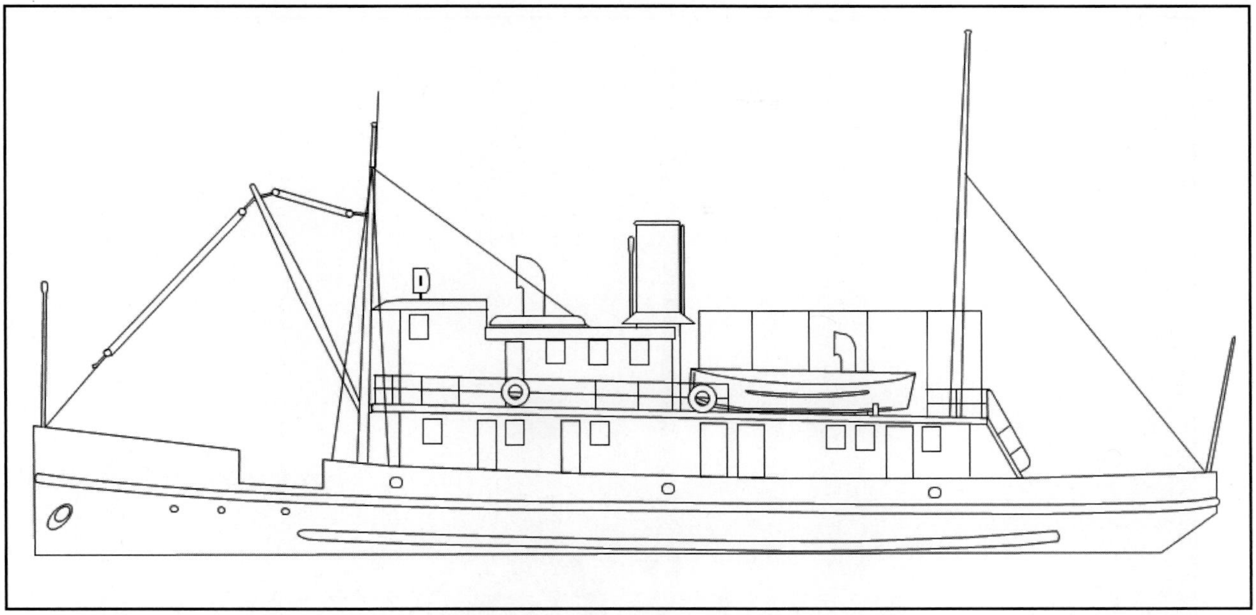

U.S.A.J.M.P. ***Lt. Col. Herman C. Schumm*** (Coast Defenses of Long Island Sound)

Station—Fort H.G. Wright, NY, 1921-31; Fort Sherman, CZ, 1931-41

Built by Defoe Shipbuilding Company and launched in 1919 at Bay City MI. Accepted for service by the Quartermaster Corps on 30 June 1921. Named in honor of Lt. Col. Herman C. Schumm. Stationed at Fort H.G. Wright, NY, in 1921 and assigned to the Coast Defenses of Long Island Sound. Served as a junior mine planter and as a freight and passenger craft in the Harbor Boat Service at Fort H.G. Wright, NY, 1919-31. Transferred in January 1931 to the Harbor Defenses of Cristobal. Arrived at Cristobal 18 January 1931 and took station at Fort Sherman, CZ. Location 7 Dec 41—Fort Sherman, CZ.

Status: Unknown.

Length: 98.5 ft.	Beam: 22 ft.	Draft: 12.8 ft.	Displacement: 170 tons

Author's Collection

U.S.A.J.M.P. ***Gen. Robert Swartwout*** (Coast Defenses of Pensacola)

Station—Fort Barrancas, FL, 1919-20

Built by Neafie and Levy Shipbuilding Company and launched 23 March 1905 at Philadelphia, PA. Named in honor of General Robert Swartwout, Quartermaster General of the US Army, 1813-1816. Accepted for service by the U.S. Army Quartermaster Corps in June 1905. Stationed at Fort Barrancas, FL, as of January 1919 and assigned to the Coast Defenses of Pensacola. Sold about 1920.

Status: Unknown.

Length: 110 ft. Beam: 2420 ft. Draft: 130 ft. Displacement: 430 tons

US Army Transportation Museum, Fort Eustis, VA

U.S.A.J.M.P. *Maj. Evan Thomas* (Coast Defenses of Puget Sound)

Station—Fort Worden, WA 1919-24; Fort MacArthur, CA, 1924-30

Built by the Heffernan Engine Works and launched about June 1904 at Ballard, WA. Accepted for service by the Quartermaster Department in August 1904. Named in honor of Maj. Evan Thomas, who was killed in action with Modoc Indians 26 Apr 1873 at the Lava Beds, CA. Stationed at Fort Worden, WA, as of January 1919 and assigned to the Coast Defenses of Puget Sound. Served as an artillery steamer and part-time freight and passenger craft in the Harbor Boat Service in Puget Sound, WA, 1919-24. Transferred to Fort MacArthur, CA in 1924, and assigned to the Coast Defenses of Los Angeles. Served as a freight and passenger craft in the Harbor Boat Service in Los Angeles Harbor 1924-30. Sold in 1932 to the Pacific Tow Boat Company of Los Angeles and renamed as the *Retriever*.

Status: Unknown.

Length: 105 ft. Beam: 20 ft. Draft: 6 ft. Displacement: 212 tons

No image available

U.S.A.J.M.P. ***Capt. A.M. Wetherill*** (Coast Defenses of the Potomac)

Station—Fort Washington, MD, 1919-29

Built by T. S. Marvel Shipbuilding Company and launched about June 1907 at Newburgh, NY. Named in honor of Capt. Alexander M. Wetherill, 6th Infantry, killed 1 July 1898 at the battle of San Juan Hill, Cuba. Accepted for service by the Quartermaster Department in August 1907. Stationed at Fort Washington, MD, as of January 1919 and assigned to the Coast Defenses of the Potomac. Typically docked at the Fort Washington pier. Sold 28 June 1923 at Norfolk, VA, and renamed as the tug *H.M. Hoodless*.

Status: Ran aground 17 Jan 29 at Smith Jetty, Georgetown, SC; declared a total loss and dropped off the list of US Merchant Vessels.

Length: 80 ft. Beam: 20 ft. Draft: 10 ft. Displacement: 128 tons

GPO U.S. GOVERNMENT PRINTING OFFICE: 2010—653-506